MW00561991

BAYESIAN DATA ANALYSIS FOR THE BEHAVIORAL AND NEURAL SCIENCES

Non-Calculus Fundamentals

This textbook bypasses the need for advanced mathematics by providing in-text computer code, allowing students to explore Bayesian data analysis without the calculus background normally considered a prerequisite for this material. Now, students can use the best methods without needing advanced mathematical techniques. This approach goes beyond 'frequentist' concepts of p-values and null hypothesis testing, using the full power of modern probability theory to solve real-world problems. The book offers a fully self-contained course, and demonstrates analysis techniques using over 100 worked examples crafted specifically for students in the behavioral and neural sciences. The book presents two general algorithms that help students solve the measurement and model selection (also called 'hypothesis testing') problems most frequently encountered in real-world applications.

Todd E. Hudson is a professor of rehabilitation medicine at New York University's Grossman School of Medicine, holding cross-appointments in neurology, and also in the Department of Biomedical Engineering at the New York University Tandon School of Engineering. Dr. Hudson has taught statistics, perception and sensory processes, experimental design, and/or advanced topics in neurobiology and behavior at several major universities, including Brandeis University and Columbia University. He co-founded, and serves as Chief Scientific Advisor to, Tactile Navigation Tools, LLC, which develops navigation aids for the visually impaired.

Bayesian Data Analysis for the Behavioral and Neural Sciences

NON-CALCULUS FUNDAMENTALS

TODD E. HUDSON

New York University

CAMBRIDGE
UNIVERSITY PRESS

CAMBRIDGE
UNIVERSITY PRESS

University Printing House, Cambridge CB2 8BS, United Kingdom

One Liberty Plaza, 20th Floor, New York, NY 10006, USA

477 Williamstown Road, Port Melbourne, VIC 3207, Australia

314–321, 3rd Floor, Plot 3, Splendor Forum, Jasola District Centre, New Delhi – 110025, India

103 Penang Road, #05–06/07, Visioncrest Commercial, Singapore 238467

Cambridge University Press is part of the University of Cambridge.

It furthers the University's mission by disseminating knowledge in the pursuit of education, learning, and research at the highest international levels of excellence.

www.cambridge.org
Information on this title: www.cambridge.org/9781108835565
DOI: 10.1017/9781108890984

First published 2021

Printed in the United Kingdom by TJ Books Limited, Padstow, Cornwall 2021

A catalogue record for this publication is available from the British Library.

Library of Congress Cataloging-in-Publication Data
Names: Hudson, Todd Erik, author.
Title: Bayesian data analysis for the behavioral and neural sciences : non-calculus fundamentals / Todd E. Hudson.
Description: Cambridge ; New York, NY : Cambridge University Press, 2021. | Includes bibliographical references and index.
Identifiers: LCCN 2020052398 | ISBN 9781108835565 (hardback) | ISBN 9781108812900 (paperback) | ISBN 9781108890984 (ebook)
Subjects: LCSH: Social sciences – Statistical methods. | Social sciences – Data processing. | Psychology – Statistical methods. | Psychology – Data processing. | Neurosciences – Statistical methods. | Neurosciences – Data processing. | Bayesian statistical decision theory.
Classification: LCC HA29 .H813 2021 | DDC 519.5/42–dc23
LC record available at https://lccn.loc.gov/2020052398

ISBN 978-1-108-83556-5 Hardback
ISBN 978-1-108-81290-0 Paperback

Additional resources for this publication at www.cambridge.org/hudsonbayesian

To my wife, Elizabeth, and my sons,
Gabriel William and Julian Leonard,
who showed me there was even more to life

Contents

Appendices

Preface

A scientist should live two lifetimes: one studying the empirical results and experimental methods of a scientific or medical specialty area, and the other spent studying the art and science of extracting information from data. In this text I will assume that you have made a start on the first, and have learned something of neuroscience, education, economics, psychology, and/or medical research. Here, we will take the first steps toward completing your training, and begin a study of modern data analysis.

Why is data analysis so important? The reason for the extreme importance of data analysis is twofold: First, a working knowledge of the logically valid techniques for extracting information from data will naturally provide insights into experimental design, and allow you to create experiments that are well suited to answering the scientific questions in which you are interested. Second, it gives you the ability to take the data you have obtained, and efficiently extract *all* of the information contained therein. Neither of these is truly possible without a solid understanding of data analysis, and by extension probability.

This text is meant to be either a first or a second exposure to data analysis. First contact occasionally occurs prior to the university level, and occasionally waits until graduate school. As a first exposure (that is, prior to any other course that would have need of the concept of probability), this text is meant to provide a self-contained treatment of the basics of data analysis ***without the need for calculus.***[1] This, in fact, was my motivation for writing a textbook at all. There are certainly other excellent, probably more

[1] Here is a quick test to know if you have the mathematics background for this text:

Choose the lowest row of the table with an equation you can confidently solve:	
$x + x$	(a) $2x$ (b) $x/2$ (c) x^2 (d) x^{-2}
$\sum_{i=1}^{5} 2i$	(a) 2 (b) 30 (c) 5 (d) 10
$e^0 + \ln(1)$	(a) 0+1 (b) $1 - 1$ (c) 1+0 (d) $-1 + 1$
$\int d\theta \cos(\theta) + \int d\vartheta \sec^2(\vartheta)$	(a) $\sin\theta + \cos\vartheta$ (b) $\cos - \sin\vartheta$ (c) $\tan(\theta) - \sin(\vartheta)$ (d) $\sin(\theta) + \tan(\vartheta)$

The correct answers progress from (a) to (d) by row from top to bottom. If you can solve all rows' equations, you are ready for the current text, including the optional calculus-based material. If you solved the first three, you are fully prepared for the current text. If you solved only one equation from the first or second row, but were familiar with the elements of the equation on the third row (even if you could not immediately solve it), you should do fine with this text after a little refamiliarization with the concept of a logarithm (a refresher is provided in **Appendix B**). If you were unable to solve either of the first two rows' equations, you will need to take an algebra and/or precalculus course before attempting this text.

complete and certainly more rigorously mathematical textbooks on the topics of probability and Bayesian data analysis already available. They are simply not appropriate as a first exposure because they require advanced calculus *as their starting point.*

If this is *not* your first course in data analysis, it is likely that first contact was provided by a 'frequentist statistics' course (most typically a single-term course in the second university year, although such courses are now more common at the preuniversity level). These courses focus on memorizing a series of 'frequentist statistical tests,' with little or no attempt at explaining their origins, along with a cookbook-style recipe for application; for example, *if your data consist of two sets of continuous observations, you test for a difference in their means using thus-and-so statistical test; if the result is greater than a particular value, the meaning of the frequentist test is....* Because the cookbook approach avoids any attempt at explaining the origins of tests (the most commonly used explanations require advanced mathematics), there is always a great deal of confusion on the part of students. This has, inevitably, led to large-scale misuse of frequentist statistical tests – this is true even in a professional setting, because the majority of frequentist tests are computed via software package, where the user of that software need not be aware of the subtleties that went into producing the output, or whether the match between analysis and data was truly appropriate. This has led to no end of problems and confusion, as you might imagine. Confusion is exacerbated by the fact that frequentist statistics courses are based on a definition of probability that is incompatible with modern probability theory, and that ultimately leads to logical inconsistency.[2]

To avoid the problems of a frequentist statistics course and still provide a text that can be used by undergraduate students, I have done three things: First, I use the modern formulation of the concept of probability, which allows a unified and logical treatment of both probability theory and data analysis. This allows also for straightforward explanation of the origins of each of the resulting concepts and analyses. Second, I avoid the requirement of advanced calculus-based methods. Third, in lieu of advanced mathematics[3] I make use of computer-based approximation techniques. Approximate techniques are suitable both for the student who has not yet taken calculus, as well as the professional performing calculations for which no analytical solution exists; approximate techniques are therefore useful regardless of your level of mathematics training. Although many of the same mathematical topics are covered in several other excellent texts on probability and data analysis, applications here are geared toward students in the behavioral, neural, and biomedical sciences (i.e., psychology, education, neuroscience, biomedical engineering, economics, biology, and medicine).

For students who have taken a frequentist statistics course, it is my hope that the information presented here will provide a useful counterpoint to what you have been

2 One such inconsistency, the 'optional stopping problem,' is demonstrated in Chapter 2.

3 Although I have taken pains to eliminate calculus-based techniques in this text (which constitutes a self-contained course in the basic elements of Bayesian data analysis), you should still be prepared for what is to come: there will be equations. Familiarity with the use of equations is fundamental for any real understanding of data analysis, even in a non-calculus introduction. Indeed, since data analysis and probability theory are topics in mathematics, there will in fact be a fair number of equations. If you are not yet comfortable with them, just keep in mind that there are no equations in this text that will require anything of you beyond basic arithmetic (i.e., addition, subtraction, multiplication, division, and by extension exponents and logarithms); a refresher of exponents and logarithms is provided in **Appendix B**, and an in-depth demonstration of how to solve marginalization equations in terms of sums and multiplications can be found in **Appendix C**.

previously taught, and give you the skills necessary to perform the analyses most suited to extracting information from your experimental data. With this in mind, I have attempted to provide explicit comparisons between modern methods and some of those taught in an old-fashioned frequentist statistics course, at least to the extent possible without becoming bogged down in digression.

What, you should ask, makes this text different and useful? Aside from presenting techniques of Bayesian data analysis in a non-calculus context, I have also based my presentation of the course material on *applying* the concepts to realistic problems of data analysis. This is very different from the commonly seen 'cookbook approach,' where the student's goal is to memorize a flowchart in which the data and experiment are put into categories (e.g., 'a multifactorial design with repeated measurements'), and this categorization dictates the test to be performed: the focus is therefore on memorizing the mapping from experiment and categorization to frequentist test.[4] Here, we will focus on the *process* through which one must pass in understanding a dataset, rather than in presenting a set of ready-made equations to memorize and use in predefined circumstances. To this end, the culmination of this text is a pair of data-analytic algorithms that are meant to *guide our thinking* when analyzing data. The steps of these algorithms will guide us as we construct each analysis, whether or not the data conform to a prepackaged set of descriptors (e.g., the deliberately mysterious 'repeated-measures multifactorial design' mentioned above). The initial chapters will focus on building these algorithms up from Bayes' theorem, and the final chapters demonstrate their use in a set of worked problems.

Two final points must be made before we begin: First, data analysis is always an exercise in logic. This logic is fundamental to the portion of the scientific enterprise that uses data of any variety, because it provides the set of rules that tell us what can be reasonably concluded from the data we have collected. Probability theory encodes this logic, and gives the mathematics that allows us to optimally extract information from data; this is in part a purely formal exercise, and in part based on our information about the data and the scientific hypotheses under investigation. Second (and finally), I must emphasize that the analysis of data is *not* entirely a mechanical exercise (i.e., 'plug-and-chug,' 'turn-the-crank'): it will require some thought. In consequence, you will sometimes struggle to construct the best analysis, and you will sometimes make mistakes. To understand your data and analyze it fully, you must be willing to try, make mistakes, revise, and

[4] This 'cookbook approach' has led to the proliferation of frequentist statistical software packages that are meant to be used by those without the requisite training to understand their inner workings (rather than simply to relieve a trained expert of the need to perform seemingly endless tedious calculations). In one recent example that appeared in my e-mail, the package was advertised with the headline: *You don't need to be a statistician to perform statistical analysis on your data*, which I assume is meant to imply that you don't need to understand statistical data analysis to generate results from the software. This view is supported by their further claims regarding the product:
- *Ease of use!*
- *Stat Wizard runs the right tests*
- *Interprets the results for you*
- *Creates charts to visualize results*
- *Accurate results without worry*
Apparently, one need only feed in numbers, and the software will do all the work ... including **interpret the results for you!** The software is meant to generate reports that look as if they were produced by a knowledgable expert who had thought through and tailored an analysis to the problem at hand, rather than automatic outputs that could have been generated by a monkey with a keyboard. Such statistical packages are the second ingredient in a recipe for disaster. That disaster is currently playing itself out in the scientific journals, and is a major contributor to the 'crisis of reproducibility' in the behavioral and neural sciences.

try again. There is an increasingly persistent misperception, even among professionals, that a 'good' scientist should never make mistakes – a belief that leads to a constellation of negative consequences, the most insidious being a fear of simply *getting started and trying something*. We will learn in the following pages, however, that crafting just the right analysis for the scientific question we are interested in answering will generally require trial-and-error. Trial-and-error is fundamental to the actual practice of the professional scientist; it is how we learn what works in the real world, on real datasets, and allows us to hone our skills and further the scientific enterprise. The good scientist must learn to understand the logic that connects data to theory and theory to experiment, and you will find a good deal of trial and error along the way. I encourage you to keep this in mind as you begin your journey into the sometimes challenging, but ever rewarding study of data analysis.

Acknowledgments

I am grateful to my colleagues for their interest in my work, especially Leonard Matin, Michael Landy, Kateri McRae, Peter Sokol-Hessner, John Martone, Janet Rucker, and JR Rizzo, who encouraged me during the writing process and motivated me to simplify and focus my presentation of the material.

CHAPTER ONE

LOGIC AND DATA ANALYSIS

In any scientific discipline, the goal is to **infer** underlying world-states and the rules by which those world-states change, based on observed data. In the biosciences, particularly the behavioral and neural sciences, this involves inferring the rules by which organisms acquire and process environmental inputs to produce **behavior**; that is, to infer the fundamental rules by which neural circuits and systems process environmental inputs to govern behavior. In some cases the behavior of interest is defined in terms of the organism as a whole, while in other cases our interest is in behavior at a more fine-grained level, such as the behavior of the thyroid or the behavior of the superior colliculus (a paired structure of the mammalian midbrain). In medical research, the goal is to understand the behaviors of organs and organ systems in healthy and disease states, knowledge that is applied to develop treatments; treatment efficacies are compared via the same logic used to compare scientific theories (see Box 1.1). If these are our goals as scientists, our next question must be: How are inferences made? What is the logic relating experimental data and our **hypotheses**? As we will see throughout this text, the logic relating experimental data to scientific inference permeates every aspect of the scientific process: it tells us how best to test existing theories, how to design experiments, how to improve current theories, and how to test new medical treatments. **Data analysis** is nothing but an exercise in this logic.

Much of this text will be concerned with testing scientific models (Fig. 1.1) of the behavior of organisms or their components, and for this purpose we will ultimately develop procedures for both measurement and hypothesis testing. Hypothesis testing is done in two stages. Initially, when we become interested in explaining some aspect of behavior, we have performed no formal **experiments**. We know only that there is some behavior that has certain characteristics – whatever it is that piqued our interest, whether that be some disease state or an aspect of normal economic, psychological or neurophysiological behavior that we find interesting in its own right. At this stage, we

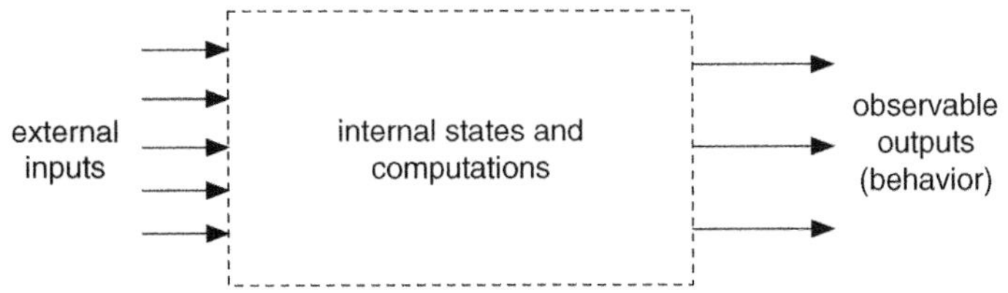

Figure 1.1 Basic anatomy of a behavioral theory. Behavioral theories must describe the interaction between observable external inputs to a system, the internal states and computations of that system, and the observable outputs (behaviors) produced by interaction of the preceding.

BOX 1.1 The Anatomy of a Scientific Theory: Examples from Psychology, Economics, Medicine, and Neuroscience

Theories are, to put it in terms of the logical arguments described in Section 1.1, statements/propositions. Scientific hypotheses are a special class of proposition, because they are testable. The basic criterion for a testable behavioral theory is that it makes predictions that can be compared to observations of behavior. A typical example from neuroscience might be the hypothesis that posits a particular population of neurons in primary motor cortex that controls arm movements. This theory is straightforward in the sense that there must be neurons that are active before an arm movement, and whose firing tells us about the type of movement that will be made (e.g., move the hand 5 cm forward); ideally, we could artificially stimulate those neurons to produce predictable arm movements.

If theories are simply statements that represent a testable guess or belief about some system's behavior, then what is the minimal structure of a testable behavioral theory? A behavioral theory must describe a behavior, and it must describe the causes/determinants of that behavior. In other words, a behavioral theory will describe the interaction of three elements (shown graphically in Fig. 1.1): external inputs to a system, the internal states and computations of that system, and an observable output or behavior of the system. Furthermore, that description must be specific enough to allow us to say which combinations of external inputs along with internal states and computations will produce the behavior, and also how changes to these precursors will affect behavior: it is this specificity that makes a theory testable.

We will encounter a range of behavioral theories in this text, from behavioral economic theories, to sensory/motor neuroscience, medicine, and theories of personality and social psychology. In these various cases we will be interested in different 'systems,' whether that be the visual system, the enteric nervous system, a single neuron, or the entire organism (human, rat, rabbit, etc.). In all of these cases, we will expect to define a set of inputs to the system (a system which may, e.g., in the case of a single-neuron system, be entirely contained within the body), a set of internal structures and computations relevant to the underlying theory, and a behavioral response mediated by those inputs and internal computations. Within the realm of motor control, we may want to examine a theory that makes predictions regarding which cells will and will not cause arm movements (primary motor neurons will, but for example primary visual neurons won't), as well as how patterns of neural activity (one type of behavior) will relate to arm movements (another type of behavior). In medicine, many theories attempt to relate treatment to behavioral outcomes that involve recovery from illness or injury. The most common examples come from drug development, such as medications designed to delay the progression of Alzheimer's disease. Here, a test of the drug (and therefore the theory that the drug has the desired effect) would involve comparison of the timecourse of disease progression in individuals taking versus not taking the drug. In the field of economics a classical theory of economic choice is the rational choice model, in which it is predicted that human economic decisions will tend to maximize expected monetary gain. Here a test of the model involves comparison of human economic choices with those of an ideal (rational) decider that maximizes expected gain (we define expected gain and an ideal decision-maker in several later chapters). Finally, within the field of personality psychology, many theories involve identifying stable characteristics of cognition and emotion that predict chronic emotional responses and social behaviors. A typical experiment might use a pencil-and-paper 'personality test' to classify individuals into categories that are subsequently used to predict questionnaire answers by the same individuals, indicating their likely emotional responses and decisions in emotionally charged circumstances.

Every testable scientific theory must make predictions, because models are compared and tested by comparing the predictions of competing models against observed data. Each experimentally observed datum contributes to our ability to discriminate among competing models, because it will be more consistent with one model over its competitors. A good behavioral theory will always posit *specific* predictable relationships between the internal states of the system (e.g., current firing of sensory neurons, chronic cognitive or emotional activation, intramuscular lactic acid levels), inputs to the system (e.g., sensory inputs, social or emotional circumstances, or monetary decision scenarios), and the behaviors produced by that system. The states of the system that mediate between inputs and outputs are characterized by both physical constants and neural response functions, both of which can be measured in terms their characteristic parameters. In the case of the visual system, one such parameter would be the focal length of the corneal lens relative to the depth of the eyeball (which is used to predict image sharpness/blur), whereas in the case of monetary decision-making an important parameter is 'risk aversion,' which describes the degree to which one will trade or forego high potential monetary gains in favor of lower gains because the lower-gain choice is also less likely to lead to a loss (predicting, among other things, the types of stock investments one is comfortable making). When we have a theory that posits these types of internal parameters, we may choose to **measure** the values of those parameters, perhaps within a certain subset of the human population (e.g., those who have or have not suffered a concussion). Measurements of those parameters represent a common type of to-be-tested proposition (i.e., 'the value of the parameter is'). These measurement problems, in addition to being useful in their own right, form the basis for more advanced calculations used within Bayesian statistics.

The most straightforward of these extensions is **model selection**, which is used to differentiate among competing models (theories) of a given behavior; thus, when we are testing a scientific theory we are performing model selection. Scientific theories progress when we have multiple competing models *of a single behavior*. Tests of these theories constitute a model selection problem, where our goal is to select the model that is most consistent with our experimental data. So whereas the solution to a parameter estimation problem takes data and uses it to provide the best estimate for the numerical value of some parameter from a single model, the solution to a model selection problem tells us which of several competing scientific theories (models) provides the most reasonable fit to our experimental data (often without worrying about the exact values of model parameters).

generate new theories by noting regularities in behavior. That is, observed regularities in behavior allow us to generate an initial set of informed guesses (hypotheses) concerning underlying rules governing behavior. This set of initial hypotheses is formed based on the fact that our initial data (observed regularities) will be logically consistent with certain underlying rules governing behavior, but not others. Once we have defined an initial set of hypotheses, one narrows the field of *most-plausible* hypotheses by performing experiments. Experiments are designed to discriminate among hypotheses. If properly designed, they will produce data that is logically *more* consistent with some hypotheses than with others. Notice that both parts of the process require us to analyze data – either to determine what initial hypotheses are tenable, given the initially observed regularities in behavior, or to later discriminate among those initial hypotheses, given the results of our experiments. The details of this practice of data analysis will occupy us for the remainder of the text.

As we will see below, there are two methods of assessing the impact of data on theory: **deduction** and **induction**. If one has previous basic coursework in logic, symbolic logic, or Boolean algebra, the topic was deduction. And while deduction is a useful and well-known method of scientific inference, it is only applicable in a very limited set of circumstances: those circumstances in which one is eliminating impossible theories that *conflict with known facts*. That is, it eliminates the *impossibilities*; it cannot, however, be used when choosing among several competing *possibilities*. When we have gone as far as we can with deduction, we must narrow the field of possibilities using inductive, rather than deductive, inferences that connect data to theory. Until recently, the **frequentist approach** was the most common method of inductive inference; but advances in the foundations of probability theory since the mid-twentieth century have shown that the only logically consistent method of induction that meets basic criteria of rationality is the approach based on probability theory. Any other method that is not ultimately identical to probability theory will be logically flawed, in the sense that it will be internally inconsistent or show other logically undesirable behavior. Here, we will demonstrate and explore the two most basic applications of probability theory to data analysis: measurement and hypothesis testing.

There are four major goals to accomplish in the remainder of this introductory chapter. The first is to provide a general introduction to scientific inference, as it relates data to hypotheses (Section 1.1). Next, in Section 1.2, we examine the concept of **uncertainty**, which is central to the distinction between inductive and deductive inference, and data analysis generally. In Section 1.3 we introduce the logic of data analysis via probability theory, whose details will occupy us for the remainder of this text. In addition to introducing you to the theoretical landscape of formal data analysis (Sections 1.1–1.3), the final goal of this chapter is to introduce the practice of **data visualization**. The critical, albeit relatively unstructured process of data visualization gives us our first look at any new dataset. The goal in data visualization is to verify that we have obtained data that, on the whole 'makes sense' given what we already know about the phenomenon under study. Data visualization allows us both to identify when errors might have been committed during collection, import, transcription, storage, retrieval, etc. of the data, as well as to identify possible unexpected mechanisms and characteristics of the object of study (e.g., a previously unrecognized input to a particular neural circuit); this is the topic of Section 1.4.

1.1 The Logic of Inference

The real-world analysis of experimental data depends on the interplay of deductive and inductive inference. **Inductive inference** is the reasoning used to select among competing alternative hypotheses when none directly conflicts with known facts; it is the topic that will occupy us for the remainder of this text. **Deductive inference**, by contrast, is used to eliminate impossible theories that are in conflict with known facts. Deduction is most applied during the initial stages of investigation when initial hypotheses are being examined.

1.1.1 Deductive Inference and Rational Belief Networks

Deductive inference occurs in two forms, the *modus ponens* and *modus tollens* types. We first state these deductive arguments (where 'A' and 'B' represent statements that could potentially be true or false, such as scientific hypotheses, usually termed **propositions** within the context of a logical argument), written both symbolically and in words:

Modus Ponens ('mode of affirmation'):

$A \Rightarrow B$ [If A is true, then B must also be true]
A [A is affirmed – that is, A is declared true]
$\therefore B$ [Therefore B is true]

Modus Tollens ('mode of denial'):

$A \Rightarrow B$ [If A is true, then B must also be true]
$\bar{B}$ [$\bar{B}$ denotes the negation[1] of B – in other words, the truth of B is denied]
$\therefore \bar{A}$ [Therefore A is false]

The logic of these deductive **arguments** is as follows: In the ***modus ponens*** case, it is first assumed that there is a logical connection whereby the truth of the proposition A guarantees the truth of the proposition B (this is stated on the first line of the argument). In addition, the second line of the argument asserts A to be true. The truth of proposition B is the logical consequence of the assertions made on lines 1 and 2, because if B is always true when A is true (line 1), and we assume that A is true (line 2), it follows that we must also assume that B is true (line 3). In the ***modus tollens*** case line 1 is identical, but the negation[1] of B is asserted on line 2. Since the rule given on line 1 requires B to *always* be true when A is true, the denial of B implies the denial of A (because B would have been true if A had been true). Notice that while both of these deductive arguments are **valid** regardless of the meanings of A and B, the truth of the conclusions in both argument forms is conditional on the truth of the statements, or **premises** given on lines 1 and 2. A valid argument form in which the premises are true is called a **sound argument.**

[1] Negation is the logical operation by which the proposition is asserted to be untrue. Thus the negation of a compound proposition, $A \equiv$ Harvey is a blind cat, is correctly given as 'it is not true that Harvey is a blind cat.' While this could

Programming Aside: IF Else and the Modus Ponens Deduction

We can use the built-in if . . . then logical evaluation to explore the modus ponens argument. Let's create the proposition, rabbitsAreFluffy and the proposition rabbitsAreSoft, and further assert: *rabbitsAreFluffy* ⇒ *rabbitsAreSoft*. We can write a quick program to explore this:

```
rabbitsAreFluffy=1;

%implication defined below
if rabbitsAreFluffy,
    rabbitsAreSoft=1;
else rabbitsAreSoft=nan;

%conclusion
rabbitsAreSoft
```

The proposition following *if* can either be true or false, and the next line defines the second part of the implication *rabbitsAreFluffy* ⇒ *rabbitsAreSoft*, by telling us what is also true if rabbitsAreFluffy=true. If run as is, the final line (query of the rabbitsAreSoft proposition) will yield a 1 (true). If we change rabbitsAreFluffy to false, then the rabbitsAreSoft proposition has an undefined value based on the implication *rabbitsAreFluffy* ⇒ *rabbitsAreSoft*, and so we assign it nan.

There are also **invalid** (and therefore **unsound**) argument forms that look quite similar to the deductive forms above. For example, the argument

$A \Rightarrow B$	[If A is true, then B must also be true]
B	[B is affirmed]
$\therefore A$	[Therefore A is fallaciously declared true]

is not deductively valid; it is a logical **fallacy**. This argument (called *affirming the consequent*) is invalid because the third line does not *necessarily* follow in all cases where the premises (lines 1–2) are true. Consider the example: A = 'we are reading a Socratic dialogue,' and B = 'we are reading ancient Greek philosophy.' In this example, further assume both A and B are true. Despite this, line 3 still doesn't logically (deductively) follow: the second line could be true reading any number of philosophers (Zeno, Pythagoreas, Parmenides, Aristotle, etc.), so this argument form (affirming the consequent), is not a valid deductive argument.

OK, now let's assume we have constructed a valid argument, such as a *modus ponens* deduction. Is this argument, being valid, guaranteed to yield a true conclusion? Perhaps surprisingly, the answer is no. A valid argument does not guarantee anything about the real-world truth of its conclusion: the conclusion may be true or untrue, despite having resulted from a valid argument. To see why this is so, and also to gain a better understanding of why deduction is nevertheless useful in the face of these facts, let's define the two true premises, A = 'Blind cats catch prey auditorily,' and B = 'Sockeye is a salmon variety,' and consider these premises in the *modus ponens* argument. We see

mean that Harvey is neither cat nor blind, it could also mean that Harvey is not a cat but is in fact blind, or it could mean that Harvey is a sighted cat. Elementary propositional logic is reviewed at the start of Chapter 2.

that because the first line of the argument may not be true (i.e., there is no logical connection between blind cats' hunting methods and salmon varieties), the conclusion of the argument may not be true (it is not *logically necessary* that it be true). However, the logical form of the argument is unaffected by these considerations: *If* the first two lines of the argument *were* true, then the conclusion *must* follow. Indeed, one could think of a deductive argument as defining a **rational belief network**, where *if* one believes A to be true, and also believes that A implies B, then a rational being *must also* believe B. The job of the scientist is to construct belief networks (both deductive and, as we will see below, inductive) involving behavioral theories, and extract experimental facts regarding the world to either support or disprove those theories via the logical connections of those networks.

Exercises

1) What can be concluded from the following arguments, if we define:
   $C = A \Rightarrow B$ (C is defined as: if A, then B)
   $D = B \Rightarrow \bar{A}$
   a. C, A, therefore ______.
   b. $C, \bar{B}$, therefore ______.
   c. D, A, therefore ______.
   d. D, B, therefore ______.
2) You are given four cards, two front-up, and two front-down. You are told that on every card with an even number on its front, there is a vowel printed on its back. There is a 2 and an 11 printed on the two front-up cards, and a 'q' and 'u' visible on the backs of the two face down cards. Which cards, if turned over, provide a test of the assertion given above concerning what is printed on the fronts and backs of individual cards?

1.1.2 Plausible Inference

All deductive conclusions are known with certainty. They are true or false, not 'likely true' or 'probably false.' This is the beauty of a deductive argument, and is a consequence of the certainty inherent in the implication (if A is true, B ***must*** also be true). Once such a 'certain implication' can be defined, we need only agree upon one of the premises (that A is true or that B is false), and from this we can determine what also *must* be true or *must* be false. There is no ambiguity or uncertainty in the conclusion of a deductive argument. Interestingly, this very same beautiful certainty is also the drawback of a deductive argument, because a deductive argument has nothing to say about 'uncertain implication'; i.e., when it is only known that if A is true it provides ***evidence*** that B is also true, but nevertheless does not *logically guarantee* that B be true. Given that our information regarding the connection between theory and data will rarely define a **certain implication**, the rules of deductive inference cannot be applied without caveat. It was therefore a breakthrough for scientific inference when Richard Cox showed that probability theory, as originally developed by Pascal and Fermat in the seventeenth century, Bernoulli and most completely by Laplace is the unique method of consistent reasoning with **uncertain** information.

BOX 1.2 What Is Probability?

Two types of deductive argument were described: the conclusion of a *sound* deductive argument describes the state of the world; the conclusion of a *valid* deductive argument is a statement of our information; that is, in a *valid* deductive argument, the conclusion tells us whether or not a proposition is true, *assuming* the statements in the argument are also true. Probabilities, and the inductive inferences they support, are of the second kind. Probabilities quantify the strength of logical support – given as a number between 0 and 1, favoring the truth of the object of the probability statement that can be asserted *assuming* conditioning statements are true. The important point is that, just as with a valid deductive argument, we do not require that conditioning statements be true in order to draw valid conclusions, only that we treat them as true for the purpose of computing probabilities; those probabilities tell us the evidence available for the object of the probability statement, *if* the conditioning statements *were* true. This is very different from the frequency definition of probability, defined in terms of observed frequencies, which must, by definition, be true.

Probabilities defined in terms of information are an extension of the 'logical belief network' described for deductive reasoning that defines not just what a logical agent/being *must believe* (when probabilities are 0 or 1), but also what a logical agent *should believe* (what is more or less likely, defined as probabilities *between* 0 and 1). It describes the extent to which a logical agent should hold certain beliefs, given other logically related beliefs. Understood in this way, assignment of numerical values for probabilities is purely an exercise in logic; subjectivity does not enter into the calculation any more than it enters into a deductive argument. This information-based definition of probability allows the broadest use of probability, not limiting the scope of application the way the frequency definition would.

Why does the frequency definition limit the scope of probability theory? Because there is no frequency-definition way to assign probabilities to the class of proposition that is most important to a scientist: hypotheses and models. The most common example of such a proposition is meteorological: tomorrow's weather. The weather on any given day or time has only one value, because a statement such as 'it will rain tomorrow at 9 AM' is not the type of thing that can sometimes be true and sometimes be false. Tomorrow's weather is not the type of event that can have 'an infinite series of identical repetitions' (as could be theoretically achieved with coin tosses). Rather, it's truth-value (rain/no-rain) is constant and unchanging. The same is true of any scientific hypothesis, because they belong to a class of proposition that cannot, for example, be true 8 times out of 10 and false 2. Once we lose the ability to define the probabilities of hypotheses, we also lose the ability to test hypotheses in the most straightforward way – comparing their probabilities.

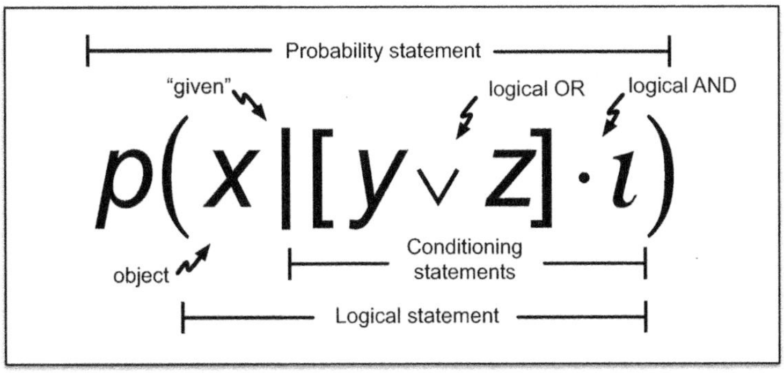

Figure 1.2 Written format for probability statements. In words, this expression represents the probability of the truth of the proposition represented by x, *given* (that is, *under the assumption*) that both the general background information about the problem (which we will represent by the Greek iota, ι) *and either* the proposition y *or* z is true.

Cox showed that any **inductive**, or **plausible inference** based on uncertain information is equivalent to a series of applications of the **sum and/or product rules of probability theory**. Probability statements are written symbolically in the form shown in Figure 1.2, and the **degrees of certainty** represented by probabilities, where each probability, $p(\bullet \mid \bullet)$, is a real number assigned to the logical statement in parentheses (the $\bullet$ are simply placeholders, indicating where logical propositions will appear).
The sum and product rules of probability theory are used to combine probabilities:

$$\text{Sum Rule:} \quad p(A \vee \bar{A} \mid \iota) = p(A \mid \iota) + p(\bar{A} \mid \iota) = 1 \tag{1.1}$$

$$\text{Product Rule:} \quad \begin{aligned} p(A \cdot B \mid \iota) &= p(A \mid \iota)p(B \mid A \cdot \iota) \\ &= p(B \mid \iota)p(A \mid B \cdot \iota) \end{aligned} \tag{1.2}$$

In this framework, complete certainty of truth (e.g., truth of the proposition x in Fig. 1.2) is represented by setting the value of the probability statement to $p(\bullet \mid \bullet) = 1$. Complete disbelief of the truth of the object is represented by $p(\bullet \mid \bullet) = 0$. The proposition preceding the vertical bar will be referred to as the **object** of the probability statement, and the statement(s) following the vertical bar are **conditioning statements.** The numerical probability value indicates the degree of certainty one can reasonably attribute to the object logical statement. Therefore, probabilities indicate how much evidence there is for asserting the truth of the proposition that is the object of the probability statement; they give the 'weight of evidence' available in the conditioning statements for supporting the truth of the object of the probability statement (see Box 1.2).

Both the object and conditioning parts of the probability statement consist of a proposition or combination of propositions connected by logical OR[2] (written '∨') or logical AND[3] (written '·'). Propositions following the vertical bar represent a state of information under which the numerical probability assignment is justified. For example, (1.1)

[2] A proposition which is itself composed of two propositions connected by logical OR is true if either one or both of the two composing propositions is true. Thus, the proposition $D = E \vee F$ is true if either the proposition E is true or the proposition F is true, or if both are true simultaneously.

[3] A compound statement composed of two propositions connected by logical AND is true only if both of the composing propositions are simultaneously true.

can be read as: The truth of one out of a pair of mutually exclusive and exhaustive possibilities (given background knowledge $\imath$) is guaranteed. Notice that all of the probabilities listed above are conditional on (at least) the background information represented by the proposition $\imath$. For example, in (1.1) this information would include statements indicating that the proposition A can be either true or false, as well as the conditions necessary to give a numerical value to the two individual statements, $p(A \mid \imath)$ and $p(\bar{A} \mid \imath)$. It is true in general that a probability statement lacking **conditioning statements** is not technically a meaningful expression, because the state of information justifying a particular numerical assignment has not been given. For example, writing $p(h)$ for the probability that a flipped coin will come up heads is indeterminate because as written it could be assigned a probability 0, ½, 1, or any intermediate value, depending on whether none, one, or both of the coin's faces is known to be stamped with a head, our information about the distribution of mass within the coin, and in what manner the coin is to be flipped. In other words, the statement $p(h)$ fails to include the background information necessary to assign a unique probability.

Exercises

1) Write the following in words:
   a. $p(A \vee \bar{A} \vee B \mid C \cdot \imath) = x$
   b. $p([A \vee B] \cdot C \mid \imath) = y$
   c. $p(A \cdot \bar{A} \cdot B \mid \imath) = z$
   d. $p(A \cdot B \mid \imath) = p(A \mid \imath)p(B \mid A \cdot \imath)$
   e. $p(A \cdot B \mid \imath) = p(B \mid \imath)p(A \mid B \cdot \imath)$
2) What is the numerical value of x in 1a?
3) What is the numerical value of z in 1c?
4) The probability of the proposition B (given $\imath$) is said to be independent of the proposition A if $p(A \cdot B \mid \imath) = p(A \mid \imath)p(B \mid \imath)$. Explain why equation (1.2) above could not (as a general rule) have been: $p(A \cdot B \mid \imath) = p(A \mid \imath)p(B \mid \imath)$.

Example: Deduction and Plausible Inference

How does probability-theory-based inference relate to the deductive forms?[4] Could one, for example, create a theory of plausible inference in which induction is a type of deduction? This would seem desirable, since it is generally agreed that deduction is *the* paradigm method of logical inference. Not only is the answer 'no,' but it turns out that the situation is reversed: deduction is contained in the rules of probability theory as a special case. First, consider the probability $p(B \mid A \cdot \imath)$, from the product rule:

$$p(B \mid A \cdot \imath) = \frac{p(A \cdot B \mid \imath)}{p(A \mid \imath)} \tag{1.3}$$

where we define the proposition $\imath$ to include the logical implication $A \Rightarrow B$, and will also assert $p(A \mid \imath)$. Under these assumptions, the probability of the **conjunction** of A and B is always 1 when the probability of A alone is 1. Thus, the ratio $\frac{p(A \cdot B \mid \imath)}{p(A \mid \imath)}$ in (1.3), and therefore $p(B \mid A \cdot \imath)$ must also be 1 in this case. This is the *modus ponens* argument – simultaneously asserting A and $\imath$ guarantees the truth of B.

[4] This example is adapted from Jaynes (2003).

BOX 1.3 A Brief History of the Development of Probability Theory

There were several mathematicians who made important initial headway in developing the theory, including Pascal, Fermat, and Bernoulli. However, the theory was developed to nearly its modern form by Pierre Laplace, who used it extensively to analyze scientific data. The problem that spurred the initial development of modern probability theory was a gambling question posed to Pascal by the Chevalier de Méré called the problem of points. The game involves two players who alternate throwing two dice. A point is awarded for each throw in which a six appears. Each player contributes an equal stake, and the first player who scores a predetermined number of points wins the combined pot. The question posed to Pascal was to determine the most equitable division of the pot when the game is interrupted and neither player has yet won. One possible solution to this problem was to divide the pot based on the proportion of points currently won by each player. Thus, if both players had won 3 points in a game to 10, each would have won 3/6 of the total points awarded, and each would be given half the pot. A problem with this solution can be seen if only one point has been awarded before the game is interrupted. In this scenario, the player to whom 1/1 points were awarded would be given the entire pot. This is clearly unfair, given that the game could have easily unfolded in a way that would have favored either player by its conclusion. Indeed, this insight leads one quickly to Pascal and Fermat's solution, based on the probability that each player would earn the points necessary to win. Thus, in a game where one participant had been awarded one and the other zero points, partial winnings are determined by the agreed-upon length of the game. If the game had been to a total of two points, then there are twice as many ways the game could have unfolded that would have favored the first player. However, if the game had been to a total of 1000 points, winning the first point changes your eventual probability of winning by nearly zero, and division of the pot would be nearly equal. Pascal and Fermat expressed their solution in terms of the expected winnings of each player, a concept we examine in Chapter 4. The concept of expectation was taken up and developed by the mathematician and physicist Christiaan Huygens in his *De Ratiociniis in Ludo Aleae* (On Reasoning in Games and Chance) in 1657, and also by James Bernoulli (1654–1705) in his *Ars Conjectandi* (published eight years after his death). The latter is most notable for the development of the Bernoulli theorem, now called the law of large numbers. Finally, Pierre Simon Laplace (1749–1827) published his *Théorie analytique des probabilités* in 1812. In it, Laplace describes the two fundamental rules of probability theory, the sum and product rules, as well as providing a clear definition of the concept of probability itself, along with extensive explanations and examples. Development was stalled following Laplace's death (much of the nineteenth and twentieth centuries) as the frequentist approach became the dominant force in academic statistics departments worldwide. Indeed, modern developments, including a deeper understanding of the foundations of probability theory and advancements in our understanding of prior probability distributions, had to wait for the work of physicists and econometricians, notably Harold Jeffries (1891–1989), Richard Cox (1898–1991), Arnold Zellner (1927–2010), and Edwin Jaynes (1922–1998). Jaynes, in particular, reignited interest in the foundations of probability theory with his work, including a landmark textbook (Jaynes, 2004) and a pair of publications appearing in the *Physical Review* in 1957, in which he posits a relationship between entropy, probability, and thermodynamics.

Also, consider the combination of the product rule, written

$$p(A \mid \bar{B} \cdot \imath) = \frac{p(A \cdot \bar{B} \mid \imath)}{p(\bar{B} \mid \imath)}$$

and (from the sum rule[5]),

$$p(A \mid \bar{B} \cdot \imath) + p(\bar{A} \mid \bar{B} \cdot \imath) = 1$$

Producing

$$p(\bar{A} \mid \bar{B} \cdot \imath) = 1 - \frac{p(A \cdot \bar{B} \mid t}{p(\bar{B} \mid \imath)} \tag{1.4}$$

Our assumption of the truth of the logical implication defined by t and the assertion $p(\bar{B} \mid \imath) = 1$, means that it is impossible for $\bar{B}$ and A to be simultaneously true. That is, the term in the numerator of (1.4) is $p(A \cdot \bar{B} \mid \imath) = 0$. From this we conclude $p(\bar{A} \mid \bar{B} \cdot \imath) = 1$, which is the *modus tollens* argument – asserting $\bar{B}$ and $\imath$ simultaneously requires that we also assert truth of $\bar{A}$.

Cox was the first[6] to clearly provide the missing mathematical basis, the so-called first principles, justifying the rules of probability theory (see Box 1.3) initially outlined by Pascal and Fermat (in a series of letters exchanged primarily in 1654), as well as Bernoulli (in his *Ars Conjectandi*, 1713), and nearly fully developed in its modern form by Laplace in his *Théorie des probabilités* (1812) and *A Philosophical Essay on Probabilities* (1825). Ultimately, Cox demonstrated that any system of inference which cannot be reduced to the sum and product rules (i.e., identical to probability theory) must eventually exhibit some inconsistency. We have provided an important demonstration of this above by showing that deduction is simply a special case of the product and sum rules of probability theory (where background information is of a particular type). In addition we have shown that of the two forms of reasoning, deductive reasoning is vastly more restricted in its scope than plausible reasoning. Why 'more restricted'? Exactly because it is a special case. The equations (1.3) and (1.4) are identical with deduction only when 'certain implication' is assumed (contained in the background information, t), and it is only when we can define a certain implication that deduction can be used for data analysis.

[5] In (1.1) it is stated that the probability of two mutually exclusive and exhaustive possibilities is given by $p(A \vee \bar{A} \mid \imath) = 1$. An important implication of (1.1) is a logical consequence of the mutual exclusivity of the two propositions, A and $\bar{A}$. If we know that $p(A \mid \imath) = x$, then conversely $p(\bar{A} \mid \imath) = 1 - x$: The proportion of the total probability referring to A cannot also refer to $\bar{A}$, and therefore the two probabilities must sum to the total. More compactly, $p(A \vee \bar{A} \mid \imath) = 1$ implies $p(A \mid \imath) + P(\bar{A} \mid \imath) = 1$.

[6] More recently, Zellner (1986) has provided a proof that the mathematical rules of probability theory can be derived from considerations of optimal information processing. He proved that any system of inference that is not identical to probability theory either adds information that is not properly part of the problem, ignores relevant information, or both.

Exercises

1) Which equation above describes the *modus tollens* deductive argument? What happens to the output of this equation if all of the inputs are not 0 or 1?
2) Which equation above describes the *modus ponens* deductive argument? What happens to the output of this equation if all of the inputs are not 0 or 1?
3) What can be concluded deductively in the Holmes example if there are only three coins (only the first three described), and seven flips yield: *TTTTTTT*?

1.1.3 Uncertainty

A typical introduction to probability theory will make liberal use of the terms 'random' and 'randomness' (as in 'random event,' 'random variable,' and even 'random experiment'). By definition, these terms indicate that the event, variable, etc. has no cause that could reproduce it. Although the distinction may appear one of semantics, we will instead prefer to be concerned with 'uncertainty,' which is a measure of our own ignorance. That is, a statement of uncertainty is a statement about available information, and the *degree* of uncertainty indicates the *strength* of the available information.

Example: The Die Is Cast

A probability distribution provides a numerical representation of our uncertainty about the object of a probability statement (Fig. 1.2), such as the uncertainty regarding the outcome of the roll of a die. The outcome of a die roll is an event that has well-known causes. In the usual situation, we are ignorant of the relevant physical parameters (the die's orientation and thrown height at the time of the roll, forces acting on it and the material properties of the die and surface, etc.). It turns out, however, that even when these physical parameters are unknown, we are not helpless to predict aspects of its behavior, based on partial information about dice and die-rollers.

A Deductive Case

First imagine knowing that a die is stamped with a single dot on all six sides. If we define d_n the proposition that there will be n dots on the upward-facing die face, then we feel certain d_1 is true [i.e., $p(d_1 \mid \iota) = 1$] because our background information says this is the only possible outcome. Although simple, notice that this example demonstrates how reliable predictions may be possible even without knowing all the parameters describing the physical system.

One or Two Dots

Consider next a case where each of the six die faces is stamped with either one or two dots. In this example, we will assume that all faces are stamped with either one or two dots. Let's consider two levels of information about the die that lead to different predictions. At the first level, we are only told that the die faces will either be stamped with one or two dots, but not how many faces will be stamped with each. In this case, what can we infer regarding the outcome of a die-roll? The logic here is based on symmetry: Our information about the outcome of any die-roll is symmetrical, because all we know is that two outcomes are possible. This should not allow us to prefer to predict either of the outcomes over the other. If we add information about the number of one- and two-dot sides, this might provide the information needed to predict one over the other outcome. If we were told that half of the sides are stamped with one and half with two dots, this would be another form of symmetrical information and we would still have no reason to prefer predicting one over the other outcome [i.e., $p(d_1 \mid \imath) = p(d_2 \mid \imath) = 0.5$]. However, if we are told that *more* sides are stamped with one dot than two, we should now prefer to predict one dot. Furthermore, if we are told that only one side is stamped with two dots, then we should strongly prefer one dot: $p(d_1 \mid \imath) = 5/6$, $p(d_2 \mid \imath) = 1/6$, because we now have reason to believe that there are more opportunities for one versus two dots (five of six faces), but no reason to believe that any particular face will land upward more often than the others (and therefore, again because of symmetry, must treat them equally). Thus, if each face is to be treated equally but there are five of six stamped with one dot, then the 5/6 and 1/6 probability assignments are demanded by our background information. Notice that in none of these examples did the physics of the die-roll enter our calculations; our calculations were, in fact, based on *not knowing* anything about the physics of the die-roll. If were were additionally informed that the die were being thrown by an extremely precise robotic hand, and that this hand could always cause the two-dot side to face up, we would again change our probability assignment to: $p(d_1 \mid \imath) = 0$, $p(d_2 \mid \imath) = 1$.

Notice that the situations above were described in terms such as 'we are told that all but one of the six faces is stamped with two dots.' These descriptions were used to emphasize the fact that our probability assignments are based simply on a state of information;[7] this state of information may or may not eventually be shown to map directly onto the state of the world. Indeed, it may be the case that although we were *told* the die was stamped with two dots on a single face, it may have actually had one face stamped with one dot, and the remainder stamped with two. The correct probability assignment in this situation is still $p(d_1 \mid \imath) = 5/6$ and $p(d_2 \mid \imath) = 1/6$, even if *in reality* some other configuration of dots was stamped on the die. Our probability assignment *always* represents our information, because we can only assign probabilities based on the information available to us. Of course as scientists it is up to us to bring our information into register with the facts of the physical world through observation and experiment.

The Essence of Hypothesis Testing

If our probability assignments only reflect our information and not the physical world, then you will surely ask: what use are they for describing the world? The short answer is that we will attempt to put our information into register with the physical world by collecting data. The long answer brings us to the idea of scientific hypothesis testing (see Box 1.5). Statements such as 'we are told that n faces are stamped with one dot' could easily be replaced with 'we *hypothesize* that n faces are stamped with one dot.' Hypotheses lead us to make *predictions* about what we might observe in an experiment involving the die (e.g., the average number of dots that will appear in many rolls of the die). For example, if we hypothesize that all faces are stamped with a single dot, we predict that the average number of dots shown over many rolls of the

[7] That is, there was no mention of frequencies, or a hypothetical infinite series of die-throws. These types of thought experiment are simply unnecessary for an understanding of the concept of probability, or its practical application (see Box 1.4).

die will be 1. Compare the hypothesis that half the faces are stamped with one and half with two dots, where we predict that the average number of faces showing over many rolls would be about 1.5. We can compare another hypothesis that only a single face is stamped with two dots, where we predict that the average number of dots shown over many rolls will be about 7/6. Comparing these predictions, we notice that observing even a single instance of two dots deductively eliminates the first hypothesis (this corresponds with the first step of the scientific process described in Box 1.1). Comparing the remaining hypothesis, if the observed die-rolls more closely match one prediction over the other, that gives us more confidence in the underlying hypothesis, where a closer match corresponds to a greater increase in confidence. Conversely, consistent deviations between the predicted values of experimental variables (here, the average number of dots per roll) and the experimentally observed values of those variables alert us to deficiencies in our hypotheses. This process of hypothesis-prediction-experiment-compare-update is the essence of the scientific process (revisited in Fig. 1.3).

Exercises

1) If your are told that the probabilities of observing faces 1–6 are $p = [0.15, 0.25, 0.1, 0.2, 0.1, 0.2]$, respectively, what is the probability of:
   a. the die landing with its second face upward?
   b. either the third or fifth face landing up?
   c. both the first and third face landing up?
2) What is the probability of observing two dots when you are told that faces 1–6 are stamped with the following numbers of dots (respectively)?
   a. $d_n = [1, 2, 1, 2, 1, 2]$
   b. $d_n = [1, 1, 1, 2, 2, 2]$
   c. $d_n = [1, 2, 2, 2, 2, 2]$
   d. $d_n = [2, 2, 2, 1, 1, 2]$
3) If you are told that the probabilities of observing faces 1–6 are $p = [.25, .15, .1, .1, .1, .15, .25]$, (respectively), what is the probability of observing a single dot when you are also told that faces 1–6 are stamped with the following numbers of dots (respectively)?
   a. $d_n = [1, 2, 1, 2, 1, 2]$
   b. $d_n = [1, 1, 1, 2, 2, 2]$
   c. $d_n = [1, 2, 2, 2, 2, 2]$
   d. $d_n = [2, 2, 2, 1, 1, 2]$
4) How many dots per roll would you expect to observe in many rolls of the die when all that is known about the die is that:
   a. Five of the faces have two dots and one has one dot?
   b. Four faces have one dot and two have two dots?
   c. The probabilities of faces 1–6 are $p = [0.25, 0.15, 0.1, 0.1, 0.1, 0.15, 0.25]$, respectively, and the first two faces have one dot while the remaining faces have one.
   d. The probabilities of faces 1–6 are $p = [0.15, 0.25, 0.1, 0.2, 0.1, 0.2]$, respectively, and the first five faces have two dots while the final face has one.

5) Describe the logic of your probability assignment in the following situation: You are told that the robot hand is rolling the die with all but one face showing a single dot, but you do not know which face the hand is programmed to yield.

1.1.4 The Logic of Data Analysis

Now that we have examined the idea of probability, inference, and hypothesis testing generally, we can proceed to the heart of the data-analytic enterprise – the series of steps (i.e., the **algorithm**) used to make measurements and to test hypotheses. Our goal is to assign the following set of probabilities: $p(\boldsymbol{h} \mid \boldsymbol{d} \cdot \iota) = p([h_1, h_2, \ldots, h_n] \mid \boldsymbol{d} \cdot \iota)$. This set of probabilities (one each for n hypotheses), is called the **probability distribution** over $\boldsymbol{h}$, and is assigned based having observed the dataset $\boldsymbol{d}$. To select from among competing hypotheses (e.g., the number of one- versus two-dot faces on a die), we must compare the probabilities associated with each hypothesis, allowing us to make a decision about which hypothesis to consider most plausible, and which hypotheses we may either consider less plausible or even cease to think of as reasonable at all (see Box 1.6 for an alternative view based on the frequentist definition of probability).

Hypothesis testing is a straightforward application of the two basic rules of probability theory, the sum and product rules (equations 1.1 and 1.2 above). The basic algorithm is as follows:

1. A set of two or more competing hypotheses is defined.

The hypotheses of interest ($\boldsymbol{h}$) will either represent values of a parameter (e.g., a physical constant or other variable describing a system), or a set of models representing hypotheses about the internal structure of a system (see Box 1.1). In the first case we are interested in solving a measurement (or parameter estimation) problem, and in the second we are answering a model selection question. Note that the bold letter indicates that $\boldsymbol{h}$ contains not one, but rather several propositions, indexed from 1 to H (i.e., $\boldsymbol{h} = [h_1\ h_2\ \cdots\ h_H]$), and therefore H associated probabilities upon which to base our parameter estimate or model comparison.

What kinds of propositions are these? First, let's consider a measurement problem from physics: At what rate does a dropped stone fall to Earth? To measure the acceleration due to gravity, we would obtain observations of distances traveled by the stone in 1, 2, 3 etc. seconds. Our calculation would yield a single number: $g = 9.81\ \text{m/s}^2$. Notice that we already have a model of the phenomenon, namely, that the stone undergoes constant acceleration, and our goal is to measure a parameter of that model. But how do we choose among models? What if we wanted to compare a model in which all stones at the Earth's surface fall at the same acceleration (i.e., Newtonian universal gravitation) and one in which more massive stones fall at higher acceleration? This model selection problem is agnostic regarding parameter values; rather, we want to compare the *patterns* predicted by the two models against experimental data (equal vs. increasing accelerations for increasing stone masses), regardless of what the exact values of the measured accelerations happen to be.

2. The probabilities of the hypotheses, conditional on one's current state of knowledge (e.g., past and current experimental data), are assigned and compared.

How do we assign probabilities to hypotheses? We recognize that in this situation, our information will consist of the hypotheses we have defined (the list of H hypotheses,

BOX 1.4 Frequency, Probability, and the Many Flavors of Bayesianism

We have defined probabilities in the most general sense of encoding information. This takes us out of the realm of 'Frequentist' statistics, where probabilities can only be defined as frequencies (aka, the rate of heads in coin-tossing). For the Frequentist, it makes no sense to say things like 'there is a 50 percent chance of rain tomorrow' or 'there is a 10 percent chance that this hypothesis is false,' because the first statement cannot be reduced to a count of instances when it rains versus doesn't rain tomorrow and the second statement cannot be reduced to a count of instances when the hypothesis is true versus false. Contemporary statistical thought has rejected the Frequentist paradigm in part because this definition of probability is unnecessarily limiting: there is no way to directly assess our hypotheses and models by assigning them probabilities.

Within the Bayesian paradigm, there are multiple 'flavors' that differ in what is considered most important to compute (e.g., various alternatives to model comparison), and also with how probabilities are assigned. The main three branches seem to be the 'objective,' 'subjective,' and what I will call the 'classical mixture' branches. The objective school will attempt to assign initial probabilities based on whatever small amounts of information may be available using consistent rules (such as Jeffreys' rule, or the principle of maximum entropy, to be discussed later). The subjective school will (within some variants, but not all) allow human experts to assign initial probabilities based on their subjective sense of the available information (e.g., book-making for the result of a game between little-known teams). The classical mixture school of thought finds value in both classical ('frequentist') statistical methods and Bayesian methods. This is often seen in an applied machine learning setting, where one is more interested in finding methods that seem most useful regardless of the theoretical school that produced them.

Here, we favor the objective approach over the subjective on the grounds that it fulfills a basic requirement of the scientific method, that results from one laboratory should be reproducible at another laboratory; this would not be the case if probabilities were assigned subjectively. We favor the Bayesian approach over the frequentist approach on theoretical grounds, because the frequentist approach leads to null-hypothesis testing, which is an approach that is well known to be logically flawed (Box 1.6). This latter is partially based on the belief that, even when the frequentist approach yields practically useful results, development of a more logically sound (Bayesian) approach will ultimately produce superior results.

We will pursue the objective Bayesian approach here, with a focus on developing its two most straightforward applications: parameter estimation and model selection. However, there are many further applications and alternative viewpoints on best procedures that are held, and yet to be developed. Therefore, part of your goal in learning this material should be to make your own choices regarding what is ultimately the best approach to analyzing data in any given situation.

$\boldsymbol{h} = [h_1\ h_2\ \cdots\ h_H]$), and the data we obtain experimentally (the list of n numbers, $\boldsymbol{d} = [d_1\ d_2\ \cdots\ d_n]$). The trick is to write their *joint* probability using (1.2):

$$\begin{aligned} p(\boldsymbol{h} \cdot \boldsymbol{d} \mid \iota) &= p(\boldsymbol{h} \mid \boldsymbol{d} \cdot \iota)p(\boldsymbol{d} \mid \iota) \\ &= p(\boldsymbol{d} \mid \boldsymbol{h} \cdot \iota)p(h \mid \iota) \end{aligned}$$

therefore,

$$p(\boldsymbol{h} \mid \boldsymbol{d} \cdot \iota) = \frac{p(\boldsymbol{h} \mid \iota)p(\boldsymbol{d} \mid \boldsymbol{h} \cdot \iota)}{p(d \mid \iota)} = \frac{\varpi(\boldsymbol{h})\mathcal{L}(\boldsymbol{h})}{\mathcal{L}(\iota)} \tag{1.5}$$

This general logic will dictate two basic procedures, one for comparing scientific models or theories, and one for measuring model parameters. When measuring model parameters the list $\boldsymbol{h}$ describes the possible values of the parameter, whereas when comparing models $\boldsymbol{h}$ is a list of models being compared. Model selection will usually be performed prior to making measurements: the measurement procedure is used to estimate some parameter(s) of a single model, whereas model selection is used to compare multiple models.

Outline of the Logic

Equation (1.5) is generally called Bayes' theorem, and is one consequence of the product rule of probability theory. The answer to the inference question in a probabilistic analysis is contained in the final left-hand term of (1.5), called the **posterior probability**, or simply the posterior, $p(\boldsymbol{h} \mid \boldsymbol{d} \cdot \iota)$. There are three probabilities that compose the posterior, and each is named: The first, $p(\boldsymbol{h} \mid \iota)$ [which we will write $\varpi(\boldsymbol{h})$ using the Greek pi[8]], called the **prior probability** or simply the **prior**, is the probability assigned to each of the hypotheses in the vector $\boldsymbol{h}$, and represents the plausibility of each hypothesis before taking the current data into account. Prior probabilities can be assigned based on our general background information and any previous experimental data pertinent to that hypothesis. Methods for assigning priors are introduced in Chapter 3. The second term, $p(\boldsymbol{d} \mid h \cdot \iota)$, called the **likelihood** [written $\mathcal{L}(\boldsymbol{h})$], gives the probability of the dataset under the hypotheses in $\boldsymbol{h}$. The final term, $p(\boldsymbol{d} \mid \iota)$, is the **global likelihood**, or **model likelihood** and gives the probability of the data under the current background information ι, independent of which $\boldsymbol{h}$ is correct. The global likelihood acts as a **normalization constant**, forcing the sum of probabilities in the posterior to 1; that is, the set of posterior probabilities forms a **normalized distribution of probabilities** over the set of hypotheses.[9]

Calculation of the posterior concludes the inferential portion of the data-analytic algorithm. The distribution of posterior probabilities over the set of hypotheses lets one answer the inference question, always of the form: What probabilities should be assigned to the hypotheses, given my current state of knowledge? There is often also a decision stage at the end of the algorithm, where one must decide which of the candidate

[8] Notice that I attempt to avoid confusion by using the alternate form, ϖ, of the Greek 'pi' to refer to the *prior* probability distribution. I have often instead seen the symbol π used in this capacity, even though this is universally also used to refer to the ratio of a circle's circumference to its diameter: a quantity used generally in scientific contexts, including this text.

[9] As a technical point that will be better understood later, we are assuming that the set of hypotheses under consideration is exhaustive, because if there were additional reasonable hypotheses available, they should be added to the list of 'hypotheses under consideration.' Therefore, both the set of prior and posterior probabilities (each of which is a probability distribution over hypotheses) must sum to one.

BOX 1.5 What Is the Difference between Estimation and Hypothesis Testing?

Figure 1.1 describes the anatomy of a scientific model, including the parameters that define the elements of a model. The first use of probability theory we will develop in this text is parameter estimation, or measurement, where we will learn to make the best estimates of parameters. The second way we will employ probability theory in data analysis is to use experimental data to choose among competing theories, what we will refer to as model selection.

This second use of probability theory requires that we have defined multiple models, and compare the predictions of these multiple models against observed data. When we perform model selection, our primary interest is not in measuring the values of any of the models' parameters. Instead, we are interested in assessing the fitness of the models themselves in explaining data. Parameter estimation, on the other hand, is primarily interested only in measuring the values of parameters. Here, however, the model whose parameters we are estimating is generally accepted as true – this is the reason we are interested in measuring parameters. The specific values of model parameters are usually only interesting when the values tell us about a model that we believe is true.

The short answer to the question, 'What is the difference between estimation and hypothesis testing?' is that hypothesis tests are used to select among several competing models, and parameter estimation is used to determine best estimates of the parameters of a single specific model. There is a common mistake, however, in which the parameter estimation procedure is erroneously used for model selection. As we will see in Chapter 6 when we study hypothesis testing in greater detail, there are many experimental scenarios designed to differentiate between two models whose only difference is that one model assumes that a parameter value is zero (let's call it $\alpha = 0$), whereas another model predicts that the same parameter has a nonzero value (i.e., $\alpha \neq 0$). In such circumstances, it is often reasoned that we can provide evidence in favor of the second model by estimating that value of the parameter in question: If it is nonzero, we can reject the $\alpha = 0$ hypothesis. It is through this sleight of hand that 'a hypothesis test is converted into a parameter estimation problem.' We can see the error in this line of reasoning by recognizing that we measure the value of the parameter by first computing the probability of observing the experimental data (the likelihood of the parameter taking any given value), $p(\mathbf{d} \mid \alpha \cdot \iota)$. Simply writing this expression tells us the problem, because the likelihood statement that must be used to estimate the value of α is ***incompatible with both hypotheses***. This statement allows α to take any value, and neither hypothesis allows this. Under the first hypothesis, the value of α must be zero, and under the second hypothesis the parameter can take any value except zero. Parameter estimation and model selection are distinct procedures, and shouldn't be conflated.

hypotheses is worth further consideration and experimental investigation. This requires that some decision rule be adopted, by which hypotheses with substantially greater probability than the competitors are provisionally accepted as being most likely. Notice also what this algorithm does not do. It does not label hypotheses as true or false, but rather

BOX 1.6 Null-Hypothesis Testing Algorithm

Rejecting the original Laplace–Bernoulli definition of probability had wide-ranging consequences for how experimental data could be analyzed and hypotheses tested. Denied the ability to use probability theory in its most general form, and therefore also the ability to calculate the probabilities of hypotheses, a more circuitous method was devised. The frequentist algorithm is modeled on the *modus tollens* form of deductive logic, which in modern mathematics is called 'proof by contradiction,' and has the following form: One defines the 'null' hypothesis, H_0. One assumes H_0 to be true, and generates *deductive* arguments based on H_0 that lead to testable predictions. If deductive inference from H_0 leads to anything untrue, it can be concluded that the null hypothesis cannot be true.

On its face, this is certainly a reasonable way to proceed. It basically states that if what you observe experimentally is incompatible with your theoretical prediction, the hypothesis on which that theoretical prediction was made must be incorrect (we will refer to the frequentist algorithm as a 'null-hypothesis' testing algorithm because it is designed to reject H_0). Indeed, when it is possible to deductively reject hypotheses via the modus *tollens* argument, we will happily do so. But if we approve of the *modus tollens* argument, what is the problem with the statistical argument?

The problem is that, in practice, null-hypothesis testing deviates from the correct form of the *modus tollens* argument. The experimental result need not actually be an *impossible* consequence of H_0 to be rejected. In fact, the observed experimental result is predicted by the null hypothesis, but H_0 is rejected when the experimentally observed dataset is more extreme than a criterion; that is, it is determined to be a 'low-frequency' result. So instead of rejecting hypotheses based on having observed a dataset that would have been *impossible* under H_0, the statistical algorithm is left to reject hypotheses when the observed data (along with unobserved datasets less likely than the observed dataset) are merely less likely than some cutoff value (criterion).

Finally we must point out that the null hypothesis is not generally the hypothesis of true scientific interest. So the null-hypothesis test never defines the hypothesis of actual interest – the specific alternative to H_0 that we believe is correct. The Bayesian test, by comparison, selects among competing hypotheses by directly comparing their probabilities (which are assigned based on experimental data in the way defined in the main text). The statistical algorithm defines only a single hypothesis (H_0) and attempts to reject it by noting whether the experimental dataset is relatively more or less commonly expected than a preset criterion; thus it requires computations based on assuming H_0 but never compares it to the result of computations based on any alternative hypothesis (i.e., there is no comparison of hypotheses). The 'logic' of the null-hypothesis test leads to well-known paradoxes of scientific inference, including the 'optional stopping problem,'[10] which we examine in detail in Chapter 2.

[10] *Optional stopping* refers to the practice of performing a preliminary analysis of the data partway through data collection to determine whether it is worth continuing with the experiment and collecting the full dataset.

as more or less likely, given our current state of knowledge. As stated above, probabilities are a measure of the reasonable degree of certainty one can ascribe to a proposition (each individual hypothesis, $\boldsymbol{h}_i$) based on one's current state of knowledge. Notice the final caveat: current state of knowledge. One would not fault the weatherman for changing his prediction for snow if new information became available, and similarly the scientist should not be faulted for changing his assessments of hypotheses if new or better information becomes available. Rather, we must be held to a basic requirement of rationality: that the information available can lead to only one set of inferences, only one set of probabilities. If the available information changes, probabilities can and should be updated. In fact, it is often pointed out that (1.5) is a formula for updating our information (regarding the hypotheses, $\boldsymbol{h}$) based on experimental data. Put another way, what you know about the set of hypotheses $\boldsymbol{h}$ after obtaining data is a combination of what you knew about them before the current experiment (the prior), what the experiment tells you (the likelihood) and a normalization term (global likelihood).

The overview of the data-analytic enterprise given above should serve as a framework from which we can begin to build a better understanding of the role of probability theory in data analysis. In what follows we will expand our understanding of probability in general, and of the roles and characteristics of the prior, likelihood, and posterior distributions. Once we have gained a deeper understanding of these elements, we will revisit the general data analytic structure outlined above and define two elaborated data processing algorithms: the ***measurement algorithm*** and the ***model selection algorithm***. These will be the focus of Chapters 5 and 6, and will be used to solve a series of the core measurement and model selection problems encountered in behavioral research.

Exercises

1) You are given two coins, and told that they have the following rates of showing heads: $r_1 = .15$ and $r_2 = .55$, respectively. You choose one of the coins and flip it 10 times; it shows heads 3 times.
   a. Without doing any calculations, which coin are you more likely to have chosen?
   b. Explain your answer to (a).
2) Based on the two-coin scenario above, and the likelihood function $p(S \mid N \cdot r \cdot \iota) = \frac{N}{S!(N-S)!} r^S (1-r)^{N-S}$, which describes the probability of observing S heads in N tosses when the underlying rate of heads is r, what is the probability:
   a. of observing the 10-flip experimental data if the first coin had been used?
   b. of observing the 10-flip experimental data if the second coin had been used?
3) Based on the two-coin scenario above, and the following prior probabilities, compute the posterior probability of having flipped the first second coin:
   a. $\varpi_1 = 0.95$, $\varpi_2 = 0.05$
   b. $\varpi_1 = 0.8$
   c. $\varpi_1 = 0.3$
   d. $\varpi_1 = 0.1$
4) In the two-coin scenario, the prior probability is most accurately described as $\varpi = 0.5$ for both coins.
   a. Compute the posterior probability for the two coins based on this prior.
   b. Explain why the prior should be 0.5 for the two coins?

5) Compute the mean and variance statistics of the following datasets:
   a. $d = [5, 6, 7, 8, 9, 10, 11, 12, 13, 14, 15]$.
   b. $d = [1, 3, 5, 7, 9, 11, 13, 15, 17, 19]$.
   c. $d = [8, 9, 10, 11, 12]$.

1.2 Data Visualization

We have spent a good deal of time discussing hypothesis testing, and this is appropriate since it lies at the heart of the scientific enterprise. However, our first task after we obtain data will *not* usually be to jump right into the process of testing hypotheses. Rather, we want first to become familiar with our dataset, plotting it in (at least) the obvious ways we have at our disposal. This initial familiarization procedure is dual purpose: First, we want to be certain we understand the basic character of the dataset, to properly inform our formal data analysis. In addition, by taking the time to get familiar with a dataset, we may avoid many mistakes – either because we have inadvertently introduced an error while transforming data (e.g., erroneously dividing by 10 to convert between meters and millimeters), or because the raw data may display certain awkward qualities that can

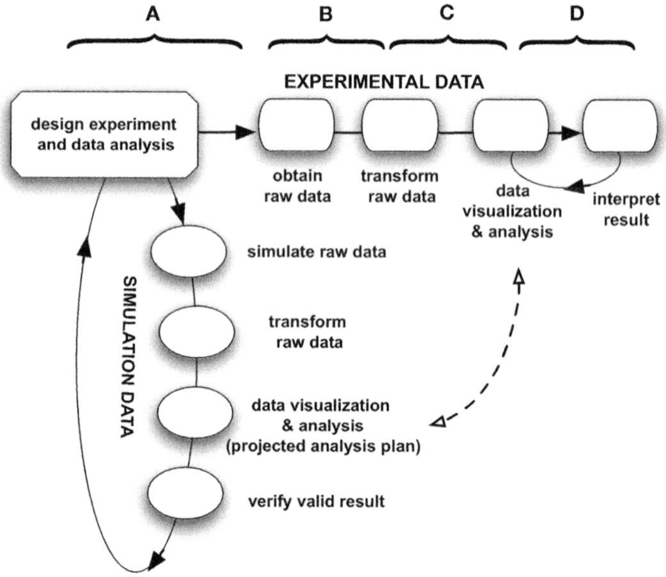

Figure 1.3 Analysis steps and recursions. When designing new research and associated analyses, there are several steps that one generally follows. The experimental design is first finalized, and a preliminary data analysis plan is worked out. Ideally, this plan serves first as the starting point for a simulation study of the expected experimental data. This simulation study will allow you to generate the appropriate code for the final analysis of (real) experimental data and to sharpen the final analysis itself, by verifying that the experimental data are capable of answering the scientific questions of interest (final step in simulation flow). If it is not, the experimental design should be updated and a new analysis plan devised. Following a successful simulation study, the experimental data are collected. Here, again, there is the opportunity to refine your analysis, as you discover the pecularities of real data. Note that consistent differences between the behavior of real and simulated data may provide insight into the underlying character of the data-generating process (i.e., the underlying behavioral, chemical, or biological process).

BOX 1.7 The Importance of Description and Visualization

In Figure 1.3 we describe the process of analyzing experiments in terms of a co-mingling of both informal description and visualization on the one hand, and formal analysis procedures on the other. At one level, we can identify inference procedures with our formal analyses based on (1.5) and descriptive procedures based on plot visualizations and computing descriptive statistics (mean, correlation, etc.). However, there is an important theoretical distinction between the two. Descriptive techniques produce exactly that: descriptions of your *dataset*. They do not provide direct information regarding the purpose of your experiment: to measure the parameters of a scientific model or to test one scientific model against another. The use of visualization and description allow you to get a feel for your dataset, and compare what you find to your expectations regarding the data you are collecting. In other words, description allows you to make an informal comparison between your expectations regarding data values and patterns that you may have held going into your experiment, and the data you actually observe.

Thus, at the completion of an experiment, we should have a set of observable data that we will analyze. These data are related to the scientific hypothesis or model under consideration because they are the *output* of an internal process, where that internal process is described by our model. Notice that the model is an *unobservable*, mathematical object (Fig. 1.1), whereas our data are *observable outputs* of a neuron or neural system. In later chapters we will see that these observable data are linked to the mathematical models that describe our scientific theories through the *predictions* made by our models.

Our goal in this text will be to develop the techniques to complete a formal analysis, an analysis that will indicate the evidence available from our data in support of scientific hypotheses. These techniques are designed to compare the predictions of a model with the observed data, to tell us about the underlying parameters of the scientific model we are testing, where these parameters are *unobservable* aspects of a scientific model. Our observable data also (and most directly) tell us about the specific experiment that we conducted, and visualizations and statistical descriptions of those data are therefore most relevant as a way to see that our experiments have yielded the type of data that we had intended: that our experiment 'worked.' It is only after verifying that we have conducted our experiment in the intended manner, and have successfully manipulated experimental variables or successfully measured certain behavioral variables that we can confidently proceed to the heart of the scientific enterprise: testing scientific models through formal analysis techniques.

be addressed when their presence is known (e.g., when there are 'outliers' in the data, described below, as might be caused by imperfect experimental control). We will consider several such circumstances here.

We can conceptualize the total process of data analysis as an intermingling of the two complimentary processes of formal analysis and data visualization (see Box 1.7), as depicted in Figure 1.3. One begins this journey prior to collecting data (**A**), when the experiment is designed. Once an experiment is planned and executed (**B**), one must typically compute various transformations or other functions of the raw data: examples include (1) converting a computer monitor's pixel positions into centimeter positions relative to screen center, or (2) in a different context converting neural action potential ('spike') counts into firing rates (i.e., count/time). This step is typically co-mingled with data visualization, because it is important to verify the transformation of the raw data by plotting it. At this point (**C**), we can begin becoming familiar with the results of our experiment by plotting them (data visualization) in various ways, and also by computing summary statistics. Until we have become familiar with the data, visualization/plotting activities will at first be performed in isolation. However, as we gain confidence that the data have been acquired and transformed successfully, the formal analysis should begin (**D**). For the remainder of the analysis we will oscillate between performing formal analyses (as we will discuss in subsequent chapters) and devising visualizations of the data that illustrate important features of that formal analysis – as shown in Figure 1.3, segment D. Note that the diagram hints at additional steps involving numerical simulations that might be taken prior to executing your experiment. We will see worked examples in later chapters that involve simulated experimental data.

1.2.1 The Goal of Data Visualization

Many would say there is an 'art' to plotting a complex dataset, where the object is to produce plots that will allow us to extract unexpected insights and detect any errors that may have been made during data collection – but without becoming hypersensitive and overinterpreting every little blip and bump in the data. The art is in understanding, based on the look of the raw data and previous experience in analyzing similar datasets, which general characteristics of the data are reproducible, incidental, and 'artifact.' Indeed, a common mistake made by the novice analyst is overinterpreting the inevitable bumps in a histogram or other basic plot-type. The trick, therefore, is to go into the process of data visualization with the goal of 'getting a feel' for the data, comparing the broad strokes of the result to what we should expect to see for a dataset of the type we have observed.

There are two things to look for while comparing observed data to our expectations of that data: ***mistakes*** and ***unexpected features***. The search for these can be thought of as two stages of the initial data-visualization step of an analysis. In the first, we want to examine the data for mistakes in the collection, transcription, and transformation operations that went into producing the to-be-analyzed dataset. This consists of plotting data in all ways that will provide verification that these data have the characteristics that they *must* have, based on the experiment that produced them (e.g., that data describing human motor behavior, human perception, neural spike trains, etc. stay within the known bounds of human physiology). The second stage involves plotting the data in ways that may allow us to gain some insight concerning questions or hypotheses we may have about the data. This second-stage search for unexpected features does not constitute a formal analysis or test of hypotheses, but it can help us to get a feel for the dataset, and possibly discover features of the data that we had not anticipated. This stage involves plotting the data in ways that will allow us to see whether the data conform to what we *expect* to see, particularly for data characteristics that have been previously investigated and therefore have previously measured (published) values. If the data generally conform to both *required* and *expected* characteristics, we can confidently begin our formal analysis. If there are unexpected features of the data, we should first attempt to understand whether they have arisen due to a mistake or whether they are true features of the data before we begin our formal analysis (and, of course, either expand our analysis or perform additional experiments if we suspect the presence of interesting and previously unexpected features of the behavior under study).

1.2.2 Histograms

A histogram tells us how data values cluster, and uses the concept of **binning** (where nearby data values are put into the same 'bucket' or bin, and bin height grows by one as each new data value is placed within a bin). Binning allows us to see how often similar data values are occurring, and what the most oft-occurring data values are. By observing patterns in the way data clusters, we gain a better sense of our dataset.

To understand the content of a histogram, we must first create an example scenario that we can use to illustrate data visualization. For example, we might consider a dataset consisting of times. There are many different types of timing data, and the particular type

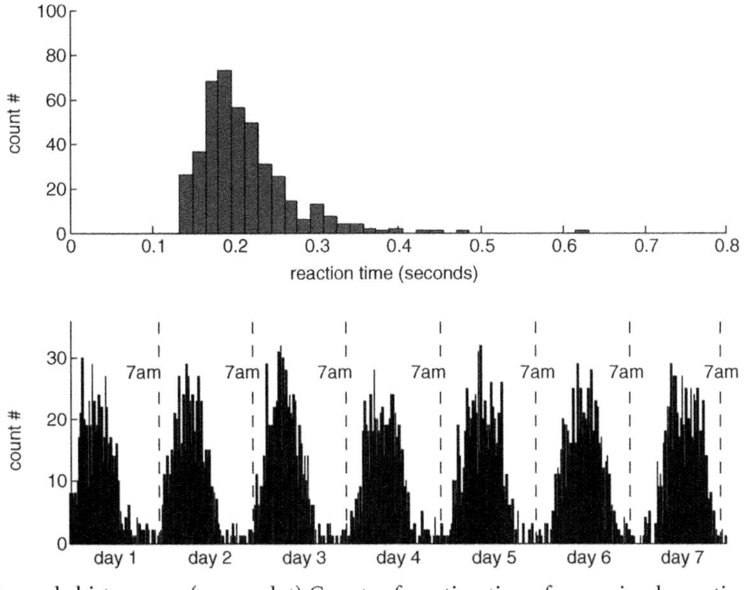

Figure 1.4 Example histograms. (upper plot) Counts of reaction times from a simple reaction time experiment (described in the main text). The height of each bin indicates the number of reaction times (of the 421 repetitions of responses to the 'go beep') that fall within the bin's time bounds on the abscissa. (lower plot) Counts of accelerometer readings that exceeded a minimum threshold, observed over the course of seven days without external day/night cues; 7 AM is indicated for each day.

Programming Aside: Histograms

We will create histograms of simulated data from both of the examples described in the main text. The first is the easiest to quantify and describe: that of a reaction time experiment. Such experiments usually have a go-signal (auditory or visual) to signal that the movement should be made as quickly as possible, and whose timing is unpredictable (when the go-signal is given, the movement – most commonly a button-press or saccadic eye movement – is initiated). The timing data of interest here is the time elapsed between the go-signal and movement. A typical dataset in this experiment will often look skewed, with more data occurring to the right (longer reaction times) of the peak than to its left. This occurs because there is a physical limit to the fastest reaction time that can occur, owing to neural transduction and transmission speeds, muscle recruitment, and the impedance of the arm or eye. The same is not true for long reaction times, because there is no analogous limiting factor on the opposite side of the timing spectrum. In addition, because reaction times are intended to be fast relative to the minimum possible time, the peak of the histogram should be near the low end of the range of observed times. One can simulate reaction-time data with the rtrnd function:

```
dt=rtrnd(500);
```

where the function's input is the desired number of simulated rt data. The output is a set of 500 (in this instance) numbers, given in seconds. We can get a sense of the distribution of simulated reaction times by plotting their histogram:

```
figure; subplot(2,1,1); hist(dt,31)
```

In the plot it is clear that the data do not occur symmetrically about the peak of the histogram, suggesting that they arise from a skewed distribution.

The second example involved sleep/wake cycles. There are several ways to obtain information about sleep/wake cycles, including simply asking when one sleeps and wakes. However, in the scenario described above it would be necessary to obtain data without asking subjects to report times. One possible alternative would be to monitor their activity levels using accelerometers placed on limbs and torso. One could simply count the number of acceleration readings above a particular threshold. These would tend to display cycles that correspond to the sleep/wake times. Analysis of these cycles would allow us to determine whether the normal cycle was disturbed when external time signals were eliminated. First, we plot the histogram:

```
[times activitycount]=getactivitytimes(7); %7 days of activity
                                           %recording
subplot(2,1,2); bar(times,activitycount,1);
axis([times(1) times(end) 0 max(activitycount)+4])
```

Note the difference in the way the two histogram plots were created. In the first, the raw dataset was a list of times, and the 'hist' command sorts through those times to place them into a set of bins. The final histogram gives the counts representing the number of time-data whose values fall into each bin. In the second case, the raw data are the number of accelerometer readings exceeding a particular threshold, where the bins are still time-bins but are now simply a time-segmentation of the seven-day period shown in the plot.

In this case the data need not be sorted, because the times simply occur along with accelerometer data, and are counted as they occur. Because these data have both times and corresponding counts, they are plotted using the 'bar' function rather than 'hist.' You can obtain more information on these commands by typing:

```
> help hist
> help bar
```

As a final note regarding the relationship between the hist and bar functions, we can ask the hist function for the set of bin-centers and counts that it used to create its histogram of times. This list of bin-centers and corresponding counts can then be used in the bar function to create the same histogram that was created originally by the hist function. The advantage to creating a histogram with the bar function in this indirect way is that the bar function allows greater control over the final look of the plot. In particular, we can easily change the widths of the bar (to make them overlap or to have a bit of space between them) or the colors of the bars (we have separate control over the edge and fill colors). Thus, we could make a nicer-looking version of our first plot by typing

```
[counts, bincenters]=hist(dt,31);
Ecolor=[0 0 0]; %RGB coordinates of the color black
Fcolor=[.2 .2 .2]; %RBG coordinates of dark grey
barwidth=1; %width of 1 exactly fills the space between bins
figure; bar(bincenters, counts,1,'FaceColor',Fcolor,'EdgeColor',Ecolor)
```

Or, if you prefer, a rather garish-looking version can be created with the commands

```
Ecolor=[.8 .5 .4]; %RGB coordinates (indicating mix of Red, Green, and Blue light)
Fcolor=[.3 .3 .8]; %RBG coordinates
figure; bar(C,N,.8,'FaceColor',[.3 .3 .8],'EdgeColor',[.8 .3 .3],'LineWidth',1.1)
```

may suggest interesting avenues for visualizations. Your timing data could represent reaction times, perhaps from an experiment where auditory beeps are played and the task is to press a button as quickly as possible on hearing the sound. In this case, we would likely be interested to determine when, in general, button-presses occur relative to the beep time. On the other hand, your timing data may correspond to the sleep/wake times of experimental subjects living without any external cues to time (sunlight, clocks, other people, etc.). In this scenario you may be interested in whether light-deprived people will, in general, naturally continue to sleep and wake on a 24-hour day-length or whether their sleep-wake cycle will drift from this externally driven day/night norm. Once timing data have been collected, our first step in examining them will be to create a histogram. Simulated data from these two scenarios are shown in Figure 1.4, where the histograms consist of a group of bars, and each bar represents the number of data whose values fall within a prescribed range, that is, a data-'bin.' Bins are usually equally spaced across the range of possible data-values, where each datum is assigned to the bin whose center is nearest the data-value.

Because a histogram tells us about the occurrence and pattern of data-clusters, it provides an excellent opportunity to discuss one of the fundamental questions that arises in data analysis: if a new dataset were collected under the same experimental conditions, would it have the same clustering characteristics? Obviously, any feature of a histogram consisting of only two or three data-values is unlikely to be reproducible because the data are likely to fluctuate (that is, the heights of histogram bars are likely to vary slightly) by two or three counts at a minimum from one dataset to another when repeating an experiment. Will the bump in Figure 1.4a at about 300 ms reappear or will it be smooth there, but other little bumps in the histogram appear at different locations? If the bump reappears in a convincing way, we should think about what that bump might mean and whether there is an existing theory or new theory that incorporates this data.

Another method of visually identifying the major features of a dataset is via a 'raster plot,' which historically has been the standard method of plotting neural spike data. Figure 1.5 shows an idealized example of the timing of neuronal firing organized as a raster plot, in which each spike time is indicated as a vertical dash, and rows of such dashes represent multiple repetitions of nominally identical recordings. Plots organized in this way are called 'raster plots' (as in the raster lines of an old-style CRT television, where quickly stacking a set of such lines creates an image). Here, stacking a set of spike traces gives an impression of the overall timing, rates, and clustering of neural firing. For example, Figure 1.5 represents the spiking of a visually sensitive neuron following presentation of a visual stimulus. We can see that the spike rate is noticeably higher within the first 50 ms following presentation of the stimulus than in the period prior to stimulus onset. Perhaps most noticeable is the dip in spike rate at about 100 ms. Indeed, while our eyes can immediately grasp the shape of the changes in spiking that occur in the figure, to help quantify the spike rate (and its change with time) we can create a moving window (here, 20 or 30 ms wide) and simply count the number of spikes in the window as it moves from left to right. This moving spike-count is shown as a solid gray line in the lower panel. One can also convert the raster plot into a histogram by simply creating bins as described above and counting the spike events contained within each bin (lower portion of the plot).

In creating a histogram or raster plot the idea is to gain familiarity with, and extract some of the main elements of a dataset. What aspects of the histogram or raster plot, as described above, should we expect are stable and reproducible? That is, if we were to obtain a new dataset under the same conditions that produced the first, would we see the identical plot? Certainly not identical in the precise spike counts and histogram bin heights, but likely similar. The reproducible features of the dataset will be expected to be quite similar from one dataset to another whereas the incidental (unreproducible) features will not. The reproducible features are usually such things as the mean or median (i.e., some measure of the location of a datacluster), but not the details of exact heights and placements of individual bars of a histogram created to depict that datacluster. For example, we might expect that the median will be (nearly) the same in the two datasets (original and replication), or we may expect that if there is only a single cluster in the original that there will be only a single cluster in a replication. In the raster plot, we may expect the timing of the major peaks and dips to remain stable as well.

This idea of reproducibility will be an important concept when we consider exactly what to compute when analyzing a dataset, and also what types of probability distributions characterize our information about the data. For the moment, however, it is most important to recognize that only the stable characteristics of a dataset will likely

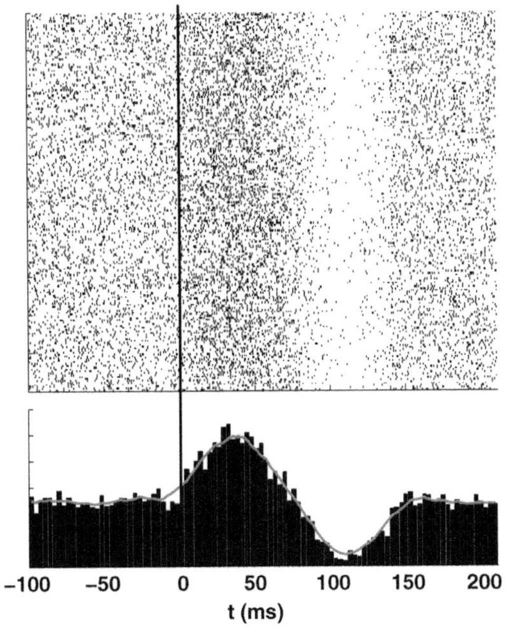

Figure 1.5 Raster plot and associated histogram. Idealized spike-timing data demonstrating baseline firing, followed by increased firing subsequent to an event at time 0 (such as presentation of a visual stimulus) and, finally, a refractory period and return to baseline firing. The upper plot is an example of a raster plot, and the lower panel shows what the histogram of the spike-timing data would look like. The solid line overlaid on the histogram is a windowed mean of spike counts at each instant of time. This line is effectively a smoothed version of the histogram.

Programming Aside: Raster Plots

The raster plot describes the spike trains recorded from a neuron during the performance of some behavioral task (e.g., before and during an eye or arm movement). The raster plot is a bit more complicated to make than, for example, the histogram, because we need to plot each row of the raster plot separately (where each row corresponds to a repetition of the neural recording, obtained by repeating the experiment multiple times). By repeating the experiment and making multiple recordings of spike trains from the same neuron, we can get a sense of the stable characteristics of the spike timing (relative to a behavior or to an experimental manipulation), even though the exact timing of neural firing will vary slightly from one repetition of the experiment to another.

We will plot simulated data inspired by the experiments of Porter et al. (2007), in which single neurons from the inferior colliculus of macaque were recorded during an eye movement task. In this task, the monkey sat in complete darkness until a single LED (light-emitting diode) was turned on at one of several possible locations. The monkey was required to fixate the LED as soon as it appeared (note that, because the eye position of the monkey was being monitored, the LED could be chosen to have a particular position relative to the monkey's point of regard as it sat in the dark room, and therefore required an eye movement to fixate). After fixating the LED for a brief period (600–900 ms) a 200-ms-long tone was played. The tone indicated that juice reward would be given in 300–600 ms if the monkey continued to fixate the LED. If either the monkey failed to look at the LED within 3 s of it being turned on, or failed to maintain fixation as described above, no reward was given and the data from that trial was discarded. However, monkeys love juice, and so they soon learn to perform this task.

A typical repetition ('trial') of this experiment will last about 4 s (1–3 s to look at the LED, 1.5 s to fixate, hear the sound, and continue fixation till reward is given), and during that time the data will consist of two types of number. The first is simply the eye position, which we will use to extract the time of the saccade and to verify fixation. The other is the spiking produced by the IC neuron being recorded. This latter data will simply be a list of times, starting at −0.5 (one would start recording 500 ms prior to turning on the LED) and running until juice is delivered at a variable time later (usually about 3–4 s).

How do we take a set of spike times and try to understand what this neuron is 'saying,' or what its output represents? With data of this type, our initial step is to create a set of raster plots. The first of these that we will create to examine the data described above will be raster plots of the spikes, when aligned to the onset of the LED (time zero in the description above).

To create the first plot, we open the raster function:

```
> open raster
```

and manually change the `exampletype` variable to 1 (this is not its default value), then in the command window, type

```
> [Tcell]=raster;
```

With no inputs, this function generates preprogrammed example data, `Tcell`.

Just looking at the data this way, we might get the impression that this IC neuron responds fairly reliably to the LED, but not much else (there are no obvious features beyond a prolonged increase in firing just after time zero). However, there is a variable time between the LED onset and the corresponding saccade in each trial, and another variable length of time between fixating the LED and the tone (and also between the tone and juice reward). Without aligning the data to each of these experimental events, we cannot tell if there is a reliable neural response corresponding to them. The data are already naturally aligned to the LED onset, so we simply take this plot and reproduce it (after truncating it a bit).

```
[Tcell0 Tbar]=raster(Tcell(:,1),[-50 300],0,2);
figure(3); bar(Tbar(:,1),Tbar(:,2);
```

This command generates a raster plot from the `Tcell` data (first column of cells from the `Tcell` cell array) aligned at time 0 (third input), and plots rasters starting 200 ms prior to time zero, and continuing for 300 ms after time zero (second input); the last input to the raster function specifies the figure number to plot into. The second line uses the bar function to make the histogram positioned above this raster plot in Figure 1.5. The second plot should be realigned to correspond to saccade onset. Thus, we must look in the eye position data to find the time (within each trial) that the eye begins to move. We then relabel the spike times in that trial so that the start of the eye movement is at time 0 (for example, eye movement occurred at one second following LED onset, then the relabeled times would put saccade onset at time −1 s and the start of the trial at −1.5 s). After shifting the spike times for each trial individually based on saccade onset times (these times are contained in the third column of the `Tcell` cell array), we obtain a new plot:

```
[Tcell0 Tbar]=raster(Tcell(:,1),[-200 300],Tcell(:,3),4);
figure(5); bar(Tbar(:,1),Tbar(:,2);
```

Finally, we perform the same time-shifting procedure on all spikes in the various trials once more, this time to put the onset of the auditory tone at time zero (i.e., for each trial, find the time of the auditory tone and subtract it from the LED-referenced spike times in that trial). The raster plot resulting from this second time-shift is:

```
[Tcell0 Tbar]=raster(Tcell(:,1),[-200 300],Tcell(:,4),6);
figure(7); bar(Tbar(:,1),Tbar(:,2);
```

Note that here the times of the auditory tones are contained in the fourth column of the `Tcell` cell array.

We can see from the last two plots that there is consistent structure in the spiking of this IC neuron that was not initially obvious in the 'raw' (unshifted) data. Of course, this need not have been the case: The data may have looked like a raster plot obtained by again generating preprogrammed example data (but manually setting the `exampletype` variable to 2) using

```
[Tcell]=raster;
```

where the overall data appear to have no obvious structure, and also several of the subplots constructed by rezeroing the data in each trial also have no consistent response above baseline (we will analyze these data in the exercises). The fact that we do find a consistent response to all three experimental events suggests that the neuron is either responding to these events (e.g., detecting them) or is computing something relative to them. For example, the spiking at saccade onset would generally be taken as evidence that this neuron is involved in saccade planning and/or execution.

reproduce themselves in a replication (new dataset obtained under nominally identical conditions). Thus, we can only expect that a stable aspect of the data is informative about the underlying mechanisms that generated those data, in the sense that we can expect to see those elements in a new dataset obtained under similar conditions. Furthermore, recognizing which aspects of the data are stable may allow us to perform more powerful analyses, as we will see in later chapters.

Exercises

1) Create histograms using the following positions (x) and counts (N):
   a. $x = 1:10$; and $\boldsymbol{N} = [0,0,0,1,5,7,6,2,0,0]$
   b. $x = 11:20$; and $\boldsymbol{N} = [0,0,0,1,5,7,6,2,0,0]$
   c. $x = 1:10$; and $\boldsymbol{N} = [12,7,3,1,5,7,6,2,0,0]$
2) Interpret the histograms (describe their features) from ex. 1.

3) Create and interpret histograms from the raw data generated by:
   a. $d = randn(500, 1)$
   b. $d = rand(250, 1)$
   c. $d = randn(10, 1)$
   d. $d = randn(10, 2)$
   e. $d = randn(10, 5)$
4) Reproduce the plot in Figure 1.5 using the instructions in the raster programming aside [note that spike times are contained in Tcell(:,1), whereas the timing of the three experimental events, LED saccade and tone, are contained in Tcell(:,2), Tcell(:,3), and Tcell(:,4), respectively].
   a. Reproduce the b-d subplots shown in Figure 1.5 for these (Tcell) data.
   b. What is the average firing rate in panel (b)?
   c. What is the peak firing rate in panel (c), and at what time does it occur?
   d. What is the average firing rate in panel (d)?
   e. Given that the peak firing rate occurs prior to the saccade in panel (c), speculate regarding the possible cause of elevated firing in this simulation.

1.2.3 Scatterplots

Are there any interesting spatial or temporal relationships that you expect to see in your data? Suppose you are using a tablet, and reach out to touch an icon on the screen. Your touchpoint will probably be relatively accurate. We further predict that if you repeated the same reach multiple times, your touchpoints will cluster together, because if this experiment is repeated we expect essentially the same result (it would not be very useful to have a reach control system that is highly variable and produced results that only weakly corresponded with what was intended).

The scatterplots in Figure 1.6 show possible spatial endpoints associated with reaches to your tablet. The plots shows spatial errors, where the origin (0,0) is the intended reach endpoint (location of the icon). After obtaining data of this type, we will often perform a visual inspection of the data by creating a plot of this type. If the data are similar to the (a) panel, it would suggest something important was occurring (i.e., you are either observing pathology, a possibly unexpected feature of the data, or a glitch in the data collection). In Figure 1.6a the data are clustered reasonably tightly, but that datacluster is low (vertically) relative to the target (every single datum is below the target). Is this a problem with the tablet (e.g., poor calibration)? Were these data from normal control subjects, or neurologically compromised individuals with possibly pathological motor control? The data from panel (b) appear more like what we would expect, where the center of the cluster is located in a reasonable position (near the actual target position, but the scatter is also larger. Since our background information suggests that movements will be relatively consistent and reproducible, we should consider the possible causes of such scatter before we simply accept that the data are 'noisier than expected.' Indeed, any consistent data features that are unexpected should be examined before proceeding with the formal data analysis – thus ensuring that any findings from the final analysis will

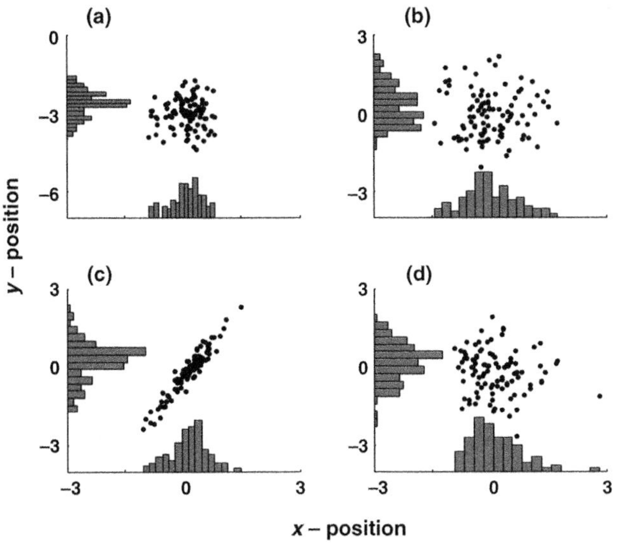

Figure 1.6 Four scatterplots of endpoint data. (a) Datacluster with low standard deviation, circular distribution. (b) Datacluster with larger circular standard deviation. (c) Correlated 2D datacluster with very similar marginal histograms as those produced by the circular datacluster in (b). (d) Datacluster skewed in the *x*- but not the *y*-dimension. Histograms plotted along each axis ('margins') allow us to clearly see the marginal standard deviations of these 2D scatterplots. Because marginal histograms are created by projecting data onto each axis, they are not informative about possible correlations in the 2D data.

PA: Scatterplots

In Figure 1.6 the *x-y* positions of a hypothetical fingertip were displayed. To create this plot our first step will be to define an N × 2 set of *x-y* positions. Lacking real experimental data, we will generate simulated data by typing (at the command line):

```
> XYdat=mvnrand([0 0],[1 .8; .8 1],50);
```

This command creates a 50 × 2 matrix of points where the mean of the first column of 50 numbers has an average near 5 and the second column of 50 numbers has an average near 1. We will have more to say about random number generators in Chapter 3, but you should examine the help file associated with this command now (by typing `help mvnrand` at the command line).

To create a scatterplot with these data, we simply plot the N × 2 matrix of numbers (here representing *x-y* positions), where the *x*-component of the data is contained in the first column of the matrix and the *y*-component of the data is contained in the second column of the matrix, making use of the plot.m function. The plot command takes at least two arguments, the first is the vector of *x*-data and the second is the vector of *y*-data. There are also optional arguments for the type of plot symbol and the size and desired colors of the edges and centers of plot symbols. So, for example, to plot start position at the origin, we type

```
>> figure; hold on; plot(0,0,'o','MarkerSize',12,'MarkerFaceColor',
   [0 0 0],'MarkerEdgeColor',[0 0 0])
```

where the third argument ('o') is the marker type (a circle), and the remaining arguments are pairs of argument identifiers in text and corresponding values. Thus, for example, the input pair that allows us to specify the size of the plotted circle is 'MarkerSize' followed by the size of the marker (12). The [0 0 0] are [R G B] triplets, where 0 injects none of a component and 1 injects 100% of that component.

Finally, we plot the scatter of movement endpoint locations:

```
plot(XYdat(:,1),XYdat(:,2),'.','Color',[.4 .4 .4])
```

Here, the marker is a darker gray. Note that when the plot symbol is the dot ('.'), we do not specify edge and face colors separately, since the dot is always a single solid color without a separate edge and face. Similarly, we do not specify a size for the dot symbol, which has a standard unmodifiable size.

make sense in light of the experimental procedure and data collection, and not be caused by errors introduced through poor use of equipment or initial mishandling of the data.

Similar thoughts should occupy us after obtaining spatiotemporal data, such as decay rates, spike trains, oculomotor saccade or pursuit velocity trajectories, etc. In these cases, instead of a scatterplot of 2D or 3D spatial positions, we will have a time axis that will allow us to visualize how variables (eye position, hand position, emotional response, concussion severity, spike count, etc.) fluctuate and change as time progresses.

Programming Aside: Temporal Profile Plots

There are two common types of spatiotemporal plot: one showing the temporal evolution of an experimental variable (e.g., showing fingertip or eye position as a function of time), and a raster plot. Temporal evolution plots can be created as a straightforward scatterplot using the plot command. For example, we could create a simulated eye movement ('saccade') in the following way: First we define an acceleration profile. A saccade acceleration profile describes the acceleration-deceleration pair of a single saccade. We can roughly simulate this with one cycle of a sine wave:

```
t=linspace(0,.1,101); %100ms saccade duration
```

where, we first create a time variable (t) that contains a linearly spaced set of 101 values from 0 to 0.1 (i.e., we will simulate acceleration values at times from 0 to 0.1 s in 1 ms intervals). A single 100 ms cycle of a sinewave can be created with the command

```
at=7400*sin(2*pi*t/.1); %simulated acceleration profile
figure; subplot(3,1,1); plot(t,at,'k:','LineWidth',1.2);
```

The velocity profile associated with this sinusoidal acceleration profile is

```
vt=cumtrapz(at)*.001; %simulated velocity profile
```

where the function cumtrapz.m computes the cumulative trapezoidal approximation to the integral of the input vector (at), allowing us to convert from acceleration to velocity,

```
subplot(3,1,2); plot(t,vt,'k--','LineWidth',1.2); %plot of velocity profile
```

and then again from velocity to position:

```
pt=cumtrapz(vt)*.001; %simulated position profile
subplot(3,1,3); plot(t,pt,'k-','LineWidth',1.2); %plot of position profile
```

In the velocity profile we see velocity starts at zero, rises to a single peak at the middle of the movement, and returns to zero at the end of the movement. The position plot describes the change in eye position created by the above velocity profile, and has a characteristic 's' shape.

Exercises

1) You observe that for a 2° saccade to the right the saccade endpoint is at about 1°. You collect new data for a 2° saccade to the left. In each case below, speculate about the possible calibration error(s) that could account for the (combined) result of the previous (undershoot) and new recording, if the new recording showed:
   a. saccades landing about 1° to the left.
   b. saccades landing about 3° to the left.
   c. saccades landing about 2° to the left.
2) Suppose you observe consistent saccade undershoots (as in a, above) using equipment that you know to be properly calibrated. Saccades might tend to undershoot as an energy-saving strategy. If so, then it would be more important to plan a saccade undershoot for larger than smaller saccades (where energy savings could be more substantial). Create a scatterplot of predicted saccade endpoints from an experiment where saccades are made to targets at .5° intervals from .5° to 10.5° from initial fixation. Explain the shape of the scatter.
3) Describe the relative scatter of the upper subplots of Figure 1.6.
4) Given the scatterplot of Figure 1.6a, would you consider it more likely that the data display a shift or a scale miscalibration? Why?
5) Assuming that saccades are essentially accurate, is there a single miscalibration error (scale, shift, sign error) that can explain the scatterplot of Figure 1.6b? If not, which pair of miscalibration errors, and in what combination, can explain the data?

1.2.4 Descriptive Statistics

The term 'statistic' comes from the single-number data summaries often used to describe data. Examples of statistics are the mean of a set of numbers, or a political poll percentage. Statistics can be quite useful during data visualization and to provide a data summary, and in particular have an important use during the exploratory phase of an analysis.

Location

While histograms and scatterplots give a sense of data clustering, the sample mean and median tell us only about the most typical data value in the dataset, where typicality is defined slightly differently in the two cases. The **mean** is the average of the data; it gives the center of mass, or point along the x-axis where a scatterplot of the data would just balance (if each datapoint were a mass). The **median** is the middle value; half the dataset is composed of numbers greater than, and half less than the median. The mean and median of a dataset will be roughly the same when the data histogram is symmetrical. The mean, however, gets shifted more by skew (nonsymmetry, as in Fig. 1.4a) and outliers (datapoints far from the main datacluster, as in Fig. 1.6d) than does the median. These statistics are called measures of location because they give an indication of the location of the typical value in a dataset. They are, in other words, reasonable answers to questions regarding the best guess at data values (as in 'how much taller are 17-year-old boys than girls?', if you were analyzing a dataset of the the heights of girls and boys in a particular city). In addition to the mean and median, a third useful measure of location is the peak of a frequency distribution, which corresponds to the location of the tallest bar in the data histogram (when dealing with histogram-counts, this location is called the **mode**).

Although the mean, median, and peak/mode are all reasonable choices for a location measure, notice that each uses the information in the dataset quite differently. The mean uses all of the information in the dataset and adjusts its value to some extent based on each. The median, however, throws some of this information away: consider a case where there are only three data: $x = [-1,\ 0,\ 1]$. Both the mean and median in this case are zero (the mean is $\bar{x} = (\Sigma x_i)/n = (-1 + 0 + 1)/3 = 0$, and the median is zero because half the data values are above and half below zero). If the third datum were changed so that the dataset were $x = [-1, 0, 10]$ the mean would change ($\bar{x} = (\Sigma x_i)/n = 9/3 = 3$) in response to this change in the dataset. The median would remain zero because the median is defined only as the datum that has an equal *number* of (other) data above and below it; he exact numerical values of those other data are irrelevant. The mode is only useful if there is a very large dataset or when the data are discrete, because otherwise no data values are likely to repeat often enough (or even approximately repeat as in a histogram bin) for the mode to be particularly informative. The unusual aspect of the mode, however, is that if a data histogram is peaked at one end or the other of its range (see Fig. 1.5b), then this peak is the location of the mode: whereas both the mean and median would be nearer the center of the range (unless that peak contained the vast majority of the data in the dataset). These differences are the reason that each of the three location measures provides a slightly different feel for the data – each tells us about a representative value in the dataset, but does so based on a different definition of 'representative value.'

Scale

Aside from measures of location, the most common descriptive statistics are measures of dispersion (also called spread or scale). These numbers provide a representation of the extent to which data cluster near a single location. Perhaps the most obvious solution to representing dispersion is the average distance ($\bar{d}$) between each datum and the mean of the dataset:

$$\bar{d} = \frac{\Sigma_i \sqrt{(x_i - \bar{x})^2}}{n}$$

Unfortunately, the distance statistic has the awkward property that its plot takes the shape of a 'v,' and therefore does not curve smoothly near zero (see exercises). A similar statistic that varies smoothly throughout its domain is obtained by instead computing the average squared distance:

$$v = \frac{\Sigma_i (x_i - \bar{x})^2}{n}$$

which is called the variance of the dataset. Because it is a smooth function (see exercises), the variance is mathematically preferable to the average distance. Notice, however, that variance is in squared units (e.g., if the x-data are measured in mm, then the variance is given in mm^2), and so one must take its square root if we would like a dispersion statistic that has the same units as the original variable. This statistic is called the standard deviation (s) of the dataset:

$$s = \sqrt{v} = \sqrt{\frac{\Sigma_i (x_i - \bar{x})^2}{n}}$$

Figure 1.6 shows four data clusters. All four panels show data clusters, some of which are more spread out than others. The upper two panels of Figure 1.6 show two possible scales for the scatter in the data. In panel (a) the scatter is noticeably smaller than in panel (b), although the shape of the 2D distribution is the same in both: approximately a circle. Contrariwise, looking at the histograms plotted along each of the axes in panels (c) and (d) we see that the scale of the scatter is not notably different from that in panel (b), although the shapes of the 2D scatter in these panels differ markedly from the circular shapes of panels (a) and (b). In panel (c) the 2D distribution of datapoints is clustered along a line oriented between the x- and y-axes. Because of this additional structure in the data in panel (c) relative to that in (b), we can see that there is less overall variation in the data in the oriented dataset relative to the roughly circular scatterplot in (b) that shares the same range of data values, because the data values do not stray as far from the center of the scatter in (c) relative to data in (b). This decrease in overall scatter in the (c) dataset is the consequence of a **correlation** between the simulated latency and gain values in this plot.

Correlation

The shape of a 2D (or higher-dimensional) scatterplot is also informative. A scatterplot of data that is either roughly circular or aligned to one of the Cartesian axes (e.g., x- or y-axis as above, Fig. 1.7a) is said to be **uncorrelated.** If the scatterplot displays a correlation (Fig. 1.7b) this conveys additional information in the following way: Imagine choosing one of the 2D data values of Figure 1.7a, and being told the x-value of the selected datum is between -5 and -10. What is your best guess of the datum's y-value? For correlated data, your best guess is the mean of y-values *corresponding to those x-values*, which will be different from the mean of data from another range of x-values (such as those between 10 and 15). For uncorrelated data, the mean of y-values corresponding to that x-range (Fig. 1.7b) is the same as the mean of all y-values, because y-values do not change systematically with different x-values. Thus, knowing the x-value

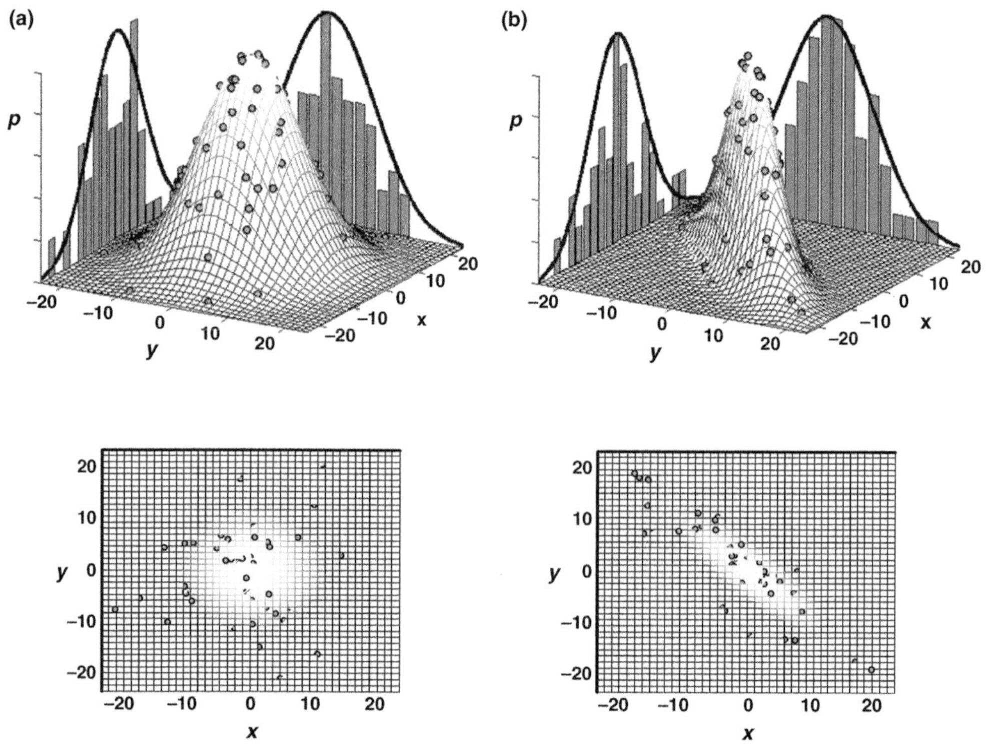

Figure 1.7 Correlated and uncorrelated 2D probability distributions with corresponding data. The two left-hand plots (a) display uncorrelated probability distributions and data, whereas the two right-hand plots (b) display correlated probability distributions and data. Upper plots show 2D data overlaid on their corresponding 2D probability distributions. The margins of these plots show data histograms and 1D probability distributions corresponding to the x- and y-coordinates of the 2D data. Note that the 1D probability distributions in the correlated and uncorrelated cases are identical (e.g., the two 1D probability distributions on the x-axis are identical). Similarly, data histograms are nearly identical as well. Lower plots show an aerial view of each corresponding upper plot.

does not increase your ability to guess the corresponding y-value[11] for uncorrelated data. This last statement tells us about the probability of any particular 2D location, which is defined by the probability expression: $p(x \cdot y \mid \iota) = p(y \mid x \cdot \iota)p(x \mid \iota)$. In this expression, the term $p(y \mid x \cdot \iota)$ encodes the dependence relation, whereby information regarding the identity of the y-coordinate may depend on that datum's x-coordinate value (or vice versa, if we had written the joint probability as $p(x \cdot y \mid \iota) = p(x \mid y \cdot \iota)p(y \mid \iota)$. Uncorrelated x- and y-coordinate values are described by the simplification $p(y \mid x \cdot \iota) = p(y \mid \iota)$, or $p(x \mid y \cdot \iota) = p(x \mid \iota)$, which removes the dependence relation wherein our information about the value of y is conditional on our information about the value of x. An interesting consequence of this uncorrelated state is that we can build the 2D probability distribution corresponding to our information about these data, $p(y \cdot x \mid \iota)$, directly from the two marginal 1D distributions, $p(x \mid \iota)$ and $p(y \mid \iota)$. This can be

[11] There is a caveat here, that the joint probability distribution must be of the shape described by the 2D probability distributions shown in Figure 1.7. Otherwise, one can construct certain counterexamples to the statement that lack of correlation implies independent probabilities. Here, however, we are describing the intuitive meaning of the statistic, which corresponds to the situation depicted in Figure 1.7.

seen, for example, in the 2D and marginal distributions that are plotted in Figure 1.7. In Figure 1.7a, where two 1D probability distributions are shown along the x- and y-axes (solid line), the 2D joint distribution over x and y (the 2D probability bubble) can be built by multiplying the x- and y-probabilities corresponding to the components of each x-y coordinate pair. This procedure (multiplying marginal probabilities to create a 2D distribution) will always produce a 2D distribution that is aligned to the two coordinate axes (or is circular; Fig. 1.7a), and never a distribution that is oriented relative to the two axes (as in Fig. 1.7b). When there is a correlation between the two data variables, the scatterplot will develop an orientation relative to the x- and y-axes. We can see in the (b) panels of Figure 1.7 that if the 2D scatterplot (note the these have approximately the same 1D histograms, drawn from marginal distributions identical to the (a) panels) are given a correlation, the resulting 2D probability distribution can no longer be constructed *only* from the 1D marginal distributions as previously. Instead, one requires additional information regarding the relationship between the two variables before the 2D probability distribution can be constructed. The part of this additional information that describes the strength of the predictive relationship is contained in the correlation coefficient, which is a number from -1 to 1. Positive correlations correspond to 2D scatter rotated into the first and third quadrants of the x-y coordinate plane, and negative correlations to 2D scatter rotated into the second and fourth quadrants. Correlations closer to 1 or -1 correspond to data that cluster very tightly around the rotated line that defines the oriented scatter. The correlation statistic describing a relationship between the x- and y-dimensions of a 2D dataset is given by

$$r = \frac{\Sigma x_i y_i - n\overline{xy}}{n s_x s_y}$$

where the term s_x is the standard deviation along the x dimension, and $\bar{y}$ indicates the mean of the y coordinate data, etc.

Why are correlations important in science? Because they are the most common case in which the value of one variable can be used to predict changes in the values of other variables. First, consider the uncorrelated case shown in Figure 1.7a. Imagine there is one additional datum whose value we do not yet know. If we were to predict the y-value of an unknown datum for a continuation of the dataset shown in panel (a), our best prediction is the mean of the y-values from the dataset (or the median or peak probability location, if you prefer). But what about if we are told the x-value of this new datum? Even if we are now told the x-value of this datum, the (circularly symmetric) shape of this 2D probability distribution does not us to use the x-value to better predict the unknown value of y. This is because each vertical slice through the probability distribution (i.e., the vertical slice through the circular probability distribution at the given x-value) will be centered at $\bar{y}$, and so our best prediction ($\bar{y}$) does not change for different x-values. Now consider the correlated 2D dataset and probability distribution shown in panel (b). Here again our best guess for the y-value of an unknown datum is $\bar{y}$, the mean of the y-values. But the situation is quite different if we are told the x-value of this new datum. Knowing the x-coordinate of the new datum allows us to make a much better prediction about the likely value of its y-coordinate, because each slice through the correlated probability distribution defines a 1D probability distribution whose mean changes location for different x-values. For example, if we were told that the x-coordinate of a new datum in the correlated 2D dataset were about 4, we would be able to guess fairly confidently that the corresponding y-value is close to the mean, $\bar{y} = -4$, of that vertical slice; similarly our best guess about the y-coordinate of datapoints whose x-coordinates are $-20, -10$, and 20 would be 20, 10, and -20, respectively. These guesses regarding y-coordinate values clearly depend on the value of the corresponding x-coordinate, whereas similar guesses based on Figure 1.7a are independent of the x-coordinate, because regardless of the x-coordinate our best guess regarding the corresponding y-coordinate, in this uncorrelated case, does not change.

Finally, we must mention **causality**. The predictability conferred by observing a correlation is itself important because it suggests the possibility that a causal relation exists between those two variables. To take this a step further, we would say that it seems rather unlikely that changes in variable x cause any changes in variable y when the x-y data look like the plot in Figure 1.7a, but we would consider it much more likely that such a causal relationship exists (whereby changes in one variable cause changes in another) if the data look like the plot in Figure 1.7b. However, while a correlated dataset gives the appearance of a causal relationship, any proposed chain of causation must be investigated either through additional experiments or logical arguments (or both). Can we say with certainty that changes in the x-dimension cause changes in the y-values in Figure 1.7b? We would have to consider how likely we consider such a causal chain, depending on what the data represent – direct causality between two correlated variables cannot be determined only based on the presence of the correlation between them (Fig. 1.8a).

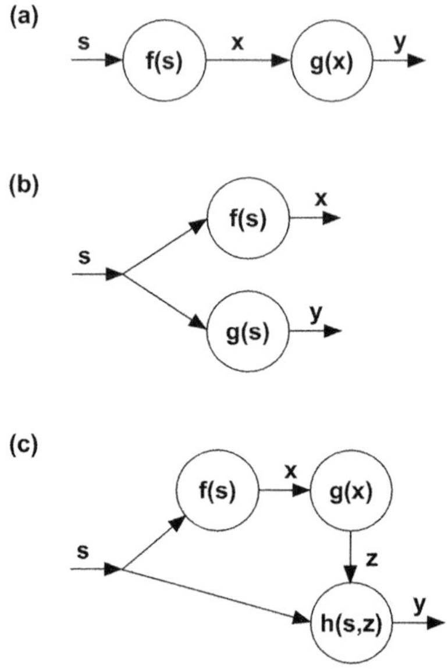

Figure 1.8 Causal chains that begin with an external stimulus s and produce correlated x, y, or z variables. (a) Direct causal chain in which the y variable is a direct function of the x variable. (b) Causal chain in which x and y variables are both functions of the same input (stimulus) variable, s. (c) Indirect causal chain in which the output z variable is indirectly (through y) a function of both x and the input variable s. As an aside, if the functions f, g, and h are linear, the variables s, x, y, and z in all three panels must be correlated.

PA: Mean, Median, Variance, and Correlation

Here we will use MATLAB® to simulate data from a pair of correlated variables, and then compute the mean, median, variance and correlation of these variables. We begin with the internal psuedorandom multivariate Gaussian number generator, mvnrand (multivariate normal rand):

```
mu=[0 0]; V1=1; V2=2^2; r=.85; N=100;
xy=mvnrand([0 0],[V1 r*sqrt(V1*V2); r*sqrt(V1*V2) V2],N);
```

These commands produce 100 xy data-pairs (the size of the xy matrix is 100 x 2), where the variance in the x-dimension is V1 and the variance in the *y*-dimension is V2. We can get a sense of the distribution of simulated data by plotting their scatter and histograms:

```
GaussPoints(xy,mu,[V1 r*sqrt(V1*V2); r*sqrt(V1*V2) V2]);
```

This plot command produces a 2D scatterplot with histograms of each of the two dimensions along each of the axes, as in Figure 1.7. We can see from the plot that the data are roughly centered on the origin (we specified that mu should be [0 0] when we generated the data), and that the spread of the data is larger on the *y*-axis than on the *x*-axis. Also, there is a clear positive correlation between the data values along the two axes, with values in the 2D scatter adhering closely to a straight line of positive slope. We can compute the mean and median of the data with the commands

```
mubar=mean(xy)
muhat=median(xy)
```

Both commands produce a 2-element vector output, where the first element is the mean or median in the *x*-dimension and the second the mean or median in the *y*-dimension. Use of the var command produces a similar 2-element output that describes the variance of the two dimensions:

```
Vhat=var(xy)
```

Finally, we compute the correlation of the 2D scatter with the command:

```
rhat=corrcoef(xy)
```

Nevertheless, while direct causal chains between correlated variables (x and y in Fig. 1.8) cannot be assumed, we can usually assume there is indirect causality based on more complex causal chains (e.g., Fig. 1.8c) that will also likely produce correlated data. In all of these cases, the mere fact that a correlation exists cannot tell us which variables are causally related, and therefore we must be cautious when inferring the nature of a causal chain based on correlation data. In an introductory text this caution is often replaced by the slogan 'correlation does not equal causation,' which unfortunately gives the impression that correlations occur when *no* causation exists. This is misleading because the slogan does not express the more important, subtler point, that a *direct* causal chain (Fig. 1.8a) is not necessarily implied by a correlation, although a persistent correlation is generally produced by *some* causal chain – indirect though it may be.

Once we have spent some time visualizing our data, we will usually also want to characterize the main aspects of the data in terms of their location, spread, etc. The summary, or descriptive statistics outlined in this and the previous two subsections will therefore contribute to a gestalt of our dataset that we would like to obtain before embarking on a formal data analysis. For example, once we have collected a new dataset, we might want to ask several questions, such as, Does it cluster tightly, or spread out? What values are most likely? Are the sample mean and the sample median similar? If not, is there evidence of substantial skew in the data? Answering questions like these will help us gain a 'feel' for the data we have collected. These descriptive statistics also come in handy when we perform the final step of our preanalysis routine, data checks.

Exercises

1) Plot histograms and compute the mean, median, and s of the following:
   a. d = randn([300 1])
   b. d = crand(0, 1, [300 1])
   c. d = rand(0, 300)
   d. d = randi(30, 300)
   e. d = rrand(2, [300 1])
   f. d = randn([300 1])*3
   g. d = randn([300 1])*5
2) Plot 2D histograms and compute the marginal means, standard deviations, and correlations using x=sort(randn([300 1])); and:
   a. y = x + 3*randn([300 1])
   b. y = sort(randn([300]))
   c. y = sort(randn([300 2])*10)
3) Define the time vector t=linspace(0,1,101); and then compute correlations between x, y, and (possibly) z in the (a), (b), and (c) configurations of Figure 1.7 with the following functions:
   a. f(t) = 2t + randn(101, 1); g(t) = .5t + randn(101, 1)*3; z(t) = t.*randn(101, 1)
   b. f(t) = 3t + randn(101, 1); g(t) = 10t.*randn(101, 1); z(t) = t + randn(101, 1)
4) Show that the distance statistic has the shape of a 'v,' as mentioned in the text (by plotting distance as a function of position from the origin, with position ranging from -5 to 5), and that the variance is a smooth function (by plotting squared distance as a function of position over the same range).

1.2.5 Data Checks: Expected versus Unexpected Data Values and Patterns

Before we begin a formal data analysis, we would like to verify that the data do not contain any errors, and that they have the characteristics we expect from data of the type associated with our particular experiment. This is an important step in getting a feel for your dataset, because we would like to verify that the data contain features known to occur in datasets of the type we are about to analyze – or if not, to determine whether substantial deviations are due to experimenter error. For example, arm movements have characteristic latencies, movement trajectories, and movement accuracy, and these differ from the analogous characteristics of eye movements (eye movements can be initiated faster, often reach higher peak velocities, etc.). Thus, while your experiment will surely differ from the conditions that elicit textbook arm or eye movement (assuming you are advancing knowledge in the field), their typical characteristics can often serve as a guide in determining whether we should be concerned that there has been an error in our data collection or in the execution of our experiment that could have produced spurious results.

If expectations are violated, we must consider several possibilities: First, it is possible that we have made a mistake in constructing our experiment such that, for example, stimuli do not occur with the desired temporal or spatial parameters, or that the data collection equipment was not set up properly and the data recording is in error, etc. A second possibility is that the behavior (e.g., eye movements made to peripheral targets) dose not operate according to our general expectation; in other words, we have made an erroneous assumption about how the behavior is generated, controlled, internally monitored, etc. under current experimental conditions. Testing the first option simply requires a tedious check of the physical apparatus and computer code used for stimulus display and data collection. The second option, however, offers an opportunity for scientific discovery. For example, you may discover that some of your experimental subjects display a distinct pattern of results: perhaps their movements are initiated much faster than normal, which would have been evident in a histogram of latencies. Once the anomaly is detected, we could determine if it occurs in a particular subset of experimental subjects. Further probing might reveal that these anomalous subjects had all previously suffered a stroke, or were all elderly, suffer from sleep disturbance, or have some other distinguishing characteristic relative to the population at large. A new experiment might then be performed to test the idea that this distinguishing characteristic was the cause of the difference in saccade onset times.

Our data checks correspond to (some subset of) our prior information about the data we will be collecting. It is simply always true that we have at least a bit of useful prior information in a scientific setting: even if it is just a tiny iota. Or, to put it another way: If you were to collect distance data and discover a reading of a billion meters, or collect count data and discover a reading of -2 observations, you should feel the need to do some checking – because some aspect of your prior information/expectation about the data was violated. And while the correspondence between which data types and which numbers will look surprising may take some thought, the simple fact that there are *some* data values that would look surprising tells us that we are not *completely uninformed* regarding what kinds of data values we should expect in our experiments. This realization will become an important theoretical consideration when we construct probability distributions for various data types, and will be an important practical consideration when we design the computer code that will implement our probability calculations (starting in Chapter 2). The following are several features whose presence in a dataset should particularly lead to data checks.

Unexpected Correlation (or Lack of Correlation)

During initial data visualization we will often plot the scatter of a 2D dataset, and check that the spread of the data is within reasonable bounds. In many such cases, we expect that the shape of the scatter will be similar to that seen in the left-hand column of Figure 1.7, that is, aligned to the coordinate axes. If the data are instead arranged along an oriented line (e.g., right-hand column of Fig. 1.7), this indicates that there is some 'force' or causal chain causing data-value-pairs to prefer certain locations in the space of 2D coordinates and avoid others. This 'something' could be an error in the design or execution of the experiment, or could be a previously unknown mechanism: both possibilities deserve further exploration.

The converse is also true; it is important to check on predicted correlations. If theory and previous experimental results predict that a correlation should be present in part of the data and it clearly is not, we must also consider whether there is some aspect of our current experimental design that differs from previous studies. Such a difference could help inform the underlying theory, by delineating conditions that produce and those that inhibit a particular correlation.

Bimodality

Although we can always compute the mean and standard deviation of a dataset, the validity of our intuitive interpretation of these descriptive statistics is compromised in certain circumstances. One of the more common ways in which the value of a descriptive statistic will be somewhat misleading is when data are multimodal, meaning there is more than one 'bump' in the probability distribution or histogram based on those data. For example, consider the histograms plotted in Figures 1.9a,b. Figure 1.9a shows a typical, symmetrical, unimodal histogram. Here, the mean and standard deviation of the data describe what a typical value of the dataset might be, and how widely the data are likely to stray from that typical value. In Figure 1.9b there is a histogram with two clearly separate bumps. If we were to take the mean of these data and not plot their histogram, we might be led to believe that the location of a typical datum is at $x = 0$, which is partway between the two peaks, and actually describes very little of the observed data (only about five data points have values near $x = 0$). Similar cautions can be applied to the standard deviation computed from these data. The data are spread over two distinct regions, and the value of a standard deviation measured from these data will reflect both the widths of the two regions and their separation. This is in contrast to our intuitive understanding of the standard deviation, which is only a function of the former element when the data are unimodal.

Unexpected Sign

The sign of the data found in a dataset, positive or negative, is an important piece of information that should be monitored when inspecting our data. A common case in which the sign of the data provide an alert during data visualization is when signs are reversed relative to expectation. Perhaps the most common case involves positions along the vertical dimension for data related to visually presented stimuli, due to an oddity in

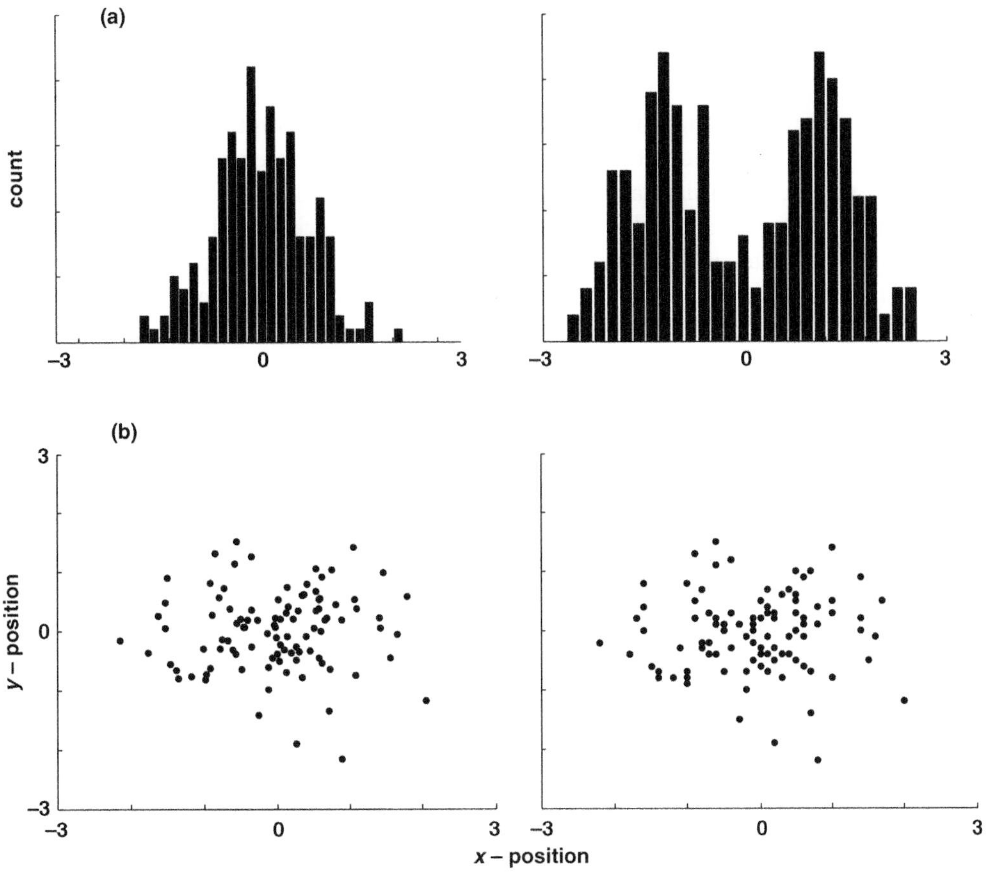

Figure 1.9 Data checks. (a) Unimodal (left) and bimodal (right) histograms centered on $x = 0$. (b) Demonstration of discretized data in a 2D spatial plot. The data on the left and right are identical except for rounding. Notice that right-hand data look as if they are aligned on regular grid points, with different datapoints sharing identical repeated x- and y-values.

the way screen/monitor (pixel) coordinates are defined. When presenting stimuli on a screen, it is often the case that the origin in screen-pixel coordinates is defined as the upper left corner of the screen, and positions below the origin are labeled positive (e.g., +5 pixels down from the origin, and +15 pixels to the right of the origin[12]). However, when computing the spatial position of the stimulus (in real-world coordinates), it is positions above, not below the origin that are defined as positive (and the origin in real-world coordinates is usually defined as the screen center). Thus, when relating real-world and pixel coordinates there is a danger that the signs of vertical positions will become inadvertently flipped. Such flips are readily detected during data visualization by plotting the scatter for data from a set of known locations whose sign will be positive if data were processed correctly and negative if flipped (or vice versa).

[12] Notice that it is not possible to have pixel coordinates to the left, or above, the origin when it is defined as the upper left-hand corner of the screen, so all pixel coordinates must be positive using this scheme.

Identical Repeated Values

When collecting data via computer, there is usually a smallest possible number that can be represented. In the current version of MATLAB®, for example, this number is 10^{-306}. Thus, all data must be represented as discrete multiples of this smallest number. If data are rounded or truncated, this smallest-represented number is much larger. For example, if all data are truncated at the thousandths position, then all data must be represented as multiples of 10^{-3}. The level at which rounding or truncation occurs should be quite small relative to the size of the to-be-detected signal in the data. Or, if the size of the to-be-detected signal is unknown, then it should be small relative to the noise in the data (on the assumption that the signal strength may not be much larger than the noise); this means that if data with a spread of a few meters is rounded at the millionths (10^{-6}) position the discretization will typically not affect any analysis of the data, and discretization will not be seen in a plot or histogram (Fig. 1.9a, left). However, if rounding or truncation occurs at the ones position, there will be discretization as seen in Fig. 1.9b (right), and this will affect means, medians, etc. computed from these data. One way that we will detect a situation in which there has been unwanted or inadvertent rounding or truncation at an unacceptably course level is if we observe identical repeated values in a plot. This can be seen directly in the scatterplot in Fig. 1.9b (right). When this occurs, it is important to examine the data collection procedure in detail and eliminate any unwanted rounding, if possible. In some cases it is possible to fix the problem, but in others it is not. The most common instance in which it is not possible to fix unwanted discretization is when it is due to the sampling rate of data collection. When eye position data are acquired through an eyetracker, for example, the currently available technology allows eye position to be sampled at a rate of between 30 and 2000 Hz. At the low end of this range (30 Hz), data are only available once every 33 ms. This acquisition rate is a rather low if our goal is to characterize an eye movement, which can be completed in as little as 10 ms, and a plot of the timecourses of eye movements will clearly show gaps that the same plot with 2000 Hz data collection will not. The problem with low-sampling-rate data is that you can easily lose details in the data, when those details occur between samples. Indeed, the shortest-duration saccades last only 20–30 ms, which would make it impossible to detect any of the details of the timecourse of the saccade profile. Thus, it is best if your data obey the rule-of-thumb criterion that, when plotted, discretization is not obvious on the scale at which the signal is visible.

Although all of the above alerts should be examined carefully, we must not assume that they always occur because of a mistake, or always occur because of a previously unknown mechanism. Both of these possibilities are important to consider whenever we encounter one of the above alerts, but we should also consider one last possibility: that the unusual element of our data is the result of a relatively small sample size. It is obvious from the definitions of means and standard deviations that if we would like to compute a mean or standard deviation, more data are better - larger datasets lead to more stable estimates of means and standard deviations computed from noisy data. Small sample sizes also cause issues for correlations and bi-modality. Consider that any two-element dataset will display a correlation of one (either positive or negative), because a straight line drawn exactly through two datapoints will (a) not be horizontal (it is essentially impossible that the straight line between two noisy datapoints would be perfectly horizontal or vertical; see Exercises), and (b) will be perfectly predictive (the data will not deviate at all from the straight line drawn through them). Similarly, a two-element dataset will always be bi-modal (at lest for continuous data such as times or positions, because it is essentially impossible that two such data values will be exactly identical). Spurious correlations, bimodality, and differences from expectation are more likely to occur when dealing with small datasets.

Exercises

1) You collect data in which subjects were asked to place their fingertip over a target. The targets were arranged on a desktop. The data you obtain are d = [10.1 15.2 -15.5 121.2 22.1 -19.2]; all in cm. Compute the mean and standard deviation of the dataset. Do these values make sense given the background information? Why or why not?
2) Compute the mean and standard deviation of the dataset d=randn([101 2]). Round the dataset separately to the one-hundredths, tens, and ones positions, and recompute the means and standard deviations

1.3 Summary

Here, we have glimpsed the data-analytic algorithm that will occupy our attention for the remainder of the text – Bayesian data analysis. This was briefly contrasted with the now thoroughly discredited frequentist program of null hypothesis testing in an attempt to highlight some of the advantages, both theoretical and practical, of a probability-theory-based analysis of data over those outdated methods, as well as to put the modern method into historical context. Along the way, we have exposed some of the flaws in the statistical algorithm, and how they are corrected in the data-analytic algorithm of probability theory. Of these, we will find that the most important when dealing with applications is the inability of the statistical algorithm to deal with 'nuisance parameters' (first defined and examined in Chapter 2; you can think of them as parameters that, while present in the theory under test, are not directly relevant to our current test of the theory). Indeed, since there are virtually no (interesting) problems of scientific inference that do not require one to deal with nuisance parameters, we find that behavioral and neural scientists who have failed to move beyond the statistical algorithm are unable to make accurate quantitative comparisons when testing many of their most interesting hypotheses.

1.3.1 Emphasis on Worked Examples

Our exploration of data analysis in the remainder of the text will take a decidedly hands-on approach. This doesn't mean there will be any shortage of equations in later chapters, or that theory is de-emphasized. Rather, it means that I have included a great many example problems with worked solutions, including sample MATLAB® code for working through the examples yourself. I find that this is the only route to a deep understanding of the concepts introduced here: to experience them for yourself through example problems. And after that, a few more example problems.

A second reason for some emphasis on worked examples and learning to follow along on the computer (and some facility with coding) is to become familiar with trial and error. After completing this text, you should understand the theory, and be able to justify your ultimate analysis; but any real-world experimental data will require you to engage in trial-and-error before you come to that final analysis. It is easy to think that the mathematical derivations/analyses you see in this text and other published work have come about via a straightforward approach whereby one follows a linear progression from problem to solution. This is almost never the case. With interesting problems of data analysis there are often several attempts at a 'most appropriate analysis' before one hits upon the best approach. At each intermediate stage, one realizes that there are additional complexities to a problem, and these must be taken into account before the desired solution can be achieved. Each iteration of this process brings us closer to a more realistic and appropriate solution for the specifics of the particular problem at hand, whatever it may be. These trial-and-error iterations on our final analysis of data can be seen in sections A and D of Fig. 1.3, where loops are drawn to indicate that multiple iterations may be required, and the dashed two-way arrow indicates that the outcome of a data visualization may prompt us to revisit data simulations and our assumptions about the experimental data generally (which naturally leads to a new cycle of simulations, data visualizations, and analyses). This process of trial and error is virtually impossible without coding the analysis ourselves. Because while there is certainly no shortage of software intended for data analysis, prepackaged analyses almost never have the flexibility and power to deal with the complexities of real data; and even when they do, they stunt your thinking about the data because they simply spit out the result of an analysis without forcing you to think through the logical process of building the posterior distribution from (1.5). Without this process, it is easy to miss important nuances in a particular experiment or dataset that would otherwise let you know that the best analysis of your data is not what your first guess might have led you to expect. This process of trial and error, and of getting to know your data incrementally over the course of the analysis, is also the reason that so much space in this initial chapter has been devoted to data visualization (which is not properly part of a formal data analysis). Data visualization is a crucial part of any applied data analysis, and the trial-and-error involved in plotting, data-checking, etc. will supplement and guide your formal analyses, as delineated in Fig. 1.3.

So while the organization and logical flow of the text is driven by an exposition of the theory underlying formal data analysis, we will also take the time to provide you with the skills and experience to engage in trial and error, both via data visualization and the probability theory algorithm, in a variety of experimental circumstances. This is done with the goal of providing both a deeper understanding of the material, and a level of comfort with modern tools for data analysis and visualization (i.e., probability theory and coding).

1.3.2 Comment on Reality

Before moving on to applications, it is important to clarify what probability calculations can and cannot tell us. As with any branch of mathematics, all we can extract from probability equations is what we put into them to begin with; the information content never changes. But if this is the case, then you may be left wondering how it is that the probability equations [such as (1.5)] from which our analyses are forged can have any connection with reality. As we will see in later chapters, that connection exists when we include data in our calculations. Predata calculations are purely products of our assumptions and prior information (although some of these may be based on having generated data in previous experiments or having made other real-world observations). Furthermore, if the information put into a probability calculation is found not to reflect reality, the output of the corresponding probability analysis using this incorrect information should also not be expected to reflect reality.

These caveats are basic to all logical inference: We cannot extract from the mathematics that which is not already present at the start of the analysis. Mathematics only transforms what we know at the start of the analysis into a form that is, hopefully, more directly useful and understandable. But there is no magic here. No new information can suddenly occur as the result of our analyses. This is exactly as it should be. After all, did the deductive inferences at the beginning of the chapter reveal new information in their conclusions? Absolutely not. They simply assimilated what was already known and put it into a different form – one that presumably directly addressed a question we wanted to answer. The importance of understanding these connections is that we cannot fault probability theory for giving incorrect answers when we have given it incorrect/inaccurate information with which to produce inferences. The posterior distribution (the inference resulting from a probability-theory-based data analysis) is always the exactly correct answer to the question posed mathematically in (1.5), given the information that was put into the equations. The object of performing an experiment is to obtain the best possible information to inject into that analysis. We then transform that information (data) via (1.5) to directly answer questions of scientific interest.

1.3.3 Outline of the Text

The remainder of the text will be focused on acquiring the skills necessary to perform basic data analyses using (1.5). Chapter 2 examines how probability statements are manipulated and rearranged to answer basic questions, and ends with a discussion of the most common probability distributions used to describe discrete events (e.g., coin tosses and card draws). Chapter 3 examines the information contained in some of the most common probability distributions. This chapter is intended to expand your repertoire of probability distributions, and to consider what the information contained in various likelihood functions might imply about the best choice of prior distribution. Once you have encountered all the elements of the probability calculation in (1.5), you must gain some familiarity with the details of how these probability statements are converted to equations that can be used to generate useful analyses; these are the topics of the remaining chapters. These chapters offer many example problems in which the full probability algorithm is examined step by step (particularly Chapters 5 and 6).

CHAPTER TWO

MECHANICS OF PROBABILITY CALCULATIONS

The goal of this chapter is to provide the practical machinery needed for making probability calculations and assigning probability distributions. This involves both algebraically manipulating probability statements and manipulating the logical expressions *within* those probability statements. We therefore begin with a discussion of symbolic logic, which will provide us the necessary skill in interpreting and manipulating the logical expressions within probability statements. By the end of the chapter we will use this machinery to assign probability distributions, and investigate the role of sampling distributions and likelihood functions – two types of probability function – in scientific inference. Along the way (Section 2.1), we discuss the rationale for the conditioning statements found in the product rule that can sometimes seem opaque, and introduce the concepts of *marginalization* and *extending the question* in an applied context. Section 2.2 provides an introduction to assigning probability distributions, focusing on sampling distributions that describe sequences of coin tosses and other two-outcome processes (called Bernoulli trials). Section 2.3 describes the relationship between the sampling distribution, which is the crucial element in the null-hypothesis testing algorithm, and the likelihood function, used in Bayesian statistics. This section also provides a comparison of the potential for error when inferences are based on sampling distributions as compared to when they are based on likelihood functions.

As with any area of mathematics, your understanding of probability will improve with practice. This chapter includes many worked examples for this purpose, four of which are of special note: (1) an interesting example of probabilistic intuition gone awry – a version of the infamous Monty Hall problem; (2) a paradox of apparent sex bias in Berkeley admissions data; (3) medical decision-making, which highlights the potentially disastrous consequences of relying on frequentist statistics instead of the posterior; and (4) a simple example in which the null-hypothesis testing algorithm displays a logical inconsistency (Section 2.3.2), the optional stopping 'paradox.'

2.1 Symbolic Manipulations

Symbolic statements describing probabilities were discussed briefly in Chapter 1. These statements are defined by a two-part symbolic expression (Figure 1.2). The first part, the object of the statement, is the proposition to which the numerical probability is assigned. The second part, the conditioning statement(s), tells us the state of information under which the assigned probability is valid.

Logical expressions of any kind are formed from the combination of some set of propositions (denoted A, B, x, y, etc., and representing statements that may be true or false, such as 'it will rain tomorrow' or 'there are 25 hours in a day') combined by the logical operators AND (denoted ·), OR (denoted $\vee$), and NOT (denoted either by $\sim$ in front of the negated proposition, or by a bar over the negated proposition). For example, one would write $C = \sim A$ to indicate that C is simply the proposition that is the negation of whatever is expressed by A. We write $C = A \vee B$ to indicate that C is true whenever the proposition expressed by A is true or the proposition B is true, or when both are true. And finally, one would write $C = A \cdot B$ to indicate that C is true whenever the propositions expressed by both A and B are true simultaneously, but false if either A or B is false.

2.1.1 Formal Symbolic Operations for Logical Expressions

Each part of the logical statement may be manipulated via the rules of symbolic logic, or Boolean algebra.

Basic symbolic logic: The list of valid symbolic operations is as follows:

Associativity:
$$(A \vee B) \vee C = A \vee (B \vee C)$$
$$(A \cdot B) \cdot C = A \cdot (B \cdot C)$$

Commutativity:
$$A \vee B = B \vee A$$
$$A \cdot B = B \cdot A$$

Distributivity:
$$(A \cdot B) \vee C = (A \vee C) \cdot (B \vee C)$$
$$(A \vee B) \cdot C = (A \cdot C) \vee (B \cdot C)$$

Idempotence:
$$A \vee A = A$$
$$A \cdot A = A$$

Let's take a few examples of these attributes of logical statements, and relate them to their analogous properties from basic arithmetic. In each of the following examples we will construct a **truth table** of a compound logical proposition (i.e., a proposition composed of multiple subpropositions that are connected by the logical operators · or $\vee$). A truth table lists the possible true-false values of the propositions that compose a compound logical statement, and for each combination of truth values of its constituents also lists the truth value of the total statement.

Example: Commutative Property of Logical OR and AND
Of the first three properties, commutativity is the simplest: the **commutative property** states that it is irrelevant how we order two propositions joined by the logical operations $\vee$ (OR) or ·(AND). We see the same property in addition and multiplication, because it is irrelevant to the result whether we multiply 5×2 or 2×5. In multiplication we verify the commutative property by noticing that multiplication of any two numbers will yield the same answer when the order of the two numbers is reversed. To verify the commutative property for logical propositions, we create a truth table of a two-proposition logical statement connected by $\vee$ or and confirm that the table remains unchanged when the order of the logical statements is reversed. The truth table for logical OR is given in Table 2.1A, and if we reverse the order of the inputs, the truth table remains identical (note the equality of two symbolic statements is demonstrated if the truth tables are identical). The last two columns of the table show the commutative property for logical AND.

TABLE 2.1A Truth table for commutative property

A value	*B* value	$A \vee B$	$B \vee A$	$A \cdot B$	$B \cdot A$
true (1)	*true* (1)	$[1 \vee 1] = 1$	$[1 \vee 1] = 1$	$[1 \cdot 1] = 1$	$[1 \cdot 1] = 1$
true (1)	*false* (0)	$[1 \vee 0] = 1$	$[0 \vee 1] = 1$	$[1 \cdot 0] = 0$	$[1 \cdot 0] = 0$
false (0)	*true* (1)	$[0 \vee 1] = 1$	$[1 \vee 0] = 1$	$[0 \cdot 1] = 0$	$[0 \cdot 1] = 0$
false (0)	*false* (0)	$[0 \vee 0] = 1$	$[0 \vee 0] = 1$	$[0 \cdot 0] = 0$	$[0 \cdot 0] = 0$

TABLE 2.1B Truth table for associative property

(*a*, b, c) values	$(a \cdot b) \cdot c$	$a \cdot (b \cdot c)$	$(a \cdot c) \cdot b$
(1,1,1)	$(1) \cdot 1 = 1$	$1 \cdot (1) = 1$	$(1) \cdot 1 = 1$
(1,1,0)	$(1) \cdot 0 = 0$	$1 \cdot (0) = 0$	$(0) \cdot 1 = 0$
(1,0,1)	$(0) \cdot 1 = 0$	$1 \cdot (0) = 0$	$(1) \cdot 0 = 0$
(0,1,1)	$(0) \cdot 1 = 0$	$0 \cdot (1) = 0$	$(0) \cdot 1 = 0$
(0,0,0)	$(0) \cdot 0 = 0$	$0 \cdot (0) = 0$	$(0) \cdot 0 = 0$
(0,0,1)	$(0) \cdot 1 = 0$	$0 \cdot (0) = 0$	$(0) \cdot 0 = 0$
(0,1,0)	$(0) \cdot 0 = 0$	$0 \cdot (0) = 0$	$(0) \cdot 1 = 0$
(1,0,0)	$(0) \cdot 0 = 0$	$1 \cdot (0) = 0$	$(0) \cdot 0 = 0$

Now that we have seen an example showing equality of truth tables, it is important to also see an example of truth tables that are not identical. To do this note the basic inequality of the logical operations AND ($\cdot$) and OR ($\vee$), demonstrated by comparing an OR column to an AND column of Table 2.1A. Logical expressions are unequal when any row of the table gives unequal truth-values for the two expressions. That is, if any input produces unequal outputs in the two logical expressions, the logical expressions cannot be the same. We see in Table 2.1A that logical AND can only be true when all of its inputs are true. On the other hand, logical OR[1] can only be false when all of its inputs are false.

Exercises

1) Construct a truth table for $a \cdot (b \vee c)$, and compare it to the truth table for $(a \cdot b) \vee (a \cdot c)$.
2) Construct a truth table for $a \vee (b \cdot c)$, and compare it to the truth table for $(a \vee b) \cdot (a \vee c)$.

Example: Associative Property of Logical Expressions

The associative property of logical expressions states that one may group multiple expressions connected by one of the two logical operators in any way one likes. This matches

[1] We should also point out, that the standard version of logical OR, and the one we use here, can is also referred to as inclusive or, and either-or-both. This is in contrast to exclusive or, also called XOR. The truth table for XOR is slightly different than that of OR, because whereas inclusive or is true when *either one* or *both* of its inputs is true, exclusive or is true when *only one* if its inputs is true. In other words, you can think of XOR as a kind of a difference detector. It is false when the truth-values of A and B are identical (either both true or both false), and it is true when the truth-values of the two inputs are different.

the associative property of addition and multiplication: If we must multiply N numbers, for example the product of three numbers $d = abc$, we may group that series of multiplications in any convenient way without changing the outcome. For example, we may first multiply a and b, and then take that product and multiply it by c to obtain the final result $d = (ab)c$. Alternatively, we may have initially multiplied b and c, and taken that product to multiply by a to obtain the final result $d = a(bc)$. The same insensitivity to grouping also applies to a series of additions, but notice that associativity applies to arbitrary groupings so long as one is *only* adding or *only* multiplying. When we mix additions and multiplications, we may *not* change the grouping of the suboperations and still expect to end with the same answer.

As with addition and multiplication, we may group a series of propositions connected *only* by logical $\vee$ or *only* by logical $\cdot$ in any convenient way without changing the final truth-value of the compound proposition. Thus, if we have the compound proposition, $a \cdot b \cdot c$, we may first evaluate any pair, $(a \cdot b, b \cdot c, a \cdot c)$, for its truth value, and then complete the analysis of the three-element compound proposition by combining this value with the truth value of the remaining proposition $[(a \cdot b) \cdot c, a \cdot (b \cdot c), (a \cdot c) \cdot b]$. We can see this also in the truth table, Table 2.1B, showing the possible input truth-values for the three-value compound proposition for the three configurations discussed.

Notice that as the length of the series of propositions increases in length, the proportion of rows in the $\cdot$ truth table that are true decreases dramatically (one of four in a two-element compound $\cdot$ proposition, one of eight for a three element proposition, etc.). The opposite is true of a series of propositions all connected by $\vee$, because the only way for such a series to be false is when all constituents are false.

Exercises

1) Construct a truth table for $a \cdot b \cdot c \cdot d$, demonstrating the associative property.
2) What is the ratio of true to false compound propositions in the truth table for $a \cdot b \cdot c \cdot d$?

Example: Distributive Property of Logical Expressions

The associative property applies when there are multiple propositions connected only by logical $\cdot$ or only by logical $\vee$; but what happens when we have propositions connected by mixed combinations of these two logical operators? The distributive property of logical expressions describes the way propositions connected by mixed combinations of logical $\vee$ and logical $\cdot$ are evaluated. Again, we will use the analogy with addition and multiplication to demonstrate distributivity.

The distributive property in addition and multiplication tells us that when we have mixed combinations of addition and multiplication, we may distribute the multiplications across a combined set of additions, as in: $a(b + c) = ab + ac$. Thus, we may take an example where we are computing $5(2 + 3)$, and equivalently compute $5(2) + 5(3)$.

This property holds for *both* the logical $\vee$ and logical $\cdot$ operators. Thus we may distribute an OR-connected proposition that pairs with a set of AND-connected propositions, as in:

$$a \cdot (b \vee c) = (a \cdot b) \vee (a \cdot c)$$

and also the inverse, as in

$$a \vee (b \cdot c) = (a \vee b) \cdot (a \vee c)$$

The distributive property of logical expressions will allow us to combine and simplify complex logical operations, just as the distributive property in basic mathematics can allow us to simplify algebraic expressions.

Exercises

1) Construct a truth table for $a \cdot (b \vee c)$, and compare it to the truth table for $(a \cdot b) \vee (a \cdot c)$.
2) Construct a truth table for $a \vee (b \cdot c)$, and compare it to the truth table for $(a \vee b) \cdot (a \vee c)$.

Example: Equality of Expressions Differing Only by Idempotent Expressions
The idempotent property simply tells us that redundant information does not change the truth value of a logical expression. Thus, if we assert the proposition A, it is no different than asserting that proposition twice – via *either* of the two logical operators (i.e., $A = A \vee A = A \cdot A$). This simple example may seem so obvious that it may appear unnecessary to spend time on idempotence, but in more complex relations proper application of the idempotent property may be more difficult to intuit. As an example note the identity of the two logical expressions, $C = [A \vee B]$ and $C = [(A \cdot A) \vee B]$, that differ by the idempotent relation, $A \cdot A$.

Here, the analogy with basic mathematical properties is less exact, which is why this comparison is left to the end. However, the idempotent property is a bit like the additive or multiplicative identity properties (i.e., $a + 0 = a$ and $ax1 = a$), where applying the addition or multiplication operators (respectively) does not change the result. Here, we may add as many zeros as we like to an initial number and not change that initial number ($3+0+0+\cdots+0 = 3$), or we may multiply an initial number by as many ones ($5 \times 1 \times 1 \times \cdots \times 1 = 5$) as we like without changing that initial number. The idempotent property for logical expressions applies slightly differently, because we are applying the operator (logical $\cdot$ or logical $\vee$) to sets of the *identical* proposition. The basic rule being that adding redundancy to a statement does not change the truth value of your assertion. If A is true, then A AND A as well as A OR A must also be true; further, if A is false then A OR A (as well as A AND A) is also false. Whenever we find a redundancy in a complex logical statement, the idempotent property allows us to simplify that statement by removing the redundancy.

Exercises

1) Construct a truth table for
   a. $C = [A \vee B]$
   b. $C = [(A \cdot A) \vee B]$
   c. $C = [(A \cdot A) \vee (B \vee B)] \ldots$
2) Evaluate the expression, $a \cdot (a \vee \bar{a})$, and explain in words why it has the result it does.

Duality
In addition to the list of symbolic operations given above, there is a property called duality which allows one to interchange all $\cdot$ operations with $\vee$ operations, and vice versa, where (a) each element of the resulting expression has the opposite truth value, and (b) the overall expression has the opposite truth value of the original. For example, recall

Programming Aside: Logical Statements

The flow of information through a program is often determined by a set of logical statements, such as

```
if A,
        {execute commands based on truth of A}
else if B,
        {execute commands based on truth of B}
else if C,
        {execute commands based on truth of C}
else
        {execute default commands}
end
```

The series of statements enclosed by if...else...elseif...elseif...end are executed differentially depending on whether the logical statements A or B or C are TRUE. A, B, C are propositions whose truth values we set earlier in the program. Here we will use the built-in random number generator to practice using the if...else...elseif logical structure.

```
N=rand([1 2]);
if and(N>.5), ['option 1']
  elseif and(N<.5), [option 2']
  else ['default option'], end
```

The output will be one of the three options. Which is least likely? What happens if it is possible for more than one option to be true?

that $A \vee \bar{A} = 1$. The dual, $\overline{A \vee \bar{A}} = \bar{A} \cdot \bar{\bar{A}} = \bar{A} \cdot A = 0$, is also a valid expression. Duality is often useful when an entire logical expression is negated, because the dual lets us break up the solid overbar negating the entire expression, allowing each element of the expression to be further manipulated and combined. For example, the negation of the U term in $F = A \vee \bar{U}$, where $U = \bar{A} \cdot (\bar{B} \vee C)$, causes the full expression to be written: $F = A \vee \overline{\bar{A} \cdot (\bar{B} \vee C)}$. This is difficult to work with, because all three elements are being negated simultaneously. The dual, $\bar{\bar{A}} \vee (\bar{\bar{B}} \cdot \bar{c})$, is simpler to deal with and allows us to easily reduce the resulting expression to: $F = A \vee (B \cdot \bar{C})$.

The dual is also naturally indicated when we are dealing with a mutually exclusive and exhaustive set (such as $A_1 \vee A_2 \vee A_3 = 1$), because every expression in the set, for example, A_2, can be written either as itself, A_2, or as the complement of the remaining propositions, $A_2 = 1 - (A_1 \vee A_3) = \overline{A_1 \vee A_3} = \bar{A}_1 \cdot \bar{A}_3$. Several examples of this line of reasoning will be a crucial element of our logical analysis of signal detection problems in later chapters.

Exercises

1) Construct a truth table for
   a. $A \cdot B \cdot (C \vee A)$

b. $A \vee C \cdot (B \vee \bar{A})$
c. $\overline{A \vee B \cdot (C \vee \bar{D})}$

2) Give the dual of 1c, and show that the truth tables are exactly opposite, and therefore equal to the expression under the large negation bar of 1c.
3) Evaluate F. Assume that sets of A_i are mutually exclusive and exhaustive, which means that the disjunction of the entire set A_i always has a truth value of 1. For example, in the case of $i = [1\ 2]$, this reduces to $A_1 \vee A_2 = A \vee \bar{A} = 1$.
   a. $F = B \vee C \vee A_1 \vee A_2$
   b. $F = C \cdot (A_1 \vee A_2)$
   c. $F = (A_1 \vee A_2 \vee A_3 \vee \ldots \vee A_n) \cdot B$
   d. $F = (A_1 \vee A_2) \cdot (B \vee A_3)$
   e. $F = E \vee (A_1 \cdot A_2)s$

2.1.2 Intuitive Rationale behind the Basic Rules of Probability Theory

There was some discussion of the sum and product rules of probability theory in Chapter 1, but in that chapter we simply rearranged these probability statements algebraically, without any modification of the logical expressions within those probability statements. In this section, we will present an intuitive rationale for these rules, focusing on the structure of the logical expressions *within* probability statements. These are not formal proofs, but will help to educate your intuitions about the sum and product rules.

The **sum rule** is relatively straightforward: the probability that one or the other of two propositions is true is just the sum of the probabilities assigned the two propositions, minus the probability corresponding to any overlap between the two. The only potential issue here is the reason behind subtracting the probability corresponding to the overlap (i.e., the probability that *both* a and b are true). In short, it is because computing the sum of probabilities for two propositions double-counts any overlap in the two, and subtracting the overlap therefore removes this double-counted probability mass. This is illustrated in Figure 2.1, where we show the universe of possibilities consistent with our

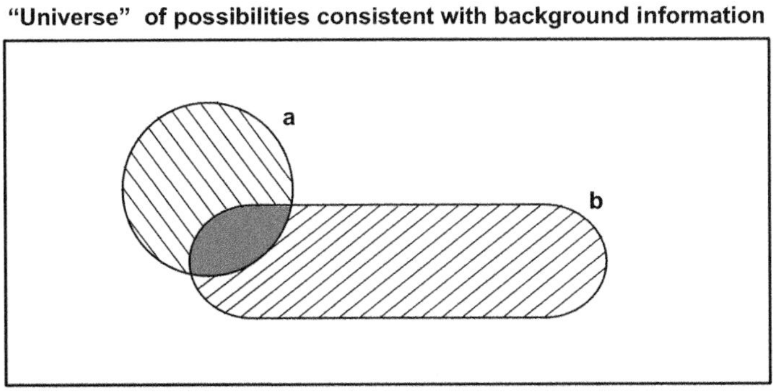

Figure 2.1 Venn diagram of the compound proposition $a \vee b$. The rectangle represents logical space consistent with our background information; the circle is the portion of that space consistent with the proposition a, and the oblong with b; $p(a \vee b \mid \iota)$ is the probability representing the combined circle–oblong space. This probability must be computed $p(a \mid \iota) + p(b \mid \iota) - p(a \cdot b \mid \iota)$. The probability of the common region, $p(a \cdot b \mid \iota)$, must be subtracted from the sum $p(a \mid \iota) + p(b \mid \iota)$ or it will be counted twice.

BOX 2.1 Independent Probabilities

The term 'independent' or 'independence' is found in several scientific and data-analytic contexts. As applied to probabilities, it simply means that information regarding the outcome of one event (call it a) does not affect your probability assignment for another event (b); in other words, the statement that 'b is independent of a' means that your probability assignment for proposition b is unaffected by having observed a.

In an equation we might represent the background information leading to an assignment of independent probabilities as ι_i, where that statement of independent probabilities is $p(b|a \cdot \iota_i) = p(b|\iota_i)$, or $p(a \cdot b|\iota_i) = p(a|\iota_i)p(b|\iota_i)$ which are both consequences of the other:

$$\begin{aligned} p(b|a \cdot \iota_i) &= \frac{p(a \cdot b|\iota_i)}{p(a|\iota_i)} \\ &= \frac{p(b|\iota_i)p(a|\iota_i)}{p(a|\iota_i)} \\ &= p(b|\iota_i) \end{aligned}$$

$$\begin{aligned} p(a \cdot b|\iota_i) &= p(b|a \cdot \iota_i)p(a|\iota_i) \\ &= p(b|\iota_i)p(a|\iota_i) \end{aligned}$$

Graphically, it is easiest to examine nonindependence and independence in a 2D probability surface (e.g., Figures 1.6 and 1.7), by taking 'slices' parallel to either axis. Any slice through y_j parallel to the x-axis defines a 1D probability distribution, $p(x|y_i \cdot \iota)$, and slices through any point x_i parallel to the y-axis will define a 1D distribution $p(y|x_i \cdot \iota)$. In the uncorrelated case, our best guess about the value of y is unaffected by having been told the x-value of a new datum. In the correlated case, we can make better guesses about the y-value of a new datum.

An additional important point here is that 'independent probabilities' is a statement about our information, where knowing the value of a does not allow us to update our information about b. There are two basic scenarios that lead us to assert independent probabilities: based either on the absence or presence of information about a and b. In one type of situation, exemplified by die rolls with a perfectly symmetrical die and constantly changing method of rolling, there is no way to predict the outcome of the next roll of the die based on the outcomes of past rolls. The outcomes of a die roll can also be assigned independent probabilities simply on ignorance about the physical characteristics of the die and its method of rolling: here we have no reason to treat die faces asymmetrically on the second roll based on the first, and therefore must also assign independent probabilities.

Finally, recognize that probabilistic dependence is not the same as causality; indeed, neither implies the other. Two events may in fact be causally dependent, but the probabilities must remain independent until we discover this fact. On the other hand, pairs of events (e.g., total Queen Anne and Hudson cherry crop yields) do not directly cause one another, but are nevertheless logically dependent (information about one should influence our information about the other). Misunderstanding regarding the difference between causal and logical dependence can comes from the (correct) notion that when there is a logical dependence, this often implies participation in a shared causal network, but in also failing to recognize that this causal link need not be direct (recall Fig. 1.8; Queen Anne and Hudson cherries do not physically influence *one another directly*, but yields are nevertheless part of a causal network because both are directly influenced by many similar factors (temperature, soil, rainfall, bees, etc.).

background information, as well as the regions within that universe of possibility consistent with the propositions a and b The sum rule, $p(a \vee b|\imath)$, should tell us the probability encompassed by those regions (circle and oval) relative to the total in the rectangle. This area is *not*, however, just the sum of the probabilities of the a and b regions, because the solid-filled area would be counted twice: once as part of the circular region, and once as part of the oblong region. Subtracting the joint probability of the two propositions simply removes this double counting.

In the special case where there is no overlap between two propositions (for a mutually exclusive pair of propositions), the probability that one or the other proposition is true is simply the sum of their individual probabilities. In the case where these nonoverlapping propositions also have probabilities that sum to one, that is, for a mutually exclusive *and* exhaustive set of possibilities such as A and $\bar{A}$ (that together fill the entire rectangle in Fig. 2.1), one option must be true and both cannot be.

Although the sum rule was relatively straightforward, the **product rule** is less so. This is perhaps because the majority of our thoughts about assigning probabilities involve situations such as coin tossing and dice rolling, and it happens to be true that most of the time these activities can be described by probabilities that are independent of one another (see Box 2.1) which is a special case in which the outcome of one event (e.g., the ith coin toss) does not help us guess the outcome of another event (i + nth) toss.

When the probability of one event (A) does not provide information relevant to assigning the probability of another event (B), the product rule reduces to $p(A \cdot B|\imath) = p(A|\imath)p(B|\imath)$. As a general rule, however, this is not the correct expression of a joint probability; the general case must take account of an influence of information about A or B on the other member of the pair. Consider the example

$T_i \equiv$ The ith toss of the coin comes up tails.

$H_i \equiv$ The ith toss of the coin comes up heads.

$\imath_0 \equiv$ The coin is either two-headed, or two-tailed.

On the first toss, the probability of heads is equal to the probability of tails: $p(H_1|\imath_0) = p(T_1|\imath_0) = 0.5$. Even though we know that heads and tails are not *both* possible outcomes of this first toss, we do not know which type of coin we are flipping, and so have no way to prefer heads versus tails: we can only assign them equal probabilities. However, on the second toss, we have a different situation: the outcome of the first toss is now quite relevant to our probability assignment. Now, the probability of heads will be assigned either a 1 or 0, depending on the outcome of the first toss:

$$p(H_1 \cdot H_2|\imath_0) = p(H_2|H_1 \cdot \imath_0)p(H_1|\imath_0) = 1 \text{ or}$$
$$p(T_1 \cdot H_2|\imath_0) = p(H_2|T_1 \cdot \imath_0)p(T_1|\imath_0) = 0$$

We use this general case of the product rule, taking account of conditioning information, whenever information about the one proposition is relevant to the value of the other proposition in a joint probability.

Exercises

1) The following is the derivation of the sum rule for two propositions that are neither mutually exclusive nor exhaustive:
   Starting with the sum rule for the compound proposition $A \vee B$

$$p(A \vee B|\imath) + p(\overline{A \vee B}|\imath) = 1$$
$$p(A \vee B|\imath) = 1 - p(\overline{A \vee B}|\imath)$$
$$= 1 - p(\bar{A} \cdot \bar{B}|\imath)$$

   and by the product rule (1.2)

$$= 1 - p(\bar{A}|\imath)p(\bar{B}|\bar{A} \cdot \imath)$$
$$= 1 - p(\bar{A}|\imath)[1 - p(B|\bar{A} \cdot \imath)]$$
$$= 1 - p(\bar{A}|\imath) + p(\bar{A}|\imath)p(\bar{B}|\bar{A} \cdot \imath)$$

   and by the sum rule (1.1)

$$= p(A|\imath) + p(\bar{A}|\imath)p(B|\bar{A} \cdot \imath)$$

   and after another set of applications of the product and sum rules

$$= p(A|\imath) + p(B|\imath) - p(A \cdot B|\imath)$$

   Using repeated application of the sum and product rules:
2) Fill in the details of the final step ('another set of applications of the product and sum rules' in the derivation of $p(A \vee B|\imath)$ above.
3) Derive an analogous expression for two propositions, where they are known to be mutually exclusive but not exhaustive: $p(A \vee B|\imath_{\text{ME}\cdot\sim\text{EX}})$.
4) Derive an extended sum rule for any three propositions: $p(A \vee B \vee C|\imath)$.
5) Derive an expression for a 3-term joint probability $p(A \cdot B \cdot C|\imath)$
   a. where $\imath$ indicates that the probabilities assigned to A, B, C are independent.
   b. in which $\imath$ indicates that the probabilities assigned to A, B, C are not necessarily independent.
6) Derive an expression for a 4-term joint probability $p(A \cdot B \cdot C \cdot D|\imath)$
   a. in which $\imath$ indicates that the probabilities assigned to A, B, C, D are independent.
   b. where $\imath$ indicates that the probabilities assigned to A, B, C, D are not necessarily independent.
7) Comment on the conditions that would allow one to assert that the correct frequency distribution of heads in a coin-tossing 'experiment' had been assigned (i.e., under the frequency definition of probability).
8) In the two-headed or two-tailed coin example, imagine that you have tossed the coin twice, but only your friend observes the outcome. Based only on *your* information, expand the following probabilities via the product rule and assign them probabilities:

a. $p(H_1 \cdot H_2|\iota_0)$
b. $p(H_1 \cdot T_2|\iota_0)$
c. $p(T_1 \cdot H_2|\iota_0)$
d. $p(T_1 \cdot T_2|\iota_0)$

2.1.3 Extending the Question

'Extending the question' is a technique that is a consequence of the sum rule and the logical statement $B = B \cdot 1$, and we will see is closely related to marginalization. The technique is used when we would like to *add* a variable to a probability statement. For example, we could add the variable A (which, from background information we know can take on n possible values) to the probability statement $p(B|\iota)$ by writing: $p(B|\iota) = p(B \cdot 1|\iota) = p(B \cdot [A_1 \vee A_2 \vee \cdots \vee A_n]|\iota)$. Indeed, the name 'extending the question' comes from the fact that we have extended the probability statement to include an additional variable.

We will return to coin tossing to illustrate the concept of extending the question. Instead of the usual case of a single toss, let's use the following scenario:

$\iota_0 \equiv$ The coin is tossed 100 times, with each toss recorded as $T = 0$, or $H = 1$).

The above considerations lead us to the general algorithm: to assign a probability in which a relevant but unknown term (such as O_2 above) must be one of several mutually exclusive outcomes we must (A) construct a joint probability statement with the unknown term ($H_3 = 1 \cdot H_3 = O_2 \cdot H_3$), and $p(H_3|\iota_1 = p(O_2 \cdot H_3|\iota_1)$, where the constituents of O_i can be any of ($o_1 \;\; o_2 \ldots o_n$), and (B), assign the value of the unknown term as a disjunction of the possibilities. Thus a general equation, where $O = (o_1 \vee o_2 \vee \cdots \vee o_n)$, is

$$
\begin{aligned}
p(A|\iota) &= p(A \cdot 1|\iota) \\
&= p(A \cdot O|\iota) \\
&= p(A \cdot [o_1 \vee o_2 \vee \cdots \vee o_n|\iota) \\
&= p(A \cdot o_1 \vee A \cdot o_2 \vee \cdots \vee A \cdot o_n|\iota) \\
&= p(A \cdot o_1|\iota) + p(A \cdot o_2|\iota) + \cdots + p(A \cdot o_n|\iota)
\end{aligned}
\qquad (2.1).
$$

Exercises

1) Show the calculations for predictions of the first through fifth tosses, all under information ι_m, m=1.
2) ι_u: There are 100 jelly beans in an urn, each of 3 possible flavors (10 strawberry, 50 mint, 40 blueberry). While blindfolded, you choose beans from the urn (without replacing them). Assign the following probabilities:
   a. $p(M_1 \cdot S_2|\iota_u)$
   b. $p([M_1 \vee B_1] \cdot S_2|\iota_u)$
   c. $p(M_3|\iota_u)$
3) In Chapter 1 several examples were given that were predicated on the idea that the six sides of a die might each be stamped with either one or two dots. Each of these examples then went on to provide a statement about how many of the faces were

stamped with one and with two dots. If, however, the statement of the problem had stopped with the first statement, and all we knew is that each face might have one or two dots, we still have enough information to assign $p(d_1|\iota)$. Starting from $p(d_1|\iota) = p(d_1 \cdot 1|\iota)$, solve this problem.

2.1.4 Marginalization

The basic concept of marginalization is a consequence of the sum rule (1.1), which states that the probability of a set of mutually exclusive propositions (e.g., $a_1, a_2, \ldots, a_n$) is the sum of the probabilities assigned to those propositions. We will use this basic idea of marginalization to remove unwanted dimensions from multidimensional distributions, as well as to combine theoretically equivalent values of variables.

Marginalizing over Nuisance Variables

The ability to marginalize over an entire dimension of a multidimensional distribution is a consequence of the logical rule: $A \cdot (B \vee \bar{B}) = A \cdot 1 = A$. In words, any proposition, A, in conjunction with certainty (e.g., the disjunction of a mutually exclusive and exhaustive set such as $(B \vee \bar{B})$ has a truth value equal to A. Let's convince ourselves of this with a simple example before moving to more realistic applications. First, let's define the independent probabilities, $p(A|\iota) = 0.2, p(B|\iota) = 0.6$, and then insert numbers into $A \cdot (B \vee \bar{B}) = A \cdot 1 = A$:

$$p(A \cdot [B \vee \bar{B}]|\iota) = p(A \cdot B|\iota) + p(A \cdot \bar{B}|\iota) = (.2)(.6) + (.2)(.4) = .2$$

The most common scientific application of marginalization occurs when our theoretical model naturally includes multiple variables whose values are unknown, and we would like to compute probability distributions over one of these variables individually (Fig. C.3). For example, we will come across many instances of the Gaussian sampling distribution (giving the probability of observing data d, and is a bell-shaped distribution),

$$p(d|\mu \cdot \sigma \cdot \iota) = (\sigma\sqrt{2\pi})^{-1} e^{-\frac{1}{2}\frac{(d-\mu)^2}{\sigma^2}}$$

which requires that we provide location (μ) and scale (σ) parameters, and dataset (d). This Gaussian function is also our likelihood when we use Bayes' rule (1.5) to compute the posterior over the Gaussian parameters: $p(\mu \cdot \sigma|d \cdot \iota)$. This two-dimensional posterior (Fig. 2.2) describes our information about the two Gaussian parameters after collecting data (d). In the end, however, we are generally only interested in the value of the location parameter, and want to compute the 1D probability distribution over μ based on d, regardless of the value of σ. We compute the desired 1D posterior by marginalizing the σ-axis out of the 2D posterior.

To demonstrate this marginalization, let's start by simplifying the problem a bit. First, assume we have information (given in ι) about the possible range of values of μ and σ: $-10 \leq \mu \leq 10$, and $0 < \sigma \leq 15$. Furthermore, assume that within their respective ranges the variables are discrete, with μ taking the 40 equally spaced discrete values $[\mu_1 = -9.75, \mu_2 = -9.25, \ldots, \mu_{40} = 9.75]$, and σ taking 30 equally spaced discrete

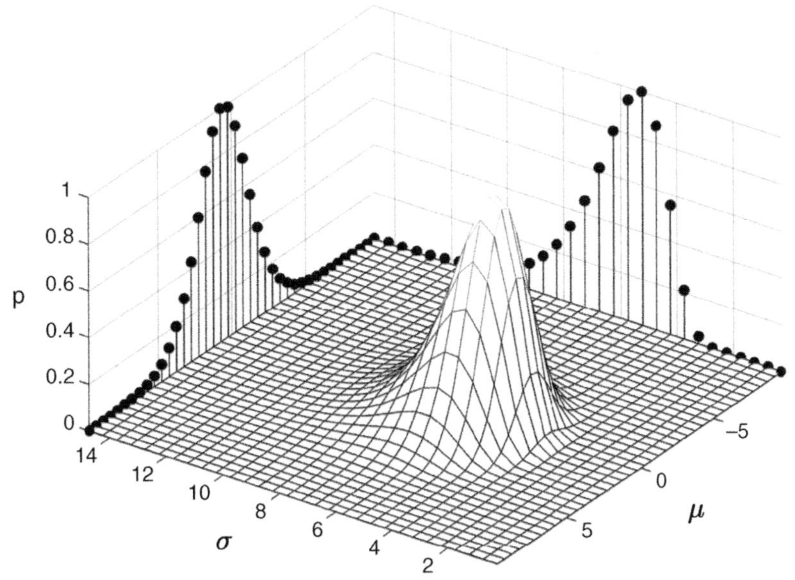

Figure 2.2 Marginalization over uninteresting ('nuisance') parameters. The figure shows both a 2D probability surface for a joint probability $p(\mu_i \cdot \sigma_j|d \cdot \imath)$, and the two corresponding 1D marginalized probability distributions (plotted in the margins). The two 1D distributions describe our information about the variable along the parallel axis, *regardless of* the true value of the variable along the perpendicular axis.

values $[\sigma_1 = 0.25, \sigma_2 = 0.75, \ldots, \sigma_{30} = 14.75]$. These sets of μ and σ values are each mutually exclusive and exhaustive; so for example $p([\sigma_1 \vee \sigma_2 \vee \cdots \vee \sigma_{30}]|\imath) = 1$.

We now marginalize to answer the question, 'What is the probability distribution over μ based on the data (d), regardless of the value of σ?' That is, we want the 1D posterior whose ith element is $p(\mu_i|d \cdot \imath)$, which after extending the question we see is equal to $p(\mu_i \cdot [1]|d \cdot \imath) = p(\mu_i \cdot [\sigma_1 \vee \sigma_2 \vee \cdots \vee \sigma_{30}]|d \cdot \imath)$, Thus, we obtain the desired probability by computing

$$\begin{aligned} p(\mu_i|d \cdot \imath) &= p(\mu_i \cdot [\sigma_1 \vee \sigma_2 \vee \cdots \vee \sigma_{30}]|d \cdot \imath) \\ &= p(\mu_i \cdot \sigma_1|d \cdot \imath) + p(\mu_i \cdot \sigma_2]|d \cdot \imath) + \cdots + p(\mu_i \cdot \sigma_{30}|d \cdot \imath) \\ &= \sum_j p(\mu_i \cdot \sigma_j|d \cdot \imath). \end{aligned} \qquad (2.2a).$$

To obtain the marginal distributions in Figure 2.2 we made the simplifying assumption of discrete μ and σ parameters. However, in most applications we will be concerned with continuous parameters, and marginalization over continuous parameters is often accomplished via calculus-based methods:

$$P(\mu|d \cdot \imath) = \int_0^{15} d\sigma \; p(\mu \cdot \sigma|d \cdot \imath) \qquad (2.2b).$$

Programming Aside: Marginalization over Nuisance Parameters (Fig. 2.2)

We begin by computing the 2D posterior over the Gaussian parameters:

```
mu=linspace(-10,10,41); mu=mu(2:end)-diff(mu(1:2))/2; %equally-spaced mu values
sig=linspace(0,15,31); sig=sig(2:end)-diff(sig(1:2))/2; %sigmas
D=nrand(0,5,11);
p=nan(length(mu),length(sig)); %initialize 2D-probsurface
```

The dataset (D) stays constant while we compute the posterior probabilities of (μ, σ) -pairs:

```
for snow=1:length(sig), %for each value of sigma
    for mnow=1:length(mu), %for each value of mu
        Lnow=1; %reset p for ith mu and jth sig
        for dnow=1:length(D), %for each datum
            %gaussian likelihood
            Lnow=Lnow/(sqrt(2*pi)*sig(snow))*exp(-.5*(D(dnow)...
                -mu(mnow))^2/sig(snow)^2); end
        p(mnow,snow)=Lnow;end, end %put p at ith mu and jth sig into 2D matrix
figure; meshc(sig,mu,p/max(max(p))); colormap bone
view(-145,45); r=axis; hold on
```

Note the innermost for-loop computes the likelihood, and the other two loops step through (μ, σ)-pairs. Next marginalize over σ axis, yielding the desired 1D distribution over μ:

```
pmu=sum(p,2); pmu=pmu/max(pmu); %marginalize over SIGMAs
for mnow=1:length(mu), %plotting
    plot3(sig(end)*[1 1],mu(mnow)*[1 1],[0 pmu(mnow)],'k-');
    plot3(sig(end),mu(mnow),pmu(mnow),'ko','MarkerFaceColor','k'); end
```

Appendix C shows that the approximate solution to the continuous marginalization problem, and therefore the integral in (2.2b), is identical to the solution just given for the discretized problem (if we use 30 and 40 sampled densities; the approximation improves if we use several hundred). Thus, when we see an integral equation, even if you are unfamiliar with calculus, you can still understand what the equation is asking you to do and compute a numerical solution. Not only is this method of approximate solution useful when you are unsure how to solve a particular integral, but it is also the format for numerical evaluation via computer, and will allow us to avoid use of the Calculus in this text. If you are unfamiliar with this procedure, please complete the exercises in **Appendix C** before continuing. In the remainder of the text we will write marginalizations over continuous variables in the calculus format (2.2b), and assume that you are using the numerical methods described in **Appendix C** for their solution.

Marginalizing over Theoretically Equivalent Values of Variables

In some cases, one is interested in comparing the probabilities associated with different subsets of the possible values of a parameter. As an example, one may be interested in the rate at which heads turns up when flipping a coin in a particular manner. Perhaps a friend has told you about a method of flipping coins that she assures you will increase the theoretical rate of heads, relative to the one-half that you yourself observe when flipping the same coin, to at least two-thirds. Denote the true rate of obtaining heads θ. We will be interested in probabilities of rates, $p(\theta|d \cdot m \cdot \imath)$, where m is the new method of tossing the coin devised by your friend, and the full set of possible θ values ranges from 0 to 1.

Notice that here we do not wish to calculate a probability after removing the entire θ parameter, as in the example above. Rather, we are interested in calculating the probability of the rate parameter within the range consistent with our friend's assertion, $\theta > 2/3$. We combine probabilities associated with this range of rates because under our friend's claim all rates above 2/3 support her claim. To marginalize over this range, we write

$$p(\theta > 2/3|d \cdot m \cdot \Delta_\theta \cdot \imath) = \int_{2/3}^{1} d\theta p(\theta|d \cdot m \cdot \Delta_\theta \cdot \imath) \quad (2.3).$$

We will wait until Chapter 6 for a full answer to this problem. However, as a preview of one important issue to be dealt with in detail in Chapter 6, notice that our friend begins with an unfair advantage, because there is a range of rates consistent with her claim but only $\theta = 0.5$ consistent with the counter-claim of 'regular coin flipping.' Therefore, when we attempt to compare evidence for and against our friend's claim, we will want a method that does not ignore the different volumes of parameter space covered by the competing claims.

Exercises

1) $\imath$: A, B, C are not mutually exclusive.
   Assign probabilities to
   a. $p(\mu_i \cdot [\sigma_1 \vee \sigma_2 \vee \cdots \vee \sigma_{11}]|d \cdot \imath)$
   b. $p(A \cdot B \cdot [C \vee A]|\imath)$
   c. $p(A \vee C \cdot [B \vee A]|\imath)$
   d. $p(A \vee B \cdot [C \vee D]|\imath)$
2) $\imath$: sets of A_i are mutually exclusive and exhaustive, which means that the disjunction of the entire set $A_i = \{A_1\ A_2 \ldots A_n\}$ always has a truth value of 1. For example, in the case of $i = \{1\ 2\}$, this reduces to: $A_1 \vee A_2 = A \vee \bar{A} = 1$. Assign the probabilities
   a. $p(B \vee C \vee [A_1 \vee A_2]|\imath \cdot n = 2)$
   b. $p(C \cdot [A_1 \vee A_2]|\imath \cdot n = 2)$
   c. $p([A_1 \vee A_2 \vee A_3 \vee \cdots \vee A_m] \cdot B|\imath \cdot n = m)$
   d. $p([A_1 \cdot A_2 \cdot A_3] \cdot B|\imath \cdot n = 3)$
   e. $p(E \vee [A_1 \cdot A_2]|\imath \cdot n = 2)$
3) $\imath$: You are given an urn with 100 jellybeans inside. 17 are vanilla flavored (F_0), 41 are blueberry (F_1) and the remainder are strawberry (F_2). In addition, each is either scented ($O; n = 32$) or unscented ($\bar{O}$). You cannot smell the jellybeans while they are inside the urn. What probabilities should be assigned to
   a. Drawing a berry-flavored, unscented bean.
   b. Drawing a blueberry flavored bean, regardless of odor.
   c. Drawing an odiferous bean, regardless of flavor.
4) Load the file Ch2margin1. The values for x_1 range between 0 and 10 in increments of 0.2 (50 values of x_1), and the values for x_2 range between −4 and 4 in increments of 0.1 (80 total values of x_2). For this dataset,

a. Plot the 2D likelihood and prior contained in the file.
b. Compute the posterior from the likelihood and prior using (1.2).
c. Compute the probability distribution for x_1, regardless of the value of x_2.
d. From (c), compute the odds of x_1 being greater than 8.
e. Compute the probability distribution for x_2, regardless of the value of x_1.
f. From (e), compute odds of x_2 being less than 0.

5) Load the file Ch2margin2. The values for x_1 range between −40 and 40 in increments of 0.1 (800 total values of x_1), and the values for x_2 range between 0 and 30 in increments of 0.2 (150 values of x_2). For this dataset,
a. Plot the 2D likelihood and prior contained in the dataset.
b. Compute the posterior from the likelihood and prior using (1.2).
c. Compute probability distribution for x_1, regardless of the value of x_2.
d. From (c), compute odds of x1 being greater than 0.
e. Compute the probability distribution for x_2, regardless of the value of x_1.
f. From (e), compute odds of x_2 being greater than 0.

6) Load the file Ch2margin3. The values for x_1 range between 0 and 20 in increments of 0.2 (100 values of x_1), and the values for x_2 range between −10 and 10 in increments of 0.1 (200 total values of x_2). For this dataset,
a. Plot the 2D likelihood and prior contained in the dataset.
b. Compute the posterior from the likelihood and prior using (1.2).
c. Compute probability distribution for x_1, regardless of the value of x_2.
d. From (c), compute odds of x_1 being greater than 10.
e. Compute the probability distribution for x_2, regardless of the value of x_1.
f. From (e), compute odds of x_2 being less than 0.

2.1.5 The Five-Card Monty Hall Problem

We will now work the first of the examples alluded to in the introduction to this chapter, that use the calculations described above. This first problem, the Monty Hall problem, highlights how very wrong our unaided and untrained intuitions will often be. The original version of the Monty Hall problem was made famous by its appearance in the *Ask Marilyn* column of *Parade* magazine in 1991, and the ensuing debate in which even professionals very publicly displayed their erroneous intuitions. The original question was stimulated by the television game show *Let's Make a Deal*, hosted by Monty Hall. As one part of the show, Monty Hall would choose audience members to participate in a game in which they could choose one of three doors. Behind one door was usually a new car, and the other two hid less desirable items (behind one was usually a donkey). After contestants had chosen one of the three doors, Monty Hall might show them that a door they had *not* picked did *not* contain the car, and then allow them one of two options. He would offer them a sum of cash to quit the game, or allow them to continue and either switch doors or, of course, keep their original door choice. The debate sparked by the *Ask Marilyn* column centered around the question of whether there was any advantage to staying with the original door, or switching, in this type of scenario. Although analysis of Monty Hall's actual game-show scenario may be complicated by the fact that the host could choose to offer the additional options only to a subset of the contestants, such as those who had originally chosen the correct door, we can avoid ambiguity by considering a modified version of the problem that involves choosing from among five cards:

The Problem

You are shown five cards: the queen of clubs and of spades, and three kings. The cards are placed face down on a table and shuffled about so quickly that you cannot tell where the cards end up. You have placed a \$50 bet on your ability to find one of the queens. You are told in advance that after you pick a card, one of the three kings will be revealed. You will then be asked if you would like to stick with your original choice, or change your mind and switch to one of the remaining face-down cards.

Are you more likely, equally likely, or less likely to walk away with an extra \$50 if you stay with your original choice? If the answer is 'less likely' or 'more likely,' give a numerical estimate of how much more or less.

To answer these questions, we first define the propositions:

$Q_t \equiv$ You select a face-down queen at time $t = 1$ (initial choice) or $t = 2$ (choice after a king is revealed).

$S \equiv$ You stay with your original choice when asked to switch at $t = 2$.

ι_{5CMH} Background information describing the cards and rules of the Five-Card Monty Hall scenario.

It is clear that, under the definition of ι_{5CMH}, we should assign $p(Q_1|\iota_{5CMH}) = \frac{2}{5}$. And, because at $t = 1$ neither your private thoughts concerning whether eventually to switch nor those of the dealer concerning which of the nonqueens to uncover can change your chances of having originally picked a queen, we write

$$p(Q_1|S \cdot \iota_{5CMH}) = p(Q_1|\bar{S} \cdot \iota_{5CMH}) = p(Q_1|\iota_{5CMH}) = \frac{2}{5} \qquad (2.4).$$

We would like to calculate the two probabilities

$$p(Q_2|S \cdot \iota_{5CMH}) = p(Q_2 \cdot [Q_1 \vee \bar{Q}_1]|S \cdot \iota_{5CMH}) \qquad (2.5)$$

$$p(Q_2|\bar{S} \cdot \iota_{5CMH}) = p(Q_2 \cdot [Q_1 \vee \bar{Q}_1]|\bar{S} \cdot \iota_{5CMH}) \qquad (2.6).$$

That is, we are interested in our probability of winning the bet when we stay with our original choice (2.5) and when we don't stay with our original choice (2.6). Notice that in both of these equations, we are interested in the probability of finding a queen at the end, not whether one was found on the first guess. Symbolically, this corresponds to the logical statement: $Q_2 \cdot (Q_1 \vee \bar{Q}_1)$. Thus, the logical situation is one where we extend the question to include the outcome of the first guess [as is done on the right-hand side [rhs] of (2.5) and (2.6)], and then marginalize over the outcome of that choice. Expanding (2.5), we have

$$\begin{aligned} p(Q_2 \cdot [Q_1 \vee \bar{Q}_1]S \cdot \iota_{5CMH}) &= p([Q_2 \cdot Q_1] \vee [Q_2 \cdot \bar{Q}_1]|S \cdot \iota_{5CMH}) \\ &= p(Q_2 \cdot Q_1|S \cdot \iota_{5CMH}) + p(Q_2 \cdot \overline{Q_1}|S \cdot \iota_{5CMH}) \qquad (2.7). \end{aligned}$$

Expanding the first term of (2.7), we have

$$p(Q_2 \cdot Q_1|S \cdot \iota_{5CMH}) = p(Q_1|S \cdot \iota_{5CMH})p(Q_2|Q_1 \cdot S \cdot \iota_{5CMH}) \qquad (2.8).$$

We can assign both of these rhs probabilities. They are

$$p(Q_1|S \cdot \iota_{5CMH}) = p(Q_1|\iota_{5CMH}) = \frac{2}{5} \qquad (2.8a)$$

and

$$p(Q_2|Q_1 \cdot S \cdot \imath_{5CMH}) = 1 \qquad (2.8b).$$

The first, (2.8a), follows from (2.4). The second, (2.8b), is the result of the first two propositions following the vertical bar. Given that you stay with your first choice, and that you chose a queen in your original guess, you are certain to find the queen at $t = 2$.

Expanding the remaining term of (2.7), we have

$$p(Q_2 \cdot \bar{Q}_1|S \cdot \imath_{5CMH}) = p(\bar{Q}_1|S \cdot \imath_{5CMH})p(Q_2|\bar{Q}_1 \cdot S \cdot \imath_{5CMH}) \qquad (2.9)$$

to which we can assign

$$p(\bar{Q}_1|S \cdot \imath_{5CMH}) = 1 - p(Q_1|\imath_{5CMH}) = \frac{3}{5} \qquad (2.9a)$$

and

$$p(Q_2 \mid \bar{Q}_1 \cdot S \cdot \imath_{5CMH}) = 0 \qquad (2.9b).$$

Notice that (2.9a) is just the complement of (2.8a), which follows from (2.4). Furthermore, (2.9b) is impossible because one cannot stay with an original choice that was not a queen, and still end up (at time $t = 2$) holding a queen.

We therefore find that (2.7), expanded in (2.8) and (2.9), compels us to assign $p(Q_2|S \cdot \imath_{5CMH}) = \frac{2}{5} + 0 = \frac{2}{5}$, which is what most people guess intuitively. Once the choice to stay with the original guess is made, the mere offer of a switch cannot change the probabilities involved.

Next, we consider (2.6), which expresses the probability of winning the bet by switching at $t = 2$. Expanding (2.6) gives

$$\begin{aligned} p(Q_2 \cdot [Q_1 \vee \bar{Q}_1]|\bar{S} \cdot \imath_{5CMH}) &= p([Q_2 \cdot Q_1] \vee [Q_2 \cdot \bar{Q}_1]|\bar{S} \cdot \imath_{5CMH}) \\ &= p(Q_2 \cdot \bar{Q}_1|\bar{S} \cdot \imath_{5CMH}) + p(Q_2 \cdot Q_1|\bar{S} \cdot \imath_{5CMH}) \end{aligned} \qquad (2.10).$$

Expanding the first term of (2.10), we have

$$p(Q_2 \cdot \bar{Q}_1|\bar{S} \cdot \imath_{5CMH}) = p(\bar{Q}_1|\bar{S} \cdot \imath_{5CMH})p(Q_2|\bar{Q}_1 \cdot \bar{S} \cdot \imath_{5CMH}) \qquad (2.11)$$

to which we can assign

$$p(\bar{Q}_1|\bar{S} \cdot \imath_{5CMH}) = 1 - p(Q_1|\imath_{5CMH}) = \frac{3}{5} \qquad (2.11a)$$

and

$$p(Q_2|\bar{Q}_1 \cdot \bar{S} \cdot \imath_{5CMH}) = \frac{2}{3} \qquad (2.11b).$$

Equation (2.11a) follows from (2.4); (2.11b) follows from two constraints. First, $\imath_{5CMH}$ tells us that the dealer cannot turn over a queen (it is against the rules, and it would spoil the game), and second, your initial choice was incorrect (a king). This leaves the dealer only the remaining kings to turn over. Once the dealer turns over a king, two of the three remaining cards to which you may switch are queens.

Expanding the second term of (2.10), we have

$$p(Q_2 \cdot Q_1|\bar{S} \cdot \imath_{5CMH}) = p(Q_1|\bar{S} \cdot \imath_{5CMH})p(Q_2|Q_1 \cdot \bar{S} \cdot \imath_{5CMH}) \tag{2.12}$$

to which we can assign

$$p(Q_1|\bar{S} \cdot \imath_{5CMH}) = p(Q_1|\imath_{5CMH}) = \frac{2}{5} \tag{2.12a}$$

and

$$p(Q_2|Q_1 \cdot \bar{S} \cdot \imath_{5CMH}) = \frac{1}{3} \tag{2.12b}$$

Equation (2.12a) follows from (2.4); (2.12b) is the result of the same two constraints detailed above, leading to the assignment of (2.11b), except that because you found one of the queens at $t = 1$, only one of the three remaining cards is a queen.

Equation (2.10) therefore compels us to assign : $p(Q_2|\bar{S} \cdot \imath_{5CMH}) = \frac{8}{15}$, which is *greater* than the probability of finding the queen using the strategy of staying with your original choice by a factor of $1\frac{1}{3}$.

Because our intuitions are usually wrong in this example, an additional few words may be useful to help educate those intuitions. Consider a modified version of the game just described, where there are initially 1,000,000 kings and a single queen. When the cards have been spread on the table and shuffled about and you make a selection, your odds of blindly discovering the queen are virtually nonexistent (a million to one against, in fact). The dealer then removes all cards but your selection and one other, *one of which is guaranteed to be the queen.* Are you better off switching now? The game is the same, but the difference in probabilities has been exaggerated. Since there is almost no chance that you found the queen by accident when there were 1,000,001 cards on the table, the only card to which you may switch in the second stage is virtually certain to be the queen. Switching is clearly the superior strategy.

Exercises

1) How much have your odds improved after the cards are removed in the million kings example above?
2) Derive a general formula for the probability of finding the queen if there are N cards originally, Nq queens, and n cards are revealed/removed at the end of $t = 1$.
3) Under what conditions is it advantageous to stay with your original choice, and under which conditions is switching irrelevant [Hint: Characterize the conditions of the switch points in the general equation from Exercise 2 above]?
4) Consider a game where you place a bet on your ability to find the queen among 100 kings. At the start of the game, you choose a card. On each round of the game the dealer removes one king and gives you three options: (1) keep your card as your final guess; (2) switch to another card, which is then your final guess; (3) postpone final decisions another round.

   When you choose option 1 or 2 and guess correctly, play ends and your payoff is: $bet(\alpha[\mathbf{N}_{cards} - 2])$, where $\mathbf{N}_{cards}$ is the number of cards remaining (including your original guess) and α is a positive multiplier. So, waiting until only your original guess and one other card remain before choosing option 1 or 2 (whether or not you find the queen) causes you to lose your original bet.

a. Should your final choice be option #1 or #2?
b. How many turns should you wait before finalizing your guess for $\alpha = .5$ and $\alpha = 5$?
c. What is the optimal stopping time for any α (i.e., as a function of α)?
d. How much money should you expect to win (beyond your original bet) for $\alpha = .5$ and $\alpha = 5$?

2.1.6 Inverse Probability

The term inverse probability was quite popular in the eighteenth, nineteenth, and early twentieth centuries for describing a probability statement such as $p(D_{rh}|\boldsymbol{d} \cdot \imath)$, where D_{rh} is some rather horrible disease and $\boldsymbol{d}$ is the observed data, such as the signs and symptoms of a patient whose physician is considering the applicability of a D_{rh} diagnosis. This is to be contrasted with what was at the time called **direct probability**,[2] and referred to statements such as $p(\boldsymbol{d}|D_{rh} \cdot \imath)$ indicating the probability of observing certain data given that one indeed has D_{rh}. In other words, these were posterior and sampling probabilities. The early terminology points to a stage in the development of probability theory when people felt perfectly comfortable with assigning sampling distributions (they were 'directly available' or 'directly observable') but not posteriors; this posed a problem for its application in science, because it is the inverse, not the direct probability that is of most interest to a scientist. This problem arose because scientific hypotheses usually involve unobservable parameters that are the causes of observable events, and the scientific enterprise usually involves attempting to infer those unobservable causes.

It was the Reverend Thomas Bayes (1701–1761) who, using a method of solution specific to success-rate data [as in $p(C_{fair}|hth \cdot \imath)$, for describing coin tosses], was the first[3] to publish equations equivalent to (1.5). Bayes' solution provided an avenue for computing inverse probability in success-rate problems, although he never actually wrote the general equation we call Bayes' theorem [i.e., (1.5)]. It was Laplace who independently recognized (1.5) as a general method for hypothesis testing. Laplace went on to develop, virtually *ex nihilo*, the core elements of probability theory needed for scientific inquiry. The general solution to the inverse probability problem is quite simple, once it is known. As was indicated in the previous chapter, we can write the product rule, which indicates the probability of the propositions A and B being jointly true based on certain background information [i.e., $p(A \cdot B|\imath)$], in two equivalent ways:

1. In terms of the probability that A is true given that B is assumed to be true, and the prior probability that B is true: $p(A \cdot B|\imath) = p(A|B \cdot \imath)p(B|\imath)$.
2. In terms of the probability that B is true given that A is assumed to be true, and the prior probability that A is true: $p(A \cdot B|\imath) = p(B|A \cdot \imath)p(A|\imath)$.

[2] We will not use the terms 'inverse' and 'direct' probability in the remainder of this text, preferring the more modern terms 'sampling' and 'posterior' probability.

[3] There is some debate here, but it is certainly customary to attach his name to the solution.

Since both expressions share the identical left-hand term, $p(A \cdot B|\imath)$, we can also equate the two rhs expressions, giving $p(B|A \cdot \imath)p(A|\imath) = p(A|B \cdot \imath)p(B|\imath)$. Finally, this can be rearranged to the form given in (1.5), $p(B|A \cdot \imath) = p(A|B \cdot \imath)p(B|\imath)/p(A|\imath)$. The connection to inverse probability (i.e., 'the probability of unobservable causes') discovered by Laplace is highlighted by changing the names of the terms to: $p(h|\boldsymbol{d} \cdot \imath) = p(\boldsymbol{d}|h \cdot \imath)p(h|\imath)/p(\boldsymbol{d}|\imath)$, where h is an hypothesis, and $\boldsymbol{d}$ is a dataset relevant to h.

As an algebraic manipulation repeating what was shown in Chapter 1, this 'derivation' of (1.5) is unremarkable. However, (1.5) was considered revolutionary when it was proposed by Laplace as a general solution to the problem of inverse probability. The perception of (1.5) as a revolutionary advance was likely amplified by the fact that humans have naturally rather poor intuitions concerning problems where it must be applied. Thus, as an aid to understanding as well as to practice basic programming, we will next examine a series of intuitively difficult examples that make use of (1.5) via simulation - with the hope that when the logic is not intuitively clear the simulation may provide insight, and we may thus educate our logical intuitions as well as gain practice coding.

Example: Basic Simulation Strategies – A Return to the Urn

For the simulations to be discussed in this section, we will return to the idea of drawing differently colored balls from an urn, and use this situation to further emphasize the differences and similarities between sampling and posterior probabilities. Let us define the situation and several related propositions:

$\imath \equiv$ There are two urns containing balls of different colors. The first urn contains 54 red and 64 black ball, while the second contains 74 red and 64 black balls.
$U_{r \cdot b} \equiv$ Balls are drawn from the urn containing r red and b black balls.
$r_n \equiv n$ red balls are observed.
$b_n \equiv n$ black balls are observed.

First, we will compute some sampling probabilities: The first being the probability of observing two red balls (in the first two draws from an urn), given that you are drawing from the first urn. This probability is obtained by enumerating the possible sets of two balls that might be drawn from the first urn. However, instead of enumeration, we will use the following programming shortcut: We will draw pseudorandom samples of pairs of balls, and count the number of times r_2 occurs in those draws. By drawing pairs of balls we are assuming that, had each two-ball simulation run occurred by first selecting one ball and then selecting a second ball, the first ball would not be replaced in the urn until after the second ball of the pair was drawn - at which point both would be replaced in preparation for the next simulation run (all simulation runs must begin with the same number of balls in the urn).

Since the urn has 54 red and 64 black balls, we can create a list of numbers from 1 to 118, where the first 54 of these will be considered red. For each draw of two balls, we will pseudorandomly shuffle this list of numbers and take the first two as our draw from the urn. One such draw represents a simulation run. Repeating this sequence of shuffling and selecting the first two numbers from the reshuffled list many times constitutes our simulation.

Programming Aside: Urn Probabilities #1

To program the simulation, we first define the number of repetitions, the number of balls in the urn, and the list of balls (from 1 to the number of balls) in the urn:

```
REPS=10000; %number of repetitions in the simulation
Nballs=118; %number of balls
URN=1:Nballs; %define the urn [first 54 are red]
```

We next make a matrix of NaN ('not a number') values whose size is equal to the number of simulation repetitions x the number of observations per repetition:

```
D=nan(REPS,2); %'empty' observation matrix
```

Finally, we write a for-loop that executes the simulation (fills the matrix with simulated observations, replacing nan's), and find the simulation runs that meet the criterion that both observations are red (i.e., less than or equal to 54). The length of the list (rows in `D`) found to match this criterion, divided by the total number of simulation runs (`REPS`, is our simulation-based approximation to the desired probability calculation:

```
for n=1:REPS, Unow=URN(randperm(Nballs)); D(n,:)=Unow(1:2); end
sum(and(D(:,1)<=54,D(:,2)<=54))/REPS
```

Or, we could write a version of the loop that does not explicitly simulate the mixing of the balls using the RANDPERM command, instead using the `RANDI` command:

```
for n=1:REPS, D(n,1)=randi(Nballs); unow=exclude(URN,D(n,1));
   D(n,2)=unow(randi(Nballs-1)); end
sum(and(D(:,1)<=54,D(:,2)<=54))/REPS
```

An alternate formulation using RANDI and EXCLUDE is

```
D(:,1)=randi(Nballs,[REPS 1]);
for n=1:REPS, D(n,2)=exclude(URN,D(n,1),randi(Nballs-1)); end
sum(and(D(:,1)<=54,D(:,2)<=54))/REPS
```

Of course, this was a great deal of work to estimate the value of $p(r_2|U_{54.64}\cdot\iota)$. The probability calculation is

$$p(r_2|U_{54.64}\cdot\iota) = p(r_1|U_{54.64}\cdot\iota)p(r_1|U_{53.64}\cdot\iota)$$
$$= \frac{54}{54+64}\frac{53}{53+64} = 0.207.$$

In other words, this situation is exactly like flipping a (differently) biased coin twice. On the first flip of the coin, you have a $\frac{54}{54+64}$ chance of obtaining a red, and given that a red ball is indeed observed (i.e., one red ball is now missing), you have a $\frac{53}{53+64}$ chance of obtaining a red on the next flip.

Our next simulation will be for the probability, $p(r_2\cdot b_1|U_{74.64}\cdot\iota)$, that is, the probability of observing two red and one black ball (in the first three draws) from the second urn. This simulation problem has an interesting difference from our first simulation in that we have not specified the order of the two red and one black ball – only their occurrence. In the previous simulation, our program did not have to take account of different

Programming Aside: Urn Probabilities #2

To create this simulation, we first write

```
REPS=100000; %number of repetitions in the simulation
Nballs=138; %number of balls
URN=1:Nballs; %define the urn
D=nan(REPS,3); %initialize a data matrix with NaN values
```

where we have redefined `Nballs` and `D` because we are dealing with the second urn, and because each simulation run will contain three draws. The for-loop that executes the simulation is

```
for n=1:REPS,
for nn=1:3, Unow=URN(randperm(Nballs)); D(n,nn)=Unow(1); end, end
sum(or(or(...
    and(D(:,1)>74,and(D(:,2)<=74,D(:,3)<=74)),...
    and(D(:,2)>74,and(D(:,1)<=74,D(:,3)<=74))),...
    and(D(:,3)>74,and(D(:,1)<=74,D(:,2)<=74)))...
    )/REPS
```

possible orders of balls, because both balls were the same color. Here, we must find all instances of one black and two red, regardless of the order; that is, we are looking for the sum of the simulated instances of *brr*, *rbr*, and *rrb*. In this simulation we will also assume that, after each draw (within each simulation run), the drawn ball is returned to the urn.

Notice that the definition used in the above logical expression has increased considerably in complexity. We have nested three copies of a logical expression that asks whether sets of three balls meet a certain set of criteria; either *rrb*, *rbr* or *brr*, one set for each copy.

Programming Aside: Speeding Your Simulations

As a programming side-note, we can increase the speed of this simulation by eliminating the for-loops and replace them instead with multiple draws from `RANDI`:

```
D=randi(Nballs,[REPS 3]);
```

where the above logical expression again evaluates whether the draws meet our criterion and approximates the probability calculation. Or, using a slightly different logical expression to evaluate the draws, the same could have been obtained from `RAND` instead of `RANDI`:

```
D=rand(REPS,3);
sum(or(or(...
    and(D(:,1)>74/Nballs,and(D(:,2)<=74/Nballs,D(:,3)<=74/Nballs)),...
    and(D(:,2)>74/Nballs,and(D(:,1)<=74/Nballs,D(:,3)<=74/Nballs))),...
    and(D(:,3)>74/Nballs,and(D(:,1)<=74/Nballs,D(:,2)<=74/Nballs)))...
    )/REPS
```

We can verify that these simulations produce approximately the correct answer by noting that for every single draw from the urn, there is the probability $\theta = 74/(74+64) = 0.536$ of obtaining a red ball and the probability $1-\theta = 0.464$ of obtaining a black ball. This means that any one of the three combinations of two red and one black ball have the probability $p = \theta^2(1-\theta)^1 = 0.133$. And since there are three such combinations, the probability of observing any of the three is $p(r_2 \cdot b_1|U_{74\text{-}64} \cdot \imath) = 3[\theta^2(1-\theta)^1] = 0.4$.

In our final sampling simulation we will approximate $p(b_1|\imath)$. The interesting aspect of this probability is that the logical expression does not specify from which urn we are drawing; the expression would be read: 'the probability of drawing a black ball from one of the two urns.'

The above simulations make the assumption that both urns are equally likely to have balls to have been drawn from them, the first by explicitly tossing a coin to determine the urn and the second by drawing half of the S vector from each urn. The equal likelihood assumption is essentially determined by the fact that no alternative weighting can be justified by the statement of the problem. If there had been an explicit specification of the relative probability that balls had been drawn from one or the other urn, we could have flipped a biased coin with that relative likelihood of heads and tails. But when we have no information about which of two alternatives has been chosen, we have no information that would allow us to prefer to believe that one or the other had been the urn from which balls were drawn. The only way to express that symmetry is with 50-50 chances.

If we had obtained an explicit solution via the sum and product rules, the realization that we were selecting a flat prior probability over which urn had produced the black ball would also have forced itself upon us from the equations. The solution requires that we extend the question to the two mutually exclusive and exhaustive possibilities ($\imath$) that we draw from the first or second urn, $p(b_1|[U_{54\text{-}44} \vee U_{74\text{-}74}] \cdot \imath)$. We can then use the product rule to expand this to

$$p(b_1|[U_{54\text{-}44} \vee U_{74\text{-}74}] \cdot \imath) = \frac{p([U_{54\text{-}44} \vee U_{74\text{-}74}] \cdot b_1|\imath)}{p([U_{54\text{-}44} \vee U_{74\text{-}74}]|\imath)} \tag{2.13}$$

Programming Aside: Posterior over Urns

To perform this simulation we will simply add a layer of complexity to existing simulations, inserting a coin toss at the start of each simulation run. The outcome of the coin toss will then determine from which of the two simulated urns we draw:

```
REPS=100000;
Nballs1=98; Nballs2=148;
S=nan(REPS,1); %initialize success vector with NaN values
for n=1:REPS,
    if rand<.5, S(n)=randi(Nballs1)>54;
    else S(n)=randi(Nballs2)>74; end, end
mean(S)
```

Alternately, we could use the `randi` discrete pseudorandom number generator to produce simulated observations:

```
S=[randi(Nballs1,[REPS/2 1])>54; randi(Nballs2,[REPS/2 1])>74];
mean(S)
```

Then, recognizing that the denominator is unity and rearranging the numerator:

$$\begin{aligned} p(b_1|[U_{54\cdot44} \vee U_{74\cdot74}] \cdot \iota) &= p([b_1 \cdot U_{54\cdot44}] \vee [b_1 \cdot U_{74\cdot74}]|\iota) \\ &= p(b_1 \cdot U_{54\cdot44}|\iota) + p(b_1 \cdot U_{74\cdot74}|\iota) \\ &= p(U_{54\cdot44}|\iota)p(b_1|U_{54\cdot44} \cdot \iota) \\ &\quad + p(U_{74\cdot74}|\iota)p(b_1|U_{74\cdot74} \cdot \iota) \end{aligned}$$

That is, the solution, $p(b_1|\iota) = .475$, is the weighted sum of (a) the probability that, when drawing from the first urn, a black ball will be drawn and (b) the probability, when drawing from the second urn, a black ball will be drawn.

These simulation examples may seem to embrace the frequency definition of probability – the very definition we have so strenuously argued against both in the present and the previous chapter. This is not the case. What we have argued against above is *not* that a frequency is *never* useful in assigning probabilities, only that it is incorrect to think that there is an *identity of frequency and probability*. However, as we will see in many examples, when our information is in the form of counts or frequencies, those frequencies inform our probability assignments.

We will now use the same simulation techniques to numerically approximate a posterior probability. The difference between sampling probabilities, simulated above, and posterior probabilities is that for the latter we are interested in the probability of something that is not directly observable in the data. Thus, we will simulate the probability that balls are being drawn from the first urn, given that the data available to us indicate only that we have drawn two red balls, $p(U_{54\cdot44}|r_2 \cdot \iota)$. Notice that this probability is something we could not validly simulate when using the frequency definition of probability, since there is in fact only one correct answer to the question (assuming we in fact had two urns and had drawn from one of them).

Notice that we have made use of a counter vector, `C`, with two elements. Both elements of the counter start at zero, and the appropriate element is iterated each time a pair of

Programming Aside: Approximate Posterior via Simulation

To simulate this probability, and represent our *information* regarding the balls' urn or origin, we will simply draw pairs of balls from both urns. After drawing balls, we then determine, of all the pairs that were both red, what proportion had come from the first urn. To guarantee that we will have drawn a minimum number of pairs that meet our criterion, we will make use of a while-loop:

```
C=[0 0]; %initialize counter vector with zeros
REPS=100000; Nballs1=98; Nballs2=148;
while sum(C)<REPS,
    D1=randperm(Nballs1); D2=randperm(Nballs2);
    C(1)=C(1)+and(D1(1)<=54,D1(2)<=54);
    C(2)=C(2)+and(D2(1)<=74,D2(2)<=74); end
C(1)/sum(C)
```

red balls is drawn from the first or second urn. The desired value is the probability that the first urn produced the observed data (two red balls), which is therefore the ratio of the number of times the first urn produced this data to the number of times the dataset is observed overall (from either urn).

To obtain the exact solution, we use (1.5) to expand the probability expression:

$$p(U_{54.64}|r_2 \cdot \imath) = \frac{p(U_{54.64}|\imath)p(r_2|U_{54.64} \cdot \imath)}{p(r_2|\imath)}$$

$$= \frac{p(U_{54.44}|\imath)p(r_2|U_{54.44} \cdot \imath)}{p(U_{54.44}|\imath)p(r_2|U_{54.44} \cdot \imath) + p(U_{74.74}|\imath)p(r_2|U_{74.74} \cdot \imath)}$$

$$= \frac{\frac{54}{98}\frac{53}{97}}{\frac{54}{98}\frac{53}{97} + \frac{74}{148}\frac{73}{147}} = 0.548$$

The techniques used for these example simulations will form the basic tools that we will use in the remaining examples of the use of (1.5) below.

Exercises

1) Based on the example above, you draw three balls from one of the two urns, all of which are red. What is the probability that the urn you drew from contains 64 black balls?
2) Simulate the following sampling probabilities, where the proposition $\bar{R}$ indicates that balls are not replaced until each simulation run is finished, and the proposition R indicates that each ball is replaced after it is drawn (i.e., all draws are made with all balls in the urn):
   a. $p(r_2|U_{22\cdot 33} \cdot \overline{R} \cdot \imath)$
   b. $p(r_2 \cdot b_{22}|U_{55\cdot 10} \cdot R \cdot \imath)$
   c. $p(b_2|[U_{22\cdot 11} \vee U_{11\cdot 22}] \cdot R \cdot \imath)$, where $p(U_{22\cdot 11} \vee U_{11\cdot 22}|\imath) = 1$
   d. $p(r_2 \cdot b_2|[U_{22\cdot 11} \vee U_{11\cdot 11} \vee U_{11\cdot 22}] \cdot R \cdot \imath)$, where $p(U_{22\cdot 11} \vee U_{11\cdot 11} \vee U_{11\cdot 22}|\imath) = 1$
3) Simulate the following posterior probabilities:
   a. $p(U_{14\cdot 771}|r_1 \cdot R \cdot \imath)$, where $p(U_{14\cdot 771} \vee U_{14\cdot 1}|\imath) = 1$
   b. $p(U_{14\cdot 1}|(r_1 \cdot R \cdot \imath)$, where $p(U_{14\cdot 771} \vee U_{14\cdot 1}|\imath) = 1$
   c. $p(U_{14\cdot 1}|(r_1 \cdot b_{15} \cdot R \cdot \imath)$, where $p(U_{14\cdot 771} \vee U_{14\cdot 1}|\imath) = 1$
   d. $p(U_{88\cdot 88}|(r_3 \cdot b_3 \cdot R \cdot \imath)$, where $p(U_{66\cdot 55} \vee U_{88\cdot 88}|\imath) = 1$
   e. $p(U_{44\cdot 44}|(r_3 \cdot b_3 \cdot R \cdot \imath)$, where $p(U_{66\cdot 55} \vee U_{44\cdot 44}|\imath) = 1$
   f. $p(U_{44\cdot 44}|(r_1 \cdot b_3 \cdot R \cdot \imath)$, where $p(U_{66\cdot 55} \vee U_{44\cdot 44} \vee U_{101\cdot 226}|\imath) = 1$

Example: The Monty Hall Problem Simulated

We have already hopefully educated our intuitions somewhat concerning the Monty Hall problem, so this problem will serve nicely as an introduction to the kind of simulation we will be using in subsequent examples.

The first stage of the simulation simply generates a great number of repetitions of the game, where the simulated contestant's choice of card location (1 through 5) at each

Programming Aside: Two-Stage Simulation for N-Card, M-Queen Monty Hall

For the modified Monty Hall problem described above, there are two stages. In the first stage of our simulation we will generate a large set of pseudorandom orders of numbers between 1 and 5, and use the first two from each order to indicate which cards contain queens. The second stage involves removing one of the nonqueen cards, and determining whether a queen would have been found by our simulated 'contestant' by switching. The logic of the simulation is that at completion we can simply count the number of winning simulation runs when the contestant switches versus the wins from staying.

```
REPS=100000;
Ncards=5; Nqueens=2;
D=1:Ncards; %define the 'deck' of cards
C=[0 0]; %initialize counter vector
for n=1:REPS,
    Pick1=randi(Ncards); %End of stage 1
    Dnow=find(D~=Pick1); %Remove chosen card from list
    ind=randi(Ncards-2); %Select new card
    Pick2=Dnow(ind(1));
    C(1)=C(1)+any(Pick1==[1 Nqueens]); %Stay wins
    C(2)=C(2)+any(Pick2==[1 Nqueens]); end %Switch wins
C/REPS
```

stage is based on the discrete pseudorandom number generator, randi. The second stage does the real work, and removes one of the unchosen, nonqueen cards, which are always at the end of the list of cards (since the queens are located at positions 1 through the number of queens in our simulation).

The simulation, as we have written it, highlights the fact that it does not matter which cards are chosen at each stage, only whether a switch is made. This fact is a consequence of our symmetrical information about the three cards in the first stage, and the cards to which we could switch in the second stage. The only asymmetrical information concerning the cards occurs at the start of the second stage, when we are offered the chance to switch. At that point, our information about the card corresponding to our original choice is different than the remaining (nonremoved) cards, because of the condition that only nonqueens can be removed. It is this asymmetry in our information that is reflected in the unequal probabilities of finding the queen upon switching versus staying.

Exercises

1) Notice that in the two-queens modification of the problem, it is possible to show contestants a queen at the close of stage 1, and still allow them the opportunity to stay or switch to ultimately win the game (uncovering a queen at the close of stage 2). (a) Make a guess about the outcome, and why, and then (b) simulate this further modification of the game.

2) Explain why it does not matter that the locations of the queens are not chosen by randi in the two-queens simulation.
3) Simulate the 100-queens, 2-kings problem. Here the intuition should be that not switching is to be preferred, and the simulation will tell us by about what odds this is.
4) Do the intermediate cases, 5q 5k and 5q 6k. How do these compare with 500q, 500k and 500q, 501k? Why is there a difference?
5) It should now be relatively straightforward to answer a simplified version of the above optional exercise, involving a general relation between number of kings, number of queens and relative probability following a switch.

Example: Coins

The following is a problem posed by Joseph Bertrand in the nineteenth century:

$\iota \equiv$ There are three identical boxes, each with two drawers, with each drawer containing one coin. The first box contains two gold coins, the second box contains a gold and a silver coin, and the third box contains two silver coins.

In addition to this background information, you are told that a silver coin has been found in one drawer of one of the boxes (call it box '*B*'). The problem is the following: what is the probability that there is a silver coin in the other drawer of box B?

To solve this problem analytically, one defines the following propositions:

$d_s \equiv$ A silver coin is found in one drawer of box *B*.
$d_{ss} \equiv$ A silver coin is found in both drawers of box *B*.

Programming Aside: Coins Simulation

To simulate this situation, label the drawers 1 through 6 and (to simplify the programming) assume the first half of the drawers contain gold coins and the latter half silver; then choose drawers using the pseudorandom number generator. First, find those instances in which the chosen drawer number is greater than or equal to 4. These cases satisfy your background information that a silver coin was found in one drawer; only these will be used to compute the final probability. Second, for each of these instances determine whether the drawer number is greater than 4. When this latter condition is satisfied, both drawers contain silver coins. The ratio of the number of instances in which the drawer number is greater than or equal to 4 (corresponding to the given background information), and instances in which the drawer number is greater than 4 (both drawers contain silver) is then the desired probability.

```
REPS=100000;
Dsamp=randi(6,[REPS 1]); %vector of pseudorandom numbers bet 1 and 6
S1=sum(Dsamp>=4); %which Dsamp numbers are at least 4?
S2=sum(Dsamp>4); %which Dsamp numbers are at least 5?
p=S2/S1 %approximation to probability that both drawers contain silver
```

where the selection process leading to the choice of box B is unknown to you. The solution then follows from (1.5), by writing the probability question symbolically:

$$p(d_{ss}|d_s \cdot \imath) = \frac{p(d_{ss}|\imath)p(d_s|d_{ss} \cdot \imath)}{p(d_s|\imath)}$$

All the elements of the right-hand side (RHS) of the equation were given in the statement of the problem: we know that only one of the three boxes has two silver coins [$p(d_{ss}|\imath) = 1/3$], that one-half of the drawers contain a silver coin [$p(d_s|\imath) = 1/2$], and that you are certain to find a silver coin in one drawer of a chest that contains a silver coin in each drawer [$p(d_s|d_{ss} \cdot \imath) = 1$]. Thus the solution is $p(d_{ss}|d_s \cdot \imath) = 2/3$, which should be approximately what was found numerically via simulation.

Exercises

1) Expand the Coins simulation to include pseudorandom selection of the locations of the three chests and drawers. Are the probabilities different? Why, or why not?
2) The simulation in the Coins problem does not require that we initially select drawers with equal probability, because the given information is that one of the last three was chosen. Rewrite the above simulation by first selecting from the last three drawers with equal probability. Run the original and the new simulations several times. What is the difference in the outputs?
3) Here is a problem involving a simplified genetics example: eye color phenotypes come in two varieties: blue and brown, with three accompanying genotypes – BB, Bb, and bb – where the brown (B) allele is dominant. Assuming the two alleles have no combination preferences, and ignoring the possibility of mutation,
   a. What is the probability that two blue-eyed parents produce a Bb genotype (brown-eyed) child?
   b. What is the probability that three blue-eyed siblings have one Bb and one bb parent?
   c. What is the probability that three blue-eyed siblings have two Bb parents?
   d. With two brown-eyed children, what is the highest-probability genotype for the two parents?
   e. How would your answer in (d) change if the same parents produced a third, blue-eyed, child?
4) A treasure fleet of three ships was lost at sea. Records indicate that one ship carried two chests of gold, while another ship carried a chest of gold and also a chest of silver; the final ship carried two chests containing silver. On a dive, you find two of the three ships, each with its two chests. One of these four chests has broken open, and contained gold, but none of the other chests can be opened until they are retrieved. Unfortunately, weather reports indicate a storm is approaching, and there is time to retrieve only one chest (but not the broken chest, whose contents would take too long to collect). Knowing that other divers may retrieve anything left behind before you can return, you face a difficult decision.
   a. Should you retrieve the chest from the same ship as the broken chest, or should you switch ships and retrieve one of the remaining two chests?

```
REPS=10000; Nchests=6; Ngold=3;
D=1:Nchests; PickList=[2 1 4]';
```

```
C=[0 0];
for n=1:REPS,
    Broken=randi(Ngold); %Pick one of the 3 gold chests as 'broken'
    Pick1=PickList(Broken); %End of stage 1
    Dnow=find(and(D~=Pick1,D~=Broken)); %Remove broken and Pick1
    ind=randi(Nchests-2); %Select new chest
    Pick2=Dnow(ind);
    C(1)=C(1)+any(Pick1==[1:Ngold]); %Stay finds gold
    C(2)=C(2)+any(Pick2==[1:Ngold]); end %Switch finds gold
C/REPS
```

b. How would your answer change if all three ships had been found, but otherwise the situation was identical?
c. How would your answer change if the broken chest contained silver?
d. Solve a, b, or c analytically.

Example: Simpson's Paradox and Sex Bias at UC Berkeley

Here we have an example based on actual graduate school admissions data at UC Berkeley from 1973. This example demonstrates a well-known paradox of probability theory, Simpson's paradox, wherein trends that appear *within subsets* of the data can show the exact opposite trend in the aggregate, simply due to the *number of instances* of various data subtypes.

Looking at the dataset, the obvious thing to notice is the totals, which show an almost 20 percent higher acceptance rate for men than women to Berkeley graduate programs in 1970. This massive difference in acceptance rates (exaggerated here relative to the actual acceptance numbers for effect) is in line with the modern notion of 'unconscious bias': the theory that just seeing a female applicant's name would prompt the

Programming Aside: Berkeley Simulation

We first shuffle the rows of the table using the custom Shuffle.m function:

```
Ntable=[5125 940; 1625 2965; 2510 1123; 955 1965; 2085 1875; 1265 1705];
%Num of male and female applicants
Ptable=[73 83; 27 28; 64 68; 15 18; 35 37; 6 7]/100; %Num of male and
                                                      female acceptances
Dept={'engineering','english','chemistry','communication','psychology','philosophy'}';
ilist=Shuffle(1:6); %vector of pseudorandom numbers bet 1 and 6
Ntablenew=Ntable(ilist,:); %new table
p=sum(Ntablenew.*Ptable)./sum(Ntablenew) %probabilities
pcoin=bpdf(sum(Ptable(:,2)>=Ptable(:,1)),6,.5);
%binomial probability
table(Dept(:),Ptable(:,1),Ptable(:,2),'VariableNames',{'Dept' ,...
    'MaleAccept','FemaleAccept'})
disp('Total proportion accepted:')
disp([num2str(p(1))': Male'])
disp([num2str(p(2))': Female'])
```

The pcoin variable shows the probability of flipping a fair coin 6 times (once per department) and having the result show heads each time. This is also the probability of having a result in which either mens or women's applications are favored in every single department by accident (without looking at the sex of the applicant).

committee to view the application less favorably than if the name had been male. Given that this type of discrepancy actually occurred, we would obviously like to know: *did the discrepancy result from unconscious bias against women?*

Our simulation will take the form of a shuffling algorithm, wherein we change the size of the applicant pool to each of the graduate disciplines listed. In all cases, admittance rates will remain the same (within disciplines). In this way, we can try to develop a sense of the effect of changes in pool sizes, independently of departmental acceptance rate.

If you explore the simulation for a few iterations you will see the trick: women applied preferentially to the most selective graduate departments. This made their overall acceptance numbers lower than those of the men, who applied more often to less selective departments. Thus, even though *every single graduate department favored female applicants* (in these data by as much as 10 percent), the *overall* number of male acceptances was higher. This phenomenon, wherein the numbers of items contributing to each cell of the table causes the overall trend to flip direction relative to the actual trends seen within the table, is known as Simpson's paradox. This is in part why, when we are designing a study involving comparisons between groups (such as male/female or placebo/treatment) on multiple dimensions or multiple levels of a treatment (e.g., different doses of an experimental drug), we prefer to have equal numbers of individuals in each group.

Exercises

1) Create a table of the modified Berkeley data given in the PA with columns for male, female, and overall acceptance/rejection numbers within each discipline.
2) Explain whether the admissions table data are consistent with the claim that the admissions process is biased. If so, for whom was it biased?
3) Create a simulation using the same acceptance rates for men and women per department, but with 1000 men and 1000 women applying to every department. How does this simulation (a) change or (b) reinforce your answer to Ex. 2?
4) Our analysis of the Berkeley data has so far only looked for evidence of a discrepancy in admission rates. The claim of bias requires an additional component: causal factors that are (1) imposed externally on applicants and (2) based explicitly on the sex of the applicant rather than factors pertinent to the application itself.
   a) List as many internal factors (controlled by applicants) and factors external to the applicants that could have caused the observed discrepancy in acceptance rates.
   b) Choose one of each type of factor and describe the data you would need if you wanted to test whether it might have played a causal role in the discrepant rates.
   c) If such data exists, describe whether it supports the existence of a causal factor. If it does not, create mock data and explain how it supports the existence or non-existence of a causal factor.
5) In addition to a discrepancy in admission rates, there was a discrepancy in the number of male and female applicants to Berkeley in 1973, and in particular a difference in the number of male and female applicants to mathematical (e.g., engineering, chemistry) and non-mathematical (e.g., english, philosophy) departments.

a) Describe as many internal and external factors that might have contributed to this discrepancy.
b) Choose one of each and describe the data you would need to assess whether it played a causal role in application numbers.
c) Using either existing data or simulation data, explain how such a dataset supports the existence / non-existence of the proposed causal link.

Example: Medical Decision-Making

Less famous, though rather more important to most, are examples where intuitions regarding probabilities have gone awry in the context of medical decisions. Here we will focus on binary classification tests used in medical diagnostics, demonstrating that interpretation of these tests can be just as difficult as the Simpson, Coins, and Monty Hall problems.

When a diagnostic or screening test is developed, the producer of the test is interested in reporting its **sensitivity** and **specificity**. The sensitivity and specificity of a test tell us something about the test as a discriminative tool, and are computed by jury-rigging the sample of testees. The sensitivity tells us the probability that the test will correctly diagnose those with the underlying disease, out of the group selected because they have the disease: $Sensitivity = p(+|Disease)$. The specificity is the converse, telling us the probability that the test will correctly reject the diagnosis in those without the disease: $Specificity = p(-|\overline{Disease})$

Intuitively, it would seem that sensitivity and specificity provide us with all the information to interpret the result of a diagnostic test, when it comes in positive or negative for a given patient. To understand why this is not entirely correct we will examine several examples, wherein the results are those of a binary classification test, with four possible outcomes (those with the disease can be correctly or incorrectly classified, and similarly for those without the disease). One could create a matrix containing the four possible outcomes of such a binary classification test, called a contingency table. This graphical representation, shown in Figure 2.3a, is often a useful aid to reasoning about the results of this type of test. For those with the disease, the test can give either a positive or negative result; that is, correctly identify or incorrectly reject the diagnosis ('hits' and 'misses,' respectively). In addition, the test can give a positive or negative result for individuals without the disease (yielding a 'false alarm' or 'correct rejection,' respectively).

Sensitivity and Specificity

Let us first take a moment to examine a simulation for sensitivity and specificity. Consider a scenario in which you have developed a test to detect the presence of a hypothetical developmental disorder of the enteric nervous system (D_{ENS}) causing chronic childhood abdominal pain, from proteins expressed in amniotic fluid as early as 3 months gestational age (mga). You have also developed a treatment for D_{ENS} that is effective in 60 percent of cases for treatment at 3 mga, but causes sickness and a hospital stay for the mother in 80 percent of cases if administered when D_{ENS} is absent. Effectiveness increases in 10 percent increments in the three months between 3 and 6 months (i.e., to 90 percent at 6 months), but the required hospital stay when administered unnecessarily increases by 10 days per month from 5 to 35 over the same three months. At 3, 4,

(a)

result of hypothesis test	truth-value of null hypothesis: false	truth-value of null hypothesis: true
reject (+)	HIT reject actually–false null hypothesis	FA reject actually–true null hypothesis
fail to reject (–)	MISS fail to reject actually–false null hypothesis	CR fail to reject actually–true null hypothesis

(b)

test result (3 mos.)	underlying condition: present	underlying condition: absent
positive (+)	45	923
negative (–)	5	9027

test result (4 mos.)	underlying condition: present	underlying condition: absent
positive (+)	45	791
negative (–)	5	9159

test result (5 mos.)	underlying condition: present	underlying condition: absent
positive (+)	46	713
negative (–)	4	9237

test result (6 mos.)	underlying condition: present	underlying condition: absent
positive (+)	47	680
negative (–)	3	9270

(c)

test result	underlying condition: present (D)	underlying condition: absent ($\bar{D}$)
positive (+)	20 hit	400 false positive
negative (–)	2000 (miss)	40,000 (correct rejection)

Figure 2.3 Contingency tables. (a) Binary classification test. (b) Tables for the example diagnostic test administered between 3 and 6 months gestational latency (mga), arranged from left to right. (c) Counterexample to the 'SpIn' rule for interpreting diagnostic test results. By the Spin rule, a positive test should allow us to reliably rule in the tested-for disease, but a positive result here is consistent with only a 5 percent chance of having the underlying disease.

5, and 6 months, contingency tables of diagnostic results are given in Figure 2.3b. Results remain unchanged past 6 months, although unnecessary treatment becomes dangerous to the mother after this point.

where we must simply input the four cells of the appropriate contingency table (HIT, MISS, CR, and FA) to obtain our best estimates of the sensitivity, S(1), and specificity, S(2), of the test at each time. Analytically, the sensitivity is given by

$$Sensitivity = p(+|D_{EVS} \cdot \iota) = \frac{\#pos|disease\ present}{\#disease\ present} = \frac{HIT}{HIT + MISS}$$

whereas the specificity is

$$Specificity = p(-|\bar{D}_{EVS} \cdot \iota) = \frac{\#neg|disease\ absent}{\#disease\ absent} = \frac{CR}{CR + FA}$$

and indicate that both measures are quite good, even at 3 months: Colloquially stated, at 3 mga the test correctly identifies those both with and without the disease about 90 percent of the time.

Programming Aside: Simulated Sensitivity and Specificity

We can simulate the sensitivity and specificity of the test at these four gestational latencies in the following way:

```
URNall=HIT+MISS+CR+FA; %size of urn containing all tests
URNhm=HIT+MISS; %urn containing all testees with disease
URNcf=CR+FA; %urn containing all testees without disease
HCR=[0 0]; PN=[0 0]; %simulated numbers of hits/CR and pos/neg results
REPS=40000;
for n=1:REPS,
    PNind=1+(randi(URNall)>URNhm); PN(PNind)=PN(PNind)+1;
    if PNind==1, HCR(1)=HCR(1)+(randi(URNhm)<=HIT);
    else HCR(2)=HCR(2)+(randi(URNcf)<=CR); end, end
S=HCR./PN
```

Posterior Probability of Disease

The sensitivity and specificity numbers are clearly useful in assessing the test, and indicate that it becomes better with increasing gestational latency – particularly its sensitivity. However, take a moment to consider the application of these numbers for the main purpose of the test: diagnosis. What do sensitivity and specificity have to say for someone who has had the test, and been given a positive (or negative) result?

As someone to whom the test has been applied, our interest is rather different than specificity and sensitivity. We are not interested in the probability that the test was positive on the *assumption* that we have (or do not have) the underlying disease: In a real-world scenario we do not know beforehand whether we have the disease. If we have had a positive test result we want to know the probability of actually having the underlying disease (**positive predictive value**). Or if we have been given a negative result, we want the probability that we indeed do not the disease (**negative predictive value**).

Analytically, the positive predictive value is the posterior probability of the disease, having observed a positive result,

$$PPV = p(D_{ENS}| + \cdot\iota) = \frac{p(D_{ENS}|\iota)p(+|D_{ENS}\cdot\iota)}{p(+|\iota)}$$

and the negative predictive value is the posterior probability of not having the disease, having observed a negative test result,

$$NPV = p(\bar{D}_{ENS}| - \cdot\iota) = \frac{p(\bar{D}_{ENS}|\iota)p(-|\bar{D}_{ENS}\cdot\iota)}{p(-|\iota)}$$

and finally the probability of disease presence after a negative test result is

$$p(D_{ENS}| - \cdot\iota) = 1 - \frac{p(\bar{D}_{ENS}|\iota)p(-|\bar{D}_{ENS}\cdot\iota)}{p(-|\iota)}$$

Programming Aside: Positive Predictive Value at 3 Months Gestational Latency

We can update our earlier simulation to accomplish this (continuing with the 3-month contingency table):

```
PN=[0 0]; %simulated number positive and negative results
HCR=[0 0]; FAM=[0 0]; %simulated numbers of hit/CR and FA/Miss results
for n=1:REPS,
    PNind=1+(randi(URNall)>URNhm); PN(PNind)=PN(PNind)+1;
    if PNind==1,
        if randi(URNhm)<=HIT, HCR(1)=HCR(1)+1;
  else FAM(2)=FAM(2)+1; end
    else
        if randi(URNcf)<=CR, HCR(2)=HCR(2)+1;
  else FAM(1)=FAM(1)+1; end, end, end
PNpv=HCR./(HCR+FAM)
```

where we now see that the sensitivity and specificity act as the likelihood elements of these posterior probabilities. In other words, a positive test result could be thought of as one symptom of a disease, but (unless the test gives 100 percent specificity and sensitivity) not definitive of disease presence or absence.

The posterior probabilities tell a drastically different story: After having tested negative for D_{ENS}, the probability of instead having the disease, is $p(D_{ENS}| - \cdot\iota) = 0.00055$; and somewhat surprisingly there is only a probability, after having tested positive for D_{ENS}, of having the disease of $p(D_{ENS}| + \cdot\iota) = 0.0465$. That is, there is very little probability of having the disease whether or not one tests positive, despite this probability being 100 times greater after a positive result. This is due to the fact that D_{ENS} has a rather small prior probability $[p(D_{ENS}|\iota)]$. This prior probability, also called the **base-rate** or disease **prevalence**, scales the likelihood terms (e.g., the sensitivity), such that an improbable prior can swamp the information present in the likelihood. Base-rate neglect appears to be the source of much confusion in problems with informative priors.

Programming Aside: Effect of Base-Rate on Posterior Predictive Result

For example, if the contingency table data had instead been:

```
URNall=100;
HIT=45; MISS=5; CR=47; FA=3;
URNhm=HIT+MISS;
URNcf=CR+FA;
```

it would change the disease base-rate from $p(D_{ENS}|\iota) = 0.005$ to $p(D_{ENS}|\iota) = 0.5$, and the posterior probabilities to $p(D_{ENS}|+\cdot\iota) = 0.9375$ and $p(D_{ENS}|-\cdot\iota) = 0.0962$.

Decision Rules

With this information, we can examine some criteria for deciding to administer treatment. For example, one criterion might be that we want a decision rule that incorrectly withholds treatment in no more than 1 out of every 2000 cases in which the disease is present. The relevant information is then the probability, given a negative test result, that the disease is actually present.

Another criterion might be that we want a decision rule that risks, on average, no more than a two-week hospital stay per treatment administered.

Under this criterion, the decision rule would be to treat on positive test only during the 3- to 4-month gestational window.

Example: Sensitivity, Specificity, Spin, and Snout

Now that we have encountered both the sensitivity/specificity and positive/negative predictive values, we are equipped to examine one of the clinical rules of thumb that is commonly taught in medical schools: 'SpIn' and 'SnOut.' These mnemonics are intended to suggest that tests with high **sp**ecificity are useful for 'ruling **in**' a disease, whereas tests with high **sen**sitivity are useful for 'ruling **out**' disease.

One can find the following logic used to explain the SnOut rule: 'The sensitivity describes the ability of a diagnostic test to identify true disease without missing anyone by leaving the disease undiagnosed. Thus, a high-sensitivity test has few false negatives and is effective at ruling conditions out (SnOut).' Similarly, one can find the following logic used to explain the SpIn rule: 'Specificity describes the ability of a diagnostic test to be correctly negative in the absence of disease, without mislabeling anyone. Thus, a high-specificity test has few false positives and is effective in ruling conditions in (SpIn).'

Programming Aside: Negative Predictive Value

This is simulated by sampling from all cases with negative results at the rate at which misses occur:

```
REPS=100000000;
HIT=[45 45 46 47]; %Hit data at each testing time
MISS=[5 5 4 3];
CR=[9027 9159 9237 9270];
FA=[923 791 713 680];
URNall=HIT+MISS+CR+FA; %size of urn containing all tests
URNhm=HIT+MISS; %urn containing all testees with disease
URNcf=CR+FA; %urn containing all testees without disease

for n=1:4,
    Nlist=randi(URNall(n),[REPS 1])>(HIT(n)+FA(n)); %negative tests
    Mlist=randi(CR(n)+MISS(n),[REPS 1])>CR(n); %Misses | neg test
    pM(n)=sum(and(Nlist,Mlist))./sum(Nlist); end
disp(num2str(pM))
```

which yields posterior probabilities of $p(D_{ENS}|-\cdot\iota) = [0.00056\ 0.00054\ 0.00043\ 0.00032]$, and shows that the rate of incorrectly administering the treatment based on positive test results falls below 1 in 2000 after the 4-month testing period, and the decision rule would be to treat on positive test result only for pregnancies past the 4-month point.

Programming Aside: Decision Rule for Risking No More than a Two-Week Hospital Stay per Treatment

To obtain the relevant information, we would simulate the possible outcomes from administering treatment on testing positive at the four gestational latencies, keeping track of the length of hospital stay in each case. Since the length of stay is related only to the time of inappropriate treatment, we can simply multiply the probability of receiving treatment incorrectly $p(\overline{D_{ENS}}|+\cdot\iota)$ by the length of stay at each treatment time (reusing the variable definitions from the previous simulation):

```
FAs=[0 0 0 0];  %initialize list of simulated false alarms at each month
Hs=[0 0 0 0];  %initialize list of simulated hits at each of 4 months
for M=1:4,
    for n=1:REPS,
        if randi(URNall(M))>URNhm(M),   %disease absent
            FAs(M)=FAs(M)+(randi(URNcf(M))>CR(M));
        else Hs(M)=Hs(M)+(randi(URNhm(M))>MISS(M)); end, end, end
.8*[5:10:35].*[FAs./(FAs+Hs)]
```

which shows that the probabilities of incorrectly administering treatment based on a positive test result are $p(\overline{D_{ENS}}|+\cdot\iota) = [0.954\ 0.946\ 0.939\ 0.935]$, and the only times that meet the criterion are at 3 and 4 months.

The mistake made in the SpIn and SnOut rules is that the rationale above effectively ignores the conditioning statements in $p(+|D\cdot\iota)$ and $p(-|\bar{D}\cdot\iota)$. That is, sensitivity is a probability statement that is *valid only for cases where the disease is present.* It has nothing to say about the case where disease is absent, so it cannot be used to infer disease absence (i.e., ruling the disease out). Similarly, specificity defines a probability that is *valid only when the disease is absent*; it has nothing to tell us in cases when disease is present, and so cannot be used to rule the disease in.

To assure ourselves of this error, we can return to the contingency table of Figure 2.3c, which shows a counterexample to the SpIn rule. This diagnostic test has high specificity $[p(-|\bar{D}\cdot\iota) = 0.99]$, but this does not allow us to rule the disease in on observing a positive test result. To repeat the logic above, 'a high-specificity test has few false positives and is effective in ruling conditions in.' This statement is misleading – a better statement would be that the test has *relatively few* false positives *in relation to all disease-absent cases.* Seen in this light, we would be less likely to erroneously conclude that a positive result is generally a good indicator of disease presence, because having relatively few of something is meaningless unless we know the number of all disease-absent cases (the base-rate). We see from the contingency table that in fact a positive test result indicates only a 5 percent chance of having the disease – by no means the type of number that should be used to 'reliably rule the disease in.' The identical case can be made against the SnOut rule: Simply switch the two columns of numbers in the contingency table of Figure 2.3c, so that the disease is high-prevalence instead of low-prevalence. Now, a negative test result would be consistent with a 95 percent chance of nevertheless having the disease, despite the test's high sensitivity [after switching numbers in the columns, $p(+|D\cdot\iota) = 0.99)$].

Programming Aside: Simulation of Positive Result from a High-Specificity Diagnostic Test

If you were a physician given a positive test result from

```
REPS=42420; %[first 20 are hits, next 400 are FA, next 2000 are misses,
          and last 40000 are CR]
keepgoing=1;
while keepgoing, counter=0;
    samp=randi(REPS); %select a person from among all those tested
    while samp>421, samp=randi(REPS); counter=counter+1; end
    disp([num2str(counter) 'patients have received negative results'])

    % Construct a questdlg with three options
    choice = questdlg('You have a patient with a positive test result.
              Is the disease present?','',{'Yes','No','Cancel'}); % Handle response
    switch choice
        case 'Yes'
            if samp<21, disp(['You''re right!! disease WAS present'])
            else disp(['wrong!! no disease here']); end
        case 'No'
            if samp>20, disp(['You''re right!! no disease here'])
            else disp(['wrong!! disease was present after all']); end
        case 'Cancel'
            keepgoing=0; end, end
```

A negative result from a high-sensitivity test does not allow us to reliably rule the disease out (SnOut), because a high base-rate of disease means that almost everyone has it – regardless of test result.

Exercises

1) Within medicine:
   a. how do sensitivity and specificity relate to Bayes' rule?
   b. relate sensitivity and specificity to PPV and NPV.
   c. show how PPV and NPV combine to yield the posterior in a mock example.
2) Serologic testing for herpes produces the following contingency table: 95 Hits, 11 Misses, 18 FA, 408 CR.
   a. What are the sensitivity and specificity of the test?
   b. What do positive and negative test results mean?
3) Fecal occult blood test results in the following contingency table for colorectal cancer: 17 Hits, 36 Misses, 2998 FA, 96949 CR.
   a. What are the sensitivity and specificity of the test?
   b. What do positive and negative test results mean?
   c. The above contingency table gave the results for men. For women, the results are: 13 H, 20 M, 2999 FA, 96961 CR. How do your answers for (a) and (b) change if the patient is a woman?

4) Prostate specific antigen screening for prostate cancer produces the following contingency table for men under age 40: 3 Hits, 7 Misses, 36899 FA, 63101 CR.
   a. What are the sensitivity and specificity of the test?
   b. What do positive and negative test results mean?
   c. How do the results in (a) and (b) change for men between 60 and 70 [349 H, 651 M, 5535 FA, 9465 CR]?
5) An ultrasonographic screening of pregnant women under the age of 30 for a Down syndrome baby produces the following results: 7 Hits, 8 Misses, 120 FA, 1966 CR.
   a. What is the probability of having a DS baby after getting a positive test result?
   b. After a negative test result?
   c. How do (a) and (b) change if the screening results are for a woman over the age of 35: 49 H, 60 M, 999 FA, 18978 CR?
6) Show the calculations involved in disproving the pan-applicability of the SpIn and SnOut rules based on Figure 2.3c.
7) Alter the contingency table in Figure 2.3c so that the SpIn rule applies. What is the critical difference between the two contingency tables that allows SpIn to apply in one but not the other?

2.2 Probabilities and Probability Distributions

In previous sections we were primarily concerned with calculating single probabilities, such as the probability of obtaining heads on a given coin flip, or a given series of coin flips. In order to solve most problems of scientific inference, however, we must deal with full distributions of probabilities (as in Figure 2.4), instead of their individual constituents. This section provides our first systematic look at assigning full probability distributions. Here, we will focus primarily on distributions based on the probabilities that describe coin tossing and other two-outcome experimental trials. These two-outcome experiments are called Bernoulli trials, named for James Bernoulli (1655–1705) who used them extensively in his *Ars Conjectandi* (published posthumously in 1713). One of the outcomes is usually referred to as a 'success,' and the total number of successes is denoted S. We will define background information specifying Bernoulli trials as:

$\iota_B \equiv$ there are exactly two outcomes possible on each trial of the 'experiment,'[4] the probability of a success is constant across repetitions, and the outcomes of repeated experiments are logically independent.

2.2.1 Multiplicity Factors

We have already encountered part of the mathematical framework for calculating the probability distributions describing Bernoulli trials. If the rate of heads is $\theta = 0.5$ and

[4] It always strikes me as odd to use the word 'experiment' to refer to the act of tossing a coin. It is, however, technically correct; an experiment describes any test or procedure performed under controlled conditions to generate data. Perhaps it is because coin tossing is such a boring example of an experiment that it may appear not to fit the mold. However, it is the traditional (and correct) description, and will be used here – hopefully without confusion.

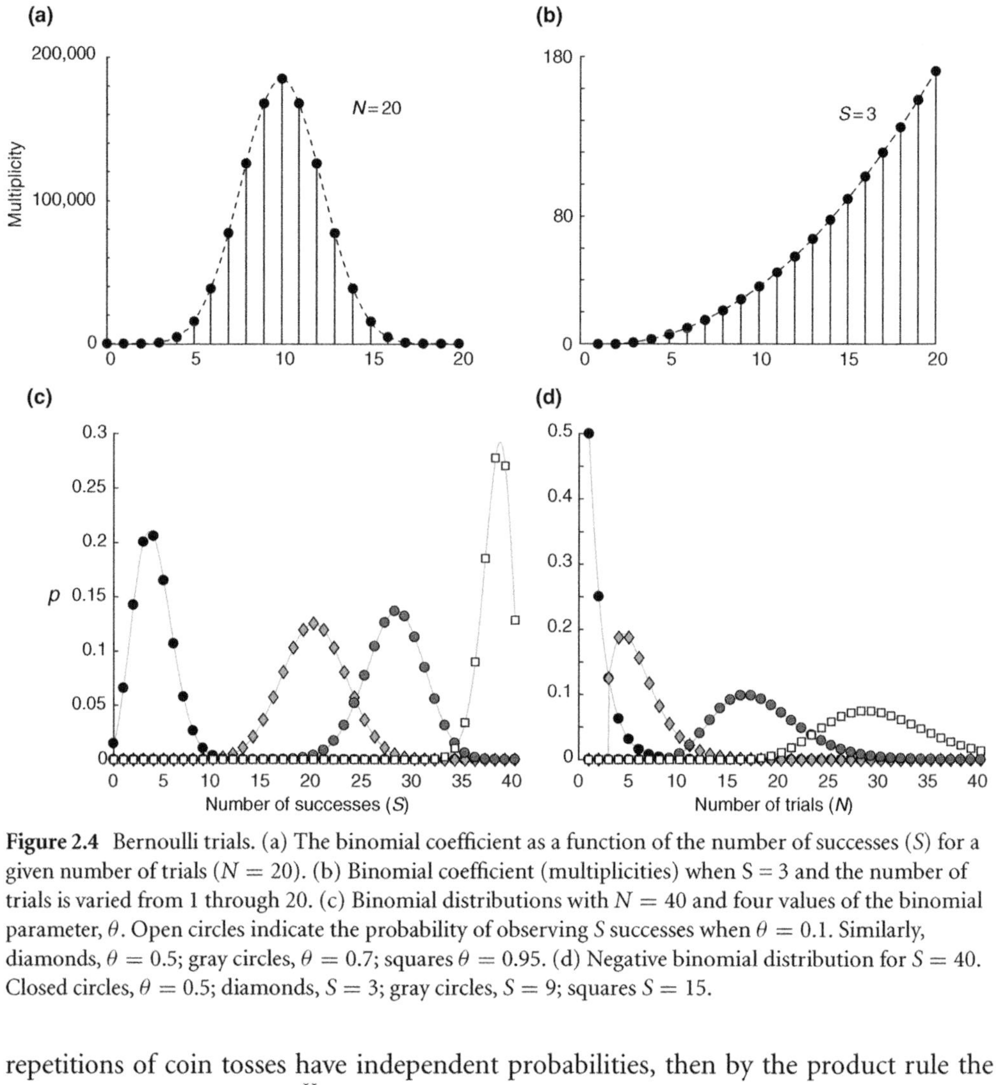

Figure 2.4 Bernoulli trials. (a) The binomial coefficient as a function of the number of successes (S) for a given number of trials ($N = 20$). (b) Binomial coefficient (multiplicities) when $S = 3$ and the number of trials is varied from 1 through 20. (c) Binomial distributions with $N = 40$ and four values of the binomial parameter, θ. Open circles indicate the probability of observing S successes when $\theta = 0.1$. Similarly, diamonds, $\theta = 0.5$; gray circles, $\theta = 0.7$; squares $\theta = 0.95$. (d) Negative binomial distribution for $S = 40$. Closed circles, $\theta = 0.5$; diamonds, $S = 3$; gray circles, $S = 9$; squares $S = 15$.

repetitions of coin tosses have independent probabilities, then by the product rule the probability of H heads is θ^H. With two possible outcomes and N repetitions, S successes ($N - S$ failures) were calculated to have probability $\theta^s(1-\theta)^{N-S}$. In previous applications we assumed that all differently ordered N-repetition sets with the same number of successes and failures were different outcomes. For example, we assumed the two pairs of coin tosses HT and TH were different – their order mattered. However, in many applications the order of outcomes is irrelevant; the outcomes HT and TH are not discriminated because they contain identical numbers of T and H results. In these cases, we will lump together (summate) the probabilities of sequences that are equivalent, disregarding order. This requires considering the number of ways S successes and $N - S$ failures could possibly occur. We generally call this number the **multiplicity** of the result, and with two potential outcomes (e.g., H or T), the multiplicity of S successes in N trials is given by the binomial coefficient:

$$\binom{N}{S} = \frac{N!}{S!(N-S)!} \qquad (2.14).$$

Figure 2.4 a plots the binomial coefficient for the possible outcomes of 20 Bernoulli trials. Take a moment to notice the tremendous range of numbers here. The maximum is nearly 2×10^6 (when $S = N/2 = 10$) and falls to a minimum of 1 (when either $S = 0$ or $S = N$). Notice also that the binomial coefficient is always a maximum when $S = N/2$, and that the vast majority of ways in which the set of Bernoulli trials could occur are within a small range centered on the maximum: In this example about 90 percent of the possible results of 20 Bernoulli trials occur within 3 successes of the maximum-multiplicity outcome (i.e., near 10 successes). Exercise 4 demonstrates that this concentration of outcomes near the maximum of the distribution becomes more pronounced as N increases.

For example, when we multiply the probability, $\theta^3(1-\theta)^3$, of any specific three-tail/three-head sequence (e.g., *THTHTH*) by the multiplicity of three-tails/three-head sequences we obtain the order-irrelevant probability:

$$
\begin{aligned}
p(T^3H^3|\theta = 0.5 \cdot \iota_b) &= \binom{N}{S}\theta^s(1-\theta)^{N-S} \\
&= \frac{N!}{S!(N-S)!}\theta^s(1-\theta)^{N-S} \\
&= \frac{6!}{3!3!}0.5^3 0.5^3 = \frac{6!}{3!3!}0.5^6 = (20)(0.015625) = 0.3125
\end{aligned}
$$

The multiplicity function shown in Figure 2.4a may be thought of as expressing the 'stability' of the outcome, because out of all the ways one could choose sets of 20 heads/tails, nearly 70 percent of all possible configurations are within two abscissa positions (10 percent of the range) of the 50-50 split. This stability improves dramatically as N increases; with $N = 50$, only 13 percent of possible configurations are further than 10 percent of the range from the 50-50 split, and this drops to 4 percent when $N = 100$.

Exercises

1) In 12 flips of a coin stamped with a head on one side and tail on the other, how many ways can _____ occur?
   a. 2 tails
   b. 10 heads
   c. 8 heads
   d. 4 tails
2) You flip a coin until the Sth success, which takes N total flips. How many ways can the sequence of trials prior to the final success (and therefore final flip of the coin) occur? [Hint: the last coin flip must be a success, so it's position in the order of successes/failures cannot vary.]
3) Consider the differences in our state of information when a sequence of two-outcome trials does and does not consider order information. Give examples of real-world situations in which each of these states of information is more plausible than the other.

4) Calculate a multiplicity function as in Figure 2.4 for $N = 14$ through 100 Bernoulli trials (in increments of 2). For each distribution, calculate the density of multiplicities within n outcomes of the maximum-multiplicity outcome (where n is the minimum number of outcomes containing 90 percent of the total multiplicity: $\delta = N/n$ [$\delta = 3.3$ for $N = 20$ trials (see above)]. Plot δ as a function of N.
5) For the same set of multiplicity distributions computed in Ex.4, compute the proportion of possible ordered distributions that fall within two of the 50-50 point (i.e., $N/2 + [-2 : 2]$). Plot this proportion as a function of N.

2.2.2 Bernoulli Trials: The Binomial Distribution

As noted above, the probability assigned to S successes in N trials, when the order of 'successes' and 'failures' is irrelevant (or unknown), is given by the equation

$$p(S|N \cdot \theta \cdot \imath_b) = \frac{N!}{S!(N-S)!}\theta^s(1-\theta)^{N-S} = \binom{N}{s}\theta^s(1-\theta)^{N-S} \qquad (2.15).$$

This formulation makes a great deal of intuitive sense: it says that (for N trials) the probability of observing an instance of the category S can be obtained by noting that each ordered outcome in this category is assigned probability $\theta^s(1-\theta)^{N-S}$; and the probability that *some* member of the category S is observed is just this probability, summed over the number of ways this category could occur. This is simply the sum rule, and exactly the logic we used to compute marginalizations in previous sections.

Written as in (2.15), this distribution answers the question, 'What is the probability of observing S successes in a given number (N) of Bernoulli trials and a known success rate, θ?'. Equation (2.15) defines a probability distribution, called the binomial distribution, where one probability is assigned to each possible value of S. When does this distribution occur, aside from coin flipping and thermal physics? One relevant case is that of neural spiking, where a given observation epoch of time T produces a single spike. Without knowing when during the observation epoch that the spike occurred, we can break the observation epoch into subintervals of length Δt. We can then compute the probability of finding it within any subinterval, which is equal to the rate, $\theta = \Delta t/T$, at which (upon repetition of this 'experiment') the spike would be found in that subinterval. If instead there are N total spikes in the observation epoch, then the probability of a particular subinterval of the total epoch T containing S spikes is given by (2.15), where again $\theta = \Delta t/T$ is the probability that a given spike will fall within a particular subinterval.

Figure 2.4b shows four binomial distributions, where each differs in its success rate. Notice that the binomial distribution is flattest when θ is near 0.5 and becomes more sharply peaked as θ moves toward either 1 or 0. This means that one is better able to make predictions about S for extreme values of , with perfect predictability occurring at the limits $\theta = 0$ and $\theta = 1$. Notice also that the shape of the binomial distribution, which tells us the probabilities of different experimental outcomes (numbers of successes) for a

Programming Aside: Binomial and Negative Binomial Multiplicity Plots (Fig.2.4)

The plots shown in the upper panels of Figure 2.4 are binomial and negative binomial multiplicities. Each of these requires us to compute factorials, which are defined as:

$$N! = factorial(N) = N \times (N-1) \times (N-2) \times \cdots \times 1.$$

The binomial multiplicity, $M - \binom{N}{S} = N![S!(N-S)!]$, is written:

```
Mb=nchoosek(N,S)
n=20; for k=0:20, Mb(k+1)=nchoosek(n,k); end %binomial multiplicity
clf; hold on; box off
plot(0:20,Mb,'k--');
stem(0:20,Mb,'ko','MarkerFaceColor','k','MarkerSize',11)
```

The negative binomial multiplicity, $M = \binom{N-1}{S-1} = (N-1)!/[(S-1)!(N-S)!]$, is:

```
k=3; for n=1:20,
      if n<k, Mnb(n)=0; else Mnb(n)=nchoosek(n-1,k-1); end, end
      %neg bin multiplicity
clf; hold on; box off
plot(1:20,Mb,'k--');
stem(1:20,Mb,'ko','MarkerFaceColor','k','MarkerSize',11)
```

where the factorials are computed in the nchoosek function. Notice that the negative binomial uses a constant number of successes (S=3) and the binomial a constant number of trials (N=20).

fixed binomial rate θ, is a combination of both the multiplicity and the term $\theta^s(1-\theta)^{N-S}$. However, for a given dataset the multiplicity is a constant. Thus, when we are interested in which of several binomial rates best describes an observed dataset, we are interested in computing the binomial likelihood, which treats the rate as unknown and the data as fixed, that is, $\mathcal{L}_b = M[\theta^s(1-\theta)^{N-S}]$, where $M = \binom{N}{S}$ is a constant. We will often be interested in writing the likelihood function for a given application as a proportional relation and dropping constant scale factors. Written as a proportional relation whose constant scale factors have been removed, the binomial likelihood is $\mathcal{L}_b = M[\theta^s(1-\theta)^{N-S}] \propto \theta^s(1-\theta)^{N-S}$

Exercises

1) Plot the binomial distribution for $\theta = 0.0$ and $N = 20$.
2) Plot the binomial distribution for $\theta = 0.9$ and $N = 40$, and relate it to the binomial distributions shown in Figure 2.4.
3) Using (2.15) construct five binomial distributions, all with $\theta = 0.2$, but with $N = [10\ 20\ 30\ 40\ 50]$.
4) For $N = 15, 25$, and 35, plot the binomial multiplicity, normalized such that the maximum value is 1. Compare this to the likelihood for $\theta = 0.1, 0.35$, and 0.95 by plotting

these binomial cores on the same axis (also normalized to max = 1) as each multiplicity plot. Describe the contributions of the two components to the shape of the resulting binomial distribution.

2.2.3 Bernoulli Trials: The Negative Binomial Distribution

In addition to answering the questions defined above, for which (2.15) was the answer, there is a second type of question that may be asked of the identical dataset consisting of Bernoulli trials: 'What is the probability of observing the Sth success on the Nth repetition in a series of Bernoulli trials for which the success rate is θ?' The answer to this question is provided by the negative binomial distribution:

$$p(N|S\cdot\theta\cdot\imath_{nb}) = \frac{(N-1)!}{(S-1)!(N-S)!}\theta^S(1-\theta)^{N-S} = \binom{N-1}{S-1}\theta^S(1-\theta)^{N-S} \quad (2.16).$$

Notice the similarity between the conditions necessary to assign binomial and negative binomial distributions. Both are based on observing a series of Bernoulli trials. The binomial distribution describes situations where the total number of trials is known and there is uncertainty concerning the number of successes that will be observed within those N trials. The negative binomial describes when the number of successes (S) is known and there is uncertainty concerning the number of total trials that occur before the final success is observed (N). Several negative binomial distributions with different rate parameters are shown in Figure 2.4b.

Given the similarities in the definitions of the two distributions, why does the multiplicity term of the negative binomial, $\frac{(N-1)!}{(S-1)![(N-1)-(S-1)]!} = \frac{(N-1)!}{(S-1)![N-S]!} = \binom{N-1}{S-1}$, contain terms with $N-1$ and $S-1$, in place of the N and S terms found in the multiplicity of the binomial? These substitutions are both a result of the fact that we intend to compute the probability of the Sth success, which is constrained to fall on the Nth trial. The reason for subtracting 1 from both N and S is that the multiplicity in this problem refers to the number of sequences that have the final of S success occurring on the last of N trials - the outcome of the final trial is fixed. If we know that one of the successes will always occur in the final trial, then we have $S-1$ successes still unaccounted for in the remaining $N-1$ trials. It is these reduced-by-one numbers that are the basis for our multiplicity calculation when using the negative binomial distribution.

The binomial and negative binomial distributions are called sampling distributions because they describe the probabilities of possible data samples. One would use the binomial distribution to assign the probabilities of possible data for an experiment that is equivalent to flipping a coin with success rate θ (e.g., constant neural spiking rate) a known number of times (N); here the data to be observed are the total number of successes (S). On the other hand, one would use the negative binomial distribution to assign the probabilities of possible data samples for an experiment equivalent to flipping a coin with a known success rate θ an unknown number of times (N) until the Sth success is observed; here, the data to be observed are the total number of repetitions (N).

Programming Aside: Binomial and Negative Binomial Plots (Fig. 2.4)

To generate the plots shown in Figure 2.4 we must first calculate binomial and negative binomial probabilities. Each of these requires us to compute factorials, which are defined as:

$$N! = factorial(N) = N \times (N-1) \times (N-2) \times \cdots \times 1.$$

These computations can easily lead to an underflow or overflow problem (see Appendix B), and we should make it a practice to compute factorials using the logarithmic gamma function. Without worrying about how the gamma function is computed, we can use the built-in MATLAB® gamma function to compute factorials:

$$N! = factorial(N) = N \times (N-1) \times (N-2) \times \cdots \times 1 = gamma(N+1),$$

where the log-factorial is therefore:

$$\ln(N!) = \ln[N \times (N-1) \times (N-2) \times \cdots \times 1] = gammaln(N+1).$$

Furthermore, we create a function called lnfactorial.m. This is done by creating a blank function under 'New,' and filling the blank function with

```
%lnfactorial.m

% USAGE: GF=lnfactorial(n)
% uses gamma functio to compute n!
%
%EXAMPLES:
% exp(lnfactorial(3)) %=6
% exp(lnfactorial(3.123) %=7

function GF=lnfactorial(n)
GF=gammaln(n+1);
```

and then saving the function with the name lnfactorial.

Furthermore, we see that the factorials appearing in (2.15) and (2.16) are used to compute the multiplicities, $\binom{N}{S}$ and $\binom{N-1}{S-1}$, which enumerate the number of sequences of length N from which you can choose S successes (often abbreviated 'N choose K,' where K stands in for the number of successes). Thus, we would also like to create a function lnchoosek.m that computes the log of the multiplicity:

```
% LNCHOOSEK.m
% USAGE: lnM=lnchoosek(N,K)
%  computes lnM=ln[N!/K!(N-K)!], that is: ln[Binomial Coefficient],
   using the gammaln function
%  [note that gammln supports fractional inputs N,K)
%
% OUTPUT: BC=ln[N!/K!(N-K)!]=ln(N!)-ln(K!)-ln([N-K]!)
%           [the number of distinct configurations that have N
%           successes in N observations]
% INPUTS: N=number of observations
%         K=number of successes

function lnM=lnchoosek(n,k)
NUM=lnfactorial(n);
```

```
DEN=lnfactorial(k)+lnfactorial(n-k);
lnM=NUM-DEN; end
```

We can then use these functions to produce the binomial and negative binomial plots. We begin by computing the set of four binomial distributions shown in Figure 2.4:

```
%%% Binomial distributions
Lbin=@(N,S,theta) lnchoosek(N,S)+S*log(theta)+(N-S)*log(1-theta);

Nnow=40;
thetas=[.1 .5 .7 .95];
Slist=cell(1,2); Lprob=cell(1,2);
Slist{1}=linspace(0,Nnow,Nnow+1)';
Slist{2}=linspace(0,Nnow,10*Nnow+1)';
Lprob{1}=Lbin(Nnow,Slist{1},thetas);
Lprob{2}=Lbin(Nnow,Slist{2},thetas);
```

We then plot the distributions on a single plot using 'hold on':

```
figure(1); clf; hold on
for n=1:4,
    plot(Slist{2},exp(Lprob{2}(:,n)),'-','Color',.7*[1 1 1],'LineWidth',1); end
plot(Slist{1},exp(Lprob{1}(:,1)),'ko','MarkerFaceColor','k','MarkerSize',10)
plot(Slist{1},exp(Lprob{1}(:,2)),'kd','MarkerFaceColor',.65*[1 1 1],'MarkerSize',10)
plot(Slist{1},exp(Lprob{1}(:,3)),'ko','MarkerFaceColor',.35*[1 1 1],'MarkerSize',10)
plot(Slist{1},exp(Lprob{1}(:,4)),'ks','MarkerFaceColor','w','MarkerSize',10)
```

Similarly, we compute a set of negative binomial distributions, now holding the success rate constant at $\theta = 0.5$ and varying the number of total trials (N) on the abscissa for each of four target-numbers of successes, S:

```
%%% Negative binomial distributions
%%% selecting 4 S-values
Lnbin=@(N,S,theta) lnchoosek(N-1,S-1)+S*log(theta)+(N-S)*log(1-theta);
Nlist=cell(1,2); Lprob=cell(1,2);
Snow=[1 3 9 15];
thetas=0.5;

Nlist{1}=linspace(1,Nnow,Nnow)'; Nlist{2}=linspace(1,Nnow,10*Nnow)';
for n=1:length(Snow),
    ntmp=Nlist{1}; ntmp(ntmp<Snow(n))=nan; Lprob{1}(:,n)=Lnbin(ntmp, Snow(n),thetas);
    ntmp=Nlist{2}; ntmp(ntmp<Snow(n))=nan; Lprob{2}(:,n)=Lnbin(ntmp,...
    Snow(n),thetas); end
Lprob{1}(isnan(Lprob{1}))=-inf; Lprob{2}(isnan(Lprob{2}))=-inf;

figure(2); clf; hold on
for n=1:4,
    plot(Nlist{2},exp(Lprob{2}(:,n)),'-','Color',.7*[1 1 1],'LineWidth',1); end
plot(Nlist{1},exp(Lprob{1}(:,1)),'ko','MarkerFaceColor','k','MarkerSize',10)
plot(Nlist{1},exp(Lprob{1}(:,2)),'kd','MarkerFaceColor',.65*[1 1 1],'MarkerSize',10)
plot(Nlist{1},exp(Lprob{1}(:,3)),'ko','MarkerFaceColor',.35*[1 1 1],'MarkerSize',10)
plot(Nlist{1},exp(Lprob{1}(:,4)),'ks','MarkerFaceColor','w','MarkerSize',10)
```

Exercises

1) Plot the negative binomial sampling distribution for $\theta = 1.0$ and $S = 20$.
2) Using (2.16) construct four negative binomial sampling distributions, all with $S = 10$, but with $\theta = [0.25\ 0.5\ 0.7\ 0.95]$.

3) For $N = 15, 25$, and 35, plot the negative binomial multiplicity, normalized such that the maximum value is 1. Compare the cores for $\theta = 0.1, 0.35$, and 0.95 by plotting these negative binomial cores on the same axis (also normalized to max = 1) as each multiplicity plot. Describe the contributions of the two components to the shape of the resulting negative binomial distribution.
4) Write the equation for the negative binomial likelihood, with and without constant scale factors removed.
5) Compute the binomial and negative binomial likelihoods for two successes in 20 trials, with $\theta = [0.1, 0.4, 0.6, 0.9]$
   a. with constant scale factors
   b. with constant scale factors removed.

2.3 Sampling Distributions and Likelihood Functions

In the figures and exercises above we calculated the probabilities of various possible datasets that might be obtained from sets of Bernoulli trials; that is, we calculated sampling distributions. When we compute a sampling distribution, we are implicitly asking a question about potential datasets. In the binomial case, the question was, 'What is the probability of observing S successes in N Bernoulli trials?' This does not, however, directly address the question of scientific interest, which involves an inference regarding an *unobservable parameter*, such as, 'After observing S successes in N Bernoulli trials, what can I say about the value of the binomial rate parameter, θ?' These inferences are always based on calculating a posterior distribution, whose definition was given in Chapter 1. From (1.5) we define the posterior probability over possible values of the binomial rate parameter as

$$
\begin{aligned}
p(\theta|N \cdot S \cdot \imath) &= \frac{p(\theta|\imath)p(N \cdot S|\theta \cdot \imath)}{p(N \cdot S|\imath)} \\
&\propto p(\theta|\imath)p(N \cdot S|\theta \cdot \imath)
\end{aligned}
$$

The posterior distribution is proportional to the product of two other probabilities, $p(\theta|\imath)$ and $p(N \cdot S|\theta \cdot \imath)$ [the last term, $p(N \cdot S|\imath)$, does not include θ and is a constant when (N, S) is assumed known]. The first is the prior probability distribution over possible values of θ, and the second probability comes from the sampling distribution, $p(N \cdot S|\theta \cdot \imath)$. Because this is a bivariate distribution, it can be decomposed using the product rule

$$
\begin{aligned}
&p(N \cdot S|\theta \cdot \imath) \\
&\quad = p(S|\theta \cdot \imath)p(N|S \cdot \theta \cdot \imath) \\
&\quad = p(N|\theta \cdot \imath)p(S|N \cdot \theta \cdot \imath)
\end{aligned}
$$

In the first case, we may have forced S to a prespecified constant experimentally, by stopping the experiment when the final s is observed, regardless of N. In this case, the probability reduces to $p(N \cdot S|\theta \cdot \imath_{nb}) = (1)p(N|S \cdot \theta \cdot \imath_{nb})$ and leads to the expression for the negative binomial distribution. Alternatively, we could utilize a stopping rule whereby the experiment is terminated after N observations, regardless of the value of S.

In this second case the probability is $p(N \cdot S|\theta \cdot \imath_b) = (1)p(S|N \cdot \theta \cdot \imath_b)$ and leads to the expression for the binomial sampling distribution.

To compute a posterior distribution over θ in, for example, the negative binomial case, we first select a set of θ values, where the probability of the $\imath^{\text{th}}$ value of the binomial rate parameter is: $p(\theta_i|N \cdot S \cdot \imath_{nb}) \propto p(\theta_i|\imath_b)p(N|S \cdot \theta_i \cdot \imath_{nb})$, which is proportional to the product of the prior probability for the $\imath^{\text{th}}$ value of θ and the probability of observing the data (S successes in N observations) under the hypothesis that the ith value of θ is the true rate. The former is an element of a prior probability distribution, and the latter is a probability taken from the negative binomial sampling distribution; both are elements of normalized probability distributions. However, when we iterate over the i index to compute the set of $p(\theta_i|N \cdot S \cdot \imath_{nb})$ elements from pairs of prior and sampling probabilities, we see that while all of the $p(\theta_i|\imath_{nb})$ are elements of the *same* prior distribution, each of the sampling probabilities $p(N|S \cdot \theta_i \cdot \imath_{nb})$ is taken from a *different* sampling distribution. This set of sampling probabilities, each taken from different sampling distributions, is the likelihood function. That is, the likelihood function is constructed by plucking probabilities from many *different* sampling distributions; each probability describes the dataset that was actually observed, but under different possible values of the unknown parameter (θ). In the current section, we will explore the relationship between sampling distributions and the likelihood function, using sampling distributions derived from Bernoulli trials.

2.3.1 Constructing Likelihood Functions from Sampling Distributions

What is the relationship between the sampling distribution and the likelihood function? We will see below that the likelihood function is derived from *a set of sampling distributions* – but only the part of the sampling distributions relevant to the observed data. That is, even though only one dataset is ever observed in an experiment, a sampling distribution describes all possible datasets that might be observed experimentally under one particular hypothesis about the underlying parameters (e.g., under the assumption that the true binomial rate parameter is $\theta = 0.5$). In contrast, the likelihood function is built from a set of sampling distributions, by extracting only those probabilities (one from each distribution) that describe the dataset that was actually observed in the experiment (S successes in N Bernoulli trials).

To begin our example, that of estimating a binomial rate parameter θ from coin tosses, we first return to (1.5). The posterior distribution over the binomial rate parameter is

$$p(\theta_i|N \cdot S \cdot \imath_b) \propto p(\theta_i|\imath_b)p(S|N \cdot \theta_i \cdot \imath_b)$$

and the second term on the right-hand side is just (2.15)

$$p(S|N \cdot \theta_i \cdot \imath_b) = \binom{N}{S}\theta^s(1-\theta)^{N-S}$$

To understand how the sampling distribution is related to the likelihood function, we will consider our information relating data to hypothesis when data are collected, which in this example is encoded by (2.15). Now, prior to collecting data, there are two unknowns on the right-hand side of this equation: S and θ (N is constrained experimentally and therefore known beforehand). Corresponding to these two unknowns, we can plot a 2D surface of the sampling probabilities under various values of the rate parameter and the possible data that might be observed. For the binomial distribution this 2D surface is shown in the upper panel of Figure 2.5.

We note that each slice through the upper panel of Figure 2.5, when that slice is taken parallel to the data axis (e.g., open circles), corresponds to a particular sampling distribution (e.g., Fig. 2.4a). In Figure 2.4a the plots correspond to slices taken parallel to the data axis at $\theta = 0.1, 0.5, 0.7$, and 0.95. The most important of sampling distribution for the null-hypothesis testing algorithm is the slice at the null hypothesis, $\theta_0 = 0.5$. Notice, however, that once the experiment has been conducted there is only one dataset

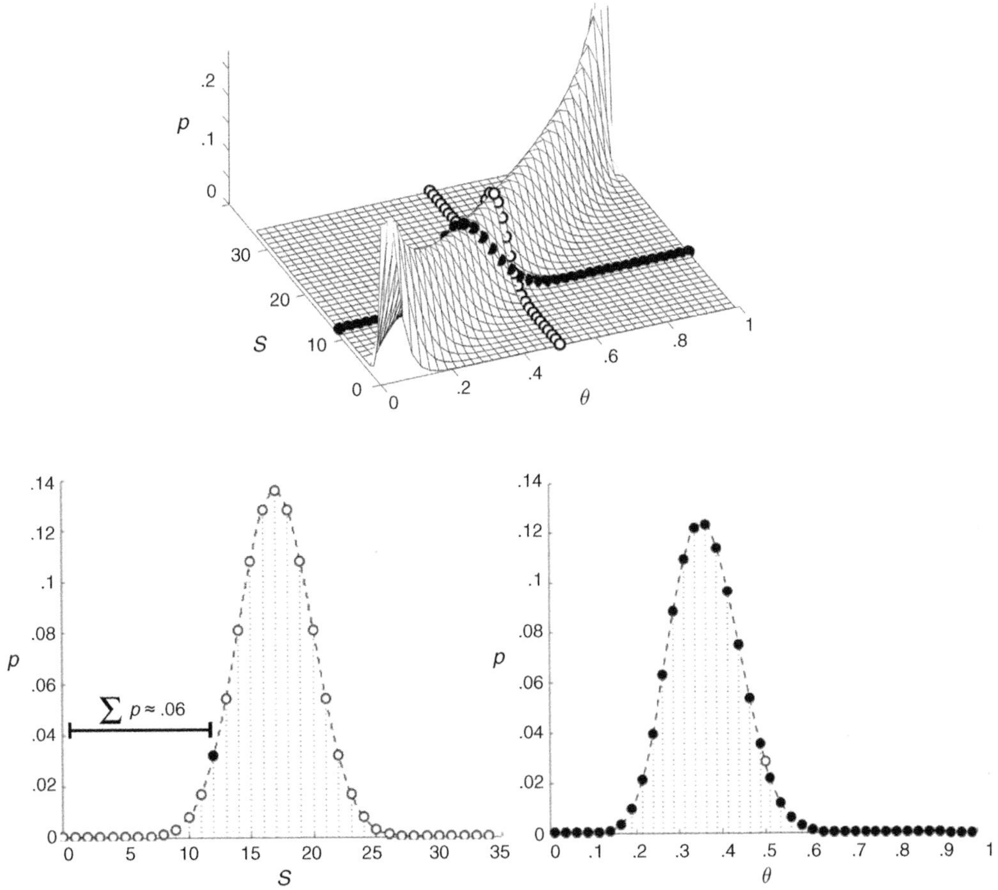

Figure 2.5 Relationship between sampling distributions and the likelihood function for the binomial distribution. The likelihood function is constructed from the sampling probabilities corresponding to a series of theta values (hypotheses). The sampling distribution for the null hypothesis is shown in open circles in the three panels, and the sampling probabilities associated with the observed data (the likelihood function) are shown in closed circles in all three panels.

along the data axes relevant to a scientist: the data actually observed in the experiment. Correspondingly, there is only one slice through the 2D data-hypothesis surface of relevance to our calculations: the slice parallel to the θ axis (closed circles) that intersects the coordinates that represent 12 successes in 34 trials (the hypothetical dataset for our example).

By passing a slice through each of the 2D surfaces at the observed dataset ($S = 12, N = 34$) on the data axis, we have selected only those sampling probabilities that correspond to our post-data-collection information. However, because those sampling probabilities all correspond to different sampling distributions (i.e., each element of the filled-circles lower-right plots is taken from a separate sampling distribution), the set of values extracted by hypothesis-axis-parallel slices will not necessarily form a normalized probability distribution (i.e., will not generally sum to 1). These slices are referred to as likelihood functions, written $\mathcal{L}(\theta)$ to emphasize the fact that this is a function of the parameter θ rather than a function of the data, and is not a proper probability distribution because it is not a normalized distribution the way that sampling distributions are.

Once the data are known, it is possible to generate likelihood functions more directly than via the 'slicing' method just described. Instead of generating all possible sampling distributions and taking a slice through the observed data, we can compute the likelihood function in the lower right panel of Figures 2.5 directly, using $p(S|N \cdot \boldsymbol{\theta} \cdot \iota_B) = \binom{N}{S}\boldsymbol{\theta}^S(1-\boldsymbol{\theta})^{N-S}$ or $\mathcal{L}(\theta) = \boldsymbol{\theta}^S(1-\boldsymbol{\theta})^{N-S}$, where $\boldsymbol{\theta}$ is the list $\boldsymbol{\theta} = [\theta_1, \theta_2, \ldots]$ of discretized parameter values and S, N are the experimentally observed data (therefore constants). This method simply eliminates the multiplicity term $\binom{N}{S}$ when calculating the likelihood, which is a constant scale-factor in $\mathcal{L}(\theta)$ and is therefore irrelevant because it will be accounted for when we normalize the final posterior distribution. A similar direct calculation of the likelihood is possible for the lower right-hand panel of Figure 2.6. Here the likelihood is computed directly by calculating the negative binomial likelihood, $\mathcal{L}(\theta) = \binom{N-1}{S-1}\boldsymbol{\theta}^S(1-\boldsymbol{\theta})^{N-S} \propto \boldsymbol{\theta}^S(1-\boldsymbol{\theta})^{N-S}$, over the discretized list of possible parameters $\boldsymbol{\theta}$.

By writing the likelihood as $\mathcal{L}(\theta) = \boldsymbol{\theta}^S(1-\boldsymbol{\theta})^{N-S}$, we have dropped all constant terms from the sampling equation: any terms that do not contain the parameter θ (such as any term that depends only on the data). When it is not necessary to use a normalized likelihood function,[5] we will often simplify our calculations by using the core of the likelihood function, eliminating all constant factors that scale the overall height of the function but do not change its shape. When the core of the likelihood is used instead of a normalized likelihood, the shape of the posterior distribution will not be affected, although the resulting likelihood function will no longer consist of normalized probability values. The equation describing the posterior distribution simply changes from the exact form, given in (1.5):

$$p(H_i|\boldsymbol{d} \cdot \iota) = \frac{p(H_i|\iota)p(\boldsymbol{d}|H_i \cdot \iota)}{p(\boldsymbol{d}|\iota)}$$

[5] We sometimes use the term *normalized likelihood* to refer to a likelihood equation that retains all its constant terms, such that it looks identical to the corresponding normalized sampling distribution.

Programming Aside: Plotting Sampling Surfaces

It will be useful to gain some experience with creating sampling surfaces such as those shown in Figures 2.5 and 2.6. These figures are produced by the `BuildLikelihoodBin.m` and the `BuildLikelihoodNBin.m` functions. To use these functions, we simply need to provide the observed data and null hypothesis. The help file tells us that the outputs are the likelihood function ('`lx`'), the sampling distribution ('`px`') and the pvalue ('`pval`').
To generate Figures 2.5 and 2.6 the observed data are $N = 34$ and $S = 13$. Thus we write

```
N=34; S=13; H0=.5;
[lx px pval]=BuildLikelihoodBin(S,N,H0); pval
[lx px pval]=BuildLikelihoodNBin(S,N,H0); pval
```

The two p-val outputs should match those shown on the figures. You can manually generate the likelihood and sampling probabilities with the commands

```
figure; plot(lx(:,2),lx(:,1),'k.')
figure; plot(px(:,2),px(:,1),'.')
```

We can also verify that the p-values are correct by first generating the three plots:

```
[lx px pval]=BuildLikelihoodBin(S,N,H0); pval
```

and comparing the sum

```
sum(px(px(:,2)<=S),1)
```

and similarly for the negative binomial

```
[lx px pval]=BuildLikelihoodBin(S,N,H0); pval
```

and comparing the sum

```
sum(px(px(:,2)<=S),1)
```

Use these functions to find an even more egregious example of the optional stopping problem involving 11 successes, by trying values of N in the two programs (N>S):

```
S=11; H0=.5;
for N=S:3*S,
    [lx px pvalBin]=BuildLikelihoodBin(S,N,H0);
    [lx px pvalNBin]=BuildLikelihoodNBin(S,N,H0);
    [N pvalBin pvalNBin], end
```

Finally, you should examine the code in the BuildLikelihood... functions to familiarize yourself with the plotting functions and the computations that were made to generate those figures.

to the proportional form

$$p(H_i|\mathbf{d}\cdot\iota) \propto p(H_i|\iota)p(\mathbf{d}|H_i\cdot\iota) = \varpi(H_i)\mathcal{L}(H_i) \tag{2.17}$$

where constants that would normalize the sampling distribution have been dropped from $p(\mathbf{d}|H_i\cdot\iota)$, as has the global likelihood term $[p(\mathbf{d}|\iota)]$ in the denominator of (1.5), which would ordinarily serve to normalize the posterior distribution. Later we will substitute

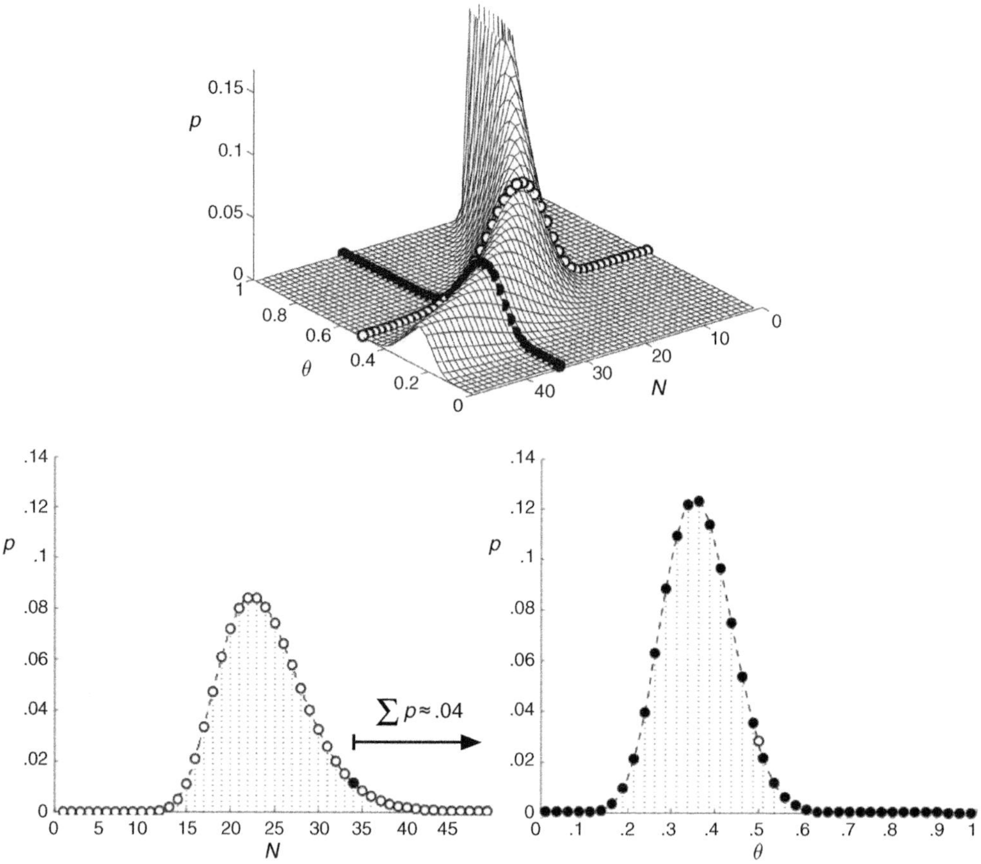

Figure 2.6 Relationship between sampling distributions and the likelihood function for the negative binomial. The likelihood function is constructed from sampling probabilities corresponding to a set of theta values (hypotheses about theta). The sampling distribution for the null hypothesis $\theta = 0.5$ is shown in open circles, and sampling probabilities associated with the observed data (likelihood function) are in closed circles.

these 'cores' for the corresponding normalized functions in measurement problems, but not in model selection problems.

Exercises

1) Which parameters are varied, and which are held constant in the:
   a. binomial sampling distribution
   b. negative binomial likelihood
   c. negative binomial sampling distribution
   d. binomial likelihood function
2) Compare the core of the likelihood function for the binomial and negative binomial distributions, both graphically and in a short statement.
3) Compute $p(\boldsymbol{\theta}|N \cdot S \cdot \imath)$ from the normalized binomial likelihood, $p(S|N \cdot \boldsymbol{\theta} \cdot \imath_b)$, and from the core of the binomial likelihood, $\mathcal{L}(\theta)$. In both cases first compute the terms in

the numerator if (1.5), and then normalize the result. Plot the two results on the same figure.

4) Compute $p(\boldsymbol{\theta}|N \cdot S \cdot \imath)$ from the normalized negative binomial likelihood, $p(N|S \cdot \boldsymbol{\theta} \cdot \imath_b)$, and from the core of the negative binomial likelihood, $\mathcal{L}(\theta)$ as above. Plot the two results on the same figure.
5) The sampling distribution for the standard Gaussian distribution (i.e., the Gaussian distribution with $\mu = 0$ and $\sigma = 1$), described briefly in Chapter 1, is: $p(x|\mu \cdot \imath) = \sqrt{2\pi}^{-1} e^{-\frac{x^2}{2}}$. On a single x-p axis, create a plot of the normalized likelihood and the corresponding core for the standard Gaussian. Describe any differences between the plots.

2.3.2 The Optional Stopping Problem

Optional stopping refers to the practice of performing a preliminary analysis of the data partway through data collection to determine whether it is worth continuing with the experiment and collecting more data. This creates a problem for null-hypothesis testing or any other algorithm whose result depends on the probabilities of unobserved data. In the above plots we have an example of this phenomenon, which will allow us to explore in detail what it means when the result of an hypothesis test depends on unobserved data, and why this does not occur in a Bayesian analysis.

Figures 2.5 and 2.6 describe null-hypothesis tests using the binomial and negative binomial distributions for exactly the same dataset, here $S = 12$ in 34 trials. Remember that a frequentist inference is based on the probability of observing a dataset at least as extreme as the one that was actually observed. This probability, called the 'p-value,' is compared to the 'alpha level' that was set prior to the experiment (usually $\alpha = 0.05$); the null hypothesis is rejected if $p < \alpha$. These 'tail-area' probabilities (see Box 2.2) are shown graphically in Figures 2.5 and 2.6.

From the differences in the shapes of the two distributions, it should be clear that the sums of the two tail-area probabilities (p-values) will generally differ. In the specific case shown in the figures, the tail-area probability starting at the observed dataset is $p(N \geq 34|S = 12 \cdot \theta_o \cdot \imath_{nb}) \approx .040$ with the negative binomial, and $p(S \leq 12|N = 34 \cdot \theta_o \cdot \imath_b) \approx .061$ for the binomial distribution. Thus, we obtain different frequentist inferences ('reject' and 'don't reject' the null hypothesis) using the binomial and negative binomial distributions, because the probabilities of *unobserved* datasets (the tail-areas) are different in the two distributions.

Although these two p-values may not seem massively different, it is clearly a problem that the identical data result in different inferences, and that the difference derives essentially from the thoughts of the analyst (in one case you think of the data as coming from an experiment that ended after $N = 34$ observations and in the other you think of the experiment as continuing until $S = 12$ successes were observed). To have a consistent program of statistical inference, one should obtain the same inferences when the data are identical.

BOX 2.2 Interpreting the Statistical *p*-Value

The statistical *p*-value, as highlighted by the optional stopping problem, is notoriously misunderstood. This is likely a consequence of a combination of factors, including the fact that the statistical algorithm is used to test hypotheses, and that the exact *p*-value is often reported in a way to make it seem that the lower the p-value the more statistically significant the result. These two factors combine to suggest that the *p*-value is a kind of evidence measure for your hypothesis, when in fact the convoluted logic of the statistical algorithm guarantees that it is nothing of the kind: recall that a *p*-value is: 'the probability of observing a dataset that is at least as extreme as the one you observe in your experiment (see Figures 2.5 and 2.6), *on the assumption that the null hypothesis is in fact true*.' The *p*-value was only ever designed to be a comparison to your predefined α-level (usually $\alpha = 0.05$), as a way to control the type-I error rate; *it is not a description of a particular dataset*. When exact *p*-values are reported in published research in relation to a particular dataset, it generally serves only to further confuse readers regarding the logical foundations of the statistical algorithm. While keeping this in mind, consider the following (adapted from: Oakes, 1986; Haller and Krauss, 2002):

You have developed a treatment for the common cold, and collect data on recovery times in both untreated patients and patients who are given your new treatment. In your analysis, the *p*-value corresponding to the observed difference in recovery times of the two groups was $\boldsymbol{p = 0.015}$ (average recovery time for patients receiving your new treatment that was 1 day shorter than controls). Given this, which of the following statements are true:

1. You have disproved the null hypothesis (the hypothesis that there is no difference in recovery time).
2. You have obtained more evidence against the null than if the *p*-value were 0.045.
3. You have found the probability of the null hypothesis being true.
4. You have proved your hypothesis that there is a reliable difference in recovery time.
5. The *p*-value allows you to deduce the probability of the experimental hypothesis being true.
6. You are able to lower your α – criterion and report this effect as significant at the 0.02 level (i.e., $p < 0.02$).
7. If you decide to reject the null hypothesis, you can deduce the probability that you are making the wrong decision.
8. You have a reliable experimental finding in the sense that a great many repetitions of the experiment would be significant 98.5% of the time.
9. The *p*-value can tell you the probability of the alternative hypothesis being false.

The vast majority of participants in the Oakes (1986) and the Haller and Krauss (2002) studies, professors and students alike, believed at least one of these statements was true. In fact, none of these statements is true, although many are the kinds of statements we would *expect* to apply to a measure of evidence produced by a useful hypothesis testing algorithm. This confusion surrounding the interpretation of the statistical *p*-value contrasts sharply with the posterior probabilities we are computing: the probabilities of hypotheses. The probability that your hypothesis is true is exactly the sort of information you would like to obtain from your analysis of experimental data, because it has exactly the intuitive meaning you would expect: it tells you the extent to which you should believe that your hypothesis is true, based on your current knowledge (i.e., your data).

Does the Bayesian algorithm suffer from the same problem? If we look at the probabilities associated with different hypotheses (rates) based on the observed dataset (i.e., the likelihood function) calculated from the binomial and the negative binomial distributions, we see that they are identical, as shown by identical distributions in the bottom right panels (filled circles) in both Figures 2.5 and 2.6. This equality will hold generally, because the likelihood is never determined by unobserved datasets, only on the probability of observing $S = 12$ in $N = 34$ trials. The fact that the Bayesian algorithm will produce identical results is, of course, assured because the cores of the two likelihoods are identical: $\mathcal{L}(\theta) = \theta^S(1-\theta)^{N-S}$.

Gaussian Sampling Distribution

After having been exposed to such a basic logical error contained in the null-hypothesis testing algorithm, one may wonder why this method has enjoyed any credibility at all as a system of scientific inference. The answer is that it has done so *due to a mathematical accident.* This accident involves the Gaussian sampling distribution, which is used in many – indeed most – situations with continuous data, such as positions and times. We will explore the Gaussian probability distribution in some detail in later chapters. Here, however, it will suffice to recall the form of the Gaussian sampling distribution:

$$p(x|\mu\cdot\sigma\cdot\imath_G) = \left(\sigma\sqrt{2\pi}\right)^{-1} e^{-\frac{1}{2}(\varepsilon/\sigma)^2} \qquad (2.18),$$

where $\epsilon = x - \mu$, and defines the difference between a single observed datum (x) and a location parameter, μ. Note that μ and σ are unobservable parameters corresponding to the location of the peak of the probability distribution and the width of the probability distribution; that is, conjectures concerning their values represent hypotheses one might like to test. Such a test will generally take the form of collecting a dataset of n data, $\boldsymbol{d} = (x_1, x_2, \ldots, x_n)$, whose sampling probability, based on assuming particular values of μ and σ, is[6]

$$\begin{aligned} p(\boldsymbol{d}|\mu\cdot\sigma\cdot\imath_G) &= p(x_1\cdot x_2\cdot\ldots\cdot x_n|\mu\cdot\sigma\cdot\imath_G) \\ &= p(x_1|\mu\cdot\sigma\cdot\imath_G)p(x_2|\mu\cdot\sigma\cdot\imath_G)\ldots p(x_n|\mu\cdot\sigma\cdot\imath_G) \\ &= (\sigma\sqrt{2\pi})^{-1}e^{-\frac{1}{2}\left(\frac{x_1-\mu}{\sigma}\right)^2}(\sigma\sqrt{2\pi})^{-1}e^{-\frac{1}{2}\left(\frac{X_2-\mu}{\sigma}\right)^2}\ldots(\sigma\sqrt{2\pi})^{-1}e^{-\frac{1}{2}\left(\frac{X_n-\mu}{\sigma}\right)^2} \qquad (2.19), \\ &= (\sigma\sqrt{2\pi})^{-n}e^{-\frac{\Sigma_i(x_i-\mu)^2}{2\sigma^2}} \propto \sigma^{-n}e^{-\frac{n}{2}\frac{\overline{x^2}-\bar{x}^2}{\sigma^2}}e^{-\frac{n}{2}\frac{(\bar{x}-\mu)^2}{\sigma^2}} \end{aligned}$$

[6] Note our use of the product rule with independent probabilities:

$$p(x_1\cdot x_2\cdot\ldots\cdot x_n|\imath) = p(x_1|\imath)p(x_2|\imath)\ldots p(x_n|\imath)$$

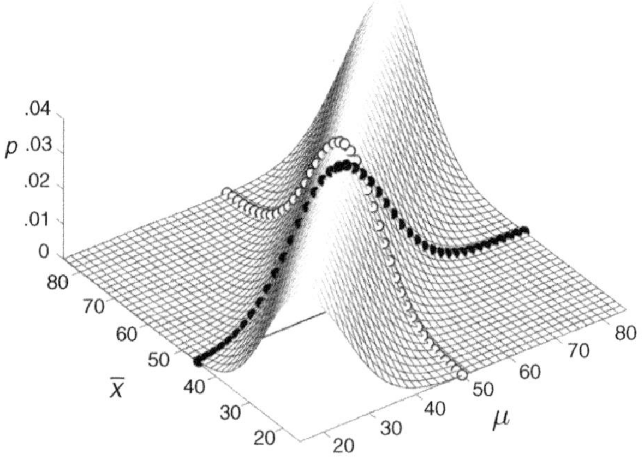

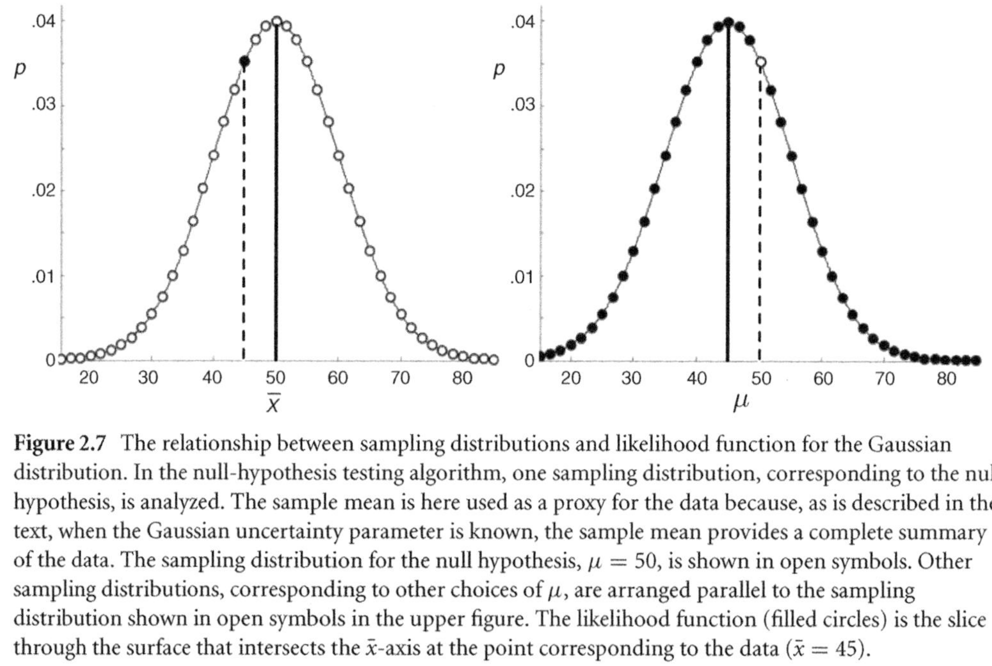

Figure 2.7 The relationship between sampling distributions and likelihood function for the Gaussian distribution. In the null-hypothesis testing algorithm, one sampling distribution, corresponding to the null hypothesis, is analyzed. The sample mean is here used as a proxy for the data because, as is described in the text, when the Gaussian uncertainty parameter is known, the sample mean provides a complete summary of the data. The sampling distribution for the null hypothesis, $\mu = 50$, is shown in open symbols. Other sampling distributions, corresponding to other choices of μ, are arranged parallel to the sampling distribution shown in open symbols in the upper figure. The likelihood function (filled circles) is the slice through the surface that intersects the $\bar{x}$-axis at the point corresponding to the data ($\bar{x} = 45$).

The Gaussian is one of the most common probability distributions used in analyzing data, primarily because it corresponds to one of the most conservative states of information when one is collecting continuous data. For example, if one were to measure the time required for the single-synapse patellar reflex to occur, one might reasonably assume that reflex latency has a particular nonzero value and that the uncertainty (σ) of measured values (due to unaccounted-for causes of variation in measured reflex times, such as uncontrolled fluctuations in calcium, sodium, neurotransmitter levels, unknown numbers of available binding sites at the postsynaptic neuron, etc.) is much lower than the reflex time. The state of knowledge[7] represented by these two pieces of information, that the unknown latency value lies on a continuous scale and uncertainty is consistent with a finite width parameter σ, can be used to define a Gaussian probability distribution. The **statistic** describing the location of this type of dataset (of n data) on the time axis is the arithmetic mean of the sample, $\bar{x}$; in other words, if we repeat the experiment n times, the best description of the location of the corresponding n time observations is their mean. The mean is also our best estimate of the unknown μ parameter based on the likelihood function. We can see this from inspection of the Gaussian likelihood (2.19). Only the last term of the equation contains the μ parameter. Thus, for a given dataset and σ value, the core will be: $\mathcal{L}(\mu) \propto e^{\frac{n(\bar{x}-\mu)^2}{2\sigma^2}}$, which is a Gaussian function peaking at $\mu = \bar{\boldsymbol{x}}$ (Fig.2.7, at $\bar{\boldsymbol{x}} = 45$).

For this example we will treat the theoretical Gaussian width parameter σ as a known constant, allowing us to create a 2D sampling-likelihood surface analogous to those plotted for Bernoulli trials. This also means that the only unknown parameter is μ, which occurs in the final term of (2.19). When σ is a known constant, the first two terms of (2.19) contain only constants, and simply serve to normalize the sampling distribution. We can ignore these constants in what follows, as they do not change anything in Figure 2.7. As above, each sampling distribution is a slice through the surface running parallel to the data axis representing observed latency. The height of the distribution indicates the probability of observing a latency of a given duration under an assumed value of the unobservable parameter θ. The sampling distribution corresponding to the null hypothesis, here $\mu = 50$ ms, is shown in the lower left-hand panel of Figure 2.7.

The likelihood function is constructed from a set of these sampling distributions, one sampling distribution corresponding to each discretized μ value, by selecting the probabilities associated with the datum actually observed in the experiment (in this dataset, $\bar{x} = 45$ ms) from each sampling distribution. This slice through the surface is enlarged in the lower right-hand panel of Figure 2.7. Inspection of the sampling and likelihood functions reveals the nature of the mathematical accident alluded to above. The Gaussian distribution happens to be symmetrical in hypothesis and data, and the sampling distribution and likelihood function have the same mathematical form. So, although hypotheses and data are not logically equivalent, the mathematical form of a Gaussian distribution creates a situation where they are interchangeable. Of course, recognizing the cause of the mathematical accident that produces acceptable frequentist results in this particular case does not give us more confidence in the null-hypothesis testing algorithm generally. Rather, this information makes us even more dubious about the general appropriateness of a frequentist analysis of experimental data, because we are now aware

[7] In Chapter 3 we discuss the role of information in assigning probability distributions. In fact, a strict analysis of only the information available in this example based on the principle of maximum entropy would lead to a different (non-Gaussian) probability assignment, because reaction times violate the requirement that data can theoretically fall anywhere on the number line (durations must be positive). However, because the error uncertainty (σ) will be very small relative to the reflex time (i.e., the probability mass will be almost all above 0 on the abscissa with a Gaussian probability assignment), the Gaussian probability assignment still provides a reasonable approximation to our state of information in this problem.

Programming Aside: Gaussian Sampling-Likelihood Surface (Fig. 2.7)

To generate the sampling-likelihood surface and the sliced sampling and likelihood plots (Fig. 2.7), we need to first compute a large set of probabilities for combinations of average datum ($\bar{x}$) and location parameter (μ), allowing us to plot the 2D surface. Then we select one average datum (corresponding to experimental observations) and compute the likelihood (taking a slice through the surface at the experimental observation). Similarly, we select one hypothetical location parameter (corresponding to the frequentist 'null hypothesis') and compute the sampling distribution (taking a slice through the surface at the null hypothesis).

```
H0=50; murange=[15 85]; sig=10; Xbar=45; dv=2;
N=round(murange(2)/dv);

figure(1); clf; hold on
x=linspace(murange(1),murange(2),N);
[X Y]=meshgrid(x,x); GA=[];
for n=1:length(x),
    GA(:,n)=npdf(x,x(n),sig); end
mesh(X,Y,GA); colormap(bone); view(-36,58);
r=axis; axis([murange murange 0 r(end)])

GA=npdf(x,H0,sig);
plot3(ones(size(x))*H0,x,zeros(size(x)),'k','LineWidth',.9)
for n=length(x):-1:1,plot3(H0,x(n),GA(n)+up,'ko','MarkerFaceColor','w',...
    'MarkerSize',8, 'LineWidth',.9), end

figure(2); clf; hold on %stem(x,GA,'ko','MarkerFaceColor','w',...
    'MarkerSize',8,'LineWidth',.8)
GAi=interp1(x,GA,[x(1):1/(length(x)*5):x(end)],'pchip');
plot([x(1):1/(length(x)*5):x(end)],GAi,'k-','LineWidth',.9)
plot(x,GA,'ko','MarkerFaceColor','w','MarkerSize',8,'LineWidth',1.5)
GAt=interp1(x,GA,H0,'pchip');
plot(H0*[1 1],[0 GAt],'k-','LineWidth',1.3)
plot(H0,GAt,'ko','MarkerFaceColor','w','MarkerSize',8,'LineWidth',1.5)
GAt=interp1(x,GA,Xbar,'pchip');
plot(Xbar*[1 1],[0 GAt],'k--','LineWidth',1.3)
plot(Xbar,GAt,'ko','MarkerFaceColor','k','MarkerSize',8,'LineWidth',1.5)
r=axis; axis([murange 0 r(end)*1.05])

figure(1); GA=npdf(Xbar,x,sig);
plot3(x,ones(size(x))*Xbar,GA+up,'ko','MarkerFaceColor','k',...
    'MarkerSize',8,'LineWidth',.8)
plot3(x,ones(size(x))*Xbar,zeros(size(x)),'k-','LineWidth',.9)

figure(3); clf; hold on %stem(x,GA,'ko','MarkerFaceColor','k',...
    'MarkerSize',8,'LineWidth',.8)
GAi=interp1(x,GA,[x(1):1/(length(x)*5):x(end)]);
plot([x(1):1/(length(x)*5):x(end)],GAi,'k-','LineWidth',.9)
plot(x,GA,'ko','MarkerFaceColor','k','MarkerSize',8,'LineWidth',1.5)
GAt=interp1(x,GA,H0,'pchip');
plot(H0*[1 1],[0 GAt],'k--','LineWidth',1.3)
plot(H0,GAt,'ko','MarkerFaceColor','w','MarkerSize',8,'LineWidth',1.5)
GAt=interp1(x,GA,Xbar,'pchip');
plot(Xbar*[1 1],[0 GAt],'k-','LineWidth',1.3)
plot(Xbar,GAt,'ko','MarkerFaceColor','k','MarkerSize',8,'LineWidth',1.5)
r=axis; axis([murange 0 r(end)*1.05])
```

of just how exceptional the circumstances must be before the null-hypothesis testing algorithm will be expected to provide us with the information we seek. In particular, the symmetry is broken when the variance of the distribution is unknown, and in this case we would not necessarily expect the frequentist program to continue to yield acceptable results.

Exercises

1) For each of the following datasets, determine whether the optional stopping problem exists:
   a) $D = [HHHTTHHHHHHHHHT]$
   b) $D = [TTTTTTTHHHHTTTTHTHTHTHTHTTTTTTT]$
   c) $D = [TTHHHTTTTHHHHHTHTHTHTHTTTTTTT]$
   d) $D = [HTHHTTHHHTTTHHHHTTTTHHHHHTTTTTHHHHHHTTTTTT]$
2) Plot the normalized likelihood for each of the datasets above.
3) After collecting the data, $D = [4.32, 4.47, 4.38, 4.22, 4.09, 4.39, 4.29, 4.44]$, and under the null hypothesis $H_0 = (\mu_0, \sigma_0) = (4, .75)$, which of the following variables are known, and which are constants, assuming we will describe the data using a Gaussian distribution:
   a. $\bar{x} = \frac{1}{n} \sum_i x_i$
   b. $\overline{x^2} = \frac{1}{n} \sum_i x_i^2$
   c. σ
   d. $S = \sqrt{\overline{x^2} - \bar{x}^2}$
   e. μ
4) Plot a mesh of the 'sampling surface' that described (2.19) based on the information given in 3, over possible values of the two unknown parameters in the Gaussian sampling distribution.

2.4 Distributions Derived from Bernoulli Trials

We can extend the logic described above, used to assign the binomial distributions from sets of Bernoulli trials, to assign two new probability distributions – the Poisson and the multinomial distributions.

2.4.1 Multinomial Distribution

Recall that we assigned the binomial distributions by calculating probabilities of sets of Bernoulli trials. Now consider the following extension of that scenario in which there are more than two possible outcomes. First, consider a three-outcome experiment with the possible outcomes R, G, B; perhaps red, green, and blue balls in an urn. On each trial of the experiment, a ball is drawn from an urn containing particular proportions r, g, and b $(r + g + b = 1)$ of the three colors of balls, respectively. If we had N urns with the same proportions of the three types of balls (one urn for each trial of the experiment), we could calculate the probability of any particular sequence of N balls. For example, the sequence RRGBRGR has probability $p = rrgbrgr = r^4g^2b^1$. Of course, we can generalize this calculation by noting that the probability of drawing any specific sequence of N_r red, N_g green, and N_b blue balls $(N_r + N_g + N_b = N)$ is $p = r^{N_r}g^{N_g}b^{N_b}$.

Now, in most situations we will be uninterested in the order in which the R, G, and B outcomes occur. To generate the probability distribution that describes this state of information (in which any ordering of the same number of r, g, and b outcomes is considered identical) we group sequences of observations that are considered identical, multiplying by the multiplicity. For our example with three outcomes, this is simply $M = \frac{N!}{N_r!N_g!N_b!}$. We see the relation to the binomial coefficient clearly if we take the case where there are only two possible outcomes. For example, if there had been only red and green balls, the multinomial coefficient would reduce to $M = \frac{N!}{N_r!N_g!}$, which could also be written $\frac{N!}{N_r!(N-N_r)!}$, and is the binomial coefficient. Recognizing the pattern, we can extend the multinomial coefficient to any number, n, of possible observation types: $M = \frac{N!}{N_1!N_2!\ldots N_n!}$. The multinomial distribution is then written

$$p(N_1 \cdot N_2 \cdot \ldots \cdot N_n|\theta_1 \cdot \theta_2 \cdot \ldots \cdot \theta_n \cdot N \cdot \imath_M) = \frac{N!}{N_1!N_2!\ldots N_n!}\theta_1^{N_1} \cdot \theta_2^{N_2} \cdot K \cdot \theta_n^{N_n} \quad (2.20)$$

and describes our expectations about the number of different possible observation types when each type is observed at a known rate $(\theta_1, \theta_2, \ldots, \theta_n)$, and we do not wish to discriminate among different orderings of the various observations, caring only about the total number of each *type* of observation.

Now we will construct a likelihood surface for the multinomial distribution in a manner analogous to what was done above for the binomial distributions, by creating a set of sampling distributions, and organizing them according to the values of the unobservable parameters that are assumed by each. When we did this for the binomial distribution, we calculated a set of sampling distributions $p(S|N \cdot \theta \cdot \imath_b)$, where S was the number of successes in a constant number (N) of Bernoulli trials and a rate parameter θ that differed in each of the sampling distributions. To be concrete, our example calculations will be based on the observation of $N_1 = 22$ out of 44 observations. For the multinomial distribution with three possible outcomes, $p(N_1 \cdot N_2 \cdot N_3|\theta_1 \cdot \theta_2 \cdot \theta_3 \cdot N \cdot \imath_M)$, each sampling distribution would give the probabilities of observing N_1, N_2, N_3 from N total trials, given known values of $\theta_1, \theta_2, \theta_3$. We see immediately that each such sampling distribution will require one probability axis and one dimension for all but one of the outcome variables (N_i) and all but one unobservable parameter (θ_i), for a total of 5 dimensions. Although this is impossible to render on the page, we can imagine that one of the three θ-variables and the total number of trials (N) are assumed known. This will allow us to calculate $\Sigma_{N_2,N_3}p(N_1 \cdot N_2 \cdot N_3|\theta_1 \cdot \theta_2 = 1 - .2 - \theta_1 \cdot \theta_3 = .2 \cdot N = 44 \cdot \imath_M)$

Programming Aside: Multinomial Sampling-Likelihood Surface (Fig. 2.8)

The multinomial distribution only differs from the binomial distribution when there are more than two count-types (as would occur when tracking the occurrence of multiple behavior types, such as the set of symptoms that correspond to a particular disease). This creates a bit of a problem for us, because we can only represent a 2D probability surface on the page, so adding count-dimensions in addition to what was needed to represent the binomial in Figure 2.5 is not possible. We can, however, circumvent the issue by setting some of the additional variables constant. To create the surface in Figure 2.8a, we limit the total number of trials to 44, and the first rate constant to 0.2.

```
%set constants
THETA=[.2 0 0]; N=22; Nmax=44; Htheta=.4125;
thetadeltsize=.025;
sumtheta=sum(THETA); offtheta=THETA(find(THETA~=0));
theta=[thetadeltsize/2:thetadeltsize:1-sumtheta-thetadeltsize/2]';
thetacomp=1-theta-sumtheta;
Ns=0:Nmax; Nstr='Ns'; Xstr='X{1}'; Istr='i(:,1)'; INstr='i(n,1)';
for n=2:length(THETA),
    Nstr=[Nstr ',Ns'];
    Xstr=[Xstr 'X{' num2str(n) '}'];
    Istr=[Istr ' i(:,' num2str(n) ')'];
    INstr=[INstr ',i(n,' num2str(n) ')']; end
eval(['[' Xstr ']=meshgrid(' Nstr ');']); %allows us to compute
                        %meshgrid for different numbers of multinomial counts

Z=X{1}; for n=2:length(THETA), Z=Z+X{n}; end

[ijk]=find(Z~=Nmax); [i j k]=ind2sub(size(Z),ijk);
for n=1:length(ijk), X{1}(i(n),j(n),k(n))=-1; end
eval('NX=size(X{1}); i=[]; ijk=[];');

THETA=[theta thetacomp];
for n=1:length(offtheta), THETA(:,end+1)=offtheta(n)*ones(size (theta)); end
for Nrun=Ns, eval('i=[];')
    [ijk]=find(X{1}==Nrun);
    eval(['[' Istr ']=ind2sub(NX,ijk);']);
    MDtemp=[];
    for n=1:length(ijk),
        for nn=1:size(i,2), eval(['Nnow(1,nn)=Xnn(' INstr ');']); end
        MDtemp(n,:)=mnpdf(repmat(Nnow,[length(theta) 1]),THETA); end
    MD(Nrun+1,:)=sum(MDtemp,1); end
check1=sum(MD,2);
figure(1); hold on
[X1 X2]=meshgrid(theta,Ns);
mesh(X1,X2,MD); colormap(bone); brighten(-1); view(-32,32); axis([0 1 0 Nmax 0 .35])

delttheta=abs(theta-Htheta); deltN=abs(Ns-N);
indTheta=min(find(delttheta==min(delttheta)));
indN=min(find(deltN==min(deltN)));

plot3(X1(:,indTheta),X2(:,indTheta),max(max(MD))*.005+MD(:,indTheta),...
    'ko','MarkerFaceColor','w','MarkerSize',8,'LineWidth',1.4)
plot3(X1(:,indTheta),X2(:,indTheta),zeros(size(X1(:,indTheta))),'k-','LineWidth',2)
plot3(X1(indN,:),X2(indN,:),max(max(MD))*.005+MD(indN,:),'ko',...
```

```
        'MarkerFaceColor','k','MarkerSize',8,'LineWidth',1.4)
    plot3(X1(indN,:),X2(indN,:),zeros(size(X1(indN,:))),'k-','LineWidth',2)
    xlabel('\theta_1','FontName",'Times','FontSize',14)
    ylabel('N_1','FontName','Times','FontSize',14)
    zlabel('probability','FontName','Times','FontSize',14)

    figure(2); hold on
    aleph=sum(MD(:,indTheta));
    for n=1:length(Ns),
        plot([Ns(n) Ns(n)],[0 MD(n,indTheta)/aleph],'k:','LineWidth',1.7); end
    plot(Ns,MD(:,indTheta)/aleph,'ko','MarkerFaceColor','w','MarkerSize',8, 'LineWidth',1.9)
    plot(indN-1,MD(indN,indTheta)/aleph,'ko','MarkerFaceColor','k',...
        'MarkerSize',8,'LineWidth',1.9)
    xlabel('N_1','FontName','Times','FontSize',14)
    r=axis; mprob=r(4);

    figure(3); hold on
    aleph=trapz(MD(indN,:));
    for n=1:length(theta),
        plot([theta(n) theta(n)],[0 MD(indN,n)/aleph],'k:', 'LineWidth',1.7); end
    plot(theta,MD(indN,:)/aleph,'ko','MarkerFaceColor','k','MarkerSize',8,'LineWidth',1.9)
    xlabel('\theta','FontSize',16)
    r=axis;
    mprob=max([mprob r(4)]);
    axis([0 1 0 mprob])
    figure(2); r=axis; axis([r(1) r(2) r(3) mprob])
```

The resulting figure is essentially a 2D 'slice' through the full multinomial probability distribution.

and requires only three axes to plot, shown in Figure 2.8a. Here again we see that a likelihood function corresponds to a 'slice' taken through the 2D surface of sampling distributions passing through a value on the N_1 axis corresponding to our experimental data ($N_1 = 22$).

Exercises

1) Calculate the probability of observing $p(N_1 = 4 \cdot N_2 = 3 \cdot N_3 = 6|\theta_1 \cdot \theta_2 \cdot \theta_3 \cdot \iota_M)$, when
   a. $\theta_1 = .4 \cdot \theta_2 = .3 \cdot \theta_3 = .3$
   b. $\theta_1 = .1 \cdot \theta_2 = .2 \cdot \theta_3 = .7$
   c. $\theta_1 = .8 \cdot \theta_2 = .1 \cdot \theta_3 = .1$
2) Plot the (2D) sampling distribution [one abscissa for each of the outcome variables, N_1 and N_2] for $p(N_1 = 4 \cdot N_2 \cdot N_3|\theta_1 = .2 \cdot \theta_2 = .4 \cdot \theta_3 = .4 \cdot N = 22 \cdot \iota_M)$.
3) Plot the (2D) likelihood function [one abscissa for each of the unobservable θ variables, θ_1 and θ_2] for $p(N_1 = 4 \cdot N_2 = 10 \cdot N_3 = 8|\theta_1 \cdot \theta_2 \cdot \theta_3 = .4 \cdot \iota_M)$. [Hint: The θ-parameters must sum to 1]
4) Describe the relationship between the 2D surface of multinomial sampling distributions shown in Figure 2.8a, and the 2D surface of binomial sampling distributions shown in Figure 2.6.

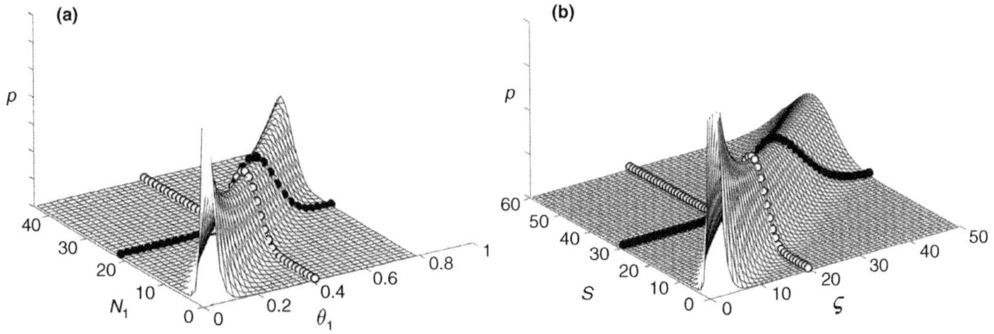

Figure 2.8 Sampling-likelihood surfaces for multinomial and Poisson distributions. (a) Relationship between multinomial sampling distributions and likelihood functions shown under the restricted condition that θ_3 is held constant at 0.2 and the total number of trials (N) is fixed at 44. By restricting ourselves to these conditions, it is possible to plot the probability of (N_1) for various values of θ_1, summing over the probabilities of the possible values of N_2 and N_3. Note that, by assuming θ_3 is held constant at 0.2, the value of θ_2 is determined by $\theta_2 = 1 - \theta_1 - \theta_3$ for any value of θ_1. (b) Relationship between sampling distributions and likelihood functions for the Poisson distribution. Sampling distributions for each possible source strength (ς) between 0 and 50 are plotted perpendicular to the N-axis. Each of these sampling distributions is a probability distribution indicating the probability of observing S occurrences given that ς is known. Arranging these sampling distributions as a 2D probability surface allows us to take 'slices' through the ς-axis (to recover the original sampling distributions that went into the construction of the 2D surface). Taking a slice of the 2D surface perpendicular to the ς-axis generates a likelihood function corresponding to a particular value of S. When analyzing data, the only value of S that is of interest corresponds to the experimentally observed data. The filled-circle slice through the 2D surface corresponds to the likelihood function generated when the results of an experiment yield data corresponding to $S = 30$.

2.4.2 Poisson Distribution

The binomial distribution $[p(S|N \cdot \theta \cdot \iota_B) = \binom{N}{S}\theta^S(1-\theta)^{N-S}]$ describes the number of successes expected in N Bernoulli trials with success rate θ. In other words, the binomial distribution assumes that there are N Bernoulli trials with a constant success rate θ, but has nothing to say about the relative values of N or θ. In the correct circumstances, however, we could modify this case by adding information about their relative values.

To derive these equations, we will return to the neural spiking example from Section 2.2.2. Recall from that example that we were concerned with an observation epoch of time T. When a single spike is contained in T, the probability of finding it within any subinterval of length Δt is $\Delta t/T$, whereas if there are N total spikes in the observation epoch the probability of observing S of them in the Δt subinterval is given by (2.15), the binomial distribution. Here, the binomial rate parameter is $\theta = \Delta t/T$, the probability of observing a single spike in the Δt subinterval. Now imagine increasing N and T, while keeping the product $\varsigma(\Delta t) = N\theta = N\left(\frac{\Delta t}{T}\right)$, $\varsigma = \frac{N}{T}$ constant. If we allow N to approach infinity while keeping ς constant, we would define the Poisson distribution. The Poisson rate parameter, ς, also called the **source strength**, which in the neural spiking example is the expected firing rate.

Under the assumptions of the Poisson distribution, the first two terms of the binomial equation become

$$\frac{N!}{S!(N-S)!}\theta^S = N(N-1)(N-2)\ldots(N-S+1)\left(\frac{\varsigma(\Delta t)}{N}\right)^S \frac{1}{S!}$$

$$= \frac{N}{N}\frac{N-1}{N}\frac{N-2}{N}\cdots\frac{N-S+1}{N}\frac{[\varsigma(\Delta t)]^S}{S!}$$

$$= \left(1-\frac{1}{N}\right)\left(1-\frac{2}{N}\right)\cdots\left(1-\frac{S-1}{N}\right)\frac{[\varsigma(\Delta t)]^S}{S!}$$

and as N becomes large this approaches the value $\frac{[\varsigma(\Delta t)]^S}{S!}$. The final term of the equation is

$$(1-\theta)^{N-S} = \left(1-\frac{\varsigma(\Delta t)}{N}\right)^{N-S} = \left(1-\frac{\varsigma(\Delta t)}{N}\right)^{N}\left(1-\frac{\varsigma(\Delta t)}{N}\right)^{-S}$$

and as N approaches infinity this approaches[8] the value $(1)(e^{-\varsigma(\Delta t)}) = e^{-\varsigma(\Delta t)}$. The Poisson distribution is

$$P(S|\varsigma \cdot \Delta t \cdot \imath_p) = \frac{e^{-\varsigma(\Delta t)}[\varsigma(\Delta t)]^S}{S!} \qquad (2.21a),$$

or, using the typical assumption that $(\Delta t) = 1$,

$$P(S|\varsigma \cdot \imath_P) = \frac{e^{-\varsigma}\varsigma^S}{S!} \qquad (2.21b).$$

Again, we must belabor a point. The distribution we just derived is based only on a combination of logical analysis and a set of equations that describe our assumptions. The Poisson distribution describes a certain state of information about the data we are analyzing, just as every distribution we have encountered in this chapter has done. As such, it can be assigned purely on logical grounds, before we have examined the data. We simply note that when the state of information embodied by the Poisson is the same as our current information about the data, then the Poisson represents what we currently know about the data, and can therefore be of use in our analysis of the data.

We have gone to a good deal of trouble to construct (2.21), and we should now take a step back and ask ourselves what it has bought us. The interesting thing about the Poisson, relative to the binomial distribution, is that it does not contain a separate term relating to the number of possible successes (i.e., the number of discrete trials, such as coin flips, whether successes or failures). This is the appeal of the Poisson in analyzing spike rates. Because whereas the binomial distribution would require us to enumerate the possible times at which a spike could have occurred before we are able to compute the posterior distribution over theoretical spike rates, the Poisson distribution has no

[8] $(1+c/x)^x$ approaches e^c as x becomes very large.

Programming Aside: Poisson Sampling-Likelihood Surface

The Poisson distribution has a naturally 2D sampling-likelihood surface, so we need not make any assumptions beyond what is necessary to define the Poisson. The 2D sampling-likelihood surface requires us to compute Poisson probabilities of a range of combinations of observed count (data) and theoretical count rates.

```
function [X Y PD]=BuildLikelihoodPoisson(ThetaLimits,Nmax,Hlambda,Hn)
if nargin==0, thetadeltsize=1; ThetaLimits=[0 50]; Nmax=round(ThetaLimits
    (2)*1.2); Hlambda=20; Hn=30; end
ThetaMIN=ThetaLimits(1); ThetaMAX=ThetaLimits(2);
Lambda=ThetaMIN+thetadeltsize/2:thetadeltsize:ThetaMAX-thetadeltsize/2;
N=0:Nmax;
[X Y]=meshgrid(Lambda,N); PD=[];
for n=1:length(Lambda),
    PD(:,n)=ppdf(N,Lambda(n)); end

figure(1); hold on
mesh(X,Y,PD); colormap(bone); brighten(-1); view(-33,40);
deltlambda=abs(Lambda-Hlambda); deltN=abs(N-Hn);
indLambda=min(find(deltlambda==min(deltlambda)));
indN=min(find(deltN==min(deltN)));
plot3(X(:,indLambda),Y(:,indLambda),max(max(PD))*.005+PD(:,indLambda),...
    'ko','MarkerFaceColor','w','MarkerSize',8,'LineWidth',1.4);
plot3(X(:,indLambda),Y(:,indLambda),zeros(size(Y(:,indLambda))),'k-','LineWidth',2);
plot3(X(indN,:),Y(indN,:),max(max(PD))*.005+PD(indN,:),'ko',...
    'MarkerFaceColor','k','MarkerSize',8,'LineWidth',1.4);
plot3(X(indN,:),Y(indN,:),zeros(size(Y(indN,:))),'k-','LineWidth',2);
xlabel('lambda','FontName','Times','FontSize',14);
ylabel('N','FontName','Times','FontSize',14);
zlabel('probability','FontName','Times','FontSize',14);
r=axis; axis([r(1:5) .2]);

figure(2); hold on
aleph=trapz(PD(:,indLambda));
for n=1:length(N), plot([N(n) N(n)],[0 PD(n,indLambda)/aleph],'k:','LineWidth',1.7);
end
plot(N,PD(:,indLambda)/aleph,'ko','MarkerFaceColor','w','MarkerSize',8,...
    'LineWidth',1.9);
plot(Hn,PD(indN,indLambda)/aleph,'ko','MarkerFaceColor','k','MarkerSize',8,...
    'LineWidth',1.9);
xlabel('N','FontName','Times','FontSize',14);
r=axis; mprob=r(4);

figure(3); hold on
aleph=trapz(PD(indN,:));
for n=1:length(Lambda), plot([Lambda(n) Lambda(n)],[0 PD(indN,n)/aleph],'k:',...
    'LineWidth',1.7); end
plot(Lambda,PD(indN,:)/aleph,'ko','MarkerFaceColor','k','MarkerSize',8,...
    'LineWidth',1.9);
xlabel('\lambda','FontSize',16);
r=axis; mprob=max([mprob r(4)]);
axis([r(1:3) mprob]);
figure(2); r=axis; axis([r(1:3) mprob]);
```

such requirement. We can estimate the one unknown parameter, the spike rate (ς), from the experimentally observed number of spikes within the continuous-time observation epoch.

As before, we can construct a surface of Poisson sampling distributions based on (2.21). This surface is shown in Figure 2.8b, and represents the probabilities of observing N of a particular outcome (e.g., neural action potentials) for a given source strength (ς, representing the underlying neural firing rate, radioactive decay rate, etc.). Each of the sampling distributions used to construct this 2D surface of probability distributions describes our information about the possible datasets that might be observed when the source strength is known – a scenario that is usually irrelevant to a scientist, because in the sampling distribution what is known (the unobservable source-strength parameter, ς) and what is unknown (the experimental data) is the opposite of the situation we face in the laboratory. However, by taking slices through the surface parallel to the ς axis of Figure 2.8b we define a likelihood function, which defines our information about the possible unobservable source-strength parameters (ς) that are indicated by the data – exactly the situation found in the laboratory. It is the likelihood function, not the sampling distribution, which we will use in later chapters as the basis for our inferences concerning which unobservable parameters (our hypotheses) are best indicated by the experimental data.

Exercises

1) Explain why the $N \to \infty$ condition makes the Poisson distribution appropriate to model neural spiking in a way that the binomial distribution is not.
2) Calculate the probability of observing $p(S = 5|\varsigma \cdot \imath_P)$, when
   a. $\varsigma = 1$
   b. $\varsigma = 27$
   c. $\varsigma = 100$
3) Calculate and plot the probability distribution $p(S \leq 30|\varsigma = 12 \cdot \imath_p)$.
4) Evaluate and plot the likelihood function $p(S = 7|\varsigma \cdot \imath_p)$ at all values of the source strength parameter $\varsigma = \{0.5\ 1\ 1.5\ 2\ \cdots 21\}$.

2.5 Summary

We began this chapter by manipulating the logical propositions within probability statements, and the consequent individual probabilities indicated by those statements. In particular, applications of marginalization and extending the question were explored. These techniques will form the basis for much of our future analyses of real experimental data.

2.5.1 Marginalization: The Core of Advanced Techniques

Although basic to the probabilistic analysis of experimental data, the techniques of marginalization and extending the question are unavailable within the frequentist program. Marginalization, in particular, is a powerful technique that will allow us to tackle many problems that are not properly analyzable under the null-hypothesis testing algorithm. Although marginalization is straightforward conceptually, it is also the major barrier to presenting probabilistic data analysis in a non-calculus context, because most applications benefit from calculus-based techniques for solving integrals. The connections between marginalization, integrals and their non-calculus-based solution in terms of summations are discussed in **Appendix C**. In later chapters we will see many examples of the use of marginalization in the two major types of analysis we will undertake: measurement and model selection.

2.5.2 Single Probabilities

The first half of the chapter focused on single probabilities. Initially, these single-probability calculations were exercises in basic sum- and product-rule applications. After some experience with these applications, we were introduced to the sometimes surprising level of difference between our expectations regarding the outcome of a probability calculation and the correct outcome. This realization led to a series of examples meant both to educate our intuitions, and to obtain much-needed practice in converting a probability problem into code.

The first half of the chapter ended with a brief introduction to the idea of decision, and its relationship to probability. Here, we examined a series of examples from medical decision-making, showing in particular the mistakes that can be made with a common 'rule of thumb' used to interpret the results of diagnostic tests.

2.5.3 Probability Distributions

After consideration of single probabilities, we were introduced to the concept of assigning normalized probability distributions, focusing on the probability distributions describing Bernoulli trials. This allowed us to explore relationships among sampling distributions, which describe our prior information concerning the occurrence of possible datasets, to likelihood functions, which describe the information contained in data concerning the truth of the hypotheses under consideration. With the definition of the likelihood function, the first major break of the null-hypothesis testing and Bayesian algorithms could be explored in detail – their use of the sampling distribution function instead of the likelihood function for analyzing data.

2.5.4 More to Come

In the following chapter we will become familiar with an expanded set of likelihood functions (beyond those derived here from Bernoulli trials) and learn to assign prior probabilies distributions to the parameters of these likelihood functions. Chapter 4 will introduce the final two elements of our basic data-analytic toolbox: prediction and decision. Once we are able to assign both prior probability distributions and likelihood functions, and to compute predictive distributions and make optimal decisions from posterior distributions, we will be in a position to explore basic applications of the Bayesian algorithm to realistic inference problems, which are the topics of Chapters 5 and 6.

CHAPTER THREE

PROBABILITY AND INFORMATION: FROM PRIORS TO POSTERIORS

In Chapter 2 we encountered several discrete probability distributions, derived based on the concept of Bernoulli trials: either based on purely combinatorial considerations (e.g., binomial distributions), or in conjunction with additional simplifying assumptions (e.g., the Poisson distribution). We also took our first look at the continuous Gaussian distribution, extending the range of data types for which we can assign probabilities. These distributions are important because they describe the probabilities of observing different datasets, and can therefore be used to construct a likelihood function – which is in turn one of the three basic components of Bayes' theorem:

$$p(\boldsymbol{h} \mid \boldsymbol{d} \cdot \iota) = \frac{p(\boldsymbol{h} \mid \iota)p(\boldsymbol{d} \mid \boldsymbol{h} \cdot \iota)}{p(\boldsymbol{d} \mid \iota)} \propto \varpi(\boldsymbol{h})\mathcal{L}(\boldsymbol{h}) \qquad (1.5).$$

We also saw in Chapter 2 that the likelihood, $p(\boldsymbol{d} \mid \boldsymbol{h} \cdot \iota) = \mathcal{L}(\boldsymbol{h})$, is composed of elements from a series of sampling distributions. Sampling distributions are a type of prior probability distribution, in that they represent our information about data we might observe, computed prior to observing data. The other type of prior probability distribution that we encounter in Bayesian statistics is the prior, $p(\boldsymbol{h} \mid \iota) = \varpi(\boldsymbol{h})$, which describes our information about the set of plausible hypotheses (models or parameter values, $\boldsymbol{h}$), also assigned prior to observing data.

The purpose of the present chapter is to expand our understanding of how to relate prior information to probability distributions. We will take a closer look at the two types of prior probability distribution that occur in Bayesian statistics: sampling and prior distributions. Our goal will be to understand the role of these distribution types in (1.5) for constructing a posterior distribution over hypotheses, and also to gain a better understanding of when to assign different types of sampling distributions and priors.

Usually, the first step in understanding a new distribution is to generate single-number summaries of that distribution, where those summaries are meant to represent stable information carried by the distribution. In Sections 3.2–3.3 we will focus on the first few 'moments' of sampling distributions (the first moment, or mean, of a distribution was already encountered) as summaries.

We will also begin to consider how to assign prior probabilities over parameters ($\varpi(h)$; Section 3.4). Our discussion of the prior will focus on 'maximally uninformative' distributions over parameters, designed to encode only the information used to assign a corresponding sampling distribution that contains those parameters. Section 3.4 concludes with a discussion of prior probability distributions for the parameters in likelihood functions based on Jeffreys' rule. Jeffreys' rule uses a measure of the information contained in the likelihood function (**Fisher information**) to assign **maximally uninformed** prior distributions for the parameters of interest from the likelihood (e.g., the rate parameter, θ, in the binomial distribution or the location parameter, μ, of the Gaussian distribution), and these distributions have the property of **transformation invariance** (Section 3.5). 'Uninformative' priors are useful when a line of inquiry is in its initial stages, and we have very little information about the likely values of the parameters contained in the likelihood function. At the close of Section 3.5 we will not only have the ability to assign likelihood functions for the most common data types, but also basic uninformed prior probability distributions for the parameters of those likelihoods. In Section 3.6, prior probabilities and likelihood functions will be combined to produce posterior distributions in a series of in-depth applications of Bayesian statistics.

3.1 Probability Distributions: Definition and Characteristics

Probability distributions, both discrete and continuous, are carriers of information. The information they carry relates to the propositions Θ asserted along the abscissa of a probability plot $p(\Theta \mid \imath)$. For each proposition, the probability shown on the ordinate indicates the relative strength by which the corresponding proposition found along the abscissa may be reasonably asserted. For example, the coordinate $N = 2$ in Figure 2.4b corresponds to the proposition 'the value of N is 2', and the truth of this proposition is asserted with strength $p(N = 10 \mid S = 3 \cdot \imath_{nb}) = 0$, meaning we find it impossible that $N = 2$ (after having observed $S = 3$). Of course, we find values of $N \geq 3$ possible, and each nonzero probability value represents our information about the truth of the corresponding proposition on the abscissa of that plot. The set of probabilities, p_i, corresponding to all propositions $x = x_i$ is called a probability distribution, and represents the totality of our information concerning the truth of the propositions x_i; that is, $\sum p_i = 1$.

3.1.1 Probability and Information

While we will often represent our information at the close of an experiment by plotting the full posterior distribution, we also find it useful when characterizing the information contained in a probability distribution to find single-number summaries of the information contained in that probability distribution. The most common summaries of probability distributions are meant to convey (1) the location of its peak and (2) the spread of its mass around that peak. One will often report one or more of the **moments** of the distribution when such summaries are desired. The moments of a probability distribution for x are defined in terms of the expectation operator ($\mathrm{E}[\bullet]$), where the expectation of the nth power of x is defined as (also recall Box 1.1):

$$\mathrm{E}[x^n] = \sum_i (x_i)^n p(x_i \mid \imath) \text{ for discrete } x \qquad (3.1a),$$

and

$$\mathrm{E}[x^n] = \int dx\, x^n\, p(x \mid \imath) \text{ for continuous } x \qquad (3.1b).$$

The first moment of the probability distribution for x is its **mean** (also written $\mathrm{E}[x] = \langle x \rangle$, and $\bar{x}$), and is the expectation of the first power of x. The mean of the probability distribution indicates a location along the abscissa that is strongly indicated, or 'expected,' given the shape of the probability distribution. Other measures of location that are strongly indicated by the distribution are the **median** (written $\hat{x}$), which is the location along the abscissa (x value) that splits the probability mass of the distribution in half $[\int_{-\infty}^{x} dx\, p(x \mid \iota) = \int_{x}^{\infty} dx\, p(x \mid \iota) = 0.5]$, and the **maximum** of the probability distribution, which is the location along the abscissa at the peak of the distribution (written $\check{x}$).

Rather than continue to use (3.1), higher moments (beyond the mean) of a probability distribution[1] for x are given by the expectation of the nth power of the *difference* between x and its mean [i.e., $(x-\mu)^n$],

$$\mathrm{E}\left[(x-\mu)^n\right] = \mathrm{E}\left[\varepsilon^n\right] = \sum_i (\varepsilon_i)^n p(\varepsilon_i \mid \iota) \text{ for discrete } x \qquad (3.2\text{a}),$$

and

$$\mathrm{E}[(x-\mu)^n] = \mathrm{E}[\varepsilon^n] = \int d\varepsilon\, \varepsilon^n\, p(\varepsilon \mid \iota) \text{ for continuous } x \qquad (3.2\text{b}).$$

In addition to the mean we will make extensive use of the second central moment defined by (3.2), called the **variance**, in describing probability distributions. The variance of a probability distribution is commonly used to represent our **uncertainty** about the true value of x, since it gives an indication of the width of a singly peaked distribution. When computing variances we will often make use of the linearity of the expectation operator, $\mathrm{E}[a + bx] = a + b\mathrm{E}[x]$, and derive expressions for the variance using the identity

$$\begin{aligned} V[x] &= \mathrm{E}[\varepsilon^2] = \mathrm{E}[(x-\mathrm{E}[x])^2] = \mathrm{E}[(x-\mu)^2] \\ &= \mathrm{E}[(x-\mathrm{E}[x])^2] = \mathrm{E}[x^2] - 2x\mathrm{E}[x] + \mathrm{E}[x]^2 = \mathrm{E}[x^2] - 2\mathrm{E}[x]\mathrm{E}[x] + \mathrm{E}[x^2] \\ &= \mathrm{E}[x^2] - \mathrm{E}[x]^2 = \mathrm{E}[x^2] - \mu^2 \end{aligned} \qquad (3.3).$$

Note that it is important to distinguish between the mean and variance of a probability distribution, and a sample mean and variance. The mean and variance of a data sample are given by

$$\bar{x} = \frac{1}{n}\sum_{i=1}^{n} x_i \qquad (3.4)$$

$$\text{var} = s^2 = \frac{1}{n}\sum_{i=1}^{n} (x_i - \bar{x})^2 \qquad (3.5)$$

[1] You may run across the names of some of the higher moments of a probability distribution: the second moment, the variance, is the topic of some discussion below. The third moment, the skewness, describes the 'lopsidedness' of a distribution (which may be positive or negative, lopsided to the left or right, respectively). The skewness of a symmetric distribution is zero. The fourth moment of a distribution, its 'kurtosis,' describes the heaviness (thickness) of its tails.

Programming Aside: Computing the Mean of a Distribution

The function `meandef.m` returns the mean (*M*) of a probability distribution, calculated using the definition of the expectation of a probability distribution [eq. (3.1)]. This function takes the set of probabilities (*p*) and abscissa values (*X*) as inputs:

```
>> M=meandef(p,X);
```

The probability input must be a vector arranged as a column. There is the option to arrange the probability input as a matrix of column vectors. In this case, the *X* input can be either a single column vector – if all probability vectors use the same abscissa – or an equally sized matrix.

To obtain a plot of the probability distribution and its calculated mean value, type

```
>> M=meandef(p,X,1);
```

or the set of probabilities and a start (`strt`) and increment value (`inc`):

```
>> M=meandef(p,strt,inc,1);
```

The mean of a discrete variable can also be computed with the function `meandef.m`. For example, we can construct the sampling distribution for the binomial distribution ($N = 20, = .8$):

```
>> S=0:20;
>> p=bpdf(S,S(end),.8);
```

and use these variables as inputs to `meandef.m`:

```
>> M=meandef(p,S,1)
```

We can then verify that the program gives the expected value derived in the text [eq. (3.8)] by typing

```
>> .8*20
```

Now, try the same thing for a continuous variable. From the definition of the exponential distribution (3.18), compute (scaled) probabilities for t = 0 to t = 10 when the exponential time constant (tau) is 1 (thus allowing the probabilities to become very small in the tail).

```
>> t=0.01:10;
>> p=exp(-t/1);
```

The meandef program assumes that the `p` input is the full probability distribution, and will normalize if it was not already done. We can simply type

```
>> M=meandef(p,0,.01,1);
```

respectively, and are measures of the location of the dataset along the *x*-axis, and the dispersion of the dataset around that center point. The mean and variance of a probability distribution, on the other hand, refer to the location and spread of that probability distribution. When summarizing empirical data with a mean and variance there is no uncertainty – our data are one of the few things about which we have *zero uncertainty*.

Programming Aside: Computing the Variance of a Probability Distribution

The function `vardef.m` returns the variance (V) of a probability distribution, calculated using the definition of the second moment of a probability distribution about its mean [eq. (3.2)]. This function, just as with `meandef.m`, takes the set of probabilities (p) and abscissa values (X) as inputs:

```
>> V=vardef(p,X);
```

The probability input must be a vector arranged as a column. There is the option to arrange the probability input as a matrix of column vectors. In this case, the X input can be either a single column vector – if all probability vectors use the same abscissa – or an equally sized matrix.

To obtain a plot of the probability distribution and its calculated variance, type

```
>> V=vardef(p,X,1);
```

The variance of a discrete variable can also be computed with the function `vardef.m`, and uses the same inputs. For example, we can construct the sampling distribution for the binomial distribution ($N = 20, \theta = 0.8$):

```
>> S=0:20;
>> p=bpdf(S,S(end),.8);
```

and use these variables as inputs to `vardef.m`:

```
>> V=vardef(p,S,1)
```

We can then verify that the program gives the expected value derived in the text [eq. (3.9)] by typing

```
>> 20(1-.8)*.8
```

When summarizing an inference by reporting the mean and variance of a posterior distribution, we are reporting a reasonable guess (the expected value) as to the underlying true value of some parameter (x), and a measure of our uncertainty concerning that guess (the variance); this is also true of the mean and variance of the prior, since the prior conveys the same type of information as the posterior distribution, minus the information conveyed by your current data. The mean and variance of a sampling distribution, on the other hand, are a guess concerning the sample that might be obtained from that distribution, and the uncertainty of that guess. Note that one can also define the data-sample analog of the **median** of a probability distribution: the median of a data sample is the x-axis position of the datum[2] that splits the data sample, so that half of the data lie above and half the data lie below that position. The data-sample analog of the maximum of a probability distribution is called the **mode** of the sample, and is the datum that occurs most often in the sample; for example, the value 5 in the dataset $D = \{1, 3, 3, 5, 5, 5, 7, 9, 9\}$. The mode is useful when characterizing

[2] For even-length datasets the median is the average of the two middle values of the dataset.

large discrete datasets, and if we consider bin-locations in a histogram of continuous data-values as repetitions of the same value, is also the location of the peak of a histogram.

In keeping with our goal of providing a calculus-free introduction to this material, we also point out that one may compute a sampled approximation to the continuous mean and variance equations given in (3.1b) and (3.2b), as discussed in the corresponding Programming Asides, and make use only of (3.1a) and (3.2a).

Exercises

1) Compute (by hand) the mean values of the following probability densities defined at $x = 1$ through 11 in increments of 1:
   a) $p = [0.2, 0.6, 0.2, 0, 0, 0, 0, 0, 0, 0, 0]$
   b) $p = [0.1, 0.1, 0.1, 0.1, 0.1, 0, 0.1, 0.1, 0.1, 0.1, 0.1]$
   c) $p = [0.05, 0.1, 0.15, 0.2, 0, 0, 0, 0.2, 0.15, 0.1, 0.05]$
   d) $p = [0.0086, 0.0087, 0.0172, 0.0258, 0.0344, 0.0431, 0.0862, 0.129, 0.172, 0.216, 0.259]$
2) Compute (by hand) the variance of each of the distributions from (1).
3) Plot the Gaussian sampling distribution associated with a nine-element dataset discretized at intervals of 0.01 from −4 to 4 with the parameters: $\mu = 0, \sigma = 1$. Below is a pseudorandomly drawn dataset using these parameters (also see Box 3.1):

   $$d = [0.6715\ -1.2075\ 0.7172\ 1.6302\ 0.4889\ 1.0347\ 0.7269\ -0.1241\ -1.3499]$$

   Compute the mean of the dataset.
4) Create Gaussian pseudorandom datasets of 11, 101, and 1001 elements ($\sigma = 1$) with any mean you choose. Plot the sampling distributions associated with the parameters you chose for drawing the three datasets. Overlay a plot of the datapoints on the sampling distribution, and (referring to this plot) explain why the mean of the Gaussian probability distribution and the mean of the sample will nearly coincide.
5) Create a discrete probability mass function with a mean of 0 and a variance of 10. What is the easiest way to modify your mass function to transform it into a distribution with mean 0 and variance 100?
6) Are there distributions with a mean of 0 and variance of 10 other than the one you give in (5)? If so, give an example. If not, explain why not.

3.2 Discrete Distributions

3.2.1 Uniform Distribution

If some quantity x can conceivably take on one of n distinct values, and each outcome (value of x) is equally likely, a discrete uniform distribution is assigned to represent our information about the potential outcomes. For example, consider tossing a die. If it is known that the die is a perfectly symmetrical six-sided cube and the mass of the material removed from each face by the number of holes used to indicate its face-number is offset by the paint filling those holes, and it is further known that a different person will throw the die each time, then on any one toss we have no reason to expect any particular face more than another. Under these conditions the only logically consistent set of probabilities for any particular face showing up is described by a uniform distribution (Fig. 3.1a). If we extend the example to a 'die' of n faces, then for each toss (or 'repetition of the experiment')

$$p(x_i \mid \imath) = \begin{cases} 1/n, & x = x_i \\ 0, & \text{otherwise} \end{cases} \quad (3.6).$$

Moments: The expected value of this distribution is

$$\begin{aligned} \mathrm{E}[x] &= \sum\nolimits_i (x_i) p(x_i \mid n \cdot \imath) \\ &= \frac{1}{n} \sum\nolimits_{i=1}^{n} x_i = \bar{x}_i \end{aligned} \quad (3.7a).$$

Notice here that we have just defined a relationship between mathematical expectation and the **arithmetic average** of the n possible outcomes: the average is the expectation of n equally likely outcomes (x_i). The average also has an important connection to the Gaussian distribution, as we will see below. For equally likely *and* equally spaced values of x with any separation, the expectation can also be written

$$\begin{aligned} &= \sum\nolimits_i (x_i) p(x_i \mid n \cdot \imath) = \frac{1}{n} \sum\nolimits_{i=1}^{n} x_i \\ &= x_1 + \frac{x_n - x_1}{2} = \frac{x_1 + x_n}{2} \end{aligned} \quad (3.7b).$$

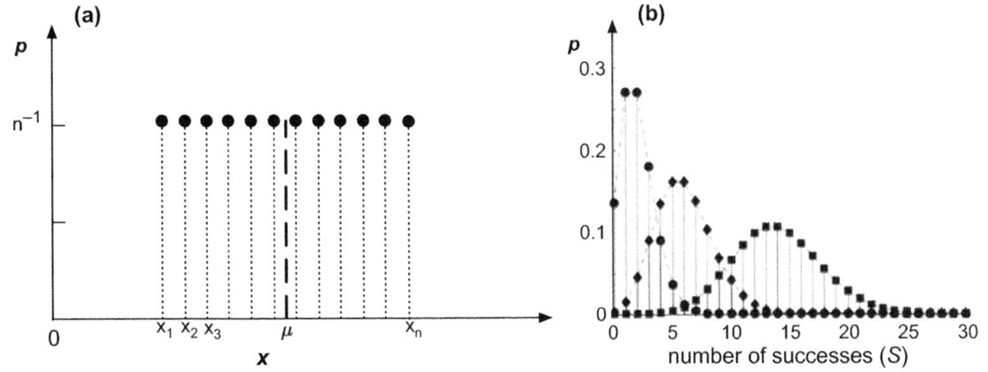

Figure 3.1 Discrete sampling distributions. (a) In the discrete case, the probability mass associated with each of the possible values of x (x_1, x_2, etc.) is concentrated exactly at those particular values of x. Normalization requires that the probability of each of the outcomes (x_i) be inversely proportional to the number of possible outcomes, n. Notice that if the x are evenly spaced and n is even, the mean of the distribution corresponds to an impossible value of x. (b) Poisson sampling distributions for $\zeta = [2\ 6\ 14]$. The probability distributions for the smallest values of ζ display a marked asymmetry, which lessens as ζ increases.

Programming Aside: Uniform Stem Plot (Fig.3.1a)

```
xs=1:12; MS=[11];
ps=ones(size(xs))./length(xs);

figure; clf; hold on
for L=1:length(xs),
    plot(mean(xs)*[1 1],[0 ps(1)],'k--')
    stem(xs(L),ps(L),'ko','MarkerFaceColor', 'k','MarkerSize',MS), end
xlim([0 13]);
```

The first moment of a distribution is, by definition, always found at the distribution's geometric center of mass. For a uniform distribution with equispaced mass points it doesn't matter how many points are found between the minimum *(a)* and maximum *(b)* values of *x*, the center of mass (or average position) is always halfway between the lowest (x_1) and highest (x_n) mass-coordinate.

To derive an expression for the variance [see (3.2a)], we will make use of the fact that the sum of the squares of the first N natural numbers is: $\sum_{n-1}^{N} n^2 = N(N+1)(2N+1)/6$ in the definition of the second moment:

$$\mathsf{V}[x] = \mathsf{E}[\varepsilon^2] = \sum_i (\varepsilon_i)^2 p(x_i \mid a \cdot b \cdot n \cdot \imath)$$

$$= \frac{1}{n}\sum_{i=1}^{n}(x_i - \mu)^2 = \frac{2}{n}\sum_{i=1}^{\frac{n-1}{2}} i$$

In this last step we assume that n is odd, and recognize that the sum of the squared deviations from the mean is twice the sum of the first $\frac{n-1}{2}$ natural numbers squared. The second moment is then written

$$\mathsf{V}[x] = \frac{1}{3n}\left(\frac{n-1}{2}\right)\left(\frac{n-1}{2}+1\right)\left(2\frac{n-1}{2}+1\right)$$

$$= \frac{n^2-1}{12} \qquad (3.8).$$

When n is even the variance is also given by (3.8). The derivation of this result starting with even n is left as an exercise.

Exercises

1) Calculate, from (3.7), the expected values of the following discrete uniform distributions, when your background information indicates that Δ is constant, and that the bounds (R = [a b]) on possible values of x are
   a) R = [−20 20]
   b) R = [−3 10]
   c) R = [−223 − 230]
   d) R = [0 150]

2) Use meandef.m to calculate the expected values from Ex. 1 above assuming $\Delta = 1$.
3) In which of the above (a–d) did the expected value correspond to a possible value of x?
4) Calculate [both from (3.8) and vardef.m] the second moments of the above probability distributions (1a–d), assuming $\Delta = 1$.
5) Show that (3.8) gives the second moment of a uniform distribution when n is even. [Hint: Use the result that the sum of the squares of the odd natural numbers between 1 and $N-1$ (where N is even) is given by: $N(N^2-1)/6$.]
6) Generalize (3.8) to account for the case: $\Delta \neq 1$. [Hint: Compare the outputs of (3.2a) and (3.8) for uniform distribution from 1a above, when $\Delta \neq 1$.]

3.2.2 Binomial Distribution

If our background information (ι_B) indicates that there is a series of Bernoulli trials, a binomial distribution (Fig. 2.4) is most often assigned. Bernoulli trials are discrete events for which two outcomes are possible (s and $\bar{s}$, often referred to as 'success' and 'failure'), the rate of s outcomes is constant (equal to θ),and the occurrence of s on one trial provides no information about whether an s outcome will occur on another trial (i.e., the probabilities of successes are independent across trials). The probability assigned to S occurrences of the outcome s [S=*count(s)*] in a total of N trials is given by

$$p(S_i \mid N \cdot \theta \cdot \iota_B) = \frac{N!}{S_i!(N-S_i)!}\theta^{S_i}(1-\theta)^{N-S_i} = \binom{N}{S_i}\theta^{S_i}(1-\theta)^{N-S_i} \qquad (2.15).$$

Notice from (2.15) that the binomial distribution is flattest when θ is near 0.5, and becomes more sharply peaked as θ approaches the limits of its range, 1 or 0 (Fig. 2.4). This means that one is better able to make predictions about S for extreme values of θ, with perfect predictability occurring in the 0/1 limit.

Moments: The first moment of the binomial distribution (its mean) is given by

$$\begin{aligned} \mathrm{E}[S] &= \sum\nolimits_S S_i p(S_i \mid N \cdot \theta \cdot \iota_B) \\ &= \sum\nolimits_{S=0}^{N} S_i p(S_i \mid N \cdot \theta \cdot \iota_B) = round(\theta N) \end{aligned} \qquad (3.9).$$

That is, if there are N repetitions (such as N tosses of a coin) and each repetition has a probability θ of being an occurrence of $s = heads$, then one would expect that the number of heads observed in the set of N repetitions would be equal to the nearest integer value of the product θN.

The variance of a binomial distribution is

$$\begin{aligned} \mathrm{V}[S] &= \sum\nolimits_S (\varepsilon_i)^2 p(S_i \mid N \cdot \theta \cdot \iota_B) \\ &= \sum\nolimits_{S=0}^{N} (S_i - \theta N)^2 p(S_i \mid N \cdot \theta \cdot \iota_B) = N(1-\theta)\theta \end{aligned} \qquad (3.10).$$

Programming Aside: Binomial Stem Plots

```
symb=['oods'];
fll=['kwkw'];
theta=[.1 .95 .7 .5];
MS=[11 11 11.5 11.5];

N=40;
S=0:N;
Sinterp=0:.1:N;
M=gamma(N+1)./(gamma(S+1).*gamma(N-S+1));
Minterp=gamma(N+1)./(gamma(Sinterp+1).*gamma(N-Sinterp+1));

figure; clf; hold on
for L=1:length(theta),
    b=theta(L).^S.*(1-theta(L)).^(N-S);
    binterp=theta(L).^Sinterp.*(1-theta(L)).^(N-Sinterp);
    plot(Sinterp,Minterp.*binterp,'k--')
    stem(S,M.*b,['k' symb(L)],'MarkerFaceColor',fll(L),'MarkerSize',MS(L)), end
```

This result can be seen intuitively by noting the variance for a single trial. For a single Bernoulli trial (N=1), it is possible that $S = 0$ and $S = 1$. From (3.3), this gives

$$\begin{aligned} \mathrm{V}[S] &= \sum_{S=0}^{1} \left[S_i^2 \binom{N}{S_i} \theta^{S_i}(1-\theta)^{N-S_i} \right] - (\theta N)^2 \\ &= \left[0^2(1)\theta^0(1-\theta)^1 + 1^2(1)\theta^1(1-\theta)^0\right] - (\theta)^2 \\ &= \theta - \theta^2 = \theta(1-\theta) \end{aligned}$$

which for N repetitions yields the result (3.10).

Exercises

1) Calculate the expected values of the following binomial distributions, when your information is
   a) $\theta = .1, \mathrm{N} = 10$
   b) $\theta = .1, \mathrm{N} = 12$
   c) $\theta = .4, \mathrm{N} = 20$
   d) $\theta = .7, \mathrm{N} = 20$
2) Calculate the variance of the probability distributions from Ex. 1a–d.
3) Use meandef and vardef to recompute the values from Ex. 1 and 2.
4) Compute the posterior distributions for θ obtained from the equation: $p(\theta_i \mid S \cdot N \cdot \iota_b) = \frac{p(\theta_i|N\cdot\iota_b)p(S|N\cdot\theta_i\cdot\iota_b)}{p(S|N\cdot\iota_b)} = \frac{p(\theta_i|\iota_b)p(S|N\cdot\theta_i\cdot\iota_b)}{p(S|N\cdot\iota_b)}$, where the denominator is $p(S \mid N \cdot \iota_b) = \sum_i p(\theta_i \mid N \cdot \iota_b) p(S \mid N \cdot \theta_i \cdot \iota_b) = \sum_i p(\theta_i \mid \iota_b) p(S \mid N \cdot \theta_i \cdot \iota_b)$(assume a uniform prior for θ_i, and use $\theta_i = [0.005, 0.015, 0.025, \cdots, 0.985, 0.995]$ successes/trial).

Notice that in both equations $p(\theta_i \mid N \cdot \imath_b)$ is simplified to $p(\theta_i \mid \imath_b)$, because the underlying rate parameter would not logically depend on how many total Bernoulli trials were performed.

a) $N = 100, S = 10$
b) $N = 120, S = 12$
c) $N = 200, S = 40$
d) $N = 200, S = 70$

3.2.3 Poisson Distribution

The Poisson distribution results from a binomial distribution under the assumption that a 'source strength' parameter ς (the firing rate, when modeling neuronal spiking), proportional to $N\theta$ is kept constant as N approaches infinity and θ approaches 0. The Poisson distribution gives the probability of S successes (e.g., neural spikes) as

$$p(S_i \mid \varsigma \cdot \imath_p) = \frac{e^{-\varsigma}\varsigma^{S_i}}{S_i!} \qquad (2.22).$$

Moments: The mean of the Poisson distribution is defined as

$$\mathrm{E}[S] = \sum_{S=0}^{\infty} S_i P(S_i \mid \varsigma \cdot \imath_p)$$

The expression under the summation is clearly 0 when $S = 0$, which allows us to write

$$\mathrm{E}[S] = \sum_{S=1}^{\infty} S_i P(S_i \mid \varsigma \cdot \imath_p) = \sum_{s=1}^{\infty} S_i \frac{e^{-\varsigma}\varsigma^{S_i}}{S_i!} = \sum_{s=1}^{\infty} \frac{e^{-\varsigma}\varsigma^{S_i}}{(S_i - 1)!}$$

Now, defining $m_i = (S_i - 1)$, we write

$$\mathrm{E}[S] = \sum_{m=0}^{\infty} \frac{e^{-\varsigma}\varsigma^{m_i+1}}{m_i!} = \varsigma \sum_{m=0}^{\infty} \frac{e^{-\varsigma}\varsigma^{m_i}}{m_i!} = \varsigma \qquad (3.11).$$

For the Poisson distribution, the source strength parameter is the mean of the probability distribution. We could have also noticed this fact from the definition of the Poisson as the limit of the binomial distribution in which $N \to \infty$ and $\theta \to 0$ such that their product is always constant $N\theta = \varsigma$. Given that the source strength cannot be negative, the Poisson distribution must be skewed for small values of ς. This is shown in Figure 3.1b.

We can derive the variance of the Poisson distribution in much the same way we found its mean. Using the definition for the variance given in (3.3), we first write

$$\mathrm{V}[S] = \sum_{s=0}^{\infty} (S_i - \varsigma)^2 p(S_i \mid \varsigma \cdot \imath_p) = \mathrm{E}[s^2] - (\mathrm{E}[s])^2$$

and use linearity to expand this to

$$\begin{aligned}\mathrm{V}[S] &= (\mathrm{E}[S(S\text{–}1)]) + \mathrm{E}[S]) - (\mathrm{E}[S])^2 \\ &= (\mathrm{E}[S(S\text{–}1)] + \varsigma) - \varsigma^2\end{aligned}$$

Programming Aside: Poisson Stem Plots (Fig. 3.1b)

```
symb=['ods'];
lambda=[2 6 14];
MS=[11 11.5 11.5];

figure; hold on
for L=1:length(lambda),
    plot(0:30,ppdf([0:30],lambda(L)),'k--')
    stem(0:30,ppdf([0:30],lambda(L)),['k' symb(L)],...
        'MarkerFaceColor','k','MarkerSize',MS(L)), end
```

Now, expanding the first term (while recognizing that the expression under the summation is 0 both when $S = 0$ and when $S = 1$) gives

$$\mathrm{E}[S(S-1)] = \sum\nolimits_{S=0}^{\infty} S_i(S_i - 1)\frac{e^{-\varsigma}\varsigma^{S_i}}{S_i!} = \sum\nolimits_{S=2}^{\infty} \frac{e^{-\varsigma}\varsigma^{S_i}}{(S_i-2)!}$$

and making the substitution $m = S - 2$,

$$= \sum\nolimits_{m=0}^{\infty} \frac{e^{-\varsigma}\varsigma^{m_i+2}}{m_i!} = \varsigma^2 \sum\nolimits_{m=0}^{\infty} \frac{e^{-\varsigma}\varsigma^{m_i}}{m_i!} = \varsigma^2$$

the expression for the second moment is

$$\mathrm{V}[S] = (\mathrm{E}[S(S-1)]) + (\mathrm{E}[S]) - (\mathrm{E}[S])^2 = \varsigma^2 + \varsigma - \varsigma^2 = \varsigma \qquad (3.12).$$

Again, we see that this could have been anticipated from the relationship of the Poisson to the binomial: if $N\theta = \varsigma$ as $N \to \infty$ and $\theta \to 0$ $(N\theta)(1-\theta) = \varsigma(1-0) = \varsigma$.

Properties

The Poisson has the remarkable property that the first two moments are always equal. This distribution is also routinely used as a first-approximation model of neural firing. Why does this model present a useful way to describe neural firing, but the binomial distribution does not? The answer lies in the specialized condition that gave rise to the Poisson: instead of counting successes over a set of discreet 'trials' the Poisson counts successes over epochs of continuous time (due to the $N \to \infty$ condition).

Exercises

1) Aside from neural firing, name three other types of experimental data that are better described by a Poisson than a binomial distribution, and three data types that are better described by the binomial sampling distribution.
2) Plot the Poisson sampling distributions with $\varsigma = 1, 5$ and 10, and S between 0 and 20.
   a. over the course of $\Delta t = 1$ s
   b. over the course of $\Delta t = 3$ s
3) Calculate $p(S \mid \varsigma \cdot \imath_p)$for S between 0 and 30 and $\varsigma = 3$ and 12 ($\Delta t = 1$). Use the definition of the mean and variance of the number of Poisson-distributed successes

from (3.1a) and (3.2a) to verify that their ratio is approximately 1 for these two sets of probabilities.

4) From their definitions, calculate the mean and variance of the posterior distributions for ς_i obtained from $p(\varsigma_i \mid S \cdot \iota_p) = \frac{p(\varsigma_i|\iota_p)p(S|\varsigma_i \cdot \iota_p)}{p(S|\iota_p)}$, where the denominator is $p(D \mid \iota_p) = \sum_i p(\varsigma_i \mid \iota_p)p(D \mid \varsigma_i \cdot \iota_p)$ [assume a uniform prior for the ς_i, and use $\varsigma_i = [0.005, 0.015, 0.025, \cdots, 9.985, 9.995]$ successes/ms, and $\Delta t = 10$ ms]:
   a. $S = 10$
   b. $S = 12$
   c. $S = 40$
   d. $S = 70$

3.3 Continuous Distributions

In the previous section we were concerned with various discrete distributions, and derived single-number summaries to describe their locations and scales. We would like to do the same here for several important continuous distributions. However, unlike the derivations above for the means and variances of discrete distributions, the derivations for the means and variances of continuous probability distributions require that we recall the difference between a **probability mass** function and a **probability density** function detailed in Appendix C. Thus, while the moments of the previous distributions could be obtained via (3.1a) and (3.2a), the following distributions must be analyzed via (3.1b) and (3.2b). For an introduction to continuous distributions that avoids calculus-based derivations, we will simply note the properties of each distribution, and verify that the derived moments are accurately approximated by the included programs meandef.m and vardef.m.[3]

As above, each distribution may be assigned on purely logical arguments, based on one's current state of information. Although we reserve those arguments because of their mathematical complexity, we note that the properties described for each distribution form part of the basis for those arguments. For now, therefore, it will suffice to note the properties of each distribution, keeping in mind that each corresponds (though not uniquely) to the description of a particular type of data that might be obtained experimentally.

3.3.1 Uniform Distribution

If our iota of background information (ι) indicates a continuous variable (x), there are two possibilities for assigning a uniform probability distribution for the possible values of x. Either we assign a continuous density between a and b, or we sample the continuous uniform distribution at regular intervals between a and b. Both cases are shown graphically in Figure 3.2a, where the fully continuous case is that in which Δ, the separation between possible x values, approaches zero. When approximating a continuous quantity, the exact values of x_i used will depend on the method of discretization. The simplest of these methods is shown in Figure 3.2a, in which the probability density associated with the range x_{i-1} to x_i is approximated by the value of the density at x_i.

[3] These sections, which define the moments of the continuous distributions, are marked with an asterisk.

*Moments**: If x is assigned a uniform probability the expectation of x is

$$\mathsf{E}[x] = \int_a^b dx\, xp(x \mid a \cdot b \cdot \imath) = \frac{[x^2]_a^b}{2(b-a)} = \frac{[b^2 - a^2]}{2(b-a)} = \frac{a+b}{2} = \mu \quad (3.13),$$

which is exactly the center of the range of possible abscissa values.

When we discretize the uniform distribution via the scheme shown in Figure 3.2 (placing the probability masses at the centers of each discretized interval), we also get

$$\begin{aligned}\mathsf{E}[x] &= \sum\nolimits_x xp(x \mid a \cdot b \cdot \Delta \cdot \imath) \\ &= \frac{\sum_{i=1}^n x_i}{n} = \frac{a+b}{2} = \mu \end{aligned} \quad (3.14).$$

In general, positioning the probability mass at the center of the region over which the probability mass would have been spread in a continuous distribution conforms most closely to our common-sense expectations about the discrete approximation.

The expectation of the square of $\varepsilon = (x_i - \mu)$ for the discrete case described above is

$$\begin{aligned}\mathsf{V}[x] &= \sum\nolimits_i (\varepsilon_i)^2 p(x_i \mid a \cdot b \cdot \imath) \\ &= \frac{1}{n}\sum_{i=1}^{n}(x_i - \mu)^2 = \frac{(b-a)^2}{12}(1 - \frac{1}{n^2}) \end{aligned} \quad (3.15),$$

which, as the width of Δ approaches 0 over the interval from a to b, and therefore $n \to \infty$, becomes $\frac{(b-a)^2}{12}(1)$, which is the variance of the continuous distribution. This is most easily shown by shifting the distribution to $\mu = 0$, giving

$$\begin{aligned}\mathsf{V}[x] &= \int_{-\frac{\Delta_{ab}}{2}}^{\frac{\Delta_{ab}}{2}} dx\, x^2 p(x \mid a \cdot b \cdot \imath) \\ &= \frac{1}{b-a}\int_{-\frac{b-a}{2}}^{\frac{b-a}{2}} dx\, x^2 = \frac{1}{3(b-a)}[x^3]_{-\frac{b-a}{2}}^{\frac{b-a}{2}} = \frac{1}{3(b-a)}\left[2\frac{(b-a)^3}{8}\right] = \frac{(b-a)^2}{12} \end{aligned} \quad (3.16).$$

Properties: For a singly peaked distribution, the variance provides a measure of the width of the 'high-density zone' of that probability distribution.[4] The width of the distribution indicates how precisely some particular value of a variable is selected by that distribution, or how well values near the peak are discriminated. A sharply peaked probability distribution discriminates values of the variable (x) very near the peak of the distribution from neighboring values of x more strongly than a shallower distribution could. For the uniform distribution, the entire range of the probability function (i.e., wherever the probability is nonzero) is the high-density zone. The uniform distribution does not select any value over any other, beyond the categorical possible/impossible distinction produced by having a distribution with a finite range.

[4] In saying that the variance is a measure of the width of the high-density zone of the distribution, we must assume that the distribution is singly peaked. This is because the variance is measured about the mean of the distribution, which is always at the geometric center of the distribution's probability mass. If there are two peaks, the center of probability mass may be at a very low-probability region; in which case the variance is probably an inappropriate measure of the discriminating power of the distribution.

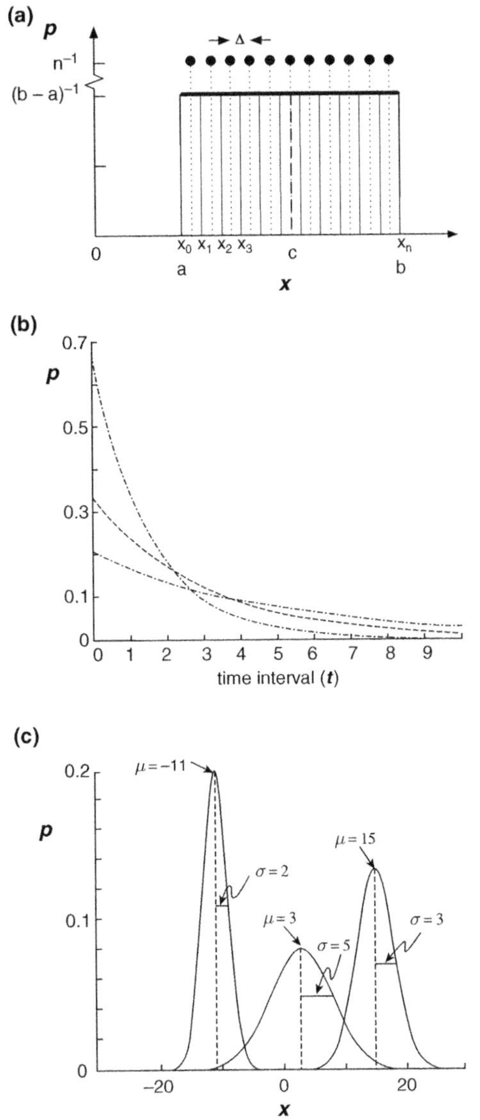

Figure 3.2 Continuous sampling distributions. (a) The continuous distribution allows any outcome (x-value) between a and b. In the discrete approximation to the continuous case, the probability mass associated with each of the possible values of x (x_1, x_2, etc.) is concentrated exactly at the center of each range $a + (i - 1)\Delta$ to $a + i\Delta$ (where the index i runs from 1 to n). We can make Δ as small as we like to improve the approximation (note there is always one more segment edge than probability mass). (b) Three exponential distributions. Each of the exponential probability distributions differs in its mean value. The three mean values are $\tau = [1.5, 3, 5]$, with the higher mean values corresponding to flatter distributions. (c) Three Gaussian distributions. Each of the exponential probability distributions differs in its mean value. The three mean values are $\tau = [1.5, 3, 5]$, with the higher mean values corresponding to flatter distributions.

For a very wide domain, the uniform distribution is the distribution that would be constructed if you were indifferent to shifts of position along the abscissa. For example, imagine that you want to assign probabilities to a set of possible locations, but you are unsure of the exact location of the origin of the coordinate system. If, within the range of your uncertainty (between a and b), you are entirely indifferent to shifts in the coordinate system then the uniform distribution encodes your prior information about location (more correctly the lack thereof). Note also that we may use the continuous uniform distribution to generate pseudo-random numbers from other distribution-types, both discrete and continuous (see Box 3.1 and Fig. 3.3).

Exercises

1) Calculate the values of p, and expected values of the following discrete uniform distributions, when the bounds ($R = [a\ b]$) on possible values of x are:
   a. R = [−20 20]
   b. R = [−3 10]
   c. R = [−223 − 243]
   d. R = [0 150]
2) Calculate the variances of the above uniform distributions. Comment on the effect of the shift in mean on the variance in (a)and (c).
3) Use meandef and vardef to repeat Ex. 1 & 2, verifying that the results approximate (3.14) and (3.16)
4) Compare the variances obtained in Exercise 2 with the variances from discrete uniform distributions ($\Delta = 1$) with the same bounds.
5) For discrete approximations to 1) and 2), show the effect, on approximating (3.14) and (3.16), of different numbers of equally spaced discrete abscissa values: $N =$ [5 10 20 40 80].

3.3.2 Exponential Distribution

Waiting time variables are often modeled with an exponential distribution (Fig. 3.2b). For example, the time between auto accidents on a stretch of road, time elapsed between neural action potentials, time for the next particle within a mass of radioactive material to decay, etc. have all been modeled as an exponential waiting-time distribution. In fact, any repeatable events that occurs at an average rate of $\varsigma = \frac{1}{\tau}$ (where one occurrence is logically independent of another, in the sense that one occurrence does not provide information relevant for predicting the occurrence of the next) can be modeled as an exponential waiting-time distribution. Based on the exponential distribution, the probability of the relevant event occurring t ms from its last occurrence is

$$p(t|\tau \cdot \iota) = \frac{e^{-\frac{t}{\tau}}}{\tau} = \varsigma e^{-\varsigma t} \quad (3.17).$$

The continuous uniform distribution discussed above, and the Gaussian distribution to be discussed next, can both be located at any point along the real line, $-\infty < t < \infty$; this is not true of an exponential distribution, however. Waiting times cannot be negative, and so the exponential distribution has nonzero probability only for nonnegative time intervals, $0 \le t < \infty$, and for positive decay-rate parameters $\varsigma = \frac{1}{\tau} > 0$.

*Moments**: Derivations of the first two moments of the exponential distribution require a technique known as integration by parts.[5] To find the mean of the exponential distribution, we use the following substitutions: $du = \frac{1}{\tau}e^{-\frac{t}{\tau}}dt, u = -e^{-\frac{t}{\tau}}$, and $dv = dt, v = t$. These give

$$\begin{aligned} \mathrm{E}[t] &= \int_0^\infty dt \frac{t}{\tau} e^{-\frac{t}{\tau}} \\ &= \left[-te^{-\frac{t}{\tau}}\right]_0^\infty + \int_0^\infty dt\, e^{-\frac{t}{\tau}} \end{aligned}$$

where solution of the bracketed term makes use of a result due to L'Hopital,[6] giving

$$= (0-0) + \left[-\frac{1}{\tau}e^{-\frac{t}{\tau}}\right]_0^\infty = [0-(-\tau)] = \tau \qquad (3.18).$$

This result makes intuitive sense in our waiting-time examples: If accidents occur along a particular stretch of road during evening commuting hours at an average rate of 1 every 10 minutes, then we would expect to wait about 10 minutes between accidents.

Derivation of the second moment of the exponential distribution follows a pattern very similar to that followed above in the derivation of the mean. We again make use of integration by parts, now using the following substitutions: $du = \frac{1}{\tau}e^{-\frac{t}{\tau}}dt, u = -e^{-\frac{t}{\tau}}$, and $dv = 2t\,dt, v = t^2$. These give

$$\mathrm{V}[t] = \mathrm{E}[t^2] - \mathrm{E}[t]^2$$

where

$$\begin{aligned} \mathrm{E}[t^2] &= \int_0^\infty dt \frac{t^2}{\tau} e^{-\frac{t}{\tau}} \\ &= \left[-t^2 e^{-\frac{t}{\tau}}\right]_0^\infty + 2\int_0^\infty dt\, te^{-\frac{t}{\tau}}, \end{aligned}$$

and solution of the bracketed term makes use of another result due to L'Hopital,[7] here giving

$$= [0-0] + 2\tau \int_0^\infty dt \frac{t}{\tau} e^{-\frac{t}{\tau}} = (2\tau)\mathrm{E}[t] = 2\tau^2$$

and the variance is

$$\mathrm{V}[t] = \mathrm{E}[t^2] - \mathrm{E}[t]^2 = 2\tau^2 - \tau^2 = \tau^2 \qquad (3.19).$$

[5] Integration by parts follows the formula $\int_a^b du\, v = [uv]_a^b - \int_a^b dv\, u$.
[6] $Lim_{x\to\infty} \frac{-x}{e^{\alpha x}} = Lim_{x\to\infty} \frac{-l}{\alpha e^{\alpha x}} = 0$
[7] $Lim_{x\to\infty} \frac{-x^2}{e^{\alpha x}} = 0$

Exercises

1) What are the expected values and variances of the following exponential distributions:
   a) $\tau = 1$
   b) $\tau = 12$
   c) $\tau = 4$
   d) $\tau = 8$
2) Calculate the means and variances of discretized versions of the above exponential distributions, using the definition of the mean and variance. Discretize t using:

```
> t=[0:.2:20];
```

   Comment on the effect of the discretization.
3) Consider an extension of the exponential distribution where the maximum probability is located at some arbitrary position along the time line, $t = t_0$, rather than simply at $t = 0$. This can be accomplished by replacing the exponential term, $\frac{t}{\tau}$, with $\frac{t-t_0}{\tau}$, where t is assigned nonzero probability over the range: $t_0 \le t < \infty$. Using:

```
> t0=[-3, -1, 0, 1, 3]; tau=3;
```

   for each of the i values of t_0, calculate $p(t \mid \tau \cdot t_{x0}) = \frac{1}{\tau}e^{-\frac{t-t_0}{\tau}}$ at the t-values:

```
> t=t0(i)+[0:.25:25];
```

   use the definition of the first and second moments to compute the means and variances of these 5 probability distributions.
   a. For the distribution computed from $t_0 = 0$, explain any differences between the computed mean and variance, and the theoretically predicted values derived above.
   b. Describe any changes in mean between the 5 distributions. What is the relationship between the means computed using $t_0 = 0$,and the other t_0 values?
   c. Describe any changes in variance between the 5 distributions. What is the relationship between the variances computed using $t_0 = 0$,and the other t_0 values? Why did/didn't variance change?
4) Consider an extension of the exponential distribution, called the *double-exponential* or sometimes *Laplacian* distribution, where the maximum probability is located at some arbitrary position along the time line, $t = t_0$, rather than simply at $t = 0$, *and* where t is assigned nonzero probability at all values along the time line. This can be accomplished by replacing the exponential term, $\frac{t}{\tau}$, with $\left|\frac{t-t_0}{\tau}\right|$, where t is now assigned nonzero probability over the range: $-\infty < t < \infty$. Using:

```
> t0=[-15, -5, 0, 5, 15]; tau=5;
```

   for each of the i values of t_0, calculate $p(t \mid \tau \cdot \iota_{x_2}) \propto e^{-\frac{|t-t_0|}{\tau}}$ at the t-values:

```
> t=t0(i)+[-50:.5:50];
```

   Use the definition of the second moment to compute the variances of these 5 probability distributions.
   a. Plot the 5 double exponential distributions.
   b. Describe any changes in variance between the 5 distributions and the variance of the exponential distribution.

3.3.3 Gaussian Distribution

Over all fields of inquiry, the Gaussian probability distribution (often called the 'normal' distribution) is perhaps the most oft-assigned probability distribution for scientific inference. Historically, the Gaussian has been successfully assigned as a 'default' distribution, usually without any analysis of the type of (continuous, and sometimes even discrete) data being collected. Until the mid-twentieth century there was some discussion surrounding the success of this default use of the Gaussian in data analysis. Although an understanding of the information-theoretic basis for the success of the Gaussian probability assignment requires advanced calculus, here we can simply note the direct connection between the free parameters of the Gaussian distribution and our intuitive understanding of a mean and a variance.

Intuitively, the mean of a distribution is at the distribution's geometric center of mass. While this is always true by definition, we have noticed that the means of previous distributions encountered in this chapter didn't quite live up to some of our other intuitive expectations: That the mean be the highest-probability value of x, and that x-values above and below the mean be assigned symmetrically lower probabilities. While the means of previous continuous and discrete uniform distributions indicated the location of the distribution along the real line, they failed to indicate a value of x that was more probable than any other value; similarly, the mean of the exponential distribution was often nowhere near the maximum probability value, which was always located at the origin. And while the means of the binomial and Poisson distributions were always high-probability locations, it was not always a highest-probability value surrounded on both sides by symmetrically decreasing lower-probability values. The mean of a Gaussian distribution, on the other hand, conforms to our intuitive notions: It represents the highest-probability location of the distribution along the real line, and is surrounded on each side by symmetrically decreasing lower-probability values of x. It also has the nice property that the mean and variance are dissociated (compare the Poisson), allowing each to be set independently.

Programming Aside: Gaussian Distribution Plots (Fig. 3.2c)

```
makeGaussian

symb={'--',':','-.'};
sigma=[2 5 3];
mu=[-11 3 15];
x=[-30:.05:30];

figure; hold on
for L=1:length(sigma),
    plot(x,npdf(x,mu(L),sigma(L)),['k' symb{L}],'LineWidth',1.5); end
```

*Moments**: The Gaussian probability distribution is usually written

$$p(x \mid \imath_G) = \frac{1}{\sigma\sqrt{2\pi}} e^{\frac{-(x-\mu)^2}{2\sigma^2}} = \left(\sigma\sqrt{2\pi}\right)^{-1} e^{-\frac{1}{2}\left(\frac{x-\mu}{\sigma}\right)^2} \qquad (3.20),$$

and its expectation is

$$\mathsf{E}[x] = \int_{-\infty}^{\infty} dx\, xp(x \mid \mu \cdot \sigma \cdot \imath_G) = \left(\sigma\sqrt{2\pi}\right)^{-1} \int_{-\infty}^{\infty} dx\, xe^{-\frac{1}{2}\left(\frac{x-\mu}{\sigma}\right)^2}$$

which, after the substitutions $\alpha = (x - \mu)/\sigma$ and $d\alpha = dx/\sigma$ becomes

$$= (2\pi)^{-1/2} \int_{-\infty}^{\infty} d\alpha(\sigma\alpha + \mu)e^{-\frac{1}{2}\alpha^2} = \sigma(2\pi)^{-1/2} \int_{-\infty}^{\infty} d\alpha\, \alpha e^{-\frac{1}{2}\alpha^2} + \mu(2\pi)^{-1/2} \int_{-\infty}^{\infty} d\alpha\, e^{-\frac{1}{2}\alpha^2}.$$

The first term is an odd function, whose integral must be 0. Removing this term, the expectation is, finally,

$$\mathsf{E}[x] = [0] + \mu(2\pi)^{-1/2} \int_{-\infty}^{\infty} d\alpha\, e^{-\frac{1}{2}\alpha^2} = \mu(2\pi)^{-1/2}\left[\sqrt{2\pi}\right] = \mu \qquad (3.21).$$

We can see just from inspection of (3.20) that μ is the peak of the distribution because of all values of x, $x = \mu$ maximizes $e^{-\frac{1}{2}\left(\frac{x-\mu}{\sigma}\right)^2}$, regardless of the value of σ. So in addition to being the mean value, μ is also the maximum probability value of a Gaussian. And given that positive and negative deviations in x from the maximum probability value at μ produce identical values of $e^{-\frac{1}{2}\left(\frac{x-\mu}{\sigma}\right)^2}$, we can also see that the mean is always located at a point of symmetry such that values of x greater or less than μ have symmetrically decreasing probabilities relative to the maximum.

Indeed, given the symmetry of the Gaussian distribution, we could have guessed the expectation of the Gaussian given in (3.21) above. This is because the center of mass of any symmetrical distribution (for which a mean can be defined mathematically) will always be located at the center of the distribution. For the Gaussian, that point of symmetry is located at μ, because the μ parameter shifts the entire Gaussian distribution from the origin.

The second moment of the Gaussian distribution is

$$\mathsf{E}[\varepsilon^2] = \int_{-\infty}^{\infty} dx(x - \mu)^2 p(x \mid \mu \cdot \sigma \cdot \imath_G)$$

which, assuming[8] $\mu = 0$ and setting $\sigma\alpha = x - \mu$ and $\sigma d\alpha = dx$, is $\mathsf{E}[\varepsilon^2] = \frac{\sigma^2}{\sqrt{2\pi}} \int_{-\infty}^{\infty} d\alpha\, \alpha^2 e^{-\frac{1}{2}\alpha^2}$. The solution of this equation again involves integration by parts, here using the following substitutions: $du = \alpha e^{-\alpha^2/2} d\alpha$, $u = -e^{-\alpha^2/2}$, and $dv = d\alpha$, $v = \alpha$, giving

$$\begin{aligned}
\mathsf{E}[\varepsilon^2] &= \frac{\sigma^2}{\sqrt{2\pi}}\left(\int_{-\infty}^{\infty} du\, v\right) \\
&= \frac{\sigma^2}{\sqrt{2\pi}}\left(\left[-\alpha e^{-\alpha^2/2}\right]_{-\infty}^{\infty} + \int_{-\infty}^{\infty} d\alpha\, e^{-\alpha^2/2}\right) \\
&= \frac{\sigma^2}{\sqrt{2\pi}}\left([0 - 0] + \int_{-\infty}^{\infty} \sqrt{2\pi}\right) = \sigma^2 \qquad (3.22).
\end{aligned}$$

[8] If you are concerned about this simplification, take a moment to plot several Gaussians, as in Figure 3.2c, but that differ only in their μ-value. Notice that the shape of the distribution does not vary with changes in μ. This guarantees that, when μ is the only variable that is changed, the variance will remain unchanged.

Properties: Examination of (3.20) tells us that if σ^2 is the value of the second moment (variance) of the Gaussian when $\mu = 0$, then it will remain equal to σ^2 if the distribution is shifted along the real line ($\mu \neq 0$). The second moment of the Gaussian and its square root, σ, are often referred to as the uncertainty of the Gaussian distribution, because intuitively, they represent one's uncertainty regarding the position of the location parameter, μ.

We showed above that the first moment conforms to our intuitive expectations about the mean. For the variance, our major intuitive expectation is that it be independent of the mean – that knowing the mean tells us nothing about what the variance might be. The variance of the Gaussian conforms to this intuitive expectation, in sharp contrast to other nonuniform distributions encountered in this chapter, such as the Poisson, exponential, or binomial, where the variance depends strongly on the mean of the distribution.

Our intuitive expectations regarding the Gaussian are further supported when we examine the maximum point of the 2D Gaussian likelihood (as a function of μ and σ). This is most easily done by taking the first partial derivatives of the Gaussian likelihood with respect to its unknown parameter values. Before doing so, we first rearrange the terms in the exponential when the likelihood describes n data as in (2.19):

$$p(x_i \mid \iota_G) = \prod\nolimits_{i=1}^{n} \frac{1}{\sigma\sqrt{2\pi}} e^{\frac{-(x_i-\mu)^2}{2\sigma^2}}$$

$$= (\sigma\sqrt{2\pi})^{-n} e^{\frac{-\sum_{i=1}^{n}(x_i-\mu)^2}{2\sigma^2}} = (\sigma\sqrt{2\pi})^{-n} e^{-\frac{n}{2}\left(\frac{\bar{x}-\mu}{\sigma}\right)^2} e^{-\frac{n}{2}\left(\frac{s}{\sigma}\right)^2}.$$

We then take the log of this likelihood function,

$$\Lambda = \ln\left[p(\bar{x}\cdot s \mid \mu\cdot\sigma\cdot\iota_G)\right] \propto \left[-n\ln\sigma - \frac{n}{2}\left(\frac{\bar{x}-\mu}{\sigma}\right)^2 - \frac{n}{2}\left(\frac{s}{\sigma}\right)^2\right]$$

which does not change the location of the peak, but simplifies the calculation

$$\frac{\partial\Lambda}{\partial\mu} = \left[-\frac{n}{\sigma^2}(\bar{x}-\mu)\right] = 0$$

$$\mu = \bar{x}$$

and

$$\frac{\partial\Lambda}{\partial\sigma} = \left[-\frac{n}{\sigma} + \frac{n}{\sigma^3}(\bar{x}-\mu)^2 + \frac{n}{\sigma^3}(s)^2\right] = 0$$

$$\sigma^2 = (\bar{x}-\mu)^2 + s^2 \quad \left\{ s^2 = \frac{1}{n}\sum\nolimits_{i=1}^{n}(x_i-\bar{x})^2 = \overline{x^2} - \bar{x}^2 \right.$$

Here we see that the peak of the 2D likelihood is located at the arithmetic average of the n data values. This is perhaps what we would have predicted – that the maximum likelihood estimate of the mean of the probability distribution should correspond to the arithmetic average of a data sample drawn from that distribution. Extending this idea, we might expect that the maximum likelihood estimate of the second moment of the distribution should correspond to the variance of the data sample, $s^2 = \overline{x^2} - \bar{x}^2$, because of the identity given in (3.3): $\sigma^2 = \mathrm{E}[x^2] - \mathrm{E}[x]^2$. When the data mean is identical to the mean of the probability distribution, $\bar{x} = \mu$, s^2 is indeed the maximum likelihood estimate of the variance.

Exercises

1) Use meandef and vardef to compute the means and variances of the following Gaussian distributions:
   a. $\mu = 0, \sigma = 1$
   b. $\mu = 0, \sigma = 10$
   c. $\mu = 4, \sigma = 3$
   d. $\mu = -7.2, \sigma = .1$
2) Plot two pairs of distributions, one Gaussian and one Poisson distribution: One pair with mean, variance and $\varsigma = 10$, and one pair with mean, variance, and $\varsigma = 45$. For each of the two pairs:
   a. Which distribution has the higher-probability mean location?
   b. Which distribution has thicker tails?

BOX 3.1 Pseudo-random Number Generation

In exploring applications of (1.5) we will sample from various distributions, both discrete and continuous. Here we will learn to sample from these distributions, taking examples from the distributions described in Sections 3.2 and 3.3, and starting only from the continuous uniform random number generator (examine the help file for the rand function). This will allow us to simulate different data types and use them to explore later example problems in prediction, decision, measurement, and model selection, regardless of whether there is a built-in pseudo-random number generator for the specific sampling distribution needed in a given application.

Discrete Distributions

Of the discrete distributions, the discrete uniform is the easiest to implement, because it only involves rounding a scaled and shifted version of the output of a uniform density (rand function). For example, 10 samples from a discrete uniform distribution from between 0 and 20 is accomplished with

```
> sample=round(rand([10 1])*21-.5;
```

and a 500000 x 2 set of samples from the same distribution with

```
> sample=round(rand([500000 2])*21-.5;
```

We can verify that these samples are from the desired distribution with

```
>figure; hist(sample,20);
```

Samples from the binomial and Poisson distributions are somewhat more difficult to compute. The two included functions randB and randP produce the desired samples. Type

```
>help(randB)
>help(randP)
```

to see the inputs needed to run these programs.

Both programs work in the same way, illustrated by Figure 3.3a.

The lower left-hand panel is the continuous uniform random density. Using the pseudo-random number generator in the MATLAB® function rand, a number between 0 and 1 is drawn.

The upper left-hand panel shows the running total of the area under the uniform density to the left of a given abscissa value (i.e., there is no probability mass to the left of 0, but all of the probability mass is to the left of 1). The cumulative probability of the random sample is indicated here.

The lower right-hand panel shows the Poisson distribution, and the upper right-hand panel is the cumulated probability distribution corresponding to the Poisson.

The arrow between the upper panels indicates that we can find the cumulative probability corresponding to the sample from the uniform distribution on the cumulated probability distribution corresponding to the Poisson distribution. The arrow between the right-hand panels shows the final step of the algorithm: finding the Poisson probability corresponding to the sample.

The program first selects a sample from the uniform density (lower left), and computes the percentile of the cumulative uniform distribution at which the sample falls (upper left). We then find the sample at the same percentile of the target cumulative distribution (binomial, Poisson, etc.; upper right), and this yields the location of the sample, and its probability, in the coordinates of the target distribution.

Continuous Distributions

Continuous distributions are sampled using nearly the identical method as above. Check the help files from the included functions randE and randG to see the inputs for samples drawn from the exponential and Gaussian distributions. A schematic of the procedure is given in Figure 3.3b. The configuration of the panels is the same as in Figure 3.3a. The lower right-hand panel now corresponds to the probability density for the exponential distribution, and the upper right-hand panel now corresponds to the cumulated density function for the exponential.

3.4 Assigning Prior Probabilities over Parameters

Because prior probabilities provide a quantitative expression of the information we currently have (concerning a parameter or a dataset), they are often assigned based on measures of information.[9] Two types of probability distribution must be assigned before we will be able to compute the full answer to an inference question (that is, the posterior): The first is the prior,[10] and the second is the sampling distribution, which is used to define the likelihood.

9 Two of the methods of assigning probability distributions in most common use, Jeffreys' rule (described here) and the principle of maximum entropy are both based on information measures. Jeffreys' rule uses the Fisher information matrix I_{ϖ}. PME is, as the name suggests, based on Shannon's logarithmic information measure, entropy.

10 Some authors will exchange the term prior distribution (referring to a prior probability distribution over hypotheses) for the far fancier Latin '*a priori*.' Unfortunately, this is incorrect: *a priori* means 'knowledge gained

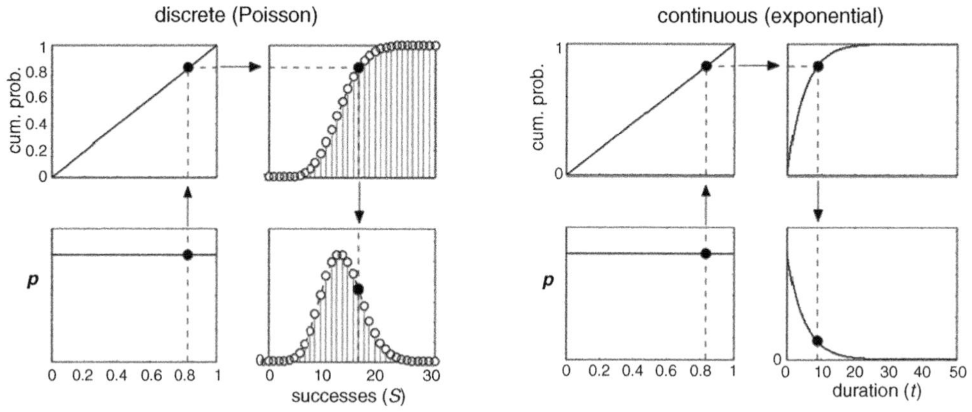

Figure 3.3 Pseudo-random number generation. Demonstration of how to build a random number generator for the sampling distributions discussed here using just the uniform number generator. Schematic of the algorithm used to generate 'random' draws from the Poisson and exponential distributions.

3.4.1 Three Types of Prior over Parameter Values

In this section we will examine the topic of assigning prior probability distributions over hypotheses. This topic has historically been a difficult one for many reasons. One of the more lingering difficulties has been an uncertainty about how to begin. Here, we will begin by defining a null point against which we might make comparisons. In this context we would like an uninformative prior against which we can compare distributions that contain information regarding hypotheses of interest (models in the case of model selection, or parameter values in the case of measurement). In this respect, the concept of a probability distribution expressing 'complete ignorance' of the value of a parameter is needed. But what distribution is maximally uninformative, and does this depend on the type of parameter you are measuring (e.g., Poisson vs. binomial rate parameter)?

The obvious choice for an uninformative distribution is uniform. Unlike, for example the Gaussian distribution, which identifies one region of the abscissa as being more likely than others, the uniform distribution over $(-\infty, \infty)$ contains no suggestion that one region should be preferred to any other. In this respect the uniform distribution does, in fact, represent complete ignorance. There are, however, problems with indiscriminate use of the uniform prior. One such problem is **transformation invariance** (i.e., a uniform distribution over a parameter will not generally remain uniform under transformations of that parameter; see **Appendix C**). Transformation invariance is problematic because, if the original and transformed variables convey the same type of information, then to be uninformed about one is to be similarly uninformed about the other. If the prior over one variable conveys a different state of information than the prior

independent of experience or sense data.' Prior probability distributions are always assigned based on experience – just not on the experience of having seen the current experimental data.

over an equivalent variable, then they both cannot be maximally uninformative. Another problem is that an unbounded uniform distribution is improper, and this can create problems in situations where it is necessary to normalize the prior.

An alternative, and in a way complimentary, type of prior distribution to the unbounded uniform distribution is the **conjugate prior distribution**. A conjugate prior distribution is characterized by the property that posterior distributions produced with the conjugate prior have the identical mathematical form as the prior - as opposed to taking the mathematical form of the likelihood, as do posteriors derived from the uniform prior. Note that the conjugacy referred to in this type of prior distribution is with the likelihood function, and each likelihood function has its own corresponding conjugate prior distribution. Although the mathematical form of a conjugate prior is always also the mathematical form of the resulting posterior, the best fits to parameter values will be updated when it is combined with information from the likelihood (i.e., the prior is updated by data); conjugate priors therefore have the benefit that solutions to basic problems are mathematically tractable.

A final type of prior distribution that will be examined in this chapter (Section 3.3.4) is the **Jeffreys prior**, named for Harold Jeffreys who defined this class of prior distribution in his 1948 paper, An Invariant Form for the Prior Probability in Estimation Problems. As we will see below, Jeffreys priors are special cases of the conjugate prior to a given likelihood. Jeffreys priors have the property that they solve the problem of transformation invariance. They are obtained by deriving a distribution that contains only information about the *type* of parameter whose value we are interested in measuring, while remaining agnostic concerning the numerical values of those parameters. Although Jeffreys priors are always improper priors, we will use them extensively throughout this text because they are a natural choice in situations where little background information is available.

3.4.2 Uniform Priors

The uniform distribution, $p \propto const$, $x \in (-\infty, \infty)$, has the pleasant feature that its combination with any likelihood function produces a posterior that is mathematically identical to the original likelihood. Of course, a uniform distribution over the entire real line cannot be normalized; that is, it is an improper prior. If we require a proper prior distribution, such as when we are solving a model comparison problem (Chapter 6), we might modify the improper uniform prior by truncating it so that it contains as wide a portion of the real line as we might reasonably expect to contain the true value of the parameter; that is, we impose bounds on the prior large enough to contain the plausible domain of the parameters. It is often the case that we will have prior information about maximum and minimum bounds on a parameter value. For example, the value of a position measurement could not be outside the building that houses your experimental equipment; or the value of a speed measurement cannot exceed c. This method of normalizing an improper prior can be used in many instances, including with nonuniform priors.

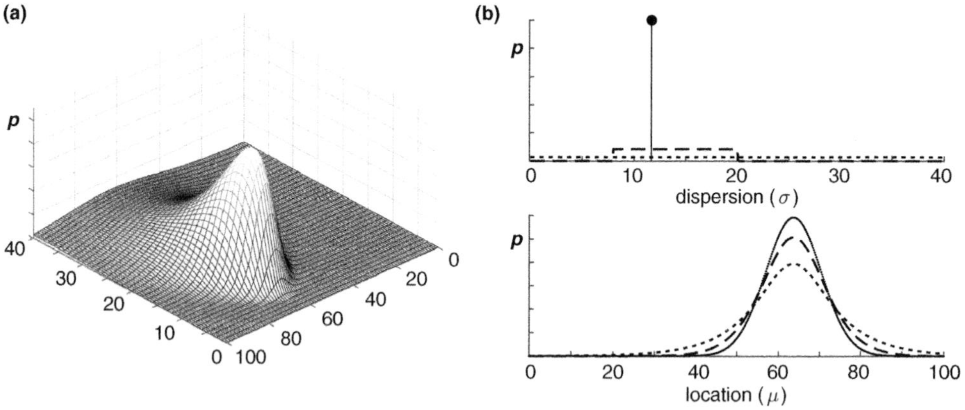

Figure 3.4 Uniform prior. The Gaussian likelihood is paired with the uniform prior to show the effect of truncation. (a) 2D Gaussian posterior over location (μ) and dispersion (σ). (b) 2D Gaussian posterior over location (μ) and dispersion (σ).

Programming Aside: Uninformed and Informed Uniform Priors over Gaussian Parameters

```
d=[67 48 76]; n=length(d);
mus=linspace(0,100,501);
sigs=linspace(0,40,401); sigs=sigs(2:end);

mumin=0; mumax=100;
sigmin=0.5; sigmax=40;
primu=zeros(length(mus),1); primu(and(mus>=mumin,mus<=mumax))=1;

prisig=zeros(1,length(sigs)); prisig(and(sigs>=sigmin,sigs<=sigmax))=1;
pri=primu*prisig; pri=pri/sum(sum(pri));
avg=mean(d); s2=mean(d.^2)-avg^2;
like=@(muin,sigin) sigin^-n*exp(-n/2*(avg-muin)^2/sigin^2)*exp(-n/2*s2/sigin^2);
p=nan(length(mus),length(sigs)); %initialize posterior matrix

for mnow=1:length(mus),
    for snow=1:length(sigs),
        p(mnow,snow)=pri(mnow,snow)*like(mus(mnow),sigs(snow)); end, end
figure(1); meshc(sigs,mus,p); colormap bone

figure(2);
subplot(2,1,1); hold on
plot(sigs,prisig/(sigmax-sigmin),'k:','LineWidth',2)
subplot(2,1,2); hold on
plot(mus,sum(p,2)/sum(sum(p)),'k:','LineWidth',2)
```

In our examination of prior probability distributions we therefore take as our starting point the intuitive assignment of uniform prior probability distributions over unknown parameters. We will explore truncated uniform priors and the effect of truncation on the resulting posterior. We then examine the idea of an uninformative prior by transforming uniform priors in particular ways. Specifically, we will transform uniform priors after re-parameterizing the likelihood into an equivalent form. By starting with a uniform prior, we can clearly see the effect of the transformation, and this will provide us some insight into the kinds of nonuniform priors that might be invariant under a change of variables, foreshadowing our discussion of Jeffreys priors at the close of Section 3.4.

Example: Truncated Uniform Priors for the Parameters of the Gaussian Likelihood
Consider an observed dataset $\boldsymbol{d} = [67, 48, 76]$ that we will describe with a Gaussian likelihood. If we further assign uniform priors over the location and scale parameters of the Gaussian likelihood function the resulting posterior distribution is proportional to the Gaussian likelihood itself:

$$p(\mu \cdot \sigma \mid \boldsymbol{d} \cdot \imath) = \frac{p(\mu \cdot \sigma \mid \imath)p(\boldsymbol{d} \mid \mu \cdot \sigma \cdot \imath)}{p(\boldsymbol{d} \mid \imath)}$$

$$\propto p(\mu \cdot \sigma \mid \imath)p(\boldsymbol{d} \mid \mu \cdot \sigma \cdot \imath)$$

$$= p(\mu \cdot \sigma \mid \imath)\left(\sigma\sqrt{2\pi}\right)^{-n} e^{-\frac{n}{2}\left[\left(\frac{s}{\sigma}\right)^2+\left(\frac{\bar{\mathrm{d}}-\mu}{\sigma}\right)^2\right]}$$

$$\propto \sigma^{-n} e^{-\frac{n}{2}\left[\left(\frac{s}{\sigma}\right)^2+\left(\frac{\bar{\mathrm{d}}-\mu}{\sigma}\right)^2\right]} \qquad \begin{cases} \mu_{\min} \leq \mu \leq \mu_{\max} \\ \sigma_{\min} \leq \sigma \leq \sigma_{max} \end{cases}$$

$$\bar{x} = n^{-1}\sum\nolimits_{i=1}^{n} x_i$$

$$s^2 = \frac{1}{n}\sum\nolimits_{i=1}^{n}(x_i - \bar{x})^2 = \overline{x^2} - \bar{x}^2$$

over the prior ranges of the location and scale parameter. This 2D posterior, for an unbounded prior range, is plotted in Figure 3.4 (left).

Note we always constrain the range of a scale parameter to the positive real line, since these are the only values that a scale parameter can take. However, imagine we have additional information concerning the value of the scale parameter. Suppose that we have made similar previous measurements and know that this parameter is never larger than 20, and is never less than 5, and we first truncate the uniform prior at $\sigma_{\min} = 0.5$ and $\sigma_{\max} = 40$; a conservative range given our prior information, which has almost no effect on the resulting posterior (Fig. 3.4b). If we further truncate the prior, at $\sigma_{\min} = 8$ and $\sigma_{\max} = 20$, and finally using the value s as if it were the correct theoretical value, $\sigma = s$, we can see the effect of truncation on the resulting posterior. Using a conservative bound, covering the plausible range of values suggested by our prior information, produces a posterior that is essentially indistinguishable from that produced with the unbounded uniform prior. If, however, our prior information is informative, it may allow us to produce a more precise posterior than would have been possible otherwise. This is the situation shown when the bounds are set closer and closer together. Of course, once we cross over from the realm of truncated priors that are essentially indistinguishable in their effect on the posterior from an unbounded prior and into the realm of priors whose truncation bounds obviously affect the posterior, we must

Programming Aside: The Squaring Transform for Conversion between Variance and Standard Deviation

The squaring transform (i.e., $\vartheta = f(\sigma) = \sigma^2$) changes a distribution in standard deviation units to one in variance units. Starting with a uniform distribution over standard deviation, we arrive at the (approximate sampled) transformed distribution via the MATLAB® commands:

```
SDs=.005:.01:1-.005; %create vector of SD values
pSD=ones(size(SDs)); %uniform probability dist over SD values
vTX=@(x) x.^2; %linking function for variance units
PvTX=pTX(SDs,pSD,vTX); %compute squaring transform of sd probs
```

Similarly, we can compute a transformed distribution over SD starting from a distribution over possible variance values:

```
Vs=.005:.01:1; %create vector of var values
pV=ones(size(Vs)); %uniform probability dist over var values
sdTX=@(x) sqrt(x); %linking function for SD units
PsdTX=pTX(Vs,pV,sdTX); %compute sqrt transform of var probabilities
```

take care to be sure that the information leading to those bounds is accurate. Indeed, in the limit of assuming that sigma is a known value (Fig. 3.4b, stem and solid line), there would be a clear overestimate of the precision of the corresponding estimate of μ if the value of the dispersion parameter were treated as known when in fact it was unknown.

Exercises

1) Give two specific instances of prior information that could be translated into a bound on the variance of a Gaussian likelihood function.
2) Is it justified to use $\sigma = s$ as a known value when estimating μ? Why / why not?

Example: The effect of transformed uniform priors over the standard deviation and variance parameters on posteriors derived from the Gaussian likelihood

Consider a dataset that we will describe with a Gaussian likelihood. This likelihood information can be combined with a uniform prior over the standard deviation or variance of the likelihood, depending on whether the Gaussian distribution is parameterized as

$$p(x \mid \mu \cdot \sigma \cdot \iota) = \left(\sigma\sqrt{2\pi}\right)^{-1} e^{-\frac{1}{2}\frac{(x-\mu)^2}{\sigma^2}}$$

or

$$p(x \mid \mu \cdot v \cdot \iota) = \sqrt{2\pi v}^{-1} e^{-\frac{1}{2}\frac{(x-\mu)^2}{v}}$$

Either scenario is quite common when we are interested in computing a prior over the scale parameter of the Gaussian distribution. These two cases are plotted as solid lines in Figure 3.5a.

Notice that the uniform priors do not even enter the above calculations, because multiplying these distributions by a vector of ones (or any other constant) will not affect the shape of the posterior; remember that as a final step we divide the posterior by its maximum value to force the ordinate to range between zero and one, and this division effectively discards any constants that scale the height of the posterior.

In addition to the posteriors described above, we have also plotted the posterior that results from switching between one parameterization of the Gaussian and another, and transforming the uniform prior in each of these cases to produce the new posteriors.

Here, posteriors based on transformed uniform priors do no match posteriors over the same parameters based on untransformed uniform priors. This type of discrepancy was the source of an early controversy concerning prior distributions. This controversy surrounded the topic of prior probabilities, and was specifically concerned with the assignment of an uninformative distribution for the Gaussian uncertainty parameter. The problem concerned whether to use the standard deviation of the Gaussian (σ), the variance of the Gaussian ($\nu = \sigma^2$), or the precision of the Gaussian ($\rho = 1/2\sigma^2$) when defining the uninformative prior probability distribution for the uncertainty parameter that scales the width of the Gaussian. For if we were truly uninformed, then it should also not matter which parameterization was used – the resulting posterior would carry the same information. However, as we can see in Figure 3.5a, this is not generally the case. When a uniform prior is used to represent ignorance of a Gaussian standard deviation, and the likelihood is reparameterized in terms of the variance, this reparameterization yields a posterior distribution over ν that is not related to the original posterior (over σ) by the same squaring transform that defined the reparameterization. This suggests that a uniform prior encodes different information

Programming Aside: Scale Parameters (Fig 3.5a)

The left- and right-hand solid-line plots are obtained in MATLAB® with the commands

```
%create data vector
N=8; d=randn([N 1]); d=(d-mean(d))*3/std(d); %data (mean=0, std=3)
%Fig 1 (SD units)
SDs=.005:.01:7-.005; %create vector of possible SD values
poSD=exp(-N/2*(mean(d.^2)-mean(d)^2)./SDs.^2).*SDs.^-N; %posterior
figure(1); plot(SDs,poSD/max(poSD),'k.'); hold on; axis([0 7 0 1])
%Fig 2 (variance units)
Vs=SDs.^2; %create vector of possible variance values
poV=exp(-N/2*(mean(d.^2)-mean(d)^2)./Vs).*Vs.^(-N/2); %posterior
figure(2); plot(Vs, poV/max(poV),'k.'); hold on; axis([0 15 0 1])
```

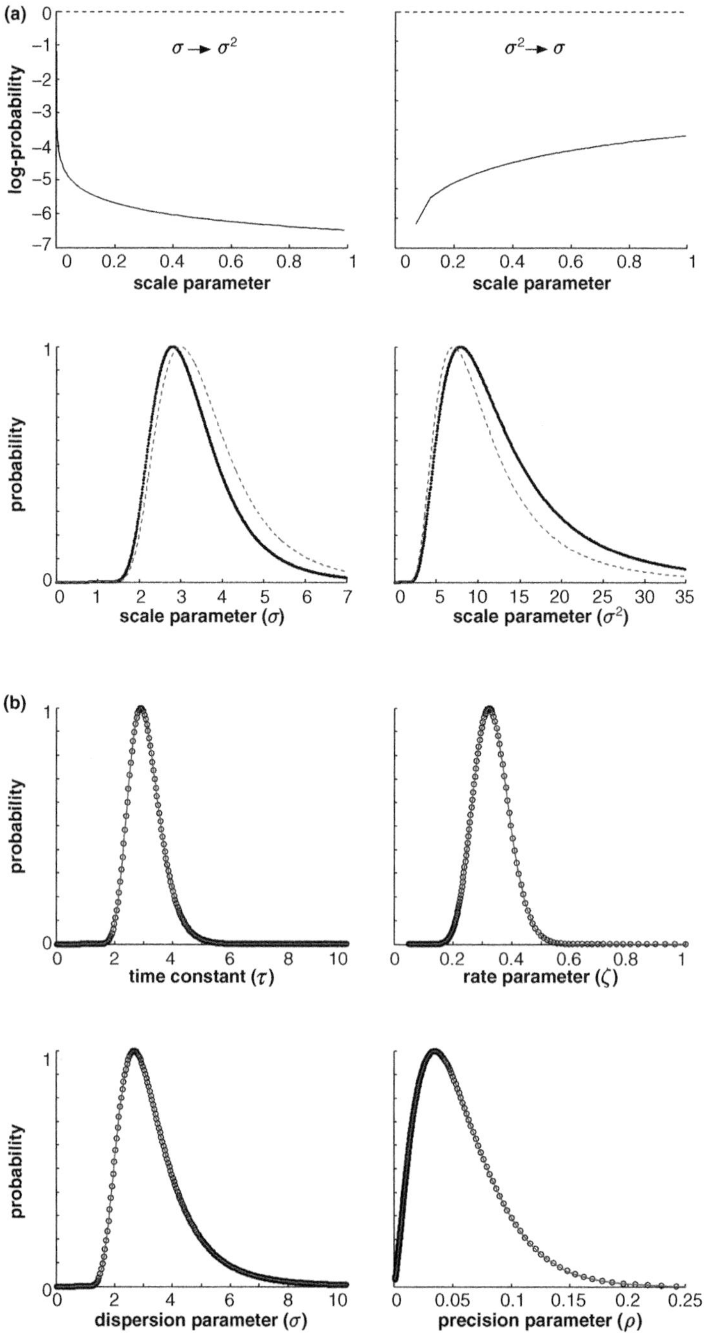

Figure 3.5 Transforms and transformation invariance. (a) Uniform priors. Upper panels show the result of transforming uniform priors over the Gaussian dispersion parameters σ and σ^2 into the other form. Lower panels show the effect of these transforms on the resulting posteriors. (b) Jeffreys priors. Upper panels show transforms between time and rate parameterizations of the exponential distribution. Lower panels show transforms between dispersion and precision parameterizations of the Gaussian distribution.

Programming Aside: Reparameterized Scale Parameters (Fig. 3.5a)

The posteriors produced by reparameterization are shown as dashed blue lines in Figure 3.5a, and are obtained from the MATLAB® code:

```
%Fig 1 (SD units)
piV=ones(size(Vs)); %uniform prior over variances
sdTX=@(x) sqrt(x); %linking function transforming to SD units
PIsdTX=pTX(Vs,piV,sdTX); %transform of uniform var prior to SD
POsdTX=PIsdTX(:,1)'.*exp(-N/2*(mean(d.^2)-mean(d)^2)./SDs.^2).*SDs.^-N;
figure(1); plot(SDs,POsdTX/max(POsdTX),'b--','LineWidth',2.4)
%Fig 2 (variance units)
piSD=ones(size(SDs)); %uniform prior over SDs
vTX=@(x) x.^2; %linking function for transformation into var units
PIvTX=pTX(SDs,piSD,vTX); %transform of unif SD prior to var
POvTX=PIvTX(:,1)'.*exp(-N/2*(mean(d.^2)-mean(d)^2)./SDs.^2).*SDs.^(-N);
figure(2); plot(Vs,POvTX/max(POvTX),'b--','LineWidth',2.4)
```

in the case of the different parameterizations of the Gaussian scale parameter, and therefore at least one cannot be completely uninformative. Conversely, if we were able to find a prior distribution that produced equivalent posteriors (i.e., posteriors that become equal following reparameterization by the transformation relating the two scale parameters) this would solve the problem of transformation invariance. The Jeffreys prior, which we examine in Section 3.3.3, was designed to be equally uninformed regardless of parameterization.

Exercises

1) Plot the transformed priors that are used to create the posteriors plotted in dashed blue lines in Figure 3.5a. Describe how transformation changes the originally uniform priors.
2) Comment on what it means for the transformed prior that was originally in variance units (used to create the left-hand blue-dashed plot in Figure 3.5a) to be different than the uniform prior over SD (used to create the left-hand solid plot) for the idea of a 'completely uninformed' prior over the Gaussian scale variable.
3) Recall the difference between sampling distributions and likelihoods (Chapter 2), and explain why we numerically transform between posteriors (coordinate transform, as described in Appendix C) but simply change parameterization without coordinate transform when changing between one form of the likelihood and another.
4*) Using the same initial data above, plot the posterior over the Gaussian location variable (μ; assuming now that it is unknown), assuming a known value of $\sigma = 3$ and a uniform prior over μ (assume a broad truncated range of $-20 \leq \mu \leq 20$ to create the prior).

5*) Transform the prior from Ex. 3 by shifting the uniform prior by 2 location units using the equation:

```
muTX=@(x) (x+2); % function transformaing into shifted location units
```

Plot the posterior corresponding to this transformed prior. Does the mean of the posterior differ from the mean of the posterior from Ex. 3? Express the difference as a proportion of the prior range. Expand the prior range in 5 steps of 20, and plot the difference between posteriors derived from original and transformed priors (again as a proportion of the prior range). Comment on this difference as the truncated uniform prior approaches the improper uniform prior.

3.4.3 Conjugate Priors

Above we considered the uniform prior, which leaves the likelihood intact so that the posterior is simply a normalized form of the likelihood. A conjugate prior is the flip-side of this idea: the posterior maintains the mathematical form of the prior instead of the likelihood. The only difference between prior and posterior is that the best estimates of their parameters (Gaussian location, Poisson rate, etc.) are updated based on the information contained in the likelihood. This is very reasonable in the sense that the prior and the posterior are both distributions over the same parameter(s), and (1.5) is often thought of as a way to update the prior based on data.

Conjugate priors are defined both in terms of the parameter of interest for our scientific problem (unknown parameters of the likelihood: Gaussian location, binomial rate, etc.) and also a set of **hyperparameters**. The conjugate prior produces what is, in a certain mathematical sense, the simplest type of update; only the values of hyperparameters change as a result of the update process, not the mathematical form of the distribution itself. Because only the values of hyperparameters change as we transition from prior to posterior, the analytical expression for the posterior can usually be written immediately in terms of updated hyperparameters through a set of update equations specific to each prior. For example, when the conjugate prior is a beta distribution (as we will see below for the binomial likelihood), the expression for the prior is $\frac{1}{\beta(a,b)}\theta^{a-1}(1-\theta)^{b-1}$ with hyperparameters a, b. The expression for the posterior is identical, but with values $a' = a + \sum_{i=1}^{N} S_i$ and $b' = b + \sum_{i=1}^{N}(n_i - S_i)$ derived from success-count data. Thus, the combination of update equation (for the hyperparameter values) and prior distribution become a time-saving shortcut for finding the analytical expression for the posterior.

The idea that one can find priors which, when combined with a partner likelihood, produce posterior distributions with the same functional form as the prior is an attractive quality for a prior distribution to have, because it dovetails nicely with the idea of data analysis as updating prior information with data. Updated prior information (i.e., the posterior) is also our new prior information to be combined with data from yet another round of experimental observations.

The most common conjugate priors and hyperparameter updates (categorized by their partner likelihood) are binomial:

$$p(\theta \mid a \cdot b \cdot \imath) = \frac{1}{\beta(a,b)}\theta^{a-1}(1-\theta)^{b-1} \propto \theta^{a-1}(1-\theta)^{b-1} \quad \{0 \le \theta \le 1 \tag{3.23a}$$

$$\text{update:} \quad \begin{aligned} a' &= a + \textstyle\sum_{i=1}^{N} S_i \\ b' &= b + \textstyle\sum_{i=1}^{N} (n_i - S_i) \end{aligned} \tag{3.23b}$$

negative binomial:

$$p(\theta \mid a \cdot b \cdot \imath) = \frac{1}{\beta(a,b)}\theta^{a-1}(1-\theta)^{b-1} \propto \theta^{a-1}(1-\theta)^{b-1} \; \{0 \le \theta \le 1 \tag{3.24a}$$

$$\text{update:} \quad \begin{aligned} \alpha' &= \alpha + \textstyle\sum_{i=1}^{N} S_i \\ \beta' &= \beta + F\textstyle\sum_{i=1}^{N} n_i = \beta + FN \end{aligned} \tag{3.24b}$$

Poisson:

$$p(\varsigma \mid a \cdot b \cdot \imath) = \frac{b^a \varsigma^{a-1}}{\Gamma(a)e^{-b\varsigma}} \propto \varsigma^{a-1}e^{-b\varsigma}$$

$$\Gamma(s) = \int_0^1 dt\; e^{-t}t^{s-1} \tag{3.25a}$$

$$\text{update:} \quad \begin{aligned} a' &= a + \textstyle\sum_{i=1}^{N} S_i \\ b' &= b + N \end{aligned} \tag{3.25b}$$

exponential:

$$p(\tau \mid a \cdot b \cdot \imath) = \frac{b^a e^{-b/\tau}}{\Gamma(a)\tau^{a+1}} \propto \tau^{-(a+1)}e^{-b/\tau} \quad \{\tau > 0 \tag{3.26a}$$

$$\text{update:} \quad \begin{aligned} a' &= a + N \\ b' &= b + \textstyle\sum_{i=1}^{N} t_i = b + N\bar{t} \end{aligned} \tag{3.26b}$$

Gaussian location:

$$p(\mu \mid \mu_0 \cdot \sigma_0 \cdot \imath) = \left[\sigma_0\sqrt{2\pi}\right]^{-1} e^{-\frac{1}{2}\frac{(\mu_0-\mu)^2}{\sigma_0^2}} \propto e^{-\frac{1}{2}\frac{(\mu_0-\mu)^2}{\sigma_0^2}} \tag{3.27a}$$

$$\text{update:} \quad \begin{aligned} \mu' &= \left[\tfrac{\mu_0}{\sigma_0^2} + \tfrac{\sum_{i=1}^{N} X_i}{\sigma^2}\right](\sigma')^{-2} = \left[\tfrac{\mu_0}{\sigma_0^2} + N\tfrac{\bar{x}}{\sigma^2}\right](\sigma')^{-2} \\ \sigma' &= \sqrt{\sigma_0^{-2} + N(\sigma^{-2})^{-1}} \end{aligned} \tag{3.27b}$$

Gaussian precision:

$$p(\tau \mid a \cdot b) = \frac{b^a \tau^{a-1}}{\Gamma(a)e^{-b\tau}} \propto \tau^{a-1}e^{-b\tau} \tag{3.28a}$$

$$\text{update:} \quad \begin{aligned} a' &= a + \tfrac{n}{2} \\ b' &= b + \tfrac{n}{2}\overline{\Delta X^2} \end{aligned} \tag{3.28b}$$

Gaussian variance:

$$p(\upsilon \mid a \cdot b \cdot \iota) = \frac{b^a e^{-b/\upsilon}}{\Gamma(a)\upsilon^{a+1}} \propto \upsilon^{-(a+1)} e^{-b/\upsilon} \{\upsilon = \sigma^2 > 0 \tag{3.29a}$$

$$\text{update:} \quad \begin{aligned} a' &= a + \tfrac{N}{2} \\ b' &= b + \tfrac{\sum_{i=1}^{N}(x_i - \mu)^2}{2} = b + \tfrac{n\overline{\Delta x^2}}{2} \end{aligned} \tag{3.29b}$$

Gaussian standard deviation:

$$p(\sigma \mid a \cdot b \cdot \iota) = \frac{2b^a e^{-\frac{b}{\sigma^2}}}{\Gamma(a)\sigma^{-(2a+1)}} \propto \sigma^{-2a+1} e^{-\frac{b}{\sigma^2}} \quad \{\sigma > 0 \tag{3.30a}$$

$$\text{update:} \quad \begin{aligned} a' &= a + \tfrac{N}{2} \\ b' &= b + \tfrac{\sum_{i=1}^{N}(x_i - \mu)^2}{2} = b + \tfrac{n\overline{\Delta x^2}}{2} \end{aligned} \tag{3.30b}$$

Example: Poisson

The Poisson likelihood (2.22), in which S is the observed number of successes and ς is the unknown true source strength, is

$$\mathcal{L}(\varsigma) \propto e^{-\varsigma} \varsigma^s$$

and the conjugate prior over the unknown source strength parameter is

$$p(\varsigma \mid a \cdot b \cdot \iota) = \frac{b^a \varsigma^{a-1}}{\Gamma(a) e^{-b_\varsigma}} \propto \varsigma^{a-1} e^{-b_\varsigma} \tag{3.25a}$$

that is, a gamma distribution[11] with hyperparameters $a \geq 0,\ b \geq 0$. The hyperparameters are updated by the likelihood via the equations

$$\begin{aligned} a' &= a + \sum\nolimits_{i=1}^{N} s_i \\ b' &= b + N \end{aligned} \tag{3.25b}$$

where we now have a natural interpretation of a as the total number of occurrences in b observation epochs.

If we start with an initial gamma prior over the source strength parameter, and combine this with the Poisson likelihood we obtain

[11] The gamma distribution is partly normalized by the gamma function, $\Gamma(s) = \int_0^1 dt\, e^{-t} t^{s-1}$, which is a constant in this context.

$$
\begin{aligned}
p(\varsigma \mid S \cdot a \cdot b \cdot \imath) &= \varpi(\varsigma)\mathcal{L}(\varsigma) \\
&\propto \left[\varsigma^{a-1}e^{-b\varsigma}\right]\left[e^{\varsigma}\varsigma^{S}\right] \\
&\propto \varsigma^{S+a-1}e^{-(b+1)\varsigma}
\end{aligned}
$$

where the posterior again has the same form as the prior, but with new hyperparameters based on the content of the likelihood function. Updating this prior with new likelihood information yields

$$
\begin{aligned}
p(\varsigma \mid S_1 \cdot S_2 \cdot a \cdot b \cdot \imath) &= \varpi(\varsigma)\mathcal{L}(\varsigma) \\
&\propto \left[\varsigma^{S_1+a-1}e^{-(b+1)\varsigma}\right]\left[e^{-\varsigma}\varsigma^{S_2}\right] \\
&\propto \varsigma^{S_1+S_2+a-1}e^{-(b+2)\varsigma}
\end{aligned}
$$

The updated a and b hyperparameters that define the posterior could also have been obtained in a single step using (3.25).

Example: Gaussian Standard Deviation

The Gaussian standard deviation likelihood (3.20), in which x is the observed dataset of length and n with known location μ, where σ is the unknown standard deviation parameter, is

$$
\begin{aligned}
\mathcal{L}(\sigma) &\propto \sigma^{-n}e^{-\frac{1}{2\sigma^2}\sum_{i=1}^{n}(x_i-\mu)^2} \\
&= \sigma^{-n}e^{-\frac{1}{\sigma^2}\frac{n\overline{\Delta x^2}}{2}}
\end{aligned}
$$

and the conjugate prior over the unknown standard deviation parameter is

$$
\begin{aligned}
p(\sigma \mid a \cdot b \cdot \imath) &= \frac{2b^a e^{-\frac{b}{\sigma^2}}}{\Gamma(a)\sigma^{2a+1}} \\
&\propto \sigma^{-(2a+1)}e^{-\frac{b}{\sigma^2}} \quad \{\sigma > 0
\end{aligned}
\qquad (3.30a),
$$

which has hyperparameters $a > 0, b > 0$. Combining prior and likelihood updates the hyperparameters so that the new values are

$$
\begin{aligned}
a' &= a + \frac{N}{2} \\
b' &= b + \frac{\sum_{i=1}^{N}(x_i-\mu)^2}{2} = b + \frac{n\overline{\Delta x^2}}{2}
\end{aligned}
\qquad (3.30b).
$$

The hyperparameters a, b can be interpreted in terms of a prior estimate of variance; an estimate based on $2a$ observations in which the sum of the squared deviations of those prior observations from the known location parameter was $2b$ (i.e., a prior variance estimate of b/a).

To update the information in (3.30) with the Gaussian location likelihood based on the observation of $x_1 = 5$, we write

$$\begin{aligned} p(\sigma \mid x \cdot \mu \cdot a \cdot b \cdot \imath) &\propto \varpi(\sigma)\mathcal{L}(\sigma) \\ &= \left[\sigma^{-(2a+1)} e^{-\frac{b}{\sigma^2}}\right]\left[\sigma^{-1} e^{-\frac{1}{\sigma^2}\frac{\Delta x_1^2}{2}}\right] \\ &= \sigma^{-\left(2\left[a+\frac{1}{2}\right]+1\right)} e^{-\frac{b+\frac{\Delta x_1^2}{2}}{\sigma^2}} \\ &= \sigma^{-(2\acute{a}+1)} e^{-\frac{\acute{a}}{\sigma^2}} \end{aligned}$$

and after an additional two datapoints, $x_2 = 6$ and $x_3 = 4.5$, the posterior is

$$\begin{aligned} p(\sigma^2 \mid x \cdot \mu \cdot a \cdot b \cdot \imath) &\propto \varpi(\sigma^2)\mathcal{L}(\sigma^2) \\ &= \left[\sigma^{-(2a+1)} e^{-\frac{b}{\sigma^2}}\right]\left[\sigma^{-n} e^{-\frac{1}{\sigma^2}\frac{\Delta x_1^2+\Delta x_2^2+\Delta x_3^2}{2}}\right] \\ &= \sigma^{-\left(\left[a+\frac{n}{2}\right]+1\right)} e^{-\frac{\left[b+\frac{\sum \Delta x^2}{2}\right]}{\sigma^2}} \end{aligned}$$

where the hyperparameters could be obtained directly from the update equation (3.30b).

Exercises

1) For $a = 1, b = 1$ and $S = 10, n = 15$, compute and plot the posterior distribution based on the binomial likelihood and conjugate prior.
2) For the data in Ex. 1, compute and plot the posterior if the prior is based on $a = 30$ and $b = 30$? How would this change (plot a new posterior atop the previous one) if the data were S=200, n=300?
3) Start with a binomial conjugate prior based on $a = 2$ and $b = 2$.
   a. Update it using the definition of the binomial (2.15) with the following datasets and plot the posterior for each:
      n_1=10, S=5
      n_2=7, S=2
      n_3=12, S=5
      n_4=21, S=10.
   b. Compute and plot the posterior for the combination of datasets using (3.23).
   c. Compare the final plot in (a) with that in (b).
4) Write the expression for the posteriors in Ex. 1-2.
5) For a=1, b=1 and S=10, n=15, compute and plot the posterior distribution over the negative binomial parameter, θ.
6) For the data in Ex. 5, compute and plot the posterior if the prior is based on $a = 30$ and $b = 30$? How would this change (plot a new posterior atop the previous one) if the data were S=200, n=300?

7) Start with a conjugate prior for the negative binomial based on $a = 2$ and $b = 2$.
   a. Update it using the definition of the negative binomial distribution (2.16) with the following datasets and plot the posterior for each:
      $n_1=10, S=5$
      $n_2=7, S=2$
      $n_3=12, S=5$
      $n_4=21, S=10$.
   b. Compute and plot the posterior for the combination of datasets using (3.24).
   c. Compare the final plot in (a) with that in (b).
8) Write the expression for the posteriors in Ex. 5-6.
9) For $a = 3, b = 1$, and $S = 21$, compute and plot the posterior based on the Poisson likelihood and conjugate prior over the range from $\varsigma = 0$ to 50.
10) For the data in Ex. 9, compute and plot the posterior if the prior is based on $a = 155$ and $b = 8$? How would this change (plot a new posterior atop the previous one) if there had instead been 25 observation epochs with an average of $S = 21$ occurrences?
11) Start with the Poisson conjugate prior based on $a = 10$ and $b = 1$.
    a. Update it with the following datasets using the Poisson likelihood and plot the posterior for each:
       $S = 12$
       $S = 13$
       $S = 11$
       $S = 14$.
    b. Compute and plot the posterior for the combination of datasets using (3.25).
    c. Compare the final plot in (a) with that in (b).
12) Write the expression for the posteriors in Ex. 9-10.
13) For $a = 1, b = 1$ and $t = [2, 4, 5, 3, 1]$, compute and plot the posterior distribution resulting from the exponential likelihood and conjugate prior.
14) For the data in Ex. 13, compute and plot the posterior if the prior is based on $a = 30$ and $b = 63$? How would this change (plot a new posterior atop the previous one) if the data were $\bar{t} = 3, n = 300$?
15) Start with the exponential conjugate prior based on $a = 1$ and $b = 2$.
    a. Update it with the following datasets using the exponential likelihood and plot the posterior for each:
       $t_1 = 1.2$
       $t_2 = 1.3$
       $t_3 = 1.1$
       $t_4 = 1.4$.
    b. Compute and plot the posterior for the combination of datasets using (3.26).
    c. Compare the final plot in (a) with that in (b).
16) Write the expression for the posterior in Ex. 13-14.
17) For $\mu_0 = 0, \sigma_0 = 100$ and $x_1 = 1, \sigma = 10$, compute and plot the posterior distribution over the Gaussian location.
18) For the data in Ex. 1, compute and plot the posterior if the prior is based on $\mu_0 = 0, \sigma_0 = 1$? How would this change (plot a new posterior atop the previous one) if the data were $n = 100$, $\bar{x}_1 = 1, \sigma = 10$?

19) Start with the Gaussian location conjugate prior based on $\mu_0 = 0, \sigma_0 = 100$.
    a. Update it using the Gaussian likelihood with the following datasets, assuming $\sigma = 1$, and plot the posterior for each:
    $x_1 = 1.2$
    $x_2 = 1.3$
    $x_3 = 1.1$
    $x_4 = 1.4$
    b. Compute and plot the posterior for the combination of datasets using (3.27).
    c. Compare the final plot in (a) with that in (b).
20) Write the closed-form expression for the posterior in Ex. 17-18.

3.4.4 Jeffreys Priors

Assignment of prior distributions has been, historically, the subject of some concern because of the lack of invariance under transformation of variables. This lack of invariance was demonstrated for the uniform prior in Section 3.3.2. The invariance we refer to here has to do with the shape of the posterior; for example, we showed in Section 3.4.2 that a uniform prior over the Gaussian precision parameter (τ) yields a particular posterior distribution, but that if we first start with a uniform prior over the Gaussian scale parameter (σ) and transform this into a prior over the Gaussian precision parameter, the identical data yields a *different* posterior over the precision parameter. This lack of invariance with regard to inference (inequality of the resulting posteriors) led to some early concern regarding Bayesian statistical analysis. However, in 1946 Harold Jeffreys showed that it is possible to construct prior distributions that are invariant to certain classes of transformation. In particular, he solved a problem for the Gaussian likelihood function, showing that a prior with the desired invariance property does indeed exist; for the Gaussian scale parameter (σ) it is proportional to σ^{-1}, or for a precision parameter (τ) is proportional to τ^{-1}. We will first give the (calculus-based) algorithm for constructing transformation-invariant priors using Jeffreys' rule, along with a list of the Jeffreys priors corresponding to the most common likelihood functions. We then explore these in a series of examples highlighting the use and characteristics of this class of prior distribution.

The algorithm for constructing a Jeffreys prior for some parameter, ϑ, is as follows:

1. Take the logarithm (to any base) of the likelihood function for ϑ, $\mathcal{L}(\vartheta)$.
2. Take the second partial derivative with respect to the parameter of interest.
3. Take the negative of the expected value.
4. Take the square root.

Steps 1–3 produce a measure of information associated with the likelihood function called the Fisher information. A Jeffreys prior is proportional to the result of step 4, and is therefore proportional to the square root of the Fisher information: Fisher information measures the information about some parameter ϑ that is contained in the likelihood function,[12] and is written I_ϑ. The Jeffreys prior for a parameter ϑ is

$$p(\vartheta \mid \iota) \propto I_\vartheta^{\frac{1}{2}} = \left[-\left\langle \frac{\partial^2}{\partial \vartheta^2} \log(\mathcal{L}(\vartheta)) \right\rangle \right]^{\frac{1}{2}} \qquad (3.31).$$

[12] This is another way to write the expectation, or mean of x: $\langle x \rangle = \mathrm{E}[x]$.

We will make use of Jeffreys priors for the parameters of the most common likelihood functions in later chapters. Section 3.4.5 contains a demonstration of the invariance property of Jeffreys priors using two versions of the Gaussian dispersion parameter, σ and ρ. Although an initial study of this material does not require the student to become proficient in constructing Jeffreys priors, the numbered equations presented in the list below should be examined in anticipation of their use. We will see several simple examples of full inference problems calculated from simulated data using Jeffreys priors at the close of this chapter.

Jeffreys Priors for Common Likelihood Functions

In Section 3.1 we derived expressions for the mean and variance most common sampling distributions. For convenience, we list the Jeffreys priors for the parameters of the likelihood functions associated with those sampling distributions here:

$$\text{binomial / negative binomial: } \varpi_J(\theta) \propto [\theta(1-\theta)]^{\frac{-1}{2}} \{0 \leq \theta \leq 1 \quad (3.32)$$

$$\text{Poisson: } \varpi_J(\varsigma) \propto \varsigma^{-1/2}\{\varsigma > 0 \quad (3.33)$$

$$\text{exponential: } \varpi_J(\tau) \propto \tau^{-1}\{\tau > 0 \quad (3.34a)$$

$$\varpi_J(\varsigma) \propto \varsigma^{-1}\{\varsigma > 0 \quad (3.34b)$$

$$\text{Gaussian: } \varpi_J(\mu) \propto \mu^0 = const \quad (3.35)$$

$$\varpi_J(\sigma) \propto \sigma^1\{\sigma > 0 \quad (3.36a)$$

$$\varpi_J(\sigma^2) = \varpi_J(\vartheta) \propto \vartheta^1\{\vartheta > 0 \quad (3.36b)$$

$$\varpi_J(\rho) \propto \rho^{-1}\{\rho > 0 \quad (3.36c).$$

The priors are written here in the format, $\varpi(\bullet)$, *proportional* to some function of the parameter of interest. This is because Jeffreys priors are improper distributions, and not normalized. In some applications we will need to use normalized priors; in those cases normalization is often easiest to achieve by selecting suitable bounds on the range of possible parameter values, and truncating the distribution beyond those bounds. The resulting bounded distribution is then easily normalized by dividing the distribution by the probability mass contained within the chosen bounds. Note however, when the purpose of the analysis is parameter estimation, as it will be in the examples below, it is possible to use improper priors and base parameter estimates on the shape of the posterior (the shape of the posterior is proportional to the product of the prior and likelihood).

Recall that the major drawback of the conjugate prior is that using conjugate priors does not fully solve the problem of how to assign priors to a given likelihood: we still need a method of assigning hyperparameter values. Jeffreys priors solve this problem. Jeffreys priors are related to the conjugate priors studied in the previous section because the Jeffreys prior turns out to be a special case of the analogous conjugate prior.[13] The Jeffreys

[13] For example, the binomial conjugate prior with $a = 0.5, b = 0.5$ is equivalent to the Jeffreys prior. The conjugate prior is: $\varpi(\theta) \propto \theta^{a-1}(1-\theta)^{b-1}$, and inserting the values of a and b gives

$$\varpi\left(\theta; a = \frac{1}{2}, b = \frac{1}{2}\right) \propto \theta^{\frac{1}{2}-1}(1-\theta)^{\frac{1}{2}-1}$$
$$= [\theta(1-\theta)]^{-\frac{1}{2}} = \varpi_J(\theta)$$

prior solves the problem of assigning priors in two ways: they have no hyperparameters that need to be set, and they solve the problem of transformation invariance.

Exercises

1) Are there parameter values for other conjugate priors in Section 3.4.3 that would transform them into Jeffreys priors? If so, for which conjugate priors is this possible?
2) For the conjugate priors that can become Jeffreys priors with the appropriate choice of hyperparameters, what are those hyperparameter values?
3) Plot the Jeffreys prior for the binomial, and show how it changes as alternate 0/1 data are observed.

3.4.5 Inference under Reparameterization

The hallmark of the Jeffreys prior is that it should produce equivalent inferences under reparameterization of the likelihood. We will explore this property in several examples below, deriving posterior distributions for two parameterizations of several likelihoods, and then comparing transformed versions of the resulting posteriors. Once a prior distribution is defined, we can determine whether the resulting *posterior* is changed under reparameterization. We first define two equivalent parameterizations of a likelihood, and their corresponding priors. After computing the posterior based on the two prior-likelihood pairs *for the same dataset*, we transform between the two parameterizations of the posterior. This can be compared to examples in the section above on uniform priors, which demonstrated nonequivalence under the same transformations.

Priors that maintain transformation invariance such as the Jeffreys prior maintain the inferences drawn from data (i.e., the resulting posterior) across different parameterizations. By focusing on the effect of different priors on the resulting posteriors we hope to emphasize our ultimate goal in examining the Jeffreys prior, in addition to testing transformation invariance.

Exercises

1) Give two equivalent parameterizations of the following:
   a. exponential likelihood
   b. Poisson likelihood
   c. Gaussian scale likelihood
   d. Gaussian location likelihood
2) Using a uniform prior (and the given data), derive posteriors for the two parameterizations of (always use a large range over the unknown parameter such that the likelihood drops to near 0 at the edge of the truncated range):
   a. exponential likelihood, $t = [2.4, 3.2, 4.4, 4.7, 3.5, 3.3]$
   b. Poisson likelihood, $S = 44$
   c. Gaussian scale likelihood, $x = [2.4, 3.2, 4.4, 4.7, 3.5, 3.3]$
   d. Gaussian location likeliood, $x = [2.4, 3.2, 4.4, 4.7, 3.5, 3.3]$

3) Numerically transform between the two parameterizations of the posteriors derived in Ex. 2.
4*) Show, based on (1.5), that one could also express transformation invariance directly on the priors, by first defining uninformative priors for the two parameterizations of some likelihood function, and then simply transforming between those two priors.

Example: Equivalence of Inferences for Exponential τ and $\varsigma = \tau^{-1}$ Using Jeffreys Priors

We first examine the exponential distribution with rate parameter, ς, as compared to the exponential distribution parameterized in terms of a time constant, τ. In both cases, we will assume a dataset of $n = 30$ observations with mean observed time between events of $\bar{t} = 3$ ms.

When parameterized as a time constant, the likelihood is $\mathcal{L}(\tau) \propto \frac{1}{\tau} e^{\frac{-n\bar{t}}{\tau}}$, and when this likelihood is combined with the Jeffreys prior, $\varpi(\tau) \propto \tau^{-1}$, it yields the posterior

$$\begin{aligned} p(\tau \mid d \cdot \iota) &\propto \varpi(\tau)\mathcal{L}(\tau) \\ &= \frac{\tau^{-n}}{\tau} e^{-(\Sigma_i t_i)/\tau} \\ &= \tau^{-(n+1)} e^{-15/\tau} \end{aligned}$$

which is plotted in Figure 3.5b (upper) in open circles. When the prior over τ is transformed via the function $\varsigma = \tau^{-1}$ (i.e., approximate transformation of the posterior distribution over time constants to the equivalent posterior over rate) it combines with the ς-likelihood (described below) to yield the posterior shown in Figure 3.5b as a grey line.

As noted above, the most common alternate parameterization of the exponential distribution is in terms of a rate parameter. When parameterized in terms of an unknown recurrence rate, the exponential likelihood is $\mathcal{L}(\varsigma) \propto \varsigma e^{-\varsigma n\bar{t}}$, and when combined with the Jeffreys prior, $\varpi(\varsigma) \propto \varsigma^{-1}$, yields the posterior:

$$\begin{aligned} P(\varsigma \mid d \cdot \iota) &\propto \varpi(\varsigma)\mathcal{L}(\varsigma) \\ &= \varsigma^{-1}\varsigma^{-n} e^{-\varsigma(\Sigma|_i t_i)} \\ &= \varsigma^{-(n+1)} e^{-15\varsigma} \end{aligned}$$

This is plotted in Figure 3.5b in open circles. To plot the posterior based on the transformed Jeffreys prior, we take $\varpi_J(\varsigma)$ and numerically transform it via $\tau = \varsigma^{-1}$. Combining this with the τ-likelihood (described above) yields the transformed posterior, which is shown in Figure 3.5b as a grey line. The important thing to note is that the two posteriors are identical, as expected by our use of the Jeffreys prior.

Programming Aside: Exponential Posteriors Derived from Jeffreys Priors (Fig. 3.5b, upper)

The function pTX.m returns the approximate transformation of a probability distribution, pORIG in original coordinates (cOrig) via the linking function f. This function was used extensively to create plots in Appendix C. Here, it will be used to compare different parameterizations of the same posteriors derived from Jeffreys priors. To do so, we must first create pOrig based on both parameterizations of the exponential distribution.

```
n=30; tbar=3; tdat=n*tbar;
tau=linspace(0,20,502); tau=tau(2:end); sig=1./tau;
pritau=tau.^-1; Ltau=tau.^-n.*exp(-tdat./tau); ptau=pritau.*Ltau;
prisig=sig.^-1; Lsig=sig.^+n.*exp(-tdat*sig); psig=prisig.*Lsig;
```

Once the posterior distributions in their original coordinates (ptau and psig) have been computed, we are in a position to compute the approximate transformed versions of each of these. We first define the linking function:

```
f=@(x) x.^-1;
```

to be used in pTX.m. We then define the two transformed priors and posteriors.

```
prisigx=pTX(tau,pritau,f); psigx=prisigx(:,1).*Lsig';
pritaux=pTX(sig,prisig,f); ptaux=pritaux(:,1).*Ltau';
```

From here, we can create plots:

```
figure(1); clf; hold on; box off;
plot(tau,ptau/max(ptau),'ko','MarkerFaceColor','k','MarkerSize',8,'LineWidth',2);
plot(pritaux(:,2),ptaux/max(ptaux),'-','LineWidth',2)
axis([0 10 0 1])
figure(2); clf; hold on; box off
plot(sig,psig/max(psig),'ko','MarkerFaceColor','k','MarkerSize',8,'LineWidth',2);
plot(prisigx(:,2),psigx/max(psigx),'-','LineWidth',2)
axis([0 10 0 1])
```

Exercises

1) Use of the Jeffreys prior guarantees the identity of the alternately parameterized posteriors derived from the identical data. Show that if we had instead used a uniform prior that this would not have been the case.
2) Show that using a conjugate prior instead of the Jeffreys prior, for at least one choice of hyperparameters except for the special case that yields the Jeffreys prior, produces unequal posteriors under reparameterization of the exponential distribution.
3) In the PA for this section, we plotted the transformed posteriors against the ordinate values given by pritaux(:,2) and prisigx(:,2) [the outputs of the pTX.m function]. Would it have also been possible to plot tau and sig on the ordinates? Why or why not?

Programming Aside: Gaussian Posteriors Derived from Jeffreys Priors (Fig. 3.5b, lower)

We will use two steps to demonstrate transformation invariance. First, we plot the originalcoordinates posteriors for the two parameterizations of the likelihood (here, in terms of standard deviation and precision). Then, we numerically transform each of these priors in the other coordinates and compute (and plot) the resulting transformed posteriors.

Step 1: Plot original-coordinates posteriors:

```
sig=linspace(0,20,52); sig=sig(2:end); rho=sort(sig.^-2); %rho
%reverse order unless sorted
d=[-2.25 -1.02 4.13 2.48 -3.71]; n=length(d);
```

sigma:

```
figure(19); clf; hold on; box off;
prisig=sig.^-1; Lsig=sig.^-n.* exp(-.5*(sig.^-2)*sum(d.^2));
psig=prisig.*Lsig;
plot(sig,psig./max(psig),'ko','MarkerSize',8,'LineWidth',2);
```

rho:

```
figure(20); clf; hold on; box off
prirho=rho.^-1; Lrho=rho.^(n/2).*exp(-.5*rho* sum(d.^2));
prho=prirho.*Lrho;
plot(rho,prho./max(prho),'ko','MarkerSize',8,'LineWidth',2);
```

Step 2: Plot transformed posteriors: First define the transforms:

```
f1=@(x) (x).^-(1/2); f2=@(x) x.^-2;
```

Then plot each transformed posterior atop the original:

SIG:

```
figure(19); axis([0 10 0 1])
prisigx=pTX(rho,prirho,f1); psigx=prisigx(:,1).*Lsig';
plot(prisigx(:,2),psigx/max(psigx),'-','LineWidth',2);
```

RHO:

```
figure(20); axis([0 .25 0 1])
prirhox=pTX(sig,prisig,f2); prhox=prirhox(:,1).*Lrho';
plot(prirhox(:,2),prhox/max(prhox),'-','LineWidth',2)
```

Example: Equivalence of Inferences for Gaussian σ and ρ and Using Jeffreys Priors

Remember the reason Jeffreys developed his rule for deriving uninformative prior distributions: He was solving the invariance problem for representing equivalent states of prior information. Below, we will verify his solution, by showing that the prior probability distributions for two of the Gaussian dispersion parameters [σ and ρ] obtained using Jeffreys' rule, will lead to identical inferences about those parameters when they are combined with identical likelihood information from data. To demonstrate this identity, we first look at the shape of the posterior for inferences about σ. The posterior over the Gaussian standard deviation is

$$
\begin{aligned}
p(\sigma \mid d \cdot \mu \cdot \iota) &\propto \varpi(\sigma)\mathcal{L}(\sigma) \\
&= [\sigma^{-1}]\left[\sigma^{-n} e^{-\sigma^{-2}\Sigma(\mu-d_i)^2/2}\right] \\
&= \sigma^{-n-1} e^{-\sigma^{-2}\Sigma(\mu-d_i)^2/2}
\end{aligned}
$$

which is plotted in the lower panels of Figure 3.5b (open circles).

Now, the analogous posterior distribution describing our information about the precision (inverse dispersion)[14] parameter based on these data can be derived by combining the precision prior with the same Gaussian likelihood parameterized in terms of precision:

$$
\begin{aligned}
p(\rho \mid \boldsymbol{d} \cdot \mu \cdot \iota) &\propto \varpi(\rho)\mathcal{L}(\rho) \\
&= [\rho^{-1}]\left[\rho^{n/2} e^{-\rho\Sigma(\mu-d_i)^2/2}\right] \quad \{\rho = \sigma^{-2} \\
&= \rho^{\frac{n}{2}-1} e^{-\frac{\rho}{2}\Sigma(\mu-d_i)^2}
\end{aligned}
$$

which is plotted in Figure 3.5b (open circles). Finally, to make the comparison required to assess transformation invariance, we numerically transform each of the priors above into the other coordinate system; that is, we transform the prior over ρ into a prior over σ, combine this with the σ-likelihood, and plot the resulting posterior in Figure 3.5b as a solid line. Similarly, we transform prior over σ into a prior over ρ, combine this with the ρ-likelihood, and plot the resulting transformed posterior in Figure 3.5b as a solid line. Since these plots are identical (i.e., they overlap when plotted by forcing the peak to a value of 1 as in Fig. 3.5b), these posteriors must normalize in exactly the same way in both cases to produce identical posterior probability distributions. And given that the open-circles plots were derived from a direct application of (1.5) and the solid-line plots were obtained via a transformation of variables, we have demonstrated the invariance of these posterior distributions to transformations when using Jeffreys priors, the implication being that information expressed by those Jeffreys priors must be equivalent for the two parameterizations.

Exercises

1) Use of the Jeffreys prior guarantees the identity of the alternately parameterized posteriors derived from the identical data. Show that if we had instead used a uniform prior that this would not have been the case.
2) Show that using a conjugate prior instead of the Jeffreys prior, for any choice of parameters except for the special case that yields the Jeffreys prior, produces unequal posteriors under reparameterization of the Gaussian likelihood.
3) Use the argument above to create plots similar to those in Figure 3.5b for the Gaussian location parameter, that is, create posteriors for original and shifted coordinates of the Gaussian location parameter.
4*) Another way to state the condition of transformation invariance for assigning prior probability distributions is to say that the shape of the distribution must be unaffected

[14] Note that precision is usually defined as $\rho = \sigma^{-2}$, but is also sometimes defined as $\rho = \frac{1}{2\sigma^2}$. In either case, the Jeffreys prior is $\varpi_J(x) \propto x^{-1}$.

by a certain class of transformation, because our information is such that we have no reason to prefer the original or transformed distribution to represent our current state of knowledge. For example, the uniform distribution is unaffected by translations of the coordinate axis, because the transformed distribution is again uniform (in transformed coordinates). Similarly, the Jeffreys prior for the Gaussian scale parameter is uniform in log-coordinates because it is invariant to a change in units.

a. Plot a segment of the real line describing distances from 1 to 100 m in log units, after transforming the units to: (1) m, (2) mm, (3) yards, (4) furlongs, and explain why a uniform distribution in one log-transformed unit will be uniform in the other log-transformed units.
b. What is the probability that a given bank account's balance (from an unspecified country, and therefore an unspecified currency) will have a leading digit of 1? 2? 3? ⋯ 9?
c. If money were expressed in base-7 instead of base-10, what is the probability that a given bank account's balance (country unspecified) will have a leading digit of 1? 2? ⋯ 7?

3.5 Updating Information Based on Data: The Effect of Prior Information

The purpose of the Section 3.4 was to gain some understanding of the issues involved in assigning prior probability distributions over parameters. We focused particularly on 'ignorance priors' – priors that contain no information about the *value* of a parameter, but *do* contain information about the *type* of parameter being measured. Here, we will gain some practice setting up problems of scientific inference using various priors, including Jeffreys priors, and observe how information is added to priors as data are observed.

We will also take this opportunity to examine what happens to posteriors as large numbers of data are observed, and how this is affected by the prior distribution we assigned at the outset of the analysis. We will see that while the prior can have a great deal of influence over the posterior when few data have been obtained, this influence generally becomes insignificant as more data are observed. Thus, while the topic of selecting the most appropriate prior is always of theoretical importance, its practical importance typically diminishes once a substantial number of data have been observed.

Example: Poisson Conjugate and Jeffreys Priors

Above it was noted that a Jeffreys prior is often a special case of a conjugate prior. Here, we will explore that idea a bit further in an example. First, we will examine how the information in a series of datasets updates a Jeffreys prior. We compare this Jeffreys-prior-based analysis to a series of analyses based on conjugate priors, allowing us to compare the informativeness of each prior by noticing its effect on the resulting posteriors.

Suppose you have conducted an experiment counting the number of synapses at the neuromuscular junction of the medial rectus (eye) muscle during synaptogenesis. The observed data (in counts per epoch) are $S = [15\ \ 12\ \ 13]$, counted in four animals. When we combine the Jeffreys prior for an unknown Poisson parameter, $\varpi_j(\varsigma) \propto \varsigma^{-\frac{1}{2}}$ with the Poisson likelihood we obtain the following four posteriors corresponding to the first four observed counts (indexed by i):

$$p(\varsigma \mid d \cdot \iota) \propto \varpi(\varsigma)\mathcal{L}(\varsigma)$$
$$\propto \left[\varsigma^{-\frac{1}{2}}\right]\left[e^{-n\varsigma}\varsigma^{\Sigma_i S_i}\right] = e^{-n\varsigma}\varsigma^{(\Sigma_i S_i)-\frac{1}{2}}$$

which peak at $\varsigma = [14.5 \;\; 13.3 \;\; 10.5 \;\; 11.1]$ after observing the first through fourth count, respectively. Thus, after having observed several sets of counts the posterior begins to converge toward the true value of the Poisson parameter($\varsigma = 11$).

The conjugate prior corresponding to the Poisson likelihood becomes the Jeffreys prior when the hyperparameters of the Poisson conjugate prior are $a = \frac{1}{2}, b = 0$. Setting hyperparameter values such that $a > 1, b \geq 1$ will indicate that prior counts had been observed (or perhaps more accurately, information equivalent to prior counts having been observed). For example, if we had set the hyperparameters to $[a-1] = 14.5, b = 1$ (i.e., $a - 1$ prior counts in b previous observation epochs) we would obtain the following expression for the posterior:

$$p(\varsigma \mid d \cdot a \cdot b \cdot \iota) \propto \varpi(\varsigma)\mathcal{L}(\varsigma)$$
$$= [\varsigma^{a-1}e^{-b\varsigma}]\left[e^{-n\varsigma}\varsigma^{\Sigma_{i=2}^{4} S_i}\right]$$
$$= e^{-(n+1)\varsigma}\varsigma^{14.5+\Sigma_{i=2}^{4} S_i}$$

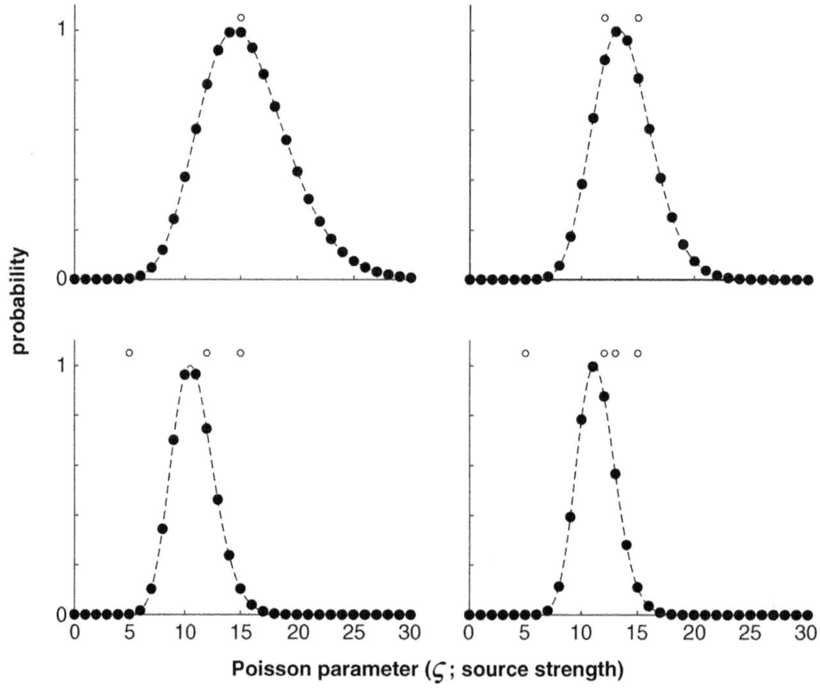

Figure 3.6 Conjugate and Jeffreys priors for the Poisson parameter. Each of the four panels represents an updated state of knowledge about the value of the Poisson parameter, each update occurring after observing new counts. The data (open circles) are drawn from a pseudorandom Poisson count generator with a source strength of 11. The two conjugate priors yield the identical posteriors from the last three panels (conjugate prior 1) or last panel (conjugate prior 2), from fewer counts.

Programming Aside: Conjugate and Jeffreys Priors for the Poisson Parameter (Fig. 3.6)

Jeffreys prior

```
d=[15, 12, 5, 13]; n=length(d); pmax=nan(n,1);
SS=linspace(0,30,301); inds=find(rem(SS,1)==0);
f=@(nvar) exp(-nvar.*SS).*SS.^(sum(d(1:nvar))-.5);
for nnow=1:n, figure(20+nnow); clf, hold on; box off; axis([0 max(SS) 0 1.1]);
    pSS=f(nnow); pmax(nnow)=median(SS(pSS==max(pSS)));
    plot(SS,pSS/max(pSS),'k--','LineWidth',1.5);
    plot(SS(inds),pSS(inds)/max(pSS),'ko','MarkerFaceColor','k','MarkerSize',12)
    plot(d(1:nnow),1.05,'ko','MarkerSize',8,'LineWidth',1.7); end
```

Conjugate prior #1

```
d2=[12, 5, 13]; n2=length(d2);
f2=@(nvar) exp(-(nvar+1).*SS).*SS.^(14.5+sum(d2(1:nvar)));
for nnow=0:n2, figure(20+n+nnow); clf, hold on; box off; axis([0 max(SS) 0 1.1]);
    pSS=f2(nnow); pmax(nnow+1)=median(SS(pSS==max(pSS)));
    plot(SS,pSS/max(pSS),'k--','LineWidth',1.5);
    plot(SS(inds),pSS(inds)/max(pSS),'ko','MarkerFaceColor','k','MarkerSize',12)
    if ~isempty(d(1:nnow)), plot(d(1:nnow),1.05,'ko','MarkerSize',8,...
    'LineWidth',1.7); end, end
```

Conjugate prior #2

```
d3=[13]; n3=length(d3);
f3=@(nvar) exp(-(nvar+diff([n3 n])).*SS).*SS.^(diff([n3 3])*10.5+sum(d3(1:nvar)));
for nnow=0:n3, figure(20+n+n2+nnow); clf, hold on; box off; axis([0 max(SS) 0 1.1]);
    pSS=f3(nnow); pmax(nnow+1)=median(SS(pSS==max(pSS)));
    plot(SS,pSS/max(pSS),'k--','LineWidth',1.5);
    plot(SS(inds),pSS(inds)/max(pSS),'ko','MarkerFaceColor','k','MarkerSize',12)
    if ~isempty(d(1:nnow)), plot(d(1:nnow),1.05,'ko','MarkerSize',8,...
    'LineWidth',1.7); end, end
```

The prior and the three posteriors corresponding to data-based updates of this prior are computed in the PA, and are identical to the four posteriors from Figure 3.6 based on the Jeffreys prior after adding data through the likelihood. In other words, the initial conjugate prior carries the same information as we would obtain from having observed the first success-count based on the Jeffreys prior. To take this a step further, we could subsume the information gleaned from the first three observation epochs (based on a Jeffreys prior) under a single informative conjugate prior. Thus the prior looks exactly like the lower left panel of Figure 3.6, and only a single success-count brings us to the same state of information as in the final (lower-right) panel.

Exercises

1) Note that the number of 'pseudo-observations' used to create the two informed conjugate priors are not the actual numbers of observations that produce the equivalent posterior in Figure 3.6 How are the numbers of pseudo-observations chosen?

2) Write the expression fore the informed conjugate prior that:
   a) reproduces the bottom left-hand plot of Figure 3.6
   b) reproduces the upper right-hand plot of Figure 3.6
3) Compare the statistical properties of the Jeffreys prior and the two conjugate priors for the Poisson parameter:
   a. $a = 1, b = 0$.
   b. $a = 0, b = 0$.

   In all three cases, generate 100,000 repetitions each of 1 through 10 pseudorandom Poisson success-counts. For each 100,000 repetitions of a given number of counts, find the peak of the resulting posterior distribution and take the average of these. Plot these averages as a function of the number of observation-epochs (1 through 10) for each of the three types of prior. Discuss the differences in these three functions.

Example: Consequences of Different Types of Binomial Prior Information

Writing a grant to study balance in the elderly, we must report to the grant agency about the impact on health and/or quality of life due to compromised balance in the elderly. We would like to report how often loss of balance currently causes serious injury in older individuals. To estimate the underlying rate at which injury results from a fall in the elderly, we consult hospital records on patients over the age of 70 who present with balance complaints. Our goal is to estimate the rate at which hospitalization of the elderly is the result of a fall – that is, we want to infer the value of the binomial rate parameter describing this rate of fall-related hospitalization.

We will compute the posterior probability for the binomial rate parameter, θ, from the likelihood function $P(S \cdot N \mid \theta \cdot \iota_B) = \binom{N}{S} \theta^S (1-\theta)^{N-S}$, and each of four different prior probability distributions over θ: The Jeffreys prior (3.32), a uniform prior $[p(\theta \mid \iota_{B0}) = \theta^0]$, a shallowly peaked prior with its maximum at $\theta = .5$, and a sharply peaked prior with its maximum at $\theta = .5$. The latter two informative priors are given by: $p(\theta \mid \iota_{B1}) \propto \theta - \theta^2$ and $p(\theta \mid \iota_{B2}) \propto \theta^{15}(1-\theta)^{15}$, and represent what one might assign if prior information consisted of knowledge that there had been one occurrence of h (fall-related hospitalization) and one occurrence of t (non-fall-related hospitalization), or represented prior knowledge of 15 occurrences each of both h and t.

Our analysis will consist of computing the mean of the posterior distribution derived from the observed data and these four priors. The posterior distribution for the parameter θ is proportional to the product of the prior and the likelihood (see eq. 1.5):

$$p(\theta \mid D \cdot \iota) = \frac{p(\theta \mid \iota)p(D \mid \theta \cdot \iota)}{\int d\theta p(\theta \mid \iota)p(D \mid \theta \cdot \iota)} \propto p(\theta \mid \iota)p(D \mid \theta \cdot \iota) = \varpi(\theta)\mathcal{L}(\theta)$$

Figure 3.7 shows the results of the analysis for simulated data obtained from a sampling distribution with $\theta = .75$. The top two rows of plots are posterior distributions obtained as the first 5 data are recorded (the first plot is the prior probability distribution). Notice that the first datum necessarily causes the symmetrical priors to become asymmetric, although this effect of the first datum on the posterior clearly depends on how informative the prior had been concerning the value of θ. The Jeffreys prior

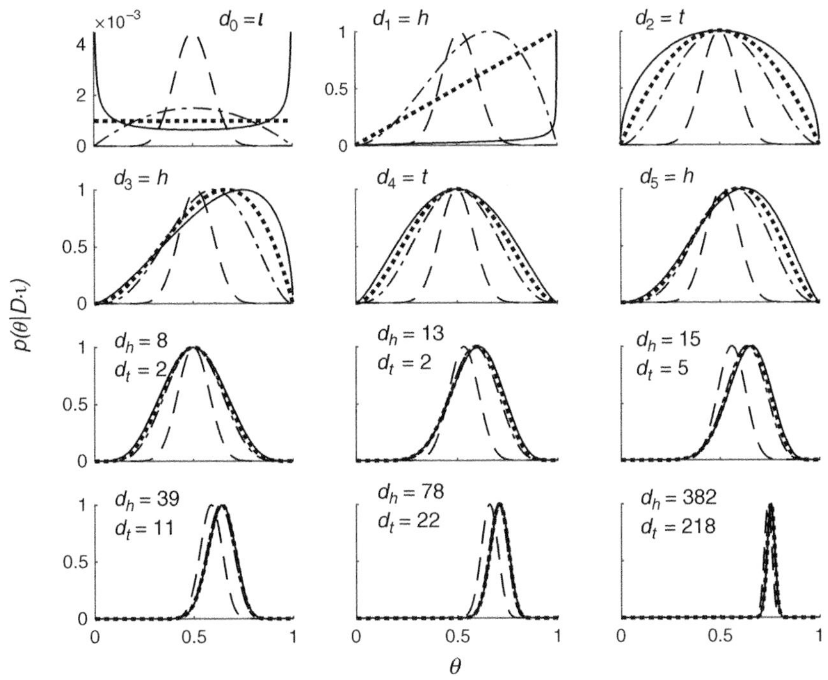

Figure 3.7 Conjugate and Jeffreys priors for the binomial parameter. Inferring a binomial rate parameter starting from four different priors. Each of the four priors represents a different state of prior knowledge about the value of the binomial rate parameter. Of these, the Jeffreys prior is the most conservative, in the sense described in the text.

(solid line) is most affected, and its average shifts from of $\theta = 0.5$ to $\theta = 0.75$. The sharply peaked prior (dashed line) is least affected, shifting only to $\theta = 0.52$. The remaining two priors, the uniform (dotted line) and the prior with the shallow peak (dash-dotted line) show intermediate effects, shifting to $\theta = 0.67$ and $\theta = 0.6$, respectively.

The first 5 data alternate between h and t. This allows us to see the shape of the posterior at two values of N when the numbers of h and t observations are equal. Notice that the Jeffreys prior is always wider than the other prior distributions. One way to quantify the width of these posteriors is to calculate the **standard deviation** ($\sigma = \sqrt{\mathrm{E}[\epsilon^2]} = \sqrt{\mathrm{V}[\theta]}$) of each of the distributions within the plots at $N = 2$ and $N = 4$. When $N = 2$, we see that $\sigma = 0.25$ for the Jeffreys prior, $\sigma = 0.22$ for the uniform, and $\sigma = 0.19$ and 0.085 for the two peaked priors. This ordering of the standard deviations remains the same in the plot showing $N = 4$, when again all four posterior distributions are symmetrical about the point $\theta = 0.5$. In both plots, not only is the standard deviation somewhat larger, but the distribution derived from the Jeffreys prior is visibly wider than the other three distributions – that is, it provides the most conservative estimate of θ, in the sense that it assigns larger probabilities to a wider range of possible θ values than the other posteriors. As a consequence, the Jeffreys-derived posterior also has the property that its mean is most affected by the odd-numbered data

Programming Aside: Priors for the Binomial Likelihood (Fig. 3.7)

```
beta1=.5; beta2=2;
stepsize=.001; Rtheta=[0 1];
theta=Rtheta(1)+stepsize/2:stepsize:Rtheta(2)-stepsize/2;
fpriorJ=@(t) (t.*(1-t)).^(-.5);
fpriorC=@(t,beta) (t.^(beta-1)).*((1-t).^(beta-1));
fpriorU=@(t) ones(length(t),1)./length(t);
flike=@(t,N,S) (t.^S).*(1-t).^(N-S);
fprior3015=flike(theta,30,15);

Ns=[1:5 10:5:20 50 100 500];

figure; subplot(4,3,1); hold on
fpJ=fpriorJ(theta); fpC1=fpriorC(theta,beta1); fpC2=fpriorC(theta,beta2);
fpU=fpriorU(theta);
piJ=fpJ/sum(fpJ); piC=fpC2/sum(fpC2); piU=fpU/sum(fpU);
pi3015=fprior3015/sum(fprior3015);

pis=[piJ(:) piC(:) piU(:) pi3015(:)];

plot(theta,pis(:,1),'k-','LineWidth',1.05)
plot(theta,pis(:,2),'k-.','LineWidth',1.1)
plot(theta,pis(:,3),'k:','LineWidth',2.1)
plot(theta,pis(:,4),'k--','LineWidth',1.1)

axis([0 1 0 max(pi3015)])

for n=1:length(Ns),
    N=Ns(n); S=sum(Bdraw(1:N));
    fnow=flike(theta,N,S); fnow=fnow(:)*ones(1,size(pis,2));
    post=fnow.*pis; pnorm=max(post); post=post./(ones(size(post,1),1)* pnorm);
    subplot(4,3,n+1), hold on
    plot(theta,post(:,1),'k-','LineWidth',1.05)
    plot(theta,post(:,2),'k-.','LineWidth',1.1)
    plot(theta,post(:,3),'k:','LineWidth',2.1)
    plot(theta,post(:,4),'k--','LineWidth',1.1)
    meandef(post,theta)
    sqrt(vardef(post,theta))
    axis([0 1 0 1]); end
```

in these first six panels. That is, its mean (and also its peak) most closely follows the changes in the data, as can be seen in the panels showing d_1, d_3, and d_5 (it is always the most skewed of the distributions in these plots).

What are the advantages and disadvantages of using these four prior probability distributions in our inference? The answer will depend on whether we have reliable information about θ prior to data collection, and also on the *amount* of data that we ultimately collect. If we collect a large to moderate amount of data, then a highly informative prior based on reliable information can significantly improve the precision of our measurements. For example, suppose that we had prior information leading to the sharply peaked prior in the first panel; this prior would protect the final estimate from deviations (in the mean and peak of the distribution) caused by a short run of h or t

observations, when the true value of θ is near the mean of the prior. Conversely, if we have very little information prior to data collection, then we would like our data to influence our final estimate of θ as much as possible, and a relatively uninformed prior should be preferred. But what about when we ultimately collect a great deal of data? As we see from the later panels of the figure, the more data, the less influence the prior will have on the posterior. In the final panel, for example, there is almost no discernible difference between the four posterior distributions, and we can imagine that with double or triple the 600 observations used to construct the distributions in that panel, there would be no detectable differences caused by the four priors to be found, regardless of the prior used.

Exercises

1) Why is the Jeffreys prior most affected by the initial observations?
2) Describe how you might assign hyperparameters for a conjugate prior in this example.
3) Describe the difference between the uniform and the Jeffreys priors in this example. Which would you prefer to use, and why?

Example: Priors over 1D and 2D Gaussian Parameters

Now let's consider an example using a continuous sampling distribution. Imagine that we are interested in characterizing the average corrective shift (in diopters) required by children when they are first prescribed corrective lenses. We will model the data with a Gaussian likelihood function whose mean value is equal to the unknown parameter value. We will further assume that the standard deviation of the Gaussian is a known constant, $\sigma = 1.0$. The posterior is given by

$$p(\mu \mid \boldsymbol{d} \cdot \sigma \cdot \imath) \propto p(\boldsymbol{d} \mid \mu \cdot \sigma \cdot \imath) p(\mu \mid \sigma \cdot \imath) = \varpi(\mu)\mathcal{L}(\mu)$$

From Section 3.4.1, we see that the Jeffreys prior for this example is the uniform distribution, which had been a mildly informative prior in the previous example concerning the binomial rate. Of course, we are unlikely to be totally uninformed about the value of the underlying true value of the μ parameter: we will likely be aware of a range, $R_\mu = [\mu_{\text{min}}, \mu_{\text{max}}]$, over which the parameter will fall – based on such things as the fact that the vast majority of early-age corrective lenses are for 'nearsightedness' (negative-diopter correction) and that corrections cannot be infinitely powerful. These two uniform distributions, the totally uninformed prior given by $p(\mu_i \mid \imath_0') = \Delta = const$, and the mildly informed uniform prior containing range information given by $p(\mu_i \mid R_\mu \cdot \imath_0) = \frac{1}{\mu_{\text{max}} - \mu_{\text{min}}}$ will be our usual choice for uninformed prior distributions for a Gaussian location parameter, because they are uniform over the allowed range of parameter values.

Another possible choice of prior for such a parameter is a generalization of one of the peaked priors used above for the binomial rate parameter, stretched to fit over the range of possible parameter values (R_μ), and forced to peak at a previous 'best estimate' of μ, such as

$$p(\mu \mid R_\mu \cdot \imath_B) \propto \vartheta^{u/\beta}(1 - \vartheta)^{v/\beta}$$

where $\vartheta = \frac{\mu - \mu_{\min}}{\mu_{\max} - \mu_{\min}}$. This prior over μ encodes a preference for parameter values centered at the abscissa location: $\frac{u\mu_{\min} + v\mu_{\max}}{u+v}$, with a width proportional to β. We will use a mildly informed, singly peaked prior with $u/\beta = v/\beta = 5$. Finally, although not a plausible representation of prior information in most situations, we will examine a bimodal distribution, given by

$$p(\mu_i \mid R_\mu \cdot \imath_{2x}) \propto \vartheta^{10}(1-\vartheta)^{20} + \vartheta^{20}(1-\vartheta)^{10}$$

Where ϑ is defined as in the previous singly peaked informative prior. This bimodal prior peaks at one-third and two-thirds of the total range of μ values. These priors are plotted in Figure 3.8a.

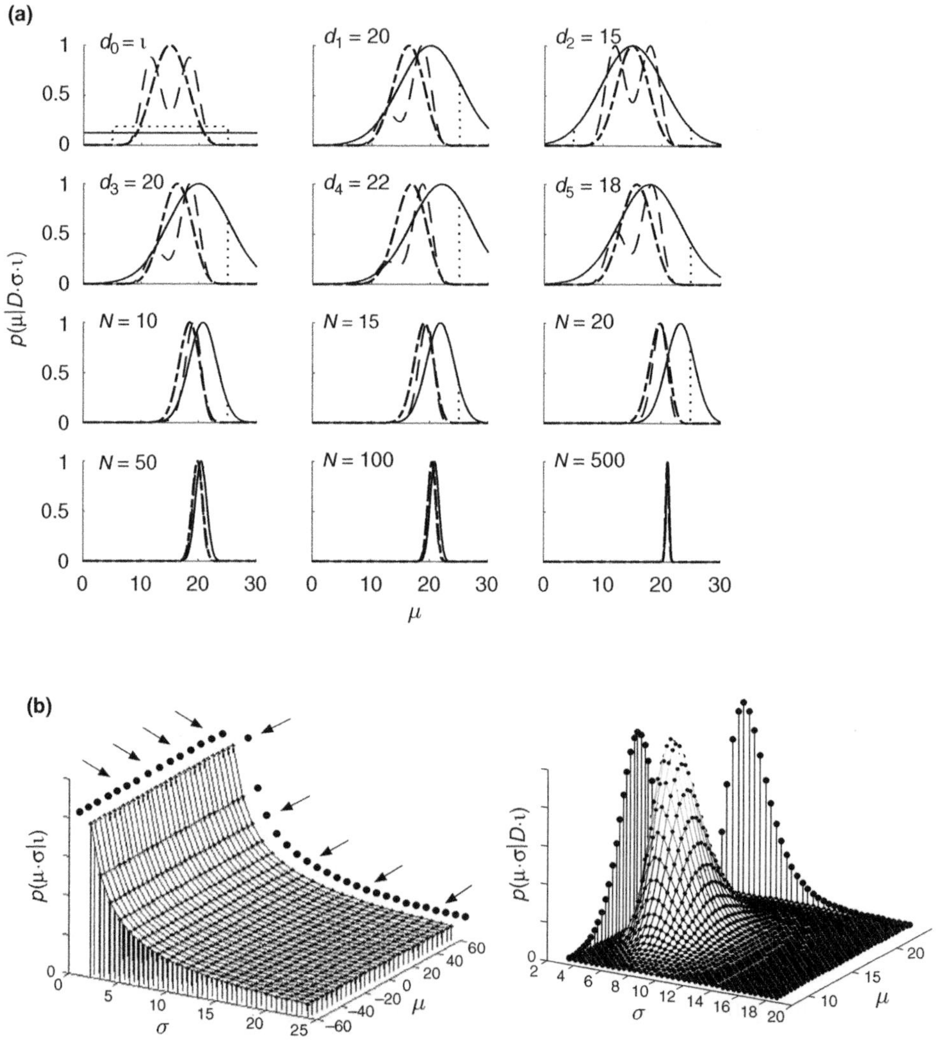

Figure 3.8 Conjugate and Jeffreys priors for the Gaussian. The Gaussian likelihood with Jeffreys priors to show the effect of increasing numbers of data. (a) Posterior distributions for the Gaussian location (μ) derived from four priors: unrestricted uniform (solid), truncated uniform (dotted), unimodal informative prior (dash-dotted), and a bimodal informative prior (dashed). (b) 2D Gaussian posterior over location (μ) and dispersion (σ).

Programming Aside: Posterior Distributions for the Gaussian Mean (Fig. 3.8a)

```
mureal=21; sd=7.5;
Gdraw=nrand(mureal,sd,[500 1]); Gdraw(1:5)=[20 15 20 22 18];

mumin=5; mumax=25;
mu0=mumin-5:.001:mumax+5;
mu=mumin:.001:mumax;
ld=(length(mu0)-length(mu))/2;
theta=(mu-mumin)/(mumax-mumin);
pbi=theta.^10.*(1-theta).^20+theta.^20.*(1-theta).^10;
pbi=[zeros(ld,1); pbi(:)/sum(pbi); zeros(ld,1)];
pmi=theta.^5.*(1-theta).^5; pmi=[zeros(ld,1); pmi(:)/sum(pmi); zeros(ld,1)];
pu=ones(size(mu))/length(mu); pu=[zeros(ld,1); pu(:)/sum(pu); zeros(ld,1)];
pu0=ones(size(mu0))/length(mu0); pu0=pu0(:)/sum(pu0);

floglike=@(mus,D) (-(D(:)*ones(1,length(mus))-ones(length(D),1)*mus).^2/sd^2);

Ns=[0:5 10:5:20 50 100 500];

figure; subplot(4,3,1); hold on
pis=[pu0 pu pmi pbi]/max(pmi);

plot(mu0,pis(:,1),'k-','LineWidth',1.05)
plot(mu0,pis(:,2),'k:','LineWidth',1.1)
plot(mu0,2*pis(:,3),'k-.','LineWidth',2.1)
plot(mu0,2*pis(:,4),'k--','LineWidth',1.1)

for n=2:length(Ns),
    N=Ns(n-1)+1:Ns(n); D=Gdraw(N);
    fnow=sum(floglike(mu0,D),1);
    fnow=exp(fnow-max(fnow));
    fnow=fnow(:)*ones(1,size(pis,2));
    post=fnow.*pis;
    pnorm=max(post);
    post=post./(ones(size(post,1),1)*pnorm);
    subplot(4,3,n), hold on
    plot(mu0,post(:,1),'k-','LineWidth',1.05)
    plot(mu0,post(:,2),'k:','LineWidth',1.1)
    plot(mu0,post(:,3),'k-.','LineWidth',2.1)
    plot(mu0,post(:,4),'k--','LineWidth',1.1)
    axis([min(mu0) max(mu0) 0 1]); end
```

After the first datum, notice that the two uniform priors' peaks shift exactly to the location of that datum, but the peaks of the two distributions derived from the informative priors do not. This has to happen in the case of the unbounded uniform prior (peak at -2 diopters), because this prior acts exactly as if it did not exist in this problem. The bounded prior acts similarly, also shifting its peak to -2, and is truncated at the ends of the range vector, $\mu_{\min}$ and $\mu_{\max}$. The bounds of the prior do have an effect, however. They cause a shift in the mean of the posterior distribution relative to the peak. So whereas the mean of the posterior derived from the unbounded prior will always

Programming Aside: Posterior Distributions for the Gaussian Mean and Dispersion (Fig. 3.8b)

```
mureal=-2.1; sdreal=1;
load GaussDat.mat

mumin=-6.0; mumax=6.0;
sigmin=.1; sigmax=2.5;
muvec=mumin:.1:mumax; sigvec=sigmin:.1:sigmax;
pmu=ones(length(muvec),1)/length(muvec);
psig=1./sigvec; psig=psig/max(psig);
pi1=pmu(:)*psig(:)';

floglike=@(mus,sigs,D) (-(D-mus(:)*ones(1,length(sigs))).^2./...
    (2*(ones(length(mus),1)*sigs).^2))-log(ones(length(mus),1)*sigs);

Ns=[0 10 20 50 100 500];
%Ns=[0 10 15 20 25 30];

[M V]=meshgrid(sigvec,muvec);
steps1=1; steps2=4;

figure(1); clf; hold on
mesh(M(1:steps2:end,3:steps1:end),V(1:steps2:end,3:steps1:end),...
    pi1(1:steps2:end,3:steps1:end)), colormap(bone), brighten(-.8)
plot3(M(1:end,3),V(1:end,3),pi1(1:end,3),'k-','LineWidth',.8)
for n=1:steps2:length(muvec), plot3(M(n,[3 3+steps1]),V(n,[3 3+...
        steps1]),pi1(n,[3 3+steps1]),'k-','LineWidth',1.2), end
stem3(M(1:steps2:end,3:steps1:end),V(1:steps2:end,3:steps1:end),...
     pi1(1:steps2:end,3:steps1:end),'k.')
r=axis; axis([r(1:4) 0 .00275]), view(30,25)


pi1=log(pi1)-log(max(max(pi1)));
muvec=mumin:.01:mumax; sigvec=sigmin:.01:sigmax; sigind=find(sigvec==sdreal);
[M V]=meshgrid(sigvec,muvec);

pmu=ones(length(muvec),1)/length(muvec);
psig=1./sigvec; psig=psig/max(psig);
pi1=log(pmu(:)*psig(:)'); pi1=pi1-max(max(pi1));
fnow=zeros(length(muvec),length(sigvec));

for n=2:length(Ns),
    Nnew=Ns(n-1)+1:Ns(n); Dnew=Gdraw(Nnew);

    fnew=zeros(length(muvec),length(sigvec),length(Dnew));
    for nn=1:length(Dnew),
        fnew(:,:,nn)=floglike(muvec,sigvec,Dnew(nn)); end

    fnow=fnow+sum(fnew,3);
    post1=fnow+pi1; post1=exp(post1-max(max(post1)));

    Ncut=150; skips=4;
    if n==2, xs=[]; cutoff=1; preal=sum(post1,2)/max(sum(post1,2));
        while length(xs)<Ncut, cutoff=cutoff/2;
            xs=find(preal>cutoff); end
        ys=[]; cutoff=1; preal=sum(post1,1)/max(sum(post1,1));
        while length(ys)<Ncut, cutoff=cutoff/2;
            ys=find(sum(preal,1)>cutoff); end, end
    figure(n); clf; hold on
```

```
mesh(M(xs(1:skips:end),ys(1:skips:end)),V(xs(1:skips:end),...
ys(1:skips:end)),post1(xs(1:skips:end),ys(1:skips:end))), colormap(bone)

stem3(M(xs(1:skips:end),ys(1:skips:end)),V(xs(1:skips:end),ys(1:skips:end)),...
      post1(xs(1:skips:end),ys(1:skips:end)),'k.'); r=axis;

stem3(ones(1,length(xs(1:skips:end)))*sigvec(ys(1)),...
     muvec(xs(1:skips:end)),sum(post1(xs(1:skips:end),:),2)/max...
     (sum(post1(xs(1:skips:end),:),2)),'ko','filled','k')

stem3(sigvec(ys(1:skips:end)),ones(1,length(ys(1:skips:end)))*muvec(xs...
        (end)),sum(post1(:,ys(1:skips:end)),1)/max(sum(post1(:,ys(1:...
        skips:end)),1)),'ko','filled','k')
    axis([r(1:4) 0 1]), view(30,25); end
```

correspond exactly to the peak of that posterior (calculated using the infinite bounds that define the prior), the mean of the bounded posterior is shifted relative to its peak, due to the fact that the mean is calculated only over the range of nonzero prior probability that defines the bounded prior. The mean of the bounded prior is therefore -1.74 instead of -2 diopters, after collecting the first datum.

The behavior of the dotted distribution derived from the bounded uniform prior should let us know that the prior range specified by R_μ was sufficient to encode our information about μ. If this had not been the case, the unbounded and bounded distributions would have different shapes, as would happen, for example, if the data all fell outside of R_μ. In this case, the bounded posterior would be zero everywhere, because all of the probability mass (which would be represented correctly in the unbounded posterior) would fall outside the bounds defined by R_μ. Indeed, if we had been more conservative in our selection of $\mu_{\min}$ and $\mu_{\max}$, such as $R_\mu = [-6\ 6]$, then there would be no appreciable difference between the bounded and unbounded uniform priors, in both their peak locations and their means.

Posteriors derived from the two informative priors show a different pattern of changes as data are acquired. This in particular is true of the bimodal prior, which first loses its lower-valued peak as the first 50 data are collected. After the first 50 data, the bimodal- and unimodal-prior-derived posteriors are practically identical.

Notice that the above example makes an assumption that is not usually true – namely, that the standard deviation of the likelihood function is known with certainty. In our next example, we will move beyond this assumption and use a joint prior distribution over both Gaussian parameters (μ and σ) to estimate the same mean value. This time, the uncertainty in our information concerning σ requires us to use the joint prior to marginalize over the unknown value of σ to estimate μ. This estimate will have realistic confidence intervals that, unlike in the current example, reflect our uncertain knowledge of the parameters - both μ *and* σ. Therefore, we will need to generate a joint prior for the μ and σ parameters, and marginalize over the σ-axis of the resulting joint posterior distribution for μ and σ to obtain a posterior for μ alone. We can then generate a single-value estimate from the one-dimensional posterior for μ, such as the mean or peak of that posterior.

Rather than derive the 2D joint prior over the unknown values of the μ and σ parameters, we will simply construct a 2D prior out of the two 1D Jeffreys priors over μ

and σ. How do we generate the required 2D joint prior from the two individual 1D Jeffreys priors for μ and σ? We can simply use the distributions given in (3.35) and (3.36) to compute the probability in the ij^{th} position on the 2D surface as the product $p(\mu_i \cdot \sigma_j \mid \imath) = p(\mu_i \mid \imath)p(\sigma_j \mid \imath)$, or the product of the ith and j^{th} probabilities from the right-hand equations. This is shown graphically in the first (upper left-hand) panel of Figure 3.8b, where $p(\mu_i \cdot \sigma_j \mid R_{\mu\sigma} \cdot \imath) = p(\mu_i \mid R_{\mu\sigma} \cdot \imath)p(\sigma_j \mid R_{\mu\sigma} \cdot \imath)$ is plotted, using $R_\mu = [-6, 6]$ and $R_\sigma = [0.1, 2.5]$ -although notice that the range is compressed in all but the first panel to show more of the detail in these 2D probability surfaces.

Now we can compare the marginal distributions over μ obtained from the 2D surfaces from Figure 3.8b to the distributions derived from the uniform prior shown in Figure 3.8a. The distributions derived from the same portions of the full dataset in these two figures always have identical mean values. This is a consequence of the symmetry of the Gaussian function, which is computed from the square of the ratio of $\mu_i - D$ to σ_j; and therefore the peak of the likelihood function will always be identical, regardless of the value of σ.

Exercises

1) Plot the three Gaussian priors using reasonable bounds and plot increments. In each plot, normalize the prior using:
   a. The maximum of the prior.
   b. The total probability.
2) Recompute the plot of Figure 3.8 for the 10-datum case by modifying the program GaussianExample2.m, using (a) σ^2. and (b) ρ in place of σ as the Gaussian uncertainty/-precision parameter. In each case, use vardef.m to compare the marginal distributions for μ to that obtained above from marginalizing over σ.

Example: Effects of Priors and Data for Inference on the 1D Cauchy Distribution
Our final example concerns the continuous Cauchy sampling distribution. The Cauchy density is defined as

$$p(r \mid \mu \cdot \alpha\imath) = \frac{1}{\pi} \frac{\alpha}{\alpha^2 + (r - \mu)^2} \quad \{ -\infty < r < \infty$$

which has a singly peaked shape (centered at μ, with width parameter α) that is visually similar to the Gaussian distribution, but with a sharper falloff in the immediate vicinity of its peak probability value (at μ) and also thicker tails. The unit Cauchy sampling distribution,

$$p(\Delta r \mid \imath) = \left[\pi(1 + \Delta r^2)\right]^1$$

will be used for our first example. This sampling distribution displays behavior different from that of the Gaussian sampling distribution as data are collected, so it provides an interesting counterpoint.

This distribution has a very unusual property: the mean of N Cauchy-distributed samples has a sampling distribution that is no narrower than the distribution of the individual samples composing the mean. This is at odds with what we observed for the Gaussian distribution, where the sampling distribution of the mean of N samples displays a distinct narrowing relative to the width of the distribution of the individual Gaussian-sample elements. Here, we will examine an example of this phenomenon and its consequences for inference.

First, let us remind ourselves of the Gaussian example: As more data are collected, the probability distribution over the mean of the dataset becomes narrower. This is demonstrated in the left-hand column of Figure 3.9a. The upper two plots show a series of samples drawn from a $\sigma = 1$ Gaussian centered at $\mu = 0$. The lower plot shows the standard deviation of the sample, divided by the square root of the number of samples, $\sigma \mid \sqrt{N}$, referred to as the **standard error**. For the mean of these 10,000 Gaussian samples, $\sigma \mid \sqrt{N}$, should drop steadily from 1 to 0.001, which we can see happens in the plot.

Why do the data and corresponding standard deviations behave differently in the second, relative to the first plot? In the upper-left plot, we see the behavior of Gaussian samples, which stay relatively close to zero at all times. In contrast, the upper-right plot displays a series of samples reasonably near zero, and also a noticeable number of samples that are off the edges of the plot (as shown in the middle-left plot). In the Gaussian plot the mean of the samples is expected to approach zero more and more closely. This 'homing-in' of the mean is demonstrated in the lower-left plot representing the width of the sampling distribution of the mean of Gaussian samples, which becomes narrower as the number of samples increases. Indeed, the mean falls reliably to one-third of its original value after only about 10 samples. In contrast, the means of the Cauchy samples do not approach the true location parameter in the same way as Gaussian samples do. This is because a substantial number of samples are drawn very far from the peak (these are shown in the middle plot in each column), the mean of samples jumps away from zero at each of these 'outliers.' Due to these jumps, the standard deviation of the estimated mean of Cauchy samples stays the same regardless of the number of samples used to compute it. This odd fact is a consequence of the thicker tails of the Cauchy as compared to the Gaussian. The more probability mass that is located in the tails, the more likely you will observe samples that are far from the location parameter of the distribution (thus pushing the mean and spread of the sample away from zero). In the Cauchy, the area in the tails causes the tendency for the sample mean to jump away from zero, and the central peak creates the tendency for the sample mean to gravitate toward zero; the trade-off between these two combine to yield a distribution for the mean of samples that maintains an exactly constant width regardless of the number of samples present (lower-right plot of Fig.3.9a).

If the mean of a dataset yields an estimate that is no better than any individual member of that dataset, then it may appear that attempting to estimate the location or scale parameter of the Cauchy would be a lost cause – or at least that estimation of the Cauchy location parameter would not benefit from observing multiple samples. As we will see, this is not the case. We are perfectly capable of estimating the location (and scale) parameter of the Cauchy, and this estimate does indeed benefit from observing multiple data samples. We simply do not make that estimate based on the mean of the observed sample. We will first examine an example problem, and then discuss the relationship between estimators, such as the sample mean, and the parameters of a sampling distribution.

Programming Aside: Sampling and Posterior Distributions for the Cauchy (Fig. 3.9b)

We begin with (3.37), and compute the posterior with respect to a uniform prior over the unknown location parameter. We will utilize a known width parameter in this example, of $\alpha = 3$:

```
% Cauchy sampling example

%D=crand(0,3,[401 1]);
%save Cdat D
load Cdat.mat
rdat=D';
Ns=[1 10 100];
mus=linspace(-25,25,1201)';
alpha=3; Om=ones(size(mus));
COL=[zeros(1,3); .5*[1 1 1]; [.3 .4 .7]];
SYM={':','--','-'};

figure(2); clf
for iN=1:length(Ns), Nnow=Ns(iN);
    rdatnow=D(1:Nnow)'; Or=ones(1,Nnow);
    floglike=sum(log(alpha)-log((alpha.^2+(Om*rdatnow-mus*Or).^2)),2)-log(pi);
    floglike=floglike-max(floglike);

    subplot(2,1,1); hold on; plot(mus, floglike, SYM{iN},'Color',COL(iN,:),'LineWidth',2);
    subplot(2,1,2); hold on; plot(mus,exp(floglike),SYM{iN},'Color',...
        COL(iN,:),'LineWidth',2); end
subplot(2,1,1); axis([mus(1) mus(end) -10 0])
subplot(2,1,2); axis([mus(1) mus(end) 0 1])
```

The Cauchy distribution describes the sampling distribution of the ratio of two Gaussian-distributed samples. Thus, if we were taking the the ratio, $r = \frac{x_1}{x_2}$ of samples from the distributions,

$$p(x_i \mid \mu_j \cdot \sigma_j \cdot \imath) = \left[\sigma_j\sqrt{2\pi}\right]^{-1} e^{-\frac{1}{2}\frac{(x_i-\mu_j)^2}{\sigma_j^2}}$$

then the Cauchy distribution describes the ratio of these samples:

$$p(r \mid \mu \cdot \alpha \cdot \imath) = \frac{1}{\pi}\frac{[\sigma_1/\sigma_2]}{[\sigma_1/\sigma_2]^2 + (r-\mu)^2}$$

To estimate the ratio $\mu = \frac{\mu_1}{\mu_2}$ from the samples $r_i = (x_1/x_2)_i$, we do not blindly compute the mean of samples. Instead, we return to (1.5):

$$\begin{aligned} p(\mu \mid \mathbf{r} \cdot \alpha \cdot \imath) &\propto \varpi(\mu)\mathcal{L}(\mu) \\ &= p(\mu \mid \imath)p(r \mid \mu \cdot \alpha \cdot \imath) \\ &= p(\mu \mid \imath)\frac{1}{\pi}\prod_i \frac{\alpha}{\alpha^2 + (r_i-\mu)^2} \qquad (3.37). \end{aligned}$$

Below we examine the result with the uniform Cauchy prior, $\varpi(\mu)$. Figure 3.9b shows the data and progression of the posterior distribution over possible ratios as the size of the dataset increases. Clearly, the posterior homes in on the theoretical ratio value, $\mu = 0$, as the size of the dataset $\boldsymbol{r}$ increases. The posterior also becomes thinner at the same time, consistent with an improved estimate of the theoretical ratio value with sample size. So what is the difference between the lack of improved estimates that we observed in Figure 3.9a and the clearly improved estimate we observe in Figure 3.9b? We are doing very different things in the two cases. In the first, we are using a shortcut-estimate of the probability location, but a given shortcut-estimate (the mean, in this case) is not

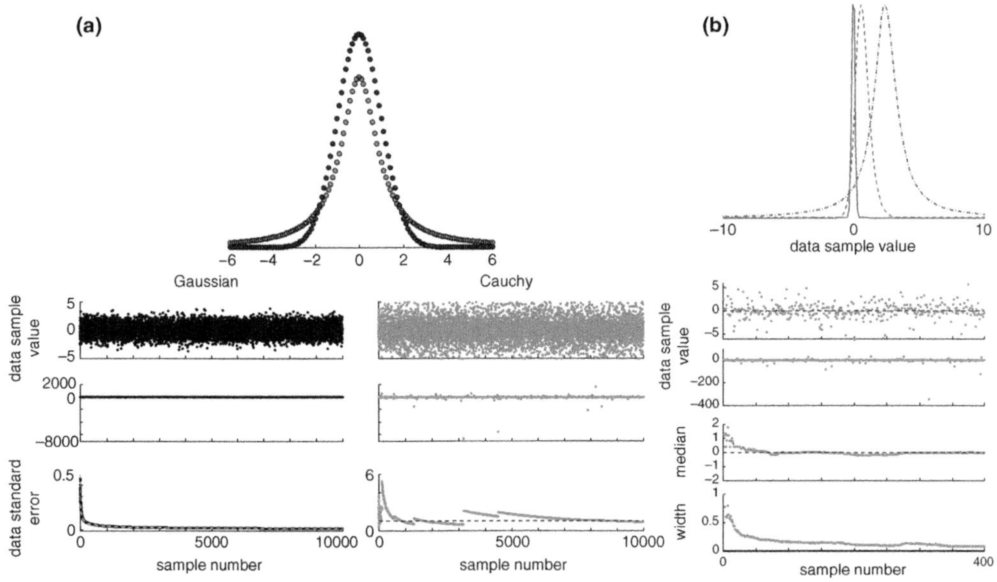

Figure 3.9 Priors and estimation for the Cauchy distribution. (a) Cauchy versus Gaussian samples. Uppermost plot shows overlaid Gaussian (black) and Cauchy (gray) sampling distributions. (left-hand column) Samples and standard errors of samples from the Gaussian distribution. (right-hand column) Samples and standard errors of samples from the Cauchy distribution. The upper two plots in each column show samples from the corresponding distribution. The uppermost of these truncates the range to ± 5, and the lower expands the range to capture all Cauchy samples. The Gaussian samples all fall within the range ± 4. The Cauchy samples have a range that is orders of magnitude larger than for the Gaussian samples, but notice that the densest central portion of samples is slightly narrower in the uppermost Cauchy plot relative to the uppermost Gaussian plot; this is predicted by the shapes of the sampling densities above. The standard error plot derived from Cauchy samples is quite irregular relative to that derived from the Gaussian samples, which is due to the occasional large departures from the median value (at zero). It is these departures that keep the standard error of the mean from decreasing as the number of samples increases, as is the case with Gaussian samples. (b) Cauchy-distributed samples and parameter estimates. Three posterior distributions are shown for the value of the Cauchy location variable after 1 (dash-dotted line), 10 (dashed line), and 100 (solid line) samples. Data samples are shown in the same format as in panel (a). The bottom two plots show parameter estimates for Cauchy location and the width of the distribution of that estimate as a function of sample number. Note that the location parameter estimate 'homes in' on the correct value at zero, and the uncertainty of that estimate decreases regularly as more data are collected. This behavior is quite similar to that observed with Gaussian data samples, estimating the Gaussian mean and standard error of the mean.

guaranteed to work in all situations. In the second case we are correctly estimating the theoretical parameter, μ directly from Bayes theorem. The use of (1.5) is will always produce the correct estimate, when such an estimate exists. The confusion arises because in many cases (e.g., the case of the Gaussian sampling distributions), it happens that the best estimate of the theoretical location parameter is given by the mean of the observed sample:

$$p(\mu \mid d \cdot \imath) \propto \mathcal{L}(\mu) = \prod_i [\sigma\sqrt{2\pi}]^{-1} e^{-\frac{1}{2}\frac{(x_i-\mu)^2}{\sigma^2}}$$

$$\propto e^{-\frac{N}{2\sigma^2}\left[\overline{x^2}-\bar{x}^2\right]} = e^{-\frac{1}{2}\left[\frac{\sigma}{\sqrt{N}}\right]^{-2}\left[\overline{x^2}-\bar{x}^2\right]}$$

where the maximum of the posterior must occur at the mean, and the width of the posterior is $\sqrt{N^{-1}}$ of the width of the (single-datum) sampling distribution.

In the case of the Cauchy distribution, the peak location (again for the uniform prior) occurs near the median, not he mean, of the sample. If the prior had been a Cauchy instead of a uniform prior, the estimate would be near that of the median of the dataset plus an additional 'datum' at the location of the prior. In either case the exact equation of the Cauchy location derived from a given dataset should be obtained directly from (3.37) rather than through the use of a shortcut-estimate, such as an assumption of the mean or median.

We see from Figure 3.9b that it is perfectly reasonable to estimate the location parameter when data are Cauchy distributed, even though the mean of the distribution is undefined and the standard error of the mean of samples fails to decrease as more data are collected. Despite these anomalies of the Cauchy distribution, if we proceed via Bayes' theorem as the basis for our data analysis we will extract the information that is available from Cauchy data.

Exercises

1) Plot the three Cauchy priors using reasonable plot increments. In each plot, normalize the prior using:
   a. The maximum of the prior.
   b. The total probability.
2) Write and execute a program to draw samples from a Cauchy distribution using the random number generator crand.m in the following steps.
   a. write a loop to run $N = 1000$ times
   b. draw n samples from the Cauchy random number generator
   c. compute the standard error of those numbers
   d. find the median of those standard errors

   Run this loop once with n = 10 and once with n = 100. Does the result at (c) differ in the two cases? Run the loop with n = 10 and n = 100 again, but replacing the Cauchy random number generator with the Gaussian number generator. Does the result change?

3.6 Summary

In the second chapter we learned how to use the likelihood function as the basis for inferences from data, and the superiority of basing inferences on the likelihood function as opposed to the sampling distribution was demonstrated with an in-depth look at an example of the optional-stopping problem. Here, we have completed the training needed to perform full Bayesian measurements of parameter values, including assigning uninformed priors over parameters. Section 3.5 in particular computed posterior distributions over parameter values based on the combination of prior and likelihood, and examined the effects of different types of prior information on the final measurement. In the next chapter we will take a step beyond the minimal elements of a Bayesian analysis, expanding our toolbox to include decisions and predictions from posterior distributions.

3.6.1 Prior Paralysis: Don't Be a Victim

The topic of selecting a prior probability distribution over a parameter is still an area of active research, and different researchers and analysts have differing opinions on how to proceed. We should not be paralyzed by such controversy, however, because as we demonstrated in Section 3.5, the form of the prior becomes less and less relevant as more data are collected. In the remainder of the text we will focus on Jeffreys priors, recognizing that they will generally have minimal impact on our final inferences. Further more, the extent of any impact is lessened considerably by a moderately sized dataset ($\sim 20 - 100$ observations); and is practically nonexistent for a large-sized (> 100 observations) dataset.

Indeed, we can always check the effect of different types of prior information, recomputing a posterior distribution based on Jeffreys, uniform, conjugate or informed priors. This allows us to see just how important our choice of prior distribution really was. When it is relatively unimportant (e.g., parameter estimates differ by much less than the width of any of the candidate posteriors), we can simply note this and proceed. When we have very little or poor-quality data, our conclusions must necessarily be tentative. In such a case, we can again examine a range of plausible (or implausible!) prior-distribution options, and note the possible variations of our conclusions due to this in our analysis. In neither case (a great deal or small amount of data), however, should we be paralyzed by the choice of prior and fail to complete the analysis. If we are forced to do the best we can with limited data, we cannot expect to make the same highly precise inferences that we would if there were a great deal of data. In these cases one can still often draw tentative conclusions, or perhaps conclude that nothing can be inferred even tentatively – all of which is important information to have in order to move forward with a research program. At the very least, such an analysis will point the direction toward the type or amount of data that *should* be collected in future to support the level of certainty we desire.

3.6.2 Comparison to the Frequentist Algorithm

Here we have developed the capability to use information about the problem that is *not* contained in the current experimental data – our prior information. Although the most common source of prior information is prior experiments and the outcomes of those experiments, we have focused here on the extreme case of prior information specifying complete ignorance of the value of the parameter of interest. Notice, though, that this does not mean we are totally ignorant about everything concerning the variable of interest – just its numerical value. In fact, it is precisely by taking advantage of our prior information concerning the type of information conveyed by a particular variable within the likelihood function that we can construct the Jeffreys prior to encode complete ignorance of a parameter's numerical value.

There are two major advantages gained by a system of inference that can encode and use prior information. The first is the obvious advantage described above, obtained by using all of the available information: indeed, ignoring information except that contained in the current dataset is simply wasteful, because using more relevant information necessarily improves our inferences. The second advantage is less obvious, and was demonstrated in the Gaussian example of the previous section. Encoding our prior information concerning several unknown variables allows us to derive an expression for the joint posterior over multiple variables, from which we can use marginalization to eliminate theoretically uninteresting, or 'nuisance' parameters from our final inference. The width of the marginalized posterior for the remaining parameter of interest gives an accurate representation of the precision of our information concerning the value of that parameter. Not only is marginalizing over nuisance parameters the most honest way to proceed when there is uncertainty concerning more than one model variable, but it can also improve the precision of the final estimate of one of the variables of interest when we marginalize over the remaining parameters, as we saw in the final worked example of the Gaussian example problem.

In the realm of frequentist null-hypothesis testing, there is only one probability distribution that need be assigned - the sampling distribution. This distribution can be assigned prior to data analysis, and in this sense is a prior probability distribution - about possible datasets. But as far as prior probability distributions concerning possible *parameter* values are concerned, it is not admissible to even talk about such prior (or posterior) probability distributions under the frequentist program, because all probabilities must be interpretable as frequencies. This means that we cannot incorporate information from prior experiments in the same principled way that is allowed within Bayesian statistics. Nor it is possible to marginalize over nuisance parameters, which bars us from separating the effects of each parameter within the model, as demonstrated above, to see the precision with which each can be estimated on its own.

3.6.3 What's Next?

In a sense, we have completed our training: we have gained an understanding of the two main elements of Bayes' theorem (prior and likelihood), and learned to apply (1.5) in basic realistic applications that included marginalizing over nuisance parameters. Despite this, there are two elements of the Bayesian statistical program that we have still to explore: prediction and decision.

As part of our understanding of any neural circuit or system, we will generally want to predict its behavior in future experiments and contexts. Prediction is also an integral part of the simulation-experiment-analysis cycle described in Figure 1.3. This is the topic of the first half of Chapter 4.

One of the reasons we may want to predict future states of a system is to use our information about the system to make decisions. Once we understand how a particular system or organism will behave in various circumstances, we are in a position to make decisions about which circumstances (potential inputs to the system) will produce the most beneficial outcomes. Our exploration of the topic of Bayesian decision theory (second half of Chapter 4) will touch on both the probabilities that are required to make optimal decisions, and also on what it means to produce beneficial outcomes. There we will see that decision theory incorporates the first truly subjective elements into our calculations. After completing our examination of these final two elements of the theory underlying Bayesian statistics, we will take an in-depth look at measurement (Chapter 5) and model selection (Chapter 6).

CHAPTER FOUR

PREDICTION AND DECISION

Now that we have examined each of the constituents of our basic data-processing equation (1.5), as well as its application in a few example problems, we are in a position to extend our analytical range beyond basic scientific inference (encoded in the posterior distribution), and into the realms of prediction and decision. As we will see, both of these subjects simply build upon our previous results involving the posterior distribution as encoded by (1.5):

$$p(\boldsymbol{\mu}|\boldsymbol{d}\cdot\imath)=\frac{p(\boldsymbol{\mu}|\imath)p(\boldsymbol{d}|\boldsymbol{\mu}\cdot\imath)}{p(\boldsymbol{d}|\imath)}\propto\varpi(\boldsymbol{\mu})\mathcal{L}(\boldsymbol{\mu}) \qquad (1.5).$$

Our discussion of prediction will have a dual focus: first, we will explore the types of data we can expect to observe in the future, based on any previously observed data and our underlying model of that data. We will then examine the topic of state estimation, which incorporates the idea of a system that displays dynamic behavior and whose internal state can be best described by considering both our current observations of the system and also our predictions regarding the current state of the system derived from past observations of the system (you can think of this in terms of the act of tracking a thrown ball, combining current visual information indicating a moving ball's location with a prediction about its current location based on having seen the ball in motion and general physical knowledge of moving objects). Finally, we will take a closer look at the concept of a loss function (first introduced in Chapter 2) and relate loss functions and probability distributions to final decisions, such as the choice to hurry down a flight of stairs, or the choice of a particular single-number summary that best conveys the result of a scientific experiment.

Roughly, we can think of prediction as an exercise in taking our previous knowledge of an underlying system or phenomenon to assign a sampling distribution for future observations from that system. Given that prediction relies heavily on our previous information regarding the system whose behavior is to be predicted, any posterior distributions that we might have computed for the system's parameters will be of obvious relevance to the predictive enterprise. Decision-making takes this a step further, making use of our knowledge of the underlying system parameters and our ability to predict system-outputs when that system is given different inputs. If you know how the system will behave when you give it different inputs, then you can give it the input that will, with highest probability, produce the most desirable outputs; the essence of decision-making is in selecting the inputs (decisions) that will produce the most advantageous outputs, or that will make the best compromises when the output can only be predicted imprecisely. These rough descriptions of prediction and decision clearly reference the posterior distribution, as well as several of the operations on probability distributions we have encountered in previous chapters.

Prediction and decision are defined:

(1) **Prediction:** There are two general types of prediction with which we will be concerned: predictions of future datasets when the system parameters are stable, and predictions of the future parameters of a time-evolving system.

In the first case, we are asking a question such as: After observing my current dataset ($\boldsymbol{d}$), what is the probability of observing a new dataset, $\boldsymbol{d}'$? We will see below that, starting with an N-dimensional posterior over the parameters of the likelihood, the desired probability is the N-dimensional integral of the $N+D$ dimensional probability volume describing the new (unknown) D-element dataset ($\boldsymbol{d}'$) and the N parameters (μ) underlying data generation (as per our background information, $\imath$):

$$\begin{aligned} p(\tilde{\boldsymbol{d}}|\boldsymbol{d}\cdot\imath) &= \int d\mu p(\mu\cdot\tilde{\boldsymbol{d}}|\boldsymbol{d}\cdot\imath) \\ &= \int d\mu p(\mu|\boldsymbol{d}\cdot\imath)p(\tilde{\boldsymbol{d}}|\mu\cdot\boldsymbol{d}\cdot\imath) = \int d\mu p(\mu|\boldsymbol{d}\cdot\imath)p(\tilde{\boldsymbol{d}}|\mu\cdot\imath) \\ &= \int d\mu\varpi(\mu)p(\tilde{\boldsymbol{d}}|\mu\cdot\imath) \end{aligned}$$

In other words, observing experimental data tells us about the parameters of our underlying model of the data, and this model should be a valid description not just of the data already observed, but also new as-yet-unobserved data.[1] The fact that old and new data share a common underlying model of their generation is what allows us to make predictions for future data.

When this is not the case, and we are dealing with a time-evolving system (a moving limb, a growing body, a brain reorganizing itself following stroke or TBI), we are likely to be interested in predicting future states (sets of parameters) describing the system rather than in predicting future datasets. These future states will be related to previous states of the system through a set of equations called state evolution or state update functions, $\boldsymbol{\Phi}_{\Delta t}$, that define changes that occur in the state variables, $\boldsymbol{\vartheta}$ during the time interval Δt:

$$\begin{aligned} \vartheta_{t(1)} &= \Phi_{\Delta t(1)}(\vartheta_{t-1(1)}) \\ &\vdots \\ \vartheta_{t(n)} &= \Phi_{\Delta t(n)}(\vartheta_{t-1(n)}) \end{aligned}$$

and we will see how to apply state evolution functions to a posterior distribution describing previous states of the system to make predictions regarding later states of the system.

(2) **Decision:** What is the best decision regarding some hypothesis, policy, etc. that can be made after observing the data? Previously, we have only been concerned with the best possible inference: Inferences are based on information only, and therefore are equated with probability distributions alone. Decisions, on the other hand, depend on potential outcomes, and we have individual preferences regarding outcomes.

[1] Also, notice that the final term $p(\boldsymbol{d}'|\mu\cdot\imath) \neq \mathcal{L}(\mu)$, because the data are yet to be observed and a likelihood function describes a known dataset and unknown parameter.

For example, the decision to hurry down a short flight of stairs can have positive or negative outcomes (safely reaching the bottom in time to to catch the subway train vs. falling down those same steps) that are very little different when one is young (such falls do not usually result in long-term injury), but can have disastrously different outcomes for an elderly person or to one suffering from osteogenesis imperfecta (falls often result in broken bones, long and costly hospitalization, even death). So even when there is precisely the same probability of falling (if our information suggests the same likelihoods of the various outcomes), the decision to hurry down a flight of stairs will also depend on the **value**, which can be positive (**gain**) or negative (**loss**), we assign to each of those possible outcomes. The basic decision equation is conditioned on the action to be taken, because different actions will naturally result in certain outcomes being more or less probable. It uses the information in the posterior regarding possible states of the world, states that might result from our action, as a weight function for averaging over the values (v) of those world-states,

$$\langle V_a \rangle = \int d\boldsymbol{\mu}\, v(\boldsymbol{\mu}, a) p(\boldsymbol{\mu}|\boldsymbol{d} \cdot a \cdot \imath)$$

This computation provides the *expectation* of the value associated with possible outcomes of choosing the action a, where outcomes that are more probable (based on our previous experience) should obviously contribute more to the expected value than outcomes judged less likely. The expected value of an action tells us the overall positive or negative value of an *action* weighted by the likely outcomes of the action, and can be used as a metric for comparing the utility of choosing one action over another.

4.1 Predictive Sampling Distributions

Prediction in this context refers to a sampling distribution that encodes our predictions regarding the likely values of observed (future) data. There are two types of predictive distribution: the prior and posterior predictive distribution, where the difference is determined by the information used to define the predictive sampling distribution – either the prior or posterior probability distribution over the parameters of that sampling distribution. The former for example is a prediction of future datasets based on the information contained in the prior over the parameters, and defines the sampling distribution of the data (which is itself our prior information regarding future possible datasets). Here, data values should have a higher probability in the prior predictive sampling distribution if the parameters that produce those data values are considered more likely in the prior. The equation describing the prior predictive sampling distribution is

$$\begin{aligned} p(\tilde{\boldsymbol{d}}|\imath) &= \int d\Theta p(\tilde{\boldsymbol{d}} \cdot \Theta|\imath) \\ &= \int d\Theta p(\Theta|\imath) p(\tilde{\boldsymbol{d}}|\Theta \cdot \imath) \\ &= \int d\theta_1 d\theta_2 \cdots d\theta_N p(\theta_1 \cdot \theta_2 \cdot \cdots \theta_N \cdot |\imath) p(\tilde{\boldsymbol{d}}|\theta_1 \cdot \theta_2 \cdot \cdots \theta_N \cdot \imath) \end{aligned}$$

The first line starts with the joint probability over possible future datasets $\tilde{\boldsymbol{d}}$ and the parameters of the sampling distribution (which itself encodes the relationship between theoretical parameters, Θ, and those data). The second line expands that joint probability using the product rule, and the last line expands the parameter term to make it clear that Θ can contain many different parameter values, $\theta_1\theta_2 \cdots \theta_N$, depending on the complexity of the sampling distribution. Taking this logic a step further, we have the posterior predictive (sampling) distribution if we have already observed some data. These data will allow us to refine our prior knowledge of the parameters, Θ; that is, observed data allows us to update the prior and compute a posterior distribution over Θ. The prior predictive then becomes the posterior predictive distribution:

$$
\begin{aligned}
p(\tilde{\boldsymbol{d}}|\boldsymbol{d} \cdot \iota) &= \int d\Theta p(\tilde{\boldsymbol{d}} \cdot \Theta|\boldsymbol{d} \cdot \iota) \\
&= \int d\Theta p(\Theta|\boldsymbol{d} \cdot \iota)P(\tilde{\boldsymbol{d}}|\Theta \cdot \iota) \\
&= \int d\theta_1 d\theta_2 \cdots d\theta_N p(\theta_1 \cdot \theta_2 \cdot \cdots \cdot \theta_N|\boldsymbol{d} \cdot \iota)p(\tilde{\boldsymbol{d}}|\Theta \cdot \boldsymbol{d} \cdot \iota)
\end{aligned}
$$

This series of equations uses the same sequence of steps as above.[2]

Now you might be thinking: once we have assigned a sampling distribution, why can't we just use that as our prediction of future data samples? The answer is that we could, if the Θ parameters of the sampling distribution were known. Since our knowledge of the values of the Θ parameters is unlikely to be certain, we cannot simply use the sampling distribution, with known Θ parameters inserted, to generate predictions for future data. Instead, we compute a weighted average of all possible sampling distributions (parameters inserted into the sampling distribution), weighting each possible sampling distribution [$p(\tilde{x}|\Theta \cdot x \cdot \iota) = p(\tilde{x}|\Theta \cdot \iota)$ term above] by the probability that a particular set of system parameters (set of values contained in Θ) is the correct set. This scaling is given by the posterior distribution over $\Theta, p(\Theta|x \cdot \iota)$, which tells us about which of the Θ parameter values is likely to be correct, and by extension which sampling distributions will yield the most accurate predictions of future data. Since the definition of the average of x-values is $\langle x \rangle = \int dx\, xp(x|\iota)$, where each possible x-value is weighted by the corresponding probabilities $p(x|t)$, we can see by analogy that the average of sampling distributions is $\int d\Theta p(\tilde{\boldsymbol{d}}|\Theta \cdot \iota)p(\Theta|\boldsymbol{d} \cdot \iota)$, where the sampling distributions $p(\tilde{\boldsymbol{d}}|\Theta \cdot \iota)$ (whose identities depend on the value of Θ) are weighted by the posterior probabilities over Θ parameters. The same logic applies to the prior predictive distribution, but here it is our prior information regarding parameter values [$p(\Theta)|\iota$] that is used to weight each possible sampling distribution in the weighted average, $\int d\Theta p(\Theta|\iota)p(\tilde{\boldsymbol{d}}|\Theta \cdot \iota)$. These calculations can also give predictions about any function of the data such as its mean, dispersion, or other more ad hoc measures, through a coordinate transform (see Appendix C).

In the remainder of this section we will examine a series of examples of both predicting new datasets, and functions of those datasets. First, we will examine a prediction for

[2] Here we also make use of the fact that, when the parameters Θ are known, $p(\tilde{\boldsymbol{d}}|\Theta \cdot \iota) = p(\tilde{\boldsymbol{d}}|\Theta \cdot \boldsymbol{d} \cdot \iota)$. In other words, knowing $\boldsymbol{d}$ will not help us to predict $\tilde{\boldsymbol{d}}$ when the Θ parameters are also known.

a new dataset (i.e., sampling distribution of new data) based on data observed in an experiment where we have assigned a Gaussian error distribution. From there, we will move on to prediction of the mean and dispersion of new datasets. This sequence of first finding the sampling distribution for new data, and then predicting functions of new data, will be duplicated for different error functions and observed datasets. Finally, we will examine how prediction can be used for optimal state estimation in time-varying systems.

Exercises

1) Describe the difference between a predictive sampling distribution and a 'regular' sampling distribution (the distributions described at the start of Chapter 3).
2) Describe the predictive distribution in terms of averages of sampling distributions.
3) For what is the posterior predictive distribution used?

4.1.1 Prior Predictive

The prior predictive distribution is defined as the expectation over the space of sampling distributions indicated by prior information, with respect to the prior over the unknown parameter values used to define that space of sampling distributions. Although that's a mouthful, the idea is relatively straightforward: the sampling distribution, $p(\tilde{\boldsymbol{d}}|\Theta \cdot \imath)$, is agnostic regarding the actual value(s) of the parameter θ – it simply states that the probability of a specific dataset requires knowledge of the value of the θ parameter. But when this parameter is itself unknown, how do we go about generating samples from the distribution? The answer is that we can marginalize over unknown parameter values by recognizing that we are describing a case in which both the (future, as-yet-unobserved) dataset $\tilde{\boldsymbol{d}}$ and the parameter θ are unknown: $p(\tilde{\boldsymbol{d}}|\imath)$. Marginalization over the unknown θ parameter then proceeds as expected, with respect to the prior over the θ parameter:

$$
\begin{aligned}
p(\tilde{\boldsymbol{d}}|\imath) &= \int d\theta p(\tilde{\boldsymbol{d}} \cdot \theta|\imath) \\
&= \int d\theta p(\theta|\imath) p(\tilde{\boldsymbol{d}}|\theta \cdot \imath)
\end{aligned}
$$

The result is a sampling distribution, $p(\tilde{\boldsymbol{d}}|\imath)$, that depends only on our prior information, having marginalized over all unknown variables. Because it contains no unknown terms, it can be used to simulate datasets in the manner described in Chapter 3. These simulated datasets are primarily of use in thinking about the data you would expect to see experimentally, based on your prior information about the problem at hand, and qualitatively assessing whether samples generated from the prior predictive have the expected character (and if not, to think about the prior parameters that might do a better job of capturing your intuitions about the data, and how/why they differ from the prior parameters you had previously set). Of course, it is often possible to perform this exercise mentally, once the prior predictive distribution is plotted, assuming you are dealing with one- and two-dimensional distributions. The benefit of sampling occurs in cases where the unknown parameter is high-dimensional, as in $p(\tilde{\boldsymbol{d}}|\Theta \cdot \iota)$, where $\Theta = \theta_1 \cdot \theta_2 \cdot \dots \cdot \theta_N$. In these cases it is often difficult to represent a sampling distribution graphically, let alone produce a mental image, and data samples drawn from the distribution can be used to this purpose.

In addition, the prior predictive appears naturally within model comparison, because for a particular observed dataset it gives the likelihood of the data model (i.e., the model of the data encoded in ι, used to construct the prior predictive). Although we will wait until Chapter 6 to examine model comparison in detail, we should understand the effect of having a broad, uninformed versus an informed prior for these computations. The last example of this subsection will therefore examine the effect of restricting the prior range on the prior predictive sampling distribution.

Exercises

1) How does a prior distribution over parameters enter the prior predictive sampling distribution?
2) What type of probability distribution is the prior predictive (prior, posterior, sampling, likelihood), and why?
3) In computing the prior predictive, which of the quantities are known:
   a. parameter values, Θ
   b. previous data, $\boldsymbol{d}$
   c. future data, $\tilde{\boldsymbol{d}}$
4) How does the prior predictive differ from the likelihood, including how they are used?

Example: Simulating from the Binomial Prior Predictive

The binomial distribution is one of the most oft-encountered distributions in data analysis because of the ubiquity of dichotomous outcomes: success or failure, life or death, detected or undetected, favorable or unfavorable, win or loss. Despite its commonplace nature, we often have difficulty picturing the correspondence between the continuously scaled binomial rate parameter, θ, and dichotomous outcomes that are reasonably associated with a given rate. This is particularly true of rates that deviate from $\theta = 0.5$, because they are more likely to produce long runs of 1s ($\theta \gg 0.5$) or 0s ($\theta \ll 0.5$), and these are often seen as 'unnatural' by the human eye.

We will begin with the simplest case: the scenario in which your prior information is uniform over the range of possible values of the binomial rate parameter. In this case, the problem is

$$
\begin{aligned}
p(\tilde{\boldsymbol{d}}|\iota) &= \int_0^1 d\theta p(\tilde{\boldsymbol{d}} \cdot \theta|\iota) \\
&= \int_0^1 d\theta p(\theta|\iota) p(\tilde{\boldsymbol{d}}|\theta \cdot \iota)
\end{aligned}
$$

$$= \int_0^1 d\theta(1)\left[\binom{N}{S}\theta^s(1-\theta)^{N-S}\right]$$
$$\propto \int_0^1 d\theta \frac{N!}{S!(N-S)!}\theta^S(1-\theta)^{N-S}$$

where notice that we have not dropped the multiplicity term as we would have when computing (1.5). The reason for this difference is that $p(\tilde{\boldsymbol{d}}|\theta \cdot \iota)$ is a sampling distribution, and the shape of the 2D sampling probability with coordinates (θ, S) depends on the binomial coefficient which itself is a function of N (here a constant) and S (here unknown).

We can stop here, because we will, throughout this chapter, use numerical techniques to analyze predictive distributions and to draw samples from those distributions. We start, therefore, by constructing a 2D distribution over (θ, S) assuming a constant N (or, for the negative binomial, over (θ, N) with constant S). This 2D probability surface ($N = 30$) is shown in Figure 4.1a. Next, numerical integration over the θ axis with respect to a uniform prior (Fig. 4.1b) yields the prior predictive distribution (Fig. 4.1c).

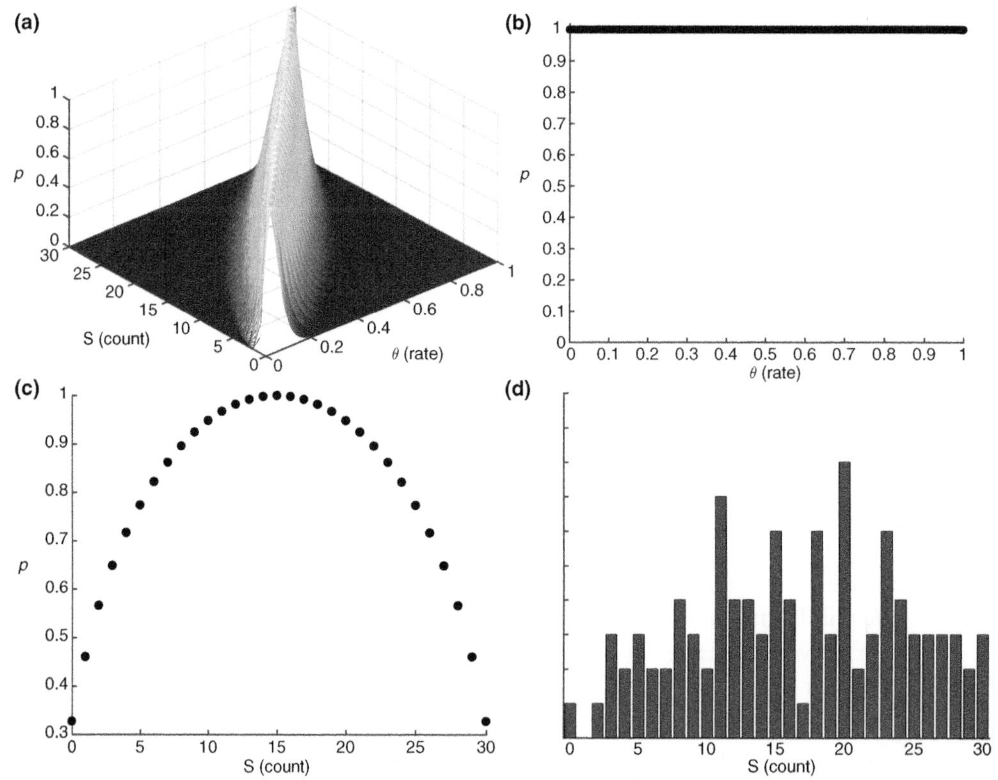

Figure 4.1 Prior predictive and sampling for the binomial. (a) Set of sampling distributions (over S) forming a 2D probability surface. The high-probability ridge traces the relation $S = N\theta$. (b) Uniform prior distribution over the unknown binomial rate parameter, θ. (c) Prior predictive sampling distribution over binomial counts, S, after 30 Bernoulli trials. The uniform prior yields a symmetrical prior predictive sampling distribution. (d) Samples drawn from the prior predictive distribution.

Programming Aside: Binomial Prior Predictive and Sampling (Fig. 4.1)

```
%%%%%%%%%%%%%%%%%%%%%%%%%%%%%%%%%%%%%%%%
%%% Binomial Prior Predictive (F4.1) %%%
N=30; Slist=[0:N]'*ones(1,301); thetas=ones(size(Slist,1),1)* linspace(0,1,301);


%%% F4.1a %%%
Lnow=lnfactorial(N)-(lnfactorial(Slist)+lnfactorial(N-Slist))+...
     Slist.*log(thetas)+(N-Slist).*log(1-thetas);
Lnow(isnan(Lnow))=0; Lnow=Lnow-max(Lnow);  %nan generated when p=1
figure(5); clf;
mesh(thetas(1,2:end-1),Slist(:,1),exp(Lnow(:,2: end-1)));
xlabel('\theta; (rate)','FontName','Arial','FontSize',13)
ylabel('S (count)','FontName','Arial','FontSize',13)
zlabel('p','FontName','Arial','FontSize',13)
view(-41,44.5)


%%% F4.1b %%%
pri=zeros(1,size(thetas,2))-log(N+1);
figure(6); clf;
plot(thetas,exp(pri),'ko','MarkerFaceColor','k','MarkerSize',8);
r=axis; axis([r(1:2) 0 .05]); box off
xlabel('\theta; (rate)','FontName','Arial','FontSize',13)
ylabel('p','FontName','Arial','FontSize',13)


%%% F4.1c %%%
Lnow=logsum(Lnow+ones(size(Slist,1),1)*pri,2,diff(thetas(1,1:2)));
figure(7); clf;
plot(Slist(:,1),exp(Lnow),'ko','MarkerFaceColor','k','MarkerSize',8); box off;
ylabel('p','FontName','Arial','FontSize',13)
xlabel('S (count)','FontName','Arial','FontSize',13)


%%% F4.1d %%%
BinTrials=N;
N=101;
tdraw=rand(N,1);
cumpdrawn=tdraw;
tevald=0:BinTrials;

Bevald=exp(Lnow);
sumBevald=sum(Bevald);
cumpevald=cumsum(Bevald./sumBevald);

cumind=nan(1,N);
for nbr=1:N,
cumind(nbr)=findnearestN(cumpevald,cumpdrawn(nbr),1); end
Bdraw=tevald(cumind);

figure(8); clf; hold on
[N X]=hist(Bdraw,Slist(:,1));
bar(X,N,'FaceColor',.25*[1 1 1])
box off; axis([-.5 30.5 0 10])
xlabel('S (count)','FontName','Arial','FontSize',13)
```

Finally, we sample from this distribution via the method outlined in the first section of Chapter 3. Notice that the output of our numerical integration over the θ parameter feeds directly into the sampling algorithm, so there is no need for further processing of that output before it can be used for sampling (see Programming Aside: 'Binomial Prior Predictive and Sampling'). One hundred one such samples of $N = 30$ coin flips using the prior predictive sampling distribution are plotted in Figure 4.1d.

The other case we should consider is that of the uninformed Jeffreys prior, $\varpi_J(\theta) \propto [\theta(1-\theta)]^{-1/2}$ assigned over the range of possible values of the binomial rate parameter, $0 < \theta < 1$. This calculation, based on negative binomial sampling,

Programming Aside: Negative Binomial Prior Predictive and Sampling

```
%%%%%%%%%%%%%%%%%%%%%%%%%%%%%%%%%%%%%%%%%
%%% NegBinom Prior Predictive %%%
S=12; Nlist=[S:1200]'*ones(1,301);
thetas=ones(size(S,1),1)*linspace(0,1,301);

%%% a %%%
Lnow=lnfactorial(Nlist-1)-(lnfactorial(S-1)+lnfactorial(Nlist-S))+...
    S.*log(thetas)+(Nlist-S).*log(1-thetas);
Lnow(isnan(Lnow))=0; Lnow=Lnow-max(Lnow);  %nan generated when p=1
Lnow(isnan(Lnow))=0;

figure(5); clf;
mesh(thetas(1,2:end),Nlist(:,1),exp(Lnow(:,2:end))); view(-9.8,67.6)
xlabel('\theta; (rate)','FontName','Arial','FontSize',13)
ylabel('N (count)','FontName','Arial','FontSize',13)
zlabel('p','FontName','Arial','FontSize',13)

%%% b %%%
pri=-.5*(log(thetas(1,:))+log(1-thetas(1,:))); pri(isinf(pri))=nan;
pri=pri-max(max(pri)); pri(isnan(pri))=0;
figure(6); clf;
plot(thetas,exp(pri),'ko','MarkerFaceColor','k',...
    'MarkerSize',8); r=axis; axis([r(1:2) 0 1]); box off
xlabel('\theta; (rate)','FontName','Arial','FontSize',13)
ylabel('p','FontName','Arial','FontSize',13)

%%% c %%%
Lnow=logsum(Lnow+ones(size(Nlist,1),1)*pri,2,diff(thetas(1,1:2)));
figure(7); clf;
plot(Nlist(:,1),exp(Lnow),'ko','MarkerFaceColor','k','MarkerSize',8); box off;
ylabel('p','FontName','Arial','FontSize',13)
xlabel('N (count)','FontName','Arial','FontSize',13)

%%% d %%%
reps=101;
tdraw=rand(reps,1);
cumpdrawn=tdraw;
tevald=Nlist(:,1);

Bevald=exp(Lnow);
sumBevald=sum(Bevald);
cumpevald=cumsum(Bevald./sumBevald);
```

```
cumind=nan(1,reps);
for nbr=1:reps,
        cumind(nbr)=findnearestN(cumpevald,
        cumpdrawn(nbr),1); end
Bdraw=tevald(cumind);

figure(8); clf; hold on
[N X]=hist(Bdraw,Nlist(:,1));
bar(X,N,'FaceColor',.25*[1 1 1])
box off; axis([min(min(Nlist))-.5 max(max(Nlist))+.5 0 3])
xlabel('N (count)','FontName','Arial','FontSize',13)
```

$$P(N \mid S \cdot \theta \cdot \imath_{nb}) = \frac{(N-1)!}{(S-1)!(N-S)!}\,\theta^S\,(1-\theta)^{N-S} = \binom{N\ -1}{S_i\ -1}\theta^S\,(1-\theta)^{N-S}$$

is performed in the PA. We have truncated the Jeffreys prior at the extreme ends, $\theta = 0$ and $\theta = 1$, and renormalized to avoid the infinities that would otherwise occur at these points in the parameter space with the Jeffreys prior (which, you will recall, is the identical distribution whether we are using the binomial or the negative binomial sampling distribution.

Exercises

1) In Figure 4.1, which underlying value of the Binomial rate parameter θ is used to simulate coin flips?
2) Describe the transition from panel a→b→c→d in Figure 4.1.
3) Perform prior predictive sampling for the Binomial using the Jeffreys prior instead of the uniform prior.
4) Run the program for generating samples 100 times. For each run, draw 101 samples and compute the mean. Describe whether the mean of samples closely follows the mean of the sampling distribution. Explain why or why not.

Example: Gaussian Sampling Distribution with Truncated Jeffreys Priors

A common measurement example involves the Gaussian sampling distribution and Jeffreys priors over unknown parameters. We can take the same two probability distributions, the Gaussian sampling distribution and Jeffreys prior, and predict the datasets we would be likely to see in this scenario.

We will examine two cases: that of a known and unknown dispersion parameter, σ. In the first case, knowledge of the dispersion parameter simplifies the problem because we must marginalize only over the Gaussian location parameter, μ:

$$\begin{aligned} p(\tilde{\boldsymbol{d}}|\sigma \cdot \imath) &= \int_a^b d\mu\; p(\tilde{\boldsymbol{d}} \cdot \mu|\sigma \cdot \imath) \\ &= \int_a^b d\mu\; p(\mu|\sigma \cdot \imath)\; p(\tilde{\boldsymbol{d}}|\mu \cdot \sigma \cdot \imath) \end{aligned}$$

$$= \int_a^b d\mu (const) \left[(\sigma\sqrt{2\pi})^{-N} e^{-\frac{1}{2}\frac{\sum(\tilde{d}-\mu)^2}{\sigma^2}} \right]$$

$$\propto \int_a^b d\mu e^{-\frac{1}{2}\frac{\sum(\tilde{d}-\mu)^2}{\sigma^2}}$$

where we must choose the range (a, b) over which we will marginalize based on our background knowledge of the problem. This need not be a small range, so long as it is finite (a requirement for numerical integration); such information is always available, or we would not be able to choose recording equipment for our experiment (e.g., eyetracker, fMRI machine), as any physical device must have a finite range over which it functions. In our example problem we will use the range $(a, b) = (-10, 10)$. Notice that if we were unsure of the range that best matches our prior information, which may in part represent the prior experience of a scientist who has conducted similar experiments in the past, we may perform simulations with a range of a and b values, both to understand the effect of small changes in these variables on the final prior predictive sampling distribution and to determine whether samples produced by one set of a and b values matches our prior expectations better than those produced by another set of a and b values. In general, of course, we would like parameters such as variable ranges to be set by the underlying scientific theory.

Having set the prior range of the location parameter, and using a known dispersion ($\sigma = 3$), we can plot the 2D distribution over (μ, x), which represents the observed datum in a single observation:

$$p(\tilde{d}|\sigma \cdot \imath) \propto \int_{-10}^{10} d\mu \, e^{-\frac{1}{2}\frac{(\tilde{d}-\mu)^2}{(3)^2}}$$

Notice that, whereas the μ parameter was truncated at $(-10, 10)$ we have not discussed the possible values of x. If the prior range of the μ parameter was set based on the physical limits of a recording device (i.e., responses are positions on a computer monitor), and no responses can occur that are not within the $(-10, 10)$ range that defines the monitor, then x-values must share the same truncated range. If, however, we have set the range of μ based on past experience rather than physical limitations, then individual observations may take on values outside the range set for μ. We will assume the latter, and allow for x to take a wide range of values.

The underlying model in this example can be expanded to accommodate an unknown dispersion parameter, σ:

$$p(\tilde{d}|\imath) = \int_a^b d\mu \int_0^c d\sigma \, p(\tilde{d} \cdot \mu \cdot \sigma \cdot |\imath)$$

$$= \int_a^b d\mu \int_0^c d\sigma \, p(\mu \cdot \sigma |\imath) p(\tilde{d}|\mu \cdot \sigma \cdot \imath)$$

Programming Aside: Gaussian Prior Predictive and Sampling

```
%%%%%%%%%%%%%%%%%%%%%%%%%%%%%%%%%
%%% Gaussian Prior Predictive %%%
Nx=300; Nm=200;
Mlist=linspace(-20,20,Nm)'*ones(1,Nx);
Slist=3; xlist=ones(Nm,1)*linspace(-15,15,Nx);

%%% a %%%
Lnow=-log(Slist)-.5*log(2*pi)-.5*(Mlist-xlist).^2/Slist^2;
figure(5); clf; mesh(xlist(1,:),Mlist(:,1),exp(Lnow)); view(-61,48.5)
xlabel('x (data)','FontName','Arial','FontSize',13)
ylabel('\mu; (parameter)','FontName','Arial','FontSize',13)
zlabel('p','FontName','Arial','FontSize',13)

%%% b %%%
pri=zeros(size(Mlist(:,1)))-log(diff(Mlist([1 end])));
figure(6); clf;
plot(Mlist(:,1),exp(pri),'ko','MarkerFaceColor','k',...
    'MarkerSize',8); r=axis; axis([r(1:2) 0 .03]); box off
xlabel('\mu; (parameter)','FontName','Arial','FontSize',13)
ylabel('p','FontName','Arial','FontSize',13)

%%% c %%%
Lnow=logsum(Lnow+pri*ones(1,Nx)+log(diff(Mlist(1:2,1))),1);
figure(7); clf;
plot(xlist(1,:),exp(Lnow),'ko','MarkerFaceColor','k','MarkerSize',8);
box off; axis([min(min(xlist))-.5 max(max(xlist))+.5 0 1.04*max(exp(Lnow))])
ylabel('p','FontName','Arial','FontSize',13)
xlabel('x (data)','FontName','Arial','FontSize',13)

%%% d %%%
N=101; %sig=Slist; mu=0;
cumpdrawn=rand(N,1);
tevald=xlist(1,:);
cumpevald=cumsum(exp(Lnow));

cumind=nan(N,1);
for nbr=1:N,
  cumind(nbr)=findnearestN(cumpevald,cumpdrawn(nbr),1); end
Gdraw=tevald(cumind);

figure(8); clf; hold on
[N X]=hist(Gdraw,51);
bar(X,N,'FaceColor',.25*[1 1 1])
box off; axis([min(tevald) max(tevald) 0 10])
xlabel('x (location)','FontName','Arial','FontSize',13)
```

$$= \int_a^b d\mu \int_0^c d\sigma\, \sigma^{-1}\left[(\sigma\sqrt{2\pi})^{-1} e^{-\frac{1}{2}\frac{(\tilde{d}-\mu)^2}{\sigma^2}}\right]$$

$$\propto \int_a^b d\mu \int_0^c d\sigma\, \sigma^{-2} e^{-\frac{1}{2}\frac{(\tilde{d}-\mu)^2}{\sigma^2}}$$

where we must now also choose an upper limit for the dispersion parameter.

Programming Aside: Gaussian Prior Predictive with Unknown Dispersion Parameter and Sampling

```
%%%%%%%%%%%%%%%%%%%%%%%%%%%%%%%%%%%%%%%%%%%%%%%%%%%%%%%%%%%%%%%%%%
%%% Gaussian Prior Predictive with unknown dispersion %%%
Nx=300; Ns=201; Nm=201; c=10;
xlist=linspace(-15,15,Nx); Mlist=linspace(-20,20,Nm);
Slist=linspace(0,c,Ns+1); Slist=Slist(2:end);

Mnow=ones(Nx,1)*Mlist; xnow=xlist'*ones(1,Nm); Lnow=nan(Nx,Nm,Ns);
for i=1:Ns, Lnow(:,:,i)=-.5*(Mnow-xnow).^2/Slist(i)^2; end
Lnow(isnan(Lnow))=0; Lnow=Lnow-max(max(Lnow)); %nan generated when p=1

%%% a %%%
figure(5); clf;
mesh(Mlist,Slist,exp(squeeze(Lnow(10,:,:)))); view(-100,35)
xlabel('x (data)','FontName','Arial','FontSize',13)
ylabel('\mu; (parameter)','FontName','Arial','FontSize',13)
zlabel('p','FontName','Arial','FontSize',13)

%%% b %%%
pri=zeros(Nm,Ns)-ones(Nm,1)*log(Slist); pri=pri-max(max(pri));
figure(6); clf; mesh(Slist,Mlist,exp(pri)); view(-133.5,35);
r=axis; axis([r(1:4) 0 1]);
xlabel('\sigma; (parameter)','FontName','Arial','FontSize',13)
ylabel('\mu; (parameter)','FontName','Arial','FontSize',13)
zlabel('p','FontName','Arial','FontSize',13)

%%% c %%%
pri=pri-logsum(pri,[1 2]); Pri=nan(size(Lnow));
for n=1:Nx, Pri(n,:,:)=pri; end; Pri=logsum(Pri,[1 2 3]);
Pnow=logsum(Lnow+Pri,[2 3]); Pnow=Pnow-logsum(Pnow);
figure(7); clf;
plot(xlist,exp(Pnow),'ko','MarkerFaceColor','k','MarkerSize',8);
box off; axis([min(xlist)-.5 max(xlist)+.5 0 1.04*max(exp(Pnow))]);
ylabel('p','FontName','Arial','FontSize',13)
xlabel('x (data)','FontName','Arial','FontSize',13)

%%% d %%%
N=101; sig=Slist; mu=0;
cumpdrawn=rand(N,1);
tevald=xlist;

Pevald=Pnow;
sumPevald=sum(Pevald);
cumpevald=cumsum(exp(Pnow));

cumind=nan(N,1);
for nbr=1:N, cumind(nbr)=findnearestN(cumpevald,cumpdrawn(nbr),1); end
Gdraw=tevald(cumind);

figure(8); clf; hold on
[N X]=hist(Gdraw,51);
bar(X,N,'FaceColor',.25*[1 1 1])
box off; axis([min(tevald) max(tevald) 0 max(N)+1])
xlabel('x (location)','FontName','Arial','FontSize',13)
```

Exercises

1) Use truncated Gaussian prior over θ, with $(\mu, \theta) = (.8, .1)$
2) Characterize the difference induced in the prior predictive by using a known versus unknown dispersion parameter in the Gaussian sampling model.
3) Compare the empirical σs of the histograms of the Gaussian samples in the known versus unknown dispersion cases above.
4) Describe any changes in the parameters needed to sample from the Gaussian (see Chapter 3), and the Gaussian prior predictive.
   a. What are the advantages or disadvantages of this change for the process of sampling?
   b. What are the implications of this change in terms of the information content of the underlying distributions?

4.1.2 Posterior Predictive

The posterior predictive distribution is a straight forward extension of the prior predictive distribution, substituting the posterior distribution $p(\theta|\boldsymbol{d} \cdot \imath)$, for the prior distribution $p(\theta|\imath)$. So whereas the prior predictive is defined by the marginalization

$$p(\tilde{\boldsymbol{d}}|\imath) = \int d\theta p(\tilde{\boldsymbol{d}} \cdot \theta|\imath)$$

$$= \int d\theta p(\theta|\imath) p(\tilde{\boldsymbol{d}}|\theta \cdot \imath)$$

the posterior predictive is defined by the analogous marginalization

$$p(\tilde{\boldsymbol{d}}|d \cdot \imath) = \int d\theta p(\tilde{\boldsymbol{d}} \cdot \theta|d \cdot \imath)$$

$$= \int d\theta p(\theta|\boldsymbol{d} \cdot \imath) p(\tilde{\boldsymbol{d}}|\theta \cdot \imath)$$

The posterior distribution will be more informative than the prior distribution over the same parameter space, and should lead to a tighter clustering of the predictive distribution and samples than the prior predictive.

The most common use of the posterior predictive distribution is in simulated 'posterior predictive data checking' where samples from the posterior predictive are compared to experimental data in an effort to provide a check on the underlying model. This practice has the drawback of using a single dataset twice; once to compute the posterior, and once as part of a procedure to verify the underlying model. This use of the posterior predictive is a bastardization of the method in which a model is fitted with the help of one dataset, and predictions of the model are compared to *new* experimental data, as a test of the model. Attempting to bypass the time-consuming task of designing a new experiment and collecting additional data to be used as a test of the underlying model results in a violation of the likelihood principle, and therefore this common use of the posterior predictive should only be employed as a coarse 'sanity-check' rather than a formal test of the underlying model. The idea is that, even with incorrect model equations, one can nevertheless usually produce a best fit to observed data. A posterior predictive check may alert you to this scenario (incorrect model equations that nevertheless yield a valid fit to the data). If this coarse check fails, it may be necessary to conduct additional experiments to provide a formal test of the model in question. Formal model testing is the topic of Chapter 6.

Exercises

1) How does the posterior predictive differ from the prior predictive, and what do you predict this will mean for the shapes of the corresponding sampling distributions?
2) How is data incorporated into the posterior predictive?
3) How do the uses of the posterior predictive differ from those of the prior predictive?

Example: Binomial Rate Model

Returning to the binomial rate, and the dichotomous outcome data associated with such rates, we revisit the binomial sampling model. Here, the posterior predictive distribution is

$$
\begin{aligned}
p(\tilde{\boldsymbol{d}}|\boldsymbol{d}\cdot\imath) &= \int d\theta p(\tilde{\boldsymbol{d}}\cdot\theta|\boldsymbol{d}\cdot\imath) \\
&= \int d\theta\ p(\theta|\boldsymbol{d}\cdot\imath)p(\tilde{\boldsymbol{d}}|\theta\cdot\imath) \\
&\propto \int d\theta\ p(\theta|\imath)p(\boldsymbol{d}|\theta\cdot\imath)p(\tilde{\boldsymbol{d}}|\theta\cdot\imath) = \int d\theta\ \varpi(\theta)\mathcal{L}(\theta)p(\tilde{\boldsymbol{d}}|\theta\cdot\imath)
\end{aligned}
$$

where notice that there are two distributions written in the form $p(D|\Theta\cdot\imath)$. The first of these describes an already-observed dataset, and is therefore a likelihood function, $p(\boldsymbol{d}|\theta\cdot\imath) = \mathcal{L}(\theta)$; the second describes the probabilities of as-yet-unobserved data samples given various possible values of the rate parameter, $p(\tilde{\boldsymbol{d}}|\theta\cdot\imath)$, and is therefore a (set of) sampling distribution(s). The likelihood function is a 1D function of θ, whereas the set of sampling distributions is a 2D probability surface with coordinates $(\theta,\tilde{\boldsymbol{d}})$ where each slice through the surface parallel to the $\tilde{\boldsymbol{d}}$ axis is a sampling distribution over $\tilde{\boldsymbol{d}}$ contingent on a particular choice of θ parameter.

Here we would like again to construct an equation that will allow us to sample binary outcomes in a manner consistent with the binomial sampling distribution, but now with θ parameter chosen in a way that is informed by having observed a previous dataset ($\boldsymbol{d}$). We will again use the uniform prior, but here assume that 30 data have been observed, and that 20 of 30 were successes. From this starting point, we can expand the equation above:

$$
\begin{aligned}
p(\tilde{\boldsymbol{d}}|\boldsymbol{d} \cdot \iota) &\propto \int d\theta p(\tilde{\boldsymbol{d}} \cdot \theta|d \cdot \iota) \\
&= \int d\theta \varpi(\theta)\mathcal{L}(\theta)p(\tilde{\boldsymbol{d}}|\theta \cdot \iota) \\
&\propto \int d\theta p(\tilde{\boldsymbol{d}} \cdot \theta|\boldsymbol{d} \cdot \iota) \\
&\propto \int d\theta (const)(\theta^S[1-\theta]^{N-S}) \left(\frac{\tilde{N}!}{\tilde{S}!(\tilde{N}-\tilde{S})!}\theta^{\tilde{S}}[1-\theta]^{\tilde{N}-\tilde{S}}\right) \{N = 30, S = 20
\end{aligned}
$$

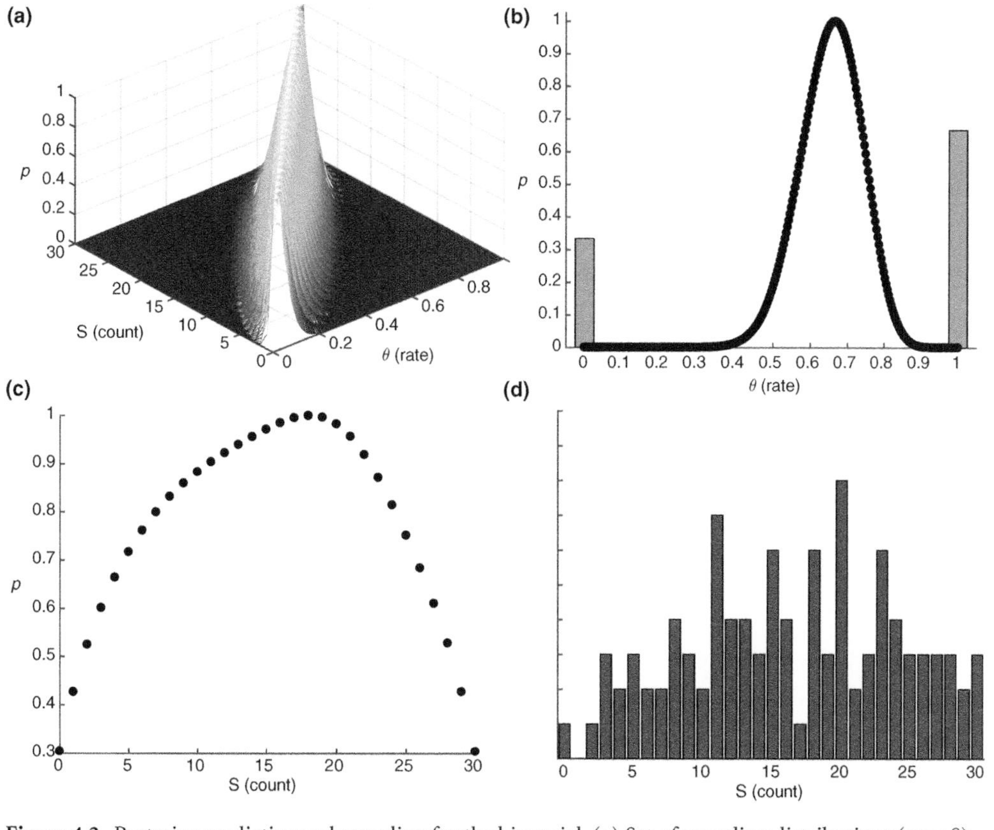

Figure 4.2 Posterior predictive and sampling for the binomial. (a) Set of sampling distributions (over S) forming a 2D probability surface, identical to that shown in 4.1a. (b) Posterior distribution over the unknown binomial rate variable, θ, based on observing 20 successes in 30 Bernoulli trials. (c) Posterior predictive sampling distribution over binomial counts, S, based on the posterior panel (b). Because the posterior indicates a rate parameter $\theta > 0.5$, the predictive distribution is asymmetrical with a peak location $S > N/2$. (d) Samples drawn from the prior predictive distribution are skewed toward higher success counts.

Programming Aside: Binomial with Sampling (Fig 4.2)

```
%%% Binomial Prior Predictive %%
Sprior=20; Nprior=30;
N=30; Slist=[0:N]; thetas=linspace(0,1,301);

%%% a %%%
Snow=Slist'*ones(1,301); thetanow=ones(size(Slist,1),1)*thetas;
Lnow=lnfactorial(N)-(lnfactorial(Snow)+lnfactorial(N-Snow))+...
     Snow.*log(thetanow)+(N-Snow).*log(1-thetanow);
Lnow(isnan(Lnow))=0; Lnow=Lnow-max(Lnow);  %nan generated when p=1
figure(5); clf;
mesh(thetas(2:end-1),Slist,exp(Lnow(:,2:end-1))); view(-41,44.5)
xlabel('\theta; (rate)','FontName','Arial','FontSize',13)
ylabel('S (count)','FontName','Arial','FontSize',13)
zlabel('p','FontName','Arial','FontSize',13)

%%% b %%%
pri=bpdf(Sprior,Nprior,thetas);
figure(6); clf;
plot(thetas,pri,'ko','MarkerFaceColor','k',...
'MarkerSize',8); r=axis; axis([r(1:2) 0 1.05*max(pri)]); box off
xlabel('\theta; (rate)','FontName','Arial','FontSize',13)
ylabel('p','FontName','Arial','FontSize',13)

%%% c %%%
pri=pri-logsum(pri,diff(thetas(1:2)));
Lnow=logsum(Lnow+ones(N+1,1)*pri,2,diff(thetas(1:2)));
Lnow=Lnow-logsum(Lnow);
figure(7); clf;
plot(Slist,exp(Lnow),'ko','MarkerFaceColor','k','MarkerSize',8);
box off; ylabel('p','FontName','Arial','FontSize',13);
xlabel('S (count)','FontName','Arial','FontSize',13);

%%% d %%%
N=101;
cumpdrawn=rand(N,1);
Bevald=exp(Lnow);
cumpevald=cumsum(Bevald);

cumind=nan(1,N);
for nbr=1:N,
    cumind(nbr)=findnearestN(cumpevald,cumpdrawn(nbr),1); end
Bdraw=Slist(cumind);

figure(8); clf; hold on
[N X]=hist(Bdraw,Slist); bar(X,N,'FaceColor',.25*[1 1 1])
box off; axis([-.5 30.5 0 10])
xlabel('S (count)','FontName','Arial','FontSize',13)
```

where we must maintain the binomial coefficient term in the sampling distribution, $p(\tilde{\boldsymbol{d}}|\theta \cdot \iota)$. On the other hand, the likelihood term, $\mathcal{L}(\theta)$, can drop the binomial coefficient because it is constant for a known (previously observed) dataset.

Thus, for a given number, say 100, of samples we can write the equation for the sampling distribution of those as-yet-unobserved 100 data:

$$p(\tilde{\boldsymbol{d}}|\boldsymbol{d}\cdot\iota) \propto \int d\theta\, \varpi(\theta)\mathcal{L}(\theta)p(\tilde{\boldsymbol{d}}|\theta\cdot\iota)$$

$$\propto \int d\theta(\theta^{S}[1-\theta]^{N-S})\left(\frac{\tilde{N}!}{\tilde{S}!(\tilde{N}-\tilde{S})!}\theta^{\tilde{S}}[1-\theta]^{\tilde{N}-\tilde{S}}\right)\{N=30, S=20, \tilde{N}=100$$

and use this to create the histogram shown in Figure 4.2. Notice that in this figure the expectation is that coin flips (or whatever binary variable is being observed) will be highly biased, despite having the identical prior information used in the binomial-based prior predictive sampling example in the previous section. The difference here is that we have obtained additional information regarding the true underlying rate of successes, in the form of prior observations of the system. These prior observations of system outputs allow us to compute a posterior over possible values of the underlying rate parameter. This in turn can be used to generate predictions, in the form of draws from the posterior predictive sampling distribution. These predictions are more likely to accurately reflect the system under study (coin/coin flipping, in this example) in the sense that they are based on more information about the system (observed data *in addition* to our prior information, instead of simply our prior information in the examples from the previous section).

Exercises

1) Describe the axes of the surface of sampling distributions, $p(\tilde{\boldsymbol{d}}|\theta\cdot\iota)$.
2) How does the prior distribution interact with the surface described by $p(\tilde{\boldsymbol{d}}|\theta\cdot\iota)$ to yield the posterior predictive?
3) How would the distribution shown in Figure 4.2c change if there were no prior data?

Example: Gaussian Model

The essence of updating your information regarding the underlying parameters of a model is to continue to refine your estimates of those parameters as more data become available. Thus, we progress from the prior predictive to the posterior predictive for generating samples from a Gaussian sampling model as new datasets become available that each pertain to the same model and underlying model parameters, thus allowing us to update our information regarding the unknown location and/or dispersion parameters of the underlying Gaussian model of the data.

When we examine the case of known dispersion in the Gaussian model the posterior predictive sampling distribution, which must only integrate over the remaining unknown (location) parameter, is

$$p(\tilde{d}|\boldsymbol{d}\cdot\sigma\cdot\iota) = \int_a^b d\mu\, p(\tilde{d}\cdot\mu|\boldsymbol{d}\cdot\sigma\cdot\iota)$$

$$= \int_a^b d\mu\, p(\mu|\boldsymbol{d}\cdot\sigma\cdot\iota)p(\tilde{d}|\mu\cdot\sigma\cdot\iota)$$

$$\propto \int_a^b d\mu\, e^{-\frac{1}{2}\frac{\sum(\boldsymbol{d}-\mu)^2}{\sigma^2}}e^{-\frac{1}{2}\frac{(\tilde{d}-\mu)^2}{\sigma^2}}$$

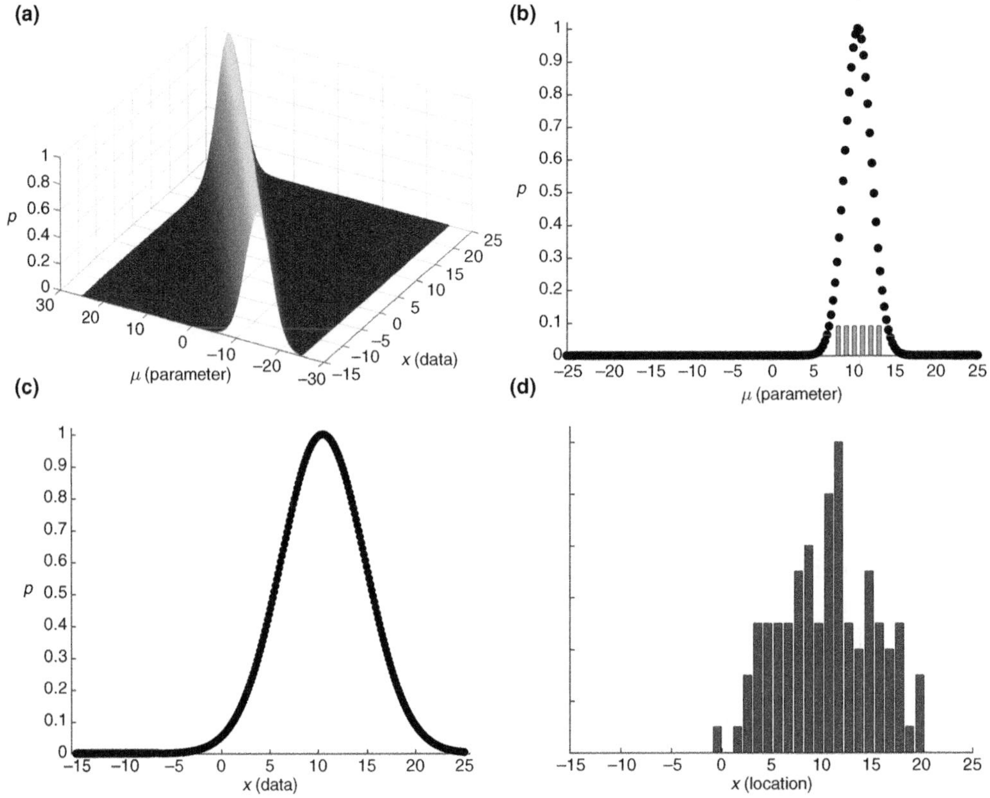

Figure 4.3 Prior predictive and sampling for the Gaussian. (a) Set of sampling distributions (over x) forming a 2D probability surface with the Gaussian location parameter μ. The high-probability ridge traces the relation $x = \mu$. (b) Posterior distribution over the unknown Gaussian location parameter, μ. The posterior peaks at just above $\mu = 10$, giving reasonably precise information regarding the location parameter. (c) Posterior predictive sampling distribution over Gaussian samples, x. The posterior yields a symmetrical prior predictive sampling distribution that is shifted toward positive sample values. (d) Samples drawn from the posterior predictive distribution are shifted toward positive sample values.

where again we choose the limits of integration (a, b) based on our background knowledge of the problem. The summation indicates that the prior dataset will usually contain multiple data, and the joint probability of all data is obtained via this sum.

For example, Figure 4.3 describes the posterior predictive distribution that results when the prior dataset is $d = [8,\ 12.5]$, and the prior range is $(a, b) = (-20,\ 20)$.

The posterior predictive distribution should not surprise us, in the sense that we should expect that it would peak at the posterior mean, given that this is the information contained in the previously observed dataset. Furthermore, as we collect further data to allow us to refine the posterior over a stable pair of Gaussian parameters, we should *expect* that those observed data will tend to support the true parameter values, and this will in turn allow us to refine our predictions regarding possible future unobserved datasets (Fig. 4.3d).

Programming Aside: Normal with Known Variance and Sampling (Fig 4.3)

```
%%%%%%%%%%%%%%%%%%%%%%%%%%%%%%%%%%%%%%%%%%%
%%% Gaussian Prior Predictive (F4.3) %%%
Xpri=nrand(10,3,[2 1]);
Nx=300; Nm=200;
Mlist=linspace(-25,25,Nm); Slist=3; xlist=linspace(-15,25,Nx);

xnow=ones(Nm,1)*xlist; Mnow=Mlist'*ones(1,Nx);
Lnow=-.5*(Mnow-xnow).^2/Slist^2; Lnow(isnan(Lnow))=0;
Lnow=Lnow-max(Lnow);  %nan generated when p=1;
figure(5); clf; mesh(xlist,Mlist,exp(Lnow)); view(-61,48.5);
xlabel('x (data)','FontName','Arial','FontSize',13);
ylabel('\mu; (parameter)','FontName','Arial','FontSize',13);
zlabel('p','FontName','Arial','FontSize',13);

pri=zeros(size(Mlist));
for n=1:length(Xpri),
  pri=pri+log(npdf(Xpri(n),
  Mlist,Slist)); end
pri=pri-logsum(pri,diff(Mlist(1:2)));
figure(6); clf;
plot(Mlist,exp(pri),'ko','MarkerFaceColor','k','MarkerSize',8);
r=axis; axis([r(1:2) 0 1.05*max(exp(pri))]); box off
xlabel('\mu; (parameter)','FontName','Arial','FontSize',13);
ylabel('p','FontName','Arial','FontSize',13);

%%% c %%%
Pri=nan(Nm,Nx);
for n=1:length(xlist), Pri(:,n)=pri'; end
Lnow=logsum(Lnow+Pri,1,diff(Mlist(1:2))); Lnow=Lnow-logsum(Lnow);
figure(7); clf;
plot(xlist(1,:),exp(Lnow),'ko','MarkerFaceColor','k','MarkerSize',8); box off;
axis([min(min(xlist))-.5 max(max(xlist))+.5 0 1.04*max(exp(Lnow))]);
ylabel('p','FontName','Arial','FontSize',13);
xlabel('x (data)','FontName','Arial','FontSize',13);

N=101;
cumpdrawn=rand(N,1);
cumpevald=cumsum(exp(Lnow));

cumind=nan(N,1);
for nbr=1:N,
  cumind(nbr)=findnearestN(cumpevald,
  cumpdrawn(nbr),1); end
Gdraw=xlist(cumind);

figure(8); clf; hold on
[N X]=hist(Gdraw,21);
bar(X,N,'FaceColor',.25*[1 1 1])
box off; axis([min(xlist) max(xlist) 0 1.05*max(N)])
xlabel('x (location)','FontName','Arial','FontSize',13)
```

Exercises

1) Notice that the data in Figure 4.3b are not really drawn from a Gaussian sampling distribution: they are simply a sequence of equally spaced values. If the data were instead drawn from a Gaussian sampling distribution (but retain the current sample's mean and standard deviation), what effect would this have on the outcome?
2) The 2D parameter space over x and μ describes an elongated 'bump' centered on the unity line. Describe the significance of the orientation of this bump (as being centered on the unity line), and what it would mean if it were differently oriented.
3) Given the general discussion of model comparison and its use of the prior predictive sampling distribution, give an example of how the posterior predictive sampling distribution might be used in a model comparison setting.

4.2 Prediction in Time-Varying Systems

In our previous examples of prediction, the focus was one predicting new datasets from our (imperfect) information regarding the unobserved state of the world (e.g., location and scale parameters of a Gaussian distribution that perhaps describe the location and scatter of dart endpoints in an experiment exploring human motor performance). These previous examples hinged on the assumption that values of variables describing the state of the world ('state variables') were constant over the relevant window of time between measuring those variables from previous observations, and the future time at which our predictions would be used. Here, we will consider cases in which (1) the state of the world is no longer constant but changes in some lawful way and (2) we are interested in predicting the time evolution of state variables based on past and current observations (rather than in predicting future observations from past observations).

State estimation will require us to combine predictions of possible values *of the state variables* suggested by prior observations with those values suggested by current observations; this combination will yield a guess, or estimate, regarding the current state of the system. Note that, using slightly different terminology, this is similar to the way our brains are thought to control the skeletal muscles of the body: motor commands are issued, and a combination of the expected consequences of our motor commands and any available sensory information are used to monitor and also correct the motion of possibly errant end-effectors (limbs, digits, etc.). State estimation will rely on two aspects of our information regarding a state and its time evolution. First, we must have a function relating our observations to the unobservable states of the system, or an **observation function.** Thus, defining $\boldsymbol{o}_t$ as the vector comprising our observations of the system at time t, we define the observation function,

$$\boldsymbol{o}_t = g(\boldsymbol{\vartheta}_t, \boldsymbol{\varepsilon}_o) \tag{4.1}$$

relating the unobservable state variables defining the system at time t (encoded in $\boldsymbol{\vartheta}_t$) to our noise-corrupted observations of that system ($\boldsymbol{o}_t$; our current dataset), where the noise sample corrupting our observations is $\boldsymbol{\varepsilon}_0$. Notice that observation noise is in the units of the observation variable(s), which will not necessarily be the units of the state variable(s) encoded in $\boldsymbol{\vartheta}$. In the current scenario we have a second source of information, because we have an expectation of the unfolding state of the system based on our prior knowledge regarding its time evolution. This second source of information allows us to make predictions, based on past states and observations, about future states of the system. Thus, if our interest is in estimating the current state of the system we can predict the current state based on previous observations of the system and its known (possibly noisy) time evolution. We define a **state transition** (or **state evolution**) **function,**

$$\boldsymbol{\vartheta}_t = f(\boldsymbol{\Theta}_{t-\Delta t}, \boldsymbol{\Phi}_t, \boldsymbol{\varepsilon}_t)$$

where the current state of the system ($\boldsymbol{\vartheta}_t$) is defined in terms of all previous states of the system (denoted $\boldsymbol{\Theta}_t$; notice that in the current sections we will adopt the convention that uppercase variables represent the totality of all times up until, and including the subscripted time), any internal or external forcing (denoted $\boldsymbol{\Phi}_t$; again, the uppercase indicates that we should consider not just the current time interval, but also all previous time intervals), and the noise sample corrupting these state variables during the state update (denoted ε_t, where the lowercase refers only to the subscripted time step). In what follows we will assume a linear first-order system (where state variables are additive and the dynamics memoryless), so that, following each time step, the new state is simply the sum of the immediately previous state and any forcing and error that occurs during the current time step:

$$\begin{aligned} \boldsymbol{\vartheta}_t &= f(\boldsymbol{\vartheta}_{t-\Delta t}, \boldsymbol{\phi}_t, \boldsymbol{\varepsilon}_t) \\ &= \boldsymbol{\vartheta}_{t-\Delta t} + \boldsymbol{\phi}_t + \boldsymbol{\varepsilon}_t \end{aligned} \qquad (4.2a),$$

which we have now written in all lowercase to indicate that we need only consider the immediately previous state (ignoring older previous states) and any forcing during the Δt interval. In addition to the simplification brought about by assuming an additive memoryless update, we may also in some circumstances not be concerned with possible noise contamination (from, for example, a noisily implemented state update as described by the state evolution function).

Noisy state estimation involves using the observation function in conjunction with the state evolution function to predict future states of the system, as well as to make our best guesses regarding the current state of the system. Notice that both of these state estimation problems (making our best guess regarding current and future states of the system) require understanding and using the state evolution function. Before we examine noisy state estimation, therefore, we should understand the dynamics of a time-evolving system, based only on state evolution. The state evolution can be based either on the internal dynamics of the system alone, or may also involve an internal control signal or external forcing that act to drive the system dynamics. We begin with an example of the former based on cell division.

Example: Cell Division

Perhaps the simplest of all dynamic systems is found in the petri dish, in the form of the progression over time of the division of cells. Sticking with simplest cases, we will begin with the example of prokaryotic cell division, such as might be observed in bacteria. In these simple organisms, cell division is accomplished via binary fission: Their single chromosome containing a single circular DNA molecule first replicates to produce two identical copies, which then migrate to opposite ends of the organism, at which point the cytoplasm divides to produce two daughter cells, genetically identical to the original.

Programming Aside: Cell Division

Each cell divides at each time step following the initial time, t_0. We begin by defining this initial value:

```
n0=3;
```

At each subsequent time step we double the previous count, which yields the recursive relation

$$n_{t+1} = 2n_t$$

or

```
fdiv=@(Nprev) 2*Nprev;
```

As we saw in the text, this corresponds to the closed-form solution

```
fdivcf=@(N0,t) N0*2^t;
```

Thus, we expect the same output from the two functions, which we verify here for the first 4 time steps starting from n0:

```
nnow=n0*[1 1];
for t=1:4, nnow=[fdiv(nnow(1)) fdivcf(n0,t)];
    disp(['t:' num2str(t) '; n:[' num2str(nnow(1)) ', ' num2str(nnow(2)) ']']); end;
```

Part of the background information for this problem stipulated that no cells die during our counting 'experiment.' However, we can imagine how cell death might work. For example, we might assume that a proportion, α, of the previous population dies during the time separating the current and previous time step. To see the effect of deaths, we subtract the cells that die during the interval between the previous and current time step from the original (at the end of the previous time step) count, assuming deaths always occur after dividing. This yields a new recursive relation:

$$n_{t+1} = 2n_t - \alpha n_t = (2 - \alpha)n_t$$

We can further run this relation forward from t_0 to death-adjusted cell counts for the first few time steps:

```
fdie=@(Nprev,alpha) round((2-alpha)*Nprev);
n0=1; alpha=.1; nnow=n0*[1 1]; for n=1:5, nnow=[fdiv(nnow(1)) fdie(nnow(2),alpha)], end
```

At which time step do we see the effect of the cell-death term of the new equation? why?

In this example we will assume that cell division occurs at regular intervals, Δt, that all cells divide during each interval (whether they are brand-new or old), and that no cells die during our experiment. Based on these simplifying assumptions, we should recognize that our recursive state-update equation is

$$\begin{aligned}\vartheta_t &= f(\vartheta_{t-\Delta t}, \phi_t)\\ &= \vartheta_{t-\Delta t} + \phi_t\\ &= 2n_{t-1} + \phi_t\end{aligned}$$

which in the absence of any perturbation (artificially adding or removing cells from our population) is

$$\vartheta_t = 2n_{t-1} + \phi_t = 2n_{t-1}$$

and predicts the number of daughter cells in the upcoming time step, n_t, based only on the number of cells counted during the previous time step, n_{t-1}, (i.e., it is a recursive relationship). To see this in an example, we will start with a single cell and observe the following sequence of cell-counts during the first three time steps:

$$t_0 : \vartheta_0 = n_0 = 1$$
$$t_1 : \vartheta_1 = 2n_{t-1} = 2n_0$$
$$t_2 : \vartheta_2 = 2n_{t-1} = 2[2n_0] = 4n_0$$
$$t_3 : \vartheta_3 = 2n_{t-1} = 2[2[2n_0]] = 8n_0$$

There are two things to notice about this example and sequence. First, we could have started with any initial number of cells, n_0, and we would have arrived at the same sequence (substituting for the new n_0. Second, we should notice that the number of doublings is always equal to the time step: so at time step t_4 there will have been four doublings, and the number of cells will be $\vartheta_4 = 2[2[2[2n_0]]] = n_0 2^4$. Indeed, in this example we should notice the pattern

$$\vartheta_t = n_t = n_0 2^t$$

gives an analytical solution for the number of cells at any given time step, and allows us to write the prediction for the number of cells at any time step based only on the initial population count, n_0. Analytical solutions are typically unavailable except when modeling the simplest systems:[3] So while it is nice to have the option of an analytical solution, such solutions are not necessary for the analysis of time-varying systems, as we will see in the several examples to follow.

Exercises

1) Using the log function, compute the predicted cell population size after 10 time steps, assuming you start with 30 cells.
2) How are cell deaths incorporated into the cell division model in the programming aside? What aspects of the lifecycle and reproduction of bacteria does this augmented model capture? How is it unrealistic?

4.2.1 Optimal State Estimation

Optimal state estimation is, in terms of (1.5), a combination of two elements: (1) the *prediction* of the current state of a system based on a combination of *previous sensor readings* and the (assumed known) state evolution function; (2) the likelihood of the current state of the system based on *current sensor readings*. These combine to yield a most-informed current measurement of the state of the system, where in terms of (1.5) the first (predictive) element serves as the prior and the second element as the likelihood.

[3] This is the study of difference and differential equations, which we will not pursue here.

The prior in this application of (1.5) represents a prediction of the current state. Recalling our use of (1.5) in the previous chapter, notice that our priors were based on background information regarding the type of variable whose value is to be measured, usually in the form of the Jeffreys prior. Although the Jeffreys prior is based on a logical analysis rather than empirical observation, we also know that the prior probability term of (1.5) can just as easily be used to represent information contained in past observations or experiments (assuming they are relevant to estimating the parameters of a current experiment); that is, the posterior from one observation can be used in the prior for a subsequent observation. This is why (1.5) is often thought of as a way to refine or update our information about the value of a parameter, because it can take information extracted from past experiments or observations and combine it with information extracted from our current observations. This is also the sense in which it is used for optimal state estimation. The twist here is that the posterior over the current system state at t must be transformed into a prediction for the future state at $t+1$ before it can be used as the prior for that future state.

The interesting new element of optimal state estimation, therefore, is in the mathematical form of the prior term. Here, the prior encodes our *expectations* for future values of the state variable, as computed from previous observations of the system and projected forward in time via the temporal dynamics encoded in the state evolution functions defining the system under study. So whereas our definition of the prior has until now generally been based on being maximally uninformed regarding the values of state variables (i.e., we have typically used the Jeffreys prior), we will now consider an uncertain but informed prediction regarding the current system or model (and its state variables / parameters). This prior, just like the Jeffreys prior, is not based on *current* sensory or observation data. It is obtained by first defining a state transition (or evolution) function,

$$\boldsymbol{\vartheta}_t = f(\boldsymbol{\vartheta}_{t-\Delta t}, \boldsymbol{\phi}_t, \boldsymbol{\varepsilon}_t)$$

where the current state of the system ($\boldsymbol{\vartheta}_t$) is defined in terms of the previous state of the system and any forcing ($\boldsymbol{\phi}_t$) of state variables during the transition from time $t-\Delta t$ to time t, and f encodes system dynamics. The state transition may be implemented noisily and include an error term, ε_t that perturbs the state at each time point, t. The state evolution function is combined with the posterior over the previous state to define the prior over the current state.

After having computed the prior over the present state (in terms of the previous state's posterior propagated forward in time via state evolution), we have but one element of the posterior left to assign: the state likelihood, $\mathcal{L}(\boldsymbol{\vartheta})$. The likelihood is defined in terms of an observation function,

$$\mathbf{o}_t = g(\boldsymbol{\vartheta}_t, \boldsymbol{\varepsilon}_o)$$

such that[4] $\mathcal{L}(\boldsymbol{\vartheta}_t) = p(\mathbf{o}_t|\vartheta_t \cdot \iota)$

To start we will use (1.5) to define the posterior over state at t, $p(\boldsymbol{\vartheta}_t|\mathbf{O}_t \cdot \iota)$. We separate the current observations, which are directly relevant only to the likelihood of possible *current* states, from past observations:

[4] One final reminder: In the current section capitals, such as in the observation term, $\mathbf{O}_t$, refer to all observation vectors up to and including the subscripted time point, such as $\mathbf{O}_t = [\mathbf{O}_t, \mathbf{O}_{t-1}, \ldots, \mathbf{O}_1]$

$$p(\boldsymbol{\vartheta}_t|\boldsymbol{O}_t \cdot \iota) = \{p(\boldsymbol{\vartheta}_t|\boldsymbol{o}_t \cdot \boldsymbol{O}_{t-\Delta t} \cdot \iota)\}$$

This is important because each time step refers to a separate state, and previous observations are not *directly* relevant to computing the posterior over the current state. Next, we obtain an explicit expression defining the prior and likelihood via (1.5):

$$\begin{aligned} p(\boldsymbol{\vartheta}_t|\boldsymbol{O}_t \cdot \iota) &\propto \varpi(\boldsymbol{\vartheta}_t)\mathcal{L}(\boldsymbol{\vartheta}_t) \\ &= [p(\boldsymbol{\vartheta}_t|\boldsymbol{O}_{t-\Delta t} \cdot \iota)]p(\boldsymbol{o}_t|\boldsymbol{\vartheta}_t \cdot \boldsymbol{O}_{t-\Delta t} \cdot \iota) \end{aligned}$$

Here, we must decide what to do with the square-bracketed prior term. You might be tempted to drop the conditioning on previous observations ($\boldsymbol{O}_{t-\Delta t}$) from the prior, since these are not directly informative regarding the current state. However, if we recall that the previous state is directly relevant to inferring the present state, and that the previous observation is in turn directly relevant to inferring the previous state, we should instead find a way to incorporate an explicit representation of the previous state into the prior to complete this logical bridge. We therefore extend the question to, as part of the prior (bracketed term), include an explicit reference to the previous state,

$$= p(\boldsymbol{o}_t|\boldsymbol{\vartheta}_t \cdot \iota)\left[\int d\boldsymbol{\vartheta}_{t-\Delta t}\, p(\boldsymbol{\vartheta}_{t-\Delta t} \cdot \boldsymbol{\vartheta}_t|\boldsymbol{O}_{t-\Delta t} \cdot \iota)\right]$$

and expand this expression via the product rule:

$$= p(\boldsymbol{o}_t|\boldsymbol{\vartheta}_t \cdot \iota)\int d\boldsymbol{\vartheta}_{t-\Delta t}\, p(\boldsymbol{\vartheta}_t|\boldsymbol{\vartheta}_{t-\Delta t} \cdot \boldsymbol{O}_{t-\Delta t} \cdot \iota)p(\boldsymbol{\vartheta}_{t-\Delta t}|\boldsymbol{O}_{t-\Delta t} \cdot \iota)$$

Finally, we notice that the last term in the expression has the same form as that of the desired posterior, but for the previous time step. We therefore separate observations directly relevant to the state at the previous time step from even older observations, yielding our final expression for the current state:

$$\begin{aligned} p(\boldsymbol{\vartheta}_t|\boldsymbol{O}_t \cdot \iota) &= \{p(\boldsymbol{\vartheta}_t|\boldsymbol{o}_t \cdot \boldsymbol{O}_{t-\Delta t} \cdot \iota)\} \\ &= p(\boldsymbol{o}_t|\boldsymbol{\vartheta}_t \cdot \iota)\int d\boldsymbol{\vartheta}_{t-\Delta t} p(\boldsymbol{\vartheta}_t|\boldsymbol{\vartheta}_{t-\Delta t} \cdot \iota)\{p(\boldsymbol{\vartheta}_{t-\Delta t}|\boldsymbol{o}_{t-\Delta t} \cdot \boldsymbol{O}_{t-2\Delta t} \cdot \iota)\} \end{aligned} \tag{4.3}$$

where the prediction term that encodes our information regarding state evolution, $p(\boldsymbol{\vartheta}_t|\boldsymbol{\vartheta}_{t-\Delta t} \cdot \boldsymbol{O}_{t-\Delta t} \cdot \iota)$, reduces to $p(\boldsymbol{\vartheta}_t|\boldsymbol{\vartheta}_{t-\Delta t} \cdot \iota)$ because knowing the previous state ($\boldsymbol{\vartheta}_{t-\Delta t}$) makes it irrelevant what observations ($\boldsymbol{O}_{t-\Delta t}$) led to it. Similarly, the likelihood term $p(\boldsymbol{o}_t|\boldsymbol{\vartheta}_t \cdot \boldsymbol{O}_{t-\Delta t} \cdot \iota)$ reduces to $\mathcal{L}(\boldsymbol{\vartheta}_t) = p(\boldsymbol{o}_t|\boldsymbol{\vartheta}_t \cdot \iota)$ because knowing the current state ($\boldsymbol{\vartheta}_t$) allows us to compute the probability of current observations ($\boldsymbol{o}_t$) regardless of previous observation ($\boldsymbol{O}_{t-\Delta t}$). It is worth reiterating here that the important difference between the current measurement problem and problems in previous chapters is that the state is changing, and we are now measuring its time evolution. If the state were constant across time steps, all observations would be relevant to measuring that constant state, and the posterior would have simply been $p(\boldsymbol{\vartheta}|\boldsymbol{O} \cdot \iota) \propto \varpi(\boldsymbol{\vartheta})\mathcal{L}(\boldsymbol{\vartheta})$ across all time steps, obviating the need for state updating and separate predictions/priors at each time step (see Box 4.1).

BOX 4.1 Random Walks and Markov Chains

A random walk is a process or algorithm whose output forms a series. A simple example occurs when a variable updates at each time step from its previous value by one of the integers, $-9, -8, \ldots, 9$, sampled via some probability distribution. The update rule and distribution can become arbitrarily complicated and can involve multiple previous time steps, or indeed the entire time evolution of the system. The probabilities that characterize the transition from one state to another (or that characterize state differences) are called the transition probabilities. Transition probabilities can be fixed or changing, depending on the type of system and particulars of the problem under consideration.

To get an intuitive understanding of transition probabilities, consider the transition from one word to another in written English. Taking this book as an example, we could create a corpus of all words used herein, and then report the frequency of the transition from each word to the next (i.e., a square array in which each word occurs both on the ordinate and abscissa, and at the intersection of each word pair would be given the frequency of one word followed by the other). This transition table (or transition matrix) characterizes the transition from one word to the other, without taking account of any other element of the context in which these words were found. We could also imagine that a more accurate characterization of the transitions might be had by taking account of not just the current word (in predicting the next) but looking back some number of additional words (first- or second-order transition probabilities that look back an additional word or two, respectively). However, staying with the simplest (zeroth-order) transition table we can gain some further understanding. If we were to look at the transition from the word 'the' to the word 'probability' and compare this transition probability to that found in the New York Times, we would see that it is surprisingly high. Indeed, this transition would be higher here than from many other sources, or even from my own writing on other topics. This is largely a function of the topic of this text, which necessarily features the word 'probability' at a much higher frequency than other sources (and transitions to and from the word 'probability' are generally higher than normal). However, we could imagine that there are other transitions that describe the *style* of the writer. We could for example find several newspaper articles on similar topics, and that shared very similar base frequencies of word usage, but nevertheless had distinct writing styles. These articles, despite their similar base word frequencies, would have distinct transition tables. Another example of this phenomenon can be found among composers, where the transitions would reflect the ordering of notes used in their compositions.

As far as our current interest in random walks and transition probabilities, we will be primarily interested in a simple form of random walk called a Markov process or Markov chain (named after the Russian mathematician Andrey Markov, 1856–1922). The Markov chain includes the additional constraint that it obeys the Markov property. This property, which can be thought of as 'memorylessness,' is a form of conditional independence whereby any system exhibiting the Markov property evolves such that each new system state depends *only* on the current state (in terms of the progression from the current to the next state, it is as if the system retains no 'memories' of previous states that would serve to alter its progression through state space). This property is expressed as: $p(s_{k+1}|s_k \cdot s_{k-1} \cdot \cdots \cdot s_0 \cdot \iota) = p(s_{k+1}|s_k \cdot \iota)$.

The Markov property is important because it allows us to simplify calculations in many instances, turning what might seem an intractable problem into one that is easily solved. Now, predicting s_{k+1} need not require us to deal with the ever-increasing multiplicity of previous states, as in $p(s_{k+1}|s_k \cdot s_{k-1} \cdot \cdots \cdot s_0 \cdot \iota)$, and instead becomes simply $p(s_{k+1}|s_k \cdot \iota) = \frac{p(s_{k+1} \cdot s_k|\iota)}{p(s_k|\iota)}$.

In closing we must emphasize a fundamental difference between a stationary system and the random-walk system defined here. In the former, system state is unchanging and therefore all observations of the data are directly relevant to inferring a **single** system state. This has been the case with all our previous problems; each datum contributed to estimating a single set of underlying system parameters, regardless of when those data were observed. Thus the previous n observations are no less relevant to inferring the current system state as the current observation, because the system state was stationary, and therefore identical at each of those times. In a random-walk system, the system state changes with each time step, and because the system state is *not* the same from one time step to another ('nonstationary'), each time step's observations are only directly relevant to inferring that time step's state.

Because the current posterior over state, $p(\boldsymbol{\vartheta}_t|\mathbf{O}_t \cdot \iota)$, includes a term for the previous posterior, $p(\boldsymbol{\vartheta}_{t-\Delta t}|\mathbf{O}_{t-\Delta t} \cdot \iota)$, we see that (4.3) defines a **recursive relation**. The full solution, therefore, requires us to start with an expression for the prior at t_0 and continue computations forward until the current time, t. The time step that we label t_0 is somewhat arbitrary: it can be any time at which an expression for the posterior over the system state is available, which in our hands will usually be a time at which no observations have yet been made (i.e., the 'initial' system state) and the state is known with certainty.

To give an example of optimal state estimation, we can write the expression for the posterior over state at t_2:

$$p(\boldsymbol{\vartheta}_2|\mathbf{O}_2 \cdot \iota) \propto p(\mathbf{o}_2|\boldsymbol{\vartheta}_2 \cdot \iota) \int d\boldsymbol{\vartheta}_1 p(\boldsymbol{\vartheta}_2|\boldsymbol{\vartheta}_1 \cdot \iota)\{p(\boldsymbol{\vartheta}_1|\mathbf{O}_1 \cdot \iota)\}$$

where notice we have enclosed the posterior for the previous time step, t_1, in curly brackets. We replace the curly-bracketed term with a replica of the t_2 expression for the posterior, except that we reduce all subscripts by one and also ultimately drop the O_0 term (which by definition is an empty set at t_0):

$$p(\boldsymbol{\vartheta}_2|\mathbf{O}_2 \cdot \iota) \propto p(\mathbf{o}_2|\boldsymbol{\vartheta}_2 \cdot \iota) \int d\boldsymbol{\vartheta}_1 p(\boldsymbol{\vartheta}_2|\boldsymbol{\vartheta}_1 \cdot \iota)\Big\{p(\mathbf{o}_1|\boldsymbol{\vartheta}_1 \cdot \iota) \int d\boldsymbol{\vartheta}_0 p(\boldsymbol{\vartheta}_1|\boldsymbol{\vartheta}_0 \cdot \iota)\{p(\boldsymbol{\vartheta}_0|\iota)\}\Big\}$$

Here, because the innermost curly-bracketed term is for the posterior over state at t_0, we replace this term with the probability over the state variable that is based only on prior information about the system, $p(\boldsymbol{\vartheta}_0|\iota)$, rather than on any prior observations of system outputs, $\mathbf{O}$. This backward progression to t_0 is necessary for an initial computation of the posterior at time t. Notice, however that once the posterior at t has been computed, this can be inserted directly into the expression for the posterior at the next time step, $t + 1$, without any reference to earlier time steps; in other words, the computations can begin at any arbitrary initial time at which an expression for the posterior over state is available (or can be derived/assigned). If, for example, we were to wait for a third time step and rerun our algorithm, the above expression for the posterior at t_2 will be propagated forward into this expression as the new curly-bracketed term:

$$p(\vartheta_3|O_3 \cdot \iota) \propto p(o_3|\vartheta_3 \cdot \iota) \int d\vartheta_2 p(\vartheta_3|\vartheta_2 \cdot \iota)\{p(\vartheta_2|O_2 \cdot \iota)\},$$

and since an expression for the previous time step's posterior, $p(\vartheta_2|O_2 \cdot \iota)$, had been available there is no need to run the equations any further backward in time (and, indeed, these time steps could be renamed t_0 and t_1 instead of t_2 and t_3). This stepping-forward procedure can continue indefinitely, or for as long as the state evolution function continues to be a valid description of the system dynamics and as long as observations continue to become available. To put these equations into practice, we must first define a state-evolution and an observation function, which are particular to the system under study.

Exercises

1) Describe the predictive aspect of optimal state estimation, and how it inserts itself into the normal course of parameter estimation/measurement.
2) What is a recursion, and how does it occur within optimal state estimation?
3) What is the Markov property, and how is it used in optimal state estimation?
4) Describe the difference between a random walk and a Markov chain. Why is this property useful in state estimation?

4.2.2 Range Effects

The context in which an event occurs is a powerful mediator of many behavioral responses, including learning and memory, addictive responses, social interactions, etc. Indeed, even basic sensory and other neural responses, such as the responses of retinal ganglion cells to changes in light intensity, are context-sensitive. One type of context effect that can be seen in a wide array of behaviors is the **range effect**, wherein the magnitude of the behavioral response is scaled not just to the proximal stimulus eliciting the response, but the larger context within which that stimulus is experienced.

To understand why this might occur, and the form it takes, consider the familiar phenomenon of light adaptation; the retinal ganglion response to light intensity. The ganglion cell has a finite dynamic range that is quite small compared with the levels of light intensity to which we are capable of responding: a full range starting at just a few light quanta in near-complete darkness up to the bright sunshine of a sunny noontime picnic, and gradations in-between as small as the transient dimming of indoor lighting that occurs when there is a small dip in supplied current. How do we manage to see in this wide range of lighting conditions? Light adaptation is a form of range effect, made possible by adjusting the dynamic range of the cone system. Shifting the dynamic range of our visual system makes it possible to see and discriminate among small gradations in brightness within different lighting contexts, from dim indoor lighting to bright outdoor sunshine. In each case, an input (light intensity) that is well outside the current functional range (i.e., a very dim light in the bright context) elicits a behavioral response that is much less (if at all) useful than what would occur if the same stimulus were presented after shifting the system's functional range to include that stimulus (i.e., shifting the dynamic range down to low lighting). In our light perception example, presenting a very dim flash of light in the brightly lit outdoor environment will produce no perception of the flash, whereas presenting the same light stimulus in a near-dark environment will produce a clear perceptual impression.

As in our light-perception example, the essence of a range effect is that it modifies responding based on the'context' within which the current stimulus is embedded. This can take many additional forms, and we will here explore the simplest state model which also happens to display range effects. This model has a state that may drift slowly over time in an unpredictable way, which simplifies the model considerably because the prediction used to project each state forward in time consists simply of a (noisy) copy of the current state, as defined by the state evolution function:

$$\begin{aligned}\boldsymbol{\vartheta}_t &= f(\boldsymbol{\vartheta}_{t-\Delta t}, \boldsymbol{\phi}_t, \boldsymbol{\varepsilon}_{\vartheta}) \\ &= \boldsymbol{\vartheta}_{t-\Delta t} + \boldsymbol{\phi}_t + \boldsymbol{\varepsilon}_{\vartheta} \quad \{\boldsymbol{\phi}_t = \mathbf{0} \\ &= \boldsymbol{\vartheta}_{t-\Delta t} + \boldsymbol{\varepsilon}_{\vartheta}\end{aligned}$$

Because there is no predictable 'trajectory' to these state transitions (i.e., $\boldsymbol{\phi}_t = \mathbf{0}$), the state will bounce around in a Brownian or random-walk fashion. In this model, the main constraint on state changes is in their magnitude: it is more likely that the state change will be small than large, where the exact definition of 'small' and 'large' are inferred from the distribution of the noise term, ε_s (and therefore on the particulars of the system under consideration).

The probability of each new state, after having observed the latest sensor readings, is

$$\begin{aligned}p(\boldsymbol{\vartheta}_t|\mathbf{O}_t \cdot \iota) &= \{p(\boldsymbol{\vartheta}_t|\mathbf{o}_t \cdot \mathbf{O}_{t-\Delta t} \cdot \iota)\} \\ &\propto \varpi(\boldsymbol{\vartheta}_t)\mathcal{L}(\boldsymbol{\vartheta}_t) \\ &= [p(\boldsymbol{\vartheta}_t|\mathbf{O}_{t-\Delta t} \cdot \iota)]p(\mathbf{o}_t|\boldsymbol{\vartheta}_t \cdot \mathbf{O}_{t-\Delta t} \cdot \iota) \\ &= p(\mathbf{o}_t|\boldsymbol{\vartheta}_t \cdot \iota)\left[\int d\boldsymbol{\vartheta}_{t-\Delta t} p(\boldsymbol{\vartheta}_{t-\Delta t} \cdot \boldsymbol{\vartheta}_t|\mathbf{O}_{t-\Delta t} \cdot \iota)\right] \\ &= p(\mathbf{o}_t|\boldsymbol{\vartheta}_t \cdot \iota)\int d\boldsymbol{\vartheta}_{t-\Delta t} p(\boldsymbol{\vartheta}_t|\boldsymbol{\vartheta}_{t-\Delta t} \cdot \mathbf{O}_{t-\Delta t} \cdot \iota)p(\boldsymbol{\vartheta}_{t-\Delta t}|\mathbf{O}_{t-\Delta t} \cdot \iota)\end{aligned}$$

This series of equations begins as we always do with (1.5), defining the posterior distribution: the relation between what is desired (knowledge of the current state, $\boldsymbol{\vartheta}_t$) and what is known (the sensory inputs, $\mathbf{O}_t$, and prior, $\varpi(\boldsymbol{\vartheta}_t)$). The prior has a slightly different flavor in the context of state estimation, because the prior is clearly characterized as our *prediction*[5] regarding the state of the system at the time that the newest sensory information is scheduled to arrive, t:

[5] Although it is always true that the prior represents our best prediction, prior to observing data, of the state of the system under study, this characterization of the prior is particularly apt when that predictive aspect of the prior is a temporal prediction based on past states of the system.

$$
\begin{aligned}
\varpi(\vartheta_t) &= p(\vartheta_t|\mathbf{O}_{t-\Delta t}\cdot\iota)\\
&= \int d\vartheta_{t-\Delta t}p(\vartheta_{t-\Delta t}\cdot\vartheta_t|\mathbf{O}_{t-\Delta t}\cdot\iota)\\
&= \int d\vartheta_{t-\Delta t}p(\vartheta_t|\vartheta_{t-\Delta t}\cdot\mathbf{O}_{t-\Delta t}\cdot\iota)p(\vartheta_{t-\Delta t}|\mathbf{O}_{t-\Delta t}\cdot\iota)\\
&= \int d\vartheta_{t-\Delta t}p(\vartheta_t|\vartheta_{t-\Delta t}\cdot\iota)p(\vartheta_{t-\Delta t}|\mathbf{O}_{t-\Delta t}\cdot\iota)
\end{aligned}
$$

The last line of the definition of the prior tells us that to obtain our prediction of the current state we start with the previous state of the system (or if it is uncertain, our posterior $p(\vartheta_{t-\Delta t}|\mathbf{O}_{t-\Delta t}\cdot\iota)$ over that state), and combine it with the probability distribution over transitions *away from that previous state*, $p(\boldsymbol{\varepsilon}_\vartheta|\iota) = p(\vartheta_t|\vartheta_{t-\Delta t}\cdot\iota)$ [where note that we can always simplify $p(\vartheta_t|\vartheta_{t-\Delta t}\cdot\mathbf{O}_{t-\Delta t}\cdot\iota)$ to $p(\vartheta_t|\vartheta_{t-\Delta t}\cdot\iota)$, because previous sensory signals, $\mathbf{O}_{t-\Delta t}$, are irrelevant to predicting a Markov state progression when the previous state, $\vartheta_{t-\Delta t}$, also appears to the right of the '|' in the probability statement]. This combination yields $p(\vartheta_t|\vartheta_{t-\Delta t}\cdot\iota)p(\vartheta_{t-\Delta t}|\mathbf{O}_{t-\Delta t}\cdot\iota) = p(\vartheta_{t-\Delta}\cdot\vartheta_t|\mathbf{O}_{t-\Delta}\cdot\iota)$, which is the 2D distribution over previous-state/current-state pairs, taking account of our knowledge of both the likely values of the previous state and the most likely state transitions away from those previous states. Our final prediction of the current state of the system is obtained by marginalizing over the possible previous states of the system, yielding the prior: $\varpi(\vartheta_t) = \int d\vartheta_{t-\Delta t}p(\vartheta_{t-\Delta}\cdot\vartheta_t|\mathbf{O}_{t-\Delta}\cdot\iota)$

We should pay special attention to the fact that the definition of the prior is a recursive relation: our information regarding the previous state of the system $p(\vartheta_{t-\Delta t}|\mathbf{O}_{t-\Delta}\cdot\iota)$, is the posterior at the previous time step. However, just because we have defined a recursive relation, which can theoretically be stepped backward indefinitely, does not mean we have no place to start, or that our starting point must be at a time step when we have certain knowledge of the system state. Rather, our starting point can be at any time point at which we can define a prior. Once that prior is defined, we are not *required* to examine further prior time steps as a prerequisite for computing the desired model states and posteriors over those states, because these will not improve our estimates – a direct consequence of the Markov property. Note that because the prior simply expresses our information about possible current states, the circumstance may dictate that the initial time step's prior be uniform (or some other relatively uninformed shape), such as when no previous sensory inputs are known or available.

We will use the basic model described above as a way to explore range effects from the domain of memory research. The state model we will use to model memory is the simplest state model, involving a state update based only on the most recent previous state, because there are no applied forces or perturbations to the system, and instead there is only drift in the form of noise accumulation. It is important to thoroughly understand this simplest of state updates, so that we may develop our intuitions regarding what properties of a given system might be due to noise accumulation alone and which might be due to perturbations and forces applied during state evolution.

Example: Memory for Temporal Intervals

Memory is one of the topics in neuroscience that early captured the attention of scientists. Indeed, as early as 1868 Vierordt was performing experiments on temporal reproduction, measuring the ability of humans to remember and subsequently make use of previously heard temporal intervals. Vierord's data demonstrated two important properties of memory for temporal intervals:

1. A consistent pattern of errors in which short durations are overestimated and longer intervals underestimated.
2. The 'scalar property' describing time-dependent reproduction noise in which longer intervals are more difficult to reproduce precisely (i.e., the scale of the error is proportional to the scale of the temporal interval).

We will first examine a simplified model of temporal memory: one that we might have proposed without having seen the Vierordt's data. This model surprisingly captures neither of the two properties of that data, even if we specifically encode the scalar property in the variance term of the likelihood function. In this and the following example we will examine the general class of model that encodes the assumption that 'new temporal intervals will be noisy copies of previous intervals':

$$\tau_t = \tau_{t-1} + \varepsilon_\tau$$

Here we have *not* built a model that predicts a particular trajectory of changes in temporal interval or of the intervals themselves; rather, we are simply encoding the fact that we expect each temporal interval to be, on average, similar to the one before it. The distribution over ε_τ, the change of interval (world state) from one time step to another, encodes our information about the expected size of the possible changes in true interval. This updating of the true temporal interval based on the previous interval yields the following prior over interval for the current time step:

$$\begin{aligned}\varpi(\tau_t) &= \int d\tau_{t-1} p(\tau_{t-1} \cdot \tau_t | [\iota_t]) \\ &= \int d\tau_{t-1} p(\tau_{t-1} \cdot \tau_t | [T_{t-1} \cdot \sigma_\tau \cdot \iota_t]) \\ &= \int d\tau_{t-1} p(\tau_t | \tau_{t-1} \cdot \sigma_\tau \cdot \iota) p(\tau_{t-1} | T_{t-1} \cdot \sigma_\tau \cdot \iota)\end{aligned}$$

which encodes the fact that our best prediction for the upcoming interval (τ_t) depends on the possible values of the previous time step's temporal interval.

The joint probability of the previous and upcoming temporal interval, $p(\tau_{t-1} \cdot \tau_t | \iota_t)$, controls the extent to which the previous interval will predict the next interval. At the limit of perfect predictability, only the first temporal interval in a series (when there is no prior interval) would be based on the observed data. Every subsequent estimate would be perfectly predicted by the previous, and under this model would therefore be identical. This is obviously not useful for a system that is expected to deal with more than one temporal interval over its lifetime, and we will therefore first examine the opposite extreme: the uniform limit of $p(\tau_{t-1} \cdot \tau_t | \iota_t)$ for which the previous interval (τ_{t-1}) does not help us to predict the current interval (τ_t). This version of $p(\tau_{t-1} \cdot \tau_t | \iota_t)$ is shown in Figure 4.4a. Furthermore, because the joint probability over the previous and current temporal interval is uniform over a large range compared to the reproduced interval values, the marginalized prior $\varpi(\tau_t) = \int d\tau_{t-1} p(\tau_{t-1} \cdot \tau_t | [\iota_t])$ over previous intervals will also be (nearly) uniform, and therefore provides essentially no guidance when estimating the upcoming interval.

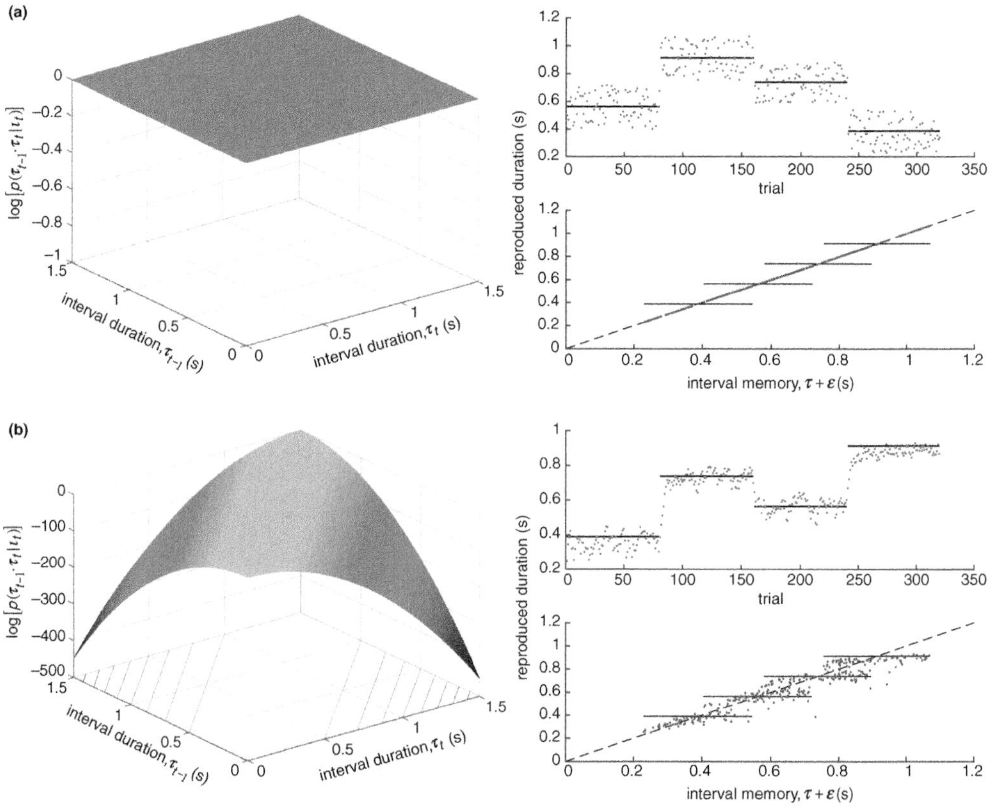

Figure 4.4 Basic temporal reproduction model. (a) (left) Log likelihood of consecutive pairs of temporal intervals (at $t-1$ and t). The fact that this 2D distribution is flat tells us that if one interval is long, the next is no more expected to be long as it is expected to be short. (right) Temporal reproduction data. In the upper plot, four different average temporal intervals are given, with a small range around each, and simulated reproduction data are shown for each. Notice that the transition between the different average temporal intervals is gradual rather than immediate, indicative of an automatic (unconscious) as opposed to a cognitive effect. The lower plot shows reproduction intervals associated with each given (sensory) interval. The four groups of average intervals are easily distinguished based on their average duration. However, notice that the identical (true) interval at the limit of each range will be reproduced repeatably differently, depending on the range within which it was encountered. So, for example, the longest interval of each range overlaps slightly with the shortest interval of the next highest range, and yet the reproduction of these intervals depends reliably on the range of other durations from each set that was presented. This is the range effect, and it occurs over the relatively short timescale seen in this example.
(b) Range effect in temporal memory. (left) Log-likelihood of pairs of temporal intervals. The shape of this 2D distribution tells us that if one interval is long, the next is expected to be long, and if the previous interval was short, the next interval is expected to be short. This is simply a restatement of the assumption that the intervals will maintain the same approximate scale from one time step to the next. This assumption produces the range effect seen in the temporal reproduction data. (right) Temporal reproduction data. In the upper plot, four different average temporal intervals are given, with a small range around each, and simulated reproduction data are shown for each. Notice that the transition between the different average temporal intervals is gradual rather than immediate, indicative of an automatic (unconscious) as opposed to a cognitive effect. The lower plot shows reproduction intervals associated with each given (sensory) interval. The four groups of average intervals are easily distinguished based on their average duration. However, notice that the identical (true) interval at the limit of each range will be reproduced repeatably differently depending on the range within which it was encountered. So, for example, the longest interval of each range overlaps slightly with the shortest interval of the next highest range, and yet the reproduction of these intervals depends reliably on the range of other durations from each set that was presented. This is the range effect, and it occurs over the relatively short timescale seen in this example.

Programming Aside: Limit of Zero Weight Given to Previous Temporal Intervals (Fig. 4.4a)

```
clear %#ok<*UNRCH>
%%%%%%%%%%%%%
%%% Flags %%%
reset=false;

%%%%%%%%%%%%%%%%%%%%%%%%%
%%% Timing with drift %%%
L=801;
Ngroups=4; Nper=80; T=Ngroups*Nper;
trange=[.3 1]; drange=.1*diff(trange); dvar=.05;

taus=linspace(0,1.5,L)';
pri=zeros(L,1);
if and(~reset,exist(['timedat2.mat'],'file'))
    load(['timedat2.mat'])
else
    disp('generating temporal intervals');

    tmat=linspace(trange(1),trange(2),Ngroups+1);
    tmat=[str8n(tmat(1:Ngroups))-drange str8n(tmat(2:end))+drange];
    %matrix of overlapping timing ranges

    tnow=nan(size(tmat,1),Nper);
    like=@(t,sig) -log(sig)-.5*(t-taus).^2./sig^2;
    tset=nan(size(tmat));

    drange=.2;
    for n=1:Ngroups,
        inow=randi(size(tmat,1));
        tset(n,:)=tmat(inow,:);
        tmat=RFL(tmat,inow);
        tnow(n,:)=diff(tset(n,:))*(rand([1 Nper])-.5)+mean(tset(n,:)); end
tnow=str8n(tnow'); signow=tnow/17; save('timedat2.mat'); end %scalar property

%time differences and likelihood over differences
dtaus=taus*ones(1,L)-ones(L,1)*taus';
LtauD=0*(-.5*dtaus.^2./dvar^2);

%likelihood computation
Like=@(onow,snow) -log(snow)-.5*(onow-taus).^2/snow^2;

%initialize likelihood and estimate
Lnow=zeros(L,1); tauest=nan(T,1); tic
for t=1:T,
    Llastpostsum=logsum(Lnow*ones(1,L)+LtauD,1,diff(taus(1:2)));
    Lnow=like(tnow(t),signow(t))+Llastpostsum;
    tauest(t)=logpeakval([Lnow taus]);
    if rem(t,Nper)==0, toc; end, end

%%%%%%%%%%%%%%%%
%%% PLOTTING %%%
figure(1); clf; %est by trial
subplot(2,1,1); hold on
for n=1:Ngroups,
    plot((n-1)*Nper+[1 Nper],mean(tset(n,:))*[1 1],'k-','LineWidth',2); end
plot(tauest,'.')
```

```
%%% remembered / estimated
subplot(2,1,2); hold on
plot([0 1.2],[0 1.2],'k--')
for n=1:Ngroups,
    plot(tset(n,:),mean(tset(n,:))*[1 1],'k-','LineWidth',1.3); end
plot(tnow,tauest,'.','Color',[.2 .3 .7]);
punderover=[]; %proportional error
for n=1:Ngroups,
    ilist=Nper*(n-1)+round(.5*Nper):Nper;
    punderover=[punderover; [tnow(ilist)-tset(n,1) (tauest(ilist)-...
        tnow(ilist))/diff(tset(n,:))]]; end
%#ok<AGROW>
figure(2); clf; plotmat(punderover,'ko','MarkerFaceColor','k','MarkerSize',6)
figure(3); clf; meshc(taus,taus,LtauD)
```

Figure 4.4a shows the output of the model, represented in two ways. In the upper right panel, a series of reproduced temporal intervals is plotted in the sequence given in the 'experiment.' Notice there are four large-scale 'levels' of temporal interval, plotted as horizontal black lines. In addition there are small variations in the reproduced intervals around these four levels. In the lower right panel we see the same reproduced temporal intervals plotted against the raw duration 'data' (presumably a noisy internal encoding of a duration) that generated them. The interesting and useful property of this temporal interval reproduction model is that intervals reproduced (represented) by this model of temporal memory are generally quite close to the raw interval data, as shown in the lower right panel of the figure. This is, of course, useful because errors between the data and memory representation of any given temporal interval are quite small. In fact, because the joint probability $p(\tau_{t-1} \cdot \tau_t|\imath_t)$ is uniform, this model ends up ignoring *all* past information and therefore represents a special case that reduces to the standard use of (1.5), with no predictive element: It simply estimates each interval based only on the current raw duration data without taking the context of previous data/intervals into account.

To move beyond this model, we should consider the particulars of the experiment that generated Figure 4.4a. In this experiment there are four large-scale levels of temporal interval, plotted as horizontal black lines in the upper right panel of the figure. In addition there are small variations in the memory for intervals around these four levels. This trial-to-trial variation can be interpreted in two ways. Either these differences around the four levels of temporal interval are just additional experimentally imposed variation, or they represent the internal noise-corrupted input data. The difference is important because in the first scenario the correct temporal reproduction will match those small variations in interval around the four levels. In the second scenario there are only four temporal intervals that are correct to reproduce, and reproducing the additional variation around those four intervals means that the system is reproducing the noise in the internal memory for those intervals.

To the extent that we expect there to be noise in the internal memory for, and likely also in the encoding of temporal intervals, we would like our temporal reproduction model to learn the four levels of temporal interval from the noisy repetition of those intervals. That does not happen in the current model, because the data fall essentially along the unity line in the lower panel of Figure 4.4a. A model that tracks the variation in individual intervals also displays no learning, which would manifest as a tendency to discover the durations of the four overall levels and (over the course of each quarter of the experiment) bias reproduced intervals toward these durations. Such learning would cause the data to tend to match the horizontal black lines in both righthand panels of Figure 4.4a.

Exercises

1) What aspects of the Vierordt data were reproduced by the model? Which were not?
2) Why would a model that displays range effects tend to produce data that matches the horizontal lines in the lower panel of Figure 4.4a?
3) What evidence is there for/against the presence of a range effect in these data?
4) How might we modify the model to better reproduce the two elements of Vierordt's data described in the main text?

Example: Distorted Memory for Temporal Intervals

The previous model of temporal memory was a limiting case of the general class of model that encodes the assumption that 'new temporal intervals will be noisy copies of previous interval,' where knowing the previous temporal interval provides so little information regarding the upcoming interval that predictions of upcoming interval lengths are unaffected. Here, we will examine a case that is somewhere between the limiting case of the previous example and the limiting case at the opposite end of the spectrum, the perfectly predictable model. A partially predictable model, in which each temporal interval provides partial information regarding the duration of the next interval:

$$\tau_t = \tau_{t-1} + \varepsilon_\tau$$

where the joint probability over the previous and upcoming temporal intervals, $p(\tau_{t-1} \cdot \tau_t | \iota_t)$, controls the predictability of one interval to another. In this model, the predictability of the next interval from the last also encodes the expectation that the interval will change. To encode the expectation that intervals will change *slowly*, this joint distribution will be relatively sharply peaked (Fig. 4.4b), whereas we encode the expectation that intervals will be unstable and change relatively *quickly* with a distribution that is closer to being flat (Fig. 4.4a).

In the previous version of the model, each new datum was treated as if it was a noisy representation of an entirely different temporal interval from what produced any previous datum. This leads to reproduced intervals that are related much more to the data than to the four levels of temporal interval that produced those data: each new reproduced interval uses only the current datum, and so has no capacity to 'discover' the duration of the stable true interval. In the current version of the model, it will tend to discover the repeated true duration of the temporal intervals, because there is an expectation encoded in $p(\tau_{t-1} \cdot \tau_t | \iota_t)$ that multiple data observations will represent similar true durations. This expectation is critical because it allows us to use multiple data to estimate the length of each reproduced interval, much like when making multiple observations to estimate a single temperature on a thermometer or a single weight with multiple

Programming Aside: Memory Distortion Based on Previous Temporal Interval (Fig. 4.4b)

```
clear %#ok<*UNRCH>
%%%%%%%%%%%%%
%%% Flags %%%
reset=false;

%%%%%%%%%%%%%%%%%%%%%%%%%%
%%% Timing with drift %%%
L=801;
Ngroups=4; Nper=80; T=Ngroups*Nper;
trange=[.3 1]; drange=.1*diff(trange); dvar=.05;
taus=linspace(0,1.5,L)';
pri=zeros(L,1);
if and(~reset,exist(['timedat.mat'],'file')),
    load(['timedat.mat'])
else
    disp('generating temporal intervals');

    tmat=linspace(trange(1),trange(2),Ngroups+1);
    tmat=[str8n(tmat(1:Ngroups))-drange str8n(tmat(2:end))+...
        drange]; %matrix of overlapping timing ranges

    tnow=nan(size(tmat,1),Nper);
    like=@(t,sig) -log(sig)-.5*(t-taus).^2./sig^2;
    tset=nan(size(tmat));

    drange=.2;
    for n=1:Ngroups,
        inow=randi(size(tmat,1));
        tset(n,:)=tmat(inow,:);
        tmat=RFL(tmat,inow);
        tnow(n,:)=diff(tset(n,:))*(rand([1 Nper])-.5)+mean(tset(n,:)); end
        tnow=str8n(tnow'); signow=tnow/17; save'timedat.mat'); end %scalar property

%time differences and likelihood over differences
dtaus=taus*ones(1,L)-ones(L,1)*taus';
LtauD=-.5*dtaus.^2./dvar^2;

%likelihood computation
Like=@(onow,snow) -log(snow)-.5*(onow-taus).^2/snow^2;

%initialize likelihood and estimate
Lnow=zeros(L,1); tauest=nan(T,1); tic
for t=1:T
    Llastpostsum=logsum(Lnow*ones(1,L)+LtauD,1,diff(taus(1:2)));
    Lnow=like(tnow(t),signow(t)*3)+Llastpostsum;
    tauest(t)=logpeakval([Lnow taus]);
    if rem(t,Nper)==0, toc; end, end

%%%%%%%%%%%%%%%%
%%% PLOTTING %%%
figure(1); clf; %est by trial
subplot(2,1,1); hold on
for n=1:Ngroups,
    plot((n-1)*Nper+[1 Nper],mean(tset(n,:))*[1 1],'k-','LineWidth',2); end
plot(tauest,'.')
```

```
%%% remembered / estimated
subplot(2,1,2); hold on
plot([0 1.2],[0 1.2],'k-')
for n=1:Ngroups,
    plot(tset(n,:),mean(tset(n,:))*[1 1],'k-','LineWidth',1.3); end
plot(tnow,tauest,'.','Color',[.2 .3 .7]);

punderover=[]; %proportional error
for n=1:Ngroups,
    ilist=Nper*(n-1)+round(.5*Nper):Nper;
    punderover=[punderover; [tnow(ilist)-tset(n,1) ...
          (tauest(ilist)-tnow(ilist))/diff(tset(n,:))]]; end
%#ok<AGROW>
figure(2); clf;
plotmat(punderover,'ko','MarkerFaceColor','k','MarkerSize',6)
figure(3); clf; meshc(taus,taus,LtauD)
```

observations of scale readings. The estimate is better because if the underlying truth does not change, multiple observations can be combined. When estimates are only partially stable, we can exploit this partial stability by using a limited number of recent observations in combination for estimating the partially stable duration. Because we expect temporal intervals to change slowly, the change of interval (state) from one time step to another, encodes our information about the expected size of the possible changes from one interval to another. To keep changes in these intervals small, we will assume a Gaussian prior over changes in interval with a narrow width, $(\sigma\sqrt{2})e^{-\frac{1}{2}(\tau_t-\tau_{t-1})^2/\sigma^2}$, ($\sigma$ small). This updating of the true temporal interval based on the previous interval yields the following prior over interval for the current time step:

$$
\begin{aligned}
\varpi(\tau_t) &= \int d\tau_{t-1} p(\tau_{t-1}\cdot\tau_t \| [\imath_t]) \\
&= \int d\tau_{t-1} p(\tau_{t-1}\cdot\tau_t \| [T_{t-1}\cdot\sigma_\tau\cdot\imath_t]) \\
&= \int d\tau_{t-1} p(\tau_t | \tau_{t-1}\cdot\sigma_\tau\cdot\imath) p(\tau_{t-1} | T_{t-1}\cdot\sigma_\tau\cdot\imath) \\
&\propto \int d\tau_{t-1} (\sigma e^{-\frac{1}{2}(\tau_t-\tau_{t-1})^2/\sigma^2} p(\tau_{t-1} | T_{t-1}\cdot\sigma_\tau\cdot\imath)
\end{aligned}
$$

In the model explored above, we treated the memory for time intervals as if it were a prediction of the current state of a noisy external system that generated time intervals, where we assumed that sensory information regarding the system state is acquired at discrete times, and that during the interval between one sensory signal and another we update our information regarding the state via an internal model of possible state changes (i.e., the state evolution function). During each of these cycles of acquiring sensory information (which we can think of as a noisy observation of the state) and then allowing the state to change unobserved, the width of the posterior will cycle as well. Observing the state will typically narrow our posterior (we have acquired information), whereas leaving the state to change unobserved (where our only information regarding the state comes from predictions based on the state evolution function) will tend to widen that posterior.

In addition to the implications on our estimates of system state of this cycling of observations and corresponding cycling of information, we should also consider the implications of the width of the prior on range effects generally. The width of the prior sets, effectively, the range of 'natural variation' within the system state. Within this range, the state update will match changes in state with higher fidelity than outside the range. At the limit of a uniform (infinite) prior, the state update will precisely match the likelihood of the incoming observation, whereas at the limit of the punctate prior, the state cannot update, regardless of the likelihood of the incoming observation. The width of the prior depends critically on the uncertainty associated with state transitions: in other words, on the probability of the state 'drifting' from its current value during any future time step. Thus in designing a state estimator of this type, we would like to set the width of the prior to the size of the typical change in system state. By doing so, our overall estimates of state will be more stable than could be obtained by simply choosing the maximum state likelihood based on the observations obtained at each time step (this difference is illustrated by comparing Figure 4.4a and Figure 4.4b from the examples in this section).

For the simple model here where the state is supposed to remain relatively constant, a sharper prior will yield estimates that change slowly (you give more weight to the prior) and a wider less informative prior will yield estimates that change more quickly (you give less weight to the prior).

Exercises

1) What aspects of the Vierordt data were reproduced by the model? Which were not?
2) How does a relatively flat versus peaked prior change the model? Why
3) What evidence is there for/against the presence of a range effect in these data?

4.3 Decision

Decision-making should, *prima facia*, embody an attempt to acquire preferred outcomes and avoid nonpreferred outcomes. In quantitative terms, we would say that decisions are based on the *values* that we assign to the possible outcomes of our actions, and we should prefer decisions that yield the 'best' possible outcomes. Thus, before we can understand and optimize the decision-making enterprise, we must first think about value and how value can be combined with probability.

Think for a moment what decision-making would be like if the outcomes of our actions were always known. In this hypothetical world, one would confidently choose the course of action whose eventual outcome were the most desirable. An example of a micro-world with this property might be a bush whose berries were green up until the exact moment of peak flavor, at which time they turn red, and then blue when flavor has passed its peak. For a bunny interested in selecting a tasty berry to eat, the decision to choose the red berry hardly deserves the name decision: there is no uncertainty regarding whsiether the chosen berry would be at its tastiest – its color leaves no room for doubt.

To move beyond this simplest case, we should assign some numbers: For a hedonistic bunny, green berries (with their astringent, unripe flavor) are the least valued (to give a number, we will say the bunny rates them -5), whereas blue berries are good but not most desirable (it rates them a 1), and red berries are most desirable (rated 2).

Now because there is no uncertainty in this current hypothetical world, the *value of the choice to* eat red berries is, unsurprisingly, $+2$. How does uncertainty affect this value, however? Suppose we relax the certainty of the hypothetical relationship between berry color and taste, and suppose that 14 percent of red berries are not yet at peak flavor and still have the taste of green berries, whereas blue berries maintain their consistency of taste in all cases. Now, the choice to eat red berries might be called into question because our bunny cannot count unambiguously on red berries having the best flavor (rated a 2): 14 percent will have a taste rated -5. With no way of separating the red berries that have the taste rated -5 from those with the taste rated 2 means that a bunny choosing to eat red berries can expect to eat 14 percent astringent red berries and only 86 percent of the most-desired red, delicious berries.

Which berry should the bunny choose in this case? Should it stay with the red berry and put up with eating a small proportion of unripe berries, or should it change its decision and go with the still-yummy but less delicious blue berry?

Exercises

1) If given the choice between only the blue and green berries, which will the bunny choose? Why?
2) By what criterion should the bunny choose among the three berry colors in the uncertain-taste example? Give two possible criteria, and explain which decision is favored by each criterion.

4.3.1 The Mathematics of Decision Theory

The examples above will hopefully have primed our thoughts and intuitions regarding the correct method of combining value and probability: when we are uncertain regarding the value that will be realized from a given decision, the *possible* outcomes and their associated values are enumerated, and each outcome's value is scaled by the probability that it will actually be realized. This defines the scaled value function: $sv = p(t|\iota)v(t)$, where the probability and value both vary as functions of t (which describes some world-state, such as berry taste). Thus, if the hypothetical bunny in our earlier example chooses the blue berry, the calculation is trivial: there is one possible outcome (a taste value of $v(blue) = 1$), and because there is only one outcome it must occur with probability 1 [scaled $value = (p)(v) = (1)(1) = 1$]. However, if the red berry is chosen, the scaled value function becomes a bit more interesting: $sv = (p)(v) = [0.14(-5), 0.86(2)]$, representing the two possible values of the choice to eat a red berry.

The scaled value function is the basis for decision-making in the same way that the probability distribution is the basis for inference. And just as with probability functions used for inference, our first step toward characterizing the scaled value function is via the expectation operator (recall Chapter 3).

Example: Expected Value in the Bunnies and Berries Scenario

Once we have made a decision, that decision determines the probabilities of the outcomes of that decision and therefore also the values of the possible outcomes of our action. In the bunnies and berries example, choosing the blue berry has exactly one possible value-outcome, $v = 1$, whereas choosing the red berry has two possible value-outcomes, $v = \{-5, 2\}$. Furthermore, these outcomes are expected to occur with different probabilities, and these probabilities may in general change for different choices: so in the bunnies and berries example choosing a green berry yields $v = -5$ with probability 1, but choosing the red berry yields a value-outcome of $v = -5$ with probability 0.14.

The expectation of the value of a given decision can be computed by scaling the values assigned to the possible true world-states consistent with your decision by their corresponding probabilities, and taking the sum. In other words, the expectation of the value function is computed in exactly the same way as the expectation of any other variable. The interesting difference is that the probabilities assigned to different value-outcomes change with choices. As described above, the expected value of choosing a green berry is $EV = pv = (1)(-5) = -5$, whereas the expected value of choosing a red berry is $EV = \Sigma pv = (.14)(-5)+(.86)(2) = 1.02$.

In general, we will be concerned with a value function (v) that is contingent on both your belief regarding the state of the world ($\hat{\theta}$), and the true world-state, θ' [i.e., $v(\hat{\theta}, \theta')$]. For example, one common value function simply equates the value of any guess/belief regarding the state of the world $\hat{\theta}$ with the numerical difference $v(\hat{\theta}, \theta') = \Delta\theta = |\hat{\theta} - \theta'|$ between the predicted parameter $\hat{\theta}$ and the true parameter value, θ', describing the true world-state. The expected value is just the mean over possible value-outcomes computed as the sum or integral over the product of the values assigned to possible outcomes and the probabilities of those outcomes,

$$EV = E_{\hat{\theta}}\left[v(\hat{\theta}, \theta')\right] = \int dt\, v(\hat{\theta}, \theta')p(\theta'|\hat{\theta} \cdot \iota)$$

which we have encountered in its discrete form on several previous occasions above:

$$EV_i = E_{\hat{\theta}}\left[v(\hat{\theta}, \theta')\right] = \sum\nolimits_k \left[v(\hat{\theta}_i, \theta'_k)\right] p(\theta'_k|\hat{\theta}_i \cdot \iota)$$
$$= \sum\nolimits_k v_{i,k}p_k$$

Here, i indexes the choice or decision, $\hat{\theta}_i$, and k indexes the possible outcomes (true worldstates), θ'_k.

Making decisions based on less than certain information (also known as making a real-world decision) is always exactly equivalent to gambling. This insight appears to have been the motivation for the two-volume treatise on probability theory written by the Italian mathematician Bruno de Finetti (1906–1985) of the University of Rome, who famously based his exposition of probability theory on games of chance. In other words, he took a decision-theoretic approach to understanding probability and statistics, just as did the early American statistician Abraham Wald of Columbia University (1902–1950). The equivalence between decisions and gambles arises because we are uncertain about either the world states that bear on our decisions, the connection between decision and outcome, or both. The type of world state relevant to decision-making is exemplified by the bunnies and berries example described at the start of this section. If there were a known, one-to-one relationship between some berry characteristic (e.g., color) and value, the decision would be trivial – hardly worth the name. The cases with which we will be concerned, those in which the *possible* outcomes are known and can be enumerated, are uncertain because it is not known that the world is in a particular state (e.g., the chosen berry is at its peak ripeness). Choosing a red berry corresponds to a gamble wherein the bunny 'wins' two 'points' with probability 0.86, and 'loses' five 'points' with probability 0.14, as opposed to choosing the blue berry and winning 1 point with certainty. This yields the expected value calculation:

$$EV(red) = .14(-5)+.86(2) = 1.02$$

In other words, choosing to eat red berries is still the best average choice because any bunny choosing to eat blue berries can expect to have a very slightly less desirable average gastronomic experience ($EV = 1$).

To describe the jth choice we can generalize the berry example to the sum of outcome-values multiplied by their corresponding probabilities:

$$EV_j = \sum_i P_{ij} V_i$$

In the most general case we could also imagine that both probabilities *and* the values of outcomes might vary with the choice (i.e., replace v_i, where the value assigned to the ith possible outcome is independent of choice, with v_{ij}), although we will not explore such situations.

Exercises

1) Explain why it is useful to have a value function be based on the difference between your belief about the state of the world and the true world-state.
2) How is the value function described in Ex1 different from the bunnies & berries example value function? Explain how these two types of value function (lookup table vs. function based on differences) are likely to relate to different types of world-state parameters, and give two examples of each type of value function (and corresponding probability distribution).

Example: Fundamental Subjectivity of Decision Theory

Value, unlike probability, is intrinsically subjective. When we assign a probability function, we do so objectively in the sense that anyone with the same information *must* assign the *identical* probabilities. Not so with value: value is subjective, and the same world states or decision outcomes might hold very different intrinsic value for different people (just as not all bunnies will have the same taste preferences for berries). Indeed, if we look at the most strongly entrenched political and ethical debates that occur in our society, you will notice that the difference between people on one side of the debate and the other is usually *not* intelligence or moral integrity, but rather a different set of values placed on various world-states. If you value personal needs or safety over the rule of law you might turn to theft during a time of need; that is, you side with Valjean. On the other hand, if you value the rule of law above personal wants or needs, you side with

Javert. There are reasoned arguments to be made on both sides, and your decisions and actions will be dictated by your personal preferences on these issues (the result of a combination of factors, including patterns of reinforcement experienced over a lifetime, and one's cultural background – both that imposed by your particular 'accident of birth,' and that chosen in adulthood). The fundamentally subjective nature of value holds whether we are dealing with important life-and-death issues such as starvation versus the stability of society, or whether we are dealing with more mundane situations such as the small decisions encountered during your daily routine: all are dictated by the values we subjectively assign to various preferred and nonpreferred world-states (outcomes). The following group of examples is intended to highlight this in instances where value is equated with uncontroversial monetary sums.

In the scenario to be explored below, the year is 1999, and you have been hired by the hypothetically re-formed Pan-American airline company. To allow the company to overbook their flights, and acquire profit that would otherwise be lost due to no-shows, the company is in need of a consultant to do the calculations necessary to tell them how many no-shows to expect on a given flight. The newly re-formed airline will initially provide flights between New York and Boston, using a 200-passenger plane. You are hired to consult on the no-show issue, given an initial fee for your services, and promised a performance bonus once flights commence.

Since there is no data available from your employer that could help you assess the likely numbers of no-shows for a flight of this type, you make a trip to JFK airport. In 1999 it is possible to sit at any of the departure gates and monitor the number of passengers boarding planes. Focusing on flights from the various airlines that utilize the same size plane for flights to Boston, you compile the following frequency histogram [6] of the proportion of no-shows (zero through 5): $[8, 3, 4, 6, 12, 24]^{-1}$. This means that, for example, one-third of the flights you observed had a single no-show.

At this point, what is the best possible estimate of the number of no-shows that you can give to your employer? You might want to report the number with the highest frequency of occurrence (1), or you might report the number closest to the mean number of occurrences (2). There is in fact no definitive guiding principle at this point that would allow us to choose among the various single-number best guesses that might be given. As we will see below, the logical choice of decision when choosing among such alternatives is based on the value that each such choice yields. That is, your answer regarding the predicted number of no-shows per flight should, at this point, be 'it depends on the details of the performance bonus.' To illustrate why this is the case, we will consider the most commonly encountered *types* of estimate.

Example: Bonus Based on Number of Correct Estimates

In this and subsequent examples, keep in mind that we cannot expect to provide the correct number of no-shows for every Pan-Am flight; therefore, 100 percent correct estimation cannot be your goal. Instead, your goal is to maximize the amount you can expect

[6] We've compiled a frequency histogram, despite our warnings against using a frequency histogram in place of a probability distribution in the previous chapters. In this particular case (estimating a binomial rate), however, there is clear justification for the procedure. Such justification, the Glivenko–Cantelli theorem, depends on the number of observations that have gone into our frequency histogram. We will assume that our dataset is large enough that the frequency histogram provides a good estimate of no-show rates.

to be paid. Or, in the technical language of decision theory, to maximize your **expected gain** (where gain here refers to the monetary value represented by your paycheck). Given that your base pay is constant, the only way to maximize expected gain is to provide an estimate of the number of no-shows that will maximize the amount of bonus you can expect to receive.

With this in mind, consider a scenario in which your initial fee is $30,041.67, and you are offered a bonus of $100 for every flight within the first year of operation whose number of no-shows matches your prediction (and given that they plan to offer five flights per day, your bonus could become substantial). Intuitively, the answer might seem straightforward, but let's start with a few computations. First, we will ask ourselves what our expected bonus would be if we gave an estimate of zero no-shows. Based on our data and the assumption that rates of no-shows will be approximately constant over the course of the next year, we can reasonably expect this prediction to be correct in 12.5 percent of flights. This would yield a bonus of $(365*5*\$100)/8 = \$22,812$; of course, this is just shorthand for the full sum $(365*5*\$100)/8 + 0 + 0 + 0 + 0 + 0$ that corresponds to the expected proportion of no-shows multiplied by the bonus associated with those numbers of no-shows. At the other end of the spectrum, by providing a best estimate of 5 no-shows per flight you should expect a bonus of $(365*5*\$100)/24 = \$7,604$. Since the only difference between these two estimates of your bonus pay is the number in the denominator corresponding to the frequency of previously observed no-shows, it is clear that your maximum bonus should be achieved by telling the airline to expect to have a single no-show per flight.

Example: Bonus Proportional to Predicted-Actual No-Show Mismatch

In this scenario, your bonus is again highest when your prediction matches the actual number of no-shows in any given flight. Now, however, there is a penalty imposed when your prediction fails and that penalty is larger for larger mismatches. In this version of your consulting contract, the bonus for an exact match is now $80, it is $40 when there is a one-passenger difference between your estimate and the number of no-shows, $0 for a two-passenger difference, −$40 (bonus is reduced) for a three-passenger difference, −$80 for a four-passenger difference, and −$120 for a 5-passenger difference.

As a first step in our analysis, let's take a moment and consider how this example is different from the previous. First, the maximum bonus per flight is lower. In addition, when there is a large discrepancy between your estimate and the actual number of no-shows, your bonus is reduced – remember that the company will lose money whenever there is a discrepancy, so they would naturally like to encourage you to keep this discrepancy low.

Given the fact that there is no single estimate that will be correct for all flights, your bonus will be affected by all of the potential discrepancies between your estimate and actual number of no-shows (and therefore by every single flight). In this scenario we cannot choose our estimate based solely on the proportion of flights that should exactly match a given estimate (i.e., the shorthand calculation used above is not appropriate here). Now, to calculate the expected gain associated with each of the no-show estimates we might want to give our employer, we compute the sum of the products of the previously observed proportions of no-shows and the bonus associated with those numbers of no-shows under each possible best estimate; this is the expected gain calculation. So, if we tell PanAm that they should expect five no-shows per flight, the expected gain is

$$EG_5 = [p_0 G_{|0-5|} + p_1 G_{|1-5|} p_2 G_{|2-5|} p_3 G_{|3-5|} p_4 G_{|4-5|} p_5 G_{|5-5|}]^* 5^* 365$$
$$= [8^{-1}(-120) + 3^{-1}(-80) + 4^{-1}(-40) + 6^{-1}(0) + 12^{-1}(40) + 24^{-1}(80)]^* 5^* 365$$
$$= -\$82,125$$

It would clearly be a spectacularly bad idea to tell your employer to expect five no-shows per flight, because by the terms of your contract you would owe them just over $52*K* at the end of the first year (after returning your initial paycheck)! There are better options, however: if, for example, you had told them to expect three no-shows per flight, the calculation is now

$$EG_3 = [p_0 G_{|0-3|} + p_1 G_{|1-3|} p_2 G_{|2-3|} p_3 G_{|3-3|} p_4 G_{|4-3|} p_5 G_{|5-3|}]^* 5^* 365$$
$$= [8^{-1}(-40) + 3^{-1}(0) + 4^{-1}(40) + 6^{-1}(80) + 12^{-1}(40) + 24^{-1}(0)]^* 5^* 365$$
$$= \$39,541.67$$

which yields a positive bonus the end of the first year of operation. As an aside, notice that the above two calculations could be rewritten in terms of the discrepancy between the predicted and observed number of no-shows:

$$EG_n = [p_0 G_{|0-n|} + p_1 G_{|1-n|} p_2 G_{|2-n|} p_3 G_{|3-n|} p_4 G_{|4-n|} p_5 G_{|5-n|}]^* 5^* 365$$
$$= \begin{bmatrix} 8^{-1}(80-40|0-n|) + 3^{-1}(80-40|1-n|) + 4^{-1}(80-40|2-n|) \\ +6^{-1}(80-40|3-n|) + 12^{-1}(80-40|4-n|) + 24^{-1}(80-40|5-n|) \end{bmatrix}^* 5^* 365$$

These calculations should tell us that there is a clear difference between the two scenarios so far examined. We should further notice that these differences are based solely on the structure of the performance bonus, since none of the data that we have used to estimate the probable numbers of occurrences of flights with 0, 1, 2, etc. numbers of no-shows has changed.

Example: Bonus Based on the Squared Discrepancy in No-Show Passengers

Finally, we will take a look at the performance of a bonus structure in which you are penalized in proportion to the square of the discrepancy between your estimate and the actual number of no-show passengers.

In this scenario, computing expected gain is a bit less intuitive than in the previous examples. We have to square the *discrepancy* and use this as a multiplier to reduce a base-level bonus (the bonus given for an exact match). Thus, it is best to start by modifying the long form of the expected gain equation from the previous scenario, and modify it to use the square of the discrepancy instead of the absolute value of the discrepancy:

$$EG_n = [p_0 G_{[0-n]^2} + p_1 G_{[1-n]^2} p_2 G_{[2-n]^2} p_3 G_{[3-n]^2} p_4 G_{[4-n]^2} p_5 G_{[5-n]^2}]^* 5^* 365$$
$$= \begin{bmatrix} 8^{-1}(120 - 50[0-n]^2) + 3^{-1}(120 - 50[1-n]^2) \\ +4^{-1}(120 - 50[2-n]^2) + 6^{-1}(120 - 50[3-n]^2) \\ +12^{-1}(120 - 50[4-n]^2) + 24^{-1}(120 - 50[5-n]^2) \end{bmatrix}^* 5^* 365$$

BOX 4.2 The Minimum Risk Criterion

In the airline example we computed the maximum expected gain, or minimum loss, for each possible choice of predicted number of no-shows. In discussing the squared-error loss function, we considered that while the bonus structure in this example did not yield the best possible scenario for the consultant (the *predicted–actual no-show mismatch* example did), there were good reasons for the airline to impose such a bonus structure. If given the choice, however, you might opt for the second bonus scenario – even if the maximum expected gain were slightly smaller in the squared-error example than in the predicted-actual mismatch example. The reason is that we can be more confident that we will end up *without a major loss* by avoiding the squared-error loss function in this set of examples. This aversion to possible losses must be weighed against the lure of higher potential gains. The minimum-risk criterion is precisely one solution to this trade-off, because ***risk*, defined as the expectation of negative gain**, is an *average* of the possible outcomes. That average does not have a separate weighting factor that penalizes risk functions with greater spreads between the maximum and the minimum *possible losses*.

To attempt a more intuitive understanding of the averaging that is the basis for the minimum risk criterion, let's return for a moment to the (second) bunnies and berries example. If we recall, there were three taste sensations that could be elicited when eating a berry: an unpleasant acid-unripe flavor (rated −5), a sweet berry flavor (rated 1) and a peak-of-ripeness sweet berry flavor (rated 2). There is information in the color of the berry that allows bunnies to at least partially predict what flavor he will experience when eating any particular berry. The values, here given as losses, and probabilities associated with the three colors of berry (green, blue, red) are

$$\ell_r = 5, -1, -2, p(v_j|r \cdot \imath) = 0.14, 0, 0.86$$
$$\ell_b = 5, -1, -2, p(v_j|b \cdot \imath) = 0, 1.0$$
$$\ell_g = 5, -1, -2, p(v_j|g \cdot \imath) = 1, 0, 0$$

or written shorthand,

$$\ell = 5, -1, -2p(v_j|c \cdot \imath)$$

where c indexes the *color* of the chosen berry and j indexes its *taste*.

We compute the minimum-risk choice of berry color by computing the three-element risk function:

$$\boldsymbol{r} = r_r, r_b, r_g = r_c \left[\begin{array}{l} c = r, b, g \\ r_c = (\ell_j)p(\ell_j|c \cdot \imath) \end{array} \right. .$$
$$= -1.02, -1, +5$$

This loss function clearly tells us to avoid choosing the green berry (*maximum loss* = 5), but what about our choice between the red and blue berries? Based on the computation above, the minimum-risk criterion tells us that we should eat the red berries: but let's think a bit further about what this choice buys us. The risk is higher for the blue berry, certainly, but only slightly so. Furthermore, the magnitude of the improvement in risk when choosing the red berry must be weighed against the fact that the risk computation does not encode the fact that blue berries will be uniformly sweet, whereas red berries will be sometimes sweet and sometimes very unpleasant-tasting. That is, we can be certain of a desirable outcome when choosing the blue berry, but there is some volatility in the outcome when choosing a red berry. Therefore, although the risk is higher, our bunny might intuitively prefer to nevertheless *avoid* the red berries in favor of the slightly higher-risk blue berry. Choosing the red berry will expose the bunny to a noticeable proportion of unpleasant-tasting berries, all to end up with an overall (averaged over all berries) taste experience that is probably not discriminably better (in terms of just-noticeable difference in taste, especially averaged over time) than what would have been achieved by simply choosing the blue berry.

The intuition is that a bunny might prefer to choose berries that are *all* tasty, albeit slightly less than maximally tasty, instead of eating 14 percent unpleasant-tasting berries mixed in with the maximally tasty red berries that would over time yield an average taste sensation that is slightly superior to the blue berry. In this case, the bunny is attempting to maximize taste sensation while simultaneously minimizing contact with unpleasant-tasting berries. One strategy of avoiding potential losses is to use 'minimax' decision strategy, wherein (1) a list of worst-case scenarios corresponding to each choice/action is made, and (2) the action corresponding to the smallest loss from this list is chosen. Minimax procedures are useful when one is focused on choosing a decision that will minimize potential losses. Aside from minimum risk (maximum expected gain) and minimax decision strategies, one could define any number of other decision strategies. For example one could define a value function that is the sum of the usual gain function and the negative of some proportion of the variance of the gain function. This would also tend to move decisions away from those with high average gain but also high variance.

In this vein, it has been found that individuals have stable preferences for either focusing on achieving gains or avoiding losses, called a *promotion* and *prevention* focus, respectively. Individuals with a promotion focus appear to downplay potential negative consequences, focusing instead on all the good things that might come about under various decisions (such as eating the best-tasting berry); in contrast, individuals with a prevention focus tend to focus on potential negative consequences, and allocate decisions based on avoiding those undesired outcomes (such as avoiding the worst-tasting berry). In terms of losses and risk, this suggests there is a psychological sensitization to gains (in the case of promotion focused individuals) or losses (prevention focus) such that an individual may experience a real-world gain (say, of $5000) differently than (the negative of) a real-world loss of the same real-world item. These types of asymmetric gain/loss function can yield complex and interesting patterns of behavior, and much research in psychology and neuroscience is devoted to understanding stable patters of decision-making within this context.

This scenario provides a higher base level of bonus ($120 when your prediction is exactly correct), but squaring the discrepancy when computing penalties will lead to an overall larger penalty in case of a large discrepancy.

When we compute expected gain for this scenario, we see that making mistakes is indeed highly costly. For example, whereas predicting five no-show passengers per flight in the previous scenario would have cost a bit over \$82K in negative bonus, here it leads to an expected gain of

$$
\begin{aligned}
EG_5 &= [p_0 G_{[0-5]^2} + p_1 G_{[1-5]^2} p_2 G_{[2-5]^2} p_3 G_{[3-5]^2} p_4 G_{[4-5]^2} p_5 G_{[5-5]^2}]^* 5^* 365 \\
&= \begin{bmatrix} 8^{-1}(120 - 50[-5]^2) + 3^{-1}(120 - 50[-4]^2) \\ +4^{-1}(120 - 50[-3]^2) + 6^{-1}(120 - 50[-2]^2) \\ +12^{-1}(120 - 50[-1]^2) + 24^{-1}(120 - 50[0]) \end{bmatrix}^* 5^* 365 \\
&= -\$826,573
\end{aligned}
$$

In other words, you would owe the airline nearly a million dollars. Why would you negotiate a contract with a clause specifying such a penalty system? Again, the airline will argue that this bonus structure is intended to both motivate you and to offset some of the lost revenue due to unfilled seats, and also from compensating irate customers with free meals and/or flight vouchers. The amount of this compensation may become particularly large in cases where there are *groups* of customers bumped from their seats, because such a group will realize that the airline had overbooked and will in consequence be more likely to extract not only fair compensation for their time and disrupted plans, but also a bit of social media revenge. And while the consequences of choosing the wrong prediction is in this case extreme, choosing the best prediction should yield a reasonably nice bonus.

Example: Meta-level Decisions and Overall Best Choices

Hopefully these examples have piqued your interest as well as jumpstarted your intuitions regarding the influence of gains and losses on decision-making. To close this initial section on decision theory, we should not fail to report the best possible decisions to be made by the consultant in these hypothetical examples. That is, we should decide on the best-estimate number of no-shows in each scenario. In the first, our best choice is clearly to predict a single no-show per flight. In the second scenario, our best choice is to predict two no-show passengers per flight. This is also the best choice in the final of the three scenarios. If you have not done so already, you should take a moment and compute the expected gain for each of the six numbers of no-show passengers, and verify for yourself that the maximum expected gain corresponds to the choice of prediction just given.

Now let's assume for a moment that we are capable of making, by means of the expected gain calculation, the best choice of prediction in each scenario. Does this mean that your total bonus will be the same in each of the three scenarios outlined above? If you performed the expected gain calculations requested in the previous paragraph, you will know that each of these contracts will be expected to yield different bonuses at the end of the first year – even after maximizing your bonus in each (if you did not complete those calculations, please do so now). Given that this is the case, we can ask an additional question: of the three contracts, for which should we have negotiated? The contract that could have paid you the highest bonus at the close of the first year of operation was the second. This contract should be strongly preferred, not only because your expected gain under this contract is nearly \$7K higher than in either of the other two contracts. You should also feel uneasy about the squared-error contract, since a single flight with an unusually large number of no-shows could easily decimate your bonus. This is worrying because, while your observations of other airlines found no flights with more than five no-shows, there are good reasons to believe that there might be a small number of flights with more. For example, problems with electronic ticketing, or problems with passengers finding the correct gate could, in the first weeks of operation, cause additional passengers to miss their flights on a new airline. Even a small number of such unusual events could completely wipe out your bonus, when you consider that a single flight with 12 no-shows (*vs.* your prediction of 2 no-shows) would reduce your bonus by $120 - 50[10]^2$, and just 7 such events (or their equivalent) would force you to return your initial fee (and then some)!

Exercises

1) Perform the expected gain computations in each of the three scenarios, under all six possible choices of prediction. Show your work.
2) Which of the predictions yield positive expected gains under each of the three contracts? Which is the best contract, in terms of yielding a report to your employer with the highest expected gain? Are there any potential disadvantages to choosing this 'highest-gain' contract?
3) If the airline lost \$100 in revenue for each unfilled seat and gave every bumped passenger a \$100 flight voucher, by how many seats should the airline overbook each flight to maximize their expected gain?
4) If the airline lost \$100 in revenue for each unfilled seat, but simply directed irate (bumped) passengers to the ticket's fine print warning them to arrive early or they could be bumped, by how many seats should the airline overbook each flight?
5) How do the best interests of the airline and the best interests of the consultant differ in (2),(3) and (4), if at all? Explain.
6) Under what circumstance might you choose an estimate that favors the airline's bottom line over your own highest expected bonus?

Example: Loss and Risk

In the previous example we were concerned with maximizing gain, in the form of a bonus paid to a hypothetical airline consultant. In many circumstances it may be more natural to focus on the loss function, which is simply the negative of the gain. We write the loss function, $\ell(\hat{\theta},\theta)$, and it encodes the loss incurred when we have chosen $\hat{\theta}$ (or predicted $\hat{\theta}$, or acted as if the state of the world were $\hat{\theta}$), when in fact the true state of the world is θ.

Risk[7] is then defined as the expected value of the loss function, $\ell(\hat{\theta},\theta)$, under a given choice, $\hat{\theta}$, which we will recall from Chapter 3 is defined:

$$r(\hat{\theta}) = E_{\hat{\theta}}(\ell) = \int d\theta\, \ell(\hat{\theta},\theta)p(\theta|\imath)$$

where the subscript indicates that the expectation is computed holding $\hat{\theta}$ constant within the loss function. Furthermore, we can expand this to define the risk as a function of the vector of all possible choices, $\hat{\boldsymbol{\theta}}$:

[7] Be aware that there are instances where risk is defined in terms of a sampling distribution (i.e., a frequentist concept), rather than using the Bayesian decision-theoretic definition.

$$r(\hat{\boldsymbol{\theta}}) = \int d\theta \ell(\hat{\boldsymbol{\theta}}, \theta) p(\theta | \imath)$$

We were computing a discrete form of the (negative) risk function in the airline example to find the best choice of estimated number of no-show passengers to predict. In each case, you computed the negative of the risk (i.e., the expected gain) for each possible choice of no-show, such that for each element of the vector of possible choices, $\hat{\boldsymbol{\theta}}$, there was a corresponding expected gain. The set of these expected gains (negative expected losses), gives us the risk function, $r(\hat{\boldsymbol{\theta}}) = -[EG_{\hat{\theta}=0}, EG_{\hat{\theta}=1}, \ldots, EG_{\hat{\theta}=5}]$, which we then minimized to find the best of the expected bonuses under each contract (see Box 4.2). This general method can be used to compute the risk associated with any individual decision, $\hat{\theta}$, under a discrete probability distribution over possible outcomes, θ,

$$E_{\hat{\theta}}(\ell) = \Sigma_{\theta} \ell(\hat{\theta}, \theta) p(\theta | \hat{\theta} \cdot \imath)$$

with an associated risk function over possible decisions,

$$r(\hat{\boldsymbol{\theta}}) = [E_1(\ell), E_2(\ell), \ldots, E_N(\ell)]$$

Referring again to no-show behavior in the airline example above, we can also consider the expected gain from the best choice of $\hat{\theta}$ that can be derived from each contract to construct the vector of minimized risks ($\vartheta = min[r_c(\hat{\boldsymbol{\theta}})]$) over the possible choices of contract (c), which yields the risk function:

$$r(\boldsymbol{\vartheta}) = [r_1(\hat{\boldsymbol{\theta}}), \ldots, r_4(\hat{\boldsymbol{\theta}})],$$

which we minimized intuitively to form the meta-decision to prefer the second contract.

Exercises

1) How is expected gain related to risk?
2) Why are there two inputs to the loss function, $\ell(\hat{\theta}, \theta')$? Write a valid loss function described by $\ell(\hat{\theta})$.
3) Write a program to compute the risk function over possible contracts in the airline example.

4.3.2 Decision and Measurement

A decision can be thought of as a shorthand way of saying that we will *act as if* the true world-state is described by the parameter vector $\boldsymbol{\theta}' = (\theta'_1, \theta'_2, \ldots, \theta'_N)$, where the chosen action is advantageous when the parameters of that vector (θ'_1, θ'_2, etc.) correctly parameterize the world. One of the simplest applications of decision theory is usually referred to as ***point estimation***, which is just another way of saying the final best estimate of a parameter based on a corresponding posterior distribution (i.e., the activity that has occupied much of our time so far). In previous chapters we have calculated posterior distributions over various parameters, and have also given our best estimates of those parameter values based on the computed posteriors. Although we have not made it explicit until now, the transition between the posterior distribution and a single-number summary or best estimate involves a decision. As a linguistic point it is obviously true that *choosing* a single best-guess value is clearly a *decision*, but it is also true in the fundamental decision-theoretic sense: the difference between choosing one particular best-guess value of a parameter over another possible value of that parameter is a decision problem. The three most common best-guess choices are the estimates represented by the posterior mean, the posterior median, and the peak of the posterior. You may have previously wondered about the difference, practically speaking, of using each of these three best-estimate values when characterizing the information in the posterior, $p(\theta|d \cdot \imath)$, regarding the true value of θ. We are now finally in a position to quench your curiosity on this matter: It turns out that the difference lies in the *values* assigned to choosing an estimate $\hat{\theta}$ when in fact the true value is θ'; each estimate (mean, median, peak) results from a different definition of *the extent to which we dislike errors of various kinds.*

The estimate $\hat{\theta}$ that we ultimately choose from among the possible true values of the parameter will, of course, be based on the posterior distribution and thus ultimately (1.5). We will refer to this single-number best-estimate value as our ***measurement*** of the value of that parameter. If, however, we intend to remain within the objective realm of probability theory without venturing into the intrinsically subjective domain of decisions, we may also refer to the posterior itself as our measurement of the parameter (this will be the topic of Chapter 5), since any single-number best estimate will be chosen based on the posterior. There should be no ambiguity between these uses, because a posterior distribution must by definition contain multiple values whereas decisions based on applying a cost function will usually settle on a single best value.

In the following examples we will explore the scenario of an archer shooting at a target. Our hypothetical archer will select one from among a range of possible combinations of bow tension, grip position, bow angle, muscular contraction, etc., parameterized by α_i. This selection (a choice α_i, which we will refer to with the shorthand: the ith 'aimpoint') will cause the shot to unfold in a particular way, and defines a set of possible landing positions - some of which will be more likely than others. That is, it defines a probability distribution, $p(\theta|\alpha_i \cdot \imath)$, over possible landing positions, θ. Because there is uncertainty regarding the ultimate landing position of the arrow along the θ dimension (vertical position through the bull's-eye) for any given aimpoint, we represent the archer's information regarding the ultimate landing location of the arrow as the probability distribution, $p(\theta|\alpha_i \cdot \imath)$, where we will assume that the bull's-eye is at $\theta = \theta' = 0$. For any chosen aimpoint, the arrow may end up at the center of the bull's-eye, $\hat{\theta} = \theta'$, slightly above or below but still on the extended bull's-eye target $0 < |\hat{\theta} - \theta'| < T$, outside the extended bull's-eye but still on the target hanging on the wall $T < |\hat{\theta} - \theta'| < R$, or it may end up far enough from the bull's-eye that the arrow completely misses the target $|\hat{\theta} - \theta'| > R$, and instead hits the wall to which the target is attached.

There are two ways that we will want to apply decision theory in the context of the archer example. (1) Planning problem: we want to select the index corresponding to the aimpoint, α_i, that will be most likely to yield a maximally favorable outcome, $EG_i = \max(EG)$. Notice that we must first compute the risk of each aimpoint (loss associated with the set of endpoints, θ, predicted by the posterior distribution, $p(\theta|\alpha_i \cdot \iota)$, that are associated with the ith aimpoint). We then select the best choice of aimpoint by comparing elements of the risk function,

$$r(\alpha_i) = -EG_{\alpha_i} = \int d\theta \ell(\theta \cdot \alpha_i) p(\theta|\alpha_i \cdot \iota)$$

from the set of aimpoints. Here the archer's goal is to choose the aimpoint that leads to the most advantageous probability distribution over arrow endpoint, which we will assume is the minimum risk aimpoint.

Notice that in the scenario above, each individual aimpoint (α_i) yields a *single* risk, where risk is defined in terms of a loss function, $\ell(\theta, \alpha_i)$, that encodes the loss associated with arrow endpoints that deviate from the bull's-eye. (2) Estimation problem: the second application of decision theory in the archer example is designed to allow us to decide, for a single aimpoint, which is the best *prediction* of the arrow's landing position. We might imagine this scenario as one in which we loosed the arrow and watched its initial flight path (i.e., obtained some relevant data, $\boldsymbol{d}$), and want to use this data (and our background information about the aimpoint) to estimate where the arrow will land. By focusing on a single aimpoint (e.g., α_3) and its corresponding posterior distribution $p(\theta|\boldsymbol{d}\cdot\alpha_3\cdot\iota)$, we can apply a loss function that encodes the loss associated with predicting that the arrow will land at $\hat{\theta}$ when it in fact lands at one of the θ locations [i.e., $\ell(\theta, \hat{\theta})$], to select the best prediction of arrow landing position. At its conclusion we will have constructed, for this *single* aimpoint (i.e., α_i), a risk function over the set of predictions indexed by $j, \hat{\theta}_j$, within the range of possible landing positions, θ:

$$r_i(\hat{\theta}_j) = -EG_{\hat{\theta}_j} = \int d\theta \ell(\theta, \hat{\theta}_j) p(\theta|\boldsymbol{d} \cdot \alpha_i \cdot \iota)$$

where the minimum of this function will be chosen as the best prediction (or 'estimate,' or 'measurement') of the arrow's landing position.

Notice that all behaviors can be thought of in terms of decision theory. This is obvious in fields such as social or cognitive neuroscience, where behaviors are obviously decisions. But it is also true of the more basic fields of motor control and perception, where the selection of a movement plan for something as mundane as typing on a keyboard involves a decision (Planning problem), and where the brain must perceptually interpret its noisy sensory stimulation in terms of the possible real-world causes of sensory stimulation (Estimation problem).

In the examples below we will examine these planning and estimation applications of decision theory within the archer scenario for the three most common loss functions: zero-one, absolute error, and squared-error losses.

Example: Uniform Loss (Zero-One Loss; Binary Loss)

Of the available scenarios, zero-one loss makes the most sense in practice when there are discrete categories of desired/undesired outcome. Here, a small circular target of radius T at the bull's-eye would separate the outcome space into discrete desired/undesired outcomes, where arrows landing within the target earn some reward, and missing the target results in a penalty. We can, however, simplify the mathematics a bit by subtracting the

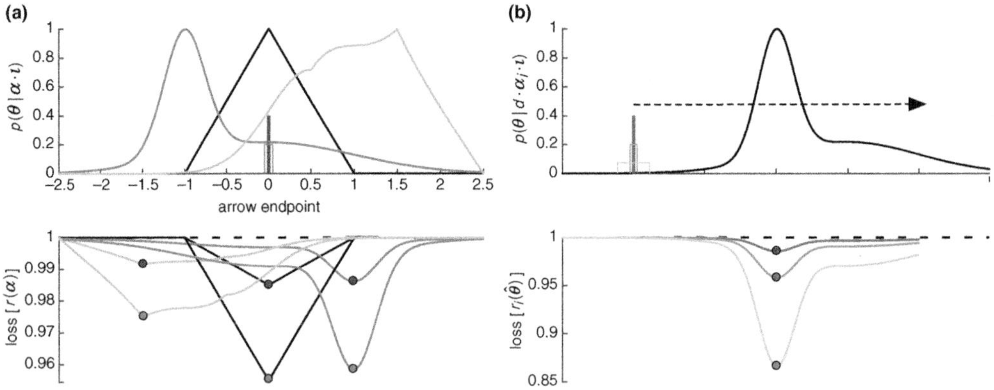

Figure 4.5 Zero-one loss and risk. (a) The upper panel shows three probability distributions that each represent the landing probabilities for a different 'method' of shooting the arrow directly at the target, and two target widths superimposed (rectangles). The lower panel shows the risk functions associated with different choices of aimpoint, where minimum risk aimpoints are marked with a circle. (b) The upper panel shows a probability distribution over the unknown landing position of the arrow along the θ parameter (black line) for a particular aimpoint, plotted along with three differently sized binary reward regions. The loss function associated with predicting that the arrow will land at any given location (symbolized by moving the reward region across the parameter space) is shown in the lower panel. The minimum-risk choices of predicted endpoint are shown as circles for the three widths of the reward region. A punctate reward always dictates that the peak of the distribution be chosen as the best estimate.

reward off of both penalty and reward, to leave a loss function containing only a nonzero penalty component:[8]

$$\ell(\theta', \theta) = \begin{cases} 0, |\theta' - \theta| \leq T \\ A, |\theta' - \theta| > T \end{cases}$$

This allows us to deal only with positive losses, and ignore the negative part of the loss function that describes hitting the target. In terms of choosing the aimpoint α to hit the target, this yields a risk of

$$\begin{aligned} r(\alpha) &= \int_{-\infty}^{\infty} d\theta \ell(\theta, \theta') p(\theta\,|\alpha \cdot \iota) \\ &= \int_{-\infty}^{\infty} d\theta A p(|\theta - \theta'| > T|\alpha \cdot \iota) \\ &= A\left[\int_{-\infty}^{\theta'-T} d\theta p(\theta\,|\alpha \cdot \iota) + \int_{\theta'+T}^{\infty} d\theta p(\theta\,|\alpha \cdot \iota\right] \end{aligned}$$

Notice that in the planning application of decision theory to the archer problem we are focused on comparing the outcome of the shot, the arrow's landing position along the θ dimension, to the location of the bull's-eye, θ'. In the final equation we have broken the original integral into two parts that exclude the region immediately surrounding our chosen estimate of the bull's-eye's location, because only θ values in the ranges

[8] Or, if we were optimists, we could subtract out the penalty, and deal only with the reward. This would yield a gain function, $g = -\ell$. Aside from their shorter descriptions, loss and risk (as opposed to gain and expected gain) are somewhat more common, although you will see both sets of value functions used in the scientific literature.

$(-\infty, \theta' - T)$ and $(\theta'+T, \infty)$ will be associated with nonzero loss when the criterion is satisfied. Recognizing this, we can also define the risk in terms of the difference between total probability and the mass *within* a target-radius of the bull's-eye:

$$\begin{aligned} r(\alpha) &= A \int_{-\infty}^{\infty} d\theta p(|\theta - \theta'| > T|\alpha \cdot \iota) \\ &= A\left[1 - \int d\theta p(|\theta - \theta'| \leq T|\alpha \cdot \iota\right] \\ &\propto 1 - \int_{\theta'-T}^{\theta'+T} d\theta p(\theta|\alpha \cdot \iota) \end{aligned}$$

where we have dropped the irrelevant A multiplier because it changes nothing in this case, when our purpose is only to find the minimum of the risk function. The final line states that risk is minimized when the probability mass contained *within* a target-radius of the bull's-eye is greatest, which occurs when we have chosen α so that we are enclosing the largest part of the high-density region of the probability distribution $p(\theta'|d \cdot \iota)$ within the range $[\theta' - T, \theta'+T]$. Taking this statement to its limit in the case of smaller and smaller target radii (Fig. 4.5), we see that for a punctate target the best choice of α will place the peak of the probability distribution (its point of highest density) at the punctate target location. In keeping with this, if we then reduce the width of T such that $T \to 0$ we find that the choice of $\hat{\theta}$ that minimizes risk is, $\hat{\theta} = \breve{\theta}$, at the peak of the posterior, $p(\breve{\theta}|d \cdot \iota)$. This makes sense, because an infinitesimally small target radius will enclose the greatest probability mass if it is centered at the highest density point, $\hat{\theta} = \breve{\theta}$. Here, missing the straw hay-bale on which the target is affixed is no worse than missing the bull's-eye of the target by one fiber-width. It is an odd loss function when gradations in error are meaningful, but a sensible loss function when the relevant outcome variable is binary (hit/miss, yes/no, on/off, etc.), as the archer/target examples in Figure 4.5 demonstrate.

We can also use a binary-valued loss function when choosing our best estimate of the arrow's landing location, θ. This is analogous to saying that you are only interested in the estimate of the underlying parameter that is *most representative*, based on the information in the posterior. Figure 4.5b shows a series of loss functions, each corresponding to a different width of such a binary-valued loss function. Thus, a given posterior distribution (which we will assume is a product of having chosen the α_i aimpoint) will assign probabilities $p(\theta|\mathbf{d} \cdot \alpha_i \cdot \iota)$ to a set of possible arrow landing positions, θ, and each value of this parameter may be chosen as its measured value (choosing the jth such value will be written $\hat{\theta}_j$). Choosing the jth value of θ as our measured value has associated with it the risk

$$r_i(\hat{\theta}_j) = \int d\theta \ell(\theta, \hat{\theta}_j) p(\theta|\mathbf{d} \cdot \alpha_i \cdot \iota)$$

which reflects the probabilities of the possible arrow endpoints, and the loss associated with having chosen $\hat{\theta}_j$) as our measured value when in fact some other value of θ may be the true endpoint:

$$\ell(\hat{\theta}, \theta) = \begin{cases} 0, |\hat{\theta} - \theta| \leq T \\ A, |\hat{\theta} - \theta| > T \end{cases}$$

Programming Aside: Zero-One Loss/Risk (Fig 4.5)

In the left-hand column of plots (a), we define three posterior distributions for landing positions of the arrow, when the location of the aimpoint is nominally zero (upper plot). We then ask, via a decision-theoretic analysis making use of the zero-one loss function, 'by how much should we shift these (nominally unshifted) probability distributions to minimize risk?'. We see (lower plot) that the triangular posterior need not be shifted, because its minimum risk point is at zero. To minimize risk with the other two distributions, one must be shifted positively and one negatively (by 1 and −1.5 units, respectively).

```
%zero-one loss / risk lefthand (a) panel
figure(1); clf
thetas=linspace(-3,3,1200);
Tlist=[.01 .025]; hlist=[.4 .2]; grylist=[.0 .5 .75];
collist=[.2 .3 .6; .4 .5 .9];
LW=1.4; xminmax=[-2.5 2.5];
for iT=1:length(Tlist), T=Tlist(iT); subplot(2,1,1), hold on
    plist=[zeros(1,sum(thetas<-1)) linspace(0,1,sum(and(thetas<=0,thetas>=-1)))
      linspace(1,0,sum(and(thetas<=1,thetas>0))) zeros(1,sum(thetas>1))];
    plot(thetas,plist,'.','Color',grylist(1)*[1 1 1])

    plot(-T*iT*[1 1],[0 hlist(iT)],'-','Color',collist(iT,:),'LineWidth',LW);
    plot(T*iT*[1 1],[0 hlist(iT)],'-','Color',collist(iT,:),'LineWidth',LW);
    plot([-T T]*iT,hlist(iT)*[1 1],'-','Color',collist(iT,:),'LineWidth',LW);

    subplot(2,1,2); hold on
    ptot=sum(plist);
    plot(xminmax,[1 1],'k--','LineWidth',1.8)
    r=nan(size(plist));
    for inow=1:length(thetas), dtheta=thetas(inow);
        iset=find(abs(thetas+dtheta)<=T);
        r(inow)=ptot-sum(plist(iset)); end
    plot(thetas,r/ptot,'.','Color',grylist(1)*[1 1 1]);
    rmin=mean(r(isnear(r,min(r))))/ptot;
    plot(mean(thetas(isnear(r,min(r)))),rmin,'ko',...
        'MarkerFaceColor',collist(iT,:),'MarkerSize',8);

    subplot(2,1,1); hold on
    plist=npdf(thetas,0,1);
    plist=plist+npdf(thetas,-1,.25); plist=plist/max(plist);
    plot(thetas,plist,'.','Color',grylist(2)*[1 1 1]);

    subplot(2,1,2); hold on
    ptot=sum(plist);
    plot(xminmax,[1 1],'k--','LineWidth',1.8)
    r=nan(size(plist));
    for inow=1:length(thetas), dtheta=thetas(inow);
        iset=find(abs(thetas+dtheta)<T);
        r(inow)=ptot-sum(plist(iset)); end
    plot(thetas,r/ptot,'.','Color',grylist(2)*[1 1 1]);
    plot(thetas(isnear(r,min(r))),r(isnear(r,min(r)))/ptot,...
      'ko','MarkerFaceColor',collist(iT,:),'MarkerSize',8);

    subplot(2,1,1), hold on
    thetas=linspace(-3,3,1200);
    plist=[zeros(1,700) linspace(0,1,200)];
    plist=[plist(1:end-1) linspace(1,0,201) zeros(1,100)];
```

```
    plist=plist+npdf(thetas,.5,.5); plist=plist/max(plist);
    plot(thetas,plist,'.','Color',grylist(3)*[1 1 1]);

    subplot(2,1,2); hold on
    ptot=sum(plist);
    plot(xminmax,[1 1],'k--','LineWidth',1.8)
    for inow=1:length(thetas), dtheta=thetas(inow);
        iset=find(abs(thetas+dtheta)<T);
        r(inow)=ptot-sum(plist(iset)); end
    plot(thetas,r/ptot,'.','Color',grylist(3)*[1 1 1]);
    plot(thetas(isnear(r,min(r))),r(isnear(r,min(r)))/ptot,...
    'ko','MarkerFaceColor',collist(iT,:),'MarkerSize',8); end

subplot(2,1,1); axis([-2.5 2.5 0 1])
subplot(2,1,2); axis([-2.5 2.5 .999*rmin 1])
```

In the right-hand column of plots (b) we plot three risk functions, each one associated with a different target-width but with the same posterior probability over arrow endpoints, and all using the zero-one loss function. Here, the minimum risk point tells us which location along the theta axis to choose as our measurement of the (as-yet unseen) arrow endpoint.

```
%zero-one loss / risk righthand (b) panel
%estimate = peak
Tlist=[.01 .025 .075]; hlist=[.4 .2 .075]; grylist=[.4 .6 .8];
collist=[.2 .3 .6; .3 .4 .8; .4 .5 .9];
LW=1.4; xminmax=[-3 3];
thetas=linspace(-3,3,1200);
plist=npdf(thetas,1,1); plist=plist+npdf(thetas,-0,.25); plist=plist/max(plist);

figure(1); clf;
subplot(2,1,1); hold on
plot(thetas,plist/max(plist),'k.')

%plot rectangles for target radii
for iT=1:length(Tlist), T=Tlist(iT);
   plot(-T*iT*[1 1]-2,[0 hlist(iT)],'-','Color',grylist(iT)*[1 1 1],'LineWidth',LW);
   plot(T*iT*[1 1]-2,[0 hlist(iT)],'-','Color',grylist(iT)*[1 1 1],'LineWidth',LW);
   plot([-T T]*iT-2,hlist(iT)*[1 1],'-','Color',grylist(iT)*[1 1 1],'LineWidth',LW); end
axis([xminmax 0 1])

%plot risk function for each target
subplot(2,1,2); hold on
ptot=sum(plist);
plot(xminmax,[1 1],'k--','LineWidth',1.8)
for iT=1:length(Tlist), T=Tlist(iT);
    ir=find(abs(thetas<=2));r=nan(size(ir));
    for inow=1:length(ir), dtheta=thetas(ir(inow));
        iset=find(and(thetas>=dtheta-T,thetas<=dtheta+T));
        r(inow)=ptot-sum(plist(iset)); end
    plot(thetas(ir),r/ptot,'.','Color',grylist(iT)*[1 1 1]);
    plot(mean(thetas(isnear(r,min(r)))),r(isnear(r,min(r)))/ptot,
       'ko','MarkerFaceColor',collist(iT,:),'MarkerSize',8); end
axis([xminmax .85 1]); axis off
```

Graphically, the expectation that defines the risk $[r_i(\hat{\theta}_j)]$ is computed by moving the reward region (T) along the abscissa: at each location $\hat{\theta}_j$ to which the reward region is moved we obtain $r_i(\hat{\theta}_j)$ by multiplying the loss at all θ values by the corresponding probability at those θ values and take the sum of those products (as indicated by the arrow in the righthand plot). We note that the minimum loss (indicated by the circle on each loss function of the lower plot), regardless of target width, is found at the location of the peak of the posterior.

Why is it the case that this loss function causes us to choose the peak of the posterior as our measurement? Consider what happens as we move the reward region from it's location in Figure 4.5b along the abscissa, as indicated by the arrow in the figure. When the reward region is far from the peak of the distribution, the product of the high probability region and the loss function will be nearly 1, in that you have *not* contained any of the high probability region of the posterior within the reward region of the loss function. As the loss function is moved along the abscissa toward the center of the figure, there will be more and more overlap between the reward region of the loss function and the high-probability region of the posterior: this will *decrease* the risk. This decrease will be maximal when the reward region is at (for the smallest-width reward function) or near (for a wide loss function) the peak of the posterior shown in Figure 4.5b. Indeed, the risk will be essentially zero when the reward region is large enough to encompass the entire high-probability region of the posterior. Notice, however, that as we become less discriminating about what constitutes a good measurement (choose wider and wider reward regions), the difference between the best estimate and the worst estimates decreases; even the small increase in width seen in the figure causes this difference to drop to almost nothing.

Exercises

1) Describe the logic of choosing a best estimate of θ at the peak of the probability function, $p(\theta|d \cdot \imath)$ under zero-one loss.
2) Figure 4.5b shows that the peak of the distribution is selected under zero-one loss, at least for the widths of the reward region shown in the figure. Are there any widths of the reward region that will change this? If so, why not?
3) Construct a probability distribution with the shape,
   $p(\theta|d \cdot \imath) \propto e^{-\frac{1}{2}\theta^2} + e^{-\frac{1}{2}\frac{[\theta-(-1)]^2}{.25^2}}$ and:
   a. plot its risk function for zero-one loss (any $T > 0$)
   b. find the estimate $\hat{\theta}$, yielding minimum risk.
4) Construct a triangular probability distribution:
   a. plot its risk function for zero-one loss (any $T > 0$)
   b. find the estimate $\hat{\theta}$, yielding minimum risk.
5) Construct a distribution that is the sum of a triangular probability distribution and a Gaussian:
   a. plot its risk function for zero-one loss (any $T > 0$)
   b. find the estimate $\hat{\theta}$, yielding minimum risk.

Example: Absolute-Error Loss

Although the zero-one loss function makes sense when there is a single target and one's goal is simply to hit the target, so that missing only a bit is in practical terms no different than missing by quite a lot. In shooting at an archery target, this is typically not

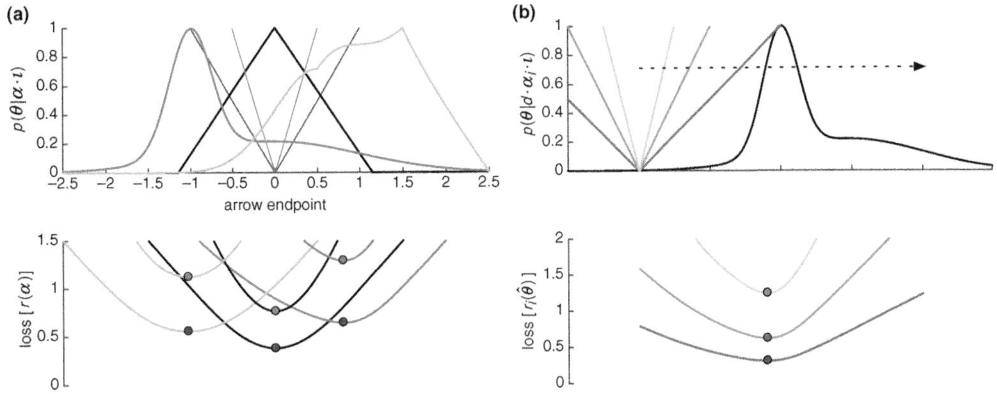

Figure 4.6 Linear loss and risk. (a) The upper panel shows three probability distributions that each represent the result of a different 'method' of shooting the arrow directly at the target (and therefore impact the shape of the posterior over landing position). We consider two point-structures for hitting near the bull's-eye, both v-shaped. These structures indicate that you lose more 'points' the further your arrow lands from the bull's-eye. The lower panel shows the risk functions associated with different choices of 'adjustment' of the aimpoint, where minimum risk aimpoints are marked with a blue circle. (b) The upper panel shows a probability distribution over the unknown landing position of the arrow along the θ parameter (black line) for a particular aimpoint, plotted along with three differently sized v-shaped loss functions. The risk function associated with predicting that the arrow will land at any given location (symbolized by moving the loss function across the parameter space) is shown in the lower panel. The minimum-risk choices of predicted endpoint are shown as circles for the three widths of the reward region. A linear loss function always dictates that the median of the distribution be chosen as the best estimate.

the case. Instead, shots landing on the bull's-eye of the target are treated as the best possible outcome, but missing by a just bit is certainly preferred to missing the target altogether. The most straightforward loss function with this property is the absolute-error loss function. Here, the value of the shot declines linearly with distance from the bull's-eye:

$$\ell(\hat{\theta}, \theta') = A|\hat{\theta} - \theta'|$$

Thus, it is twice the cost to miss by two units than to miss by one unit. This linear option may be the unspoken assumption in many decision problems with a continuous space of outcomes. As in the previous example, the bull's-eye is located at the origin along the θ dimension, and we have developed three methods of shooting the arrow (e.g., different grips on the arrow/bow, different positioning of the arm relative to the bow). These three methods result in three different posterior probabilities over the arrow's landing position at the target, $p(\theta|\alpha \cdot \imath)$ [where note we are assuming that these posteriors have been learned from our previous shooting experience while developing these three methods of making the shot, and could therefore be written $p(\theta|d \cdot \alpha \cdot \imath)$].

The risk associated with absolute-error loss is

$$r(\theta) = A \int_{-\infty}^{\infty} d\theta' \ell(\hat{\theta}, \theta') p(\theta = \theta'|d \cdot \imath)$$

$$= A \int_{-\infty}^{\infty} d\theta' |\hat{\theta} - \theta'| p(\theta'|d \cdot \imath)$$

Programming Aside: Linear Loss/Risk (Fig 4.6)

In the left-hand column (a) of plots, we define three posterior distributions for landing positions of the arrow, when the location of the aimpoint is nominally zero (upper plot). We then ask, via a decision-theoretic analysis making use of the linear loss function, 'by how much should we shift these (nominally unshifted) probability distributions to minimize risk?'. We see (lower plot) that the triangular posterior need not be shifted (its minimum risk point is at zero). To minimize risk with the other two distributions, one must be shifted positively and one negatively (by about 0.8 and just over −1 units, respectively) so that the median of the distribution is at the bull's-eye.

```
%absolute loss / risk
%aimpoint calculations
%
figure(3); clf
thetas=linspace(-3,3,1200);
Tlist=[1 2]; grylist=[.0 .5 .75]; collist=[.2 .3 .6; .4 .5 .9];
LW=1.4; xminmax=[-2.5 2.5];
for iT=1:length(Tlist), subplot(2,1,1), hold on
    plist=[zeros(1,sum(thetas<-1.15)) linspace(0,1,sum(and(thetas<=0,thetas>=-1.15)))
       linspace(1,0,sum(and(thetas<=1.15,thetas>0))) zeros(1,sum(thetas>1.15))];
    plot(thetas,plist,'.','Color',grylist(1)*[1 1 1])

    %loss function
    plot(thetas,Tlist(iT)*abs(thetas),'-','Color',collist(iT,:),'LineWidth',LW);

    subplot(2,1,2); hold on
    ptot=sum(plist);
    r=nan(size(plist));
    for inow=1:length(thetas), dtheta=thetas(inow);
        loss=Tlist(iT)*abs(dtheta+thetas);
        r(inow)=sum(plist.*loss); end
    plot(thetas,r/ptot,'.','Color',grylist(1)*[1 1 1]);
    rmin=mean(r(isnear(r,min(r))))/ptot;
    plot(mean(thetas(isnear(r,min(r)))),rmin,'ko',...
       'MarkerFaceColor',collist(iT,:),'MarkerSize',8);


    subplot(2,1,1); hold on
    plist=npdf(thetas,0,1);
    plist=plist+npdf(thetas,-1,.25); plist=plist/max(plist);
    plot(thetas,plist,'.','Color',grylist(2)*[1 1 1]);

    subplot(2,1,2); hold on
    ptot=sum(plist);
    r=nan(size(plist));
    for inow=1:length(thetas), dtheta=thetas(inow);
        loss=Tlist(iT)*abs(dtheta+thetas);
        r(inow)=sum(plist.*loss); end
    plot(thetas,r/ptot,'.','Color',grylist(2)*[1 1 1]);
    plot(thetas(isnear(r,min(r))),r(isnear(r,min(r)))/ptot,'ko',...
       'MarkerFaceColor',collist(iT,:),'MarkerSize',8);


    subplot(2,1,1), hold on
    thetas=linspace(-3,3,1200);
    plist=[zeros(1,700) linspace(0,1,200)];
```

```
    plist=[plist(1:end-1) linspace(1,0,201) zeros(1,100)];
    plist=plist+npdf(thetas,.5,.5); plist=plist/max(plist);
    plot(thetas,plist,'.','Color',grylist(3)*[1 1 1]);

    subplot(2,1,2); hold on
    ptot=sum(plist);
    for inow=1:length(thetas), dtheta=thetas(inow);
        loss=Tlist(iT)*abs(dtheta+thetas);
        r(inow)=sum(plist.*loss); end
    plot(thetas,r/ptot,'.','Color',grylist(3)*[1 1 1]);
    plot(thetas(isnear(r,min(r))),r(isnear(r,min(r)))/ptot,...
        'ko','MarkerFaceColor',collist(iT,:),'MarkerSize',8); end
subplot(2,1,1); axis([-2.5 2.5 0 1])
subplot(2,1,2); axis([-2.5 2.5 0 1.5])
```

In the right-hand column of plots (b) we plot three risk functions, each one associated with a different target-width but with the same posterior probability over arrow endpoints, and all using the absolute loss function. Here, the minimum risk point tells us which location along the theta axis to choose as our measurement of the (as-yet unseen) arrow endpoint.

```
%absolute loss / risk
Tlist=[.5 1 2]; grylist=[.4 .6 .8];
collist=[.2 .3 .6; .3 .4 .8; .4 .5 .9]; LW=1.4; xminmax=[-3 3];
thetas=linspace(-3,3,1200);
plist=npdf(thetas,1,1); plist=plist+npdf(thetas,-0,.25); plist=plist/max(plist);

figure(4); clf;
%plot distributions
subplot(2,1,1); hold on
plot(thetas,plist/max(plist),'k.')

%plot squares for target radii
for iT=1:length(Tlist),
    plot(thetas,Tlist(iT)*abs(thetas+2),'.','Color',grylist(iT)*[1 1 1]); end
axis([xminmax 0 1])

%plot risk function for each target
subplot(2,1,2); hold on
ptot=sum(plist);
tlist=find(abs(thetas)<=2);
for iT=1:length(Tlist), T=Tlist(iT); r=nan(size(tlist));
    for inow=1:length(tlist), dtheta=thetas(tlist(inow));
        loss=T*abs(thetas-dtheta);
        r(inow)=sum(plist.*loss)/ptot; end
    plot(thetas(tlist),r,'.','Color',grylist(iT)*[1 1 1]);
    imax=find(isnear(r,min(r)));
    plot(mean(thetas(tlist(imax))),mean(r(imax)),'ko',...
        'MarkerFaceColor',collist(iT,:),'MarkerSize',8); end
axis([xminmax 0 2])
```

$$\propto \int_{-\infty}^{\infty} d\theta'[\hat{\theta} - \theta']p(\theta'|d \cdot \imath) + \int_{\hat{\theta}}^{\infty} d\theta'[\theta' - \hat{\theta}]p(\theta'|d \cdot \imath)$$

$$= \hat{\theta} \int_{-\infty}^{\hat{\theta}} d\theta' p(\theta'|d \cdot \imath) - \int_{\hat{\theta}}^{\infty} d\theta'\theta' p(\theta'|d \cdot \imath)$$

$$+ \int_{\hat{\theta}}^{\infty} d\theta'\theta' p(\theta'|d \cdot \imath) - \hat{\theta} \int_{\hat{\theta}}^{\infty} d\theta' p(\theta'|d \cdot \imath)$$

We can intuit the minimizer for the absolute-error loss scenario[9] if we imagine a symmetric triangular probability distribution, $p(\theta'|d \cdot \iota)$, as in Figure 4.6. In this case, we can see from the equation and the figure that the risk is minimized when θ' is centered on the probability mass -when it splits the mass in two. As we will see in the examples in the programming aside (see Fig. 4.6), it is also the case for probability distributions with other shapes that the median of the probability distribution is the location estimate that minimizes the risk function based on absolute-error loss.

Exercises

1) What criterion defines the median of a probability distribution?
2) What shape is the absolute-error loss function?
3) For a symmetric distribution, which is closer to the peak of the distribution, the mean or median?
4) Is the mean or median of a distribution typically more affected by skew?

Example: Squared-Error Loss

Although absolute-error loss captures the notion that errors relative to the true location of a parameter or world-state should be preferred less the further removed they are from that true value, there are obvious gradations in how *much* less preferred such values should be. Is an error of two units *twice* as bad as an error or one unit, or do you value such errors *even less* (such as rating them three or four times as bad)? One such value function, defining a set of losses that increase supra-linearly, is squared-error loss (quadratic loss). Applying the quadratic loss function to our archer, the value of the shot would decline as the square of the distance from the bull's-eye. That is, it is $4\times$ the cost to miss by two units than to miss by one unit. This squared-error loss function,

$$\ell(\hat{\theta},\theta') = A(\hat{\theta} - \theta')^2$$

[9] For readers with a calculus background, we know that the minimum value of risk, which is a function of $\hat{\theta}$, is found by taking the derivative of the risk function with respect to $\hat{\theta}$,

$$\frac{dr}{d\hat{\theta}} = \frac{d}{d\hat{\theta}}\left[\ \hat{\theta}\textstyle\int_{-\infty}^{\hat{\theta}} d\theta' p(\theta'|d\cdot\iota) - \int_{\infty}^{\hat{\theta}} d\theta'\theta' p(\theta'|d\cdot\iota) + \int_{\hat{\theta}}^{\infty} d\theta'\theta' p(\theta'|d\cdot\iota) - \int_{\hat{\theta}}^{\infty} d\theta' p(\theta'|d\cdot\iota)\ \right]$$
$$= \int_{\infty}^{\hat{\theta}} d\theta' p(\theta'|d\cdot\iota) - \int_{\hat{\theta}}^{\infty} d\theta'\theta' p(\theta'|d\cdot\iota)$$

and setting the result equal to zero:

$$\int_{\infty}^{\hat{\theta}} d\theta' p(\theta'|d\cdot\iota) - \int_{\hat{\theta}}^{\infty} d\theta'\theta' p(\theta'|d\cdot\iota = 0$$

or

$$\int_{\infty}^{\hat{\theta}} d\theta' p(\theta'|d\cdot\iota) = \int_{\hat{\theta}}^{\infty} d\theta'\theta' p(\theta'|d\cdot\iota$$

That is, the minimum-loss estimate is the estimate that splits the probability mass equally; this location is, by definition, the estimate $\hat{\theta}$ at the median of the probability distribution.

yields a risk of

$$
\begin{aligned}
r(\hat{\theta}) &= A \int d\theta' \ell(\hat{\theta}, \theta') p(\theta' | d \cdot \imath) \\
&= A \int d\theta' \ell(\hat{\theta} - \theta')^2 p(\theta' | d \cdot \imath) \\
&\propto \hat{\theta}^2 \int d\theta' p(\theta' | d \cdot \imath) - 2\hat{\theta} \int d\theta' \theta' p(\theta' | d \cdot \imath) + \int d\theta' \theta'^2 p(\theta' | d \cdot \imath) \\
&= \hat{\theta}^2 - 2\hat{\theta}\mathrm{E}[\theta'] + \mathrm{E}[\theta'^2] \\
&= \hat{\theta}^2 - 2\theta'\mathrm{E}[\theta'] + \mathrm{E}[\theta'^2] + \mathrm{E}[\theta']^2 - \mathrm{E}[\theta']^2 \\
&= (\hat{\theta} - \mathrm{E}[\theta'])^2 + (\mathrm{E}[\theta'^2] - \mathrm{E}[\theta']^2)
\end{aligned}
$$

This function is minimized when ($\hat{\theta} = \mathrm{E}(\theta')$, which we can see by recognizing that the second term in the risk function, $\mathrm{V} = \mathrm{E}[\theta'^2] - \mathrm{E}[\theta']^2$, is the risk variance (see Chapter 3 to review the definition of variance) and does not impact the location of the minimum (only how strongly that minimum is indicated) because it is constant for a given probability distribution over possible θ' values. Therefore the only way to minimize the risk function is to minimize the first term, $[(\hat{\theta} - \mathrm{E}[\theta']]^2$, which can be as small as zero when $\hat{\theta} = \mathrm{E}(\theta')$.

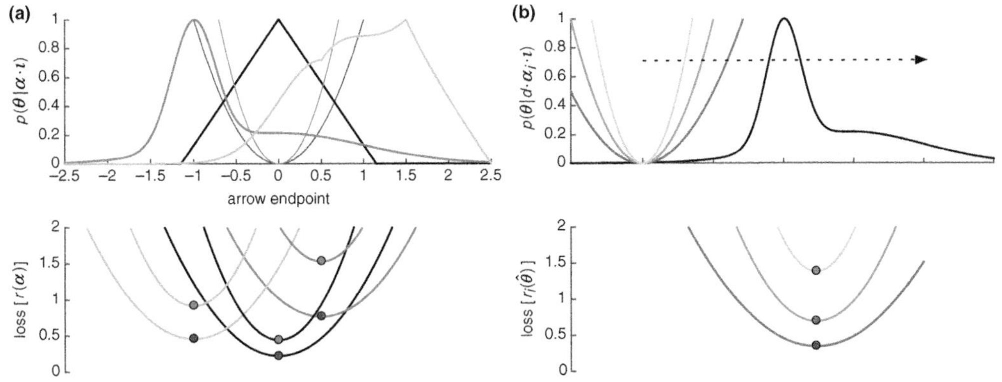

Figure 4.7 Quadratic loss and risk. (a) The upper panel shows three probability distributions (grayscale) that each represents the result of a different 'method' of shooting the arrow *directly* at the target. We consider two point-structures for hitting near the bull's-eye, both u-shaped. These structures indicate that you lose more 'points' the further your arrow lands from the bull's-eye. The lower panel shows the risk functions associated with different choices of 'adjustment' of the aimpoint, where minimum risk aimpoints are marked with a circle. (b) The upper panel shows a probability distribution over the unknown landing position of the arrow along the θ parameter (black line) for a single particular aimpoint, plotted along with three differently sized u-shaped reward structures. The risk function associated with predicting that the arrow will land at any given location (symbolized by computing risk at each point while moving the loss function across the parameter space) is shown in the lower panel. The minimum-risk choices of predicted endpoint are shown as circles for the three widths of the loss function. A quadratic loss function always dictates that the mean of the distribution be chosen as the best estimate.

Programming Aside: Squared-Error Loss/Risk (Fig 4.7)

In the left-hand column (a) of plots, we define three posterior distributions for landing positions of the arrow, when the location of the aimpoint is nominally zero (upper plot). We then ask, via a decision-theoretic analysis making use of the quadratic loss function, 'by how much should we shift these (nominally unshifted) probability distributions to minimize risk?' We see (lower plot) that the triangular posterior need not be shifted (its minimum risk point is at zero). To minimize risk with the other two distributions, one must be shifted positively and one negatively (by about 0.5 and −1 units, respectively) so that the mean of the distribution is at the bull's-eye.

```
%quadratic loss / risk
%aimpoint calculations
%
figure(5); clf
thetas=linspace(-3,3,1200);
Tlist=[1 2]; grylist=[.0 .5 .75];
collist=[.2 .3 .6; .4 .5 .9]; LW=1.4; xminmax=[-2.5 2.5];
for iT=1:length(Tlist), subplot(2,1,1), hold on
    plist=[zeros(1,sum(thetas<-1.15)) linspace(0,1,sum(and(thetas<=0,thetas>=-1.15)))...
         linspace(1,0,sum(and(thetas<=1.15,thetas>0))) zeros(1,sum(thetas>1.15))];
    plot(thetas,plist,'.','Color',grylist(1)*[1 1 1])

    %loss function
    plot(thetas,Tlist(iT)*(thetas).^2,'-','Color',collist(iT,:),'LineWidth',LW);

    subplot(2,1,2); hold on
    ptot=sum(plist);
    r=nan(size(plist));
    for inow=1:length(thetas), dtheta=thetas(inow);
        loss=Tlist(iT)*abs(dtheta+thetas).^2;
        r(inow)=sum(plist.*loss); end
    plot(thetas,r/ptot,'.','Color',grylist(1)*[1 1 1]);
    rmin=mean(r(isnear(r,min(r))))/ptot;
    plot(mean(thetas(isnear(r,min(r)))),rmin,'ko',...
        'MarkerFaceColor',collist(iT,:),'MarkerSize',8);

    subplot(2,1,1); hold on
    plist=npdf(thetas,0,1);
    plist=plist+npdf(thetas,-1,.25); plist=plist/max(plist);
    plot(thetas,plist,'.','Color',grylist(2)*[1 1 1]);

    subplot(2,1,2); hold on
    ptot=sum(plist);
    r=nan(size(plist));
    for inow=1:length(thetas), dtheta=thetas(inow);
        loss=Tlist(iT)*abs(dtheta+thetas).^2;
        r(inow)=sum(plist.*loss); end
    plot(thetas,r/ptot,'.','Color',grylist(2)*[1 1 1]);
    plot(thetas(isnear(r,min(r))),r(isnear(r,min(r)))/ptot,...
        'ko','MarkerFaceColor',collist(iT,:),'MarkerSize',8);

    subplot(2,1,1), hold on
    thetas=linspace(-3,3,1200);
    plist=[zeros(1,700) linspace(0,1,200)]; plist=[plist(1:end-1) ...
          linspace(1,0,201) zeros(1,100)];
    plist=plist+npdf(thetas,.5,.5); plist=plist/max(plist);
    plot(thetas,plist,'.','Color',grylist(3)*[1 1 1]);
```

```
    subplot(2,1,2); hold on
    ptot=sum(plist);
    for inow=1:length(thetas), dtheta=thetas(inow);
        loss=Tlist(iT)*abs(dtheta+thetas).^2;
        r(inow)=sum(plist.*loss); end
    plot(thetas,r/ptot,'.','Color',grylist(3)*[1 1 1]);
    plot(thetas(isnear(r,min(r))),r(isnear(r,min(r)))/ptot,...
        'ko','MarkerFaceColor',collist(iT,:),'MarkerSize',8); end

subplot(2,1,1); axis([-2.5 2.5 0 1])
subplot(2,1,2); axis([-2.5 2.5 0 1.5])
```

In the right-hand column of plots (b) we plot three risk functions, each one associated with a different target-width but with the same posterior probability over arrow endpoints, and all using the quadratic loss function. Here, the minimum risk point tells us which location along the theta axis to choose as our measurement of the (as-yet unseen) arrow endpoint. This point is always the mean of the distribution, and the extent to which the mean is preferred over other choices (predictions) is given by the width of the loss function.

```
%quadratic loss / risk
%estimate = mean
Tlist=[.5 1 2]; grylist=[.4 .6 .8];
collist=[.2 .3 .6; .3 .4 .8; .4 .5 .9]; LW=1.4; xminmax=[-3 3];
thetas=linspace(-3,3,1200);
plist=npdf(thetas,1,1);
plist=plist+npdf(thetas,-0,.25); plist=plist/max(plist);

figure(6); clf;

%plot distributions
subplot(2,1,1); hold on
plot(thetas,plist/max(plist),'k.')

%plot squares for target radii
for iT=1:length(Tlist),
    plot(thetas,Tlist(iT)*(thetas+2).^2,'.','Color',grylist(iT)*[1 1 1]); end
axis([xminmax 0 1])

%plot risk function for each target
subplot(2,1,2); hold on
ptot=sum(plist);
tlist=find(abs(thetas)<=2);
for iT=1:length(Tlist), T=Tlist(iT); r=nan(size(tlist));
    for inow=1:length(tlist), dtheta=thetas(tlist(inow));
        loss=T*abs(thetas-dtheta).^2;
        r(inow)=sum(plist.*loss)/ptot; end
    plot(thetas(tlist),r,'.','Color',grylist(iT)*[1 1 1]);
    imax=find(isnear(r,min(r)));
    plot(mean(thetas(tlist(imax))),mean(r(imax)),'ko',...
        'MarkerFaceColor',collist(iT,:),'MarkerSize',8); end
axis([xminmax 0 2])
```

The mean of a probability distribution shifts from its peak when that distribution is either skewed or when it is multimodal, as in Figure 4.7 for the two nonsymmetric distributions. In these cases, it is possible that the mean is found within a low-density region of the probability distribution. In Figure 4.7, for example, the mean of the distribution is computed in the lower portion of panel b. Comparing the location of the mean to the probability distribution itself (upper portion of panel b), we see that it is located at almost the center of a dip in the function, where probability drops to a local low point. In such cases, it may be desirable to reevaluate your choice of loss function, and/or the assumptions that led you to it.

Exercises

1) What is the shape of the squared-error loss function?
2) For a symmetric distribution, where is the minimum-loss estimate based on squared-error loss?
3) Describe the differences between the risk functions in the lower right-hand panel of Figure 4.7. What causes these differences?
4) Define the mean of a probability distribution.
5) By comparing the definitions of the mean and median of a probability distribution, explain why one is shifted more relative to the peak of a skewed distribution than the other.
6) One might imagine that, when practice-shooting, an archer has an internal value function that is a combination of either absolute-error or squared-error loss for positions on the target (the sheet of paper including the bull's-eye and sever outer concentric circles), and uniform loss for positions off the target. With this loss function, the relative position of your shot matters to you much more when it is close to the center of the target (based on the absolute or squared error), but if you miss the target altogether it really doesn't matter by how much (uniform loss beyond the target's edge assigns the same value to all such errors).
   a. Write a program that plots this loss function (linear or squared) for a 1-unit radius target.
   b. Modify the code from the programming aside to plot the risk functions associated with the three probability distributions shown in Figure 4.7 and this hybrid loss function.
   c. Plot the corresponding risk functions, and their minima.
   d. Where are these minima relative to those of the corresponding (linear or squared) 'pure' loss function?
7) Box 4.3.2 describes the unbiased estimator fallacy. Given the nature of the fallacy, explain why replacing the unbiased estimator with the UMVUE does not solve the problem

4.3.3 Clinically Relevant Differences

In the bunnies and berries example we show that there is an improved overall gustatory experience expected from choosing the red berries over the blue berries. Nevertheless, there are two problems with choosing the red over the blue berries: the volatility of the taste experience from the red-colored berries versus the blue-colored berries, discussed above, and the very slim margin by which the overall taste experience of the red berry is expected to surpass that of the blue. The latter issue is, in short, that the boost in gain expected from choosing a red berry is so small that it may be insignificant, and the overall taste of the two may be considered by many bunnies to be indistinguishable.

BOX 4.3 The "Unbiased-Estimator" Fallacy

It is sometimes suggested that estimators should be chosen to be ***unbiased***. The concept of an unbiased estimator is taken from frequentist statistical practice; unbiased in this context simply means that best-guess estimates of this type will be, in the long run, neither consistently larger nor smaller than the true value you are attempting to estimate. In statistical practice, it is generally taken as a matter of course that unbiased estimators should always be preferred (should they exist). Indeed, frequentist texts provide something akin to the following proscription:[1]

For practical statistics problems, it is important to determine the unbiased estimator if one exists, since less-than-optimal procedures would naturally be avoided.

This suggestion occurs despite the the obvious fact that, if a measurement results from your loss function, it will naturally fit the criteria you most value (i.e., your loss function).

First note that the very definition of unbiasedness relies on the frequentist notion of an infinite set of repetitions (the underlying meaning of 'in the long run'), which we are likely to reject as unimportant when faced with our *current experiment* and our *current data*; after all, should we care that the current estimate, when combined with an infinity of other estimates from similar experiments, will yield a set of symmetrical errors around the true value? There is nothing in the definition of the unbiased estimator that prevents it from being as far as you please from the true parameter value for the *single* dataset that we care about: our *current* data. It only tells us that in the unattainable infinite future, and if we repeated our experiment indefinitely into that future, the set of results will be symmetrical around the true value. An example of an unbiased estimator is the mean of a sample drawn from a Gaussian, which provides an estimate of the location of the probability distribution describing that data, and has the further property that the distribution of data means (the estimator), computed from many repeated draws from the same Gaussian, will not be systematically biased relative to the true mean of that distribution.

Now, we have certainly used the mean as an estimate, and it works well – so why all the fuss? The problem is that there is nothing *primary* about the property of being unbiased – so despite the quote at the opening of this box, there is no reason to expect an unbiased estimator to be *optimal*. Indeed, even within the frequentist regime, the unbiased estimator is demonstrably *not* optimal. To see why, we first note that the bias is only one of the two components of the long-run error: there is the expected constant offset (bias) component and the expected variable (variance, or spread) component. This bias-variance decomposition of the expected long-run behavior of the estimator is defined by the mean-squared-error:

$$
\begin{aligned}
MSE &= \mathrm{E}[\epsilon]^2 \ \{\epsilon = \hat{\theta} - \theta' \\
&= \mathrm{E}[\epsilon^2] + \{\mathrm{E}[\epsilon]^2 - \mathrm{E}[\epsilon]^2\} \\
&= \mathrm{E}[\epsilon]^2 + (\mathrm{E}[\epsilon^2] - \mathrm{E}[\epsilon]^2) \\
&= b^2(\hat{\theta}) + \mathrm{V}(\hat{\theta})
\end{aligned}
$$

where bias is

$$
\begin{aligned}
b &= \mathrm{E}[\epsilon] = \mathrm{E}[\hat{\theta} - \theta'] \\
&= \mathrm{E}[\hat{\theta}] - \theta' \qquad \{\mathrm{E}[const] = const
\end{aligned}
$$

and variance is

$$
\begin{aligned}
\mathrm{V} &= \mathrm{E}[\epsilon]^2 = \mathrm{E}[(\hat{\theta} - \theta')^2] \\
&= \mathrm{E}[\hat{\theta}^2 + \theta'^2 - 2\theta'\hat{\theta}] \\
&= \mathrm{E}[\hat{\theta}^2] + \mathrm{E}[\theta'^2] - 2[\theta']\mathrm{E}[\hat{\theta}] \\
&= \mathrm{E}(\hat{\theta}^2) + [\theta']^2 - 2[\theta']\mathrm{E}[\hat{\theta}]
\end{aligned}
$$

Thus we can use these definitions to more easily compute the MSE of an estimator. Now within statistical practice, an estimator is a function of data that is used to estimate an underlying parameter. So, for example, the mean of a dataset is used to estimate the mean of the underlying distribution (which in the frequentist paradigm is always a sampling distribution).

The function

$$\hat{s}^2 = (n-1)^{-1} \sum_{i=1}^{n} (x_i - \mu)^2$$

is the unbiased estimator for the variance, σ^2, of a Gaussian. To see this, we write

$$
\begin{aligned}
\mathrm{E}[\hat{s}^2] &= (n-1)^{-1}\mathrm{E}\left[\sum_{i=1}^{n} (x_i - \bar{x})^2\right] \\
&= (n-1)^{-1}\mathrm{E}\left[\sum_{i=1}^{n} (x_i^2 + \bar{x}^2 - 2x_i\bar{x})\right] \\
&= (n-1)^{-1}\mathrm{E}\left[\sum_{i=1}^{n} x_i^2 - n\bar{x}^2 - 2\bar{x}\sum_{i=1}^{n} x_i\right] \\
&= (n-1)^{-1}\left(n\mathrm{E}[x^2] - n\mathrm{E}[\bar{x}^2]\right) \\
&= (n-1)^{-1}\left(n[\mu^2 + \sigma^2] - n[\mu^2 + \sigma^2/n]\right) \\
&= (n-1)^{-1}\left([n-1]\sigma^2\right) = \sigma^2
\end{aligned}
$$

which is by definition unbiased. Because its bias is zero, the MSE[2] of this variance estimator, $MSE = b^2(\hat{s}^2) + \mathrm{V}(\hat{s}^2)$, is equal to its variance component only:

$$
\begin{aligned}
MSE &= b^2(\hat{s}^2) + \mathrm{V}(\hat{s}^2) = 0 + \mathrm{V}(\hat{s}^2) \\
&= (n-1)^{-2}\mathrm{V}\left[\sum_{i=1}^{n} (x_i - \bar{x})^2\right] \\
&= (n-1)^{-2}\mathrm{V}\left[\frac{\sigma^2 \sum_{i=1}^{n} (x_i - \bar{x})^2}{\sigma^2}\right]
\end{aligned}
$$

$$= \frac{\sigma^4}{(n-1)^2}[2(n-1)]$$
$$= \frac{2\sigma^4}{n-1}$$

We want to compare this with the MSE of the variance estimate, $\hat{v} = n^{-1}\left[\sum_{i=1}^{n}(x_i - \bar{x})^2\right]$, defining the mean squared deviation from the mean. The bias of this estimator is

$$b(\hat{v}) = n^{-1}\mathrm{E}\left[\sum_{i=1}^{n}(x_i - \bar{x})^2\right] - \sigma^2$$
$$= n^{-1}[(n-1)\sigma^2] - \sigma^2 = \frac{-\sigma^2}{n}$$

and its variance is

$$\mathrm{V}[\hat{v}] = n^{-2}\mathrm{V}\left[\sum_{i=1}^{n}(x_i - \bar{x})^2\right]$$
$$= n^{-2}\mathrm{V}\left[\frac{\sigma^2 \sum_{i=1}^{n}(x_i - \bar{x})^2}{\sigma^2}\right] = \frac{2\sigma^4(n-1)}{n^2}$$

The MSE is therefore

$$MSE = b^2(\hat{v}) + \mathrm{V}(\hat{v})$$
$$= \left[\frac{-\sigma^2}{n}\right]^2 + \frac{2\sigma^4(n-1)}{n^2} = \sigma^4\frac{2n-1}{n^2}$$

and is always at least as small as the MSE of the unbiased estimator (Fig. 4.8).

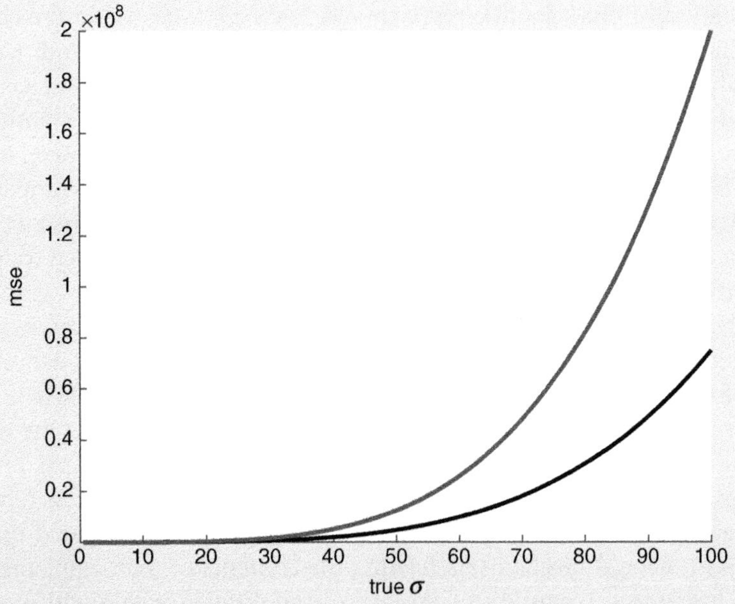

Figure 4.8 Unbiased estimator fallacy. The unbiased estimator is always outperformed by a biased estimator in this example.

```
sig=linspace(0,100,202)'; sig=sig(2:end);N=2;
mse=(2*sig.^4)*(N-1).^-1;
mse(:,2)=sig.^4*(2*N-1)./N.^2;

figure
plot(sig,mse(:,2),'k-','LineWidth',3)
hold on; plot(sig,mse(:,1),'b-','LineWidth',3)
N=1:20;
mse1=(2*sig.^4)*(N-1).^-1;
mse2=sig.^4*(2*N-1)./N.^2;

figure; hold on
meshc(N,sig,mse1)
meshc(N,sig,mse2); colormap bone
```

Although we agree that optimal procedures should be preferred, optimal can only be defined with reference to a particular situation, as it is based on maximizing some gain or loss function.

1 For purposes of the point made here, unbiased estimator can be used interchangeably with the UMVUE, or uniformly minimum-variance unbiased estimator. The UMVUE is the estimator that has the two properties given in its name: it is unbiased and it has minimum variance relative to other unbiased estimators. We will focus here on the property of being unbiased, since that is primary in both types of estimator.

2 Making use of a well-known identity, where for a normal distribution:

$$\mathrm{V}\left[\frac{\sum(x_i-\bar{x})^2}{\sigma^2}\right]=2(n-1)$$

We can think of this second issue with the bunnies and berries example in terms of the application of our scientific research and findings: their use in the clinic. We might be deciding between two drugs or other therapeutic modalities, both with different costs, availabilities, efficacies, and side effects. How do we make this decision? Typically, we would try to put the cost, availability, etc. into monetary units, and then decide if the difference in cost, if any, outweighs any difference in efficacy between the two treatments. This is the type of analysis often performed by an insurance company when deciding which therapies to reimburse, and at what rate, although of course such decisions should be made in conjunction with medical professionals who have been trained to understand the probabilities involved.

When describing the results of our research and their significance, we might consider the decisions that might be made in response to those results, as well as whether they are of scientific significance, of clinical significance, or both. When we find a reliable pattern in our data, that pattern will be of scientific interest to the extent that it hints at underlying mechanisms responsible for the behavior or process under investigation. This is true regardless of the sizes of the effects seen in our data. Thus, if we measure a reliable correlation between a nutritional supplement and blood pressure, it logically hints at potential mechanisms relating the contents of that supplement and cardiovascular function – regardless of the size of the difference in blood pressure achieved by taking that supplement. However, if the difference is quite small, an honest report of the scientific finding would acknowledge its limited clinical effectiveness.

When considering the clinical effectiveness of your work, it is useful to put it into a decision-theoretic context, and outline the circumstances under which different decisions might be made. In the bunnies and berries example, we can imagine a range of scenarios in which the red berries were in fact at peak ripeness in 85 percent, 86 percent, 87 percent, 88 percent, or some higher proportion of cases. If it were the 85 percent case, all bunnies should prefer the blue berry, but at some point (perhaps at 90 percent or 95 percent), the red berry should begin to be preferred. The switch point will have to do with the extent to which a bunny prioritizes consistency of taste (preferably in terms relative to its excellence-of-taste preference). For example, we might report this result by stating that a bunny who values consistency of taste as much as a 1-point difference in overall taste value will want to choose the blue berry, but a bunny who only values consistency as much as a 0.1-point difference in taste-value should prefer the red berry. Describing results in this way allows us to put the data into context, and to convey the clinical decision-making significance of our results clearly. If we were describing the clinical import of an experiment comparing radiation and chemotherapy versus radiation alone in the treatment of a particular cancer, we must weigh any difference in efficacy against differences in cost, availability, side-effect severity, etc. In reporting the results, we should indicate that the first has debilitating side effects but higher efficacy, and therefore we may want to keep it in reserve, until first trying the somewhat less effective but more easily tolerated treatment (radiation alone).

Without considering their clinical significance, many scientific discoveries have been erroneously heralded as 'healthcare breakthroughs' only to be shown later to have been based on consistent-but-minuscule differences between treatment and comparison/placebo groups. Only later, after much wasted effort, research dollars, not to mention the lasting negative effect of misinformation in the public domain, does it finally become clear the the true clinical effects do not live up to early hype. Such effects are probably worth knowing about, but may not be worth acting on in a clinical setting.

While it is always a decision problem to evaluate scientific results, we must stress that clinical significance is not always the same as scientific importance (simply peruse the list of scientific discoveries that have won Nobel prizes, but have yet to yield direct application). Within the domain of clinical research, we assess the importance of our experiments and experimental findings based on their clinical merit. How much would your proposed therapy cost to treat an underlying clinical issue (disease, injury, etc.)? How much longer/shorter is the proposed treatment, and what is its probability of success/side effects? Questions like these are important to consider when you explore the significance of your experimental findings, which findings are most important to follow up on, and which are most likely to yield important health/societal benefits. Within scientific practice, we must also decide which experiments and experimental results are worth caring about. Scientific inquiry is typically undertaken in an attempt to *understand* the behavior of a biological system rather than in finding safer and more effective ways to *modify/repair/protect* the health of an individual. This difference means that it is just as important, within a scientific context, to perform a series of experiments that discriminates among competing models whose differences lie in the smaller details of the theory rather than just the broad strokes. Changing the broad strokes of a model will tend to translate into the largest improvements in clinical significance, but it is often in the details that we truly grasp the interconnected workings of a system under study.

Exercises

1) What are the risks associated with the 85 percent, 86 percent, etc. proportions discussed in the text?
2) Describe a volatility-to-gain trade-off that seems reasonable to you. Justify your trade-off.
3) Describe a scenario (real or fictitious) in which the clinical import of a scientific finding is markedly different from its scientific merit.
4) How might the concept of a clinically significant difference appear within the context of medical decision-making, as discussed in Chapter 2?

Trade-offs between Cost and Efficacy: Diminishing Returns

One of the more important intersections of decision theory and clinical practice involves the trade-off seen to occur between cost and efficacy, particularly given that a more expensive treatment is often intuitively associated with more advantageous outcomes. To examine this trade-off, the pertinent questions are: How much greater is the expense, to what size increase is it associated, and what constraints are imposed on our selection of an 'optimal' cost/efficacy trade-off?

The truth of the matter is that most increases in the strength or intensity of an intervention (e.g., medication dose, rehabilitation sessions, or other costly goods/services) eventually show a diminishing return, which we will characterize by the shape of the ***dose/response curve***. A dose/response curve describes the effect of varying amounts and/or intensities of an intervention (Fig. 4.9a), where we expect that a useful intervention will produce a positively sloped dose/response curve (i.e., 'response' is usually considered positive). A diminishing return on intervention strength can therefore take one of two general forms: either decelerating increases in efficacy, usually asymptoting to a steady peak value (Fig. 4.9a), or an inverted 'u'-shaped function that shows increased efficacy with initial increases in the strength of intervention, but a peak and eventual numerical decrease in efficacy as intervention strength increases further (Fig. 4.9b). In the first case we have a diminishing return because the same size increase in intervention strength along the abscissa produces a smaller and smaller increase in efficacy. These ever-smaller increases always stay above zero, and so the response asymptotes at some maximal value. However, in the second case (Fig. 4.9b) increases in response to a single size increase in intervention strength first decrease to zero, and then becomes negative. Adding a negative-going portion to the first case produces the inverted 'u' shape characteristic of the dose/response curve in the second case.

Exercises

1) What is a dose/response curve?
2) What characterizes a diminishing return in a dose/response curve?
3) If there were no diminishing return for the dose/response curve of a drug's effective relative to its dose, what would be the appropriate dose of the drug to administer?

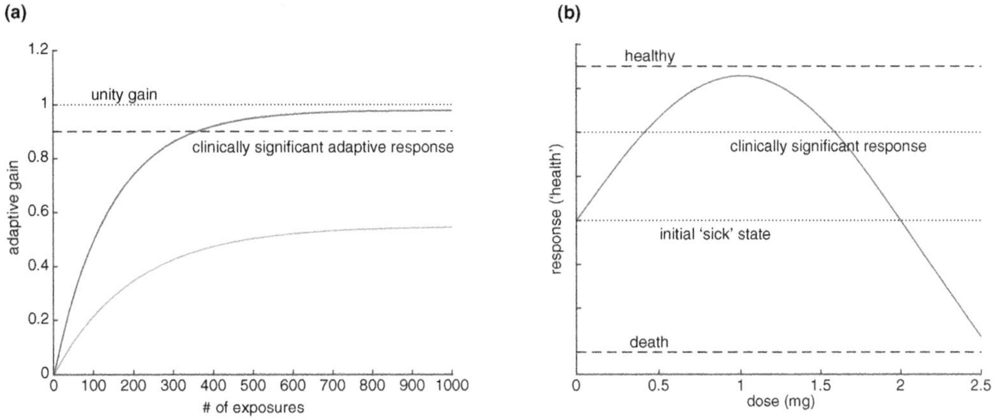

Figure 4.9 Clinically relevant differences. (a) Exponentially diminishing returns. An adaptive response to the chromatic aberration seen when wearing a new pair of prescription glasses will tend to reduce the perceived aberration. If the aberration is completely eliminated from perception, the exponential will saturate at the unity line. On the other hand the aberration may be partly eliminated from perception (a statistically significant reduction is achieved by both lines). Partial correction may not reach the level of a clinically significant adaptive correction; this occurs for the red but not the gray curve. (b) U-shaped diminishing returns. As the dose of the drug is increased, we see a positive response, improving health from the initial 'sick' state (0–1-mg). At some dosage this response function peaks and begins to decrease (1–1.5 mg). Eventually, the effect of the drug is to do more harm than good, leading to death (2–2.5 mg). Note that peak response need *not* reach the level of clinical significance in either plot.

4.4 Summary

In this chapter we have explored two of the final elements of probability and decision theory that are in common use in scientific contexts: prediction and decision. Prediction of samples (prior and posterior predictive sampling distributions) can be useful in understanding what we might expect samples to look like when we go ahead and collect data in an experiment. The concept of prediction in optimal state estimation is an important tool when analyzing time-evolving systems. This is a relatively advanced and involved technique, as we saw in the temporal memory model examples, but is indicated when the underlying model parameters may change over time, and particularly when model parameters change in partially predictable ways.

4.4.1 Integrating Basic Measurement and Predictive Distributions

In this chapter we introduced the topic of measurement, considered both as a decision-theoretic single-number estimate derived from a posterior distribution, as well as a shorthand for referring to the posterior distribution itself. When thinking in terms of the posterior proper, we realize that the topic of measurement has been our focus so far throughout this text. Thus, when computing the posterior over some underlying parameter, such as an object's elevation from the ground based on ruler observations, this is our measurement of that parameter – whether we take that measurement to be the entire posterior or a single-number representation of the information contained in that posterior.

Our concept of measurement (taking forms such as 'neural excitation' or 'perceived position') was expanded in the current chapter through our understanding of predictive distributions. We learned that, by proposing a model of neural firing that depends on certain system inputs (e.g., light intensity or visual contrast for a visually sensitive neuron) and computing measurements of firing rate based on both those variables and past observations, we create a time-varying measurement model. This new measurement model, expanded through our use of predictive probabilities, allows us to report measurements of neural excitation (parameterized as the model's rate parameter rather than observed spikes/s) at times ***interpolated between*** measurements made while observing the neuron.

How is this type of time-varying measurement model useful in the bio-behavioral sciences? To usefully apply these ideas we must have an interest in modeling time-varying systems, such as a moving appendage. Clearly, when we move an arm, leg, or eye we may need to apply muscular control to that moving system (to avoid obstacles in the case of arms or legs, and also generally because muscular forces are applied throughout a movement to keep movements on target). In other research domains, predictive distributions can be useful to scientists interested in predicting e.g., the attitudes of voters between polls, but after societal events that tend to change political views (natural disaster, pandemic, economic recession, election cycles, etc.). It can also be useful for tracking the progress of therapeutic modalities, where there is relative inertia of a patient's condition generally, but also tendencies for organic improvement or deterioration over time (depending on the particular condition). Indeed, while predictive models are necessarily more complex and therefore require more time to develop, there is essentially no applied setting that could not employ these techniques to some advantage.

By modeling time-varying systems we accomplish two things in general: First we improve our scientific understanding of the system being modeled, by observing where the predictive model performs best and worst. Second, we allow ourselves better measurements to the extent that the information in our predictive model is truly predictive. Further, in combination with decision theory, predictive modeling can be a powerful tool in applied settings by allowing us to determine cutoffs and schedules for interventions based on the desired cost/benefit criteria of the patient, therapist, and/or hospital.

4.4.2 Decision theory Is everywhere

Decision theory is an extension of probability theory that allows us to quantify the process of decision-making by defining value functions, either as gain or loss functions. Unlike probability, value is entirely subjective, but by recognizing and explicitly defining the value functions used to make decisions we can add to our understanding of those decisions.

Although there are a few examples of decision-making given above, we should also be aware of the incredible generality of decision within both our interpretations of experimental and clinical data, but also within the data themselves. The former was reviewed above, where we saw that the single-number measurements we report necessarily define a type of loss function and decision corresponding to minimizing that loss (e.g., for measurements consistent with the mean, median, and peak of the posterior). We must be aware of this type of decision when we report our experimental findings. The second type, decisions within the data themselves show the generality for applying decision theory to behavior. For example, we hinted above at the fact that every movement is a decision made by the nervous system, wherein the parameters of the movement are chosen based on an internal loss function. The same can be said of perceptual experiences (they can be described as an internal decision about the probable state of the world), as well as our social, political, and economic behaviors. Indeed, every behavior that we observe or elicit experimentally can be thought of as a decision from among the possible behaviors that might be chosen in that situation, and understanding those behaviors in terms of the loss functions and probability functions that elicit them can be an instructive exercise for theory development.

In addition to the use of decision theory within the context of interpreting and reporting our experimental results, we can also explore the decision-theoretic context in which science operates more generally. This includes the types of research groups we form, the collaborations that are made, publication decisions, grant applications and reviews, and the use of science in society. The latter can be particularly important when making policy decisions and recommendations based on experimental data, because if we are not aware of the potential forces that may be working to skew measurements and/or recommendations, we may under- or overestimate the importance of research findings.

This skewing of research findings seems nowhere more prevalent than when science is reported in the popular press. Indeed, it seems that not a week passes when we do not hear about the next 'medical miracle' to ease the suffering of those afflicted with some disease or other condition - miracles that very rarely live up to the hype. These reports suffer from a particularly egregious pattern of skewing because, like the awful auditory screech caused by a microphone and speaker trapped in a feedback loop, multiple steps in the process of producing such reports each tend to skew the description of data/findings in the same direction - toward the miraculous. It starts when findings are selected for publication, because 'high-profile' scientific journals are likely only to publish the 'most fantastic' results, and such results seem to suffer more from being either overblown or entirely unreplicable. Knowing this bias toward fantastic-sounding results, scientists who would like to further their careers by publishing in high-profile journals may feel pressure to write scientific findings in ways that are more likely to 'make a splash' and gain the attention of editors from these journals. Regardless of where these findings end up being published, when they are written to make a splash over being meticulous and accurate (what scientists are known for), they are more likely to catch the eye of journalists. Not having the technical background to understand the details of the scientific work, both experimentally and analytically, they report their own narrative of the science – a narrative that is more likely to be picked up by other news outlets if, again, it is written specifically to make a splash. The important point to understand is that this incrementally more and more skewed description of the result is entirely predictable once we understand the loss function, or motives, of each entity contributing to the process.

Exercises

1) Find a current, high-profile journal article from *Science* or *Nature*, and one from the same field published prior to 1970. Describe two ways that the articles differ and speculate about changes in loss function that may have contributed to these differences.
2) Number of publications is often one of the metrics used to rank departments and individuals engaged in research. How might this number be increased without conducting additional research of your own? What is the average page length of an article from *Journal of Physiology* from 1960 versus today? Discuss the loss function that might be responsible for of this shift, and its potential impact on scientific discovery.
3) Describe two ways you would suggest to improve the scientific culture and guard against inappropriate external influences.
4) Propose a way one might alter the way scientists interact with the media, or forms of compensation to scientists or journalists that could improve the accuracy of reporting.

CHAPTER FIVE

MODELS AND MEASUREMENTS

In the previous four chapters we have been concerned with the computational details of the calculations we will need to make when analyzing data. Now that we have gained some proficiency with these calculations, we will need to learn to use them appropriately within the context of a wide range of problems. The present chapter takes a step-by step approach to several conceptual issues that must be understood before the mathematics learned in previous chapters can be correctly applied to problems beyond the most basic applications. In particular, we examine the relationship of **data** to **measurement** and **uncertainty**, and introduce the concepts of an **observation model** and a **noise model** (or sometimes, **statistical model**), which form the basis for a best-guess **measurement** of an unknown parameter. The difference between data and measurement is an important conceptual distinction, relating what we know with certainty (data values) to unknown quantities we would like to infer (parameter values). Indeed, the concept of measurement is at the heart of all data analyses, and the distinction between data and measurement must be thoroughly understood before measurement equations can be properly applied. We will define a measurement in terms of the posterior distribution, $p(\boldsymbol{\mu}|\boldsymbol{d}\cdot\imath)$, which in turn is obtained via the equation we have returned to time and again in previous chapters to guide our exploration of data analysis:

$$p(\boldsymbol{\mu}|\boldsymbol{d}\cdot\imath)=\frac{p(\boldsymbol{\mu}|\imath)p(\boldsymbol{d}|\boldsymbol{\mu}\cdot\imath)}{p(\boldsymbol{d}|\imath)}\propto\varpi(\boldsymbol{\mu})\mathcal{L}(\boldsymbol{\mu}) \tag{1.5}$$

Measurement, as we will see below, refers simply to the posterior distribution over the parameter or parameters ($\boldsymbol{\mu}$) of interest. Colloquially, of course, one sees the term 'measurement' used to indicate a single-number 'best guess' concerning a parameter or hypothesis of interest, and we will take advantage of this usage when that single-number estimate is the peak of the posterior. The reason for complicating our lives with an additional term that refers to the posterior is that a measurement involves application of an observation function or forward operator to model the data, rather than simply the mechanical application of (1.5), as was primarily the case in previous chapters. The observation function is a key addition to our data analytic toolbox; it will allow us to examine complex theoretical constructs that go beyond the dimensions of the observations themselves.

The goal of the present chapter is twofold. First, we will build the background necessary to introduce the **measurement algorithm**, which will codify the steps we have so far used informally to solve measurement problems. The measurement algorithm is

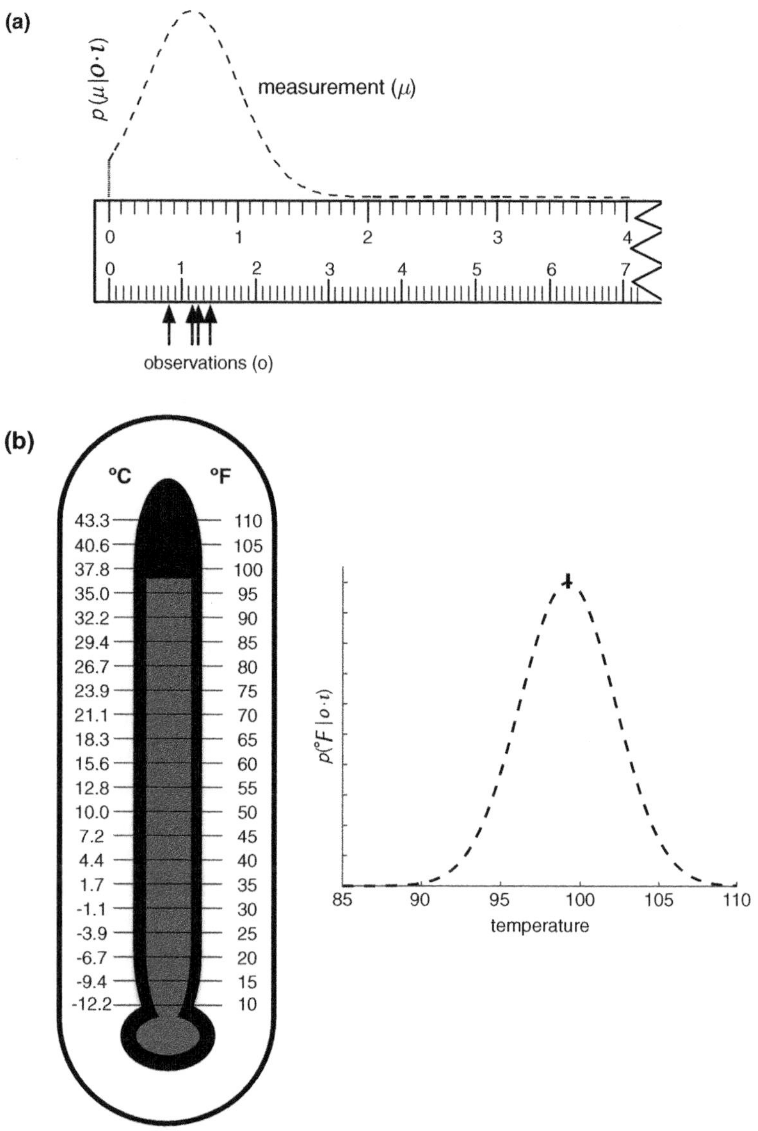

Figure 5.1 Measurement. (a) Measurement is the output of (1.5), after taking account of experimental observations and noise (dashed posteriors). Ruler measurement is performed by observing tick-marks on a ruler (arrows) and one or more observations, inferring the true length of what is being measured. Measurement may also incorporate a coordinate transformation, such as converting from cm to in. (b) The thermometer (left) reads 98.6°F, and we would like to infer the true body temperature from this observation. (right) The posterior distribution over (i.e., measurement of) temperature in the plot is based on seven such thermometer observations.

designed to organize and guide our thinking[1] regarding the underlying model of the measurement and how it relates to the computations necessary to generate a posterior distribution over a to-be-measured parameter. Along the way we will explore the

[1] Do not take this to mean that the measurement algorithm is a recipe that if followed to the letter, will always present us with the correct solution. Rather, it represents the logic of the solution in the vast majority of cases, and can therefore serve as a framework for thinking about measurements.

relationship of uncertainty to measurement, the distinction between data and parameter coordinates, and the use of a graphical model to clarify the details of the measurement. After introducing the measurement algorithm, we will complete a set of examples, to both gain experience using the measurement algorithm and to demonstrate many of the core measurements that are encountered in behavioral data analysis.

5.1 Observables, Models, and Measurements

In previous chapters we learned the mechanical practice of manipulating probability statements in ways that will be necessary to solve measurement, prediction and decision problems. In those chapters, we returned time and again to the idea that probability distributions are carriers of information. In this section we will be primarily concerned with the information that observations yield regarding parameters, that is, about the relationship of data and noise to our ultimate measurements.

5.1.1 Measurement and Uncertainty

In an experiment we are often interested in measuring some quantity of theoretical interest: Retinal photoreceptor density of short-wavelength cones in a color anomalous patient, reaction times following peripheral nerve damage, and D_2 dopamine receptor density in substantia nigra before and after administration of certain drugs are all examples. After data have been collected, however, there is almost always uncertainty associated with the values inferred for such variables. This, in fact, brings us to the crux of at least one facet of the issue: Why are our inferences uncertain when data are known with certainty? To answer this question we should return to our goal in collecting and analyzing data. In the current chapter, our goal is to infer some model parameter. Our interest is not, therefore, in the data themselves (we do not want to infer something about the data), but in what the data can tell us about the parameter (usually not directly observable) whose value we are ultimately interested in inferring. If we were interested in the data themselves, our job would be substantially easier, because the data are known with certainty. Thus, an understanding of the data would require only the descriptive statistics discussed in Chapter 1 (a report of the data range, mean, median, variance, etc.). When our goal is to infer the value of a parameter, the process is different because our information concerning the parameter is uncertain due to the fact that we can only infer its value *indirectly* from data. In this first section we will focus on both the relationship between experimental data, measurement, and the concept of uncertainty in terms of its relation to our final single-number measurements and inferences.

Mathematically, a **measurement** is just a parameter estimate based on (1.5). Note, however, that whereas (1.5) can be used for any application that calls for combination of probabilities, our goal here is restricted to inferring parameter values (e.g., the Gaussian location, $\boldsymbol{\mu}$) from data. A measurement therefore consists of three critical parts: data, a likelihood function describing the relationship between data and the underlying theoretical variables of interest, and prior information regarding parameter values (that informs our assignment of prior probabilities to model parameters). In focusing on measurement, we will often separate elements of the likelihood function and prior into parts associated with an **observation model** that describes the relationship between (1) our experimentally controlled variables & data (observables) and (2) the hypothesized **signal** present in the data, and also a **noise** model that captures our information regarding contamination of that signal. We can think of these elements in terms of a communication problem. When we speak to a friend, sound travels through the air and into the listener's ear, producing a spike train in the cochlear nerve that ultimately gets decoded in the CNS. The information in that spike train gets corrupted by ambient sounds, as well as by noise in the auditory system (e.g., imperfect sensory transduction). The noise-corrupted nerve impulses produced by that imperfectly transduced stream of sounds serves as the raw data fed into the central nervous system, which plays the role of the data analyst in this analogy. But what is this 'true signal' whose noise corrupted image constitutes the raw data? That signal is the set of nerve impulses that *would* be produced if the intended message were *not* corrupted by ambient noise while traveling through the air as sound, and if that intended message were *not* corrupted by noise in the peripheral auditory and central nervous systems. It is the *ideal* dataset (nerve-impulse-train), produced if the intended message were transmitted and transduced flawlessly. The noise model encodes our information about likely errors that might corrupt that signal to produce the raw data, and the observation model is/are the formal equation/s that translate between the parameters of your hypothesis and ideal signal (here, the translation from intended message to nerve-impulse-train).

This is exactly analogous to our problem: there is a signal (ideal dataset predicted by the model via the observation function), and a noise-corrupted raw dataset that is a noisy image of that signal. Our job is to decode and infer (measure) the parameters of the signal based on those data. The data are, of course, just the observations (e.g., the thermometer observations in Fig. 5.1b) that we will use in making our measurement. Data will always consist of a set of numbers; either representing continuous values (such as observations of ruler markings, clock positions, thermometer readings, etc.) or counts (such as the number of deceased subjects in a drug trial, or action potentials generated by a neuron). Noise, on the other hand, tends to obscure the presence and character of the underlying signal, and can be thought of as the component(s) of our observations with unmodeled causes, or due to causes with unknown effects on our observations. Our final measurement is based on computing a posterior over the possible values of the unknown parameters (see Box 5.1). This is accomplished via a probabilistic noise model (e.g., the Poisson or Gaussian likelihood) that describes the relationship between noise-contaminated data and the underlying signal. This noise model is the likelihood function, where in a data analytic context the likelihood encodes the relationship between data ($\boldsymbol{d}$), experimentally controlled variables ($\mathbf{X}$), and theoretically relevant parameters $\boldsymbol{\Theta}$ (where one or more elements of the parameters contained in $\boldsymbol{\Theta}$ are to be measured):

$$\mathcal{L} = n(s; d, \boldsymbol{\Theta}) \tag{5.1a}$$

We define the theoretical signal as the ideal (noiseless) dataset predicted by a particular combination of model parameters (the subset of parameters relating to the signal, $\boldsymbol{\Theta}_s$, as opposed to the noise, $\boldsymbol{\Theta}_n$) and values of experimenter-controlled variables ($\mathbf{X}$) used in obtaining the data:

$$s = m(\boldsymbol{\Theta}_s, \mathbf{X}) \tag{5.2}$$

In most situations it is also convenient to define noise corruption explicitly as part of the noise model; that is, define term(s) withi the noise model to describe the components of the observed data ($\boldsymbol{d}$) that are unrelated to the underlying signal (s). For example, the most common form of noise corruption is additive:

$$\boldsymbol{d} = \boldsymbol{s} + \boldsymbol{\varepsilon} \tag{5.3}$$

where noise corruption occurs after the signal is formed ('late noise'), and is additive.

In (5.2) we refer to the observation function m that defines the theoretical signal, describing the theoretically predicted (noiseless) data in terms of the parameters ($\boldsymbol{\Theta}$) and the experimentally controlled variables ($\boldsymbol{X}$). The set of parameters defined by $\boldsymbol{\Theta}$ is a list, such as $\boldsymbol{\Theta} = \{\boldsymbol{\vartheta}_1, \boldsymbol{\vartheta}_2, \ldots, \boldsymbol{\mu}_1, \boldsymbol{\mu}_2, \ldots, \boldsymbol{\rho}_1, \ldots, \boldsymbol{\varsigma}_1, \ldots\}$, where each parameter can possibly take on some set of values, for example, $\boldsymbol{\mu}_1 = [\mu_{11}, \mu_{12}, \ldots \mu_{1n}]$. Parameters are the theoretical constructs whose values we either assume we know or that we would like to measure, whereas experimentally controlled variables $\mathbf{X} = \{\boldsymbol{x}_1, \boldsymbol{x}_2, \boldsymbol{x}_3 \ldots\}$ are manipulated during an experiment (and are therefore known). For example, one might wish to measure the neural firing rates, $\boldsymbol{\varsigma}$, produced within a neuron when we experimentally control the amount of current ($\boldsymbol{x}$) injected into another population of neurons that synapse onto the recorded neuron. In this example, the data ($\boldsymbol{d}$) would consist of a set of counts, one spike count per experimental condition (i.e., each element of the vector $\boldsymbol{d}$ corresponds to an element of the the experimental-condition vector $\boldsymbol{x}$, where in this example each condition or value of $\boldsymbol{x}$ is a magnitude of injected current).

The purpose of the observation function (5.2) is to define the theoretical signal we believe exists, along with noise, in the data; it tells us what data would ideally be produced by any given set of signal parameters. Once defined, an observation function is the basis for simulating ideal datasets (i.e., predictions) that we can compare to our observations. And perhaps more to the point, they represent our predictions for the observations that might be made if the true values of the unknown parameters took on particular numerical values. Then, by simply trying all possible parameter values and applying the noise model to the observed data, we can assess how likely it is that a particular set of parameters gave rise to those data – this is the likelihood function, which we combine with the prior to yield the desired measurement.

The important point regarding the observation and likelihood function being made here is the following: There is at least one element of the set of parameters ($\boldsymbol{\Theta}$) that we would like to measure, and the likelihood encodes, via (5.1), the relationship between between possible parameter values, the set of experimentally controlled variables ($\boldsymbol{X}$), and ideal (noiseless) data ($\boldsymbol{s}$). Furthermore, because the likelihood provides a ranking of how well each parameter value matches possible observations via the predictions encoded by the ideal dataset ($\boldsymbol{s}$), it provides an important input for our inference – it tells us which parameter values are most consistent with the current data. In the remainder of this chapter we will take a closer look at the particular types of connection between parameters and data that occur when making basic measurements, and the details of how those measurements are made – paying special attention to the role played by uncertainty or noise.

In addition to its dependence on the observation function, a measurement is integrally connected with the fact that repeated, nominally identical observations will *not*

BOX 5.1 Single- and Multiple-Observation Temperature or Ruler Measurements

First taking the case of a multiple-observation length measurement, we begin with the observations, $d = [8.2, 11.5, 12.1, 13.9]$, all in mm. From these ruler readings we would like to make a measurement of length. Our first step is to apply the observation model. Based on our background information concerning the conditions under which the observations were made (we assume there was a the short temporal separation between readings and that the environment was not purposely altered during the course of taking readings), we will assume that there is a single, constant underlying length that has generated our data. That is, the underlying signal we wish to measure is a constant: $s = m(\mu) = \mu$, and we will refer to the scalar parameter μ as the true length underlying our ruler readings.

A single length measurement, and the full set of four observations, are shown in Figure 5.1. Notice that we are able to plot the scatter of ruler readings along the ruler itself in Figure 5.1 as a set of tic-marks, even though these tic-marks represent observations, not theoretical underlying length measurements (which is what is represented by the probability distribution). The probability plot is meant to help in selecting a number to represent the true length, based on the observed readings. The only question remaining is: 'at what position do we draw that line?' This is where the error model comes into play: for the present we will use a Gaussian error model,

$$p(\varepsilon|\mu \cdot \imath) = (\sigma\sqrt{2\pi})^{-N} e^{-\frac{1}{2\sigma^2}\sum \varepsilon_i^2} = (\sigma\sqrt{2\pi})^{-N} e^{-\frac{1}{2\sigma^1}\sum [d_i - \mu]^2}.$$

The error and observation models combine to form the likelihood function, which allows us to determine the highest-probability choice of the underlying signal, based on the observed data (i.e., yields the posterior) via (1.5):

$$p(\mu|d \cdot \imath) = p(\mu|\imath)\frac{p(d|\mu \cdot \imath)}{p(d|\imath)} = p(\mu|\imath)\frac{p(\varepsilon|\mu \cdot \imath)}{p(\varepsilon|\imath)}.$$

For simplicity we will assign a prior that is a continuous uniform distribution over the unknown location parameter, μ; this uniform prior distribution can be dropped from the calculation because it will not affect the outcome (i.e., location of the peak of the posterior does not change):

$$p(\mu|d \cdot \imath) \propto p(\mu|\imath)p(\varepsilon|\mu \cdot \imath) = (const)\, p(\varepsilon|\mu \cdot \imath) \propto p(\varepsilon|\mu \cdot \imath).$$

We will further assume that the value of the σ parameter of this error model is known to be $\sigma = 1$ (i.e., it is part of the background information $\imath$ in this problem), giving:

$$p(\mu|d \cdot \imath) = (\sigma\sqrt{2\pi})^{-N} e^{-\frac{1}{2\sigma^2}\sum [d_i - \mu]^2} \propto e^{-\frac{1}{2}\sum \varepsilon_i^2}.$$

The form of this Gaussian density tells us that the highest-probability choice of the parameter μ will be that which minimizes the squared sum of differences between observed data values and μ (since e^{-x^2} will be at its maximum when x is zero – or as close to zero as it can be); we will write this as, $\check{\mu}$, defined as the value of μ that minimizes the exponential term, $\sum[d_i - \mu]^2$. For our dataset, the value of μ that minimizes the term in the exponential is equal to the arithmetic mean of the observations, $\breve{\mu} = \bar{d} = 11.4$mm. The probability distribution corresponding to our measurement, $p(\mu|d \cdot \iota)$, is shown in Figure 5.1 as a dashed line. This distribution is obtained by computing the probabilities of equally spaced elements of the displayed range of possible parameter values using (5.3). Each new candidate parameter value μ changes the error vector posited to have produced the observed dataset. Each new error vector posited to have produced our observations defines a single probability based on (5.3). The resulting set of probabilities, defined over the set of different possible choices of μ, defines the posterior probability distribution that is the focus of our computation; this distribution peaks at the mean of the dataset. For example, consider a theoretical length of 25. For this to be the true length, the observed dataset would have had to have been contaminated by the error vector:

$$\begin{aligned} \varepsilon &= [8.2, 11.5, 12.1, 13.9] - 25 \\ &= [-16.8, -13.5, -12.9, -11.1]. \end{aligned}$$

Note that every element of this hypothetical dataset, having been generated by the identical true value, must have an error that yields the true value when added to that observed datum; thus there is only one possible noise vector associated with any candidate length. Also note that, because the Gaussian noise model is symmetrical about zero, we deem it rather unlikely that a noise vector (of reasonable size) with all negative values would ever occur (as described in eq. 2.16) – and therefore it is unlikely that the true temperature would be one that requires the noise vector to be all negative values (or, equally unlikely, all positive values). This basic observation explains why the probability distribution drops symmetrically toward zero as the numerical value of μ deviates from the mean of the dataset.

In the same figure, we also show the probability distribution (dashed line) corresponding to the temperature measurement that would have been made if we had taken only a single reading: 99.2°. For the case of a single reading, the measurement process is identical to that described above for the multiple-observation dataset. Here, however, there is no summation in the exponential because there is only a single datum. It is clear that the peak of the probability distribution will always be equal to the observed datum, because this value defines an error equal to zero in (5.3), and the exponential defined by the Gaussian density above, will always be at its peak when the value in the exponent is zero.

yield identical data; data are 'noisy.' The final measurement that results from observing data will make use of both an observation and a noise model. The function of the noise model is to allow us to assign probabilities to parameter values, by comparing the signal values predicted by a given set of parameters applied to the observation model, ultimately allowing us to rank those parameter values in their match to the observed data (see Box 5.2). These rankings become the likelihood, for use in (1.5) to complete the measurement.

Exercises

1) Compute $\boldsymbol{\varepsilon} = \boldsymbol{d} - \mathbf{s}$ for the following:
   a. $\boldsymbol{d}$ = [.435, .479, .496, .69, 1.23, 1.37, 1.30, 1.14, .807, .844, 1.05]
      $\mathbf{s}$ = [0, .1, .2, .3, .4, .5, .6, .7, .8, .8, .8]
   b. $\boldsymbol{d}$ = [.14, -.08, 1.11, .288, -.157, .404, .419, .899, .233, .634, .65]
      $\mathbf{s}$ = [0, .1, .2, .3, .4, .5, .6, .7, .8, .8, .8]
   c. $\boldsymbol{d}$ = [.546, .239, -1.04, .095, .233, 1.45, .527, .267, .269, .824, 1.14]
      $\mathbf{s}$ = [0, .1, .2, .3, .4, .5, .6, .7, .8, .8, .8]
   d. $\boldsymbol{d}$ = [-.342, .107, .172, .082, .487, .463, .676, .886, .617, .746, .769]
      $\mathbf{s}$ = [0, .1, .2, .3, .4, .5, .6, .7, .8, .8, .8]
2) Compute s from the following observation functions for $\boldsymbol{\mu} = [10, 11, 12, 13, 14, 15]$:
   a. $\mathbf{s} = \boldsymbol{\mu}$
   b. $\mathbf{s} = 2\boldsymbol{\mu}/3$
   c. $\mathbf{s} = \boldsymbol{\mu}^{2/3}/10$
   d. $\mathbf{s} = 2\cos(20\pi t + \boldsymbol{\mu})\ \{0 \leq t \leq 10$
   e. $\mathbf{s} = 2t\boldsymbol{\mu}\{0 \leq t \leq 1$
3) Compute the mean and standard deviation of $\boldsymbol{\varepsilon} = \boldsymbol{d} - s$ for the dataset of repeated observations $\boldsymbol{d}$ = [10 15 12 7], and observation function $s = .5\mu$ if:
   a) $\mu = 15$
   b) $\mu = 20$
   c) $\mu = 25$
   d) $\mu = 30$
4) Re-produce the plot in Figure 5.1a, if $d = 10$ and the observation function is $s = \mu$.
5) Why it will always be true that $\breve{\mu} = \bar{\boldsymbol{d}}$ for the examples depicted in Figure 5.1?
6) How are the noise distribution, observed data, and parameter values connected to the concept of uncertainty?
7) Describe the connection between the data and parameters. Which is uncertain, and why?
8) How does noise corruption affect the certainty of our data? Parameters? What difference is there, if any – and why?

5.1.2 Data versus Parameter Coordinates

The apparently new element of our discussion in this chapter has been the observation function, which allows us to partition and extract the information relevant to each parameter that is contained in the data. How does the observation function enhance our ability to make measurements? An observation function allows us to make predictions for models that are more complex than estimating a simple Gaussian location or Poisson rate. In these simple cases, the observation function is transparent, in the sense that we don't even notice its existence:

$$\begin{aligned} s &= m(\mu) \\ &= \mu \end{aligned}$$

Cases of transparent measurement rely on data that have the identical coordinates (see Box 5.3) to the parameter we wish to measure. For example, consider the behavioral response to infection, which includes elevated body temperature. If we were to take thermometer readings from 30 patients diagnosed with Dengue fever, it would allow us to measure the population temperature in this group. The likelihood component of that measurement would be

$$\mathcal{L}(\mu) = (\sigma\sqrt{2\pi})^{-n} e^{-\frac{1}{2}\frac{\sum \varepsilon_i^2}{\sigma^2}} = (\sigma\sqrt{2\pi})^{-n} e^{-\frac{1}{2}\frac{\sum_i (d_i - s)^2}{\sigma^2}} = (\sigma\sqrt{2\pi})^{-n} e^{-\frac{1}{2}\frac{\sum_i (d_i - \mu)^2}{\sigma^2}}$$

where the signal is simply the Gaussian location parameter (the true population temperature), and each thermometer observation is a noisy copy ('image') of the unobservable temperature value, μ. The procedure would be the same if you had only ever seen a single case of Dengue: you would simply use that single observation for the unobservable population temperature measurement.

Despite being basic to the practice of data analysis, there is a conceptual subtlety in this temperature example that may create confusion in applying the same logic and equations to more complex examples: The simplification that occurs when the desired parameter estimate is identical with the ideal datum. We will call this simplified case **transparent** measurement, and contrast it below to **indirect** or **complex** measurement. That difficulty occurs if we collapse the separate concepts of model parameter, signal and datum (i.e., incorrectly believing $d = s = \mu$). Thinking of the measurement as the data (or the mean of the data) is possible only because the unknown parameter and the data share the same coordinates: both in degrees Fahrenheit. However, it is a mistake to think of a measurement as equal to the data because it obscures the purpose of the observation function, which is to partition the components of the data and assign them to the various parameters of the model.

At the other end of the spectrum are **complex models**, and measurements of the parameters of those models. A complex model might posit that temperature is dynamic, cycling over the course of a day between a minimum and maximum value that is centered on the daily 'base' temperature seen in Dengue patients. This more complex model would involve additional parameters:

$$\begin{aligned} s &= m(\mu, \alpha, \varphi) \\ &= \mu + A\sin(\alpha t + \varphi) \end{aligned}$$

and would not suffer from the collapse of concepts described above. Here, the likelihood becomes

$$\mathcal{L}(\mu) = (\sigma\sqrt{2\pi})^{-n} e^{-\frac{1}{2}\frac{\sum (\varepsilon_i)_t^2}{\sigma^2}} = (\sigma\sqrt{2\pi})^{-n} e^{-\frac{1}{2}\frac{\sum_i (d_i - s)_t^2}{\sigma^2}} = (\sigma\sqrt{2\pi})^{-n} e^{-\frac{1}{2}\frac{\sum_i (d_i - [\mu + A\sin(\alpha t + \varphi)])_t^2}{\sigma^2}}$$

The observation function partitions the data into signal and noise by assuming the existence of stable cycles of higher and lower temperature over the course of a day that are superimposed on an individual's base body temperature (near 98.6° F). Under the first model, a thermometer reading of 99.5° F in mid-afternoon could be evidence of fever, whereas under the second model could simply represent a normal base temperature of 98.6° F with the addition of a second component that is part of a normal circadian cycle.

BOX 5.2 Error Distributions and Information

The importance of the observation function is primarily in defining the transform between unknown parameter values and observed data. However, one consequence of this transform is that it forces us to recognize that error distributions are determined by our information about the problem at hand, and reinforces what we learned in Chapter 1: probability distributions are defined by our information.

To see why this is the case, we must recognize that any variation in the data that is not predicted by the observation model is interpreted as noise. This statement is easily seen in the definition of the Gaussian likelihood, $\mathcal{L}(\mu) \propto e^{-\frac{1}{2}\frac{\sum_i \varepsilon^2}{\sigma^2}}$ $= e^{-\frac{1}{2}\frac{\sum[s-d]^2}{\sigma^2}}$. The noiseless signal that is predicted to occur in the data, s, is simply the observation function defined by our theoretical model (and its parameters). Any change in the theoretical model will therefore change the error term of this likelihood, because we will have redefined what part of the data is signal (and therefore what is noise).

Now, you may argue that if we change the model then the earlier theory was not defining the 'real' signal, and so we were simply mistaken when we defined the first likelihood. However, by the same argument, we are also mistaken about the updated observation model: After all, models are by their nature approximations and therefore always mistaken to an extent. To want to wait until our model is perfect before we can define the 'real' signal simply ignores the reality of the scientific program. Our job is always to make the best inferences that are possible *now*, based on our *current* state of information – not to wait for some future never-to-be-realized perfect state of information before getting down to work. Probability theory allows us to make the best inferences possible with the information at hand. The quality of those inferences is certainly determined by the quality of our current state of information, and scientific progress is made when we improve our model of the data. So while it is true that progress is slower when our models are imperfect, the alternative is to never make a start.

Our goal in this final subsection before outlining the measurement algorithm is to highlight the fact that all measurements rely on an observation function in exactly the same way, whether that observation function is complex (when the presence of the observation function, and the distinction between data and parameter coordinates, is unambiguous) or transparent (when the presence of the observation function is often ignored). The distinction between data and parameter coordinates is an important one for understanding the unity of the measurement procedure, regardless of the circumstances of the measurement. In most cases, we think of 'taking a measurement' as using some piece of equipment such as a ruler, voltmeter, ammeter, etc. to directly measure μ. However, we have hopefully seen above that the procedure, even when it is transparent, involves an underlying set of operations wherein we define the connection between the unknown parameters and the data expected from specific values of those parameters. In other words, it is important to think of measurement primarily in terms of the indirect case, and not the simpler transparent case.

BOX 5.3 Dimensional Analysis

In an additive error model, the units of s and d will be identical (e.g., when making a time measurement, both will be in ms, or both in s). This must always be the case, because we cannot subtract values with different units; to do so would violate the prohibition against 'comparing apples and oranges.' If the noise model relies on the difference $\varepsilon = d - f(\theta)$, then either it is a transparent observation function $f(\theta) = \theta + c$ (where c is a constant), or θ and d are in incommensurate units. In the latter case, the observation function must define a relationship that relates data coordinates to parameter coordinates. This fact is important because it can alert us to problems with our observation function through an analysis of the dimensions of each model element.

Dimensional analysis simply looks at the units of each variable in an equation, an allows us to (a) verify that the components of the equation combine units logically, and (b) that the observation function will correctly combine units in its parameters to ultimately yield data coordinates.

For example, imagine that you have distance data, but your unknown parameter μ has units of speed (e.g., cm/s). This means that $s = m(\mu)$ must define a transform between speed units and time units. This transform requires multiplying the μ variable by a time. For example:

$$\begin{aligned} s_1 &= m(\mu) \\ &= \mu T \end{aligned}$$

where T may be a known time value that is part of our background information (e.g., an experimentally controlled variable). A second possibility would be:

$$\begin{aligned} s_2 &= m(\mu) \\ &= \mu T + x_0 \end{aligned}$$

where x_0 is an initial distance.

A dimensional analysis simply requires us to replace each variable with its units, and cancel. For s_1 this yields: $\frac{cm}{s}s = \frac{cm}{\not s}\not s = cm$. For s_2 this yields: $\frac{cm}{\not s}\not s + cm = cm$. Both of these have the correct output dimensions of cm, but s_2 demonstrates the rule that any variables combined through addition or subtraction must have the same units. For example it is not valid to add a length to a time, or even a length in cm to a length in mm (without first converting cm to mm or vice versa).

What if T in the s_1 equation above had been given in ms rather than s? There are $1000ms$ in a second, so while the dimensions of: $\frac{cm}{s}ms$ do not cancel, we can convert T to have units of s with the conversion:

$$s_1 = \mu(T/1000)$$

whose dimensional analysis now correctly yields:

$$\frac{cm}{s}\frac{ms}{1000} = cm$$

As a variation on the above, imagine your data were in time units (e.g., ms). Here, your observation function would have to involve dividing a distance variable by μ, for example:

$$s_3 = x/\mu,$$

where x is given in cm. The dimensions are now: $cm/\frac{cm}{ms} = \not{cm}\frac{ms}{\not{cm}} = ms$.

As a final example, we convert Celsius to Fahrenheit temperature:

$$s_4 = \mu\rho_{CF} + F_0$$

where the unknown variable, μ is given in degrees Celsius, $\rho_{CF} = \Delta_F/\Delta_C$ is a conversion factor that relates the change in degrees F for an equal-temperature change in degrees C (the conversion factor has units F / C). For example, the change in Fahrenheit-scaled temperature between the freezing and boiling point of water is $\Delta_F = 212 - 32$, whereas the Celsius-scaled temperature between the freezing and boiling point of water is $\Delta_C = 100 - 0$. The ratio of these, $\rho_{CF} = \Delta_F/\Delta_C = (212 - 32)/100$, tells us the conversion factor between changes in Fahrenheit and Celsius-scaled temperatures: a change of 1°C corresponds to a change of (212 − 32)/100°F. And since the zero point of the Celsius scale corresponds to $F_0 = 32$°F, we have to add this to the converted Celsius value to shift the Fahrenheit scale to the correct zero point. As an initial check on this observation function, our dimensional analysis shows that we correctly transform from Celsius to Fahrenheit scales of temperature: $°\not{C}\frac{°F}{°\not{C}} +° F =° F$. A second-level check on your observation function would verify that the value $\mu = 0$ C corresponds to $s_4 = 32$°F, and the value $\mu = 100$°C corresponds to the signal $s_4 = 212$°F.

It is usually a good idea, when constructing any nontrivial observation function, to perform a dimensional analysis to verify that the observation function correctly transforms between data units and parameter units.

Exercises

1) Certain observation functions can also serve as linking functions for a coordinate transform of a posterior distribution. These include transforming distance into speed for a given time, or transforming Celsius into Fahrenheit temperature (examples of these can be found in Appendix C). These transforms are capable of serving this dual purpose because there is an initial (transparent) observation function that allows a posterior to be computed based on the data. After this initial posterior is computed based on the transparent observation function, one can use the speed equation or the relation between Celsius and Fahrenheit temperature to transform the posterior into different coordinates. Based on a uniform prior over Celsius temperature, the thermometer readings, 67° and 69°F, and a standard deviation of 2.2°:
   a. compute the posterior over F-ruled temperature and perform a change of coordinates to convert the posterior into Celsius scaled temperature.
   b. compute the posterior over Celsius-ruled temperature by inserting the observation function, $s = m(\mu) = \mu(212 - 32)/100 + 32$ into the Gaussian likelihood.
2) Categorize the following in terms of transparent or indirect measurement. If the case is indeterminate without describing the data, say so as well:

a) temperature	b) duration	c) Neural spike count
d) Poisson rate	e) speed	f) distance
g) binomial rate	h) acceleration	

3) How do transparent and other measurements differ? Write the transparent observation function.
4) What is the purpose of dimensional analysis? Perform such an analysis for any transform you choose (other than the example above) and describe each part of the analysis in words.

5.1.3 Graphical Models

So far, we have described the components of the underlying relationships between the parameters of an observation model, noise model, and observable data. We will now take a closer look at how these elements function together. In doing so, we will gain a better understanding of how to concretely state the desired measurement in any given experimental situation.

To define interrelationships among the parameters of the observation and noise models, and how they produce observed data, we will learn to create a graphical representation of the underlying process or model that generates our data. As such, a graphical model must represent elements of both the observation and noise models discussed above, as well as any background information that is directly relevant to our model of how the data are generated.

The graphical models we will use here define the connections among observable (experimentally controlled variables, and data) and 'hidden' (unknown parameters) elements of the model, and as such it may appear that these models simply reiterate what we have already stated when defining observation and noise models. This is true to an extent. However, a graphical model allows us to quickly and clearly grasp the interrelationships among model variables, and therefore helps to avoid the confusions that arise when our understanding of these interconnections is a bit hazy. Such confusions occur particularly when we look up (i.e., in a reference text) the equations necessary for a particular analysis, on the assumption that those equations will be appropriate for the analysis of a dataset we have recently collected. This situation occurs often (i.e., looking up a standard analysis), and yet without a clear understanding of the assumptions that have gone into the looked-up equations, it could easily be the case that the analysis is actually quite inappropriate for the data at hand. By constructing a graphical model of both the reference analysis and of the current dataset we can avoid most such errors. As an added bonus, the graphical models we will construct can be converted into other types of graphical model, such as 'Bayes networks,' which are designed to provide a basis for many of the computer-aided analysis programs that are able to compute approximate solutions to high-dimensional measurement problems (e.g., those involving marginalization over tens or hundreds of nuisance variables), but which require computational techniques beyond the scope of the present text.

Our models will be composed of three basic building blocks: lines (or connections), variable nodes, and function blocks. Lines carry information (such as the value of a particular variable) from one part of the model to another. Variables that are not the result of a model-defined computation are introduced into the model via nodes; this,

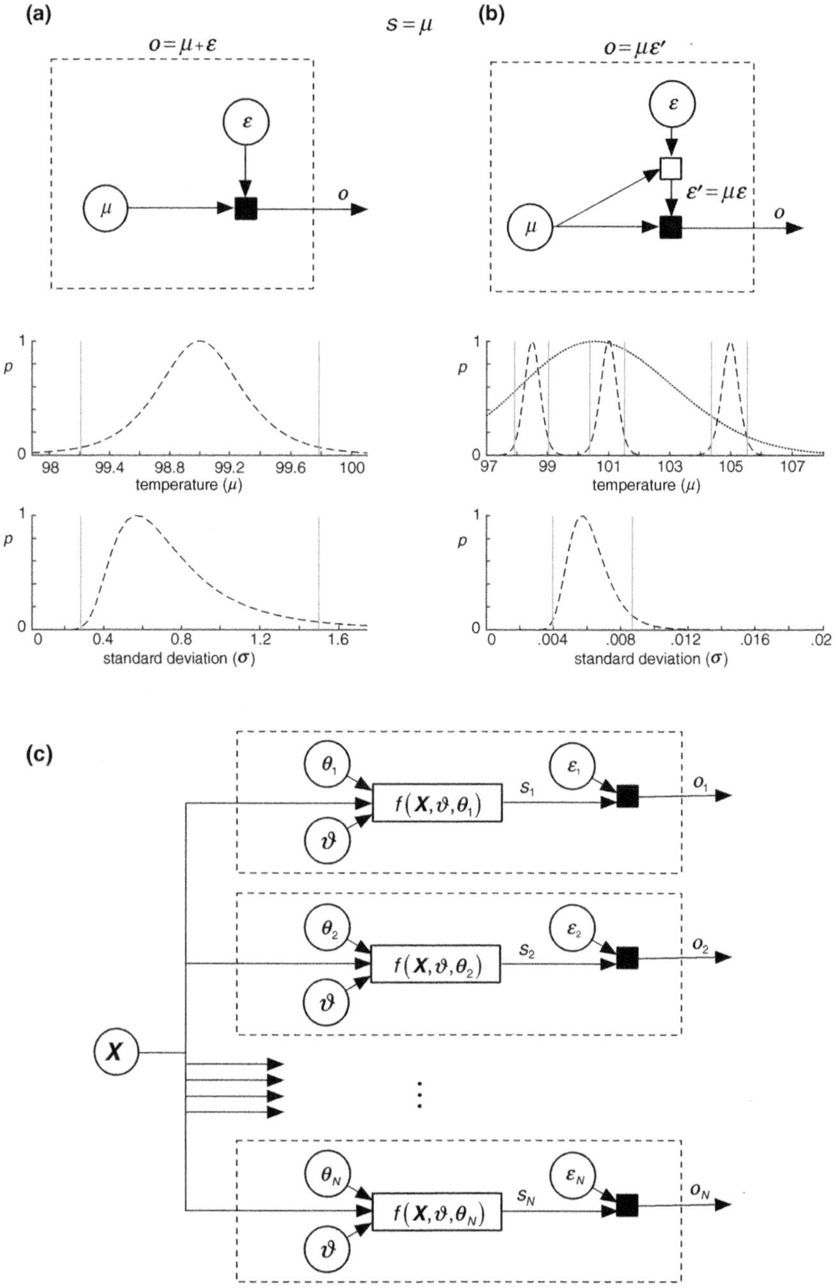

Figure 5.2 Transparent measurement models. (a) Constant-variance additive noise model (upper) and body temperature measurement (lower), including the marginalized posterior probability distribution over the unknown parameter μ and separately over σ. Marginalized distributions are shown along with 95 percent shortest confidence interval(dashed vertical lines). (b) Multiplicative noise model, where added noise is scaled by the size of the signal, μ, and marginalized posteriors. (c) Multi-source additive model, where each source is influenced by independent noise sources but a common external input variable (X).

for example, is often the case with the error term that perturbs the underlying signal we wish to measure. Function blocks define functions that convert input information, such as might be derived from a variable node, to model-relevant output(s), such as the theoretical signal for a given measurement problem. Note that we will also take advantage of two special function blocks. We will use a small filled square to indicate that inputs to the block are added and an open square to indicate that inputs are multiplied; other function blocks will contain a description of the function being computed. A few examples will help to clarify.

Example: Transparent Measurement

The graphical models in Figure 5.2 describe a common measurement scenario: They encode a transparent measurement where the observation model is $s = m(\mu) = \mu$. In Figure 5.2a the noise model describes a Gaussian probability distribution over possible values of ε:

$$p(\boldsymbol{\varepsilon}|s \cdot \nu) = \sqrt{2\nu\pi}^{-N} e^{-\frac{1}{2}\frac{\sum \varepsilon^2}{\nu}} = \sqrt{2\nu\pi}^{-N} e^{-\frac{N}{2}\frac{\overline{\varepsilon^2}}{\nu}}.$$

Note that Gaussian noise is commonly assumed with additive noise models.

Following the flow of information in Figure 5.2a: The left-hand node introduces the unknown μ parameter, which is connected to additive noise. The observed data are the sum of the value of μ and the particular sample of noise that occurs during the experiment: that is, they are the sum of a constant signal and a sample-dependent noise term:

$$\boldsymbol{d} = s + \boldsymbol{\varepsilon},$$

where the error and data terms are vectors (one element per observation) and the signal (μ) is a constant. The additive error term above is assigned the Gaussian distribution, where the variance is $\nu = \sigma^2$ and the error vector is defined $\boldsymbol{\varepsilon} = s - \boldsymbol{d}$. Note that a dashed box surrounds the unobservable variables and functions. This is useful to highlight the difference between observable and theoretical variables.

Figure 5.2b encodes a transparent observation model with additive noise that is scaled by μ. Here, the flow of information through the model takes a more complicated path, such that the size of the signal affects noise level. Again, there is a node introducing the μ parameter on the far left. This node has an output that connects to a multiplicative combination of itself and the output of the error node. The second output from the μ node adds the μ-multiplied noise to itself to produce the observed output, o. These observations are described by the signal added to a noise term, although here the noise term is scaled by the signal strength.

The data in this case can also be described with a Gaussian noise model. The noise combines with the parameter μ additively just before observation, so that our observation of μ is perturbed by an error (ε) that is added to μ, just as above. However, these added errors scale with the value of μ. Thus, the Gaussian noise model that describes the output of the error node (ε') is:

$$p(\varepsilon'|\nu \cdot \iota) = \sqrt{2\nu\pi}^{-1} e^{-\frac{1}{2}\frac{(\varepsilon')^2}{\nu}},$$

but the variance term (ν) is scaled by the size of μ

$$\begin{aligned} p(\varepsilon'|\sigma \cdot \iota) &= p([\mu\varepsilon]|\sigma \cdot \iota) \\ &= \left[\mu\sigma\sqrt{2\pi}\right]^{-1} e^{-\frac{1}{2}\frac{(\mu-d)^2}{(\mu\sigma)^2}} \end{aligned}$$

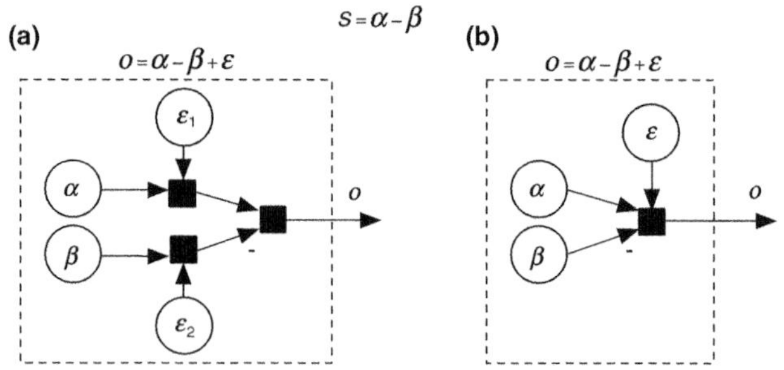

Figure 5.3 Function of two unobserved variables. (a) Each variable has a separate late-noise term. (b) Lumped-noise version of (a).

To understand why added errors have this form, consider that $[p(\varepsilon'|\sigma \cdot \imath)]$ is still expected to be at the origin, and the upper term in the exponential will therefore be $(\mu - d)^2$, just as above. The scale parameter, however, increases by a factor of μ. This is due to the linearity of the expectation operator:

$$\mathrm{V} = \mathrm{E}\left[(\varepsilon)^2\right] = \mathrm{E}\left[(\mu\varepsilon')^2\right] = \mathrm{E}\left[(\mu^2(\varepsilon')^2\right] = (\mu\sigma)^2,$$

which defines the denominator of the exponential, and thereby also the normalization term of the Gaussian. The graphical representation in both cases describes the connections among parameters of the observation and noise models in generating data. The first case is straightforward, with constant-variance noise added after whatever process (not modeled) might have generated μ. The second case also features late noise, but the noise term scales with μ.

Exercises

1) Simulate data from 5 subjects based on Figure 5.3 (left), using $\mu_1 = 1, \mu_2 = 2$, etc. For each subject, 25 trials of observations are recorded. Draw noise samples (values of $\boldsymbol{\varepsilon}$) from a standard Gaussian (zero-mean, with variance of one) random number generator. Plot the data.
2) Simulate data from 5 subjects based on Figure 5.3 (right), using $\mu_1 = 1, \mu_2 = 2$, etc. For each subject, 25 trials of observations are recorded. Draw noise samples (values of $\boldsymbol{\varepsilon}$) from a standard Gaussian random number generator. Plot the data.
3) Describe the major differences between the plots in (1) and (2).

Example: Function of Multiple Hidden Variables

Instead of a single hidden variable, observations may be based on multiple hidden variables, as shown in Figures 5.2c and 5.3. In Figure 5.3 the theoretical signal is the difference of two unknown variables, $s = m(\alpha, \beta)$. However, there is nothing in this model that allows us to separate the effects of the two hidden variables; we cannot differentiate anything about the effect of α relative to that of β in the output. Because there is no way to know the separate effects of the two hidden variables, we can only measure their combination (combined here as a difference).

The model shown in Figure 5.3b differs from that in Figure 5.3a in that the former contains a single (lumped) noise element and in the latter separate noise elements perturb the components of the difference signal. However, even in Figure 5.3a both noise elements are unobserved, and so the best we can do in modeling them is to lump them together as $\varepsilon = \varepsilon_1 - \varepsilon_2$.

This example highlights several important functions of the graphical model: First, to help us see when a particular measurement problem is equivalent to another, and second to show us when model elements are not individually identifiable in terms of our ability to measure their individual values.

Exercises

1) Simulate data from 12 subjects based on 5.3b, using $\alpha_1 = 1, \alpha_2 = 2$, etc. and $\beta_1 = 11, \beta_2 = 12$, etc. For each subject, 25 trials of observations are recorded. Draw noise samples (values of $\boldsymbol{\varepsilon}$) from a standard Gaussian (zero-mean, with variance of one) random number generator. Plot the average (α, β)-pairs of the simulated subject pool.
2) What is the variance of the output of Figure 5.3a, in terms of ν_1 and ν_2? Explain your answer.
3) Describe an experimental scenario in which we might be able to separately measure α and β in either of the models shown in Figure 5.3, for some real-world observation o and possible underlying causes α and β.
4) Construct an equivalent version of Figure 5.3 (right) with a single addition node. What are the advantages and disadvantages of drawing the model in these ways?

Example: Straight-Line Model Dependent on an Experimentally Controlled Variable
Unlike the previous models, the model shown in Figure 5.4 features an experimentally controlled input variable, x. Because the values of x are known, it appears outside the dashed box. The values of x are scaled by the hidden variable, β, to produce the theoretical signal. Here we have the strictly proportional straight-line model,

$$s = \beta x$$

in which the signal is a straight line that passes through the origin when plotted against x-values. The strictly proportional functional relationship generalizes to a proportional change model when it is augmented to include a stable offset (bias, α) term:

$$s = \alpha + \beta x$$

shifting the entire line up or down relative to the origin. Data are observed at a known set of experimentally controlled x-values, and constitute a noisy image of this straight-line model.

The straight-line model is the second most common signal used in behavioral science, after the constant-signal model (Fig. 5.2). For this reason, there are a great many variants of the straight-line model, including late-noise, early-noise, strictly proportional (as here), proportional change, and subject-specific variants in which the slope parameter (β) is assumed stable across subjects but offsets (α) vary.

Exercises

1) a. Plot a straight-line with constant offset version of the plot in Figure 5.4a.
   b. What is the difference between graphical models producing the plot in Figure 5.4a and a constant-offset plot?

c. Are both the scale factor and constant offset parameters able to be separately estimated? Explain why or why not.

2) a. Build a multiplicative (early) noise version of Figure 5.4a.
 b. Simulate and plot data from your model.
 c. How does the plot differ from that in (1)?
 d. How does it differ from the plot in Figure 5.3b?

3) Plot sample datasets (o vs. x) for Figure 5.4a with the parameters ($x = [-5 : 5]$):
 a. $\alpha = 1, \sigma = 1$
 b. $\alpha = .5, \sigma = .1$
 c. $\alpha = 1, \sigma = 5$

Example: Two Outputs Derived from the Same Input

One of the complications of the straight-line model occurs when several outputs vary linearly with the value of a single input variable. Two versions of this situation are shown in Fig. 5.4b: one in which the outputs are each dependent on the input but independent of one another, and one in which the outputs are both dependent on the input and there is also a direct relationship between parameters that underlie the two outputs.

In the left-hand model, outputs are determined independently by x. In the right-hand model the slopes of the two outputs are related to one another via the function block, $\beta_2 = \kappa - \beta_1$. Thus, while the two output variables will have a straight-line relationship (analogous to the plot in Fig. 5.4a) to variations in x whether the underlying mechanism is of the type described in the left- or right-hand plot, there is a direct relationship between the two outputs (via their slopes) in the right-hand model that is *not* present in the left-hand model. Note that in all cases where there are multiple outputs that are linearly related to the same input, the outputs themselves will display a straight-line relationship to one another (i.e., a plot of o_1 vs. o_2 will look like a straight-line relationship), whether (right-hand model) or not (left-hand model) there is a direct relationship between the outputs themselves. This fact is obvious if we write expressions for the two underlying signals in the independent case:

$$s_1 = \alpha_1 + \beta_1 x$$
$$s_2 = \alpha_2 + \beta_2 x$$

and substitute the x in the expression for s_1 into the expression for s_2:

$$\begin{aligned} s_2 &= \alpha_2 + \beta_2 \frac{s_1 - \alpha_1}{\beta_1} \\ &= \left[\alpha_2 - \frac{\beta_2}{\beta_1}\alpha_1\right] + \frac{\beta_2}{\beta_1} s_1 \\ &= \alpha + \beta s_1 \end{aligned}$$

where the slope of the relationship between s_2 and s_1 will be $\beta = \beta_2/\beta_1$. Notice that while the individually measured values β_1 and β_2 always provide a measurement of the slope of the o_1 versus o_2 plot regardless of whether data are produced by the mechanism shown in the two models shown in Figure 5.4b, only in the right-hand model can we measure the slope of the o_1 versus o_2 plot from the measured value of β_1 alone (making use of the *theoretical* relationship between the two slopes, $\kappa = \beta_1 + \beta_2$).

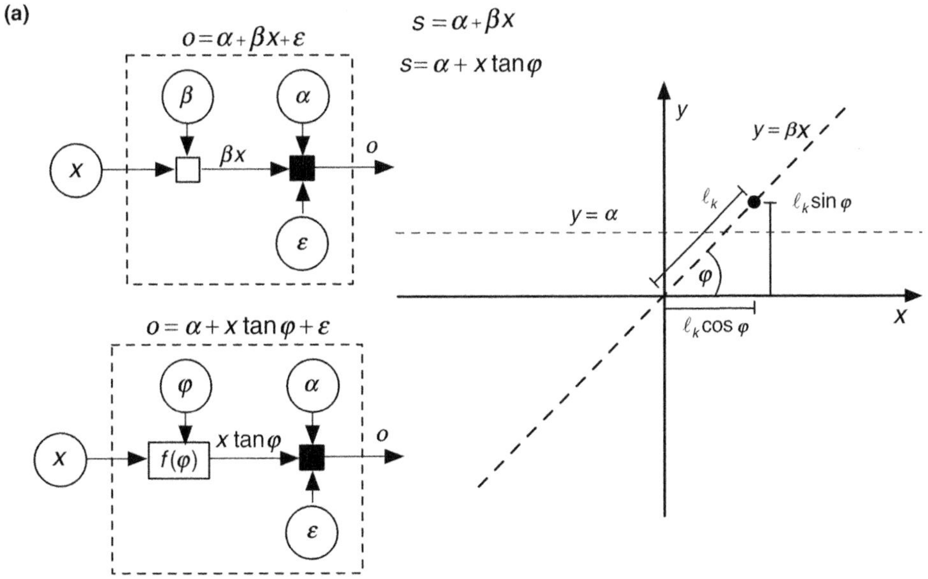

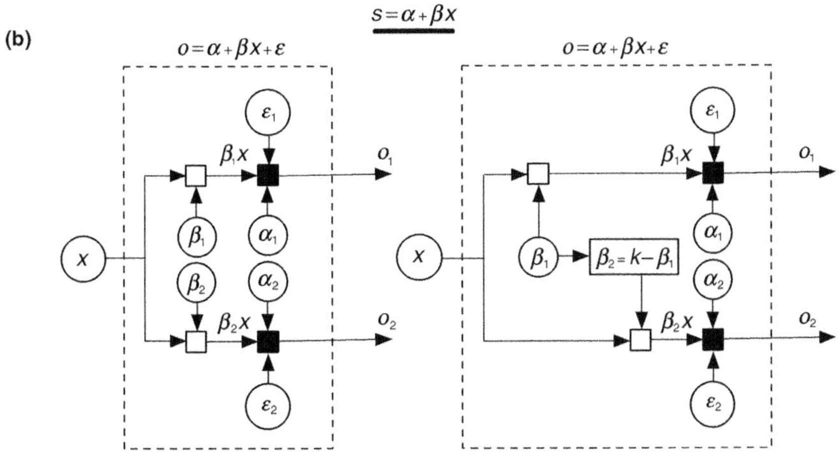

Figure 5.4 Straight-line models. (a) Three of the most common equations used to model experimental data: the constant-value model (light dashed horizontal line), the constant-proportion straight-line model (dark dashed line), and a combination of the two. Whereas the first model predicts the same measurement ($y = \alpha$) for all values of the x variable, this straight-line model predicts changes in the observed value of y that are proportional to changes in the input variable, x [i.e.,$y = \beta X$]. Note that one can think of the ultimate effect of fitting a straight line to 2D data as reducing the dimensionality of observed data from two dimensions to one. The one remaining dimension can be parameterized by distance along the line (l) relative to its intersection with $X = 0$, which is the origin of this 1D coordinate system (right). Observed data (circles) are plotted against values of the experimental variable (x) along with the theoretical straight line. (b) In a dual-output straight-line model, all outputs depend on the value of x and may either be independent of one another (left) or one output may be dependent on the other, such that one slope is a function of the other slope.

Now that we have constructed models for several different measurements, let's take a quick look back at the models that involve the slopes of lines. In the *straight-line model dependent on an experimentally controlled variable* example, individual data values were a function of a known (experimentally manipulated) x-value. In the *two outputs derived from the same input* examples, the individual data values were also functions of a known x-value, but in these situations it is often the relationship between the two parameters themselves that is of interest (i.e., we are interested in a possible direct connection between the unobservable elements within the model). For example, we might want to measure the slope of the relationship[2] between o_1 and o_2. In this respect, the graphical models point to an important difference between the model depicted in Figure 5.4a and those in Figure 5.4b: Figure 5.4a has noise in the output o only, whereas when comparing o_1 and o_2 (Fig. 5.4b) there is noise in both outputs. In terms of data plots, there is only uncertainty along the ordinate in the plot shown in Figure 5.4a, but there is uncertainty along both axes in an analogous straight-line plot of o_1 versus o_2 based on Figure 5.4b. This distinction between straight-line models (whose plot has uncertainty along one vs. two axes) is often overlooked, and they are lumped together and analyzed with no regard for this distinction. They are, however, distinct forms of the straight-line measurement problem and require different analyses. Because it is critical that we think carefully about sources of error and the interrelationships among the variables that go into observation and noise models, we will always attempt to construct as detailed a graphical model as possible in our application of the measurement algorithm.

Exercises

1) Plot sample datasets (o_1 vs. o_2) for Figure 5.4b (left). In the sample datasets use $x = [-5 : 5]$, and assume there are 5 different subjects in the experiment. Each subject has a slightly different set of β parameters (assume all $\alpha = 0$, and all $\sigma = .5$), where the means of the slopes are:
   a. $\bar{\beta}_1 = 1, \bar{\beta}_2 = 1$
   b. $\bar{\beta}_1 = .5, \bar{\beta}_2 = 2$
2) Plot sample datasets (o_1 vs. o_2) for Figure 5.4b (right). In the sample datasets use $x = [-5 : 5]$, and assume there are 5 different subjects in the experiment. Each subject has a slightly different set of β parameters (assume $k = 1$, all $\alpha = 0$, and all $\sigma = .5$), where the means of the slopes are:
   a. $\bar{\beta}_1 = 1.1$
   b. $\bar{\beta}_1 = .5$
   c. $\bar{\beta}_1 = .8$
3) Describe the differences in the plots of (1a) and (2a) above.
4) Plot o_1 versus o_2 for the data used to simulate
   a. Data from Ex. 1
   b. Data from Ex. 2

[2] It is tempting to believe that the mere existence of a straight-line relationship between o_1 and o_2 is evidence of the right-hand, 'causal' or 'dependent,' version of the model shown in Figure 5.4. This is absolutely false. Both versions of Figure 5.4 *must always* (so long as both outputs display a straight-line relationship to x) yield a straight-line relationship between o_1 and o_2, and more involved analyses must be undertaken to differentiate the two versions of the model.

c. Describe the plots from (a) and (b) relative to one another. Is there any reason to prefer one or the other as a causal or noncausal description of the underlying parameters? Why?

5) Plot β_1 versus β_2 for the parameters that were used to simulate Ex 1a and 2a. Describe the two plots relative to one another. Describe the connection between the two model variants and the these two plots of slopes.

5.2 The Measurement Algorithm

In the next several sections we will consider in detail the solution to a series of measurement problems, the majority based on nontrivial observation functions. Although these are not the first measurement problems we have so far encountered, our emphasis in previous chapters was on the mechanics of manipulating probability expressions and of assigning priors and likelihoods. When solving the current problems we will pay special attention to how the measurement algorithm is implemented at each step of the solution.

We will see that all measurement problems, although different in the details of the final numerical calculations required for their solution, are nearly identical in terms of the logical sequence of steps needed to generate those final calculations. This is one of the great strengths of our method. There is generally no question about what constitutes the solution to a problem. The correct *inference* is always identical with the appropriate portion (marginalized over nuisance parameters) of a posterior distribution, and that posterior distribution is always obtained via the same manipulations of probability statements introduced in Chapter 2, beginning with Bayes' theorem (1.5).

5.2.1 Logic

In general, the initial equation with which we will analyze hypotheses about an unknown parameter value (υ) is Bayes' theorem:

$$\begin{aligned} p(\upsilon \cdot \boldsymbol{d}|\imath) &= p(\upsilon|\boldsymbol{d} \cdot \imath)p(\boldsymbol{d}|\imath) \\ &= p(\boldsymbol{d}|\upsilon \cdot \imath)p(\upsilon|\imath), \end{aligned} \tag{1.5}$$

where we have written (1.5) in terms of a single unknown parameter value, υ, a dataset, $\boldsymbol{d}$, where the dataset corresponding to a single unknown parameter will usually be a length-N vector, with one datum for each of N sources (although it is not entirely uncommon that each source may yield m observations, making $\boldsymbol{d}$ an N x m matrix). The posterior, obtained by re-arranging the above into the form given in (1.5), is the 1D probability distribution over the unknown parameter value υ:

$$p(\upsilon|\boldsymbol{d} \cdot \imath) = \frac{p(\upsilon|\imath)p(\boldsymbol{d}|\upsilon \cdot \imath)}{p(\boldsymbol{d}|\imath)} = \frac{\varpi(\upsilon)\mathcal{L}(\upsilon)}{\mathcal{L}(\imath)} \propto \varpi(\upsilon)\mathcal{L}(\upsilon)$$

If we further introduce additional unknown parameters $\boldsymbol{\Theta}$, we can incorporate them into (1.5):

$$p(\upsilon \cdot \boldsymbol{\Theta}|\boldsymbol{d} \cdot \imath) = \frac{p(\upsilon \cdot \boldsymbol{\Theta}|\imath)p(\boldsymbol{d}|\upsilon \cdot \boldsymbol{\Theta} \cdot \imath)}{p(\boldsymbol{d}|\imath)} = \frac{\varpi(\upsilon \cdot \boldsymbol{\Theta})\mathcal{L}(\upsilon \cdot \boldsymbol{\Theta})}{\mathcal{L}(\imath)} \propto \varpi(\upsilon \cdot \boldsymbol{\Theta})\mathcal{L}(\upsilon \cdot \boldsymbol{\Theta}),$$

where the posterior now represents an $M + 1$-dimensional surface formed by the $N = n + m$ elements of the unknown parameter vector $\boldsymbol{\Theta} = [\vartheta_1, \vartheta_2, \ldots, \vartheta_n, \sigma_1, \ldots, \sigma_m]$, and each element of the vector $\boldsymbol{\Theta}$ is one unknown parameter, and each unknown parameter has associated with it a range of possible parameter values, thus defining a multidimensional posterior distribution. These additional parameters are considered 'nuisance' parameters, defined as parameters whose values are not of interest, but that are nevertheless part of our computations. Nuisance parameters are removed from the final posterior through marginalization, $p(\upsilon|\boldsymbol{d}\cdot\iota) = \int d\boldsymbol{\Theta} p(\upsilon\cdot\boldsymbol{\Theta}|\boldsymbol{d}\cdot\iota)$.

In practical applications, the quantity in the denominator of Bayes' theorem need not be computed, but is computable by recognizing that it is a likelihood term that describes the likelihood of the background information (i.e., the underlying model). For example, assuming we are computing $p(\upsilon|\boldsymbol{d}\cdot\iota) = \varpi(\upsilon)\mathcal{L}(\upsilon)/\mathcal{L}(\iota)$, we can solve for the $\mathcal{L}(\iota)$ term via:

$$\begin{aligned}\mathcal{L}(\iota) &= p(\boldsymbol{d}|\iota)\\ &= \int d\upsilon\, p(\upsilon\cdot\boldsymbol{d}|\iota)\\ &= \int d\upsilon\, p(\upsilon|\iota)p(\boldsymbol{d}|\upsilon\cdot\iota)\\ &= \int d\upsilon\, \varpi(\upsilon)\mathcal{L}(\upsilon)\end{aligned}$$

where $\mathcal{L}(\iota)$, referred to as the global or **model likelihood**, is the sum over probabilities in the unnormalized posterior distribution. $\mathcal{L}(\iota)$ therefore acts as a normalization constant for the posterior. In measurement problems it is unnecessary to normalize the posterior distribution, because division by a constant cannot change the shape of the posterior and therefore will not change inferences based on the shape of the posterior (mean, median, or maximum probability location). We will ignore $\mathcal{L}(\iota)$ in measurement problems, although this term is critical for the solution of signal detection and other model comparison problems[3] (Chapter 6).

5.2.2 The Algorithm

A. *Define the posterior distribution that corresponds to the desired measurement.*
B. *Define observation and noise models and their interrelationships.*
C. *Assign priors over unknown parameter values.*
D. *Compute the posterior distribution (normalizing if necessary), single-number measurements, and associated confidence intervals.*

The first step is to define the posterior for the desired measurement. This will allow us to determine what prior and likelihood functions will need to be assigned. This step will also include construction of a graphical model of the interrelationships of the known and unknown parameters of the model, such that it is clear how observed and unobserved parameters will interact to produce the hypothetical signal. The second step requires us to define observation and noise models appropriate to the current problem. This step involves filling out the graphical model, by assigning the appropriate priors and likelihoods, and the observation and model equations that interconnect them. Inference requires that we define priors over any unknown parameters, and this is the purpose of the third step. Priors will, in many cases, be informed by the likelihood equations

[3] Since it represents the likelihood of the model, M, underlying a particular choice of observation and noise function, that is normally hidden in the background information term of our equations [that is, $\mathcal{L}(\iota) = \mathcal{L}(M\cdot\iota)$].

defined in the previous step (e.g., Jeffreys priors). In the final step we compute the posterior distribution over the unknown parameters whose values we wish to measure. In the simplest applications this step is trivial because the combined observation and noise model contain only a single unknown parameter, as exemplified when estimating the binomial rate:

$$p(\theta|S \cdot N \cdot \imath) \propto \varpi(\theta)\mathcal{L}(\theta) \propto \sqrt{\theta(1-\theta)}[\theta^s(1-\theta)^{N-s}]$$

A common example that is only slightly more complicated involves the Gaussian likelihood:

$$p(\mu|\boldsymbol{d} \cdot \sigma \cdot \imath) \propto \varpi(\mu)\mathcal{L}(\mu) = \varpi(\mu) \int d\sigma \, \varpi(\sigma)\mathcal{L}(\mu,\sigma),$$

where there is a single nuisance parameter, the dispersion. This posterior, in other words, contains one to-be-measured parameter (location, μ) embedded in a noise model with an unknown noise parameter (σ). In more complicated cases, a number of unknown variables will need to be marginalized out of the expression to obtain the desired posterior:

$$p(\mu|\boldsymbol{d} \cdot \imath) = \int d\boldsymbol{\Theta} p(\mu \cdot \boldsymbol{\Theta}|\boldsymbol{d} \cdot \imath),$$

where $\boldsymbol{\Theta} = (\boldsymbol{\vartheta}, \boldsymbol{\sigma})$ represents both the set of observation-model parameters, $\boldsymbol{\vartheta} = (\vartheta_1, \vartheta_2, \ldots, \vartheta_n)$, and noise-model parameters, $\boldsymbol{\sigma} = (\sigma_1, \sigma_2, \ldots, \sigma_m)$, that are usually considered nuisance variables and will be marginalized out of the probability equations to yield the final measurement over μ. This can become arbitrarily complicated depending on the details of the observation and noise models. Our example problems will begin with 'transparent' measurements that make use of the simplest possible observation function (so simple that it's existence might normally go unnoticed) and end with several cases of relatively complex observation functions that highlight the power and generality of the Bayesian approach.

A. Define the Posterior Distribution That Corresponds to the Desired Measurement

Progression through the measurement algorithm may seem backward, in that we start with a definition of the desired posterior distribution, and work our way toward defining the prior distribution before actually computing the measurement. However, this starting point is important because it is often easier to define the marginalizations required to solve the problem if we begin with the desired endpoint of the calculation. To define the posterior distribution for a given measurement, we will need to marginalize over nuisance parameters via the sum rule. Marginalization is both the most useful and most difficult aspect of a Bayesian data analysis. In the examples we will encounter in the remainder we will content ourselves with numerically marginalizing over nuisance parameters via the simplest method of numerical integration - a practice that is made possible by the advent of fast computers and the fact that we will restrict ourselves to problems with at most only a handful of nuisance parameters. Once the number of nuisance parameters increases beyond this level (the exact number will depend on the speed of your computer, and any tricks for speeding computer calculations that you may have up your sleeve) this practice becomes untenable, and we must resort to approximate solutions using Markov chain Monte Carlo methods.

The result of this step of the algorithm will be a set of equations. If there are M unknown parameter values we wish to estimate and a set of nuisance variables $\mathbf{\Theta}$, the solution will in general involve marginalizations of the form:

$$
\begin{aligned}
p(\mu_1|d\cdot\imath) &= \int d\mu_2\ldots d\mu_M d\mathbf{\Theta} p(\mu_1\cdot[\mu_2\cdot\ldots\cdot\mu_M]\cdot\mathbf{\Theta}|d\cdot\imath)\\
p(\mu_2|d\cdot\imath) &= \int d\mu_1 d\mu_3\ldots d\mu_M d\mathbf{\Theta} p(\mu_1\cdot[\mu_2\cdot\ldots\cdot\mu_M]\cdot\mathbf{\Theta}|d\cdot\imath)\\
&\vdots \\
p(\mu_M|d\cdot\imath) &= \int d\mu_2\ldots d\mu_{M-1} d\mathbf{\Theta} p(\mu_M\cdot[\mu_1\cdot\ldots\cdot\mu_{M-1}]\cdot\mathbf{\Theta}|d\cdot\imath),
\end{aligned}
\tag{5.4}
$$

where the joint posterior over all unknown variables is $p(\boldsymbol{\mu}\cdot\mathbf{\Theta}|d\cdot\imath)$.

Note that in order to define these marginalizations, we must have some idea of the variables that are used in the noise and observation models. If this is not the case, we will simply write out the desired posteriors [e.g., $p(\mu_1|d\cdot\imath),\ldots,p(\mu_M|d\cdot\imath)$] here, and wait until completion of the next step to fill in the details of any needed marginalizations.

B. Define Observation Models, Noise Models, and Their Interrelationships

The second step involves defining the details of the observation and noise models of the data. In the temperature example, we can see that we deconstruct the desired posterior, for example, $p(°F|d\cdot\imath)$, into the prior $\varpi(F)$ and likelihood $\mathcal{L}(F)$. The likelihood function is defined in this step, which requires us to consider the appropriate noise model, the observation model, and the interrelationships among these as encoded in the graphical model of the measurement.

It is important to recognize that there is some fluidity between the first and second steps; in particular, we may sometimes need the graphical model in the first step while we define the posterior, and in some cases it is more natural to examine the graphical model in this step. Indeed, one may need to cycle through the first and second steps for an iteration or two (or more) before a satisfactory definition of posterior and likelihood functions is achieved. For example, we may not initially be aware of all the nuisance variables that will affect our measurement. In such a case the equation we write at the close of (**A**) [e.g., $p(\mu|d\cdot\imath) = \int d\mathbf{\Theta}\rho(\mu_1\cdot\mathbf{\Theta}|d\cdot\imath)$] will use $\mathbf{\Theta}$ as a placeholder to be fleshed out here as we construct the graphical, observation, and noise models.

In this step we ask two questions. First, we ask 'what is the underlying signal that is the basis for our observations?', and then: 'what varieties of noise contaminate our observations?'. Here, we will combine the skills developed in previous chapters, guided by a graphical model of the interrelationships among the variables, to define the specific measurement problem at hand. One of the more common examples is given by the transparent measurement with constant noise. The graphical model describing this problem is given in Figure 5.2a. The flow of information within the graphical model describes a noise-added unobservable variable (μ) yielding the observed data, $d = s + \varepsilon$. In this example the observation, error and noise models are:

$$
\begin{aligned}
s &= m(\mu) = \mu,\\
\varepsilon &= d - \mu,\\
\mathcal{L}(\mu) &= p(\mathbf{d}|\mu\cdot\sigma\cdot\imath) = (\sigma\sqrt{2\pi})^{-N} e^{-\frac{\sum(\mathbf{d}-s)^2}{2\sigma^2}} \propto \sigma^{-N} e^{-\frac{\sum(\mathbf{d}-\mu)^2}{2\sigma^2}}
\end{aligned}
$$

Programming Aside: Computing Confidence Intervals

To understand the basic character of the shortest 95 percent confidence range (interval), we will develop a 'brute-force' method. This method will essentially step through each point in the posterior distribution, and from there compute the length along the abscissa needed to encompass 95 percent of the probability mass. The shortest of these is our approximation of the shortest 95 percent confidence interval. The approximation is limited by increment size.

```
mu=10; sd=12;
mus=linspace(-60,60,1001)';
post=npdf(mus,mu,sd);
Ninterp=201;

%%% step through the posterior
cs=cumtrapz(mus,post);
post=post./cs(end);
itest=0; inow=0; iend=zeros(size(cs)); c0=zeros(size(cs));
%initialize index
while inow<length(mus), cnow=c0;
    cnow(inow+1:end)=cumtrapz(mus(inow+1:end),post(inow+1:end));
    itest=find(cnow>=.95,1,'first')-1;
    if and(itest<length(mus),~isempty(itest)),
        inow=inow+1;
        iend(inow)=itest;
    else break; end, end
startend=[[1:inow]' iend(1:inow)];
ranges=diff(startend,1,2);

imins=find(ranges==min(ranges)); Ushaped=0;
for nmin=1:length(imins),
    iminmax=startend(imins(nmin),1); iminmax(1,2)=iminmax(1)+1;

    vmins=linspace(mus(iminmax(1)),mus(iminmax(2)),Ninterp+2); vmins=vmins(2:end-1)';
    vmaxs=nan(Ninterp,1);
    pmins=interp1(mus,post,vmins);
    for inow=1:Ninterp,
        ctrap=cumtrapz([vmins(inow); mus(imins(2):end)],...
              [pmins(inow); post(imins(2):end)]);
        vmaxs(inow,1)=interp1(ctrap,[vmins(inow); mus(imins(2):end)],0.95); end

    lens=vmaxs-vmins;
    indmin=find(lens==min(lens));
    if ~or(indmin==1,indmin==length(lens)),
        Ushaped=1; break; end, end

if Ushaped, ['success'], else ['error: no min found'], end
CIapprox=[vmins(indmin) vmaxs(indmin)];
CI=icdf('normal',[.025 .975],mu,sd);
figure(1); clf;
subplot(2,1,1); plot(vmins,lens,'ko:','MarkerSize',8);
subplot(2,1,2); hold on; plot(mus,post/max(post),'k.');
for n=1:2, plot(CI(n)*[1 1],[0 1],'b:');
    plot(CIapprox(n)*[1 1],[0 1],'k--'); end
```

respectively. The signal (s) term in the likelihood may encode a complex set of interconnected variables as our observation models (the function m) become more elaborate. If, for example, the signal were that of a straight-line model, $s = \alpha x + \beta$ (Fig. 5.4a), the likelihood term becomes:

$$\mathcal{L}(\alpha, \beta) = p(\boldsymbol{d}|\alpha \cdot \beta \cdot x \cdot \imath) = (\sigma\sqrt{2\pi})^{-N} e^{-\frac{\sum(\boldsymbol{d}-s)^2}{2\sigma^2}} \propto \sigma^{-N} e^{-\frac{\sum[\boldsymbol{d}-(\alpha x+\beta)]^2}{2\sigma^2}}$$

C. Assign Priors over Unknown Parameter Values

This step requires us to think about our state of information regarding any unknown parameters of the model at the time of data collection. If we have already collected data relevant to the measurement, then the posterior distribution over the desired parameter (obtained from those earlier experiments) may constitute our prior information. If no earlier experimental results are available, or if we wish to make the current measurement as if no prior data had been analyzed, we may start by defining the relevant Jeffreys priors over unknown parameters. This step should be done thoughtfully, however. It is easy to simply assign a uniform prior over any unknown variables and drop those uniform priors from the resulting posterior without considering whether a uniform prior is truly appropriate in a given situation.

D. Compute the Desired Measurement

In the final step of the algorithm we make the computations described in the previous step, and identify a single number best-guess estimate, along with a confidence range associated with that guess. The two most common best-guess estimates correspond to the peak of the posterior and the mean of the posterior, whereas the confidence interval we will use in reporting our measurements is the shortest range encompassing 95% of the posterior probability mass. Note that this is the first and only step of the algorithm where experimental data are used.

Exercises

1) Generate sample datasets for Figures 5.2a and 5.2b with the parameters:
   a. $\mu = 5, \sigma = 1$
   b. $\mu = 1, \sigma = 1$
   c. $\mu = 1, \sigma = 5$
2) Plot the data generated above in (1).
3) Construct an equivalent version of Figure 5.3b with a single addition node. What are the advantages and disadvantages of drawing the model in these ways?
4) Using (5.4) as a guide, write the marginalizations necessary to describe the posterior for the Gaussian likelihood with unknown location and scale parameters.
5) Change the number of elements in the μ variable of the confidence interval PA to 61. How does this affect the estimate? Why?
6) Change the range of the μ variable of the PA on computing confidence intervals to [-45,45]. Does this affect the estimate? Why?

5.3 Single-Source Measurements

We begin our discussion of measurement with single-source measurements, which we differentiate from multiple-source measurements. This difference between single-and multi-source measurement is straightforward: multisource measurements require us to combine information across data sources. When the model parameters of all sources are identical, we may combine the posteriors produced by each individual source without special arrangement. Below we will consider a range of single-source measurements, from basic transparent measurements of temperature to measurements of detection thresholds from binary response data. Once we have mastered single-source measurement, we will learn how to combine posteriors across sources in the most common multisource measurement scenarios.

5.3.1 Transparent Measurement

We will examine both transparent measurement scenarios described in Figure 5.2. These examples will form an important comparison to the more complex models examined in Section 5.3.2, and also against the same models when used for multiple-source measurement in Section 5.4.

Example: Body Temperature Measurement with Constant Noise
Working in a mosquito-borne pathogens lab to investigate ways to block mosquito sensory detection of humans and curtail the spread of mosquito-borne viruses, you notice while working that you have an itch on your hand. Having been potentially exposed to the Dengue fever virus, which produces a spike in temperature after three to five days, you monitor your temperature three days later. To be certain of the outcome of the measurement, you take a set of N thermometer readings, assuming a Gaussian sampling distribution with unknown location and scale parameters.

A. Define the Posterior Distribution That Corresponds to the Desired Measurement
Using (5.4) as a guide, there are two unknown variables and therefore two marginal posteriors of potential interest. The posterior distribution corresponding to the desired temperature measurement is

$$\begin{aligned} p(\mu|\boldsymbol{d}\cdot\iota) &= \int d\sigma\, p(\mu\cdot\sigma\,|\,\boldsymbol{d}\cdot\iota) \\ &\propto \varpi(\mu)\int d\sigma\varpi(\sigma)\mathcal{L}(\mu,\sigma). \end{aligned}$$

which marginalizes over the σ axis of the 2D posterior distribution, $p(\mu\cdot\sigma\,|\,\boldsymbol{d}\cdot\iota)$, and the posterior over the dispersion parameter,

$$\begin{aligned} p(\sigma|\boldsymbol{d}\cdot\iota) &= \int d\sigma\, p(\mu\cdot\sigma\,|\,\boldsymbol{d}\cdot\iota) \\ &\propto \varpi(\sigma)\int d\mu\varpi(\mu)\mathcal{L}(\mu,\sigma) \end{aligned}$$

B. Define Observation and Noise Models and Their Interrelationships

The graphical model representing these temperature readings is shown in Figure 5.2a. The additive noise term is assigned a Gaussian sampling distribution. This assignment is technically inaccurate since a Gaussian distribution can take any value on the real line, but a temperature reading cannot occur at levels below absolute zero. Nevertheless, when the standard deviation of the noise (σ) is much smaller than the distance between observed temperature readings and absolute zero, this becomes irrelevant. Here, for example, we are measuring a human body temperature. If it were low <98.6, then we won't worry about having a fever. If it were too high >106 you would likely be unconscious, and the fever would be obvious without looking at the thermometer. The flow of information within the graphical model suggests that there is a noise-added unobservable variable ('true temperature,' μ) that yields our thermometer readings, the observations $o = \mu + \varepsilon$. If the noise power (σ^2) is unknown, then the observation and noise models are

$$s = m(\mu) = \mu$$

$$\mathcal{L}(\mu, \sigma) = p(\mathbf{d}|\mu \cdot \sigma \cdot \iota) = (\sigma\sqrt{2\pi})^{-N} e^{-\frac{\sum(\mathbf{d}-s)^2}{2\sigma^2}} \propto \sigma^{-N} e^{-\frac{\sum(\mathbf{d}-\mu)^2}{2\sigma^2}}$$

respectively. Note that all terms containing unknown parameters must be kept in the likelihood function; since the σ is unknown in this example, it cannot be dropped from the likelihood as it was in some previous examples.

C. Assign Priors over Unknown Parameter Values

We will assume again that the true temperature is in the range that supports human life:

$$\varpi(\mu) = \begin{cases} 0 & 90 \geq \mu \leq 110 \\ 20^{-1} & 90 < \mu < 110 \end{cases}$$

We will further assume that the sampling distribution of temperature observations is relatively narrow compared to the range of possible temperature values. For example, if the standard deviation of the sampling distribution of observations were larger than 20° F we would need to replace our equipment and start over, so we will define the prior over σ values as

$$\varpi(\sigma) \propto \begin{cases} 0 & 20 > \sigma \\ \sigma^{-1} & 0 < \sigma \leq 20 \end{cases}.$$

The only caveat here is that, in addition to μ, we might also measure σ. Our σ measurement will be a check on the prior, such that if the measured σ value is close to 20, we may also need to reexamine the data collection equipment and/or procedure that led to such noisy observations.

Finally we define the joint prior over the two unknown parameters:

$$\varpi(\mu, \sigma) = \varpi(\mu)\varpi(\sigma),$$

which defines independence of the location and dispersion probabilities.

Programming Aside: Body Temperature Measurement (Fig. 5.2a)

This is the most common problem in all of measurement, with a constant signal and added noise. We start with the data, which involves one or more observations of thermometer mercury level.

```
d=[98.4 98.8 98.5 99.4 99.9];

mus=linspace(90,110,3001)';
sigmas=linspace(0,20,501); sigmas=sigmas(2:end);
N=length(d);

%%% 2d mu-sigma distribution
Lms=-(N/2*((mean(d.^2)-mean(d)^2)*(sigmas.^-2)+...
     (mus-mean(d)).^2*(sigmas.^-2))+(N+1)*ones(size(mus))*log(sigmas));
figure; meshc(sigmas,mus,exp(Lms)); colormap bone

%%% marginal alpha distribution
Lm=logsum(Lms,2,diff(sigmas(1:2))); Lm=Lm-max(Lm);
ciM=CIp(mus,Lm);

%%% marginal sigma distribution
Ls=logsum(Lms,1,diff(mus(1:2))); Ls=Ls-max(Ls);
ciS=CIp(sigmas(:),Ls);

figure
%%% plot marginal alpha distribution
subplot(2,1,1); hold on
plot(mus,exp(Lm),'k--','LineWidth',1.75);
dciM=diff(ciM(1:2)); axis([ciM(1)-.2*dciM ciM(2)+.2*dciM 0 1])
for n=1:2, plot(ciM(n)*[1 1],[0 1],'-','Color',.65*[1 1 1],'LineWidth',.7); end

%%% plot marginal sigma distribution
subplot(2,1,2); hold on
plot(sigmas,exp(Ls),'k--','LineWidth',1.75); dciS=diff(ciS(1:2));
axis([ciS(1)-.2*dciS ciS(2)+.2*dciS 0 1])
for n=1:2, plot(ciS(n)*[1 1],[0 1],'-','Color',.65*[1 1 1],'LineWidth',.7); end
```

D. Compute the Desired Measurement

To compute the desired measurements, we first compose the equations for the full marginalized posterior over both μ and σ. The measurement over μ is:

$$\begin{aligned} p(\mu|\boldsymbol{d}\cdot\iota) &\propto \int d(\sigma)\varpi(\sigma)\mathcal{L}(\mu,\sigma) \\ &\propto \int d\sigma(\sigma)^{-(N+1)}e^{-\frac{1}{2}\frac{\sum_{i=1}^{N}(d_i-\mu)^2}{\sigma^2}} \\ &= \int d\sigma(\sigma)^{-(N+1)}e^{-\frac{N}{2}\frac{\overline{d^2}-\bar{d}^2}{\sigma^2}}e^{-\frac{N}{2}\frac{(\mu-\bar{d})^2}{\sigma^2}}\{90\le\mu\le 110, 0<\sigma\le 20 \end{aligned}$$

and the posterior over σ is:

$$
\begin{aligned}
p(\sigma|\boldsymbol{d}\cdot\iota) &\propto \varpi(\sigma)\int d\mu\varpi(\mu)\mathcal{L}(\mu,\sigma) \\
&\propto (\sigma)^{-(N+1)}\int d\mu e^{-\frac{1}{2}\frac{\sum_{i=1}^{N}(d_i-\mu)^2}{\sigma^2}} \\
&= \sigma^{-(N+1)}e^{-\frac{N}{2}\frac{\overline{d^2}-\bar{d}^2}{\sigma^2}}\int d\mu e^{-\frac{N}{2}\frac{(\mu-\bar{d})^2}{\sigma^2}}\{90<\mu<110, 0<\sigma\leq 20
\end{aligned}
$$

Once computed, the marginal posterior over μ can be used to obtain our measurement of the theoretical parameter μ and a confidence interval around that estimate. Often, for the Gaussian location parameter, the best estimate is equated with the expected value, $<\mu>$, and the confidence interval is obtained by finding the shortest range of μ values that are covered 95 percent of the probability mass of the marginalized posterior.

It should be stressed here that observation and measurement are not the same, even in this simplest case of a constant signal in noise (i.e., where the observation model is $s = m(\mu) = \mu$). This is perhaps a counterintuitive point given that in the above example, as with many of the most common examples of measurement (thermometers, rulers, etc.), the value of the datum is numerically identical to the resulting best-guess measurement and therefore have the same dimensions (observation and measurement are given in the same units, such as °C). However, a measurement is the result of applying observation and error models to data. In the case of a length measurement from a single ruler observation or single temperature reading, (1.5) typically yields a posterior probability distribution over possible true values of the underlying parameter that has its peak at the value of the observation, thus giving the impression that the *processes* of observation and of measurement are also identical. This will become increasingly clear as the examples become more complex and the data and measurement dimensions differ.

Exercises

1) Generate sample datasets for Figure 5.2a with the parameters:
   a. $\mu = 5, \sigma = 1$
   b. $\mu = 1, \sigma = 1$
   c. $\mu = 1, \sigma = 5$
2) Plot the data generated above in (1).
3) Perform measurements of μ and σ with these new datasets, and plot the resulting posteriors.
4) Find the means, medians and peaks of these distributions.
5) Why is it useful, if you want to be certain of your measurement, to take multiple temperature readings? Compute the posterior over the Gaussian μ parameter with 1 through 10 simulated data with true parameter values $\mu = 100, \sigma = 5$.

Example: Body Temperature Measurement with Multiplicative Noise

The Dengue virus you may have contracted in the previous example does not produce an immediate fever: it takes 3-5 days. In this circumstance, you would likely want to obtain more than one measurement. You might start by measuring your temperature immediately, as a baseline value. Then a new measurement on days 3 and 5 to look for a spike. To generate a single measurement we obtain N readings, and for m measurements we obtain $N_1, \ldots, N_m$ readings.

Here we will also add an additional complication to our measurement model. The previous measurement used an additive noise model, but often it is true that devices will display multiplicative noise (Fig. 5.2b) where the noise is scaled to the value of μ.

A. Define the Posterior Distribution That Corresponds to the Desired Measurement
For this problem we will compute posteriors over more than one underlying temperature, using the same subject, apparatus and experimental procedure. The 3D posterior over these temperature measurements is:

$$\begin{aligned} p(\mu_1 \cdot \mu_2 \cdot \mu_3 | \boldsymbol{d} \cdot \imath) &= \int d\sigma p(\mu_1 \cdot \mu_2 \cdot \mu_3 \cdot \sigma | \boldsymbol{d} \cdot \imath) \\ &\propto \int d\sigma \varpi(\sigma) \mathcal{L}(\mu_1, \mu_2, \mu_3, \sigma) \end{aligned}$$

where there is a new copy of the μ-prior and likelihood for each temperature, but a single copy of the σ-prior for the entire problem because the same measurement equipment, procedure and subject are used. Although the μ-prior is a constant and can be dropped from the calculation, the σ-prior is not constant and must be retained.

Also, as a check on our assignment of the σ range, we would also like to compute the posterior:

$$\begin{aligned} p(\sigma | \boldsymbol{d} \cdot \imath) &= \int d\mu_1 d\mu_2 d\mu_2 p(\mu_1 \cdot \mu_2 \cdot \mu_3 \cdot \sigma | \boldsymbol{d} \cdot \imath) \\ &\propto \varpi(\sigma) \int d\mu_1 d\mu_2 d\mu_2 \varpi(\mu_1 \cdot \mu_2 \cdot \mu_3) \mathcal{L}(\mu_1, \mu_2, \mu_3, \sigma) \end{aligned}$$

which marginalizes over the μ axes of the 4D posterior distribution. This check will simply consist of verifying that the peak of the posterior describing the σ-parameter is within the prescribed range. If the peak of the posterior over the σ parameter were outside the prior bounds we would be wise to reevaluate our prior information and the logic of the argument that led to the assigned prior, as well as the resulting computations, for possible errors. At the least we would need to understand why the peak is outside the prior range before proceeding.

B. Define Observation and Noise Models and Their Interrelationships
The graphical model representing these temperature readings is shown in Figure 5.2b. The noise term is assigned a Gaussian sampling distribution. Unlike in the previous example, however, noise is scaled by the value of μ before being added to the theoretical signal. Because of the linearity of the variance function, the variance of the scaled noise is:

$$(\sigma')^2 = E(\epsilon'^2) = E([\mu\epsilon^2]) = \mu^2 E(\epsilon^2) = (\mu\sigma)^2$$

The flow of information within the graphical model suggests that there is a noisy constant signal $s = \mu$ that determines our observations, $o = \mu + \epsilon$. If the noise power is unknown, then for a single temperature the noise model is:

$$\mathcal{L}(\mu, \sigma) = p(\boldsymbol{d} | \mu \cdot \sigma \cdot \imath) = (\sigma' \sqrt{2\pi})^{-N} e^{-\frac{1}{2} \frac{\sum(\boldsymbol{d}-\mu)^2}{(\sigma')^2}} \propto (\mu\sigma)^{-N} e^{-\frac{1}{2} \frac{\sum(\boldsymbol{d}-\mu)^2}{(\mu\sigma)^2}}$$

Note that, as always, terms that do not contain one of the unknown parameters can be dropped from the likelihood. The likelihood for m different temperatures, an (m+1)-dimensional likelihood, maintains a shared σ parameter and is:

$$\mathcal{L}(\mu_1,\ldots,\mu_m,\sigma) \propto (\mu_1\sigma)^{-N_1} e^{-\frac{1}{2}\frac{\sum(\mathbf{d}_1-\mu_1)^2}{(\mu_1\sigma)^2}} \ldots (\mu_m\sigma)^{-N_m} e^{-\frac{1}{2}\frac{\sum(\mathbf{d}_m-\mu_m)^2}{(\mu_m\sigma)^2}}$$

C. Assign Priors over Unknown Parameter Values

We will assume again that the true temperature is in the range for a live human, between 90° and 110° F:

$$\varpi(\mu_i) = \begin{cases} 0 & 90 \geq \mu_i > 110 \\ 20^{-1} & 90 < \mu_i \leq 110 \end{cases},$$

We will again truncate the range of possible variances, but here the maximum value has to be consistent with the multiplicative factor, μ. If μ were at its maximum value, then a σ of 0.035 would correspond to data with a standard deviation just above 3.5°F, which is substantially larger than our previous estimate. We will define the prior over σ values as:

$$\varpi(\sigma) \propto \begin{cases} 0 & 0.0035 < \sigma \leq 0 \\ \sigma^{-1} & 0 < \sigma \leq 0.035 \end{cases}.$$

As noted above we will, in addition to μ, also measure σ as a check on the prior, such that if the measured σ value is very close to 0.035 we will need to reexamine the data collection equipment and/or procedure.

Finally we define the joint prior over the two unknown parameters:

$$\varpi(\mu_1,\mu_2,\mu_3,\sigma) = \varpi(\mu_1)\varpi(\mu_2)\varpi(\mu_3)\varpi(\sigma),$$

which defines independence of μ and σ probabilities.

D. Compute the Desired Measurement

The $(m+1)$-dimensional posterior incorporates priors over the unknown temperatures and the shared dispersion:

$$\begin{aligned} p(\mu_1\cdot\ldots\cdot\mu_m\cdot\sigma|\mathbf{d}\cdot\imath) &\propto \varpi(\mu_1\cdot\ldots\cdot\mu_m\cdot\sigma)\mathcal{L}(\mu_1,\ldots\cdot\mu_m,\sigma) \\ &= \varpi(\mu_1\cdot\ldots\cdot\mu_m\cdot\sigma)\mathcal{L}(\mu_1,\sigma)\ldots\mathcal{L}(\mu_m,\sigma), \end{aligned}$$

and for any single measurement of the jth temperature we marginalize over the remaining temperatures and unknown dispersion:

$$p(\mu_j|d\cdot\imath) = \int d\sigma\, d\mu_1\ldots d\mu_{j-1}\mu_{j+1}\ldots d\mu_m p(\mu_1\cdot\ldots\cdot\mu_j\cdot\ldots\cdot\mu_m\cdot\sigma|\mathbf{d}\cdot\imath),$$

which for the first of three sets of temperature readings is:

$$\begin{aligned} p(\mu_1|\mathbf{d}\cdot\imath) &= \int d\sigma\, d\mu_3 d\mu_2 p(\mu_1\cdot\mu_2\cdot\mu_3\cdot\sigma|\mathbf{d}\cdot\imath) \\ &\propto \int d\sigma\, d\mu_3 d\mu_2 \varpi(\mu_1\cdot\mu_2\cdot\mu_3\cdot\sigma)\mathcal{L}(\mu_1,\sigma)\mathcal{L}(\mu_2,\sigma)\mathcal{L}(\mu_3,\sigma) \\ &\propto \mu_1^{-N1}\int d\sigma\, d\mu_3 d\mu_2 \sigma^{-(N_1+N_2+N_3+1)} e^{-\frac{1}{2}\frac{\sum(\mathbf{d}_1-\mu_1)^2}{(\mu_1\sigma)^2}} \mu_2^{-N_2} e^{-\frac{1}{2}\frac{\sum(\mathbf{d}_2-\mu_2)^2}{(\mu_2\sigma)^2}} \mu_3^{-N_3} e^{-\frac{1}{2}\frac{\sum(\mathbf{d}_3-\mu_3)^2}{(\mu_3\sigma)^2}} \end{aligned}$$

Programming Aside: Temperature Measurement with Multiplicative Noise (Fig. 5.2b)

First we measure a single temperature that lumps the three datasets, and then we simultaneously measure three temperatures under the multiplicative noise assumption. The multiplicative noise parameter (σ)is measured more reliably with multiple datasets at multiple separate temperatures, because it remains constant across temperatures.

Single-Location Measurement

In the case of making observations at a single location (single true temperature), the two unknowns in the model require us to simultaneously compute the 2D location-scale posterior, and then marginalize over each in turn to obtain the relevant 1D posteriors.

```
d1=[98.4 97.5 98.8 98.6 99.2];
d2=[100.4 100.8 100.5 101.4 101.9];
d3=[105.5 104.5 104.2 104.9 105.8];
d=[d1 d2 d3];

Nmu=151; Nsigma=51;
mus=linspace(90,110,Nmu)';
sigmas=linspace(0,5,Nsigma+1); sigmas=sigmas(2:end);
N=[length(d1) length(d2) length(d3)];
Nd=sum(N);

%%% plot marginal sigma distribution
Lms=-(Nd/2*((mean(d.^2)-mean(d)^2)*((mus*sigmas).^-2)+...
    (mus*ones(size(sigmas))-mean(d)).^2.*((mus*sigmas).^-2))+(Nd+1)*log((mus*sigmas)));
Lm=logsum(Lms,2,diff(sigmas(1:2))); Lm=Lm-max(Lm);
figure(1); subplot(2,1,1); cla; hold on
plot(mus,exp(Lm),'k:','LineWidth',2);
```

Mulitlocation Measurement

Contrast the above with a separate measurement for each of the three datasets.

```
Nmu=151; Nsigma=101;
mus=linspace(96,108,Nmu)';
sigmas=linspace(0,2,Nsigma+1)/100; sigmas=sigmas(2:end);

%%% 4d mu1-mu2-sigma distribution
Lm123s=zeros(Nmu,Nmu,Nmu,Nsigma);
for m=1:Nmu, if m==round(Nmu/3), disp('1/3'); elseif m==round(Nmu/2), disp('1/2');
elseif m==round(2*Nmu/3),disp('2/3'); end
for s=1:Nsigma,
    Lm123s(m,:,:,s)=...
        -(N(1)/2*((mean(d1.^2)-mean(d1)^2)*((mus(m)*sigmas(s))^-2)+...
        (mus(m)-mean(d1)).^2./(mus(m)*sigmas(s)).^2)+(N(1)+1)...
        *log((mus(m)*sigmas(s))))-(N(2)/2*((mean(d2.^2)...
        -mean(d2)^2)*((mus*ones(size(mus'))*sigmas(s)).^-2)...
        +(mus*ones(size(mus'))-mean(d2)).^2./(mus*ones(size(mus'))*sigmas(s)).^2)...
        +(N(1)+1)*log((mus*ones(size(mus'))*sigmas(s))))...
        -(N(3)/2*((mean(d3.^2)-mean(d3)^2)*(ones(size(mus))*mus'*...
        sigmas(s)).^-2)+(ones(size(mus))*mus'-mean(d3)).^2./...
        (ones(size(mus))*mus'*sigmas(s)).^2)...
        +(N(2)+1)*log((ones(size(mus))*mus'*sigmas(s)))); end, end
Lm123=logsum(Lm123s,4,diff(sigmas(1:2)));
```

```
%%% marginal mu1 distribution
Lm1=logsum(Lm123,2:3,diff(mus(1:2))*[1 1]); Lm1=Lm1-max(Lm1);
subplot(2,1,1); hold on
ciM=CIp(mus,Lm1);
plot(mus,exp(Lm1),'k--','LineWidth',1.75); axis([97 108 0 1])
for n=1:2, plot(ciM(n)*[1 1],[0 1],'-','Color',.65*[1 1 1],'LineWidth',.7); end

%%% marginal mu2 distribution
Lm2=logsum(Lm123,[1 3],diff(mus(1:2))*[1 1]); Lm2=Lm2-max(Lm2);
subplot(2,1,1); hold on
ciM=CIp(mus,Lm2);
plot(mus,exp(Lm2),'k--','LineWidth',1.75); axis([97 108 0 1])
for n=1:2, plot(ciM(n)*[1 1],[0 1],'-','Color',.65*[1 1 1],'LineWidth',.7); end

%%% marginal mu3 distribution
Lm3=logsum(Lm123,[1:2],diff(mus(1:2))*[1 1]); Lm3=Lm3-max(Lm3);
subplot(2,1,1); hold on
ciM=CIp(mus,Lm3);
plot(mus,exp(Lm3),'k--','LineWidth',1.75); axis([97 108 0 1])
for n=1:2, plot(ciM(n)*[1 1],[0 1],'-','Color',.65*[1 1 1],'LineWidth',.7); end

%%% marginal sig distribution
Ls=logsum(Lm123s,[1:3],diff(mus(1:2))*[1 1 1]); Ls=Ls-max(Ls);
subplot(2,1,2); cla; hold on
ciS=CIp(sigmas,Ls);
plot(sigmas,exp(Ls),'k--','LineWidth',1.75); axis([0 0.02 0 1])
for n=1:2, plot(ciS(n)*[1 1],[0 1],'-','Color',.65*[1 1 1],'LineWidth',.7); end
```

whereas if we are interested in measuring the shared dispersion parameter we compute:

$$
\begin{aligned}
p(\sigma|\boldsymbol{d}\cdot\iota) &= \int d\mu_1\dots d\mu_m p(\mu_1\cdot\ldots\cdot\mu_j\cdot\ldots\cdot\mu_m\cdot\sigma|\boldsymbol{d}\cdot\iota)\\
&= \sigma^{-(N_1+N_2+N_3+1)}\int d\sigma\, d\mu_3 d\mu_2 \mu_1^{-N1} e^{-\frac{1}{2}\frac{\sum(\mathbf{d}_1-\mu_1)^2}{(\mu_1\sigma)^2}} \mu_2^{-N_2} e^{-\frac{1}{2}\frac{\sum(\mathbf{d}_2-\mu_2)^2}{(\mu_2\sigma)^2}} \mu_3^{-N_3} e^{-\frac{1}{2}\frac{\sum(\mathbf{d}_3-\mu_3)^2}{(\mu_3\sigma)^2}}
\end{aligned}
$$

The three sets of thermometer readings yield the marginal distributions over μ and σ shown in Figure 5.2b. We have performed the temperature measurement twice, first by lumping all data together (dotted curves) and a second time separating each dataset as a potentially separate temperature (dashed curves).

The marginal posterior over σ is different here than in the last example because the three μ-distributions share a common σ parameter, and that parameter acts as a scale factor for the multiplicative noise model. The posterior over σ suggests that noise in these temperature measurements increases by a factor of about 0.006 per degree.

Exercises

1) Show that the posterior probability function for a Gaussian location parameter (μ; assuming known dispersion) is essentially identical to the Gaussian likelihood function when a Jeffreys prior with wide bounds is used, by assuming a wider and wider bound (for any simulated dataset).

2) What does the dotted posterior mean, in terms of the concept of an underlying true temperature parameter? To what extent does the same critique apply to the dashed measurements? Why/why not?
3) The form of the multiplicative noise model predicts zero noise at 0°F. Comment on whether this is realistic given that we are using a Fahrenheit temperature scale. List two ways this multiplicative noise model could be updated, and how the updates change the nature of the model.
4) If the standard deviation of the Gaussian likelihood function from Ex1 were unknown, it would be necessary to extend the location measurement question to include a range of possible standard deviation values, and marginalize over them. Describe any differences in the posterior for μ in these two cases (known and unknown σ)
5) Compare the posterior over dispersion computed from each of the three datasets separately to the marginal posterior shown in Figure 5.2b. What is the origin of the major difference?

5.3.2 Rate Measurement

Rate measurement is a common goal in many scientific contexts, some of the more well known being rates associated with radioactive decay, heart beats, respiration, response rates on a questionnaire, and neural firing. Rates can also be used to create a coarse measure of certain behaviors: for example, instead of creating an error metric that is continuous (e.g., movement error when trying to touch the center of the 'o' key while typing), one could instead define a 'target' that is 'hit' when the movement endpoint is within an arbitrarily defined target zone and missed otherwise (e.g., corresponding to depressing or not depressing the correct key). In this example, the error rate is a proxy for the average size of the error. In the same way, we can use rate of transitioning between one room and another of a house as a coarse proxy for a continuous measure of activity level, or step rate for movement speed, or recovery rate for drug efficacy.

Example: Binomial Measurement of Recovery Rate

Measuring a binomial rate is seen commonly when we are interested in quantifying the effectiveness of drugs or the success of other interventions (artificial organ, drug rehabilitation program, etc.), or the rate at which particular experimental conditions yield detection of a difficult-to-see (near-threshold) visual, auditory, or other perceptual stimulus. The binomial rate parameter encodes an expected rate of observing success outcomes (e.g., heads) in a Bernoulli trial. In this example problem, we would like to measure the rate of recovery from depression using drug X. Obviously, in this type of problem half the scientific work involves composing a suitable definition of recovery. With such a definition in place, we can simply code the outcome of each patient in the study as recovery (success) or not.

A. Define the Posterior Distribution That Corresponds to the Desired Measurement

Success rate with counting data out of a possible N discrete events is described by the binomial distribution. The desired posterior over binomial rate is therefore:

$$p(\theta|S \cdot N \cdot \iota) \propto \varpi(\theta)\mathcal{L}(\theta).$$

B. Define Observation and Noise Models and Their Interrelationships

The graphical model representing the binomial data generated in this experiment would simply have a rate parameter enclosed within the system box, producing an observed time series of success/failure outcomes. As a graphical model, this is not particularly informative in its current form; more than anything, constructing the graphical model in this example simply tells us that we do not have a very detailed model of the underlying mechanism responsible for our data. There is a binomial rate variable introduced at the top which feeds into a function that produces Bernoulli trials, yielding a successful observed outcome at a rate of θ per observation ($0 \leq \theta \leq 1$). Both the variable node and the function box represent complicated biological processes that we are not attempting to model here, although we would try to examine the structure of each of these elements as part of our research program; for example, we might attempt to describe a function $\theta = f(\Phi)$, where Φ is a set of variables related to the composition of the drug or the type of depression being treated. In any case, the structure of the probability model is clear: in N observations we expect S successes with probability:

$$p(S|N \cdot \theta \cdot \imath) = \binom{N}{S} \theta^s (1-\theta)^{N-S}.$$

For a given dataset [consisting of the number-pair, (N, S)], the likelihood of θ becomes:

$$\mathcal{L}(\theta) \propto \theta^s (1-\theta)^{N-S},$$

where we have dropped the binomial coefficient $\binom{N}{S}$ from the likelihood because it is a constant term that does not contain the θ parameter.

C. Assign Priors over Unknown Parameter Values

The only unknown parameter in this model is the binomial rate, θ. The Jeffreys prior over a binomial rate is:

$$\varpi(\theta) \propto \sqrt{\theta(1-\theta)}^{\,-1}.$$

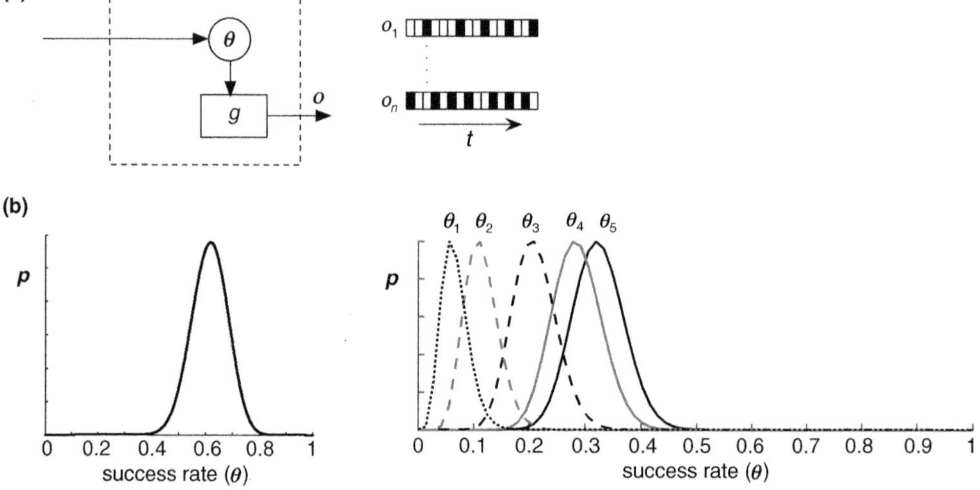

Figure 5.5 Rate measurement. (a) Posterior probability distribution over the unknown binomial rate, θ. (b) Rate measurement for each possible response for one item of a Likert-scaled questionnaire.

Note that we will often be concerned with assigning an appropriate range of values which it is possible for the unknown model parameters to take (recall we truncated the range of possible temperature values in the example above). By defining a finite range of possible parameter values we make it possible to compute a posterior even for variables that can (mathematically) vary over an infinite range. The binomial rate is special – its range is already finite. However, the binomial rate has a different problem in that if we assign a Jeffreys prior, the points at the edge of the range are infinite – and we usually end up truncating the range anyway, by eliminating $\theta = 0$ and $\theta = 1$ from the list of possible rates. This typically will not matter, because we can make the range approach these bounds as closely as we like by reducing the separation between θ values when we discretize this continuous rate parameter. If the peak of the posterior is too close to the bounds, we can switch to a uniform prior over rate, removing this issue altogether.

D. Compute the Desired Measurement

Of the 50 patients prescribed drug X during this study, a total of 31 showed enough improvement to have been classified as recoveries, while 19 did not. Recalling the posterior,

$$\begin{aligned} p(\theta|S \cdot N \cdot \iota) &\propto \varpi(\theta)\mathcal{L}(\theta) \\ &= \theta^{S-0.5}(1-\theta)^{N-S-0.5} \end{aligned}$$

these data yield the measurement of recovery rate shown in Figure 5.5a.

While our best estimate of the recovery rate is numerically larger than 0.5, we would like to be able to make a statement about whether the recovery rate for drug X is 'significantly larger' than 0.5. The two statements are different because a best estimate of $\theta = 0.5001$ is numerically larger than 0.5, but probably not in a way that we care about; the fact that $\theta = 0.5001$ is numerically larger than 0.5 is very likely a consequence of observing noisy data rather than a real effect of the drug. The question of whether a result is significantly larger than some reference value (such as 0.5, or whether the rate measured in one dataset is larger than the rate measured in another dataset) falls under the topic of *model selection*, which we will examine in Chapter 6. Note that it is not valid to use the confidence region to make a determination of whether a measured value is 'significantly different' from a reference value, because there is nothing in the statement of the posterior that would allow us to reject part of the total possible range of that parameter (i.e., all values of rate aside from 0 and 1 are possible under the posterior).

Exercises

1) List five examples of experiments where count data can be used to model an underlying rate with the binomial distribution.
2) Describe the effect of using a uniform prior instead of the Jeffreys prior described above:
   a. on small datasets.
   b. on large datasets.
3) For each of the experiments in (1), explain whether it is ameasurement or model selection problem.

Programming Aside: Binomial Rate Measurement (Fig. 5.5a)

```
S=31;
F=19;
N=S+F;
f=linspace(0,1,1201)';

%%%%%%%%%%%%%%%%%%%%%%%%%%
%%% 1d f distribution %%%
Lf=(S-.5)*log(f)+(F-.5)*log(1-f); Lf=Lf-max(Lf);
ciF=CIp(f,Lf);
figure(1); clf
subplot(2,1,1); hold on
plot(f,exp(Lf),'k--','LineWidth',1.75); dciF=diff(ciF(1:2));
axis([ciF(1)-.2*dciF ciF(2)+.2*dciF 0 1])
for n=1:2, plot(ciF(n)*[1 1],[0 1],'-','Color',.65*[1 1 1],'LineWidth',.7); end
```

Example: Multinomial Measurement of Likert-Scaled Questionnaire Item

The questionnaire has a long tradition in the fields of personality and social psychology, where the 5-element Likert scale is a common method of eliciting responses. The basic idea is to have respondents rate the extent to which they agree or disagree with a statement, or to ask the extent to which they believe a statement or the extent to which they might engage in a particular activity. A sample of respondents answers the same question, and the responses on that item can be analyzed. One part of our analysis might ask: 'for this question, at what rate was the first response chosen?', and so on for each question and response.

A. Define the Posterior Distribution That Corresponds to the Desired Measurement

After we have administered a personality questionnaire to N participants, we would like to measure the rate at which each response was chosen for a particular question. For the first question, the posterior for the rate of responding 'strongly disagree' is:

$$p(\theta_1|\boldsymbol{n}\cdot\iota) = \varpi(\theta_1)\int d\theta_5 d\theta_4 d\theta_3 d\theta_2 \varpi(\theta_2\cdot\theta_3\cdot\theta_4\cdot\theta_5)\mathcal{L}(\boldsymbol{\theta}).$$

B. Define Observation and Noise Models and Their Interrelationships

The probability of observing a set of response counts for each of the five responses on a given question is given by (2.20):

$$p(\boldsymbol{n}|\boldsymbol{\theta}\cdot N\cdot\iota_m) = \frac{N!}{n_1!n_2!n_3!n_4!n_5!}\theta_1^{n_1}\theta_2^{n_2}\theta_3^{n_3}\theta_4^{n_4}\theta_5^{n_5}$$

For a given dataset the number of responses of each of the five types $(n_1, n_2, n_3, n_4, n_5)$, the likelihood of $\boldsymbol{\theta}$ becomes:

$$\mathcal{L}(\boldsymbol{\theta}) \propto \theta_1^{n_1}\theta_2^{n_2}\theta_3^{n_3}\theta_4^{n_4}\theta_5^{n_5},$$

where we have dropped the multinomial coefficient from the likelihood because the n_i are constant.

C. Assign Priors over Unknown Parameter Values

The unknown parameters in this model are the rates, θ_i and we will initially assign them uniform priors:

$$\varpi(\boldsymbol{\theta}) \propto 1,$$

although the Jeffreys prior is explored in the exercises.

D. Compute the Desired Measurement

Of the 100 participants in this study, a total of 6 chose the first response, leading to the posterior shown in Figure 5.5b:

$$\begin{aligned} p(\theta_1|\boldsymbol{n} \cdot \iota) &\propto \varpi(\theta_1) \int d\theta_2 d\theta_3 d\theta_4 d\theta_5 \varpi(\theta_5 \cdot \theta_4 \cdot \theta_3 \cdot \theta_2)\mathcal{L}(\boldsymbol{\theta}) \\ &\propto \int d\theta_2 d\theta_3 d\theta_4 d\theta_5 \theta_5^{n_5} \theta_4^{n_4} \theta_3^{n_3} \theta_2^{n_2}, \end{aligned}$$

and rotating the indices allows us to compute posteriors over the other rates (Fig. 5.5b).

Programming Aside: Multinomial Rate Measurement (Fig. 5.5b)

```
n=[6 11 21 29 33]; N=61;
thetas=linspace(0,1,N); %theta list
lmat=-inf(N,N,N,N,N); %initialize likelihood matrix
Lf=@(tin) sum(n.*log(tin)); %n (data vec) is fixed

%%%%%%%%%%%%%%%%%%%%%%%%
%%% main comp loop %%%
for i5=1:N, imax4=findnearestN(thetas,1-thetas(i5),1);
    for i4=1:imax4, imax3=findnearestN(thetas,1-sum(thetas([i5 i4])));
        for i3=1:imax3, imax2=findnearestN(thetas,1-sum(thetas([i5 i4 i3])));
          for i2=1:imax2, i1=findnearestN(thetas,1-sum(thetas([i5 i4 i3 i2])));
              tvec=thetas([i5 i4 i3 i2 i1]);
              lmat(i1,i2,i3,i4,i5)=Lf(tvec/sum(tvec)); end, end, end, end

L1=logsum(lmat,[2:5],diff(thetas(1:2))*[1 1 1 1]);
L2=logsum(lmat,[1 3:5],diff(thetas(1:2))*[1 1 1 1]);
L3=logsum(lmat,[1:2 4:5],diff(thetas(1:2))*[1 1 1 1]);
L4=logsum(lmat,[1:3 5],diff(thetas(1:2))*[1 1 1 1]);
L5=logsum(lmat,[1:4],diff(thetas(1:2))*[1 1 1 1]);

figure; subplot(2,1,1); hold on
plot(thetas,exp(L1-max(L1)),'k-','LineWidth',2);
plot(thetas,exp(L2-max(L2)), '-','Color',[0 .45 .74],'LineWidth',2);
plot(thetas,exp(L3-max(L3)), 'k--','LineWidth',2);
plot(thetas,exp(L4-max(L4)),'--','Color',[0 .45 .74],'LineWidth',2);
plot(thetas,exp(L5-max(L5)),'k:','LineWidth',2);
```

If we were to have guessed that the rate should be equal for all five responses, we would have predicted observing 20 instances of each response being chosen. Our best estimate of the rate is numerically smaller than the 20 percent that would indicate equal rates of the five responses. As above, this does not logically disprove the underlying assumption of an equal-rate model of responding, because the comparison of an equal-rate model of responding to a model that allows a range of rates, or a model that requires $\theta < 0.2$, is the domain of model comparison rather than parameter estimation.

Exercises

1) List two additional examples of experiments where count data can be modeled based on the multinomial distribution.
2) How does the result change if the Jeffreys prior over rate is used instead of the uniform prior?
3) For each of the experiments in (1), explain whether it is a measurement or model selection problem.
4) Instead of treating the measurement of θ_1 as a problem involving a multinomial sampling distribution where θ_1 is embedded within a set of five rates, what is the result of the analysis if we treat the measurement of of θ_1 as a problem involving a binomial sampling distribution where θ_1 is embedded within a set of two rates (θ_1 vs. not θ_1)? Does this differ, and why?

5.3.3 Duration

Duration and reaction time data are often used to infer elements of decision models, as an index of priming, a biomarker indicating neurological deficit, and a range of other uses. Many analyses of reaction time data assume Gaussian errors. However, experience with such data suggests that the sampling distribution contains a substantial skew component; and although several skewed distribution types (e.g., the Fisk, Gumbel, Wald, skew-normal, recinormal, and Burr distributions) have been used to model timing (reaction time, duration) data, it is often possible to provide a reasonable fit to these data with more than one distribution. For this reason, there is not general agreement regarding the best method of fitting timing data. Here, we will examine reaction time data using the Fisk and recinormal sampling distributions, and in Chapter 6 we will learn to directly compare different noise models via model comparison techniques.

Example: QRS Duration Measurement from EKG Data
The data we will analyze in this example correspond to times derived from electrocardiograms (EKG) traces, called the QRS duration. The QRS complex is the combination of the Q wave, R wave and S wave and represents ventricular depolarization; the QRS duration is the time between the two downward dips corresponding to the points

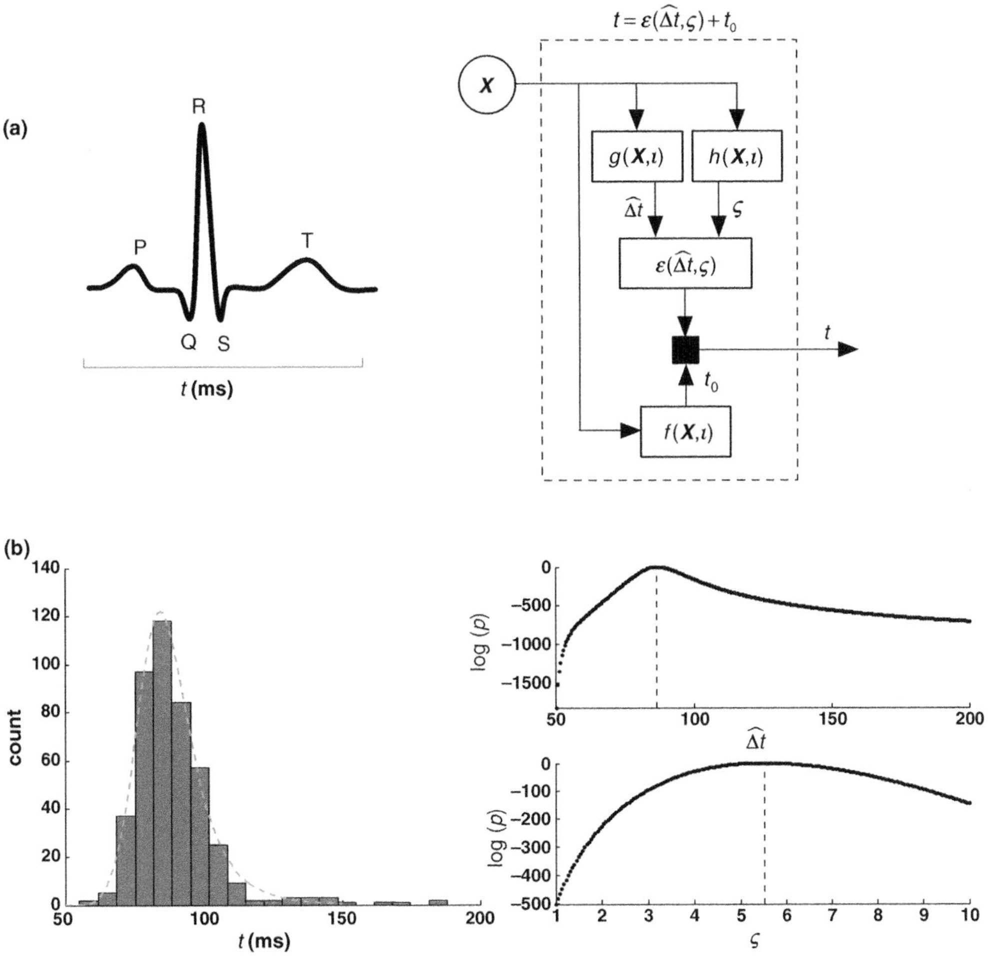

Figure 5.6 QRS duration. (a) Schematic of the QRS complex of the EKG (left). The stimulus (**X**), in combination with internal variables represented by ι, set both the median reaction time $\widehat{\Delta t}$ above the minimum and the shape of the resulting distribution of times (ς). These parameters define the Fisk error model, which is shifted by the minimum reaction time t_0 to produce the observed dataset, t (right). (b) Histogram of QRS duration data and the overlaid Fisk sampling distribution with the measured parameters (left). Parameter measurements of the median $\widehat{\Delta t}$ and shape parameter (ς) of the Fisk (right).

Q and S in Figure 5.6a (left). The normal duration of the QRS complex is between 80 and 100 ms, with durations between 100 and 120 ms considered intermediate or slightly prolonged. A QRS duration of greater than 120 ms is considered abnormal, suggesting that electrical activity is taking an abnormally long time to travel throughout the ventricular myocardium. Prolonged QRS duration occurs in right and left bundle branch block, nonspecific intraventricular conduction delay, and during ventricular arrhythmia.

A. Define the Posterior Distribution That Corresponds to the Desired Measurement

One possibility for a graphical model representing data is shown in Figure 5.6a (right). The model represents a timing mechanism in which there is a minimum possible duration $f = t_0$, as well as median $\widehat{\Delta t}$ duration defined by the g function, and an h function that represents the shape of the distribution of possible duration outputs.

We will assume that the minimum duration, t_0, is a known constant. Thus, the multidimensional posterior describing the two unknown parameters is $p(\varsigma \cdot \widehat{\Delta t}|\boldsymbol{t} \cdot t_0 \cdot \imath)$. To obtain the desired posterior over $\widehat{\Delta t}$, we compute:

$$p(\widehat{\Delta t}|\boldsymbol{t} \cdot \imath) = \int d\varsigma p(\varsigma \cdot \widehat{\Delta t}|\boldsymbol{t} \cdot t_0 \cdot \imath)$$
$$\propto \varpi(\widehat{\Delta t}) \int d\varsigma \varpi(\varsigma)\mathcal{L}(\varsigma, \widehat{\Delta t})$$

Similarly, we obtain the marginal posterior over the shape parameter, ς:

$$p(\varsigma|\boldsymbol{t} \cdot \imath) = \int d\widehat{\Delta t} p(\widehat{\Delta t} \cdot \varsigma|\boldsymbol{t} \cdot t_0 \cdot \imath)$$
$$\propto \varpi(\varsigma) \int d(\widehat{\Delta t})\varpi(\widehat{\Delta t})\mathcal{L}(\varsigma, \widehat{\Delta t})$$

B. Define Observation and Noise Models and Their Interrelationships

The Fisk distribution has good flexibility to represent skewed data, because it has both a shape parameter ς to represent the skew of the distribution (with $\varsigma = 1$ producing maximum skew with the distribution simplifying to an exponential, and large values of ς creating ever more symmetrical distributions) and a $\widehat{\Delta t}$ parameter representing the median of the distribution. The median is always slightly to the right of the peak of the distribution (which is itself located at $\widehat{\Delta t}\sqrt[\varsigma]{\frac{\varsigma-1}{\varsigma+1}}$, so that it approaches the median as $\varsigma \to \infty$; these characteristics define a right-skewed distribution).

For our purposes, we will define the density function for the Fisk distribution:

$$p(t|\widehat{\Delta t} \cdot \varsigma \cdot \imath) = \frac{\varsigma}{\widehat{\Delta t}} \left(\frac{t}{\widehat{\Delta t}}\right)^{\varsigma-1} \left[1 + \left(\frac{t}{\widehat{\Delta t}}\right)^{\varsigma}\right]^2 \quad \{\varsigma > 1, t \geq 0$$

where we have limited the range of the shape parameter so that it will never simplify to an exponential distribution (duration data will not look like an exponential). Durations will also usually have a nonzero minimum t_0, below which no data should be seen. The minimum is usually set jointly by experimental parameters ($\boldsymbol{X}$) and internal physiological and anatomical restriction ($\imath$, corresponding to, e.g., the number of synapses that are crossed, and neural conduction velocities).

C. Assign Priors over Unknown Parameter Values

We will measure the median of the response-time distribution for a known t_0, and treat the unknown shape parameter as a nuisance variable. Since the shape parameter must be greater than 1, and we can see from a few quick plots of $p(t|\widehat{\Delta t} \cdot \varsigma \cdot \imath)$ that ς values greater than 10 produce essentially symmetrical distributions, we will conservatively assign a uniform distribution over this range:

$$\varpi(\varsigma) \propto 1 \qquad \{1 < \varsigma < 10$$

Our background information on the problem tells us that the minimum possible duration is about 50 ms (i.e., $t_0 = 50$ ms), and we would not expect to see data beyond about 200 ms. We therefore assign a uniform distribution over possible median values within the appropriate range:

$$\varpi(\widehat{\Delta t}) \propto 1 \qquad \{50 < \Delta t < 200$$

Note that we have assigned uniform priors without examining the parameters of the distribution themselves, in terms of Fisher information, or the reference priors (recall Chapter 3). A more careful examination of these facets of the likelihood may yield a more sophisticated understanding of the unknown parameters and their priors, which may be pursued after this initial analysis.

D. Compute the Desired Measurement

There are several issues to consider when fitting parameters for a distribution with whose characteristics we are unfamiliar. First, we would like some familiarity with the shape of the sampling distribution, and how the parameters alter this shape. Therefore we will start by plotting the histogram of the data, and later overlay the sampling distribution with the best-fit parameters (Fig. 5.6b, left). The log of the marginal posterior distributions corresponding to our measurements of the two unknown parameters (the median QRS duration and the shape parameter of the sampling distribution over duration),

$$p(\widehat{\Delta t}|\mathbf{t}\cdot\iota) \propto \varpi(\widehat{\Delta t}) \int d\varsigma\, \varpi(\varsigma)\mathcal{L}(\varsigma,\widehat{\Delta t}) \propto \int_{\varsigma_{\min}}^{\varsigma_{\max}} d\varsigma\, \mathcal{L}(\varsigma,\widehat{\Delta t})$$

$$\propto \int_{1}^{50} d\varsigma\, \Pi \frac{\varsigma}{\widehat{\Delta t}} \left(\frac{t}{\widehat{\Delta t}}\right)^{\varsigma-1} \left[1+\left(\frac{t}{\widehat{\Delta t}}\right)^{\varsigma}\right]^{-2} \{t \geq 50$$

and

$$p(\varsigma|\mathbf{t}\cdot\iota) \propto \varpi(\varsigma) \int d\widehat{\Delta t}\, \varpi(\widehat{\Delta t})\mathcal{L}(\varsigma,\widehat{\Delta t})$$

$$\propto \int_{50}^{200} d\widehat{\Delta t}\, \Pi \frac{\varsigma}{\widehat{\Delta t}} \left(\frac{t}{\widehat{\Delta t}}\right)^{\varsigma-1} \left[1+\left(\frac{t}{\widehat{\Delta t}}\right)^{\varsigma}\right]^{-2} \{t \geq 50$$

are plotted in Figure 5.6b (right). We plot the log because the equation of the Fisk distribution has a series of exponents that is likely to cause underflow when we compute posterior probabilities based on a reasonably large dataset. To avoid this potential problem with underflow, we make computations based on the log of the Fisk likelihood.

Programming Aside: Measuring the QRS Duration (Fig. 5.6)

```
%plot the data histogram
figure(1); load('qrsdat.mat');
[n,x]=hist(tdat,20);
bar(x,n,1,'FaceColor',.45*[1 1 1]); box off; hold on

%compute the 2D (log) probability
Fpdf=@(MT,S) log(S)-log(ones(size(tdat))*(MT-50))+
    (S-1)*log((tdat-50)*(1./(MT-50)))-2*log(1+((tdat-50)*(1./(MT-50))).^S);
mt=linspace(50,200,302); mt=mt(2:end); SP=linspace(1,10,201);
Lfisk=nan(201,301);
for nSP=1:201,
    Lfisk(nSP,:)=sum(Fpdf(mt,SP(nSP)),1); end
figure(3); mesh(mt,SP,exp(Lfisk-max(max(Lfisk)))); colormap bone

%Compute and plot marginal posteriors
Lmt=logsum(Lfisk,1); Lsp=logsum(Lfisk,2); Lmt=Lmt-max(Lmt);
Lsp=Lsp-max(Lsp);
MThat=logpeakval([Lmt mt(:)]);
SPhat=logpeakval([Lsp SP(:)]);
figure(2); subplot(2,1,1); hold on
plot(mt,Lmt,'k.'); plot(MThat*[1 1],[min(Lmt) 0],'k--');
axis([50,200,min(Lmt),0]); box off
subplot(2,1,2); hold on
plot(SP,Lsp,'k.'); plot(SPhat*[1 1],[min(Lsp) 0],'k--');
axis([1,10,min(Lsp),0]); box off

%Compute sampling distribution for best-fit parameters
t=linspace(50,150,302); t=t(2:end);
LfiskT=log(SPhat)-log(MThat-50)+(SPhat-1)*log((t-50)./(MThat-50))-...
    2*log(1+((t-50)./(MThat-50)).^SPhat);
figure(1); plot(t,122*exp(LfiskT-max(LfiskT)),'--','Color',.65*[1 1 1],'LineWidth',2.5)
```

The data are consistent with a median QRS duration in the normal range, between 80 and 100 ms. In addition, the sampling distribution recovered from the measured parameter values is clearly a reasonable ('eyeball') description of these data.

Exercises

1) Examine the Fisk distribution. Program the Fisk sampling distribution, and overlay plots of:
   a. Variations of the shape parameter, from 1:5, with the median parameter fixed at 5.
   b. Variations of the median parameter, from 1:2:10, with the shape parameter fixed at 4.
2) In the computer code we compute the log of the Fisk probability distribution rather than the probability distribution itself. Why is that useful? Write the log of the Fisk distribution, based on what you see in the code, in standard format (as we usually write equations for readability).

3) Plot the Burr sampling distribution atop the data histogram for the qrs duration data:

```
figure(1); hold on
load('qrs.mat')
PD=fitdist(tdat,'burr')
Pburr=pdf('burr',t,80.45,18.925,0.449241);
plot(t,122*Pburr/max(Pburr),'--','Color',.7*[1 1 1],'LineWidth',2)
```

Describe which fit to the sampling data you prefer, and why. To what extent do you think you could discriminate whether a sample came from one or the other of the two distributions, and why?

4) Re-plot the histogram of the data, and overplot the sampling distribution based on the best-fit parameters. Plot several deviations of this by changing the shape parameter. Describe the differences, and indicate the proportion of change necessary before the sampling distribution appears to provide a poor fit to the histogram.
5) Is there any reason to prefer the Fisk versus the Burr noise model based on the underlying physiology that produces the QRS complex? Create a graphical model for QRS time that uses the Burr noise model, and attempt to label the functions in this and in the model shown in Figure 5.6 based on cardiac physiology.

Example: Saccade Latency

Saccades are the extremely fast eye movements that occur as you look from one stationary object to another. You can observe saccades by watching someone else's eyes as they look around the room or read. Interestingly, you cannot watch your own saccades in the mirror, because you are functionally blind while you make these eye movements. Saccades also occur in response to the appearance of an object ('target'), and their timing has been used to infer the properties of the neural decision and planning computations underlying movement selection and generation. The duration separating the appearance of a target and subsequent saccade, called 'saccadic latency', is usually on the order of 150–200 ms, depending on the specific experimental conditions. Saccade latencies can be prolonged in certain neurological disorders (e.g., Parkinson's disease) and also following neurological trauma (e.g., concussion).

When dealing with distributions of saccade latencies, it has been suggested that the best description is a Gaussian sampling distribution of the inverse latency. As we will see when computing posteriors, a Gaussian distribution in inverse-latency (Hz) units produces a right-skewed distribution in latency (ms) units. Thus, we will measure saccade latency in a simulated concussion patient and age-matched control, with all measurements performed using inverse-latency-transformed data (i.e., via $o_\theta = t^{-1}$).

A. Define the Posterior Distribution That Corresponds to the Desired Measurement

We want to measure the durations of saccades in both a concussion patient and an age-matched neurological control. For each subject separately, we will compute:

$$p(\theta|\mathbf{o}_\theta \cdot \imath) = \int d\sigma_\theta p(\theta \cdot \sigma_\theta|\mathbf{o}_\theta \cdot \imath)$$
$$\propto \varpi(\theta) \int d\sigma_\theta \varpi(\sigma_\theta)\mathcal{L}(\theta, \sigma_\theta).$$

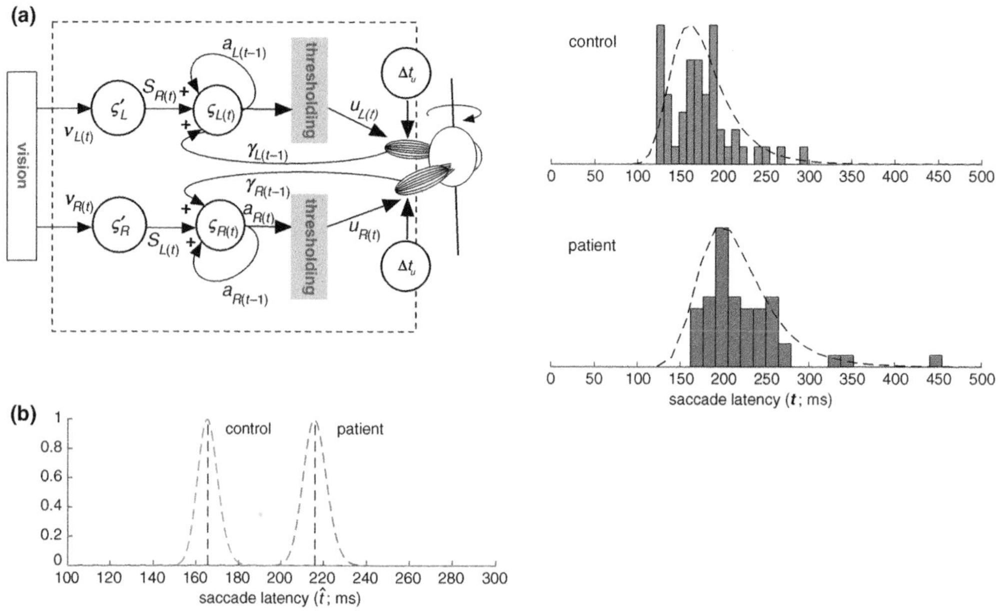

Figure 5.7 Saccade latency. (a) The graphical model (left) shows that the time needed for the eye to move to the target (presented either on the left or right) involves a decision that is based on visual stimulation (v_t) that builds activity (a_t; via a feedback loop) in cells responsible for the command to move the eye leftward ($u_{L(t)}$) or rightward ($u_{R(t)}$), until that activity reaches threshold. There is also a relatively constant muscle activation time (Δt_u) necessary to mobilize eye muscles (the schematic of the eye shows the medial and lateral rectus muscles only, along with their vertical axis of rotation). Gamma afferents help determine the location of the eye throughout this process. This model yields histograms (right) of two subjects' observed saccade latencies and overlaid sampling distributions. (b) Measurement of saccade latency for the two subjects in this experiment.

We can then compute the mean or peak of the posterior and convert these best-estimate values back into time units. We will also perform a coordinate transform of the posterior, $p(\theta|\boldsymbol{t}\cdot\imath)$ into $p(\hat{t}|\boldsymbol{d}\cdot\imath)$, via the linking function $\theta = \hat{t}^{-1}$.

B. Define Observation and Noise Models and Their Interrelationships

After we have converted all data into inverse-latency units, we use a Gaussian noise model:

$$p(\boldsymbol{o}_\theta|\theta\cdot\sigma_\theta\cdot\imath) = [\sigma_\theta\sqrt{2\pi}]^{-N} e^{-\frac{1}{2}\frac{\sum_i(o_i-\theta)^2}{\sigma_\theta^2}},$$

with an additive-noise transparent observation function:

$$\begin{aligned} o_\theta &= s + \epsilon_\theta \\ &= \theta + \epsilon_\theta \end{aligned}$$

C. Assign Priors over Unknown Parameter Values

We will compute the distribution over θ, treating the unknown dispersion parameter (σ_θ) as a nuisance variable. Since saccade latencies cannot be faster than 10ms and should

Programming Aside: Measuring Saccade Latency (Fig. 5.7)

```
load saclatdat

figure(2); clf
figure(1); clf
dtdat=dt(1:130,:); col=[.55 .45];
flink=@(x) 1./x;
hzdat=flink(dtdat);

Tmin=1/500; Tmax=1/10; Smin=.001; Smax=.01; n=size(hzdat,1);
thetas=linspace(Tmin,Tmax,1501)'; sigs=linspace(Smin,Smax,501);
Ot=ones(size(thetas)); Os=ones(size(sigs));
Lnorm=@(dnow) -Ot*log(sigs)-.5*((dnow-thetas).^2)*(sigs.^-2);

for Nsub=1:size(dtdat,2),
    %plot the data histogram
    figure(1); subplot(2,1,Nsub); cla
    [n,x]=hist(dtdat(:,Nsub),20); box off; hold on
    bar(x,n./max(n),1,'FaceColor',col(Nsub)*[1 1 1]);

    [n,x]=hist(dt(:,Nsub),140); subplot(2,1,Nsub);
    plot(x,n./max(n),'k--','LineWidth',1.4); axis([0 500 0 1.05])

    %compute the 2D (log) probability
    L=zeros(size(Ot*Os)); n=size(hzdat,1);
    for id=1:n, L=L+Lnorm(hzdat(id,Nsub)); end
    figure(2+Nsub); clf; mesh(sigs,thetas,exp(L-max(max(L)))); colormap bone

    %Compute and plot marginal posteriors
    Ltheta=logsum(L,2); Ltheta=Ltheta-max(Ltheta);
    thetahat=logpeakval([Ltheta thetas(:)]); dthat=1/thetahat;
    figure(2); subplot(2,1,Nsub); cla; hold on
    Ldt=LTX(thetas,Ltheta,flink);
    plot(Ldt(:,2),exp(Ldt(:,1)-max(Ldt(:,1))),'--',...
        'LineWidth',1.5,'Color',col(Nsub)*[1 1 1]);
    plot(dthat*[1 1],[0 1],'k--'); axis([100,300,0,1]); box off; end
```

not be longer than about 500ms, we will conservatively assign a truncated uniform distribution over the range:

$$\varpi(\theta) \propto 1\left\{500^{-1} < \theta < 10^{-1}\right.$$

Our background information derived from previous similar problems tells us that the standard deviation of rate data derived from latencies is usually between about .0005 and .0015, which is consistent with the observed data standard deviation of about 0.001 (rate coordinates). We therefore assign a uniform distribution over the range:

$$\varpi(\sigma_\theta) \propto 1\{.0001 < \sigma_\theta < .0025$$

Note that we could have assigned the truncated Jeffreys prior over the reasonable range of the dispersion parameter, but this will have very little effect on the outcome.

D. Compute the Desired Measurement

We first compute the location posterior in rate coordinates, and then transform the result into latency. The desired marginal posterior over rate is:

$$p(\theta|\boldsymbol{d}\cdot\iota) \propto \varpi(\theta)\int d\sigma_\theta \varpi(\sigma_\theta)\mathcal{L}(\theta,\sigma_\theta)$$

$$\propto \int d\sigma_\theta [\sigma_\theta\sqrt{2\Pi}]^{-N} e^{-\frac{1}{2}\frac{\sum_i (d_\theta-\theta)_i^2}{\sigma_\theta^2}}$$

The posterior over rate for the patient and age-matched control are computed in the PA, and the coordinate-transformed posteriors over latency are given in Figure 5.7. The figure shows that the two posteriors are separate, which may make use wonder if the parameters are statistically distinct. This, however, is a model comparison question and so is not directly answered by a measurement (although observing non-overlapping posteriors is often a good reason to consider performing a model comparison), because the underlying model upon which these measurements rely is the same for both measurements.

Notice that there is a great deal more in the model that may be investigated. What is the duration associated with muscle activation? What neural substrates control thresholding (which amounts to a decision to move), and what elements of the experiment might alter the threshold (e.g., number of targets, their brightness/contrast/detectability)?

Exercises

1) Perform the measurement with a truncated Jeffreys prior instead of the uniform prior used above and plot the two marginal posteriors over one another. Briefly describe any differences.
2) How would the measurement differ if it had been performed with a Gaussian sampling distribution in latency units instead of inverse-latency?
   a. Overplot the marginal posteriors from the measurement based on (transformed) inverse-latency data and latency data and comment on any differences.
   b. Which would you prefer?
   c. Why?
3) Why is the standard deviation in rate coordinates (about 0.01) so much smaller than the 1./std(dtdat) value of about 0.02 for the latency data?
4) The two measured latencies are numerically different. What evidence do you have that this difference points to an underlying difference in the saccade latencies of this patient relative to the control subject? Explain.
5) Look up articles describing experiments on saccade latencies and saccade decisions. What are some of the ways saccade latencies are modulated? Find at least one difference between control and patient populations in this regard.

5.3.4 Straight-Line Models

Our previous measurements were concerned with constant behavioral outputs, such as constant durations, constant recovery rates, constant neural firing rates, etc. However, we can imagine that these outputs need not always remain constant: of particular interest to us, they may be amenable to experimental manipulation. The simplest functional relationship $s = f(x)$ between experimental manipulation x and change in a behavioral variable (signal; s) is the straight-line relationship. The most general straight-line model is the **proportional change model**:

$$s = f(x) = \alpha + \beta x \tag{5.5}$$

where the slope (β) scales the input variable (x) and the intercept (α) shifts the straight line up/down along the y-axis. A simplification of this model is the **strictly proportional model** that passes through the origin ($\alpha = 0$).

The variety of circumstances that make use of the straight-line model is somewhat daunting, ranging from the proposal that the size of the hippocampus determines the quality of your memory (a larger hippocampus being hypothesized to underlie a better memory), to the proposal that the physical intensity of a light source determines the perceived brightness of that source (with brighter sources causing the perception of brighter sources), to the proposal that lower self-esteem leads to an increased likelihood of entering into an abusive interpersonal relationship, or that lower income parents give rise to lower school achievement in their children.

Straight-line models are found even when we do not believe that the functional relationship between an experimentally controlled variable (the x-variable) and behavior (y) is truly linear, because a straight line can often be fit as a coarse approximation to more complex functional relationships. For example, suppose the functional relationship between an experimental variable and behavior is sinusoidal (cyclical). We could take nearly any small portion of the range of that experimental variable and fit it with a straight line, and this is true for most functional relationships describing behavior, not just the sine function, making the straight-line fit one of the more common measurement problems.

Example: Auditory Space Perception

The most straightforward to analyze straight-line model is 'directly causal,' where the input (x) is an experimentally controlled variable that itself causes (i.e., directly rather than through intermediate variables; Figure 1.8a vs. 1.8c) changes in the behavior of interest (s), and the error model describes additive noise. One instance of this model is found in the field of space perception, where a straight line can be used to model the relationship between perceived and physical space. We might, for example, have data from an experiment where a subject sits at the center of a large circular array of buzzers and perceptually locates the sounds, and in this way a mapping of auditory egocentric perceptual space may be constructed.

A. Define the Posterior Distribution That Corresponds to the Desired Measurement

The graphical model representing a linear relationship between these variables is shown in Figure 5.4a, where we have assumed additive noise. The slope of the relation between visual and auditory space provides an index of the compression or expansion of perceived space. The posterior over slope is obtained by marginalizing over both the intercept (α) of the straight-line model, and any additional parameters (σ) of the noise model:

$$\begin{aligned} p(\beta|\boldsymbol{\omega} \cdot \boldsymbol{d} \cdot \imath) &= \int d\sigma\, d\alpha\, p(\alpha \cdot \beta \cdot \sigma|\boldsymbol{\omega} \cdot \boldsymbol{d} \cdot \imath) \\ &\propto \varpi(\beta) \int d\sigma\, d\alpha\, \varpi(\alpha)\varpi(\sigma)\mathcal{L}(\alpha, \sigma, \beta) \end{aligned}$$

The intercept, on the other hand, measures the bias of the mapping: the extent to which auditory space is mis-aligned with physical space:

$$p(\alpha|\boldsymbol{\omega}\cdot \boldsymbol{d}\cdot \iota) = \int d\sigma\, d\beta\, p(\alpha\cdot\beta\cdot\sigma|\boldsymbol{\omega}\cdot \boldsymbol{d}\cdot \iota)$$
$$\propto \varpi(\alpha)\int d\sigma\, d\beta\, \varpi(\beta)\varpi(\sigma)\mathcal{L}(\alpha,\sigma,\beta).$$

B. Define Observation and Noise Models and Their Interrelationships

We will apply a Gaussian noise model to the data. This noise model can be appropriately applied as long as the dispersion is low enough that we can ignore the possibility that any error will wrap around the circular array. The noise model for this experiment is:

$$p(\boldsymbol{d}|\boldsymbol{s}\cdot\sigma\cdot\iota) = (\sigma\sqrt{2\Pi})^{-n}e^{-\frac{1}{2}\frac{\sum_i(s_i-d_i)^2}{\sigma^2}} \qquad \{\sigma < 12$$
$$= (\sigma\sqrt{2\Pi})^{-n}e^{-\frac{1}{2}\frac{\sum_i([\beta x_i+\alpha]-d_i)^2}{\sigma^2}}$$

where we have limited the range of the dispersion parameter to avoid the possibility of sampling error wrapping around the circle.

Programming Aside: Straight-Line Model I

We first consider the straight-line model describing the mapping between auditory and physical space using a uniform prior over slope for a linear model written in slope-intercept form ($s = mx + b$). We will simulate buzzer locations from −40 deg (left) to +45 deg (right) relative to straight-ahead on the circular array.

```
%set constants
SD=5; buzzers=-45:15:45; Nb=length(buzzers); alpha=2; beta=.88;
alphas=linspace(-12,12,201); betas=linspace(0,2,501); sds=linspace(0,10,201);
dvec=alpha+beta*buzzers'+nrand(0,SD,[Nb 1]);
L=@(alphanow,sdnow) -(Nb+1)*sdnow-.5*sum((dvec*ones(size(betas))-...
    (alphanow+buzzers'*betas)).^2)/sdnow^2;

%main loop (uniform beta prior)
postmat=zeros(length(betas),length(alphas),length(sds));
%initialize posterior mnatrix
for na=1:length(alphas),
    for ns=1:length(sds),
        postmat(:,na,ns)=L(alphas(na),sds(ns)); end, end

Bpost=logsum(postmat,[2 3],[diff(alphas(1:2)) diff(sds(1:2))]);
Apost=logsum(postmat,[1 3],[diff(betas(1:2)) diff(sds(1:2))]);
SDpost=logsum(postmat,[1 2],[diff(betas(1:2)) diff(alphas(1:2))]);

figure(2); clf
subplot(2,1,1); plot(betas,exp(Bpost-max(Bpost)),'k--',...
    'LineWidth',1.4); axis([0 2 0 1.02]); box off
subplot(2,1,2); plot(alphas,exp(Apost-max(Apost)),'k--',...
    'LineWidth',1.4); axis([-10 10 0 1.02]); box off
```

C. Assign Priors over Unknown Parameter Values

There are two parameters to the straight-line model, the slope (β) and intercept (α). Often these will be assigned uniform priors:

$$\varpi(\alpha) \propto \begin{cases} 0, & -10 > \alpha > 10 \\ 1, & -10 \leq \alpha \leq 10 \end{cases}$$

and:

$$\varpi(\beta) \propto \begin{cases} 0, & 0 \geq \beta > 2 \\ 1, & 0 < \beta \leq 2 \end{cases}$$

and a Jeffreys prior for the unknown noise term:

$$\varpi(\sigma) \propto \sigma^{-1}.$$

We will update this uniform assignment of the slope parameter after we have made an initial analysis of this problem.

D. Compute the Desired Measurement

For uniform priors, putting the prior and likelihood into the posterior yields the following marginalized α measurement:

$$\begin{aligned} p(\alpha|\boldsymbol{X} \cdot \boldsymbol{d} \cdot \imath) &\propto \varpi(\alpha) \int d\sigma \, d\beta \varpi(\beta) \varpi(\sigma) \mathcal{L}(\alpha, \sigma, \beta) \\ &\propto \varpi(\alpha) \int d\sigma \, d\beta \sigma^{-(N+1)} e^{\frac{-\sum_1^N (\boldsymbol{d}-\boldsymbol{s})^2}{2\sigma^2}} \propto \int d\sigma \, d\beta \sigma^{-(N+1)} e^{-\frac{1}{2} \frac{-\sum_1^N (\boldsymbol{d}-\beta \boldsymbol{x}-\alpha)^2}{\sigma^2}} \end{aligned}$$

and the following measurement of β:

$$\begin{aligned} p(\beta|\boldsymbol{\omega} \cdot \boldsymbol{d} \cdot \imath) &\propto \varpi(\beta) \int d\sigma \, d\alpha \varpi(\alpha) \varpi(\sigma) \mathcal{L}(\alpha, \sigma, \beta) \\ &\propto \varpi(\beta) \int d\sigma \, d\alpha \sigma^{-(N+1)} e^{\frac{-\sum_1^N (\boldsymbol{d}-\boldsymbol{s})^2}{2\sigma^2}} \propto \int d\sigma \, d\alpha \sigma^{-(N+1)} e^{-\frac{1}{2} \frac{\sum_1^N (\boldsymbol{d}-\beta \boldsymbol{x}-\alpha)^2}{\sigma^2}} \end{aligned}$$

C. Assign Priors over Unknown Parameter Values (Con't)

The above analysis assumed a flat prior over slope values in the range, $0 < \beta \leq 2$. This was fine for a preliminary analysis. But now that we have made a preliminary measurement of slope, let us return and take a closer inspection of our prior information in this problem. In particular, we will take another look at the prior distributions assigned to the slope and intercept parameters, and recompute our measurement based on a more sophisticated understanding of our uncertainty concerning these variables.

When we assign a uniform prior over slope, we are asserting that each interval between possible slopes has equal probability mass. To get a better feel for what this implies, we plot equally-spaced slopes in Figure 5.8a (left). The plot shows us that a uniform prior over slope does not really conform to the notion of an uninformed state regarding the orientation of the model line. Indeed, if we convert slope to the orientation of the corresponding model line, we see that uniformly spaced slopes correspond to a distribution over line angle whose density is considerably higher at high slopes than near zero.

Our intuition for a completely uninformed state regarding the orientation of a model line is better expressed by the set of equally spaced model lines in the right portion of

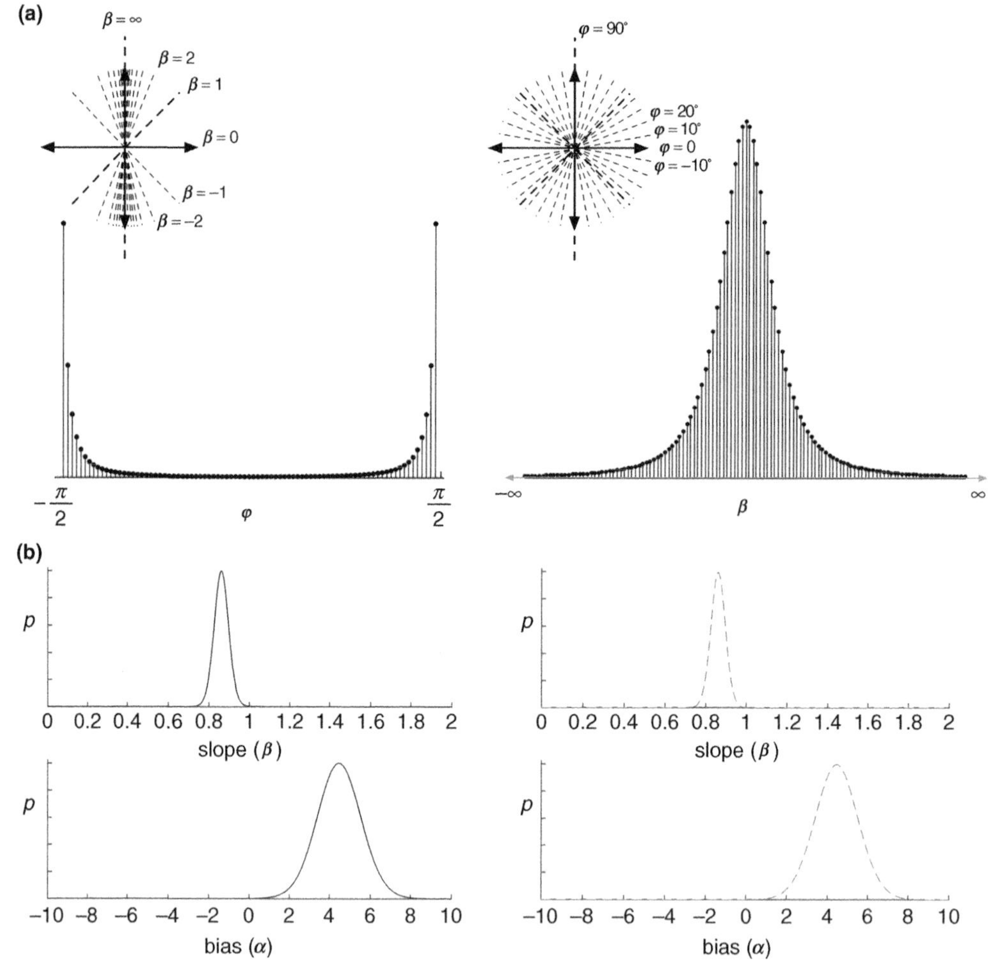

Figure 5.8 Auditory spatial localization. (a) Priors for the straight-line model. A uniform prior in slope (left) is more dense near the vertical coordinate axis, whereas a uniform prior in angle (right) is rotationally symmetric and uniformly dense along any axis. (b) Measurement of straight-line slope and bias using uniform priors when the model is parameterized in slope (left) and angle (right).

Figure 5.8a. This density of lines is uniform in angle rather than in slope, and has the feature that the resulting set of model lines is rotationally symmetric (the representation of their density is unaffected by rotating the coordinate axes). When the uniform distribution in angle is transformed to a distribution over slope (recall Appendix C), the transformed distribution has the shape of a Cauchy distribution centered on $\beta = 0$. This prior tells us that, before obtaining any data or encoding any other prior information, we assume the slope is zero.

We can incorporate this prior information into the measurement by either using a Cauchy prior of possible slopes,

$$p(\beta|\iota) \propto (1 + \beta^2)^{-1}$$

or by performing the analysis in the angle (rather than slope) domain, making use of a uniform prior. We will follow the latter course, since we did not technically derive the mathematical form of the Cauchy distribution here.

Programming Aside: Priors in Slope and Angle

To see the prior over slope that results from assigning a uniform prior over line-angle, we perform a transformation of variables (see Appendix 3).

```
alphas=linspace(-.9*pi/2,.9*pi/2,501)';
fTX=@(alphanow) tan(alphanow); %betanow=tan(alphanow)
pri=pTX(alphas,ones(size(alphas)),fTX); %transformation to angle prior
figure; plot(pri(:,2),(pri(:,1)/max(pri(:,1))),'k.'); xlim([-7 7]); box off
```

Notice this prior encodes the conservative preference for assuming that there is no relationship between the input and output variables unless the data suggest otherwise.

Programming Aside: Straight-Line Model II

Now we will measure the straight-line model parameters when describing the mapping between auditory and physical space using a uniform prior over line-agle for a linear model conceived in angle-intercept form ($s = \alpha + \tan(\varphi)$).

```
%set constants
angs=linspace(0,2*pi/3,501); %uniform prior in angle
L=@(alphanow,sdnow) -(Nb+1)*sdnow-.5*sum((dvec*ones(size(angs))-...
    (alphanow+buzzers'*tan(angs))).^2)/sdnow^2;

%main loop (uniform angle prior)
postmat=zeros(length(angs),length(alphas),length(sds));
%initialize posterior matrix
for na=1:length(alphas),
    for ns=1:length(sds),
        postmat(:,na,ns)=L(alphas(na),sds(ns)); end, end

Angpost=logsum(postmat,[2 3],[diff(alphas(1:2)) diff(sds(1:2))]);
Apost=logsum(postmat,[1 3],[diff(angs(1:2)) diff(sds(1:2))]);
SDpost=logsum(postmat,[1 2],[diff(angs(1:2)) diff(alphas(1:2))]);
Bangpost=pTX(angs,exp(Angpost-max(Angpost)),fTX);

figure(3); clf
subplot(2,1,1); plot(Bangpost(:,2),Bangpost(:,1)/...
    max(Bangpost(:,1)),'--','Color',[0 .45 .74],'LineWidth',1.4);
axis([0 2 0 1.02]); box off
subplot(2,1,2); plot(alphas,exp(Apost-max(Apost)),'--',...
     'Color',[0 .45 .74],'LineWidth',1.4); axis([-10 10 0 1.02]); box off
```

The new posterior, now using a prior uniform in straight-line angle, is written:

$$p(\beta|\boldsymbol{x}\cdot\boldsymbol{d}\cdot\iota) \propto \varpi(\varphi)\int d\sigma\, d\alpha\, \varpi(\alpha)\varpi(\sigma)\mathcal{L}(\alpha,\sigma,\varphi)$$

$$\propto \varpi(\varphi)\int d\sigma\, d\alpha\, \sigma^{-(N+1)}e^{\frac{-\sum(\boldsymbol{d}-s)^2}{2\sigma^2}} \propto \int d\sigma\, d\alpha\, \sigma^{-(N+1)}e^{-\frac{1}{2}\frac{\sum(\boldsymbol{d}-[\alpha+x\tan(\varphi)])^2}{\sigma^2}}$$

where the orientation of the line is now given in terms of the angle of the line relative to the abscissa. Notice that this version of the posterior, based on a uniform prior over the angle parameter, shifts the measurement only minimally (compare Fig. 5.8b, left and right).

The straight-line model with Gaussian additive noise is often applied in circumstances where it is not quite appropriate, either because errors are not continuous (e.g., data from a 5-point rating scale), when data are bounded (e.g., grade point averages or SAT scores), and when the numbers from both axes describe data, instead of one axis describing an experimentally controlled variable and one axis describing data. This last circumstance (observations on both axes) would have occurred in the context of the current problem if instead of comparing auditory localizations to physical locations, we had obtained auditory and visual localizations (two percepts) at each physical location in the array, and measured the slope of the visual to the auditory localization. Here, instead of a situation where our data describe the relationship between the physical location (experimentally controlled value) and the auditorily perceived location (observed data), we have a situation where we are comparing two perceptual outputs (auditorily and visually perceived spatial locations; recall Fig. 5.4b) to one another. Our example measurement tells us about any bias (intercept) or compression/expansion (slope less or greater than unity) of auditory space perception, whereas the second tells us about the the mapping of auditory-to-visual space, and whether one spatial map is shifted or scaled relative to the other internal mapping. To properly measure this second relationship, we must take account of the error inherent in having observed data along both axes. Although seemingly trivial, the addition of error along the second axis greatly complicates the analysis because the noiseless location of any datum along the 1D line is not known, creating an analysis that requires N marginalizations over N unknown locations, in addition to unknown straight-line and/or dispersion parameters that may also need to be marginalized out the analysis.

Exercises

1) Plot the discretized uniform prior over possible line-angles at the corresponding values of possible slopes that were defined in the code, and then transform and plot the corresponding prior in slope.
2) Plot the uninformed prior over possible slopes over the range defined in code, and then transform and plot the corresponding prior in angle.
3) Re-measure the slope using the Cauchy prior over the slope parameter. Compare this result to the posterior computed in terms of line orientation.
4) Staying with the assumption that there is a causal relation between these two variables, is there a way for the slope of the line to be very different from unity? What would the data mean if the slope were significantly flatter than unity?

5.3.5 Binary Classification

Our first exposure to binary classification was in Chapter 2 when we examined the interface between medical diagnostics and probability. Here we will revisit binary classification and learn the difference between measuring detectability versus detection threshold, where the former is our concern when assessing the performance of diagnostic tests or assessing object recognition in artificial visual systems and the latter is our concern when we want to know the minimum energy needed to reliably activate a given sensory system (e.g., light detection by the eye or sound detection by the ear).

Example: Measuring Stimulus Detectability

Many experiments ask questions of the form, 'How discriminable is one stimulus from another?' This type of research question involves measuring the **detectability** of the stimulus. A version of this was examined briefly in Chapter 2, when we computed posterior predictive value from hits, misses, false alarms, etc. for medical diagnostic tests. Medical diagnostic tests are used to discriminate the presence of illness from health. Such discrimination experiments yield a 'yes'/'no' binary classification indicating either the presence or absence of a signal (e.g., disease state).

Detectability can change either because signal strength changes (e.g., a sound signal becomes louder or softer relative to background noise) or because the sensitivity of the detector increases or decreases (e.g., one antibody test for Covid19 is better able to detect the body's response to the virus than another antibody test). In the binary classification paradigm, there is a series of stimulus presentations in which each stimulus is either of the signal or noise type, and the sensor correctly or incorrectly identifies each instance presented.

The detectability of a signal can be thought of in terms of Figure 5.9a (left). The dark distribution represents the sampling distribution of internal responses in the absence of the to-be-detected stimulus. The presence of the stimulus shifts this noise-only distribution to the right by an amount that represents the average internal response to the signal. Thus, these sampling distributions are responses to the noise-only and signal-plus-noise stimuli produced when trying to answer the question, 'Was the signal present?' Note that in nearly all real-world detection scenarios the sensor will sometimes register the identical stimulus strength when the signal is present and when it is not (e.g., at $\varsigma = 2$, where there is a clearly nonzero probability of observing $\varsigma = 2$ as read from both the 'A' and 'B' distributions) and *vice versa* for the noise-only stimulus, creating the opportunity for hits, misses, false alarms, and correct rejections (recall the confusion matrix of Fig. 2.3a).

The strength of the signal's detectability is encoded in the d' metric, which measures the overlap of the two distributions in Figure 5.9a. When overlap is large (bottommost row of plots), the detectability is low and the probability of registering a given strength of stimulus is similar whether from a noise trial of the experiment or a signal+noise trial. In the upper rows, detectability is higher (the two distributions are more separated laterally), and fewer values along the abscissa are strongly representative of both the noise-only and the stimulus+noise stimuli.

Let us think of a light-detection experiment, where one is presented with a single dim light that is either turned on or left off, and over multiple instances one is asked which of these events occurred. The internally registered stimulus strength elicited by these two stimuli is represented in Figure 5.9a by the two distributions. The detectability of the difference between dim and no-light stimuli is given by the overlap of the two sampling distributions in Figure 5.9a. This theoretical construct is:

$$d' = \frac{\mu_2 - \mu_1}{\sigma} = \frac{\Delta\mu}{\sigma} \tag{5.6a}$$

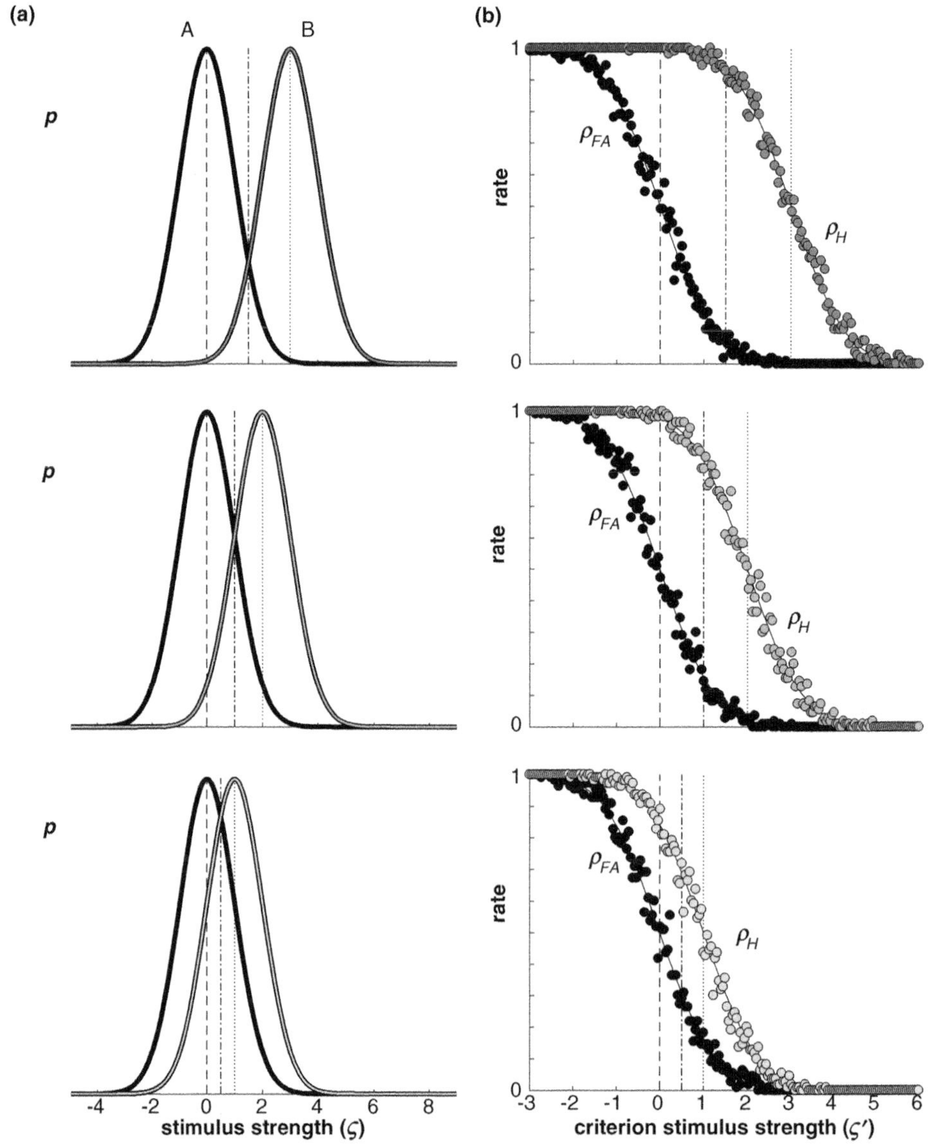

Figure 5.9 Signal detection theory. (a) Sampling distributions representing the probabilities of observing a given stimulus strength, ς, when the source is stimulus 'A' (dark lines) and when it is stimulus 'B' (light lines). Usually, these are stimulus strength values that fall along a continuum, such as light intensity; the physical stimulus could be noise-only (darkness, no light, 'A') or a stimulus+noise (dim flash of light present, 'B'). Alternatively, the two stimuli could be the horizontal locations of two auditory beeps, and we would be interested in identifying the separation necessary to discriminate the two locations. Rows show plots for stimulus pairs of increasing detectability. (b) The right-hand column shows observed (circles) and theoretically predicted (solid lines) rates of false alarms (ρ_{FA}, the rate of incorrectly labeling the stimulus as 'B' when it is actually 'A') and hits (ρ_H, the rate of correctly labeling the stimulus as 'B') pooled across all registered stimulus strengths (ς in the left-hand plots), for the criterion shown on the abscissa (in other words, you respond 'A' when the registered ς value is lower than the criterion, ς', and 'B' otherwise). Theoretical false-alarm rates (ρ_{FA}) correspond to the ratios, or proportions, of probability mass to the right of the criterion for the 'A' probability distribution in the left-hand plot of the same row; theoretical hit rates (ρ_H) correspond to the proportion of probability mass to the right of the criterion in the 'B' probability distributions of the same row. Vertical dashed and dotted lines represent three of the obvious choices for a criterion (i.e., exactly between distributions or at the peak of one or the other distribution).

where the signal strength $\Delta\mu$ is compared to the size of the noise parameter, σ, to yield the signal-to-noise ratio. The connection between the signal-to-noise ratio defined in (5.6a) and the 'yes'/'no' (or 'light'/'dark') data of this binary-classification experiment comes from the 'criterion' by which an observer (or 'receiver' in the original communications context of the theory) decides to classify a given internally registered stimulus strength as signal versus noise. Three commonly chosen criterion settings are shown in Figures 5.9a,b. In Figure 5.9a, any internal signal strength above the vertical criterion line will be labeled 'signal' and anything below 'noise.' Thus, for any criterion the probability of a hit (saying 'yes' to the presence of the stimulus) is the area under the stimulus-present distribution to the right of the criterion, and the probability of a false alarm (saying 'yes' to the absence of the physical stimulus) is the area under the noise-only distribution to the right of the criterion. Figure 5.9b shows hit and false alarm rates that would result from different criteria. These hit and false alarm rates are given on the ROC (receiver operating characteristic) plot in Figure 5.10a, and the z-transformed rates in the ROC plot of Figure 5.10b.

The signal-to-noise ratio can be estimated from the proportion of hit and false alarm data via:

$$d' = z(\rho_H) - z(\rho_{FA}) \tag{5.6b}$$

where z refers to the inverse of the standard cumulative normal density. z is the distance, in standard deviation units from the mean, that corresponds to a standard cumulative normal probability (with $\mu = 0$ and $\sigma = 1$) of ρ. Thus, $z = 0$ corresponds to a cumulative normal probability of 0.5 because one-half of the probability mass of a cumulative normal is to the left of its mean ($z = 0$ is at the mean, $\mu = 0$). Similarly, $z = 1$ corresponds to a cumulative normal probability of 0.8414 because about 84 percent of the probability mass under the standard normal distribution falls to the left of 1.

Why is the difference between the z-transformed hit and false alarm rates a constant, despite criterion? The answer hinges on the fact that for any criterion point on the abscissa of Figure 5.9a, the area to the right of that point under the sampling distribution tells us how many standard deviation units that criterion is shifted relative to the peak of the Gaussian sampling distribution. Thus, if we know how many standard deviation units the signal distribution's peak is shifted relative to the criterion, and how many standard deviation units the noise distribution's peak is shifted relative to the same criterion, then the difference between these two is the number of standard deviation units the two peaks are separated from one another. This is the definition of d'.

We see a constant value of d' in the 'iso-performance' curves of Figures 5.10a,b, which describe the hit and false-alarm rates we might see for different criterion values chosen in the three rows of Figure 5.9. In the upper row, if criterion were at 0 the noise-only stimulus would be below criterion on approximately half of trials (noise trials will produce roughly equal numbers of correct rejections and false alarms, but signal trials will almost always produce hits. The opposite pattern would result if the criterion were at 3; hits and misses would occur about equally often for signal trials, but noise trials would almost never result in false alarms. For all criteria, however, $d' = 3$. A simulation of multiple cases of this type is shown in Figure 5.10a,b, where Figure 5.10a displays the standard form of the ROC curve (plotting ρ_H relative to ρ_{FA})and a z-transformed ROC plot (i.e., $z(\rho_H)$ plotted relative to $z(\rho_{FA})$) in Figure 5.10b. The important thing to

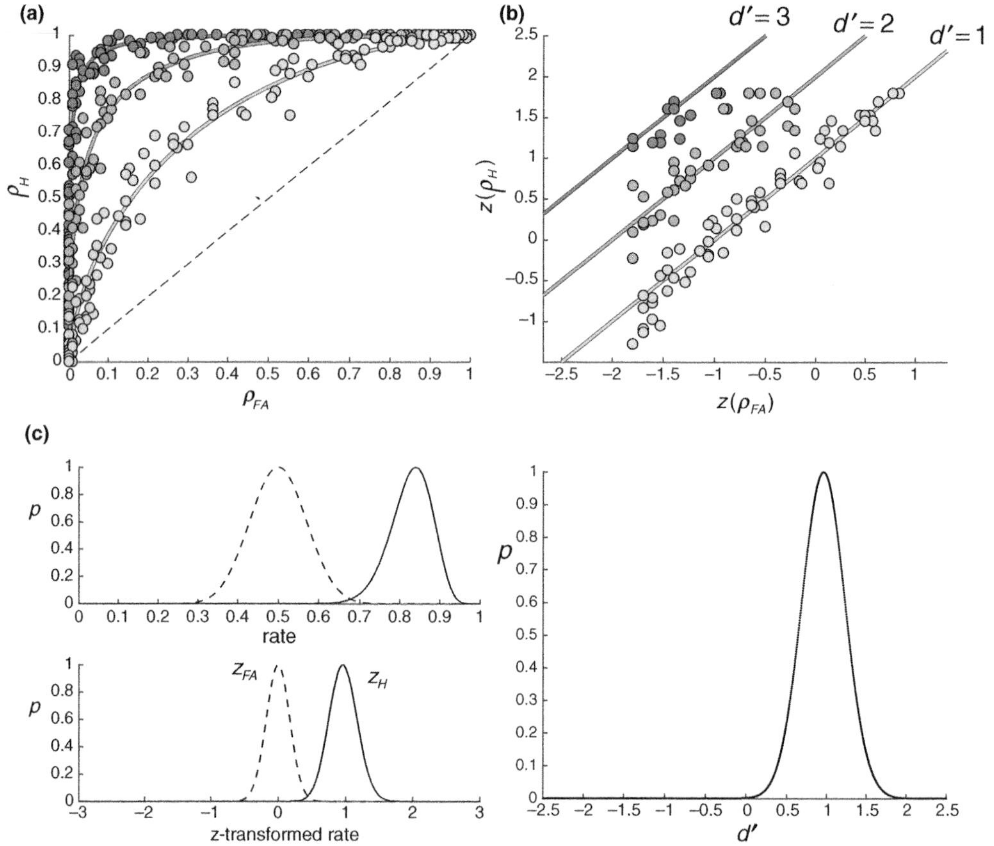

Figure 5.10 Detectability. (a) Receiver operating characteristic (ROC) plots and d' measurement. The left-hand column shows the ROC from empirical hit and false-alarm rates. The area under the ROC curve represents the discriminability of the stimulus under the given experimental conditions, because it is a measure of the overlap of the left-hand column of distributions in (a), regardless of criterion. A perfect classifier would yield an AUC of 1; classification no better than chance would yield an AUC of 0.5.
(b) Taking z-scores of the rate data yields a plot in which the data will fall along a straight line, representing a constant difference between hit and false-alarm rates, when the probability distributions representing stimulus and noise are Gaussian; d' is the difference between z-scores. In both (a) and (b) plots, points along each solid line correspond to different internal criterion values that might have been adopted (any vertical lines through the left-hand column of (a), which are also the abscissa values of the right-hand plots of the same figure). The three solid lines represent the three scenarios of Figure 5.9. The important thing to note here is that *d' does not change with changes in criterion.* (c) Measurements of rate, z, and d' corresponding to the bottom row of Figure 5.9.

notice is that, regardless of criterion, the data from each of the three cases ($d' = 3, 2, 1$) all fall along their own iso-performance curves, which have a bowed shape in Figure 5.9a, and describe a straight line following z-transformation. These straight-line relations define a constant difference of 1, 2 and 3, corresponding to the three examples in Figure 5.9.

A. Define the Posterior Distribution That Corresponds to the Desired Measurement

In the binary classification paradigm, there is a series of stimulus presentations in which each stimulus is either of the signal or noise type, and the subject indicates which stimulus-type had been presented. The most common example of measuring detectability is while assessing a clinical test or treatment, such as a concussion screen (clinical test) or new analgesic (treatment). In either case, we want to measure the efficacy of the test or treatment relative to a standard alternative. Here, we will measure efficacy of a new analgesic drug relative to placebo. We are therefore interested in computing the posterior:

$$p(d'|\boldsymbol{d} \cdot \iota) = p(\mathbf{z}_H - \mathbf{z}_{FA}|\boldsymbol{d} \cdot \iota)$$

where we recognize that we can obtain the probability of the desired difference from the cross correlation of the two posteriors (see Appendix C):

$$\begin{aligned} p(\mathbf{z}_H|\boldsymbol{d} \cdot s \cdot \iota) &= p(\rho_H|\boldsymbol{d} \cdot s \cdot \iota)\frac{d\mathbf{z}_H}{d\rho_H}, \\ p(\mathbf{z}_{FA}|\boldsymbol{d} \cdot \bar{s} \cdot \iota) &= p(\rho_{FA}|\boldsymbol{d} \cdot \bar{s} \cdot \iota)\frac{d\mathbf{z}_{FA}}{d\rho_{FA}}, \end{aligned}$$

and these are themselves distributions over z-transformed hit and false-alarm rates:

$$\begin{aligned} p(\rho_H|\boldsymbol{d} \cdot s \cdot \iota) &\propto p(\rho_H|s \cdot \iota)p(\boldsymbol{d}|\rho_H \cdot s \cdot \iota) \\ &= \varpi(\rho_H)\mathcal{L}(\rho_H) \\ p(\rho_{FA}|\boldsymbol{d} \cdot \bar{s} \cdot \iota) &\propto p(\rho_{FA}|\bar{s} \cdot \iota)p(\boldsymbol{d}|\rho_{FA} \cdot \bar{s} \cdot \iota) \\ &= \varpi(\rho_{FA})\mathcal{L}(\rho_{FA}) \end{aligned}$$

B. Define Observation and Noise Models and Their Interrelationships

The observation model must connect the theoretical rate of hits and false alarms to observed yes/no data, and we accomplish this via the binomial likelihood,

$$p(\boldsymbol{d}|\rho \cdot \iota) \propto \rho^{c}(1-\rho)^{\bar{c}},$$

where c refers to the relevant count: the number of hits (reports of reduced pain in subjects given the analgesic) in the case of $\rho = \rho_H$, and to false alarms (number of reports of reduced pain in subjects given placebo) when $\rho = \rho_{FA}$.

C. Assign Priors over Unknown Parameter Values

Here we will assign a uniform prior over the possible rate values in both cases, and leave it as an exercise to examine the effect of this choice relative to a bounded Jeffreys prior.

D. Compute the Desired Measurement

In this experiment we will give 50 subjects the analgesic and 50 placebo, counting the number of each that report noticeably reduced pain versus no apparent pain reduction. The left-hand plot of Figure 5.10c shows the posterior over ρ and the transformed posterior over $\mathbf{z}$ for the data corresponding to the lower row of Figure 5.9; the right-hand portion of Figure 5.10c gives the desired measurement of d'. Computing the posterior over d' for these data requires several steps. First, we compute the posterior over rate (hits and false alarms) via the binomial likelihood

Programming Aside: d-Prime (Fig. 5.10c)

To compute d-prime we will proceed in three steps. First we must compute probability distributions over hit and false alarm rates based on the **binomial** likelihood:

```
N=50; hits=round(N*.8414); fa=round(N*.5); %criterion at 0 for dprime=1 case
pri=@(x) ones(size(x)); %uniform prior
ftx=@(x) norminv(x); %cumulative inverse normal transform

figure(Fnum); clf
subplot(2,1,1); hold on;
[~, ~, Lhit]=Lrate([ones(hits,1);zeros(N-hits,1)],pri,Fnum);
[~, ~, Lfa]= Lrate([ones(fa,  1);zeros(N-fa,  1)],pri);

%and then z-transform these rates:
[Phit]=pTX(Lhit(:,2),exp(Lhit(:,1)),ftx);
[Pfa ]=pTX(Lfa(:,2) ,exp(Lfa(:,1)) ,ftx);
subplot(2,1,2); plot(Phit(:,2),Phit(:,1),'k-','LineWidth',2)
xlabel('z','FontName','Arial','FontSize',13,'FontWeight','Bold')

%before finally computing the probability over differences of z-transformed rates:
Phit(:,1)=Phit(:,1)/max(Phit(:,1)); Phit(isnan(Phit(:,1)),:)=[];
Pfa(:,1)=Pfa(:,1)/max(Pfa(:,1)); Pfa(isnan(Pfa(:,1)),:)=[];


%but note that here it is important to first re-linearize abscissa values
xhit=linspace(Phit(100,2),Phit(end-100,2),1001)';
xfa=linspace(Pfa(100,2),Pfa(end-100,2),1001)';

phit=interp1(Phit(100:end-100,2),Phit(100:end-100,1),xhit,'pchip');
pfa=interp1(Pfa(100:end-100,2),Pfa(100:end-100,1),xfa,'pchip');

[pS, pD, sSD]=SumDiffFig([pfa xfa],[phit xhit],[45 46],0,0);

figure(Fnum+1); clf
plot(pD(:,2),pD(:,1)/max(pD(:,1)),'k.')
axis([-3 3 0 1])
xlabel('d"','FontName','Arial','FontSize',13,'FontWeight','Bold')
ylabel('p','FontName','Arial','FontSize',13,'FontWeight','Bold')
```

conditioned on the observed data (Fig. 5.10c, upper-left). Every possible rate corresponds to an area under the Gaussian distribution to the right of criterion, as depicted in Figure 5.9, and this transform of the rate posteriors is shown in Figure 5.10c (lower-left). Finally, d' is defined as the difference of these z-transformed rates, and this lossy difference transform is depicted in Figure 5.10c, right. We can clearly see that the data corresponding to the lower row of Figure 5.9 reliably yields a measured value of $d' = 1$.

In our example experiment we knew that there were 50 of each type of subject, treatment and placebo, giving a prior probability of $\varpi = 0.5$ to each. However, the full theory of signal detectability (Signal Detection Theory, or SDT) must also account for different prior probabilities assigned to the two underlying variables. For example, recall the medical diagnostics example from Chapter 2, where we wanted to detect disease presence based on some continuous indicator (a real number, rather than the yes/no data from the example above). In this scenario you are given the result of the diagnostic test, and would like to guess whether the disease was truly present based on that number. As above, d' tells us how far apart the sampling distribution of disease-present test-scores is from the distribution of disease-absent test-scores, and therefore controls the the probability of disease presence based on having observed a particular test score, $\mathcal{L}(disease) = p(data|disease \cdot \iota)$. However, if the prior probability of disease (disease prevalence) is not 0.5, then a physician should scale the interpretation of the test, the posterior probability of disease presence $p(disease|data \cdot \iota)$, via Bayes' theorem, $p(disease|data \cdot \iota) \propto p(disease|\iota)p(data|disease \cdot \iota)$ as was discussed in Chapter 2.

Exercises

1) Define the signal-to-noise ratio in terms of Figure 5.9a.
2) What is the criterion, and how does it affect hits and false alarm rates?
3) What is the relationship between the plots in Figure 5.9b and the criterion in Figure 5.9a?
4) How is d' affected by choice of criterion value?
5) How is physical stimulus intensity reflected in the abscissa values and sampling distributions plotted in Figure 5.9a?
6) Describe the relationship between eqs. 5.6a & 5.6b.
7) Based on Figure 5.9, define the probability of a correct rejection in terms of a given criterion value.
8) Re-create the analysis of Figure 5.10c using a Jeffreys prior, and describe any differences.
9) How would Figure 5.10c change if the hit and false-alarm rates were the same but there were 500 subjects in each case instead of 50?
10) Determine the hit and false alarm rates needed to re-create data from the upper row of Figure 5.9, and recreate the measurement of d' with these data.
11) How did the unit normal distribution contribute to creating Figure 5.9c?
12) Relate what you now know about criterion and SDT to the medical decision-making example, explaining how the d' of a diagnostic test relates to the likelihood of a positive and negative test result in terms of hits, misses, false alarms, and correct rejections, as well as how these all relate to Bayes' theorem and disease prevalence.

5.3.6 Two-Alternative Forced-Choice

We learned in the previous section that d' tells us about the internally represented intensity of a physical stimulus relative to a standard (usually noise) stimulus: but what about threshold? The threshold corresponds to the physical stimulus that marks the transition from not quite strong enough to be reliably detected, to reliably detectable.[4] This is a bit tricky, because if our measure of detectability is the rate of correct responding (i.e., hits and correct rejections), it clearly depends on an unobservable criterion (and the criterion may be chosen differently by different experimental subjects, and may even change

[4] Notice the different goals when computing d' and a detection or difference threshold: When we compute detectability we are interested in measuring the signal-to-noise ratio of a *given sensory* stimulus. When we compute a threshold, we are interested in measuring the stimulus strength that is just detectable ($d' = 1$).

over the course of an experiment!). For example, in the $d' = 3$ case above, we can change our hit rate from chance ($\rho = 0.5$) to nearly perfect ($\rho = 0.95$) simply by choosing a different criterion.

Is there a way to test binary classification in a detection experiment that eliminates the influence of the criterion, and also allows us to use percent correct as our performance measure? It turns out that yes, we can effectively eliminate the influence of a criterion using the two-alternative forced-choice (2AFC) paradigm. This experimental paradigm relies on presenting one instance of the signal+noise and one instance of the noise-only stimulus (e.g., on two sides of a computer screen) in each trial. Because the subject is told that the signal will always be present, the task now becomes a matter of *choosing the larger of two internal stimulus strengths*, rather than *comparing a single internal stimulus to a constant criterion*. We eliminate the uncertainty associated with an unknown criterion setting because we have enforced this particular 'choose the larger' criterion: a criterion that will yield 50 percent correct/incorrect responses when guessing.[5] This is very different from the case we would have outside the 2AFC paradigm, when only one stimulus is given on each trial, allowing the prior rate of presenting the two stimuli to differ. We will examine an instance of the 2AFC paradigm for measuring detection threshold next.

Example: Measuring Detection Threshold

When only a single signal strength is tested, there is no guarantee that it will produce a detectable signal, and when it does, we are measuring the signal strength (signal-to-noise ratio) rather than the threshold for detecting that signal. In an experiment where we want to measure detection threshold, we will need the ability to experimentally vary signal strength, allowing us to observe data from both undetectable and detectable signals.

Thus, in a threshold experiment the stimulus strength (ς) is varied from one trial to another and we would like to estimate the lowest difference in physical stimulus intensity that can be discriminated.[6] In this example we will use visual light contrast as our physical stimulus: the parameter $\varsigma = \frac{I_s - I_b}{I_b}$ controls the strength of the physical stimulus, where I_s is the light intensity of a stimulus on a screen, I_b is the intensity of the screen background, and ς defines the light contrast between the two. In all experiments of this type there are very low stimulus strengths that should be impossible to detect (contrasts near zero, such that the correct alternative is chosen only by chance), and higher intensities that will be more easily detected (contrasts significantly above zero in this experiment). At some intermediate intensity there will be a point at which the stimulus is just detectable; this threshold level of correct responding is somewhat arbitrary, but we will use the 75 percent point because it corresponds to the halfway point between pure guessing (50 percent correct) and perfect performance (100 percent correct).

[5] With certain caveats based on assuming you have not been given information about how to guess correctly (such as presenting the noise-only stimulus on the left of the screen in 80 percent of trials).

[6] In many experiments you will be interested in the threshold for detecting a *difference* from some reference stimulus intensity. When that reference is zero intensity, the experiment is intended to determine the *absolute detection threshold*. When the reference intensity is nonzero, the experiment is intended to examine the *difference threshold*. Absolute thresholds are also commonly referred to as detection thresholds, whereas difference thresholds are often referred to as detection and/or discrimination thresholds. In the older literature you will also see the terms *limen* and *difference limen*, which translate directly to threshold and difference threshold.

A. Define the Posterior Distribution That Corresponds to the Desired Measurement
In the 2AFC version of the binary classification paradigm, there is a series of stimulus presentations in which one side of a computer monitor contains a stimulus with nonzero contrast and the other side of the screen is set at the background intensity of the first side, where the subject indicates which side contains the stimulus. Thus, performance in the experiment is determined again by the signal-to-noise ratio (Fig. 5.9), but the criterion drops out because subjects are forced to always choose the greater of the internal signals (one generated by each side of the computer monitor in this experiment).

The underlying to-be-measured signal is the binomial rate parameter (percent correct) predicted by a sigmoidal function of stimulus strength (ς), threshold stimulus strength (ς'), and lapse rate (λ) as described by the graphical model in Figure 5.11a. The noise model is, however, rather simple: it is based on the same binomial sampling distribution that describes success rates in coin tossing. Here, there is a series of theoretical coins corresponding to the various success rates predicted for strong and weak stimuli. The point of collecting data in a 2AFC experiment is to measure the detection threshold: the stimulus that is just detectable (or just detectably different from a reference stimulus). The desired measurement will therefore be identical with the posterior distribution over the threshold parameter, conditional on the observed stimulus-data pairs:

$$\begin{aligned} p(\varsigma'|\boldsymbol{d}\cdot\varsigma\cdot\rho_0\cdot\iota) &= \int d\sigma\, d\lambda\, p(\lambda\cdot\sigma\cdot\varsigma'|\boldsymbol{d}\cdot\varsigma\cdot\rho_0\cdot\iota) \\ &\propto \varpi(\varsigma')\int d\sigma\, d\lambda\, \varpi(\lambda)\varpi(\sigma)\mathcal{L}(\varsigma',\sigma,\lambda) \end{aligned}$$

where we have marginalized over two unknown parameters (dispersion, σ, and lapse-rate, λ).

B. Define Observation and Noise Models and Their Interrelationships
The observation model defines a relationship between physical stimulus strength (ς) and the theoretical signal (s), which is the expected success rate rate for responses to a given strength of stimulus:

$$\begin{aligned} s = \rho &= f(\rho_0, \delta) \\ &= (1-\rho_0)\delta + \rho_0 \left\{ \delta = g(\varsigma, \varsigma', \sigma) \right. \end{aligned} \tag{5.5a}$$

where the variables $\rho_0, \varsigma', \sigma$ encode additional parameters needed to describe most detection scenarios, and the function g is the sigmoidal (S-shaped) function describing the progression from undetectable to highly detectable as stimulus strength increases. The function g will often be a cumulative probability function (such as the cumulative Gaussian probability; see below) that transitions from 0 to 1 as stimulus strength (ς) increases. The parameter ρ_0 encodes the correct-response rate due to guessing (i.e., when no stimulus is present or the stimulus was not seen such as during lapses, which in the 2AFC paradigm is $\rho_0 = 0.5$), whereas σ is a parameter (or possibly a vector of parameters) that encodes how performance transitions from blind guessing ($\rho = \rho_0$) to threshold ($\rho = 0.5[\rho_0 + 1]$) to perfect detection ($\rho = 1$) as stimulus strength increases (i.e., it encodes the shape and/or the width of the probability distribution whose cumulative density is the sigmoid encoded by g). Note that when $\rho_0 = 0.5$ (the success rate for blind guessing), the δ term above will be scaled to a range of 0 to 0.5 instead of from 0 to 1. Adding this term to the guessing rate yields a signal (s) that has range from

0.5 (guessing) to 1 (full detectability). Finally, the parameter we are most likely to want to measure, ς', encodes the threshold stimulus strength - the value of $\varsigma = \varsigma'$ such that $\delta = 0.5$ ('detection' is at threshold).

In addition to the parameters defined above, there is the possibility that we will need a 'lapse rate' parameter (λ). The lapse rate refers to the proportion of trials in which a stimulus is unseen, perhaps as a result of blinking the eyes during stimulus presentation or due to distraction, and is usually assumed to be quite small ($\lambda \approx 0$). When lapses occur, we require a lapse-corrected observation function:

$$\begin{aligned} s &= (1-\lambda)\rho + \lambda\rho_0 \\ &= (1-\lambda)[(1-\rho_0)\delta + \rho_0] + \lambda\rho_0 \end{aligned} \tag{5.5b}$$

where the lapse rate is assumed to involve incidental aspects of either the experimental environment or the state of the subject. This distinction is important to keep in mind when, for example, we compute the expected success rate when $\lambda = 0.1$. In that case (and assuming $\rho_0 = 0.5$),we will expect to see a success rate of $s = 0.725$ instead of $s = 0.75$ in the data when the stimulus strength is at threshold (i.e., when $\delta = 0.5$).

Our background information regarding this problem contains three key assumptions: We assume that there are stimulus intensities that are too low to be detected, such that performance is necessarily at the level of blind guessing; we further assume the inverse, that there are stimulus intensities above which the stimulus is clearly detectable and performance is essentially perfect. Finally, we assume that between these two extremes performance changes smoothly, such that moving from higher to lower stimulus intensities impairs performance and *vice versa*. These three assumptions define a function relating stimulus strength and performance (percent correct) with the overall sigmoidal shape of a cumulative probability. Although any sigmoidal or ogival ('s'-shaped) function will do, the most commonly used of these is the cumulative Gaussian:

$$\delta = g_{Gauss}(\varsigma, \varsigma', \sigma) = \int_{-\infty}^{\varsigma} d\varsigma \left(\sigma\sqrt{2\pi}\right)^{-1} e^{-\frac{1}{2}\frac{[\varsigma-\varsigma']^2}{\sigma^2}} \tag{5.6a}$$

The Gaussian function is a computationally attractive option because its median (the threshold point we wish to measure), is encoded in the parameterization of (5.6a) as $\varsigma' = \varsigma$. If, however, we have additional information indicating that our stimulus strength parameter is an intensity variable (i.e., with a nonarbitrary zero point, such that zero on the intensity scale means no stimulus is present), then $\varsigma = 0$ will be the lower limit of the range of ς values (a property inconsistent with the cumulative Gaussian), and $\varsigma = 0$ will produce chance performance. In this circumstance the cumulative Weibull function is often used:

$$\delta = g_{Weibull}(t, A, B, C) = 1 - e^{-\left[\frac{t-A}{B}\right]^C} \tag{5.6b}$$

This parameterization of the Weibull, while it has an expression for the cumulative probability, does not have a single parameter that corresponds to the threshold

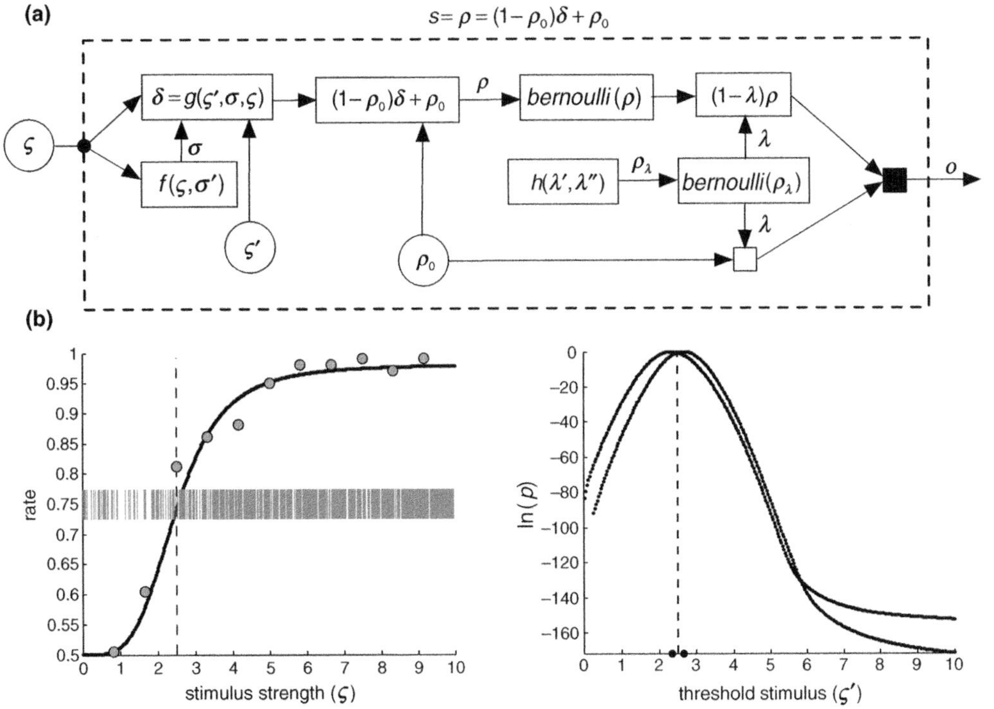

Figure 5.11 2AFC. (a) The output of the system is a binary choice that depends on the details of the experiment. Typical outputs are 'yes'/'no' or 'left'/'right' responses. Note that the lapse rate λ is presumably a function of both internal λ' and external λ'' distraction and other variables. The rate of choosing the responses coded as a 1 (ρ_0) is set internally. (b) Left-hand plot shows data simulated from the sigmoidal relationship between success rate and stimulus strength shown as circles (first dataset) and short vertical lines centered vertically in the plot (second dataset). Circles represent the ratio of correct responses to total trials at a single stimulus strength. Vertical lines represent correct (dark) and incorrect (light) responses, all at different stimulus strengths. (right) Log posterior plot depicting the threshold measurement. The two measurements are both quite close to the simulated value. True threshold is marked with a vertical dashed line in both plots.

(i.e., the median is at $\varsigma' = \boldsymbol{B}\sqrt[c]{log(2)}$). An alternative parameterization directly encodes the desired threshold, however:

$$\delta = g_{Weibull}(\varsigma, \varsigma', \sigma) = \int_0^{\varsigma} d\varsigma\,\sigma\,\varsigma'^{-\sigma}\,\varsigma^{\sigma-1} e^{-\left[\frac{\varsigma}{\varsigma'}\right]^{\sigma}} \tag{5.6c}$$

If the first parameterization were used, we would have to infer ς' via a coordinate transform performed on the joint posterior over (B,C). An alternative to the Weibull is the Fisk distribution, which has an expression for both its probability density[7] and cumulative density,

$$\delta = g_{Fisk}(\varsigma, \varsigma', \sigma) = \left[1 + \left(\tfrac{\varsigma}{\varsigma'}\right)^{-\sigma}\right]^{-1} \tag{5.6d}$$

[7] In the current parameterization (in which ς is the stimulus, ς' the threshold stimulus value, and σ a nuisance variable related to the shape and/or size of the distribution), the Fisk sampling distribution would be written $p(\varsigma|\varsigma' \cdot \sigma \cdot \iota) = \frac{\sigma}{\varsigma'}\left(\frac{\varsigma}{\varsigma'}\right)^{\sigma-1}\left[1 + \left(\frac{\varsigma}{\varsigma'}\right)^{\sigma}\right]^{-2}$.

We use a cumulative density function for (5.6) to model the transition in performance as stimulus intensity increases. As such, it is part of the theoretical signal function, not the noise model (our usual use for a probability function). Our background knowledge of this problem does, however, contain information relevant to assigning the noise model: For an experiment where the observed data look like (possibly biased) coin flips, the rate of successes is encoded in the binomial rate parameter. In this type of experiment, we assume the binomial rate parameter is equal to the theoretical rate of correct responding, s in the observation function (5.5). Thus, we assume that we are not dealing with a single 'coin', but rather a series of different coins – one for each value of the physical stimulus strength parameter. Our job is therefore to find the parameters of the cumulative Gaussian, Weibull, Fisk, etc. density function that predict binomial rate parameters at the stimulus strengths that best describe the observed rates of correct responding. This is a more complex problem than the previous examples of fitting a single best temperature measurement, single binomial rate, or difference of binomial rates. Here, instead of fitting data to the one or two parameters needed to define the observation model, we must fit our data to the pattern of rate parameters predicted by the sigmoidal shape of the cumulative Gaussian function of stimulus strength.

The probability of observing a given dataset (consisting of a string of 1s and 0s representing correct/incorrect responses for specific experimentally controlled stimulus strengths) is just the binomial sampling distribution, $p(\mathbf{d}|\varsigma \cdot s \cdot \imath)$, where the vector of expected binomial success rates, $\mathbf{s}$,is the signal defined in (5.5) for the vector of experimentally defined stimulus strength values, ς The likelihood of the three unknown variables is given in terms of the binomial sampling distribution. The usual form of the binomial likelihood can be used with the first dataset (and multiple observations are taken at each of a small set of stimulus strength values):

$$\begin{aligned}\mathcal{L}(\varsigma',\sigma,\lambda) &\propto p(\mathbf{d}|\varsigma \cdot [\varsigma' \cdot \sigma \cdot \rho_0 \cdot \lambda] \cdot \imath)\\ &= p(\mathbf{d}|\varsigma \cdot \mathbf{s} \cdot \imath)\\ &= \prod_i p(d_i|s_i \cdot \imath) \propto \prod_i s_i^{C_i}(1-s_i)^{N-C_i}\end{aligned}$$

where in the example dataset shown as circles in Figure 5.11b, the i index runs from 1 to 11 (and C represents the number of correct responses in $N = 101$ total responses for each stimulus). Note, however, that this form of the equation is just the result of taking the product of $s_i^{d_i}(1-s_i)^{1-d_i}$ for each of i data. Thus, when each observation occurs at a different stimulus strength, we write the likelihood:

$$\begin{aligned}\mathcal{L}(\varsigma',\sigma,\lambda) &\propto p(\mathbf{d}|\varsigma \cdot [\varsigma' \cdot \sigma \cdot \rho_0 \cdot \lambda] \cdot \imath)\\ &= p(\mathbf{d}|\varsigma \cdot \mathbf{s} \cdot \imath)\\ &= \prod_i p(d_i|s_i \cdot \imath) \propto \prod_i s_i^{d_i}(1-s_i)^{1-d_i}\end{aligned}$$

where in the second dataset the i index runs from 1 to 1111 (there are 1111 total observations, at 1111 possibly different stimulus strengths). In both equations the vector of stimulus strength values, ς, and the success rate when guessing, ρ_0, are known values.

Programming Aside: Complex Observation Functions in Threshold Detection (Fig. 5.11)

In this problem, more so than in many other examples so far, there are multiple parts to the solution to the measurement problem.

First, let us assume that we know the simulated lapse rate and shape parameter ($\lambda = 0.04$ and $\sigma = 4$). If these values are known, then the solution for the first dataset is, at base, just computing measurements for binomial rate constants; but whereas simply making 11 such measurements would not provide any conceptual difficulty, here the 11 rates are related by the underlying value of the sigmoid. If we were to draw a sigmoid with a median of 1 atop the circular data, the sigmoid would have an even sharper initial upturn and the rate constants predicted by this pattern would not match the 11 observed rates as well as if the median were closer to 2.5.

There are several steps to creating the plots in Figure 5.11b. First, we define a few constants:

```
load Sdat t1 d1
tlist=reshape(t2,101,11); tlist=tlist(1,:);
Nlist=sum(reshape(d2,101,11));
MT=linspace(0,10,302)'; MT=MT(2:end); Omt=ones(size(MT));
Ot=ones(size(Nlist)); ONL=Omt*Nlist;
```

We start the solution with the binomial likelihood, comparing data to a candidate rate constant:

```
L=@(Rin) ONL.*log(Rin)+(101-ONL).*log(1-Rin);
```

This equation requires the lapse-adjusted prediction of correct responding, s:

```
R=@(Din,Lin) (1-Lin)*(.5*Din+.5)+Lin*.5;
```

and this equation in turn requires the definition of the selected ogive δ:

```
D=@(Sin) 1./(1+((Omt*tlist)./(MT*Ot)).^-Sin);
```

We combine these in a loop that tests possible lapse rates (lambda), shape parameters (SP), and medians (MT):

```
SP=linspace(0,10,102); SP=SP(2:end); lambda=linspace(0,.1,101);
Lr=nan(301,101,21); %SP,MT,lambda
for nlambda=1:21,
    for nSP=1:101, Rnow=R(D(SP(nSP)),lambda(nlambda));
        Lr(:,nSP,nlambda)=sum(L(Rnow),2)-SP(nSP); end, end
LSr=logsum(Lr,3,diff(lambda(1:2)));
figure(7); mesh(SP,MT,exp(LSr-max(max(LSr)))); colormap bone
LSr=logsum(Lr,2:3,[diff(SP(1:2)) diff(lambda(1:2))]); LSr=LSr-max(LSr);
figure; plot(MT,LSr,'k.'); axis([min(MT) max(MT) min(LSr) 0])
MThat=logpeakval([LSr MT]); ind=findnearestN(MT,2.5,1);
hold on; plot(2.5*[1 1],[min(LSr) LSr(ind)],'k--','LineWidth',2)
ind=findnearestN(MT,MThat,1);
plot(MThat,min(LSr),'ko','MarkerFaceColor','k','MarkerSize',8)
```

The plotting at the end reproduces the measurement for the first dataset. The measurement for the second dataset is left as an exercise.

Now use a variant of the D function above to plot the sigmoid corresponding to the change in detection as stimulus strength increases:

```
D=@(MTnow,Sin) 1./(1+(tlist./MTnow).^-Sin);
figure; plot(tlist,D(MThat,SPhat),'k.');
```

which requires that you choose a shape parameter, SPhat. Test several and see how the result changes.

C. Assign Priors over Unknown Parameter Values

We will assume that the rate of correct responding for guesses (ρ_0) is one-half, and that the lapse rate is less than 0.1 (assigning a uniform prior over the [0,0.1) range). We will further assign a uniform prior over the unknown threshold value, and a Jeffreys prior over the unknown shape parameter σ.

D. Compute the Desired Measurement

We will analyze two datasets. In the first, the vector of stimulus strengths repeats; there are 101 repetitions of each tested contrast strength. In the second, there are no repetitions of stimulus strengths; each occurs only once in the experiment.

In the first experiment the data are numbers of successes in 101 repetitions at each of the 11 stimulus strengths. In the left-hand plot of Figure 5.11b the ratios of successes to number of trials is plotted along with a sigmoid showing the simulated relationship between stimulus strength and expected rate of correct responding. The right-hand plot shows the posterior distribution over the threshold parameter ς' associated with these data. For the first dataset (circles), it is easy to see how the data relate to the sigmoid (Fig. 5.11b, left) from inspecting the plot. However, both datasets are identical in terms of the *kind* of information they contain regarding threshold. The second dataset, however, makes it more difficult to verify that the sigmoid with the best-fit threshold parameter ς' passes close to the observed data, because the data do not visually correspond to proportions in the same way that they do in the first dataset. Nevertheless, the underlying relationship, and the analysis used to measure threshold, are the same in both cases.

Exercises

1) Dataset 1 is given as 11 rates, rate = S/N, and dataset 2 is an equal-length string of 1's and 0's. However, note that dataset 1 can also be decomposed to 1's and 0's, because the likelihood is the same whether data are combined into groups of $N > 1$ or not. Our initial analysis of dataset 1 used the binomial distribution [which takes (S,N) data] and our analysis of dataset 2 used the Bernoulli distribution [which takes (0,1) data]. Reanalyze dataset 1 using the Bernoulli distribution, and overlay the plots of your initial and reanalyzed measurement of the threshold parameter ς'.
2) Reanalyze both datasets using the cumulative Fisk (5.6d) instead of the cumulative Gaussian distribution as the underlying sigmoidal shape.
   a. Write the expression for the new likelihood.

   b. Write the expression for the marginal posterior over the threshold.
   c. Plot the posteriors over threshold.
3) Reanalyze either dataset using the cumulative Weibull (5.6d) instead of the cumulative Gaussian distribution as the underlying sigmoidal shape.
   a. Write the expression for the new likelihood.
   b. Write the expression for the joint posterior over the (B,C) parameters.
   c. Write the expression for the lossy transform necessary to convert the joint posterior over (B,C) into the marginal posterior over ς'.

5.3.7 Exponential Decay

There are many contexts in which the underlying model of our data contains an exponentially decaying observation function. There are three important parameters in these models. The first of these is the difference between the initial and final state of the system, which is often described as the amplitude of the decay. Related to this parameter are the initial and final states of the system, one of which is often known, and therefore the second of these states can be inferred via the relation, $A = |s_{init} - s_{final}|$. Finally, there is the decay rate, which describes how quickly the system travels from its initial to its final state. Of these three, either the amplitude or rate of decay is usually the parameter of interest in a scientific measurement.

Perhaps most commonly, exponential decay is used to model behavioral adaptation. Adaptation occurs when an organism is in a maladaptive state, either because it is making errors of some kind or because the state of its sensory systems are not tuned to its current environment. In the first case the organism will gradually adjust the parameters of its sensory and/or motor systems to correct errors, whereas in the second case the sensory systems that are poorly tuned to the environment will (if possible) adjust to become better able to extract environment information (images in the case of the visual system, sounds in the case of the auditory system, etc.).

In the typical adaptation experiment, there are at least the following two stages: First, an initial 'baseline' measurement is made so that the normal response of the system (motor, perceptual, cognitive subsystem, etc.) can be measured. Subsequent to baseline observations, a disturbance is introduced. In this 'adaptation stage,' the system of interest (again: motor, cognitive, etc.) responds to the disturbance. In many experiments there is also a post-adaptation or 'aftereffect stage' where the response of the system, while it returns to baseline, is also observed. Here, we will ignore the subtleties of the post-adaptation response, and concern ourselves only with a comparison of the adaptation and baseline phases of an experiment.

We will examine an example of each type of adaptation, one based on sensory-motor adaptation and one on dark adaptation, because the data and consequent analyses are quite different in the two cases.

Example: Sensory-Motor Adaptation

The classic example of sensory-motor adaptation is prism adaptation, which reach errors are introduced by placing a wedge prism in front of one eye (the other is patched or otherwise occluded); images of the external world created by light passing through the prism are shifted by an amount that depends on the refractive power of the prism. A typical experiment might proceed as follows: (a) a baseline level of reach accuracy is

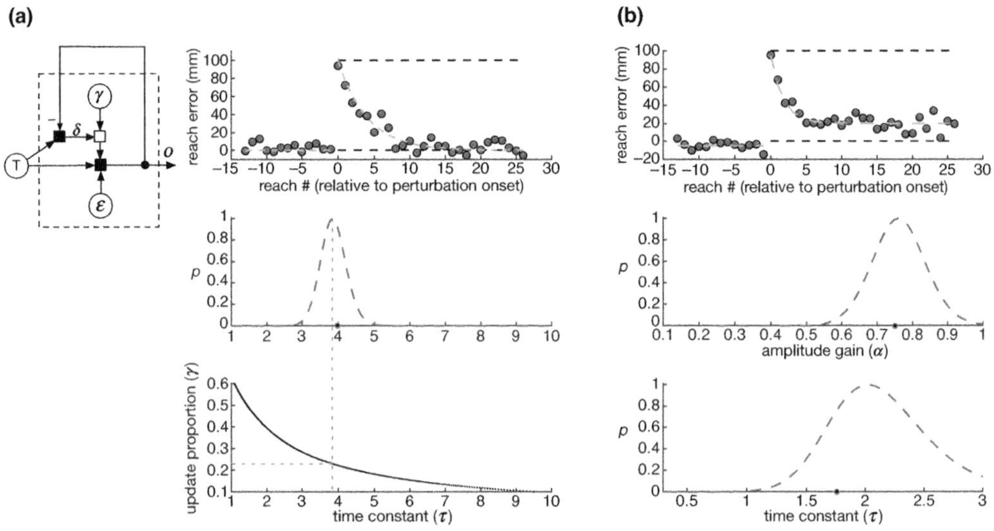

Figure 5.12 Sensory-motor adaptation. (a) The graphical model of sensory-motor adaptation shows corrective motor planning based on error feedback. Data simulated from this model (upper), and posterior over decay rate (middle) and the transform between correction and decay rate (lower). (b) Data simulated from a more complex version of adaptation, including incomplete adaptation (upper), and measurements of the extent (middle) and rate (lower) of adaptation.

measured by reaching normally (no prism) to targets presented on a screen, and then (b) the prism is placed in front of the eye and more reaches are made. Because the prism makes objects look shifted relative to their real-world locations, initial reaches will be inaccurate. Reaches become progressively more accurate after several exposures to visual feedback from one's errors while wearing the prism.

In the realm of sensory-motor adaptation, the relevant amplitude is the proportion of the movement error compensated by the nervous system in its asymptotically adapted state, and the time constant tells us how quickly maximal adaptation is achieved. We will first simulate sensory-motor adaptation experiment assuming unity adaptation gain, measuring the time constant of the adaptation (Fig. 5.12a), and then expand the example to measure both the amplitude gain and time constant when adaptation is incomplete and possibly biased (Fig. 5.12b).

A. Define the Posterior Distribution That Corresponds to the Desired Measurement

We will first explore a theoretically simplified model of sensory-motor adaptation described by the graphical model in Figure 5.12a. In this model, each error observed on one reach is used to create a correction in the reach plan for subsequent reaches. The correction is always a proportion (δ) of the reach error observed on the immediately previous reach. The reach error occurs maximally when the wedge prism is introduced into the eye's optics (introducing an error of known magnitude, A), and decays exponentially based on this correction mechanism

$$S = \begin{cases} 0 & 1 \leq t \leq T_b \\ Ae^{-[t-(T_b+1)]/\tau} & T_b < t \leq (T_b + T_p) \end{cases}$$

The two things to notice are: (1) There is a single unknown parameter, the time constant of the decay, τ. (2) The time constant is not the same as the proportion, δ (the function relating τ to δ is given in Figure 5.12a; see PA). The desired posterior is obtained by marginalizing over the dispersion parameter:

$$\begin{aligned} p(\tau|\boldsymbol{d}\cdot\iota) &= \int d\sigma\, p(\tau\cdot\sigma|\boldsymbol{d}\cdot\iota) \\ &\propto \int d\sigma\, \varpi(\tau\cdot\sigma)\mathcal{L}(\tau,\sigma) \\ &= \varpi(\tau)\int d\sigma\, \varpi(\sigma)\mathcal{L}(\tau,\sigma) \end{aligned}$$

where notice that the data term includes observations from both the baseline ($\boldsymbol{d}_b$) and perturbation ($\boldsymbol{d}_b$) phases of the experiment:

$$\boldsymbol{d} = (\boldsymbol{d}_b \cdot \boldsymbol{d}_p).$$

B. Define Observation and Noise Models and Their Interrelationships

The measurement, under the hypothesis that the underlying signal has this form, is made via the observation functions:

$$\begin{aligned} \boldsymbol{d}_b &= S_b + \epsilon_b = \epsilon_b \\ \boldsymbol{d}_b &= S_p + \epsilon_p = Ae^{-[t-(T_b+1)]/\tau} + \epsilon_p \end{aligned}$$

which, assuming Gaussian error probabilities for the $\epsilon = \boldsymbol{d} - \boldsymbol{s}$, enters the likelihood function by substituting the definition of errors within the Gaussian noise model from the data of each phase:

$$\begin{aligned} \mathcal{L}(\alpha,\tau,\beta,\sigma) &\propto \sigma^{-T_b} e^{-\frac{1}{2}\frac{\sum_{t=1}^{T_b}[\epsilon_b(t)]^2}{\sigma^2}} \sigma^{-T_p} e^{-\frac{1}{2}\frac{\sum_{t=T_b+1}^{T_b+T_p}[\epsilon_p(t)]^2}{\sigma^2}} \\ &= \sigma^{-(T_b+T_p)} e^{-\frac{1}{2}\frac{\sum_t[d_b(t)-sb(t)]^2}{\sigma^2}} e^{-\frac{1}{2}\frac{\sum_t[d_p(t)-sp(t)]^2}{\sigma^2}} \\ &= \sigma^{-(T_b+T_p)} e^{-\frac{1}{2}\frac{\sum_t[d_b(t)-0]^2}{\sigma^2}} e^{-\frac{1}{2}\frac{\sum_t[d_p(t)-Ae^{-[t-(T_b+1)]/\tau}]^2}{\sigma^2}}. \end{aligned}$$

Writing the likelihood for this example has an additional wrinkle: the observation function is different in the two different phases of the experiment, and the likelihood based on the full dataset must include separate terms for each phase.

C. Assign Priors over Unknown Parameter Values

There are two parameters in the likelihood function: we will make the conservative decision to use a Jeffreys prior over the unknown motor noise parameter, σ:

$$\varpi(\sigma) \propto \begin{cases} 0 & 0 \geq \sigma \geq 25 \\ \sigma^{-1} & 0 < \sigma < 25 \end{cases},$$

were the units are mm of error at the target. Individual differences here represent differences in manual dexterity, σ, and can range from as low as 3 or 4 mm to as high as 15 or 25 mm.

Next, we assign a prior to the time constant of the exponential adaptation function, τ. Without previous experimental data, the range of possibilities here is actually reasonably large. Sensory-motor adaptation appears to be used to adjust to changes in body morphology during childhood/adolescence, which is usually a slow process, on the order of months and years. For that reason, the time constant describing adaptation could be quite slow. On the other hand, we don't usually notice the various manifestations of adaptation (sensory, motor, and sensory-motor) that occur in our lives, which could indicate a faster timecourse. From these considerations, we might reasonably expect to see anything within the 4 log-unit range of $\tau = 0.1$ to $\tau = 1000$. However, by taking advantage of previous experimental results which show that sensory-motor adaptation is usually quit rapid in prism adaptation, we can assign a uniform prior restricted to the single log-unit range of $\tau = 1$ to $\tau = 10$:

$$\varpi(\tau) \propto \begin{cases} 0 & 1 \geq \tau \geq 10 \\ 1 & 1 < \tau < 10 \end{cases} .$$

D. Compute the Desired Measurement

The final posterior over adaptation gain will be based on the likelihood defined above, and includes both baseline and perturbation datasets:

$$p(\tau|\boldsymbol{d} \cdot \iota) \propto \varpi(\tau) \int d\sigma \varpi(\sigma) \mathcal{L}(\tau, \sigma) \propto \int d\sigma \sigma^{-(T_b+T_p+1)} e^{-\frac{1}{2}\frac{\sum_t [d_b(t)]^2}{\sigma^2}} e^{-\frac{1}{2}\frac{\sum_t [d_p(t) - Ae^{-[t-(T_b+1)]/\tau}]^2}{\sigma^2}}$$

plotted in Figure 5.12a.

Programming Aside: Measuring Exponentially Decaying Sensory-Motor Error (Fig.5.12)

```
%%% Sensory-Motor
%%%
%%%%%%%%%%%%%%%%%%
%%% Example 1 %%
%%% Create DATA
T=26; nTau=751; nSIG=201; t1=[-T/2:-1]'; t2=[0:T]';
A=100; tau=[4]; SD=7;

D1=SD*randn([T/2 1]);
D2pre=SD*randn([T+1 1]); D2pre=D2pre-mean(D2pre);
dprime=A*exp(-t2./tau);
D2=dprime+D2pre;

figure(1); clf;
subplot(2,1,1); hold on;
plot([0 T],A*[1 1],'k--','LineWidth',2)
plot([0 T],[0 0],'k--','LineWidth',2);
plot([t1; t2],[D1; D2],'ko','MarkerFaceColor',.4*[1 1 1],...
    'MarkerSize',10,'LineWidth',2.25);
plot(t1,zeros(1,T/2),'--','Color',.7*[1 1 1],'LineWidth',1.2);
plot(t2,dprime,'--','Color',.7*[1 1 1],'LineWidth',1.2);
axis([-15 30 -10 110])

Tlist=linspace(1,10,nTau+1); Tlist=Tlist(2:end);
L=zeros(nTau,nSIG);
Slist=linspace(0,25,nSIG+1); Slist=Slist(2:end);

fD2=A*[exp(-[t2*ones(1,nTau)]./[ones(T+1,1)*Tlist])];
D1now=D1; D2now=D2*ones(1,nTau);

for nSig=1:nSIG, Snow=Slist(nSig);
    L(:,nSig)=-(T+1)*log(Snow)-.5*(sum((D1now).^2)./Snow^2)...
        -.5*(sum((fD2-D2now).^2)./Snow^2); end
```

```
LT=logsum(L-max(max(L)),2,diff(Slist(1:2)));

%tau estimate
subplot(2,1,2); hold on
plot(Tlist,exp(LT-max(LT)),'--','Color',[.2 .4 .7],'LineWidth',2); axis([1 10 0 1.01])
LPVt=logpeakval([LT(:)-max(LT) Tlist(:)]);

%Convert Tau to Gamma
Ntrials=20;
gamma=linspace(.1,.6,501); tau=nan(size(gamma));
elist=1./linspace(1,10,1501); elist=elist(end:-1:1); es=exp(-[0:Ntrials]'*elist);
for n=1:length(gamma),
    err=ones(Ntrials+1,1); plot(0,err,'k.')
    for nn=2:(Ntrials+1),
        err(nn)=err(nn-1)-err(nn-1)*gamma(n); end
    %plot([0:Ntrials]',err,'ko');

    L=sum((err(:)*ones(1,length(elist))-es).^2,1);
    i=find(isnear(L,min(L)));
    tau(n)=1/mean(elist(i));
    %plot(0:Ntrials,es(:,i),'-')
end

figure(2); clf
subplot(2,1,2); hold on
plot(tau,gamma,'k.')

%%%%%%%%%%%%%%%%
%%% Example 2 %%
%%% Create DATA
T=26; nTau=91; nAlpha=351; nBeta=41; nSIG=101; t1=[-T/2:-1]'; t2=[0:T]';
A=100; alpha=[.75]; beta=[-.05]*A; tau=[1.75]; SD=7;

D1=beta+(SD*randn([T/2 1]));
D2pre=SD*randn([T+1 1]); D2pre=D2pre-mean(D2pre);
dprime=A*alpha.*exp(-t2./tau)+[A.*(1-alpha)]+beta;
D2=dprime+D2pre;

figure(3); clf;
subplot(2,1,1); hold on;
    plot([0 T],A*[1 1],'k--','LineWidth',2)
    plot([0 T],[0 0],'k--','LineWidth',2);
plot([t1; t2],[D1; D2],'ko','MarkerFaceColor',.4*[1 1 1],...
    'MarkerSize',10,'LineWidth',2.25);
plot(t1,beta*ones(1,T/2),'--','Color',.7*[1 1 1],'LineWidth',1.2);
plot(t2,dprime,'--','Color',.7*[1 1 1],'LineWidth',1.2);


Tlist=linspace(.3,3,nTau+1); Tlist=Tlist(2:end);
L=zeros(nAlpha,nBeta,nTau,nSIG);
Alist=linspace(.25,1.25,nAlpha)'; Slist=linspace(0,25,nSIG+1); Slist=Slist(2:end);
Blist=linspace(-.25*A,.25*A,nBeta)';


fD1=beta;
fD2=@(Anow,Bnow) Bnow+A*[1-Anow*(1-exp(-[t2*ones(1,nTau)]./[ones(T+1,1)*Tlist]))];
D1now=D1; D2now=D2*ones(1,nTau);
for nA=1:nAlpha, Anow=Alist(nA);
    for nB=1:nBeta, Bnow=Blist(nB);
        for nSig=1:nSIG, Snow=Slist(nSig);
            L(nA,nB,:,nSig)=-(T+1)*log(Snow)...
                -.5*(sum((fD1-D1now).^2)./Snow^2)...
                -.5*(sum((fD2(Anow,Bnow)-D2now).^2)./Snow^2); end, end, end
```

```
L2=logsum(L-max(max(max(max(L)))),[2 4],[diff(Blist(1:2)) diff(Slist(1:2))]);

%amplitude estimate
subplot(2,1,2); hold on
LA=logsum(L2-max(max(L2)),[2],[diff(Tlist(1:2))]);
plot(Alist,exp(LA-max(LA)),'--','Color',[.2 .4 .7],'LineWidth',2);
%axis([LPV+[-.1 .1] 0 1.01])
LPVa=logpeakval([LA-max(LA) Alist]); axis([.1 1 0 1.01])

%tau estimate
figure(4); clf
subplot(2,1,2); hold on
LT=logsum(L2-max(max(L2)),[1],[diff(Alist(1:2))]);
plot(Tlist,exp(LT-max(LT)),'--','Color',[.2 .4 .7],'LineWidth',2); axis([.3 3 0 1.01])
LPVt=logpeakval([LT(:)-max(LT) Tlist(:)]);
```

Notice that we have also converted our measurement of tau into a measurement of gamma, to relate our measurement to the graphical model of the adaptive response in Figure 5.12a.

This was a simplified version of an exponential decay, because the adaptive response fully corrected for the imposed prism perturbation. In a more complex scenario with incomplete correction, the signal may include an amplitude gain (α) describing the proportion of the perturbation that is ultimately corrected:

$$s = \begin{cases} 0 & 1 \leq t \leq T_b \\ (\alpha A)e^{-[t-(T_b+1)]/\tau} + \delta & T_b < t \leq (T_b + T_p) \end{cases},$$

and δ is the uncorrected portion of the prism shift ($\alpha A + \delta = A$) at asymptotic adapted performance. In addition, we make room for the possibility that there is a subject-specific bias (β) that affects all reaches, baseline and adaptive. This global bias will be included in the error term ϵ rather than in the definition of the underlying signal below, although this is not necessary (i.e., it may be included in the definition of the signal instead, without changing the final result of our analysis). Notice also that two of these are related exactly, through the relation ($\alpha A + \delta = A$), and therefore one (δ) may be removed from the probability statements.

$$\begin{aligned} p(\alpha|\boldsymbol{d}\cdot) &= \int d\sigma d\beta d\delta d\tau p(\alpha \cdot \tau \cdot \beta \cdot \sigma|\boldsymbol{d}\iota) \\ &\propto \int d\sigma d\beta d\delta d\tau \varpi(\alpha \cdot \tau \cdot \beta \cdot \sigma)\mathcal{L}(\alpha,\tau,\beta,\sigma) \\ &= \varpi(\alpha) \int d\sigma d\beta d\delta d\tau \varpi(\alpha \cdot \tau \cdot \beta \cdot \sigma)\mathcal{L}(\alpha,\tau,\beta,\sigma) \end{aligned}$$

and:

$$\begin{aligned} \mathcal{L}(\alpha,\tau,\beta,\sigma) &\propto \sigma^{-T_b} e^{-\frac{1}{2}\frac{\sum_{t=1}^{T_b}[\epsilon_b(t)]^2}{\sigma^2}} \sigma^{-T_p} e^{-\frac{1}{2}\frac{\sum_{t=T_b+1}^{T_b+T_p}[\epsilon_p(t)]^2}{\sigma^2}} \\ &= \sigma^{-(T_b+T_p} e^{-\frac{1}{2}\frac{\sum_t[d_b(t)-s_b(t)]^2}{\sigma^2}} e^{-\frac{1}{2}\frac{\sum_t[d_p(t)-s_p(t)]^2}{\sigma^2}} \end{aligned}$$

$$= \sigma^{-(T_b+T_p)} e^{-\frac{1}{2}\frac{\sum_t [d_b(t)-\beta]^2}{\sigma^2}} e^{-\frac{1}{2}\frac{\sum_t [d_p(t)-(\alpha A e^{-[t-(T_b+1)]/\tau}+\beta+\delta)]^2}{\sigma^2}}$$

$$= \sigma^{-(T_b+T_p)} e^{-\frac{1}{2}\frac{\sum_{t=1}^{T_b} [d_b(t)-\beta]^2}{\sigma^2}} e^{-\frac{1}{2}\frac{\sum_{t=T_b+1}^{T_b+T_p} [d_p(t)-(\beta+A[1-\alpha(1-e^{-[t-(T_b+1)]/\tau})])]^2}{\sigma^2}}$$

How did we deal with the redundant parameter (δ) in the observation function? We cannot simply delete this parameter from the observation function, but rather we must compute its exact value based on the combinations of its constituent variables, $\delta = (1-\alpha)A$, that are examined. It is this identity that yields the transition between the last two lines of the definition of the likelihood above.

In this expanded version of the example, the final posterior over adaptation gain will be based on the likelihood defined above, and includes both the baseline and perturbation datasets:

$$p(\alpha|\mathbf{d}\cdot\imath) = \varpi(\alpha)\int d\sigma\, d\beta\, d\delta\, d\tau\, \varpi(\tau\cdot\beta\cdot\sigma)\mathcal{L}(\alpha,\tau,\beta,\sigma)$$

$$\propto \int d\sigma\, d\beta\, d\delta\, d\tau\, \sigma^{-T_b+T_p+1} e^{-\frac{1}{2}\frac{\sum_t [d_b(t)-\beta]^2}{\sigma^2}} e^{-\frac{1}{2}\frac{\sum_t [d_p(t)-(\beta+A[1-\alpha(1-e^{-[t-(T_b+1)]/\tau})])]^2}{\sigma^2}}$$

Furthermore, an analogous posterior over adaptation rate can be easily derived:

$$p(\alpha|\mathbf{d}\cdot\imath) \propto \varpi(\alpha)\int d\sigma\, d\beta\, d\delta\, d\tau\, \varpi(\tau\cdot\beta\cdot\sigma)\mathcal{L}(\alpha,\tau,\beta,\sigma)$$

$$\propto \int d\sigma\, d\beta\, d\delta\, d\alpha\, \sigma^{-T_b+T_p+1} e^{-\frac{1}{2}\frac{\sum_t [d_b(t)-\beta]^2}{\sigma^2}} e^{-\frac{1}{2}\frac{\sum_t [d_p(t)-(\beta+A[1-\alpha(1-e^{-[t-(T_b+1)]/\tau})])]^2}{\sigma^2}},$$

and the plots of these posteriors and corresponding dataset are given in Figure 5.12b

Exercises

1) Explain how we relate τ and γ parameters in the code (Fig. 5.12a, bottom). How could we have written the observation model to directly measure γ with no intermediate measurement of τ?
2) Based on the code, what prior was used for the new α parameter? Why was this an appropriate / inappropriate choice?
3) Based on the code, what prior was used for the new β parameter? Why was this an appropriate / inappropriate choice?
4) Write a 1D marginal posterior for the β parameter, and plot it. How precisely is this variable measured? Change the size of β in the code and remeasure α and τ. Are these measurements affected by the size of β?
5) In the penultimate line of the derivation for the likelihood, $\mathcal{L}$, there is a sum of offsets, $\beta+\delta$. Normally, a sum of offsets would not be resolvable; we would not know what part of the data was caused by each element of this sum. Why can we separate these two offset terms in the current example?
6) In the above, all parameters are assessed simultaneously via the likelihood,

$$\mathcal{L}(\alpha,\tau,\beta,\sigma) \propto \sigma^{-T_b+T_p+1} e^{-\frac{1}{2}\frac{\sum_t [d_b(t)-s_b(t)]^2}{\sigma^2}} e^{-\frac{1}{2}\frac{\sum_t [d_p(t)-s_p(t)]^2}{\sigma^2}}.$$

a. Before making any computations, how would the final marginal posterior change if we had first measured the global error during the baseline phase of the experiment, and then subtracted this bias from perturbation-phase data before measuring the remaining parameters via the likelihood, $\mathcal{L}(\alpha, \tau, \sigma)$?
b. Expand the likelihood, $\mathcal{L}(\alpha, \tau, \sigma)$.
c. Assess the amplitude gain via this method, and compare the result to that computed above.

Example: Dark Adaptation

Another common source of exponentially decaying data arises from observing the change in a threshold, such as the threshold of light perception as one undergoes light or dark adaptation. This experiment type, although also making use of an exponentially decaying observation function, generates quite different data: binary yes/no data in the case of dark adaptation, as opposed to continuous error metrics in the case of sensory-motor adaptation. In addition, the dark adaptation experiment described above and a sensory-motor adaptation experiment differ in that the level of dark adaptation is controlled by a continuous time variable; adaptive responding increases to its maximum level after an exposure *duration*, rather than after a *number* of exposures to the stimulus as above.

A. Define the Posterior Distribution That Corresponds to the Desired Measurement

Figure 5.13a (right; solid line) reproduces the exponential shape of a typical dark adaptation curve (rods only). The disturbance corresponds simply to turning out the lights (at time t_0). At each of six time points following lights-out, the threshold light intensity required for detecting a short flash of light with variable intensity is measured. The exponential adaptation curve is based on a series of 2AFC data obtained at a set of six time points after t_0. These data are obtained by first keeping a subject in a brightly light environment for a fixed amount of time (e.g., 15 min). Thresholds are measured using two variable-intensity LEDs, one of which is activated and one not. At each of the six time points after t_0, four flashes are given (cued with an auditory beep, so that subjects know to guess which side the light was on). After the six time points, the subject sits in the bright light again for 15 min, and the sequence is repeated. Each cycle takes 45 min (15 min in the light, 30 min for 2AFC trials), and 12 cycles yield 48 data at each time point (the preadaptation threshold can be measured by turning out the lights, and immediately presenting the 2AFC trial). Those data yield the Fisk-based medians (thresholds) shown in Figure 5.13a; those medians in turn yield our measurement of the exponential dark-adaptation curve.

Thus, to obtain the desired posterior over the time-constant of adaptation (τ), we compute

$$\begin{aligned}
p(\tau|\boldsymbol{d}\cdot\boldsymbol{\Delta t}\cdot\iota) &= \int d\boldsymbol{\sigma}\, d\boldsymbol{I}'p(\boldsymbol{I}'\cdot\boldsymbol{\sigma}\cdot\tau|\boldsymbol{d}\cdot\boldsymbol{\Delta t}\cdot I_0'\cdot I_\infty'\cdot\iota)\\
&\propto p(\tau|\boldsymbol{\Delta t}\cdot I_0'\cdot I_\infty'\cdot\iota)\int d\boldsymbol{\sigma}\, d\boldsymbol{I}'p(\boldsymbol{I}'\cdot\boldsymbol{\sigma}|\tau\cdot\boldsymbol{\Delta t}\cdot I_0'\cdot I_\infty'\cdot\iota)p(\boldsymbol{d}|\tau\cdot\boldsymbol{I}'\cdot\boldsymbol{\sigma}\cdot\boldsymbol{\Delta t}\cdot I_0'\cdot I_\infty'\cdot\iota)\\
&\propto p(\tau|I_0'\cdot I_\infty'\cdot\iota)\int d\boldsymbol{\sigma}\, p(\boldsymbol{\sigma}|\iota)\int d\boldsymbol{I}'p(\boldsymbol{I}'|\tau\cdot\boldsymbol{\Delta t}\cdot I_0'\cdot I_\infty'\cdot\iota)p(\boldsymbol{d}|\boldsymbol{I}'\cdot\boldsymbol{\sigma}\cdot\iota)\\
&\propto \varpi(\tau)\int d\boldsymbol{\sigma}\,\varpi(\boldsymbol{\sigma})\int d\boldsymbol{I}'\mathcal{L}(\tau)\mathcal{L}(\boldsymbol{I}',\boldsymbol{\sigma})
\end{aligned}$$

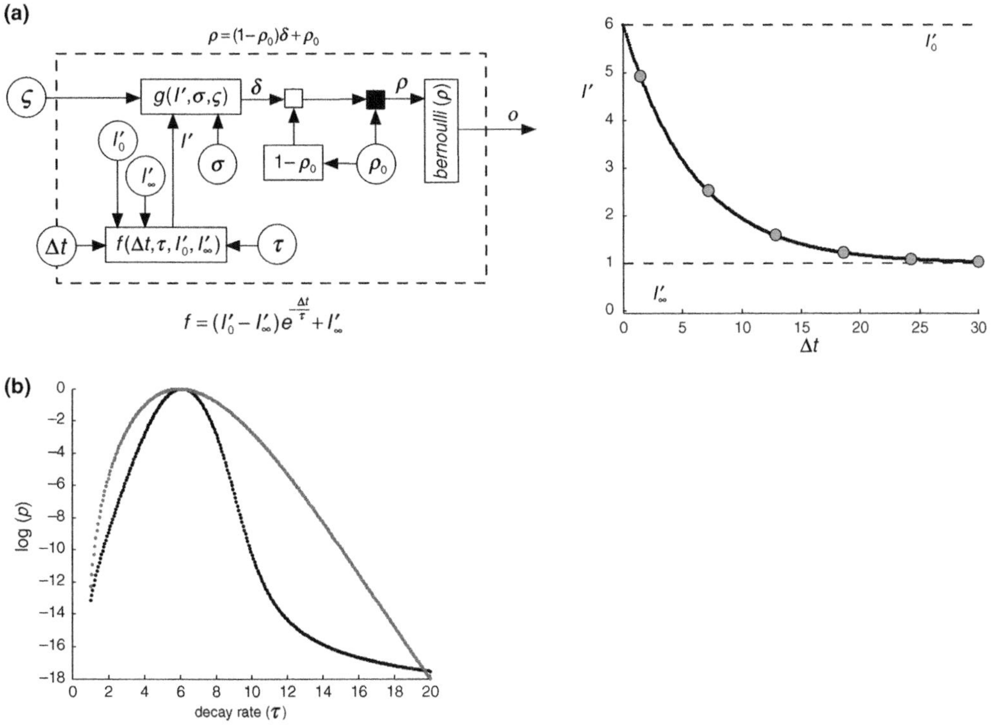

Figure 5.13 Dark adaptation. (a) Graphical model (left) and theoretical and simulated data (right) for dark adaptation. (b) Measurement of decay rate based on threshold data from both uniformly spaced light intensities (wider distribution) and adaptively chosen light intensities (narrower distribution).

where the first integral has a vector of six intensity thresholds based on six datasets each at its own time point, and could be expanded and written

$$\int d\sigma\, d\boldsymbol{I}' p(\boldsymbol{I}' \cdot \boldsymbol{\sigma} \cdot \tau | \boldsymbol{d} \cdot \boldsymbol{\Delta t} \cdot I'_0 \cdot I'_\infty \cdot \iota)$$
$$= \int dI'_1 dI'_2 \ldots dI'_7 \int d\sigma_1 \ldots d\sigma_7 p([(I'_1 \cdot \sigma_1) \cdot \ldots \cdot (I'_7 \cdot \sigma_7)] \cdot \tau | [\boldsymbol{d}_1 \cdot \cdots \cdot \boldsymbol{d}_7] \cdots [\Delta t_1 \cdot \ldots \cdot \Delta t_7] \cdot I'_0 \cdot I'_\infty \cdot \iota)$$

Notice also that the final line of the posterior contains a term for the likelihood over decay rate, $\mathcal{L}(\tau)$. This likelihood is $\mathcal{L}(\tau) = p(\boldsymbol{I}'|\tau, \boldsymbol{\Delta t}, I'_0, I'_\infty, \iota)$, which could also have been written as the prior over threshold intensity. $\varpi(\boldsymbol{I}') = p(\boldsymbol{I}'|\tau \cdot \boldsymbol{\Delta t} \cdot I'_0 \cdot I'_\infty \cdot \iota)$. This is true by definition, in that a sampling distribution $p(d|x \cdot \iota)$ is always also interpretable as the prior probability of the data.

This posterior marginalizes over the threshold-intensity (I'_1) axes of the 13-D posterior distribution, $p(\boldsymbol{I}' \cdot \boldsymbol{\sigma} \cdot \tau | \boldsymbol{d} \cdot \boldsymbol{\Delta t} \cdot I'_0 \cdot I'_\infty \cdot \iota)$. Notice there is an added wrinkle in this posterior relative to previous examples. The threshold intensity values are an intermediate measurement based on the raw datasets ($\boldsymbol{d}_i$) of correct/incorrect responses at each time point (i). As such, their exact values are marginalized out of the final measurement of the time-constant of adaptation (τ). So while the desired posterior $p(\tau|\boldsymbol{d} \cdot \boldsymbol{\Delta t} \cdot I'_0 \cdot I'_\infty \cdot \iota)$ looks very similar to posteriors from previous examples, raw data here tell us about threshold intensities, and those intensities in turn tell us about the parameter of interest, τ.

B. Define Observation and Noise Models and Their Interrelationships

The graphical model representing dark adaptation is shown in Figure 5.13a (left). Each noiseless datum is a theoretical threshold (from the exponential dark-adaptation curve) from which we simulate success-rate data. Simulated data from each threshold intensity is based on the Fisk distribution, because there is a true zero point at which the light intensity is zero. The description of this model should sound familiar. It is the threshold detection model from the previous subsection, but with a threshold measurement as the first tier of a two-tier process. In the first tier, we have threshold detection at each time point. This model is presented again here with the variable names updated for the current problem:

$$\delta_{ij} = g(I_{ij}, I_i, \sigma) = \left[(1 + \frac{I_{ij}}{I_i})^{-\sigma_i} \right]^{-1}$$

where the δ_{ij} define the sigmoidal shape that describes the transition in the rate of correct internal responses in 2AFC trials from 0 to 1, the σ variable controls the rate and shape of that transition, the I'_i variable is the threshold at the Δt_i delay, and the I_{ij} are the intensity levels tested experimentally in the ith condition. This correct response rate, in conjunction with the rate of correct guessing ($\rho = 0.5$), yields the rate of correct responding predicted at the experimentally tested light intensities:

$$s_{ij} = (1 - \rho_0)\delta_{ij} + \rho_0$$

At each level of dark adaptation, this function's parameters will change because the threshold term will change (second tier of the process), and the tested intensity levels I_{ij} at each of the Δt_i will also change. At each level of dark adaptation, the theoretically predicted threshold for detecting light in our 2AFC experiment will change as a decaying exponential function of duration in the dark, the time constant of adaptation (τ), and the unadapted and fully adapted thresholds (I'_0 and I'_∞, respectively):

$$I'_i = f(\Delta t_i, \tau, I'_0, I'_\infty) = (I'_0 - I'_\infty)e^{\frac{\Delta t}{\tau}} + I'_\infty$$

where each level of dark adaptation is indexed by i. Note that, because our experimental protocol includes an auditory cue to each 2AFC trial, lapse trials are extremely unlikely in this experiment. For that reason, we use the non-lapse-corrected likelihood for threshold detection:

$$\begin{aligned} \mathcal{L}(I'_i) &\propto p(\boldsymbol{d}|\boldsymbol{I}' \cdot \boldsymbol{\sigma} \cdot \iota) \\ &= p(\boldsymbol{d}_i|\boldsymbol{s} \cdot \iota) \\ &= \prod_i p(d_{ij}|s_{ij} \cdot \iota) \propto \prod_j s_{ij}^{d_{ij}}(1 - s_{ij})^{1-d_{ij}} \end{aligned}$$

where the data are the correct/incorrect responses (coded as 1, 0, respectively). This yields 6 likelihoods over threshold. The second tier of the analysis combines the τ -likelihoods based on each sextet of threshold intensities:

$$\begin{aligned} \mathcal{L}(\tau) &\propto p(\boldsymbol{I}'|\boldsymbol{\Delta t} \cdot I'_0 \cdot I'_\infty \cdot \iota) \\ &= \prod_i p(I'_i|\tau \cdot \Delta t_i \cdot I'_0 \cdot I'_\infty \cdot \iota). \end{aligned}$$

Thus the second tier represents the relationship between threshold in the first tier and the unknown decay constant, τ.

C. Assign Priors over Unknown Parameter Values

We will make the following simplifying assumptions in this problem: We will suppose that the thresholds T_0 and T_∞ are known, and equal to 6 and 1, respectively. These numbers are in arbitrary intensity units indicating that there is a 5-dB decrease in threshold intensity from T_0 to T_∞ (i.e., five log-units of intensity), and will help in defining priors over intensity thresholds.

In addition to our prior over intensity thresholds, we will also need to define priors for the decay rate constant τ, and for the Fisk shape parameter, δ. Given that our background information tells us that threshold decays 5 log-units over about half an hour, a decay constant of one minute would make no sense (adaptation would be complete in only a few min, not approximately 30), as would a decay constant of 20 min (the decrease in threshold would be nowhere near the total 5 log-unit drop by the end of a 30 min experiment). Thus, we will define a uniform prior over this range of values. We will also define a uniform prior over the possible shape parameters, from 1 to 10 (as in the previous example problem).

At this point, the only remaining unknowns in the model are the six threshold intensity values themselves. We will assign a uniform prior over these values, bounded between I'_0 and I'_∞.

$$\varpi(I') \propto \begin{cases} 0 & I'_\infty \geq I' \geq I'_0 \\ 1 & I'_\infty < I' < I'_0 \end{cases} .$$

The above would be fine if we were fitting only a single threshold intensity, and there were no constraints on those the unknown thresholds imposed by τ. However, we must also define the joint prior over the six unknown thresholds:

$$\varpi(I'_1 \cdot I'_2 \cdot \ldots \cdot I'_6 | I'_0 \cdot I'_\infty) = \varpi(I'_1 | I'_0 \cdot I'_\infty)\varpi(I'_2 | I'_1 \cdot I'_\infty) \ldots \varpi(I'_6 | I'_5 \cdot I'_\infty) \cdot$$

which defines a nonindependent joint prior. The probabilities in this joint prior are not independent because we have additional information in this problem that narrows the possible combinations of thresholds. In particular, while all thresholds measured in this experiment must be bounded by I'_0 to I'_∞, they are also bounded by one another: for the jth threshold, its value must be less than the j-1th threshold. Thus:

$$\varpi(I'_j) \propto \begin{cases} 0, & I'_\infty \geq I'_j \geq I'_{j-1} \\ 1, & I'_\infty < I'_j < I'_{j-1} \end{cases}$$

which states that there are segments of the range I'_0 to I'_∞ where the prior is zero.

Indeed, our prior information is even more precise than this, because there is an additional constraint imposed by the τ parameter: we know, in that it is part of the background information of this example, that the shape of the timecourse of dark adaptation is a decaying exponential. Thus, the threshold values at each time point must match the

Programming Aside: Dark Adaptation (Fig. 5.13)

This problem would be essentially impossible using the 'brute-force' method of computing probability distributions we have so far been using, if it were not for the massive computational simplification afforded us by our prior information, as encoded by the indicator function, $I(I'_i = h)$.

The first step is to load the dataset. There are two datasets. In the first, experimental light intensities used to measure threshold at each time-duration are chosen between the minimum and maximum thresholds as defined by our background information. In the second dataset, light intensities are chosen adaptively (so that if a correct response is given for one intensity, the next trial will try a lower intensity, and vice versa). You should try both.

```
load darkdatU %uniform light intensities
load darkdatA %adaptively chosen light intensities
```

The next step is to define the relevant functions. We will need a function to describe the exponentially decaying thresholds (f), a function to compute the correct-responding rates for a given underlying threshold (R), and a function to compute the log-posterior (L) associated with each possible tau value.

```
f=@(taunow) 5*exp(-Dt/taunow)+1;
R=@(Ivec,Ihat,Sin) .5./(1+(Ivec./Ihat).^-Sin)+.5;
L=@(Rin,Din) sum(Din.*log(Rin)+(1-Din).*log(1-Rin));
```

The next step is to define the list of tau and shape parameters to examine, and compute the log-probability of the result.

```
SP=linspace(0,10,102); SP=SP(2:end);
tau=linspace(1,20,303);
LT=nan(length(tau),length(SP),6);
for nT=1:length(tau), Iguess=f(tau(nT));
    for n=1:6, for nSP=1:length(SP), SPnow=SP(nSP);
            Rnow=R(Idat(:,n),Iguess(n),SPnow);
            LT(nT,nSP,n)=L(Rnow,dat(:,n)); end, end, end
```

Notice that the loop above defines tau and the 6-element Iguess vector before cycling through possible shape parameters for each time-duration. This is part of the simplification that the indicator function affords us. If we had not used this simplification, we would have had to examine a range of possible thresholds for each time-duration independently, and there would have been six for-loops, one for each of the possible thresholds at each time-duration. Finally, the combination of these would be compared to the tau values predicted by each possible combination of thresholds.

To plot the marginalized log-posterior, we first take the product of probabilities across the 6 timedurations (sum of the log of the last dimension of the LT matrix), and then marginalize over the unknown shape parameter values (logsum of the second dimension).

```
figure; LS=logsum(sum(LT,3),2,[diff(SP(1:2))]);
plot(tau,LS-max(LS),'k.'); box off
figure; hold on; box off
tauhat=logpeakval([LS(:) tau(:)]);
plot([0 30],6*[1 1],'k--','LineWidth',1.8)
plot([0 30],1*[1 1],'k--','LineWidth',1.8)
```

```
plot(dt,5*exp(-dt/tauhat)+1,'k.','LineWidth',2);
plot(Dt,Iprime,'ko','MarkerFaceColor',.6*[1 1 1],'MarkerSize',15,'LineWidth',2);
axis([-.05 30.05 -.05 6.05])
```

values predicted by the decaying exponential model:

$$\varpi(I'_j) = p(I'_j|\tau \cdot \mathbf{\Delta t} \cdot I'_0 \cdot I'_\infty \cdot \iota) \propto \begin{cases} 0 & I'_j \neq (I'_\infty - I'_0)e^{-\Delta t_j/\tau} + I'_\infty) \\ 1 & I'_j = (I'_\infty - I'_0)e^{-\Delta t_j/\tau} + I'_\infty) \end{cases}$$

which can be written as an indicator function $\mathbf{I}(I'_j = h)$ that takes the value 1 when $I'_j = h[\Delta t_j, \tau] = (I'_\infty - I'_0)e^{-\Delta t_j/\tau} + I'_\infty)$, and 0 otherwise.

This example problem is important to understand for this fact alone: thinking carefully about the prior truly matters, both for a reasonable final measurement and also because it can lead to shorter computation times. As we will see in the final subsection when we compute the posterior, we will write a script for this measurement that takes advantage of the simplification provided by our prior information. If we had not noticed this aspect of the problem, and attempted to solve it without taking advantage of the ranges of parameter space that our prior information tells us must be equal to zero, we would have to search ~27 trillion possible combinations of threshold intensities and decay rates (assuming we segmented the range of intensities into only 31 possibilities – which is a rather coarse division). Instead we will need examine only ~180 thousand threshold combinations. Notice also that there would be no way to take advantage of this information without programming our own custom analysis. This example problem is on the border between basic and intermediate (its analysis requires about ten lines of code, as we see below), and yet we have already far outstripped the capabilities of any statistical software package: imagine the disadvantage you would be at in your own work if you could not program a custom analysis of this type!

D. Compute the Desired Measurement

To make a measurement of the timecourse of changes in light-detection thresholds we will need an expression that relates possible thresholds and decay rates. This is encoded in the posterior, and includes the indicator function defined in the prior over possible threshold intensities, uniform priors over possible shape parameter values (σ) and possible decay rate constants (τ), and the likelihood functions for threshold intensity and decay rate:

$$\begin{aligned} p(\tau|\mathbf{d} \cdot \mathbf{\Delta t} \cdot I'_0 \cdot I'_\infty \cdot \iota) &= \int d\boldsymbol{\sigma}\, d\mathbf{I}' p(\mathbf{I}' \cdot \boldsymbol{\sigma} \cdot \tau|\mathbf{d} \cdot \mathbf{\Delta t} \cdot I'_0 \cdot I'_\infty \cdot \iota) \\ &= \int d\boldsymbol{\sigma}\, d\mathbf{I}' p(\mathbf{I}' \cdot \boldsymbol{\sigma}|\mathbf{d} \cdot \mathbf{\Delta t} \cdot I'_0 \cdot I'_\infty \cdot \iota) p(\tau|\mathbf{I}' \cdot \mathbf{d} \cdot \mathbf{\Delta t} \cdot I'_0 \cdot I'_\infty \cdot \iota) \\ &\propto \varpi(\tau) \int d\boldsymbol{\sigma}\, d\mathbf{I}' \varpi(\mathbf{I}', \boldsymbol{\sigma}|\tau) \mathcal{L}(\mathbf{I}', \boldsymbol{\sigma}) \mathcal{L}(\tau) \\ &\propto \varpi(\tau) \int d\sigma_1 d\sigma_2 \ldots d\sigma_6 \prod_i I(I'_i = h) \left[\prod_j s_{ij}^{d_{ij}} (1 - s_{ij})^{1-d_{ij}}\right] \end{aligned}$$

where the indicator function obviates the need to marginalize over the unknown threshold intensities (integration over an unknown parameter value occurs when there are several possible values a parameter can take – here, there is only one such value consistent with a given Δt_i and τ), and the unknown Fisk shape parameter (σ) is marginalized separately for each Δt value. The values of the S_{ij} are encoded in the six separate functions (indexed by i):

$$s_{ij} = (1 - \rho_0)\left[1 + \left(\frac{I_{ij}}{I'_i}\right)^{-\sigma_i}\right]^{-1} + \rho_0$$

where the ith function differs by the the I'_i value, as dictated by the value of τ. The posterior over possible τ values is shown in Figure 5.13b.

Exercises

1) Write the set of for-loops that would have been necessary to analyze these data if we had not simplified the analysis using our prior information. Without running the set of loops, calculate the exact number of loop cycles (revisitations of the innermost loop) would be required to run this version of the analysis.
2) Compute the variance of the decay-rate estimate derived from uniformly spaced light intensities (during threshold measurements) and from adaptively chosen light intensities. Given this level of improvement, is there any reason (downside) to designing an experiment using the adaptive technique? Describe at least one such reason.
3) Describe how you would analyze the data if you had been given measured threshold data instead of correct rates of responding in the 2AFC experiment.
   a. Write a posterior for this analysis.
   b. Expand the likelihood term of the posterior.
   c. Was it still possible to use the prior information to avoid marginalizing over unknown intensity threshold values?
   d. Did you have to make any assumptions to expand the likelihood term? Explain.
4) Find a power function that has nearly the same shape as the exponential decay in Figure 5.13a.
   a. Write a posterior for the analysis in which you are given threshold data, but based on a power function instead of the exponential function.
   b. How does this change the likelihood term?

5.4 Multiple-Source Measurements

When one has multiple sources of data, the question arises as to how these datasets should be combined. The simplest version of this problem occurs when, in a single behavioral experiment performed by a single experimenter, data from several subjects using the same experimental protocol are collected. The data obtained from each source, where here each subject is a different source, are usually combined with other sources by simply averaging the data. In the present section we will examine this and several other ways of combining data across sources for the purpose of measurement. We will see that there are cases where this averaging procedure produces the desired result, but in most cases it does not. We will offer a general procedure that can be used when combining data across multiple data sources, and examine several examples of its use.

5.4.1 Central Problem of Multiple-Source Measurement

The goal of measurement is to determine the best-guess numerical values of one or more theoretically interesting parameters of an observation model. The central problem of making these measurements is that data are often both noisy and expensive. In behavioral research, the cost may come in the form of experimental animals; in this case, it is often more likely that many data will be collected from a small set of animals. In research with human subjects the situation can be the exact opposite, it is relatively easy to get undergraduates to participate for a short behavioral experiment, but difficult to get participants where data must be collected over long periods of time or during multiple sessions. In addition, the presence of within-source variation means that measurements from a single experimental subject (person/animal) may not be representative of all such subjects, and measurements from multiple sources may need to be combined to obtain a more representative overall measurement (across individuals). In cases where it is either more experimentally expeditious, or necessary for the measurement to collect data from multiple sources, these techniques and considerations will become significant.

The important question to ask regarding multiple-source measurements is: why can't we simply treat the set of N sources as one 'supersource' with N times the data of any of the single sources? The short answer is that we could, if all N sources were identical in every way; to the extent that they are not, we must understand those differences to properly take account of them in our analysis. The fact that different sources will be identical in certain respects, but stably different in others is depicted in Figure 5.2c. All sources receive the same physical stimulation, X. Furthermore, all sources process incoming stimulation via the same function, f. The output of this function also relies on two sets of internal parameters, $\boldsymbol{\vartheta}$ and $\boldsymbol{\theta}_i$. The first set of parameters, $\boldsymbol{\vartheta}$, share the same values in all sources. The second set of parameters, $\boldsymbol{\theta}_i$, have source-specific values for the ith source. If there were no source-specific parameters, it would be possible to treat data from the N sources as if it came from a single source. However, the presence of source-specific $\boldsymbol{\theta}_i$ parameters suggests data from different sources will be observed to have a different character.

When there are both source-specific and source-independent (group-level) parameters in a multi-source measurement, calculation of the posterior proceeds in two stages. First we must marginalize over the unknown values of any source-specific parameters before we combine the posterior distributions from different sources. For example, if there were a single source-specific parameter θ_i and a single group-level parameter ϑ, the posterior would be:

$$\begin{aligned}
p(\vartheta|\boldsymbol{D}\cdot\iota) &= p(\vartheta|\boldsymbol{d}_1\cdot\ldots\cdot\boldsymbol{d}_N\cdot\iota)\\
&= \int d\theta_1\ldots d\theta_N p(\vartheta\cdot\theta_1\cdot\ldots\cdot\theta_N|\boldsymbol{d}_1\cdot\ldots\cdot\boldsymbol{d}_N\cdot\iota)\\
&\propto \int d\theta_1\ldots d\theta_N p(\vartheta\cdot\theta_1\cdot\ldots\cdot\theta_N|\iota)p(\boldsymbol{d}_1\cdot\ldots\cdot\boldsymbol{d}_N|\vartheta\cdot\ldots\cdot\theta_N\cdot\iota)\\
&= p(\vartheta|\iota)\int d\theta_1\ldots d\theta_N p(\theta_1|\iota)p(\boldsymbol{d}_1|\vartheta\cdot\theta_1\cdot\iota)\ldots p(\theta_N|\iota)p(\boldsymbol{d}_N|\vartheta\cdot\theta_N\cdot\iota)\\
&= \varpi(\vartheta)\int d\theta_1\varpi(\theta_1)\mathcal{L}(\theta_1,\vartheta)\ldots\int d\theta_N\varpi(\theta_N)\mathcal{L}(\theta_N,\vartheta)\\
&= \varpi(\vartheta)\prod_i\mathcal{L}_i(\vartheta) = \varpi(\vartheta)\mathcal{L}(\vartheta)
\end{aligned}$$

where $\mathcal{L}_1(\vartheta), \mathcal{L}_2(\vartheta) \ldots \mathcal{L}_N(\vartheta)$ are the ϑ likelihoods obtained from the datasets $\boldsymbol{d}_1, \boldsymbol{d}_2 \ldots \boldsymbol{d}_N$, respectively. On the penultimate line we marginalize the products of 2d likelihoods $\mathcal{L}(\theta_i, \vartheta)$ (one derived from each dataset) and priors over the source-specific parameter (one copy of $\varpi(\theta_i)$ per source). This marginalization yields N marginal likelihoods $[\mathcal{L}_1(\vartheta), \mathcal{L}_2(\vartheta) \ldots \mathcal{L}_N(\vartheta)]$, one derived from each dataset, over just the remaining group-level parameter, ϑ. The product of these source-specific likelihoods, now all over a single 1d parameter $[\mathcal{L}_1(\vartheta)\mathcal{L}_2(\vartheta) \ldots \mathcal{L}_N(\vartheta)]$, yields a single group-level likelihood over that parameter $[\mathcal{L}(\vartheta)]$. The desired posterior is this group-level likelihood multiplied by the prior over the group-level parameter:

$$
\begin{aligned}
p(\vartheta|\boldsymbol{D} \cdot \imath) &\propto \varpi(\vartheta)\mathcal{L}(\vartheta) \\
&= p(\vartheta|\imath)p(\boldsymbol{d}_1 \cdot \ldots \cdot \boldsymbol{d}_N|\vartheta \cdot \imath) = \varpi(\vartheta)\mathcal{L}_1(\vartheta)\mathcal{L}_2(\vartheta) \ldots \mathcal{L}_N(\vartheta)
\end{aligned}
$$

We will see below the details of accounting for these source-specific differences in two examples. The first is a multiple-source version of the basic transparent measurement, and the second is a variant of the previous dark adaptation example using data from multiple sources.

Exercises

1) Why are multiple-source measurements different from single-source measurement?
2) Describe in words the important marginalization that is allows us to combine data for multiplesource measurements.
3) Give a mock example of the type of scenario that constitutes a multiple-source measurement, and write the probability expression for the posterior.

5.4.2 Multiple Sources: Transparent I

The critical element of combining data from multiple sources is to identify those parameters of the observation and error models that are, based on our background information about the problem, identical across sources and those that are expected to display source-specific variation.

Example: All Body Temperature Parameters Assumed Equal

The prototypical case of multiple sources involves an experiment where we have collected data from multiple experimental subjects, where all experimental parameters are identical for all subjects; this is analogous to observing body temperature readings from multiple thermometers. It is only sensible to combine data across sources if each source's data provides information regarding *the same* parameter or set of parameters. If the experiment involved auditory localization or the cocktail party effect and one of the experimental subjects was hearing impaired, it would make no sense to include that subject's data because there are good reasons to think the data from that subject may provide a different *kind* of information about localization relative to the remaining subjects. By the same token, we can only combine probability distributions over the same parameters, and must always first marginalize separately over the source-specific parameters of the observation model before we can combine probability distributions corresponding to the source-independent parameters of the model

A. Define the Posterior Distribution That Corresponds to the Desired Measurement
The multi-source posterior over μ for the transparent (temperature) measurement with *no* source-specific parameters is:

$$\begin{aligned} p(\mu|\boldsymbol{D}\cdot\iota) &= p(\mu|\boldsymbol{d}_1\cdot\boldsymbol{d}_2\cdot\ldots\cdot\boldsymbol{d}_N\cdot\iota) \\ &= \int d\sigma p(\mu\cdot\sigma|\boldsymbol{d}_1\cdot\ldots\cdot\boldsymbol{d}_N\cdot\iota) \\ &\propto \int d\sigma p(\mu\cdot\sigma|\iota)p(\boldsymbol{d}_1\cdot\ldots\cdot\boldsymbol{d}_N|\mu\cdot\sigma\cdot\iota) \\ &= p(\mu|\iota)\int d\sigma p(\sigma|\iota)p(\boldsymbol{d}_1\cdot\ldots\cdot\boldsymbol{d}_N|\mu\cdot\sigma\cdot\iota) \\ &= p(\mu|\iota)\int d\sigma p(\sigma|\iota)p(\boldsymbol{d}_1|\mu\cdot\sigma\cdot\iota)\ldots p(\boldsymbol{d}_N|\mu\cdot\sigma\cdot\iota) \\ &= \varpi(\mu)\int d\sigma\,\varpi(\sigma)\prod\nolimits_i \mathcal{L}_i(\sigma,\mu) = \varpi(\mu)\mathcal{L}(\mu) \end{aligned}$$

and the analogous posterior over σ is:

$$\begin{aligned} p(\sigma|\boldsymbol{D}\cdot\iota) &= p(\sigma|\boldsymbol{d}_1\cdot\boldsymbol{d}_2\cdot\ldots\cdot\boldsymbol{d}_N\cdot\iota) \\ &= \int d\mu p(\mu\cdot\sigma|\boldsymbol{d}_1\cdot\ldots\cdot\boldsymbol{d}_N\cdot\iota) \\ &\propto p(\sigma|\iota)\int d\mu p(\mu|\iota)p(\boldsymbol{d}_1|\mu\cdot\sigma\cdot\iota)\ldots p(\boldsymbol{d}_N|\mu\cdot\sigma\cdot\iota) \\ &= \varpi(\sigma)\int d\mu\,\varpi(\mu)\prod\nolimits_i \mathcal{L}_i(\sigma,\mu) = \varpi(\sigma)\mathcal{L}(\sigma). \end{aligned}$$

With no source-specific parameters, these measurements correspond to Figure 5.2c with only $\boldsymbol{\vartheta}$ and no $\boldsymbol{\theta}_i$ parameters.

B. Define Observation and Noise Models and Their Interrelationships
The transparent observation model is:

$$s = \mu,$$

and the likelihood for the $\imath^{\text{th}}$ source is:

$$\mathcal{L}(\mu,\sigma) \propto \sigma^{-N_i} e^{-\frac{1}{2}\frac{\sum(\boldsymbol{d}_i-\mu)^2}{\sigma^2}} = \sigma^{-N_i} e^{-\frac{1}{2}\frac{\sum\boldsymbol{\varepsilon}_i^2}{\sigma^2}}$$

which includes the group-level μ and σ parameters common to all sources, and the $\boldsymbol{d}_i$ (particular observed data sample, or alternatively the particular observed noise sample $\boldsymbol{\varepsilon}_i$) specific to the $\imath^{\text{th}}$ source.

C. Assign Priors over Unknown Parameter Values
Because there is a single μ and σ parameter value common to all sources, there is only a single prior needed to describe our initial information about these unknown parameter values. We will use the Jeffreys prior over both unknown parameters,

$$\varpi(\mu) \propto \begin{cases} 0 & 90° \geq \mu \geq 110° \\ 1 & 90° < \mu < 110° \end{cases}$$

Programming Aside: Multiple-Source Transparent Measurement (Fig. 5.14a)

```
%LOAD DATA
clear
load multitemp.mat

%normal likelihood function
Ln=@(Dhat,SDhat,Nd) -Nd*log(Slist)-(Nd/2)*(((Dhat-Mlist)./Slist).^2+(SDhat./Slist).^2);

%Analysis loop
L2=-Slist; Lm=zeros(1401,1); Ls=zeros(1401,1); S=size(D,2);
for s=1:S,
    L2=L2+Ln(mean(D(:,s)),std(D(:,s)),size(D,1)); end

%plot the mu posterior
figure; hold on
LS=logsum(L2,2,diff(Slist(1,1:2)));
plot(Mlist(:,1),exp(LS-max(LS)),'k-','LineWidth',4);
axis([95 105 0 1.01]); box off
for s=1:S,
    plot(mean(D(:,s)),.95,'ko','MarkerFaceColor',[.3 .4 .7],'MarkerSize',8); end
stem(mean(D(:)),[.4],'k-','MarkerFaceColor','k','LineWidth',3.5,'MarkerSize', 11)

%plot the sigma posterior
figure; hold on
LS=logsum(L2,1,diff(Mlist(1:2,1)));
plot(Slist(1,:),exp(LS-max(LS)),'k-','LineWidth',4);
axis([0 10 0 1.01]); box off
for s=1:S,
    plot(std(D(:,s)),.95,'ko','MarkerFaceColor',[.3 .4 .7],'MarkerSize',8); end
stem(std(D(:)),.4,'k-','MarkerFaceColor','k','LineWidth',3.5,'MarkerSize',11)
```

and

$$\varpi(\sigma) \propto \begin{cases} 0 & 0^\circ \geq \sigma \geq 10^\circ \\ \sigma^{-1} & 0^\circ < \sigma < 10^\circ \end{cases} .$$

D. Compute the Desired Measurement

We will consider a set of thermometer readings with seven sources, where each source contributes 5 readings (35 readings total, contained in multitemp.mat). In this dataset, all but one source produces data near normal, with the remaining source producing an elevated temperature. Individual data means and standard deviations are plotted as colored circles in the top portion of Figure 5.14a, and the overall data mean and standard deviation is plotted as stems.

The posteriors resulting from these data are of precisely the same shape as those shown above for the single-source temperature measurements. In particular, notice that there is no indication that there is one 'outlier source' in this multisource dataset, whose temperature readings appear to be shifted relative to the remainder of the group. This topic is taken up again in the next example, where the the posteriors have source-specific variables that produce more complex effects when multiple sources are combined.

Exercises

1) Generate a new dataset with 2 sources and 7 observations for each source, based on the Gaussian sampling distribution.
   a. Use equal variances, and increase the separation between the two sources until the you reach 20 deg separation. Plot this progression of posteriors.
   b. Same as (a), but use unequal variances, 2:1 ratio. Plot this progression of posteriors.
   c. Use unequal variances, 3:1 ratio. Plot this progression of posteriors.
   d. Describe any differences between the 1:1, 2:1 and 3:1 variance-ratio datasets.
2) Generate a new dataset with two sources at different locations (20° apart), with the ratio of dispersions high enough that the posteriors (over μ) from the two datasets separately overlap. Decrease the dispersion until $\sigma = 2$. Show the progression of plots. Describe any changes in shape in either of the posteriors.

5.4.3 Multiple Sources: Transparent II

Although the previous example was technically a case of multiple source measurement, the identity of all source parameters in that example hid the power and generality of the analysis. Here, we present a second case of multiple-source transparent measurement to highlight some of the issues that arise even in the simplest case of combining data across sources with at least one source-specific parameter.

Example: Differences in Parameters

To expand the temperature measurement example to include a source-specific variable, we have relaxed the assumption of equal-variance noise sources; each thermometer may now have a different dispersion parameter describing multiple observations from that thermometer (for example because you are using digital thermometers from different manufacturers, or because the markings on a set of mercury thermometers are more or less easily read, or read from a single thermometer more or less reliably by different individuals).

A. Define the Posterior Distribution That Corresponds to the Desired Measurement

The graphical model representing these readings is shown in Figure 5.2, now with both $\boldsymbol{\vartheta}$ and $\boldsymbol{\theta}_i$ parameters. The multisource posterior for this transparent temperature measurement is:

$$
\begin{aligned}
p(\mu|\boldsymbol{D}\cdot\imath) &= p(\mu|\boldsymbol{d}_1\cdot\boldsymbol{d}_2\cdot\boldsymbol{d}_N\cdot\imath)\\
&= \int d\sigma_1 d\sigma_2\ldots d\sigma_N p(\mu\cdot\sigma_1\cdot\sigma_2\cdot\ldots\cdot\sigma_N|\boldsymbol{d}_1\cdot\ldots\cdot\boldsymbol{d}_N\cdot\imath)\\
&\propto \int d\sigma_1\ldots d\sigma_N p(\mu\cdot\sigma_1\cdot\ldots\cdot\sigma_N|\imath)p(\boldsymbol{d}_1\cdot\ldots\cdot\boldsymbol{d}_N|\mu\cdot\sigma_1\cdot\ldots\cdot\sigma_N\cdot\imath)\\
&= p(\mu|\imath)\int d\sigma_1\ldots d\sigma_N p(\sigma_1\cdot\ldots\cdot\sigma_N|\imath)p(\boldsymbol{d}_1\cdot\ldots\cdot\boldsymbol{d}_N|\mu\cdot\sigma_1\cdot\ldots\cdot\sigma_N\cdot\imath)\\
&= p(\mu|\imath)\int d\sigma_1\ldots d\sigma_N p(\sigma_1|\imath)p(\boldsymbol{d}_1|\mu\cdot\sigma_1\cdot\imath)\ldots p(\sigma_N|\imath)p(\boldsymbol{d}_N|\mu\cdot\sigma_N\cdot\imath)\\
&= \varpi(\mu)\int d\sigma_1\varpi(\sigma_1)\mathcal{L}(\sigma_1,\mu)\ldots\int d\sigma_N\varpi(\sigma_N)\mathcal{L}(\sigma_N\cdot\mu)\\
&= \varpi(\mu)\prod_i \mathcal{L}_i(\mu) = \varpi(\mu)\mathcal{L}(\mu)
\end{aligned}
$$

B. Define Observation and Noise Models and Their Interrelationships
The transparent observation model is:

$$s = \mu$$

for all sources, and the likelihood is for the ith source is:

$$\mathcal{L}(\mu, \sigma_i) \propto \sigma_i^{-N_i} e^{-\frac{1}{2}\frac{\sum(d_i-\mu)^2}{\sigma_i^2}}$$

which includes the source-specific σ_i parameter and the group-level μ parameter common to all sources.

C. Assign Priors over Unknown Parameter Values
Notice that there is only a single μ prior, but N copies of the prior. The difference between the two types of prior is that we need a separate σ prior when we integrate over each source's unknown, and perhaps different, σ value. Because there is a single μ parameter value common to all sources, only a single prior is needed to describe our predata information about this parameter value. We will use a truncated Jeffreys prior over both variables,

$$\varpi(\mu) \propto \begin{cases} 0 & 0^\circ \geq \mu \geq 100^\circ \\ 1 & 0^\circ < \mu < 100^\circ \end{cases}$$

and

$$\varpi(\sigma_i) \propto \begin{cases} 0 & 0^\circ \geq \sigma_i \geq 10^\circ \\ \sigma_i^{-1} & 0^\circ < \sigma_i < 10^\circ \end{cases}$$

D. Compute the Desired Measurement
We will consider two sets of thermometer readings. In both sets of readings there are two sources, and each source contributes 12 readings (contained in multitemp1.mat and multitemp2.mat). In each dataset, the two sources produce the likelihoods shown in Figures 5.14b,c. The data in the first dataset, whose likelihoods are shown in Figure 5.14b, is a bit noisier than the data from the second dataset (compare Figs. 5.14b,c).

The posterior that results from these data (solid line, Fig. 5.14b, right; see programming aside for details) is almost halfway between the two likelihoods. This is the expected result in most cases, because the two sources are supposed to be providing data that are both representative of a single underlying location parameter. In other words, it is only reasonable to suppose that this single location is between the two likelihoods defined by the data from the two sources. Indeed, if you had thrown all the data from the two sources together into a single supersource dataset, ignoring the identities of the two data-sources, the posterior would have been very similar. The supersource dataset has the same peak location but a slightly smaller width; this width is smaller because we have ignored the uncertainty regarding the two individual noise variances contributed by multiple sources, and instead treated the data as due to a single source (and therefore contributing a single noise variance)

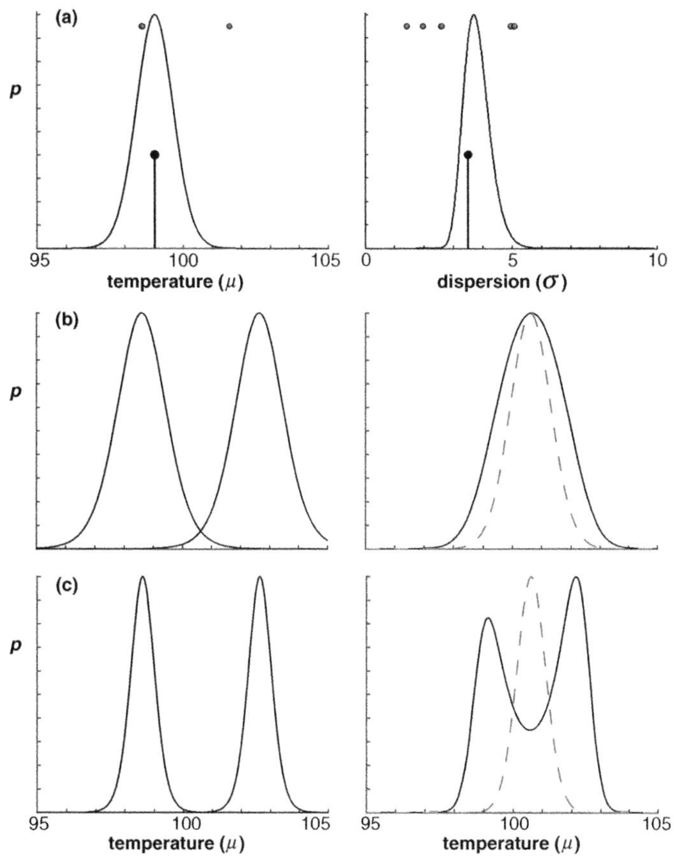

Figure 5.14 Combining sources: transparent. (a) Marginal posterior over μ based on seven sources. (b) Marginal posterior over σ for seven sources. Individual data means are plotted as circles. The overall (supersource) mean is plotted as a stem. Marginal likelihoods from two sources (left) produce the posterior (right; solid line). The dashed line shows the same posterior based on a single supersource derived from the combined data. (c) Same as in (b), but for a different pair of sources, producing lower dispersion data.

If you take a closer look at the marginal likelihoods in Figures 5.14b,c (left), you see that the shape is similar to the Gaussian, but with a 'heavier tail.' The tail portions of the marginal likelihoods are thicker than the original Gaussians because we have marginalized over the unknown dispersion parameter. A heavy-tailed likelihood behaves differently than the usual Gaussian likelihood, particularly when combining likelihoods. Most strikingly, as we will see presently, the combination of likelihoods behaves differently when the separation between peaks increases.

Even when data are generated by a single location parameter, the particular dataset observed for each source will be slightly different. These differences are due to within-source variation, and may simply reflect the unpredictable nature of the specific noise sample observed in an experiment. However, if a single group location parameter can fairly represent the members of the group, the individual likelihood locations computed from each source shouldn't be 'too different.' For example, if the dispersion of the data is 2°, then a separation of 10° might suggest there had been some kind of problem: there could have been an outlier in one dataset that is shifting its location, or data from the

Programming Aside: Temperature from Multiple Thermometers

```
%LOAD (un-comment and run one of the following two lines)

%clear; load multitemp1.mat
%clear; load multitemp2.mat
N=size(D,1);

%normal likelihood function
Ln=@(Dbar,SDbar,Nd) -(Nd+1)*log(Slist)-(Nd/2)*
(((Dbar-Mlist)./Slist).^2+(SDbar./Slist).^2);

%Analysis loop & plotting
L2=zeros(1401,201); L=zeros(1401,1); figure; hold on
for s=1:size(D,2),
    %for n=1:size(D,1), tmp=-2*log(Slist)-.5*((D(n,s)-Mlist).^2./Slist.^2); end
    tmp=Ln(mean(D(:,s)),std(D(:,s)),N);
    L2=L2+tmp;
    LS=logsum(tmp,2,diff(Slist(1,1:2))); L=L+LS;
    plot(Mlist(:,1),exp(LS-max(LS)),'k-','LineWidth',4); end
    %plot marginal likelihoods
axis([95 105 0 1]); box off

%plot the posteriors
figure; hold on
plot(Mlist(:,1),exp(L-max(L)),'k-','LineWidth',4);
axis([95 105 0 1]); box off %combine correctly
%combine across Ss (supersource)
LS=logsum(L2,2,diff(Slist(1,1:2)));
plot(Mlist(:,1),exp(LS-max(LS)),'--','Color',[.2 .4.7],'LineWidth',4)
```

two sources may not really be noisy representations of the same group-level parameter; one source may be running a slightly elevated temperature. When reasonably sized datasets from multiple sources are too far apart, the difference in location must be due to some unreliability in one of the sources, and we should tend to discount the least reliable data-source. We see this in the second dataset (Fig 5.14c), where the separation between the likelihoods computed from the two sources is large relative to the widths of the likelihoods. The posterior computed from these likelihoods is bimodal, but the peak corresponding to the more reliable of the two sources is higher. If the left-hand likelihood had been even wider, the corresponding mode in the posterior would be shorter still, until it disappeared altogether. This is particularly true if there are multiple sources clustered together, and a single 'outlier source' some distance from the cluster. Interestingly, if we assume the differences in peak location are stable attributes of the different sources, we can no longer perform the same analysis of the data. For the differences in peak to be due to stable differences between sources, the different thermometers cannot all be calibrated; they can no longer tell us about temperature in the same temperature scale, and the measurement based on a single group-level μ parameter loses its meaning.

Exercises

1) Generate a new dataset with 2 sources and 20 observations for each source, based on the Gaussian sampling distribution.
   a. Use equal variances, and increase the separation between the two sources until the posterior becomes bimodal. Plot this progression of posteriors.
   b. Use unequal variances, 2:1 ratio, and increase the separation between the two sources until the posterior becomes bimodal. Plot this progression of posteriors.
   c. Use unequal variances, 3:1 ratio, and increase the separation between the two sources until the posterior becomes bimodal. Plot this progression of posteriors.
   d. Describe any differences between the 1:1, 2:1 and 3:1 variance-ratio datasets and the transition between unimodal and bimodal posteriors.
2) Generate a new dataset with 2 sources, where one source's dispersion is twice the other, and separate them enough that the posterior shows two distinct modes. Add additional high-dispersion sources until the original low-dispersion source has been suppressed in the posterior. Show the progression of plots.
3) Generate a new dataset with two sources at different locations, with the ratio of dispersions high enough that the high-dispersion source is suppressed in the posterior. Increase the number of highdispersion sources (at the same location as the original high-dispersion source) until the location of the high-dispersion source reappears in the posterior and becomes dominant. Show the progression of plots.

5.4.4 Multiple Sources: Straight-Line Model

The logic of the multiple source measurement will be particularly important to implement when noise levels are high, and accurate measurement demands that we obtain sufficient data by combining datasets from multiple sources. When we lack the ability to collect a greater amount of data from a single source (the test produces a fixed amount of data), we must either be content with what will likely be a low-precision measurement or we can opt to improve the precision of our measurement by observing multiple sources (thus acquiring additional relevant data). Here, we will explore the nature of the multiple-source measurement in a more complex example, that of measuring the slope parameter of a straight-line model.

Example: Measuring the Rate of Temperature Change

One of the body's responses to a variety of dangerous illnesses is a rapid increase in body temperature, which we will model here as a rapid linear increase from normal temperature. Furthermore, because we will imagine that early detection is of paramount clinical importance, we will want to obtain a measure of that initial linear rise over the course of just an hour, measured at 15 min intervals (4 samples per source). We will therefore want to measure the rate of temperature increase, which is the slope (α) of the straight-line model, while treating the variance of each individual's observations (σ) as well as individual differences in baseline body temperature (β) as source-specific nuisance variables.

A. Define the Posterior Distribution That Corresponds to the Desired Measurement
The graphical model representing these adaptive responses in a multisource experiment is shown in Figure 5.15. We will assume that the slope of the temperature response (α) to illness is the only group-level variable, and that the baseline (normal) body temperature β and Gaussian dispersion parameter σ are source-specific. Here, the underlying signal is:

$$s = \alpha t + \beta$$

where t is the time variable, and therefore known. Because we will assume we have observed thermometer readings perturbed by additive Gaussian error, the posterior will involve three unknown parameter values: (α, β, σ), where both the baseline temperature and dispersion are source-specific under the current model.

$$\begin{aligned}
p(\alpha|\boldsymbol{D}\cdot\iota) &= p(\alpha|\boldsymbol{d}_1\cdot\boldsymbol{d}_2\cdot\ldots\cdot\boldsymbol{d}_N\cdot\iota)\\
&= \int d\sigma_1\ldots d\sigma_s d\beta_1\ldots d\beta_s p(\alpha\cdot\beta_1\cdot\ldots\cdot\beta_s\cdot\sigma_1\cdot\ldots\cdot\sigma_s|\boldsymbol{d}_1\cdot\ldots\cdot\boldsymbol{d}_s\cdot\iota)\\
&\propto \varpi(\alpha)\int d\sigma_1 d\beta_1\varpi(\beta_1,\sigma_1)\mathcal{L}(\beta_1,\sigma_1,\alpha)\ldots\int d\sigma_s d\beta_s\varpi(\beta_s,\sigma_s)\mathcal{L}(\beta_s,\sigma_s,\alpha)\\
&= \varpi(\alpha)\prod\nolimits_{i=1}^{S}\int d\sigma_i d\beta_i\varpi(\beta_i)\varpi(\sigma_i)\mathcal{L}(\beta_i,\sigma_i,\alpha)\\
&= \varpi(\alpha)\prod\nolimits_{i=1}^{S}\mathcal{L}_i(\alpha) = \varpi(\alpha)\mathcal{L}(\alpha)
\end{aligned}$$

B. Define Observation and Noise Models and Their Interrelationships
The measurement, under the hypothesis that the underlying signal has this exponential form, is made via the observation function:

$$\boldsymbol{d} = \boldsymbol{s} + \boldsymbol{\varepsilon} = (\alpha\boldsymbol{t} + \beta) + \boldsymbol{\varepsilon}$$

which, assuming Gaussian error probabilities for the $\boldsymbol{\varepsilon} = \boldsymbol{d} - \boldsymbol{s}$, enters the likelihood function by substituting the definition of errors within the Gaussian noise model

$$\mathcal{L}(\alpha,\beta,\sigma) \propto \sigma^{-T} e^{-\frac{1}{2}\frac{\sum_t[\varepsilon(t)]^2}{\sigma^2}} = \sigma^{-T} e^{-\frac{1}{2}\frac{\sum_t[d(t)-s(t)]^2}{\sigma^2}} = \sigma^{-T} e^{-\frac{1}{2}\frac{\sum_t[d(t)-(\alpha t+\beta)]^2}{\sigma^2}}$$

In this example, the observation function is simply the equation of the increasing-temperature straight-line signal, $s(t) = \alpha t + \beta$, because it relates data coordinates to the parameters α and β to describe the temperature increase.

C. Assign Priors over Unknown Parameter Values
There are three parameters in the likelihood function whose values require us to assign prior probabilities. We will make the conservative decision to use a Jeffreys prior over the unknown motor noise parameter, σ:

$$\varpi(\beta) \propto \begin{cases} 0 & 0 \geq \sigma \geq .25 \\ \sigma^{-1} & 0 < \sigma < .25 \end{cases},$$

were the units are degrees of error in temperature.

The rate parameter indicates the speed at which body temperature increases in response to the disease. A null rate ($\alpha = 0$) would indicate that no response to disease were present, and a negative rate would indicate dropping temperatures, which we

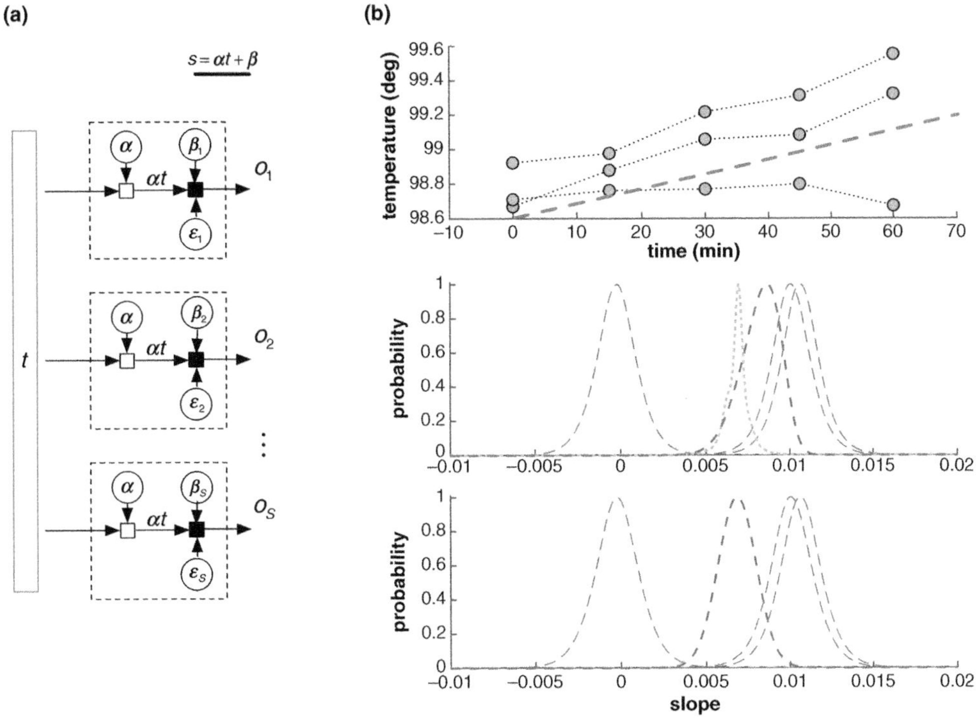

Figure 5.15 Combining sources: straight-line model. (a) Graphical model for multiple sources generating linearly increasing body temperature data. (b) Simulated data (upper) and measurement of rate of temperature increase (middle, lower).

will rule out as theoretically impossible in this scenario. We would similarly rule out any rise leading to a final temperature over the course of an hour that would exceed 104° because the 1-hour time frame was chosen to illustrate a rapidly rising temperature that is nevertheless relatively subtle to detect by the end of the recording period (a shorter recording period would therefore need to be chosen if the α parameter were likely to be above 0.1). Based on these considerations, we can confidently restrict the α parameter to a range of (0, 0.1):

$$\varpi(\alpha) \propto \begin{cases} 0 & 0 \geq \alpha \geq 0.1 \\ 1 & 0 < \alpha < 0.1 \end{cases}$$

Finally, we must assign a prior to the base body temperature parameter, β. The base temperature reading can vary in part because of individual differences in body temperature, and also because of differences in the calibration of your digital thermometer. These combined can produce a degree or two of offset from the nominal 98.6° base temperature we expect, and we therefore assign a relatively wide prior of

$$\varpi(\beta) \propto \begin{cases} 0 & 96 \leq \tau \leq 100 \\ 1 & 96 < \tau < 100 \end{cases}$$

to represent possible individual differences in base temperature.

D. Compute the Desired Measurement

As in the previous example, we will examine the difference between a multisource dataset and a supersource based on the same data (averaged across individuals), as a way of assessing some of the details of the way sources combine in this system. In the dataset plotted here, all sources had a dispersion parameter of $\sigma = 0.05$ and a randomly selected base temperature parameter within the range of the prior. Two sources had a rate parameter of $\alpha = 0.01$, and one 'outlier' source had a null rate $\alpha = 0$. The posterior was the product of a prior over the unknown rate $\varpi(\alpha)$ and three marginal likelihoods, $\prod_i \mathcal{L}_i(\alpha)$, from the three sources. These marginal likelihoods encode the information from the data about the unknown rate, after marginalizing over the source-specific parameters. This latter product, $\mathcal{L}(\alpha) = \prod_i \mathcal{L}_i(\alpha)$, is the (marginal) likelihood over the slope parameter after taking account of all datasets and nuisance parameters:

$$\begin{aligned} p(\alpha|\boldsymbol{D} \cdot \iota) &= p(\alpha|\boldsymbol{d}_1 \cdot \boldsymbol{d}_2 \cdot \ldots \cdot \boldsymbol{d}_N \cdot \iota) \\ &\propto \varpi(\alpha) \prod_{i=1}^{S} \int d\sigma_i d\beta_i \varpi(\beta_i) \varpi(\sigma_i) \mathcal{L}(\beta_i, \sigma_i, \alpha) \\ &= \varpi(\alpha) \prod_i \mathcal{L}_i(\alpha) = \varpi(\alpha) \mathcal{L}(\alpha) \end{aligned}$$

How are these sources combined, and how does this affect the multisource posterior over rate? The first plot of Figure 5.15b shows the three raw datasets and the middle plot shows the desired posterior. Notice that the outlier source tends to be ignored, because it does not fit with the results of the larger group of subjects (the two with nonzero rates), which we see in the middle panel of Figure 5.15b. In this panel, the correct posterior (dark dashed) is shifted relative to the posterior that results from treating the average data as a single supersource (dotted).

Notice that use of a single supersource defined by the average dataset leads to multiple errors: it both overestimates the precision of the estimate, and incorrectly weights the contributions of the three datasets. When we use the lumped dataset as the basis for an analysis, we have thrown out any information regarding the source of those average data, and therefore information regarding the noise present in the raw data. Without including this information in our computations, we clearly run the risk of incorrectly representing the certainty of any resulting inferences. In contrast, it is a general feature of the measurement algorithm that it correctly takes account of the relevant uncertainties when provided with all available information.

Furthermore, using the lumped dataset as our starting point hides the fact that there is a cluster of two sources whose data indicate very similar α parameters, being combined with a third source whose data point to a very different α parameter. Our analysis discounted the contribution of the outlier dataset; a feature that results from integrating over the unknown dispersion parameter. Our posterior was the result of combining three marginal likelihoods, obtained by integrating over the unknown dispersion and bias parameters. If we had not integrated over dispersion as a source-specific parameter (i.e., treated instead as a group-level nuisance parameter):

Programming Aside: Measuring Multiple-Source Slope Parameter (Fig. 5.15)

```
%%%
%%% Temperature increase
%%%

%%% Create DATA
S=3;
T=5; xmin=0; xmax=60; x=linspace(xmin,xmax,T)';
nAlpha=1551; amin=-.025; amax=.025; alpha=[.01 .01 0];
nBeta=101; bmin=97; bmax=100; beta=98.6+.5*(rand(1,S)-.25);
nSig=451; smin=0; smax=.1; SD=.05;

if length(alpha)==1, alpha=alpha*ones(1,S); end; alpha=alpha(1:S);
if length(beta)==1, beta=beta*ones(1,S); end; beta=beta(1:S);
if length(SD)==1, SD=SD*ones(1,S); end; SD=SD(1:S);

noise=nan(T,S);
tmpnoise=rand([T,1]); tmpnoise=tmpnoise-mean(tmpnoise);
tmpnoise=tmpnoise/std(tmpnoise);
for s=1:S, noise(:,s)=SD(s)*jumble(tmpnoise,1); end
D=[ones(T,1)*alpha].*[x*ones(1,S)]+[ones(T,1)*beta]+noise;

figure(1); clf; subplot(2,1,1); hold on;
for s=1:S,
  plot(x,D(:,s),'ko:','MarkerFaceColor',.7*[1 1 1],'MarkerSize',10,'LineWidth',1.25); end
xlim([-10 70]);

tic
L=zeros(nAlpha,nBeta,nSig,S);
Alist=linspace(amin,amax,nAlpha);
Blist=linspace(bmin,bmax,nBeta);
Slist=linspace(smin,smax,nSig+1); Slist=Slist(2:end);
fD=@(Bnow) Bnow+[x*Alist];
for s=1:S+1-(S==1), if s==S+1, Dnow=mean(D,2); else Dnow=D(:,s); end
        for nB=1:nBeta, Bnow=Blist(nB);
            for nSig=1:nSig, Snow=Slist(nSig);
                L(:,nB,nSig,s)=-(T+1)*log(Snow)...
                        -.5*(sum((fD(Bnow)-Dnow).^2,1)./Snow^2)2); end, end, toc, end

    if S>1, L1=nan(nAlpha,S);
        for snow=1:S,
            dprime=alpha(snow)*[0 65]+beta(snow);
            plot(x,D(:,snow),'ko:','MarkerFaceColor',.2*[1 1 ...
                1],'MarkerSize',10,'LineWidth', 2.25);
            plot([0 65],dprime,'-','Color',.2*[1 1 1],'LineWidth',2.1);
            L1(:,snow)=logsum(L(:,:,:,snow)-max(max(max(L(:,:,:,snow)))),...
                [2 3],[diff(Blist(1:2)) diff(Slist(1:2))]); end
            Lavg=logsum(L(:,:,:,end)-max(max(max(L(:,:,:,end)))),[2 3],...
                [diff(Blist(1:2)) diff(Slist(1:2))]);
            Lall=sum(logsum(L(:,:,:,1:S)-max(max(max(max(L(:,:,:,1:S))))),...
                [2 3],[diff(Blist(1:2)) diff(Slist(1:2))]),2);
            else Lall=logsum(L(:,:,:,1)-max(max(max(L(:,:,:,1)))),[2 3],...
                [diff(Blist(1:2)) diff(Slist(1:2))]); end

figure(2); clf
%amplitude estimate
subplot(2,1,1); hold on
if S>1,
```

```
    for snow=1:S, plot(Alist,exp(L1(:,snow)-max(L1(:,snow))),'--',...
        'Color',[.2 .4 .7]); end
    plot(Alist,exp(Lavg-max(Lavg)),':','Color',.7*[1 1 1],'LineWidth',2);
    LPVamean=logpeakval([Lavg-max(Lavg) Alist']);
    plot(alpha,0,'ko','MarkerFaceColor',.7*[1 1 1]); end
plot(Alist,exp(Lall-max(Lall)),'--','Color',[.2 .4 .7], 'LineWidth',2);
LPVa=logpeakval([Lall-max(Lall) Alist']);
plot(alpha,0,'ko','MarkerFaceColor',[.2 .4 .7])
plot([0 0],[0 1],'k--'); axis([-.025 .025 0 1.01])

figure(1); subplot(2,1,2); hold on
dclean=zeros(T,1); Bdelt=mean(D)-mean(x)*LPVa-98.6;
for s=1:S, dclean=dclean+[D(:,s)-Bdelt(s)]; end
plot(x,dclean/S,'ko','MarkerFaceColor',[.2 .3.6],'MarkerSize',10,'LineWidth',2.25);
plot([-5 0],98.6*[1 1],'-','Color',.5*[1 1 1],'LineWidth',1.2);
dprime=[0 65]*LPVa+98.6; plot([0 65],dprime,'-','Color',.5*[1 11],'LineWidth',1.2);
axis([-10 70 98.3 99.5])
```

$$
\begin{aligned}
p(\alpha|\boldsymbol{D}\cdot\iota) &= p(\alpha|\boldsymbol{d}_1\cdot\boldsymbol{d}_2\cdot\ldots\cdot\boldsymbol{d}_N\cdot\iota)\\
&\propto \varpi(\alpha)\int d\sigma\,\varpi(\sigma)\prod\nolimits_{i=1}^{S}\int d\beta_i\varpi(\beta_i)\mathcal{L}(\beta_i,\sigma,\alpha),\\
&= \varpi(\alpha)\int d\sigma\,\varpi(\sigma)\prod\nolimits_i \mathcal{L}_i(\sigma,\alpha) = \varpi(\alpha)\mathcal{L}(\alpha)
\end{aligned}
$$

the posterior would no longer display this behavior, and would instead be located at the identical position as the posterior resulting from the supersource data (lower panel). Notice that even this modification of the posterior in the lower panel does not overestimate the precision of the result in the way that the analysis based on the supersource dataset does, and should therefore be preferred.

Finally, notice that all observed data values are within the range of the prior over base temperature, which would make any of these variations difficult, if not impossible, to detect with a single temperature reading (i.e., a single temperature reading taken at the end of an hour-long wait period). This is the advantage of detecting a subtle signal based on its rate of increase (slope parameter, α) over the course of time, instead of on observing that change at a single time point. The logic and practice of signal detection is presented in the next chapter.

Exercises

1) What should happen if there are only two sources in the dataset with slopes $\alpha = [0, 0.01]$; explain your reasoning.
2) Modify the PA to have only the two sources in [1], and plot the resulting posterior over slope. How does it compare to your prediction?
3) The text describes a case where dispersion is a group-level nuisance parameter.
   a. Write the likelihood for this case.
   b. Update the code from the text to reflect this case

c. plot the new posterior over rate (see Fig. 5.15b, bottom panel)
d. Why does this posterior peak at the same value as the single-source posterior computed from the average (across-source) data?

4) What happens to the posterior in the case where dispersion is a group-level nuisance parameter, and the outlier source is substantially noisier than the other two sources? Update the code and plot the slope posterior in this case.

5.4.5 Multiple Sources: Summary

As we can see from just the few examples above, the topic of combining data from multiple sources is a complex one, and it is clear that each such case deserves an in-depth analysis. Indeed, this topic is often called **meta-analysis**, and there are entire textbooks devoted to it. However, the term meta-analysis is typically only used to refer to combining across several datasets obtained from different laboratories, and collected under different (though hopefully similar) experimental conditions. Thus, while meta-analysis is certainly one form of multiplesource measurement, we have seen that there are also important related issues to consider when data from different sources (experimental subjects or animals) are combined within the same experiment, in the same laboratory, and under the identical experimental conditions.

Tracing the effect of marginalization on the multisource posterior is perhaps the most important issue involved in the combination of data from multiple sources. For example, in the first multisource transparent measurement example, closer examination of the posterior would have revealed the near-equivalence of the multisource measurement and the supersource measurement, without the need for data simulation. Recall that

$$\begin{aligned} p(\mu|\boldsymbol{D}\cdot\imath) &= \int d\sigma p(\mu\cdot\sigma|\boldsymbol{D}\cdot\imath) \\ &\propto p(\mu|\imath)\int d\sigma p(\sigma|\imath)p(\boldsymbol{d}_1\cdot\ldots\cdot\boldsymbol{d}_N|\mu\cdot\sigma\cdot\imath) \\ &= p(\mu|\imath)\int d\sigma p(\sigma|\imath)p(\boldsymbol{d}_1|\mu\cdot\sigma\cdot\imath)\ldots p(\boldsymbol{d}_N|\mu\cdot\sigma\cdot\imath) \\ &= \varpi(\mu)\int d\sigma\varpi(\sigma)\prod\nolimits_i\mathcal{L}_i(\sigma,\mu) = \varpi(\mu)\mathcal{L}(\mu) \end{aligned}$$

where the third line separates the likelihood based on the full dataset into the source-specific likelihoods. The product of these source-specific likelihoods is combined with priors over μ and σ to produce the desired posterior. However, that problem required no source-specific operations to be performed on the source-specific likelihoods – before they are combined again in the last line, into the multisource likelihood, $\prod_i\mathcal{L}_i(\sigma,\mu)$. When there are no source-specific operations performed on the probability equations before we define the multisource likelihood, we could have computed the multisource likelihood directly as the likelihood over all data, regardless of source or order, using $p(\boldsymbol{d}_1\cdot\ldots\cdot\boldsymbol{d}_N|\mu\cdot\sigma\cdot\imath) = \prod_{ij}p(d_{ij}|\mu\cdot\sigma\cdot\imath)$. The equivalence between the two expressions defining multisource likelihoods is due to the fact that all parameters across sources are identical.

Although the first multisource example does not have source-specific marginalization, we still marginalize over the unknown σ parameter. We also marginalize over unknown

σ parameters in the second example. The key difference between the first and second transparent multisource examples is that marginalization over the unknown σ parameter occurs once for all sources (they share the same dispersion parameter) in the first, and occurs once for each source (each source has its own dispersion parameter) in the second example. Thus, when likelihoods are combined in the first example, the result still has the shape of the Gaussian sampling distribution. In the second example the combination of likelihoods has the shape that results from marginalizing the Gaussian sampling distribution over the σ axis:

$$\int d\sigma_i \varpi(\sigma_i) \mathcal{L}(\sigma_i \cdot \mu) \propto \int d\sigma_i \sigma_i^{-(N+1)} e^{-\frac{1}{2}\frac{\sum_{k=1}^{N}(d_k-\mu)^2}{\sigma_i^2}} \quad \text{[marginal likelihood for the } i^{th} \text{source]}.$$

This shape is the Cauchy distribution,

$$p(x|\alpha \cdot \beta) = \left(\pi\beta\left[1 + \frac{(x-\alpha)^2}{\beta^2}\right]\right)^{-1}$$

where α and β are the location and scale parameters, respectively, of the Cauchy distribution. This distribution is heavy-tailed, as we saw in Chapter 3, and that fact has important implications for how data are combined when your dataset contains more than one observation. In other words, marginal likelihoods from N sources each have the Cauchy shape, so and the combination of the sources is like having several datapoints in a Cauchy-distributed dataset:

Knowing that the marginal likelihood has a Cauchy distribution therefore tells us about the behavior of the combination of sources in the multisource measurement. Similar analyses can be performed for other measurement scenarios to glean additional insight into the way data is processed in each case by the measurement algorithm.

Exercises

1) Write a function to plot points from the Cauchy pdf, $p(\boldsymbol{X}|\alpha \cdot \beta)$, defined above. Change the values of the α and β parameters and describe the effect of each on the plots. [ANS: α is the location of the peak, and β is the HWHH]
2) Use the function from (1) as a likelihood, and describe the following datasets (plot each)
   a. $\boldsymbol{d} = [22.5, 22.3, 22.4, 22.2]$ $\beta = 1$
   b. $\boldsymbol{d} = [22.5, 22.3, 22.4, 23.6]$ $\beta = 1$
   c. $\boldsymbol{d} = [22.5, 23.7, 20.3]$ $\beta = 5$
   d. $\boldsymbol{d} = [22.5, 23.7, 20.3]$ $\beta = 9$

5.5 Summary

Here we have acquired the final technical abilities required to solve real problems in probabilistic data analysis (the observation equation, error model, graphical model, etc.), and have examined some of the conceptual intricacies involved in the measurement algorithm. After this introduction to the measurement algorithm, it may seem that we have completed our tour of the basic problem types to be encountered in analyzing scientific data. However, Chapter 6 introduces a final problem type that is philosophically and practically even more basic than measurement, albeit somewhat more mathematically intensive: model selection. Model selection refers to the process of selecting among competing observation and error models (also often referred to as hypothesis testing, since the full specification of a model usually defines a particular hypothesis about the underlying structure of the system under study). In all previous applications we have simply assumed that we are in possession of the correct underlying model of the system, as described by the graphical models and associated equations used in the '*B: Define observation and noise models and their interrelationships*' portion of the measurement algorithm. By doing so (i.e., making some assumptions regarding the appropriate observation and error models for a given problem) we were able to examine the mathematically simpler topic of measurement before moving on to the more complex topic of model selection. In the laboratory we will see that many of the assumptions made above in the example measurement problems will need to be tested, and indeed are the primary focus of a research program; this testing process amounts to model selection. In these cases, our primary interest will not be in the measurement algorithm as presented here, but rather the model selection material to be covered in the next chapter.

5.5.1 Common Mistakes

As measurement is one of the most common analysis types seen in a scientific context, there are common mistakes associated with, not to mention deliberate adulterations of, the measurement algorithm that occur with some regularity in the scientific literature. We should become familiar with these mistakes and adulterations.

The Frequentist Null-Hypothesis Testing Algorithm

Although the frequentist null-hypothesis testing algorithm is designed for hypothesis testing, it is nevertheless based on a corruption of the measurement algorithm. Recall from Chapter 2 that the null hypothesis of the frequentist algorithm is typically a statement that no effect or difference exists between groups: such as between personality test results from introverts and extroverts. Or when testing for a linear relationship between two variables (such as testing increasing dosages of a drug to measure its effectiveness with dose, or testing for the presence of a temperature spike as in the final multisource example in the text), the null hypothesis would posit that no relationship exists (i.e., zero correlation). Of all possible examples, the most common null hypothesis test is designed to determine whether group A (e.g., saccade reaction times from concussed patients) differs from group B (e.g., reaction times from neurologically intact controls). In all of these cases, the frequentist test is based on estimating (measuring) the value of a statistic, such as the average difference between reaction times, or a correlation between personality test results and introverted/extroverted behavior, from data.

If we would like to reject an underlying model of the data, we could proceed via a *proof by contradiction* argument, and show that the observed statistic is impossible based on that model (as when we reject the suggestion that we are flipping a two-headed coin upon observing a tails result). The frequentist algorithm is an adulteration of this argument, and rejects the underlying model of the data when the total probability of values of the statistic (e.g., correlation statistic) that are more extreme than the observed value are less probable (under that model of the data) than a preset criterion. This logic (described in detail in Chapter 2) falls short of a **proof by contradiction** whenever the experimentally observed value of the statistic is not a zero-probability event. In other words, computing $p(d|h_0 \cdot \imath)$ does not tell us the value of $p(d|h_1 \cdot \imath)$, let alone $p(h_1|d \cdot \imath)$.

Confidence Intervals

The frequentist confidence interval is often interpreted as the range of values that are the most likely choices for the true, underlying value of the parameter we are attempting to measure. This interpretation is quite incorrect. In fact, the frequentist confidence interval is relatively meaningless in this regard because under the frequentist regime parameter values are dictated by the null hypothesis, and any parameter values inconsistent with those assumed by the null hypothesis are impossible by definition.

The frequentist confidence interval is based on the sampling distribution and therefore tells us something about possible samples: specifically, it tells us the range of samples that would be most likely under the null hypothesis. On the other hand, the confidence interval generated using the Bayesian algorithm is capable of being interpreted in the desired manner. The shortest range covering 95 percent of the posterior probability mass (also called a Bayesian confidence or credible interval) gives the range of *parameter values* with $p = 0.95$ of containing the true parameter value under the specified model (Gaussian error function with unknown location and scale parameters, for example) and observed data. This is because probability mass in the posterior distribution is associated with *possible parameter* values under assumptions defining likelihood and prior probability functions for the unknown parameters of a given model, and not with *alternative datasets* defined only with respect to a sampling distribution that is based on the assumption of a true null model.

Fitting versus Testing

In the current chapter we have focused on measurement, which is a parameter fitting procedure when the model is known. We will see in the final chapter that measurement/fitting is a distinct enterprise from hypothesis testing, and requires that the data be processed differently.[8] It is nevertheless easy to blur the line between the two in the following way:

Suppose you have made two measurements, one for a patient population and one for a control group, using the same priors, and find that the posteriors are quite separate, as in Figure 5.7. Although you have made the measurement under a model that includes the parameters of both measured values, the data seem to suggest that those measured values are distinct.

Logically, there is merit to this argument. However, the measurement equations do not allow us to take the next step, and conclude that we have statistically demonstrated that these populations are described *by distinct models with different parameters*. Measurement is not what is logically indicated when we want to take this step. It is, however, certainly capable of giving us the indication that we should consider there might be distinct models underlying the two sets of observed data (i.e., go back to the model building and simulation stage of the flowchart in Fig. 1.3). A formal model comparison, ideally based on a dedicated experiment designed to yield data tailored to model comparison computations, could then be planned.

[8] Although both the measurement and model selection algorithms start from (1.5), they evolve into different sets of equations specific to the distinct enterprises embodied by fitting (measurement) and testing (model selection).

Select-Predict Model Validation

In the previous chapter under the heading of the posterior predictive distribution (Section 5.1.2) we discussed briefly the process of testing scientific hypotheses: in particular we described the process of first selecting a model via formal model selection/comparison techniques (introduced in Chapter 6) using one dataset, and then testing or validating that model via further model comparison calculations by comparing the predictions of that model to new, as-yet-unobserved experimental data. In such a situation, measurements consistent with the predictions of a model can be taken as support for the model. We will refer to this method as 'select-predict validation,' and recognize that science progresses by postulating models either based on previous experience or previous experiments, and then performing further tests to validate those models – ideally tests that are decisive because they make substantially different predictions for each of the competing models.

Although the correct progression seems to require multiple experiments before one can properly test most hypotheses, it is a mathematical truism that it is twice as difficult to design and execute pairs of experiments (one to suggest the set of competing models and generate predictions, and one to test those predictions), than it is to perform single experiments. It should not surprise us, therefore, that many shortcuts have been attempted that might allow one to use the data from a single experiment to perform both the function of initially defining a model, and also of validating the predictions of that model. In addition, the primary methods used to accomplish this rely on the frequentist algorithm and therefore conflate measurement and model selection, thus adding a layer of complexity when unraveling the logical errors underlying these methods.

The most obvious, and clearly invalid, method is to simply reuse the data from one experiment for the two purposes. The subtlety seen in practice is that this single experiment is usually *described* as a test of a selected model's prediction – that is, it is presented as if it were the second stage in the test of the hypothesis (after model selection procedures had been performed in an earlier experiment) when in fact the hypothesis was generated by looking at the same dataset used to 'test' those predictions. This is usually the culmination of a 'fishing expedition'; one performs an experiment with many uncontrolled variables but little to no theoretical justification linking them to a phenomenon of interest, examines the data to construct an hypothesis to explain some of those data, and then presents that hypothesis as the rationale for having performed the experiment in the first place (see Chapter 6 for more on the fishing expedition). The data are then formally analyzed as a test of the predictions of the hypothesis. By using the same data to both generate *and* test hypotheses, we are creating a situation where many invalid hypotheses will be supported.[9] This type of fishing-expedition-style of research is all too common in the neural, biomedical and social sciences, and it has the pernicious long-term effect of inserting false findings into the scientific literature, which produce obvious negative consequences.

[9] Recall the coin-flipping probabilities we examined in Chapter 2: if we think of every hypothesis test as a coin flip with some (hopefully small) rate of falsely supporting an hypothesis, then it is easy to see how a given experiment (which may generate quite a few tests for differences between variables, correlations between variables, etc.) might falsely support an hypothesis. If the result of that experiment is then used to make further predictions based on the favored hypothesis, and a new experiment is executed, it is highly unlikely that the false hypothesis will be supported a second time by accident. However, when that first experiment is represented as *if* it were the second in the select-predict model validation chain, it helps to proliferate false hypotheses.

One must, of course, start somewhere. In this regard the fishing expedition style of experiment is useful, because it can help to suggest new theories. However, it is a mistake to use the same data to generate a new theory and also to support (verify) that theory. Instead, new experiments must be used for the second step. This is also true of the model selection procedure to be discussed in the next chapter. If the data from a fishing expedition suggest a set of plausible models for some effect, then the predictions of those models should be mined, and new experiments designed based on those predictions. In particular, experiments should be designed such that competing models will predict widely divergent results, and the observed results can decisively discriminate among those competing hypotheses via model comparison computations.

Thus the remedy is, of course, to take the slower and surer approach, designing multiple experiments testing new theories. Each separate experiment provides an independent test, as well as providing evidence of the repeatability and robustness of the original results/model (when the original result is repeated as one of the experimental conditions examined in follow-up experiments).

5.5.2 Measurement: Summary

Although the details can become arbitrarily complex, we have seen the procedure by which problems are solved using the measurement algorithm. One always begins by computing the joint posterior probability for the unknown model parameters in light of the data and prior information about parameter values; if necessary, extending the question and/or marginalizing over nuisance parameters.

One of the advantages of the probability approach to measurement is that there is never a question of what 'test' to perform to ask a question of one's data. The answer is always contained in the posterior distribution, and the posterior distribution is always calculated from the product rule and Bayes' theorem. Complication arises in formulating an appropriate observation function, and in assigning the constituent probability distributions (priors and likelihoods) based on realistic background information about the problem and the data.

As mentioned previously, measurement problems ask the question, 'Which parameter values are most consistent with the data and prior information, under the current model of the problem?' and can be thought of as comparing a specific type of proposition where each 'proposes' different parameter values for a known model of behavior. This is a bit different from what is generally meant when one talks about hypothesis testing in a scientific context. Instead, hypotheses are traditionally thought of in terms of the underlying mechanisms and causes that produce a given phenomenon, and testing hypotheses of this type begins with selecting among possible models that might encode and predict the details of the behavior in question. These ask the question, 'Which among several models of the problem provides the best *explanation* of the data, regardless of the parameter values that are used to fit the model?' and are the topic of Chapter 6.

CHAPTER SIX

MODEL COMPARISON

In Chapter 5 we took an in-depth look at the problem of measurement, defining measurement and noise models of the data. When measuring the parameters of a model, there is the critical assumption that our model provides the correct description of the data. However, a great deal of scientific inquiry falls under the heading of **hypothesis testing**, in which two or more models describing potential mechanisms, each proposed to underlie a behavior, are compared. Hypothesis testing problems ask a more basic question than measurement problems: Which of several *models* provides the best description of observed data? Like all inferences derived from Bayes' theorem, our goal will be to construct a posterior probability distribution – here, over the models of interest. The posterior over models provides a direct comparison of the probabilities of those models, allowing us to compare and select among the hypotheses encoded by alternative models.

The first step required to implement model comparison computations is to reexamine (1.5), to see how we may interpret this basic method of computing the probabilities of propositions in terms of hypothesis testing for models. That is, instead of a measurement problem where we are estimating parameters, we are interested in comparing different underlying models of the data. To write this posterior we simply change the parameter term, $\boldsymbol{\vartheta}$, in (1.5) to a term describing the set of to-be-compared models, $\boldsymbol{M}$:

$$p(\boldsymbol{M} \mid \boldsymbol{d} \cdot \imath) = \frac{p(\boldsymbol{M} \mid \imath)p(\boldsymbol{d} \mid \boldsymbol{M} \cdot \imath)}{p(\boldsymbol{d} \mid \imath)} \qquad (1.5).$$

This equation is used to identify the best model from among the candidates $\boldsymbol{M} = [M_1, M_2, \ldots, M_m]$, rather than measure the parameter values of a particular model (as in Chapter 5). As such, an analysis based on (1.5) for the vector $\boldsymbol{M}$ should occur at the start of any line of scientific inquiry. Once we have identified a best model of the measurement, we can then move on to estimate the parameters of that model. Indeed, we should not fail to recognize that the probability expressions used for measurement problems [i.e., (1.5) for parameters] always contain a background information term that includes a description of the model (i.e., an element of the vector $\boldsymbol{M}$; where that element, the particular model we use to describe the data, is here labeled M). It is this model's parameters ($\boldsymbol{\vartheta}$) we are estimating in a measurement problem. Our previous expressions for (1.5) defining measurement problems could therefore be expanded to

$$\begin{aligned} p(\boldsymbol{\vartheta} \mid \boldsymbol{d} \cdot [\imath]) &= \frac{p(\boldsymbol{d} \mid \boldsymbol{\vartheta} \cdot [\imath])p(\boldsymbol{\vartheta} \mid [\imath])}{p(\boldsymbol{d} \mid [\imath])} \\ &= \frac{p(\boldsymbol{d} \mid \boldsymbol{\vartheta} \cdot [M \cdot \imath])p(\boldsymbol{\vartheta} \mid [M \cdot \imath])}{p(\boldsymbol{d} \mid [M \cdot \imath])}. \end{aligned} \qquad (1.5).$$

Written this way, it emphasizes the fact that in measurement problems [i.e., computing $p(\vartheta \mid \boldsymbol{d} \cdot M \cdot \iota)$] we assume that we are in possession of the correct model of the data (M). This expanded expression for measurement also shows us the first point of connection between what we have done previously and our goal here: model comparison [i.e., computing $p(\boldsymbol{M} \mid \boldsymbol{d} \cdot \iota)$ to select the model that best explains the data from the list of viable models].

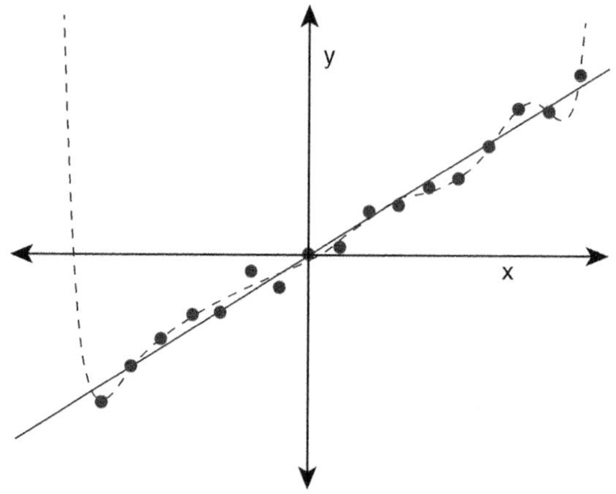

Figure 6.1 Over-fitting. Data are plotted along with the theoretical fits from two models. The first model assumes the data can be described by a straight line through the origin (solid line). The second model assumes the data are described by a tenth-order polynomial (also through the origin). Although the more complicated polynomial model fits the data better than the straight-line model in the sense that the dashed line passes closer to the center of more data, we instinctively reject this model as an overly complicated description of the data.

Model comparison problems begin with the definition of two or more competing **hypotheses** that we would like to compare. Hypotheses are word-based descriptions of laws or mechanisms that operate in the world. Each of these hypotheses must be translated into a mathematical **model** of the underlying mechanism, which represents a combination of observation, noise and graphical models (the models and model elements introduced in the previous chapter). For example, one might hypothesize that all of our personal preferences (such as preferences in food or clothing) are genetically determined. A competing hypothesis might be that our past experiences, not our genetics, determine personal preferences (and, keeping with historical tradition, we will at first ignore the possibility of a third option implicating some combination of genetics and experiences), and the hypothesis that best explains experimental data should be preferred. Thus, while hypotheses are usually a set of words that describe the causal or law-like relationships that we envision might operate in the world, we must construct a mathematical model of the predictions made by each hypothesis in order to test them. In the food-preference example, our experiment might involve collecting data on the food preferences of two sets of identical twins: the first set raised in the same home and the second set of twins raised in different homes (typically through adoption). The model implied by the 'genetics hypothesis' is that all twins (in both groups) will have identical preferences. The model implied by the 'experiences hypothesis' is that only the twins in the first group will have similar preferences (assuming similar exposure to foods while growing up in a single home).

What data might be generated by these models? It will, of course, depend on the specific experiments performed. For example, one might give these twins a questionnaire where they rate preferences, for example numerically from 1 to 10, for a long list of food items. For these data, the 'genetics' model predicts that, because of their identical genetics, all twins' rankings will match. The 'experiences' model predicts that the first group of twins' rankings will *mostly* match, to the extent that their homes provided more similar circumstances and experiences relative to the second group (whose rankings will not match, except by chance). This is straightforward as far as it goes, but there is a hidden snag. Two groups of rankings can match in exactly one[1] way (the prediction for both groups of twins under the genetics model), but there are a great many ways for two groups of rankings to partially match (the prediction for the same-home group under the experiences model), and an even greater number of ways to mismatch (the prediction of the different-homes group under the experiences model). That is, the hypotheses allow for a great many more ways for the data to fit with the 'experiences' model, relative to the number of possible datasets that might fit with the 'genetics' model. This difference in the range of acceptable fittings that are available to the two models is one instance of the central problem we must solve to perform a proper hypothesis test, because without accounting for this difference we are essentially doomed to choose the model with more fitting power regardless of its fitness as a description of the data.

Exactly *how* does this central problem affect our ability to compare hypotheses? The 'how' question is perhaps better illustrated by a different situation: that depicted in Figure 6.1. This figure plots a single dataset, along with the model predictions from two hypotheses of the underlying phenomenon. For the moment, let's not worry about what those hypotheses or data represent, and consider the different levels of complexity represented by the two model fits. The first model fits the data to a straight line:

$$y = \alpha x$$

In this model, there is a single unknown parameter, α. The second model fits the data to a 10th- order polynomial:

$$y = \alpha_1 x + \alpha_2 x^2 + \alpha_3 x^3 + \alpha_4 x^4 + \alpha_5 x^5 + \alpha_6 x^6 + \alpha_7 x^7 + \alpha_8 x^8 + \alpha_9 x^9 + \alpha_{10} x^{10}$$

where there are 10 unknown parameters $\boldsymbol{\alpha}$. The second model is much more complex, and in consequence more flexible in its ability to fit data. It can provide a good fit to data that wiggle and wander around in a way that the first model, which can only form a straight line at some angle through the origin, cannot. For a given dataset, the *less flexible* model will never be able to provide a better fit to the data, in the sense that the straight-line model is *never* able to pass closer to the centers of the 17 datapoints than the *more flexible* tenth-order polynomial model. At best, the straight-line model could only just match the quality of the fit of the polynomial model (and then only in extraordinary circumstances, such as if the data were to fall exactly along a line through the origin) – it can never surpass it. 'Quality of fit' therefore seems a poor metric for deciding among models, because inspection of Figure 6.1 suggests that the polynomial model is likely

[1] That is, for a given first set of rankings, the second set can match in exactly one way.

overly complex, and should *not* be preferred. These considerations bring us to the central problem of hypothesis testing: by what data-based criterion can we ever select a simpler model in favor of a more flexible (and usually more complex) model? If we were to rely only on how well the simpler and more complicated models fit the data, we would always be forced to choose the more complicated model, even in the situation depicted in Figure 6.1 where it seems obvious that this model is overly complex. The more complex model is better able to construct a signal that passes through the data, but it nevertheless seems obvious that the data are not *really* the noisy image of such a contrived signal – a signal with a complex set of small wiggles and then large positive excursions just outside the range of the data. The main focus of our initial exploration of hypothesis testing will be to define the model comparison algorithm that is derived most straightforwardly from Bayes' theorem, and see how our algorithm selects among models while also avoiding this central problem.

Section 6.1 describes the logic of Bayesian hypothesis testing, and provides several examples of elementary model comparison problems. Two new concepts will be introduced and defined: the Occam factor, and evidence. Evidence is a useful transformation of the posterior probability distribution over models, and encodes in a single number *how much* we should prefer any particular model over the entire group of alternatives. Evidence is a logarithmic transformation of the odds ratio, and provides an intuitive measure of the information contained in the posterior probability distribution, given in decibels (dB) – the same intuitively useful measure used to describe sound intensity and signal-to-noise ratios. The second new concept, the Occam factor, is explored in Section 6.2. The Occam factor arises naturally as a consequence of the mathematics of Bayesian hypothesis testing, and encodes the relative explanatory power of the competing models. Greater explanatory power is usually thought of as a function of the number of free parameters, but is also influenced by the range of parameter values considered possible under a given model. The idea of a model's prior explanatory power was introduced in an intuitive way in Chapter 1, and described again above in connection with the personal preferences example and with Figure 6.1. In Section 6.2.2 we provide a quantitative description of the Occam factor.

As in the previous chapter, our focus when solving example problems (Sections 6.3, 6.4, and 6.5) will be implementing each step of the the model comparison algorithm. Section 6.4 expands the basic algorithm to include the modifications necessary to incorporate multiple data sources into an analysis, whereas Section 6.5 expands the logic of hypothesis testing to include testing multiple (more than two) hypotheses against one another simultaneously. This extension will allow us to examine problems involving three or more competing hypotheses, and use experimental data to select among them. We end with a comparison between Bayesian hypothesis testing and other methods that have historically been used to test hypotheses, notably the frequentist hypothesis-testing algorithm. We explore the errors and limitations of hypothesis testing methods that deviate from our algorithm, particularly those errors produced by ignoring the Occam factor.

6.1 Model Comparison Algorithm

6.1.1 Models and Measurement

To better draw important connections between measurement and hypothesis testing we will begin with a recap of measurement. The measurement problems considered in

Chapter 5 required that the form of the underlying model, its noise and observation equations, be known. Because the underlying model of the measurement and noise was considered known, no explicit term representing the model was included in our probability statements – it was simply subsumed within the background information terms (ι) contained in (1.5). Here we bring out of the background information of (1.5) an explicit term, M, representing one possible model of the data:

$$p(\boldsymbol{\vartheta} \mid \boldsymbol{d} \cdot [\iota]) = \frac{p(\boldsymbol{\vartheta} \mid [\iota])p(\boldsymbol{d} \mid \boldsymbol{\vartheta} \cdot [\iota])}{p(\boldsymbol{d} \mid [\iota])}$$
$$= \frac{p(\boldsymbol{\vartheta} \mid [M \cdot \iota])p(\boldsymbol{d} \mid \boldsymbol{\vartheta} \cdot [M \cdot \iota])}{p(\boldsymbol{d} \mid [M \cdot \iota])} = p(\boldsymbol{\vartheta} \mid \boldsymbol{d} \cdot [M \cdot \iota])$$

The numerator of the first line is usually written in terms of the prior over the set of unknown parameter values $\boldsymbol{\vartheta}$ [i.e., $p(\boldsymbol{\vartheta} \mid \iota) = \varpi(\boldsymbol{\vartheta})$] and the likelihood of the parameter set $p(\boldsymbol{d} \mid \boldsymbol{\vartheta} \cdot \iota) = \mathcal{L}(\boldsymbol{\vartheta})$. When we make explicit mention of the theoretical model that defines our measurement, we may write the prior, $p(\boldsymbol{\vartheta} \mid M \cdot \iota) = \varpi_M(\boldsymbol{\vartheta})$, and the likelihood of the parameter set, $p(\boldsymbol{d} \mid \boldsymbol{\vartheta} \cdot M \cdot \iota) = \mathcal{L}_M(\boldsymbol{\vartheta})$. Thus, in words, the numerator of (1.5), $\varpi_M(\boldsymbol{\vartheta})\mathcal{L}_M(\boldsymbol{\vartheta})$, is the product of the prior and likelihood of the set of unknown parameters $\boldsymbol{\vartheta}$, under model M. By analogy with the likelihood of the parameters in the numerator, notice that the denominator of (1.5) is the likelihood of the model, $\mathcal{L}(M)$. Thus, we will write

$$p(\boldsymbol{\vartheta} \mid \boldsymbol{d} \cdot M \cdot \iota) = \frac{\varpi_M(\boldsymbol{\vartheta})\mathcal{L}_M(\boldsymbol{\vartheta})}{\mathcal{L}(M)} = \frac{\varpi_M(\boldsymbol{\vartheta})\mathcal{L}_M(\boldsymbol{\vartheta})}{\int d\boldsymbol{\vartheta}\, \varpi_M(\boldsymbol{\vartheta})\mathcal{L}_M(\boldsymbol{\vartheta})}$$

These equations are not new: they are the same equations we used in previous chapters to solve measurement problems, now written to highlight the fact that all computations depend on the details of the underlying model of the data. For example, the simplest transparent measurement considered in Chapter 5 uses a model containing a single unknown location parameter (μ) and additive noise with constant and known dispersion (σ); the point of our analysis of this model was to measure μ, the unknown location parameter. These equations might describe a dart-throwing experiment, where our goal is to characterize the vertical bias in dart end-position relative to the intended endpoint (the bull's-eye, at the origin); such measurements have been made in relation to theories of both the biomechanics of throwing and the neural computations related to movement planning. Defined relative to the aimed-for end position, the unknown bias term μ is measured by combining the observation model $s = \mu$ (of the underlying true signal) and Gaussian noise model:

$$\mathcal{L}_1(\mu) = p\left(\boldsymbol{d} \mid \mu \cdot \sigma \cdot M_1 \cdot \iota\right) = (\sigma\sqrt{2\pi})^{-N} e^{-\frac{1}{2}\frac{\sum e^2}{\sigma^2}} = (\sigma\sqrt{2\pi})^{-N} e^{-\frac{1}{2}\frac{\sum(\boldsymbol{d}-s)^2}{\sigma^2}}.$$

We apply (1.5) to complete the desired measurement of μ:

$$p\left(\mu \mid \boldsymbol{d} \cdot \sigma \cdot M_1 \cdot \iota\right) = \frac{p\left(\mu \mid \sigma \cdot M_1 \cdot \iota\right) p\left(\boldsymbol{d} \mid \mu \cdot \sigma \cdot M_1 \cdot \iota\right)}{p\left(\boldsymbol{d} \mid \sigma \cdot M_1 \cdot \iota\right)} \propto \varpi_1(\mu)\mathcal{L}_1(\mu).$$

Notice that the measurement could be quite different under a different model of the data. In an extreme example we might hypothesize that a high-powered magnetic field placed behind the target will prevent the dart from landing above the bull's-eye and vertical landing errors follow an exponential distribution of points below the bull's-eye:

$$\mathcal{L}_2(\mu) = p\left(\boldsymbol{d} \mid \mu \cdot M_2 \cdot \imath\right) = \mu^{-1} e^{-d\mu^{-1}}$$

which leads to measurement

$$p\left(\mu \mid \boldsymbol{d} \cdot M_2 \cdot \imath\right) = \frac{p\left(\mu \mid M_2 \cdot \imath\right) p\left(\boldsymbol{d} \mid \mu \cdot M_2 \cdot \imath\right)}{p\left(\boldsymbol{d} \mid M_2 \cdot \imath\right)} \propto \varpi_2(\mu)\mathcal{L}_2(\mu)$$

of the mean bias term, μ

The above equations, although written to bring out the involvement of the underlying model, nevertheless still each define a measurement of μ – the type of problem considered in detail in Chapter 5. More must be done to perform a test of models relevant to the value of μ, however. The first step in testing models relevant to a particular measurement scenario is to enunciate possible variations in the definition of the measurement model, noise model, or prior over model parameters that could define a set of viable alternative models, $\boldsymbol{M} = [M_1, M_2, \ldots, M_m]$, of the underlying phenomenon. These variations in the underlying model are the hypotheses that we will subsequently compare, with the goal that our hypothesis test will select the model that best describes the observed data – even if this is the simplest of the possible models in our set of competing alternatives, $\boldsymbol{M}$.

6.1.2 Hypotheses and Models

In the dart-endpoint measurement scenario above, the likelihood and prior probability functions governing the desired measurement are assumed known, and our goal in collecting data and making calculations is to measure the value of μ in the particular conditions under which the data were collected. In hypothesis testing problems, we are interested in comparing several different mathematical models of the phenomenon under investigation; that is, different competing prior probability functions, noise and/or measurement models that might provide a description of the dataset(s) under consideration. In the dart-throwing scenario we might wish to test the hypothesis that throws made under normal conditions will overcompensate for the effect of gravity - a hypothesis we will compare against one positing that throws *not* overcompensate for the effect of gravity. To compare these models, we translate each into a prior probability, measurement and noise model. The two hypotheses can be translated into the following two models, both based on a transparent measurement:

M_1: The vertical bias value (μ) is positive, $\mu > 0$ ($\sigma = 1$ is a known constant).
M_2: The vertical bias value (μ) is not positive, $\mu \leq 0$ ($\sigma = 1$ is a known constant).

Both of these models contain the same bias parameter, and neither contains an additional unknown parameter. Thus, the likelihood term is the same in the two models:

$$\mathcal{L}_1(\mu) = \mathcal{L}_2(\mu) = p\left(\boldsymbol{d} \mid \mu \cdot \sigma \cdot M_i \cdot \iota\right) = (\sigma\sqrt{2\pi})^{-N} e^{-\frac{1}{2}\frac{\sum_j \left(d_j-\mu\right)^2}{\sigma^2}}$$

Their priors, by contrast, *do* differ: The first model only allows values of μ greater than 0, corresponding to overcompensation for the effect of gravity:

$$p\left(\mu \mid M_1 \cdot \iota\right) = \varpi_1(\mu) \propto \begin{cases} 0 : \mu \leq 0 \\ 1 : \mu > 0 \end{cases}$$

whereas the second model allows only the complimentary range of μ values:

$$p\left(\mu \mid M_2 \cdot \iota\right) = \varpi_2(\mu) \propto \begin{cases} 1 : \mu \leq 0 \\ 0 : \mu > 0 \end{cases}$$

The above equations represent a mathematical translation of the two hypotheses we wish to test regarding compensation for gravity during dart-throws, and give expressions of the probability statements necessary to compute the relevant posterior probabilities:

$$p\left(\mu \mid \boldsymbol{d} \cdot \sigma \cdot M_1 \cdot \iota\right) \propto \varpi_1(\mu)\mathcal{L}(\mu)$$

and

$$p\left(\mu \mid \boldsymbol{d} \cdot \sigma \cdot M_2 \cdot \iota\right) \propto \varpi_2(\mu)\mathcal{L}(\mu)$$

Under this particular pair of hypotheses, the model equations segment the space of possible μ values into two discrete groups.

The above represents an example of the type of activity that will form the first step in our hypothesis-testing algorithm: we must translate each hypothesis into model equations. These equations will in turn allow us to compute posterior distributions over the parameters of each model. The equations developed in this step of the process will be exactly the equations used in the measurement problems of Chapter 5, but there will be one set of measurement and noise equations for each of the to-be-compared models. These model equations may differ in their likelihoods, their priors, or both.

Exercises

1) Based on the dart-throwing example scenario described above, translate the following hypotheses into model equations: equations:
   H_1: Throwers will overestimate the gravity correction necessary to hit the target.
   H_2: Throwers will underestimate the gravity correction by 10 percent (of the throwing distance).
2) Imagine an experiment in which a new antidepressant drug is being tested. Both before and after 6 months of administering the new drug, subjects are tested for depression on a test yielding a score of -5 to 5 for each subject (negative values indicate less depression relative to baseline values before the start of the experiment). Translate the following hypotheses into model equations:

H_1: The new drug is effective for relieving depression.
H_2: The new drug is ineffective.

3) In the drug-testing experiment from Ex. 2 above, imagine you are testing two such drugs against one another, where drug1 is an established antidepressant and drug2 is a new experimental drug. Translate the following hypotheses into model equations:
   a. H_1: Drug2 is at least as effective as drug1.
      H_2: Drug2 is less effective than drug1.
   b. H_1: Drug2 is more effective than drug1.
      H_2: Drug2 is less effective than drug1.
4) Taking the dart-throwing example from Ex. 1, translate the following two hypotheses into model equations:
   H_1: Throwers will overestimate the effect of gravity by more than 10 percent (of gravity).
   H_2: Throwers will not overestimate the effect of gravity by more than 10 percent.

6.1.3 Logic: General

In hypothesis testing, our interest is in making inferences about m models, each encoding one viable competing hypothesis, represented by the vector $\boldsymbol{M} = [M_1, M_2, \ldots, M_m]$. The posterior over that set of possible models is then simply defined by (1.5), but now written with the vector $\boldsymbol{M}$ substituted for the usual parameter variable ($\boldsymbol{\vartheta}$):

$$p(\boldsymbol{M} \mid \boldsymbol{d} \cdot \imath) = \frac{p(\boldsymbol{M} \mid \imath) p(\boldsymbol{d} \mid \boldsymbol{M} \cdot \imath)}{p(\boldsymbol{d}|\imath)} \propto \varpi(\boldsymbol{M})\mathcal{L}(\boldsymbol{M}) = \varpi_{\boldsymbol{M}}\mathcal{L}_{\boldsymbol{M}}.$$

Here, the background information term ($\imath$) represents our information concerning the set of m models (i.e., how they might differ in their parametric form, priors, etc.). This form of (1.5) will require us to define a prior over possible models, $\varpi(\boldsymbol{M})$, and a set of model likelihoods, $\mathcal{L}(\boldsymbol{M})$. We will avoid calculation of $p(\boldsymbol{d}|\imath)$ by representing the output of our model comparison algorithm not in terms of the posterior probability distribution over models, but rather in terms of their odds ratio.

Most measurement problems involve computing a posterior over a continuous model parameter, such as the Gaussian location or scale parameter, or the Poisson rate parameter: in other words, a measurement usually involves selecting among an infinity of possible parameter values. Model comparison, on the other hand, is always a comparison among a finite, discrete, and usually small set of well-defined models. Furthermore, these must represent the *complete* set of competing alternatives. These criteria have two important consequences: First, each candidate model must be spelled out in full detail before its predictions can be compared to those of its competitors. Second, the set of competing models must includes all viable models; this is equivalent to stating that the posterior over models can be normalized $\left(\sum p(\boldsymbol{M} \mid \boldsymbol{d} \cdot \imath) = 1\right)$. This second fact allows us to, instead of computing a posterior probability distribution over models, base our model comparison on the odds ratio,

$$\boldsymbol{O}(M_1) = \frac{p\left(M_1 \mid \boldsymbol{d} \cdot \imath\right)}{p\left(\overline{M}_1 \mid \boldsymbol{d} \cdot \imath\right)}$$

which for two models is just the ratio of the model posterior probabilities,

$$\begin{aligned} \boldsymbol{O}(M_1) &= \frac{p(M_1 \mid \boldsymbol{d}\cdot \iota)}{p(M_2 \mid \boldsymbol{d}\cdot \iota)} \\ &= \frac{\varpi(M_1)\,\mathcal{L}(M_1)}{\varpi(M_2)\,\mathcal{L}(M_2)} = \frac{\varpi_1\mathcal{L}_1}{\varpi_2\mathcal{L}_2} \end{aligned}$$

where the $p(\boldsymbol{d}|\iota)$ terms drop out of the odds, simplifying its calculation. We will examine the logic of model comparisons first when there are just two competing models, and then when there are multiple competing models. Finally, notice that we will use the shorthand of writing $\varpi_i = \varpi(M_i)$ and $\mathcal{L}_i = \mathcal{L}(M_i)$ to refer to the prior and likelihood of the ith model, which should not be confused with the shorthand for the prior and likelihood of the parameter sets, $\boldsymbol{\Theta}$, under the ith model, $\varpi_i(\boldsymbol{\Theta}) = p(\boldsymbol{\Theta}|M_i\cdot\iota)$ and $\mathcal{L}_i(\boldsymbol{\Theta}) = p(\boldsymbol{d}|\boldsymbol{\Theta}\cdot M_i\cdot\iota)$.

Two Competing Models

The odds ratio over model posteriors is based on computing ϖ_i and $\mathcal{L}_i$ for each of m models. The first of these is relatively straightforward: the prior over possible models is simply a vector of m numbers, one per model, corresponding to our initial evidence regarding the truth of the m competing hypotheses. The second term, the vector of m numbers, one per model, giving the model likelihoods, $\mathcal{L}(\boldsymbol{M})$, is more complicated but not unfamiliar. The model likelihood for the ith model, $\mathcal{L}(M_i)$ is the denominator of (1.5) when it is written as a measurement based the ith model. To see why this is, let us write (1.5) as we did in the previous chapter, but expand the background information term to include explicit mention of the model, M. We start with

$$p(\boldsymbol{\vartheta} \mid \boldsymbol{d}\cdot[\iota]) = \frac{p(\boldsymbol{\vartheta} \mid [\iota])p(\boldsymbol{d} \mid \boldsymbol{\vartheta}\cdot[\iota])}{p(\boldsymbol{d} \mid [\iota])}$$

and expand this into

$$\begin{aligned} p(\boldsymbol{\vartheta} \mid \boldsymbol{d}\cdot[M\cdot\iota]) &= \frac{p(\boldsymbol{\vartheta} \mid [M\cdot\iota])p(\boldsymbol{d} \mid \boldsymbol{\vartheta}\cdot[M\cdot\iota])}{p(\boldsymbol{d} \mid [M\cdot\iota])} \\ &= \frac{\varpi_M(\boldsymbol{\vartheta})\mathcal{L}_M(\boldsymbol{\vartheta})}{\mathcal{L}(M)} = \frac{\varpi_M(\boldsymbol{\vartheta})\mathcal{L}_M(\boldsymbol{\vartheta})}{\int d\boldsymbol{\vartheta}\,\varpi_M(\boldsymbol{\vartheta})\mathcal{L}_M(\boldsymbol{\vartheta})} \end{aligned}$$

This expansion of (1.5) leaves all calculations unchanged relative to what was done previously in a measurement scenario – we have simply made explicit mention of the model (M) that we have assumed all along was part of our background information. Notice that the last line of (1.5) written in this way gives us the definition of the model likelihood:

$$\begin{aligned} \mathcal{L}_M = \mathcal{L}(M) = p(\boldsymbol{d} \mid M\cdot l) &= \int d\boldsymbol{\vartheta}\,p(\boldsymbol{\vartheta}\cdot\boldsymbol{d} \mid M\cdot\iota) \\ &= \int d\boldsymbol{\vartheta}\,p(\boldsymbol{\vartheta} \mid M\cdot\iota)p(\boldsymbol{d} \mid \boldsymbol{\vartheta}\cdot M\cdot\iota) = \int d\boldsymbol{\vartheta}\,\varpi_M(\boldsymbol{\vartheta})\mathcal{L}_M(\boldsymbol{\vartheta}) \end{aligned} \tag{6.1}$$

To compare two models [$\boldsymbol{M} = (M_1, M_2)$], we will need to define two versions of (6.1), one for each to-be-tested model:

$$\mathcal{L}_1 = \mathcal{L}(M_1) = p\left(\boldsymbol{d} \mid M_1 \cdot \imath\right) = \int d\boldsymbol{\vartheta}_1 \varpi_1(\boldsymbol{\vartheta}_1)\,\mathcal{L}_1(\boldsymbol{\vartheta}_1)$$

$$\mathcal{L}_2 = \mathcal{L}(M_2) = p\left(\boldsymbol{d} \mid M_2 \cdot \imath\right) = \int d\boldsymbol{\vartheta}_2 \varpi_2(\boldsymbol{\vartheta}_2)\,\mathcal{L}_2(\boldsymbol{\vartheta}_2)$$

Notice that both the parametric form of a model (its observation function, noise model, etc.) and its parameter values ($\boldsymbol{\vartheta}$) may be different in each model, which is why parameter vectors are subscripted to match their respective models. Because the likelihoods for each of the two alternative models are obtained by marginalizing over all parameter values ($\boldsymbol{\vartheta}_i$) considered possible under the model M_i, we effectively eliminate those parameters from consideration via the sum rule, in that we have computed the probability of the model, independent of its parameter values (i.e., marginalized over all parameters).

Now that we have defined two competing models' likelihoods, we must compare them. Any two models can be compared by considering their posterior odds ratio (i.e., the ratio of their posterior probabilities). The odds in favor of M_1 is

$$\boldsymbol{O}(M_1) = \frac{p\left(M_1 \mid \boldsymbol{d} \cdot \imath\right)}{p\left(\overline{M}_1 \mid \boldsymbol{d} \cdot \imath\right)} \tag{6.2}$$

And, again, in the simple case of two alternative models M_1 and M_2, (6.2) expands to

$$\begin{aligned}
\boldsymbol{O}(M_1) &= \frac{p\left(M_1 \mid \boldsymbol{d} \cdot \imath\right)}{p\left(M_2 \mid \boldsymbol{d} \cdot \imath\right)} \\
&= \frac{\dfrac{p(M_1 \mid \imath)\,p\left(\boldsymbol{d} \mid M_1 \cdot \imath\right)}{p(\boldsymbol{d} \mid \imath)}}{\dfrac{p(M_2 \mid \imath)\,p\left(\boldsymbol{d} \mid M_2 \cdot \imath\right)}{p(\boldsymbol{d} \mid \imath)}} \\
&= \frac{p(M_1 \mid \imath)\,p\left(\boldsymbol{d} \mid M_1 \cdot \imath\right)}{p(M_2 \mid \imath)\,p\left(\boldsymbol{d} \mid M_2 \cdot \imath\right)} = \frac{\varpi(M_1)\,\mathcal{L}(M_1)}{\varpi(M_2)\,\mathcal{L}(M_2)}
\end{aligned}$$

where the transition between the denominator of the first and the second line takes advantage of the fact that, when there are only two models, it will be true that $\overline{M}_1 = M_2$.

A further elaboration of the odds, called the **evidence** for model M_1, is given by

$$\boldsymbol{e}(M_1) = 10 \log\left[\boldsymbol{O}(M_1)\right] \tag{6.3}$$

and is a decibel (dB) measure of the relative support for model M_1 compared to any alternatives (here, M_2). A decibel measure of the evidence for a model is convenient because the decibel scale is often more intuitive than a linear scale (such as for probabilities), and is familiar to most scientists. For example, sound intensity, noise power in a circuit, and signal-to-noise ratios are all decibel measures.

Before moving on to applications, it is important to recognize several characteristics of the hypothesis-testing calculations outlined above. First, most of the experimental questions that behavioral and neural scientists are interested in answering are hypothesis-testing questions, making (6.1)–(6.3) our most important equations for practical applications. Why is this? In a scientific setting we are less often interested in measuring specific parameter values within a known model, than in selecting the best model of a particular phenomenon; our scientific goal is usually to select the best model from among a group of competing models, not to select the best parameter values under a model that is already known to be true. Second, we note that the model likelihood, the central element of hypothesis testing computations, is a function of both the likelihood and the prior probability distribution over model parameters, marginalized over all parameters. As such, it is impossible to perform model comparison calculations under the frequentist algorithm, which has no way to define the probabilities of hypotheses and therefore also no way to perform the requisite marginalizations. This is an important point that will be revisited several times throughout this chapter, including in the summary where we compare other methods that have historically been used to compare hypotheses and models.

Finally, we must make special note of a difference in our treatment of the priors and likelihoods used to describe parameters for purposes of hypothesis testing versus when they were used for measurement. In the previous (measurement) scenario we did *not* require priors and likelihood functions to be normalized, and were able to drop constant terms that only scaled our measurement equations. Although this practice allowed us to simplify equations and computations without affecting the outcome of our measurements, this convenient mathematical shortcut will cause errors when computing posteriors over models. Why is normalization important here, where we are using the measurement equations to compute model likelihoods, but unimportant for measurements themselves? In the measurement problems of the previous chapter we did not marginalize over all model parameters, so the final marginalized result (for a single model – since that's all we care about in measurement problems) was a posterior *distribution over a parameter value* (e.g., $\boldsymbol{\vartheta}_1$ in Fig. 6.2a); here, however, the final result is a single-number model likelihood (marginalization over *all* parameters from both models, see Fig. 6.2b), and single-number posterior for each model. Scaling the model likelihood equation for each of the models corresponds to changing the height (but not the shape) of the distribution in Figure 6.2a. However, scaling one model likelihood will not scale the likelihoods of any other models, and will differentially change the height of the stem (Fig. 6.2b) corresponding to that one model only – therefore artificially altering the shape of the distribution over models in Figure 6.2b. It is for this reason that the computation of model likelihoods for model comparison must be made using equations that contain all the terms of the corresponding normalized sampling distribution for that model.

For example, we might compare a Gaussian and a Poisson model of the mechanism that produced a particular dataset. The likelihood of the Gaussian location parameter is

$$\mathcal{L}_1(\mu) = p\left(\boldsymbol{d} \mid \mu \cdot \sigma \cdot M_1 \cdot \iota\right) = (\sigma\sqrt{2})^{-N} e^{-\frac{1}{2}\frac{\sum(\boldsymbol{d}-\mu)^2}{\sigma^2}} \propto e^{-\frac{1}{2}\frac{\sum(\boldsymbol{d}-\mu)^2}{\sigma^2}}$$

whereas the likelihood of the Poisson model parameters is

$$\mathcal{L}_2(\varsigma) = p\left(\boldsymbol{d} \mid \varsigma \cdot M_2 \cdot \iota_P\right) = \prod_i \frac{e^{-\varsigma}\varsigma^{d_i}}{d_i!} \propto e^{-\varsigma} \prod_i \varsigma^{d_i}$$

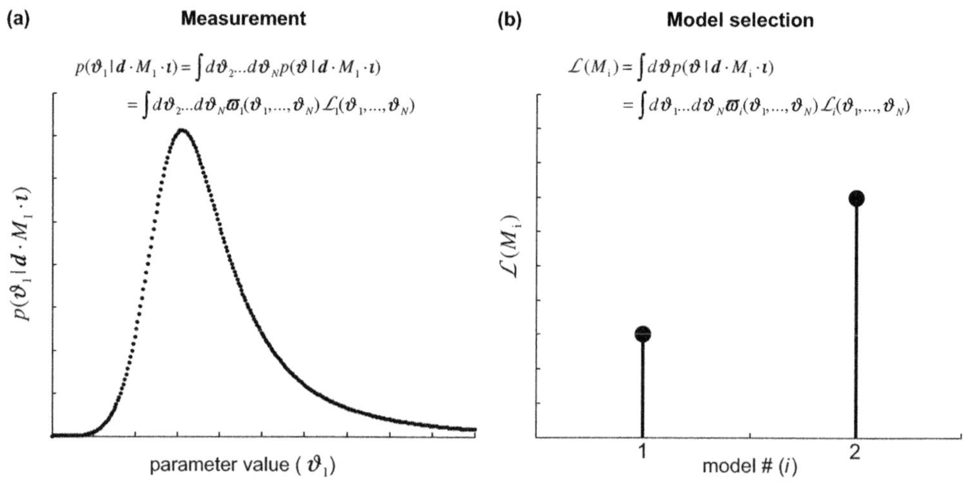

Figure 6.2 Outputs of measurement and model selection analyses. (a) A measurement yields a posterior over a single parameter of one model [here, ϑ_1], and that model is assumed to correctly describe the measurement. All other model parameters [here, $\vartheta_2, \vartheta_3, \cdots, \vartheta_N$] are marginalized out of the joint posterior, $p(\boldsymbol{\vartheta}|\boldsymbol{d}\cdot M_1\cdot\iota)$. (b) A model comparison starts with marginalization over the same joint posterior $p(\boldsymbol{\vartheta}|\boldsymbol{d}\cdot M_1\cdot\iota)$ but integrates over the entire set of parameters. The (a) plot might correspond to the shape of the posterior for one parameter from one of the to-be-compared models, whose likelihood is $\mathcal{L}(M_1)=\int d\boldsymbol{\vartheta}p(\boldsymbol{\vartheta}|\boldsymbol{d}\cdot M_1\cdot\iota)$. A second model's likelihood, $\mathcal{L}(M_2)=\int d\boldsymbol{\vartheta}p(\boldsymbol{\vartheta}|\boldsymbol{d}\cdot M_2\cdot\iota)$, is computed from the same data.

The shapes of these two distributions will be unchanged if they are scaled by the constants, $k_1 = \sigma\sqrt{2}$ and $k_2 = \prod_i(d_i!)$, and so measurements based on them will not change with such scaling. However, scaling the two distributions will alter the ratio of their model likelihoods,

$$\frac{\mathcal{L}\,(M_1)}{\mathcal{L}\,(M_2)}=\frac{\int d\mu d\sigma\,\varpi_1(\mu,\sigma)\mathcal{L}_1(\mu,\sigma)}{\int d\varsigma\varpi_2(\varsigma)\mathcal{L}_2(\varsigma)}\neq\frac{k_1}{k_2}\frac{\int d\mu d\sigma\,\varpi_1(\mu,\sigma)\mathcal{L}_1(\mu,\sigma)}{\int d\varsigma\varpi_2(\varsigma)\mathcal{L}_2(\varsigma)}$$

and will therefore alter odds $\mathbf{O}(M_1)=\frac{\varpi(M_1)\mathcal{L}(M_1)}{\varpi(M_2)\mathcal{L}(M_2)}$ and evidence $\boldsymbol{e}(M_1)=10log[\mathbf{O}(M_1)]$ calculations based on those ratios.

For this reason, we must always[2] use the normalized expressions for priors and likelihoods over model parameters, a requirement that may appear problematic when using Jeffreys priors. For example, consider the Jeffreys prior for σ used above [$\varpi(\sigma)\propto\sigma^{-1}$], which is designed to be uninformative about the scale of the dispersion of errors, σ. This is an improper distribution extending over the entire positive real line, and is therefore not normalizable. In real applications, however, this is not likely to be an honest description of one's prior information concerning dispersion. For example, range information is generally available – some set of reasonable bounds over which we would accept the value of the parameter as possible, and outside of which we would, if that value were indicated by data, think there had been an equipment failure or other mistake in

[2] The inevitable exception being a case where *all* models contain the same scale factor, such as when all models utilize the Gaussian likelihood and therefore contain the scale factor $\sqrt{2}$.

generating it.[3] Range information is readily incorporated into probability distributions. One simply truncates the distribution at the desired bounds and (re-) normalizes. The new posterior generated in this way contains range information that it did not previously. Our inferences, however, will not necessarily change. That only occurs if the new information is relevant. But probability theory tells us exactly when this is so, because a comparison of posteriors and model likelihoods with and without the new range information reveals differences only if the information was relevant to the inference.[4] We will typically use a normalized truncated Jeffreys prior to describe our prior information over parameters in the remainder of the chapter.

Exercises

1) Create a table of dB values for a list of common sound intensities (bird-chirps, leaves rustling, lawnmower, etc.), and arrange them relative to the sound intensity at which damage to hearing can begin to occur. Make sure to include common causes of hearing loss such as listening to music with earbuds, concerts, subway trains, etc.
2) Find three other examples of domains in which dB measures are used, and a benchmark dB value that is important within each domain.

Multiple Model Comparison

The previous section defined the odds ratio as it is used to compare two competing models. There, the odds ratio was defined simply as the ratio of the posterior probabilities of the two models; for example the odds ratio in favor of the first of two models is

$$O(M_1) = \frac{p(M_1 \mid \boldsymbol{d} \cdot \iota)}{p(\overline{M}_1 \mid \boldsymbol{d} \cdot \iota)} = \frac{p(M_1 \mid \boldsymbol{d} \cdot \iota)}{p(M_2 \mid \boldsymbol{d} \cdot \iota)}$$

How do we extend this to multiple models? The key is in the definition of the denominator term, $p(\overline{M}_1|\boldsymbol{d} \cdot \iota)$. In the case of comparing two models, this term is defined $p(\overline{M}_1|\boldsymbol{d} \cdot \iota) = p(\overline{M}_2|\boldsymbol{d} \cdot \iota)$, because of the condition, $\sum_i p(M_i|\boldsymbol{d} \cdot \iota) = 1$, which is always part of our background information when comparing models; this allows us to further define $p(\overline{M}_1|\boldsymbol{d} \cdot \iota) = 1 - p(M_1|\boldsymbol{d} \cdot \iota) = p(M_2|\boldsymbol{d} \cdot \iota)$. When comparing multiple models, we have to return to the definition of $p(\overline{M}_1|\boldsymbol{d} \cdot \iota)$, and reconsider its expansion when there are multiple models in the vector $\boldsymbol{M}$ of m possible models, as in $p(\overline{M}_i|\boldsymbol{d} \cdot \iota) = 1 - p(M_i|\boldsymbol{d} \cdot \iota) = \sum_{j \neq i} p(M_j|\boldsymbol{d} \cdot \iota)$. When there are three or more alternative models, the term $\overline{M}_1$ contains the disjunction of all the alternative models ($\overline{M}_1 = M_2 \vee \ldots \vee M_m$), and we will need a more elaborate version of (6.2) to compute

[3] For example, it is not possible to have a noiseless physical system (zero variance). Similarly, the upper bound on a variance parameter can usually be defined by truncating below the point where the value of the variance could only be obtained from data that are impossible. An example would be a position measurement, where the variance parameter of the position likelihood cannot be so large that it could only have occurred with position data outside the room in which the data were recorded.

[4] This procedure, of considering the relevance of various types of prior information, also allows us to consider what would happen to our inferences if we had various types of additional prior knowledge, which may suggest further experiments that are capable of providing that information.

the odds. As an example, the second of four possible models uses the odds computation

$$O(M_{i=2}) = \frac{p(M_i \mid \boldsymbol{d} \cdot \iota)}{p(\overline{M}_i \mid \boldsymbol{d} \cdot \iota)} = \frac{p(M_2 \mid \boldsymbol{d} \cdot \iota)}{p(M_1 \vee M_3 \vee M_4 \mid \boldsymbol{d} \cdot \iota)}$$

$$= \frac{\dfrac{p(M_2 \mid \iota)\, p(\boldsymbol{d} \mid M_2 \cdot \iota)}{p(\boldsymbol{d} \mid \iota)}}{\dfrac{\sum_{j \neq 2} p(M_j \mid \iota)\, p(\boldsymbol{d} \mid M_j \cdot \iota)}{p(\boldsymbol{d} \mid \iota)}}$$

$$= \frac{p(M_2 \mid \iota)\, p(\boldsymbol{d} \mid M_2 \cdot \iota)}{\sum_{j \neq 2} p(M_j \mid \iota)\, p(\boldsymbol{d} \mid M_j \cdot \iota)} = \frac{\varpi(M_2)\,\mathcal{L}(M_2)}{\sum_{j \neq 2} \varpi(M_j)\,\mathcal{L}(M_j)} = \frac{\varpi_2 \mathcal{L}_2}{\sum_{j \neq 2} \varpi_j \mathcal{L}_j}$$

and for arbitrary m, the odds computation for the ith model is

$$O(M_i) = \frac{p(M_i \mid \boldsymbol{d} \cdot \iota)}{p(\overline{M}_i \mid \boldsymbol{d} \cdot \iota)} = \frac{p(M_i \mid \iota)\, p(\boldsymbol{d} \mid M_i \cdot \iota)}{\sum_{j \neq i} p(M_j \mid \iota)\, p(\boldsymbol{d} \mid M_j \cdot \iota)} = \frac{\varpi_i \mathcal{L}_i}{\sum_{j \neq i} \varpi_j \mathcal{L}_j} \qquad (6.2b).$$

where this more general version of (6.2) allows us to compute the odds of one model relative to the conglomerate of its competitors. This reduces to $\boldsymbol{O}(M_i) = \mathcal{L}_i / \sum_{j \neq i} \mathcal{L}_j$ when we assign equal priors to the set of m possible models, $\varpi_1 = \varpi_2 = \ldots = \varpi_m$.

One's initial reaction to the odds ratio for multiple simultaneous model comparison may be that it seems unfair to compare one model to the conglomerate of its competitors. However, this is precisely the comparison we will want to make when trying to select the best model from a set of m alternatives, because the best model will not simply outperform one of the alternatives from the set, but simultaneously outperform all competing alternative models.

The evidence computed from a multiple model comparison can produce a more interesting result than evidence computed from a two-model comparison. When there are only two models being compared, the evidence for one model is simply the opposite of the evidence for the other, $\boldsymbol{e}(M_1) = -\boldsymbol{e}(M_2)$. With multiple models, however, this is not the case; each new addition to our dataset will distribute its evidence to each of the available models, adding evidence to some models and reducing the overall evidence in favor of other models. This timecourse of evidence as new data are collected can yield interesting effects with as few as three models.

Exercises

1) In multiple model comparison, is it possible to compute the odds in favor of a model without computing the normalization term, $p(\boldsymbol{d}|\iota)$? If so, how; or if not, why not?
2) True or false?
   a. The sum of evidence values across the set of possible models is always unity.
   b. The evidence in favor of one model is always the opposite of the evidence favoring the the second of two models.
   c. The evidence in favor of one model is always the opposite of the least probable of the set of possible models.
   d. A uniform prior probability over models drops out of the evidence calculation when there are two competing models.

e. A uniform prior probability over models does not drop out of the evidence calculation when there are m competing models.
f. The prior probability over parameters never drops out of the evidence calculation.

6.1.4 The Algorithm

In the previous chapter we defined the measurement algorithm, and used it as a guide to solving measurement problems. Here, we would like to perform hypothesis tests by comparing the evidence, contained in experimental data, for each element of the set of competing alternative models that formally describe those hypotheses. For this, we would like an analogous algorithm for selecting the best model from a set of competing alternative models. The outcome of such an algorithm would allow us to compare the evidence in favor of each competing model, such that we can make a judgment about which hypothesis is best supported by data, and by how much.

The answer to this question requires us to translate hypotheses into model equations, and then to compare the probabilities of those models. This **model comparison algorithm** will take us through the following steps, similar to those used for measurement in the previous chapter:

A. ***Translate hypotheses into model equations.***
B. ***Compute model likelihoods.***
C. ***Assign prior probabilities to hypotheses.***
D. ***Compute the evidence.***

A. Translate Hypotheses into Model Equations

This step is perhaps the most critical element of the model comparison algorithm, because a precise mathematical statement of each to-be-tested hypothesis is *the* basic requirement for comparing those hypotheses. Hypotheses start out as our intuitions regarding the inner workings of physical, chemical, or biological systems. For our purposes, the only important element of defining hypotheses is that they must be definite, precise statements. Any vagueness in the statement of our hypotheses will likely make it difficult to successfully pass through the remaining steps in the algorithm. For example, a statement in regard to the dart-throwing example above such as 'some darts might land near the target' is difficult to translate into a testable set of model equations. Hypotheses require more specificity to be testable, such as 'darts will land on target,' or 'darts will be at least 10 percent (of the throwing distance) too high' – both of which can be translated into testable model equations.

Note that this step of the model comparison algorithm requires us to complete the first two steps of the measurement algorithm m times, once for each of the m competing hypotheses. To facilitate construction of a precise set of noise-model and prior probability statements for each of the m competing hypotheses, we will construct a graphical model, or set of graphical models, as required by a given model comparison problem.

B. Compute Model Likelihoods

After defining the posterior, likelihood, and measurement functions that link the parameters of each model to the data, we next use these functions to compute model likelihoods, $\mathcal{L}_m = \mathcal{L}(M_m)$. The remaining steps in this process are to (a) assign prior probabilities over model parameters (step 3 of the *measurement* algorithm), and to marginalize the product of these priors $[\varpi_m(\boldsymbol{\vartheta}_m)]$ and likelihoods $[\mathcal{L}_m(\boldsymbol{\vartheta}_m)]$ over the set of all model parameters:

$$\mathcal{L}_1 = \int d\boldsymbol{\vartheta}\, \varpi_1 (\boldsymbol{\vartheta}_1)\, \mathcal{L}_1 (\boldsymbol{\vartheta}_1)$$
$$\mathcal{L}_2 = \int d\boldsymbol{\vartheta}\, \varpi_2 (\boldsymbol{\vartheta}_2)\, \mathcal{L}_2 (\boldsymbol{\vartheta}_2)$$
$$\ldots\ \mathcal{L}_m = \int d\boldsymbol{\vartheta}\, \varpi_m (\boldsymbol{\vartheta}_m)\, \mathcal{L}_m (\boldsymbol{\vartheta}_m)\,. \qquad (6.1).$$

Note that the marginalization is over *all* variables defined within the models. These model-specific parameters, $\boldsymbol{\vartheta}_i$, correspond to the set of parameters defined within the ith model; $\mathcal{L}_i(\boldsymbol{\vartheta}_i)$ is the multidimensional likelihood function over all model parameters corresponding to the ith model; and $\mathcal{L}_i$ is a single number model likelihood for the ith model. Thus, we see from (6.1) that the m model likelihoods resulting from this step will yield m single numbers; these model likelihoods express the relative support contained within the data for each to-be-tested model.

C. Assign Prior Probabilities to Hypotheses

We assigned prior probability *distributions* over the *parameters* contained within the various to-be-compared models in the previous step, because mathematically we must assign priors over those parameter values before we can marginalize those parameters out of the model likelihood. Here, we assign single-number prior probabilities to the models themselves. This step is similar to the analogous step in the measurement algorithm, although somewhat simpler. Unlike most *parameters*, models are not continuous. Models will form a small, discrete set of mutually exclusive and exhaustive alternatives. As such, the prior model probabilities will be a discrete set of probabilities, $\sum_i \varpi_i = 1$.

When we assign these prior probabilities, we will often find ourselves in one of two situations: Either we will have definite probability assignments imposed by our prior information, or we would like to remain agnostic regarding the prior weights given to each of the competing hypotheses. The former case must be dictated by the specifics of a particular hypothesis testing situation, and we will examine several examples of this in what follows. The latter case, however, is simplest: we encode the prior probabilities of the set of hypotheses by assigning each hypothesis the same prior probability, $\varpi_i = m^{-1}$.

How should we think about the case where we have definite information upon which to assign prior probabilities to our competing hypotheses? This situation will arise when our hypotheses concern events whose general rates of occurrence are known, and the substance of the hypothesis test concerns which of those events has caused a *particular* dataset. We can imagine that this is the situation faced by a mouse in an experimental chamber with two levers; pressing these levers will sometimes deliver a food pellet, and each lever delivers food at a different rate, one high ($\theta_\uparrow = 0.9$) and one lower ($\theta_\downarrow = 0.5$). Each time the mouse is placed in this environment it would like to find the lever with the higher rate of food delivery (and press it). If the mouse had never been placed in this chamber before, it would have no information about which is likely to be the high-rate lever, and if it were a logical mouse it would assign $\varpi_i = m^{-1}$. However, because the mouse has had extensive experience in this experiment, we will assume it knows that the left-hand lever is more likely to be the high-rate lever (say odds of 2:1); a clever mouse would seek to exploit that information. In other words, the animal's state of information *prior to any lever-presses* would be modeled as ϖ_i, containing a term for the high-rate lever being on the left, $\varpi_{L=\uparrow} = 2/3$ [i.e., 2:1 in favor], and a term for the high-rate lever being on the right, $\varpi_{R=\uparrow} = 1/3$ [i.e., 2:1 against], as detailed in Figure 6.3.

D. Compute the Evidence

Once we have assigned model priors $[\varpi_m]$ and likelihoods $[\mathcal{L}_m]$, we can define an expression for the probability of the mth model,

$$p(M_m|\boldsymbol{d} \cdot \iota) \propto \varpi_m \mathcal{L}_m \quad (1.5),$$

and choose the model with the highest posterior probability as the most likely of the set.

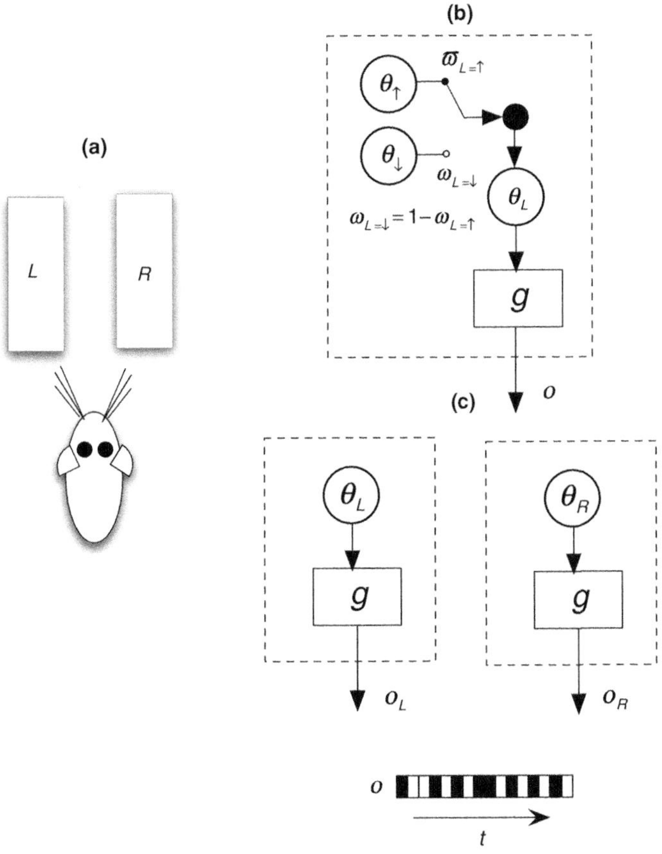

Figure 6.3 Mouse lever-pressing scenario. (a) There are two levers the mouse can theoretically choose, one delivering food reward at a high rate ($\theta \uparrow= 0.9$) and one at a lower rate ($\theta \downarrow= 0.5$). (b) A mouse that has learned that there is a high reward rate and a low reward rate lever, and that the high-rate lever occurs most often on the left, will begin a new trial by pressing the left-hand lever (a preference that should be stronger for higher $\varpi_{L=\uparrow}$). After each left-hand lever press, it should consider the time series of rewarded and unrewarded lever presses (the output, o) and attempt to discern whether the high- or low-rate lever is being pressed. If at some point it rejects the model assuming the high-rate lever on the left, it should switch to pressing the other lever. (c) Model of the stimulus (reward) generation for the left- and right-hand levers, one of which produces the high- and one the low-reward rate. The mouse uses the observed data stream (o) to identify the left-hand lever's reward rate (θ_L) with one of two underlying binomial rate constants ($\theta \uparrow$ or $\theta \downarrow$).

In terms of the lever-pressing scenario above, the mouse takes the role of a scientist, and must interpret the data from its lever presses to select the best model. There are two models of interest: whether the high rate of food delivery comes from the left-hand or from the right-hand lever. Each model will have a single-number likelihood, based on how many lever presses were successful at each of the two locations, and a single-number prior probability, $\varpi(M_L) = \varpi_{L=\uparrow} = 2/3$ and $\varpi(M_R) = \varpi_{R=\uparrow} = 1/3$, based on the past experience. Computing the posterior over the set of models is equivalent to asking the model comparison question, 'Am I in the scenario where the left- or right-hand lever delivers food reward at the higher rate?' We answer this question by looking at the predictions of each model to determine which is more likely to have caused the observed data. Intuitively, we should recognize that when there is no evidence (i.e., before either lever has been pressed), we should default to the largest of the prior probabilities as our best model (and, as per our example, choose the left-hand-lever model). Following each press of the left-hand lever, we recompute the evidence favoring a model where the left-hand lever delivers the higher rate of reward; a logical mouse will switch levers if it obtains enough evidence that it was pressing the lower-rate ($\theta_\downarrow$) lever. Notice also that because the choice of best model utilizes the entire dataset up to the current time point, the prior over models will have less and less influence on the final decision as more data are acquired.

The odds ratio favoring the ith model is written:

$$\boldsymbol{O}(M_i) = \frac{p\left(M_i \mid \boldsymbol{d}\cdot\imath\right)}{p\left(\overline{M}_i \mid \boldsymbol{d}\cdot\imath\right)} = \frac{\varpi_i \mathcal{L}_i}{\sum_{j\neq i}\varpi_j\mathcal{L}_j} \tag{6.2}$$

where the term $\overline{M}_i$ stands in for the set of models *other* than M_i being considered in the hypothesis test. We will report the result of our hypothesis test in terms of **evidence**, which we define as the log transform of the odds favoring the ith model:

$$\boldsymbol{e}(M_m) = 10\log\left[\boldsymbol{O}(M_m)\right] \tag{6.3}$$

Evidence is a decibel measure; for example, if the odds are 2:1 in favor of M_1, this translates to just about 3 dB of evidence. Thought of in terms of sound intensity, 1 dB of evidence is about the smallest increment of sound that is detectible to the human ear (i.e., the detection threshold), whereas 3 dB is equivalent to the sound of a bird softly tweeting or leaves rustling in the wind: quite detectable, but by no means loud. Unless otherwise noted, we will use this 3 dB value as a just-significant difference favoring one model over its competitors, although real-world applications should also consider clinical significance in setting thresholds.

This step of the algorithm will also include simulations to check your assumptions and code (verify that the model comparison will yield evidence for/against hypotheses as the data become more/less favorable for that hypothesis), and to evaluate the stability (e.g., lack of singularities, oscillations, or other features that may be inconsistent with the known properties of your models) of the model comparison you have defined. Such simulations can also be used, for example, to determine how much and which types of data will be required to find a significant amount of evidence for or against particular hypotheses.

Exercises

1) Taking the dart-throwing example above, translate the following two hypotheses into model equations:
   $H1$: Throwers will overestimate the gravity correction necessary to hit the target.
   $H2$: Throwers will underestimate the gravity correction by 10 percent.
2) Imagine an experiment in which a new antidepressant drug is being tested. Both before and after 6 months of administering the new drug, subjects are tested for depression on a test yielding a score of -5 to 5 for each subject (negative values indicate less depression relative to baseline values before the start of the experiment). Translate the following hypotheses into model equations:
   $H1$: The new drug is effective for relieving depression.
   $H2$: The new drug is not effective.
3) In the drug-testing experiment from Ex. 2 above, imagine you are testing two such drugs against one another, where drug1 is an established antidepressant and drug2 is a new experimental drug. Translate the following hypotheses into model equations:
   a. $H1$: Drug2 is at least as effective as drug1.
      $H2$: Drug2 is less effective than drug1.
   b. $H1$: Drug2 is more effective than drug1.
      $H2$: Drug2 is less effective than drug1.

Example: Basic Lever Pressing
At this point it should be instructive to walk through an example of the above algorithm for a simple hypothesis-testing example. To that end, we will set up equations describing the lever-pressing scenario outlined above.

A. Translate Hypotheses into Model Equations
This example is based on an experiment in which a mouse is presented with two levers (lever- pressing delivers reward, but only intermittently and unpredictably), and the animal must allocate time and energy in a way that brings the most reward (reward is usually food or water).

ι_A: There are two levers that the mouse can press (Fig. 6.3) on the left and right, and a food pellet is delivered after some of the lever presses that occur when a light between the two levers is lit (these light-on times are the trials of the experiment and last for several seconds, giving the mouse time to execute multiple lever presses during each trial). The Bernoulli rate of reward is fixed during a trial, but varies between trials in the following way: There is one high-rate ($\theta_\uparrow = 0.3$) and one low-rate ($\theta_\downarrow = 0.1$) lever, and the identity of each is assigned unpredictably from trial to trial. The mouse has to choose between two hypotheses. We will assume the mouse is able to do the math and compare the following models, and does so only by pressing the left-hand lever (a simplification):
M_H: The high-reward lever is on the left in the current trial.
M_L: The low-reward lever is on the left in the current trial.

The graphical model that describes these data is for the most part straightforward (Fig. 6.3). The success/failure input (s) simultaneously feeds a module that identifies the model, and also the module that estimates the Bernoulli rate (θ) based on the same data and the model. The output is a vector indicating both the estimated rate (θ) and the selected model (M). For the moment we will ignore the rate estimate and focus entirely on the output of the first module that selects from among the available models of the current lever-pressing scenario (M).

In the current scenario, there are two levers, and we will compare two models of the rate of reward delivery at the left-hand lever. The evidence (6.3) and odds (6.2) calculations for these two models are

$$\boldsymbol{e}(M_H) = 10 \log [O(M_H)]$$

and

$$\begin{aligned} O(M_H) &= \frac{p(M_H \mid \boldsymbol{d} \cdot \imath)}{p(\overline{M}_H \mid \boldsymbol{d} \cdot \imath)} = \frac{\varpi_H \mathcal{L}_\mathrm{H}}{\varpi_L \mathcal{L}_\mathrm{L}} \\ &= \frac{\varpi(M_H) \sum_i p(\theta_{\uparrow_i} \mid \imath) p(\boldsymbol{d} \mid \theta_{\uparrow_i} \cdot \imath)}{\varpi(M_L) \sum_j p(\theta_{\downarrow j} \mid \imath) p(\boldsymbol{d} \mid \theta_{\downarrow j} \cdot \imath)} = \frac{\varpi_H \sum_i \varpi(\theta_{\uparrow_i}) \mathcal{L}(\theta_{\uparrow_i})}{\varpi_L \sum_j \varpi(\theta_{\downarrow j}) \mathcal{L}(\theta_{\downarrow j})} \end{aligned}$$

where we have used the summation sign instead of the integral sign to define model likelihoods because the possible rate parameters in this experiment form a discrete set (i.e., each model predicts specific rates, rather than a continuous range).

As a next step, we assign the (parameter) likelihood terms, $\mathcal{L}(\theta)$. Both models are based on the binomial likelihood, and therefore the form of this likelihood over the unknown constant θ is identical in the two models:

$$\mathcal{L}(\theta) = \binom{N}{S} \theta^S (1-\theta)^{N-S} = \frac{N}{S!(N-S)!} \theta^S (1-\theta)^{N-S}$$

The only difference between the two models is whether the left-hand lever will theoretically yield a high rate of reward. Now since we have assumed a mathematically inclined mouse, we will further assume it has, over the course of the experiment, become aware that there are only two rates being used, $\theta_H = 0.3$ and $\theta_L = 0.1$. This is useful information, because it dramatically restricts the range of possible rate constants under each model:

$$\varpi_H(\theta) = \begin{cases} 0 & \theta \neq 0.3 \\ 1 & \theta = 0.3 \end{cases}$$

and

$$\varpi_L(\theta) = \begin{cases} 0 & \theta \neq 0.1 \\ 1 & \theta = 0.1 \end{cases}$$

In fact, the possible rate constants under each model have been reduced to a *single* value (rather than, say, a set of N possible values), based on our prior information regarding the mouse and its experience with the model parameters. With this simplification, we can drop the summation altogether in the odds computation and write

$$O(M_H) = \frac{\varpi_H \mathcal{L}_\mathrm{H}}{\varpi_L \mathcal{L}_\mathrm{L}} = \frac{\varpi_H \left[\varpi(\theta_\uparrow) \mathcal{L}(\theta_\uparrow)\right]}{\varpi_L \left[\varpi(\theta_\downarrow) \mathcal{L}(\theta_\downarrow)\right]}$$

B. Compute Model Likelihoods

The model likelihoods occur in the previous equation in square brackets. These terms are

$$\mathcal{L}_H = \sum\nolimits_i p\left(\theta_{\uparrow_i} \mid \imath\right) p\left(\boldsymbol{d} \mid \theta_{\uparrow_i} \cdot \imath\right) = p\left(\theta_{\uparrow} \mid \imath\right) p\left(\boldsymbol{d} \mid \theta_{\uparrow} \cdot \imath\right)$$

for the high-rate model and

$$\mathcal{L}_L = \sum\nolimits_j p\left(\theta_{\downarrow j} \mid \imath\right) p\left(\boldsymbol{d} \mid \theta_{\downarrow j} \cdot \imath\right) = p\left(\theta_{\downarrow} \mid \imath\right) p\left(\boldsymbol{d} \mid \theta_{\downarrow} \cdot \imath\right)$$

for the low-rate model. Continuing the analysis with the specific numbers defined by our background information, we assign $p(s|\theta_{\uparrow} \cdot \imath) = 0.3$ and $p(\bar{s}|\theta_{\uparrow} \cdot \imath) = 0.7$ to describe our expectations for a lever press that delivers food (s) or not ($\bar{s}$) when that lever is on the high-rate side, and we assign $p(s|\theta_{\downarrow} \cdot \imath) = 0.1$ and $p(\bar{s}|\theta_{\downarrow} \cdot \imath) = 0.9$ to describe our expectation of the same data from the low-rate lever; from this we see that the model likelihood will always depend on the observed data. On food-present lever presses the high-rate model likelihood is

$$\mathcal{L}_{\mathrm{H}} = \varpi\left(\theta_{\uparrow}\right) \mathcal{L}\left(\theta_{\uparrow}\right) = p\left(\theta_{\uparrow} \mid M_H \cdot \imath\right) p\left(s \mid \theta_{\uparrow} \cdot \imath\right) = (1)(0.3)$$

and the low-rate model likelihood is

$$\mathcal{L}_{\mathrm{L}} = \varpi\left(\theta_{\downarrow}\right) \mathcal{L}\left(\theta_{\downarrow}\right) = p\left(\theta_{\downarrow} \mid M_L \cdot \imath\right) p\left(s \mid \theta_{\downarrow} \cdot \imath\right) = (1)(0.1)$$

On observing a food-absent lever press, the model likelihoods are

$$\begin{aligned} \mathcal{L}_{\mathrm{H}} &= p\left(\theta_{\uparrow} \mid \boldsymbol{M}_H \cdot \imath\right) p\left(\bar{s} \mid \theta_{\uparrow} \cdot \imath\right) = (1)(0.7) \\ \mathcal{L}_{\mathrm{L}} &= p\left(\theta_{\downarrow} \mid \boldsymbol{M}_L \cdot \imath\right) p\left(\bar{s} \mid \theta_{\downarrow} \cdot \imath\right) = (1)(0.9) \end{aligned}$$

Note that while we have dropped the summation over rates (indexed by i and j above) in the definitions of these model likelihoods, there are nevertheless multiple terms in the model likelihood when the data vector ($\boldsymbol{d}$) contains multiple observations. Thus, for example, observing $\boldsymbol{d} = [s, \bar{s}, \bar{s}, s, \bar{s}]$ would yield the model likelihood:

$$\begin{aligned} \mathcal{L}_{\mathrm{H}} &= p\left(\theta_H \mid M_H \cdot \imath\right) p\left(\boldsymbol{d} \mid \theta_H \cdot \imath\right) = (1)[(0.3)(0.7)(0.7)(0.3)(0.7)], \\ \mathcal{L}_{\mathrm{L}} &= p\left(\theta_L \mid M_L \cdot \imath\right) p\left(\boldsymbol{d} \mid \theta_L \cdot \imath\right) = (1)[(0.1)(0.9)(0.9)(0.1)(0.9)] \end{aligned}$$

for high- and low-rate levers, respectively. Finally, notice that while there are four model likelihoods, there are only two ratios of these numbers that we will see in our odds and evidence calculations: those corresponding to the food-present outcome ($\mathcal{L}_{\mathrm{H}}/\mathcal{L}_{\mathrm{L}} = 0.3/0.1 = 3$), and those corresponding to the food-absent outcome (e.g., $\mathcal{L}_{\mathrm{H}}/\mathcal{L}_{\mathrm{L}} = 0.7/0.9 \approx 0.78$).

C. Assign Prior Probabilities to Hypotheses

The prior probabilities are easy to assign in this example problem because we were told that the high- and low-rate levers appear unpredictably on the left-hand side. Thus, because we have no information that would allow us to assign a greater chance for either lever to appear on the right, the only logical course of action is to assign them equal probability. If, however, the experiment is designed to have the high-rate lever appear on the left in 90 percent of trials (and the mouse has learned this), this information should be encoded in the model prior probabilities. When the two models are equally likely (or equivalently, the mouse is unaware of any reason to assign higher probability to either), we write: $\varpi_H = \varpi_L = 0.5$; but in the hypothetical example of a mouse believing there is a 90-10 split of high-to-low appearing on the left, model priors are assigned: $\varpi_H = 0.9$, $\varpi_L = 0.1$.

D. Compute the Evidence

Once we have assigned model priors $[\varpi_m = \varpi(M_m)]$ and likelihoods $[\mathcal{L}_m = \mathcal{L}(M_m)]$, we have all the pieces in place for computing evidence, $\boldsymbol{e}(M_H) = 10log[\mathbf{O}(M_H)]$, in favor of the model in which the high-rate lever is on the left-hand side. Expanding the odds term of this equation yields

$$\mathbf{O}(M_H) = \frac{\varpi_H \mathcal{L}_\mathrm{H}}{\varpi_L \mathcal{L}_\mathrm{L}} = \frac{\varpi_H \left[\varpi(\theta_\uparrow)\,\mathcal{L}(\theta_\uparrow)\right]}{\varpi_L \left[\varpi(\theta_\downarrow)\,\mathcal{L}(\theta_\downarrow)\right]}$$

and the logarithmic form of the evidence function allows to further write

$$\boldsymbol{e}(M_H) = 10\log\left[\frac{\varpi_H \mathcal{L}_\mathrm{H}}{\varpi_L \mathcal{L}_\mathrm{L}}\right] = 10\log\left[\frac{\varpi_H}{\varpi_L}\right] + 10\log\left[\frac{\mathcal{L}_\mathrm{H}}{\mathcal{L}_\mathrm{L}}\right]$$

which allows for easy separation of prior evidence, $\boldsymbol{e}_H^{(0)} = 10\log[\varpi_H/\varpi_L]$, and the evidence change that occurs as each datum is acquired, $\Delta\boldsymbol{e}_H = 10\log[\mathcal{L}_H/\mathcal{L}_L]$. In fact, because each lever press has an independent probability of delivering food under both models, we can separate the *increment* of evidence produced by each new datum. For trials in which the left-hand lever yields no food reward, the evidence in favor of that lever being high-rate is

$$\Delta\boldsymbol{e}_H^{-} = 10\log\left[\frac{p(\bar{s} \mid M_H \cdot \imath)}{p(\bar{s} \mid M_L \cdot \imath)}\right] = 10\log(7/9) \approx -1.1,$$

whereas when the left-hand lever yields a food reward the evidence changes by

$$\Delta\boldsymbol{e}_H^{+} = 10\log\left[\frac{p(s \mid M_H \cdot \imath)}{p(s \mid M_L \cdot \imath)}\right] = 10\log(3) \approx 4.8$$

How does this translate into a total evidence calculation for an example dataset? Let's return to the hypothetical dataset, $d = [s, \bar{s}, \bar{s}, s, \bar{s}]$, from above. Because of the independence of probabilities describing multiple lever presses from both the high- and low-rate levers, we can write the probability of the dataset under either model as

$$\begin{aligned} p(\boldsymbol{d} \mid M_\bullet \cdot \imath) &= p(\bar{s} \mid [s, \bar{s}, \bar{s}, s] \cdot M_\bullet \cdot \imath)p(s \mid [s, \bar{s}, \bar{s}] \cdot M_\bullet \cdot \imath) \ldots p(s \mid M_\bullet \cdot \imath) \\ &= p(\bar{s} \mid M_\bullet \cdot \imath)p(s \mid M_\bullet \cdot \imath)p(\bar{s} \mid M_\bullet \cdot \imath)p(\bar{s} \mid M_\bullet \cdot \imath)p(s \mid M_\bullet \cdot \imath) \end{aligned}$$

and the total evidence (in dB) favoring the high-rate hypothesis in our example is

$$\begin{aligned} \boldsymbol{e}_H &= \boldsymbol{e}_H^{(0)} + \sum\nolimits_i \boldsymbol{e}_H^{i} = \boldsymbol{e}_H^{(0)} + \left[\boldsymbol{e}_H^{+} + \boldsymbol{e}_H^{-} + \boldsymbol{e}_H^{-} + \boldsymbol{e}_H^{+} + \boldsymbol{e}_H^{-}\right] \\ &= \boldsymbol{e}_H^{(0)} + n_{-}\boldsymbol{e}_H^{-} + n_{+}\boldsymbol{e}_H^{+} \\ &= 0 + 3\boldsymbol{e}_H^{-} + 2\boldsymbol{e}_H^{+} \approx 6.3 \text{ dB} \end{aligned}$$

Programming Aside: Basic Lever-Pressing Example

We will perform the calculations based on observing three failed (no-food) lever presses and two successful lever presses in two ways. First, we will iteratively compute the evidence based on the binomial probabilities for single observations of successful and unsuccessful lever presses (the definitions of $\Delta \mathbf{e}_H^+$ and $\Delta \mathbf{e}_H^-$ given in the main text), and then we will arrive at the same result using an all-at-once calculation based on the binomial probabilities describing the full dataset under each of the two models.

```
%%% press-by-press calculation
> dat=[0 0 1 0 1];
> dEpos=10*log10(3/1); %evidence change (high-rate hypothesis)
following successful press
> dEneg=10*log10(7/9); %evidence change (high-rate hypothesis)
following unsuccessful press
> EV=0;
> for i=1:length(dat),
       if dat(i)==1, EV=EV+dEpos;
       else EV=EV+dEneg; end, end

%%% all-at-once calculation
> EV(2)=sum(dat==1)*dEpos+sum(dat==0)*dEneg;
%%% alternate all-at-once calculation
> rhoH=.3; rhoL=.1;
> Lh=bpdf(sum(dat),length(dat),rhoH);
> Ll=bpdf(sum(dat),length(dat),rhoL);
> EV(3)=10*log10(Lh/Ll);

%%% compare the three calculations
> isnear(EV(1),EV(2))
> isnear(EV(2),EV(3))
```

When repeating this calculation please note the number of simplifications that went into the final formula, $\mathbf{e}_H = n_-\mathbf{e}_H^- + n_+\mathbf{e}_H^+$. We dropped the $\mathbf{e}_H^{(0)}$ term because of the equal prior probabilities of the two models ($\log[1] = 0$), each term of $\sum_i \mathbf{e}_H^{(i)}$ was the log of a simple ratio of the probabilities generated by the two models (because $\overline{M}_1 = M_2$ when there are only two models), and $\sum_i \mathbf{e}_H^{(i)} = n_-\mathbf{e}_H^- + n_+\mathbf{e}_H^+$ because probabilities were independent in this lever-pressing example problem. Other problems will not simplify so extremely.

Exercises

1) Write the expression for evidence in favor of M_L based on the same example dataset used above.
2) Compute the odds in favor of both M_H and M_L if the model likelihoods in the above equations (based on some particular dataset you generate) had been
   a) $\mathcal{L}_1 = 5$ and $\mathcal{L}_2 = 1$
   b) $\mathcal{L}_1 = 1$ and $\mathcal{L}_2 = 5$
   c) $\mathcal{L}_1 = 3.22$ and $\mathcal{L}_2 = 1.48$.

3) Compute and plot evidence in favor of both M_H and M_L for the model likelihoods in the main text, when all lever presses yield
   a) successes
   b) failures
4) In the above examples we assume there is a single rate associated with the high and low-rate levers. Instead, assume the second model allowed two possible rates, M_L: A low-reward lever is on the left in the current trial $[\theta_L = \theta_2 \vee \theta_3]$, and compute evidence from the same data as above.
5) Assume the mouse had previously observed N trials of food or no-food from the two levers described in the example, and had developed a prior over rate based on this information. Make the evidence calculation based on the same experimental data, after the mouse had observed N previous trials and correctly measured the two rates based on this information.
   a. $N_\uparrow = 5$ and $N_\downarrow = 5$
   b. $N_\uparrow = 25$ and $N_\downarrow = 5$
   c. $N_\uparrow = 5$ and $N_\downarrow = 25$
6*) Simulate 10,000 repetitions of the experiment above. In each repetition, make the number of lever presses that the mouse executes (on the left) a sample from a Poisson distribution with Poisson parameter $\zeta = 10$, and use your simulation results to determine the evidence threshold (for when the mouse choses which is the high-yield lever) that yields maximum expected gain in total food pellets.

6.2 Occam Factor

A key element of model comparison is something we will refer to as the **Occam factor**. The Occam factor penalizes models relative to their flexibility (usually due to imprecision in predictions). The Occam factor is generated as a natural consequence of Bayesian model comparison, due to the integral defined in (6.1). That integral (or summation) causes hypotheses with more prior ability to explain data to be penalized. The upshot of the Occam factor is that, without having to formulate any ad hoc rules governing a 'preference for simpler hypotheses,' our analysis will naturally select the most inflexible (i.e., 'simplest') hypothesis that is still able to provide a good explanation of the data. In other words, referring back to the start of the chapter and Figure 6.1, where a straight-line fit and a tenth-order polynomial fit to an approximately straight-line 17-point dataset were compared, our analysis based on (6.1)–(6.3) will naturally reject the *over*-complicated model in favor of the more realistic and simpler straight-line model.

6.2.1 Occam's Razor: History and Implementation

The preference for simplicity in logical and scientific explanation appears to have been first expressed in its most popular form, *Entia non sunt multiplicanda praeter necessitatem*, by John Duns Scotus (1265–1308), although it bears the name of a later and perhaps more fervent proponent, William of Ockham (1285–1349). This preference, Occam's razor, is used as an heuristic when deciding amongst scientific hypotheses, such that the 'simplest' hypothesis should be chosen over those with apparently unnecessary features and adornments.

What exactly are we guarding against, that Occam's razor is intended to prevent? We are essentially guarding against the Ptolemaic model of the solar system – the modern poster child for an unnecessarily complex explanation in science. At base, the Ptolemaic model is an elaboration of the Aristotelian geocentric model, wherein the Earth was considered the stationary center of the solar system, and the Sun and planets were assumed to orbit the Earth in a set of concentric circular orbits. The geocentric nature of this model was likely motivated by two observations: First, the Earth feels quite stationary. Second, the planets, Sun and other stars appear to revolve around the Earth. The details of the motions of the planets were problematic, however. This was particularly true of 'retrograde motion,' wherein the path of a planet across the sky will, on occasion, slow and reverse direction. Retrograde motion cannot be predicted by the Aristotelian model. The theory-building response to retrograde motion was the near-universal response in this type of situation (i.e., when one is faced with data that do not fit within your preferred model): Rather than undertake a radical reformulation of the model, an attempt was made to formulate an updated model that kept the basic character of the Aristotelian model, including the two observations that presumably first motivated it, but contained additional mechanisms to account for the discrepant data. This is not only the most common response, it is also a sensible one. The fact of retrograde motion does not change our observation that the Earth feels stable and stationary, or that celestial bodies appear to rotate approximately about the Earth. Introducing some clever geometrical additions to the Aristotelian model, Ptolemy developed the required update. The conspicuous new element of the Ptolemaic model was its use of epicycles, or small circular orbits contained *within* the overall circular orbits followed by each planet around the Earth. The Ptolemaic model was incredibly successful, both predictively and socially: it both does an excellent job of predicting planetary motion, and was the accepted model for well over a thousand years. The problem, of course, is that the Ptolemaic model is incorrect, and posits epicycle orbits that are unmotivated by any underlying theoretical construct, but rather only by inconvenient elements of the then-extant astronomical data.

The problem of 'unnecessarily complex' model elements is straightforward to articulate, but difficult to resolve: How do we decide what is an 'unnecessary' element of a model that serves no theoretical purpose, but is only present to deal with 'inconvenient' data? By what criterion do we interpret Occam's razor? Should the number of variables in the model be counted? The range of the variables? Should we make allowances for mathematical or theoretical 'elegance' in deciding which models are 'simplest'? For example, the Copernican model (and its Keplerian extension) is in some respects *more*, not less complicated than the Ptolemaic model. The Ptolemaic orbits are all circles, and so one need not be concerned with their orientation or elongation as one must be with an elliptical orbit. The Keplerian model requires one to measure variables involving the orientation and elongation of elliptical orbits – additional variables that, on the surface, allow us to provide a better fit to the data, just as adding epicycles to circular orbits allowed Ptolemy to better fit the data. The problem with using Occam's razor as an heuristic device is that, while it may seem intuitively obvious that we should prefer a simple explanation to one that is *unnecessarily* complex, stating the problem and solution in this way is actually quite fuzzy, leaving the definition of 'simple,' 'complex,' and 'unnecessary' open to interpretation. Indeed, it is only through hindsight that we mock the complexity of the Ptolemaic model. It still fits the data, and thus as a 'mechanical engine' to predict planetary motion works quite well (and is, in fact, the mathematical model often implemented in the projection systems used by planetariums). Our ultimate preference for the Copernican system came through years of additional observations solidifying our belief in modern physics, to which the Copernican system naturally conforms and the Ptolemaic model does not. However, we do not normally have the luxury of this type of hindsight when comparing models, and it seems that an *ad hoc* rule, incapable of rigorous application, will provide an inconsistent guide to the desired outcome.

All this is *not* to say that there is no place for well-thought-out arguments of the relative merits of one hypothesis over another, including arguments based on complexity, or even 'elegance.' However, we would ideally prefer that our hypothesis-testing algorithm have a formal computation that embodies Occam's razor, rather than an amorphous heuristic whose implementation is open to debate. As an example of a formal computation based on logical principles, consider the Bayesian analyses we've developed so far. Posterior probabilities, computed via (1.5), were described in detail in the first two chapters, and such computations are based entirely on the rules of probability theory. We would like something similar to implement Occam's razor when comparing hypotheses. We will see below that this is exactly what we get, entirely for free, within the Bayesian model comparison framework described above. When comparing hypotheses via the model comparison algorithm, we compute the probability of each model. We've seen that one element of that computation is the marginalization over model parameters that yields the model likelihood, $\mathcal{L}(M_i)$ of the ith model. It turns out that a byproduct of computing the model likelihood term of the posterior is the generation of a natural penalty for the *prior explanatory power of a model*, called the **Occam factor**. This penalty is based on the total volume of parameter space over which each model is allowed to search for a good fit to the data. In other words, the Occam factor basically penalizes models that are vague. The more vague a model is, the more diffuse its predictions; an extremely vague model can be made to predict virtually any observation – an undesirable state when we would ideally like to make very definite predictions. Penalizing based on prior explanatory power solves the central problem of hypothesis testing – it will allow us to select a simpler model in preference to a more complex one when the data are inconsistent with the need for the greater explanatory power (additional complexity) of the 'complex' model. Finally, we should note that hypothesis-testing calculations, because they contain an Occam factor that is defined in part by the prior distributions over each model's parameters, cannot be performed within the frequentist framework (which has no concept of prior probability, or marginalization over parameters).

Another advantage of the Occam factor in the model comparison algorithm to be explored below is that it is more general than the quote above regarding 'unnecessary complexity': it will also penalize *flexible hypotheses*. A flexible hypothesis is one that might not be described as 'complex' in the usual sense, but which nevertheless has greater prior explanatory power (than specific, inflexible, hypotheses). These flexible hypotheses are not optimal scientific hypotheses because they are *vague*, and are therefore consistent with a wide range of results. For example, one might hypothesize that a particular drug has 'some effect' on 'mood.' This hypothesis is quite vague, allowing it to be true in a wide variety of circumstances; the hypothesis predicts no specific direction for the change, or even the specific affective dimension (e.g., feeling more anxious, less optimistic, or more calm are all possibilities). A less flexible hypothesis regarding the drug would be that it 'elevates mood.' Now, the prediction is more specific in that it predicts a particular direction for the change; it still fails, however to predict the affective dimension of change. A less flexible hypothesis than the last might be that the drug elevates levels of optimism. A still less flexible hypothesis might be that the drug reduces self-reported anxiety levels by at least 40 percent. Notice how each subsequent hypothesis in this list would be consistent with fewer and fewer experimental outcomes. As a final thought regarding flexible hypotheses, it should be pointed out that each of the hypotheses listed above could be the most appropriate hypothesis to test at a given stage of investigation into the effects of taking a new drug. When we are curious about a new mood disorder, and we are in a situation where general previous experiences point to broad groups of chemical compounds as possibly effective in altering the effects of that disorder, it would be silly to require an extremely specific hypothesis regarding the outcome of an experiment looking for such an effect (i.e., simply separating various candidate compounds into possible modulator vs. inactive groups is a useful first step). However, as your research program matures, and you learn more about the neural substrates involved in the disorder, your hypotheses regarding the effects of various drugs should become more specific. Thus, it is important to always choose competing hypotheses (for your model comparisons) that are all viable candidates for the truth, and are appropriate to the stage of your research program.

Exercises

1) Describe either a current scientific hypothesis that appears overly complicated (and why), or an historical hypothesis that has been altered to reduce its complexity (and the evidence that prompted the change).
2) Discuss some problems that might arise if hypothesis complexity were defined only in terms of the number of free parameters in the model, and how this might negatively affect our ability to compare scientific hypotheses.

6.2.2 Occam Factor: Examples

Here, we will consider a series of examples comparing pairs of models. These examples will not emphasize the model comparison algorithm, but rather are meant to highlight the nature of the Occam factor and its relationship to the prior explanatory power of the to-be-compared hypotheses. Thus, our focus will be on the evidence calculation, and the ways model likelihoods of two to-be-compared models can each contribute an 'Occam penalty' that serves ultimately to reduce the contribution of the data toward evidence favoring that model. We will recall that the two-model evidence function [expanding (6.2) and (6.3)] is

$$
\begin{aligned}
\boldsymbol{e}(M_2) &= 10\log[\mathbf{O}(M_2)] \\
&= 10\log\left[\frac{p(M_2 \mid \boldsymbol{d}\cdot\imath)}{p(\overline{M_2} \mid \boldsymbol{d}\cdot\imath)}\right] \\
&= 10\log\left[\frac{\varpi(M_2)\,\mathcal{L}(M_2)}{\varpi(M_1)\,\mathcal{L}(M_1)}\right]
\end{aligned}
$$

Which, when we set $\varpi(M_1) = \varpi(M_2)$ (equal model priors), simplifies to

$$
= 10\log\left[\frac{\varpi(M_2)\,\mathcal{L}(M_2)}{\varpi(M_1)\,\mathcal{L}(M_1)}\right] = 10\log\left[\frac{\mathcal{L}(M_2)}{\mathcal{L}(M_1)}\right] \tag{6.4}
$$

The last line of the solution is written in terms of the two model likelihoods; recall that the model likelihood, $\mathcal{L}(M_m)$, is the marginalization over all model parameters, Θ, of the mth model,

$$\mathcal{L}(M_m) = \int d\Theta \varpi(\Theta)\mathcal{L}(\Theta)$$

that serves as the normalization constant in the measurement:

$$\begin{aligned} p(\theta_1 \cdot \theta_2 \ldots \mid \boldsymbol{d} \cdot M_i \cdot \iota) &= \frac{p(\theta_1 \cdot \theta_2 \ldots \mid M_i \cdot \iota)\, p\left(\boldsymbol{d} \mid \theta_1 \cdot \theta_2 \ldots \cdot M_i \cdot \iota\right)}{\int d\theta_1 d\theta_2 \ldots p(\theta_1 \cdot \theta_2 \ldots \mid M_i \cdot \iota)\, p\left(\boldsymbol{d} \mid \theta_1 \cdot \theta_2 \cdots \cdot M_i \cdot \iota\right)} \\ &= \frac{\varpi(\Theta)\mathcal{L}(\Theta)}{\int d\Theta \varpi(\Theta)\mathcal{L}(\Theta)} \end{aligned}$$

where model M_i contains the set of adjustable parameters $\Theta = \{\theta_1, \theta_2, \ldots\}$. The normalization constant that defines the model likelihood is the marginalization over all adjustable θ parameters.

In each example, you will see that models able to search a large volume of parameter space for a good fit to data, *either* because the model has a great many parameters *or* because the model does not impose stringent limits on the range of its parameters, are more likely to fit the noise *in addition to* the underlying signal (this was the problem with the 10th-order polynomial fit in Fig. 6.1). We would prefer a model that only fits the underlying signal, effectively suppressing the noise in the data rather than treating parts of the noise as signal. Thus, there is a trade-off between the 'prior explanatory power' of a model (the volume of parameter space it is able to use when finding a fit to the data), and the extent to which that search yields a substantially better explanation of the data relative to a simpler model, arguing for the necessity of that additional model complexity. The Occam factor performs this function.

Exercises

1) Describe 'overfitting' in terms of the concepts 'signal' and 'noise.'
2) Give examples of 'parameter space' in terms of a measurement problem involving a binomial rate and also in terms of a Gaussian location with unknown variance.
3) What is the connection between the model likelihood and (1.5) written in terms of measurement?
4) Define the two elements that contribute to the size of a parameter space.

Comparing Specific Models for the Binomial Location Parameter

Here we will examine a pair of models in which each predicts a single possible location parameter, each with a different location. In M_1 it is hypothesized that the location parameter μ is equal to μ_1; a single, punctate prediction for the true location parameter. In M_2, it is hypothesized that the location parameter μ is equal to μ_2, defining a second (different) punctate prediction for the true location parameter. This type of model comparison problem can occur when remission rates or success rates or death rates are predicted based on two competing models of the underlying causes of the success, death, remission, etc.

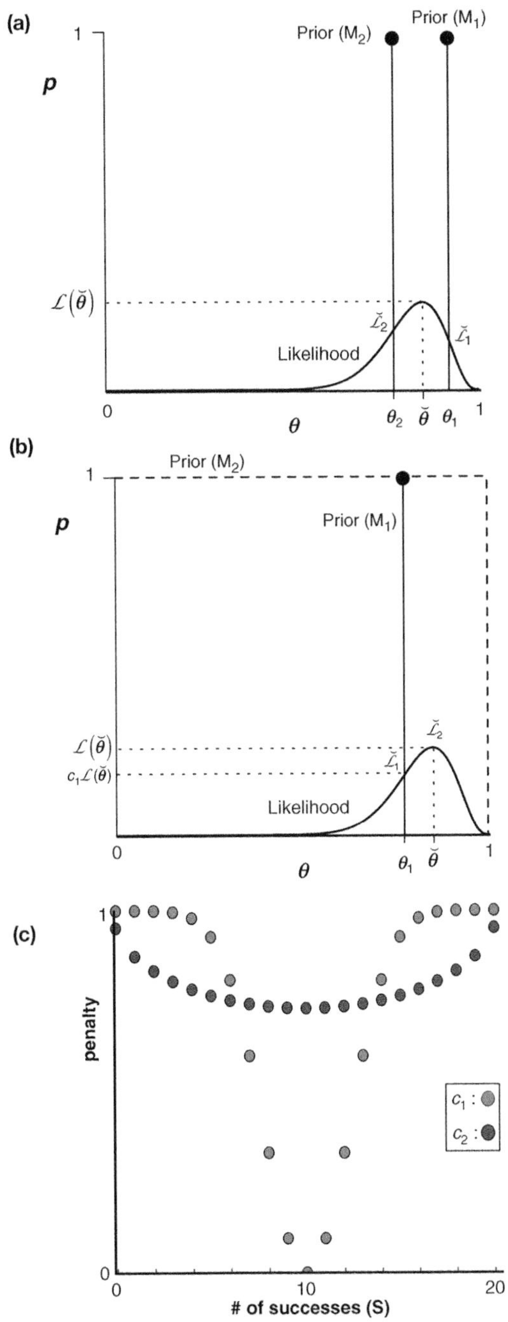

Figure 6.4 Occam Factor: binomial likelihood. (a) Prior and likelihood for the binomial location (rate) parameter, θ. Stems display the punctate predictions of the two models, M_1 and M_2, corresponding to the rates $\theta_1 = 0.9$ and $\theta_2 = 0.8$. The average observed rate, θ, is also the rate corresponding to the peak of the likelihood function, θ, and is observed at $\theta = 0.85$. (b) Likelihood function over rate (θ) and prior probabilities of the rate variable under the two models. The first model allows only a single, discrete rate to explain the data; the second model allows any possible rate [i.e., it can 'choose' the best rate within its prior range, which here is $\mathcal{L}_2 = \mathcal{L}(\theta)$] when attempting to explain the data. The data are modeled by the same likelihood under both models. (c) When writing the model likelihoods in terms of penalized ratios of the maximum Binomial likelihood, $\mathcal{L}_i = (1 - c_i)\mathcal{L}(\theta)$, with penalty c_i, the final odds ratio is simply $O_i = (1 - c_i)/(1 - c_{\bar{i}})$. The model with the lower penalty will be preferred. This is shown here for the case where the punctate model predicts $\theta = 0.5$. For other predictions, the penalty function over possible datasets will differ.

Example: Parameter-Free Models Comparing Recovery Rates

Your company has developed a new orally delivered type-II diabetes medication. Your colleague's analysis of the the chemical and biophysical properties of your new medication leads to a predicted remission rate of $\theta_1 = 0.9$; you disagree, hypothesizing instead that its properties, in conjunction with their interaction with gut flora, will result in a remission rate of only $\theta_2 = 0.8$.

The following statements define our two models (whose likelihoods are plotted in Fig 6.4a):

ι: We are observing counts, and are interested in selecting among models that make predictions about the rate of desirable versus undesirable outcomes. Therefore, we can plot both the observed rate $\hat{\theta}$ of desirable/undesirable outcomes and predicted rates on the same axes. We assume for the moment that there is no reason to have a prior preference for one model over the other, defining a prior over models of $\varpi(M_1) = \varpi(M_2)$.

M_1: $\theta = \theta_1$

M_2: $\theta = \theta_2$

In testing the new drug with 20 patients, we observe 17 cases of remission (i.e., $N = 20, S = 17$) and 3 with no change. This is an interesting case because the observed rate $\hat{\theta} = 0.85$ is exactly halfway between the two predicted rates, and one might predict that it should give no indication of a preference between the two models. We will complete the calculation to verify.

Returning to (6.4), we define the two model likelihoods for M_1 and M_2, which we will recognize are just the single-number parameter likelihoods used for measurement in this case (as in the lever-pressing example above), due to the single-value priors that define each model.

In the first model this likelihood is

$$\begin{aligned}\mathcal{L}(M_1) &= \varpi(\theta_1)\,\mathcal{L}(\theta_1) = \mathcal{L}(\theta_1)\\ &= \binom{N}{S}\theta_1^s(1-\theta_1)^{N-s} = 0.1901\end{aligned}$$

whereas for M_2 the model likelihood is

$$\begin{aligned}\mathcal{L}(M_2) &= \varpi(\theta_2)\,\mathcal{L}(\theta_2) = \mathcal{L}(\theta_2)\\ &= \binom{N}{S}\theta_2{}^s(1-\theta_2)^{N-S} = 0.2054\end{aligned}$$

Finally notice that, as always, the data ($N = 20, S = 17$) are the same in the two model likelihood calculations.

The evidence in this example problem (with equal model priors) is simply a log-transform of the ratio of the model likelihoods, or [from (6.4)]

$$\boldsymbol{e}(M_2) = 10\log\left[\frac{\mathcal{L}(M_2)}{\mathcal{L}(M_1)}\right] = 0.34\text{ dB}$$

Evidence in the Balanced Case

When the prior probabilities of each model allow for only a single point in the parameter space, the evidence calculation reduces to a log-transform of the likelihood ratio based on the maximum attainable likelihoods under the two models. This was exactly the lever-pressing example from the rat experiment above.

```
%%% press-by-press calculation
rho1=.9; rho2=.8;
N=20; S=17; dat=permlist([ones(1,S) zeros(N-S)]);
EV=cell(2,1);
for i=1:length(dat),
        datnow=dat(1:i); %for the first i data
        B1=rho1.^sum(datnow).*(1-rho1).^sum(~datnow);
        %Bernoulli prob: high-rate
        B2=rho2.^sum(datnow).*(1-rho2).^sum(~datnow);
        %Bernoulli prob: high-rate
        EV{1}(i)=10*log10(B1/B2); end %the i'th evidence value

%%% all-at-once calculation
B1=rho1.^sum(dat).*(1-rho1).^sum(~dat);
%Bernoulli prob: high-rate
B2=rho2.^sum(dat).*(1-rho2).^sum(~dat);
%Bernoulli prob: high-rate
EV(2)=10*log10(B1/B2);

%%% compare the two calculations
isnear(EV{1}(end),EV{2})
```

Although this is very little evidence, it nevertheless favors the second model (predicting $\theta = 0.8$). If you had instead made 180 tests of the new medication (rather than 20), and observed 153 successful outcomes (thus maintaining the identical rate, $\hat{\theta} = 0.85$), the final evidence calculation would have just exceeded the 3 dB threshold for a minimally detectable signal, as we will discover in the exercises.

As the most basic case where two models have balanced predictive power, and therefore no Occam penalty, this model will serve as a base comparison for the examples that follow, both of which have unbalanced predictive power and therefore produce an Occam penalty.

Exercises

1) Explain why it was that the observed maximum-likelihood value, $\check{\theta} = 0.85$, was able to yield evidence in favor of the second model, despite being exactly equidistant from the rates predicted by the two models, $\theta_1 = 0.8$ and $\theta_1 = 0.9$?
2) Make the evidence calculation for the dataset above, and for the 180/153 dataset. What element(s) of the equations creates the difference in computed evidence in the two cases?
3) Change hypotheses to $\theta = 0.45$ and 0.55, and have $\theta_{obs} = 0.5$. Is there any number of observations with $\theta_{obs} = 0.5$ that favors one of the two hypotheses. Why?
4) Find the smallest N where $\hat{\theta}$ of 0.65 favors the $\theta_2 = 0.7$ over the $\theta_1 = 0.6$ model with evidence >3 dB.

5) Update the definition of the model predicting the lower rate to include two possible rates, 0.6 and 0.8.
   a. Based on Figure 6.4a, what do you predict will happen to the evidence for the two models?
   b. Show the updated model likelihood equations and compute the model likelihoods for the updated models
   c. Based on the updated model likelihood equations, explain why the evidence changed in the way that it did.

Comparing General and Specific Models

The previous example compared models where each allowed for a single punctate binomial rate. Because these models permit the same number of hypotheses in the same parameter space, the model comparison was 'balanced' in the sense that neither had a prior advantage over the other; the final evidence contained no Occam penalty because neither was less precise than its competitor. We will now examine an 'imbalanced' comparison to see how such a penalty is generated automatically by the application of Bayes' theorem to model comparison.

Example: 'Imbalanced' Models Comparing Recovery Rates

A more common situation is one in which the two competing models are 'imbalanced,' due to less precision in the predictions of one relative to its competitor. The most extreme version of this occurs when one model makes a single punctate rate prediction as above ($\theta = \theta_1$), and one model allows for any possible rate (i.e., $0 \leq \theta \leq 1$). The following statements define our two models (whose likelihood and priors are plotted in Figure 6.4b):

ι: We are collecting data whose dimension is the same as μ (i.e., we can plot them on the same axes). We assume that the sampling dispersion σ is a known constant, and we have no prior preference for one model over the other, $\varpi(M_1) = \varpi(M_2)$.

M_1: $\theta = \theta_1$

M_2: $0 \leq \theta_2 \leq 1$

The only difference between these models is in the predicted value of the location (rate) parameter, θ. In both cases, the likelihood over the unknown rate is

$$\mathcal{L} = \binom{N}{S} (1-\theta)^{(N-S)}\theta^S$$

The prior over the unknown rate differs in the two models. In the first model, we allow only a single rate, concentrating the entire prior probability mass at the single point, θ_1 :

$$\begin{aligned}\mathcal{L}_1 &= \varpi(\theta_1)\,\mathcal{L}(\theta_1) \\ &= \binom{N}{S}(1-\theta_1)^{(N-S)}\,\theta_1^S \\ &= \left(\frac{N!}{S!(N-S)!}\right)(1-\theta_1)^{(N-S)}\,\theta_1^S = \breve{\mathcal{L}}_1\end{aligned}$$

where the prior restricts the range to a single rate, θ_1, and therefore drops out of the calculation (i.e., $\varpi(\theta_1) = 1$).

In the second model, the prior probability mass is spread evenly over the entire range of rate parameter (from 0 to 1), and the model likelihood for M_2 is computed by marginalizing over this unknown rate:[5]

$$\begin{aligned}
\mathcal{L}_2 &= \int_0^1 d\theta\, \varpi(\theta)\mathcal{L}(\theta) \\
&= \int_0^1 d\theta \begin{pmatrix} N \\ S \end{pmatrix} (1-\theta)^{(N-S+1)-1}\theta^{(S+1)-1} \\
&= \left(\frac{N!}{S!(N-S)!}\right)\frac{(S)!(N-S)!}{(N+1)!} \\
&= \left(\frac{N!}{S!(N-S)!}\right)\frac{(S)!(N-S)!}{(N+1)!}\frac{(1-\breve{\theta})^{(N-S)}\breve{\theta}^S}{(1-\breve{\theta})^{(N-S)}\breve{\theta}^S} \\
&= \frac{(S)!(N-S)!}{(N+1)!}\left[(1-\breve{\theta})^{(N-S)}\breve{\theta}^S\right]^{-1}\left(\frac{N!}{S!(N-S)!}\right)\left[(1-\breve{\theta})^{(N-S)}\breve{\theta}^S\right] \\
&= \frac{(S)!(N-S)!}{(N+1)!}\left[(1-\breve{\theta})^{(N-S)}\breve{\theta}^S\right]^{-1}\breve{\mathcal{L}}_2 = (1-c)\breve{\mathcal{L}}_2 = (1-c)\mathcal{L}(\breve{\theta}) \\
&= \frac{(S)!(N-S)!}{(N+1)!}\left[(1-\breve{\theta})^{(N-S)}\breve{\theta}^S\right]^{-1}\breve{\mathcal{L}}_2 = \breve{\mathcal{L}}_2\breve{\mathcal{L}}_2^{-1}(N+1)^{-1} = (N+1)^{-1}
\end{aligned}$$

From what we know about factorials, the ratio $\frac{(S)!(N-S)!}{(N+1)!}$ will always be less than 1. Furthermore, the product of this ratio with the $(1-\breve{\theta})^{(N-S)}\breve{\theta}^S$ term will remain less than 1 because $\breve{\theta} = S/N$.

We can define a penalty term based on the relation, $\mathcal{L}_i = (1-c_i)\mathcal{L}(\breve{\theta})$, which yields $c_i = 1 - \mathcal{L}_i/\mathcal{L}(\breve{\theta})$ or $c_i = 1 - [\mathcal{L}(\breve{\theta})(N+1)]^{-1}$, and is lowest when the observed rate is centrally located (near $\breve{\theta} = 0.5$) as opposed to when it is 'extreme' (near 0 or 1).

For the observed data ($N = 20, S = 17$), the two likelihood calculations yield

$$\mathcal{L}_1 = \breve{\mathcal{L}}_1 = \frac{20!}{17!3!}0.2^3\,0.8^{17} = .2054$$

and

$$\mathcal{L}_2 = (1-c)\breve{\mathcal{L}}_2 = (1-c)\left[\frac{20!}{17!3!}\left(\frac{3}{20}\right)^3\left(\frac{17}{20}\right)^{17}\right] = .1961[.2428] = .0476$$

The evidence is a log-transform of the ratio of the model likelihoods [from (6.4)]:

$$\begin{aligned}
\mathbf{e}(M_2) &= 10\log\left[\frac{\mathcal{L}_2}{\mathcal{L}_1}\right] = 10\log\left[\frac{(1-c_2)\breve{\mathcal{L}}_2}{\breve{\mathcal{L}}_1}\right] \\
&= -6.35dB
\end{aligned}$$

[5] The solution of the integral in the definition of $\mathcal{L}_2$ makes use of a known result called the 'beta integral:

$$B(a,b) = \int_0^1 d\theta(1-\theta)^{b-1}\theta^{a-1} = \frac{(S)!(N-S)!}{(N+1)!} \quad \{0 \le \theta \le 1$$

with the substitutions $a = S+1$ and $b = (N-S)+1$.

Programming Aside: Create Penalty Plot (Fig. 6.4c)

The penalized-maximum-likelihood form of the model likelihoods allows us to see when we should expect each model to perform well, and when it has a large penalty.

```
N=20; Lmax=nan(N+1,1); L1=nan(N+1,1); theta=.5;
for k=0:1:20,
    L1(k+1)=bpdf(k,20,theta);
    Lmax(k+1)=bpdf(k,20,k/20); end
rMaxLike=1-L1./Lmax; c=1-1./[Lmax*(N+1)];
figure; box off; hold on
plot([0:N],rMaxLike,'ko','MarkerFaceColor',.5*[1 1 1],'MarkerSize',11)
plot([0:N],c,'ko','MarkerFaceColor',.25*[1 1 1],'MarkerSize',11)
axis([-.5 20.5 0 1])
```

This calculation clearly favors the first model (predicting $\theta = 0.8$), despite the fact that the second model contains the maximum of the likelihood function. Why would we prefer a model that makes a distinct (punctate), but somewhat off-the-mark prediction over a model that can fit any observed rate exactly? We do so because the second model is nonspecific in its predictions, relative to the first model. The model comparison algorithm balances model specificity with its ability to also fit currently known data; note that an evidence calculation based only on the ratio of maximum likelihoods, and which contained no penalty for less-specific models, would be *incapable* of selecting the first model (it is essentially impossible for real data to match punctate predictions).

Our final preference for the more precise, but off-the-mark hypothesis (M_1) or for the hypothesis yielding less precise predictions but precise fits to data will depend on the trade-off between the max-likelihood ratio and c, which defines the odds ratio and therefore the final evidence calculation. The important point to understand is that when the punctate prediction of M_1 is 'close enough' to the peak of the likelihood function (i.e., $|\theta_1 - \breve{\theta}|$ is 'small'), the ratio of maximum likelihoods will favor M_2 to *less* of an extent than the penalizing effect of c on M_2, and the evidence will favor M_1; otherwise, it will favor M_2. This is obviously in sharp contrast to the situation we would find ourselves in if we had simply used the maximum likelihood ratio, which could never favor M_1.

Although it is useful to think in terms of penalized model likelihoods when trying to understand the Occam factor and how it influences the result of the evidence calculation, the evidence calculation itself can here be simplified to

$$\mathbf{e}(M_2) = 10\log\left[\frac{\mathcal{L}_2}{\mathcal{L}_1}\right] = 10\log\left(\left[\breve{\mathcal{L}}_1(N+1)\right]^{-1}\right)$$

because the model likelihood for the second, imprecise model can be simplified to $\mathcal{L}_2 = (N+1)^{-1}$.

Programming Aside: Evidence Calculation

The penalized-maximum-likelihood form of the model likelihoods allows us to see when we should expect each model to perform well, and when it has a large penalty. These penalties are computed here for the case shown in Figure 6.4b:

```
N=20; S=17; dat=permlist([ones(1,S) zeros(1,N-S)]); theta=.8;

%%% compute evidence from raw dataset
rMaxLike=bpdf(sum(dat),length(dat),sum(dat)/length(dat))/...
        bpdf(sum(dat),length(dat),theta);
c=1-(bpdf(sum(dat),length(dat),sum(dat)/length(dat))*(length(dat)+1))^-1;
EV=10*log10((rMaxLike*[1-c])^-1)

%%% compute evidence from N and S
rMaxLike=bpdf(S,N,S/N)/bpdf(S,N,theta);
c=1-(bpdf(S,N,S/N)*(N+1))^-1;
EV(2)=10*log10((rMaxLike*[1-c])^-1)

%%% simplified all-in-one computation
L1=bpdf(S,N,theta); L2=(N+1)^-1;
EV(3)=10*log10(L1/L2);

%%% compare the two calculations
isnear(EV(1),EV(2))
isnear(EV(2),EV(3))
```

Exercises

1) Explain why it is impossible for the maximum likelihood ratio to favor M_1.
2) Compute the evidence for the first model when its predicted location parameter matches the peak of the binomial likelihood, and its prediction is
   a. $\theta_1 = 0.5$
   b. $\theta_1 = 0.8$
   c. $\theta_1 = 0.95$
3) When computing binomial coefficients and other factorial-based measures, it is easy to encounter overflow/underflow problems. For example, try computing $N!/[S!(N-S)!]$, where the number of observations is between 150 and 200, and $S = N/2$:
   [bc=[]; for N=150:2:200, bc(end+1)=factorial(N)/(factorial(N/2)^2); end]
   a. At what value of N does overflow occur?
   If instead you compute the log of the factorial using the gammaln.m function, the above calculation will be [bc=[]; for N=150:2:200, bc(end+1)=gammaln(N+1)-2*gammaln(N/2+1)^2); end]
   b. Use the gammaln.m function to compute the binomial coefficients for N=150:2:200. Plot these against the log of the binomial coefficients computed in (a).
4) Create a plot of the two model likelihoods ($\theta_1 = 0.8$), over the 21 possible numbers of observed successes (for $N = 20$).
5) Explain why the model likelihood for M_2 is always $\mathcal{L}_2 = (N+1)^{-1}$.
6) Explain why the preference for M_2 is greatest when the data show N successes. What factor might mitigate this preference?

Example: Different Prior Ranges over the Gaussian Location Parameter
Here we will examine a pair of models with different prior ranges for the Gaussian location parameter. In M_1 it is hypothesized that the location parameter μ is equal to μ_1; a single, punctate prediction for the true location parameter. In M_2, it is hypothesized that μ lies within the range between μ_a and μ_b. The following statements define our two models (whose likelihoods are plotted in Figure 6.5):

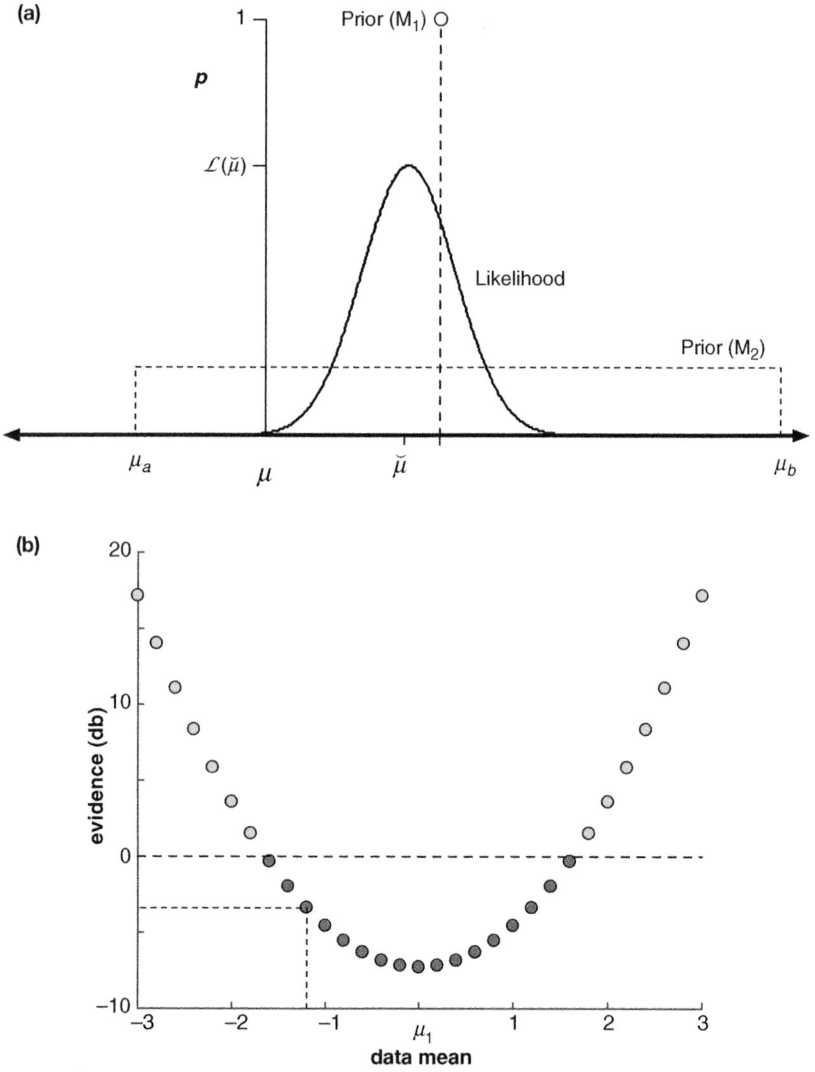

Figure 6.5 Occam Factor: Gaussian location. (a) Prior and likelihood for the Gaussian location parameter, μ. (solid line) Likelihood function for the dataset, D. (open circle) Prior probability for the location parameter under M_1. (dashed line) Prior over μ under M_2. (b) When the data are relatively close to the prediction of the punctate model (dark circles), it is preferred. This preference is due to the Occam penalty assessed to the general model, because the ratio of the maximum likelihoods never favors the punctate model for any observed dataset.

$\imath$: We are making observations of data whose dimension is the same as μ. We assume that the sampling dispersion σ is a known constant that is small compared to $\Delta\mu = \mu_b - \mu_a$.
M_1: $\mu = \mu_1$.
M_2: $\mu_a \leq \mu \leq \mu_b$, and $\sigma = \Delta\mu$).

The difference between these models is only in the priors over the location parameter, μ. In M_1, the prior is concentrated entirely at $\mu = \mu_1$. M_2 allows a range of μ values, including μ_1 (Fig. 6.5). In both cases, the Gaussian error function describing deviations of observed data values from the theoretical μ value is the same, where the width of that function is parameterized by the standard deviation, σ.

Our goal in this analysis is to compute the evidence favoring M_2 over M_1. To do this we start with (6.3):

$$\begin{aligned} \boldsymbol{e}(M_2) &= 10\log[\boldsymbol{O}(M_2)] \\ &= 10\log\left[\frac{\varpi(M_2)\mathcal{L}(M_2)}{\varpi(M_1)\mathcal{L}(M_1)}\right] = 10\log\left[\frac{\mathcal{L}(M_2)}{\mathcal{L}(M_1)}\right] \end{aligned}$$

where we have assigned equal model prior probabilities $\varpi(M_1) = \varpi(M_2)$, and their ratio drops out of the calculation. Next we compute the model likelihoods, $\mathcal{L}_i = p(\boldsymbol{d}|M_i \cdot \imath)$.

Model M1

When there are no adjustable parameters, the model likelihood is simply the likelihood computed at the single point in parameter space available to that model (multiplied by its unity prior). Here, that likelihood is the Gaussian probability:

$$\begin{aligned} \mathcal{L}_1 &= p(\mu_1|\sigma \cdot \imath)p(\boldsymbol{d}|\mu_1 \cdot \sigma \cdot \imath) \\ &= p(\boldsymbol{d}|\mu_1 \cdot \imath) \quad \{p(\mu_1|\imath) = 1 \end{aligned}$$

Notice that this probability also represents the maximum of the likelihood over the μ parameter under M_1, or $p(\boldsymbol{d}|\mu_1 \cdot \imath) = \breve{\mathcal{L}}_1$, since this model allows only one possible value of μ. Thus, we can also write the model likelihood for the first model:

$$\begin{aligned} \mathcal{L}_1 = \breve{\mathcal{L}}_1 &= [\sigma\sqrt{2\pi}]^{-N} e^{-\frac{1}{2}\frac{\sum_i (d_i - \mu_1)^2}{\sigma^2}} \\ &= [\sigma\sqrt{2\pi}]^{-N} e^{-\frac{N}{2}\frac{\overline{d^2} - \bar{d}^2}{\sigma^2}} e^{-\frac{N}{2}\frac{[\bar{d}-\mu_1]^2}{\sigma^2}} = [\sigma\sqrt{2\pi}]^{-N} e^{-\frac{N}{2}\frac{s^2}{\sigma^2}} e^{-\frac{N}{2}\frac{[\bar{d}-\mu_1]^2}{\sigma^2}} \end{aligned}$$

Model M2

For the model likelihood associated with M_2, the only unknown parameter is the Gaussian location μ, whose range is infinite, but is restricted by prior information to $\mu_a \leq \mu \leq \mu_b$. This range and parameter-type point to a Jeffreys prior over the parameter space:

$$p(\mu \mid \mu_{\mathrm{a}} \cdot \mu_b \cdot \imath) = \Delta_\mu^{-1}$$

Using the same sampling assignment as in M_1, and given $\sigma \ll \Delta$, we compute the model likelihood by integrating over the full range of the parameter:

$$\begin{aligned} \mathcal{L}_2 &= \int d\mu\varpi(\mu)\mathcal{L}(\mu) \\ &= \int d\mu p(\mu \mid \mu_{\mathrm{a}} \cdot \mu_b \cdot \imath)\left[p\left(\boldsymbol{d} \mid \mu \cdot \mu_{\mathrm{a}} \cdot \mu_b \cdot \sigma \cdot \imath\right)\right] \end{aligned}$$

$$= \int d\mu \Delta_\mu^{-1} \left[(\sigma\sqrt{2\pi})^{-1} e^{-\frac{1}{2}\frac{\sum_i (d_i-\mu)^2}{\sigma^2}} \right]$$

$$= \Delta_\mu^{-1} \left[(\sigma\sqrt{2\pi})^{-1} e^{-\frac{N}{2}\frac{s^2}{\sigma^2}} \int d\mu e^{-\frac{N}{2}\frac{[\bar{d}-\mu]^2}{\sigma^2}} \right]$$

To make further progress we must think about the exponential term under the integral. This term is a Gaussian function, $e^{-\alpha[\bar{d}-\mu]^2}$, and will therefore peak at $\breve{\mu} = \bar{d}$. Furthermore, the height of the peak is $e^{-\alpha[\bar{d}-(\breve{\mu}=\bar{d})]^2} = e^0 = 1$. Thus, the remaining bracketed terms must scale the height of this Gaussian function such that it will match the peak of the likelihood function, $\mathcal{L}(\breve{\mu}) = p(\boldsymbol{d}|\mu = \breve{\mu} \cdot \sigma \cdot \imath)$. For convenience we will represent this maximum-likelihood value as $\mathcal{L}(\breve{\mu}) = \breve{\mathcal{L}}$.

Finally, recall that all Gaussian functions have the mathematical form $e^{-\alpha\Delta x^2}$, and that Gaussian sampling distributions, which are just normalized versions of Gaussian functions, have the mathematical form: $p = \sqrt{\frac{\alpha}{\pi}} e^{-\alpha\Delta x^2}$. From this we can deduce the normalization constant of the Gaussian distribution above: $\alpha = N/(2\sigma^2)$. Finally, we write the expression for the second model likelihood:

$$\mathcal{L}_2 = \breve{\mathcal{L}}_2 \Delta_\mu^{-1} \int d\mu e^{-\frac{N}{2\sigma^2}(\bar{\mathbf{d}}-\mu)^2}$$

$$= \breve{\mathcal{L}}_2 \left(\Delta_\mu\sqrt{N}\right)^{-1} \sigma\sqrt{2\pi}$$

The Evidence Calculation

Reviewing the argument above, the evidence favoring the second model over the first (where negative evidence favors the first model) is

$$\boldsymbol{e}(M_2) = 10\log[\boldsymbol{O}(M_2)]$$

$$= 10\log\left[\frac{\mathcal{L}(M_2)}{\mathcal{L}(M_1)}\right]$$

$$= 10\log\left[\frac{\breve{\mathcal{L}}_2 \frac{\sigma\sqrt{2\pi}}{\Delta_\mu\sqrt{N}}}{\breve{\mathcal{L}}_1}\right]$$

$$= 10\log\left[\frac{\breve{\mathcal{L}}_1}{\breve{\mathcal{L}}_2}\frac{\sigma\sqrt{2\pi}}{\Delta_\mu\sqrt{N}}\right] = 10\left[\log\left(\frac{\breve{\mathcal{L}}_2}{\Delta_\mu\sqrt{N}}\right) - \log\left(\frac{\breve{\mathcal{L}}_1}{\sigma\sqrt{2\pi}}\right)\right]$$

The last line of this solution shows that the odds calculation is based on two ratios: first on the ratio of the maximum likelihoods attained by the two models, and second on the ratio of the Gaussian normalization constant, $\sigma\sqrt{2\pi}$, to the product of the range of the second model's prior and the square root of the number of observed data, $\Delta_\mu\sqrt{N}$. The first ratio will never favor the simpler model, M_1; the two maximum likelihoods can be equal only if the data happen to match perfectly the theoretical prediction for location made by the first model, encoded in the value μ_1 (an event with probability 0). The second ratio will always favor the first (simpler) model, because when $\sigma \ll \Delta_\mu$ it is safe to assume that the prior range Δ will be (at least) 4x the width of the dispersion σ (so that the mass under the likelihood function over μ is essentially all contained within that prior range). With $N = 1$ the second ratio becomes $\frac{\sigma\sqrt{2\pi}}{4\sigma\sqrt{1}} = \frac{\sqrt{\pi}}{2\sqrt{2}} < 1$; this ratio decreases to favor the first model even more strongly when more data are collected (the N term in the denominator of the ratio increases) or if the prior width of M_2 were to expand (if the model becomes even less precise in its prediction of the location parameter) independently of the the dispersion, σ.

With the evidence written as the difference between two logs, the emphasis is in comparing penalized maximum-likelihoods: the maximum likelihood value of each model is penalized, by $\sigma\sqrt{2\pi}$ in the case of the first model and by $\Delta_\mu\sqrt{N}$ in the case of the second model, and the difference between the logs of these penalized likelihoods (multiplied by 10) yields the final evidence value. This penalized-likelihood form of the calculation calls attention to the fact that if the two maximum-likelihoods are the same (they predict the data equally well, because the data mean is equal to μ_1), then the evidence will favor the model that was more specific in its predictions (as opposed to the model that can search a larger volume of parameter space to find its best fit). Furthermore, if the two likelihoods have the same penalty, then the evidence will in this case favor the model that fits the data best. This second possibility (equal penalties) could only occur if the two models had *different* predictions regarding the location parameter μ. A larger range of possible μ values that is searchable by the second model generates a disadvantageous Occam factor precisely because it is allowed to search over a larger volume of parameter space to find its maximum likelihood fit to the data.

It is also true that adding extra parameters to a model, as occurs in the comparison of a straight-line fit to a tenth-order polynomial fit shown in Figure 6.1, will generate an Occam factor that favors the simpler (straight-line) model, even if the two models allow the same range of intercept and linear slope parameters (the parameters present in both models). The tenth-order polynomial fit still has a greater total volume of parameter space over which to search for a good fit to the data.[6] So we see that the Occam factor, rather than providing a way to *implement* Occam's razor quantitatively in data analysis, is simply the *quantitative definition* of Occam's razor. The 'simpler' model, regardless of the details of the number of parameters and the relative ranges of shared parameters, is the model with the smaller Occam factor.

When calculating the final result of an hypothesis test, there is also a question of what prior probabilities to assign to the models themselves (the left-hand term in the numerator of eq. 6.2). The easiest method is to assign them equal probability for purposes of the initial analysis. However, once we have finished our initial analysis, it is informative to consider also what kinds of prior information might substantially *alter* the result found with the initial uniform probability assignment. The simplest example of this occurs when an hypothesis test using the initial default value of 0 prior evidence (prior probability of 0.5 assigned to two models) suggests that there is 20 dB of posterior evidence favoring M_2. Here, anyone who did not have at least 20 dB of prior evidence favoring M_1 would have to, based on the result of the experiment, now prefer M_2 (to an extent determined by the exact amount of prior evidence that was available). Thus, when thinking about the final result of your model comparison, it may be useful to consider what types of additional information might produce prior evidence that would lead to a change of preference, in addition to the posterior evidence available under equal priors assigned to the models.

[6] What is the effect of having additional (spurious) parameters, allowing us to search a larger volume of parameter space than if we had only the parameters necessary to capture the underlying (true) signal? If the true state of nature were generating noisy straight-line data, for example, then we can see from Figure 6.1 that extra parameters can only serve to fit the noise in the data.

Programming Aside: Penalized Ratio of Gaussian Likelihoods (Fig. 6.5c)

In the 'balanced' example the two model likelihoods were weighted equally, as neither model allowed a search over the Binomial parameter space. Here, the situation is different, in that the second model searches a large prior range of μ values to find the best fit to the data. This ability to search the parameter space for a good fit downweights M_2 in the evidence calculation; that is, it defines an Occam penalty.

```
%%% Model likelihoods and evidence
dat=[1.1,2.75,-.12,-1.23,3.84]; dat0=dat-mean(dat); Nx=length(dat);
sig=2; murange=[-3*sig 3*sig]; Dmu=diff(murange);
mu1=0;

x=linspace(x(1),murange(2),1201);
L=ones(size(x));
for n=1:Nx, L=L.*npdf(dat(n),x,sig); end

figure(3); clf; hold on;
plot(x,L,'k-','LineWidth',2.2);

L1=nan(Nx,1); L2=nan(Nx,1); EV=nan(Nx,1);
Nx=31; xlist=linspace(-3,3,Nx);
for i=1:Nx; xnow=xlist(i);
    dnow=dat0+xnow; mu2=mean(dnow);
    L1(i)=prod(npdf(dnow,mu1,sig)); %uncertain model
    L2(i)=prod(npdf(dnow,mu2,sig)); %single-mu model

    %%% compute evidence
    EV(i)=10*(log10(L2(i)./(Dmu*sqrt(Nx)))-log10(L1(i)./
    (sig*sqrt(2*pi)))); end

%%% plotting
COL={.4*[1 1 1],.8*[1 1 1]};
ind=findnearestN(xlist,mean(dat),1);

figure(3);
stem(mu1,L1(ind),'k--','LineWidth',1.2);
plot(mu1,L1(ind),'ko','MarkerFaceColor',COL{1},'MarkerSize',12,'LineWidth',1);
stem(mean(dat),L2(ind),'k--','LineWidth',1.2);
plot(mean(dat),L2,'ko','MarkerFaceColor',COL{2},'MarkerSize',12,'LineWidth',1);
xlabel(['location parameter (\mu)'],'FontName','Arial','FontSize',15)
ylabel('likelihood','FontName','Arial','FontSize',15)

figure(4); clf; hold on
plot(xlist,L2./L1,'ko','MarkerFaceColor',.7*[1 1 1],'MarkerSize',8)
plot(xlist([1 end]),[1 1]./(sig*sqrt(2*pi)/(Dmu*sqrt(Nx))),'k--','LineWidth',2)

figure(5); clf; hold on
for n=1:Nx,
    plot(xlist(n),EV(n),'ko','MarkerFaceColor',COL{(EV(n)>0)+1},...
        'MarkerSize',9,'LineWidth',1); end
plot(xlist([1 end]),[0 0],'k--','LineWidth',2)
xlabel(['data mean'],'FontSize',15)
ylabel('evidence (db)','FontName','Arial','FontSize',15)
```

Exercises

1) Evaluate the evidence when the likelihood over μ peaks at 5 with $\sigma = 2$, and:
   a. $\mu_1 = 2, \mu_2 = 6$
   b. $\mu_1 = 3, \mu_2 = 6$
   c. $\mu_1 = 4, \mu_2 = 6$
   d. $\mu_1 = 5, \mu_2 = 5$
2) Evaluate the evidence when the likelihood over μ peaks at 0 with $\sigma = 2$, and:
   e. $\mu_1 = -1, \mu_2 = 3$
   f. $\mu_1 = -1, \mu_2 = 2$
   g. $\mu_1 = -1, \mu_2 = 1$
   h. $\mu_1 = 0, \mu_2 = 0$
3) Marginalize over the μ dimension between -3 and 3 in a version of the worked problem in which the data are:
   i. $d = [-3, -2, -1, 0, 1, 2, 3]$
   j. $d = [-13, -12, -11, -10, -9, 9, 10, 11, 12]$
   Plot the full 2D density and the marginalized density in each case.
4) Above, we note that when the prior range of M_2 is large and the data provide only diffuse information regarding the location of the best μ value, the penalty is small. Create a plot of the Occam factor as σ increases in the above example. Why does the magnitude of the Occam factor asymptote for large σ? What is its smallest value?
5) Find the exact data mean yielding zero evidence favoring either model.

6.3 Model Comparison

In the previous section, examples were chosen so that the final evidence expressions could be written in terms of the Occam penalties that favor models making specific predictions over models that make more general predictions but are better at fitting an experimental dataset. Now that we can be confident that the Occam factor occurs spontaneously as part of model comparison computations, we will present additional examples of model comparisons without attempting to highlight the Occam factor. These examples are meant instead to highlight the model comparison algorithm and provide practice with its implementation, and will therefore be taken step-by-step through the model comparison algorithm.

6.3.1 Binomial Rates

The binomial rate parameter is often used in model comparisons when the underlying model contains a rate parameter describing the frequency of some event, and different hypotheses predict the event occurring at either different specific rates or ranges of rates. This rate could, for example, describe recovery following administration of a drug. In another example, you might be interested in the effect of negative emotional feedback on problem-solving ability. In such a scenario, we will make use of puzzles that have 'normative data' (previous data showing performance in a similar cohort of experimental subjects), to select puzzles that are known to be completed correctly within the allotted time by 50 percent of subjects. In the experiment we would administer two such

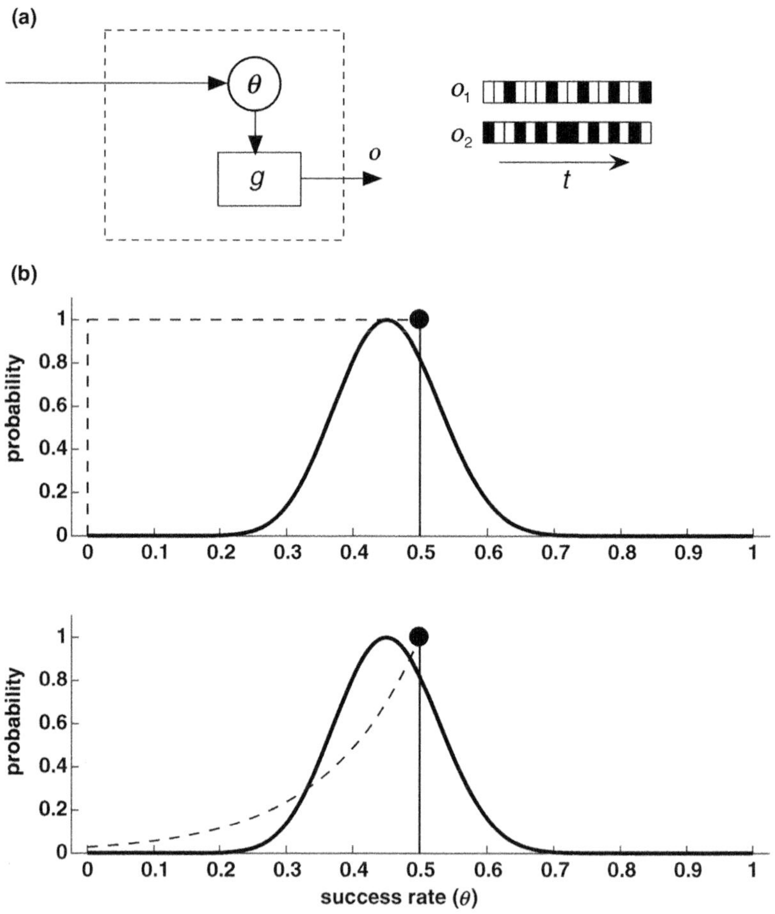

Figure 6.6 Binomial rates (a) Binomial data model, in which there is an outside influence on the success rate parameter, θ. The rate parameter feeds into a function g, that produces either a success or a failure output. Although we will not model the g function, we note that the binomial data that are produced by this model, as shown on the right for output O_1 with a rate of success less than $\theta = 0.5$ and a second output O_2 whose rate of success is $\theta = 0.5$, are a by-trial process – meaning it is clear not only how many successes have occurred but also the number of total outcomes, success or failure. (b) Binomial likelihood shown with uniform (upper) and exponential (lower) priors for M_1 and a discrete prior at $\theta = 0.5$ for M_2.

puzzles, and would give negative-valence feedback (e.g., 'It looks like you're not very good at these. At least there's just one more.') upon completing the first. There are three hypotheses that one might care to test. We will consider the first two here: first, we will verify that the success rate in the first puzzle is $\theta = 0.5$; we will also consider whether the success rate in the second puzzle conforms to the obvious prediction that discouraging feedback leads to poorer performance ($\theta < 0.5$) on the second puzzle.

Example: Test for Reduced Success Rate ($\theta < 0.5$)
A. Translate Hypotheses into Model Equations

In the previous example we had a specific prediction, namely, that the success rate would be $\theta = 0.5$. Here, however, we are predicting that the success rate will be below $\theta = 0.5$, with no specific prediction regarding the exact rate beyond this. The model could therefore be written:

M_1: The puzzle is completed correctly at a rate below $\theta = 0.5$ [$\theta_1 < 0.5$].

As before, we must be concerned with the comparison we would like to make with this hypothesis. For example, we might simply compare this to the model in which the success rate is exactly $\theta = 0.5$, as was reported in the normative study by the distributor. This would make the second model:

M_2: The puzzle is completed correctly at a rate of $\theta = 0.5$ [$\theta_2 = 0.5$]

However, if we define the odds ratio as $\boldsymbol{O}(M_1) = \frac{p(M_1|\boldsymbol{d}\cdot\iota)}{p(\overline{M}_1|\boldsymbol{d}\cdot\iota)}$, the negation of M_1 is any model parameter that is *not* less than 0.5; in other words, the comparison should be made against all possible rates that are inconsistent with the first model; this is an interesting scenario for exactly that reason. Logically, we would never predict that this feedback would lead to *improved* performance, but while constructing the model $\overline{M}_1$ we must address these rates. In the present case, it seems most reasonable to use the comparison $\overline{M}_1 = M_2$, and stipulate that rates above $\theta = 0.5$ are not possible: this is equivalent to using the discrete hypothesis, $\theta = 0.5$, which naturally excludes all values of the rate parameter other than this single specific rate. The alternative would be to allow for improvements caused by the previous feedback, and define a model M_2 in which higher rates are allowed, although the prior over these rates need not be uniform). The important thing to recognize is that the alternative to M_1 encoded in $\overline{M}_1$ must be, by your hypotheses and background information, the total of the allowable hypothetical outcomes that are not defined by the first hypothesis. If we intend to define M_2 as allowing only a subset of the states in $\overline{M}_1$, the disallowed states must be explicitly excluded as part of the prior information defining M_2.

Here again we have a Bernoulli-trial-based experiment, and the likelihood is given by

$$\mathcal{L} = \binom{N}{S} (1-\theta)^{(N-S)} \theta^S$$

where the prior probabilities over these rate parameters for the two models are

$$\varpi_1(\theta) = \begin{cases} 0 & \theta \geq 0.5 \\ 1 & \theta < 0.5 \end{cases}$$

whereas the second model defines the prior probabilities:

$$\varpi_2(\theta) = \begin{cases} 0 & \theta \neq 0.5 \\ 1 & \theta = 0.5 \end{cases}$$

These priors and binomial likelihood over the rate parameter, θ, based on the current background information, are shown graphically in Figure 6.6b. Notice that we have chosen a definition of M_2 in which we exclude all probabilities above $\theta = 0.5$. We have also chosen a definition of M_1 in which all probabilities below $\theta = 0.5$ are assigned equal prior probabilities. The latter choice was one of convenience; we will use this as a starting point for a more complex analysis, since it does not quite represent our information regarding M_1. Specifically, we would not really want to assign the same prior probabilities to $\theta = 0$ and $\theta = 0.49$, and yet this is the situation described above by the uniform prior. A better choice of prior, and one explored in the programming aside below, might assign lower and lower prior probabilities to greater deviations from the nominal rate of $\theta = 0.5$, as encoded by the exponential distribution[7] shown in Figure 6.6b.

The odds ratio that will define our model comparison is

$$O(M_1) = \frac{p(M_1 \mid \cdot \boldsymbol{d} \cdot \iota)}{p(\overline{M_1} \mid \boldsymbol{d} \cdot \iota)} = \frac{\varpi(M_1)\int_{M_1} d\theta\, \varpi_1(\theta)\mathcal{L}(\theta)}{\varpi(M_2)\left[\varpi_2(\theta)\mathcal{L}(\theta)\right]}$$

Notice that whereas in the previous example the primary model of interest, M_1, was a discrete hypothesis, it is now the secondary (comparison) hypothesis that is discrete. Thus, we must integrate over possible model parameters in the first model to obtain a ratio of scalars for the odds computation. To continue expanding this odds computation, our next step is to think about the prior probabilities of the two models.

B. Assign Prior Probabilities to Hypotheses

Here the experimental hypotheses will be assigned equal prior probabilities, $\varpi_1 = \varpi_2$. As we have discussed previously, we will examine other possible assignments to the prior over hypotheses as part of our discussion of the result of the model comparison.

C. Compute Model Likelihoods

Success rate is described by the Bernoulli constant whose unknown value we assign the variable θ, and we are interested in distinguishing between two models that differ in terms of the predicted success rate. Here, the two models represent one discrete probability, and one integral over half the parameter space, $0 \leq \theta < 0.5$. From (**A**), we recall that the odds ratio for these two models, describing the weight of evidence favoring the first of the two models, is the product of the prior odds ratio and the model likelihood ratio:

$$\boldsymbol{O}(M_1) = \frac{p(M_1 \mid \boldsymbol{d} \cdot \iota)}{p(\overline{M_1} \mid \boldsymbol{d} \cdot \iota)} = \frac{\varpi(M_1)\int_{\theta_1} d\theta\, \varpi_1(\theta)\mathcal{L}(\theta)}{\varpi(M_2)\left[\varpi_2(\theta)\mathcal{L}(\theta)\right]} = \frac{\varpi_1}{\varpi_2}\frac{\mathcal{L}_1}{\mathcal{L}_2}$$

These ratios are, as ever, ratios of scalars. In the case of the likelihood ratio, the first term (denoting the range of possible parameter values allowed by the first model with an M_1 subscript on the integral, the likelihood of the first model is

$$\mathcal{L}_1 = \int_{M_1} d\theta\, \varpi_1(\theta)\mathcal{L}(\theta) = \int_0^{0.5} d\theta\, \varpi_1(\theta)\mathcal{L}(\theta)$$

This integral has no closed-form solution (as the integral over the entire range had, in the Beta function), and so we will compute this likelihood numerically (note that while there is no closed-form solution for an integral over part of the binomial parameter space, there is nevertheless an incomplete Beta function[8] that has a fast built-in algorithm for its solution using MATLAB® or other computational programming language. This solution is also demonstrated).

[7] This exponential is defined by the equation, $\varpi_2(\theta) = \lambda e^{-\lambda\theta}/[1 - e^{-\lambda\theta_{\max}}]$, with $\lambda = -7.187$ and $\theta_{\max} = 0.5$.

[8] The incomplete Beta function is very similar to the Beta function, and includes the Beta function as a normalizing factor:

$$I_x = \frac{1}{\mathrm{B}(a,b)}\int_0^x d\theta(1-\theta)^{b-1}\theta^{a-1} \quad \{0 \leq \theta \leq 1$$

As above, our use of the incomplete beta function to solve the current integral depends on the substitutions $a = S + 1$ and $b = (N - S) + 1$.

Programming Aside: Evidence Based on a Truncated Range of Possible Rate Parameters

In the previous example, we demonstrated numerical calculation of the model likelihood when the model allowed the full range of possible rate parameters (i.e., the possible rates spanned the full binomial range, [0,1]). Here we will numerically compute the likelihood for both a model that uses a uniform and one that uses an exponential prior range, both now over only half the binomial range.

```
%%% prelim
N=40; S=14; thetas=linspace(0,.5,1201); theta2=0.5;
like2=bpdf(S,N,theta2);
EV=nan(1,2);

%%% numerical solution for Fig. 6.6b,upper
pri=2*ones(size(thetas));
like1=trapz(thetas,pri.*bpdf(S,N,thetas));
EV(1)=10*(log10(like1)-log10(like2));

%%% numerical solution for Fig. 6.6b,lower
lambda=-7.187; Tmax=.5;
pri=lambda.*exp(-lambda.*thetas)./(1-exp(-lambda.*Tmax));
like1=trapz(thetas,pri.*bpdf(S,N,thetas));
EV(2)=10*(log10(like1)-log10(like2));

%%% compare the two calculations
EV
```

Evaluation of the model likelihood for the second model is straightforward,

$$\begin{aligned}\mathcal{L}_2 &= \varpi_2(\theta)\mathcal{L}(\theta) = \mathcal{L}(\theta_2) \\ &= \left(\frac{N!}{S!(N-S)!}\right)\left(1-\theta'\right)^{(N-S)}\theta'^{S} = \breve{\mathcal{L}}_2\end{aligned}$$

and is just the binomial likelihood evaluated at the discrete prediction of the second model, $\theta_2 = 0.5$.

D. Compute the Evidence

Recalling the odds ratio that defines our evidence calculation (and assuming equal prior odds, which drops the prior odds ratio from the calculation), we will want to compute the odds of the first model:

$$\begin{aligned}\boldsymbol{O}(M_1) &= \frac{p\left(M_1 \mid \boldsymbol{d}\cdot\iota\right)}{p\left(\overline{M}_1 \mid \boldsymbol{d}\cdot\iota\right)} \\ &= \frac{\mathcal{L}_1}{\mathcal{L}_2} = \breve{\mathcal{L}}_2^{-1}\int_0^{0.5} d\theta\,\varpi_1(\theta)\mathcal{L}(\theta)\end{aligned}$$

which we will compute via the numerical integration techniques of Appendix C. This solution is described in the programming aside and yields evidence of

Programming Aside: Evidence Calculation Using the Incomplete Beta Function

If we are prepared to use the uniform prior over the possible rates of the first model, we have the option of using the incomplete beta function to evaluate the evidence. We require the uniform prior in this instance because this prior allows us to simply scale the result of the integral rather than integrate the product of the likelihood and prior over the rate parameter.

```
%%% prelim
a=S+1; b=N-S+1;

%%% solution using the incomplete beta
like1=2*betainc(.5,a,b)/(N+1);
EV(3)=10*(log10(like1)-log10(like2))
```

$$
\begin{aligned}
e(M_1) &= 10\log_{10} O(M_1) \\
&= \log_{10}[\mathcal{L}_1] - \log_{10}[\mathcal{L}_2] \\
&= \log_{10}\left[\int_0^{0.5} d\theta\, \varpi_1(\theta)\mathcal{L}(\theta)\right] - \log_{10}\left[\check{\mathcal{L}}_2\right] \\
&= 3.5dB \quad [uniform] \\
&= 5.1dB \quad [exponential]
\end{aligned}
$$

The second method of solution for this model comparison, which is valid for the uniform-distribution version of the definition of M_1, is to use the Beta and the incomplete Beta functions:

$$
\begin{aligned}
e(M_1) &= \log_{10}\left[\int_0^{0.5} d\theta\, \varpi_1(\theta)\mathcal{L}(\theta)\right] - \log_{10}\left[\check{\mathcal{L}}_2\right] \\
&= \log_{10}\left[(2)\left(\frac{I_x(a,b)}{N+1}\right)\right] - \log_{10}\left[\check{\mathcal{L}}_2\right] \\
&= 3.5\, dB
\end{aligned}
$$

This method is demonstrated in the second programming aside.

Exercises

1) Why is the method of solution using Beta functions only valid for the uniform-distribution version of the definition of M_1?
2) Based on the example give above write the expression for, and compute the evidence in favor of M_2. Show your work, using numerical integration over the unknown binomial rate.

3) Compute the two model likelihoods if the success rate had been:
   a. $S = 12$ and $N = 40$
   b. $S = 18$ and $N = 40$
   c. $S = 22$ and $N = 40$
4) Compute the evidence in favor of both M_1 and M_2 if the data had been:
   a. $S = 18$ and $N = 30$
   b. $S = 23$ and $N = 40$
   c. $S = 28$ and $N = 50$.
5) The current test of the hypothesis that there is a negative effect on performance of a second puzzle following the negative-valence feedback resulting from a first puzzle is somewhat indirect. It relies on the assumption that there is a true $\theta = 0.5$ success rate for these puzzles under 'normal' conditions. Describe an experiment, and model comparison for the resulting data, that is a more direct test of this hypothesis.
6) If we were comparing models to verify the nominal 0.5 success rate, write the expression for, and compute the evidence in favor of each. Show your work, including any numerical integration over binomial rate.
7) If we were comparing models to verify the nominal 0.5 success rate, compute the two model likelihoods if the success rate had been:
   a. $S = 12$ and $N = 40$
   b. $S = 18$ and $N = 40$
   c. $S = 22$ and $N = 40$
8) If we were comparing models to verify the nominal 0.5 success rate, compute the evidence in favor of both M_1 and M_2 if the data had been:
   a. $S = 18$ and $N = 30$
   b. $S = 23$ and $N = 40$
   c. $S = 28$ and $N = 50$

6.3.2 Rate Differences

In the previous example we saw that the evidence equation naturally reduced to a form that tested whether the difference between the observed rates matched the expected source strength difference between the click-streams at the two ears. In the present example we would like to ask a different, and more general question: we would like to test whether one quantity/signal is larger/stronger than another, regardless of rate.

Example: Difference in Recovery Rate

In our first example, the specific experimental context will be that of drug development, where we are interested in whether the rate of symptom reduction from a new anti-anxiolytic drug is equal to, or whether it is better than the symptom reduction ('recovery') rate resulting from the current standard of care.

A. Translate Hypotheses into Model Equations

This is a model comparison question, where the two possible models: one for which both rate parameters are assumed equal, and one in which the new drug displays superior performance; further there is no constraint on the absolute rate of recovery (if they are equal), or on the recovery rate produced by the current standard of care (θ_1, if they are unequal). Experimental data show seventy-eight cases of symptom reduction with the

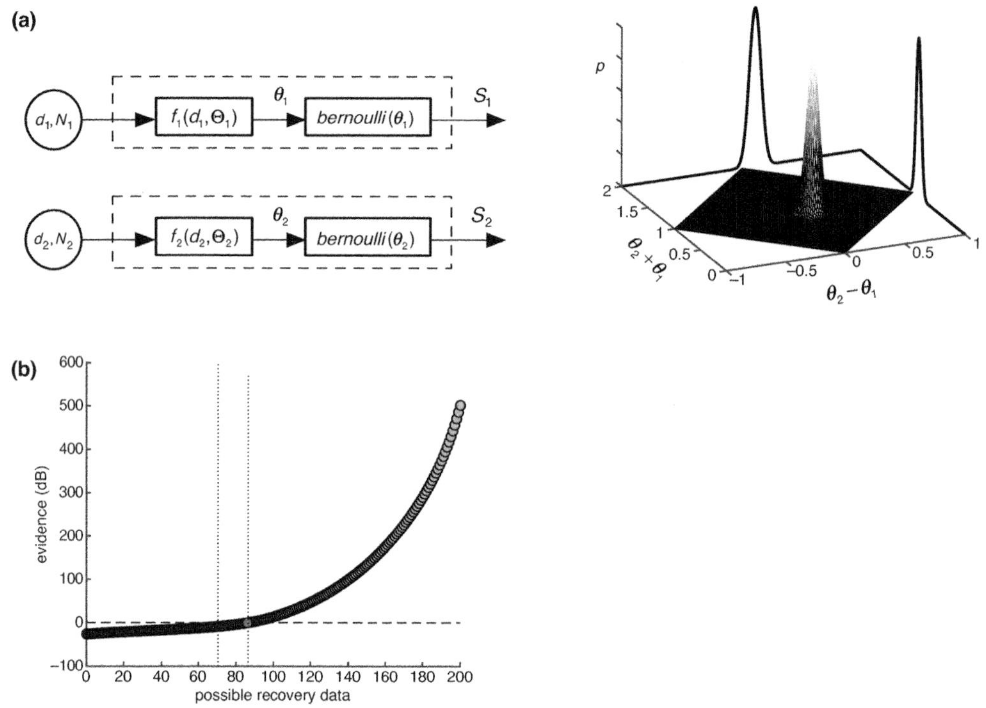

Figure 6.7 Rate difference. (a) Graphical model suggesting the difference of rates (left). The 2D distribution over sums and differences of binomial rates (right; see Appendix C) contains all the information in the 2D distribution over the binomial success rates for the two medications. Marginal distributions are also shown, which marginalize over possible sums and differences of binomial rates. (b) Evidence as a function of the number of recoveries observed in the new-drug group.

old drug ($S_1 = 78$), and ninety with the new drug ($S_2 = 90$), out of 200 patients in both groups ($N_1 = N_2 = 200$).

M_1 : The recovery rates from the two treatments are equal $[\theta_1 = \theta_2]$.
M_2 : The recovery rate produced by the new treatment is greater than that of the old treatment $[\theta_2 > \theta_1]$.

On the surface this may seem quite similar to previous problems involving binomial rates in which we tested, for example whether the rate was $\theta = 0.5$ as compared to $\theta > 0.5$. These problems are similar, but the current problem is a much-expanded version; we now have two rates, θ_1 and θ_2, *neither of which is uniquely specified.* Here, instead of testing just one contingency ($\theta = 0.5$ vs. $\theta > 0.5$), we are testing all contingencies of the form: $\theta_1 = q$ *and* $\theta_2 > q$ versus $\theta_1 = q$ *and* $\theta_2 = q$, where the q variable can take on any value, $0 \leq q \leq 1$. The current problem therefore corresponds to choosing between a model in which the *difference* ($\Delta = \theta_2 - \theta_1$) between the rate parameters is $\Delta = 0$ versus the model in which the difference is $\Delta > 0$. This formulation of the problem in terms of Δ predictions, while equivalent to that stated above in terms of the two separate rates, makes explicit our need of the probability distribution over differences of rate parameters. This, as we will recall from Appendix C, relies on the cross-correlation operation applied to the probability distributions over the two rate parameters computed individually. For the model comparison problem, we will then need to integrate over the unknown difference parameter, $\Delta > 0$, to obtain the model likelihood of the second model (which allows for any delta in this range), and compare it to the model likelihood for the first model that allows only a single value of the difference parameter, $\Delta = 0$.

The outcome of this analysis will be the odds ratio,

$$\boldsymbol{O}(M_2) = \frac{p(M_2 \mid \boldsymbol{d} \cdot \iota)}{p(\overline{M}_2 \mid \boldsymbol{d} \cdot \iota)} = \frac{\varpi(M_2)}{\varpi(M_1)} \frac{\left[\int_{\Delta>0} d\Delta \varpi_2(\Delta)\mathcal{L}(\Delta)\right]}{[\varpi_1(\Delta)\mathcal{L}(\Delta)]} = \frac{\varpi_2 \mathcal{L}_2}{\varpi_1 \mathcal{L}_1}$$

based on the two model likelihoods. These will be needed below to compute the evidence in favor of model M_2, which states that the binomial success rate corresponding to the new anti-anxiolytic medication is higher than that of the standard medication.

B. Assign Prior Probabilities to Hypotheses

Initially in each analysis we have assumed that the prior probability distribution over models was uniform. This assumption can be replaced with a more informed prior, if additional prior information is available. Here, we should have access to preliminary data indicating the range of success rates that would be reasonable to expect of the new medication, as well as the published success rates of the old medication. At present, however, we will begin with equal model priors:

$$\varpi(M_s) = \varpi(M_d) = 0.5.$$

C. Compute Model Likelihoods

The model likelihood is always the joint posterior over all unknown parameters in the model, marginalized over all possible values of each of the unknown parameters, given by (6.1). We must therefore set up the measurement question, and then marginalize over all parameters to obtain a single number, which is the model likelihood. For the two models considered here, the measurement problem is solved easily for the no-difference model (M_1), because the only allowable parameter estimate is $\Delta = 0$, which allows us to simply select that likelihood.

The model likelihood for the second model depends on the prior over the unknown model parameters, θ_1 and θ_2. Any 2D prior over differences of these variables must be confined to the range, $0 < \Delta \leq 1$, but may otherwise incorporate prior information regarding the more or less likely parameter values (either the $\Delta = \theta_2 - \theta_1$ parameter, or of the initial θ_1 and θ_2 parameters). For example, one might just default to a uniform prior over either the difference parameter (Δ), or over the two θ parameters. Neither of these is particularly appropriate to the current model, because if we are attempting to encode an uninformed state, the Jeffreys prior over the two θ parameters would be more appropriate; further, we should expect a smaller rather than a larger Δ parameter, both because uninformed priors over the two θ parameters will yield a prior over the Δ parameter that peaks near $\Delta = 0$, but also because it is more likely that a new drug will be an incremental (as opposed to a massive) improvement over an existing drug. To encode this we might use an exponential prior over the Δ parameter. This exponential is similar to the prior over the Δ parameter that results from use of the least-informed (Jeffreys) prior over the two unknown model parameters, θ_1 and θ_2.

Programming Aside: Difference of Binomial Rates (Fig. 6.7)

Recalling the method of computing differences of probability coordinates described in Appendix C, we will use that routine to obtain the posterior over differences to compute the model likelihoods and evidence for the current problem.

```
clear
plotFLAG=0; %#ok<*UNRCH>
N=200; S=[80 71]; Ntics=101; lambda=2.6721; Tmax=1;
thetas=linspace(0,1,Ntics+2)'; thetas=thetas(2:end-1);
s=struct;

%compute 2D Jeffreys prior over differences of rates
jef=[(thetas.*(1-thetas)).^-.5 thetas]; [~, ~, s.priJ]=pSumDiff(jef,jef,[],1,1);
eval(s.priJ.evalprep('s.priJ')); priSDj=pSD; %extract pSD, icell,
%Dmat, Smat

%%% separate prior; I0 consistent with M1, Ip consistent with M2
Ip=Dmat>0; I0=Dmat==0; In=Dmat<=0;
priSDJ0=priSDj.*I0/sum(sum(priSDj.*I0)); pmax=max(max(priSDJ0));
priSDJp=priSDj.*Ip/sum(sum(priSDj.*Ip)); pmax(2)=max(max(priSDJp));

if plotFLAG, figure(3); clf; hold on
    mesh(Dmat,Smat,priSDJ0); colormap(bone)
    plotmat([Dmat(:),Smat(:),priSDJ0(:)],'k.'); r0=axis;
    figure(4); clf; hold on
    mesh(Dmat,Smat,priSDJp); colormap(bone)
    plotmat([Dmat(:),Smat(:),priSDJp(:)],'k.'); rp=axis;
    for f=3:4, figure(f); axis([r0(1:4) 0 .01]); view(-20,10); end, end

Stest=0:N;
EVtest=nan(size(Stest));
for Snow=0:200,
    vbp1=[bpdf(Snow,N,thetas) thetas];
    vbp2=[bpdf(S(2),N,thetas) thetas];

    %%% compute likelihoods of differences and sums of binomial
    rates
    [~,~, s.like]=pSumDiff(vbp1,vbp2,[],1,1);
    eval(s.like.evalprep('s.like')); likeSD=pSD;

    pSD=priSDJ0.*likeSD; pSDJ0=pSD;
    eval(s.like.evals{2}); pDJ=pD(:,1); %compute pD from pSD, Dmat

    pSD=priSDJp.*likeSD; pSDJp=pSD;
    eval(s.like.evals{2}); pDJ=[pDJ pD]; %compute pD from pSD, Dmat

    ML=sum(pDJ(:,1:2));

    %odds computation
    o=ML(:,2)./ML(:,1);

    %%% evidence
    EVtest(Snow+1)=10*log10(o);
    if and(plotFLAG,Snow==S(1)),
        EV=10*log10(o); %EV(1)=.73, for uniform over delta
        figure(5); clf; hold on
        mesh(Dmat,Smat,pSDJ0); colormap(bone); plot3(Dmat(:),Smat(:),pSDJ0(:),'k.');
        plot3(str8n(Dmat(I0)),str8n(Smat(I0)),pSDJ0(I0),'o',...
            'MarkerFaceColor',.65*[1 1 1],'MarkerEdgeColor',.6*[1 1 1],'MarkerSize',4)
```

```
        plotmat([pDJ(:,3) max(Smat(:))*ones(size(pDJ(:,3))) ...
                max(max(pSDJ0))*pDJ(:,1)/max(pDJ(:,1))],'ko',...
                'MarkerFaceColor','k','MarkerSize',10);
        plot3([0 0],max(Smat(:))*[1 1], [0 max(max(pSDJ0))],'k-')
                ind0=find(pDJ(:,3)~=0); plotmat([pDJ(ind0,3) max(Smat(:))...
                *ones(size(ind0)) ...
        zeros(size(ind0))],'ko','MarkerFaceColor',.65*[1 1 1],...
        'MarkerSize',8);
        a=6.5; b=48.5;
        view(a,b); r2=axis; r2(1:2)=[-.8 .8]; axis(r2)

        figure(6); clf; hold on
        mesh(Dmat,Smat,max(max(pSDJ0))*pSDJp/max(max(pSDJp))); colormap(bone);
        plot3(Dmat(:),Smat(:),max(max(pSDJ0))*pSDJp(:)/max(max(pSDJp)),'k.');
        plot3(str8n(Dmat(Ip)),str8n(Smat(Ip)),zeros(sum(Ip(:))),...
        'o','MarkerFaceColor',.6*[1 11],'MarkerEdgeColor',
        .65*[1 1 1],'MarkerSize',4)
        plotmat([pDJ(:,3) max(Smat(:))*ones(size(pDJ(:,3)))
        max(max(pSDJ0))*pDJ(:,2)/max(pDJ(:,2))],'ko',
        'MarkerFaceColor','k','MarkerSize',8);
        ind0=find(pDJ(:,3)<=0); plotmat([pDJ(ind0,3) max(Smat(:))*ones(size(ind0)) ...
             zeros(size(ind0))],'ko','MarkerFaceColor',.65*[1 1 1],'MarkerSize',8);
        view(-a,b); axis(r2)

        figure(7); clf; stem([-1 1],ML,'ko','MarkerFaceColor','k','MarkerSize',15)
        r=axis; axis([-1.5 1.5 r(3:4)]); box off; end, end

figure(8); clf; hold on
plot([0 N],[0 0],'k--')
plot(Stest(EVtest>0),EVtest(EVtest>0),'ko','MarkerFaceColor',.7*[1 1 1],'MarkerSize',11)
plot(Stest(EVtest<0),EVtest(EVtest<0),'ko','MarkerFaceColor',.4*[1 1 1],'MarkerSize',11)
r=axis;
plot((Stest(find(EVtest>0,1))-.5)*[1 1],r(3:4),'k:')
plot((Stest(Stest==S(2))-.5)*[1 1],r(3:4),'k:')
xlabel('possible recovery data','FontName','Arial','FontSize',14)
ylabel('evidence (dB)','FontName','Arial','FontSize',14)
```

D. Compute the Evidence

The evidence is computed based on the odds, which will in turn depend on the prior over the Δ parameter. The odds is computed using the values defined above under (**A**):

$$\begin{aligned}
\boldsymbol{e}(M_2) &= 10\log_{10}\left[\frac{p(M_2 \mid \boldsymbol{d}\cdot\iota)}{p(\overline{M}_2 \mid \boldsymbol{d}\cdot\iota)}\right] \\
&= 10\log_{10}\left[\frac{\varpi_2\mathcal{L}_2}{\varpi_1\mathcal{L}_1}\right] = 10\log_{10}\left[\frac{\mathcal{L}_2}{\mathcal{L}_1}\right] \\
&= 10\log_{10}\left[\frac{\int d\Delta\varpi_2(\Delta>0)\mathcal{L}(\Delta)}{\varpi_1(\Delta=0)\mathcal{L}(\Delta)}\right]
\end{aligned}$$

Under the integral we find the prior over the Δ parameter, which we will either assign directly (as in the uniform and exponential priors over Δ in the programming aside, shown graphically in Figure 6.7b), or provide an assignment of priors over the 'raw' θ parameters coupled with lossy parameter transform. This integral is the area under the product of the likelihood over Δ, and one of the priors over Δ (any of the priors with positive probability extending over the range $0 < \Delta \leq 1$). The evidence computations corresponding to each of the priors are demonstrated graphically in the PA. Note that each represents the solution to a different problem, where each problem asserts a different type of prior information regarding the probable values of θ, Δ, or both.

The evidence calculation, as always, provides us with a single number. However, when we are simulating our experiment prior to collecting data, it is often useful to get a broader sense of the bounds at which our experiment will be likely to produce useful results, and what kinds of data we should collect to produce the strongest case for or against the models/hypotheses under consideration. One way to do this is to repeat the evidence calculation for a range of potential datasets. Figure 6.7b demonstrates this calculation, assuming a constant 200 observations in each of the control and new-drug groups, and a constant number of recoveries in the control group (control data may have been collected in an earlier experiment, or possibly by the drug company that produces the original drug).

Exercises

1) Plot the 2D Jeffreys prior over sums and differences of the θ parameters.
2) What are the assumptions regarding possible rates, and possible differences of rates? Are these assumptions reasonable in this drug-testing scenario? Explain.
3) Compute the evidence for M_2 based on $N = 200$ and $S = [70, 92]$.
4) What is the smallest difference, with $\bar{\theta} = 81.5$, that will yield evidence in favor of M_2, using any choice of prior you prefer.
5) In Section 6.3.1 above, it is mentioned that there are three ways to examine the possible decrease in success rate for solving the second of the two puzzles, following negative-valence feedback on the first puzzle. One could also look at whether there is decrease in the success rate, modeled as a difference between success on the first puzzle and success on the second puzzle (which can be justified based on the fact that the normative data shows equal success for the two puzzles; though a preferable experiment would be one in which there are two groups of subjects, one-half receive no feedback and one-half receive negative-valence feedback, and the difference in success rates between the two groups was tested).
   Compute the difference in success rate between the two puzzles, and perform a model comparison of these data. Describe this result with respect to the outcome of the model comparisons performed in Section 3.1.2.
6) Convert the problem to one involving spike rates (based on a Poisson sampling distribution), and compare models predicting no difference between spike rates and one predicting a greater rate in one of the two neurons.

6.3.3 Model Comparison for the Gaussian Likelihood

Here we will examine a series of models involving Gaussian likelihoods that are similar to models considered above that feature discrete sampling distributions. Previous models involved success rates, and therefore were focused on experiments that could yield only discrete outcomes, either yes/no, or success/failure. For the remainder of this section we will be primarily concerned with continuous data types (data that can take any value on the real line, rather than data consisting only of discrete counts and the counting numbers). Thus, whereas in a previous model comparison problem we observed the number of subjects successfully completing a puzzle or the number of rewarded lever presses made by an experimental animal, we might here observe data from a memory-based Vernier setting in the following experiment (see Fig. 6.8a): A vertical line is briefly presented just above the half-height of a computer screen. After a short delay, a second vertical line is presented just below the half-height line, and subjects are required to adjust this (lower) second line to match the horizontal position of the first (upper, briefly presented) line.

It should not be surprising that the precision of the adjustment will be affected by the length of the memory delay (as well as the length of the first line. If the two lines are presented simultaneously, we have the well-known Vernier acuity test, and precision is within the visual-angle width of a retinal cone. With an imposed memory delay, precision will be degraded, and we might also expect that settings would become biased, perhaps toward the initial position of the adjustable second line. We will examine both hypotheses (separately) in examples below.

Example: Bias in Gaussian Model

Since we know that bias is defined as a consistent offset between the true value and an estimate, we can extrapolate and define bias in the Vernier discrimination to mean that there is nonzero error in the settings made with the lower vertical bar in Figure 6.8a.

A. Translate Hypotheses into Model Equations

Translating the definition of bias as it relates to the Vernier discrimination described above, we define the following:

ι: Vernier perceptual settings of the alignment of vertical line segments are performed with an imposed memory delay.

M_0: The bias of Vernier settings is $b = 0$, indicating an unbiased perceptual discrimination.

M_b: The bias of Vernier settings is $b \neq 0$, indicating a biased perceptual discrimination

In this problem we will simulate Vernier settings, s_i, and compute the evidence in favor of an underlying model of those settings in which they are biased (i.e., nonzero) versus unbiased. This evidence calculation[9] is one of the most basic that we will encounter, and is found in various guises in a great many contexts.

We will simulate Vernier perceptual settings from a Gaussian sampling distribution that is either biased or unbiased relative to the true position μ of the upper bar:

M_0: $s_i = nrand(\mu, \sigma)$
M_b: $s_i = nrand(\mu + b, \sigma)$

[9] This is essentially the calculation demonstrated above when we examined the concept of the Occam penalty.

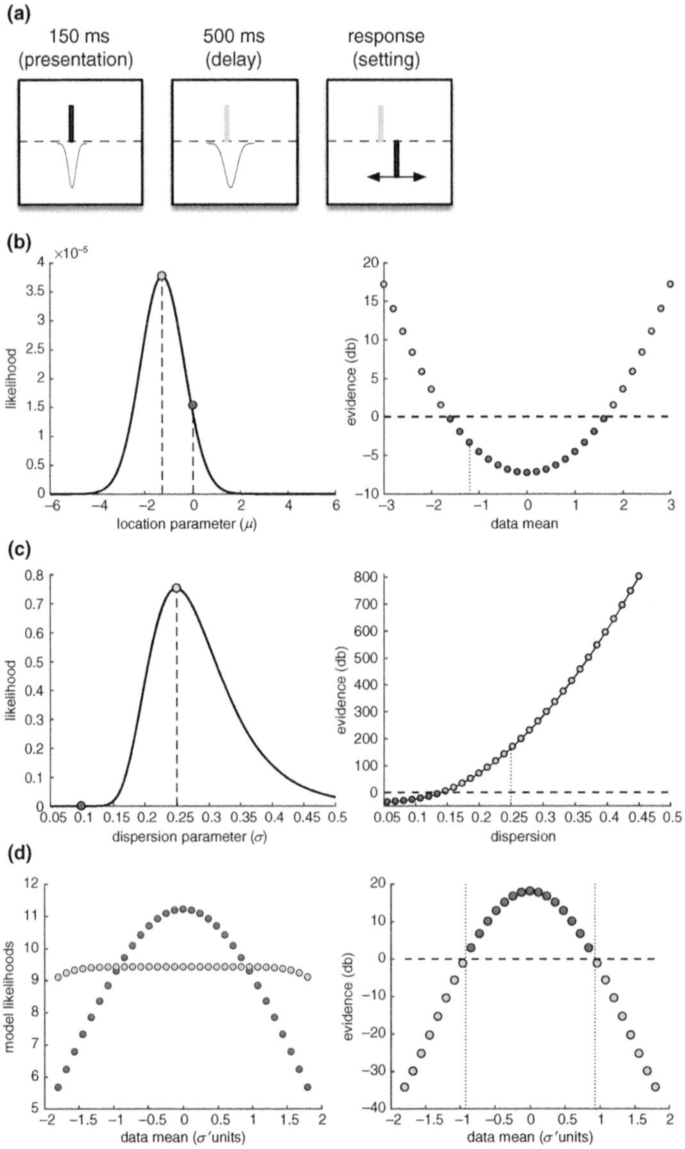

Figure 6.8 Vernier acuity. (a) Vernier acuity setting in a delayed matching paradigm. The three panels are arranged chronologically, as they would be presented in the experiment, with only the black bars actually shown: light bars, arrows, and dashed lines are for descriptive purposes only. Thus, a vertical bar is briefly presented at some horizontal position just above the half-height of the screen. A blank screen is then presented for some fixed time, introducing a memory delay, during which the subject is expected to maintain a memory representation of the position of the bar (gray bar; presumably with some uncertainty, as represented by the Gaussian). Finally, a black bar is presented just below the half-height of the computer screen, and this is adjusted until it appears to match the remembered location of the first bar. (b) Example likelihood function with the maximum of the likelihood available to the two models highlighted (left). Evidence as a function of the data mean (right). (c) Likelihood for the dispersion parameter based on a single observed dataset, with model predictions highlighted (left). Evidence for the variable-dispersion model as a function of the simulated data dispersion (right). (d) Model likelihoods for the equality (dark) and inequality (light) models. The likelihood of the inequality model remains relatively constant throughout the simulated range of possible comparison means, whereas the equality model peaks sharply at a mean of zero (i.e., when the comparison mean is equal to the standard mean; left). Evidence is computed from these model likelihoods, also plotted as a function of comparison mean value (right).

where we label the ith setting of the lower bar s_i, and its error $\varepsilon = s - \mu$. Simulated experimental data will allow us to analyze the evidence in favor of the two competing models. The outcome of this analysis will be the odds ratio,

$$\begin{aligned} \boldsymbol{O}(M_0) &= \frac{p\left(M_0 \mid \boldsymbol{d} \cdot \iota\right)}{p\left(\bar{M}_0 \mid \boldsymbol{d} \cdot \iota\right)} = \frac{\varpi\,(M_0)\left[\int_{-\infty}^{\infty} db\, \varpi_0(b)\mathcal{L}(b)\right]}{\varpi\,(M_b)\left[\int_{-\infty}^{\infty} db\, \varpi_b(b)\mathcal{L}(b)\right]} \\ &= \frac{\varpi_0 \int_{-\infty}^{\infty} db\, \sigma_0(b)\mathcal{L}(b)}{\varpi_b \int_{-\infty}^{\infty} db\, \sigma_b(b)\mathcal{L}(b)} = \frac{\varpi_0\mathcal{L}_0}{\varpi_b\mathcal{L}_b} \end{aligned}$$

which will be applied below to compute the evidence in favor of the unbiased model (M_0).

B. Assign Prior Probabilities to Hypotheses

In this experiment, we will make use of the uniform prior. Although use of the uniform prior is often by default, here it might be used because there are competing reasons for predicting both models. On the one hand, this discrimination is a spatial perception of alignment, and we might expect that such basic perceptions are typically veridical for any organism evolved to live and move within a physical environment. On the other hand, there are well-known examples where similar spatial perceptions are indeed biased, such as in line bisection. Without direct previous evidence for or against bias in the Vernier task, therefore, we assign

$$\varpi\,(M_b) = \varpi\,(M_0) = 0.5$$

C. Compute Model Likelihoods

Here we have a Gaussian likelihood model parameterized by the known Gaussian location and dispersion parameters (μ, σ) and the unknown bias term (b). Thus in both models the likelihood term describing these parameters is

$$\mathcal{L}(b) = (\sigma\sqrt{2\pi})^{-N} e^{-\frac{1}{2}\frac{\sum_i [s_i - (b+\mu)]^2}{\sigma^2}}$$

where the bias term of the sum $(b + \mu)$ is **resolvable** because μ is known.

In the unbiased model, our background information regarding the model defines it with a known bias $(b = 0)$, and so the integral over b drops out of the calculation:

$$\begin{aligned} \mathcal{L}_0 &= \int_{-\infty}^{\infty} db\varpi_0(b)\mathcal{L}(b) \\ &= \int_{-\infty}^{\infty} db\varpi_0(b)p(s \mid b \cdot \mu \cdot \sigma \cdot \iota) \\ &= p(s \mid b = 0 \cdot \mu \cdot \sigma \cdot \iota) \end{aligned}$$

Programming Aside: Vernier Bias (Fig. 6.8b)

To understand how the evidence for a bias follows the size of the true bias, we will simulate a dataset and vary its mean from left to right of no bias, computing and plotting the evidence in each case.

```
%%% Model likelihoods and evidence
sig=.1; dat=randn([10,1])*sig; dat=dat-mean(dat); N=length(dat);
COL={.4*[1 1 1],.8*[1 1 1]};
murange=[-2*sig 2*sig]; Dmu=diff(murange(1:2)); %don't expect any large biases
Nmu=101; mu2=linspace(murange(1),murange(2),Nmu);

mu1=0; Lpri1=0; Lpri2=-log(Dmu); %normalized log-priors
x=linspace(murange(1),murange(2),301); L=ones(size(x));
ind=[findnearestN(x,0,1) findnearestN(x,.05,1)];
for n=1:N, L=L.*npdf(dat(n)+.05,x,sig); end
figure(3); clf; hold on; plot(x,L,'k','LineWidth',2.2);
stem(x(ind(1)),L(ind(1)),'k--','LineWidth',1.2);
plot(x(ind(1)),L(ind(1)),'ko','MarkerFaceColor',COL{1},'MarkerSize',12,'LineWidth',1);
stem(.05,L(ind(2)),'k--','LineWidth',1.2);
plot(.05,L(ind(2)),'ko','MarkerFaceColor',COL{2},'MarkerSize',12,'LineWidth',1);
xlabel(['location parameter (\mu)'],'FontName','Arial','FontSize',15)
ylabel('likelihood','FontName','Arial','FontSize',15)

L1=nan(Nx,1); L2=nan(Nx,1); EV=nan(Nx,1);
Nx=31; xlist=linspace(.9*mu2(1),.9*mu2(end),Nx);
for i=1:Nx; xnow=xlist(i);
    dnow=dat+xnow;
    L1(i)=sum(log(npdf(dnow,mu1,sig)))+Lpri1; %single-mu model
    L2tmp=zeros(size(mu2));
    for n=1:length(dnow),
        L2tmp=L2tmp+log(npdf(dnow(n),mu2,sig)); end %uncertain model
    L2(i)=logsum(L2tmp+Lpri2-log(Nmu)); %last term is to approximate integration

    %%% compute evidence
    EV(i)=10*(L2(i)-L1(i)); end

%%% plotting
figure(4); clf; hold on ind=findnearestN(xlist,.05,1);
plot(xlist,L1,'ko','MarkerFaceColor',COL{1},'MarkerSize',8)
plot(xlist,L2,'ko','MarkerFaceColor',COL{2},'MarkerSize',8)
xlabel(['data mean'],'FontSize',15);
ylabel('model likelihood','FontName','Arial','FontSize',15);

figure(5); clf; hold on
plot(.05*[1 1],[-10 EV(ind)],'k:')
plot(xlist(EV<0),EV(EV<0),'ko','MarkerFaceColor',COL{1},...
    'MarkerSize',9,'LineWidth',1);
plot(xlist(EV>0),EV(EV>0),'ko','MarkerFaceColor',COL{2},...
    'MarkerSize',9,'LineWidth',1);
plot(xlist([1 end]),[0 0],'k--','LineWidth',2);
axis([murange -10 100]);
xlabel(['data mean'],'FontSize',15);
ylabel('evidence (db)','FontName','Arial','FontSize',15);
```

The biased model retains the integral to marginalize over the unknown bias term, yielding the marginal likelihood:

$$\mathcal{L}_b = \int_{-\infty}^{\infty} db\varpi_b(b)\mathcal{L}(b)$$

$$= [b_{\max} - b_{\min}]^{-1} \int_{b\min}^{b\max} dbp(s \mid b \cdot \mu \cdot \sigma \cdot \imath)$$

$$= [b_{\max} - b_{\min}]^{-1} (\sigma\sqrt{2\pi})^{-N} \int_{b_{\min}}^{b_{\max}} dbe^{-\frac{1}{2}\frac{\sum_i [s_i-(b+\mu)]^2}{\sigma^2}}$$

Notice that both models assume known (and equal) uncertainty and location terms. While it makes sense that whatever Gaussian uncertainty we would use to describe the first model is the uncertainty we would use in the second model when comparing the two, it is not clear that we would necessarily have a known value for that dispersion term. We will nevertheless first make a known-dispersion assumption to simplify the computations, as an unknown dispersion term would require us to incorporate an additional marginalization over that unknown term in both models, complicating our calculations.

D. Compute the Evidence

Having defined all the elements, we are now able to compute the model evidence values defined above under (**A**):

$$\boldsymbol{e}(M_0) = 10\log_{10}[\mathbf{O}(M_0)] = 10\log_{10}\left[\frac{\varpi_0\mathcal{L}_0}{\varpi_b\mathcal{L}_b}\right]$$

$$= 10\log_{10}\left[\frac{\varpi_0}{\varpi_b}\frac{\varpi_0(b)\mathcal{L}(b)}{\int_{b\neq 0} db\varpi_b(b)\mathcal{L}(b)}\right]$$

Note that although we would observe only a single dataset in our experiment, such as the dataset whose mean was $\bar{x} = .05$, we have plotted the evidence calculation for multiple datasets to get as sense of the large picture of how the computation turns out in different contexts. To remind ourselves that there is only a single result from our experiment, however, we have placed a vertical dashed line at the above-mentioned result on the evidence plot.

$$= 10\log_{10}\left[\frac{\varpi_0}{\varpi_b}\frac{[b_{\max} - b_{\min}]\, e^{-\frac{1}{2}\frac{\sum_i[s_i-\mu]^2}{\sigma^2}}}{\int_{b_{\min}}^{b_{\max}} dbe^{-\frac{1}{2}\frac{\sum_i[s_i-(b+\mu)]^2}{\sigma^2}}}\right]$$

To get a sense of the evidence produced by real data, we simulate from the Gaussian:

$$X \propto e^{-\frac{1}{2}\frac{\sum_i[s_i-(b+\mu)]^2}{\sigma^2}}$$

plotting the average evidence computed after 100 simulation runs. This is done while varying the size of the bias term over a range from zero to positive bias equal to $b_{\max}/2$. The result of these calculations is plotted in Figure 6.8b (dark circles; see Programming Aside).

If we compare the result of this Gaussian model comparison to the very similar model comparison performed above when examining the properties of the Occam factor, we should notice that the punctate model does not perform as well, because the more forgiving of the two models is nevertheless more specific than in the earlier example. Here, we have more information about the expected range of biases, because we know that if there is a bias in the Vernier discrimination, it will be quite small. By sharpening our alternative to the punctate model, it becomes better able to predict the data that will be seen experimentally, and therefore a more formidable alternative.

Exercises

1) Write the evidence equation that arises when the biased model allows only positive (rightward) biases, as compared to the zero-bias model.
2) Fill in steps A–D, and compute the evidence associated with the model comparison described in Ex1 for a single simulated dataset.
3) Without making the computation, explain why the biased, unbiased, neither or both models would yield higher evidence if the mean of the dataset were to the *left* of the standard bar for the model defined in Ex1.
4*) Write out step (A) for a model that predicts that the sign of the Vernier bias will be equal to the sign of the start position of the adjustable pointer relative to the standard bar (i.e., imagine an experiment that yields the to-be-analyzed data as having an adjustable bar with an initial position to the left or right of the standard, where experimental subjects are instructed to move it to match the position of the standard), and an alternative that is a no-bias model.

Example: Precision Relative to a Known Standard

The basic Vernier task is usually performed while simultaneously viewing both the standard and the comparison bars. The scenario described above gives a slightly more complex version of the task with a memory component: The observer is asked to remember the location of the standard bar, and then adjust the position of the comparison bar after some time interval following the disappearance of the standard bar. We might imagine that there is an underlying exponential decay of the memory trace, or in other words an exponential relation between increasing memory delay and decreasing precision of Vernier setting. This, of course, can only be true over a small range of delays, because uncertainty would eventually be limited by cognitive mechanisms that allow us to encode the approximate location of the bar (i.e., subjects will verbally encode that the line was 'in the right-hand quarter of the screen'), and override purely sensory/memory uncertainty. We will therefore use 1/4 of the screen width as the upper bound of the range for possible values of the uncertainty of the Vernier setting in a model comparison problem where we test whether the standard deviation of Vernier settings increases with a memory delay (relative to a known standard value that describes Vernier settings made with simultaneous viewing of standard and comparison bars).

A. Translate Hypotheses into Model Equations

Translating the definition of precision as it relates to the Vernier discrimination described above, we define the following:

ι: Vernier perceptual settings of the alignment of vertical line segments are performed with an imposed memory delay (as in Fig. 6.8a). The standard deviation of Vernier settings when there is no memory delay (i.e., the simultaneous viewing paradigm), is $\sigma' = 0.2$. The maximum possible standard deviation is .25w, where w is the screen width.

M_0: The standard deviation of memory-based Vernier settings is $\sigma = \sigma'$, equal to that observed during the 'simultaneous viewing' paradigm.

$M_>$: The standard deviation of memory-based Vernier settings is $\sigma > \sigma'$, which translates into the range, $\sigma' < \sigma < w/4$.

As before we will simulate Vernier settings, s_i, and compute the evidence in favor of an underlying model of those settings in which the uncertainty of settings increases versus does not increase.

We will simulate Vernier perceptual settings from a Gaussian sampling distribution that is either the same or wider than the known 'simultaneous viewing' uncertainty:

$\mathbf{M_0}$: $s_i = nrand(\mu, \sigma')$
$\mathbf{M_>}$: $s_i = nrand(\mu, \sigma > \sigma')$

where we label the ith setting of the lower bar s_i, and its error $\varepsilon = s - \mu$. Simulated experimental data will allow us to analyze the evidence in favor of the two competing models. The outcome of this analysis will be the odds ratio,

$$\boldsymbol{O}(M_0) = \frac{p\left(M_0 \mid \boldsymbol{d} \cdot \iota\right)}{p\left(\overline{M}_0 \mid \boldsymbol{d} \cdot \iota\right)} = \frac{\varpi\,(M_0)\left[\int d\sigma\, db\, \varpi_0(b,\sigma)\mathcal{L}(b,\sigma)\right]}{\varpi\,(M_>)\left[\int d\sigma\, db\, \varpi_>(b,\sigma)\mathcal{L}(b,\sigma)\right]}$$
$$= \frac{\varpi_0}{\varpi_>} \frac{\int_{-\infty}^{\infty} db\, \varpi_0\left(b,\sigma'\right)\mathcal{L}\left(b,\sigma'\right)}{\int_0^{\infty} d\sigma \int_{-\infty}^{\infty} db\, \varpi_>(b,\sigma)\mathcal{L}(b,\sigma)} = \frac{\varpi_0\mathcal{L}_0}{\varpi_>\mathcal{L}_>}$$

which will be applied below to compute the evidence in favor of M_0.

B. Assign Prior Probabilities to Hypotheses

In this experiment, we have strong theoretical reasons to assume that there will be increased uncertainty with a memory delay. However, we will nevertheless assign:

$$\varpi\,(M_0) = \varpi\,(M_>) = 0.5,$$

to ensure that any evidence in favor of increased variance is not due to our prior expectation of such an effect. We can then, at a later time or when reporting the results of the experiment in a published forum, assess whether a more realistic evidence measure should include such a prior expectation.

C. Compute Model Likelihoods

Here we have a Gaussian likelihood model parameterized by the Gaussian location and dispersion parameters (μ, σ) and the unknown bias term (b), where the μ parameter is known. Thus in both models the likelihood term describing unknown parameter values is:

$$\mathcal{L}(b,\sigma) = (\sigma\sqrt{2\pi})^{-N} e^{-\frac{1}{2}\frac{\sum_i [s_i-(b+\mu)]^2}{\sigma^2}},$$

where our primary interest will be in the value of the dispersion parameter, and we will therefore marginalize over the unknown bias.

Programming Aside: Vernier Setting Precision (Fig. 6.8c)

To understand how the evidence for a bias follows the size of the true bias, we will simulate a dataset and vary its mean from left to right of the no-bias point, computing and plotting the evidence in each case.

```
%%% Model likelihoods and evidence
sig0=.1; sigprime=2.5*sig0; dat=randn([10,1]);
dat=dat-mean(dat); N=length(dat);
COL={.4*[1 1 1],.8*[1 1 1]};
murange=[-2*sig0 2*sig0]; Dmu=diff(murange); %don't expect any large biases
sigrange=[sig0/2 10*sig0/2]; dlsig=diff(log(sigrange));
Nmu=201; mus=linspace(murange(1),murange(2),Nmu);
Nsig=201; sigs=linspace(sigrange(1),sigrange(2),Nsig)';

lgpdf=@(x,munow,signow) -log(signow*ones(1,Nmu))-.5*log(2*pi)-.5*...
    ((x-ones(Nsig,1)*munow).^2./ (signow*ones(1,Nmu)).^2);

Lprim=-log(Dmu); Lpris=-log(dlsig); %normalized log-priors
s=linspace(sigrange(1),sigrange(2),301); L=ones(size(s));
ind=[findnearestN(s,sig0,1) findnearestN(s,sigprime,1)];
for n=1:N, L=L.*npdf(dat(n)*sigprime,0,s); end

figure(3); clf; hold on;
plot(s,L,'k-','LineWidth',2.2);
stem(s(ind(1)),L(ind(1)),'k--','LineWidth',1.2);
plot(s(ind(1)),L(ind(1)),'ko','MarkerFaceColor',COL{1},'MarkerSize',12,'LineWidth',1);
stem(s(ind(2)),L(ind(2)),'k--','LineWidth',1.2);
plot(s(ind(2)),L(ind(2)),'ko','MarkerFaceColor',COL{2},'MarkerSize',12,'LineWidth',1);
xlabel(['dispersion parameter (\sigma)'],'FontName','Arial','FontSize',15)
ylabel('likelihood','FontName','Arial','FontSize',15)

Ns=31;
L1=nan(Ns,1); L2=nan(Ns,1); EV=nan(Ns,1);
slist=linspace(1.1*sigrange(1),.9*sigrange(2),Ns);
for i=1:Ns; snow=slist(i);
    dnow=dat*snow;
    L1tmp=zeros(1,Nmu); L2tmp=zeros(Nsig,Nmu);
    for n=1:length(dnow),
        L1tmp=L1tmp+lgpdf(dnow(n),mus,sig0); %single-sigma model
        L2tmp=L2tmp+lgpdf(dnow(n),mus,sigs); end %uncertain-sigma model
    L1(i)=logsum(L1tmp,[1 2]); %last term is to approximate integration
    L2(i)=logsum(L2tmp+Lpris,[1 2]);

%%% compute evidence
EV(i)=10*(L2(i)-L1(i)); end

%%% plotting
figure(4); clf; hold on
ind=findnearestN(slist,sigprime,1);
plot(slist,L1,'ko','MarkerFaceColor',COL{1},'MarkerSize',8)
plot(slist,L2,'ko','MarkerFaceColor',COL{2},'MarkerSize',8)
xlabel(['dispersion'],'FontSize',15);
ylabel('model likelihood','FontName','Arial','FontSize',15);

figure(5); clf; hold on
plot(sigprime*[1 1],[-30 EV(ind)],'k:')
plot(slist(EV<0),EV(EV<0),'ko-','MarkerFaceColor',COL{1},...
    'MarkerSize',9,'LineWidth',1);
plot(slist(EV>0),EV(EV>0),'ko-','MarkerFaceColor',COL{2},...
    'MarkerSize',9,'LineWidth',1);
```

```
plot(sigrange,[0 0],'k--','LineWidth',2);
axis([sigrange -30 1000]);
xlabel(['dispersion'],'FontSize',15);
ylabel('evidence (db)','FontName','Arial','FontSize',15);
```

In the first model, the dispersion parameter is fixed at the theoretical value of simultaneous settings, leaving only a marginalization over the unknown bias term:

$$\begin{aligned}
\mathcal{L}_0 &= \int dbd\sigma\, \varpi_0(b,\sigma)\mathcal{L}(b,\sigma) \\
&= \int_{-\infty}^{\infty} db\varpi_0\left(b,\sigma'\right)\mathcal{L}\left(b,\sigma'\right) \\
&= [b_{\max} - b_{\min}]^{-1} \int_{b\min}^{b\max} dbp\left(s \mid b \cdot \mu \cdot \sigma' \cdot \iota\right) \\
&= \sqrt{2\pi}^{-N} [b_{\max} - b_{\min}]^{-1} \left(\sigma'\sqrt{2\pi}\right)^{-N} \int_{b_{\min}}^{b_{\max}} dbe^{-\frac{1}{2}\frac{\sum_i [s_i-(b+\mu)]^2}{\sigma'^2}}
\end{aligned}$$

where we have expanded the prior, $\varpi_0(b,\sigma) = p(b|\iota)p(\sigma|\iota)$, and assigned the uniform (Jeffreys) prior over the bias, $p(b|\iota) = [b_{\max} - b_{\min}]^{-1}$.

The increased-uncertainty model retains both marginalizations, to eliminate both the unknown bias and uncertainty terms and produce the marginal likelihood:

$$\begin{aligned}
\mathcal{L}_> &= \int dbd\sigma\, \varpi_>(b,\sigma)\mathcal{L}(b,\sigma) \\
&= \left[\ln\sigma_{\max} - \ln\sigma'\right]^{-1} [b_{\max} - b_{\min}]^{-1} \int_{\sigma'}^{\sigma_{\max}} d\sigma p(\sigma \mid \iota) \int_{b_{\min}}^{b_{\max}} dbp(s \mid b \cdot \mu \cdot \sigma \cdot \iota) \\
&= \left[\ln\sigma_{\max} - \ln\sigma'\right]^{-1} [b_{\max} - b_{\min}]^{-1} \sqrt{2\pi}^{-N} \int_{\sigma'}^{\sigma_{\max}} d\sigma \left[\sigma^{-(N+1)}\right] \int_{b_{\min}}^{b_{\max}} dbe^{-\frac{1}{2}\frac{\sum_i [s_i-(b+\mu)]^2}{\sigma^2}},
\end{aligned}$$

where notice the normalization of the (Jeffreys) σ-prior, $p(\sigma|\iota) \propto \sigma^{-1}$ is $[ln\ \sigma_{\max} - \ln\sigma']^{-1}$, or $p(\sigma|\iota) = [ln\ \sigma_{\max} - \ln\sigma']^{-1}\sigma^{-1}$. These models both require marginalizations over unknown variables. The simpler of the two models, the known-variance model, requires a single marginalization while the more complex model requires two. Thus in both models there is the identical prior over the unknown bias, featuring the same range over the minimum and maximum allowable bias values.

D. Compute the Evidence

Having defined all the elements, we are now able to compute the model evidence values defined above under (**A**).

$$\begin{aligned}
\boldsymbol{e}(M_0) &= 10\log_{10}[\mathbf{O}(M_0)] = 10\log_{10}\left[\frac{\varpi_0\mathcal{L}_0}{\varpi_>\mathcal{L}_>}\right] \\
&= 10\log_{10}\left[\frac{\varpi_0}{\varpi_>}\frac{\int_{-\infty}^{\infty} db\varpi_0\left(b,\sigma'\right)\mathcal{L}\left(b,\sigma'\right)}{\int_0^{\infty} d\sigma \int_{-\infty}^{\infty} db\varpi_>(b,\sigma)\mathcal{L}(b,\sigma)}\right]
\end{aligned}$$

$$= 10\log_{10}\left[\frac{\varpi_0}{\varpi_>}\frac{[\sigma']^{-N}\int_{b_{\min}}^{b_{\max}} db e^{-\frac{1}{2}\frac{\sum_i[s_i-(b+\mu)]^2}{\sigma'^2}}}{[\ln\sigma_{\max}-\ln\sigma']^{-1}\int_{\sigma'}^{\sigma_{\max}} d\sigma\left[\sigma^{-(N+1)}\right]\int_{b_{\min}}^{b_{\max}} db e^{-\frac{1}{2}\frac{\sum_i[s_i-(b+\mu))^2}{\sigma^2}}}\right]$$

We should take note of the fact that, by having equal priors over the unknown bias term, that the prior range of the unknown bias cancels out of the evidence ratio, along with the usual cancellation of the $2\pi^{-\frac{N}{2}}$ factor from the shared Gaussian likelihood.

There are three interesting differences between the current and previous examples. First, there are unknown parameter values within each model that are irrelevant to the question being asked, but must nevertheless be removed via marginalization. This increases the overall permissiveness of these models, even though the difference between the models will ultimately be between one model that specifies the value of the critical parameter σ and one that allows it to take a range of values – just as it was in the previous example. Second, the integration is over a variable that cannot be negative – this changes the prior range in the sense that there is a logically imposed lower bound that cannot be broken by theoretical considerations based on the models being tested. Third, this change in the *type* of variable also changes the least-informed (Jeffreys) prior associated with it, and this affects only the more general (greater-than) model.

Exercises

1) What is the likelihood of the dispersion parameter at $\sigma = -.2$?
2) Characterize the transition from negative to positive evidence in Figure 6.8c in terms of the underlying models being compared.
3) Sketch the shape of the evidence function analogous to that in Figure 6.8c if the evidence for M_0 were being computed.
4) There were σ^{-N} terms in the model likelihoods of the previous example that do not appear in the final evidence calculation derived from them.
   a. Why do those terms fail to appear in the evidence calculation of the previous example?
   b. Why do similar terms remain in the evidence calculation of the current example?

Example: Equality of Two Constant Signals

The previous example examined the most obvious effect of introducing a memory delay into the Vernier discrimination task: increased setting uncertainty. However, we might also imagine that introducing the memory delay also produces a change in the bias of Vernier settings relative to what is seen for Vernier settings made during simultaneous viewing of standard and comparison bars. This should sound very much like the bias example examined above, because it is almost exactly that model comparison except that here the original bias of Vernier settings (simultaneous viewing) is unknown, and we have two datasets: one for the simultaneous viewing case and one for the delayed-viewing (memory) case. When the bias of the simultaneous-viewing Verner discrimination is unknown, we have a model comparison in which one model asserts that two measurements must be the same, and one that asserts they will be different. In both cases the value of the bias will be assumed unknown, and the dispersion known and constant across the two viewing situations.

A. Translate Hypotheses into Model Equations

Translating the same/different model specification as it relates to the Vernier discrimination described above, we define the following:

ι: Vernier perceptual settings of the alignment of vertical line segments are performed once with simultaneous viewing and once with an imposed memory delay. To simplify this case we will assume that there is no change in dispersion with memory delay, and the standard deviation of settings is $\sigma' = 0.2$. The bias of Vernier settings will be assumed unknown in all circumstances, simultaneous-viewing and memory-delayed.

M_0 : The bias of Vernier settings under memory delay is equal to that observed during simultaneous viewing, $b = b_0$.

$M_{\neq}$: The bias of Vernier settings changes under memory delay relative to what is observed during simultaneous viewing, $b \neq b_0$.

As before we will simulate Vernier settings, s_i, and compute the evidence in favor of an underlying model of those settings in which the bias changes in the memory-delayed condition. Here, simulated experimental data must consist of two datasets, one for the simultaneous viewing case and one for the memory-delayed case.

We will simulate Vernier perceptual settings from a Gaussian sampling distribution that is either the same or different than the unknown 'simultaneous viewing' bias (which in the simulation is set to 0):

M_0: $s_{1i} = nrand(b = 0, \sigma'), s_{2i} = nrand(b = 0, \sigma')$
$M_{\neq}$: $s_{1i} = nrand(b = 0, \sigma'), s_{2i} = nrand(b \neq 0, \sigma')$

where we label the ith setting of the lower bar s_i, and its error $\varepsilon = s - \mu$. Simulated experimental data will allow us to analyze the evidence in favor of the two competing models. Notice also that we have simplified the simulation by setting the theoretical bias of the simultaneous-viewing data to 0, giving us a concrete value for setting the memory delayed bias in simulated data; this is irrelevant for the analysis because the bias of both datasets will be assumed unknown. The outcome of this analysis will be the odds ratio, which will be applied below to compute the odds in favor of the equal-bias model (M_0):

$$\mathbf{O}(M_0) = \frac{p\left(M_0 \mid \boldsymbol{d} \cdot \iota\right)}{p\left(\overline{M}_0 | \boldsymbol{d} \cdot \iota\right)} = \frac{\varpi\,(M_0)\left[\int_{-\infty}^{\infty} db\,\varpi_0(b)\mathcal{L}(b)\right]}{\varpi\,\left(M_{\neq}\right)\left[\int_{-\infty}^{\infty} db\,\varpi_{\neq}(b)\mathcal{L}(b)\right]}$$
$$= \frac{\varpi_0}{\varpi_{\neq}} \frac{\int_{-\infty}^{\infty} db\,\varpi_0(b)\mathcal{L}(b)}{\int_{-\infty}^{\infty} db\,\varpi_{\neq}(b)\mathcal{L}(b)} = \frac{\varpi_0\mathcal{L}_0}{\varpi_{\neq}\mathcal{L}_{\neq}}$$

B. Assign Prior Probabilities to Hypotheses

In this experiment, we have strong theoretical reasons to assume that there will be increased uncertainty with a memory delay. However, we will nevertheless assign:

$$\varpi\,(M_0) = \varpi\,\left(M_{\neq}\right) = 0.5,$$

to ensure that any evidence in favor of increased variance is not due to our prior expectation of such an effect. We can then, at a later time or when reporting the results of the experiment in a published forum, assess whether a more realistic evidence measure should include such a prior expectation.

C. Compute Model Likelihoods

Here we have a Gaussian likelihood model parameterized by the Gaussian location and dispersion parameters (μ,σ) and the unknown bias term (b), where the μ parameter is known. Thus in both models the likelihood term describing unknown parameter values is:

$$\mathcal{L}(b) = (\sigma\sqrt{2\pi})^{-N} e^{-\frac{1}{2}\frac{\sum_i [s_i-(b+\mu)]^2}{\sigma^2}},$$

where we will marginalize over the unknown bias term in slightly different ways to capture the essence of the two models.

In the first model, the unknown bias term is equal in the two datasets:

$$\begin{aligned}\mathcal{L}_0 &= \int db d\sigma\, \varpi_0(b,\sigma)\mathcal{L}(b,\sigma)\\ &= \int_0^{\infty} d\sigma \int_{-\infty}^{\infty} db\varpi_0\left(b,\sigma'\right)\mathcal{L}\left(b,\sigma'\right)\\ &= [\Delta b]^{-2}[\Delta \ln\sigma]^{-1}\int_{\sigma_{\min}}^{\sigma_{\max}} d\sigma\sigma^{-1}\int_{b\min}^{b\max} dbp\left(\mathbf{s}\mid b\cdot\mu\cdot\sigma'\cdot\iota\right)\\ &= (2\pi)^{-2N}[\Delta b]^{-1}[\Delta \ln\sigma]^{-1}\int_{\sigma_{\min}}^{\sigma_{\max}} d\sigma\sigma^{-(2N+1)}\int_{b_{\min}}^{b_{\max}} dbe^{-\frac{1}{2}\frac{\sum_i\left[s_{1i}-(b+\mu)\right]^2}{\sigma'^2}}e^{-\frac{1}{2}\frac{\sum_i\left[s_{2i}-(b+\mu)\right]^2}{\sigma'^2}}\end{aligned}$$

which allows us to simply define the two likelihoods with this one bias term, and marginalize it out of the joint likelihood of the two datasets and the single prior that describes the possible values of that bias. Note also that $\Delta b = [b_{\max} - b_{\min}]$, and $\Delta \ln \sigma = [\ln(\sigma_{\max}) - \ln(\sigma_{\min})]$.

The altered-bias model retains separate bias terms in the two likelihoods, and therefore requires two marginalizations to eliminate both unknown bias terms (one per dataset):

$$\begin{aligned}\mathcal{L}_{\neq} &= \int_{b_2\min}^{b_{2\max}} db_2 \int_{b_{1\min}}^{b_{1\max}} db_1\varpi_{\neq}(b_1)\,\mathcal{L}(b_1)\,\varpi_{\neq}(b_2)\,\mathcal{L}(b_2)\\ &= [\Delta b]^{-2}[\Delta\ln\sigma]^{-1}\int_{\sigma_{\min}}^{\sigma_{\max}} d\sigma\sigma^{-1}\int_{b_{2\min}}^{b_{2\max}} db_2\int_{b_{1\min}}^{b_{1\max}} db_1 p(s_1\mid b_1\cdot\mu\cdot\sigma\cdot\iota)\,p(s_2\mid b_2\cdot\mu\cdot\sigma\cdot\iota)\\ &= (2\pi)^{-2N}[\Delta b]^{-2}[\Delta\ln\sigma]^{-1}\int_{\sigma_{\min}}^{\sigma_{\max}} d\sigma\sigma^{-(2N+1)}\int_{b_{2\min}}^{b_{2\max}} db_2\int_{b_{1\min}}^{b_{1\max}} db_1 e^{-\frac{1}{2}\frac{\sum_i[s_{1i}-(b_1+\mu)]^2}{\sigma^2}}e^{-\frac{1}{2}\frac{\sum_i[s_{2i}-(b_2+\mu)]^2}{\sigma^2}}\end{aligned}$$

Unlike in the previous model comparison, the models here both require marginalizations over unknown variables. The simpler of the two models, the known-variance model, requires a single marginalization while the more complex model requires two marginalizations. Thus in both models there is the identical prior over the unknown bias, featuring the same range over the minimum and maximum allowable bias values.

Evidence for Signal Equality (Fig. 6.8d)

To examine the changes in evidence for a difference in Vernier bias with change in data mean, we simulate a series of comparison datasets whose mean changes with each simulation while keeping the no-delay dataset constant at zero mean.

```
clear
%%% Model likelihoods and evidence
sigprime=.3; N=10; Nvern=51; murange=[-2*sigprime 2*sigprime];
e0=randn([1 N])*sigprime; e0=e0-mean(e0); mu0=0;
e1=randn([1 N])*sigprime; e1=e1-mean(e1);

Lpri0=-log(diff(murange)); Lpri1=-2*log(diff(murange)); %normalized log-priors
Nmu=301; Nsig=201;
mulist=linspace(murange(1),murange(2),Nmu)';
slist=linspace(0,1,Nsig+1); slist=slist(2:end);
diffs0=[diff(mulist(1:2)) diff(slist(1:2))];
diffs1=[diff(mulist(1:2))*[1 1] diff(slist(1:2))];
Nx=31; xlist=linspace(.9*mulist(1),.9*mulist(end),Nx);
mumat=mulist*ones(1,N); Ltmp0=nan(Nx,1); Ltmp1=nan(Nx,1);
EV=nan(Nx,1);
for ix=1:Nx, Lall0=zeros(Nmu,1,Nsig); Lall1=zeros(Nmu,Nmu,Nsig);
    mutrue=xlist(ix);

    %%%%%%%%R%%%%%%%%%%%%%%%%%%%%%%%%%%%%%%
    %%% DATA SIM using rotation ratio %%%
    d1=ones(Nmu,1)*(e0+mu0);
    d2=ones(Nmu,1)*(e1+mutrue);

    likeFN0=@(snow) [-(N/2)*((mean((d1-mumat).^2,2)/snow^2)+...
        (mean((d2-mumat).^2,2)/snow^2) )-(2*N+1)*log(snow)]; %output is Nb x 1
    likeFN1=@(snow) [-(N/2)*((mean((d1-mumat).^2,2)/snow^2)*ones(1,Nmu)+ones(Nmu,1)*...
        (mean((d2-mumat).^2,2)/snow^2)')-(2*N+1)*log(snow)]; %output is Nb x Nb

    %%%%%%%%%%%%%%%%%%%%%%%%%%%%%%%%%%%%%%%
    %%% param likelihood by condition %%%
    for is=1:Nsig, snow=slist(is);
        Lall0(:,1,is)=squeeze(Lall0(:,1,is))+likeFN0(snow);
        Lall1(:,:,is)=squeeze(Lall1(:,:,is))+likeFN1(snow); end

    %%% compute likelihoods
    Ltmp0(ix)=logsum(squeeze(Lall0),[1 2],diffs0); %unif prior range cancels
    Ltmp1(ix)=logsum(Lall1,[1 2 3],diffs1)-10*log10(diff(murange));
    %%% compute evidence
    EV(ix)=10*(Ltmp0(ix)-Ltmp1(ix)); end

%find EV zero-crossings
Ltmp0mat=[Ltmp0(1:end-1) Ltmp0(2:end)]; Ltmp1mat=[Ltmp1(1:end-1) Ltmp1(2:end)];
inds=[find(and(Ltmp0mat(:,1)<Ltmp1mat(:,1),Ltmp0mat(:,2)>Ltmp1mat(:,2))) ...
find(and(Ltmp0mat(:,1)>Ltmp1mat(:, 1),Ltmp0mat(:,2)<Ltmp1mat(:,2)))];
xcrit=[interp1(Ltmp0(inds(1)+[0:1]),xlist(inds(1)+[0:1]),mean(Ltmp1(inds(1)+[0:1])))...
interp1(Ltmp0(inds(2)+[0:1]),xlist(inds(2)+[0:1]),mean(Ltmp1(inds(2)+[0:1])))];

%%% plotting
COL={.4*[1 1 1],.8*[1 1 1]};
xlist=xlist/sigprime;

figure(4); clf; hold on
plot(xlist,Ltmp0,'ko','MarkerFaceColor',COL{1},'MarkerSize',10)
plot(xlist,Ltmp1,'ko','MarkerFaceColor',COL{2},'MarkerSize',10)
```

```
xlabel(['data mean (\sigma\prime units)'],'FontSize',15);
ylabel('model likelihoods','FontName','Arial','FontSize',15);

figure(5); clf; hold on
EVrange=[-40 20];
plot(xcrit(1)*[1 1],EVrange,'k:')
plot(xcrit(2)*[1 1],EVrange,'k:')
plot(xlist(EV>0),EV(EV>0),'ko','MarkerFaceColor',COL{1},...
     'MarkerSize',12,'LineWidth',1);
plot(xlist(EV<0),EV(EV<0),'ko','MarkerFaceColor',COL{2},...
     'MarkerSize',12,'LineWidth',1);
plot(xlist([1 end]),[0 0],'k--','LineWidth',2);
axis([murange/sigprime EVrange]);
xlabel(['data mean (\sigma\prime units)'],'FontSize',15);
ylabel('evidence (db)','FontName','Arial','FontSize',15);
```

Notice that we have ignored the zero-width mathematical line, $b_1 = b_2$ in the 2D probability space, $p(b_1 \cdot b_2 | s_1 \cdot s_1 \cdot \mu \cdot \sigma \cdot \iota)$. This is because any punctate point or line in this 2D space has probability zero (see Appendix C for further clarification), and therefore requires no special handling. In fact, because one model allows all differences and one model defines a punctate difference (of zero), we need not transform into difference coordinates as we did above when the two models predicted partial ranges of the difference dimension (such as positive vs. negative differences of spike rates). We instead have simply defined $\mathcal{L}_0$ in terms of two likelihoods with the same bias parameters (and therefore zero difference between bias terms), and defined $\mathcal{L}_{\neq}$ in terms of two likelihoods with separate bias parameters (and therefore, in terms of probability mass devoted to any combination of b_1 and b_2, also unequal bias parameters).

D. Compute the Evidence

Having defined all the elements, we are now able to compute the model evidence values defined above under (**A**).

$$
\begin{aligned}
\boldsymbol{e}(M_b) &= 10\log_{10}[\boldsymbol{O}(M_b)] = 10\log_{10}\left[\frac{\varpi_0\mathcal{L}_0}{\varpi_{\neq}\mathcal{L}_{\neq}}\right] \\
&= 10\log_{10}\left[\frac{\varpi_0}{\varpi_{\neq}}\frac{\int_0^\infty d\sigma \int_{-\infty}^{\infty} db\varpi_0(b,\sigma)\mathcal{L}(b,\sigma)}{\int_0^\infty d\sigma \int_{-\infty}^{\infty} db_2 db_1 \varpi_{\neq}(b_1,b_2,\sigma)\,\mathcal{L}(b_1,b_2,\sigma)}\right] \\
&= 10\log_{10}\left[\frac{\varpi_0}{\varpi_{\neq}}\frac{\int_{\sigma_{\min}}^{\sigma_{\max}} d\sigma\sigma^{-(2N+1)}\int_{b_{\min}}^{b_{\max}} dbe^{-\frac{1}{2}\frac{\sum_i[s_{1i}-(b+\mu)]^2}{\sigma^2}} e^{-\frac{1}{2}\frac{\sum_i[s_{2i}-(b+\mu)]^2}{\sigma'^2}}}{[\Delta b]^{-1}\int_{\sigma_{\min}}^{\sigma_{\max}} d\sigma\sigma^{-(2N+1)}\int_{b_{2\min}}^{b_{2\max}} db_2\int_{b_{1\min}}^{b_{1\max}} db_1 e^{-\frac{1}{2}\frac{\sum_i[s_{1i}-(b_1+\mu)]^2}{\sigma^2}} e^{-\frac{1}{2}\frac{\sum_i[s_{2i}-(b_2+\mu)]^2}{\sigma^2}}}\right].
\end{aligned}
$$

To get a sense of the evidence produced by real data, we simulate from the Gaussian:

$$x \propto e^{-\frac{1}{2}\frac{\sum_j[s_j-(b+\mu)]^2}{\sigma^2}}$$

plotting the evidence computed for each simulation run. Each simulation run has a slightly different comparison (memory-delay) mean bias, which allows us to examine how evidence for signal equality changes with the size of the comparison bias. This also allows us to estimate the size of the difference that would have to be observed experimentally before we could expect to see significant evidence in favor of a difference between the two biases, shown as vertical dotted lines in Figure 6.8d.

Exercises

1) What is the normalization for the σ prior, and where does it appear in the final evidence equation?
2) The example above assumes a constant dispersion for the no-delay and the delay conditions of the experiment. How would the evidence calculation change if this restriction were relaxed and the two conditions were allowed separate dispersions?
3) Explain why was it possible to bypass the step, used above in the spike rate and rate of recovery examples, of transforming the two bias parameters into sums and differences of biases?
4) Why does the model likelihood for the equality model (Fig. 6.8d) peak at 0, as opposed to some other location?
5) Why is it that the model likelihood for the inequality model is relatively constant across possible data means, whereas the model likelihood for the equality model is sharply peaked at 0?

6.3.4 Straight-Line Models

The straight line model is the second most popular model of change that we encounter in a scientific context, after the 'something changed' model whose variants ('change in location,' 'change in dispersion,' and 'change in rates' models) were explored above. The straight-line model expands those 'something changed' models by offering a ***quantitative, functional description*** **of the change**. Such functional relationships describe how observed changes (in an output variable, usually y, or o) are ***lawfully related*** to an input variable, (usually x, or ω). By proposing a functional relationship describing change, it is possible for us predict the *size* of a change as a function of the the input variable, which you will see referred to as an **explanatory variable.**

The description of this relationship between variables ω and y has so far been kept deliberately vague, to keep it as general as possible. However, in a scientific context the types of relationship we are generally most interested in are **direct causal relationships** (Fig. 6.9a, left) whereby changes in one aspect of the controlled (physical) variable ω_1 produce changes in afferent stimulation (s) which cause changes in the observed variable y; this is in contrast to the 'spurious relationship' schematized in Figure 6.9a (right) in which another aspect of the larger physical stimulus (ω_2) produces a second type of afferent stimulation (s_2) that mediates the changes seen in y: such relationships are referred

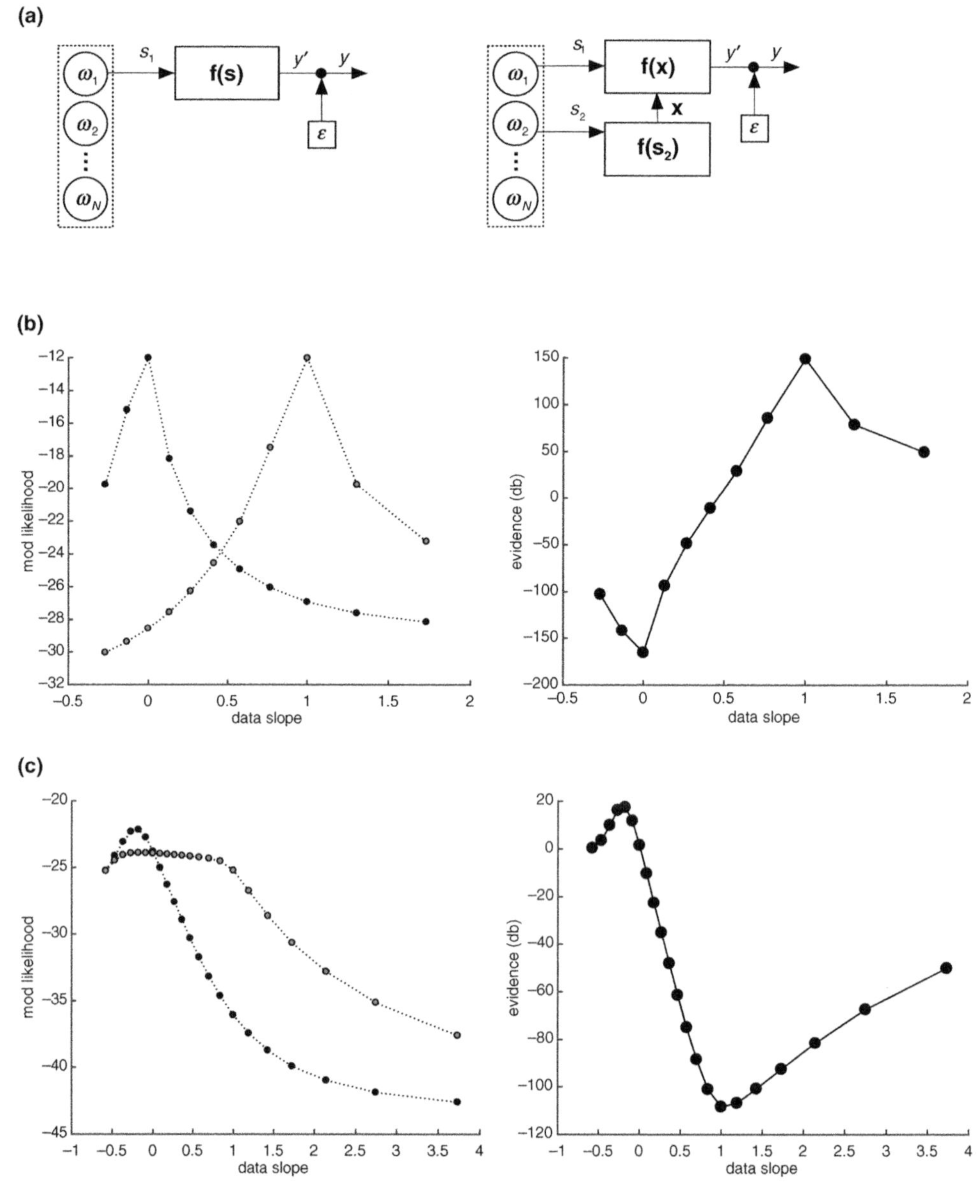

Figure 6.9 Straight-line model (a) A causal mechanism (left) is modulated by an aspect of the physical environment (ω_1) known to produce an output, y, with additive noise, whereas a spuriously causal model (right) is erroneously thought to be described by the same causal chain from ω_1 to y, when in reality the chain of causality originates with ω_2. (b) Model likelihood and evidence for comparing slopes to a known standard. (left) Model likelihoods for the two straight-line models with known slopes of 0 and 1. Each model likelihood function peaks when the data slope matches the prediction of the model. (right) Evidence values clearly separate the two models when the underlying data match the model; otherwise, evidence falls toward zero. (c) Model likelihood and evidence for the hypothesis that there is no consistent slope to the data. (left) Model likelihoods for the zero-slope and variable-slope models. The zero-slope model likelihood is highest when the data slope is near zero. (right) Evidence values clearly separate the two models when the underlying data match the model; otherwise, evidence falls toward zero. Notice that the evidence has an inflection at a slope of 1 due to the data slope falling outside both models' predictions.

to as 'spuriously causal' because the causal source is incorrectly attributed to ω_1 or s_1. There are two straight-line relationship types, **strictly proportional**:

$$y' = f(\omega) = \beta\omega \tag{6.5}$$

and **proportional change**:

$$y' = f(\omega) = \alpha + \beta\omega \tag{6.6}$$

where the two differ by a constant shift (α) along the y-axis.

The variety of such causal relationships is daunting, ranging from the proposal that the size of the hippocampus determines the quality of your memory to the proposal that the physical intensity of a light source determines the perceived brightness of that source to the proposal that lower self-esteem leads to an increased likelihood of entering into an abusive interpersonal relationship, or that lower income parents produce lower school achievement in their children.

Although some of these are clearly more easily quantified than others, there is a second consideration that is controlling for the purpose of choosing examples: only the first of these examples fits the description above, in which an experimentally controlled variable is thought to produce changes in the theoretical value of the outcome variable. This is an important consideration, because when the input to the functional relationship (ω) is an experimentally controlled variable, we can assume its values are *known* (they have been set by the experimenter). Whereas when the input is simply *observed*, its true value must be considered uncertain, just as the observed value of the outcome variable, y, is a noisy and uncertain image of the theoretical construct, y'. We will first deal with the simpler case in which values of a causal input variable are known[10] and only the outcome variable has appreciable uncertainty. In this case, when the known value of an experimentally controlled variable produces changes in an outcome variable, the equations above are most easily implemented for predicting the outcome variable; we simply enter the known ω, and the outcome value is a scaled ($\beta\omega$) and shifted ($+\alpha$) transform of this value. If the true value of ω were unknown we would have to infer its value from data (such as household income, hippocampus volume) and use this inferred value to predict outcomes, y.

On the outcome dimension, we will assign a Gaussian distribution to describe our uncertainty regarding the true value (y') of the observed outcome, y. In terms of our brightness experiment, this might correspond to presenting a range of physical brightnesses, ω_i, to the observer and asking for a numerical estimate of each brightness, y_i. We assume that the physical stimulus impinges on the retina and produces the proximal stimulus: sensory transduction at the retinal receptors, activity passing through the retina, and a set of firing rates in the retinal ganglion cells of the optic nerve. This proximal stimulus produces the ultimate perceptual sensation of brightness, and that sensation will change somewhat from one presentation of the identical physical stimulus to another. Noise in this system guarantees that a single physical brightness will produce a noisy range of responses (y). We can think of these as noisy representations of a theoretical noiseless brightness percept (y') that would be produced by that physical

[10] Of course there is always some small amount of uncertainty in any setting or value of a controlled (experimental) variable. However, compared to the uncertainty associated with observational (uncontrolled) variables, this will in most cases be vanishingly small and can be safely ignored.

stimulus if sensory transduction, neural transmission, etc. were all operating at nominal levels. This line of reasoning leads to:

$$\begin{aligned} y_k &= y'_k + \varepsilon_k \\ &= \beta\omega_k + \varepsilon_k \end{aligned}$$

as a description of the transition between the noiseless percept and observed data for the kth experimental condition (level of physical brightness; see Figure 6.9a showing the graphical model and representation of additive noise), and to the following probability statement describing our prior information regarding errors (i.e., the sampling distribution):

$$\begin{aligned} p\left(y_k \mid y'_k \cdot \sigma \cdot \iota\right) &= [\sigma\sqrt{2\pi}]^{-1} e^{-\frac{1}{2}\frac{\left[y_k - y'_k\right]^2}{\sigma^2}} \\ &= [\sigma\sqrt{2\pi}]^{-1} e^{-\frac{1}{2}\frac{[y_k - \beta\omega_k]^2}{\sigma^2}} \end{aligned} \tag{6.5a}$$

where σ is the unknown standard deviation of the Gaussian sampling distribution. It will be important later to note that (6.5) is written in terms of the difference between the predicted and observed y-value, and is applicable to all experimental conditions (indexed by k). This allows us to process data from all experimental conditions simultaneously:

$$p\left(y \mid y' \cdot \sigma \cdot \iota\right) = [\sigma\sqrt{2\pi}]^{-N} e^{-\frac{1}{2}\frac{\sum_{k=1}^{N}\left[y_k - y'_k\right]^2}{\sigma^2}} \tag{6.5b}$$

Example: Slope Relative to Known Standards

A. Translate Hypotheses into Model Equations

In many problems of this type we will be testing the 'veridical percept model' against a model in which the observer cannot detect changes in the physical stimulus at all. In other words, between a model in which we expect that changes in the physical stimulus will be mirrored, one-to-one, by changes in the percept. By definition, this model clearly predicts unity slope[11] ($\beta = 1$), which we will compare to the 'no perceived modulation' model which predicts that changes in the physical brightness of the light go undetected by experimental subjects (and predicts a slope $\beta = 0$). Such a prediction might be made when we suspect that retinal receptors (either of a particular individual or of humans generally) are unable to detect the particular frequency of light being presented, or if downstream neurons are unresponsive to changes in the physical stimulus.

ι: Brightness judgments are made in response to a range of physical brightnesses, where the physical light stimulus is a single-frequency light presented in an otherwise completely dark room. Five different brightnesses were shown, all known to be above the known light detection threshold for white light.

M_0 : The slope of the relationship between physical brightness presented visually and the corresponding judged brightness is zero, $\beta = 0$.

M_1 : The slope of the relationship between physical brightness presented visually and the corresponding judged brightness is one, $\beta = 1$.

[11] We are hiding an important step in the logic here: we assume that the scaling of the internal brightness percept is equal to the physical scaling of brightness units used to represent the physical variable. This is a common problem, although with some perceptual judgments the issue may be bypassed, such as when equating the perception of depth with physical depth, where the perceptual judgment can be conveyed by holding the hands apart side-to-side to match the seen depth.

Simulated brightness judgments are generated by first choosing an underlying slope value. If this value is $\beta = 1$, then for each condition of the experiment we set $y' = \omega$ from which to simulate brightness judgments:

$M_1: y_k = nrand(\omega_k, \sigma)$,

whereas if $\beta = 0$ then $y' = 0$ for all physical brightnesses:

$M_0: y_k = nrand(0, \sigma)$.

These simulated observation values mimic a system with additive noise, $y = y' + \varepsilon$, as dictated by the underlying model (Fig. 6.9a).

From these simulated data, we will compare the two models outlined above based on the odds ratio, where the odds ratio favoring M_0 is:

$$\begin{aligned} \boldsymbol{O}(M_0) &= \frac{p\left(M_0 \mid \boldsymbol{d} \cdot \iota\right)}{p\left(\overline{M}_0 \mid \boldsymbol{d} \cdot \iota\right)} = \frac{\varpi\,(M_0)\left[\int_{-\infty}^{\infty} d b \varpi_0(\beta)\mathcal{L}(\beta)\right]}{\varpi\,(M_1)\left[\int_{-\infty}^{\infty} d b \varpi_1(\beta)\mathcal{L}(\beta)\right]} \\ &= \frac{\varpi_0}{\varpi_1}\frac{\int_{-\infty}^{\infty} d b \varpi_0(\beta)\mathcal{L}(\beta)}{\int_{-\infty}^{\infty} d b \varpi_1(\beta)\mathcal{L}(\beta)} = \frac{\varpi_0 \mathcal{L}_0}{\varpi_1 \mathcal{L}_1} \end{aligned}$$

B. Assign Prior Probabilities to Hypotheses

This experimental scenario is a bit unusual for the straight-line model in that it is so distinct: the two predictions are for two punctate slope values, and nothing in between or more general. This is unlikely to be the case in the majority of your research, but is an important first-case scenario that we should address. Although in reality such a pair of hypotheses would likely come with a strong theoretical bias toward one or the other, we will as before assign:

$$\varpi\,(M_0) = \varpi\,(M_1) = 0.5,$$

to ensure that the final outcome is not due to our prior expectation. We can then, at a later time or when reporting the results of the experiment in a published forum, assess whether a more realistic evidence measure should include a prior expectation.

C. Compute Model Likelihoods

Here we have a Gaussian likelihood model parameterized by the Gaussian location and dispersion parameters ($y' = \beta\omega, \sigma$) and the unknown slope term (β), where y' is dependent on the product $\beta\omega$ and the set of experimentally controlled values of $\boldsymbol{\omega}$ is known. Thus in both models the likelihood term describing unknown parameter values is:

$$\begin{aligned} \mathcal{L}(\beta) &= p\left(\boldsymbol{y} \mid \boldsymbol{y}' \cdot \iota\right) \\ &= p\left(\boldsymbol{y} \mid \beta \cdot \boldsymbol{\omega} \cdot \iota\right) \\ &= (\sigma\sqrt{2\pi})^{-N} e^{-\frac{1}{2}\frac{\sum_k [y_k - (\beta\omega_k)]^2}{\sigma^2}}. \end{aligned}$$

This likelihood is parsimonious because it applies to *all* brightness judgments, regardless of the physical brightness used to elicit them; this is an important point for our purposes because it means that this single likelihood equation can process the entire dataset, consisting of multiple levels of physical brightness and corresponding judgments, in terms of a single theoretical value of the slope, β.

In the first model (M_0) the slope parameter is set to zero by our prior, $\varpi(\beta) = \begin{cases} 0 & \beta \neq 0 \\ 1 & \beta = 0 \end{cases}$, and the dispersion term will be assigned a truncated Jeffreys prior which yields the model likelihood:

$$\mathcal{L}_0 = \int d\sigma\, \varpi_0(\beta,\sigma)\mathcal{L}(\beta,\sigma),$$

which would reduce to $\mathcal{L}_0 = \mathcal{L}_0(\beta = 0)$ if the dispersion parameter of the Gaussian likelihood were known. Instead, this model likelihood marginalizes over the unknown value of the dispersion (describing individual brightness judgments, y_k):

$$\begin{aligned}\mathcal{L}_0 &= \int_0^\infty d\sigma\, \varpi_0(\beta,\sigma)\mathcal{L}(\beta,\sigma) \\ &= \left(\log\sigma_{\max} - \log\sigma_{\min}\right)^{-1} \int_{\sigma_{\max}}^{\sigma_{\max}} d\sigma\sigma^{-1}(\sigma\sqrt{2\pi})^{-N} e^{-\frac{1}{2}\frac{\sum_k [y_k-(\beta\omega_k)]^2}{\sigma^2}} \\ &= (\Delta \log\sigma)^{-1} \int_{\sigma_{\max}}^{\sigma_{\max}} d\sigma\sigma^{-1}(\sigma\sqrt{2\pi})^{-N} e^{-\frac{1}{2}\frac{\sum_k [y_k]^2}{\sigma^2}},\end{aligned}$$

where notice that the leading difference-of-logs term normalizes the truncated Jeffreys prior:

$$\int_{\sigma_{\max}}^{\sigma_{\max}} d\sigma\sigma^{-1} = \left(\log\sigma_{\max} - \log\sigma_{\min}\right)^{-1},$$

and that the theoretical slope-value, $\beta = 0$, simplifies the exponential term. The model likelihood for the unity-slope model is almost identical, except that it simplifies less extremely:

$$\begin{aligned}\mathcal{L}_1 &= \int_0^\infty d\sigma\, \varpi_1(\beta,\sigma)\mathcal{L}(\beta,\sigma) \\ &= \left(\log\sigma_{\max} - \log\sigma_{\min}\right)^{-1} \int_{\sigma_{\max}}^{\sigma_{\max}} d\sigma\sigma^{-1}(\sigma\sqrt{2\pi})^{-N} e^{-\frac{1}{2}\frac{\sum_k [y_k-(\beta\omega_k)]^2}{\sigma^2}} \\ &= (\Delta \log\sigma)^{-1} \int_{\sigma_{\max}}^{\sigma_{\max}} d\sigma\sigma^{-1}(\sigma\sqrt{2\pi})^{-N} e^{-\frac{1}{2}\frac{\sum_k [y_k-\omega_k]^2}{\sigma^2}}.\end{aligned}$$

D. Compute the Evidence

Having defined all the elements, we are now able to compute the model evidence values defined above under (**A**).

$$\begin{aligned}\boldsymbol{e}(M_0) &= 10\log_{10}\left[\boldsymbol{O}(M_0)\right] = 10\log_{10}\left[\frac{\varpi_0\mathcal{L}_0}{\varpi_1\mathcal{L}_1}\right] \\ &= 10\log_{10}\left[\frac{\varpi_0 \int_0^\infty d\sigma\,\varpi_0(\beta,\sigma)\mathcal{L}(\beta,\sigma)}{\varpi_1 \int_0^\infty d\sigma\,\varpi_1(\beta,\sigma)\mathcal{L}(\beta,\sigma)}\right] \\ &= 10\log_{10}\left[\frac{\varpi_0}{\varpi_1}\frac{\int_{\sigma_{\max}}^{\sigma_{\max}} d\sigma\sigma^{-(N+1)}e^{-\frac{1}{2}\frac{\sum_k [y_k]^2}{\sigma^2}}}{\int_{\sigma_{\max}}^{\sigma_{\max}} d\sigma\sigma^{-(N+1)}e^{-\frac{1}{2}\frac{\sum_k [y_k-\omega_k]^2}{\sigma^2}}}\right]\end{aligned}$$

Programming Aside: Zero-Slope Model Evidence (Fig. 6.9b)

Evidence for the zero-slope model depends on the orientation of the dataset relative to the horizontal axis.

```
clear %#ok<*UNRCH>
reset=1; saveFLAG=0; plotFLAG=1;
COL=[.55*[1 1 1]; .3 .4 .85; .8 .5 .4];
N=6;

sig=5;
Ns=1201; slist=linspace(0,101,Ns+1)'; slist=slist(2:end); %noise level
diffs=[diff(slist(1:2))];
thetas=linspace(-100,100,N);

Nrot=11;
rotlist=linspace(-pi/12,pi/4+pi/12,Nrot);

%keep noise samples identical across simulations for clearer comparison
eorig=nrand(0,sig,[1 N]);
dorig=[thetas(:) zeros(N,1)];

margL=nan(Nrot,2); sest=zeros(Nrot,2);
for irot=1:Nrot, rotnow=rotlist(irot);

  %%%%%%%%R%%%%%%%%%%%%%%%%%%%%%%%%%%%%%%
  %%% DATA SIM using rotation ratio %%%
  dnow=rot(dorig,rotnow);
  tnow=dnow(:,1)'; dnow=dnow(:,2)'+eorig;
  likeFN0=-(N/2)*(mean( dnow.^2, 2)./slist.^2)-(N+1)*log(slist); %Ns x 1
  likeFN1=-(N/2)*(mean((dnow-tnow).^2,2)./slist.^2)-(N+1)*log(slist); %Ns x 1

  %%%%%%%%%%%%%%%%%%%%%%%%%%%%%%%%%%%%%%%
  %%% param likelihood by condition %%%
  Lall0=likeFN0;
  Lall1=likeFN1;

  %%%%%%%%%%%%%%%%%%%%%%%%%%%%%%
  %%% verify global sigma %%%
  sest(irot,1)=logpeakval([Lall0 slist]);
  ses4t(irot,2)=logpeakval([Lall1 slist]);

  %%%%%%%%%%%%%%%%%%%%%%%%%%%%
  %%% Model likelihoods %%%
  margL(irot,1)=logsum(Lall0,1,diffs);
  margL(irot,2)=logsum(Lall1,1,diffs); end
Elist=10*(margL(:,2)-margL(:,1));

if plotFLAG,
   figure(1); clf; hold on
   plot(tan(rotlist),Elist,'ko-','MarkerFaceColor','k','MarkerSize',11);
   xlabel('data slope','FontName','Arial','FontSize',15);
   ylabel('evidence (db)','FontName','Arial','FontSize',15);

   figure(2); clf; hold on; plot(tan(rotlist),margL(:,1),'ko:','MarkerFaceColor','k');
   plot(tan(rotlist),margL(:,2),'ko:','MarkerFaceColor',COL(1,:))
   xlabel('data slope','FontName','Arial','FontSize',15);
   ylabel('mod likelihood','FontName','Arial','FontSize',15); end
```

To get a sense of the evidence produced by real data, we simulate a series of datasets, each generated from simulating a different underlying slope value. Plotting the evidence as a function of these slopes, we obtain the plot in Figure 6.9. It is important to make such simulation plots because these allow us to verify that we have performed our calculations correctly, and will be making the desired model comparison when we use these functions to analyze real data (see Fig. 1.3, Section 1.2). For example, we can see in the plot that there are two important points in the relation to data slope: one at a slope of zero and the other at a slope of 1. These correspond to the peaks of the two model likelihoods (as a function of data slope), and show that the model comparison is most effective at discriminating the two models when one is actually correct. The response of the model comparison becomes muddied when neither model fits the data – as it should be.

Exercises

1) What types of perceptual models might posit a model like M1, with a slope of 1 relating physical and perceptual variables?
2) Describe the transition between the second and third lines of the evidence equation in **(D)**.
3) How do the model likelihoods differ for M_0 and M_1?
4) What is the parameter prior over possible values of the slope parameter under:
   a. M_0 ?.
   b. M_1?
5) Describe the best-fit values of the dispersion parameter for the two models in Figure 6.9.

Example: Is There a Nonzero Slope?

Continuing with the previous example scenario, perhaps a model comparison that would find better general use is the comparison between the zero-slope model, providing evidence for total insensitivity to the light in general, and a nonzero-slope model. We examine that model next.

A. Translate Hypotheses into Model Equations

By expanding the second model to allow for more slope values, how are we changing the model comparison? This question has answers at multiple levels. At the lowest level, we will see below that the final model likelihoods and evidence calculation change; this is the obvious answer. At a higher level, however, we should also recognize that whenever we change the definitions of the models being compared we change the nature of the question being answered by our model comparison algorithm. In the current incarnation of this example problem, we are asking perhaps a simpler question: not the precise question about whether the underlying perception exactly matches the changes in physical luminance or whether there are no such changes, but instead a question about whether there is any modulation in perception corresponding to the experimentally imposed changes in physical illumination. In other words, this is a signal detection problem, because we want to know if the biological system under consideration is able to detect the physical signal, the light modulation, via its sensory organs. The signal detection question is one of the more common questions that one finds in all branches of behavioral science.

ι: Brightness judgments are made in response to a range of physical brightnesses, where the physical light stimulus is a single-frequency light presented in an otherwise completely dark room. Five different brightnesses were shown, all known to be above the known light detection threshold for white light.

M_0: The slope of the relationship between physical brightness presented visually and the corresponding judged brightness is zero, $\beta = 0$.

M_1: The slope of the relationship between physical brightness presented visually and the corresponding judged brightness is nonzero, $\beta > 0$.

Simulated brightness judgments are generated as above, such that simulated observation values mimic a system with additive noise, $y = y' + \varepsilon$, as dictated by the underlying model (Fig. 6.9a).

From these simulated data, we will compare the two models outlined above based on the odds ratio, where the odds ratio favoring M_0 is:

$$\begin{aligned}\boldsymbol{O}(M_0) &= \frac{p\left(M_0 \mid \boldsymbol{d}\cdot\iota\right)}{p\left(\overline{M}_0 \mid \boldsymbol{d}\cdot\iota\right)} = \frac{\varpi\ (M_0)\left[\int_0^\infty d\sigma\,\varpi_0(\beta,\sigma)\mathcal{L}(\beta,\sigma)\right]}{\varpi\ (M_1)\left[\int_0^\infty d\sigma\int_{-\infty}^\infty d\beta\,\varpi_1(\beta,\sigma)\mathcal{L}(\beta,\sigma)\right]}\\ &= \frac{\varpi_0}{\varpi_1}\frac{\int_0^\infty d\sigma\,\varpi_0(\beta,\sigma)\mathcal{L}(\beta,\sigma)}{\int_0^\infty d\sigma\int_{-\infty}^\infty d\beta\,\varpi_1(\beta,\sigma)\mathcal{L}(\beta,\sigma)} = \frac{\varpi_0\mathcal{L}_0}{\varpi_1\mathcal{L}_1}\end{aligned}$$

B. Assign Prior Probabilities to Hypotheses

In this experimental scenario it is quite a bit more realistic to assign:

$$\varpi\ (M_0) = \varpi\ (M_1) = 0.5,$$

not only to ensure that any evidence in favor of increased variance is not due to our prior expectation of such an effect, but also because when we ask a signal detection question we often suspect, but are nevertheless unsure, of whether the system is capable of reliably detecting the signal under consideration.

C. Compute Model Likelihoods

As above, we have a Gaussian likelihood model parameterized by the Gaussian location and dispersion parameters ($y' = \beta\omega, \sigma$) and the unknown slope term (β), where y' is dependent on the product $\beta\omega$, and where the set of conditions, $\boldsymbol{\omega}$, is known. Thus in both models the likelihood term describing unknown parameter values is:

$$\begin{aligned}\mathcal{L}(\beta,\sigma) &= p\left(\boldsymbol{y} \mid \boldsymbol{y}'\cdot\sigma\cdot\iota\right)\\ &= p(\boldsymbol{y} \mid \beta\cdot\boldsymbol{\omega}\cdot\sigma\cdot\iota)\\ &= (\sigma\sqrt{2\pi})^{-N} e^{-\frac{1}{2}\frac{\sum_k[y_k-(\beta\omega_k)]^2}{\sigma^2}}.\end{aligned}$$

In the first model (M_0) the slope parameter is set to zero by our prior, $\varpi_0(\beta) = \begin{cases} 0 & \beta \neq 0 \\ 1 & \beta = 0 \end{cases}$, and the dispersion term will be assigned a truncated Jeffreys prior, yielding the model likelihood:

$$\begin{aligned}
\mathcal{L}_0 &= \int_0^\infty d\sigma\, \omega_0(\beta,\sigma)\mathcal{L}(\beta,\sigma) \\
&= \left(\log\sigma_{\max} - \log\sigma_{\min}\right)^{-1} \int_{\sigma_{\min}}^{\sigma_{\max}} d\sigma\sigma^{-1}(\sigma\sqrt{2\pi})^{-N} \mathrm{e}^{-\frac{1}{2}\frac{\sum_k [y_k-(\beta\omega_k)]^2}{\sigma^2}} \\
&= (2\pi)^{-N/2}(\Delta\log\sigma)^{-1} \int_{\sigma_{\min}}^{\sigma_{\max}} d\sigma\sigma^{-(N+1)}\mathrm{e}^{-\frac{1}{2}\frac{\sum_k [y_k]^2}{\sigma^2}}.
\end{aligned}$$

where notice that the theoretical slope value, $\beta = 0$, simplifies the exponential term.

The model likelihood for the nonzero-slope model is more complex because it does not rely on a known slope, requiring us to assign a prior over slope values. As in the previous chapter, we will follow the logic outlined in Figure 5.8 and assign:

$$\begin{aligned}
p(\beta \mid t) &= I^{-1}\left(1+\beta^2\right)^{-1} \\
&\propto \left(1+\beta^2\right)^{-1},
\end{aligned}$$

where I is the normalization constant that allows us to convert the Cauchy function, $(1+\beta^2)^{-1}$, to a probability distribution. Here, of course, we will need a normalization factor for the truncated version of this prior for slopes in the range $0 < \beta \leq 1$. Numerically, we can simply approximate this normalization, I, for the truncated range of interest in this example:

$$\begin{aligned}
I &= \int_0^1 d\beta\left(1+\beta^2\right)^{-1} \\
&\cong \pi/2
\end{aligned}$$

This leads to the normalized prior density over slope, and the model likelihood:

$$\begin{aligned}
\mathcal{L}_1 &= \int_0^\infty d\sigma\, \varpi_0(\beta,\sigma)\mathcal{L}(\beta,\sigma) \\
&= \sqrt{2\pi}^{-N}(\Delta\log\sigma)^{-1} I \int_0^1 d\beta\left(1+\beta^2\right)^{-1} \int_{\sigma_{\min}}^{\sigma_{\max}} d\sigma\sigma^{-(N+1)}e^{-\frac{1}{2}\frac{\sum_k [y_k-(\beta\omega_k)]^2}{\sigma^2}}
\end{aligned}$$

D. Compute the Evidence

Having defined all the elements, we are now able to compute the model evidence values defined above under (**A**).

Programming Aside: Evidence for Zero-Slope Model (Fig. 6.9c)

Here we will again vary the slope 111used to simulate data and compute evidence for the zero-slope model in each case.

```
clear %#ok<*UNRCH>
reset=1; plotFLAG=0;
COL=[.55*[1 1 1]; .3 .4 .85; .8 .5 .4];
N=6;

sig=30;
Nb=301; blist=linspace(-.25,1.25,Nb); %data slope
Ns=501; slist=linspace(0,50,Ns+1)'; slist=slist(2:end); %noise level
diffs=[diff(slist(1:2)) diff(blist(1:2))];
thetas=linspace(-100,100,N);

Nrot=22;
rotlist=linspace(-pi/6,pi/4+pi/6,Nrot); %rotations in radians

%keep noise samples identical across simulations for clearer
comparison
eorig=nrand(0,sig,[1 N]);
eorig=eorig-mean(eorig);
dorig=[thetas(:) thetas(:)];

margL=nan(Nrot,2); sest=zeros(Nrot,2); best=zeros(Nrot,2);
for irot=1:Nrot, rotnow=rotlist(irot);

    %%%%%%%%R%%%%%%%%%%%%%%%%%%%%%%%%%%%%%
    %%% DATA SIM using rotation ratio %%%
    dnow=rot(dorig,rotnow-pi/4); Ov=ones(Nb,1);
    slistmat=slist*ones(1,Nb); slistn2=slist.^(-2);...
        plblistmat2=pi*(1+ones(Ns,1)*blist.^2)/2;
    tnow=dnow(:,1)'; dnow=dnow(:,2)'+eorig;
    likeFN0=-(N/2)*slistn2*mean(dnow.^2, 2) -(N+1)*log(slist); %[Nsx1] output
    likeFN1=-(N/2)*slistn2*mean((Ov*dnow-blist'*tnow).^2,2)'...
        -(N+1)*log(slistmat)-log(plblistmat2);%[NsxNb]

    %%%%%%%%%%%%%%%%%%%%%%%%%%%%%%%%%%%%%%%%
    %%% param likelihood by condition %%%
    Lall0=likeFN0;
    Lall1=likeFN1;

    %%%%%%%%%%%%%%%%%%%%%%%%%%%%%%
    %%% verify global sigma %%%
    sest(irot,1)=logpeakval([Lall0 slist]);
    sest(irot,2)=logpeakval([logsum(Lall1,2,diffs(2)) slist]);
    best(irot,2)=logpeakval([logsum(Lall1,1,diffs(1)) blist']);

    %%%%%%%%%%%%%%%%%%%%%%%%%%%%%
    %%% Model likelihoods %%%
    margL(irot,1)=logsum(Lall0,1,diffs(1));
    margL(irot,2)=logsum(Lall1,[1 2],diffs); end
Elist=10*(margL(:,1)-margL(:,2));

figure(1); clf; hold on
plot(tan(rotlist),Elist,'ko-','MarkerFaceColor','k','MarkerSize',11);
xlabel('data slope','FontName','Arial','FontSize',15);
ylabel('evidence (db)','FontName','Arial','FontSize',15);
figure(30); clf; hold on;
plot(tan(rotlist),margL(:,1),'ko:','MarkerFaceColor','k');
```

```
plot(tan(rotlist),margL(:, 2),'ko:','MarkerFaceColor',COL(1,:))
xlabel('data slope','FontName','Arial','FontSize',15);
ylabel('mod likelihood','FontName','Arial','FontSize',15);
```

$$e\left(M_0\right) = 10\log_{10}\left[O\left(M_0\right)\right] = 10\log_{10}\left[\frac{\varpi_0\mathcal{L}_0}{\varpi_1\mathcal{L}_1}\right]$$

$$= 10\log_{10}\left[\frac{\varpi_0}{\varpi_1}\frac{\int_0^\infty d\sigma\,\varpi_0(\beta,\sigma)\mathcal{L}(\beta,\sigma)}{\int_0^\infty d\beta\int_0^\infty d\sigma\,\varpi_1(\beta,\sigma)\mathcal{L}(\beta,\sigma)}\right]$$

$$= 10\log_{10}\left[\frac{\varpi_0}{\varpi_1}\frac{\int_{\sigma_{\min}}^{\sigma_{\max}} d\sigma\,\sigma^{-(N+1)}e^{-\frac{1}{2}\frac{\sum_k[y_k]^2}{\sigma^2}}}{I^{-1}\int_0^1 d\beta\left(1+\beta^2\right)^{-1}\int_{\sigma_{\max}}^{\sigma_{\max}} d\sigma\,\sigma^{-(N+1)}e^{-\frac{1}{2}\frac{\sum_k[y_k-(\beta\omega_k)]^2}{\sigma^2}}}\right]$$

To get a sense of the evidence produced by real data, we simulate a series of datasets, each generated from a different underlying slope value. Plotting the evidence as a function of these slopes, we obtain the plot in Figure 6.9c. This plot has several important features, including the output of the model comparison to true data-slopes that are negative, or when greater than 1. Also pay attention to how the evidence transitions from positive to negative as the data-slopes approach 1 from the left of the plot.

Exercises

1) How does the model M_0 differ between this and the previous example? What about M_1?
2) What is the parameter prior over possible values of the slope parameter under:
   a. M_0 ?.
   b. M_1 ?
3) What considerations might have motivated the choice of upper and lower bounds for the slope parameter under model:
   a. M_0 ?.
   b. M_1?
4) Explain the calculation of I for the β prior under M_1. Change the upper and or lower bounds on this prior (while still maintaining nonzero separation between them) and recalculate I.

6.4 Multiple Sources

The previous model comparison examples and types were all tested using a single data-source (experimental subject or animal). This is not typical when conducting most analyses, and we should understand that there are certain considerations and advantages that come into play when data are collected from multiple sources. First, we will examine the logic of multiple-source model comparison, and in particular explore the influence of source-specific versus source-general model parameters. We will then explore a type of analysis that is often only available when testing multiple sources, and how this analysis can (sometimes) be translated into a single-source experiment and analysis.

6.4.1 Logic of Model Comparison with S Sources

We encountered multiple-source computations while exploring the measurement algorithm in Chapter 5. The constraints associated with multiple sources in model comparison are essentially the same as multiple source measurement. Thus in general we will be expanding the parameter likelihood terms to include multiple data sources:

$$\begin{aligned}\mathcal{L}(\mu) &= \prod_j \mathcal{L}_j(\mu)\\ &= \prod_j \int d\sigma_j \varpi(\sigma_j)\, \mathcal{L}(\sigma_j, \mu)\\ &= \int d\sigma_1 \varpi(\sigma_1)\, \mathcal{L}(\sigma_1, \mu) \int d\sigma_2 \varpi(\sigma_2)\, \mathcal{L}(\sigma_2, \mu) \ldots \int d\sigma_N \varpi(\sigma_N)\, \mathcal{L}(\sigma_N, \mu)\end{aligned}$$

where terms with the j subscript are considered source-specific and unsubscripted terms are identical across sources. As written here, there are N data sources; the data from each source will be described by the same μ parameter, but by different σ parameters.

The only potential difference separating multisource parameter estimation and model comparison is that there is no requirement that a parameter treated in one model as source specific will be treated as source-specific in another model – indeed this may be the difference being tested in the model comparison. Thus, in terms of the example above, one model in the model comparison may treat the σ parameter as source specific, while another model may treat it as identical across sources. In a model comparison context, the parameter values that are common across sources and the parameters treated as source-specific must be defined separately for each model being compared.

Example: Multisource Biased Gaussian

Here we will return to the Vernier discrimination example, and put it into the context of a multi- source model comparison. Recall in the Vernier comparison each experimental observer (i.e., data source) makes settings of a vertical line whose top falls just below the center of a computer monitor to match the horizontal position of a second (stationary) vertical line whose bottom falls just above the center of the computer monitor. As outlined in the examples above, there is the possibility that these settings of the variable (lower) line may be biased relative to the true horizontal position of the 'standard' stationary upper line.

The graphical model in Figure 6.10a expands the single-source case of this model comparison to multiple sources.

A. Translate Hypotheses into Model Equations

We will examine two versions of the multisource biased-Gaussian model. In one, the models predict source-specific, as opposed to a global (across-source) dispersion parameter. In this version of the problem, we assume all sources have a slightly different dispersion, and that this is a consistent property of their settings. These source-specific dispersion parameters must then be marginalized out of both models before these marginal likelihoods can be combined across sources to make the final evidence computation.

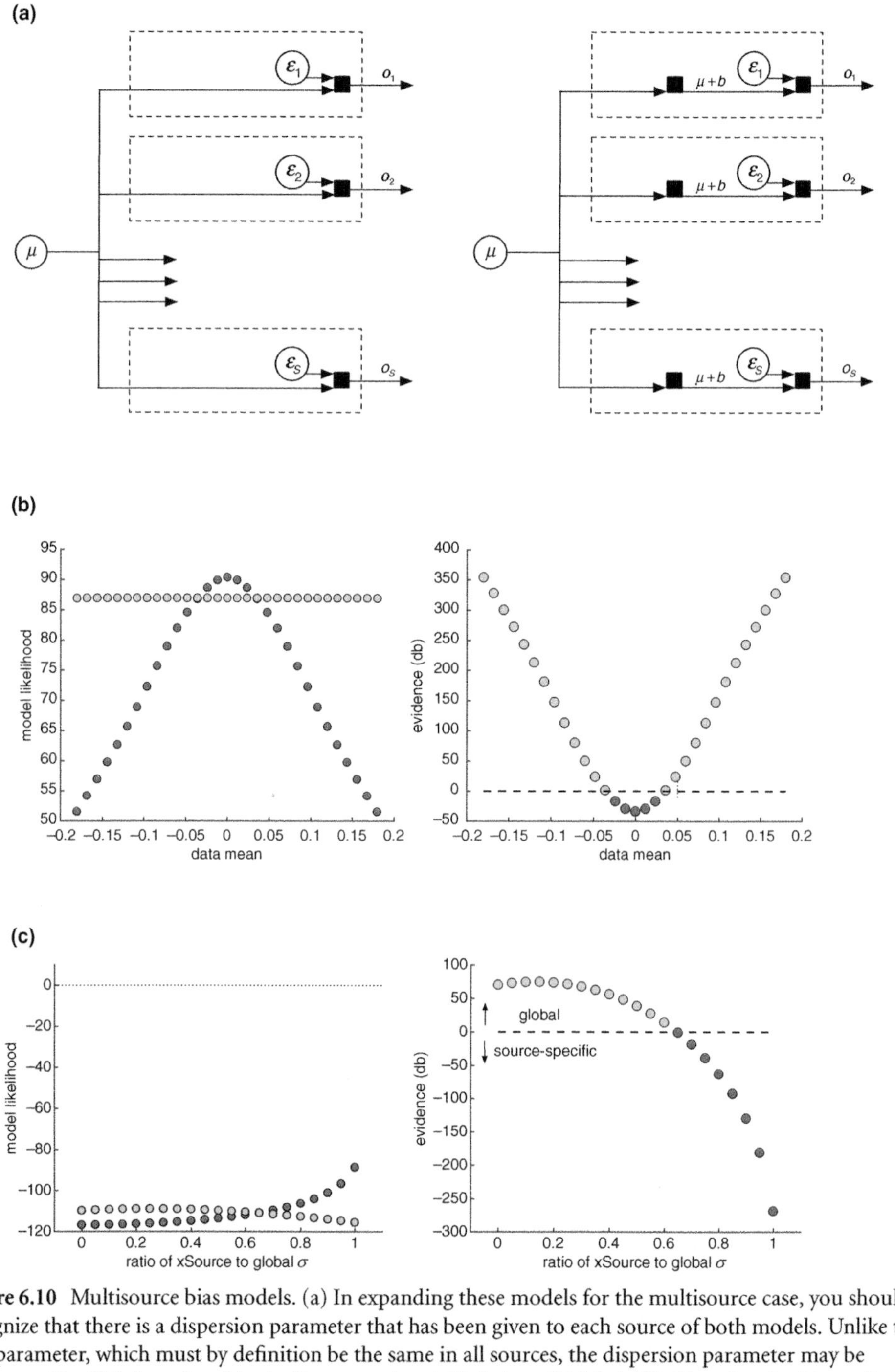

Figure 6.10 Multisource bias models. (a) In expanding these models for the multisource case, you should recognize that there is a dispersion parameter that has been given to each source of both models. Unlike the bias parameter, which must by definition be the same in all sources, the dispersion parameter may be sourcespecific. This is explored in the Programming Aside below. (b) Model likelihood and evidence for Vernier bias in the sourcespecific model. Notice that the model likelihood of the unknown-bias model is flat because the model can explain any bias equally well (left). The unbiased model can only explain data with a mean near zero and otherwise does a poor job of describing the data. Evidence favors the unbiased model when the data mean is near zero and otherwise favors the unknown-bias model (right). (c) Model likelihood and evidence for the Gaussian bias model with source-specific dispersion versus the global dispersion.

ι: Vernier perceptual settings of the alignment of vertical line segments are performed with an imposed memory delay (as in Fig. 6.10).
M_0: The bias of Vernier settings is $b = 0$, indicating an unbiased perceptual discrimination.
M_b: The bias of Vernier settings is $b \neq 0$, indicating a biased perceptual discrimination

In this problem we will simulate Vernier settings, s_{ij}, and compute the evidence in favor of an underlying model of those settings in which they are biased versus unbiased. Note that here the simulated data matrices are two-dimensional: the subscript i indexes repetitions of Vernier settings ($1 \leq i \leq N$) and the subscript j indexes the different sources ($1 \leq j \leq S$); thus each of S sources produces N Vernier settings.

We will simulate Vernier perceptual settings from a Gaussian sampling distribution that is either biased or unbiased relative to the true position μ of the upper bar:

M_0: $s_{ij} = nrand(\mu, \sigma_j)$
M_b: $s_{ij} = nrand(\mu + b, \sigma_j)$

where we label the ith setting generated by the jth source of the lower bar s_{ij}, and its error $\varepsilon = s - \mu$. Notice that the data from each source may not have the identical underlying parameters. In this particular example we allow source-specific dispersion parameters, σ_j.

The outcome of our analysis will be the odds ratio,

$$\begin{aligned}
\mathbf{O}(M_0) &= \frac{p(M_0 \mid \boldsymbol{d} \cdot \iota)}{p(\overline{M}_0 \mid \boldsymbol{d} \cdot \iota)} \\
&= \frac{\varpi_0 \int_{-\infty}^{\infty} db \varpi_0(b) \left[\prod_j \int_{-\infty}^{\infty} d\sigma_j \varpi_0(\sigma_j) \mathcal{L}_j(b, \sigma_j)\right]}{\varpi_b \int_{-\infty}^{\infty} db \varpi_b(b) \left[\prod_j \int_{-\infty}^{\infty} d\sigma_j \omega_b(\sigma_j) \mathcal{L}_j(b, \sigma_j)\right]} \\
&= \frac{\varpi_0 \int_{-\infty}^{\infty} db \varpi_0(b) \mathcal{L}(b)}{\varpi_b \int_{-\infty}^{\infty} db \varpi_b(b) \mathcal{L}(b)} = \frac{\varpi_0 \mathcal{L}_0}{\omega_b \mathcal{L}_b}
\end{aligned}$$

which will be applied below to compute the evidence in favor of either the unbiased (M_0) or biased (M_b) model.

In contrast, the second version of this problem will remain agnostic regarding whether there is a source-specific set of dispersion parameters or whether there is a single global dispersion describing all settings.

ι: Vernier perceptual settings of the alignment of vertical line segments are performed with an imposed memory delay.
M_g: The bias of Vernier settings is $b = 0$, and dispersion is a global parameter.
M_s: The bias of Vernier settings is $b = 0$, where dispersion is a source-specific parameter.

Here the simulation of data is similar, except we must choose whether to simulate a source-specific set of dispersion parameters or a single global dispersion. Notice that we have created a model comparison in which it is assumed that there is no bias. This is done to simplify the example, but it is straightforward to add a bas term to the model equations.

The outcome of this analysis will be a slightly different odds ratio,

$$\begin{aligned} O(M_s) &= \frac{p(M_s \mid \boldsymbol{d} \cdot \iota)}{p(\overline{M}_s \mid \boldsymbol{d} \cdot \iota)} \\ &= \frac{\varpi_s}{\varpi_g} \frac{\left[\prod_j \int_{-\infty}^{\infty} d\sigma_j \varpi_s(\sigma_j)\, \mathcal{L}_j(b, \sigma_j)\right]}{\int_{-\infty}^{\infty} d\sigma\, \varpi_g(\sigma) \left[\prod_j \mathcal{L}_j(\sigma)\right]} = \frac{\varpi_s \mathcal{L}_s}{\varpi_g \mathcal{L}_g} \end{aligned}$$

where the two elements of the ratio differ in the ordering of when likelihoods are combined versus when we marginalize over the unknown dispersion value(s).

B. Assign Prior Probabilities to Hypotheses

The multisource model comparison does not require special consideration of the prior over models. We will therefore maintain the argument from above and assign a uniform prior over competing models:

$$\varpi(M_b) = \varpi(M_0) = 0.5.$$

C. Compute Model Likelihoods

The key to the first model comparison is whether or not there is a bias term b in the likelihood that allows us to fit settings with a constant deviation away from the location of the standard bar, μ. When the bias term is present, we have the source-specific model likelihood:

$$\mathcal{L}_b = \int_{-\infty}^{\infty} db \varpi_b(b) \mathcal{L}(b),$$

where

$$\mathcal{L}(b) = \prod_j \mathcal{L}_j(b),$$

and

$$\mathcal{L}_j(b) = \int d\sigma_j \varpi(\sigma_j)\, \mathcal{L}(b, \sigma_j),$$

and

$$\mathcal{L}(b, \sigma_j) = \left(\sigma_j \sqrt{2\pi}\right)^{-N} e^{-\frac{1}{2} \frac{\sum_i [s_{ij} - (b+\mu)]^2}{\sigma_j^2}}$$

for the jth source.

Programming Aside: Multisource Bias (Fig. 6.10b)

To understand how the evidence for a bias follows the size of the true bias, we will simulate a dataset and vary its mean from left to right of no bias, computing and plotting the evidence in each case.

```
%%% Biased Gaussian
%%% [models compare unbiased vs. unknown bias]
clear %#ok<*UNRCH>
N=10; S=5;
COL={.4*[1 1 1],.8*[1 1 1]};

sig=.1;
Ns=201; slist=linspace(0,10,Ns)'; slist=slist(2:end); sn2=slist.^(-2);
err=randn([S,N])*sig;
for s=1:S, err(s,:)=err(s,:)-mean(err(s,:)); end

brange=[-2*sig 2*sig]; %don't expect any large biases
Nb=101; blist=linspace(brange(1),brange(2),Nb);

diffs=[diff(slist(1:2)) diff(blist(1:2))];
Nx=31; xlist=linspace(.9*brange(1),.9*brange(2),Nx);
ML1=zeros(Nx,1); ML2=zeros(Nx,1);
for ix=1:Nx, xnow=xlist(ix);
    Lall1=zeros(1); Lall2=zeros(Nb,1);

    for s=1:S,
        %%%%%%%%R%%%%%%%
        %%% DATA SIM %%%
        dnow=err(s,:)+xnow; Ov=ones(Nb,1); ON=ones(1,N);

        %%%%%%%%%%%%%%%%%%%%%%%%%%%%%%%%%%%%%%%%%
        %%% param likelihood by condition %%%
        likeFN0=-(N/2)*sn2*mean(( dnow ).^2,2)'-(N+1)*log(slist); %output is Ns x 1
        likeFNb=-(N/2)*sn2*mean((Ov*dnow-blist'*ON).^2,2)'-...
            (N+1)*log(slist); %output is Ns x Nb

        %%%%%%%%%%%%%%%%%%%%%%%%%%%%%%%%%%%%%%%%%%%%
        %%% marginalize source-specific sig %%%
        Lall1=Lall1+logsum(likeFN0,1,diffs(1));
        Lall2=Lall2+logsum(likeFNb,1,diffs(1)); end
    ML1(ix)=Lall1; ML2(ix)=logsum(Lall2,1,diffs(2)); end
%%% compute evidence
EV=10*(ML2-ML1);

%%% plotting
figure(4); clf; hold on
ind=findnearestN(xlist,.05,1);
plot(xlist,ML1,'ko','MarkerFaceColor',COL{1},'MarkerSize',10)
plot(xlist,ML2,'ko','MarkerFaceColor',COL{2},'MarkerSize',10)
xlabel(['data mean'],'FontSize',15);
ylabel('model likelihood','FontName','Arial','FontSize',15);

figure(5); clf; hold on
plot(.05*[1 1],[-10 EV(ind)],'k:')
plot(xlist(EV<0),EV(EV<0),'ko','MarkerFaceColor',COL{1},...
    'MarkerSize',12,'LineWidth',1);
plot(xlist(EV>0),EV(EV>0),'ko','MarkerFaceColor',COL{2},...
    'MarkerSize',12,'LineWidth',1);
plot(xlist([1 end]),[0 0],'k--','LineWidth',2);
```

```
axis([brange -50 400]);
xlabel(['data mean'],'FontSize',15);
ylabel('evidence (db)','FontName','Arial','FontSize',15);
```

In the unbiased case, our background information regarding the model defines it with a known bias ($b = 0$), and so the integral over b drops out of the calculation:

$$\begin{aligned}
\mathcal{L}_0 &= \int_{-\infty}^{\infty} db\varpi_0(b)\mathcal{L}(b) \\
&= \int_{-\infty}^{\infty} db\varpi_0(b)\prod_j \mathcal{L}_j(b) \\
&= \int_{-\infty}^{\infty} db\varpi_0(b)\prod_j \left[\int d\sigma_j\varpi\left(\sigma_j\right)\mathcal{L}\left(\sigma_j, b\right)\right] \\
&= \prod_j \left[\int d\sigma_j\varpi\left(\sigma_j\right)\mathcal{L}\left(\sigma_j, b=0\right)\right] \\
&= \prod_j \left[(\Delta \log\sigma)^{-1}\int_{\sigma\,\min}^{\sigma\,\max} d\sigma_j\sigma_j^{-1}\mathcal{L}\left(\sigma_j, b\right)\right] \\
&= \sqrt{2\pi}^{-SN}(\Delta\log\sigma)^{-S}\prod_j\left[\int_{\sigma\,\min}^{\sigma\,\max} d\sigma_j\sigma_j^{-(N_j+1)}\mathrm{e}^{-\frac{1}{2}\frac{\sum_i\left[s_{ij}-\mu\right]^2}{\sigma_j^2}}\right].
\end{aligned}$$

The biased model retains the outermost integral to marginalize over the unknown bias, yielding the marginal likelihood:

$$\begin{aligned}
\mathcal{L}_b &= \int_{-\infty}^{\infty} db\varpi_b(b)\mathcal{L}(b) \\
&= \int_{-\infty}^{\infty} db\varpi_b(b)\prod_j \mathcal{L}_j(b) \\
&= \int_{-\infty}^{\infty} db\varpi_b(b)\prod_j \left[\int d\sigma_j\varpi\left(\sigma_j\right)\mathcal{L}\left(\sigma_j, b\right)\right] \\
&= [b_{\max}-b_{\min}]^{-1}\int_{b\,\min}^{b\,\max} db\left(\prod_j\left[\int d\sigma_j\cdot\varpi\left(\sigma_j\right)\mathcal{L}\left(\sigma_j, b\right)\right]\right) \\
&= [\Delta b]^{-1}\int_{b\,\min}^{b\,\max} db\left(\prod_j\left[(\Delta\log\sigma)^{-1}\int_{\sigma\,\min}^{\sigma\,\max} d\sigma_j\sigma_j^{-1}\mathcal{L}\left(\sigma_j, b\right)\right]\right) \\
&= \sqrt{2\pi}^{-SN}[\Delta b]^{-1}(\Delta\log\sigma)^{-S}\int_{b\,\min}^{b\,\max} db\left(\prod_j\left[\int_{\sigma\,\min}^{\sigma\,\max} d\sigma_j\sigma_j^{-(N_j+1)}e^{-\frac{1}{2}\frac{\sum_i\left[s_{ij}-(b+\mu)\right]^2}{\sigma_j^2}}\right]\right)
\end{aligned}$$

Programming Aside: Multisource Dispersion (Fig. 6.10c)

```
%%% Biased Gaussian
%%% [models compare unbiased models that differ in whether
dispersion is source specific global]
clear %#ok<*UNRCH>
N=10; S=5;
COL={.4*[1 1 1],.8*[1 1 1]};

sigS=linspace(.2,10,S); sigG=mean(sigS)*ones(S,1);
Ns=501; slist=linspace(0,20,Ns+1)'; slist=slist(2:end);
sn2=slist.^(-2);
slnrange=log(max(slist))-log(min(slist));
err0=randn([S,N]);
for s=1:S, err0(s,:)=(err0(s,:)-mean(err0(s,:))); end

diffs=diff(slist(1:2));
ratlist=[0:.05:1]; Nrat=length(ratlist);
ML1=zeros(Nrat,1); ML2=zeros(Nrat,1);
for irat=1:Nrat, rnow=ratlist(irat);
    Lall1=zeros(1); Lall2=zeros(Ns,1);

    for s=1:S,
        %%%%%%%%R%%%%%%%
        %%% DATA SIM %%%
        dnow=err0(s,:)*(sigG(s)*(1-rnow)+sigS(s)*(rnow));

        %%%%%%%%%%%%%%%%%%%%%%%%%%%%%%%%%%%%%%%
        %%% param likelihood by condition %%%
        likeFN1=-(N/2)*sn2*mean((dnow).^2,2)'-(N+1)*log(slist); %Ns x 1
        likeFN2=-(N/2)*sn2*mean((dnow).^2,2)'-(N )*log(slist); %Ns x 1

        %%%%%%%%%%%%%%%%%%%%%%%%%%%%%%%%%%%%%%%%%
        %%% marginalize source-specific sig %%%
        Lall1=Lall1+logsum(likeFN1,1,diffs)-log(slnrange);
        Lall2=Lall2+likeFN2; end
    ML1(irat)=Lall1; ML2(irat)=logsum(Lall2-log(slist)-log(slnrange),1,diffs); end
%%% compute evidence
EV=10*(ML2-ML1);

%%% plotting
figure(4); clf; hold on
plot(ratlist,ML1,'ko','MarkerFaceColor',COL{1},'MarkerSize',10)
plot(ratlist,ML2,'ko','MarkerFaceColor',COL{2},'MarkerSize',10)
plot([ratlist(1)-.1 ratlist(end)+.1],[0 0],'k:')
xlabel(['ratio of xSource to global \sigma'],'FontSize',15);
ylabel('model likelihood','FontName','Arial','FontSize',15);
r=axis; axis([ratlist(1)-.1 ratlist(end)+.1 r(3) max([r(4) 10])])

figure(5); clf; hold on
plot(ratlist([1 end]),[0 0],'k--','LineWidth',2);
plot(ratlist(EV<0),EV(EV<0),'ko','MarkerFaceColor',COL{1},...
    'MarkerSize',12,'LineWidth',1);
plot(ratlist(EV>0),EV(EV>0),'ko','MarkerFaceColor',COL{2},...
    'MarkerSize',12,'LineWidth',1);
r=axis; axis([ratlist(1)-.1 ratlist(end)+.1 r(3:4)]);
xlabel(['ratio of xSource to global \sigma'],'FontSize',15);
ylabel('evidence (db)','FontName','Arial','FontSize',15);
```

In big-picture terms notice that the difference between the two models is just in the way the bias term is handled. In the first model, the bias term drops out of the calculations altogether because under this model the bias is the constant, $b = 0$; this causes both the integral to drop out of the likelihood, and for the bias term to drop from the exponential term of the parameter likelihood equation (because for $b = 0$, $[s_{ij} - (b + \mu)]^2 = [s_{ij} - \mu]^2$). In the second model likelihood, the integral over the bias parameter is retained, as well as its (truncated uniform) prior - although this leads to a substantially more complicated-looking expression, remember that it is basically just the first model (which requires marginalizing over each subject-specific dispersion parameter separately and combining the resulting source-specific marginal likelihoods into a single marginal likelihood for the bias term representing the data across all sources), now with the addition of a final marginalization over the unknown bias term.

The focus of the second model comparison of this type is to compare one model in which dispersion terms of the model (which now assumes no bias in both cases) is source-specific as above:

$$\mathcal{L}_s = \int_{-\infty}^{\infty} db\varpi_s(b)\mathcal{L}(b),$$

where

$$\mathcal{L}(b) = \prod\nolimits_j \mathcal{L}_j(b),$$

and

$$\mathcal{L}_j(b) = \int d\sigma_j \varpi\left(\sigma_j\right) \mathcal{L}\left(b, \sigma_j\right)$$

and

$$\mathcal{L}\left(b, \sigma_j\right) = \left(\sigma_j \sqrt{2\pi}\right)^{-N_j} e^{-\frac{1}{2}\frac{\sum_i \left[s_{ij}-(b+\mu)\right]^2}{\sigma_j^2}}$$

for the jth source. Thus, expanding these equations and dropping the outermost integral term because the bias is a known constant $b = 0$ gives

$$\begin{aligned}
\mathcal{L}_s &= \int_{-\infty}^{\infty} db\varpi_s(b)\mathcal{L}(b) \\
&= \int_{-\infty}^{\infty} db\varpi_s(b)\prod\nolimits_j \mathcal{L}_j(b) \\
&= \prod\nolimits_j \left[\int d\sigma_j \varpi\left(\sigma_j\right) \mathcal{L}\left(\sigma_j, b = 0\right)\right] \\
&= \prod\nolimits_j \left[(\Delta \log \sigma)^{-1} \int_{\sigma\,\min}^{\sigma\,\max} d\sigma_j \sigma_j^{-1} \mathcal{L}\left(\sigma_j, b\right)\right] \\
&= \sqrt{2\pi}^{-SN} (\Delta \log \sigma)^{-S} \prod\nolimits_j \left[\int_{\sigma\,\min}^{\sigma\,\max} d\sigma_j \sigma_j^{-(N_j+1)} e^{-\frac{1}{2}\frac{\sum_i \left[s_{ij}-\mu\right]^{-2}}{\sigma_j^2}}\right]
\end{aligned}$$

The alternative to this model has a global dispersion term that is constant across all sources:

$$
\begin{aligned}
\mathcal{L}_g &= \int_{-\infty}^{\infty} db\varpi_g(b)\mathcal{L}(b) \\
&= \int_{-\infty}^{\infty} db\varpi_g(b)\prod_j \mathcal{L}_j(b) \\
&= \int d\sigma\,\varpi_g(\sigma)\prod_j[\mathcal{L}_j(\sigma, b=0)] \\
&= (\Delta\log\sigma)^{-1}\int_{\sigma\min}^{\sigma\max} d\sigma\sigma^{-1}\prod_j\left[\mathcal{L}_j(\sigma, b=0)\right] \\
&= \sqrt{2\pi}^{-SN}(\Delta\log\sigma)^{-1}\int_{\sigma\min}^{\sigma\max} d\sigma\sigma^{-(S\bar{N}+1)}\prod_j\left[e^{-\frac{1}{2}\frac{\sum_i\left[s_{ij}-\mu\right]^2}{\sigma^2}}\right].
\end{aligned}
$$

D. Compute the Evidence

The first evidence calculation defined by our equations above is defined in terms of the comparison between biased/unbiased models:

$$
\begin{aligned}
\boldsymbol{e}(M_b) &= 10\log_{10}[\boldsymbol{O}(M_b)] = 10\log_{10}\left[\frac{\varpi_b\mathcal{L}_b}{\varpi_0\mathcal{L}_0}\right] \\
&= 10\log_{10}\left[\frac{\varpi_b}{\varpi_0}\frac{\int_{-\infty}^{\infty} db\varpi_b(b)\prod_j\mathcal{L}_j(b)}{\prod_j\mathcal{L}_j(b)}\right] \\
&= 10\log_{10}\left[\frac{\varpi_b}{\varpi_0}\frac{[\Delta b]^{-1}\int_{b\min}^{b\max} db\left(\prod_j\left[\int_{\sigma\min}^{\sigma\max} d\sigma_j\sigma_j^{-(N_j+1)}e^{-\frac{1}{2}\frac{\sum_i\left[s_{ij}-(b+\mu)\right]^2}{\sigma_j^2}}\right]\right)}{\prod_j\left[\int_{\sigma\min}^{\sigma\max} d\sigma_j\sigma_j^{-(N_j+1)}e^{-\frac{1}{2}\frac{\sum_i\left[s_{ij}-\mu\right]^2}{\sigma_j^2}}\right]}\right]
\end{aligned}
$$

This evidence is simulated in Figure 6.10c for the case of multiple sources, and source-specific dispersion. This figure is largely similar to the analogous figure from the single-source section above, except that multiple sources will provide additional evidence.

The comparison between source-specific and global dispersion under the Gaussian likelihood is

$$
\begin{aligned}
\boldsymbol{e}(M_g) &= 10\log_{10}\left[\boldsymbol{O}(M_g)\right] = 10\log_{10}\left[\frac{\varpi_g\mathcal{L}_g}{\varpi_s\mathcal{L}_s}\right] \\
&= 10\log_{10}\left[\frac{\varpi_g}{\varpi_s}\frac{\int_0^{\sigma} d\sigma\,\varpi_g(\sigma)\prod_j\mathcal{L}_j(b,\sigma)}{\prod_j\int_0^{\sigma} d\sigma\,\varpi_s(\sigma)\mathcal{L}_j(b,\sigma_j)}\right] \\
&= 10\log_{10}\left[\frac{\varpi_g}{\varpi_s}\frac{\int_{\sigma\min}^{\sigma\max} d\sigma\sigma^{-(S\bar{N}+1)}\prod_j\left[e^{-\frac{1}{2}\frac{\sum_i\left[s_{ij}-\mu\right]^2}{\sigma^2}}\right]}{(\Delta\log\sigma)^{-(S-1)}\prod_j\left[\int_{\sigma\min}^{\sigma\max} d\sigma_j\sigma_j^{-(N_j+1)}e^{-\frac{1}{2}\frac{\sum_i\left[s_{ij}-\mu\right]^2}{\sigma_j^2}}\right]}\right]
\end{aligned}
$$

Unlike the bias-based multiple-source model comparison, this model comparison between global and source-specific dispersion parameters (simulated in Fig. 6.10c) is inherently multisource: with a single source, there is no way to define the difference between the two models because without at least a second data source the two models are identical.

In the next example we will see how to accumulate evidence for the slope-based model comparison across sources. This multisource extension of the basic model comparison will again simply provide additional evidence relative to what can be obtained with a single-source model comparison. However, we will also examine examples that involve interrelationships of slope values between sources. This is again an inherently multisource model comparison that finds a good deal of use when attempting to establish a causal link among pairs of observed variables.

Exercises

1) Compute the evidence for the bias-based model comparison with 5 sources. Then combine the simulation data from those sources into one mega-source and recompute the evidence for the bias model. Compare the evidence calculations and the outcome of the calculation.
2) Explain why the dispersion model comparison is inherently multisource in a way that the bias- model comparison was not.
3) The model likelihood for the unbiased model varies with the bias of the data (peaking, of course, at zero bias), whereas the model likelihood of the bias model is relatively flat. Explain why one is sharply peaked while the other is relatively flat.
4) Simulate the Vernier bias experiment with 10 sources each producing 5 datapoints, and a single subject producing 50 datapoints.
   a. Are there any differences in the evidence produced by these simulations?
   b. Explain why you might prefer the multisource scenario.
   c. Explain why you might prefer the single-source scenario.

Example: Multisource Slope Comparison

Here we will return to the simplest of the slope-based straight-line model comparisons featuring two models with theoretically defined constant slope values, and expand that example by introducing individual differences in both the unknown intercept and dispersion parameters of the straight-line model.

A. Translate Hypotheses into Model Equations

The two models under consideration define theories that: (M_1) brightness perception is veridical versus (M_0) that changes in the brightness of the light shown experimentally are undetectable. We will tweak these models to allow for an unknown intercept term, defining their predictions in terms of changes only: updated models predict that *changes* in brightness will either produce equal or no *changes in perceived brightness.*

ι: Brightness judgments are made in response to a range of physical brightnesses, where the physical light stimulus is a single-frequency light presented in an otherwise completely dark room. Five different brightnesses are shown, all chosen to be above the known light detection threshold for white light.

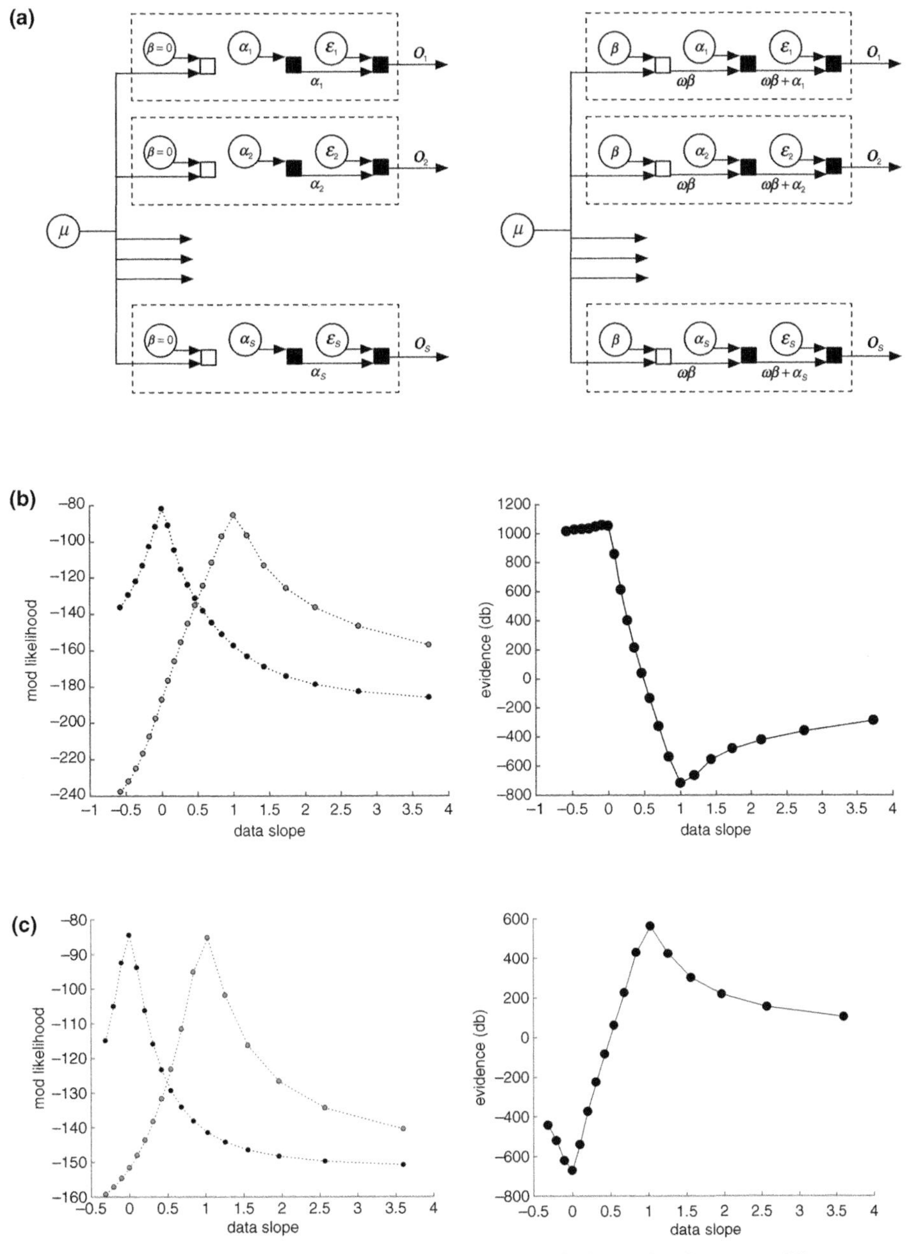

Figure 6.11 Multisource slope comparison. (a) Graphical model of causal and noncausal linear mechanisms. The noncausal ('insensitivity'; left) mechanism is described by an 'effective slope' of $\beta = 0$ because the physical light intensity has no effect on the the additive-noise output, o. The causal model (right) has, based on the theoretical prediction, a unity-slope $\beta = 1$ linking input μ to output o (i.e., the percept is veridical). Both models' outputs are shifted by a possibly source-specific intercept term, α_j. (b) Model likelihood and evidence in the global-intercept model. Model likelihood functions peak in both cases when the data slope best matches the predicted slope, at $\beta = 0$ in the insensitivity model and at $\beta = 1$ in the veridical model. Evidence in favor of the insensitivity model is maximal when the data slope matches the insensitivity prediction and at a minimum when the data slope matches the prediction of the veridical model. (c) Same as (b), except that evidence is computed for the veridical model. Compare these model likelihood and evidence functions to those presented in the global-intercept model above, noting the modulation depths of these functions and sharpness of the peaks.

M_0: The slope of the relationship between physical brightness presented visually and the corresponding judged brightness is zero, $\beta = 0$, although there is an unknown intercept term α that shifts all brightness judgments by a constant that may be subject-dependent.

M_1: The slope of the relationship between physical brightness presented visually and the corresponding judged brightness is one, $\beta = 1$, although there is an unknown intercept term α that shifts all brightness judgments by a constant that may be source-specific.

Simulated brightness judgments are generated by first choosing an underlying slope value. For these models the slope is either $\beta = 1$ or $\beta = 0$, then for each condition of the experiment we set $y'_{jk} = \omega_k + \alpha_j$ from which to simulate brightness judgments:

M_0: $y_{jk} = nrand(\alpha_j, \sigma)$, indicating that light is perceived, but no gradations in brightness are evident.

M_1: $y_{jk} = nrand(\omega_k + \alpha_j, \sigma)$, demonstrating veridical percepts, whereas if $\beta = 0$ then $y'_{jk} = \alpha_j$ for the kth physical brightness:

These simulated observation values mimic a system with additive noise, $y = y' + \varepsilon$, as dictated by the underlying model (Fig. 6.11a). From these simulated data we will compare the two models outlined above, based on the odds ratio, where the odds ratio favoring M_0 is:

$$\begin{aligned} \boldsymbol{O}(M_0) &= \frac{p(M_0 \mid \boldsymbol{d} \cdot \iota)}{p(\overline{M}_0 \mid \boldsymbol{d} \cdot \iota)} \\ &= \frac{\varpi_0 \int_0^\infty d\sigma \prod_j \int_{-\infty}^{\infty} d\alpha_j \varpi_0(\beta, \alpha) \mathcal{L}_0(\alpha, \beta)}{\varpi_1 \int_0^\infty d\sigma \prod_j \int_{-\infty}^{\infty} d\alpha_j \varpi_1(\beta, \alpha) \mathcal{L}_1(\alpha, \beta)} = \frac{\varpi_0 \mathcal{L}_0}{\varpi_1 \mathcal{L}_1} \end{aligned}$$

which will be applied below to compute the evidence in favor of either the insensitivity (M_0) or veridical (M_1) slope model. We will perform the model comparison twice, first for the case where the intercept associated with each source has a known value, $\alpha_j = 0$, and then for the case of unknown intercept values that are source-specific. In both models we will assume a constant dispersion parameter across sources – this is not particularly plausible for the current perceptual model, but will serve the purpose of demonstrating how to deal with a global nuisance parameter in this type of multisource model comparison.

B. Assign Prior Probabilities to Hypotheses

As with the previous multisource example, we simply note that multisource model comparison does not require special consideration of the prior over models, and we therefore maintain the argument from our initial analysis of this slope comparison and assign a uniform prior over competing models:

$$\varpi(M_0) = \varpi(M_1) = 0.5.$$

Programming Aside: Multisource Slope Comparisons (Fig. 6.11b)

```
%%% SLM with global dispersion and no intercepts
%%% [zero-one slope comparison]
clear %#ok<*UNRCH>
reset=1;
COL=[.55*[1 1 1]; .3 .4 .85; .8 .5 .4];
    N=6; S=5;

    sig=10;
    Ns=501; slist=linspace(0,50,Ns+1)'; slist=slist(2:end);
    slistn2=slist.^(-2); lnslist=log(slist);%noise level
    diffs=[diff(slist(1:2))];
    thetas=linspace(-100,100,N);

    Nrot=22;
    rotlist=linspace(-pi/6,pi/4+pi/6,Nrot); %rotations in radians

    %keep noise samples identical across simulations for clearer comparison
    brel=urand(-.1,.1,[S,1]);
    dorig=[thetas(:) thetas(:)]; eorig=nrand(0,sig,[S N]);
    for s=1:S, eorig(s,:)=eorig(s,:)-mean(eorig(s,:)); end

margL=zeros(Nrot,2); sest=zeros(Nrot,2);
for irot=1:Nrot, rotnow=rotlist(irot);

    %%%%%%%%%%%%%%%%%%%%%%%%%%%%%%%%%%%%%
    %%% param likelihood by condition %%%
    for s=1:S,
        %%%%%%%R%%%%%%%%%%%%%%%%%%%%%%%%%%%
        %%% DATA SIM using rotation ratio %%%
        drot=rot(dorig,rotnow-pi/4+atan(brel(s)));
        tnow=drot(:,1)'; dnow=drot(:,2)'+eorig(s,:);
        likeFN0=-(N/2)*slistn2*mean(dnow.^2, 2)-(N+1)*lnslist; %output is Ns x 1
        likeFN1=-(N/2)*slistn2*mean((dnow-tnow).^2,2)-(N+1)*lnslist; %Ns x 1

        %%%%%%%%%%%%%%%%%%%%%%%%%%%
        %%% verify global sigma %%%
        sest(irot,1)=logpeakval([likeFN0 slist]);
        sest(irot,2)=logpeakval([likeFN1 slist]);

        %%%%%%%%%%%%%%%%%%%%%%%%%
        %%% Model likelihoods %%%
        margL(irot,1)=margL(irot,1)+logsum(likeFN0,1,diffs(1));
        margL(irot,2)=margL(irot,2)+logsum(likeFN1,1,diffs(1)); end, end
Elist=10*(margL(:,1)-margL(:,2));

figure(1); clf; hold on
plot(tan(rotlist),Elist,'ko-','MarkerFaceColor','k','MarkerSize',11);
xlabel('data slope','FontName','Arial','FontSize',15);
ylabel('evidence (db)','FontName','Arial','FontSize',15);

figure(30); clf; hold on;
plot(tan(rotlist),margL(:,1),'ko:','MarkerFaceColor','k');
plot(tan(rotlist),margL(:,2),'ko:','MarkerFaceColor',COL(1,:))
xlabel('data slope','FontName','Arial','FontSize',15);
ylabel('mod likelihood','FontName','Arial','FontSize',15);
```

C. Compute Model Likelihoods

Here we have a Gaussian likelihood parameterized by location and dispersion parameters ($y' = \beta\omega + \alpha, \sigma$), where y' is dependent on the unknown slope (β) and intercept (α) terms, and the set of experimental conditions, ω, is known. Thus in both models the likelihood term describing unknown parameter values for the jth source is:

$$\begin{aligned}\mathcal{L}\left(\beta,\alpha_j,\sigma_j\right) &= p\left(y \mid y' \cdot \sigma_j \cdot \iota\right) \\ &= p\left(y \mid \alpha_j \cdot \beta \cdot \omega \cdot \sigma_j \cdot \iota\right) \\ &= \left(\sigma_j\sqrt{2\pi}\right)^{-N} \mathrm{e}^{-\frac{1}{2}\frac{\sum_k\left[y_k-\left(\beta\omega_k+\alpha_j\right)\right]^2}{\sigma_j^2}}.\end{aligned}$$

This function applies to all brightness judgments (regardless of the physical brightness used to elicit them) for the jth source only. The set of source-specific parameter likelihoods, $\mathcal{L}(\beta,\alpha_j,\sigma_j)$, can be combined across sources after marginalizing over any source-specific variables (subscripted j) to yield the marginal source-specific model likelihoods $(\mathcal{L}_0)_j$. Marginal source-specific model likelihoods require marginalization with respect to model-specific prior distributions, and so will in general be different for different models. Here, the marginal source-specific model likelihood for the insensitivity model (M_0) is

$$(\mathcal{L}_0)_j = \int d\alpha_j \varpi_0\left(\beta,\alpha_j,\sigma\right)\mathcal{L}_0\left(\beta,\alpha_j,\sigma\right)$$

The overall marginal model likelihood is then built from the set of marginalized source-specific model likelihoods and marginalized over the global dispersion:

$$\mathcal{L}_0 = \int d\sigma \prod_j (\mathcal{L}_0)_j.$$

Similarly, in the veridical model (M_1), the marginal source-specific model likelihood is

$$(\mathcal{L}_1)_j = \int d\alpha_j \varpi_0\left(\beta,\alpha_j,\sigma\right)\mathcal{L}_1\left(\beta,\alpha_j,\sigma\right)$$

and the marginal model likelihood is

$$\mathcal{L}_1 = \int d\sigma \prod_j (\mathcal{L}_1)_j.$$

The only value of the prior over β allowed by the veridical model is $\beta = 1$:

$$\varpi_1(\beta) = \begin{cases} 0 & \beta \neq 1 \\ 1 & \beta = 1 \end{cases},$$

whereas only $\beta = 0$ is allowed by the insensitivity model:

$$\varpi_0(\beta) = \begin{cases} 0 & \beta \neq 0 \\ 1 & \beta = 0 \end{cases},$$

Neither model, therefore, requires marginalization over an unknown slope value, because within each model the slope is considered known.

Programming Aside: Multisource Slope Comparisons (Fig. 6.11c)

```
%%% SLM with source-specific intercept and global dispersion
%%% [zero-one slope comparison]
clear %#ok<*UNRCH>
reset=1;
COL=[.55*[1 1 1]; .3 .4 .85; .8 .5 .4];
N=6; S=5;

sig=10;
Na=201; alist=linspace(-3*sig,3*sig,Na); %data slope
Ns=501; slist=linspace(0,125,Ns+1)'; slist=slist(2:end);
%noise level
diffs=[diff(slist(1:2)) diff(alist(1:2))];
thetas=linspace(-100,100,N);
rotlist=[-.3:.1:1.3]; %rotations in radians
Nrot=length(rotlist);

%keep noise samples identical across simulations for clearer comparison
dorig=[thetas(:) thetas(:)]; eorig=nrand(0,sig,[S N]);
alphas=urand(-2*sig,2*sig,[S 1]);
for s=1:S, eorig(s,:)=eorig(s,:)-mean(eorig(s,:))+alphas(s); end

Ov=ones(Na,1); Oh=ones(1,Ns); ON=ones(1,N);
modlike=zeros(Nrot,2);
sest0=zeros(Nrot,S); sest1=zeros(Nrot,S);
aest0=zeros(Nrot,S); aest1=zeros(Nrot,S);
Lall0=zeros(S,Ns,Na); Lall1=zeros(S,Ns,Na);
slistmat=slist*ones(1,Na); slistn2=slist.^(-2);
for irot=1:Nrot, rotnow=rotlist(irot); margL0=zeros(Ns,1); margL1=zeros(Ns,1);

    %%%%%%%R%%%%%%%%%%%%%%%%%%%%%%%%%%%%%
    %%% DATA SIM using rotation ratio %%%
    drot=rot(dorig,rotnow-pi/4); tnow=drot(:,1)';

    likeFN0=@(dnow) -(N/2)*slistn2*mean((Ov*(dnow )-...
    alist'*ON).^2,2)'-(N+1)*log(slistmat); %output: Ns x Na
    likeFN1=@(dnow) -(N/2)*slistn2*mean((Ov*(dnow-tnow)-...
    alist'*ON).^2,2)'-(N+1)*log(slistmat); %output: Ns x Na

    %%%%%%%%%%%%%%%%%%%%%%%%%%%%%%%%%%%%%%%%
    %%% param likelihood by condition %%%
    for s=1:S, dnow=drot(:,2)'+eorig(s,:);
        tmpL0=likeFN0(dnow);
        tmpL1=likeFN1(dnow);

        %%%%%%%%%%%%%%%%%%%%%%%%%%%%%%
        %%% verify global sigma %%%
        margL0=margL0+logsum(tmpL0,2,diffs(2));
        margL1=margL1+logsum(tmpL1,2,diffs(2));

        sest0(irot,s)=logpeakval([logsum(tmpL0,2,diffs(2)) slist]);
        aest0(irot,s)=logpeakval([logsum(tmpL0,1,diffs(1)) alist']);
        sest1(irot,s)=logpeakval([logsum(tmpL1,2,diffs(2)) slist]);
        aest1(irot,s)=logpeakval([logsum(tmpL1,1,diffs(1)) alist']); end

    %%%%%%%%%%%%%%%%%%%%%%%%%%%
    %%% Model likelihoods %%%
    modlike(irot,1)=logsum(margL0,1,diffs(1));
```

```
    modlike(irot,2)=logsum(margL1,1,diffs(1)); end
Elist=10*(modlike(:,2)-modlike(:,1));

figure(1); clf; hold on
plot(tan(rotlist),Elist,'ko-','MarkerFaceColor','k','MarkerSize',11);
xlabel('data slope','FontName','Arial','FontSize',15);
ylabel('evidence (db)','FontName','Arial','FontSize',15);

figure(30); clf; hold on; plot(tan(rotlist),modlike(:,1),'ko:','MarkerFaceColor','k');
plot(tan(rotlist),modlike(:,2),'ko:','MarkerFaceColor',COL(1,:))
xlabel('data slope','FontName','Arial','FontSize',15);
ylabel('mod likelihood','FontName','Arial','FontSize',15);
```

The model likelihood for the insensitivity model is:

$$\begin{aligned}
\mathcal{L}_0 &= \prod\nolimits_j (\mathcal{L}_0)_j \\
&= \int d\sigma \prod\nolimits_j \left[\int d\alpha_j \varpi_0(\beta,\alpha_j,\sigma)\, \mathcal{L}_j(\beta,\alpha_j,\sigma)\right] \\
&= \sqrt{2\pi}^{-SN} [\Delta\alpha]^{-S} [\Delta \log\sigma]^{-1} \int_{\sigma_{\min}}^{\sigma_{\max}} d\sigma\sigma^{-(NS+1)} \prod\nolimits_j \left[\int_{\alpha_{\min}}^{\alpha_{\max}} d\alpha_j e^{-\frac{1}{2}\frac{\sum_k [y_k-\alpha_j]^2}{\sigma^2}}\right]
\end{aligned}$$

where each integral in the product is evaluated separately before evaluating the final σ integral.

Similarly, the model likelihood for the veridical model is

$$\begin{aligned}
\mathcal{L}_1 &= \int d\sigma \prod\nolimits_j (\mathcal{L}_1)_j \\
&= \int d\sigma \prod\nolimits_j \left[\int d\alpha_j \varpi_1(\beta,\alpha_j,\sigma)\, \mathcal{L}_j(\beta,\alpha_j,\sigma)\right] \\
&= \sqrt{2\pi}^{-SN} [\Delta\alpha]^{-S} [\Delta \log\sigma]^{-1} \int_{\sigma_{\min}}^{\sigma_{\max}} d\sigma\sigma^{-(NS+1)} \prod\nolimits_j \left[\int_{\alpha_{\min}}^{\alpha_{\max}} d\alpha_j e^{-\frac{1}{2}\frac{\sum_k [y_k-(\omega_k+\alpha_j)]^2}{\sigma^2}}\right]
\end{aligned}$$

D. Compute the Evidence

The model comparison for the more general case with unknown source-specific intercepts, α_j, is

$$\begin{aligned}
\boldsymbol{e}(M_0) &= 10\log_{10}[\boldsymbol{O}(M_0)] = 10\log_{10}\left[\frac{\varpi_0\mathcal{L}_0}{\varpi_1\mathcal{L}_1}\right] \\
&= 10\log_{10}\left[\frac{\varpi_0}{\varpi_1}\frac{\int_{\sigma_{\min}}^{\sigma_{\max}} d\sigma\sigma^{-(NS+1)}\prod_j\left[\int_{\alpha_{\min}}^{\alpha_{\max}} d\alpha_j e^{-\frac{1}{2}\frac{\sum_k[y_k-\alpha_j]^2}{\sigma^2}}\right]}{\int_{\sigma_{\min}}^{\sigma_{\max}} d\sigma\sigma^{-(NS+1)}\prod_j\left[\int_{\alpha_{\min}}^{\alpha_{\max}} d\alpha_j e^{-\frac{1}{2}\frac{\sum_k[y_k-(\omega_k+\alpha_j)]^2}{\sigma^2}}\right]}\right],
\end{aligned}$$

whereas we can drop the marginalization over these nuisance parameters when it is known that no intercept might perturb the straight-line relation:

$$e(M_0) = 10\log_{10}[\mathbf{O}(M_0)] = 10\log_{10}\left[\frac{\varpi_0\mathcal{L}_0}{\varpi_1\mathcal{L}_1}\right]$$

$$= 10\log_{10}\left[\frac{\varpi_0}{\varpi_1}\frac{\int_{\sigma_{\min}}^{\sigma_{\max}} d\sigma\sigma^{-(NS+1)}\prod_j\left[e^{-\frac{1}{2}\frac{\sum_k[y_k]^2}{\sigma^2}}\right]}{\int_{\sigma_{\min}}^{\sigma_{\max}} d\sigma\sigma^{-(NS+1)}\prod_j\left[e^{-\frac{1}{2}\frac{\sum_k[y_k-\omega_k]^2}{\sigma^2}}\right]}\right].$$

These evidence calculations are explored in Figures 6.11b,c and demonstrate several features of this type of model comparison, in which there are punctate predictions. Most notable of these is the fact that in both the global- and the source-specific-intercept models the evidence function has its minimum and maximum values when the dataset matches that model's punctate prediction.

Exercises

1) Describe how the unknown dispersion parameter affects the final numerical values of evidence for these models. Demonstrate this effect with simulated data
2) Describe how you would go about modifying one of the two simulations and evidence calculations above to account for source-specific variation in dispersion (of unknown size), (as opposed to having modeled the data using a single global dispersion parameter in these analyses).
3) Demonstrate your answer in (2) by making the required changes in a new simulation (it need not be run if the run time is too long).
4) Give an example of a straight-line model comparison for each of the following domains:
   a. economics
   b. psychology
   c. neuroscience
   d. medicine
   e. politics

   and describe each the model parameters for each in terms of being source-specific or global.
5) Write the code and simulate one of the straight-line model comparisons from (4).

6.4.2 Interrelationships among Variables: Multisource Method of Testing

A second method of using multisource data is specific to relationships like the straight-line function, where one variable is modeled as causally dependent on another variable. Here, however, instead of each source producing a source-specific version of the straight-line function (as in the previous example), each source contributes one element to the straight-line relationship. This is shown below in Figures 6.12 and 6.13, where there are 45 and 7 sources, respectively, and each contributes one point to the dataset describing a straight-line function.

This form of source-based straight-line analysis is common in the case where we believe there is a causal connection between two *observed* variables rather than between one experimentally controlled and output variable, as in our previous straight-line models. Without experimental control, it is critical that there is 'natural variation' in the causal variable that can be used to *correlate* changes in the observed variable that is believed to be causal with changes in the second output variable.

Example: Parental Household Income and High School GPA
In this example we are testing the hypothesis that economic status, encoded in parental household income, has a causal influence on a child's academic achievement, encoded as high school GPA. This example already meets the criterion described above that there must be natural variation between sources in the causal variable, because clearly there is variation in both variables in nearly any sample of individuals in a community of parents and their high school children.

A. Translate Hypotheses into Model Equations

$\imath$: Forty-five households with high school-aged children are polled for both total household income and the corresponding child's GPA (or average of children in the household if there are multiple children). Obviously, different households (sources) will have different total incomes, and if income has a consistent effect on a child's high school GPA there will be a straight-line relationship with nonzero slope between these two variables.

M_0: There is no consistent relationship between income and GPA and therefore the model line that will best describe the plot of income versus GPA has the slope, $\gamma = 0$.

M_1: There is a consistent relationship between income and GPA and therefore the model line that will best describe the plot of income versus GPA has a stable positive slope, $\gamma > 0$.

In these models there may be an unknown global intercept term c that shifts all GPA numbers by a constant for the hypothetical household with zero income.

The graphical model shown in Figure 6.12a indicates that there are a number of internal factors, υ, λ, η, that interact with the environment to produce household income, and that may themselves be caused or influenced by the environment. In addition, GPA may be influenced through the environment in addition to the internal household income directly. These several considerations should make it clear that it is no trivial task to determine what the constituents of this model should be. In the end, however, we are testing a simplified version in the sense that we have ignored most of the detail that should logically contribute, and instead simply attempt to detect any positive relationship between a pair of parameters whose noisy images are the observed variables.

The two β parameters produce the observed data:

$$\phi_j = \beta_{1j} + \varepsilon_{1j},$$

for the household income of the jth source and

$$\varphi_j = \beta_{2j} + \varepsilon_{2j}.$$

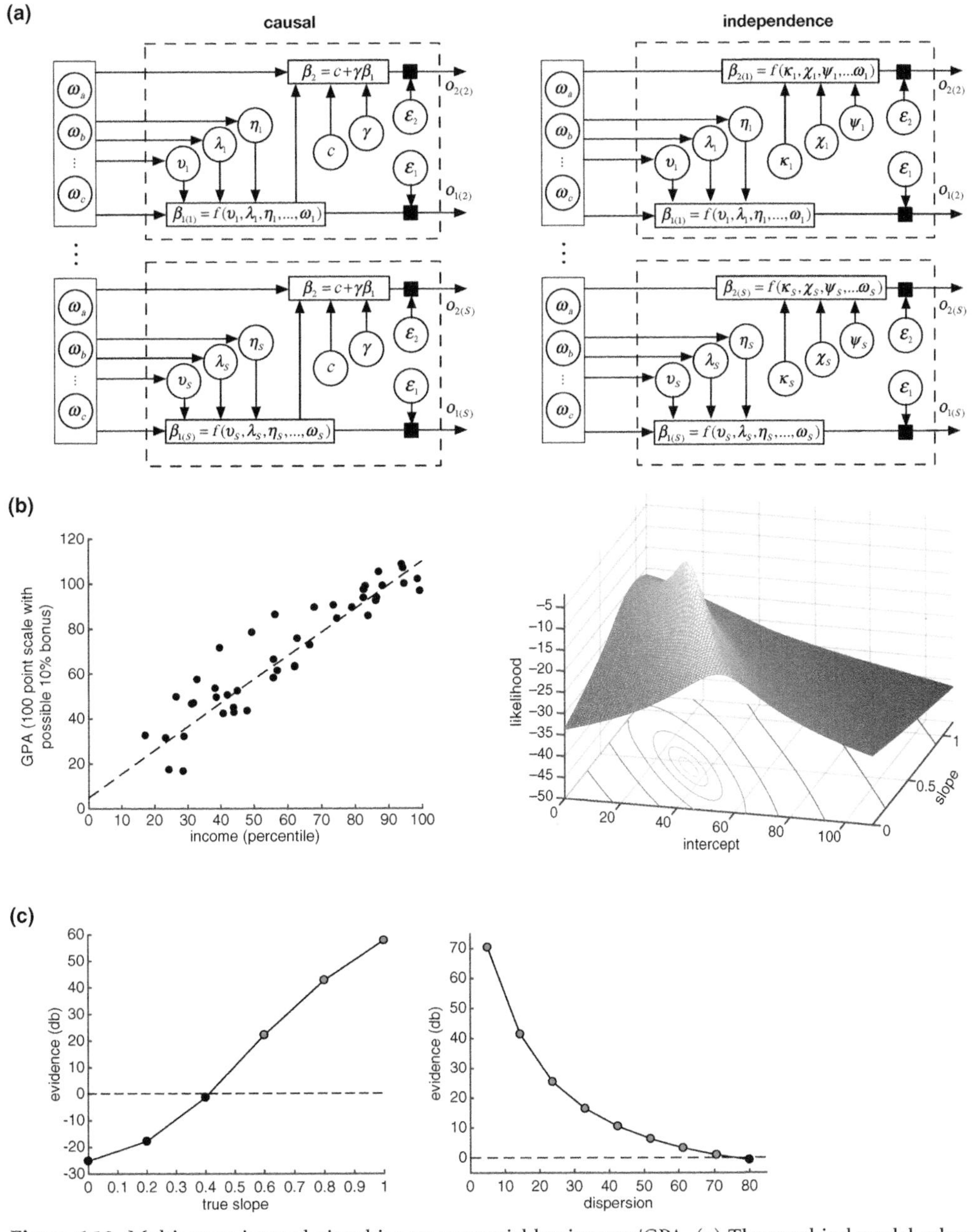

Figure 6.12 Multisource interrelationships among variables: income/GPA. (a) The graphical model, where the causal version (left) shows a linear relationship linking income and GPA variables, $\beta_2 = c + \gamma\beta_1$, where γ is the slope of this relation and β variables are noiseless representations of income and GPA. (b) The raw income and GPA data (left) are highly correlated; these data are broadly consistent with both the causal and independence models. The likelihood under the causal model (right) demonstrates a strong correlation of slope and intercept probabilities. (c) Evidence modulation via changes in the true γ underlying the connection between the two β constants (via $\beta_2 = k - \gamma\beta_1$).

for the average household GPA. Thus each source (indexed j) will generate a single data-pair in this example, and therefore each datum in the plot of Figure 6.12b represents the data obtained from one household. We simulate the observed data-pair generated by the jth source:

$$\phi_j = nrand\left(\beta_{1j}, \sigma_1\right)$$
$$\phi_j = nrand\left(\beta_{2j}, \sigma_2\right),$$

where the choice of β for each source and output dimension is model-specific:

M_0: Under the *independence model*, we predict a zero slope, $\gamma = 0$, relating the β values. Given that income is considered causal, its values (as percentiles of the range of incomes in the population) are selected from a uniform number generator:

$$\beta_{1j} = urand(0.1, 0.9)$$

but the values of the GPA variable should all be identical under this model (based on $\gamma = 0$ in the model equation), and so we select a single value for this variable:

$$\beta_{2(j=1)} = urand(0.5, 4.0),$$

and force the remaining values to match:

$$\beta_{2(j>1)} = \beta_{2(j=1)},$$

M_1: Under the *causality model*, household income has a positive causal influence on household GPA, and we can therefore sample β_1 from a uniform number generator, and then compute β_2 from this causal relation:

$$\beta_{1j} = urand(0.1, 0.9)$$
$$\beta_{2j} = \gamma\beta_{1j} + c,$$

where we will choose the parameters $\gamma = 4.375$ and $c = 0.0625$ for our simulations.

These simulated observations mimic a system with additive noise, $y = y' + \varepsilon$ in *both* output dimensions, as dictated by the graphical model (Fig. 6.12a), which is significant because the abscissa values were known in our previous examples (usually, they are experimentally controlled). In computing the odds, therefore, we must marginalize over *both* of the unknown theoretical β values that underlie the observation-pairs (β_1 is marginalized as itself, and β_2 through the identity $\beta_2 = \gamma\beta_1 + c$), as well as the global dispersion associated with each (σ_1 and σ_2):

$$\mathbf{O}(M_0) = \frac{p\left(M_0 \mid \boldsymbol{d} \cdot \iota\right)}{p\left(\bar{M}_0 \mid \boldsymbol{d} \cdot \iota\right)} = \frac{\varpi(M_0)\left[\int_{-\infty}^{\infty} d\gamma\, dc \int_0^{\infty} d\sigma_2 d\sigma_1 \varpi_0(\gamma, c)\mathcal{L}(\gamma, c)\right]}{\varpi(M_1)\left[\int_{-\infty}^{\infty} d\gamma\, dc \int_0^{\infty} d\sigma_2 d\sigma_1 \varpi_1(\gamma, c)\mathcal{L}(\gamma, c)\right]}$$
$$= \frac{\varpi_0}{\varpi_1} \frac{\left[\int_{-\infty}^{\infty} d\gamma\, dc \int_0^{\infty} d\sigma_2 d\sigma_1 \varpi_0(\gamma, c) \prod_j \int_{-\infty}^{\infty} d\beta_{1j} \mathcal{L}_j\left(\gamma, c, \beta_{1j}\right)\right]}{\left[\int_{-\infty}^{\infty} d\gamma\, dc \int_0^{\infty} d\sigma_2 d\sigma_1 \varpi_1(\gamma, c) \prod_j \int_{-\infty}^{\infty} d\beta_{1j} \mathcal{L}_j\left(\gamma, c, \beta_{1j}\right)\right]} = \frac{\varpi_0 \mathcal{L}_0}{\varpi_1 \mathcal{L}_1},$$

where notice that the β_1 is source-specific; all other variables are global and do not vary by source.

B. Assign Prior Probabilities to Hypotheses

There certainly seems to be a good deal of anecdotal evidence supporting M_1, although clearly it cannot be established outright, particularly given the additional complications that are hinted at in the graphical model. In particular, given the complexity of (likely bi-directional) influences between the environment and the individuals creating family income and high school GPA values, it is entirely possible that the anecdotal evidence may be the result of a spurious relationship. These considerations leave us with a great deal of uncertainty regarding these two models as a description of the observed data, and leaves us to assign:

$$\varpi(M_1) = \varpi(M_2) = .5$$

C. Compute Model Likelihoods

Each of the observation types, household income and average household GPA, will form its own dataset, and therefore each source will produce two data values, where different households are indexed by j. In both models, the sampling probabilities for observations along the two data dimensions are:

$$\begin{aligned} p(\phi \mid \beta_1 \cdot \sigma_1 \cdot \iota) &= \left[\sigma_1\sqrt{2\pi}\right]^{-1} e^{-\frac{1}{2}\frac{[\phi-\phi']^2}{\sigma_1^2}} \\ &= \left[\sigma_1\sqrt{2\pi}\right]^{-1} e^{-\frac{1}{2}\frac{[\phi-\beta_1]^2}{\sigma_1^2}} \\ p(\varphi \mid \beta_2 \cdot c \cdot \gamma \cdot \sigma_2 \cdot \iota) &= \left[\sigma_2\sqrt{2\pi}\right]^{-1} e^{-\frac{1}{2}\frac{[\varphi-\varphi']^2}{\sigma_2^2}} \\ &= \left[\sigma_2\sqrt{2\pi}\right]^{-1} e^{-\frac{1}{2}\frac{[\varphi-(c+\beta_1\gamma)]^2}{\sigma_2^2}} \end{aligned}$$

The β values of these equations are differentially related to one another under the independence and causality models. Under both models, however, the joint likelihood of the parameters for the jth source is:

$$\begin{aligned} \mathcal{L}_j(\beta_{1j}, \beta_{2j}) &= p(\phi_j \mid \beta_{1j} \cdot \gamma \cdot c \cdot \sigma_1 \cdot \iota)\, p(\varphi_j \mid \beta_{2j} \cdot \gamma \cdot c \cdot \sigma_2 \cdot \iota) \\ &= \sqrt{2\pi}^{-1}\sigma_1^{-1} e^{-\frac{1}{2}\left(\frac{[\phi_j-\beta_{1j}]^2}{\sigma_1^2}\right)} \sqrt{2\pi}^{-1}\sigma_2^{-1} e^{-\frac{1}{2}\left(\frac{[\varphi_j-\beta_{2j}]^2}{\sigma_2^2}\right)} \\ &= [2\pi\sigma_1\sigma_2]^{-1} e^{-\frac{1}{2}\left(\frac{[\phi_j-\beta_j]^2}{\sigma_1^2}\right)} e^{-\frac{1}{2}\left(\frac{[\varphi_j-(c+\gamma\beta_j)]^2}{\sigma_2^2}\right)}, \end{aligned}$$

where all j-subscripted parameters are unknown and source-specific. Notice that when written in terms of the model equation $\beta_2 = c + \gamma\beta_1$ the likelihood can be written in terms of the first of the β terms, allowing us to drop the additional numbered subscript; we will simply keep in mind that β_j written without a differentiating name subscript refers to β_1, household income. The above likelihood function applies to all data-pairs (regardless of the income or GPA) under both models for the jth source.

The next step is to combine data across sources. First we recall that our prior information over model parameters is:

$$M_0:$$

$$\varpi_0(\gamma) = \begin{cases} 0 & \gamma \neq 0 \\ 1 & \gamma = 0 \end{cases},$$

$$\varpi_0(c) = \begin{cases} 0 & c \neq \beta_2' \\ 1 & c = \beta_2' \end{cases},$$

where under the independence model, $\gamma = 0$, the intercept c must be set to the best overall value of β_2. One could make the argument that this value should be at the center of the possible range, $\beta_2' = 2.25$. We will begin with this assumption, but also later relax it to allow for any average GPA to be better modeled by the independence model.

Thus, under the independence model we will begin by allowing the likelihood equation to take the additional simplification provided by the known values $\gamma' = 0, c' = 2.25$, yielding.

$$\begin{aligned} \mathcal{L}(\gamma = \gamma', c = c', \sigma_1, \sigma_2) &= \prod\nolimits_j \int d\beta_j \, (\mathcal{L}_0)_j \\ &= \prod\nolimits_j \int d\beta_j \varpi_0 \left(\gamma, c, \beta_j\right) \mathcal{L}_j \left(\beta_j, \gamma, c\right) \\ &= [2\pi\sigma_1\sigma_2]^{-1} \prod\nolimits_j \int d\beta_j e^{-\frac{1}{2}\left(\frac{\left[\phi_j - \beta_j\right]^2}{\sigma_1^2}\right)} \mathrm{e}^{-\frac{1}{2}\left(\frac{\left[\varphi_j - \left(c' + \gamma'\beta_j\right)\right]^2}{\sigma_2^2}\right)} \\ &= [2\pi\sigma_1\sigma_2]^{-1} \prod\nolimits_j \int d\beta_j e^{-\frac{1}{2}\left(\frac{\left[\phi_j - \beta_j^2\right]}{\sigma_1^2}\right)} \mathrm{e}^{-\frac{1}{2}\left(\frac{\left[\varphi_j - c'\right]^2}{\sigma_2^2}\right)} \end{aligned}$$

Under the causality model these parameters are both allowed to vary within theoretical bounds:

$$M_1:$$

$$\varpi_1(\gamma) = \begin{cases} 0 & \gamma = 0 \\ 1 & \gamma > 0, \end{cases}$$

$$\varpi_1(c) = \begin{cases} 0 & 0.5 > c > 4 \\ 1 & 0.5 < c < 4, \end{cases}$$

Notice that we have assumed $\varpi_1(\gamma, c) = p(\gamma|\imath)\varpi_1(c|\imath)$ instead of $\varpi_1(\gamma, c) = p(\gamma|\imath)\varpi_1$ $(c|\gamma \cdot \imath)$. Once we look at the result we will realize that the nonindependent version of the prior makes more sense given our background scenario; we are going to ignore this information, however, to perform an analysis that is more generally applicable to other situations. We will revisit this topic in the exercises.

The set of source-specific parameter likelihoods, $\mathcal{L}_j(\gamma)$, can be combined across sources after marginalizing over any source-specific variables (subscripted j) to yield the model likelihoods $\mathcal{L}_0$ and $\mathcal{L}_1$. Here, the model likelihood for the independence model (M_0) is:

Evidence for the Causal Mechanism (Fig. 6.12)

Here we will compute evidence from simulated income and GPA data, generated by simulating natural variation in income data (as a percentile of min/max income in a given community), and then computing the associated GPA data when the slope of the relation between the two was either zero, one, or something in between.

We begin by defining constants and generating the simulated data values describing the possible relation between income and GPA:

```
clear %#ok<*UNRCH>
reset=1; plotFLAG=0;
COL=[.55*[1 1 1]; .3 .4 .85; .8 .5 .4];
S=12; N=nan;

sig=20*[1 1.5];
Ns=61; slist=linspace(min(sig)/2,max(sig)*2,Ns); Oh=ones(1,Ns);
%noise level for each observation type
slistEN2=1./slist.^2;
logpri=-(S*log(slist')*ones(1,Ns))-(S*ones(Ns,1)*log(slist));

cprime=[55 5]; gprime=[0 1.05];
Nb=45;
minI=0; maxI=100; %min/max income (percentile)
minG=0; maxG=110; %min/max gpa ans percentage (allowed to exceed 100 by 10%
blist=linspace(0,100,Nb)';

Nc=21*[1 1]; clist=linspace(0,110,max(Nc));
Ng=[1 31]; glist=linspace(0,1.15,max(Ng));
B1prime=linspace(10,90,S)'; %keep the VP slopes identical across sims
B2prime=cprime(2)+B1prime*gprime(2)-.1; %mixing endpoints (independent vs. causal)
B2now=B2prime;

Ngam=6;
gamlist=linspace(0,1,Ngam);

%keep noise samples identical across simulations for clearer comparison
d1=nan(S,1); d2prime=nan(S,1);
inds=[1:S]; while ~isempty(inds), nnow=length(inds);
    d1(inds)=B1prime(inds)+rand(nnow,1)*sig(1);
    d2prime(inds)=B2prime(inds)+rand(nnow,1)*sig(2);

    inds=find(or(any([d1<min(blist),d1>max(blist)],2),
    any([d2prime<min(clist),d2prime>max(clist)],2))); end
err=[d2prime-B2prime];
```

Next we initialize the main loop that varies the true slope of the relation between the two dimensions:

```
tmp=zeros(Ns,Ns); bss=zeros(Nb,Ns,Ns);
diffs0=[diff(clist(1:2)) diff(slist(1:2)) diff(slist(1:2))];
diffs1=[diff(glist(1:2)) diffs0];
Elist=nan(Ngam,2);

for igam=1:Ngam, gamnow=gamlist(igam); tic
    L0all=zeros(Nc(1),Ns,Ns); L1all=zeros(Ng(2),Nc(2),Ns,Ns);
    %%%%%%%%R%%%%%%%%%%%%%%%%%%%%%%%%%%%%%
    %%% DATA SIM with variable slope %%%
    if gamnow~=gprime(2),
```

```
        B2now=B1prime*gamnow; B2now=B2now-mean(B2now)+mean([minG maxG]);
        d2=B2now+err; else d2=d2prime; end
    if ~or(any(d2<clist(1)),any(d2>clist(end))),

        %%%%%%%%%%%%%%%%%%%%%%%%%%%%%%%%%%%%%%%%%%%%%
        %%% outer param likelihood by condition %%%
        for ig=1:Ng(2), gnow=glist(ig);
            for ic=1:Nc(2), cnow=clist(ic);
                gtg0=and(ig==1,ic<=Nc(1));

            %%% Likelihoods [independence, causality models]
            likeFNi=@(phi1,phi2,snow) -(1/2)*(((phi1-blist).^2)*...
                slistEN2+( phi2- cnow+ 0 ).^2/snow.^2); %output is Nb x Ns
            likeFNc=@(phi1,phi2,snow) -(1/2)*(((phi1-blist).^2)*...
                slistEN2+((phi2-(cnow+gnow*blist)).^2/snow.^2)*Oh); %output is Nb x Ns

            %%%%%%%%%%%%%%%%%%%%%%%%%%%%%%%%%%%%%%%%%%%%%
            %%% inner param likelihood by condition %%%
            tmp0=tmp; tmp1=tmp;
            for s=1:S, %by source
                if gtg0, L0bss=bss; end
                L1bss=bss;
                for is=1:Ns, snow=slist(is); %dispersion (sd)
                    if gtg0, L0bss(:,:,is)=likeFNi(d1(s),
                       d2(s),snow); end
                L1bss(:,:,is)=likeFNc(d1(s),d2(s),snow); end

                %integrate over b-vals for each sub, and combine likelihoods
                if gtg0, tmp0=tmp0+logsum(L0bss,1,diff(blist(1:2))); end
                tmp1=tmp1+logsum(L1bss,1,diff(blist(1:2)));
%              figure(20); hold on
%              plot(d1(s),logpeakval([str8n(logsum(L0bss,[2 3],
%              diff(slist(1:2))*[1 1]))blist(:)]),'ko','MarkerFaceColor','k')
%              plot(d1(s),logpeakval([str8n(logsum(L1bss,[2 3],
%              diff(slist(1:2))*[1 1]))blist(:)]),'ko','MarkerFaceColor','b')
               end
            if gtg0, L0all( ic,:,:)=tmp0+logpri; end
                     L1all(ig,ic,:,:)=tmp1+logpri; end, end
    Elist(igam,1)=logsum(L0all,[1 2 3],diffs0);
    tmpE=logsum(L1all,[2 3 4],diffs1(2:4));
    Elist(igam,2)=logsum(tmpE-log(1+glist.^2)'-log(.5*pi),1,diffs1(1));


    %%%%%%%%%%%%%%%%%%%%%%%%%
    %%% Model likelihoods %%%
    Elist(igam,3)=10*(Elist(igam,2)-Elist(igam,1));
    %Elist(:,1,2) are already in log units
    disp('');
    disp(['iGAM' num2str(igam) ':']); end, toc, end
```

Notice the ordering of the marginalizations above. First, the innermost integral involving source-specific betas is computed for each pair of dispersions and the unknown values of the model equation (gamma-slope and intercept). After these source-specific variables are marginalized out of our equations, we can combine data across sources in the overall matrices Lall and Elist.

Finally, we plot the evidence and associated model likelihood values:

```
figure(1); clf; hold on
plot(gamlist,Elist(:,3),'ko-','MarkerFaceColor','w','MarkerSize',11);
plot(gamlist(Elist(:,3)>0),Elist(Elist(:,3)>0,3),'ko',...
    'MarkerFaceColor',COL(1,:),'MarkerSize',11);
```

```
plot(gamlist(Elist(:,3)<0),Elist(Elist(:,3)<0,3),'ko',...
    'MarkerFaceColor','k','MarkerSize',11);
xlabel('true slope','FontName','Arial','FontSize',15);
ylabel('evidence (db)','FontName','Arial','FontSize',15);

figure(30); clf; hold on
plot(gamlist,Elist(:,1),'ko:','MarkerFaceColor','k'); %black
plot(gamlist,Elist(:,2),'ko:','MarkerFaceColor',COL(1,:)) %grey
xlabel('true slope','FontName','Arial','FontSize',15);
ylabel('mod likelihood','FontName','Arial','FontSize',15);
```

The above can be updated to look at variation in the underlying dispersion values, which yields the evidence and model likelihood plots of Figure 6.12.

```
clear %#ok<*UNRCH>
reset=1; plotFLAG=0;
COL=[.55*[1 1 1]; .3 .4 .85; .8 .5 .4];
S=11; N=nan;

sig0=[1 1.5]; sig=5;
Ns=81; slist=linspace(min(sig*sig0)/2,110,Ns); Oh=ones(1,Ns);
%noise level for each observation type
slistEN2=1./slist.^2;
logpri=-(S*log(slist')*ones(1,Ns))-(S*ones(Ns,1)*log(slist));

cprime=[55 25]; gprime=[0 .45];
Nb=45;
minI=0; maxI=100; %min/max income (percentile)
minG=0; maxG=110; %min/max gpa ans percentage (allowed to exceed 100 by 10%
blist=linspace(0,100,Nb)';

Nc=31*[1 1]; clist=linspace(0,110,max(Nc));
Ng=[1 41]; glist=linspace(0,1.15,max(Ng));

B1prime=linspace(10,90,S)'; %keep the VP slopes identical across sims
B2prime=cprime(2)+B1prime*gprime(2);
%mixing endpoints (independent vs. causal)

Ndisp=9;
displist=linspace(0,75,Ndisp)+sig*sig0(2);

%keep noise samples identical across simulations for clearer comparison
d1=nan(S,1); d2prime=nan(S,1); inds=[1:S]';
while ~isempty(inds), nnow=length(inds);
    d1(inds)=B1prime(inds)+rand(nnow,1)*sig*sig0(1);
    e1=d1-B1prime; d1=d1-mean(e1);
    d2prime(inds)=B2prime(inds)+rand(nnow,1)*sig*sig0(2);
    e2=d2prime-B2prime; d2prime=d2prime-mean(e2);

    inds=find(or(any([d1<min(blist),d1>max(blist)],2),...
        any([d2prime<min(clist),d2prime>max(clist)],2))); end
figure(3); clf; hold on
plot([0 100],cprime(2)+[0 100]*gprime(2),'k--')
plot(d1,d2prime,'ko','MarkerFaceColor','k','MarkerSize',8)
xlabel('income (percentile)','FontName','Arial','FontSize',15);
ylabel('gpa (100 point scale with possible 10% bonus)'
      'FontName','Arial','FontSize',15);
err=[d2prime-B2prime]/(displist(1));

tmp=zeros(Ns,Ns); bss=zeros(Nb,Ns,Ns);
diffs0=[diff(clist(1:2)) diff(slist(1:2)) diff(slist(1:2))];
diffs1=[diff(glist(1:2)) diffs0];
Elist=nan(Ndisp,2);
```

```
for idisp=1:Ndisp, dispnow=displist(idisp); tic
    L0all=zeros(Nc(1),Ns,Ns); L1all=zeros(Ng(2),Nc(2),Ns,Ns);

    %%%%%%%%R%%%%%%%%%%%%%%%%%%%%%%%%%%%%%
    %%% DATA SIM using new dispersion %%%
    B2now=B2prime+err*dispnow; d2=B2now-mean(B2now)+mean([minG maxG]);
    if ~or(any(d2<clist(1)),any(d2>clist(end))),

        %%%%%%%%%%%%%%%%%%%%%%%%%%%%%%%%%%%%%%%%%%
        %%% outer param likelihood by condition %%%
        for ig=1:Ng(2), gnow=glist(ig);
            for ic=1:Nc(2), cnow=clist(ic);
                gtg0=and(ig==1,ic<=Nc(1));

            %%% Likelihoods [independence, causality models]
            likeFNi=@(phi1,phi2,snow) -(1/2)*(((phi1-blist).^2)*...
                slistEN2+( phi2- cnow+ 0 ).^2/snow.^2); %output is Nb x Ns
            likeFNc=@(phi1,phi2,snow) -(1/2)*(((phi1-blist).^2)*...
                slistEN2+((phi2-(cnow+gnow*blist)).^2/snow.^2)*Oh); %output is Nb x Ns

            %%%%%%%%%%%%%%%%%%%%%%%%%%%%%%%%%%%%%%%%%%%
            %%% inner param likelihood by condition %%%
            tmp0=tmp; tmp1=tmp;
            for s=1:S, %by source
                if gtg0, L0bss=bss; end
                L1bss=bss;
                for is=1:Ns, snow=slist(is); %dispersion (sd)
                    if gtg0, L0bss(:,:,is)=likeFNi(d1(s),
                    d2(s),snow); end
                L1bss(:,:,is)=likeFNc(d1(s),d2(s),snow); end

                %integrate over b-vals for each sub, and combine likelihoods
                if gtg0, tmp0=tmp0+logsum(L0bss,1,diff(blist(1:2))); end
                tmp1=tmp1+logsum(L1bss,1,diff(blist(1:2)));
%               figure(20); hold on
%               plot(d1(s),logpeakval([str8n(logsum(L0bss,[2 3],...
%               diff(slist(1:2))*[1 1]))blist(:)]),'ko','MarkerFaceColor','k')
%               plot(d1(s),logpeakval([str8n(logsum(L1bss,[2 3],
%               diff(slist(1:2))*[1 1]))blist(:)]),'ko','MarkerFaceColor','b')
            end
            if gtg0, L0all( ic,:,:)=tmp0+logpri; end
                      L1all(ig,ic,:,:)=tmp1+logpri; end, end
    Elist(idisp,1)=logsum(L0all,[1 2 3],diffs0);
    tmpE=logsum(L1all,[2 3 4],diffs1(2:4));
    Elist(idisp,2)=logsum(tmpE-log(1+glist.^2)'-log(.5*pi),1,diffs1(1));

    %%%%%%%%%%%%%%%%%%%%%%%%%
    %%% Model likelihoods %%%
    Elist(idisp,3)=10*(Elist(idisp,2)-Elist(idisp,1));
    %Elist(:,1,2) are already in log units
    disp('');
    disp(['iDISP' num2str(idisp) ':']); end, toc, end

    figure(1); clf; hold on
    plot(displist(1:8),Elist(1:8,3),'ko-','MarkerFaceColor','w','MarkerSize',11);
    plot(displist(Elist(1:8,3)>0),Elist(Elist(:,3)>0,3),'ko',...
        'MarkerFaceColor',COL(1,:),'MarkerSize',11);
    plot(displist(Elist(1:8,3)<0),Elist(Elist(:,3)<0,3),'ko',...
        'MarkerFaceColor','k','MarkerSize',11);
    xlabel('dispersion','FontName','Arial','FontSize',15);
    ylabel('evidence (db)','FontName','Arial','FontSize',15);
```

```
figure(30); clf; hold on
plot(displist,Elist(:,1),'ko:','MarkerFaceColor','k'); %black
plot(displist,Elist(:,2),'ko:','MarkerFaceColor',COL(1,:)) %grey
xlabel('dispersion','FontName','Arial','FontSize',15);
ylabel('mod likelihood','FontName','Arial','FontSize',15);
```

$$\begin{aligned}\mathcal{L}_0 &= \int d\sigma_1 d\sigma_2 \prod_j (\mathcal{L}_0)_j \\ &= \int d\sigma_1 d\sigma_2 \prod_j \int d\beta_j \varpi_0\left(\sigma_1,\sigma_2,c,\gamma,\beta_j\right)\mathcal{L}_0\left(\beta_j,\gamma,c\right),\end{aligned}$$

The overall marginal model likelihood is then built from the set of marginal likelihoods, $(\mathcal{L}_0)_j$, one contributed by each source. Here the final expression must also integrate over the unknown global dispersion values associated with the two observation types:

$$\begin{aligned}\mathcal{L}_0 &= \prod_j (\mathcal{L}_0)_j \\ &= \int d\sigma_1 d\sigma_2 \varpi_0(\sigma_1,\sigma_2) \prod_j \left[\int d\beta_j \varpi_0\left(\gamma,c,\beta_j\right)\mathcal{L}_0\left(\beta_j,c,\gamma,\sigma_1,\sigma_2\right)\right] \\ &= (2\pi\,\Delta\beta)^{-S} \int d\sigma_1 d\sigma_2 (\sigma_1\sigma_2)^{-(S+1)} \prod_j \left[\int d\beta_j e^{-\frac{1}{2}\left(\frac{\phi_j-\beta_j^2}{\sigma_1^2}\right)} e^{-\frac{1}{2}\left(\frac{[\varphi_j-c']^2}{\sigma_2^2}\right)}\right]\end{aligned} \tag{6.6a}$$

Similarly, the marginal source-specific likelihood for the causality model (M_1) is:

$$(\mathcal{L}_1)_j = \int d\beta_j \varpi_0\left(\gamma,c,\sigma_1,\sigma_2,\beta_j\right)\mathcal{L}_1\left(\beta_j,\gamma,c,\sigma_1,\sigma_2\right),$$

and the model likelihood for the causality model is therefore:

$$\begin{aligned}\mathcal{L}_1 &= \prod_j (\mathcal{L}_1)_j \\ &= \int d\gamma\, dc \varpi_1(\gamma,c) \int d\sigma_1 d\sigma_2 \varpi_0(\sigma_1,\sigma_2) \prod_j \left[\int d\beta_j \varpi_1(\beta_j)\mathcal{L}_1\left(\beta_j,c,\gamma,\sigma_1,\sigma_2\right)\right] \\ &= (2\pi\,\Delta\beta)^{-S} \Delta c^{-1} A \int d\gamma\, dc \left(1+\gamma^2\right)^{-1} \int d\sigma_1 d\sigma_2 (\sigma_1\sigma_2)^{-(S+1)} \\ &\quad \times \prod_j \left[\int d\beta_j e^{-\frac{1}{2}\left(\frac{[\phi_j-\beta_j]^2}{\sigma_1^2}\right)} e^{-\frac{1}{2}\left(\frac{[\varphi_j-(c+\gamma\beta_j)]^2}{\sigma_2^2}\right)}\right]\end{aligned} \tag{6.6b}$$

In both (6.6a) and (6.6b) it is important to recognize that each of the innermost j-subscripted integrals in the product must be evaluated separately by source before combining probabilities across sources (i.e., taking the product over the j index).

D. Compute the Evidence

Having defined all the elements, we are now able to compute the model evidence values:

$$
\begin{aligned}
\boldsymbol{e}(M_1) &= 10\log\left[\boldsymbol{O}(M_1)\right] \\
&= 10\log\left[\frac{p(M_1 \mid \boldsymbol{d}\cdot\iota)}{p(\overline{M_1} \mid \boldsymbol{d}\cdot\iota)}\right] \\
&= 10\log\left[\frac{\varpi_1 \int d\sigma \prod_j \int d\beta_{1j}\varpi_0(\gamma,c,\sigma_1,\sigma_2,\beta_j)\,\mathcal{L}_1(\beta_j,c,\gamma,\sigma_1,\sigma_2)}{\varpi_0 \int d\sigma \prod_j \int d\beta_{1j}\varpi_1(\gamma,c,\sigma_1,\sigma_2,\beta_j)\,\mathcal{L}_0(\beta_j,c,\gamma,\sigma_1,\sigma_2)}\right] \\
&= 10\log_{10}\left[\frac{\varpi_1}{\varpi_0}\,\frac{(A\Delta c)^{-1}\int d\gamma\,dc\,(1+\gamma^2)^{-1}\int d\sigma_1 d\sigma_2\,(\sigma_1\sigma_2)^{-(S+1)}\prod_j\left[d\beta_j e^{-\frac{1}{2}\left(\frac{[\phi_j-\beta_j]^2}{\sigma_1^2}\right)} e^{-\frac{1}{2}\left(\frac{[\varphi_j-(c+\gamma\beta_j)]^2}{\sigma_2^2}\right)}\right]}{\int d\sigma_1 d\sigma_2\,(\sigma_1\sigma_2)^{-(S+1)}\prod_j\left[\int d\beta_j e^{-\frac{1}{2}\left(\frac{[\phi_j-\beta_j]^2}{\sigma_1^2}\right)} e^{-\frac{1}{2}\left(\frac{[\varphi_j-c']^2}{\sigma_2^2}\right)}\right]}\right]
\end{aligned}
$$

where we have dropped the leading constant that is common to both models. To get a sense of the evidence produced by real data, we simulate 45 pairs of noise samples from the β_1 and β_2 values of the corresponding 45 sources (Fig. 6.12b, left), based on the parameters of the causal mechanism. Evidence values are plotted in Figure 6.12c as a function of the true slope of the of the causal straight-line relationship (one true slope per simulation; left). We can see that evidence for the causal mechanism increases as deviation of true slope from zero increases. We can also see from the 2d likelihood in Figure 6.12b (right) that the joint likelihood of slope and intercept is clearly correlated. This correlation of the probabilities of slopes and intercepts is due to the nature of the likelihood of the straight-line model parameters: for a given dataset and given slope (or intercept), the intercept (or slope) can only fit the data well under a restricted set of its range, and this restricted set of values changes with changing slopes (or intercepts), creating a correlation.

If we allow the independence model an unknown intercept in its zero-slope straight-line relationship (i.e., $0 < c < 110$), the evidence calculation becomes:

$$
\begin{aligned}
\boldsymbol{e}(M_1) &= 10\log\left[\boldsymbol{O}(M_1)\right] \\
&= 10\log\left[\frac{p(M_1 \mid \boldsymbol{d}\cdot\iota)}{p(\overline{M_1} \mid \boldsymbol{d}\cdot\iota)}\right] \\
&= 10\log\left[\frac{\varpi_1 \int d\gamma\,dc \int d\sigma_1 d\sigma_2 \prod_j \int d\beta_{1j}\varpi_0(\gamma,c,\sigma_1,\sigma_2,\beta_j)\,\mathcal{L}_j(\beta_j,c,\gamma,\sigma_1,\sigma_2)}{\varpi_0 \int dc \int d\sigma_1 d\sigma_2 \prod_j \int d\beta_{1j}\varpi_1(\gamma,c,\sigma_1,\sigma_2,\beta_j)\,\mathcal{L}_j(\beta_j,c,\gamma,\sigma_1,\sigma_2)}\right] \\
&= 10\log_{10}\left[\frac{\varpi_1}{\varpi_0}\,\frac{A^{-1}\int d\gamma\,dc\,(1+\gamma^2)^{-1}\int d\sigma_1 d\sigma_2\,(\sigma_1\sigma_2)^{-(S+1)}\prod_j\left[\int d\beta_j e^{-\frac{1}{2}\left(\frac{[\phi_j-\beta_j]^2}{\sigma_1^2}\right)} e^{-\frac{1}{2}\left(\frac{[\varphi_j-(c+\gamma\beta_j)]^2}{\sigma_2^2}\right)}\right]}{\int d\gamma\,dc \int d\sigma_1 d\sigma_2(\sigma_1\sigma_2)^{-(S+1)}\prod_j\left[\int d\beta_j e^{-\frac{1}{2}\left(\frac{[\phi_j-\beta_j]^2}{\sigma_1^2}\right)} e^{-\frac{1}{2}\left(\frac{[\varphi_j-c]^2}{\sigma_2^2}\right)}\right]}\right]
\end{aligned}
$$

which allows for better fits to the dat by the independence model, making it a stronger contender in the comparison for all models.

In addition to plotting the evidence as a function of the underlying γ-slope (Fig. 6.12, left), we have also plotted evidence as a function of the level of dispersion (Fig. 6.12, right). This latter plot shows how the evidence approaches zero as noise increases, and can be useful during the preexperimental simulation stage of a research project when we need to determine how many sources might be needed to successfully find a straight-line relation between the variables of interest. By looking at the existing literature we can compare the expected level of dispersion in the data with simulation to make this determination.

This example should feel incomplete, in the sense that we have ignored much complexity that was present in the graphical model. That additional complexity (such as variables in the environment including crime rates, community safety, etc., or internal variables like attention span, general intelligence, emotional maturity and control) might influence or modulate the results and values of both observed variables. Next we will explore a slightly more complex example that includes just such a modulatory component.

Exercises

1) Describe what you expect to happen to the evidence plot if the noise level is reduced? increased?
2) Increase the variance of the noise from 5 to 50. How does this affect the evidence plot. Explain why.
3) If we plot the posterior over possible slopes and intercepts for the causality model, we obtain a plot such as Figure 6.12b (right), showing that these variables are correlated. Explain why this correlation might occur, and whether it is specific to the current example or should be general to all straight-line models.
4) Imagine that each source follows the same straight-line relation in terms of the slope of the income-to-GPA function (such that increments of income have the same effect on increments of GPA for all households), but differ in a source-specific way in the intercept of that relation. Simulate the current scenario [B1=linspace(25,75,S)] and with a slope of 0.6 and an intercept of 50 for all, and then run the same simulation with intercepts c=linspace(20,80,S). Compute the evidence for each simulated dataset and explain the change in evidence.
5) The dispersion parameters, σ_1 and σ_2, were modeled as global variables.
   a. What would happen to the ratio of dispersion values if we allowed source-specific dispersion values for both of the output variables?
   b. Show the 2d probability surface over σ_1 and σ_2 for a single observation-pair and a single specific value of γ and c (of your choosing). The single observation-pair should be simulated from a 2d Gaussian (mvnrand) with asymmetrical σ_s'.
   c. Compare (b) to the 2d probability surface over σ_1 and σ_2 for a a triplet of observation-pairs and a single specific value of γ and c (of your choosing). The triplet of observation-pairs should be simulated from the same 2d Gaussian (mvnrand) with asymmetrical σ_s'.
   d. Explain how the probability surfaces in (b),(c) support your answer in (a), and why this would be a general property of each instance of a source-specific pair of dispersions.

6) This analysis assumed that the 'economic status' of each household is an unknown parameter whose noisy representation is household income. Describe how this analysis would have been different if the economic status variable were considered known, and numerically identical with household income? Run this analysis and compare both the equation describing the odds and the result of the analysis with that above.

Example: Source-Specific Modulation of Variables

Another type of source-specific interrelationship occurs when source-specific elements are modulatory. The easiest examples of this type of modulatory influence are from the field of perception, although a great many subject-specific interrelationships among variables are of this type, including many thought initially to fall into the category of natural variation. Consider the following pair of perceptual variables: the perception of the height of your own eye level in external space (the same perceptual discrimination you use to decide if someone is taller/shorter than you), and the perception of the orientation of a surface in external space. Perceived eye level is usually assessed by finding the elevation on a wall appearing to correspond to your eye level. *Visual pitch* refers to the apparent rotation of a surface (such as a wall) relative to a viewer, where pitch rotation is about the horizontal axis of a surface facing the viewer. Surface pitch can be positive (with the top of the surface pitched toward the observer) or negative (top-away from the observer). Figure 6.13a shows the geometry of eye level and visual pitch.

A. Translate Hypotheses into Model Equations

It turns out that changes in both of these perceptual dimensions (perceived eye level and visual pitch) are modulated by the *physical* pitch of a surface: A slope of $\beta = 1$ describing the relationship of physical to visual pitch demonstrates veridical pitch perception, whereas a nonzero physical pitch to perceived eye level slope demonstrates a perceptual *illusion*, showing that a basic dimension of egocentric space perception, the elevation of eye level, is dependent on visual context. Furthermore, there is the possibility of an interesting subject-specific relationship between the two percepts: subjects with near-veridical pitch perception may be less influenced by the eye level illusion than those who underestimate pitch. To test this theory you want to discriminate between a causal model (Fig. 6.13b), and a noncausal version where slopes (β_p and β_v) are unrelated. The model in (Fig. 6.13b, right) shows *independent* subject-specific modulation (with strength-of-modulation encoded by the slope parameters β_p and β_v) of the two perceptual dimensions of perceived eye level and visual pitch. These perceptual dimensions are independent in the sense that β_p and β_v are not directly related to one another, and their corresponding perceptions are related only to physical pitch. In the *causal* model there is a direct relationship between β_p and β_v values, with larger β_p slopes producing smaller β_v slopes (i.e., a **negative correlation**; refer to Section 1.2.4). Thus, a plot of β_p versus β_v should show a negatively sloped straight-line relationship, such as $\beta_v = \gamma\beta_p + c\ (\gamma < 0)$, where the constants γ and c apply to all sources. These constants are critical to the theory that there is an underlying relationship between the two perceptual variables, and that this relationship can be detected via this method. Without all sources having the same constants, the predictions of a straight-line model fail, in the sense that it does us no good to have information about β_p for predictions of β_v (i.e., the definition of independence: $p(\beta_v \cdot \beta_p|\iota) = p(\beta_v|\beta_p \cdot \iota)p(\beta_p|\iota) = p(\beta_v|\iota)p(\beta_p|\iota)$.

ι: Perceptual eye level and pitch judgments are made in response to a range of physical pitches, where the physical pitch stimulus completely fills the visual field while it is being viewed. (i.e., there is no erect background that could be used as reference). Six different simulated perceptual judgments for the two perceptual dimensions are generated by first choosing source-specific slope values, β_p and β_v, and intercept values, α_p and α_v. Then, for the kth experimental conditions (physical pitch setting) we simulate the perceptual judgments of the jth source:

$$\phi_{jk} = nrand\left(\beta_{pj}\omega_k, \sigma\right)$$
$$\phi_{jk} = nrand\left(\beta_{vj}\omega_k, \sigma\right)$$

We must next select values of β for each source and perceptual dimension. This choice is model- specific:

M_0: There is no straight-line relationship connecting β_p (the slope relating physical pitch presented visually and the corresponding perceived pitch), and β_v (relating physical pitch and the perceived eye level illusion induced by variation in physical pitch), although there must be an intercept term c in the plot of β_p versus β_v that is equal to the typical β_v slope [i.e., if $\beta_v = \gamma\beta_p + c$ and $\gamma = 0$, then $c = \beta_v' = 0.6$].

Under the independence model, independence translates to an across-source slope of $\gamma = 0$; the observation that individual differences in eye level slopes are stable individual characteristics further implies that subject-specific variation in eye level slopes is due to some additional (unknown) source-specific influence. The slope values for the two perceptual dimensions may be simulated by choosing from a uniform distribution for the jth source to represent true visual pitch slopes:

$$\beta_{pj} = urand(0.5, 1.5)$$

and setting all eye level slopes to $\beta_v' = 0.6$ based on the underlying model equation, $\beta_v = \gamma\beta_p + c, \gamma = 0$ and background information on measured eye level slopes. We will therefore take $\gamma = 0$ and $c = 0.6$ as known values in this model.

M_1: Under the *causal* model (and for consistency the same range of possible perceptual slopes), we select slopes for the jth source from:

$$\beta_{pj} = urand(0.5, 1.5)$$
$$\beta_{vj} = \gamma\beta_{pj} + c.$$

Under this model we may be assured that a source producing a slope value at the minimum of the range for visual pitch, $\beta_p = 0.5$, will also produce a slope value at the maximum of the range for perceived eye level of $\beta_v = 0.9$, and similarly that $\beta_p = 1.5$ corresponds to $\beta_v = 0.3$. Thus, we may set the slope of the *model equation* to $\gamma - (0.9 - 0.3)/(0.5 - 1.5) = -0.6$ and the intercept of that relation to $c = 1.2$

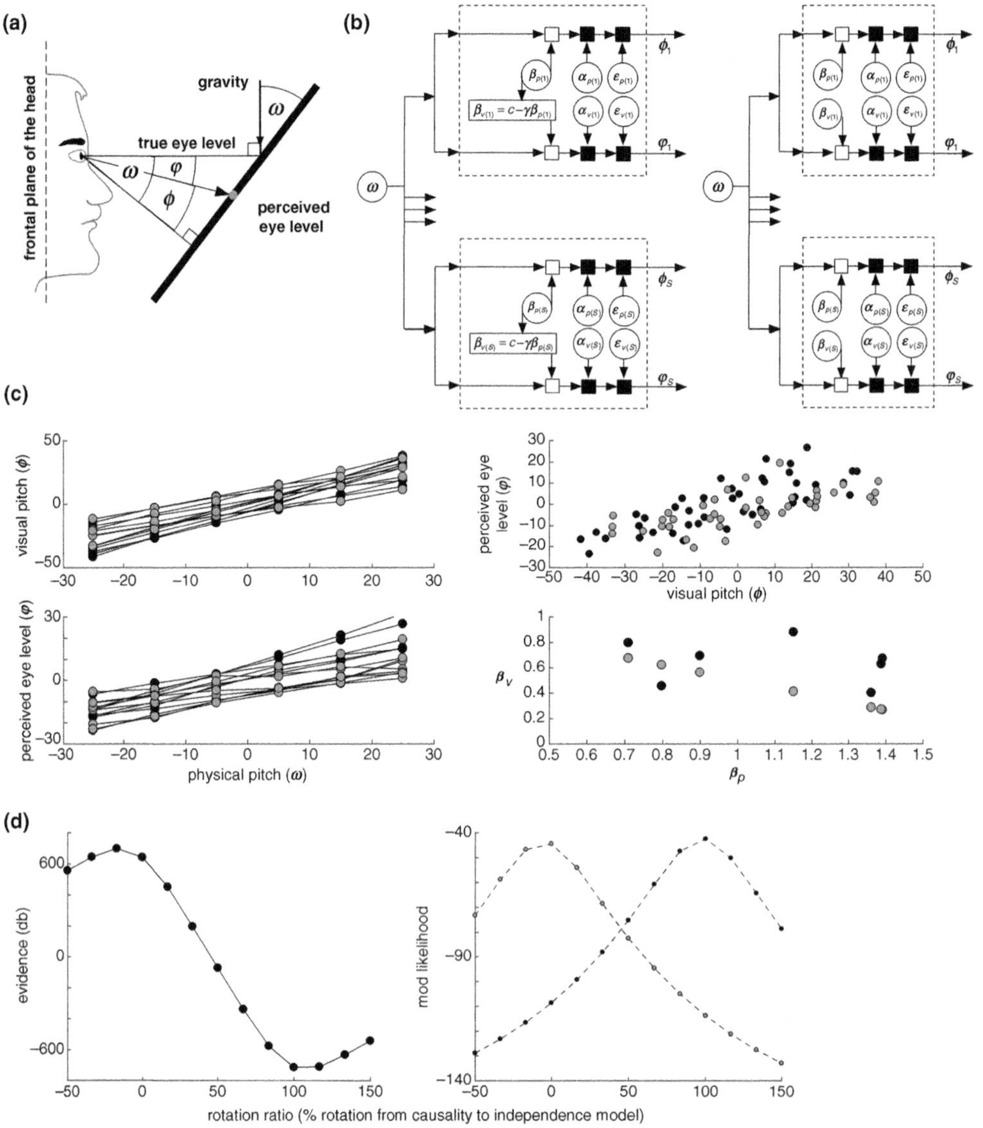

Figure 6.13 Multisource interrelationships among variables: perception. (a) Two perceptual discriminations are both influenced by the physical pitch (forward/backward tilt) of the wall: visual pitch, the percept of the wall's physical pitch, and the location on the wall corresponding to the perceived elevation of eye level. (b) Multisource graphical model of the *causal* (left) and independence (right) linear mechanism of the source specific modulation of variables' model. (c) Raw perceptual outputs (left) representing visual pitch and eye-level settings made by seven subjects while in the presence of a physically pitched visual field at various pitch angles, ω_k . (right) Plots comparing the two perceptual dimensions. The upper plot shows raw eye position settings plotted against raw visual pitch settings for the independence (black) and causal (gray) mechanisms. Both cases show a strong positive correlation between the two perceptual dimensions. The lower plot shows perceptual versus physical pitch slopes (β_P and β_V) from the two perceptual dimensions plotted against one another. Only the slopes from the causal mechanism (gray) display any correlation, here demonstrating a negative linear relation. (d) Evidence for the proposed causal relation varies with the rotation of the straight-line relation connecting slopes in the lower-right of (b).

(found by solving $(\alpha - 0.9)/(0 - 0.5) = \gamma$). We will take these to be known constants in the causal model.

The two slope parameters that describe the influence of physical pitch (ω) on the two perceptual dimensions of perceived pitch (ϕ):

$$\phi'_{jk} = \beta_{pj}\omega_k,$$

and the perception of eye level (φ):

$$\varphi'_{jk} = \beta_{vj}\omega_k.$$

where notice that the jth source will generate two datasets in this example, one for perceived pitch (Fig. 6.13c, upper-left) and one for perceived eye level (lower-left), and also that multiple physical pitch orientations must be presented to each source to generate enough data to measure β_p and β_v. These simulated perceptual observations mimic a system with additive noise, $y = y' + \varepsilon$ in *both* perceptual dimensions, as dictated by the graphical model (Fig. 6.13b), which is significant because neither the ordinate nor the abscissa values in the plot of $\beta_{vj} = \gamma\beta_{pj} + c$ are known values – whereas in a typical straight-line model the abscissa values are known because they are experimentally controlled (as are the physical pitch orientations ω_k in experimentally controlling the two perceptual outputs, $\beta_j\omega_k$). In computing the odds, therefore, we must marginalize over both of the unknown perceptual slope (β) values, as well as the global dispersion level, σ, which will be applied below to compute the evidence in favor of either the independence (M_0) or causal (M_1) slope model from simulation data.

B. Assign Prior Probabilities to Hypotheses

We will assume it is known that, on average, experimental subjects produce a perceived pitch slope that is roughly unity, around $\beta_p = 1$, and that the typical subject will display an eye level illusion that is modulated by physical pitch with a slope of about $\beta_v = 0.6$ (and further no subject ever produces a negative β_p or β_v slope. The hypothesis that the eye level illusion might be produced by perceived pitch follows from the idea that the perception of eye level is computed by first finding the surface normal, and then adjusting by an amount equal to perceived pitch (see Fig. 6.13a). The normal to a pitched surface is shifted up/down relative to the true eye level of an observer by an angle equal to the physical pitch of the surface – and if the pitch of the surface is underestimated, this could create the eye-level illusion. Thus, the average slope values are roughly consistent with this theory, and this gives us the impetus to test it, but does not give strong evidence one way or another for a causal connection between the two perceptual variables. We will start with the assignment:

$$\varpi(M_0) = \varpi(M_1) = .5.$$

C. Compute Model Likelihoods

Each of the perceptual judgments will generate its own dataset, and therefore each source will produce two datasets of perceptual settings indexed by k (one perceptual setting of each type for the ω_k physical pitches). To simplify calculations we will assume that there is a single global (but unknown) dispersion describing the two perceptual settings. This is not entirely unreasonable when the two perceptual dimensions share the same units of measure (degrees: one of surface pitch and one of visual angle).

In both models, the sampling probabilities for observations along the perceptual dimensions are:

$$p(\phi \mid \phi' \cdot \sigma \cdot \iota) = p(\phi \mid \beta_p \cdot \alpha_p \cdot \sigma \cdot \omega \cdot \iota)$$
$$= [\sigma\sqrt{2\pi}]^{-1} e^{-\frac{1}{2}\frac{[\phi-\phi']^2}{\sigma^2}} = [\sigma\sqrt{2\pi}]^{-1} e^{-\frac{1}{2}\frac{[\phi-(\beta_p\omega+\alpha_p)]^2}{\sigma^2}} = [\sigma\sqrt{2\pi}]^{-1} e^{-\frac{1}{2}\frac{[\phi-(\beta_p\omega)]^2}{\sigma^2}}$$
$$p(\varphi \mid \varphi' \cdot \sigma \cdot \iota) = p(\varphi \mid \beta_v \cdot \alpha_v \cdot \sigma \cdot \omega \cdot \iota)$$
$$= [\sigma\sqrt{2\pi}]^{-1} e^{-\frac{1}{2}\frac{[\phi-\phi']^2}{\sigma^2}} = [\sigma\sqrt{2\pi}]^{-1} e^{-\frac{1}{2}\frac{[\varphi-(\beta_v\omega+\alpha_v)]^2}{\sigma^2}} = [\sigma\sqrt{2\pi}]^{-1} e^{-\frac{1}{2}\frac{[\varphi-(\beta_v\omega)]^2}{\sigma^2}}$$

where the intercepts, α, of the straight-line functions have been dropped to simplify this example. The β values of these equations describe the strength of the influence of physical pitch on the two perceptual settings, and these β_p and β_v values are differentially related to one another under the independence and causality models.

Under both the independence and causality models the joint likelihood of the parameters for the jth source and k^{th} observation-pair is:

$$[\mathcal{L}(\beta_{pj}, \beta_{vj})]_{jk} = [\mathcal{L}(\gamma, c, \beta_j)]_{jk} =$$
$$= p(\phi_{jk} \mid \beta_{pj} \cdot \gamma \cdot c \cdot \sigma \cdot \iota)\, p(\varphi_{jk} \mid \beta_{vj} \cdot \gamma \cdot c \cdot \sigma \cdot \iota)$$
$$= \sqrt{2\pi}^{-1} \sigma^{-1} e^{-\frac{1}{2}\left(\frac{[\phi_{jk}-\beta_{pj}\omega_k]^2}{\sigma^2}\right)} \sqrt{2\pi}^{-1} \sigma^{-1} e^{-\frac{1}{2}\left(\frac{[\varphi_{jk}-\beta_{vj}\omega_k]^2}{\sigma^2}\right)}$$
$$= [2\pi]^{-1}\sigma^{-2} e^{-\frac{1}{2}\left(\frac{[\phi_{jk}-(\beta_j\omega_k)]^2}{\sigma^2}\right)} e^{-\frac{1}{2}\left(\frac{[\phi_{jk}-(c+\gamma\beta_j)\omega_k]^2}{\sigma^2}\right)},$$

where all j-subscripted parameters are unknown and source-specific. Notice that when written in terms of the model equation $\beta_v = c + \gamma\beta_p$ the likelihood is written in terms of β, dropping the additional p-subscript; we will simply keep in mind that β_j written without a differentiating name subscript refers to visual pitch slope. The above likelihood function applies to all perceptual judgments (regardless of the physical pitch used to elicit them) under both models for the jth source. Under the causality model this equation takes the additional simplification provided by known γ and c values, which we label $\gamma_1 = -0.6, c_1 = 1.2$.

The next step is to combine data across physical pitch-orientations:

$$[\mathcal{L}(\gamma, c, \beta_j)]_j = \prod_k [\mathcal{L}(\gamma, c, \beta_j)]_{jk} =$$
$$= [2\pi]^{-N}\sigma^{-2N} e^{-\frac{1}{2}\left(\frac{\sum_k [\phi_{jk}-(\beta_j)\omega_k]^2 + [\varphi_{jk}-(c+\gamma\beta_j)\omega_k]^2}{\sigma^2}\right)}.$$

Our prior information over the model parameters will be taken to be

$$M_0:$$

$$\varpi_0(\gamma) = \begin{cases} 0 & \gamma \neq 0 \\ 1 & \gamma = 0 \end{cases},$$

$$\varpi_0(c) = \begin{cases} 0 & c \neq \beta_2' \\ 1 & c = \beta_2' \end{cases},$$

where under the independence model, when $\gamma = 0$, the intercept c must be set to the central β_v value, $\beta_v' = 0.6$.

Under the causality model these parameters are set to different known constants:

$$M_1:$$

$$\varpi_1(\gamma) = \begin{cases} 0 & \gamma \neq -0.6 \\ 1 & \gamma = -0.6, \end{cases}$$

$$\varpi_1(c) = \begin{cases} 0 & c \neq 1.1 \\ 1 & c = 1.1. \end{cases}$$

Furthermore, we will simplify our final equations by treating the perceptual slopes, β_1 and β_2 as described by a uniform prior over their values, taking the prior range of each to be the range described above for the corresponding simulation.

The set of source-specific parameter likelihoods, $\mathcal{L}_j(\gamma)$, can be combined across sources after marginalizing over any source-specific variables (subscripted j) to yield the marginal source-specific model likelihoods $(\mathcal{L}_0)_j$ and $(\mathcal{L}_1)_j$. Marginal source-specific model likelihoods require marginalization with respect to model-specific prior distributions, and so will in general be different for different models. Here, the marginal source-specific model likelihood for the independence model (M_0) is:

$$(\mathcal{L}_0)_j = \int d\beta_j \varpi_0 \left(\beta_j, c, \gamma\right) \mathcal{L}_j \left(\gamma, c, \beta_j\right).$$

The overall marginal model likelihood is then built from the set of marginalized source-specific model likelihoods, where the final expression must marginalize over the unknown global dispersion:

$$\begin{aligned} \mathcal{L}_0 &= \int d\sigma \prod\nolimits_j (\mathcal{L}_0)_j \\ &= \int d\sigma \prod\nolimits_j \int d\beta_j \varpi_0 \left(c, \gamma, \beta_j\right) \mathcal{L}_0 \left(\beta_j, \gamma, c\right). \end{aligned}$$

Similarly, the marginal source-specific model likelihood for the causality model (M_1) is:

$$(\mathcal{L}_1)_j = \int d\beta_j \varpi_0 \left(\beta_j, \gamma, c\right) \mathcal{L}_1 \left(c, \gamma, \beta_j\right)$$

and the marginal model likelihood is

$$\begin{aligned} \mathcal{L}_1 &= \prod\nolimits_j (\mathcal{L}_1)_j \\ &= \int d\sigma \prod\nolimits_j \int d\beta_j \varpi_1 \left(c, \gamma, \beta_j\right) \mathcal{L}_1 \left(\beta_j, \gamma, c\right). \end{aligned}$$

Note that the parameters of the model equation are taken as known under both the causality and independence models, and marginalization is not required (they are retained in the prior and likelihood terms to remind us that these are the critical model parameters). The model likelihood for the independence model is therefore

$$
\begin{aligned}
\mathcal{L}_0 &= \prod_j (\mathcal{L}_0)_j \\
&= \int d\sigma \prod_j \left[\int d\beta_j \varpi_0(\gamma, c, \beta_j)\, \mathcal{L}_0(\beta_j, c, \gamma)\right] \\
&= 2\pi^{-SN}[\Delta\beta]^{-S} \int d\sigma\, \sigma^{-2SN} \prod_j \left[\int d\beta_j e^{-\frac{1}{2}\left(\frac{\sum_k [\phi_{jk} - (\beta_j)\omega_k]^2 + [\varphi_{jk} - (c + \gamma\beta_j)\omega_k]^2}{\sigma^2}\right)}\right]
\end{aligned}
$$

It is important to recognize that, in the model likelihood, each of the inner integrals in the product must be evaluated separately by source before taking the final product.

The model likelihood for the causality model is:

$$
\begin{aligned}
\mathcal{L}_1 &= \prod_j (\mathcal{L}_1)_j \\
&= \int d\sigma \prod_j \left[\int d\beta_j \varpi_1(\gamma, c, \beta_j)\, \mathcal{L}_1(\beta_j, c, \gamma)\right] \\
&= 2\pi^{-SN}[\Delta\beta]^{-S} \int d\sigma\, \sigma^{-2SN} \prod_j \left[\int d\beta_j e^{-\frac{1}{2}\left(\frac{\sum_k [\phi_{jk} - (\beta_j)\omega_k]^2 + [\varphi_{jk} - (c + \gamma\beta_j)\omega_k]^2}{\sigma^2}\right)}\right]
\end{aligned}
$$

Also notice that in both models the range of the visual pitch slopes, $\Delta\beta$, is known and equal for all sources, yielding the final prior normalization over possible β values of $[\Delta\beta]^{-S}$.

D. Compute the Evidence

Having defined all the elements, we are now able to compute the model evidence values:

$$
\begin{aligned}
\mathbf{e}(M_0) &= 10 \log [\mathbf{O}(M_0)] \\
&= 10 \log \left[\frac{p(M_0 \mid d \cdot \iota)}{p(\overline{M}_0 \mid d \cdot \iota)}\right] \\
&= 10 \log \left[\frac{\varpi_0 \int d\sigma \prod_j \int d\beta_{1j} \varpi_0(\gamma, c, \beta_j)\, \mathcal{L}_0(\beta_j, c, \gamma)}{\varpi_1 \int d\sigma \prod_j \int d\beta_{1j} \varpi_1(\gamma, c, \beta_j)\, \mathcal{L}_1(\beta_j, c, \gamma)}\right] \\
&= 10 \log_{10} \left[\frac{\varpi_0}{\varpi_1} \frac{\int d\sigma\, \sigma^{-2SN} \prod_j \left[\int d\beta_j e^{-\frac{1}{2}\left(\frac{\sum_k [\phi_{jk} - (\beta_j)\omega_k]^2 + [\varphi_{jk} - (c_0 + \gamma_0\beta_j)\omega_k]^2}{\sigma^2}\right)}\right]}{\int d\sigma\, \sigma^{-2SN} \prod_j \left[\int d\beta_j e^{-\frac{1}{2}\left(\frac{\sum_k [\phi_{jk} - (\beta_j)\omega_k]^2 + [\varphi_{jk} - (c_1 + \gamma_1\beta_j)\omega_k]^2}{\sigma^2}\right)}\right]}\right]
\end{aligned}
$$

Evidence for the Causal Mechanism (Fig. 6.13c,d)

Here we will compute evidence from simulated perceived eye level and perceived pitch slopes, generated by simulating perceptual settings made while varying the physical pitch of the visual field.

We begin by generating the beta values describing perceptual slopes, and generating noise samples for perceptual settings made under six physical pitch conditions, from −25° (top-backward physical pitch) to +25° (top-forward physical pitch) in 10° increments:

```
clear
reset=1;
COL=[.55*[1 1 1]; .3 .4 .85; .8 .5 .4];
S=5; N=6; %five sources, six pitch settings per source
sig=1; Ns=201; slist=linspace(.5,5,Ns); %noise level vector
Nb=201; Ov=ones(Nb,1);
minP=.8; maxP=1.2;
minE=c+gam(2)*maxP; maxE=c+gam(2)*minP;
blist=linspace(minP-.6,maxP+.6,Nb);
diffs=[diff(blist(1:2)) diff(slist(1:2))];
c=[.6 1.2]; gam=[0 -.6];
if ~isnear(mean([minE maxE]),c(1)),
error('E-slope range mismatch with known E-slope central value'); end
thetas=linspace(-25,25,N);
B1prime=linspace(.5,1.5,S)'; %keep the VP slopes identical across sims
B2c=c+gam(2)*B1prime; %mixing endpoints (independent vs. causal)
Nrat=13; r0=atan(-gam(2));
ratlist=linspace(-.5,1.5,Nrat);

%keep noise samples identical across simulations for clearer comparison
e1=nan(S,N); e2=nan(S,N);
for s=1:S,
    e1(s,:)=nrand(0,sig,[1,N]);
    e2(s,:)=nrand(0,sig,[1,N]); end
```

The above can produce the plots of Figure 6.13c (black and gray), representing data from an independence mechanism and from a causal mechanism, respectively. This plot (Figure 6.13c, upper-left) shows the raw visual pitch (perceptual) data against the raw eye level setting data (this is just all of the data for one perceptual discrimination plotted against the other, with data-pairs matched by source and physical pitch condition), and (Fig. 6.13c, lower-left) the subject-specific slopes leading to those raw data. Notice that while the raw data plot shows a straight-line relation in *both* the causal and independence models (gray and black, resp.), it is *only* the causal model *slopes* that show the theoretically predicted negative straight-line relation.

From here, we take the data from the simulated causal mechanism and compute parameter likelihoods by condition:

```
Elist=nan(Nrat,2);
for irat=1:Nrat, ratnow=ratlist(irat);
    Lall1=zeros(S,Nb,Ns); Lall2=zeros(S,Nb,Ns);

    %%%%%%%%R%%%%%%%%%%%%%%%%%%%%%%%%%%%%%%
    %%% DATA SIM using rotation ratio %%%
    B12=rot([B1prime B2c],ratnow*r0); %rotation of 2d axes
    B1=B12(:,1)+mean([minP maxP])-mean(B12(:,1));
    B2=B12(:,2)+mean([minE maxE])-mean(B12(:,2));
```

```
    d1=e1+B1*thetas;
    d2=e2+B2*thetas;
        likeFNi=@(phi1,phi2,snow) [-(N/2)*(mean((phi1-...
            (blist'*thetas)).^2,2)/snow.^2+mean((Ov*phi2-...
            ((c(1)+gam(1)*blist)'*thetas)).^2,2)/snow.^2)-2*(N+1)*...
            log(snow)]'; %output is Nb x Nb
        likeFNc=@(phi1,phi2,snow) [-(N/2)*(mean((phi1-(blist'*...
            thetas)).^2,2)/snow.^2+mean((Ov*phi2-...
            ((c(2)+gam(2)*blist)'*thetas)).^2,2)/snow.^2)-2*(N+1)*...
            log(snow)]'; %output is Nb x Nb

        %%%%%%%%%%%%%%%%%%%%%%%%%%%%%%%%%%%%%%%
        %%% param likelihood by condition %%%
        for s=1:S,
            d1now=d1(s,:); d2now=d2(s,:);
            for is=1:Ns, snow=slist(is);
                Lall1(s,:,is)=squeeze(Lall1(s,:,is))+...
                   likeFNi(d1now,d2now,snow);
                Lall2(s,:,is)=squeeze(Lall2(s,:,is))+...
                   likeFNc(d1now,d2now,snow); end, end
```

From these parameter likelihood values (by model), we would like to verify that our simulation and analysis has captured the raw perceived eye level and perceived pitch versus physical pitch slopes that underlie our analysis:

```
%%%%%%%%%%%%%%%%%%%%%%%%%%%%%%%%%%%%%%%%
%%% verify source-specific b1, b2 %%%
%%% verify global sigmas %%%
bestlist=nan(S,2); margL=zeros(Ns,2);
for s=1:S,
    tmpSdat=squeeze(Lall1(s,:,:));
    pb=logsum(tmpSdat,2,diffs(2)); bestlist(s,1)=
    logpeakval([pb(:) blist(:)]); %independence
    ps=logsum(tmpSdat,1,diffs(1)); margL(:,1)=margL(:,1)+ps;

    tmpSdat=squeeze(Lall2(s,:,:));
    pb=logsum(tmpSdat,2,diffs(2)); bestlist(s,2)=
    logpeakval([pb(:) blist(:)]); %causality
    ps=logsum(tmpSdat,1,diffs(1)); margL(:,2)=margL(:,2)+ps; end

%%% independence model plot
figure((irat-1)*2+2); clf; hold on;
plot([0 2],c+gam(2)*[0 2],'k--','LineWidth',1);
plot([0 5],[0 5],'k:'); plot([0 2],c(1)*[1 1],'k--','LineWIdth',1);
for s=1:S, plot(B1(s)*[1 1],[0 1.6],'k-','LineWidth',.2); end
    plot(B1,bestlist(:,1),'ko','MarkerFaceColor','k','MarkerSize',12);
plot(B1,bestlist(:,1),'.','Color',COL(1,:)); %dotted circles
          %fall on unity line if MEASURED BETA is accurate
plot(bestlist(:,2),ones(S,1)*c(1),'ko','MarkerFaceColor',COL(1,:),'MarkerSize',10)
plot(B1,B2,'ko','MarkerSize',6,'MarkerFaceColor',COL(3,:));
sest=logpeakval([margL(:,1) slist(:)]);
plot(sig,sest,'ko','MarkerSize',6,'MarkerFaceColor',COL(2,:));
title('independence model','FontName','Arial','FontSize',12)

%%% causality model plot figure((irat-1)*2+3); clf; hold on;
plot([0 2],c+gam(2)*[0 2],'k--','LineWidth',1);
plot([0 5],[0 5],'k:'); plot([0 2],c(1)*[1 1],'k--','LineWIdth',1);
for s=1:S, plot(B1(s)*[1 1],[0 1.6],'k-','LineWidth',.2); end
plot(B1,bestlist(:,2),'ko','MarkerFaceColor','k','MarkerSize',12);
plot(B1,bestlist(:,2),'.','Color',COL(1,:));
%dotted circles fall on unity line if MEASURED BETA1 is accurate
plot(bestlist(:,2),c+gam(2)*bestlist(:,2),'ko',...
    'MarkerFaceColor',COL(1,:),'MarkerSize',10)
```

```
plot(B1,B2,'ko','MarkerSize',6,'MarkerFaceColor',COL(3,:));
sest=logpeakval([margL(:,2) slist(:)]);
plot(sig,sest,'ko','MarkerSize',6,'MarkerFaceColor',COL(2,:));
title('causality model','FontName','Arial','FontSize',12)

%%%%%%%%%%%%%%%%%%%%%%%%%%
%%% Model likelihoods %%%
for m=1:2, Elist(irat,m)=logsum(margL(:,m),1,diffs(2)); end
Elist(irat,3)=10*(Elist(irat,2)-Elist(irat,1));
disp(' ');
disp(['iRAT' num2str(irat) ':']); end
```

Finally, we compute evidence from model likelihoods, and plot both (Fig. 6.13d):

```
figure(1); clf; hold on
plot(ratlist,Elist(:,3),'ko-','MarkerFaceColor','k','MarkerSize',11);
xlabel('rotation ratio (rot from causality to independence
    models)','FontName','Arial','FontSize',15);
ylabel('evidence (db)','FontName','Arial','FontSize',15);

figure(30); clf; hold on; plot(ratlist,Elist(:,1),'ko:','MarkerFaceColor','k');
plot(ratlist,Elist(:,2),'ko:','MarkerFaceColor',COL(1,:))
xlabel('rotation ratio (rot from causality to independence
    models)','FontName','Arial','FontSize',15);
ylabel('mod likelihood','FontName','Arial','FontSize',15);
```

where we have dropped constants[12] that are common to both models, including the prior range, $\Delta\beta = [\beta_{max} - \beta_{min}]$.

To get a sense of the evidence produced by real data, we simulate a pair of noise samples, and from these generate the data that might be produced by each of seven sources, based on each source's β_1 and β_2 slope values (such a simulated dataset is shown in Fig. 6.13c), where slopes are generated based on the parameters of the causal mechanism. This yields one evidence value, for the current experimental scenario and noise samples about 600 dB favoring the causal model. However, we would also like to see how the evidence changes as the data provide less and less support for the causal model, instead favoring the independence model. To do so here, we will rotate the linear relation between β_1 and β_2 so that instead of describing a negative-going correlation between modulations of the two perceptual variables with visual pitch, the β_1 versus β_2 relationship instead is a flat line (describing zero correlation; see PA). The variation in evidence and model likelihoods produced from this procedure are shown in Figure 6.13d. At the zero point on the 'rotation ratio' axis (i.e., no rotation away from the causal mechanism) is plotted the evidence obtained when the data are generated from the causal mechanism of Figure 6.13b (left), whereas the values plotted at 1 on the rotation ratio axis (i.e., 100 percent rotation away from causal to independence) represent the evidence and model likelihoods obtained when the same noise vectors are applied to uncorrelated β_p and β_v slopes (Fig. 6.13b, right; this the case consistent with experimental findings). The simulated raw data from these two situations (rotation ratios of 0 and 1) are plotted in gray and black in Figure 6.13c.

It is important to make simulation plots such as Figure 6.13d because these allow us to verify that we have performed our calculations correctly, and that our code will yield

[12] As a reminder, while constants cannot be dropped generally in model comparison calculations the way they can be in measurement calculations, constants that are common to all models can still be eliminated.

the desired model comparison when we use these functions to analyze real data, as well as give us insights into the evidence calculations themselves (see Fig. 1.3, Section 1.2). In particular, notice the shape of this plot, the locations of the peak and trough, the transition between these two locations, and the evidence values that are obtained with data outside the area between the peak and trough. These are all meaningful in terms of this model comparison and provide a check on both our understanding of the model comparison in this example, as well as a check on our computations. We can see in Figure 6.13d that evidence for the causal mechanism peaks approximately when the two perceptual slopes have the hypothesized relationship (evidence value at zero rotation), and falls to a minimum (supports the independence model) near a rotation proportion of 1, where the perceptual slopes fall on a flat line in accordance with the independence model's predictions. It is interesting to note, however, that the maximal positive and negative evidence values do not occur exactly at 0 and 1, as might be expected. Rather, they occur slightly *outside* the 0-1 range on the rotation-ratio axis. This is in apparent contrast to the model likelihood plot, which shows that the likelihoods of the causal and independence models peak (within the limits of simulated noise) exactly at 0 and 1. To understand the apparent paradox, consider what happens to the *ratio* of model likelihoods at rotation ratios just slightly higher and lower than 0. In both cases, the likelihood of the causal model drops slightly, and by about the same amount (again, given simulated noise). However, evidence favoring the independence model moves asymmetrically in these two cases, increasing somewhat when the rotation ratio increases slightly from 0, but falling somewhat as the rotation ratio decreases slightly from 0.

The model comparison in this example was designed to compare two very specific straight-line models relating source-specific differences – here those differences were in the strength of modulation of the two perceptual outputs, in response to changes in physical pitch (i.e., the underlying β_p and β_v values). That is, the two to-be-compared models differed in their specific pair of parameter values, (γ, c), describing the relationship between β values. In a less informed theoretical scenario, we might instead want to test whether there is *any* straight-line relationship between β values. This scenario, in which the underlying values of the parameter pair (γ, c) are unknown is also the scenario in which we would want to measure the values of those parameters (or possibly only the c parameter, if the model comparison strongly favors the independence model). If we were *measuring* the straight-line relationship between the theoretical perceptual slopes β_p and β_v, we would have a very different underlying model (i.e., neither M_0 nor M_1) in which the unknown values of the (γ, c) parameters are assigned a prior, and fitted after marginalizing over any other unknown variables (such as the source-specific intercept terms, α, that were dropped above while simplifying this example problem, and/or the global dispersion parameter).

Exercises

1) Describe what you expect to happen to the evidence plot if the noise level is reduced? increased?
2) Reduce the variance of the noise from 1 to 0.3. How does this affect the evidence plot. Explain why.

3) There appears to be a straight-line relation between the two raw perceptual settings whether or not eye level settings are determined by perceived pitch. Plot this (spurious) straight-line relationship using simulated data from both the causal *and* the independence model. Explain why this is the case, and why the current analysis is able to avoid this issue and make it possible to distinguish these two models.
4) Create a plot of eye level versus perceived pitch settings where each source contributes only a single data-pair (instead of 6), taken from a single uniform-distribution-selected physical pitch. How does the relation between the two perceptual variables differ from that shown in the left-hand portion of Figure 6.13c, if at all?
5) Add a uniformly selected intercept to each of the perceptual straight-line functions used to generate data-pairs plotted from (4). How does this affect your interpretation of the relation between the two perceptual variables relative to the plots from Figure 6.13c?
6) Describe the 'natural variation' example from above in terms of the subject-specific modulation paradigm described here [for example, in terms of an underlying 'intelligence' variable]. Given your description, is the data from the previous example more like the upper lower plot of Figure 6.13c (right)? How would you go about computing the analog of Figure 6.13c (lower-right) for the natural variation example?
7) Describe a 'natural variation' model, aside from the one above, that you think can be characterized in terms of the subject-specific modulation paradigm described here. Create a graphical model of this model. How would you go about simulating and computing the analog of Figure 6.13c for your natural variation example?

6.5 Multiple Models

Often, there are more than two viable models that must be compared in light of available evidence. For example, the experiment described above comparing two antianxiolytic agents could also include a third experimental condition in which a subset of patients received a placebo – resulting in additional models for the possible equality or inequality of the placebo group's rate parameter with those of the other groups. The odds and evidence calculations used in the majority of examples above are specific to the case in which two, and only two, models are being compared. If there are more than two competing models, the odds and evidence equations must be modified slightly to account for the additional models. This was shown for the simplest possible case when the model comparison algorithm was first described (Section 6.1.3), and we will here elaborate and expand our analysis of multiple models. We will first consider the equations governing hypothesis testing in the case of three competing models, M_1, M_2, and M_3. This will then be generalized to the case of n_m competing models.

6.5.1 Logic of m Competing Models Revisited

As discussed above when the topic of multiple model comparison was introduced briefly in Section 6.1, the reason one needs to distinguish between two and more than two competing models is simple: There was an assumption made in generating the evidence equation (6.4) that is no longer true when the number of models exceeds 2 – the assumption that $M_1 = \overline{M_2}$ and $\overline{M_1} = M_2$ is correct when there are two models, and only two models. Equations (6.3) and (6.4) described the odds and evidence in the case of two competing models, M_1 and M_2. If, in addition to models M_1 and M_2, there were a third possibility, M_3, then it would no longer be true that $M_2 = \overline{M_1}$. The odds of M_1,

$$O(M_1) = \frac{\varpi(M_1)\,\mathcal{L}(M_1)}{\varpi\left(\overline{M_1}\right)\mathcal{L}\left(\overline{M_1}\right)} \tag{6.7}$$

could in consequence no longer be written: $\frac{\varpi(M_1)\mathcal{L}(M_1)}{\varpi(M_2)\mathcal{L}(M_2)}$. We will often assume for the remainder of the section that the prior odds are 1 : 1 . . . : 1 for the n_m models. The first (prior) term of (6.7) is then always $1/(n_m - 1)$. We will now deal with the relevant model likelihoods.

The unknown term in the denominator, $\mathcal{L}(\overline{M_1}) = p(\boldsymbol{d}|\overline{M_1} \cdot \iota)$, can be expanded via the product rule to give:

$$p\left(\boldsymbol{d} \mid \overline{M_1} \cdot \iota\right) = \frac{p(\boldsymbol{d} \mid \iota)p(\overline{M_1} \mid \boldsymbol{d} \cdot \iota)}{p\left(\overline{M_1} \mid \iota\right)} \tag{6.8}$$

The second term in the numerator of (6.8) should be recognized as:

$$p\left(\overline{M_1} \mid \boldsymbol{d} \cdot \iota\right) = p\left(M_2 \vee M_3 \mid \boldsymbol{d} \cdot \iota\right) \tag{6.9}$$

and the denominator of (6.8) is:

$$p\left(\overline{M_1} \mid \iota\right) = p\left(M_2 \vee M_3 \mid \iota\right) \tag{6.10}$$

Assuming mutually exclusive models,[13] these two equations become:

$$p\left(\overline{M_1} \mid \boldsymbol{d} \cdot \iota\right) = p\left(M_2 \mid \boldsymbol{d} \cdot \iota\right) + p\left(M_3 \mid \boldsymbol{d} \cdot \iota\right) \tag{6.11}$$

and

$$p\left(\overline{M_1} \mid \iota\right) = p\left(M_2 \mid \iota\right) + p\left(M_3 \mid \iota\right) \tag{6.12}$$

Expanding (6.7) allows us to write the odds of M_1 as:

$$\begin{aligned} O(M_1) &= \frac{\varpi(M_1)\,\mathcal{L}(M_1)}{\varpi\left(\overline{M_1}\right)\mathcal{L}\left(\overline{M_1}\right)} \\ &= \frac{p(M_1 \mid \iota)}{(1 - p(M_1 \mid \iota))} \frac{p\left(\boldsymbol{d} \mid M_1 \cdot \iota\right)}{p(\boldsymbol{d} \mid \iota)\left[\dfrac{\dfrac{p\left(\boldsymbol{d} \mid M_2 \cdot \iota\right)p\left(M_2 \mid \iota\right)}{p(\boldsymbol{d} \mid \iota)} + \dfrac{p\left(\boldsymbol{d} \mid M_3 \cdot \iota\right)p\left(M_3 \mid \iota\right)}{p(\boldsymbol{d}|\iota)}}{p\left(M_2 \mid \iota\right) + p\left(M_3 \mid \iota\right)}\right]} \end{aligned}$$

which can be simplified to:

$$\begin{aligned} O(M_1) &= \frac{p(M_1 \mid \iota)}{(1 - p(M_1 \mid \iota))} \frac{p\left(\boldsymbol{d} \mid M_1 \cdot \iota\right)\left(p\left(M_2 \mid \iota\right) + p\left(M_3 \mid \iota\right)\right)}{p\left(\boldsymbol{d} \mid M_2 \cdot \iota\right)p\left(M_2 \mid \iota\right) + p\left(\boldsymbol{d} \mid M_3 \cdot \iota\right)p\left(M_3|_\iota\right)} \\ &= \frac{\varpi(M_1)\,\mathcal{L}(M_1)}{\varpi(M_2)\,\mathcal{L}(M_2) + \varpi(M_3)\,L(M_3)} \end{aligned} \tag{6.13}$$

[13] This is reasonable even in the case of 'nested' models where one model is a subset of another. For example, it cannot both be the case that a hypothetical mean can fall *anywhere* within the range [−20, 20] *and* that the mean must be equal to 10.

Similarly, by rotating indices we see that the other two odds ratios are:

$$\boldsymbol{O}(M_2) = \frac{\varpi(M_2)\,\mathcal{L}(M_2)}{\varpi(M_1)\,\mathcal{L}(M_1) + \varpi(M_3)\,L(M_3)} \qquad (6.14),$$

$$\boldsymbol{O}(M_3) = \frac{\varpi(M_3)\,\mathcal{L}(M_3)}{\varpi(M_2)\,\mathcal{L}(M_2) + \varpi(M_1)\,\mathcal{L}(M_1)} \qquad (6.15).$$

We will now derive the odds for the first of *nm* competing models, recognizing as above that the remaining odds ratios can be generated simply by rotating indices. As always, we begin by expanding the denominator of (6.7), for mutually exclusive model probabilities:

$$p\left(\boldsymbol{d} \mid \overline{M_1} \cdot \iota\right) = \frac{p\left(\boldsymbol{d}|_{I}\right) p\left(M_2 \mid \boldsymbol{d} \cdot \iota\right)}{p\left(M_2 \mid \iota\right)} + \frac{p\left(\boldsymbol{d}|_{I}\right) p\left(M_3 \mid \boldsymbol{d} \cdot \iota\right)}{p\left(M_3 \mid \iota\right)} + \ldots$$
$$\ldots + \frac{p(\boldsymbol{d} \mid I) p\left(M_{n_m} \mid \boldsymbol{d} \cdot \iota\right)}{p\left(M_{n_m} \mid \iota\right)} \qquad (6.16).$$

Expanding the second term in each numerator by the product rule and combining terms allows us to write the odds ratio for the first of n_m models:

$$\boldsymbol{O}(M_1) = \frac{p\left(\boldsymbol{d} \mid M_1 \cdot \iota\right)\left(p\left(M_2|_{\iota}\right) + \ldots + p\left(M_N \mid \iota\right)\right)}{p\left(\boldsymbol{d} \mid M_2 \cdot \iota\right) p\left(M_2|_{\iota}\right) + \ldots + p\left(\boldsymbol{d} \mid M_N \cdot \iota\right) p\left(M_N \mid \iota\right)} \frac{p\left(M_1|_{\iota}\right)}{\left(1 - p\left(M_1|_{\iota}\right)\right)}$$
$$= \frac{\varpi(M_1)\,\mathcal{L}(M_1)}{\varpi(M_2)\,\mathcal{L}(M_2) + \ldots + \varpi(M_N)\,\mathcal{L}(M_N)} \qquad (6.17).$$

Exercises

1) Based on the definition of $\varpi(\overline{M_1})$, explain why the prior term of (6.7) will always be $\varpi(M_1)/\varpi(\overline{M_1}) = 1/(n_m - 1)$ when the prior ratio is $1:1:1:\ldots:1$
2) Expand the odds ratio described in (6.17) for:
   a. $n_m = 3$
   b. $n_m = 7$
   c. $n_m = 4$
3) Show the odds calculation if both the priors and likelihoods were in the ratio $1:1:1:\ldots:1$.

Example: Multiple Models – A Melange

Previous examples all maintained separable hypothesis spaces, such as $\beta = 0$ versus $0 < \beta < 1$. This is often the case, but by no means necessary. Here we will demonstrate a model comparison in which there are overlapping hypothesis spaces, and the dimensions of the comparison are not aligned. Because this is such an unusual model set we will remain agnostic regarding the theoretical background that might have led to it, focusing only on how such a set is analyzed.

A. Translate Hypotheses into Model Equations

In this final example we will examine a range of models, beginning with a series of three models that make use of the Gaussian error function:

ι: We are making observations of data whose dimension is the same as μ (i.e., we can plot them on the same axes). We assume that the sampling dispersion σ is in the range, $\sigma = 1$ to $\sigma = 10$, and we have no prior preference for any one of the three models over another, $\varpi(M_1) = \varpi(M_2) = \varpi(M_3)$.

M_1: $0 < \mu < 1, \sigma = 5$

M_2: $\mu = 1, 1 < \sigma < 7$

M_3: $\mu = 0, 3 < \sigma < 10$

Notice that there are multiple differences between these models, in both parameters. In all cases, the Gaussian error function describing deviations of observed data values from the theoretical μ value is the same, and the models differ in their statement of allowable values of the μ and σ parameters.

Here again the odds ratio must be defined to account for multiple models, expanding the denominator of the odds ratio to a sum of possible alternative models:

$$\begin{aligned} \boldsymbol{O}(M_1) &= \frac{p(M_1 \mid \boldsymbol{d} \cdot \iota)}{p(\overline{M_1} \mid \boldsymbol{d} \cdot \iota)} \\ &= \frac{p(M_1 \mid \boldsymbol{d} \cdot \iota)}{p(M_2 \mid \boldsymbol{d} \cdot \iota) + p(M_3 \mid \boldsymbol{d} \cdot \iota)} = \frac{\varpi_1 \mathcal{L}_1}{\varpi_2 \mathcal{L}_2 + \varpi_3 \mathcal{L}_3}. \end{aligned}$$

B. Assign Prior Probabilities to Hypotheses

Because we have given no experimental scenario, our only real option for the prior over models is the uninformed choice: equal prior probabilities, m^{-1}.

C. Compute Model Likelihoods

The three models are defined by their prediction that different specific values and/or segments of the 2D Gaussian location and scale coordinates will describe data in our experiment. This example demonstrates that models need not compare data based on the same coordinates (i.e., be predictions of different segments of the same coordinate axis), and that they further need not make comparisons that collectively cover the entire range of any of the model's parameters. After we solve the three-model comparison problem, we will then explore the former point even further by adding a fourth model that posits data are described by the exponential instead of Gaussian error model.

We begin with the 2D likelihood over parameter pairs, (μ, σ), which in this example is given by the Gaussian error model:

$$\begin{aligned} \mathcal{L}(\mu,\sigma) &= (\sigma\sqrt{2\pi})^{-n} e^{-\frac{1}{2}\sum_i \left(\frac{x_i-\mu}{\sigma}\right)^2} \\ &= (\sigma\sqrt{2\pi})^{-n} e^{-\frac{n}{2}\frac{\overline{x^2}+\mu^2-2\mu\bar{x}}{\sigma^2}} = (\sigma\sqrt{2\pi})^{-n} e^{-\frac{n}{2}\frac{\overline{x^2}-\bar{x}^2+\bar{x}^2+\mu^2-2\mu\bar{x}+}{\sigma^2}} \\ &= (\sigma\sqrt{2\pi})^{-n} e^{-\frac{n}{2}\frac{(\bar{x}-\mu)^2}{\sigma^2}} e^{-\frac{n}{2}\frac{\overline{x^2}-\bar{x}^2}{\sigma^2}} = (\sigma\sqrt{2\pi})^{-n} e^{-\frac{n}{2}\frac{(\bar{x}-\mu)^2}{\sigma^2}} e^{-\frac{n}{2}\frac{\hat{s}^2}{\sigma^2}}. \end{aligned}$$

The prior probabilities over the location parameter (when it has an unknown range) is uniform, and over the dispersion parameter is the least-informed Jeffreys prior over

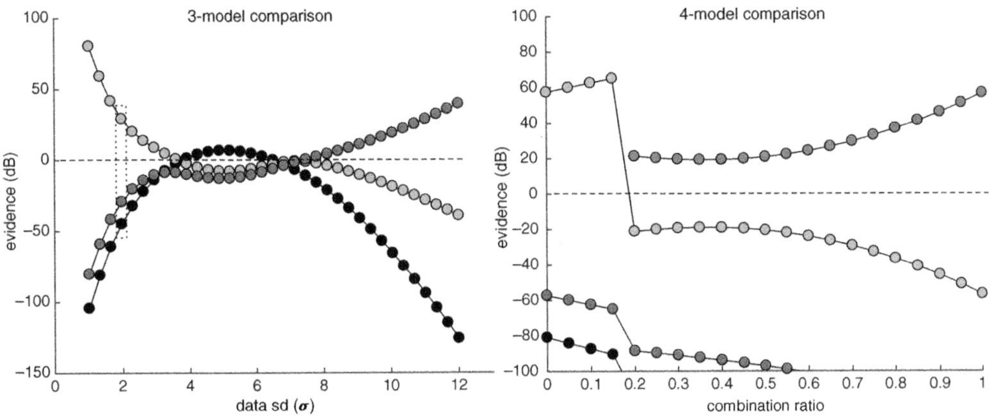

Figure 6.14 Selecting among multiple models. Evidence for three- and four-model comparisons in the potpourri example. (left) Evidence for the three models as a function of the true dispersion of the data samples. (right) Evidence in the four-model comparison as a function of the mixing ratio of a dataset sampled from the Gaussian and a dataset sampled from the exponential sampling distribution.

the allowed range. Our prior information regarding the allowed range of each of the parameter values differs in the three models, and this difference gives rise to the model likelihoods, $\mathcal{L}_1, \mathcal{L}_2,$ and $\mathcal{L}_3$ that describe the information contained in the data relevant to preferring any of the three models. The first model requires that the dispersion parameter be equal to $\sigma = 5$, but allows a range of possible locations, $0 < \mu < 1$; in other words, spreading the probability mass across multiple values along the μ axis while keeping it contained to a single position on the σ axis.

$$\begin{aligned}\mathcal{L}_1 &= \int d\mu d\sigma\, \varpi(\mu,\sigma)\mathcal{L}(\mu,\sigma) \\ &= (\sigma\sqrt{2\pi})^{-n} \int_0^1 d\mu e^{-\frac{n(\bar{x}-\mu)^2}{2\sigma'^2}} e^{-\frac{n\hat{s}^2}{2\sigma'^2}}\end{aligned}$$

In the second and third models, the prior probability mass is spread over overlapping portions of the possible range of the dispersion parameter. The model likelihoods for M_2 and M_3 are

$$\begin{aligned}\mathcal{L}_2 &= \int d\mu d\sigma\, \varpi(\mu,\sigma)\mathcal{L}(\mu,\sigma) \\ &= \log(7)^{-1}[2\pi]^{-n/2} \int_1^7 d\sigma \sigma^{-(n+1)} e^{-\frac{n}{2}\frac{(\bar{x}-\mu)^2}{\sigma^2}} e^{-\frac{n}{2}\frac{\hat{s}^2}{\sigma^2}},\end{aligned}$$

and

$$\begin{aligned}\mathcal{L}_3 &= \int d\mu d\sigma\, \varpi(\mu,\sigma)\mathcal{L}(\mu,\sigma) \\ &= [\log(10) - \log(3)]^{-1}[2\pi]^{-n/2} \int_3^{10} d\sigma \sigma^{-(n+1)} e^{-\frac{n}{2}\frac{(\bar{x}-\mu)^2}{\sigma^2}} e^{-\frac{n}{2}\frac{\hat{s}^2}{\sigma^2}}\end{aligned}$$

and will be computed numerically below.

Numerical Assessment of the Evidence (Fig. 6.14)

```
%%%%%%%%%%%%%%%%%%%%%%%%%%%
%%% 3-model comparison %%%
clear

%%% prelim
Nmus=1085; mumin=-12; mumax=12; mus=linspace(mumin,mumax,Nmus)';
Om=ones(Nmus,1);
Nsigs=204; sigmax=20; sigs=linspace(0,sigmax,Nsigs+1);
sigs=sigs(2:end); sign2=sigs.^-2;
diffs=[diff(mus(1:2)) diff(sigs(1:2))];

%%% parameter prior for three models
im1=find(and(mus>0,mus<1)); is1=findnearestN(sigs,5,1);
im2=findnearestN(mus,1,1); is2=find(and(sigs>1,sigs<7));
im3=findnearestN(mus,0,1); is3=find(and(sigs>3,sigs<10));

%keep noise constant across simulated datasets
N=24; err0=randn(N,1); err0=(err0-mean(err0))/std(err0);

%%% 2D prior and likelihood over mu / sigma
primat=-Om*log(sigs); %figure(1); clf; meshc(sigs,mus,primat)
lrange2=log(7)-log(1); lrange3=log(10)-log(3);
like=@(xbar,x2bar) -N*(log(Om*sqrt(2*pi))+log(sigs)+.5*...
    (((xbar-mus).^2)*sign2+Om*(x2bar-xbar^2)*sign2)+...
        .5*log(2*pi)); %Gaussian likelihood

mulist=linspace(-.1,1.1,57); siglist=linspace(1,12,35);
ML=zeros(length(mulist),length(siglist),3);
EV=zeros(length(mulist),length(siglist),3);
for im=1:length(mulist), munow=mulist(im);
    for is=1:length(siglist), signow=siglist(is);
        dat=err0*signow+munow;
        likenow=like(mean(dat),mean(dat.^2));
        ML(im,is,1)=logsum(likenow(im1,is1),1,diffs(1));
        ML(im,is,2)=logsum(likenow(im2,is2)+primat(im2,is2)/lrange2,2,diffs(2));
        ML(im,is,3)=logsum(likenow(im3,is3)+primat(im3,is3)/lrange3,2,diffs(2));
        EV(im,is,:)=evid(str8n(ML(im,is,:))','natural'); end, end
figure(2); clf
subplot(2,1,1); plot(mus,exp(logsum(likenow,2,diffs(2))),'k.')
subplot(2,1,2); plot(sigs,exp(logsum(likenow,1,diffs(1))),'k.')

figure(3); clf; meshc(siglist,mulist,ML(:,:,1))
figure(4); clf; meshc(siglist,mulist,ML(:,:,2))
figure(5); clf; meshc(siglist,mulist,ML(:,:,3))

figure(6); clf; meshc(siglist,mulist,EV(:,:,1))
figure(7); clf; hold on; imu=round(length(mulist));
plot(siglist,squeeze(EV(imu,:,1)),'ko-','MarkerFaceColor','k','MarkerSize',10)
plot(siglist,squeeze(EV(imu,:,2)),'ko-','MarkerFaceColor',.7*[1 1 1],'MarkerSize',10)
plot(siglist,squeeze(EV(imu,:,3)),'ko-','MarkerFaceColor',[.3 .4 .8],'MarkerSize',10)
ylabel('evidence (dB)','FontName','Arial','FontSize',16)
xlabel(['data sd \sigma'],'FontName','Arial','FontSize',16)
axis([0 13 -150 100])
```

It is not necessary, however, that the parameter likelihood be the same in all models. For example, we might have reason to propose a fourth model that predicts an exponential error function, whose mean is in the range: $0 < \tau < 5$. This yields:

```
%%%%%%%%%%%%%%%%%%%%%%%%%%%%
%%% 4-model comparison %%%

%%% add tau param and tau prior
Ntaus=501; taumin=0; taumax=5;
taus=linspace(taumin,taumax,Ntaus+1); taus=taus(2:end); ltaus=log(taus);
diffs=[diff(mus(1:2)) diff(sigs(1:2)) diff(taus(1:2))];
pritaus=-ltaus;

datasig=2; datamean=mulist(imu);
dG=1; while or(-min(dG)>.25*datamean,sum(dG<0)~=2),
dG=randn([N 1])*datasig+datamean; end
dE=0; while any(dE<=0), dE=erand(datamean,[N 1]);
dE=dE-mean(dE)+datamean; end
Nrat=21; ratlist=linspace(0,1,Nrat)';

%%% parameter likelihood for exponential model
elike=@(dset) -dset*(1./taus)-ones(N,1)*ltaus;

ML=zeros(Nrat,4);
EV=zeros(Nrat,4);
for irat=1:Nrat, ratnow=ratlist(irat);
    dnow=dG*(1-ratnow)+dE*ratnow;
    likenow=like(mean(dnow),mean(dnow.^2));
    ML(irat,1)=logsum(likenow(im1,is1),1,diffs(1));
    ML(irat,2)=logsum(likenow(im2,is2)+primat(im2,is2)/lrange2,2,diffs(2));
    ML(irat,3)=logsum(likenow(im3,is3)+primat(im3,is3)/lrange3,2,diffs(2));
    likenow=elike(dnow); likenow((dnow*ones(1,Ntaus))<=0)=-inf;
    likenow=sum(likenow,1);
    ML(irat,4)=logsum(likenow+pritaus,1,diffs(3));
    EV(irat,:)=evid(ML(irat,:),ones(1,4),'natural'); end

figure(8); clf; hold on
plot(ratlist,EV(:,1),'ko-','MarkerFaceColor','k','MarkerSize',10)
plot(ratlist,EV(:,2),'ko-','MarkerFaceColor',.7*[1 1 1],'MarkerSize',10)
plot(ratlist,EV(:,3),'ko-','MarkerFaceColor',[.3 .4 .8],'MarkerSize',10)
plot(ratlist,EV(:,4),'ko-','MarkerFaceColor',[.7 .4 .3],'MarkerSize',10)
ylabel('evidence (dB)','FontName','Arial','FontSize',16)
xlabel(['combination ratio'],'FontName','Arial','FontSize',16)
axis([0 1 -100 100])
```

Notice that this model comparison yields infinite evidence against the exponential model when any observed datum is negative. Also, you should recognize that the evidence values for the two favorable models would not change in any appreciable way if the remaining two models were removed from the analysis.

D. Compute the Evidence

Recalling the updated form of the odds ratio defined in (**A**), combined with the model prior (**B**) and the model likelihoods (**C**), the evidence computation is:

$$e(M_1) = 10\log_{10}\left[\mathbf{O}(M_1) = \frac{p(M_1 \mid d\cdot\iota)}{p(\overline{M}_1 \mid d\cdot\iota)}\right]$$

$$= 10\log_{10}\left[\frac{\varpi(M_1)\int d\mu d\sigma\, \varpi_1(\mu,\sigma)\mathcal{L}(\mu,\sigma)}{\varpi(M_2)\int d\mu d\sigma\, \varpi_2(\mu,\sigma)\mathcal{L}(\mu,\sigma) + \varpi(M_3)\int d\mu d\sigma\, \varpi_3(\mu,\sigma)\mathcal{L}(\mu,\sigma)}\right]$$

$$= 10\log_{10}\left[\frac{(\sigma\sqrt{2\pi})^{-n}\int_0^1 d\mu e^{-\frac{n}{2}\sigma-\mu)^2} e^{-\frac{n}{2}\frac{(\bar{x}-\mu)^2}{\sigma^2}} e^{-\frac{n}{2}\frac{\hat{s}^2}{\sigma^2}}}{\log(7)^{-1}[2\pi]^{-n/2}\int_1^7 d\sigma\sigma^{-(n+1)} e^{-\frac{n}{2}\frac{(\bar{x}-\mu)^2}{\sigma^2}} e^{-\frac{n}{2}\frac{\hat{s}^2}{\sigma^2}} + [\log(10)-\log(3)]^{-1}[2\pi]^{-n/2}\int_3^{10} d\sigma\sigma^{-(n+1)} e^{-\frac{n}{2}\frac{(\bar{x}-\mu)^2}{\sigma^2}} e^{-\frac{n}{2}\frac{\hat{s}^2}{\sigma^2}}}\right]$$

The evidence in favor of the other two hypotheses is computed by rotating the three terms in the ratio containing the model likelihoods:

$$e(M_2) = 10\log_{10}\left[O(M_2) = \frac{p(M_2 \mid d \cdot \iota)}{p(\overline{M_2} \mid d \cdot \iota)}\right]$$
$$= -3.73$$

and

$$e(M_3) = 10\log_{10}\left[O(M_3) = \frac{p(M_3 \mid d \cdot \iota)}{p(\overline{M_3} \mid d \cdot \iota)}\right].$$
$$= -14.03$$

As suggested above, the final part of the algorithm is open-ended, and we might examine possible sources of prior information that would modulate this result. In this example we will examine two aspects of our prior information. First, we will notice that the initial statement of the models has the second two models defined with overlapping possible ranges of their σ parameter. Now if we set the mean of the data to the halfway point between the predictions of these two models, we can see that the only reason to prefer one over the other is because of the standard deviation, $\hat{s}$, of the data. Furthermore, if we compute the evidence for the second two models when $\hat{s}$ is set to each of $\hat{s} = [0.5, 1.5, \ldots, 9.5]$, and the overlap is increased, we can see that as the overlap increases it becomes more and more difficult to discriminate between these two models. In other words, we have demonstrated the truism that when models have vanishingly small differences in their predictions, it is can be quite hard to provide experimental evidence for one that does not also fit with the other. This explains why we are often taught to work in an area, or on problems, whose models are highly distinct, because this makes it easier in general to distinguish among them.

One of the differences that we can propose for two models, and one that can create quite a sharp distinction depending on the details, is between models with different error functions. Therefore, as a final variation of this example we will amend the background information given at the outset and replace the third model above with one that requires an exponential error function whose likelihood is:

$$\mathcal{L}(\tau) = \tau^{-1}e^{-t/\tau}$$

and which restricts the allowable range of mean values to:

$$M_4 : 0 < \tau \leq 5.$$

This model has a single parameter, and therefore requires a single marginalization:

$$\mathcal{L}_4 = \int d\tau\, \varpi(\tau)\mathcal{L}(\tau)$$
$$= \left[\log(\tau_{\max}) - \log(\tau_{\min})\right]^{-1} \int_{\tau_{\min}}^{\tau_{\max}} d\tau\, \tau^{-(n+1)} e^{-\frac{x}{\tau}}$$

to yield the model likelihood, which makes use of the Jeffreys prior, $p \propto \tau^{-1}$.

Notice that because we now have two different likelihoods, we can no longer drop the 2π constant terms associated with the Gaussian that had been shared across models in the 3-model comparison. Thus we have the evidence:

$$
\begin{aligned}
e(M_3) &= 10\log_{10}\left[O(M_2) = \frac{p(M_3 \mid \boldsymbol{d}\cdot\iota)}{p(\overline{M_3} \mid \boldsymbol{d}\cdot\iota)}\right] \\
&= 10\log_{10}\left[\frac{\sigma_3 \int d\mu d\sigma\, \varpi_3(\mu,\sigma)\mathcal{L}(\mu,\sigma)}{\omega_1 \int d\mu d\sigma\, \varpi_1(\mu,\sigma)\mathcal{L}(\mu,\sigma) + \varpi_2 \int d\mu d\sigma\, \varpi_2(\mu,\sigma)\mathcal{L}(\mu,\sigma) + \varpi_4 \int d\tau\, \varpi(\tau)\mathcal{L}(\tau)}\right] \\
&= 10\log_{10}\left[\frac{[\log(10)-\log(3)]^{-1}[2\pi]^{-n/2}\int_3^{10} d\sigma\,\sigma^{-(n+1)} e^{\frac{n(\bar{x}-\mu)^2}{2\sigma^2}} e^{-\frac{n\hat{s}^2}{2\sigma^2}}}{(\sigma\sqrt{2\pi})^{-n}\int_0^1 d\mu\, e^{\frac{n(\bar{x}-\mu)^2}{2\,\sigma^2}} e^{-\frac{n}{2\sigma^2}} + \log(7)^{-1}[2\pi]^{-n/2}\int_1^7 d\sigma\,\sigma^{-(n+1)} e^{\frac{n(\bar{x}-\mu)^2}{2\sigma^2}} e^{\frac{n\hat{s}^2}{2\sigma^2}} + [\log(\tau_{max})-\log(\tau_{min})]^{-1}\int_{\tau_{min}}^{\tau_{max}} d\tau\,\tau^{-(n+1)} e^{-\frac{n\bar{x}}{\tau}}}\right]
\end{aligned}
$$

for the third model.

It is important when computing the evidence for models that do not share the same sampling distributions that we respect any differences in allowable conditions for each underlying distribution. In the current example this takes the form of monitoring whether any observed datum is negative. Negative values are disallowed under the exponential *sampling distribution*, and therefore any *dataset* containing a negative value allows us to deductively rule the exponential model out of our comparison process.

Exercises

1) Give two examples of specific scientific hypothesis sets that segment the space of the rate parameter θ based on three or more models.
2) Write the 4-model evidence expression favoring the exponential model.
3) Explain the shape of the 3-model comparison plot as the dispersion transitions from low to high.
4) Why does one evidence curve start partway through the set of combination ratios in the 4-model comparison?
5) Why is the minimum of the exponential evidence curve (4-model comparison) not at the lowest value of the combination ratio that yields noninfinite (negative) evidence?
6) Explain the function of each part of the code for the 4-model comparison on the line that begins by defining the second instance of likenow.
7) The evidence for the two best models would be unaffected if the other two models were removed from the comparison (although this comparison would only be computable for combination ratios that yield noninfinite evidence for the exponential model). Explain how you could deduce this simply based on the shapes of these evidence curves?
8) Introduce a negative value into the dataset for the example problem analyzed in Figure 6.14. How does the model comparison algorithm deal with this negative value? In particular, describe whether the exponential model is rejected automatically by the algorithm, or whether this must be done manually.
9) Write the expression for, and compute the evidence in favor of M_1 when it is compared to:
   a. a single alternative positing $\mu = 1$, $\sigma = 1$
   b. the three alternatives defined above for the dataset, d = [1.1, 2, 0.03, -0.1, 0.4, 1.8, 2.4, 1.15, 0.8, 0.4, 1, 5].

6.6 Summary

In just six chapters we have managed to take a critical step in your scientific training, beginning with the basics of probability theory, through coordinate transformations, assigning probability distributions, cost functions, and measurement - all to arrive at the the model comparison algorithm: the mathematically and logically most straightforward extrapolation of Bayes' theorem for scientific hypothesis testing. Completion of this journey puts us in possession of a form of reasoning, applicable in all experiments, for selecting among the possible scientific explanations of *any* behavior. We have focused on behavioral phenomena in this text because these are the basic units of interest when examining biological and artificial nervous systems. Such systems are typically not initially interesting because of the minutiae of the underlying mechanisms governing their internal processes, but rather because some element of the *behavior* of the system is important to us - it is only after we have taken an interest in the behavior of a system that we become interested in the details of the mechanisms, computations, and anatomy underlying that behavior. Once we have identified a behavior or set of behaviors that interests us, we must examine the 'shape' of its mechanistic underpinnings via the model comparison algorithm, and the numerical values of the parameters that define those mechanisms via the measurement algorithm, with the overall enterprise orchestrated in accordance with the schedule laid out in Figure 1.3.

Of course, we acknowledge that the program laid out in Figure 1.3 featuring the model comparison and measurement algorithms is not followed universally. Indeed, on examining the history of scientific hypothesis testing we noted that there was a substantial chunk of our history in which the frequentist approach to hypothesis testing has been the standard. Having finished our initial foray into the measurement and model comparison algorithms, we are now in a position to examine issues that arise from some of the most commonly seen deviations from the program described here.

6.6.1 Other Approaches to Hypothesis Testing

When considering the advantages of the Bayesian approach to hypothesis testing, it is instructive to make two comparisons: first, to the frequentist approach, and second, to a hybrid approach, where instead of computing p-values based on sampling distributions, we use measurement-based confidence intervals as a method of quasi-frequentist hypothesis testing. Because both alternative methods are based on the frequentist algorithm, let us take a moment to review:

1. Prior to an experiment, a null hypothesis is defined and an α-level is set. By setting the α- level, you set the rate of false positive results because you will reject the null hypothesis (rejection is considered a 'positive' result) at a rate equal to α when the null hypothesis *is actually true* (i.e., the false alarm cell of Figure 6.15). The α-level is commonly set at $\alpha = 0.05$.
2. Data are collected, and the sampling probability of the disjunction of *all datasets* more extreme than the observed dataset is computed. This probability is the p-value associated with the observed dataset. Note that the p-value *is not* the probability of observing your dataset, nor is it the probability of the null hypothesis being true or false based on your dataset.

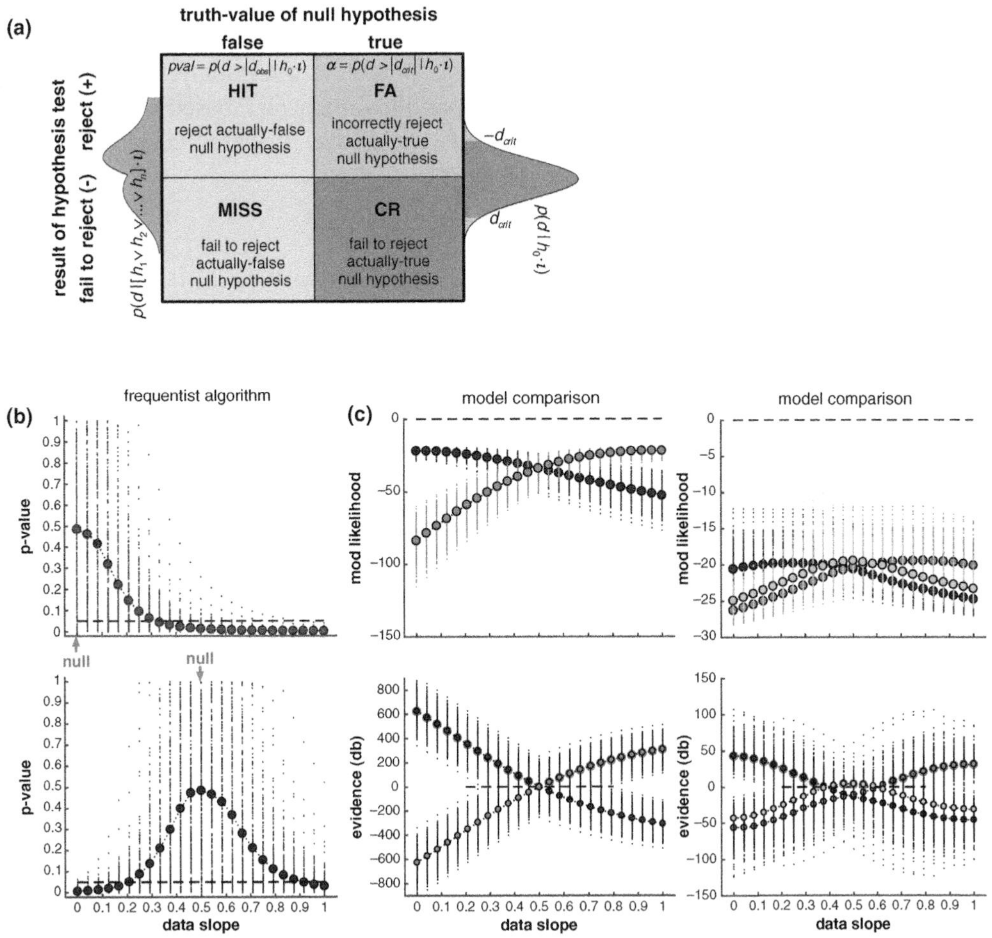

Figure 6.15 Other approaches to hypothesis testing. (a) Contingency table of possible outcomes for a frequentist hypothesis test. Compare this to Figure 2.3, describing the standard binary classification test. Note that the frequentist sampling distribution (right) applies only to the right-hand column of cells. However, a frequentist hypothesis test is declared 'significant,' corresponding to the upper *right-hand* cell ('hit'), *also based on the sampling distribution.* (b) Frequentist and (c) Bayesian model comparison results. The statistical model comparison performs particularly poorly in the lower plot, rejecting the null (and therefore asserting nothing) in nearly every case; the Bayesian analysis finds increasingly positive support for each of the three models in this case (right), as the data slope more closely matches each model's predictions.

3. The null hypothesis is rejected if the p-value is below your preset α-level (refer to **Box 2.2**).

As mentioned above, the α-level sets the rate of false-positive results (also referred to as type-I error rate). This is simply due to the definition of the α-level and p-value associated with a null hypothesis. If the null hypothesis *were* true, you would observe datasets whose associated p-values were less than the preset α-level in $100\alpha\%$ of your experimental results (thus defining a false-alarm rate equal to α). These statements about false-positive results might remind you of the contingency table and our discussions of binary-outcome experiments (as in the medical decision-making examples of Chapters 2 and 5), where we first learned about false-positives. Figure 6.15 shows a modification of the binary outcome table of Figure 2.3 specifically in terms of frequentist hypothesis testing. We see that there are four possible outcomes after analyzing the results of an experimental hypothesis test, two correct and two incorrect, based on the combination of true/false null hypothesis and whether it is rejected (declared false) or not (declared indeterminate) based on the experiment.[14]

Right-hand Column (Null Hypothesis Is True)

We should begin with the right-hand column of cells in the contingency table, as these are the only two cells in the table that correspond to the sampling distribution (plotted along the right of the table). The sampling distribution, $p(\boldsymbol{d}|h_0 \cdot \imath)$, gives the probabilities of observing different datasets, $\boldsymbol{d}$. We can think of each dataset as being very representative of the null hypothesis (datasets near the peak of the distribution, that are 'exactly what we would have expected' under the null hypothesis), or less representative of the null hypothesis (datasets that are predicted by the null hypothesis, but occur less often than the more representative datasets - these are the tails of the sampling distribution). Although in all cases the probabilities of these datasets are computed based on assuming that the null hypothesis is true (hence their applicability to the right-hand column of cells), if the dataset is less representative than a reference dataset d_{crit}, the null hypothesis is declared false. The reference dataset is chosen so that the total probability of observing datasets less representative is low (defining the α-level, usually 5 percent of the total sampling distribution), and so the *mistake* of rejecting the null hypothesis when it is actually true (upper right-hand cell) occurs at a rate equal to α (again usually $\alpha = 0.05$, or about 1 in 20 'statistically significant' experimental results). If the dataset is more representative of the null hypothesis than d_{crit}, the null hypothesis is not rejected (lower right-hand cell). This cell represents a 'correct' outcome in the sense that we should not reject the null hypothesis when it is true, but it is also a suboptimal outcome in the sense that we have not declared the null hypothesis true when in fact it is true (and are unable even to declare it 'better' when evidence suggests this is the case).

Left-hand Column (Null Hypothesis Is False)

Now that we have examined the cells that correspond to the null hypothesis being true, and therefore the cells to which the sampling distribution applies, we should notice that we still have not seen the case that (within the frequentist algorithm) is most important: the case of rejecting the null hypothesis when it is in fact false. Now, just as probabilities in the right-hand column (e.g., $p = .05$ in the upper and $p = .95$ in the lower cell) were dictated by the sampling distribution that corresponds to the null hypothesis being true, $p(\boldsymbol{d}|h_0 \cdot \imath)$, the probabilities that we will assign to cells in the left-hand column must be dictated by a sampling distribution that corresponds to the null hypothesis being false (i.e., the case where an alternative hypothesis is true $p(\boldsymbol{d}|[h_1 \vee h_2 \vee \ldots \vee h_n] \cdot \imath)])$.

[14] To reiterate, not declaring the null hypothesis false ('failing to reject') is not the same as declaring it true (accepting the null hypothesis), and so the frequentist algorithm can never accumulate direct evidence *in favor of* any hypothesis. It only gathers evidence *against* null hypotheses. This makes it particularly odd that the null hypothesis is usually formulated to make predictions that we do not believe will be true, because then the goal is apparently to find evidence against hypotheses that we already more or less knew were false.

Because no alternative sampling distribution is ever defined within the frequentist algorithm, we cannot know its shape (hence the irregular shape of the example distribution on the side). How then do we decide when to reject the null hypothesis? The null is rejected based solely on the sampling distribution that assumes the null hypothesis is true – the distribution *along the right-hand column* instead of the left-hand column.

This Is Not The Useful Contingency Table You Seek

Note that while the outcomes in the contingency table map onto the possible outcomes of the frequentist hypothesis test, we cannot assign probabilities (or frequencies) to these outcomes the way we did in the medical decision examples of Chapter 2. In those examples, based on disease detection, we found N_1 individuals known to have the disease, N_2 known to be disease free, and then count how often our test correctly and incorrectly identifies each underlying condition-type (the positive and negative outcomes per true disease state). In the hypothesis-testing case, we can know the sampling probabilities of false alarms and correct rejections because (identifying a true null hypothesis with the condition-absent case in the table), these are just the frequentist α-level and its compliment (i.e., they are known by definition). The remaining cells of the table ***cannot be known generally***. This is because: (a) we do *not* define a sampling distribution corresponding to any alternative hypothesis – indeed, we do not properly define an alternative to the null hypothesis as part of the frequentist algorithm; and (b) we cannot perform an analysis analogous to the disease-detection case above. Why? Because scientific hypotheses are either true or false, and this precludes us from finding *some* cases where the hypothesis is true and *some* where it is false (allowing us to then use our experiment to attempt to correctly detect these two cases and count the instances of each). Interestingly, it is assuming the truth of the null hypothesis (which is ultimately responsible for the issues discussed above) that also leads to the oddly convoluted nature of the frequentist argument, because it precludes us *both* from finding evidence in favor of the null, *and* finding evidence of either kind (favoring or deprecating) relative to any alternative hypotheses.

The model comparison problems considered above[15] directly compare the models of interest, taking into account both their prior probabilities (encoded as prior evidence favoring one model over another), as well as their prior explanatory power (encoded as an Occam factor). In stark contrast to the model comparison algorithm, the frequentist algorithm encodes none of this information, and in fact does not even directly compare models. The frequentist algorithm's inability to directly compare models leads to a series of problems, one of which will be paramount here. You see, it is the direct comparison of models in the model comparison algorithm that generates the Occam factor, thereby penalizing models with greater prior explanatory power. Second, and most importantly, is the fact that one cannot determine which of several models is the best available by considering only one of those models. For example, Figure 6.14 clearly

[15] We should note here that the model comparison algorithm does not quite map onto the 2x2 contingency table of Figure 6.15a, because there are always three possible outcomes of a model comparison computation: either the model is supported (evidence > 3db), there is evidence against the model (evidence < -3db), or the evidence is indeterminate (abs[evidence] < 3db).

demonstrates that the evidence for any given model is not simply a function of how well it fits the data, but rather how well it fits the data *relative to other alternative models.* When only 3 models were being considered, M_3 was clearly favored. However, in comparison to M_4, the evidence for M_3 was substantially reduced. If all alternative models are not compared directly to one another, it would be impossible to determine which to prefer. This problem is even evident in the comparison of two models with equal model-priors (prior evidence is zero), because the frequentist algorithm simply looks at the frequencies of occurrence for datasets based on the assumption of a single null hypothesis. But if the frequentist algorithm's implicitly-defined alternative hypothesis encompasses a greater number of parameter values – as is the case in comparing models in which two rate parameters are equal or unequal, the frequentist algorithm will fail to encode this information to penalize the model with greater prior explanatory power.[16]

These two issues, the inability of the frequentist algorithm to define all elements of the contingency table listed above, and its inability to generate an Occam factor to penalize models with greater prior explanatory power, will be the important points of comparison in the two examples that follow.

Example: The Frequentist Algorithm

The above shortcomings of the frequentist algorithm's approach to hypothesis testing have direct consequences in the interpretation of experimental results. The first consequence is so straightforward it required no example, and has been discussed at length: its convoluted argument structure, whose result is an algorithm that precludes us *both* from finding evidence in favor of the null, *and* finding evidence of either kind (supporting or deprecating) relative to any alternative hypotheses. In addition, we saw that it is the *direct comparison* of alternative models that forms the Occam factor, and the frequentist algorithm uses only a single 'null' model. There is a second subtler issue associated with this failure to define alternative models that can be more fully appreciated through an example.

One of the most common types of model comparison problem seen in the behavioral sciences involves discriminating among variants of a straight-line model. The simplest example of this type of problem involves just two models, such as the auditory perceptual example explored above, where one model predicts a slope of zero (insensitivity model), and the other a slope of one (veridical percept model), and here we will assume that both models have a known global dispersion and no source-specific intercept terms (we will assume all sources have a known intercept). This example is a good starting point because it involves no Occam factor (neither model has more prior predictive power than the other):

M_0**:** All sources are insensitive to variations in the input variable (e.g., perceived brightness in response to changes in illumination) and produce a constant response centered on a known value, $\alpha[\alpha = 0, \beta = 0]$.

[16] For those familiar with currently popular quasi-Bayesian model selection methods such as Akaike Information Criterion (AIC) or Bayes Information Criterion (BIC), note that these methods attempt to introduce an Occam factor 'proxy' based on differences in the *number* of uncertain variable values in to-be-compared models. Such methods fail to recognize the difference between, for example, the second and third models in the multiple model comparison example above. Occam-proxy methods ignore the important details of model comparison.

M_1: All sources are precisely sensitive to variations in the input variable and produce a unity-gain response with an intercept of zero $[\alpha = 0, \beta = 1]$.

These models define the odds ratio:

$$\mathbf{O}(M_1) = \frac{p(M_1|\boldsymbol{d} \cdot \iota)}{p(\overline{M_1}|\boldsymbol{d} \cdot \iota)} = \frac{\varpi_1}{\varpi_0}\frac{\Pi_j \varpi_1(\beta)\mathcal{L}_j(\beta_1)}{\Pi_j \varpi_0(\beta)\mathcal{L}_j(\beta_0)} = \frac{\varpi_1 \mathcal{L}_1}{\varpi_0 \mathcal{L}_0}.$$

Notice there are no free parameters and therefore no marginalizations (and *therefore also no Occam factor*) used to compute this ratio, although one must combine probability distributions across sources (indexed by j) which accounts for the multiplication over the source index. This odds ratio may be simpler to compute than it looks, because the probability $p_j = [\mathcal{L}(\beta_1)]_j$ is a scalar for each source:

$$\mathbf{O}(M_1) = \frac{\varpi_1 \prod_j \varpi_1(\beta)[\mathcal{L}_0(\beta_1)]_j}{\varpi_0 \prod_j \varpi_0(\beta)[\mathcal{L}_1(\beta_0)]_j}$$

Assuming equal prior odds of the two models this further reduces to the ratio of the product of source likelihoods under the two models. We will further simplify this example by restricting our simulations to the data of a single source:

$$\begin{aligned}\mathbf{O}(M_1) &= \prod_{j=1}^{N} e^{-\sum_{i=1}^{n}[o_{ij}-(0+x_i)]^2} \Big/ \prod_{j=1}^{N} e^{-\sum_{i=1}^{n}[o_{ij}-(0)]^2} \\ &= \prod_{j=1}^{N} e^{-\sum_{i=1}^{n}[o_{ij}-x_i]^2} \Big/ \prod_{j=1}^{N} e^{-\sum_{i=1}^{n} o_{ij}^2} \\ &= e^{-\sum_{i=1}^{n}[o_i-x_i]^2} / e^{-\sum_{i=1}^{n} o_i^2} \quad \{n = 1.\end{aligned}$$

The result can be seen for a range of 'data slopes' in Figure 6.15, which demonstrates that our analysis correctly prefers the insensitivity model when the data slope is $\beta < 0.5$ and prefers the veridical model when the data slope is $\beta > 0.5$.

How does the frequentist algorithm deal with this case? It defines its null hypothesis as the model predicting a slope of zero; this is considered the 'null' model because it conforms to the general description of a null hypothesis predicting that there is 'no effect' in behavior that results from the experimental manipulation (e.g., no perception of the experimental manipulation of light intensity in the brightness perception experiment). This null hypothesis would typically be tested in two stages: First, one would compute the best-fit slope derived from the data of each source, and then compute a 'frequentist confidence interval' on the null hypothesis, using the variance value fit from the data. The frequentist confidence interval gives the range of fitted slopes covering $100\alpha\%$ of the probability mass of *the null model*: the 'test' portion of the algorithm compares the fitted slope to see if it falls within this range. A result outside this range is taken as evidence of a difference between the fitted slope and the zero-prediction of the null hypothesis (that is, that the data do *not* conform to the insensitivity model). We can see the result of this analysis for the same series of data slopes in Figure 6.15b (upper-left). Notice that selecting the α criterion based on the fitted variance yields about $\alpha = 5$ percent false alarms: reporting a 'statistically significant result' (i.e., that the null model is incorrect) when the underlying data slope is in fact zero (points below the dashed line at data slope = 0). Notice also that the frequentist algorithm is only able to reliably reject the unity slope model when the data slope approaches 0.4, and otherwise fails to reject the null – and is effectively *unable to make any conclusion regarding the underlying model whatsoever.*

How does the model comparison algorithm's performance compare? In contrast to the frequentist algorithm, the model comparison algorithm is 100 percent accurate in preferring the zero-slope model when the underlying data slope is in fact zero. Indeed, over the range where the frequentist algorithm is unable to reliably draw *any conclusions whatsoever* regarding the models being tested, the model comparison algorithm is nearly 100 percent accurate in preferring the zero-slope model over the unity-slope model. Furthermore, when the underlying data slope is near 0.5, and there is therefore no objective reason to prefer one model over the other, the frequentist algorithm will indicate that the null model should be rejected (and indirectly used in practice to suggest support for the alternative, unity-slope model). In this $\beta = 0.5$ case the model comparison algorithm will tend to yield an evidence measure that is below the 3dB criterion, suggesting that these data cannot be taken as support for either model. As the data slope increases to match the prediction of the unity-slope model, the model comparison algorithm supplies direct support for that model (Fig. 6.15c, left).

Notice that this example was rather unrealistic, in that the models gave punctate predictions of *all* parameters: slopes (either zero or one), intercepts (always zero), and variances (somehow known to be fifteen 'units'). In a more realistic version of the problem some or all of these parameter values will be uncertain, at least to a degree. Thus, we would like to update the model comparison problem to include unknown global dispersion and slope parameters, and marginalize over them to compute the model likelihoods that go into the final odds ratio and evidence calculations.

We will define three models for this updated problem. The first two will be generalizations of the models above, such that the zero-slope model will cover the range of slopes $0 \leq \beta < 0.5$ and the unity-slope model will cover the range $0.5 < \beta \leq 1$. The third model will make the punctate prediction $\beta = 0.5$. All three new models will retain uncertainty in the variance component of the model to increase the realism of the example.

Defining these three models immediately brings out an issue with the frequentist model: it has no mechanism for incorporating this third model into the p-value metric, just as it had no mechanism for explicitly encoding the alternative hypothesis when the hypothesis test involved a comparison of just two models (Fig. 6.15b, lower). Second, even if we wanted to make the first model (the $\beta < 0.5$ model) our null hypothesis and focus on it in a frequentist hypothesis test (i.e., compute a p-value in terms of this uncertain-slope model, ignoring the other two models) there would be no useful way to do so because it involves an unknown slope parameter. The reason there is no good way to compute the p-value of any model that contains parameters whose values are uncertain is that we cannot marginalize over unknown parameters within the frequentist algorithm: instead we must fit them. The model comparison algorithm automatically solves this problem via the built-in Occam Factor, and therefore with no need to define an artificial 'null model' that may be inconsistent with any model that makes theoretical sense (nor to use vague word-based 'rules' for what a 'good' hypothesis 'looks like').

Programming Aside: Frequentist Algorithm versus 2-Model Comparison (Fig. 6.15)

```
%zero-slope vs. unity-slope model comparison: (1) no unknown
param values
clear %#ok<*UNRCH>
reset=1; saveFLAG=0; plotFLAG=1; verifysigFLAG=0;
COL=[.55*[1 1 1]; .3 .4 .85; .8 .5 .4];
    N=6; Nrep=251; Nrot=25; Nmod=2;
    sig=15; Ns=401; slist=sig; %noise level
    %betas=linspace(0,1,201); betas=betas(2:end-1);
    %diffs=[diff(slist(1:2)) diff(betas(1:2))];
    thetas=linspace(-100,100,N);
    rotlist=atan(linspace(0,1,Nrot));

    %keep noise samples identical across simulations for clearer comparison
    eorig=nrand(0,sig,[Nrep N]);
    dorig=[thetas(:) zeros(N,1)];

margL=nan(Nrot,Nmod,Nrep); Elist=nan(Nrot,Nmod,Nrep);
Plist=nan(Nrot,Nrep); if verifysigFLAG, sest=zeros(Nrot,Nmod); end
for irot=1:Nrot, rotnow=rotlist(irot);
    for irep=1:Nrep,
        %%%%%%%%R%%%%%%%
        %%% DATA SIM %%%
        dnow=rot(dorig,rotnow);
        %delta-squared is either just (deviation from 0)^2,
                %or it is (deviation from unity-line)^2
        tnow=dnow(:,1)'; dnow=dnow(:,2)'+eorig(irep,:);
        deltStr{1}='dnow.^2'; deltStr{2}='(dnow-tnow).^2';
        for nn=1:size(Elist,2),
            eval(['D2=' deltStr{nn} ';'])
            eval(['likeFN' num2str(nn-1) '=-(N/2)*...
                (mean(D2,2)./slist.^2)-(N+1)*log(slist);']); end

        %%%%%%%%%%%%%%%%%%%%%%%%%%%
        %%% Stat'l significance %%%
        tbl=table(tnow',dnow'-mean(dnow),'Variable Names',...
                {'x','y'}); %fit the null model (fitlm requires table datatype)
        ttt=fitlm(tbl,'linear'); %returns ttt struct, which
            %contains 'Coefficients' table for the fit of the null model
        Plist(irot,irep)=ttt.Coefficients.pValue(2); %p-value for null zero-slope model

        %%%%%%%%%%%%%%%%%%%%%%%%%
        %%% Model likelihoods %%%
        margL(irot,2,irep)=likeFN1; %marginal likelihood of the
                %unity-slope model, over unknown SD
        margL(irot,1,irep)=likeFN0;
        %marginal likelihood of the zero-slope model, over %unknown SD
        Elist(irot,1:2,irep)=evid(margL(irot,:,irep)); end, end
if plotFLAG,
    Hlist=Plist<.05;
    BLU=[.3 .4 .65]; Glist=[.1 .5 .75];
    figure(1); clf; hold on
    plot([.2 .8],[0 0],'k--','LineWidth',1.75);
    axis([-.05 1.05 -900 900]);
    for nn=1:Nmod, emed=median(Elist(:,nn,:),3);
        imed3=find(emed>3);
        plot(tan(rotlist(imed3))',emed(imed3),'o',...
            'MarkerFaceColor',BLU,'MarkerEdgeColor',BLU,'MarkerSize',13);
```

```
        plot(tan(rotlist)'*ones(1,Nrep),squeeze(Elist(:,nn,:)),'k.');
        plot(tan(rotlist)',emed,'ko:','MarkerFaceColor',...
            Glist(nn)*[1 1 1],'MarkerSize',9); end
    xlabel('data slope','FontName','Arial','FontSize',15);
    ylabel('evidence (db)','FontName','Arial','FontSize',15);

    figure(2); clf; hold on; plot([0 1],[0 0],'k--')
    for nn=1:Nmod,
    plot(tan(rotlist)'*ones(1,Nrep),squeeze(margL(:,nn,:)),'.','Color',Glist(nn)*[1 1 1])
    plot(tan(rotlist),median(squeeze(margL(:,nn,:)),2),
        'ko:','MarkerFaceColor',Glist(nn)*[1 1 1],'MarkerSize',13); end
    xlabel('data slope','FontName','Arial','FontSize',15); xlim([-.05 1.05])
    ylabel('mod likelihood','FontName','Arial','FontSize',15); ylim([-150 0])

    figure(3); clf; hold on
    nn=1;
    plot(tan(rotlist)'*ones(1,Nrep),Plist,'.','Color',Glist(nn)*[1 1 1])
    plot(tan(rotlist),mean(Plist,2),'ko:','MarkerFaceColor',...
        Glist(nn)*[1 1 1],'MarkerSize',13);
    plot([0 1],.05*[1 1],'k--','LineWidth',1.75)
    xlabel('data slope','FontName','Arial','FontSize',15);
    ylabel('p-value','FontName','Arial','FontSize',15);
    axis([-.05 1.05 -.02 1.02]); end
```

One option for the frequentist algorithm is to maintain the same null model as above (Fig. 6.15b, upper). This case is instructive because it emphasizes that the frequentist algorithm takes no account of the viable alternative hypotheses that could explain the data, instead focusing on a single 'null model' that we explicitly expect is *not* correct. Because this null model is identical to the null model in the previous example, a frequentist analysis yields *no change whatsoever* in its computations or outputs, as it requires that all parameter values are known and instead assumes that the data are unknown (i.e., when you base your analysis on the sampling distribution). The frequentist algorithm must still, even in this expanded case, define a single null hypothesis, and a confidence interval around this value to compare the data-fitted slope. The marginalization operation, which we have found an indispensable part of all but the simplest toy problems of data analysis, is unavailable within the frequentist algorithm. Although you might argue that a null model defined as $\beta = 0$ is not the best choice here (and we will explore a better one below), it is nevertheless telling that adding additional models to the comparison will always have absolutely no effect on the frequentist hypothesis testing algorithm across all cases in which the null model may be maintained. Notice that evidence is reduced overall under the model comparison algorithm in this case (Fig. 6.15c, right), because here we don't know the exact slope predicted in two of the models, and allowing yourself to fit this value to the data gives you additional 'explanatory power' that must be guarded against. The model comparison algorithm naturally accounts for this and lowers the evidence for these models appropriately (the ordinate covers a smaller range overall). The frequentist algorithm ignores these subtleties and uses the identical test in the two cases.

Finally, if we want to choose a null frequentist model that is at least part of the set of viable models, we may instead choose the $\beta = 0.5$ model to define the frequentist null hypothesis in this second example. It is interesting that when we choose this as the

Programming Aside: Frequentist Algorithm versus 3-Model Comparison (Fig. 6.15)

```
clear %#ok<*UNRCH>
reset=1; saveFLAG=0; plotFLAG=1; verifysigFLAG=0;
COL=[.55*[1 1 1]; .3 .4 .85; .8 .5 .4];
    N=6; Nrep=251; Nrot=25; Nmod=3;

    sig=15; Ns=401; slist=linspace(0,101,Ns+1)'; slist=slist(2:end); %noise level
    blist=linspace(0,1,201); %slopes used to approximate the
         %underlying continuous slope dimension
    rotlist=atan(linspace(0,1,Nrot));
    %slopes to use
    diffs=[diff(slist(1:2)) diff(blist(1:2))];
    thetas=linspace(-100,100,N);

    %keep noise samples identical across simulations for
    clearer comparison
    eorig=nrand(0,sig,[Nrep N]);
    dorig=[thetas(:) zeros(N,1)]; end

if verifysigFLAG, sest=zeros(Nrot,Nmod); end
margL=nan(Nrot,Nmod,Nrep); Elist=nan(Nrot,Nmod,Nrep);
Emax=nan(Nrot,Nmod); Plist=nan(Nrot,Nrep);
p1blistmat2=(1+ones(Ns,1)*blist.^2); Ipri=[.4636 .3217];
for irot=1:Nrot, rotnow=rotlist(irot);
    for irep=1:Nrep,
        %%%%%%%%R%%%%%%%
        %%% DATA SIM %%%
        dnow=rot(dorig,rotnow);
        %delta-squared is either just (deviation from 0)^2,
        %or it is (deviation from unity-line)^2
        tnow=dnow(:,1)'; dnow=dnow(:,2)'+eorig(irep,:);
        deltStr{1}='dnow.^2'; deltStr{2}='(dnow-betas(n)*tnow).^2';

        %%%%%%%%%%%%%%%%%%%%%%%%%%%%%%%%%%%%
        %%% param likelihood by condition %%%
        likeFN0=nan(Ns,sum(blist<.5)); likeFN1=nan(Ns,sum(blist>.5));
        for n=1:sum(blist<=.5),
            tmp=-(N/2)*(mean((dnow-blist(n )*tnow).^2,2)./...
                slist.^2)-(N+1)*log(slist); %L term
            likeFN0(:, n)=tmp-log(Ipri(1)*p1blistmat2(:,n)); end
            %add prior term (normalized by Ipri)
        for nn=0:sum(blist>.5)-1,
            tmp=-(N/2)*(mean((dnow-blist(nn+n+1)*tnow).^2,2)./...
                slist.^2)-(N+1)*log(slist); %L term
            likeFN1(:,nn+1)=tmp-log(Ipri(2)*p1blistmat2(:,n)); end
            %add prior term (normalized by Ipri)
%       Lall0=-(N/2)*(mean((dnow-0.0*tnow).^2,2)./slist.^2)-(N+1)*log(slist);
%       Lall1=-(N/2)*(mean((dnow-1.0*tnow).^2,2)./slist.^2)-(N+1)*log(slist);

        %%%%%%%%%%%%%%%%%%%%%%%%%%%%%%%%%%%%%
        %%% param likelihood by condition %%%
        Lall0=logsum(likeFN0,2,diffs(2));
        Lall1=logsum(likeFN1,2,diffs(2));
        Lall5=-(N/2)*(mean((dnow-0.5*tnow).^2,2)./slist.^2)-(N+1)*log(slist);

        if verifysigFLAG,
            %%%%%%%%%%%%%%%%%%%%%%%%%%%
```

```
            %%% verify global sigma %%%
            sest(irot,2)=logpeakval([Lall1 slist]);
            sest(irot,1)=logpeakval([Lall0 slist]); end

        %%%%%%%%%%%%%%%%%%%%%%%%%%%
        %%% Stat'l significance %%%
        tbl=table(tnow',dnow'-mean(dnow),'VariableNames',...
            {'x','y'}); %fit the null model (fitlm requires table datatype)
        ttt=fitlm(tbl,'linear'); %returns ttt struct, which
        %contains 'Coefficients' table for the fit of the null model
        Plist(irot,irep)=ttt.Coefficients.pValue(2);
        %p-vallue for null (zero-slope) model

        %%%%%%%%%%%%%%%%%%%%%%%%%
        %%% Model likelihoods %%%
        margL(irot,3,irep)=logsum(Lall5,1,diffs(1));
        %marginal likelihood of the 0.5-slope model
        margL(irot,2,irep)=logsum(Lall1,1,diffs(1));
        %marginal likelihood of the unity-slope model, over unknown SD and slope
        margL(irot,1,irep)=logsum(Lall0,1,diffs(1));
        %marginal likelihood of the zero-slope model, over unknown SD and slope
        Elist(irot,1:Nmod,irep)=evid(margL(irot,1:Nmod,irep)); end, end

if plotFLAG,
    Hlist=Plist<.05;
    BLU=[.3 .4 .65]; Glist=[.1 .5 .75];
    figure(1); clf; hold on
    plot([.2 .8],[0 0],'k--','LineWidth',1.75);
    axis([-.05 1.05 -150 150]);
    for nn=1:Nmod, emed=median(Elist(:,nn,:),3);
    imed3=find(emed>3);
    plot(tan(rotlist(imed3))',emed(imed3),'o',...
        'MarkerFaceColor',BLU,'MarkerEdgeColor',BLU,'MarkerSize',13);
    plot(tan(rotlist)'*ones(1,Nrep), squeeze(Elist(:,nn,:)),'k.');
    plot(tan(rotlist)',emed,'ko:','MarkerFaceColor',...
        Glist(nn)*[1 1 1],'MarkerSize',9); end
    xlabel('data slope','FontName','Arial','FontSize',15);
    ylabel('evidence (db)','FontName','Arial','FontSize',15);

    figure(2); clf; hold on; plot([0 1],[0 0],'k--')
    for nn=1:Nmod,
        plot(tan(rotlist)'*ones(1,Nrep),squeeze...
            (margL(:,nn,:)),'.','Color',Glist(nn)*[1 1 1])
        plot(tan(rotlist),median(squeeze(margL(:,nn,:)),2),...
            'ko:','MarkerFaceColor',Glist(nn)*[1 1 1],'MarkerSize',13); end
    xlabel('data slope','FontName','Arial','FontSize',15); xlim([-.05 1.05])
    ylabel('mod likelihood','FontName','Arial','FontSize',15); ylim([-30 0])

    figure(3); clf; hold on
    nn=1;
    plot(tan(rotlist)'*ones(1,Nrep),Plist,'.','Color',Glist(nn)*[1 1 1])
    plot(tan(rotlist),mean(Plist,2),'ko:','MarkerFaceColor',...
        Glist(nn)*[1 1 1],'MarkerSize',13);
    plot([0 1],.05*[1 1],'k--','LineWidth',1.75)
    xlabel('data slope','FontName','Arial','FontSize',15);
    ylabel('p-value','FontName','Arial','FontSize',15);
    xlim([-.05 1.05]); ylim([-.02 1.02])
```

frequentist 'null model,' the frequentist algorithm drifts even further from being a useful hypothesis-testing tool. Under this null model (Fig. 6.15b, lower), the frequentist algorithm is unable to find statistically reliable differences between data and the null in all but a few cases: in about the ranges $1 > \beta > 0.95$ and $0.15 > \beta > 0$.

Conceptually, the analysis of these models is quite different under the model comparison algorithm, and the poor performance of the frequentist algorithm should be contrasted with the reliably above-threshold result of the model comparison algorithm seen at all but a few cases (bottom right panel of Fig. 6.15c). Within the model comparison algorithm there is no need to formulate just the right model that we don't believe, with all punctate parameters, that we would like to disprove. Instead, we need only formulate models that are theoretically interesting and logically plausible. Is this really the big difference between the two algorithms? Although one must, of course, acknowledge subtleties in the answer to this question, I nevertheless think it is clear from a comparison of the null model results in the two examples given here what characterizes the major difference: The frequentist algorithm cannot take account of the models we actually care to test - particularly if there are multiple models worth testing, or if there are unknown parameter values in those models. In other words, it cannot correctly account for and model the subtleties involved in nearly any realistic scientific hypothesis test.

Exercises

1) Describe the difference between finding $|evid| < 3dB$ under the model comparison algorithm and $p > \alpha$ under the frequentist hypothesis testing algorithm.
2) In the 3-model comparison the $\beta = .5$ model is always at least the second-best choice. Explain why it is never the worst of the three choices.
3) In the 3-model comparison, change the variance of a noisy dataset drawn from a slope=.9 model. Plot and describe any changes in computed p-values as variance changes, as well as any changes in the evidence computed from the model comparison algorithm from the same data.

Example: Measurement as Hypothesis Testing

The outline of the frequentist algorithm relies on a method of hypothesis testing whereby a model is judged based on the sampling probabilities predicted by a 'null model.' In general, this method relies on two pieces of information: the confidence interval around the 'canonical prediction' of the null hypothesis (using the data variance) and the observed data. If the observed data are expected to occur with a lower frequency than the α-cutoff level, the null hypothesis is rejected.

One issue we have previously identified with this method is clearly its failure to move beyond sampling distributions in favor of likelihoods, priors and posteriors as dictated by (1.5). In other words, we care much more about the probabilities of the *parameters* relevant to the models we are testing than of the *datasets* under a null model. To remedy this we may, instead of comparing the observed dataset to a 'canonical dataset' predicted by the null model, compare the fitted value of a model parameter to the 'canonical parameter value' predicted by the null model. So let us examine this as a possible fix for the frequentist algorithm in the same example problem detailed above.

Programming Aside: Measurement as Model Comparison

```
S=34;
F=19;
N=S+F;
f=linspace(0,1,1201)';

%%%%%%%%%%%%%%%%%%%%%%%%%%%%
%%% 1d f distribution %%%
Lf=(S-.5)*log(f)+(F-.5)*log(1-f); Lf=Lf-max(Lf);
ciF=CIp(f,Lf);
figure(1); clf
subplot(2,1,1); hold on
plot(f,exp(Lf),'k--','LineWidth',1.75); dciF=diff(ciF(1:2));axis([0 1 0 1])
for n=1:2, plot(ciF(n)*[1 1],[0 1],'-','Color',.65*[1 1 1],'LineWidth',.7); end
```

Evidence Calculation

```
%%% compute evidence from N and S
L1=bpdf(S,N,theta); L2=(N+1)^-1;
EV=10*log10(L1/L2)
```

There will be two steps we must complete: first, we fit the parameters of the null model, and then we compare the confidence interval around this measurement to determine whether to reject this model. The logic of this Bayes-updated test is essentially that of the original frequentist algorithm, in that we are assuming the truth of a null model and then rejecting that model if the confidence bound of the fitted parameter value(s) does not encompass the 'canonical parameter value(s)' predicted by the null model. This updated frequentist testing method therefore has most of the same theoretical disadvantages of the frequentist algorithm (chiefly, its deviation from the correct logic of the 'proof by contradiction' method of deductive reasoning and failure to directly compare alternative models), but has the *practical* advantage of dealing with proper posterior probabilities and allowing us to marginalize over nuisance parameters.

This analog of the frequentist method, upgrading from sampling probabilities to posteriors, would base its hypothesis test on whether the canonical parameter value predicted by the null model is encompassed by $100(1-\alpha)$ percent of the probability mass of the posterior over the fit to the parameter based on the observed data. We will *not* expect that this modified procedure for model comparison will prove wildly successful, however, since it will nevertheless continue the frequentist algorithm's failure to compute the probabilities of to-be-compared models – now relying on proxy information contained in the probabilities from one model's parameter fit.

The major problem with this method is simple, if somewhat subtle. The posterior distribution from which the confidence interval (CI) is constructed assumes a model, and that model cannot both be M_1 and M_2 – otherwise the models would be identical. For example, if the posterior used to construct this CI assumes $\delta = 0$ (which is what happens in the frequentist hypothesis testing algorithm), the resulting CI will not also be a CI for the model in which we assume $\delta \neq 0$. Similarly, if the CI is constructed assuming $\delta \neq 0$ it cannot tell us the CI for the model in which $\delta = 0$. Finally, assuming

$0 \leq \delta \leq 1$ as a model from which the CI is constructed would be inconsistent with both M_1 and M_2.

There are discrepancies between the significance indicated by the Bayes-adjusted frequentist algorithm and the logically correct model comparison algorithm, even in this simplest case of the binomial rate parameter under the null model predicting $\theta = 0.5$ and the model predicting a rate in the set $\theta \neq 0.5$. Although each case could be different, there is little reason to expect that other model comparisons will yield results whose significance under this modified frequentist algorithm will match the evidence cutoff under the model comparison algorithm, both because this is one of the simplest model comparisons that would be expected to produce that match if anything would, and also because the two algorithms are making computations under very different assumptions. The model comparison algorithm is computing the probability of each model separately under the data and the assumptions of the to-be-compared models, whereas our modified frequentist algorithm is computing probabilities of parameters (a rate parameter in this example) under a model that matches the assumptions of *neither* of the models under consideration (it permits parameters that are disallowed by both models).

Exercises

1) Create a version of the PA where evidence just passes the 3dB criterion:
   a. what are the data, and what is the location of the peak of the rate parameter?
   b. what are the upper and lower bounds of the confidence interval?
2) Perform a Gaussian location version of the comparison above, by creating a model that assumes a location parameter at zero, and one that does not, with bounded standard deviation values.
3) Extend Ex. 2 to the case of a straight-line fit, where the null model assumes a zero slope and the alternative is a nonzero slope.

6.6.2 Pitfalls of the Frequentist Algorithm as Used in Practice

We have shown multiple arguments highlighting the failings of the frequentist algorithm on theoretical grounds. On the practical side, there are well-known difficulties implementing and interpreting its results due to the convoluted complexity of the algorithm. The combination of its theoretical failings and complex implementation and interpretation has led to certain gray-area practices. These practices have sprung up largely because it is unclear to most analysts exactly *why* they should be avoided – or at least used pointedly, and with caution. Exploitation of these gray-area practices can easily lead to large-scale unreplicability, diminishing our view of the science in the process. We will examine the two most common such practices below.

Example: The Fishing Expedition

The mathematics of the frequentist algorithm, which is intended for model comparison, is focused on 'statistical tests' for large sets of experimental variables, a paradigm that naturally yields many statistical tests per experiment – this is in contrast to an experiment-level model comparison algorithm that yields a very small number of model comparisons per experiment (often just one). In other words, the model comparison algorithm lends itself most directly to experiments that provide a single, preplanned, theoretically motivated comparison of two or more models. The antithesis of this type of experiment is the 'fishing expedition.' The fishing expedition is either an experiment that is theoretically unmotivated, except by the notion that 'some of these variables will be important for behavior *x*,' or an experiment in which there are a great many variables that are recorded in addition to a small number of theoretically motivated variables. These experiments are designed to 'test the significance of' every such variable, and the analysis is centered on determining, via a great many statistical tests, which of the experimental variables might predict 'important features' of the behavior. The nebulous goal of 'finding anything interesting' in the data is often better suited to an informal data visualization step (Fig. 1.3) of your research program than to a formal hypothesis-testing stage, because it is easy to find 'something' interesting in a dataset;[17] the important question is whether that something fits into a model or theoretical framework, and whether those model-relevant results were cherry-picked from a larger set of model-irrelevant or even model-contradictory results, and for that we need formal model comparison techniques.

When you read the scientific literature, you should be equipped with a few basic tools to identify fishing-expedition-style research, and interpret/value the results of such experiments accordingly. There are two important hallmarks of the fishing expedition: (1) Too many variables unjustified by theory, and (2) Just-so explanation: The hypothesis, while brand new, is nevertheless just complex enough to 'explain' every finding in the data.

1. When you have no *specific* model that you intend to test, your experiment is likely based on a vague impression that certain variables might be linked. In this case, you design an experiment that allows you to collect data on as many of these variables as possible, to determine which might indeed be linked. The result is very light on theoretical justification for the specific experiments performed and/or variables observed, and instead is focused on measurement of possible associations among the great many variables observed experimentally. Your first indication will therefore be that the set of observations does not seem 'on point' with respect to the model being studied, because instead of forming a coherent examination of that model, there will be many 'orphan' variables and analyses that do not contribute to the overall question being answered by the experiment.

2. The second thing to look for is a 'just-so' explanation of data, which is an indication of *post hoc* theorizing. The issue here is that the hypothesis is introduced as the motivation for the research when it is really the other way round: the hypothesis was motivated by the data. If the data you observe experimentally are used to form an hypothesis regarding interrelationships among those data, and then the experiment is reported as if it was designed to test that (data driven) hypothesis, the experiment will appear to provide support for the hypothesis - and that support will often seem 'unusually good.' The problem with post hoc theorizing is that it does not honestly report the difference between theory/model building and exploration (e.g., via the fishing expedition) and theory/model

[17] Recall again the mathematics of false-positive results: If you have 20 variables that have no interesting features themselves or pairwise connections, you nevertheless have $20 + \binom{20}{2} = 210$ opportunities for false positive results. If false positive results occur in 5 percent of cases (i.e., corresponding to a statistical α - level of 0.05), then you should expect to observe 10 positive results even if there are no real results to be found in your dataset.

testing (via tailored research), and these separate activities have their own characteristics, pitfalls, and contributions in the overall scientific enterprise.

These are obviously subjective criteria, but the issues to which they point are nevertheless surprisingly easy to spot once you are aware of them. With some experience, you will develop a strong sense of the difference between experiments that describe and test *specific* hypotheses (models and/or parameter values) that are theoretically motivated, rather than analyses that are motivated by vague and unspecific 'expectations of effects' that have no detailed underlying model or theory to support them. Similarly, you will sometimes find yourself surprised by the specificity of the predictions made at the start of a report, arising when predictions are not strongly theory-driven, nor the result of extensive earlier work, only to find that every one of those predictions is supported in the analysis (the 'just-so' theory). These situations strongly suggest a fishing expedition.

As an example of this type of problem, imagine conducting an experiment at your university's cafeteria. In this cafeteria, one pays once to enter, and may select as much food as desired. In your experiment you arrange to charge one price to some individuals and a higher price to others, looking for an effect of the price of the meal on the amount eaten. Testing this theory for a full dinner service yields a large dataset of 300 students in each group (high/low meal price). Unfortunately, your theory does not seem to hold, because the statistical test comes out with $p = 0.21$. Disappointed, you wonder if perhaps your theory would hold, but only for particular subgroups of the students: perhaps only the men or women, or freshmen, or the underweight/ overweight, or perhaps only student athletes or those who use salt/pepper. There are quite a few options for making such distinctions, and a motivated analyst could easily keep testing until *some* significant effect was found. The error of the fishing expedition is that *any* such significant result would be reported as a confirmation of the theory.

Some strongly negative statements have just been made regarding fishing-expedition style studies. Is this experiment type always bad? The truth is that, no, it is not. Sometimes, particularly at the start of a research program when a new phenomenon is just being discovered and investigated, a fishing expedition is warranted so that we can obtain a general sense of the likely determinants of the behavior, or what its general characteristics might be: that is, for early theory-building and 'pilot studies'. However, such experiments should always be followed by a series of theoretically motivated, tailored experiments that verify the results of the fishing expedition and further test the theory that was so built. Otherwise, it is easy for the fishing expedition to insert false-positive (or negative) results into the literature that go unchecked by tailored/directed research.[18]

Exercises

1) Look up the 'Framingham heart study' and argue for whether it is or is not a fishing expedition.
2) Note that there is nothing (except funding) to stop one from looking for 'interesting effects' *in addition to* testing a tailored hypothesis based on extensive previous research. Describe ways one might discriminate between a fishing expedition and this case.

[18] Also, it reeks of intellectual sloth when one specializes in these experiments, rather than executing tailored experiments designed to directly (and elegantly) test single hypotheses or perform preplanned measurements.

3) One proposal to guard against the fishing expedition is a 'registered experiment,' in which the experimental method is registered with some government or governing body that maintains an un- alterable list of such experiments. Give three pros and cons of this proposal.

Example: p-Hacking

The problem of ***p-hacking*** is very much related to the problems that occur in the fishing expedition. Here, however, the underlying issue is that multiple variants of a frequentist analysis are defined and tested with the goal of finding a variant of the analysis that yields a statistically significant result (i.e., one that yields a p-value below your predefined α-criterion; see Box 2.3.2). This phenomenon is a by-product of the fact that apparently equivalent frequentist analyses do not in general yield identical statistical conclusions, which is itself a by-product of the logical break in the frequentist algorithm (i.e., the same root cause of the optional stopping problem, as detailed in Chapter 2). To state it simply, the frequentist program offers a menu of statistical tests from which to choose when analyzing data, and alternative choices will sometimes mean the difference between being able to report a 'statistically significant' result and not. Despite this inequality of outcomes for alternative analyses, there is no real check on such selection practices,[19] because there is often no compelling reason to prefer one or another of these apparently equivalent alternative statistical tests under the frequentist program of data analysis.

This is a gray area precisely because of the apparent equivalence of the statistical tests involved. When there are multiple statistical tests that can be used for a single purpose (and it is well known that their results may differ), it is natural that several such tests will be tried. This is particularly true because, within the frequentist algorithm, one is encouraged to alter frequentist procedures based on the shape of the observed data histogram. This is done, for example when instead of appearing to be 'a Gaussian-distributed sample,'[20] the sample appears Rayleigh-distributed or perhaps F-distributed (all different sampling distributions). This additional freedom to try multiple versions of the analysis increases the tendency for false-positive results. And this problem will naturally become invisible and therefore also exacerbated when only significant results and their corresponding analyses are reported publicly.

The best example comes from our analysis of the optional stopping problem in Chapter 2, because there is essentially no simpler problem in data analysis. The binomial distribution is easily selected from prior information about the problem with little or no controversy, and under the frequentist program the analysis to be performed is clear – we are interested in whether the data differ from the (null) model prediction. Despite

[19] Although not yet widely implemented, it is possible to 'register' one's experiment and analysis with the NIH or other official body prior to performing an experiment and analysis, which (assuming the timing of the experiment and analysis is correctly reported) could serve as such a check. However, this solution relies on standards of professional conduct, just as does any prohibition against p-hacking itself, and therefore would rely on oversight from a currently nonexistent licensing body.

[20] Of course we know that the shape of the likelihood function (and coressponding sampling distribution) is more a theoretical construct than an empirical matter (and we are also aware of the fact that data samples do not have a sampling distribution of their own – they are samples *from* an underlying distribution), and should therefore ideally be determined from theoretical arguments.

all this, there is one option open to the statistician: whether to perform a hypothesis test based on the binomial or negative binomial distribution. As we saw previously, there is good reason to view these distributions as interchangeable: they have the identical likelihood distribution. However, let's imagine that you've just completed a drug trial for a vaccine against a form of malaria that kills half of infected people. Furthermore, this has been an extremely expensive and difficult experiment, because there are very few people with this particular variant of the disease. Thus, at the end of the experiment, you have vaccinated 31 individuals who have subsequently contracted this form of malaria, and of those, you have seen 11 deaths. You want to know if there is statistically significant evidence that the vaccine is effective.

You have observed 31 instances relevant to your experiment and want to determine whether 11 deaths is consistent with the null hypothesis $H_0 = 0.5$. You recall from the flowchart you memorized in your frequentist statistics course that when you have a discrete number of instances and observations, you can use the binomial sampling distribution to test null hypotheses. That is, you want to know if, among the vaccinated population, there is a death rate lower than the 50 percent seen in the general (unvaccinated) population. Computing the sampling distribution of the binomial distribution with 31 observations, you obtain plots analogous to those in Figure 2.4. Unfortunately, your result is not significant: the p-value is greater than the alpha level, at $\mathrm{p} = 0.075$. Disappointed, you consider alternative ways of looking at your data and recall that there is an analogous test against a rate of 0.5 that depends on observing S successes in N observations, but based on the negative binomial distribution. As both distributions are used to test null hypotheses about success rates, you see no harm in trying this out – they appear to test the same thing, after all. As you should have guessed, the negative binomial frequentist test against the null hypothesis $H_0 = 0.5$ is now below threshold, $p < 0.05$, and you happily publish your 'statistically significant' result.

Although this is a straightforward example of p-hacking, it is by no means particularly egregious. Clever statisticians have developed multiple versions of statistical tests, parametric and nonparametric,[21] or that assume hetero-/homoscedasticity[22] – and that's just the tip of the iceberg. Indeed, the topic of selecting the 'correct' statistical test can be quite as convoluted as the definition of the p-value or the frequentist hypothesis testing algorithm itself. It is the nature of having so many 'nearly equivalent' testing procedures that a gray area will develop, particularly for those who are unfamiliar with the differences between tests (i.e., when one only relies on prepackaged software to guide their analyses) that will lead to practices like p-hacking. Indeed, one would imagine that most instances of these gray-area practices are committed unknowingly and with no attempt to deceive.

The phenomenon of p-hacking simply does not occur when following a research program dictated by Figure 1.3, based on the measurement and model comparison algorithms. There is logically only one way to answer a given question via (1.5), whether

[21] 'Parametric' is the label given to frequentist tests that are based on a Gaussian sampling distribution. It gives some indication of the pervasive use of the Gaussian sampling distribution when we consider that the alternative to a parametric statistical test is a 'nonparametric' test, which can be based on *any* of the other sampling distributions.

[22] Homoscedasticity refers to uniform or equal variances, either between groups or across subgroups.

model comparison or measurement, and alterations of one's analysis will cause a *different question* to be asked or different model to be tested by the data, because either your model of the underlying behavior has changed or your definition of the behavior itself has changed. This is a basic principle of logical consistency: equivalent analyses must yield the same result, or they are not equivalent. Our program of analysis simply does not offer the same smorgasbord of choices, used equivalently, as under the frequentist program of data analysis, by which one could be led down the path of p-hacking. Any alteration of the analysis that changes the result does so because you have performed *different analyses* in the two instances.

Exercises

1) Define p-hacking and give two general instances of its use.
2) Develop an experimental scenario not involving the binomial distribution, and discuss how p-hacking might be used to encourage a statistically significant result.

6.6.3 The Full Monty

After surveying some of the many ways that things can go awry during hypothesis testing, it is a good idea to take a moment to reorient ourselves to the program laid out in Figure 1.3. In particular, we should consider the full course of an investigation and be aware of the various paths that might take.

The first step of the program involves model building and simulation. This is a critical component because our evidence calculations are only useful to the extent that we are comparing *all* viable models. This issue was discussed at some length in Section 6.3.1, in our first full model comparison calculations involving binomial rates, because defining the terms M_1 and $\overline{M_1}$ requires us to honestly admit that our conclusions are limited by the fact that we have excluded as impossible all models that we have not included in those two terms. The first stage of Figure 1.3, along with the first stage of the model comparison algorithm, is designed to get us thinking about potential models. The simulation stage of Figure 1.3, in particular, is designed to do this, because the simulated outputs of a model may surprise us in certain ways that will lead us to formulate additional models, or to discard a model that we had previously thought was viable, or both.

Once we feel we are comparing the full set of viable models, we proceed with the calculations that have occupied us for the bulk of this chapter. But making those calculations is by no means the end of the story. Particularly in the behavioral sciences, we can be virtually certain that any model we propose is wrong in some way, either because that model is incomplete and requires tweaking (the Ptolemaic response) or because entirely new models are needed (the Copernican response). This is the purpose of the dashed arrow in Figure 1.3 connecting the horizontal and vertical analysis arms. The end of model comparison is not simply an evidence number but rather a series of calculations that places that evidence calculation into the context of our simulations. Does the computed evidence favor neither model? How does this relate to the simulations that we performed prior to our experiments (such as those allowing us to make Figs. 6.8c, 6.9b,c, 6.10b,c, etc.)? Is this because there are aspects of the data that were unanticipated? If the evidence strongly favors one model, then which aspects of the data push the evidence calculation toward that model? Are there ways to determine if those elements of the data are stable and replicable, perhaps by analyzing extant data from other experiments? Are there patterns in the results that are ignored (i.e., not predicted) by our current crop of models?

Model comparison and measurement calculations are important elements of this overall program, but it is only in exploring the details of our result and answering these types of questions that we complete an analysis. It is this full picture, evidence and measurement computations along with the answers to questions such as those posed above, that will ultimately lead us to reset to the first stage of Figure 1.3, pitting new and/or improved models against one another in new experiments tailored to the predictions of those new models. Each cycle of this process should help us to refine our thinking about the mechanisms underlying behavior and move our state of knowledge forward – sometimes gradually through small refinements of theory, and sometimes through revolutionary rethinking of basic assumptions that produce entirely novel theories.

6.6.4 Where Do We Go from Here?

Our entrée into the arena of modern scientific data analysis began with computing simple probabilities associated with coin tosses and die throws in Chapters 1 and 2 and quickly progressed to using these probabilities to describe our information about the parameters of scientific models. We learned, in particular, how experimental data inform us regarding scientific models and how those data can be used either to estimate the parameters of a known model via the measurement algorithm or to evaluate alternative models of a given behavioral phenomenon via the model comparison algorithm.

We have also noted pitfalls of alternative hypothesis testing algorithms, particularly noting that the technical and practical pitfalls of using the frequentist algorithm do not occur as naturally when following the program outlined in Figure 1.3. Despite this, I nevertheless do not want to present the current program as a panacea against all error or abuse. Indeed, we should note that some of the in-practice misuses/abuses of the frequentist algorithm could easily occur with the model comparison algorithm, although perhaps not as naturally. How do we guard against these, and enforce standards of professional competency and conduct? The typical method of introducing such standards is via licensure (e.g., medical, dental, and nursing licenses). This would seem to be a reasonable route to take here as well for professional scientists, particularly given that behavioral and biomedical research has the potential to lead to clinical trials and drug development. However, until such time as a scientific licensing board is able to enforce standards, we can only remain vigilant against the gray-area practices defined above by being aware of their existence and methods of implementation.

Finally, we should recognize that we have really only scratched the surface of the complexity of fascinating applications based on the measurement and model comparison algorithms. Now, after having dealt with the relatively basic applications outlined here, we are ready to explore a broader range of questions for which we will find applications of Bayes' theorem, and probability theory generally, useful. One of the first problems that must be tackled is that of comparing two data samples. We examined some basic applications of this type above, but such comparisons occur in many contexts, and there are complications involved in the logic and implementation of the full analysis that can turn this into an intermediate-level problem. In addition, while we have examined several basic straight-line model problems, there are additional straight-line models that take account of important nuances in the definition of the problem (models describing discrete and other data types) that are still to be explored. Finally, with some additional mathematics, we can examine spectral models that involve sinusoidal variation in data, which are extremely important in the analysis of difficult-to-detect model parameters and cyclical phenomena.

APPENDIX A

CODING BASICS

Many students will have some familiarity with writing code: a skill which is more and more becoming an essential tool for students in engineering and the sciences. Here we will learn some of the basic programming knowledge to get you started with some of the basics that will serve us throughout this text. We will write our code in the MATLAB® programming language. This language is commonly used in neuroscience and engineering departments for signal processing and other data analysis applications.

MATLAB® is an application that you can think of as a virtual robot helper. You tell it to do things for you, and it does them quickly and without error. There are only two caveats to keep in mind when telling MATLAB® what you want: First, the things you ask for must be confined to the solutions of math problems and to drawing things (making figures). Second, you must learn to ask for what you want in just the right way - the programming equivalent of asking politely.

The first caveat will not be a problem for us, because the only things we will want it to do are solve math problems and draw plots of mathematical functions and data: exactly what MATLAB® enjoys most. The second caveat is a bit trickier, however. Just as when you visit a foreign country and want to ingratiate yourself with the locals by learning some basic phrases, MATLAB® frowns upon any request that is not given in *its* native language: MATLAB® code. Learning enough of that language to make correctly worded requests will be our first goal.

A.1 Add, Subtract, Multiply, Divide, Evaluate: How to Ask Arithmetic Questions

When you enter certain commands into MATLAB®, you might do best if you think of it as asking a question, as in: 'what is the product of 7 and 8?', or 'what is the sum of all the numbers in this list?'. These types of commands will often be the whole point of interacting with a computer to begin with, and so we will start here.

Most of these commands cast MATLAB® in the role of a fancy calculator. Thus, you can type:

```
>> 8*7
```

to find 'the product of eight and seven,' or:

```
>> 3+1
```

for 'the sum of three and one,' or:

```
>> 2^9
```

to compute 'two raised to the ninth power.'

For the multiplication-based operations, *,^, and /, there is an additional complication when you are multiplying lists of numbers. Suppose you assign the list of numbers [1, 2, 1] to the variable x:

```
>> x=[1 2 1];
```

and you want to multiply this list by the list y = [2 4 6]. You place a '.' next to the multiplication symbol to indicate that you want the products [1*2, 2*4, 1*6] rather than the matrix product x*y. The same holds true for exponentiation and division, and in most cases we will want .*, .^, and ./ instead of the matrix-based operations. To experience the difference, try the following:

```
>> y=[2 4 6];
>> x.*y
>> x*y'
>> x*y
>> y.^x
>> y./x
>> y/x
```

First, notice that one of these produces an error. This is because the matrix multiplication of a 1×3 and a 3×1 matrix (y' is the transpose of y) can be done (and produces a result with dimension 1×1), but a matrix multiply of a 1×3 and a 1×3 matrix cannot be done.

Exercises

1) Look up the 'sum' and 'prod' functions. Use them to compute:
   a. the sum of the elements in x
   b. the product of the elements of y
2) Look up the 'rand' function, and multiply a 1×2 list of random numbers with a second 1×2 list of random numbers.
3) Use the MATLAB® help to find out what operation was performed by y/x.

A.2 Assignment, Indexing, and Variable Types

Also notice the difference between ending a line with a semicolon and not. For example, the second line in the list above, which did not end in a semicolon, produced an output:

```
>> x*y'
ans =
    16
```

Ending an expression with a semicolon suppresses output, which is useful when writing a long list of connected expressions and you are only interested in the final output. In a very simple example, you might want to manually reproduce the calculations in this matrix multiply:

```
>> a=x(1)*y(1);
>> b=x(2)*y(2);
>> c=x(3)*y(3);
>> d=[a b c];
>> sum(d)
ans =
    16
```

There is a single output (answer) because we have a semicolon that suppresses the outputs on all but the last line. The first line assigns a new variable, a, the value 2. We could have had the same result by writing:

```
>> a=2;
```

We wrote this assignment the way we did to highlight the process of **indexing**, which means to select a part of a matrix by referring to its position. The first step to perform the matrix multiply is to find the product of the first elements of the x matrix and the y matrix. We next need the product of the second elements of x and y, which we assign to the variable b, and we assign the product of the third elements to the variable c. Finally, we assign the list of a, b, and c values to the variable d and ask for the sum of d as our output. Indexing can also be used to select sections of a matrix. Let's make a new matrix:

```
>> D=[1 2 3; 4 5 6; 7 8 9];
```

This is a 3×3 matrix (and is distinct from the variable d, defined above: MATLAB® is case-sensitive). Now let's try selecting portions of the matrix:

```
>> D(1:3,1)
>> D(2,1:3)
>> D(1:2,2:3)
```

You can see that the colon acts as a shorthand: it asks for the list of whole numbers that starts with the number before the colon and ends with the number after the colon. An even shorter shorthand can be used to ask for all the numbers that index a particular dimension of a matrix:

```
>> D(:,1)
>> D(2,:)
>> D(:)
```

The first two of these just repeat the longer-form indexing above (1:3). The last expression does something different. It asks for all the indices from all the dimensions of the matrix. We can also replace one of the matrix elements by putting a new value into an indexed position in the D matrix:

```
>> D(3,1)=0
```

Until now, all of our variables have been matrices (including 1×1 matrices). We created these matrices by writing numbers contained in square brackets. The second variable type with which we will want to become familiar is the cell. You can think of a cell as 'a bag of stuff.' It can contain numbers, letters, words, matrices, or even other cells. Let's create one and see how it works:

```
>> c=cell(2,3);
>> c
```

First, notice that we overwrote and erased the earlier c variable when we assigned the empty 2×3 cell to this variable name. MATLAB® doesn't warn you at all when you overwrite variables, so be careful and keep track of your variable names. Second, take a look at the new cell variable and notice that each of the cells in the cell array is contained in curly brackets. Indexing a cell array is two-tiered: first you indicate the cell, and then the position within the cell. So let's fill our cell array with some 'stuff' and give it a try:

```
>> c{1,1}=rand(2,2);
>> c{1,2}=rand(3);
>> c{1,3}=rand(4);
>> c{2,1}=cell(2);
>> c{2,2}={[],[]};
>> c{2,3}={'January','February','March'};
>> c
```

Now take a look at each cell in the array: In the first row, we've filled each cell with a matrix. You can look at what is in each cell by indexing within a curly bracket:

```
>> c{1,1}
>> c{1,2}
>> c{1,3}
```

and within each cell, you can select parts of each matrix by adding matrix indexing as above:

```
>> c{1,1}(1,:)
>> c{1,2}(2,2:3)
>> c{1,3}(2:3,3:4)
```

In the second row we've filled each cell with another cell. The first element of the second row is an empty 2×2 cell. The second element is filled with an empty 1×2 cell, but notice we've asked for these empty cells in two different ways. We can fill these cells-within-cells in the way you might have guessed: by referring to the appropriate double-curly-index. Let's put something in each of these empty cells:

```
>> c{2,1}{1,1}=zeros(2);
>> c{2,1}{1,2}=zeros(1,3);
>> c{2,1}{2,1}=ones(3);
>> c{2,1}{2,2}=3*ones(2,3);
>> c{2,2}{1}=ones(3,1)*[3 4 5 6];
>> c{2,2}{2}=[1 2 3]'*ones(1,4);
```

Now go ahead an check the contents of this second row of cells:

```
>> c{2,1}
>> c{2,1}{1,1}
>> c{2,1}{2,2}
>> c{2,2}{1}
>> c{2,2}{2}
>> c{2,3}
```

Exercises

1) Replace the elements of D(2:3,1:2) with random numbers using rand. Can this be accomplished with a single command? If so, give the command.
2) Instead of assigning a matrix to the cell within a cell, assign another cell (for a cell within a cell within a cell), and then assign a matrix within one of the innermost cells.
   a. Call the index of one of the elements within the matrix you assigned
   b. Retrieve a list of all of the matrix elements within this innermost matrix.
   c. Can you assign a cell to one of the matrix elements?
3) In what order is the output from the expression D(:)?
4) What are the sizes of the matrices in c{2,2}? What is happening with the multiplication symbol that produces this result? How is it different from matrix multiplication?

A.3 Logical Expressions, Indexing, and Flow Control

Logical expressions ask a yes/no or true/false question, and are often used as a way to allow us to make alternate computations based on if some condition is true or false. For example, suppose we want to add the two elements of a 1×2 matrix if the first element is between $+10$ and -10, and subtract the two elements if it is not. This is accomplished via the if...else...end statement sequence:

```
v=[5 6];
if abs(v)<10
    sum(v)
else
    diff(v)
end
```

Logical expressions are also used to select elements of a matrix via a form of indexing, called logical indexing. With logical indexing, we write an expression that is true or false at each index of the matrix, and treat the list of yes/no logical outputs (one for each index) as the selected (yes/true) and nonselected (no/false) indices.

```
b=rand(10,1);
tf=b>.5;
x=b(tf)
```

Or we can nest the previous two expressions:

```
y=b(b>.5)
```

We can also use logical indexing to change elements of the original matrix:

```
mean(b)
b(b>.9)=0;
mean(b)
```

Cell arrays are particularly useful when you want a single variable to hold data, but are not sure if the same amount of data will be put into each element of the array. For example, let's say you have an experiment involving a questionnaire, and you want to compute the average age of each participant who answered one of the questions (on a 5-point rating scale) with a 1, 2, 3, etc. Since there will not be an equal number of participants answering the question with a 1, 2, etc., you will end up with an uneven number of ages in each of the five groups. When inputting the data, you could create separate variables for each of the groups, but this will make life more difficult later on when writing for-loops (see 'Flow control' below). Instead, it will be better to put the data into a 1×5 cell:

```
dat=[randi(5,[1000 1]) randi([18 50],[array 1000 1])];
dat={dat(dat(:,1)==1,2), ...
  dat(dat(:,1)==2,2), ...
  dat(dat(:,1)==3,2), ...
  dat(dat(:,1)==4,2), ...
  dat(dat(:,1)==5,2)};
```

You can see that there are different numbers of elements in the cell array. Now if you want to compute the median age of each group, you will want to step through each element of the cell array in turn, and compute the median for each. To do this, we need a method of performing that 'stepping-through' operation. This is the purpose of the two flow control sequences we will use, the for-loop and the while-loop. The for-loop runs through a sequence of expressions a pre-selected number of times, whereas the while-loop runs through a sequence of expressions until a logical expression becomes false.

We will compute the medians of the dat cell array using both of these. Using a for-loop this is:

```
meds=zeros(1,5);
for i=1:length(dat),
    meds(i)=median(dat{i});
end
```

and using the while-loop it is:

```
meds=zeros(1,5); i=0;
while i<length(dat), i=i+1;
    meds(i)=median(dat{i});
end
```

We can expand each of these loops to have them tell us about the iteration as it is happening. In the for-loop we can have it output the value of i so we can see that the statement after the word 'for' creates an automatic iteration of the variable i, starting at the value 1 and ending at the value 5 (which is the length of the dat variable). In the while-loop we can add the output of the logical condition, i<length(dat), so we can see when it changes to 'false' and therefore kicks us out of the loop. These expansions are:

```
meds=zeros(1,5);
for i=1:length(dat), i
    meds(i)=median(dat{i});
end
disp('now the for-loop is done')
```

and using the while-loop it is:

```
meds=zeros(1,5); i=0;
i<length(dat)
while i<length(dat), i=i+1;
    meds(i)=median(dat{i});
i<length(dat)
end
disp('now the while-loop is done')
```

From these expanded versions we see that the for-loop iterates through the values of i that are indicated by the statement immediately following the word 'for' (e.g., 1:10, or 4:7), and for each value of i it runs through all lines of code enclosed by the words for...end. The while loop is similar: every time it gets to the word 'while' it checks if the logical statement next to the word 'while' is true. If it is, it executes the code enclosed by the words while...end, and if not it jumps to the word 'end' and executes any remaining code (in this case, the 'disp' function).

Exercises

1) What is the purpose of the length(dat) expression in the for-loop?
2) What does i=i+1 do in the while-loop?
3) When does the___-loop end? Draw a diagram describing your answer.
    a. for
    b. while
4) Add an if. . .else. . .end that executes one commend when i is less than 3 and a different command otherwise within one of the loops above.

A.4 Plotting

Plotting occurs within figure windows that MATLAB® will create for us when we give it the command 'figure.' There are two main plot types that we will use, the 2D and 3D scatterplot, and the mesh plot. First, let's make a couple figure windows, and then we can try them out:

```
figure
figure(10)
figure
figure(1)
```

Notice that each of these three figure windows is numbered. You should have figures 1, 2, and 10. If you don't specify a figure number (as we did with figure 10), it will use the lowest number that isn't already in use. Also, if you write figure(1) when that figure already exists, you are telling MATLAB® you want figure(1) to be the current figure in terms of any subsequent plotting commands.

Now let's make some scatterplots:

```
dat=[1.1,2.75,-.12,-1.23,3.84];
figure(1)
plot(dat)
figure(2)
subplot(2,1,1)
plot(1:length(dat),dat,'o','MarkerEdgeColor','k','MarkerFaceColor','b','MarkerSize',5)
subplot(2,1,2)
x=linspace(-2,2,101);
plot(x,x.^2-1,'.')
```

where notice we've specified several plot symbols, and line types. We can also create a 3d scatterplot:

```
x=linspace(-2,2,101);
y=-10:10;
z=nan(21,101);
for i=y,
    z(i+11,:)=-x.^2-abs(i); end
figure(2)
plot3(ones(21,1)*x,y'*ones(1,101),z,'k.')
view(87,12)
```

The 3D scatterplot puts punctate plot symbols, like '.', into 3D Cartesian axes. We can also create a 3D plot from the same data that interpolates a surface between those punctate positions using mesh:

```
figure(3)
mesh(x,y,z); colormap('bone')
view(70,14)
```

Finally, we can add to any plot using 'hold on.' Here we will combine the 3D scatterplot and mesh:

```
figure(3); hold on
plot3(ones(21,1)*x,y'*ones(1,101),z,'k.')
```

Exercises

1) What is the default plot symbol if none is specified in the plot command?
2) What does the subplot command do? Try making a subplot(2,2,2) on figure(1). Describe what happens.

3) What does the linspace function do?
4) What does the view command do?
5) Try the mesh plot with 'meshc' instead. What is the difference?
6) What happens if you don't use 'hold on' before final plot command in figure 3? Try this with and without first closing and re-making the entire figure.
7) What does clf do to a figure?

A.5 Functions

When we write code, we will in most cases either be directly performing operations on variables, or we will be indirectly performing those operations by calling ***functions***. We have already done this: for example, figure(), plot(), ones(), and linspace() are all functions. To write good code, we will not only need to be comfortable using functions, but we will also need to be able to write them. We will do that here for a few basic cases.

Before writing any functions, let's go ahead and save the textbook functions to your home folder. We start by downloading the textbook functions from **http://hudsonlab.org/textbook/f314a**. Then, move these files to the MATLAB® home folder (when you launch MATLAB®, this is the folder that your MATLAB® command window opens into) so that when we write code while working through the main textbook MATLAB® will be able to access them. This is also where you can download all of the 'Programming Asides' from the main text, which will allow you to easily explore the code included in the book.

Our first function is possibly the simplest function that I have ever written. The point of this function is to arrange the numbers in a variable as a single column. In MATLAB®, we can do this by writing:

```
v=[1 2 3 4]
v(:)
```

This code produces two outputs with the numbers [1 2 3 4]. On the first line, the output is arranged as a row vector, and on the second as a column. Also, notice that unlike the transpose operator:

```
v1=[1 2 3 4]
v2=[2 4 6]'
v1'
v2'
```

using the colon will arrange the numbers as a column regardless of whether it was initially a column or row vector:

```
v1=[1 2 3 4]
v2=[2 4 6]'
v1(:)
v2(:)
```

To write a function based on this colon operator, we open MATLAB®, go to the MATLAB® Editor window, and under 'new' we select 'function.' The new function template will initially look like this:

```
function [outputArg1,outputArg2] = untitled2(inputArg1,inputArg2)
%UNTITLED2 Summary of this function goes here
% Detailed explanation goes here
outputArg1 = inputArg1;
```

```
outputArg2 = inputArg2;
end
```

and we will update it to:

```
% str8n.m
%
% usage: [Vout]=str8n(Vin); %vector input
%        [Vout]=str8n(MATin); %matrix input
%
% straightens the input into a column vector
%
% INPUTS
%    Vin: vector input. may be a row or column vector
%  MATin: matrix input. output connects the bottom of each column
%   to the top of the next consecutive column
%
% OUTPUT
% Vout: Vout=Vin(:);
%
% teh wrote it [3.14.20]

function [Vout]=str8n(MATin)
Vout=MATin(:); end
```

Next, we save it in our MATLAB® home folder (overwriting the copy that should already be there from the set of functions you just downloaded). After it is saved, we can use it:

```
v1=[1 2 3 4]
v2=[2 4 6]'
str8n(v1)
str8n(v2)
```

If you're wondering about the usefulness of this function, it is primarily to shorten your code when you want to both 'straighten' a vector and simultaneously select a subset of indices from the vector:

```
str8n(v1(2:4))
```

which can happen in a single line of code using str8n, but would require two lines otherwise. Notice also that str8n can be used on a matrix:

```
M=rand(4)
str8n(M)
str8n(M(2:4,[1 3]))
```

which we will find useful in the main text.

The next function we will write is useful for removing unwanted rows of data, which can be useful if, for example, we have a data matrix and want to remove the rows that correspond to a particular condition (and then make computations on the remaining conditions). Again, we start by opening a new (blank) function in the MATLAB® Editor. Then, we update the blank function to read:

```
% RFL.m
%
function [MATout]=RFL(MATin,list) %#ok<*STOUT,*INUSL,*AGROW>
MATout=MATin;
MATout(list,:)=[]; %set desired indices to be empty (thus removing them)
```

After saving (and overwriting the downloaded version), we can test it:

```
k2=magic(4)
RFL(k2,[1 3])
RFL(k2,[2 4])
```

Now, that works as far as it goes. But what if we want pass the function a 3D matrix input:

```
k3=k2; k3(:,:,2)=k2*2 %3d matrix
RFL(k3,[1 3])
```

This does not produce an error message, but also doesn't produce the correct result because the output is 2D rather than 3D with some rows removed. Instead, the third dimension is added onto the output as additional columns. To fix this, we could add an additional colon in the function, updating it to:

```
% RFL.m
%
function [MATout]=RFL(MATin,list) %#ok<*STOUT,*INUSL,*AGROW>
MATout=MATin;
MATout(list,:,:)=[]; %set desired indices to be empty (thus removing them)
```

The problem with this, is that while it can handle the k3 input, it fails for a k4 input:

```
k4=k3; k4(:,:,:,2)=k3 %4d matrix
RFL(k4,[1 3])
```

To handle any number of dimensions (2D, 3D, 4D, etc.) in the input matrix, we make use of the eval.m function. This function reads a string of text as a command. Thus, the following two lines produce the same output:

```
mean(k2)
strng=['mean(k2)']; eval(strng)
```

This is obviously extra work for computing a mean, but we can use eval to our advantage when we do not know how many dimensions our input matrix will have:

```
% RFL.m
%
function [MATout Mremoved]=RFL(MATin,list,keeporient) %#ok<*STOUT,*INUSL,*AGROW>
nd=ndims(MATin); MATout=MATin;

Mstr='MATout(list,:'; %initialize Mstr
for n=1:nd-2, %loop to ensure number of colons is at least nd-1
    Mstr=[Mstr ',:'], end
eval([Mstr ')=[];']); %remove submatrix given by list
```

Save this function and run it with:

```
Mout=RFL(k2,[1 3]);
Mout
Mout=RFL(k4,[1 4]);
Mout
```

Notice that the function is giving an output while it runs, because we have a comma instead of a semi-colon on the line of the for-loop that we are using to construct a definition of Mstr that has the appropriate number of colons. Change the comma to a semi-colon to suppress this output once you understand how the desired Mstr string is being formed within that for-loop. Finally, when we run this function we may want to give a second output that gives us a matrix formed by the subset of rows that was removed from MATin. The complete version of the function is:

```
% RFL.m
%
% usage: [MATout]=RFL(MATin,list);
%        [MATout Mremoved]=RFL(MATin,list) %return the shortened matrix
%             (MATout) as well as submatrix of deleted rows (Mremoved)
```

```
%
% remove from list: removes a subset of rows from a matrix
%
% INPUTS
%      MATin: matrix or vector input
%        list: matrix input
%
%
% OUTPUT
%    MATout: output matrix with subset of rows removed
% Mremoved: matrix made of removed rows
%
% EXAMPLES:
% k2=magic(4) %2d input matrix
% [Mout Mremoved]=RFL(k2,[1 3])
%
% k3=k2; k3(:,:,2)=k2*2 %3d input matrix
% RFL(k3,[1,3])
%
% teh wrote it [3.14.20]

function [MATout Mremoved]=RFL(MATin,list,keeporient) %#ok<*STOUT,*INUSL,*AGROW>
nd=ndims(MATin); MATout=MATin;

Mstr='MATout(list,:'; %initialize Mstr
for n=1:nd-2, %loop to ensure number of colons is at least nd-1
    Mstr=[Mstr ',:']; end

if nargout==2, eval(['Mremoved=' Mstr ');']); end %save submatrix
eval([Mstr ')=[];']); %remove submatrix given by list
```

Again, save this version in your home folder (replacing the old version).

Notice that the final version of RFL.m makes use of the str8n.m function. That is one of the nice things about writing a simple little function like str8n.m: you can reuse it in your later work, and include it in other functions that you write. In other words, writing functions can be a great time-saver!

Exercises

1) Describe the action of str8n on a matrix input.
2) Draw a diagram to describe what happened to the k3 matrix when it was given to our first version of RFL.m.
3) Why does setting a row of a vector or matrix =[] remove that row? What happens if you set every row of a matrix = []?
4) What happens if you type `help RFL` in the command window?
5) What does the eval function do? Show how you can use eval to compute the median of [1 3 5 7].
6) What is the path to your home folder? Give the names of two functions that you downloaded to your home folder that we have not yet used, and describe their function based on their `help`.

A.6 Give It a Try and See What Happens

Here we've only just scratched the surface of writing code. The point was not to make you a proficient coder, but to get you used to typing things into MATLAB® and getting results. Throughout this text, you will be expected to type the code included in example problems, and to look at the results. After having done so, you may find that it is unclear how those results came about. Or the code you've been given may include unfamiliar symbols or MATLAB® functions. In these cases, you need to look into the parts that are unfamiliar. Try the MATLAB® help files. Type the function, and try new inputs. Play with it a little. See what works. See what gives you an error.

Having at least a familiarity with writing code is quickly becoming an essential skill for students, particularly students that come into contact with data. If this is your first exposure to writing code, or to MATLAB®, don't worry: it will come to you with a little practice. If you take the time to try things out and see what happens, you will quickly find yourself writing and understanding the code provided in this text. And when you use this new skill to explore extensions of the example problems in the text, you derive an added benefit: you will gain a much deeper understanding of the mathematics.

APPENDIX B

MATHEMATICS REVIEW: LOGARITHMIC AND EXPONENTIAL FUNCTIONS

Logarithmic and exponential functions are simply shorthand expressions for certain aspects of the usual arithmetic operations of multiplication and division. These functions occur with some regularity in probabilistic equations, and you will want to acquire familiarity with them now to avoid becoming overburdened later in the text.

B.1 Overview

In our early mathematical training we were taught important shortcuts for computing sums and differences. This started with representing counts by their corresponding digit representations; the base-10 system in particular has historically helped speed basic arithmetic computations immensely over other number-representation systems (e.g., using Roman numerals). After that, we learned rules for addition and subtraction using those digit-representations, both of whole numbers and parts of numbers. Here, having memorized the combination rules for base-10 digits (both addition, and its inverse operation, subtraction) again allowed us to speed computation, and to compute with numbers that are difficult to visualize (e.g., $10,015$). The final step in acquiring the toolbox of elementary arithmetic was to learn multiplication and its inverse, division. Multiplication is the shorthand method of computing repeated sums, much as addition with digit representations is the shorthand for repeated counting by ones. Multiplication allows, in far fewer steps relative to repeated counting by ones, to compute repeated sums such as $5 + 5 + 5 + 5 = 4 \times 5$. Division is the inverse of multiplication, and allows us to answer questions such as, 'how many 5s are in 100?'.

As we will see below, exponential and logarithmic functions are simply equations, like 4×5, that represent numbers. The exponential function is used a shorthand method of repeated multiplication, just as multiplication is a shorthand for repeated additions. And whereas division is the inverse of multiplication, the logarithmic function is the inverse of the exponential function.

B.2 Exponential Functions

Surely one of our most oft-used mathematical operations is multiplication, which is just a repeated sum. We found very early on that there were situations where we could speed the tedious computation of certain sums via multiplication. For example, when computing the square footage of a rectangular room, we multiply the width by height. Another such problem is to compute the sum of all numbers between 1 and 100. There is the obvious, tedious solution involving a sum of 100 numbers. To solve this problem efficiently, we might recognize that the first and last numbers in the list sum to 101, as do the second-to-last and the second, and third-to-last and third, and so on. The total is therefore the sum of these fifty number-pairs (101) repeated 50 times: $50 \times 101 = 5,050$. The exponential equation is the next logical step up from multiplication, and allows us to speed computations that require repeated multiplications.

The situation where we probably first encountered an exponential function was when computing the area of a square. This is simply the width multiplied by height calculation described above, but because a square has identical width and height the calculation becomes: $A = w \cdot h = W^2$. The last version of the area computation is generally referred to as '*w-squared*': this is an exponential equation that tells us to multiply w by itself: $w^2 = w \cdot w$. For the volume of a cube, we need three copies of w: $V = w \cdot w \cdot w = w^3$. We can use any base in an exponential function, such as 5^4 or π^4 or e^4. In addition, we can change the exponent to any number, including decimal numbers, such as e^2 or $2^{1.15}$.

Table B1 provides a description of the two most commonly cited rules for computing with exponential functions. In addition to the examples provided in the table, we should note a few extensions of the basic scenarios described there. First, we will often have a situation where we have the product of two exponential functions, as in: $c^a c^b$. To be concrete, if $a = 2$ and $b = 3$, and $c = 5$ the previous equation becomes: $5^a 5^b = 5^2 5^3 = (5 \cdot 5)(5 \cdot 5 \cdot 5) = 5^5$. In fact, it will generally be the case that, for any base, c, $c^a c^b = c^{a+b}$. In addition to this scenario, we will also often have situations where we want to raise an exponential equation to an exponent, as in $(c^a)^b$. To be concrete, again setting $a = 2$ and $b = 3$, and $c = 5$, we see that the equation becomes $(c^a)^b = (5^2)^3$. It tells us that we want to multiply 5^2 by itself three times, or $(5^2)^3 = (5^2)(5^2)(5^2)$. This, in turn, is a familiar set of repeated multiplications: $(5^2)^3 = (5^2)(5^2)(5^2) = (5 \cdot 5)(5 \cdot 5)(5 \cdot 5) = 5^6$. Again, a bit of thought regarding this example will tell us that the general solution is: $(c^a)^b = c^{ab}$. Finally, we will provide the rationale for a relationship that is generally just memorized without explanation: $c^0 = 1$. The rationale is based on the quotient rule: $c^0 = c^{a-a} = \frac{c^a}{c^a} = 1$. Notice that this relation holds regardless of the base, c.

Exercises

1) Compute the following exponential functions in MATLAB®:
   a. 1^2, 1^1, 1^0, 1^{-1}, 1^{-2}
   b. e^2, e^1, e^0, e^{-1}, e^{-2}
   c. 0^2, 0^1, 0^0, 0^{-1}, 0^{-2}
   d. -2^e, -1^e, -0^e, -1^e, 2^e
   e. 2^2, 2^1, 2^0, 2^{-1}, 2^{-2}
   f. 2^{-1}, $2^{-0.5}$, 2^0, $2^{-0.5}$, 2^{-1}
2) Use MATLAB® to plot a^x using several different choices of base, with abscissa values of x=linspace(−5,5,1001).
   a. Do these functions intersect? If so, where do they intersect, and why?
   b. Predict where the analogous plot of the exponential function with base 1 would intersect any of the functions you have already plotted. Explain your prediction.

B.3 Logarithmic Functions

The objective of both John Napier and Joost Burgi in (separately) inventing logs was to simplify mathematical calculation. The logarithm 'changes multiplication and division into addition and subtraction' in the sense that the log of the product of two numbers, $\log(ab)$, is equal to the sum of the logs of those numbers, $\log(ab) = \log(a) + \log(b)$ and the log of the ratio of two numbers is the difference of their logs, $\log(a/b) = \log(a) - \log(b)$. Thus, in the seventeenth, eighteenth, and nineteenth centuries, before the age of mechanical and electronic calculation, one could convert long chains of multiplications and divisions into the simpler operations of addition and subtraction; this had the desired effect of speeding calculations (and reducing errors). Pierre-Simon Laplace called logarithms '[a]n admirable artifice which, by reducing to a few days the labour of many months, doubles the life of the astronomer, and spares him the errors and disgust inseparable from long calculations' (Bryant, 1907, p. 44).

B.3.1 Computing Logarithmic Functions

What is the logarithm of a number, then? There are two answers that can be given to this question. The more mathematical of the two is that the logarithm is a mathematical operation that has the property, $\log(ab) = \log(a) + \log(b)$ (i.e., this expression is the functional equation that defines the logarithm). While this definition has the advantage that it contains all of the properties of the logarithm within it, it is less useful initially before one has gained some familiarity with the use of logs in practice. To obtain that

TABLE B.1 Rules for computing with exponential and logarithmic functions

Exponents	Definition	Example
product	$a^n = a_{(1)} \cdot a_{(2)} \cdot a_{(3)} \cdot \ldots \cdot a_{(n)}$	$5^2 = 5 \cdot 5 = 25$ $10^3 = 10 \cdot 10 \cdot 10 = 1000$ $3^{10} = 3_{(1)} \cdot 3_{(2)} \cdot \ldots \cdot 3_{(10)} = 59049$
quotient	$a^{-n} = \left[\frac{1}{a}\right]_{(1)} \cdot \left[\frac{1}{a}\right]_{(2)} \cdot \ldots \cdot \left[\frac{1}{a}\right]_{(n)}$	$2^{-2} = \frac{1}{2} \cdot \frac{1}{2} = .25$ $5^{-3} = 5^{-1} \cdot 5^{-1} \cdot 5^{-1} = 125^{-1}$

Logarithms	Definition	Example
product	$\log(ab) = \log(a) + \log(b)$	$\log_{10}(5 \cdot 2) = \log_{10}(10) = 1$ $= \log_{10}(5) + \log_{10}(2)$ $= 0.699 + 0.301 = 1$
quotient	$\log(a/b) = \log(a) - \log(b)$	$\log_{10}(20/2) = \log_{10}(10) = 1$ $= \log_{10}(20) - \log_{10}(2)$ $= 1.301 + 0.301 = 1$

practical experience and understanding, it is perhaps better to employ a less compact definition of the logarithm:

> The logarithm, $\log_c a = b$, answers the question: 'To what power (b) must we raise the base (c) to obtain (a) in the exponential equation: $c^b = a$?'

Indeed, it is advisable to memorize this definition so that it can be used whenever there is confusion or hesitation regarding the meaning of a problem or mathematical expression involving logarithms.

Table B1 provides a description of the two most commonly cited rules for computing with logarithmic functions. The product rule is the functional equation that defines the logarithmic function generally, allowing for any base (e.g., common-log base 10, binary-log base 2, natural log base e). This rule allows for many useful extensions. For example, we can take the log of a number raised to a power, such as:

$$\log(5^2) = \log(5 \cdot 5)$$

which by the product rule is:

$$\log(5) + \log(5) = 2\log(5).$$

Indeed, from this example we see that it is generally true that the log of any number (a) raised to a power (b) is simply:

$$\log(a^b) = b\log(a).$$

Knowing this, we can also derive the quotient rule,

$$\log(a/b) = \log(a \cdot b^{-1}) = \log(a) - \log(b)$$

showing that the product rule is really the only rule necessary for the use and understanding of log functions.

In addition to the product and quotient rules, there are three important relations with which we should become familiar. The first is so important it has a name: the *change of base formula*. It allows us to change the base of a logarithmic equation from a to b, regardless of the values of the two bases:

$$\log_b y = \frac{\log_a y}{\log_a b}$$

To derive the change of base formula we start with the logarithmic equation:

$$\log_b y = x$$

This equation defines the exponential function,

$$b^x = y$$

(recall the foundational question answered by the logarithm, $\log_b y = x$: 'to what power (x) must we raise the base (b) to obtain (y) in the exponential equation: $b^x = y$)?' We next take the base-a log of both sides:

$$\log_a b^x = \log_a y$$

and solve for x:

$$x = \log_a y / \log_a b.$$

Finally, we equate x in the first and last equations of the series:

$$\log_b y = \log_a y / \log_a b.$$

The change of base equation allows us to convert from a known base, such as the base-10 log that is a built-in function on most calculators (and MATLAB®), to any arbitrary base, such as the base-1.69 logarithm. For example, to compute the base-1.69 logarithm of y, we write: $\log_{1.69} y = \frac{\log_{10} y}{\log_{10} 1.69}$, for any positive value y.

The second important log identity will allow us to simplify many probability equations, and is $\log_c(c^x) = x$, for any base c and exponent x. To understand the reason for this result, let us look at the specific example, $\ln e^5$. The solution requires us to first expand the expression to $\ln(e^5) = \log_e e^5 = 5(\log_e e)$, and apply the foundational question asked by the log function to this particular equation: To what power (x) must we raise the base e to obtain the result e in the exponential equation $e^x = e$? Since the answer is 1 (regardless of the base), it turns out that the general equation relating a logarithmic equation with the form $\log_c(c^x)$ is always $\log_c(c^x) = x$.

Finally, we will see the rationale for a relationship that is generally just memorized without explanation: $\log(1) = 0$. Using the quotient rule, we see the reason for this relation, because:

$$\log(1) = \log(a/a) = \log(a) - \log(a) = 0.$$

Also, notice that none of the relations described in this subsection depend on the base of the logarithm, and therefore it is true that $\log(1) = 0$, for any base: $\log_2(1) = 0$, $\ln(1) = 0$, $\log_{10}(1) = 0$, etc.

Exercises

1) Compute the following logs in MATLAB®:
   a. $\log(2^2)$, $\log(2^1)$, $\log(2^0)$, $\log(2^{-1})$, $\log(2^{-2})$
   b. $\log(3^2)$, $\log(3^1)$, $\log(3^0)$, $\log(3^{-1})$, $\log(3^{-2})$
   c. $\log(1^2)$, $\log(1^1)$, $\log(1^0)$, $\log(1^{-1})$, $\log(1^{-2})$
2) Use the product and quotient rules to convert the following logarithmic functions:
   a. $\log(1000 \times 10)$
   b. $\ln(e^{-x^2})$
   c. $\log_2(16 \times 16 \times 4 \times 8)$
3) Compute the following natural logs, and then convert into the indicated base. Show your work.
   a. ln16 (binary)
   b. ln1000 (common)
   c. ln4 (binary)
   d. ln10 (common)
4) Use MATLAB® to plot $\log x$ using the three built-in log functions (natural or base-e, binary or base-2, and common or base-10), with abscissa values of x=linspace(.001,3,1001).

a. Do these functions intersect? If so, where do they intersect, and why?
b. Predict where the analogous plot of the log function with base 4 would intersect the common log function you have already plotted. Explain your prediction.

B.3.2 Uses of Logarithmic Functions

There are three main uses for logarithmic functions in probability theory and data analysis. The first is to simplify equations, which often have a form similar to e^{-x^2}. When we take the natural log of equations with this form we simplify the equation immensely, since $\ln(e^{-x^2}) = -x^2$, and so we will often want to work with the log of a probability equation rather than with the original. For example, the Poisson probability equation, which we encounter for the first time at the close of Chapter 2, is written:

$$p(S|\varsigma \cdot \imath_P) = \frac{e^{-\varsigma}\varsigma^S}{S!}.$$

The log of the Poisson probability is often more manageable:

$$\ln[p(S|\varsigma \cdot \imath)] = \ln\left[\frac{e^{-\varsigma}\varsigma^S}{S!}\right]$$
$$= S\ln(\varsigma) - \varsigma - \sum_{s=2}^{S} \ln(s).$$

The second major use of log functions is avoiding underflow, which occurs when we have probability calculations for very unlikely events. For example, in a coin-flipping problem we may want to compute the probability of observing N heads in N flips of a coin ($p = 0.5^N$). As N increases, this probability becomes extremely small extremely quickly. This is problematic because numerical computations will often rely on a minimum smallest number, ε, where no number (or difference between numbers) that is smaller than ε can be resolved. Underflow occurs when the results of calculations are less than ε and those results are reported (incorrectly) as zero. Underflow can be avoided in most situations by computing with log-probabilities. We can see the effect of switching from probabilities to log-probabilities in the previous example of the Poisson probability equation. In this equation, ς is a theoretical rate parameter and S is an observed number of counts; the Poisson probability equation describes the observation of discrete events such as neural spiking. If the theoretical rate is $\varsigma = 222$ spikes/s, and the observed spike-count is $S = 200$, the probability equation involves a term e^{-222}, and a term $(200!)^{-1}$. These are both extremely small, and in fact the second (factorial) term leads to underflow (i.e., computing $(200!)^{-1}$ in MATLAB® returns a result of zero). We can verify that neither term leads to underflow by computing $\ln(e^{-222}) = -222$, and $\ln(1/s!) = -\sum_{s=2}^{S} \ln(S) = -981.015$.

In other words, if we had tried to compute the probability of the observed spike count using the probability equation we would get the (incorrect) result $p = 0$, but computing via the logarithmic form of the Poisson equation (and converting from log-probability to probability units at the end of the computation) yields the result $p = 0.0091$.

Finally, we will see in Chapter 6 that the main numerical output used for comparing alternative hypotheses (i.e., for hypothesis testing) uses a logarithmic scale. This numerical output, which we will refer to as evidence, is defined as a log-transform of the odds of one hypothesis over another:

$$e(H_m) = 10\log[O(H_m)].$$

The odds is a ratio of one probability to another; in this case the odds describes the relative probabilities assigned to different hypotheses. If we were computing the odds of Hypothesis 1 to Hypothesis 2 written $O(H_1)$, the odds ratio would be:

$$O(H_1) = \frac{p(H_1|D \cdot \imath)}{p(H_2|D \cdot \imath)}.$$

Notice that, because a ratio of two positive numbers can yield any positive number, $O(M_1) > 0$, the log of this ratio has a range $(-\infty, \infty)$ where zero indicates no difference between the elements of the ratio. Furthermore, multiplying the log of a ratio of two positive numbers by ten has a special meaning: it is the way decibels are defined. Thus, evidence is a decibel measure, just as is sound intensity; for example, if the odds are 2:1 in favor of H_1, this translates into just under 3 dB of evidence. Thought of in terms of sound intensity, 1dB of evidence is about the smallest increment of sound intensity that is detectible to the human ear (i.e., the detection threshold). Three decibels is equivalent to the sound of a bird softly tweeting or leaves rustling in the wind: detectable, but not loud. Unless otherwise noted, we will use this 3 dB value as a just-significant difference in favor of one model over its competitors when comparing hypotheses/models.

Exercises

1) Compute evidence measures from the following intputs, showing your calculation and reporting the result in dB:
   a. $O(H_1) = .5$
   b. $O(H_1) = 2$
   c. $O(H_1) = 10$
   d. $p(H_1|D \cdot \imath) = .032,\ p(H_2|D \cdot \imath) = .011$
   e. $p(H_1|D \cdot \imath) = .0023,\ p(H_1|D \cdot \imath) = .0024$
2) Describe in words the meaning of positive, negative, and 0-results from the evidence calculation.
3) Write a basic MATLAB® function that computes the log of a sum for the binary log. Show that it correctly evaluates the log of the sum of the elements of [.1 .2 .3 .4], by first converting each element into its binary log, and then from the vector of log values compute the log of the sum of the original vector.

B.3.3 *Marginalization and the Logsum Problem

One of the main operations we will use while analyzing data is marginalization over one or more axes of a probability distribution (see Appendix C for details). For example, we may have the 2D probability distribution shown in Figure 2.2, and need to marginalize

* If this is your first exposure to logarithmic functions, save this section for Chapter 5, when logs have begun to be used extensively in your computations (and you've had time to get more familiar with these types of equations).

over one of the two axes to yield the 1D probability distribution shown in the margins of the same plot. This is straightforward to do: we simply compute the sums of the probabilities along each row of the plot grid, as indicated in the figure.

The marginalization computation becomes problematic when we cannot use probabilities proper (because the probability density can become so low that density values come to be too small for the computer to represent), and instead are computing with log-probabilities. When computing with log-probabilities, the marginalization computation requires us to take sums of probabilities, which is not straightforward when those numbers have been log-transformed; we will refer to this as the logsum computation:

$$\sum_i p_i = e^{\log[\sum_i p_i]}$$

We would like to make the computation based on the $\log(p_i)$ instead of the p_i. By keeping numbers log-transformed, we will make the computation in such a way that it is less likely to produce underflow errors.

Here we will derive the algorithm that allows us to make the desired logsum computation, based on the identity:

$$\log_a\left[\sum\nolimits_{i\in J} p_i\right] = \log_a(p') + \log_a\left[1 + \sum\nolimits_{k\in J'} a^{\log_a(p_k)}/a^{\log_a(p')}\right],$$

where the desired summation includes the probabilities whose subscripts are part of the set J; that is, the indices of the summed probabilities (p_i) are the indices contained in the set J. For example, with ten such probabilities, indexed 1 through 10, $J = \{1,2,3,4,5,6,7,8,9,10\}$ and the index of summation, i, runs from 1 to 10. The set J' is missing one index, corresponding to the largest probability (p') in the to-be-summed set. Note that this identity will work for log-probabilities of any base, a.

The logsum function is derived in three steps. First, we both add and subtract the log of the largest probability in the to-be-summed set:

$$\log_a\left[\sum\nolimits_{i\in J} p_i\right] = \log_a(p') + \log_a\left[\sum\nolimits_{i\in J} p_i\right] - \log_a(p')$$

Then we combine the last two terms in the above, while also separating p' from the sum in square brackets:

$$= \log_a(p') + \log_a\left[\left(p' + \sum_{k\in J'} p_i\right) p'^{-1}\right]$$

Finally, we multiply $(p')^{-1}$ through the elements in the round brackets, and convert all probabilities using the identity (described above), $p = a^{\log_a(p)}$.

$$= \log_a(p') + \log_a\left[1 + \sum\nolimits_{k\in J'} a^{\log_a(p_k)}/a^{\log_a(p')}\right]$$

$$= \log_a(p') + \log_a\left[1 + \sum\nolimits_{k\in J'} a^{\log_a(p_k)-\log_a(p')}\right].$$

Notice that no part of the final expression requires that you maintain a list of probability values, only of log-probability values. The logsum function is incredibly important in practical computations because of this property; otherwise we might be unable to marginalize over nuisance variables in cases where there was no analytical expression for the posterior probability (Appendix C).

Exercises

1) Derive the logsum equation for the specific case of the binary log.
2) Write a basic MATLAB® function that computes the log of a sum for the binary log. Show that it correctly evaluates the log of the sum of the elements of [.1 .2 .3 .4 .4 .3 .2 .1], by first converting each element into its binary log, and then from the vector of log-probability values compute the log of the sum of the original vector.
3) Derive the logsumexp expression, $\ln\left[\sum_{i\in J} e^{-x_i^2}\right] = -\widehat{x^2} + \ln\left[1 + \sum_{i\in J'} e^{-\left(x_i^2 - \widehat{x^2}\right)}\right]$
   a. Does the underflow-avoiding property of this equation require the use of the natural log?
   b. Does it allow us to retain only the values of exponentials, e^{-x^2}, or
   c. do we need to maintain a list of the corresponding x_i values?

THE BAYESIAN TOOLBOX: MARGINALIZATION AND COORDINATE TRANSFORMATION

Marginalization is surely the most important technical feature of probability theory as applied to data analysis: It is also the most problematic. The difficulty arises in two ways, with the same solution in each case. The first face of that difficulty appears because marginalization often must rely on a calculus-based technique called integration. The second appears when working in an applied setting, because techniques of integration exist for some, but not all problems one would like to solve. In both cases we must obtain an approximate answer to our marginalization problem, which relies on an alternative technique: ***numerical integration***. Here, we will examine both the origin of the need for integration techniques in marginalization, and also their approximate solution. We will then describe coordinate transformation, and the marginalization based structure of lossy coordinate transforms.

C.1 Probability Mass Functions versus Probability Density Functions

The term 'probability distribution' is ambiguous. It can refer to two conceptually similar objects that nevertheless will require different mathematical handling with regard to marginalization: discrete and continuous probability distributions. Discrete distributions are easier to understand, because its probability is in the form we intuitively expect: probability mass. A probability mass is the probability associated with discrete events, like coin tosses. A discrete probability (mass) distribution will always relate probabilities one-to-one to individual, punctate propositions. One such is the observation of thht in a sequence of four coin tosses. Another would be the observation of 11 heads in 20 coin tosses (i.e., an element of the binomial distribution). The nice thing about discrete distributions is that probability masses are the kinds of mathematical objects that you can just add up if you want to know the total mass over several different events. For example, via the sum rule you may want to know the probability of observing th *or* ht in two coin tosses, which is

$$\begin{aligned} p(th \vee ht|\iota) &= p(th|\iota) + p(ht|\iota) - p(th \cdot ht|\iota) \\ &= p(th|\iota) + p(ht|\iota) = 0.25 + 0.25 - 0 = 0.5. \end{aligned}$$

The same is not true of the probability *densities* that occur in the distributions describing continuous variables. The numerical values of a probability density indicate the probability *per unit* x. This difference has to do with the fact that, between any two parameter values in x (along the abscissa) there is an infinity of additional parameter values that we might want to assign probabilities. If these were all assigned probability *masses*, the total probability mass (obtained from taking the sum of the masses at each punctate x-value) would also be infinite.

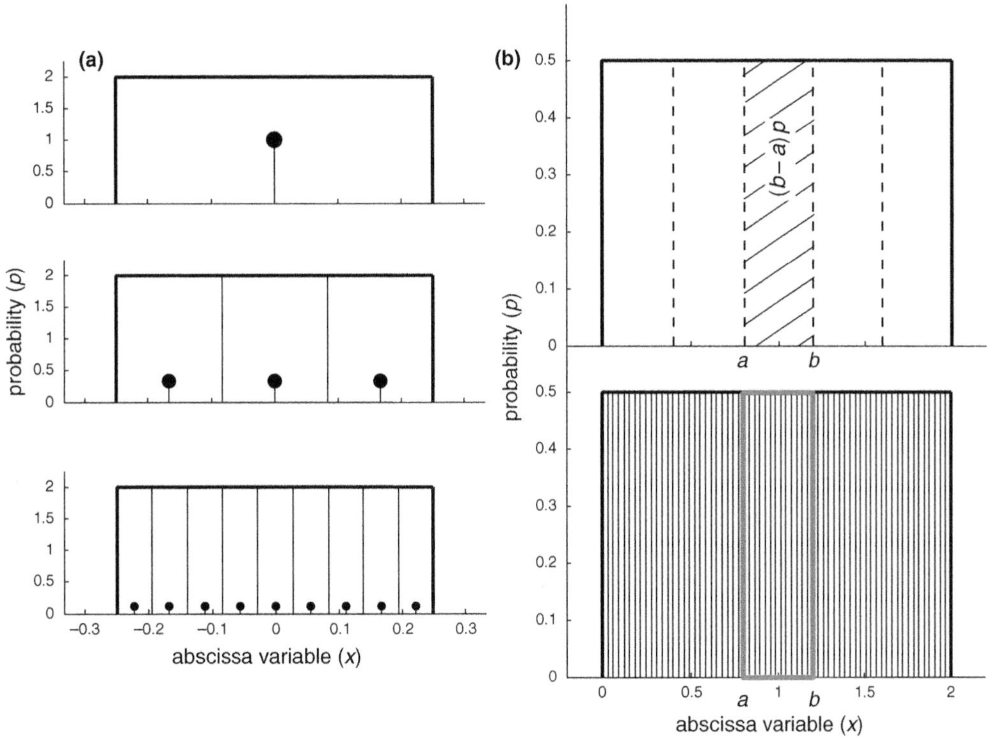

Figure C.1 Probability mass and density functions. (a) The probability density (thick solid line spanning $X_{min} = -0.25$ to $x_{max} = 0.25$) is spread evenly over its range and is defined at every point between x_{min} and x_{max}, whereas the probability mass function (stem plot) exists only at specific abscissa locations. Here, we show a series of mass functions whose average mass is always centered at the origin (at the center of the density function), with an increasing number of mass points in each. (Upper) A single mass point whose probability must be 1. (Middle) Three mass points, each with mass 1/3 and centered within an equal-sized section of the probability density. (Lower) Nine-element probability mass distribution, with each element of mass equal to 1/n and each centered within equal-sized sections of its respective probability density. (b) Note that we can continue to break the total probability mass into a greater and greater number of mass-points, while the total probability mass remains constant at 1.

C.1.1 Unity Probability Mass

Both the probability density and mass functions depicted in Figure C.1 have total probability mass of one; this is true of any normalized distribution. For example, if total probability mass is assigned to a single discrete parameter value (Fig. C.1a, upper), this would make for a boring probability distribution because the probability of the only possible abscissa value ($x = 0$) is one (unity mass). If this probability mass were broken into a set of discrete mass fragments (each fragment assigned to a different abscissa value), it is clear that the sum of these fragments is still one (Fig. C.1a, lower). This is marginalization; for example, the probability of one element from the set shown in Figure C.1a (middle) occurring is described using the sum rule: $p(-.1667 \vee 0 \vee .1667 | \iota) = 1$. Of course, we needn't always marginalize over the entire set of possibilities (yielding unity total probability mass). Instead, we may marginalize over only a small segment of the discrete distribution, such as the central three mass points in the lower plot of Figure C.1a.

From these examples we can see that probability masses behave exactly as we would expect in terms of their combination rules. They also demonstrate the attribute that will prove to be the key to numerical integration and marginalization: that total probability mass is always one, regardless of how the distribution is subdivided.

Exercises

1) Imagine you are given the plot of a probability mass function with a thousand unequally sized mass elements. By what method would you determine the total mass of these elements? What is the total mass of these elements?
2) Construct a probability mass function with 21 equally sized mass elements. What is the probability of:
   a. One of the first 5 elements?
   b. One of the last 5 elements?
   c. One out of the first, third, and last element?
3) Write the equation describing each of the computations in 2.

C.1.2 Limitless Possibilities

The more complex sister to the discrete probability distribution is the continuous probability *density*. As above, the process of marginalization will require us to determine the probability mass contained in some section of the distribution. The complexity arises because computing the probability mass contained in a subsection of the distribution requires that we first approximate the probability mass contained in smaller subsubsections of the probability distribution. Only then can we take the sum of the sub-submasses to determine the mass contained in a subsection of the probability density. The reason for this additional step is that densities at continuous abscissa locations cannot simply be summed; in a continuous density there is an infinity of abscissa locations, and any sum of densities would therefore also be infinite. In analogy with physical density and mass, the mass within a continuous density exists only over *regions* of the distribution: mass is accumulated.

This accumulation is represented mathematically by the integral. The integral over probability density in one dimension (x) is written:[1]

$$mass = p(a \leq x \leq b|\iota) = \int_a^b dx p(x|\iota) \tag{C.1}$$

and is the area under the probability density curve that represents the mass accumulation from $x = a$ to $x = b$ along the x axis of the probability density shown in Figure C.1b. On the right-hand side of the equation the integral symbol, $\int$, is an elongated 'S' meant to indicate that you will be computing a sum. The integration symbol is usually written with both a sub- and superscript to indicate the upper and lower bounds of the integral (sum), which bound the subsection of the density function whose mass we will compute; the bounds are $x = a$ and $x = b$. Finally, we have the product $dx\, p(x|\iota)$ 'under the integral.' The $p(x|\iota)$ term in the product is just the probability density we have been dealing with

[1] Notice that both summations and integrals are just sums, written in a very similar way, and both indicated by a symbol that is an 's'. Thus, if you are comfortable reading equations with a summation symbol, you will quickly learn to read and understand the meaning of equations with an integral symbol.

for several paragraphs, and should now feel familiar. The dx term of the product can be thought of as a very small segment along the x-axis (dx is analogous to Δx, meaning a small difference along the x-axis). This integral tells us that we would like to segment the probability density, $p(x|\imath)$, into a very large number of small segments (dx) along the x-axis between $x = a$ and $x = b$, and multiply the base-width of each small segment (dx) by the probability density in that segment [$p(x|\imath)$; this product yields an approximation to the mass contained within each tiny segment of the probability density, as in Figure C.1b, lower plot], and the integral sign tells us to take the sum of all these products. The sum of these many small rectangles yields the area under the probability function between a and b on the abscissa.

If you are not familiar with the calculus notation used to write integrals, let us take the mystery out of the remainder of this section, which is simply intended to familiarize you with the integral and how integrals are evaluated on a computer. These equations look daunting at first, but you will soon come to realize that they are just a shorthand way of describing an area under a curve, which in our applications will refer to the probability mass contained within some segment of a probability density function. To read these equations, we first consider the two parts of the equation *under the integral symbol*, the dx and the probability statement. Because we will be evaluating integrals numerically, you can think of this pair as an instruction: 'segment the probability function into 10,000 (or some other large number) of equally wide subsegments, and multiply the widths these subsegments (the dx portion of the equation, which must be very small to get a good approximation in most cases) by the probability *density* at the center of each sub-segment (as given by the probability statement). This procedure will yield 10,000 numbers, each approximately equal to the area of one of the rectangles formed by segmenting the probability density into subsegments (where, again, the width of each subsegment is just: $dx =$ {the width of the whole segment divided by the number of subsegments}, and the height of each rectangle is equal to the probability density at the halfway point of each rectangle's width). Finally, the integration symbol (the stylized 'S', for 'sum') tells us to take the sum of these 10,000 numbers. This sum is approximately the area under the probability density function (the probability statement under the integral) encompassed by your 10,000 thin rectangles. That's all there is to it.

Exercises

1) Make a plot of a uniform probability density over a 3-unit range, segmented into 5 subsegments. Label the probability density and probability mass of each subsegment.
2) Describe in words the probability mass described by the following equations:
   a. $\int_{-1}^{1} dx\, p(x|\imath)$ [uniform density from -3 to 1]
   b. $\int_{-1}^{1} dx\, p(x|\mu \cdot \sigma \cdot \imath)$ [Gaussian sampling density]
   c. $\int_{-3}^{1} dx\, p(x|\imath)$ [uniform density from -3 to 1]
   d. $\int_{-\infty}^{\infty} dx\, p(x|\mu \cdot \sigma \cdot \imath)$ [Gaussian sampling density]
3) Which of the equations in (2) can you solve now, without reading ahead? What are the solutions?
4) Write the integral equations for the probability masses encompassed by each of the subsegments of the distribution described in (1).

C.1.3 Area under the Curve

Each constituent of the sum that represents an integral is a volumetric element that we will refer to generically as an area, because it is the product of a base (dx) multiplied by a height (density function). The integral, $A = \int_a^b dx\, p(x|\imath)$, tells us the area under the probability density function, $p(x|\imath)$ between $x = a$ and $x = b$; this 'area under the curve' is the probability mass between $x = a$ and $x = b$ accumulated by the probability density function, $p(x|\imath)$.

In the simplest case of the 1D probability density, there is a single base element, corresponding to the abscissa variable. Thus, if the probability is $p(x|\imath)$, the base element used for marginalizing over some segment of the abscissa is dx. There are two examples of marginalization over segments of a 1D probability density shown in Figure C.2. The upper portions of the figures show a 1D Gaussian density (Fig. C.2a) and exponential probability density (Fig. C.2b), and the lower portions show the **cumulative density**

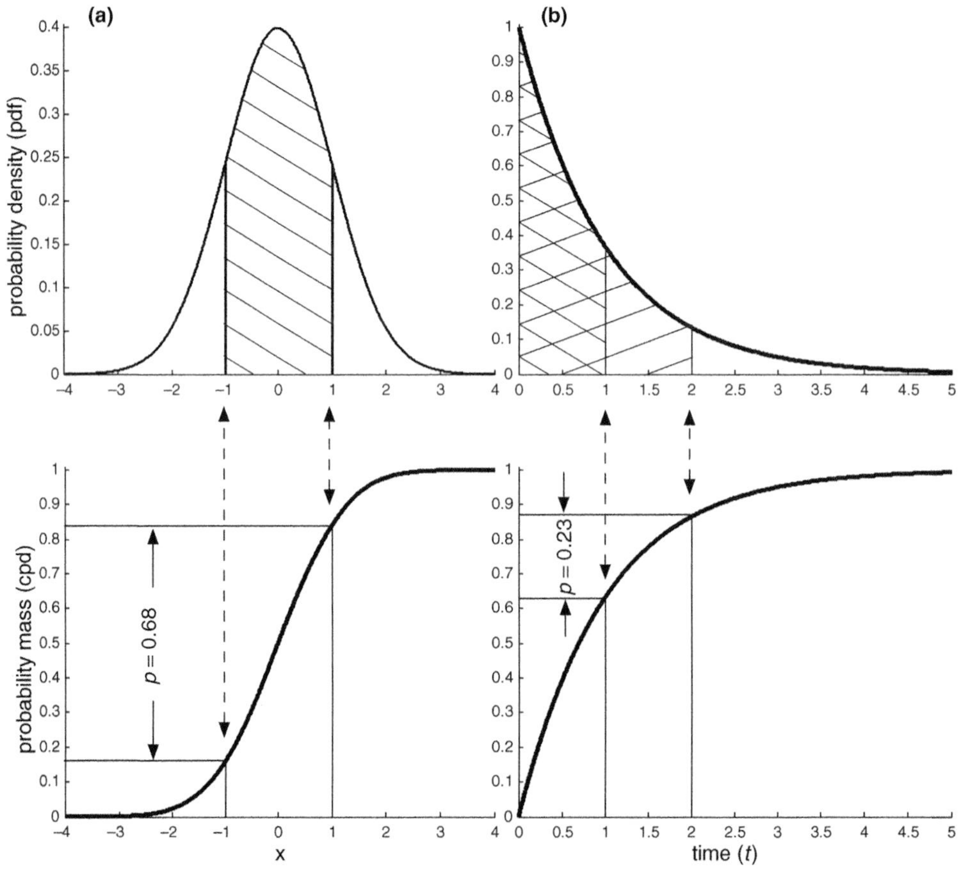

Figure C.2 Probability density functions and their corresponding cumulative probability functions. (a) Gaussian probability density function and its corresponding cumulative probability function. The hatching covers the area under the curve within one standard deviation from the mean. The accumulated probability mass from $x = -\infty$ to $x = -\sigma$ is about $p = 0.16$, and the accumulated mass from $x = -\infty$ to $x = \sigma$ is about $p = 0.84$ (lower plot). (b) Exponential distribution, pdf and cdf. The left-hatched area is the probability mass from $x = 0$ to $x = 1$, whereas the right-hatched area shows the mass accumulated between $x = 0$ and $x = 2$. These masses can be read directly off of the exponential cdf.

associated with each of these. The cumulative density displays the accumulation of probability mass, as you travel from left to right on the abscissa of the probability distributions on the upper plots. In other words, imagine that the probability density functions in the upper portions of the figure represent the thickness of the algae floating atop a small pond. If you were to take a net and skim the top of the pond, then the cumulative probability function would represent the amount of algae that would be caught in your net at any give position of the pond.

Figure C.2a shows the exponential density and the integral over $t = 0$ to $t = 2$:

$$A = \int_0^2 dt\, p(t|\tau \cdot \iota) = \int_0^2 dt\, t^{-1} e^{-\frac{t}{\tau}} = .86,$$

as well as the integral over $t = 0$ to $t = 1$:

$$A = \int_0^1 dt\, p(t|\tau \cdot \iota) = \int_0^1 dt\, t^{-1} e^{-\frac{t}{\tau}} = .63.$$

Notice that the difference between the integral from $t = 0$ to $t = 2$ and the integral from $t = 0$ to $t = 1$ is the integral from $t = 1$ to $t = 2$:

$$\int_1^2 dt\, p(t|\tau \cdot \iota) = \int_0^2 dt\, p(t|\tau \cdot \iota) - \int_0^1 dt\, p(t|\tau \cdot \iota),$$

and that it is generally true that the area under the curve between two points along the abscissa can be decomposed into the area under the curve from the leftmost possible point on the curve to the rightmost of the two bounds minus the area under the curve from the leftmost possible point on the curve to the leftmost of the two bounds. Mathematically, this is:

$$\int_a^b dx\, p(x|\iota) = \int_{\infty}^b dx\, p(x|\iota) - \int_{-\infty}^a dx\, p(x|\iota).$$

Integrals over regions of unidimensional probability densities [those with a single variable to the left of the vertical line in the probability statement, $p(x| \ldots)$] will typically be designed to determine the mass in some segment of the total range of the distribution: otherwise the result of the integration is known beforehand to be unity.

Figure C.2b highlights the area under the curve of a Gaussian density function from $x = -1$ to $x = 1$. This is the mass of a Gaussian distribution contained within 1 SD of the mean, which is about $p = 0.68$. The integral equation describing this marginalized probability mass is:

$$A = \int_{-1}^1 dx\, p(x|\mu \cdot \sigma \cdot \iota) = \int_{-1}^1 dx \left(\sigma\sqrt{2\pi}\right)^{-1} e^{-\frac{x-\mu}{2\sigma^2}} = 0.68.$$

where the first integral is the definition of the area under the Gaussian sampling distribution from $x = -1$ to $x = 1$ and the second integral replaces the probability statement with the equation for the Gaussian. Notice that the area under the upper Gaussian probability density plot can be read off of the cumulative density plot as a difference of ordinate values.

Finally, we might want to integrate over sections of probability distributions with two or more dimensions. In the 2D distribution shown in Figure C.3 this yields an area in the region from $\mu = a$ to $\mu = b$ on one abscissa and $\sigma = c$ to $\sigma = d$ on the other abscissa, and is written:

$$A = \int_c^d d\sigma \int_a^b d\mu\, p(\mu \cdot \sigma | \mathbf{d} \cdot \iota) = \int_c^d \int_a^b d\sigma\, d\mu\, p(\mu \cdot \sigma | \mathbf{d} \cdot \iota)$$

When there are two base elements, such as $d\mu$ and $d\sigma$, they form a rectangular base: and this multiplied by the probability density of that base area yields the probability mass of the volumetric element. This idea is extensible to any number of base elements (x_1 through x_N):

$$A = \int_{a_N}^{b_N} dx_N \ldots \int_{a_1}^{b_2} dx_1\, p(x_1 \cdot x_2 \cdot \ldots \cdot x_N | \mathbf{d} \cdot \iota)$$
$$= \int_{a_N}^{b_N} \ldots \int_{a_2}^{b_2} \int_{a_1}^{b_1} dx_N \ldots dx_2\, dx_1 p(x_1 \cdot x_2 \cdot \ldots \cdot x_N | \mathbf{d} \cdot \iota)$$

and yields the mass contained between $x_1(a_1)$ and $x_1(b_1)$ on the first abscissa, between $x_2(a_2)$ and $x_2(b_2)$ on the second abscissa, and so on for N abscissae. Also, we can remove all but the nth parameter from a multidimensional probability density, as in:

$$p(x_n | \mathbf{d} \cdot \iota) = \int_{-\infty}^{\infty} dx_1 \ldots \int_{-\infty}^{\infty} dx_{n-1} \int_{-\infty}^{\infty} dx_{n+1} \ldots \int_{-\infty}^{\infty} dx_N\, p(x_1 \cdot \ldots \cdot x_N | \mathbf{d} \cdot \iota).$$

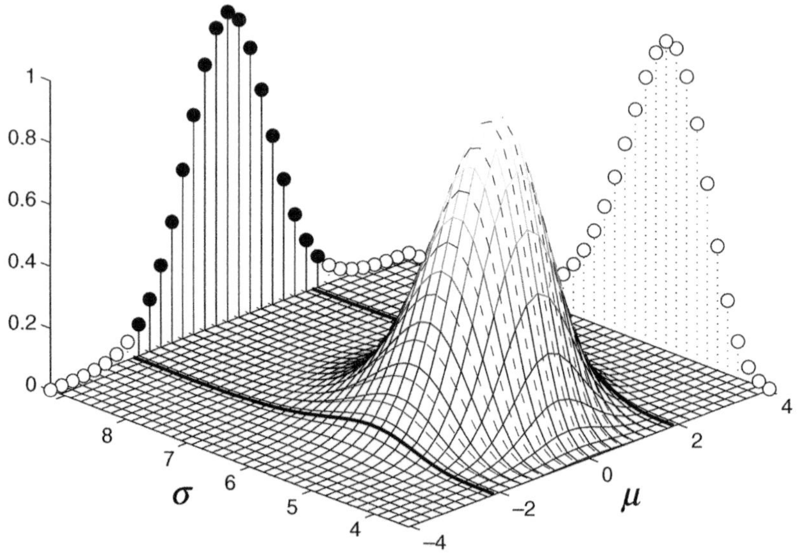

Figure C.3 Two-dimensional Gaussian density over its parameters μ and σ. The stem plots along the μ and σ margins of the plot are the discretized marginal mass distributions associated with integration over the σ and μ dimensions of the 2D density, respectively. Note that both the 2D density and the marginal distributions are scaled so that the peak of each is set to 1. This allows us to easily see the shape of each distribution; otherwise, the height of the 2D density would have been much lower than the marginal distributions, to the point where it is difficult to see its shape.

The solution of these integral equations can become quite difficult (indeed, there are many such equations that simply have no known solution). Thus, whether or not one has advanced calculus training, we must find a way to approximate solutions to these equations.

Exercises

1) Using Figure C.2a, write a single integral equation for the following segments:
   a. $-1 \leq x \leq 1$
   b. $-1 \leq x \leq 0$
   c. $0 \leq x \leq 1$
2) Break the single integrals in (1) into two integrals, each involving $-\infty$.
3) Write, either as a single integral or as the difference of two integrals, equations for the mass contained in the following intervals:
   a. $-5 \leq x \leq 5$, Figure C.2a
   b. $-\infty < x \leq -1$, Figure C.2a
   c. $-\infty < x \leq 0$, Figure C.2a
   d. $-\infty < x \leq 1$, Figure C.2a
   e. $0 \leq x \leq 0.5$, Figure C.2b
   f. $0 \leq x \leq 1$, Figure C.2b
   g. $0 \leq x \leq 2$, Figure C.2b
4) Write the integral that will reduce the 2D distribution in Figure C.3 to a 1D distribution. What is the shape of the resulting density? What is its total area?
5) Estimate the solutions to the integrals described in (1) and (3) using the cumulative densities plotted in the lower panels of Figure C.2.

C.1.4 Sequences of Areas: Discretization

The integral of a segment of a probability density tells us the area under the curve over that segment of the distribution, which is the accumulated probability mass in that segment of the distribution. If we take the areas from the set of all possible (contiguous) segments of a probability density function we find the total probability mass (always $p = 1$). The same can be said of a subset of the total-take a sequence of small areas over that subset of the total and the mass contained within the subset is the sum of the sequence of small areas. This is the essence of numerical integration.

If each small subset of a probability density contains part of the total probability mass, then we can approximate the probability masses needed to marginalize over a subset of the distribution by **discretizing** the probability distribution into a series of small segments and approximating the mass contained within each small segment. In this way, marginalization becomes addition, just as it was when we marginalized discrete mass distributions. The problem now is to approximate the mass within each small segment of the distribution.

One method of approximating the area under the curve for small segments of probability distributions is shown graphically in Figure C.4. Here, the area is broken into two

Sequences of Areas Fig. C.4

Let us verify that, for at least one example, the shaded area of Figure C.4c (as given by the accompanying equation) is equal to the sum of the right triangle formed by the points at $(p(x = e_1 | \imath), e_1)$, at $(p(x = e_2 | \imath), e_2)$, and $(p(x = e_1 | \imath), e_2)$, and the rectangle formed by the points $(p(x = e_1 | \imath), e_1)$, $(p(x = e_1 | \imath), e_2)$, $(0, e_1)$, and $(0, e_2)$, where e_1 and e_1 are the left and right edges of the shaded segment. This example will use the Gaussian pdf with $\mu = 0$ and $\sigma = 1$.

We can evaluate the Gaussian pdf with the MATLAB® function:

```
gpdf=@(xnow,munow,signow) (signow*2*pi)^{(-length(xnow)}*...
      exp((-length(xnow)/2)*((xnow-munow).^{2}/signow^{2});
```

where xnow is a vector of possible abscissa values and munow and signow are the Gaussian location and scale parameters, respectively:

```
x=-[1.1 1 .9]; mu=0; sig=1;
```

Thus, the probability density at x1 and x2 are:

```
px=gpdf(x,mu,sig);
px([1 3])
```

Now, the area of the shaded rectangle in Figure C.4b is:

```
A1=diff(x([1 3]))*px(1);
```

which is the base width multiplied by the height of the rectangle. The area of the hatched triangle atop the shaded rectangle in Figure C.4b is:

```
A2=(1/2)*diff(x([1 3]))*diff(px([1 3]));
```

which is one-half the base of the triangle multiplied by its height.

The sum of A1 and A2 should be identical to the area of the shaded region in Figure C.4c, given by:

```
A=diff(x([1 3]))*px(2);
```

which is the base width multiplied by the probability density at the center of the segment.

We can verify that these areas are equal if the logical output:

```
A==A1+A2
```

is true.

parts: the first is the rectangular shaded area, and the second is the triangular hatched area. The rectangular area is the product of the width and height of the shaded region (Fig. C.4b):

$$A_1 = h_1 \times w,$$

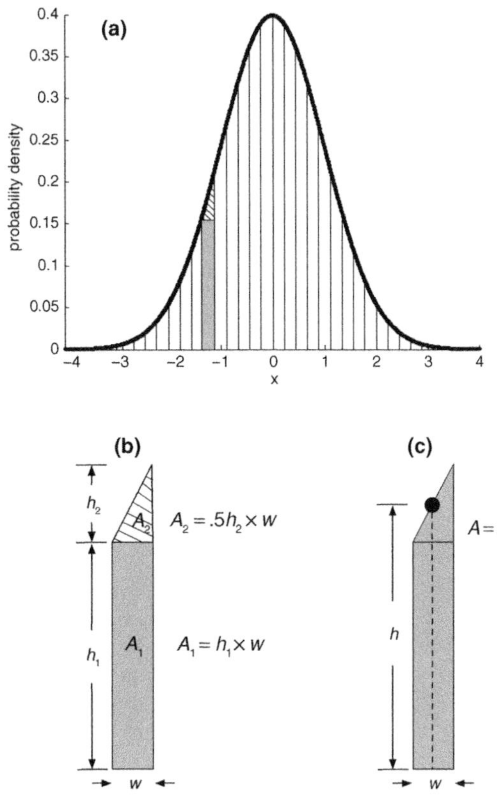

Figure C.4 Demonstration of approximate integration over the highlighted region. (a) The mass of a small segment of the Gaussian density can be found by computing the area (i.e., integrating) the highlighted region. The mass is computed by finding the area under the curve within the highlighted region. (b) To approximate this area, we can find the area in the shaded rectangular region exactly, and approximate the remaining area as a triangle, ignoring any curvature in the small region of the density curve in this small region. (c) This approximate area is equal to the density at the center of the region (stem) multiplied by the width of the region.

and the triangular area is one-half the product of the width and height of the triangle:

$$A_2 = .5(h_2 \times w).$$

The sum of these can be simplified to:

$$\begin{aligned} A_1 + A_2 &= h_1 \times w + .5(h_2 \times w) \\ &= w[h_1 + .5h_2] \\ &= \Delta x \times p(x_0|\imath), \end{aligned}$$

which is interpreted as the the probability density at the precise center of the region, $p(x_0|\imath)$ (shown as the stem in Fig. C.4c), multiplied by the width of the region (Δx in Fig. C.4c).

PA: Uniform Probability Mass (Fig. C.5)

We start by deciding on the range, and writing and computing the analytical functions for the probability density and cumulative density functions:

```
range=[0 3]; truncation=[0 3]; rangeextended=[range(1)
range(2)]+.065*diff(range)*[-1 1];
t=linspace(rangeextended(1),rangeextended(2),5001);
pdfnow=@(tnow,rangenow) ones(size(tnow))./diff(rangenow);
cdfnow=@(tnow,rangenow) (tnow-rangenow(1))/diff(rangenow);
pd=pdfnow(t,range); cpd=cdfnow(t,range);
pd(t<truncation(1))=0; pd(t>truncation(2))=0;
cpd(t<truncation(1))=0; cpd(t>truncation(2))=cpd(find(t<=truncation(2),1,'last'));
```

and continue to define the number of segments (N), the segment edges (segs) and centers (xstem), as well as the probability densities at each segment center (pstem):

```
N=4;
segs=linspace(range(1),range(2),N+1);
dx=diff(segs(1:2))/2;
xstem=dx+segs(1:N); pstem=interp1(t,pd,xstem);
masses=0; masses(end+[1:N])=(2*dx)*pstem;
```

where the masses variable encodes the approximate probability mass contained within each segment. The plots of the corresponding probability density (first subplot) and cumulative density (second subplot) are:

```
figure; subplot(2,1,1); hold on; %upper panel: pdf & approx masses
plot(t,pd,'k-','LineWidth',2.2) %analytically correct pdf
for n=1:N+1, plot(segs(n)*[1 1],[0 pd(findnearestN(t(:),segs(n),1))],'k:'); end
for n=1:N, plot(xstem(n)*[1 1],[0 masses(n+1)],'k-'); end
for n=1:N, plot(xstem(n)+dx*[-1 1],masses(n+1)*[1 1],'k-','LineWidth',5); end
axis([rangeextended 0 1.05*(max([max(pd) max(masses)]))])

subplot(2,1,2); hold on %lower panel: cdf & sums of approx masses
plot(range,[1 1],'k--') %reference line for unity total mass
plot(t,cpd,'k-','LineWidth',2.2) %analytically correct cdf
for n=1:N, plot(xstem(n)+dx*[-1 1],[sum(masses(1:n)) ...
    sum(masses(1:n+1))],'k-','LineWidth',5); end %approx masses
for n=1:N+1, plot(segs(n)*[1 1],[0 cpd(findnearestN(t(:),...
    segs(n),1))],'k:'); end %segment boundaries
axis([rangeextended 0 1.05])
```

The plot for any number of segments (e.g., the 21-segment plots) can be obtained simply by changing the value of the N variable.

Notice that when we discretize a probability density, sampling the density at regular intervals, the sampled probability densities are at the centers of small segments of the abscissa (whose widths are equal to the sampling interval). Thus, the sampled densities are approximately proportional to the probability masses at the corresponding segments centered at each sampled density (Fig. C.4). The more densely packed this regular sampling of probability densities, the more closely the resulting mass function will approximate the true masses in any given subsegment of the probability distribution.

PA: Exponential Probability Mass (Fig. C.5)

The plots shown in Figure C.5 are all simply variations of the plot described above for the uniform distribution, and we will accordingly show only what need be changed to obtain the new plots. In particular, the only necessary changes will occur in the first five lines of code from the previous PA. The remainder of the calculations and the plotting will be identical.

Thus, for the exponential function plotted in Figure C5a the range is from 0 to 5 rather than 0 to 3, and we must update the definitions of the pdfnow and cdfnow functions, along with the calls to these functions. The first five lines of code will therefore be:

```
tau=1; range=[0 5]; truncation=[0 inf];
rangeextended=[range(1) range(2)]+.065*diff(range)*[-1 1];
t=linspace(rangeextended(1),rangeextended(2),5001);
pdfnow=@(tnow,taunow) (taunow^-1)*exp(-tnow/taunow);
cdfnow=@(tnow,taunow) 1-exp(-tnow/taunow);
pd=pdfnow(t,tau); cpd=cdfnow(t,tau);
```

Where we have added a new tau variable and set it to 1. Note that here the second term of the truncation variable changes to inf, which will prevent any truncation of the right-hand side of the distribution. The second line actually has no changes; it simply must occur prior to the fifth line and so is included. Note that the second input to the pdfnow and cdfnow functions has changed to a scalar tau variable (from the two-element range variable above). Also, of course, we have changed the pdfnow and cdfnow functions to those of the exponential density.

Similar modifications to the above five lines (changing the range, adding location, scale or other appropriate variables, and changing the definitions of the pdfnow and cdfnow functions would allow us to examine other densities (e.g., the Gaussian and Cauchy densities in C5b,c).

To see how well this type of approximation works, we compare the (precisely correct) CDF to the approximation in Figure C.5 in three examples (see PAs).

In these examples (Fig. C.5) we see that the 21-element approximate CDFs obtained for these distributions are a bit poorer than that of the exponential distribution. The reason for this decreased precision in the approximation is that there is probability mass accumulated over the left-hand side of the real line that is unaccounted for in the current approximation to the Gaussian and Cauchy CDFs, and causes the approximate CDF to underestimate the total accumulated probability mass at every point on the CDF. For the Gaussian distribution this mass to the left of $x = -5$ is quite small, and has little effect on the approximate CDF. The mass to the left of $x = -5$ on the Cauchy distribution is substantially larger, and causes the approximate CDF to be shifted down relative to the correct values. However, for a symmetrical probability density such as these, we can compute a correction that will approximately eliminate this constant error in the approximate CDF. We simply note that a symmetrical distribution will have the same probability mass above and below any given range; thus we may simply compute half the difference between the total approximated probability mass in the computed range (again, assuming it is symmetrical), and add it to the start of

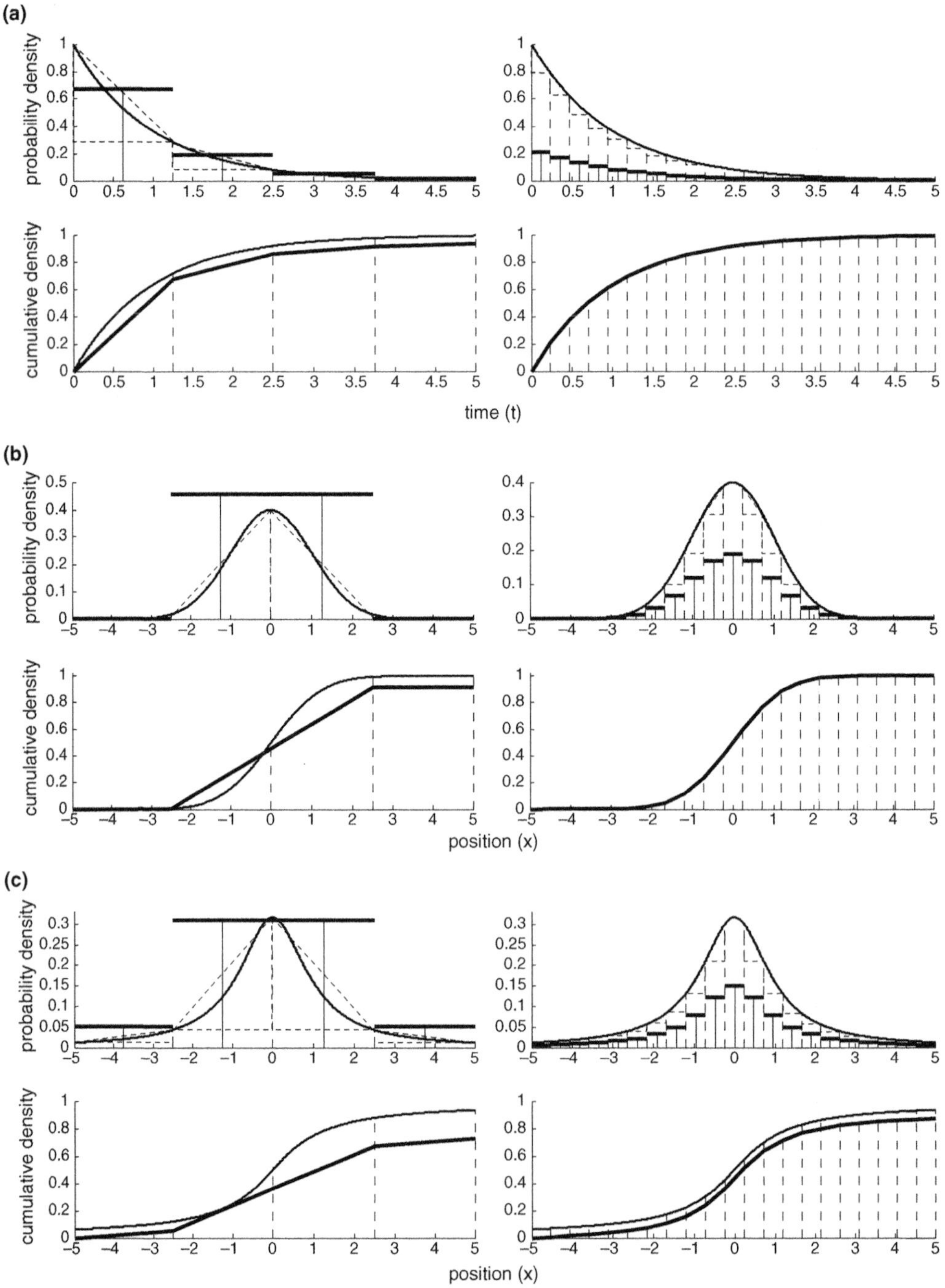

Figure C.5 Probability densities, cumulative densities, and their approximations. (a) Exponential distribution. (b) Gaussian distribution. (c) Cauchy distribution. In all plots, thin solid lines show the exact densities and cumulative densities, and thick solid lines show their approximations when there are 4 segments (left) and 21 segments (right). Vertically oriented long-dashed lines show the edges of segments, and short-dashed lines show the triangular approximations to the true density in the upper plots.

the CDF. This will, on average, eliminate the underestimate caused by ignoring the far-left of the real line when computing an approximate CDF. Obviously, it will also help to compute approximate probability masses over a large range of abscissa values, but there is a limit to this because increasing the number of computed mass points will slow our code, and we must find a balance between precision and the time required to complete our computations (we would obtain a better approximation to the CDF if we used a million segments instead of just 21, but for most applications the resulting increase in precision would not justify the additional computations, or time required to make them).

Exercises

1) Plot a uniform density over the range $3 \leq x \leq 5$, and partition the density into five equal segments.
   a. Write the integral equations that describe the mass of each segment.
   b. Compute the approximate mass in each segment using the rectangular approximation method described above.
   c. Compare this to the exact solution using the CDF of the uniform density.
2) Plot the Gaussian density with $\mu = 0$ and $\sigma = 2$ over the range $0 \leq x \leq 5$, and partition it into 7 equal segments.
   a. Write the integral equations that describe the mass of each segment.
   b. Compute the approximate mass in each segment using the rectangular approximation method described above.
   c. Compare this to the exact solution using the CDF of the Gaussian density.
3) Plot the Cauchy density with $\mu = 0$ and $\sigma = 2$ over the range $-5 \leq x \leq 0$, and partition it into 7 equal segments.
   a. Write the integral equations that describe the mass of each segment.
   b. Compute the approximate mass in each segment using the rectangular approximation method described above.
   c. Compare this to the exact solution using the CDF of the Cauchy density.
4) Why do the approximate CDFs in Figures C.5a–c fail to reach 1? Note that the answer may be different for the different distributions.

C.1.5 Approximate Marginalization of Probability Densities

Now that we have walked through the details of computing the approximate probability masses contained in segments of a probability density, we return to the original problem of marginalizing over probability densities: which occurs both over segments of a density, and over entire axes of a multidimensional density. Here we will examine a combined example, making use of our newfound facility computing approximate probability masses.

Marginalization over Part of a 2D Gaussian Distribution

When we marginalize over some range of the single dimension of a 1D density, we integrate over the density between the bounds that define the range. For example, integration over the Gaussian density over μ between the bounds, $(a, b) = (-2, 2)$ is written:

$$I = \int_a^b d\mu\, p(\mu|x \cdot \sigma \cdot \imath) = \int_{-2}^{2} d\mu (\sigma\sqrt{2\pi})^{-1} e^{-\frac{1}{2}\frac{(x-\mu)^2}{\sigma^2}}.$$

The approximate solution to this integral involves computing a set of masses over many small subranges between the bounds, -2 and 2, and finding the sum of those masses. This can be seen graphically if we imagine that the set of filled circles in the stem plot in the margin of the plot in Figure C.3 is a 1D distribution over μ.

As suggested by the plot in Figure C.3, we can obtain the same result by a slightly more extensive summation over a 2D distribution. The plot demonstrates the marginalization defined by:

$$I = \int_a^b d\mu \int_{-\infty}^{\infty} d\sigma p(\sigma \cdot \mu|x \cdot \imath); \int_{-2}^{2} d\mu \int_0^9 d\sigma (\sigma\sqrt{2\pi})^{-1} e^{-\frac{1}{2}\frac{(d-\mu)^2}{\sigma^2}},$$

in which we are computing the probability that the value of μ lies between -2 and 2, regardless of the true value of σ. This involves first creating the segments defined by the dashed lines that follow the curve of the 2D density, defining the edges of each rectangular region in the marginal 1D distribution over μ (the edges of the regions over which the stem masses are computed). Thus, the total mass of the filled stems at the far left of the discretized marginal distribution is computed by taking the sum of each 2D (volumetric) mass shown in Figure C.3 as the small black sphere at the intersection of gridlines, along the line of masses extending perpendicularly out from that stem. The approximation to the inner ($\int_0^9 d\sigma$) integral is is found by performing this summation for each stem in turn, which results in the marginal stem-plot parallel to the μ axis. The final solution to the integral is found by taking the sum of the filled stem-masses in this marginal distribution.

Note that while it is conceptually straightforward to extend the approximation techniques above to any number of dimensions, the number of computations can quickly increase beyond what is reasonable with extension to more than a few dimensions, making such extensions prohibitively time-consuming. We will limit ourselves to only a few dimensions of marginalization in this text, allowing us to continue using this approximation technique throughout.

Exercises

1) Marginalize over the μ dimension between -3 and 3 in a version of the worked problem in which the data are:
   a. $d = [-3, -2, -1, 0, 1, 2, 3]$
   b. $d = [-13, -12, -11, -10, -9, 9, 10, 11, 12]$
   Plot the full 2D density and the marginalized density in each case.
2) Marginalize over the σ dimension between 0 and 2 in a version of the worked problem where:
   a. $d = [-3, -2, -1, 1, 2, 3, 4]$
   b. $d = [-4, -3, -2, -1, 0, 1, 2]$

Plot the full 2D density and the marginalized density in each case.

C.2 Coordinate Transforms

In Chapter 2 we learned how to manipulate individual probabilities, and progressed to manipulating entire probability distributions. The goal of those computations on probability distributions was to 'transform' priors into posteriors using Bayes' theorem:

$$p(h|d \cdot \iota) = \frac{p(h|\iota)p(d|h \cdot \iota)}{p(d|\iota)} \propto \varpi(h)\mathcal{L}(h) \qquad (1.5),$$

which amounted to multiplying distributions with identical coordinate axes (Fig. C.6a). Here, we will learn how to manipulate distributions in another way: We will transform the *coordinate axes* that locate each probability in the distribution (shown for a 2d distribution in Fig. C.6b). There are two types of transform to be considered: transforming the coordinates of the distribution into a different coordinate system that continues to describe the original distribution *without loss of information*, that is, i.e., **lossless transformation.** We also consider **lossy transformation**, in which one marginalizes over equivalent combinations of inputs (as was done when we considered coin tossing for ordered vs. order-irrelevant sequences) and in the context of eliminating nuisance parameters. Whether implementing a lossy or lossless transformation, the transformation itself is always defined by a **linking function.** This linking function defines the

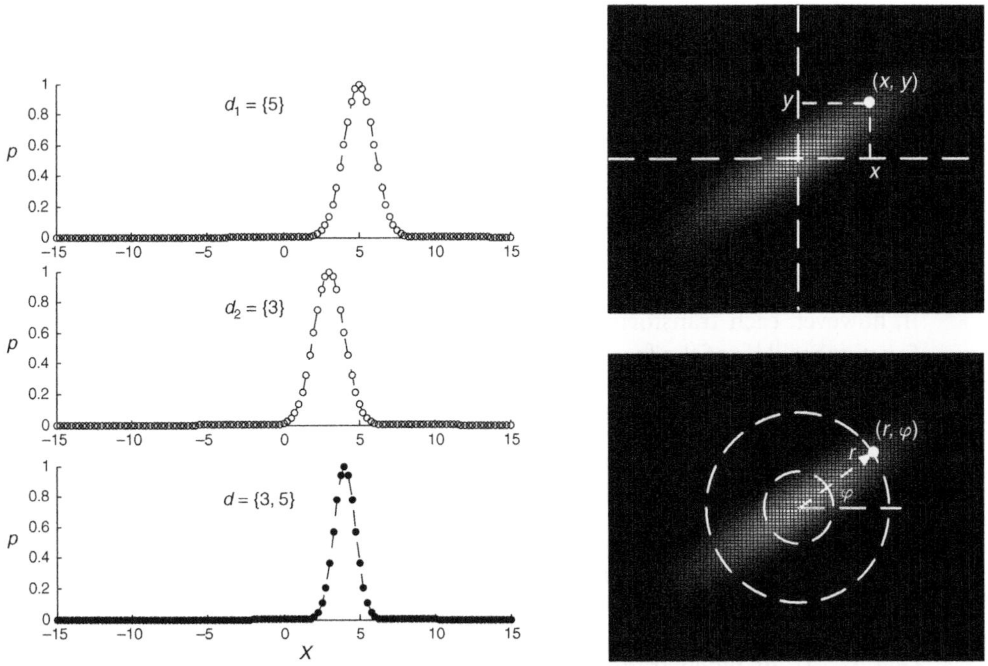

Figure C.6 Two ways to transform probability distributions. (a) Previously we have spoken about 'transformation' of prior information based on a single datum, $p(x|d_1 = 5 \cdot \iota)$, into the posterior over x that takes account of an additional datum, $p(x|\mathbf{d} = \{3, 5\} \cdot \iota)$, as described in Chapter 2. This operation leaves the coordinate axes unchanged. (b) In the current chapter we will transform probability distributions by changing the coordinate axes. This is demonstrated in a 2D distribution overlaid with Cartesian coordinates (upper), transformed into polar coordinates (lower).

mapping from original to transformed coordinates, and is a critical element of the fundamental condition that must be met when transforming probability distributions. That fundamental condition can be stated as: *probability masses must be identical when mapped from original to transformed coordinates.*

C.2.1 Linking Functions for Coordinate Transformation

We will examine three types of linking function: The simplest of these merely scale and/or shift the coordinate axes, such as when transforming from a distribution over time to a distribution over speed, and have a one-to-one relationship between elements of the original and transformed axes.

Simple One-to-One Transformations

If there is a one-to-one relationship between each of the n original and transformed axes, each axis is transformed via an independent linking function of the form:

$$\begin{aligned} x_1' &= l_1(x_1) \\ x_2' &= l_2(x_2) \\ &\vdots \\ x_n' &= l_n(x_n) \end{aligned} \quad \text{(C.2).}$$

For example, rescaling of a single axis, $x' = l(x) = kx$, has this form. In addition, rescaling of a Cartesian axis pair: $l_1 = kx_1, l_2 = kx_2$, or scaled-and-shifted Cartesian axes: $l_1 = kx_1 + c_1$, $l_2 = kx_2 + c2$ have the form (C.2). Note that the identity transform, $x_1' = x_1$, is also a one-to-one transform – indeed it is the canonical example of this class of transformation.

Complex Transformations

If, however, each transformed axis depends on the set of n original axes, then linking functions will be of the form:

$$\begin{aligned} x_1' &= l_1(x_1, x_2 \ldots, x_n) \\ x_2' &= l_2(x_1, x_2 \ldots, x_n) \\ &\vdots \\ x_n' &= l_n(x_1, x_2 \ldots, x_n) \end{aligned} \quad \text{(C.3)}$$

This occurs when rotating a distribution: $l_1 = x_1 \cos\varphi - x_2 \sin\varphi, l_2 = x_1 \sin\varphi + x_2 \cos\varphi$ (Fig. C.7d), or when transforming between Cartesian (x_1, x_2), and polar coordinates $(x_1' = r, x_2' = \varphi)$:

$$l_1 = [(x_1)^2 + (x_2)^2]^{1/2}, l_2 = \tan^{-1}\frac{x_2}{x_1}.$$

Lossy Transformations

A common element of the transforms above is that the dimensionality of the coordinate system remains constant after transformation: n-dimensional coordinates remain n-dimensional following transformation. For example, before and after undergoing a rotation transform, a 2D probability surface is still 2D (Fig. C.6b). The third type of transformation we will consider has the property that transformed probability distributions are lower-dimensional than the original (untransformed) distribution. These transformations produce information loss.

Why would we be interested in transformations that cause information loss? While loss of information sounds like a thing to be avoided, it is actually an essential element of any data analysis: Our aim in analyzing data is to extract information that is relevant to a particular question (i.e., information regarding a particular signal), while discarding (i.e., losing) irrelevant details (information not relevant to the problem). Examples of lossy transformation include transforming from probability distributions over x_1 and x_2 to a probability distribution over their sum (thus discarding information concerning the individual elements that contributed to that sum), or from a 2D distribution over position within a plane to a distribution over distance from the origin point within that plane (discarding information regarding the absolute locations of points at the same distance from the origin). In the first example one might have been interested in the average (or sum) of a set of points, working under the assumption that each individual datum is simply a noisy representation of a single constant. In the second example, one might have been interested in the probability of throwing a dart and hitting targets of various sizes (i.e., distances from target center), regardless of the absolute location of that dart within the target.

Examples of lossless transformations include transforming time observations into speeds for a known distance, Celsius into Fahrenheit temperature, frequency into wavelength, and multidimensional Cartesian into polar coordinates. Why are the latter

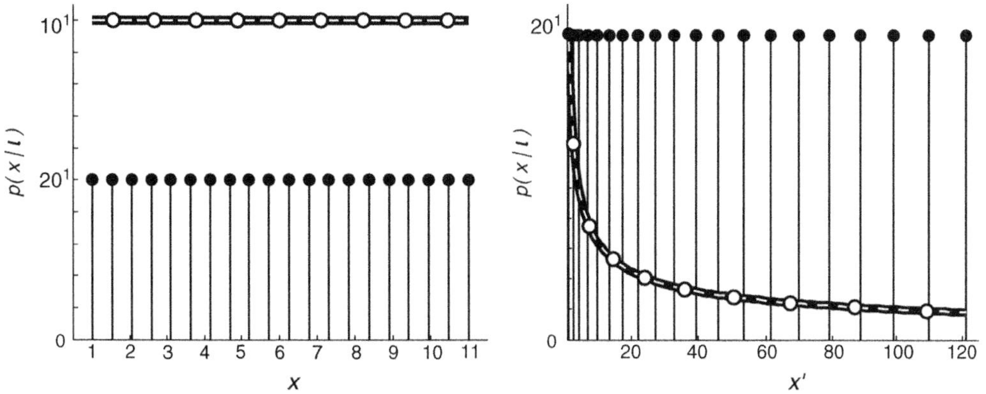

Figure C.7 Transformation of variables: $x' = x^2$. The probability distribution for x is initially uniform (continuous and discrete cases shown as line/open and closed circles, respectively). Transformation of the discrete variable returns another uniform (though unequally spaced) probability *mass* function (closed circles), but transformation of the continuous variable (solid line) returns a nonuniform *density* function for $x' = x^2$. Open circles give the discrete approximation to the density function at a small number of sample points.

lossless and the former lossy? In the former set of cases it is not possible to reverse the transformation, and recover the original (untransformed) variable or variables, because information has been lost. In the latter cases it is always possible to reverse the transformation and completely recover the original probability distribution, indicating that the original information remained intact in the transformed distributions.

Exercises

1) Give three examples of lossless and lossy transformation. What is the critical difference between the two types of transformation?
2) What is the simplest possible linking function?
3) What is the linking function relating temperature measurements on the Celsius and Fahrenheit scales?
4) State the fundamental condition for coordinate transformation.

C.2.2 Transforming Probability Mass Functions

It is the different relationship of continuous and discrete distributions to probability mass that produces slightly different computations associated with transforming the two types of distribution. Because probability mass functions have clearly defined probabilities at specific (punctate) coordinates, the fundamental condition for coordinate transformation can be applied directly – one need only transform between those specific coordinates that contain probability mass. In contrast, it is somewhat more complicated to apply the fundamental condition when dealing with a probability density function – which has no probability (mass) at specific coordinates. When transforming density functions one must take account of any stretching or deformation of the coordinates. Transformation of continuous coordinates is usually accomplished via calculus-based methods. To deal with continuous coordinates without the need for calculus-based methods, we will define the discretely sampled density in Section C.2.3. The transformed sampled density nearly exactly reproduces the transformed continuous density (the resulting distributions overlap – see Fig. C.7, continuous line vs. open circles); the sampled density simply occurs at fewer points. In the present section we will restrict our attention to proper mass functions, and consider both their lossless and lossy transformation. To distinguish between a truly discrete mass function, the discretely sampled approximation to a probability density function, and the fully continuous probability density function, we will use the shorthand terms **mass function, discretized** (or sampled) density, and **density function**, respectively, in the remainder of the text.

Lossless Transformation of Probability Mass Functions

Because discrete probabilities are defined only at punctate coordinates (the counting numbers in this case), it is clear how to satisfy the fundamental condition for transformation: one simply maps the original discrete set of coordinates onto the corresponding set of transformed coordinates, effectively relabeling the coordinates of each mass point. The fundamental condition is automatically satisfied after relabeling the coordinates because we have not changed any of the probability masses.

We can see this relabeling of mass points in the closed circles plotted in Figure C.7. The original coordinates of mass points are the 20 equally spaced coordinates from 1 to

11, and these 20 coordinates are all assigned equal probabilities of 1/20 (i.e., we have defined a uniform probability mass function). The transformation shown in the figure is the mapping of x onto x^2; all masses from the original distribution are located at the square of their original coordinates in the transformed distribution. Notice that the *shape* of the distribution remains unchanged (all probability masses are equal in both panels). Because of the squaring of coordinates, however, transformation has the effect of changing the spacing of mass points from equally spaced to nonuniformly spaced. Specifically, mass points are more densely spaced near the origin and more sparsely spaced far from the origin in the transformed distribution. In contrast, notice that the density and its approximation change shape under this same transformation, and the new shape of the density mirrors the new spacing of mass points (i.e., the density function is higher where the density of mass points is greater near the origin, and the density function is lower where mass points are sparse). This is an important clue to how density functions are transformed and will be elaborated in Section C.2.3.

Two Worked Examples

As step-by-step examples, we will consider two transforms:

$$1 = 5(x + 459.67)/9 \qquad \text{(T1)},$$

$$1 = x^{-1} \qquad \text{(T2)}.$$

T1 has the mathematical form of the transformation between Fahrenheit and Kelvin temperature scales,[2] whereas T2 is the inverse transform.

Example: Transformation between Temperature Scales

For lossless transformation of mass functions, transformation always simply consists of computing the output of the linking function at each value of x that is assigned a probability, and relocating each mass to its transformed x' coordinates. Perhaps the easiest way to visualize the transformation, especially if one is thinking in terms of an example utilizing Fahrenheit and Kelvin temperature scales, is to plot the distribution atop two abscissae; one ruled in Fahrenheit, and one in Kelvin.

Programming Aside: Linear Transforms (Temperature Scales)

A linear transform is always of the form, $x' = \alpha_0 + \alpha_1 x$, where the two constants, α_0 and α_1 shift and scale the input coordinates (x) to produce the output coordinates (x'). In the case of a temperature-scale transform, the constants take the particular values given in (T1). First, we will define these values, and then use them in the linear transform of temperature scales.

```
%%% prelim
alpha0=5*459.67/9;
alpha1=5/9;
x=41:55;
p=ones(size(x))/length(x); %fifteen copies of 1/15
```

[2] Recall that the Kelvin scale is just the Celsius scale shifted by 273.15, so we could convert Kelvin to Celsius via the formula: C=K−273.15.

```
%%% compute transformed coordinates
xprime=alpha0+alpha1*x;

%%% plotting
figure; %create blank figure
subplot(2,1,1); %create sub-figure for original plot
stem(x,p,'k-','MarkerFaceColor','k','MarkerSize',11);
%plot black(colorcode 'k') stems
subplot(2,1,2); %create second sub-figure for transformed plot
stem(xprime,p,'k-','MarkerFaceColor','b','MarkerSize',11); %plot stems
```

The first thing to note is that, as with all transformations of mass functions, none of the probability mass values have changed – only their coordinates have been altered. The second thing to notice is the spacing between mass points in the original and in the transformed coordinates. Although the size of the spaces between mass points changes, the spacing is uniform in both coordinates.

Exercises

1) Plot the distribution over distances, $p(\Delta X|\iota) \propto e^{-\frac{1}{2}\frac{(x-31)^2}{9}}$, whose mass points are located at $\Delta X = [20, 20.25, 20.5, \ldots, 40]$ mm, and the corresponding distribution over speeds if each distance corresponds to a time interval of 10s.
2) Plot the distribution over speeds, $p(\Delta X|\iota) \propto e^{-\frac{1}{2}\frac{(x-28)^2}{16}}$, whose mass points are located at $s = [15, 15.25, 15.5, \ldots, 40]$, and the corresponding distribution over distances if each speed corresponds to a time interval of 8s.
3) Plot the distribution over time intervals, $p(\Delta t|\iota) \propto e^{\frac{(x-11)^2}{2}}$, whose mass points are located at $\Delta t = [0, 0.1, 0.2, \ldots, 20]$, and the corresponding distribution over speeds if each time interval corresponds to a distance of 21mm.
4) Plot the distribution over speeds, $p(\Delta X|\iota) \propto e^{-\frac{1}{2}\frac{(x-9.5)^2}{1.44}}$, whose mass points are located at $s = [0, 0.1, 0.2, \ldots, 15]$, and the corresponding distribution over time intervals if each speed corresponds to a distance of 9mm.

Example: Inverse Transform

The inverse transform is nonlinear, and therefore provides an important contrast to the temperature-scale transform above. Here, the original probability masses will be located at the equally incremented series of 100 locations $x = \{1, 2, \ldots, 100\}$. As above, the transformed coordinates (whatever the masses associated with those coordinates) are simply the 100 coordinate locations centered on $1/50$: the locations defined by applying the linking function to the original coordinates, $x' = l(x) = \{0.01, 0.0101, \ldots, 1\}$. Here, the original distribution is a discrete uniform distribution with linearly spaced masses. The transformed distribution is also discrete and has uniform masses, but these masses are nonlinearly spaced.

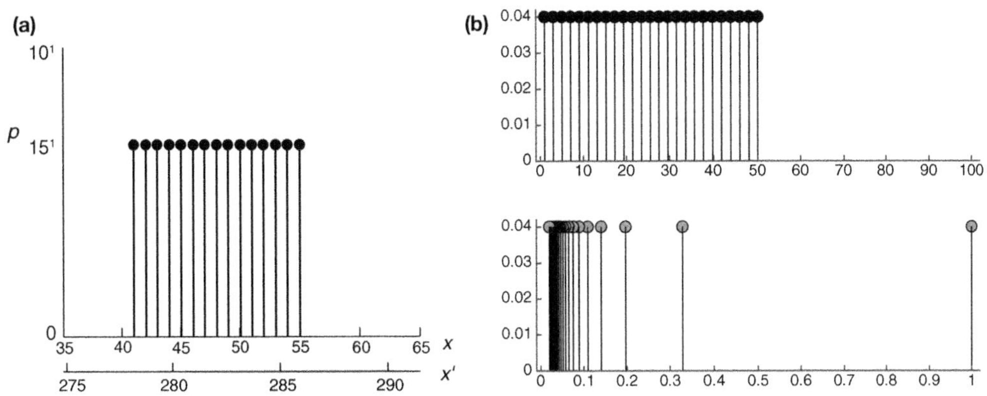

Figure C.8 Discrete transforms. (a) Transform of uniform probability mass function following T1. Both the original (upper abscissa) and transformed (lower abscissa) coordinates have probability masses at equally spaced intervals. (b) Inverse transform of a uniform probability mass function, which becomes unequally spaced after transformation.

PA: Inverse Transform

Here we demonstrate the inverse transform defined in (T2).

```
%%% prelim
x=linspace(1,100,25); %equally spaced values bet. 1 and 100
xprime=1./(x); %transformed coordinates
p=ones([length(xprime) 1])./length(xprime); %uniform distribution

%%% plotting
figure; subplot(2,1,1); %create figure and sub-figure for original plot
stem(x,p,'k-','MarkerFaceColor','k','MarkerSize',11);
%plot black (colorcode 'k') stems
axis([-1 102 0 1.05*p(1)]); box off
subplot(2,1,2); stem(xprime,p,'k-','MarkerFaceColor',.6*[1 1 1],'MarkerSize',11);
axis([-.01 1.02 0 1.05*p(1)]); box off
```

Notice that even though the uniform distribution retains its rectangular shape after nonlinear transformation with the inverse transform (Fig. C.8b), the density of the spacing changes. It was uniform in the original distribution, but becomes nonuniformly packed closer to the origin in the transformed distribution.

Exercises

1) Perform a log transform of the uniform distribution whose masses are located at unit intervals from 1 to 40.
2) Perform the T1 transform of the Gaussian distribution, $p(x|\iota) \propto e^{-(x-3.4)^2}$, whose masses are located at intervals of .1 from 0 to 9.
3) Perform a squaring transform of the Gaussian distribution, $p(x|\iota) \propto e^{-(x-3.4)^2}$, whose masses are located at intervals of .1 from 0 to 9.

Lossy Transformation of Mass Functions: Two Worked Examples

As stated briefly above, lossy transformation of probability mass functions is accomplished via marginalization over the coordinate axes that contain information irrelevant to the current problem (e.g., summing over coin-toss orderings that have the same number of heads and tails). As worked examples, we will consider two theoretically important cases: sums and differences of number-pairs:

$$x_1' = l(x_1, x_2) = x_1 + x_2 \qquad \text{(T3).}$$

$$x_2' = l(x_1, x_2) = x_2 - x_1. \qquad \text{(T4).}$$

As we will see below in these worked examples, the sum rule is much more general than simple applications of binomial probabilities; it is the basis for all lossy coordinate transforms. We will consider two examples of lossy transformation: sums and differences of coordinates. The sum transform provides the information in averages over coordinates, which has deep connections with the Gaussian distribution (whose argument, as we saw in Chapter 2, is the mean of data coordinates) and relatedly is also the basis for a famous statistical result known as the central limit theorem. The difference transform gives the information in distances between spatial positions: another commonly sought piece of information.

Example: Sums of Coordinates

There are many other reasons to be interested in sums: the simplest discrete case of this kind involves two rolls of a die. Several games of chance, such as the game of craps, involve the sum of two such rolls. For dice with six sides, we will assume that our information is uniform with respect to the different faces of each die, leading to a discrete uniform distribution for our prediction of which side of any given die will face upward on any given throw:

$$p(F|\iota) = [6^{-1}, 6^{-1}, 6^{-1}, 6^{-1}, 6^{-1}, 6^{-1}] \quad \{F = [1, 2, 3, 4, 5, 6].$$

Indicating with subscripts to which die we are referring, the joint probability of any particular two upward-facing sides must therefore be (assuming independent probabilities that is, one dieface does not provide information about the identity of the other die face): $p(F_1 \cdot F_2|\iota) = p(F_1|\iota) = p(F_2|\iota) = (6^{-1})^2 = 6^{-2}$. Although this is correct for any particular pair of *faces*, the possible *sums* are not in one-to-one correspondence with possible face-pairs, because there are multiple sets of face-pairs that yield the identical sum. Thus, as was done above, we must use the sum rule to obtain the probability of a sum that can be achieved with different facepairs. To see which sums are defined by more than one set of face-pairs, the constituents of sums may be enumerated: The smallest sum that can occur in two throws is $F_1 + F_2 = 2$, which can occur in only one way: $(F_1, F_2) = (1, 1)$. The next largest sum is $F_1 + F_2 = 3$, which can occur in two ways: $(F_1, F_2) = \{(1, 2), (2, 1)\}$, etc. Figure C.9a represents the full enumeration of possible sums, along with the appropriate corresponding face-pairs. Since the probabilities of all facepairs are equal in this example, we see that the probability of each sum is simply $p(S|\iota) = p(F_1 + F_2|\iota) = M_s p(F_1 \cdot F_2|\iota)$, where M_s is the multiplicity, or number of ways that a given sum can be achieved, and $p(F_1 \cdot F_2|\iota)$ is 6^{-2} for any values of F_1 and F_2 (based on our current background information).

(a)

$F_1 + F_2 = S$	die-faces: (F_1, F_2)	$p(F_1 + F_2 \vert \iota)$
$S = 2$	(1,1)	$p = 1(6^{-2})$
$S = 3$	(2,1) (1,2)	$p = 2(6^{-2})$
$S = 4$	(3,1) (2,2) (1,3)	$p = 3(6^{-2})$
$S = 5$	(4,1) (3,2) (2,3) (1,4)	$p = 4(6^{-2})$
$S = 6$	(5,1) (4,2) (3,3) (2,4) (1,5)	$p = 5(6^{-2})$
$S = 7$	(6,1) (5,2) (4,3) (3,4) (2,5) (1,6)	$p = 6(6^{-2})$
$S = 8$	(6,2) (5,3) (4,4) (3,5) (2,6)	$p = 5(6^{-2})$
$S = 9$	(6,3) (5,4) (4,5) (3,6)	$p = 4(6^{-2})$
$S = 10$	(6,4) (5,5) (4,6)	$p = 3(6^{-2})$
$S = 11$	(6,5) (5,6)	$p = 2(6^{-2})$
$S = 12$	(6,6)	$p = 1(6^{-2})$

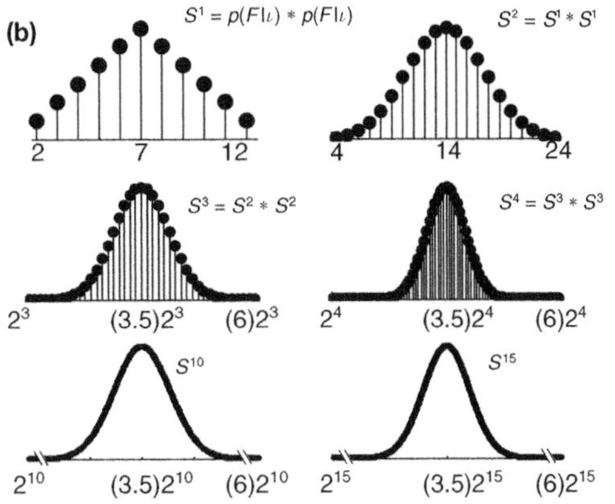

(c)

$F_2 - F_1 = D$	die-faces: (F_1, F_2)	$p(F_2 - F_1 \vert \iota)$
$D = -5$	(6,1)	$p = 1(6^{-2})$
$D = -4$	(6,2) (5,1)	$p = 2(6^{-2})$
$D = -3$	(6,3) (5,2) (4,1)	$p = 3(6^{-2})$
$D = -2$	(6,4) (5,3) (4,2) (3,1)	$p = 4(6^{-2})$
$D = -1$	(6,5) (5,4) (4,3) (3,2) (2,1)	$p = 5(6^{-2})$
$D = 0$	(6,6) (5,5) (4,4) (3,3) (2,2) (1,1)	$p = 6(6^{-2})$
$D = 1$	(1,2) (2,3) (3,4) (4,5) (5,6)	$p = 5(6^{-2})$
$D = 2$	(1,3) (2,4) (3,5) (4,6)	$p = 4(6^{-2})$
$D = 3$	(1,4) (2,5) (3,6)	$p = 3(6^{-2})$
$D = 4$	(1,5) (2,6)	$p = 2(6^{-2})$
$D = 5$	(1,6)	$p = 1(6^{-2})$

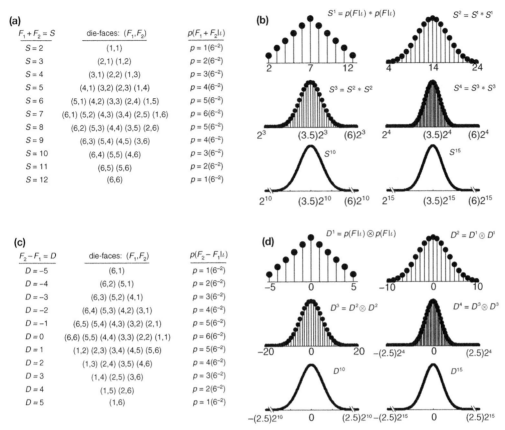

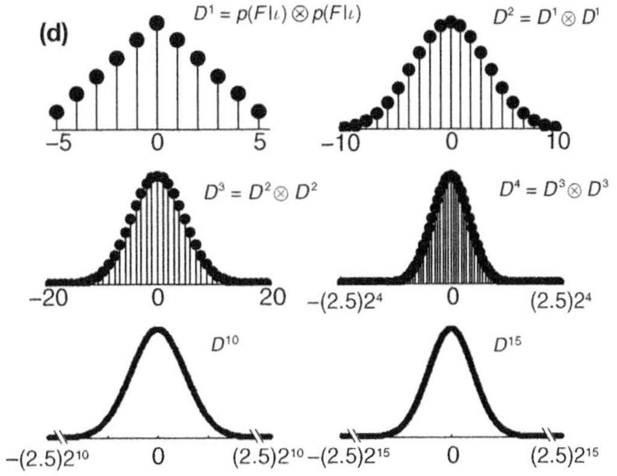

Figure C.9 Sums and differences of coordinates. (a) Full enumeration of face-pairs corresponding to the outcome of two die throws (center). To either side are listed the sums (S) corresponding to the face-pairs along a row (left) and their probabilities (right). (b) Convolutions of die-throw probabilities. The number of convolutions used to describe each sum is $2^n - 1$ for the sum S^n. A single convolution describes the sum of two die-face distributions. Note that the total range of coordinate values is discontinuous in the last two plots to allow for better comparisons between distributions. (c) Mirror of (a), enumerating differences of coordinates. (d) Higherorder cross-correlations of the uniform die-face distribution. As with higher-order convolutions of the uniform die-face distribution, these tend toward the Gaussian shape.

This enumeration of possible outcomes allows us to immediately write the discrete distribution over possible sums of two die throws. However, it becomes tedious when there are more than two throws, or each 1D distribution has more possible outcomes (e.g., a 20-sided die). A more elegant solution presents itself if we recognize two things: First, our prior information, ι, lets us write the probabilities of impossible outcomes for die faces that do not exist, for example, $p(F_1 = -3|\iota) = 0$. This is because our prior information contains the statement of the problem and any background facts, physical laws, etc. that are pertinent to the problem. Here, this includes the fact that there are six faces on a die, numbered 1 through 6. All other integer values are therefore assigned probability zero, leading to the expanded uniform distribution for die throws:

$$p(F|\iota) = [\ldots 0, 0, 6^{-1}, 6^{-1}, 6^{-1}, 6^{-1}, 6^{-1}, 6^{-1}, 0, 0, \ldots] \quad \{F = [\ldots -1, 0, 1, 2, 3, 4, 5, 6, 7, 8 \ldots].$$

Second, we recognize that the facts listed in Figure C.9a concerning die faces and sums are not all independent: Knowing any two of F_1, F_2, and S allows us to deductively determine the third. Figure C.9a was constructed by assuming that we start with F_1 and F_2 in order to determine S. However, we can also begin with F_2 and S to determine F_1. Done in this way, we can write the lossy probability of $S = 5$ as:

$$\begin{aligned}
p(S_5|\iota) &= p(F_1 + F_2 = S_5|\iota) \\
&= \sum_k p([F_2 = k] \cdot [F_1 = S_5 - k]|\iota) \\
&= \ldots + p([F_2 = k = -1] \cdot [F_1 = S_5 - F_2 = S_5 - k = 6]|\iota) \\
&\quad + p([k = 0] \cdot [F_1 = 5]|\iota) \\
&\quad + p([k = 1] \cdot [F_1 = 4]|\iota) + \ldots \\
&\quad \ldots + p([k = 6] \cdot [F_1 = -1]|\iota) \\
&\quad + p([k = 7] \cdot [F_1 = -2]|\iota) + \ldots \\
&= \ldots + 0 + 0 + 6^{-2} + \ldots + 6^{-2} + 0 + \ldots = 4(6^{-2}),
\end{aligned}$$

which is the solution we obtained by enumeration. However, this representation of the logical statement for each probability in the distribution allows us to write the lossy distribution over sums in a very succinct form:

$$\begin{aligned}
p(S_l|\iota) &= p(F_1 + F_2 = S_l|\iota) \\
&= \sum\nolimits_k p(F_2 = k \cdot F_1 = l - k|\iota) \; \{k, l \ni \mathbb{Z}
\end{aligned} \tag{C.4}$$

where the subscript l gives the coordinate of the sum, which can take any integer value from $-\infty$ to ∞; although only a small subset have nonzero probability in the example of two die throws. The subscript k is the coordinate of one of the two elements of the sum, which also takes all integer values under the summation sign for *each* value of the l subscript. Thus, one iterates the values of the l subscript only once, but the summation requires that one also iterate through the values of the k subscript once for each value of the l subscript.

This equation (C.4) for the probability of a sum is referred to as (discrete) convolution, and is often written, $p(S_1|\iota) = p(F_1|\iota) * p(F_2|\iota)$. Aside from its compact written form, convolution also has the nice property that it can be extended to the sum of any number of die throws. The probability distribution of the sum of three die throws is described by $p(F_1|\iota) * p(F_2|\iota) * p(F_3|\iota)$, and for n throws the probability distribution is given by: $p(F_1|\iota) * p(F_2|\iota) * \ldots * p(F_n|\iota)$.

The first 4 iterations in a geometric progression of convolutions are shown in Figure C.9b. This figure also shows the distribution at the 10th and 15th points in that geometric progression, to approximate the limit as the number of throws becomes very large. Interestingly, the *shape* of the distribution changes under convolution. We started with a uniform distribution and ended with a distribution having the Gaussian shape. The Gaussian shape does not change much between the 50th and 100th convolutions; many convolutions of uniform distributions (as the number of convolutions approaches infinity) approaches a stable Gaussian shape. This is also true of many other initial distribution shapes.

Exercises

1) The lossy transform from two observations to a single measurement of their sum was described above. The probability distribution over possible sums is almost identical to the distribution over possible means of the two observations, where the distribution over mean requires a second (lossless transform). Give this distribution.
2) We stated in the text that a convolution of the probability distributions describing three die throws is simply $p(F_1|\imath) * p(F_2|\imath) * p(F_3|\imath)$. Convince yourself of this by enumerating the possible outcomes in the manner of Figure C.9.
3) Perform three consecutive convolutions of $p(F|\imath)$. Compare this result to the distribution labeled S^2 in Figure C.9b.
4) Create an uniquely shaped discrete distribution, and convolve it with itself 100x. Plot and describe the shape of the result.

Example: Differences of Coordinates

As a final example involving lossy transformation of discrete distributions, we will consider differences of coordinates, which describe the possible differences of die-throws from the example in the previous subsection. Just as above, we can enumerate the full set of differences and corresponding die faces for two die throws (Fig. C.9c). Indeed, the latter are the identical set of 36 possible die faces. The differences, however, now range from -5 to 5 instead of 2 to 12 for sums. There is an interesting parallel between the probabilities of difference-defined and sum-defined coordinates (starting from two copies of the same input distribution). The transformed distributions are identical: Only their coordinates differ (compare Figs. C.9a, c). The similarity extends also to how probabilities of differences are computed, which has a very similar form to the convolution technique described above for the probabilities of sums. As above, we include impossible outcomes/coordinates:

$$p(F|\imath) = [\ldots 0, 0, 6^{-1}, 6^{-1}, 6^{-1}, 6^{-1}, 6^{-1}, 6^{-1}, 0, 0, \ldots]\ \{F = [\ldots -1, 0, 1, 2, 3, 4, 5, 6, 7, 8 \ldots],$$

and also recognize that we can write the probability of any difference of die faces, such as the difference $D = F_2 - F_1 = 4 = D_4$ in the form:

$$\begin{aligned}
p(D_4|\imath) &= p(F_2 - F_1 = 4|\imath) \\
&= \sum_k p\left([F_2 = k] \cdot [F_1 = D_4 + k]|\imath\right) \\
&= \ldots + p\left([F_1 = k = -1] \cdot [F_2 = D_4 + F_1 = D_4 + k = 3]|\imath\right) \\
&\quad + p\left([k = 0] \cdot [F_2 = 4]|\imath\right) \\
&\quad + p\left([k = 1] \cdot [F_2 = 5]|\imath\right) \\
&\quad + p\left([k = 2] \cdot [F_2 = 6]|\imath\right) \\
&\quad + p\left([k = 3] \cdot [F_2 = 7]|\imath\right) + \ldots \\
&= \ldots + 0 + 0 + 6^{-2} + 6^{-2} + 0 + \ldots = 2(6^{-2}),
\end{aligned}$$

leading to a similarly concise formula for differences:

$$p(D_l|\imath) = p(F_2 - F_1|\imath)$$
$$= \sum\nolimits_k p(F_1 = k \cdot F_2 = l + k|\imath) \quad \{k, l \ni \mathbb{Z} \qquad \text{(C.5)},$$

where the subscript l gives the coordinate of the difference, which in this example can any integer value. This formula for computing the probabilities of differences is usually referred to as the (discrete) cross-correlation function, written: $p(D_1|\imath) = p(F_1|\imath) \otimes p(F_2|\imath)$.

This parallel to the lossy sum transformation can be seen again in higher-order cross-correlations of die face probabilities. Figure C.9d shows several such distributions. These distributions are identical to those in Figure C.9b, except that the center of the distribution is always at the origin in the difference coordinate system, instead of at $3.5(2^n)$ in the sum coordinate system. It is important to note that whereas the convolution is insensitive to the order of its inputs [it is commutative, i.e., $p(F_1|\imath) * p(F_2|\imath) = p(F_2|\imath) * p(F_1|\imath)$], the cross-correlation is not, and in general $p(F_1|\imath) \otimes p(F_2|\imath) \neq p(F_2|\imath) \otimes p(F_1|\imath)$]. In addition, for the distributions shown in Figure C.9b the distribution S^1 corresponds to $2^1 - 1$ convolutions of $p(F|\imath)$, and the distribution S^2 corresponds to $2^2 - 1$ convolutions, or $S^2 = [p(F|\imath) * p(F|\imath)] * [p(F|\imath) * p(F|\imath)] = p(F|\imath) * p(F|\imath) * p(F|\imath) * p(F|\imath) * p(F|\imath)$, etc. The same is not true in Figure C.9d, because in general cross-correlations are neither commutative nor associative:

$$D^3 = D^2 \otimes D^2$$
$$= \big(p(F|\imath) \otimes p(F|\imath)\big) \otimes \big(p(F|\imath) \otimes p(F|\imath)\big).$$
$$\neq p(F|\imath) \otimes p(F|\imath) \otimes p(F|\imath) \otimes p(F|\imath)$$

The associative property is explored in the Exercises.

In addition to using the discrete convolution and cross-correlation formulas given in (C.4) and (C.5), there is another more geometric approach to computing the lossy distribution over sums and differences of two sets of die faces. This method involves two stages: First, we perform a lossless transformation into a new set of orthogonal coordinates that include the coordinates of the desired distribution (e.g., sums of die faces) as one of these orthogonal dimensions, and then marginalize over the remaining dimensions (e.g., differences of die faces). The case of sums and differences is particularly convenient because sums and differences are orthogonal dimensions that contain all of the information from any pair of numbers. That is, if you are given the sum and difference of two numbers, you can convert that sum and difference pair into the original pair of numbers and back again losslessly; that is, there is a one to one correspondence between the two pairs of numbers.

Consider, for example, the pair of die faces after two throws, which for variety we will assume each have 11 equiprobable faces. One can represent the joint probability, $p(F_1, F_2|\imath)$ as the 2D distribution in Figure C.10. As shown, one can also represent sets of equisum and equidifference coordinates by 45° lines overlaid on the 2D die face coordinates, where the intersection of any equidifference and equisum line corresponds to a unique 2D coordinate in (F_1, F_2) space. However, note that not all intersections correspond to possible (F_1, F_2) coordinates. For example, the coordinates of the intersection of the $D = 0$ and $S = 15$ lines is $(F_1, F_2) = (7.5, 7.5)$, which has probability $p(F_1, F_2) = 0$.

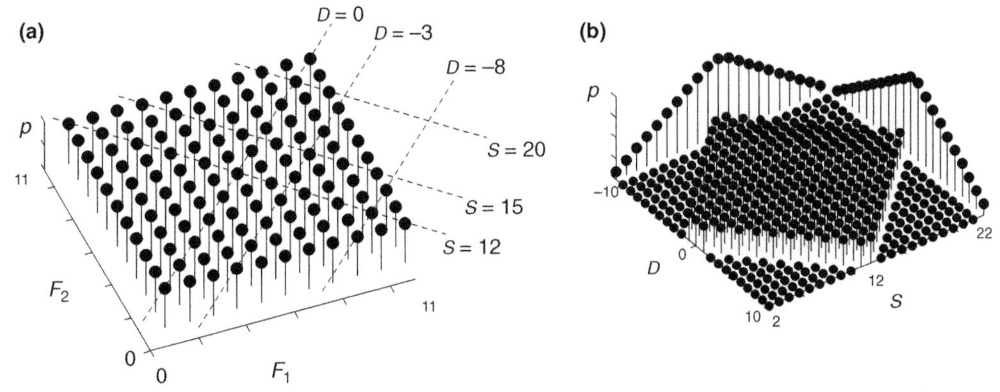

Figure C.10 Joint probability of the outcomes of two throws of an '11-sided die.' (a) Each mass-point contains an equal 11^{-2} probability. Dotted lines define slices through the 2D function corresponding to equal differences in die-faces. All equi-difference lines are parallel; the three corresponding to differences of 0, −3, and −8 are highlighted. Dashed lines define equi-sum slices through the 2D space of die-face microstates. The intersection of any equi-difference and equi-sum line corresponds to a unique 2D coordinate in (F_1, F_2) space. (b) The lossless transform of the 2D distribution with coordinates (F_1, F_2) is given in the 2D joint distribution $p(S \cdot D|\iota)$. The lossy transforms into the coordinates of *either* sums or differences are given by the (triangular) marginal distributions. The cause of the perfectly triangular shape of the lossy transform given by the first convolution and cross-correlation above is now clear – it occurs because in both cases we are marginalizing over a diamond-shaped uniform 2D distribution.

Now rotate this distribution by 45°, so the dotted and dashed lines that indicate equal differences and sums parallel the coordinate axes. This rotated distribution has the diamond-shape configuration shown in the enumeration of differences of Figure C.9c, but has the property that mass points are no longer aligned with integer axis values. This is because, in the rotated coordinates, points that had previously been separated diagonally (i.e., connected by the hypotenuse of a $1 - 1 - \sqrt{2}$ right triangle) are now aligned to the coordinate axes. Thus, an original-coordinates location of $(F_1, F_2) = (0, 1)$, whose coordinates have both a sum and difference of 1, should be located at the transformed coordinates $(S, D) = (1, 1)$; rotating the original coordinates puts this point at $\left(\sqrt{2}^{-1}, \sqrt{2}^{-1}\right)$. In other words, rotation alone creates a grid of coordinates that is too closely spaced to represent sums and differences. The desired spacing is obtained by scaling the rotated coordinates by $\sqrt{2}$. The resulting distribution is shown in Figure C.10b; the only element added to the 2D lossless transform from the distribution shown in Figure C.10a is the set of zero-probability mass points at the coordinates of impossible face-pairs (i.e., those containing an impossible die face below 1, above 11, or at noninteger values). These points do not change the distribution, but merely fill in the empty spaces on the unit-spaced grid that our background information tells us have zero probability. This allows us to specify the full 21×21 grid of unit-spaced sums and differences in each axis' respective range.

This treatment of the problem now only requires that we (separately) marginalize the two dimensions. Marginal distributions corresponding to the transformed sum-defined and difference-defined coordinates that are possible from two 11-sided die throws are shown in Figure C.10b. They are, of course, identical to the solutions defined by (C.4)

PA: Using the Built-In Convolution and Cross-Correlation Functions

One can compute the sum or difference of pairs of probability distributions using the built-in convolution and cross-correlation functions, respectively. Start with the distribution:

```
x=1:10, p=ones(1,10);
```

then compute the convolution of this with itself:

```
xS=2:20; pS=conv(p,p);
figure; subplot(2,1,1); hold on;
stem(xS,pS,'k.'); plot(xS,pS,'ko','MarkerFaceColor','k','MarkerSize',7)
```

And finally verify that the cross-correlation of this distribution with itself produces identical probabilities (but different x-coordinates):

```
subplot(2,1,2); hold on;
xD=-9:9; pD=xcorr(p,p);
stem(xD,pD,'k.'); plot(xD,pD,'ko','MarkerFaceColor','k','MarkerSize',7)
```

compute the difference

```
pS-pD
```

and (C.5) for the same problem – that is, two equal triangular distributions. This geometric approach makes it clear why the convolution and cross-correlation of the sampling distribution for two repetitions - two identical probability distributions, such as $F * F$ and $F \otimes F$, or $D^3 * D^3$ and $D^3 \otimes D^3$ – must always be identical and symmetrical: they are the marginal distributions of a rotationally symmetric 2D distribution $[p(F_1 \cdot F_2|\iota)$, or $p(D^3 \cdot D^3|\iota)]$. This must always be the case because any 2D distribution formed by 'extending the question' from identical marginals onto a 2D grid as in Figure C.10 will always be symmetrical. The next step is to rotate this symmetric distribution on a square grid by 45° and scale to restore unit spacing, thus defining a distribution over a central diamond-shaped region, and zero-probability masses over the rest of a square grid, now extended to encompass the central diamond region.

Exercises

1) The lossy transform from two observations to a single measurement of their sum was described above. The probability distribution over possible sums is almost identical to the distribution over possible means of the two observations. Give this distribution.
2) We stated in the text that the cross-correlation of the probability distributions describing three die throws does not obey the relation: $\left[p(F_1|\iota) \otimes p(F_2|\iota)\right] \otimes p(F_3|\iota) = p(F_3|\iota) \otimes \left[p(F_1|\iota) \otimes p(F_2|\iota)\right]$. Convince yourself of this by computing and plotting both. What is the relationship of the two?

3) As in Exercise 2, perform three consecutive cross-correlations of $p(F|\iota)$. Compare this result to distribution labeled D^2 in Figure C.9.
4) Using the usual case of a six-sided die, construct lossless 2D distributions and their corresponding lossy marginal distributions consistent with Figure C.10:
   a. for the case corresponding to D^1 and S^1.
   b. for the case corresponding to D^2 and S^2.
5) In terms of the two-stage process described in Figure C.10, give two reasons for the rapid reduction of probabilities near the edges of the S^n and D^n distributions in Figure C.9.

C.2.3 Approximate Transformation of Probability Densities

Until now we have restricted ourselves to probability mass functions, whose defining feature is that they contain proper probability masses, defined at specific (punctate) coordinates along the abscissae of probability distributions. These distributions are useful descriptions of things like the possible outcomes of coin tosses, where there is a discrete set of possible outcomes. However, we will often need to assign and transform probability distributions defined over a continuous range of coordinate values. This is where the concept of a *probability density* comes in. Just as with a physical density, a probability density is defined as the mass per unit volume, and has no proper probability (mass) at punctate coordinates. Rather, within a density function, the probability masses are defined only over *ranges* of coordinates. To work with probability densities on a computer, we must *discretize* them. That is, take discrete samples from the full density function and define a corresponding *sampled density function.* We then compute approximate masses contained within each sampled segment of the density function and transform coordinates using these sampled mass functions (Fig. C.7).

Exercises

1) Compute N regular segment centers and edges for the coordinate range $-10 \le x \le 10$:
   a. $N = 5$
   b. $N = 6$
   c. $N = 10$
   d. $N = 11$
   e. $N = 11$
   f. $N = 20$
2) In previous exercises (discrete distributions), we created mass functions from equations such as $p(x|\iota) \propto 1/t$ by defining a set of points at which to evaluate the equation, and then normalizing the result. This procedure is effectively the same as what one does to compute regularly sampled masses from a continuous density.
   a. Explain this equivalence, and when it does and does not hold.
   b. Show what happens if this procedure is used with irregular sampling.
3) When a continuous density is sampled with unit spacing, approximate masses and sampled densities are numerically equal. Plot a segment of any nonuniform continuous

function, and the sampled density and corresponding approximate masses when segment centers are spaced at:

a. $\Delta x > 1$

b. $\Delta x < 1$

Approximate Lossless Transformation: Probability Densities

Returning to the fundamental condition for transformation, we can use the sampled masses computed within each segment to accomplish our goal of approximate lossless transformation of probability densities. The fundamental condition for transformation states that probability mass must remain constant over original and transformed coordinates. Thus, for the ith pair of corresponding segments in the original $(\Delta x_i^{'})$ and transformed (Δx_i) coordinates, the approximate mass [the product of the density and the segment width, $p(y|\imath)\Delta y$] is equated:

$$p(x_i|\imath)\Delta x_i = p(x_i|\imath)l(\Delta x_i^{'}) = p(x_i^{'}|\imath)\Delta x_i^{'} \qquad \text{(C.6).}$$

Because probability mass does not change under coordinate transformation, we can assign the set of approximate masses to the transformed coordinates of each original mass point. These transformed masses must then be converted back to density units at their new locations. Approximate mass values were computed by multiplying the probability density values at the center of each original segment by the original segment widths. To transform from mass units back to density units within the ith transformed segment, we simply divide by the new segment lengths; that is, the widths of the transformed segments:

$$p(x^{'}|\imath) = \frac{p(x_i|\imath)\Delta x_i}{\Delta l(x_i)} \qquad \text{(C.6a),}$$

$$= \frac{p\left(l^{-1}(x_i^{'})|\imath\right) l^{-1}(\Delta x_i^{'})}{\Delta x_i^{'}} \qquad \text{(C.6b),}$$

$$= \frac{p\left(l^{-1}(x_i^{'})|\imath\right) l^{-1}(\Delta x_i^{'})}{\Delta x_i^{'}} \qquad \text{(C.6c),}$$

which is simply a restatement of the fundamental condition given in (C.6). This expression is written in two ways, depending on whether we are starting with a set of original coordinates or a set of transformed coordinates. If one has the transformation equation, and a set of probability-coordinate pairs in original coordinates, then it is easy to apply (C.6a) to obtain the transformed density $p(x_i^{'}|\imath)$. On the other hand, if one begins with a desired set of transformed coordinates, it is easiest to use the inverse transform $x_i = l^{-1}(x_i^{'})$ to choose the sample points in original coordinates, and then convert the original-coordinate sampled densities into an equivalent representation in transformed coordinates. This can be accomplished directly using the inverse transform and either original or inverse-transformed density function in (C.6b,c) to obtain sampled densities in the desired transformed coordinates.

Approximate transformation of probability density functions using (C.6) has the effect of stretching or compressing the probability mass contained within each original segment, depending on the nature of the transformation. Stretching/compressing a mass to

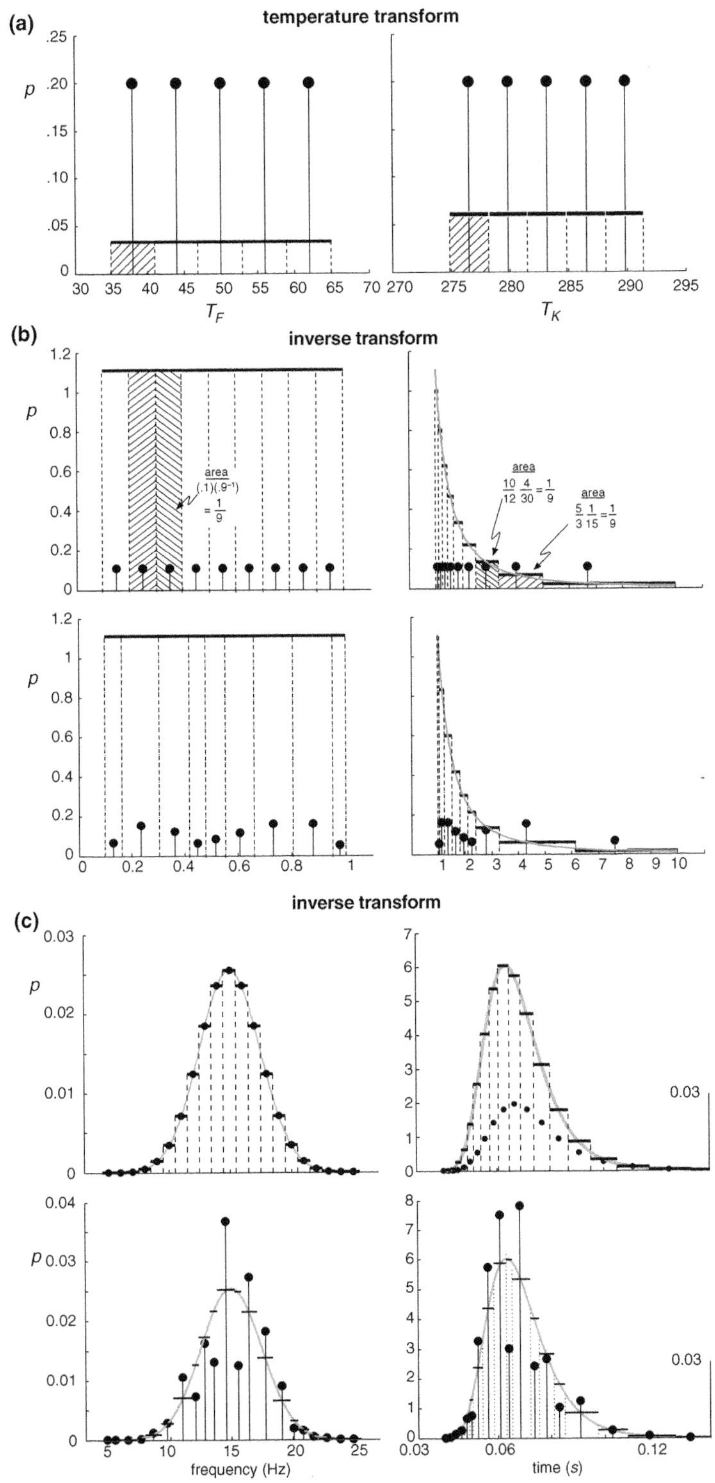

Figure C.11 Lossless transformation of continuous densities. (a) Transformed uniform density over temperature. (b) Inverse transformation of a uniform density. Approximate transformation using regularly-spacing (upper panels) and irregularly spacing (lower panels). (c) Inverse transformation of a normalized truncated Gaussian with regular spacing (upper) and irregular spacing (lower).

fill more or less transformed volume causes the density within each segment to transform simultaneously with the coordinates. For example, the distribution of uniformly spaced segments that is transformed by the inverse function in Figure C.11, has a set of equal probability masses (original distribution) that is transformed into a set of increasingly wide segments. When probability masses correspond to a discrete distribution the masses simply shift. When those discrete mass points are used to represent the probability mass over segments of a continuous distribution, those masses are shifted and are then transformed back into density units, which can change the shape of the original distribution. In general then, the shape of a continuous distribution will be different after a transformation of the coordinate system. This method of transforming 1D distributions can be extended to densities of any dimensionality. We must simply recognize that equating the probability over segments of the original and transformed coordinates requires that we take account of changes in the areas of segments within the 2D distribution, or the volumes of regions within a 3D distribution, etc.

Exercises

1) From the following sets of sampled masses (m_i) and width ratios [i.e., $r_i = \frac{\Delta x_i}{\Delta l(x_i)}$], plot the corresponding transformed (sampled) densities.
   a. $m_i = \{.0357, .0714, .1071, .1429, .1786, .2143, .25\}$
      $r_i = \{1, 1.1814, 1.3956, 1.6487, 1.9477, 2.301, 2.7183\}$
   b. $m_i = \{.2222, .1944, .1667, .1389, .111, .0833, .0556, .0278, 0\}$
      $r_i = \{2.718, 2.399, 2.117, 1.868, 1.649, 1.455, 1.284, 1.133, 1\}$
   c. $m_i = \{.04, .08, .12, .16, .2, .16, .12, .08, .04\}$
      $r_i = \{1, 1.4142, 1.7321, 2, 2.2361, 2.45, 2.646, 2.828, 3\}$
2) From the following sets of original coordinates (segment centers, x_i), compute width ratios [$r_i = \frac{\Delta x_i}{\Delta l(x_i)}$] for the given linking function:
   a. $x_i = \{-10, -9, -8, \ldots, 10\}; x' = 0.5x^3$
   b. $x_i = \{2, 6, 10, \ldots, 38\};\ x' = x^2 - x$
   c. $x_i = \{-10, -9, -8, \ldots, 10\};\ x' = lnx$
   d. $x_i = \{-11, -10, -9, \ldots, -1\};\ x' = x^{-1}$
   e. $x_i = \{-10, -9, -8, \ldots, 10\};\ x' = 5^{-1}e^{-x/5}$
3) From the following sets of original coordinates (segment centers, x_i) and sampled densities (densities evaluated at segment centers, p_i), compute transformed densities from Figure C.7 for the linking function: $x' = x^2$. Plot both the original and transformed sampled densities.
   a. $x_i = \{2, 6, 10, \ldots, 98\}$
      $p_i = \{0.04, 0.04, 0.04, \ldots, 0.04\}$
   b. $x_i = \{0.25, 0.75, 1.25, \ldots, 9.75\}$
      $$p_i = \left\{ \begin{array}{l} 0.27, 0.23, 0.21, 0.18, 0.16, 0.14, 0.12, 0.11, 0.092, 0.081, 0.071, \\ 0.062, 0.054, 0.047, 0.041, 0.036, 0.032, 0.028, 0.024, 0.021 \end{array} \right\}$$
   c. $x_i = \{1.04, 1.12, 1.19, 1.27, 1.35, 1.42, 1.5, 1.58, 1.65, 1.73, 1.81, 1.88, 1.96\}$
      $p_i = \{0.75, 0.806, 0.861, 0.917, 0.972, 1.03, 1.08, 1.14, 1.19, 1.25, 1.31, 1.36, 1.42\}$
4) Derive the inverses [$x = f^{-1}(x')$] of the following linking functions (i.e., solve the following equations for x):
   a. $t' = f(t) = 2t$
   b. $x' = f(x) = x^{-1}$

c. $y' = f(y) = y^2$
d. $z' = f(z) = \ln z$

5) From the following sets of transformed coordinates (equal-sized transformed segment centers), compute transformed densities for the transform defined by the corresponding subproblem from Exercise 3 and the original-coordinates density defined above, $p(t|\bar{t} \cdot t_{max} \cdot \iota)$:
a. $t_i' = \{1, 3, 5, \ldots, 19\}; t_{\max} = 10$
b. $t_i' = \{0.05, 0.15, \ldots, 0.95\}; t_{\max} = 10$
c. $t_i' = \{0.05, 0.15, \ldots, 0.95\}; t_{\max} = 10$

Two Worked Examples

Here, we will reexamine the two worked lossless example problems from above, assuming an underlying continuous distribution:

$$l = 5(x + 459.67)/9 \qquad \text{(T1)},$$

$$l = x_1^{-1} \qquad \text{(T2)},$$

again using the temperature (T1) and inverse (T2) transforms.

Example: Transformation between Temperature Scales

The approximate transformation of density functions following (T1) is shown graphically in Figure C.11a. First, the masses associated with each segment of the density are computed (left-hand panel). Then, we proceed exactly as if transforming a discrete mass function: those mass points are repositioned to their corresponding locations in the transformed coordinates. Each mass corresponds to one of the five segments defined in the original distribution, transformed into Kelvin-temperature coordinates. Finally, the density corresponding to each transformed segment is computed as the density that results from spreading the corresponding probability mass across the width of the transformed segment. This method represents an approximation to continuous transformation of probability density functions because it results in a set of densities whose values are constant within each segment and step discretely between segments, rather than a smooth variation of densities across and within segments.

Normally, a better approximation to the underlying continuous probability density can be obtained by sampling the original density at closer intervals. Here, however, a uniform density transformed via a linear transform yields an exact solution regardless of the number of samples of the original distribution are taken (Fig. C.11a, left). In general, however, a better approximation to the original density is obtained by sampling the original density at closer and closer-spaced intervals, and finer-grained sampling of the original density also provides a better approximation to the transformed density. We will see examples of this in the next example.

This step-by-step example using the uniform density followed the procedure defined by (C.6a). That is, we were given a set of initial-coordinate locations and associated densities, and asked what the corresponding densities at a set of transformed coordinates would be. If we had instead been given a set of desired transformed coordinates, we would find the transformed density values from (C.6b). To accomplish the transformation using

(C.6b), we begin by deriving $l^{-1}(X_i')$, to give Fahrenheit temperature as a function of Kelvin temperature:

$$x_i = l^{-1}(X_i') = 9X_i'/5 - 459.67$$

and over the ith segment, $\Delta X_i'$, this converts to:

$$l^{-1}(\Delta X_i') = l^{-1}(X_{i2}') - l^{-1}(X_{i1}') = \frac{9}{5}(X_{i2}' - X_{i1}')$$

at the X_i' locations shown in Figure C.11a (right). Furthermore, because the original-coordinates (Fahrenheit) density is uniform, the sampled densities in all original-coordinates segments are equal to: $p(x_i|\imath) = 30^{-1}$. Thus, transformed density samples are approximated by:

$$p(x_i'|\imath) = \frac{p(x_i|\imath)l^{-1}(\Delta X_i')}{\Delta X_i'} = \frac{30^{-1}\left[\frac{9}{5}(X_{i2}' - X_{i1}')\right]}{X_{i2}' - X_{i1}'} = \frac{9}{5}30^{-1},$$

at each of the uniformly sampled segments shown in Figure C.11a. Here, we also see why changing the size of the sampled segment does not improve the approximate transformed density. All terms that encode the segment size, $\Delta X_i'$, drop out of the final equation, and so choosing a finer or coarser sampling of coordinates would not have affected the outcome of the computation.

There is a second way in which one may sample from probability densities: Instead of sampling more or fewer points (i.e., a finer or coarser sampling), one may also sample at irregular intervals. For example, imagine that we had sampled the original distribution at the first, third, and last samples used in Figure C.11a. These three sampled densities would result in the three probability masses: $p = [0.20.60.2]$. Although these three masses are unequal, they will transform onto segments whose widths are in the ratio 1:3:1, and therefore will result in a transformed density that is again uniform. As we will see below, this 'conservation' of the shape of the transformed density in the face of changes in the specifics of the sampling used to produce that transformed density is a general feature of transformed densities, and not specific to uniform densities.

Exercises

1) Starting from a Gaussian density in Celsius, $p(C|\imath) = (5\sqrt{2\pi})e^{-\frac{1}{2}(\frac{x}{5})^2}$ $(-20 < x < 20$ in 81 increments), transform into a density in Kelvin. Plot both densities on the same plot.
2) Starting from a Gaussian density in Celsius, $p(C|\imath) = (5\sqrt{2\pi})e^{-\frac{1}{2}(\frac{x}{5})^2}$ $(-20 < x < 20$ in 81 increments), transform into a density in Fahrenheit. Plot both densities on the same plot.
3) Starting from a Gaussian density in speed, $p(S|\imath) = (10\sqrt{2\pi})e^{-\frac{1}{2}\left(\frac{|S-100|}{10}\right)^2}$ $(60 < x < 140$ in 81 increments), transform into a density in distance. Plot both densities on the same plot.
4) Recompute the distance density obtained in Exercise 3 using N increments:
   a. $N = 11$
   b. $N = 41$
   c. $N = 101$
   d. $N = 201$

Example: Inverse Transform

In the previous example, the scale of the coordinate system is compressed by a constant factor. This scaling does not change the shape of the transformed density relative to the original. However, when we transform using a nonuniform linking function, the shape of the resulting transformed density will generally change. Here, we will explore this effect using the inverse transform[3] (T2) transforming both a flat and a bell-shaped distribution.

The inverse transformation of a uniform distribution is shown in Figure C.11b, and demonstrates substantial nonuniform compression of small relative to large-valued coordinates (notice also the reverse ordering of the range). Smaller segment-widths (corresponding to smaller abscissa values) must have higher probability density in the transformed distribution, because all segments contain the same probability mass.

The upper panels of Figure C.11c provide a second example of the inverse transform, now applied to a density function whose original shape is nonuniform. The original density has the Gaussian shape, in this example given by:

$$p(f\,|\,\mu \cdot \iota) = .0255e^{-\frac{(f-\mu)^2}{12.5}} \; \{5 \leq f \leq 25,$$

where $\mu = 15$. Transformation causes the same skewing of the original distribution that was seen in the top panels for the uniform distribution. Here, the Gaussian shape of the original distribution causes the compressed widths at the low-coordinate end of the distribution to have less effect on density values, and the transformed density is still peaked in the interior of its range rather than at the lower edge (as occurred for the transformed uniform).

The sampled-density transformations shown in the upper panels of Figure C.11b,c used regular, equal intervals of the original coordinates to compute approximate masses for the transformation. How would the transformation change if we segmented the original coordinate axis into irregular intervals? Certainly, the set of approximating masses would no longer have the same shape as the underlying density function, as can be seen in the lower rows of Figure C.11b,c. There, we have sampled the same uniform and Gaussian densities, but now at irregular intervals within the original coordinates. In both cases the resulting approximate density has the same shape as found for uniform sampling. The transformed density values resulting from these irregular-width segments fall on exactly the same curve as the regular-width transformed densities; the curve obtained when segment-widths approach zero.

Notice that the units of the original and transformed coordinates are given as time and frequency. This is perhaps the most common use of the inverse transform; transforming from times (latencies, or time intervals) to frequencies and vice versa, which have the relation $f = 1/T$. This transform switches between units of occurrences per second (frequency, in Hz or Δs^{-1}), and the time interval between occurrences (Δs). Consistent with the idea that the inverse transform is a lossless transform between time intervals

[3] Note a possible point of confusion: the terms 'inverse function' and 'inverse transform' are used to refer both to the specific linking function $x' = l(x) = 1/x$, and the general case of a function $l^{-1}(x')$ that takes the transformed coordinate as input to return the original coordinate value. The meaning in any particular case will have to be inferred from context.

PA: Transforming a Truncated Gaussian with Regular and Irregular Spacing

We first transform a regularly spaced sampled Gaussian using the inverse transform.

```
%%% prelim
l1=@(xprime) 1./xprime; Ebase=-10.5:10.5; Tbase=-10:10;
Lt=length(Tbase); t=linspace(Ebase(1),Ebase(end),450);
load pfnfile
pt=out.p(t); mt=out.p(Tbase);
Tshift=Tbase+15; Eshift=Ebase+15; tshift=t+15;

%%% plot original Gaussian
figure(5); clf; hold on
plot(tshift,pt,'-','Color',.7*[1 1 1],'LineWidth',2.2)
plot(Eshift(1)*[1 1],[0 mt(1)],'k--','LineWidth',.75);
for n=1:(Lt),
    try plot((Eshift(n+1))*[1 1],[0 max(mt(n:n+1))],'k--','LineWidth',.75); end
    plot((Eshift(n:n+1)),mt(n)*[1 1],'k-','LineWidth',2.25);
    plot((Tshift(n)),mt(n),'ko','MarkerFaceColor','k','MarkerSize',9);end
axis([3 27 0 .03]);

%%% plot transformed Gaussian
figure(6); clf; hold on
plot(l1(Tshift),mt*100,'ko','MarkerFaceColor','k','MarkerSize',7);
[PCout]=pTX(pt,tshift,l1);
plot(PCout(:,2),PCout(:,1),'-','Color',.7*[1 1 1],'LineWidth',4)
[PCout]=pTX(mt,Tshift,l1);
for n=1:(Lt), %plot(l1(Tshift(n))*[1 1],[0 mt(n)*233.3333],'k-','LineWidth',.5);
    plot(l1(Eshift(n:n+1)),PCout(n,1)*[1 1],'k-','LineWidth',2.25);end
[PCout]=pTX(mt,Tshift,l1);
plot(l1(Eshift(1))*[1 1],[0 mt(1)],'k--','LineWidth',.75);
for n=1:(Lt),
    try plot(l1(Eshift(n+1))*[1 1],[0
          max(PCout(n:n+1,1))],'k--','LineWidth',.75); end, end
axis([0.03 .14 0 7]);
```

Then we perform this transform with irregularly spaced Gaussian.

```
%%% prelim
t=[-10.5 10.5];
ts=linspace(t(1),t(2),450); tplot=ts+15;

Lt=11; dmean=diff(t)/Lt;
dEprime=rand(Lt-1,1)*dmean+dmean/2;
Eprime=[t(1); t(1)+cumsum(dEprime); t(2)]; Eplot=Eprime+15;
Xprime=[]; m=[]; for n=2:length(Eprime),
    Xprime(n-1)=mean(Eprime(n-1:n));
    m(n-1)=out.p(Xprime(n-1))*diff(Eprime(n-1:n)); end
Xplot=Xprime+15;

%%% plot original Gaussian
figure(5); clf; hold on
plot(Xplot,m,'ko','MarkerFaceColor','k','MarkerSize',11)
plot(tplot,out.p(ts),'-','Color',[.7 .7 .7],'LineWidth',2.6)
for n=1:length(Xprime),
    plot(Xplot(n)*[1 1],[0 m(n)],'k-')
    plot(Eprime(n:n+1)+15,out.p(Xprime(n))*[1 1],'k-','LineWidth',2.1); end

%%% transform
l1=@(xprime) 1./xprime;
```

```
pmx=pTX(m,Xplot,l1); pex=pTX(out.p(Eprime),Eplot,l1);
ptx=pTX(out.p(Xprime),Xplot,l1);

%%% plot transformed Gaussian
figure(6); clf; hold on
for n=1:length(Eplot), plot(l1(Eplot(n))*[1 1],[0 pex(n)],'k:','LineWidth',.05); end
PCout=pTX(out.p(ts),tplot,l1);
plot(PCout(:,2),PCout(:,1),'-','Color',[.7 .7 .7],'LineWidth',2.6)
PCout=pTX(out.p(Xprime),Xplot,l1);
for n=1:length(Xplot),
    plot(l1(Xplot(n))*[1 1],[0 pmx(n)],'k-');
    plot(l1(Xplot(n)),pmx(n),'ko','MarkerFaceColor','k','MarkerSize',11);
    plot(l1(Eplot(n:n+1)),PCout(n,1)*[1 1],'k-','LineWidth',2.1); end
axis([0.03 .14 0 .5]);
```

and temporal frequencies, the two units are completely interchangeable, in the sense that neither provides more or less information than the other. The choice of which to use will generally be one of convenience. For example, if either the original or transformed distribution has a particularly useful shape, then the units that produce that shape will be preferred.

Exercises

1) Transform the density, $p(f|\iota) = \left(4\sqrt{2\pi}\right) e^{-\frac{1}{2}\frac{(f-8)^2}{4^2}}$, over frequency to one in time (use a 30 Hz range, incremented in steps of .25 Hz). What is the transformed density at the times corresponding to:
   a. 8 Hz
   b. 4 Hz
   c. 15 Hz
   d. 0 Hz
2) Create a transformed density over Kelvin temperature from a sampled uniform density on [5,15] C, with $N = 2, 5, 50$, and 100 samples. Plot each transformed density when samples regularly and irregularly spaced (the latter should be chosen via random number generator). Describe any differences between transformed distributions based on regular and irregular sampling schemes as N is increased.
3) Create a transformed density over time intervals from the density, $p(f|\mu \cdot \iota) = .0255e^{-\frac{(f-\mu)^2}{12.5}}, (5 \leq f \leq 25;\ \mu = 15)$ over frequency. Use $N = 2, 20, 50, 100$ samples taken both regularly and irregularly over the range. Plot both sets of transformed functions, and describe any differences between transformed distributions based on regular and irregular sampling schemes as N is increased.

Approximate Lossy Transforms: Two Worked Examples

As stated above, lossy transformation of probability mass functions is accomplished via marginalization over unwanted dimensions of a distribution. The same applies for continuous densities. Because we are dealing with approximate transforms, we will be approximating the sums necessary for lossy transformations by computing probability masses from segments of the density function as we did above for lossless transformation. The first of two worked examples will examine transformation from Cartesian to polar coordinates:

$$l = \left((x_1)^2 + (x_2)^2\right)^{\frac{1}{2}} \qquad \text{(T1a)},$$

$$l = \tan^{-1}\left(\frac{x_2}{x_1}\right) \qquad \text{(T1b)},$$

and the second examines transformation from two individual observations to sum-difference coordinates:

$$l = x_1 + x_2 \qquad \text{(T2a)},$$

$$l = x_2 + x_1 \qquad \text{(T2b)}.$$

As we will see below in these worked examples, the same algorithm that was used above for discrete distributions can be applied to lossy transformation of probability densities. We simply first create segments of regular size in the dimension of the transformed variable whose density is the desired distribution (i.e., the conserved dimension of the lossy transform).

Example: Dartboard Distance and Angle

This example describes the transform we are interested in performing when we have a target with a bull's-eye, and we want to compute the probability of observing dart distances and angles on that dartboard. The sampling probabilities of dartboard locations is assigned a 2D Gaussian density over Cartesian locations on the dartboard.

A 2D Gaussian given in a Cartesian coordinate system does not directly provide us with the probabilities associated with distances and angles from the origin of the coordinate system (bull's-eye). To obtain distance and angle probabilities, we transform from Cartesian to polar coordinates, and marginalize alternately over the distance and angle dimensions of that polar representation to obtain lossy angle and distance transforms, respectively.

Before we can perform an approximate lossy transform of a sampled probability density, it is useful to consider an appropriate regularly spaced segmentation of the transformed (polar) coordinates that will allow for the desired marginalization over transformed coordinates. This in turn will lead us to the appropriate segmentation of the original (Cartesian) coordinate system. This segmentation, based on regular spacing in polar space, is shown in Figure C.12a. We make the simplest assumption to compute probability masses associated with each segment: that each segment is approximately rectangular in shape; height equal to the range of distances covered by a segment ($h = \Delta\rho = \rho_{\max} - \rho_{\min}$), and width equal to the width of each segment at its center ($w = 2\rho\tan[\Delta\varphi/2]$). Although the width is an approximation to a constant rectangular width which is itself an approximation to the shape of a segment, these approximations become less crude as segment sizes decrease.

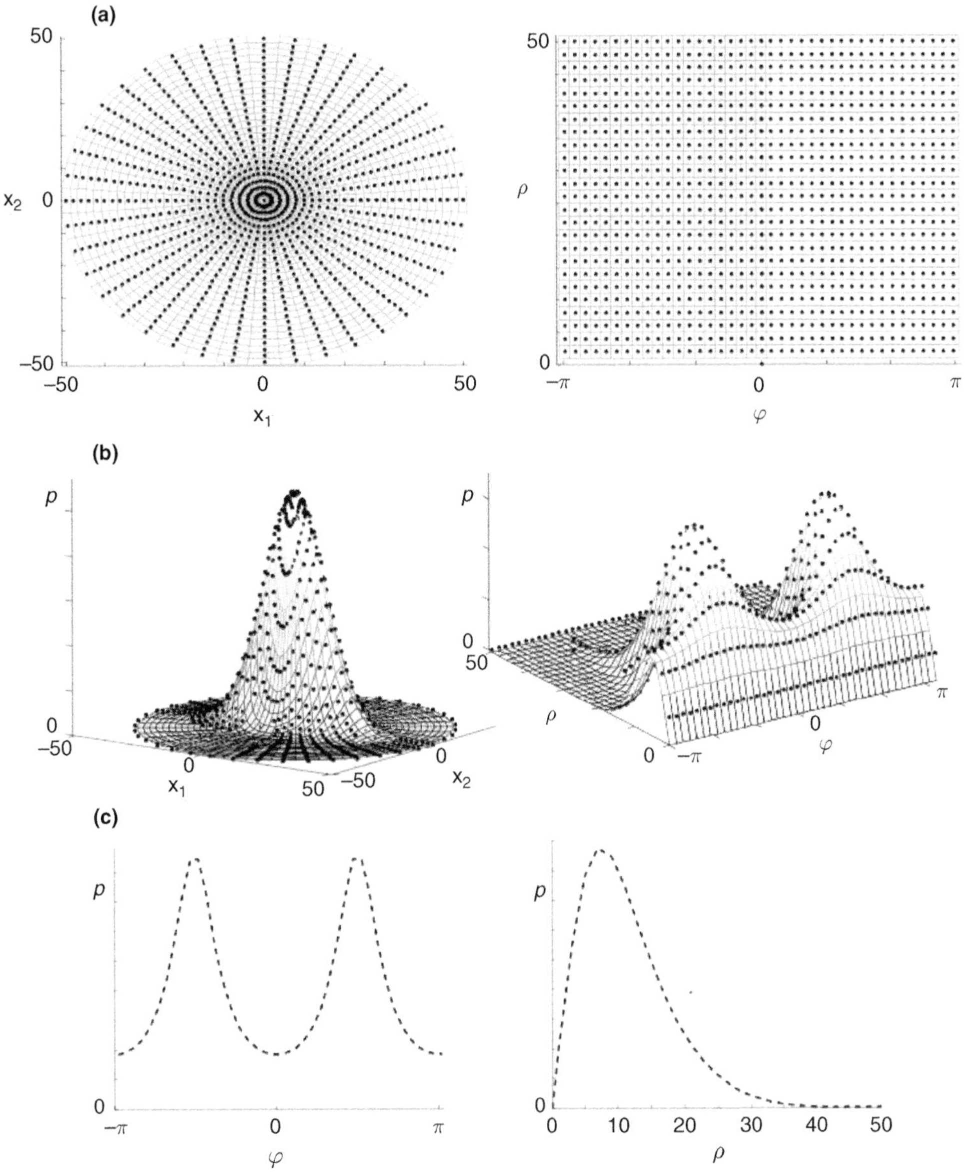

Figure C.12 Cartesian- and polar-coordinate encodings of dartboard sampled probability coordinates. (a) The sampled locations in Cartesian coordinates (left) are chosen to produce a uniform grid of sampled locations when transformed into polar coordinates (right). (b) Probability masses are plotted as circles at the centers of each segment of the original Gaussian density in Cartesian (left) and transformed polar (right) coordinates. (c) Marginal densities over the angle dimension (left) and the radius dimension (right) of the polar-coordinate distribution.

Our height-width equations tell us about the scaling that will occur when we transform between polar and Cartesian coordinates, because they indicate that whereas the area of a segment will always be equal to $(\Delta\rho)(\Delta\varphi)$ in polar space, in Cartesian space it will be approximately $2\rho\Delta\rho\tan[\Delta\varphi/2]$ -which for small values of $\Delta\varphi$ is $\rho(\Delta\rho)(\Delta\varphi)$.

To obtain a concrete set of calculations, let us suppose that we are interested in obtaining the 3 densities at $(\varphi = \varphi_1, \rho = \{\rho_1, \rho_2, \rho_2\}) = (\varphi = 0, \rho = \{1, 3, 5\})$, and the 3 densities at $\left(\varphi = \{-\frac{2\pi}{41}, 0, \frac{2\pi}{41}\}, \rho = 1\right)$; where the separations between angles and radii used to define segments are $\Delta_\rho = \frac{2\pi}{41}$ and $\Delta_\rho = 2$, as given above. The first group of three segment-centers has Cartesian coordinates at $\{(1, 0), (3, 0), (5, 0)\}$ and corresponding densities of:

$$p(x_1 = 1 \cdot x_2 = 0|\imath) = \left[\left(9.5\sqrt{2\pi}\right)^{-1} e^{-\frac{1}{2}(\frac{1}{9.5})^2}\right]\left[\left(12.6\sqrt{2\pi}\right)^{-1} e^{-\frac{1}{2}(\frac{0}{12.6})^2}\right] = 1.32 \times 10^{-3},$$

$$p(x_1 = 3 \cdot x_2 = 0|\imath) = \left[\left(9.5\sqrt{2\pi}\right)^{-1} e^{-\frac{1}{2}(\frac{3}{9.5})^2}\right]\left[\left(12.6\sqrt{2\pi}\right)^{-1} e^{-\frac{1}{2}(\frac{0}{12.6})^2}\right] = 1.26 \times 10^{-3},$$

and

$$p(x_1 = 5 \cdot x_2 = 0|\imath) = \left[\left(9.5\sqrt{2\pi}\right)^{-1} e^{-\frac{1}{2}(\frac{5}{9.5})^2}\right]\left[\left(12.6\sqrt{2\pi}\right)^{-1} e^{-\frac{1}{2}(\frac{0}{12.6})^2}\right]$$

$$= 1.16 \times 10^{-3}.$$

In the second group of three, the middle density is the same as the first density in the first group. This leaves just the two densities at the Cartesian coordinates $\left\{\left(\cos\frac{2\pi}{41}, \sin\frac{2\pi}{41}\right), \left(\cos\frac{2\pi}{41}, \sin\frac{-2\pi}{41}\right)\right\}$, which are:

$$p(x_1 = \cos\frac{2\pi}{41} \cdot x_2 = \sin\frac{2\pi}{41}|\imath) = \left[\left(9.5\sqrt{2\pi}\right)^{-1} e^{-\frac{1}{2}\left(\frac{\cos\frac{2\pi}{41}}{9.5}\right)^2}\right]\left[\left(12.6\sqrt{2\pi}\right)^{-1} e^{-\frac{1}{2}\left(\frac{\sin\frac{2\pi}{41}}{12.6}\right)^2}\right] = 1.32 \times 10^{-3}$$

$$p(x_1 = \cos\frac{2\pi}{41} \cdot x_2 = \sin\frac{-2\pi}{41}|\imath) = \left[\left(9.5\sqrt{2\pi}\right)^{-1} e^{-\frac{1}{2}\left(\frac{\cos\frac{2\pi}{41}}{9.5}\right)^2}\right]\left[\left(12.6\sqrt{2\pi}\right)^{-1} e^{-\frac{1}{2}\left(\frac{\sin\frac{-2\pi}{41}}{12.6}\right)^2}\right] = 1.32 \times 10^{-3}$$

To obtain the corresponding approximate densities in polar coordinates, we multiply these density values by the ratio of the segment areas in the two coordinate spaces. That is, we multiply by the area of each segment in Cartesian coordinates (to convert density values to approximate masses contained within each segment), and then divide by the area of each segment in polar coordinates (to convert back to density units within polar space); which is simply the ratio of the segment sizes corresponding to each original-coordinate density value. We have set the sizes of the transformed segments such that they would form a regular grid in polar space, with constant size $\Delta\varphi\Delta\rho = (\frac{2\pi}{41})(2)$ for all segments. The corresponding Cartesian-space segments whose densities we have chosen to compute are at the first, second, and third radius of the concentric-circular segmentation that results from regular-grid segments in polar space. Each radius in Cartesian space has a different segment size, which is proportional to its absolute radius, $\rho(\Delta\rho)(\Delta\varphi)$. Thus, first-radius segments all have approximate size $\rho(\Delta\rho)(\Delta\varphi) = 1(2)(\frac{2\pi}{41}) = \frac{4\pi}{41}$, second-radius segments have size $\rho(\Delta\rho)(\Delta\varphi) = 3(2)(\frac{2\pi}{41}) = \frac{12\pi}{41}$, and so on. Notice, however, that the ratios of segment sizes are always simply $\frac{\rho\Delta\rho\Delta\varphi}{\Delta\rho\Delta\varphi} = \rho$. This is a particularly nice result because the segment grid-size in polar coordinates, $\Delta\rho\Delta\varphi$, cancels out of the calculation.

PA: Approximate Dartboard Marginalizations (Fig.C.12)

We first transform a regularly spaced sampled Gaussian using the inverse transform.

```
%%% prelim
r=[2.5 4.5];
angs=linspace(0,2*pi,41); angs0=angs+angs(2)/2;
dists=0:2:50; dists0=dists+dists(2)/2;
[R0 A0]=meshgrid(dists0,angs0); [X0s Y0s]=pol2cart(A0,R0);
[R A]=meshgrid(dists,angs);      [Xs,Ys]=pol2cart(A,R);

X=[Xs(:) Ys(:)]; X0=[X0s(:) Y0s(:)];
mu=[0 0]; sigma=[30 0; 0 140];
p=mvnpdf(X,mu,sigma); p0=mvnpdf(X0,mu,sigma);
Ps=reshape(p,length(angs),length(dists));
P0s=reshape(p0,length(angs0),length(dists0));

%%% plot original distribution
figure(6); clf; hold on
mesh(Xs,Ys,Ps); colormap(bone);
plot3(X0s(:),Y0s(:),1.075*P0s(:),'k.'); axis([-51 51 -51 51])

%%% plot transformed (angle-distance) distribution
figure(7); clf; hold on
mesh(A,R,Ps.*R); colormap(bone);
plot3(A0(:),R0(:),P0s(:).*R0(:),'k.'); axis([0 2*pi 0 51])

%%% plot lossy distance transform
figure(8); clf; hold on
plot([0 dists0],[0; str8n(sum(P0s.*R0,1))],'ko--','MarkerFaceColor',...
    'k','MarkerSize',10) axis([0 50 0 .45])

%%% plot lossy angle transform
figure(9); clf; hold on
plot(angs0,str8n(sum(P0s.*R0,2)),'ko--','MarkerFaceColor','k','MarkerSize',10)
axis([0 1.02*2*pi 0 .18])
```

In applications we will be interested in seeing not only the 2D posterior (Figure C.12b), but the posterior over each dimension of the transformed distribution in isolation; these are shown, after marginalization of each unwanted dimension, in Figure C.12c.

Exercises

1) Create a regular grid of 11×1 x and y values over the region within $-40 < x < 40, -40 < y < 40$. For each segment, use a uniform random number generator to select sampled segments. Plot the grid, and the locations of sampled segments. Along the margins, plot the locations of samples in the marginal distributions.
2) Create a regular grid of 41×41 x and y values with unit spacing. For each segment, use a uniform random number generator to select sampled segments. Plot the grid, and the locations of sampled segments. Along the margins, plot the locations of samples in the marginal distributions.

3) Plot sampled densities corresponding to:

$$p(x \cdot y|\imath) = p(x|\imath)p(y|\imath),$$

$$\text{and}: \quad p(x|\imath) = \frac{1}{9\sqrt{2\pi}} e^{-\frac{1}{2}\frac{(x-12)^2}{81}}$$

$$p(y|\imath) = \frac{1}{7\sqrt{2\pi}} e^{-\frac{1}{2}\frac{(y+3)^2}{49}},$$

at the sampled locations found in Exercises 1 and 2, and their marginal distributions.
4) Compare the marginal distributions plotted in Exercise 3, with reference to the fact that the sampled segments of each 2D density should contain about the same probability mass.
5) Create a matrix of x and y coordinates at the set of (centers of) regularly spaced polar-coordinate segments using 31 angles and 31 radii, and assign them uniform probability density. Assume the density is bounded at the edges of the set of segments, which should be contained within $-40 < x < 40, -40 < y < 40$ (though, of course, not on a grid).
   a. Plot this sampled density as a 3D Cartesian plot in x, y and p.
   b. What is the value of p at $(x, y) = (0, 0)$?
6) Using the same set of 31 angles and 31 radii, assign probabilities for a 2D density described by:

$$p(x \cdot y|\imath) = p(x|\imath)p(y|\imath),$$

$$\text{and}: \quad p(x|\imath) = \frac{1}{\pi}\frac{2}{4 + x^2}$$

$$p(y|\imath) = \frac{1}{\pi}\frac{6}{36 + x^2}.$$

   a. Plot this density as a 3D Cartesian plot in x, y and p.
   b. What is the density at $(x, y) = (0, 0)$?
7) Transform the uniform density from Exercise 1 into polar coordinates, and plot the 2D polar representation of that density.
8) Transform the density from Exercise 2 into polar coordinates, and plot the 2D polar representation of that density.
9) Plot the marginal polar-coordinate densities of the 2D distributions computed in Exercises 3 and 4 (four total plots).

Example: Sums and Differences of Coordinates

Our final example involving lossy transformation of sampled densities repeats our earlier example of sums and differences. Thus we either begin with a 2D density, or, more commonly, two 1D densities. When we begin with two 1D densities, we will simply create a 2D density; either on the assumption that the probabilities along the two single axes are independent, or assuming a specific type of nonindependence between probabilities on the two axes (if such additional information were available).

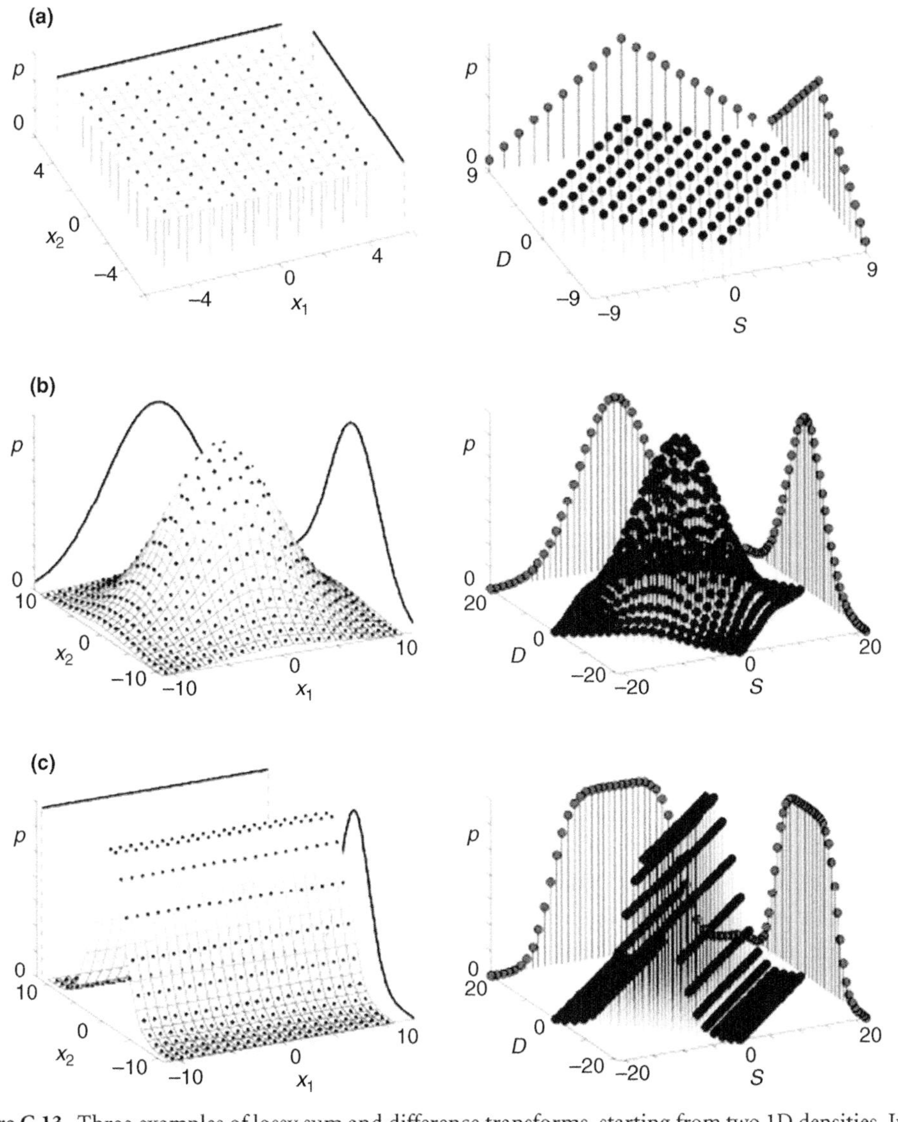

Figure C.13 Three examples of lossy sum and difference transforms, starting from two 1D densities. Initial 1D densities are plotted as solid curves along the margins of each plot in the lefthand column. 2D sampled masses in original coordinates are represented as filled circles in original coordinates (left-hand column) and stems in transformed coordinates (right-hand column). The marginalizations of these 2D mass functions onto the sum and difference axes are plotted as gray stems on the margins of right-hand plots.

Here we will begin by considering the geometric interpretation of the lossy sum/difference transform as summarized above, and then examine the convolution- and cross-correlation-based solution. Just as when we discussed sums and differences of coordinates for discrete distributions, we recognize here that constant-sum lines lie along an anti-clockwise 45° line in the original, 2D distribution. The coordinate of the intersection of that line with either axis gives the value of the sum. Similarly, equal-difference will line along a clockwise 45° line in the original coordinate system.

Transformation of the original 2D mass function into a corresponding mass function in sum/difference coordinates can be accomplished via rotation and scaling; that is,

$$S = \sqrt{2}\left(x_2 \cos\frac{\pi}{4} + x_1 \sin\frac{\pi}{4}\right)$$
$$D = \sqrt{2}\left(x_1 \cos\frac{\pi}{4} - x_2 \sin\frac{\pi}{4}\right), \tag{C.6}$$

where S and D are the sum and difference coordinates of the transformed axes shown in the right-hand column of Figure C.13.

The only difference between the discrete case and the sampled density is that we are free to choose the samples (i.e., the original-coordinate segments from which we compute approximate masses), where a closer approximation to the underlying continuous density can be achieved with a finer-grained spacing. Finally the marginalized masses along sum and difference axes (plotted as gray stems in the right-hand plots of Fig. C.13) are transformed back into densities by dividing by the width of each segment on that axis. In the examples given in Figure C.13 we have used regular spacings on all axes, and therefore the resulting marginalized density functions will have the same shape as the marginal mass functions plotted in gray stems.

The three examples of lossy sum/difference transformations given in Figure C.13 were chosen to highlight several features of this particular transformation. The first row demonstrates a continuous-density analog of the discrete example problem in Section C.2. In both cases, the uniform marginal probabilities in original coordinates transform to triangular probability distributions in sum/difference coordinates. Indeed, there is never a difference in the shape of the transformed distribution when dealing with discrete versus continuous probability functions, because there is no nonuniform scaling associated with the sum and difference transformations.

The second example demonstrates the sum/difference transformation when the original-coordinate densities are Gaussian (Fig. C.13). The interesting aspect of this example is that the transformed densities maintain the Gaussian shape of the original densities, only becoming narrower. This property is the basis for the stability of the mean relative to an individual observation. If individual observations are described by a Gaussian sampling distribution, then the mean of a set of such observations is described by a Gaussian sampling distribution as well - but the latter Gaussian is much narrower. Thus, the mean of a set of observations is usually far more statistically likely to be near the true theoretical value than any single observation.

Finally, the third example demonstrates that the transformation and marginalization procedures remain the same regardless of the shapes of the original-coordinate densities. Here, the 1D original-coordinate densities are not the same shape, as they have been in previous examples. This does not affect how we compute lossy sum/difference transformations. It is also interesting to note that, while the original-coordinate 2D density does not have the same kind of circular symmetry observed in the previous two examples, the resulting marginal densities are nevertheless symmetrical about their respective means. We will explore the conditions under which we may obtain asymmetrical marginal densities in transformed coordinates in the exercises.

PA: Approximate Sum and Difference Marginalizations (Fig.C.13)

We take each row in turn

```
% row 1
% left
a=-22; b=64; x=-5:5;
p=1/10*ones(11,1); p=p*p';
[X1 X2]=meshgrid(x,x);
figure(1); clf; hold on
mesh(X1,X2,p)

x1=-4.5:4.5; x2=-4.5:4.5;
p1=1/10*ones(10,1); p2=1/10*ones(10,1); p=p1*p2';
[X1 X2]=meshgrid(x2,x1); X1=X1(:); X2=X2(:); p=p(:);
for n=1:length(X1), plot3(X1(n)*[1 1],X2(n)*[1 1],[0 p(n)],'k-'); end
p=p1*p2'; [X1 X2]=meshgrid(x2,x1);
plot3(X1,X2,1.01*p,'k.')

plot3(6*[1 1],[-5 5],.01*[1 1],'k-','LineWidth',2)
plot3([-5 5],6*[1 1],.01*[1 1],'k-','LineWidth',2)
plot3(6*[1 1],-5*[1 1],[0 .01],'k--')
plot3(6*[1 1],5*[1 1],[0 .01],'k--')
plot3(-5*[1 1],6*[1 1],[0 .01],'k--')
plot3(5*[1 1],6*[1 1],[0 .01],'k--')
view(a,b);

% right
a=-26.5; b=28;
Fnum=2;
v=[-4.5:4.5]';
vp=[v ones(length(v),1)/length(v)];
SumDiffFig(vp,vp,Fnum,3,8)
view(a,b);

%%%%%%%%%
% row 2 %
% left
V=2.65;
a=-26.5; b=28; x=-11:11;
p=npdf(x,0,V)'; p=p*p';
[X1 X2]=meshgrid(x,x);
figure(1); clf; hold on
mesh(X1,X2,p)

x=-10.5:10.5;
p=npdf(x,0,V)'; p=p*p';
[X1 X2]=meshgrid(x,x);

X1=X1(:); X2=X2(:); p=p(:);
plot3(X1,X2,p,'k.')

plot3((max(x)+1.5)*ones(101,1),linspace(min(x)-.5,max(x)+.5,101),...
    max(p)*npdf(linspace(min(x)-.5,max(x)+.5,101),0,V)/...
    npdf(0,0,V),'k-','LineWidth',2)
plot3(linspace(min(x)-.5,max(x)+.5,101),(max(x)+1.5)*ones(101,1),max(p)*...
    npdf(linspace(min(x)-.5,max(x)+.5,101),0,V)/npdf(0,0,V),'k-','LineWidth',2)
view(a,b); axis([min(x)-.5 max(x)+1.5 min(x)-.5 max(x)+1.5 0 1.05*max(p)])

% right
a=-26.5; b=28; Fnum=2;
v=x'; vp=[v npdf(v,0,V)];
```

```
SumDiffFig(vp,vp,Fnum,1,8)
view(a,b);

%%%%%%%%%
% row 3 %
% left
V=2.65; a=-26.5; b=28; x=-11:11;
p=npdf(x,0,V)'; p=p*p';
[X1 X2]=meshgrid(x,x);
figure(1); clf; hold on
mesh(X1,X2,p)

x=-10.5:10.5;
p=npdf(x,0,V)'; p=p*p';
[X1 X2]=meshgrid(x,x);

X1=X1(:); X2=X2(:); p=p(:);
plot3(X1,X2,p,'k.')

plot3((max(x)+1.5)*ones(101,1),linspace(min(x)-.5,max(x)+.5,101),...
    max(p)*npdf(linspace(min(x)-.5,max(x)+.5,101),0,V)/npdf(0,0,V),'k-','LineWidth',2)
plot3(linspace(min(x)-.5,max(x)+.5,101),(max(x)+1.5)*ones(101,1),max(p)*...
    npdf(linspace(min(x)-.5,max(x)+.5,101),0,V)/npdf(0,0,V),'k-','LineWidth',2)
    view(a,b); axis([min(x)-.5 max(x)+1.5 min(x)-.5 max(x)+1.5 0 1.05*max(p)])

% right
a=-26.5; b=28; Fnum=2;
v=x'; vp=[v npdf(v,0,V)];
SumDiffFig(vp,vp,Fnum,1,8)
view(a,b);
```

Exercises

1) Create plots of 2D densities for the following pairs of 1D densities [assuming independent probabilities; that is, $p(x \cdot y|\iota)dxdy = p(x|\iota)p(y|\iota)dxdy$], over any reasonable range of coordinates:
   a. $p(x|\iota)dx = dx p(y|\iota)dy = dy$
   b. $p(x|\iota)dx = dx p(y|\iota)dy = y^2 dy$
   c. $p(x|\iota)dx = \ln(x)dx p(y|\iota)dy = \ln(y)dy$
   d. $p(x|\iota)dx = e^{-x^2} dx p(y|\iota)dy = \ln(y)dy$
2) Create plots of the 2D transformed densities (sum/difference transform) for the following pairs of original-coordinate 1D densities (normalized over an appropriate truncated range):
   a. $p(x|\iota)dx = dx p(y|\iota)dy = dy$
   b. $p(x|\iota)dx = (x^2 - x)dx p(y|\iota)dy = 3y dy$
   c. $p(x|\iota)dx = dx p(y|\iota)dy = y^2 dy$
   d. $p(x|\iota)dx = \ln(x)dx p(y|\iota)dy = dy$
   e. $p(x|\iota)dx = \ln(x)dx p(y|\iota)dy = \ln(y)dy$
   f. $p(x|\iota)dx = dx p(y|\iota)dy = e^y dy$
   g. $p(x|\iota)dx = e^{-x^2} dx p(y|\iota)dy = \ln(y)dy$

3) Create plots of the marginal transformed densities (sum and difference transforms) for the original-coordinate 1D densities from Exercise 2.
4) One can see that the reason for the symmetry of the transformed marginal distributions in Figure C.13 is that there is a similar symmetry along the 45° and/or −45° lines of the 2D transformed distribution. Is it possible to construct a distribution in original coordinates that produces asymmetrical marginal distributions in transformed coordinates? If so, construct such a distribution and show the asymmetrical marginals in transformed coordinates. If not, explain why not.

C.2.4 Calculus-Based Methods for Coordinate Transformation

Conversion between probability density and probability proper requires integration of the density function over the abscissa region whose probability we are interested in calculating – just as the mass of a real material is the integral of its density over some region of interest. This peculiarity of the relationship between the density function and probability proper is the result of the infinities involved in using continuous variables, as discussed at the start of Section C.2. Although the concept of a probability density makes it possible to define a normalized probability function over a continuous variable, it also requires that we consider the difference in the way probabilities *change* over small regions of the abscissa (original and transformed) when we transform a probability density function between the density representing our information about an original and a transformed variable (such as in the x and $x^{'} = x^2$ example, Fig. C.7). To obtain the exact solution, we simply recognize that the ratio of sampled segment lengths approaches the Jacobian, $|\frac{dx}{dx^{'}}|$, as the limit of the earlier approximation, $\frac{\Delta x_i}{\Delta x_i^{'}}$, as $\Delta x \rightarrow 0$. In other words, transformation via the Jacobian is identical to the method of transformation used above based on the ratio of segment- widths, as segment-widths approach zero. The new change of variable formula is:

$$p(x_i^{'}|\imath) = p(x_i|\imath)\frac{\Delta x_i}{\Delta x_i^{'}} = p\left(\imath^{-1}(x_i^{'})|\imath\right)\frac{\imath^{-1}(\Delta x_i^{'})}{\Delta x_i^{'}} \qquad \text{(C.7).}$$

Exercises

1) Write the inverses of the following linking functions:
   a. $x' = 4x$
   b. $x' = 3 - 2x$
   c. $x' = x^{-1}$
   d. $x' = x^2$
   e. $x' = \frac{x^{-2}}{2}$
   f. $x_1' = f_1(x_1, x_2) = x_1 + x_2 x_2^{'} = f_2(x_1, x_2) = x_2 - x_1$
2) Compute the Jacobians of the following linking functions:
   a. $x^{'} = x^2$
   b. $x^{'} = x^{-1}$
   c. $x^{'} = x^2$

d. $x' = e^{-x}$

e. $x_1' = f_1(x_1, x_2) = x_1 + x_2$

$x_2' = f_2(x_1, x_2) = x_2 - x_1$

***Example: Derivation of the Rayleigh Distribution and the Gaussian Integral**

The change of variable formula was used by Laplace to calculate the area under a Gaussian function,[4] $e^{-\alpha u^2}$. In the context of probability this is usually written with the parameterization $\alpha = 1/(2\sigma^2)$, or: $e^{-\frac{1}{2}\left(\frac{u}{\sigma}\right)^2}$, whereas the normalized Gaussian function, the Gaussian probability density, is most often written: $(\sigma\sqrt{2\pi})^{-1}e^{-\frac{1}{2}\left(\frac{u}{\sigma}\right)^2}$.

Inspection of this formula tells us that the area under the Gaussian function, $e^{-\alpha u^2}$, must be, $\sqrt{\pi/\alpha}$ with $\alpha = 1/(2\sigma^2)$, because the constant $(\sigma\sqrt{2\pi})^{-1}$ is used to normalize the Gaussian function and make it a probability density, as we have seen in previous examples. To see how Laplace determined the value of this constant, first assign the area under $e^{-\alpha u^2}$ a variable, $I = \int_{-\infty}^{\infty} du\ e^{-\alpha u^2}$ We then square I : $I^2 = \left[\int_{-\infty}^{\infty} du_1\ e^{-\alpha(u_1)^2}\right]\left[\int_{-\infty}^{\infty} du_2\ e^{-\alpha(u_2)^{22}}\right]$, substituting the dummy variables u_1 and u_2 for the two repetitions of the squared u. This double integral is the area under a 2-D probability bubble (as in Fig. C.3), written:

$$I^2 = \int du_1\ du_2\ e^{-\alpha\left[(u_1)^2+(u_2)^2\right]}.$$

Next, we transform from rectangular Cartesian to polar coordinates. Polar coordinates tell us the angle (θ) relative to the x-axis and distance (r) from the origin of any 2D position.

To effect this transformation, we recall that the Jacobian is defined as the magnitude (modulus) of the determinant of partial derivatives of the inverse transform. To extend this idea to a probability surface, we expand the determinant to a matrix of partial derivatives:

$$\begin{vmatrix} \dfrac{\partial u_1}{\partial u_1'} & \dfrac{\partial u_2}{\partial u_1'} \\[2ex] \dfrac{\partial u_1}{\partial u_2'} & \dfrac{\partial u_2}{\partial u_2'} \end{vmatrix} = \frac{\partial u_2}{\partial u_2'}\frac{\partial u_1}{\partial u_1'} - \frac{\partial u_1}{\partial u_2'}\frac{\partial u_2}{\partial u_1'},$$

where the subscripts 1 and 2 correspond to the variables plotted on the x- and y-axis of a probability surface whose z-axis represents probability.

In the present case, the inverse transformation equations are: $u_1 = r\cos\theta$, and $u_2 = r\sin\theta$, and the Jacobian is:

$$du_1du_2 = \begin{vmatrix} \dfrac{\partial u_1}{\partial_r} & \dfrac{\partial u_1}{\partial\theta} \\[2ex] \dfrac{\partial u_2}{\partial_r} & \dfrac{\partial u_2}{\partial\theta} \end{vmatrix} drd\theta.$$

[4] Functions with the form $e^{-\alpha u^2}$ are called Gaussian functions.

The first and last terms are the area elements in Cartesian and polar coordinates. The partial derivatives within the Jacobian are derived based on the geometric relationship between Cartesian and polar coordinates:

$$\frac{\partial u_1}{\partial_r} = \frac{\partial}{\partial_r}[r\cos\theta] = \cos\theta, \frac{\partial u_1}{\partial\theta} = \frac{\partial}{\partial\theta}[r\cos\theta] = r\sin\theta, \frac{\partial u_2}{\partial_r} = \frac{\partial}{\partial_r}[r\sin\theta] = -\sin\theta,$$
$$\frac{\partial u_2}{\partial\theta} = \frac{\partial}{\partial\theta}[r\sin\theta] = r\cos\theta.$$

Substituting the partial derivates of the transformation equations we obtain:

$$\begin{aligned} du_1 du_2 &= \begin{vmatrix} \cos\theta & -r\sin\theta \\ \sin\theta & r\cos\theta \end{vmatrix} dr d\theta \\ &= r(\cos^2\theta + \sin^2\theta) dr d\theta \\ &= r\, dr d\theta \end{aligned}$$

Notice that this is precisely the relationship for the ratio of segment widths we derived during our examination of approximate transformation from Cartesian to polar coordinates using sampled densities. Returning to the derivation, we now write I^2 in polar form:

$$\begin{aligned} I^2 &= \int_{-\infty}^{\infty} du_1 du_2 e^{-\alpha\left[(u_1)^2+(u_2)^2\right]}. \\ &= \int_0^{\infty} dr \int_0^{2\pi} d\theta\; re^{-\alpha(r^2\sin^2\theta + r^2\cos^2\theta)} \end{aligned}$$

This solution involves one integration over the angle variable (θ):

$$\begin{aligned} f(r) &= \int_0^{2\pi} d\theta\, re^{-\alpha(r^2\sin^2\theta + r^2\cos^2\theta)} \\ &= re^{-\alpha r^2}\int_0^{2\pi} d\theta = re^{-\alpha r^2}[\theta]_0^{2\pi} = re^{-\alpha r^2}[2\pi - 0] \\ &= 2\pi re^{-\alpha r^2} \end{aligned}$$

This first integral gets us halfway to our goal of deriving the area under the Gaussian. The result of integrating over the polar angle variable yields a function that is proportional to the probability that a 2D Gaussian-distributed variable is at a particular distance from the origin. We have already seen a version of this in our dartboard example, describing the probability of missing the bull's-eye by a particular amount. The normalized version is the Rayleigh distribution,[5]

$$p(r|\iota) = 2\pi\frac{\alpha}{\pi} re^{-\alpha r^2} = \frac{r}{\sigma^2}e^{-\frac{1}{2}\frac{r^2}{\sigma^2}}$$

which has been important in its own right, having application in telecommunication for describing interference in wireless signal transmission (i.e., 'Rayleigh fading'), for calculating average wind speed (regardless of wind direction), and in estimating background noise when rendering magnetic resonance images.

[5] Obtained via the integral, $\int_0^{\infty} dt\, te^{-\alpha t^2} = \sqrt{\frac{\pi}{\alpha}}$

To complete the second step and compute the desired double integral, we make use of the substitution, $v = r^2$ (and $\frac{dv}{dr} = 2r$) to obtain. [6]

$$I^2 = \int_0^\infty dr \int_0^{2\pi} d\theta re^{-\alpha(r^2 \sin^2\theta + r^2 \cos^2\theta)}$$

$$= \int_0^\infty drf(r) = 2\pi \int_0^\infty drre^{-\alpha r^2} = 2\pi \int_0^\infty \frac{dv}{2r} re^{-\alpha v}$$

$$= \pi \int_0^\infty dve^{[-\alpha]v} = -\frac{\pi}{\alpha}[e^{(-\alpha)v}]_0^\infty = -\frac{\pi}{\alpha}[e^{-\infty} - e^0] = -\frac{\pi}{\alpha}[0-1] = \frac{\pi}{\alpha}$$

Finally, taking the square root in order to return to the one-dimensional Gaussian function, we obtain $I = \sqrt{\pi/\alpha}$, where we recover the conventional form of the Gaussian distribution by defining $\alpha = (\sigma\sqrt{2})^{-2}$, and divide the Gaussian function $e^{-\alpha u^2}$ by I to normalize: $(\sigma\sqrt{2\pi})^{-1}e^{-\frac{1}{2}(\frac{u}{\sigma})^2}$.

Exercises

1) Create a Gaussian distribution representing distance:
   a. along the x-axis with $\mu = 5$ and $\sigma = 2$
   b. integrate over all directions of a 2D Gaussian $[\mu = 2, \sigma = 7]$,

   Transform these distributions over length into speed, where time is held constant $[t = 2]$.
2) Create a Gaussian distribution over time $[\mu = 2, \sigma = 0.1]$. Transform it into a probability distribution over speed, where length is held constant $[x = 5]$.
3) Using the two Gaussian distributions defined above for x and t, respectively, define a joint probability distribution, $p(x \cdot t|\iota) = p(x|\iota)p(t|\iota)$, describing possible speeds (combinations of x and t values, $s = x/t$). Can this 2D distribution describing possible combinations of x and t be collapsed into a 1D distribution describing speed only? If so, create this 1D probability plot.
4) There is a gun on a turret, located near a coastline, which can rotate 180°. The gun is fired unpredictably along the beach to discourage any unpleasant sea-based incursion. Because the gun is rotated and fired unpredictably, its orientation (φ) upon firing is not known. (a) Plot a uniform distribution describing our information about the orientation of the gun when it is fired. Now, imagine that we know the gun and turret are placed 5 km from the beach (the beach is perfectly straight). The x-location of a bullet along the beach has a definite relation to the angle of the gun when it was fired ($\tan\varphi = (x - \mu)/5$), but because that angle is unknown the bullet's location must be assigned a probability distribution. First, truncate the uniform distribution of turret orientations to cover the range (−90, 90) of angles relevant to hitting the beach, and transform this uniform distribution in angle to describe our information about possible bullet landing positions along the beach.

[6] Obtained via the integral, $\int dt\, e^{\beta t} = \beta^{-1}e^{\beta t}$

C.2.5 Summary

Coordinate transformations contribute an important functionality to our data analysis toolbox. Most prominently, in Chapter 3 we will use coordinate transformations in Harold Jeffreys' solution to the problem, alluded to in Section 4.4.1, of finding maximally uninformative prior probability densities over the parameters of a given likelihood function. This solution to the problem of assigning prior probability distributions over parameter values is based on an intuition derived from coordinate transformation. The intuition is this: transforming between equivalent parameterizations of a likelihood function, such as between $(\sigma\sqrt{2\pi})^{-1}e^{-\frac{1}{2}\left(\frac{x}{\sigma}\right)^2}$ (a Gaussian distribution centered at the origin, with width parameter σ) and $(\sigma\sqrt{2\pi})^{-1}e^{-\frac{1}{2}\frac{x^2}{\theta}}$ (a Gaussian distribution with width parameter $\theta = \sigma^2$), will not alter the posterior distribution over those parameters if alternative parameterizations of the likelihood function are combined with 'uninformative' prior distributions. In other words, if there are two equivalent parameterizations of a given likelihood function (such as the two Gaussian distributions above), combining them with an uninformative prior distribution should yield equivalent (i.e., interchangeable) posterior distributions. We will see in Chapter 3 that this requirement yields a unique prior distribution for any given likelihood function.

In Chapter 5 we will explore the concept of measurement. There, the key element is a model function that is inserted into the likelihood function to relate observed variables (i.e., data) to measured variables (i.e., parameters). The model function and the linking function are highly interrelated concepts, in that both are used to transform from one type of information (probability distribution) to another. The difference is that coordinate transformations are used to relate one coordinate representation to another, were those coordinates are *either* data variables (i.e., we were transforming sampling distributions) or parameters (i.e., transforming prior or posterior distributions). The point of the model function is to allow us to use information regarding data likelihoods to make inferences about the parameters of the likelihood function. Chapter 6 will then extend these elements to develop a model comparison algorithm, which will guide our analysis when the goal is to use data to distinguish among competing possible model functions that might describe the underlying data-generating phenomenon.

References

Abegg, M., Manoach, D. S., Barton, J. S. 'Knowing the Future: Partial Foreknowledge Effects on the Programming of Prosaccades and Antisaccades.' *Vision Research*, vol. 51, no. 1, 2011, pp. 215–221.

Anderson, A. J., Yadav, H., Carpenter, R. H. S. 'Directional Prediction by the Saccadic System.' *Current Biology*, vol. 18, no. 8, 2008, pp. 614–618.

Angelaki, D. E., Gu, Y., DeAngelis, G. C. 'Multisensory Integration: Psychophysics, Neurophysiology, and Computation.' *Current Opinion in Neurobiology*, vol. 19, no. 4, 2009, pp. 452–458.

Angelaki, D. E., Klier, E. M., Snyder, L. H. 'A Vestibular Sensation: Probabilistic Approaches to Spatial Perception.' *Neuron*, vol. 64, no. 4, 2009, pp. 448–461.

Antoniades, C. A., Altham, P. M. E., Mason, S. L., Barker, R. A., Carpenter, R. H. S. 'Saccadometry: A New Tool for Evaluating Presymptomatic Huntington Patients.' *NeuroReport*, vol. 18, no. 11, 2007, pp. 1133–1136.

Antoniades, C. A., Ober, J., Hicks S., Siuda, G., Carpenter, R. H. S., Kennard, C., Nemeth, A. H. 'Statistical Characteristics of Finger-Tapping Data in Huntington's Disease.' *Medical & Biological Engineering & Computing*, vol. 50, no. 4, 2012, pp. 341–346.

Bach-Y-Rita, P. *The Control of Eye Movements*. New York: Academic Press, 1971.

Bayes, T. 'An Essay towards Solving a Problem in the Doctrine of Chances.' *Philosophical Transactions of the Royal Society*, 53, 1763, pp. 330–418.

Beck, J. M., Ma, W. J., Kiani, R., Hanks T., Churchland, A. K., Roitman, J., Shadlen, M. N., Latham, P. E., Pouget, A. 'Probabilistic Population Codes for Bayesian Decision Making.' *Neuron*, vol. 60, no. 6, 2008, pp. 1142–1152.

Beck, J., Ma, W. J., Latham, P. E., Pouget A. 'Probabilistic Population Codes and the Exponential Family of Distributions.' *Progress in Brain Research*, vol. 165, 2007, pp. 509–19.

Bernardo, J. M., Smith, A. F. M. *Bayesian Theory*. New York: John Wiley, 1994.

Bernoulli, J. *Ars conjectandi*. Basel: Thurnisiorum, 1713.

Bertucco, M., Bdhanpuri, N. H., Sanger, T. D. 'Perceived Cost and Intrinsic Motor Variability Modulate the Speed-Accuracy Trade-Off.' *PLOS ONE*, vol. 10, no. 10, 2015, e0139988.

Boucher, L., Palmeri, T. J., Logan, G. D., Schall, J. D. 'Inhibitory Control in Mind and Brain: An Interactive Race Model of Countermanding Saccades.' *Psychological Review*, vol. 114, no. 2, 2007, pp. 376–397.

Box, G. E. P., Tiao, G. C. 'A Bayesian Approach to Some Outlier Problems.' *Biometrika*, vol. 55, 1968, pp. 119–129.

Bray, T. J. P., Carpenter, R. H. S. 'Saccadic Foraging: Reduced Reaction Time to Informative Targets.' *European Journal of Neuroscience*, vol. 41, no. 7, 2015, pp. 908–913.

Bretthorst, G. L. 'An Introduction to Model Selection Using Probability Theory as Logic.' In *Maximum Entropy and Bayesian Methods*, edited by G. Heidbreder, pp. 1–42. Berlin: Springer Science and Business Media, 1996.

Bretthorst, G. L. *Bayesian Spectrum Analysis and Parameter Estimation*. Lecture Notes in Statistics, Vol. 48. Berlin: Springer, 1988.

Bretthorst, G. L. 'Bayesian Analysis. II. Signal Detection and Model Selection.' *Journal of Magnetic Resonance*, vol. 88, no. 3, 1990, pp. 552–570.

Bretthorst, G. L. 'How Accurately Can Parameters from Exponential Models Be Estimated? A Bayesian View.' *Concepts in Magnetic Resonance*, vol. 27A, no. 2, 2005, pp. 73–83.

Bretthorst, G. L. 'The Near-Irrelevance of Sampling Frequency Distributions.' In *Maximum Entropy and Bayesian Methods*, edited by W. von der Linden et al., pp. 21–46. Netherlands: Kluwer, 1999.

Bretthorst, G. L. 'Nonuniform Sampling: Bandwidth and Aliasing.' In *Maximum Entropy and Bayesian Methods*, edited by G. Erickson, pp. 1–29. The Netherlands: Kluwer, 2000.

Bretthorst, G. L. 'On the Difference in Means.' In *Physics and Probability Essays in Honor of Edwin T. Jaynes*, edited by W. T Grandy and P. W. Milonni, pp. 177–194. Cambridge: Cambridge University Press, 1993.

Brookes, B. C., Gumbel, E. J. 'Statistical Theory of Extreme Values and Some Practical Applications.' *The Mathematical Gazette*, vol. 39, no. 330, 1955, p. 341.

Bryant, W. W. *A History of Astronomy*. London: Methuen, 1907.

Burg, J. P. (1967). 'Maximum Entropy Spectrum Analysis.' In *Proceedings of the 37th Meeting of a Society of Exploration Geophysicists*, Oklahoma City.

Carlin, B. P., Kadane, J. B., Gelfand, A. E. 'Approaches for Optimal Sequential Decision Analysis in Clinical Trials.' *Biometrics*, vol. 54, no. 3, 1998, p. 964.

Carpenter, R. H. S. 'Analysing the Detail of Saccadic Reaction Time Distributions.' *Biocybernetics and Biomedical Engineering*, vol. 32, no. 2, 2012, pp. 49–63.

Carpenter, R. H. S. 'Contrast, Probability, and Saccadic Latency.' *Current Biology*, vol. 14, no. 17, 2004, pp. 1576–1580.

Carpenter, R. H. S. 'Distribution of Quick-Phase Intervals in Optokinetic Nystagmus.' *Ophthalmic Research*, vol. 25, no. 2, 1993, pp. 91–93.

Carpenter, R. H. S., Reddi, B. A. J., Anderson, A. J. 'A Simple Two-Stage Model Predicts Response Time Distributions.' *The Journal of Physiology*, vol. 587, no. 16, 2009, pp. 4051–4062.

Carpenter, R. H. S., Williams, M. L. L. 'Neural Computation of Log Likelihood in Control of Saccadic Eye Movements.' *Nature*, vol. 377, no. 6544, 1995, pp. 59–62.

Carroll, L. *Symbolic Logic*. 1958. Mineola, NY: Dover, 2003.

Claerbout, J. F. *Fundamentals of Geophysical Data Processing: With Applications to Petroleum Prospecting*. New York: Mc-Graw Hill, 1976.

Clement, W. F., Jex, H. R., Graham, D. 'A Manual Control-Display Theory Applied to Instrument Landings of a Jet Transport.' *IEEE Transactions on Man Machine Systems*, vol. 9, no. 4, 1968, pp. 93–110.

Cornsweet, T. N. *Visual Perception*. 1970. New York: Academic Press, 1971.

Courant, R., John, F. *Introduction to Calculus and Analysis*. Vol. 1. New York: Springer, 1965.

Courant, R., John, F. *Introduction to Calculus and Analysis*. Vol. 2. Berlin: Springer, 1974.

Cox, R. T. *The Algebra of Probable Inference*. Baltimore: Johns Hopkins University Press, 1961.

Cox, R. T. (1946). 'Probability, Frequency and Reasonable Expectation.' *American Journal of Physics*, vol. 14, pp. 1–13.

Crapse, T. B, Sommer, M. A. 'The Frontal Eye Field as a Prediction Map.' *Progress in Brain Research*, Vol. 171, edited by C. Kennard and R. J. Leigh. New York: Elsevier, 2008.

Dayan, P., Abbott, L. F. *Theoretical Neuroscience: Computational and Mathematical Modeling of Neural Systems.* Cambridge, MA: MIT Press, 2009.

Dean, P., Porrill, J., Warren, P. A. 'Optimality of Position Commands to Horizontal Eye Muscles: A Test of the Minimum-Norm Rule.' *Journal of Neurophysiology*, vol. 81, no. 2, 1999, pp. 735–757.

DeFinetti, B. *Theory of Probability*. 2 vols. New York: Interscience, 1990.

de Laplace, P.-S. *A Philosophical Essay on Probabilities*. Mineola, NY: Dover, 1951.

Dettman, J. W. *Mathematical Methods in Physics and Engineering.* 2nd ed. New York: McGraw-Hill, 1969.

Deutsch, S., Deutch, A. *Understanding the Nervous System: An Engineering Perspective.* New York: IEEE Press, 1993.

Diaz, I., Abbey, C. K., Timberg, P. A. S., Eckstein, M. P., Verdun, F. R., Castella, C., Bochud, F. O. 'Derivation of an Observer Model Adapted to Irregular Signals Based on Convolution Channels.' *IEEE Transactions on Medical Imaging*, vol. 34, no. 7, 2015, pp. 1428–1435.

Dorris, M. C., Munoz, D. P. 'Saccadic Probability Influences Motor Preparation Signals and Time to Saccadic Initiation.' *The Journal of Neuroscience*, vol. 18, no. 17, 1998, pp. 7015–7026.

Dunning, A., Ghoreyshi, A., Bertucco, M., Sanger, T. D. 'The Tuning of Human Motor Response to Risk in a Dynamic Environment Task.' *PLOS ONE*, vol. 10, no. 4, 2015, e0125461.

Eckstein, M. P. 'Probabilistic Computations for Attention, Eye Movements, and Search.' *Annual Review of Vision Science*, vol. 3, no. 1, 2017, pp. 319–342.

Eckstein, M. P., Beutter, B. B., Stone, L. S. 'The Accuracy of Saccadic and Perceptual Decisions in Visual Search.' *Perception*, vol. 26, no. 1_suppl, 1997, pp. 133.

Eckstein, M. P., Mack, S. C., Liston, D. B., Bogush, L., Menzel, R., Krauzlis, R. J. 'Rethinking Human Visual Attention: Spatial Cueing Effects and Optimality of Decisions by Honeybees, Monkeys and Humans.' *Vision Research*, vol. 85, 2013, pp. 5–19.

Eckstein, M. P., Schoonveld, W., Zhang, S., Mack, S. C., Akbas, E. 'Optimal and Human Eye Movements to Clustered Low Value Cues to Increase Decision Rewards during Search.' *Vision Research*, vol. 113, 2015, pp. 137–154.

Engbert, R., Nuthmann, A., Richter, E. M., Kliegl, R. 'SWIFT: A Dynamical Model of Saccade Generation during Reading.' *Psychological Review*, vol. 112, no. 4, 2005, pp. 777–813.

Epstein, R. A. *The Theory of Gambling and Statistical Logic.* Rev. ed. Burlington, MA: Academic Press, 1995.

Everling, S. 'Where Do I Look? From Attention to Action in the Frontal Eye Field.' *Neuron*, vol. 56, no. 3, 2007, pp. 417–419.

Fischer, H. *The Central Limit Theorem from Laplace to Cauchy: Changes in Stochastic Objectives and in Analytical Methods.* Eichstätt: Katholische Universität Eichstätt, Mathematisch-Geographische Fakultät, 2001.

Gaffin-Cahn, E., Hudson, T. E., Landy, M. S. 'Did I Do That? Detecting a Perturbation to Visual Feedback in a Reaching Task.' *Journal of Vision*, vol. 19, no. 1, 2019, p. 5.

Geisler, W. S. 'Contributions of Ideal Observer Theory to Vision Research.' *Vision Research*, vol. 51, no. 7, 2011, pp. 771–781.

Gelman, A., Shalizi, C. R. 'Philosophy and the Practice of Bayesian Statistics.' *British Journal of Mathematical and Statistical Psychology*, vol. 66, no. 1, 2012, pp. 8–38.

Genest, W., Hammond, R., Carpenter, R. H. S. 'The Random Dot Tachistogram: A Novel Task That Elucidates the Functional Architecture of Decision.' *Scientific Reports*, vol. 6, no. 1, 2016, pp. 1–11.

Gold, J. I., Shadlen, M. S. 'Neural Computations That Underlie Decisions about Sensory Stimuli.' *Trends in Cognitive Sciences*, vol. 5, no. 1, 2001, pp. 10–16.

Good, I. J. 'Studies in the History of Probability and Statistics: A. M. Turing's Statistical Work in World War II.' *Biometrika*, vol. 66, no. 2, 1979, pp. 393–396.

Graf, A. B. A., Anderson, R. A. 'Inferring Eye Position from Populations of Lateral Intraparietal Neurons.' *eLife* 2014;3:e02813.

Graf, E. W., Warren, P. A., Maloney, L. T. 'Explicit Estimation of Visual Uncertainty in Human Motion Processing.' *Vision Research*, vol. 45, no. 24, 2005, pp. 3050–3059.

Graham, C. H. 'On Some Aspects of Real and Apparent Visual Movement.' *JOSA*, vol. 53, pp. 1019–1025.

Greenwald, H. S., Knill, D. C., Saunders, J. A. 'Integrating Visual Cues for Motor Control: A Matter of Time.' *Vision Research*, vol. 45, no. 15, 2005, pp. 1975–1989.

Gregory, P. C. *Bayesian Logical Data Analysis for the Physical Sciences.* Cambridge: Cambridge Univ. 2005.

Gull, S. F. 'Bayesian Data Analysis: Straight-Line Fitting.' Unpublished manuscript.

Gull, S. F. 'Bayesian Data Analysis: Straight-Line Fitting.' In *Maximum Entropy and Bayesian Methods*, edited by J. Skilling. Dordrecht: Kluwer, 1989.

Gull, S. F. 'Bayesian Inductive Inference and Maximum Entropy.' In *Maximum Entropy and Bayesian Methods in Science and Engineering*, Vol. 1, edited by G. J. Erickson and C. R. Smith, pp. 53–74. Dordrecht: Kluwer, 1988.

Gull, S. F., Daniell, G. J. 'Image Reconstruction from Incomplete and Noisy Data.' *Nature*, vol. 272, 1978, pp. 686–690.

Gull, S. F., Skilling, J. 'Maximum Entropy Image Reconstruction.' *IEE Proceedings*, vol. 131F, 1984, pp. 646–659.

Hajek, B. *Random Processes for Engineers.* Cambridge: Cambridge University Press, 2015.

Haller, H., Krauss, S. 'Misinterpretations of Significance: A Problem Students Share with Their Teachers?' Methods of Psychological Research Online, Vol. 7, No. 1, 2002. www.mpr-online.de.

Hamming, R. W. *Coding and Information Theory*. Englewood Cliffs, NJ: Prentice-Hall, 1980.

Hamming, R. W. *Digital Filters*. 3rd ed. Mineola, NY: Dover, 1998.

Hamming, R. W. *Numerical Methods for Scientists and Engineers*. New York: McGraw-Hill, 1962.

Hanes, D. P., Carpenter, R. H. S. 'Countermanding Saccades in Humans.' *Vision Research*, vol. 39, no. 16, 1999, pp. 2777–2791.

Harris, C. M. 'Does Saccadic Undershoot Minimize Saccadic Flight-Time? A Monte-Carlo Study.' *Vision Research*, vol. 35, no. 5, 1995, pp. 691–701.

Hudson, T. E., Landy, M. S. 'Sinusoidal Error Perturbation Reveals Multiple Coordinate Systems for Sensorymotor Adaptation.' *Vision Research*, vol. 119, 2016, pp. 82–98.

Hudson, T. E., Li, W., Matin, L. 'Independent Mechanisms Produce Visually Perceived Eye Level (VPEL) and Perceived Visual Pitch (PVP).' *Vision Research*, vol. 40, no. 19, 2000, pp. 2605–2619.

Hudson, T. E., Maloney, L. T., Landy, M. S. 'Movement Planning with Probabilistic Target Information.' *Journal of Neurophysiology*, vol. 98, no. 5, 2007, pp. 3034–3046.

Hudson, T. E., Maloney, L. T., Landy, M. S. 'Optimal Compensation for Temporal Uncertainty in Movement Planning.' *PLoS Computational Biology*, vol. 4, no. 7, 2008, e1000130.

Hudson, T. E., Wolfe, U., Maloney, L. T. 'Speeded Reaching Movements around Invisible Obstacles.' *PLoS Computational Biology*, vol. 8, no. 9, 2012, e1002676.

Jaynes, E. T. 'Bayesian Methods: An Introductory Tutorial.' In *Maximum Entropy and Bayesian Methods in Applied Statistics*, edited by J. H. Justice. Cambridge: Cambridge University Press, 1986.

Jaynes, E. T. 'Bayesian Methods: General Background.' In *Maximum Entropy and Bayesian Methods in Applied Statisitics*, edited by J. Justice, pp. 1–25. Cambridge: Cambridge University Press, 1986.

Jaynes, E. T. 'Clearing Up Mysteries – the Original Goal.' In *Maximum Entropy and Bayesian Methods*, edited by J. Skilling. Dordrecht: Kluwer, 1989.

Jaynes, E. T. 'Detection of Extra Solar System Planets.' In *Maximum-Entropy and Bayesian Methods in Science and Engineering: Foundations*, edited by G. J. Erickson and C. R. Smith, pp. 147–160. Berlin: Kluwer Academic, 1988.

Jaynes, E. T. 'Foundations of Probability Theory and Statistical Mechanics.' In *Delaware Seminar in Foundations of Physics*, edited by M. Bunge. Berlin: Springer, 1963.

Jaynes, E. T. 'Information Theory and Statistical Mechanics.' *Physical Review*, vol. 106, 1957, pp. 620–630; 108, 171–190.

Jaynes, E. T. 'The Intuitive Inadequacy of Classical Statistics.' *Time Series and Statistics*, 1984, pp. 43–74.

Jaynes, E. T. 'On the Rationale of Maximum-Entropy Methods.' *Proceedings of the IEEE*, vol. 70, no. 9, 1982, pp. 939–952.

Jaynes, E. T. *Papers on Probability Statistics and Statistical Physics*. Edited by R. D. Rosenkrantz. Dordrecht: Reidel, 1983.

Jaynes, E. T. 'Straight Line Fitting – A Bayesian Solution.' In *Maximum Entropy and Bayesian Methods*, edited by J. Skilling, pp. 1–17. Cambridge: Springer Science+Business Media, 1999.

Jaynes, E. T. 'The Well-Posed Problem.' In *Foundations of Physics*, pp. 477–493. Berlin: Springer, 1973.

Jaynes, E. T. 'Where Do We Stand on Maximum Entropy?' In *The Maximum Entropy Formalism*, edited by R. D. Levine and M. Tribus. Cambridge, MA: MIT Press, 1978.

Jaynes, E. T. *Probability Theory: The Logic of Science*. Cambridge: Cambridge University Press, 2003.

Jeffreys, H. *Theory of Probability*. Oxford: Clarendon Press, 1939.

Juni, M. Z., Eckstein, M .P. 'The Wisdom of Crowds for Visual Search.' *Proceedings of the National Academy of Sciences*, vol. 114, no. 21, 2017, pp. E4306–E4315.

Kadane, J. B., Larkey, P. D. 'Subjective Probability and the Theory of Games.' *Management Science*, vol. 28, no. 2, 1982, pp. 113–120.

Keynes, J. M. *A Treatise on Probability*. London: Macmillan, 1921.

Kneissler, J., Drugowitsch, J., Friston, K., Martin, V. B. 'Simultaneous Learning and Filtering without Delusions: A Bayes-Optimal Combination of Predictive Inference and Adaptive Filtering.' *Frontiers in Computational Neuroscience*, vol. 9, 2015, pp. 1–12.

Knill, D. C. 'Mixture Models and the Probabilistic Structure of Depth Cues.' *Vision Research*, vol. 43, no. 7, 2003, pp. 831–854.

Knill, D. C. 'Robust Cue Integration: A Bayesian Model and Evidence from Cue-Conflict Studies with Stereoscopic and Figure Cues to Slant.' *Journal of Vision*, vol. 7, no. 7, 2007, p. 5.

Krauzlis, R. J. 'Shared Motor Error for Multiple Eye Movements.' *Science*, vol. 276, no. 5319, 1997, pp. 1693–1695.

Kullback, S. *Information Theory and Statistics*. Mineola, NY: Dover, 1997.

Kuss, M., Jäkel, F., Wichmann, F. A. 'Bayesian Inference for Psychometric Functions.' *Journal of Vision*, vol. 5, no. 5, 2005, p. 8.

Lanczos, C. *Variational Principles of Mechanics*. 4th ed. New York: Dover, 2005.

Larkey, P., Kadane, J. B., Austin, R., Zamir, S. 'Skill in Games.' *Management Science*, vol. 43, no. 5, 1997, pp. 596–609.

Leigh, R. J., Kennard, C. 'Using Saccades as a Research Tool in the Clinical Neurosciences.' *Brain*, vol. 127, no. 3, 2004, pp. 460–477.

Leigh, R. J., Zee, D. S. *The Neurology of Eye Movements*. 4th ed. New York: Oxford University Press, 2006.

Lerch, R., Sims, C. 'A Comparison of Haptic and Visual Memory Suggests Domain General Principles in Perceptual Working Memory.' *Journal of Vision*, vol. 16, no. 12, 2016, p. 1066.

Liu, C.-L., Chiau, H.-Y., Tseng, P., Hung, D. L., Tzeng, O. J. L., Muggleton, N. G., Juan, C.-H. 'Antisaccade Cost Is Modulated by Contextual Experience of Location Probability.' *Journal of Neurophysiology*, vol. 103, no. 3, 2010, pp. 1438–1447.

Locke, S. M., Gaffin-Cahn, E., Hosseinizaveh, N., Mamassian, P., Landy, M. S. 'Priors and Payoffs in Confidence Judgments.' *Attention, Perception, & Psychophysics*, 2020.

Loredo, T. J. 'From Laplace to Supernova 1987A: Bayesian Inference in Astrophysics.' In *Maximum Entropy and Bayesian Methods*, edited by P. F. Fougere. Dordrecht: Kluwer, 1990.

Loredo, T. J. 'Promise of Bayesian Inference for Astrophysics.' In *Statistical Challenges in Modern Astronomy*, edited by P. F. Fougere and G. J. Babu. New York: Springer, 1992.

Loredo. T. J., Chernoff, D. F. 'Bayesian Adaptive Exploration.' In *Statistical Challenges in Astronomy*. New York: Springer, 2003.

Ma, W. J. 'Signal Detection Theory, Uncertainty, and Poisson-like Population Codes.' *Vision Research*, vol. 50, no. 22, 2010, pp. 2308–2319.

MacKay, D. J. C. *Information Theory, Inference, and Learning Algorithms*. Cambridge: Cambridge University Press, 2003.

Maloney, L. T., Mamassian, P. 'Bayesian Decision Theory as a Model of Human Visual Perception: Testing Bayesian Transfer.' *Visual Neuroscience*, vol. 26, no. 1, 2009, pp. 147–155.

Mamassian, P., Landy, M. S. 'Interaction of Visual Prior Constraints.' *Vision Research*, vol. 41, no. 20, 2001, pp. 2653–2668.

Matin, L., Picoult, E., Stevens, J. K., Edwards, M. W., Young, D., MacArthur, R. 'Oculoparalytic Illusion: Visual-Field Dependent Spatial Mislocalizations by Humans Partially Paralyzed with Curare.' *Science*, vol. 216, 1982, pp. 198–201.

Matin, L., Pola, J., Matin, E., Picoult, E. 'Vernier Discrimination with Sequentially-Flashed Lines: Roles of Eye Movements, Retinal Offsets, and Short-Term Memory.' *Vision Research*, vol 21, 1980, pp. 647–656.

Mcquarrie, D. A., Simon, J. D. *Physical Chemistry: A Molecular Approach*. New Delhi: Viva Books, 1998.

Mcquarrie, D. A. *Quantum Chemistry*. Mill Valley, CA: University Science Books, 1983.

McSorley, E., Gilchrist, I. D., McCloy, R. 'The Programming of Sequences of Saccades.' *Experimental Brain Research*, vol. 237, no. 4, 2019, pp. 1009–1018.

Merrison, A. F. A., Carpenter, R. H. S. 'Co-Variability of Smooth and Saccadic Latencies in Oculomotor Pursuit.' *Ophthalmic Research*, vol. 26, no. 3, 1994, pp. 158–162.

Michell, A. W., Xu, Z., Fritz, D., Lewis, S. J. G., Foltynie, T., Williams-Gray, C. H., Robbins, T. W., Carpenter, R. H. S, Barker, R. A. 'Saccadic Latency Distributions in Parkinson's Disease and the Effects of l-Dopa.' *Experimental Brain Research*, vol. 174, no. 1, 2006, pp. 7–18.

Morrison, D. F. *Multivariate Statistical Methods*. 2nd ed. New York: McGraw-Hill, 1967.

Morvan, C., Maloney, L. T. 'Human Visual Search Does Not Maximize the Post-Saccadic Probability of Identifying Targets.' *PLoS Computational Biology*, vol. 8, no. 2, 2012, e1002342.

Moscoso del Prado, F. (2008). 'A Theory of Reaction Time Distributions.' *Unpublished manuscript*.

Najemnik, J., Geisler, W. S. 'Simple Summation Rule for Optimal Fixation Selection in

Visual Search.' *Vision Research*, vol. 49, no. 10, 2009, pp. 1286–1294.

Noorani, I. 'Towards a Unifying Mechanism for Cancelling Movements.' *Philosophical Transactions of the Royal Society B: Biological Sciences*, vol. 372, no. 1718, 2017, 20160191.

Noorani, I., Carpenter, R. H. S. 'Antisaccades as Decisions: LATER Model Predicts Latency Distributions and Error Responses.' *European Journal of Neuroscience*, vol. 37, no. 2, 2012, pp. 330–338.

Noorani, I., Carpenter, R. H. S. 'The LATER Model of Reaction Time and Decision.' *Neuroscience & Biobehavioral Reviews*, vol. 64, 2016, pp. 229–251.

Noorani, I., Carpenter, R. H. S. 'Ultrafast Initiation of a Neural Race by Impending Errors.' *The Journal of Physiology*, vol. 593, no. 19, 2015, pp. 4471–4484.

Norton, E. H., Acerbi, L, Ma, W. J., Landy, M. S. 'Human Online Adaptation to Changes in Prior Probability.' *PLOS Computational Biology*, vol. 15, no. 7, 2019, e1006681.

Norwich, K. H. 'The Psychophysics of Taste from the Entropy of the Stimulus.' *Perception & Psychophysics*, vol. 35, no. 3, 1984, pp. 269–278.

Oakes, M. *Statistical Inference: A Commentary for the Social and Behavioural Sciences*. Chichester, UK: John Wiley, 1986.

Oruç, İ., Maloney, L. T., Landy, M. S. 'Weighted Linear Cue Combination with Possibly Correlated Error.' *Vision Research*, vol. 43, no. 23, 2003, pp. 2451–2468.

Oswal, A., Ogden, M., Carpenter, R. H. S. 'The Time Course of Stimulus Expectation in a Saccadic Decision Task.' *Journal of Neurophysiology*, vol. 97, no. 4, 2007, pp. 2722–2730.

Pare, M., Munoz, D. P. 'Saccadic Reaction Time in the Monkey: Advanced Preparation of Oculomotor Programs Is Primarily Responsible for Express Saccade Occurrence.' *Journal of Neurophysiology*, vol. 76, no. 6, 1996, pp. 3666–3681.

Pelli, D. G., Farell, B. 'Psychophysical Methods.' In *Handbook of Optics*, 2nd ed., vol. 1, edited by M. Bass, E. W. Van Stryland, D. R. Williams, and W. L. Wolfe, pp. 29.21–29.13. New York: McGraw-Hill, 1995.

Peng, S., Landy, M. S. 'A Two-Stage Process Model of Sensory Discrimination: An Alternative to Drift-Diffusion.' *The Journal of Neuroscience*, vol. 36, no. 44, 2016, pp. 11259–11274.

Porter, K. K., Metzger, R. R., Groh, J. M., 'Visual- and Saccade-Related Signals in the Primate Inferior Colliculus,' *PNAS*, vol. 104, no. 45, pp. 17855–17860.

Pouget, A., Beck, J. M., Ma, W. J., Latham, P. E. 'Probabilistic Brains: Knowns and Unknowns.' *Nature Neuroscience*, vol. 16, no. 9, 2013, pp. 1170–1178.

Pouget, A., Dayabn, P., Zemel, R. S. 'Inference and Computation with Population Codes.' *Annual Review of Neuroscience*, vol. 26, 2003, pp. 381–410.

Press, W. H., Flannery, B. P., Teukolsky, S. A., Vetterling, W. T. *Numerical Recipes: The Art of Scientific Computing*. Cambridge: Cambridge University Press, 1986.

Purcell, B. A., Heitz, R. P., Cohen, J. Y., Schall, J. D., Logan, G. D., Palmeri, T. J. 'Neurally Constrained Modeling of Perceptual Decision Making.' *Psychological Review*, vol. 117, no. 4, 2010, pp. 1113–1143.

Ramat, S., Shaikh, A. G. *Mathematical Modelling in Motor Neuroscience: State of the Art and Translation to the Clinic – Gaze Orienting Mechanisms and Disease*. Cambridge, MA: Academic Press, 2019.

Ratcliff, R. 'Putting Noise into Neurophysiological Models of Simple Decision Making.' *Nature Neuroscience*, vol. 4, no. 4, 2001, pp. 336.

Robertson, S. S., Watamura, S. E., Wilbourn, M. P. 'Attentional Dynamics of Infant Visual Foraging.' *Proceedings of the National Academy of Sciences*, vol. 109, no. 28, 2012, pp. 11460–11464.

Roman, J. A., Warren, B. H., Graybiel, A. 'Observation of the Elevator Illusion during Subgravity Preceded by Negative Accelerations.' Research report, U.S. Naval School of Aviation Medicine, Pensacola, FL, 1963.

Ruben, M.-B., Knill, D. C., Pouget, A. 'Bayesian Sampling in Visual Perception.' *PNAS*, vol. 108, no. 30, 2011.

Sanger, T. D. 'Bayesian Filtering of Myoelectric Signals.' *Journal of Neurophysiology*, vol. 97, no. 2, 2007, pp. 1839–1845.

Schiller, P. H., Haushofer, J., Kendall, G. 'How Do Target Predictability and Precueing Affect the Production of Express Saccades in Monkeys?' *European Journal of Neuroscience*, vol. 19, no. 7, 2004, pp. 1963–1968.

Schwarz, W. 'The Ex-Wald Distribution as a Descriptive Model of Response Times.' *Behavior Research Methods, Instruments, & Computers*, vol. 33, no. 4, 2001, pp. 457–469.

Shannon, C. E. 'A Mathematical Theory of Communication.' *Bell System Technical Journal*, vol. 27, 1948, pp. 379–423 and 623–656.

Shore, J. E., Johnson, R. W. (1980). 'Axiomatic Derivation of the Principle of Maximum Entropy and the Principle of Minimum Cross-Entropy.' *IEEE Transactions*, IT-26, pp. 26–37.

Sivia, D. 'Bayesian Inductive Inference Maximum Entropy & Neutron Scattering.' *Los Alamos Science Summer*, 1990, pp. 1–28.

Skilling, J. 'Classic Maximum Entropy.' In *Maximum Entropy and Bayesian Methods*, edited by J. Skilling. Dordrecht: Kluwer, 1989.

Skilling, H. H. *Electrical Engineering Circuits.* 2nd ed. New York: John Wiley, 1972.

Skilling, J. 'Fundamentals of MaxEnt in Data Analysis.' In *Maximum Entropy in Action*, edited by B. Buck and V. A. Macaulay. Oxford: Clarendon Press, 1991.

Skilling, J. 'Nested Sampling.' In *Maximum Entropy and Bayesian Methods in Science and Engineering*, edited by G. Erickson, J. T. Rychert, and C. R. Smith. *AIP Conference Proceedings*, vol. 735, 2004, pp. 395–405.

Skilling, J., Bryan, R. K. 'Maximum Entropy Image Reconstruction: General Algorithm.' *Monthly Notices of the Royal Astronomical Society*, vol. 211, no. 1, 1984, pp. 111–124.

Smital, J. *On Functions and Functional Equations.* Bristol: Hilger, 1988.

Sperling, G. 'The Information Available in Brief Visual Presentations.' *Psychological Monographs: General and Applied*, vol. 74, no. 11, 1960, pp. 1–29.

Stark, L. *Neurological Control Systems: Studies in Bioengineering.* New York: Plenum Press, 1968.

Tassinari, H., Hudson, T. E., Landy, M. S. 'Combining Priors and Noisy Visual Cues in a Rapid Pointing Task.' *Journal of Neuroscience*, vol. 26, no. 40, 2006, pp. 10154–10163.

Tatler, B. W., Brockmole, J. R., Carpenter, R. H. S. 'LATEST: A Model of Saccadic Decisions in Space and Time.' *Psychological Review*, vol. 124, no. 3, 2017, pp. 267–300.

Trimmer, J. D. *Response of Physical Systems.* New York: John Wiley, 1950.

van den Berg, A. V., van Loon, E. M. 'An Invariant for Timing of Saccades during Visual Search.' *Vision Research*, vol. 45, no. 12, 2005, pp. 1543–1555.

Vaziri, S., Diedrichsen, J., Shadmehr, R. 'Why Does the Brain Predict Sensory Consequences of Oculomotor Commands? Optimal Integration of Predicted and Actual Sensory Feedback.' *Journal of Neuroscience*, vol. 26, 2006, pp. 4188–197.

Verbruggen, F., Logan, G. D. 'Evidence for Capacity Sharing When Stopping.' *Cognition*, vol. 142, 2015, pp. 81–95.

von Bekesy, G. *Sensory Inhibition.* Princeton, NJ: Princeton University Press, 1967.

Wald, A. 'On Cumulative Sums of Random Variables.' *The Annals of Mathematical Statistics*, vol. 15, no. 3, 1944, pp. 283–296.

Yarbus, A. L. *Eye Movements and Vision.* New York: Plenum Press, 1967.

Yari, G., Tondpour, Z. 'The New Burr Distribution and Its Application.' *Mathematical Sciences*, vol. 11, no. 1, 2017, pp. 47–54.

Zellner, A. *An Introduction to Bayesian Inference in Econometrics.* New York: John Wiley, 1971.

Zellner, A. 'Information Processing and Bayesian Analysis.' *Journal of Econometrics*, vol. 107, no. 1, 1986, pp. 41–50.

Zellner, A. 'Generalizing the Standard Product Rule of Probability Theory and Bayes's Theorem.' *Journal of Econometrics*, vol. 138, no. 1, 2007, pp. 14–23.

Zellner, A. 'Some Aspects of the History of Bayesian Information Processing.' *Journal of Econometrics*, vol. 138, no. 2, 2007, pp. 388–404.

Ziliak, S. T., McCloskey, D. N. The Cult of Statistical Significance. Ann Arbor: University of Michigan Press, 2011.

Index

Note: Page numbers in **bold** type refer to content in **boxes**; page numbers in *italic* type refer to content in *figures*.